Psychology

CAMILLE B. WORTMAN
University of Michigan

ELIZABETH F. LOFTUS
University of Washington

MARY MARSHALL

Psychology

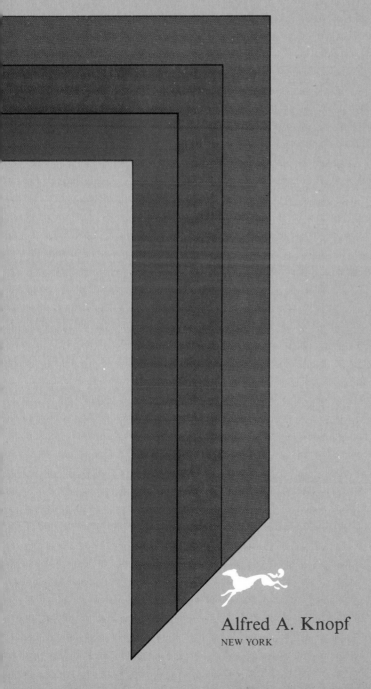

Alfred A. Knopf
NEW YORK

THIS IS A BORZOI BOOK PUBLISHED BY ALFRED A. KNOPF, INC.

First Edition
98765432
Copyright © 1981 by Alfred A. Knopf, Inc.

Library of Congress Cataloging in Publication Data

Wortman, Camille.
  Psychology.

  Bibliography: p.
  Includes index.
  1. Psychology.   I. Loftus, Elizabeth F., 1944–
joint author.   II. Marshall, Mary, joint author.   III.
Title.
BF121.W67   150   81–451
ISBN 0-394-32428-5

Manufactured in the United States of America
Cover sculpture: "Construction #107" by Jose De Rivera. The Hirshhorn Museum, Smithsonian Institution.

Preface

Teaching introductory psychology is never easy. Inevitably there seems to be a tension between the basic science instructors want to teach and the very practical information students want to learn. Different texts have dealt with this problem in different ways. Some have taken a strong research orientation, with little apparent concern for readability or student interest. Others have chosen to be research-oriented in some parts of the book, but to intersperse these parts with separate sections on applications and high interest topics. This second approach has become increasingly popular in recent years. Many authors have filled their texts with a panoply of "special features"—cartoons, news clippings, boxed inserts of all kinds, even stories and vignettes. Indeed, many current books seem based on the assumption that the only way to make scientific content palatable to students is to offer an endless array of gimmicks and titillating topics. We firmly reject this assumption. It is because of our belief that psychology can be exciting and stimulating without resorting to gimmicks or sacrificing scientific integrity that we decided to write this book.

Our major goal has been to produce a text that is rigorous and conceptually sophisticated, yet lively and engaging. We focus on central theories, classic experiments, and important psychological concepts and principles. But throughout the book we also introduce issues of concern to students to amplify and reinforce the scholarly material. More important, this integration of issues and basic science occurs entirely within the text narrative. For example, we discuss sexism in the context of social psychological theories of attitude formation and change, not in a separate boxed insert. Similarly, we explore the impact of TV violence while presenting major theories of aggression and so emphasize that much of the work in this area was inspired by competing theoretical perspectives. In addition, we try to show how attempts to apply psychological knowledge have often resulted in extensions, revisions, or elaborations of basic theories. This we demonstrate, for instance, in our discussion of Loftus's work on eyewitness testimony, which has contributed to the theoretical understanding of human memory.

In short, we believe that isolating applications from psychological theory gives a distorted view of what our discipline is all about. Accordingly, we have been guided by the principle that if something is worth including in the book it is worth discussing in the text proper. We feel that separate boxes, vignettes, and the like not only disrupt the flow and coherence of a chapter but are also based on an erroneous assumption: that students need a breather from their toils as they wearily plod through scientific material. For those who disagree with this assumption we offer an alternative view: by fully interweaving theories and applications, *all* of introductory psychology can be made fascinating, provocative, and meaningful for students.

But there is more to a good text than integration of theory and application alone. In planning our approach to writing this book we asked ourselves the following question: How can this text enhance the long-run impact of a student's first (often only) psychology course? One of the most difficult problems we as instructors have faced is that no matter how carefully and thoroughly we present material, the details of specific experiments seem to fade from students' memories as the term comes to a close. We gave this problem a great deal of discussion during the initial stages of this book. What do we want students to take away from the course? In our judgment the most important thing we can impart to students is not a body of isolated facts, but a way of thinking about science in general and psychological research in particular. For this reason we have made every effort to emphasize the *process* of scientific inquiry. Rather than simply summarizing the results of experiments, we try to convey the investigative excitement of psychology as an ongoing activity. Thus, we focus on how psychologists develop testable hypotheses, how they gather and interpret data, how they arrive at conclusions. We repeatedly try to show how early studies form the foundation for later research, which in turn often refines our understanding by ruling out alternative explanations. We believe that this approach helps to convey some of the excitement of doing scientific work. And even more important, we believe that it helps students learn both to think critically and to develop a healthy skepticism toward ideas that are unsubstantiated by scientific data. Throughout their lives our students will be exposed to a barage of "psychologizing"—everything from tests in the Sunday supplement to evaluate their marriages, to psychographs purporting to reveal their personal shortcomings, to the numerous "self-improvement" books that line drugstore shelves. We have tried to provide students with the critical skills needed to question the validity of this popularized psychology. Hopefully, these skills will remain with them long after the introductory course is through.

Of course, the goal of teaching students to think critically is certainly a difficult one. Specifically, how have we tried to accomplish it? First, we have devoted an early chapter of the book (Chapter 2) to a careful consideration of how psychologists define research objectives, select a method of inquiry, gather and interpret their data, rule out alternative explanations, and deal with the ethical dilemmas that research sometimes poses. We then carry these themes throughout the book, where we repeatedly encourage students to evaluate the theories and research we present. For example, many undergraduates are initially impressed by Rosenhan's study in which normal individuals entered mental hospitals posing as schizophrenics. Many introductory texts stop with a brief summary of this study. But in this book we encourage critical thought by guiding the reader through an analysis of what the study does and does not prove. Similarly, when presenting Schachter and Singer's classic experimental work on emotion, many introductory texts simply say that the results supported the researchers' hypothesis. In contrast, we encourage students to identify weaknesses both in the design of the original study and in the inferences Schachter and Singer drew from their data. We then try to show how these shortcomings encouraged subsequent theoretical and empirical work on emotion.

A second technique we have used to develop critical thinking is to repeatedly contrast "common sense" myths about psychology with what empirical data reveal. One of the most frustrating things about teaching introductory psychology is the large number of students who believe that psychology is merely "common sense." We try to illustrate that while empirical data sometimes support our common sense notions, they often do not. For instance, common sense might lead us to believe that the more motivated people are, the better they will perform on a task. Drawing from theoretical and empirical work, we attempt to show how simplistic this assumption is. Similarly, common sense also leads us to conclude that people's behavior can be predicted from their attitudes. We provide a full discussion of why assuming such predictability is a mistake. By highlighting the discrepancies between common sense and empirical findings, we hope to emphasize that students cannot trust their intuitions when it comes to human behavior. A careful evaluation of the available evidence is always essential.

Finally, a third and very important way we explore the process of scientific inquiry and try to encourage critical thinking is through the section in each chapter labeled "In Depth." Most of these sections present a critical discussion of one research program, chosen both for its importance to the field and for its intrinsic interest to students. For example, in the chapter on Cognition and Problem-Solving we investigate Kahneman and Tversky's program of research on the representativeness and availability heuristics, and we encourage students to evaluate whether and how these cognitive strategies affect decision making in their own lives. In addition to "In Depth" sections that concentrate on a single research program, others focus on a single critical issue, investigating how different researchers have helped to shed light on it. For instance, in the Motivation chapter, we have chosen obesity as the subject for our "In Depth" inquiry. We review the theoretical and empirical work of Schachter, Nisbett, Rodin, Herman and Polivy, and others, with particular attention to how these investigators have influenced one another's work. In the process we touch on the psychological principles underlying many current diets, why the majority of them fail in the long run, and even whether some obese people should diet at all. The many other "In Depth" sections included in the book—one in each chapter—are listed in the table of contents.

This book represents a collaborative effort between the three of us and the college publishing staff at Random House, who shared our enthusiasm about creating a conceptually sophisticated yet readable text that would emphasize process rather than facts. Our areas of expertise have nicely complemented one another. Camille Wortman, a social psychologist, has taken primary responsibility for the chapters on social psychology, personality, assessment, and abnormal psychology and its treatment. Elizabeth Loftus, an experimental psychologist by training, has worked primarily on research methods, physiology, learning, memory, and cognition. Mary Marshall has drawn from her ten years of experience in college publishing to help with decisions about how to present ideas in a manner as clear, lively, and engaging as possible. Marshall's main job, however, was to facilitate the integration of scholarly and high-interest material by ensuring high quality writing throughout the book. Alfred A. Knopf has made a number of resources available to the three of us to enhance the quality of the final product. They have provided access to the accumulated expertise and factual information resulting from their extensive background in introductory psychology publishing. Random House owns and publishes *Psychology Today*, and the ability to utilize the materials and illustrations from that text has been of great value to us, especially materials for Chapters 3, 4, 7, 8, 9, and 12.

The people at Alfred A. Knopf with whom we worked put enormous care, skill, and effort into this project. The following people deserve our special thanks: Irene Pavitt who coordinated development of the manuscript and without whose uncommon good sense we would probably still be writing and revising; Anna Marie Muskelly who put in long hours supervising the copy-editing process and illustration program and overseeing production; Jan Carr, Suzanne Thibodeau, and Sylvia Shepard who helped shape and articulate many of the ideas for this book; June Smith and Barry Fetterolf for their sound judgment and skillful orchestration behind the scenes. In addition, we would like to acknowledge three talented freelance editors who helped the book along its way, Paula Franklin, Saralyn Esh, and especially Betty Gatewood for her work on Chapters 13–16. And finally, we are grateful to our husbands for their understanding and support during the months when the writing of this book consumed so much of our time.

CBW
EFL
MM

ACKNOWLEDGMENTS

In planning and executing this book, we have worked with a carefully selected group of academic consultants: Ellen Markman from Stanford University, who helped with the Life-Span Development chapter; Robert Sekuler from Northwestern University, who aided us with the chapter on Sensation and Perception; Abigail Stewart from Boston University, who provided valuable advice on the Personality and Assessment chapters; Bonnie Spring from Harvard University and Richard Bootzin from Northwestern University, who helped with the Abnormal and Treatment chapters. In addition to asking them for guidance in selecting and organizing material, we asked these consultants to identify important new areas of research into their respective fields, as well as the directions in which the best researchers seem to be moving. All this information was extremely helpful. Finally, we are indebted to the following students from Northwestern University for their helpful advice during the planning stages of this book: Bill Buchanan, Diane Crist, Jesús Fernández, David Littrell, Evelyn Mkrtchjan, Lisa Schurer, Sharon Siegel, Rena Ugol, Kurt Walsh, and Peter

Wisch. They made a number of specific suggestions about how particular theories and empirical results could best be "brought alive" for them.

Then, when the text was finally in first draft form, a number of academic reviewers were immeasurably helpful in offering their criticisms and thoughtful ideas for improvement. We are especially grateful to David Hothersall of Ohio State University and John Somervill of the University of Northern Iowa for their careful readings of every chapter. Also providing valuable insights were the following people:

Whorton Allen
Utah State University

James Allison
Indiana University

Mary Sue Ammon
University of California at Berkeley

Jonathan Baron
University of Pennsylvania

Frank Barrios
University of Northern Iowa

Verna Barron
Stephen F. Austin State University

Ilene Bernstein
University of Washington

Michael Best
Southern Methodist University

Robert Bjork
University of California at Los Angeles

David Bolocofsky
University of Northern Colorado

Daniel Boroto
Florida State University

Nancy Breland
Trenton State College

Stephan Chorover
Massachusetts Institute of Technology

Louis Csoka
*United-States Military Academy
West Point*

Carol Diers
Western Washington State College

Edward Donnerstein
University of Wisconsin

David Edwards
Iowa State University

D. G. Forgays
University of Vermont

Margery Franklin
Sara Lawrence College

Kurt Geisinger
Fordham University

Arnold Glass
Rutgers University

Leonard Goodstein
*University Associates
Learning Resources Corporation, Inc.*

James Greeno
University of Pittsburgh

Ronald Growney
University of Connecticut

Judy Harakiewicz
Columbia University

Richard Harris
Kansas State University

Keith Holyoak
University of Michigan

Carlton James
Rutgers University

Charles Judd
Harvard University

John Keating
University of Washington

Theophile Krawiec
Skidmore College

Marianne LaFrance
*Henry A. Murry Research Center
Radcliffe College*

Marigold Linton
University of Utah

Kenneth Livingston
Vassar College

Jane Maddy
University of Minnesota—Duluth

Roslyn Mass
Middlesex County College

Donald McBurney
University of Pittsburgh

Garvin McCain
University of Texas—Arlington

Stephen McCary
(private practice) Houston, Texas

Michael McCloskey
Johns Hopkins University

Frances McSweeney
Washington State University

Fred Meeker
California State Polytechnic University

Richard Metzger
Sagamon State University

Harold Miller
Brigham Young University

Harold Moore
Bucks County Community College

Stan Moss
University of Massachusetts

Gary Olson
University of Michigan

Reed Payne
Brigham Young University

Kathy Pezdek
California State University—San Bernadino

Robert Rescorla
Yale University

Ross Rizley
Harvard University

Herbert Roitblat
Columbia University

Milton Rosenbaum
University of Iowa

Estelita Saldanha
University of Southern Maine

Allen Schneider
Swarthmore College

Marvin Schwartz
University of Cincinnati

Joan Gay Snodgrass
New York University

Mark Snyder
University of Minnesota—Minneapolis

Bernard Spilka
University of Denver

Jean Spruill
Florida State University

Joics B. Stone
California State Polytechnic University—Pomona

Sherman Tatz
C. W. Post Center—Long Island University

Geoffrey Thorpe
University of Maine

Roger Tourangeau
Connecticut College

Brian Wandell
Stanford University

Malcolm Watson
Brandeis University

A. Bond Woodruff
Northern Illinois University

Paul Wright
University of North Dakota

Philip Young
Towson State University

Sanford Zenker
State University of New York at Oneonta

Carl Zuckerman
Brooklyn College

Contents

LEARNING AND
INFORMATION PROCESSING

THE PROCESS OF DEVELOPMENT

EMOTION, MOTIVATION,
AND CONSCIOUSNESS

PART 5

PERSONALITY AND INDIVIDUALITY

PART 6

PSYCHOLOGICAL DISORDERS   PART 7

SOCIAL PSYCHOLOGY   PART 8

ABOUT THE AUTHORS

Camille B. Wortman is Associate Professor of Psychology at the University of Michigan, Ann Arbor. A social psychologist, her major research interests include reactions to uncontrollable outcomes and undesirable events, causal attribution, and reactions to stress and victimization. Wortman graduated summa cum laude from Duke University in 1969, and received her Ph.D. from Duke in 1972. Prior to joining the Michigan faculty in 1979, she was a member of the psychology faculty at Northwestern University for seven years. The introductory psychology course that she taught there was so successful that a lottery for enrollment had to be instituted because of student demand. In recognition of her excellence in undergraduate teaching, she won the Distinguished Teaching Award at Northwestern University. Since receiving her degree, Wortman has published numerous articles in every major journal in her field. She has also contributed chapters to a large number of edited books including the *Advances in Experimental Social Psychology, New Directions in Attribution Research,* and *Advances in Environmental Psychology* series. On the basis of her research, Wortman recently received the American Psychological Association's Distinguished Scientific Award for an Early Career Contribution to Psychology.

Elizabeth F. Loftus is professor of psychology at the University of Washington, Seattle. A specialist in learning and memory, she has been nationally recognized for her research on eyewitness testimony. Her book on the subject, *Eyewitness Testimony,* was published by Harvard University Press in 1979 and won an APA National Media Award in 1980. *Memory* appeared in 1980, *Essence of Statistics,* a book she coauthored, is in press, and another book on memory is also in press. Loftus received her B.A. with highest honors in mathematics and psychology from UCLA in 1966, and an M.A. (1967) and Ph.D. (1970) in psychology from Stanford University. She has been a visiting instructor at Harvard University and the National Judicial College, and was assistant professor at the New School for Social Research before moving to the University of Washington. Loftus was a Fellow at the Center for Advanced Study in the Behavioral Sciences, Stanford, 1978–79. She has published numerous articles, and travels extensively to present papers at college and university colloquia and to the legal profession. She has twice been the APA nominee for the NSF Waterman Award for outstanding contributions to science.

Until she became a psychology writer in 1979, **Mary Schieck Marshall** was manager of special projects at the college department of Random House. During her ten years in college publishing, she supervised the development of introductory texts such as *Psychology Today, Abnormal Psychology* (2d and 3d ed.), and *Understanding Psychology* (2d ed.). Marshall is a graduate with distinction of Connecticut College, Phi Beta Kappa and *magna cum laude.*

PART 1

THE SCIENCE OF PSYCHOLOGY

We begin with a discussion of psychology as an activity—its scope and its methods. Chapter 1 explores the dimensions of psychology: what psychologists do and the areas to which their activities are applied. Chapter 2 examines the methods psychologists use and the structure of psychological research.

PREVIEW

1. Psychology is the study of behavior and mental processes. It is a science, or way of collecting data, an academic discipline, or body of knowledge, and a means of promoting human welfare.

2. In psychology—as in all sciences—information is collected according to strictly defined procedures.

3. Subjects as diverse as sensation, perception, learning, memory, problem solving, communication, emotion, motivation, personality, and social interaction are investigated in psychology. The findings sometimes run counter to popular expectation.

4. When psychology emerged as a distinct discipline a hundred years ago, psychologists acted as their own subjects and studied their own thought processes. Later psychologists examined directly observable behaviors, the genetic basis for variation among individuals, and unconscious mental processes.

5. Today psychologists specialize in specific subfields and pursue careers both in and out of the academic world.

1 The dimensions of psychology

When you hear the word *psychology*, what comes to mind? Do you imagine a laboratory in which rats are run through mazes, pigeons peck at keys, and dogs salivate at the sound of a bell? Do you think of journals on such topics as learning, development, and abnormal behavior stacked on a library shelf? Or does the word conjure up images of a therapist listening to a client's problems, analyzing dreams, or providing expertise on how to raise one's children? These are common preconceptions about **psychology**, which can be defined as the study of behavior and mental processes. How accurate are they? Certainly these three images provide a very stereotyped and narrow picture of what the topic of this book is all about. Yet in a limited way each touches on an important aspect of the subject you are about to explore. First, *psychology is a science*, a set of procedures for systematically observing facts about behavior and for organizing these facts into generalizations, or laws, that seek to explain why humans and other animals act as they do. Second, *psychology is an academic discipline*, the sum of knowledge about behavior as derived from scientific research. And third, *psychology is a means of promoting human welfare*, a body of information that can be applied to help solve a variety of individual and group problems.

DEFINING PSYCHOLOGY

Psychology is a science

The hallmark of science is reliance on empirical data—that is, on information that has been systematically observed, measured, and recorded. This reliance is what differentiates science so markedly from common sense. Common sense is based on opinion, on conjecture, on conclusions drawn from personal experience. When making decisions in daily life we often appeal to common sense, and frequently this approach serves us quite well. There is one important problem, however. Because common-sense notions are never put to extensive and carefully controlled tests, we have no way of knowing when they are accurate and when they are incorrect. Science, with its emphasis on the formal testing of predictions, is designed to overcome this difficulty.

To understand the greater reliability that the methods of science afford, consider the following problem. Suppose you are teaching elementary mathematics. You are concerned about some students in your class who tend to perform poorly on math problems and who give up quickly at the first sign of failure. How could you help these students? Some teachers might try to build the children's confidence by assigning them many easy problems and thus ensuring success. In fact, many educators believe that failure experiences should be eliminated, because they only serve to elicit negative emotions on the part of the child and to make the task and/or the situation aversive.

Carol Dweck (1975) became interested in this problem. It was Dweck's hypothesis that "the way to avoid such adverse reactions to failure is not by eliminating it from the situation, but by teaching the child how to deal with it." In some of her earlier research, Dweck had found that children whose performance deteriorates under failure usually attribute their failure to factors that they are unable to change, such as their own lack of ability (Dweck and Repucci, 1973). Such children feel helpless in problem-solving situations. They believe that there is no reason to keep trying, since nothing they do will make any difference. Dweck believed that if children were taught to attribute their failure to something they could influence or control, they might respond more adaptively. In order to test her hypothesis, Dweck chose twelve children who were identified by their teachers as behaving helplessly in the face of failure. She divided the children into two equivalent groups, and gave them twenty-five days of special training involving mathematics problems. Children in one group, the "success only" condition, were assigned easy problems to solve during each training session. Those in the other group, the "attribution retraining" condition, received some easy problems. However, they were also given some very difficult problems and thus deliberately induced to fail. Each time a child failed, he or she was to attribute failure to lack of effort ("You should have tried a little harder"). At the end of the special training, both groups were tested on new arithmetic problems. The "success only" students continued to give up after each failure. But the students who had had attribution retraining improved in their reaction to failure—they persisted longer at the problems and showed much better performance in the face of failure than they had initially.

The methods of science, then, have provided important generalizations about many aspects of behavior. Yet there are still those who question whether behavior, especially human behavior, is accessible to scientific inquiry. One of psychology's most recent and widely publicized critics is William Proxmire, chairman of the Senate subcommittee that oversees the National Science Foundation (NSF). Senator Proxmire believes that certain human behaviors are too individual, too unpredictable to be studied scientifically. One of his prime targets several years ago was an NSF-funded grant for research on love. Proxmire argued:

I object to this not only because no one—not even the National Science Foundation—can argue that falling in love is a science; not only that even if they spend $84 million or $84 billion they wouldn't get an answer that anyone would believe. I am against it because I don't want the answer. I believe that 200 million other Americans want to leave some things in life a mystery, and right at the top of things we don't want to know is why a man falls in love with a woman and vice versa. (National Science Foundation Funded Projects, 1975).

Psychologists, of course, vehemently disagree. They believe that it is possible and desirable to conduct rigorous scientific research on human behavior—even on aspects of it as complex and multifaceted as love. In Chapter 17, we will include a full discussion of psychological research on love, including those research projects that Proxmire attacked. Moreover, psychologists strongly disagree that human behavior is such a mystery that it cannot possibly be understood. Psychologists believe that there are patterns underlying all phenomena in the physical universe—including human behavior. These patterns can be understood by carefully observing and measuring the ways that people respond under different conditions. From a large number of observations psychologists can then make generalizations about how human beings typically behave in a given situation. On the basis of these generalizations they can next make various predictions about how a person might act in a slightly different but related situation. By devising ways to test these predictions psychologists can further evaluate the validity of their initial generalizations, modifying them as subsequent evidence demands. This, in essence, is the process of science, and psychologists argue that it can be applied to human behavior as surely as it can be applied to the study of atoms and molecules, celestial bodies, or any aspect of the living world.

Granted, the study of human behavior often requires a great deal of ingenuity. Imagine, for example, that you wanted to know why people sometimes fail to help a stranger in distress. This is clearly an important question. We have all heard stories of city dwellers hurrying past a person who has collapsed in the street, or ignoring the victim of assault who cries for help. In 1964 this kind of behavior made headlines when a young woman was brutally stabbed to death while on her way home from work in a middle-class neighborhood of Queens, a borough of New York City. At least thirty-eight onlookers watched from their apartment windows, but nobody offered assistance. No one even called the police. Were these people heartless and uncaring, made callous by the anonymity of city life? How would you go about answering this question? Bystanders who ignore the victim of a crime or a medical emergency are seldom available for interviewing after the event has taken place. And could you even trust that the explanations they gave for their own behavior would be accurate? Psychologists John Darley and Bibb Latané circumvented these difficult problems by devising some clever experiments (Darley and Latané, 1968;

Latané and Darley, 1968). They staged a variety of "emergency" situations and recorded bystander response in each. In one experiment, smoke began pouring into a room where subjects were filling out a questionnaire; in another, subjects heard someone in the next room crash to the floor and moan in pain (actually a tape-recorded performance); in a third, a fellow subject was heard having a violent seizure (again faked); in still another, the experimenter pretended to be severely shocked by electrical equipment while subjects looked on. On the basis of these investigations, Darley and Latané made some surprising discoveries, as you will see later in this chapter.

Other aspects of human behavior are difficult to study for other reasons. How, for instance, might you investigate the role of the brain in behavior? Are different parts of the brain related to different feelings and behaviors, such as anger, aggression, and fear? Obviously, poking a person's brain with an electrode for the sole purpose of evoking an angry or a fearful response raises serious ethical questions. So psychologists interested in relationships between the brain and behavior often generalize from research done with animals other than humans. But still there is the problem of how, technically speaking, one goes about exploring the brain of a living organism. This problem baffled scientists for many generations. It is only with twentieth-century advances in technology that exploration of a living, functioning brain has come within the scientist's reach. Because the brain's activity is partly electrical, researchers have found that they can probe brain tissue with mild electrical currents. José Delgado, for example, has investigated the brains of rats, monkeys, and other animals in this way, and he has made some fascinating discoveries. In one study Delgado (as cited in Waggoner, 1970) implanted tiny electrodes in a particular part of a female monkey's brain. Now monkeys are usually devoted parents: They hold, pet, and coddle their young with great solicitude. This is why Delgado's findings were so startling. By passing a mild current through the electrodes, Delgado could provoke the mother monkey to savagely hurl her infant into the wall of the cage. When the current was turned off, the female would immediately rush to retrieve her battered offspring, once again fondling the infant tenderly. Psychologists have learned a great deal about the brain's organization and function through experiments like this one. And they have been able to apply what they have learned to a variety of human disorders. We will say much more about these procedures and their applications in Chapter 3, which focuses on the brain.

We have described just two examples of the very imaginative and diligent detective work that psychological research can entail. Throughout this book we will emphasize the theme of psychology as a creative, on-going science. You will learn much more about how psychologists formulate their theories, how they develop strategies for tracking down information, how they systematically test alternative possibilities, thereby constantly adding new dimensions to their knowledge. This theme will be especially apparent in the sections of subsequent chapters that are labeled In Depth. In these sections we will take a close-up look at particularly intriguing research problems, how investigators have tackled them, and what insights they have made. You will discover that few scientific questions are ever fully and unequivocally answered. The findings of one investigator inevitably lead to new problems, new directions, new possibilities. This is what makes the science of psychology so dynamic and exciting for researchers and students alike: there is always more to learn.

Psychology is an academic discipline

When you consider that psychology emerged as a separate discipline some hundred years ago and that today there are approximately 80,000 professional psychologists in the United States alone, you can easily imagine what a vast amount of information psychologists have already amassed. This accumulated knowledge adds another dimension to our definition of psychology: Psychology is both a science (a systematic means of obtaining reliable data) and an academic discipline (the body of information collected by these means).

The variety of topics psychologists study comes as a surprise to many people. Psychologists investigate subjects as diverse as the behavior of newborn infants, the acquisition of language, the conditions that facilitate learning, the capacity of human memory, the nature of emotion, the relationship between stress and disease, the reactions of the body during altered states of consciousness such as sleep or meditation, the factors that impede problem solving and decision making, the shaping of attitudes and prejudices, the reasons for human aggression. Psychology has something to say about many aspects of our lives. All our behavior—from the moment of conception to the moment of death—raises potential issues for psychological investigation.

One thing that makes psychology exciting as a discipline is the pace at which new knowledge is being acquired. Consider the area of physiological psychology alone. Just thirty years ago researchers knew relatively little about the function of the brain. This master control center of all behavior was viewed largely as an undifferentiated mass. Today all this has changed. Scientists have isolated some of the chemicals that help transmit information throughout the brain, and they are beginning to understand the roles these substances play in different kinds of behavior. Enormous progress has also been made in mapping the brain—that is, in identifying specific regions of brain tissue that are related to specific sensations, emotions, and behaviors. This field of investigation is changing so rapidly that it creates a problem for students—the correct answers to examination questions often change from year to year as scientists refine and improve their understanding of brain function.

Yet we are still barely at the threshold of fully understanding the brain. As tomorrow's technology makes possible even more sophisticated research techniques, even more fascinating discoveries will undoubtedly be made about this complex organ. The years ahead will offer very challenging opportunities for anyone now entering the field.

The pace at which psychological investigation is proceeding may come as a surprise to many people. But what is even more surprising to most is how much of the information gathered contradicts popular expectations about behavior. For instance, most people assume that the more highly motivated a person is, the better he or she will be at solving a complex problem (Vaughan, 1977). You probably agree with this statement yourself. However, psychologists have found that when people perform any complex task, either mental or physical, high levels of motivation usually have a detrimental effect. The highly motivated person tries to attend to too many details at once, becomes confused, and so fails to find a solution. Apparently, there is an optimum motivation level for efficient problem solving that varies with the complexity of the task. This optimum motivation level also varies with the personality of the individual, as we will discuss in Chapter 11.

For another example of insight based on psychological research consider the following statement: To change a person's negative behavior toward members of ethnic minorities, that person's prejudiced attitudes must first be changed (Vaughan, 1977). Would you say that this statement is true or false? The overwhelming majority of people believe it to be true, yet once again psychologists have challenged this common-sense assumption. In one experiment conducted many years ago, psychologists Richard LaPiere (1934) traveled around the United States with a Chinese couple, expecting to encounter anti-Oriental attitudes that would make it difficult for them to find places to eat and sleep. But this was not at all the case. "In something like ten thousand miles of motor travel," wrote LaPiere, "twice across the United States, up and down the Pacific Coast, we met definite rejection from those asked to serve us just once" (LaPiere, 1934, p. 233). Judging from the courteous reception of the innkeepers and tradespeople LaPiere and his companions encountered, one might conclude that Americans at that time were almost entirely free of prejudice against Orientals. This, however, was far from true. LaPiere followed up his travels by writing a letter to each of the 251 establishments he and his Chinese friends had visited, asking whether they would provide food or lodging to Orientals. Of the 128 who responded, more than 90 percent answered with a flat no. Thus, people do not necessarily act on their attitudes. As you will see in Chapter 17, whether a person's behavior corresponds to his or her attitudes depends in large part on the context in which that behavior occurs.

That psychology sometimes contradicts intuitive judgment about human behavior is another important theme of this book. As you both read the text and discover more about the discipline of psychology, you may be surprised to learn just how many of the "facts" about human nature that you accept as valid fail to hold up under scientific scrutiny.

Psychology is a means of promoting human welfare

Since psychology is a body of knowledge that bears on so many important aspects of our lives, it is not surprising that some psychologists are actively engaged in applying psychological principles to a variety of human problems. Such efforts are in keeping with the major goals of the American Psychological Association (APA), the principal professional organization for American psychologists. According to the APA bylaws, that organization's primary aims are to "advance scientific interests and inquiry, and the application of research findings to the promotion of the public welfare" (APA, 1968, xii).

The deliberate use of research findings to solve some practical problem or to improve the quality of human life is generally called **applied science**. Most scientific inquiry is not applied in nature. Instead, it is what researchers call **basic science**—a quest for knowledge purely for its own sake. Basic science, of course, may have important implications for the solution to a practical problem. But the specific goal of solving that problem—of effecting a "cure"—is not an aim of basic research. To illustrate the difference between applied and basic research, consider an example in the area of developmental psychology. A researcher who studies the ability of newborn infants to perceive visual patterns is doing basic research. Although she is certainly aware of the implications her findings may have for, say, the design of infants' toys, she is not directly concerned with applying these findings herself. A psychological consultant to a toy manufacturer, in contrast, focuses exclusively on the practical problems of creating play things more appealing to children. As a result, he is said to be doing applied research.

Some people have difficulty seeing the long-run benefits of basic scientific research. Consequently, they are quick to label many such studies frivolous waste of money, a criticism that is usually completely groundless. But why does the general public so easily jump to wrong conclusions? One reason is lack of understanding about how science typically progresses. What may seem at first glance to be a trivial finding can turn out to provide a small but vital clue in a larger and more important puzzle. The process of science, in other words, is largely incremental. Without the many small contributions to scientific knowledge accumulated over years of basic research, great "breakthroughs" in applied science—performing the first heart transplant, landing the first human on the moon—would certainly have never been possible.

Another reason for public underestimation of the practical value of basic research is that the full implications of a particular study are seldom spelled out for the average person. For example, a number of years ago great public outcry arose over government funding of a scientific investigation into the sexual behavior of the screwworm fly. On the surface this certainly seemed a rather trivial project for the American taxpayer to support. But closer examination revealed that it was nothing of the kind. The larvae of the screwworm fly are deadly enemies of cattle and other domesticated animals, and this study provided the information needed to develop a means of holding these insect pests in check. Apparently, the female screwworm fly mates only once in her lifetime. So by releasing many sterile males into breeding areas, the screwworm-fly population can be quite efficiently controlled. Clearly this basic research had enormous benefits to both livestock breeders and consumers.

Similar misunderstandings have occurred regarding certain kinds of psychological research. For example, consider the attempts of a number of psychologists to teach sign language to gorillas and chimpanzees. Many lay people feel that such efforts are little more than circus tricks. Of what possible value, they argue, could a "talking" chimpanzee be? But once again these critics are viewing the issue in a very narrow way. The methods developed to teach nonverbal language to apes are proving extremely helpful in efforts to teach communication skills to severely retarded children. This is not to say that the findings from research with apes are directly applicable to human subjects. But according to psychologist Richard Schiefelbusch, director of the Bureau of Child Research at the University of Kansas, apes and human children "are near enough alike for us to take advantage of the marvelous work the ape-language researchers have done" (Bazar, 1980).

One problem in judging basic research is that it is usually difficult for people to predict the ultimate significance of a particular investigator's work. For instance, many years ago the work of B. F. Skinner, who ultimately became one of the most influential psychologists in the twentieth century, was very severely attacked. Skinner was interested in the effects of rewards and punishments on an organism's behavior. He conducted a great number of experiments using such animal subjects as rats and pigeons, providing such basic rewards as food and water and such clear-cut punishments as electric shock, and observed simple learned responses such as pressing a lever or pecking at a button. The experiment on learning described earlier in this chapter as an example of the scientific approach illustrates the basic kind of study for which Skinner eventually became famous. Yet Skinner's first book, *The Behavior of Organisms* (1938), sold a mere eighty copies in its first four years in print. Much of the resistance to Skinner's early work was due to an underlying feeling that his findings had limited application. How likely was it, critics asked, for an organism as complex as a human being to respond to rewards and punishments in the same, very predictable way as a rat or a pigeon does?

Applied research in the last several decades has certainly challenged Skinner's earliest critics. Humans seem every bit as susceptible to rewards and punishments as so-called lower animals. Psychologist Nathan Azrin, for instance, who worked under Skinner as a graduate student, has divided his very productive career between basic research on learning and applied research into how the principles of reward and punishment can be used to solve human problems. Azrin began his applied work by designing procedures to teach severely retarded persons to feed and dress themselves, to use the toilet, and to refrain from such negative behaviors as bed-wetting or sprawling on the floor. These training programs proved so successful that Azrin soon expanded his efforts to alleviate common problems among intellectually normal children and adults. He has developed widely accepted therapies for problems as diverse as stuttering, nail biting, alcoholism, marital discord, and prolonged unemployment. We will say much more about such practical applications of learning theory in Chapters 5 and 16.

Much of this book will be devoted to a discussion of basic psychological research. However, we will have many occasions to mention related work being conducted by psychologists with applied orientations. These researchers have often found very creative and valuable ways to put the knowledge of basic science to practical use. In this way psychology is meeting the challenging goals set for it: to be both a science and an academic discipline, as well as a means of enhancing the welfare of all human beings.

PSYCHOLOGY YESTERDAY AND TODAY

We have briefly defined what psychology is—its aims, its methods, the fact that its knowledge is cumulative. But you may still have the feeling that you do not fully understand what psychology is about. This is probably because you have only a limited picture of exactly what psychologists study and how different psychologists have approached those topics over the years. In a sense, this entire book addresses itself to these issues. Here we simply want to step back and scan the discipline's past and present to provide an introductory overview.

Psychology's roots

Our first task is to describe the historical roots of psychology. Few things, after all, can be fully understood without some sense of the manner in which they evolved. This is true of psychology. A hundred years ago, when psychology first broke away from philosophy and physiology to emerge as a separate discipline, its subject matter and research methods were far more narrow than they are today. Psychology has grown enormously in its brief history. Perhaps the best way to appreciate this impressive growth is to examine the ideas and accomplishments of some of the people who have contributed most to it. We begin in the newly founded psychological laboratory of Professor Wilhelm Wundt at the University of Leipzig, Germany. The year is 1879.

Wundt studies conscious experience Wilhelm Wundt (1832–1920) was a meticulous and tireless scholar who devoted sixty-eight years to the study of the human mind. He was also a prolific writer, turning out more than fifty thousand pages in his long, hard-working career. Wundt's creation of a laboratory for the sole purpose of exploring the workings of human consciousness is generally considered the formal beginning of psychology as a science and a discipline (Boring, 1957). His movement, which came to be known as **structuralism**, was brought to the United States by Edward Titchener, a British psychologist who became a leading figure in American psychology in the early part of this century.

Figure 1.1 Wilhelm Wundt (1832–1920).

Wundt was impressed with the analytical approach being taken by scientists in other fields. Chemists had identified the atom as the fundamental unit of matter and were busy exploring the ways in which atoms combine with one another. Similarly, biologists had identified the cell as the basic unit of life and were beginning to learn more about the interaction of cells in living organisms. Wundt wondered if human consciousness might not also be capable of being analyzed into its constituent elements and the ways these elements were combined to form the organization, or structure, of the mind. Convinced that the answer was yes, he set out to undertake such an analysis in a systematic and scientific way.

But how can the private world of consciousness be explored scientifically? Wundt's answer was a technique called **introspection**. According to Wundt, a person properly trained to introspect can look beyond the immediate content of his or her own thoughts and focus instead on the constituent elements of consciousness. Wundt trained his young followers in introspection, and after numerous investigations under carefully controlled laboratory conditions, he came to the conclusion that conscious experience consists of three fundamental elements: sensations (the perception of external stimuli impinging on the body), images (experiences produced by the mind alone), and feelings (the emotional aspects of consciousness). All awareness, Wundt argued, consists of some combination of these three.

The frustrating aspect of Wundt's theory, critics found, was its peculiar resistance to attack. If you searched your own consciousness and arrived at conclusions different from those of Wundt, who is to say that you are right and he is wrong? Maybe the two of you are introspecting differently. Maybe you are not as keen a self-observer as Wundt. Because consciousness is such a personal realm there is no way to compare with any certainty your mental experiences with those of other people. Thus, the question of whether Wundt's ideas were right turned out to be totally unanswerable. His theories could be neither proved nor disproved.

Despite these problems, Wundt is usually considered to be the father of experimental psychology. He conducted systematic studies of the mind, in a laboratory designed specifically for that purpose, and published what was probably the first psychology journal. He also trained his students well; they started new laboratories throughout Europe. But most important, Wundt helped place psychology on a firm scientific footing by insisting that the discipline adopt the careful, rigorous methods used in the other sciences.

The Gestaltists look at the whole As psychology became recognized as a field of study, orientations different from Wundt's, and sometimes critical of it, began to emerge. One of these orientations, **Gestalt psychology**, was developed by the German psychologists Max Wertheimer (1880-1943), Kurt Koffka (1886-1941), and Wolfgang Köhler (1887-1967). The Gestaltists believed that it is impossible to divide mental life into elements, as Wundt had maintained. Although the sense organs perceive individual pieces of information, these elements are brought together by the mind and something new emerges—something different and more valuable than the individual elements of which it is composed. In other words, Gestaltists believed that "the whole is greater than the sum of its parts." When the Nazis rose to power in Germany, most of the Gestaltists fled to the United States, where they continued to study how the mind perceives and organizes information. Their work became the foundation of the study of thinking, problem solving, and sensation and perception.

The behaviorists focus on observable behavior Among Wundt's sharpest critics were a group of psychologists who came to be known as **behaviorists**. These researchers, led by the brilliant but brash young scholar John B. Watson (1878-1958), vehemently argued that subjective reports of conscious experience in no way constituted scientific evidence. By definition, they maintained, science relies only on data that can be empirically measured. Thus, if psychology was to be a science, it must banish the study of consciousness from its subject matter. Instead, psychology must be limited only to the study of observable behavior.

It is not difficult to imagine where this definition of psychology led the early behaviorists. They began to investigate how diverse environmental *stimuli* can produce a variety of *responses*. The work of Watson and his associates was strongly influenced by the pioneering studies of the great Russian physiologist Ivan Pavlov (1849-1936). In a now-famous experiement, Pavlov rang a bell a few seconds before he gave a dog some meat, a stimulus to which the dog responded by salivating profusely. After repeating this procedure many times, Pavlov found that the dog would salivate on hearing the bell alone, even though food was no longer presented. The concept of the *conditioned response*—a learned response to a previously neutral stimulus—was born. Like all behaviorists, Pavlov was accounting for present behavior (salivation) in terms of an association (bell and food) that the organism had learned in the past.

Watson took the extreme position that all behavior represents learned responses to particular environmental stimuli. Watson rejected the notion of innate, or inherited, differences in ability or temperament. He believed that by controlling environmental stimuli, he could shape an infant's character into anything one might wish. "Give me a dozen healthy infants," Watson boasted, "well-formed, and my own specified world to bring them up in and I'll guarantee to take any one at random and train him to become any type of specialist I might select—doctor, lawyer, artist, merchant-chief, and, yes, even beggar-man and thief, regardless of his talents, penchants, tendencies, abilities, vocations, and race of his ancestors" (Watson, 1924, p. 82).

Figure 1.2 John B. Watson (1878–1958).

In 1920, Watson's career came to an unfortunate end when he was forced to resign his position at Johns Hopkins University because he had divorced his wife to marry one of his former students. He engaged in a number of odd jobs, including selling coffee door-to-door and clerking in a department store. Eventually, he rose to become vice president of a New York advertising company. Yet his point of view and his writings continued to influence psychologists long after his departure from academia (McKinney, 1976).

Other American psychologists were also highly influential in directing attention to the organism's behavior. One of these was E. L. Thorndike (1874–1949), who conducted a series of innovative experiments in which cats were placed in wooden boxes that were secured from all sides. As soon as the cat performed a certain movement, such as pressing a latch or pulling a string, a door in the box opened, and the cat was given some food. Although the cats' first successful responses were largely a matter of chance, their activities became concentrated in the area of the release mechanism, and eventually they performed the correct response as soon as they were placed in the box. On the basis of this work, Thorndike became the first psychologist to emphasize the importance of rewards in learning. He argued that if an animal comes to associate a particular response with a reward, that response will be strengthened; if an animal comes to associate a particular response with some sort of punishment, the response will generally weaken (the organism will emit it less frequently).

The contemporary American psychologist B. F. Skinner (1904–) refined this view and ensured its continuation to the present day. Skinner has both narrowed the predictive claims of behaviorism and has broadened its social implications. He has tried to show how his laboratory techniques might be applied to society as a whole. His classic, still widely read novel *Walden Two* (1948) portrays what is no doubt his idea of Utopia: a small community in which every conceivable facet of life is molded through the careful application of rewards.

Like any influential person, Skinner has both critics and disciples. Some are convinced that his conditioning techniques would severely limit personal freedom. Others applaud him as a social visionary whose approach could greatly improve the quality of human life. You will probably want to reserve your own judgment until you read more about behaviorism in Chapter 5. For now, the important point to remember is that Skinner's theories and methods have had an enormous impact on both the general public and the science of psychology. Behaviorist techniques are currently vying with more traditional therapeutic approaches in the treatment of various psychological disorders. And many people now toilet-train their children, lose weight, quit smoking, and overcome phobias using Skinner-inspired methods.

Galton begins exploring individual differences Psychologists have been strongly influenced by one of the giants of modern scientific thought, Charles Darwin (1809–1882). Darwin set forth his theory of biological evolution in his famous book *The Origin of Species* (1859) and in his subsequent work *The Descent of Man* (1871). Backed by masses of biological evidence collected over many years, he proposed that all living organisms are descended from much simpler forms of life. Humans, in other words, are not above nature, as many theologians of the time believed. Instead, they are part of nature, related through distant ancestry to every other living thing. Darwin's ideas sparked an explosive controversy that has still not completely subsided. Thoughtful people everywhere were forced to revise their conceptions of humankind's place in the biological world. This included psychologists. The message of their emerging discipline was clear: The roots of human behavior may be partially found through the study of other animal species, especially our closest living relatives, the apes and monkeys. This is why the behaviorists believed they could develop general principles of behavior by studying the responses of dogs, rats, pigeons, and other "lower" animals.

Darwin's ideas also helped shape another line of psychological inquiry—investigation into the genetic basis of human variability. That human variability could have a genetic base was diametrically opposed to the views of the behaviorists, although both were influenced by Darwin. But Darwin's concepts were so provocative it is little wonder that different researchers hastened to apply them to their own particular points of view. One of these researchers was Sir Francis Galton (1822–1911), a cousin of Darwin. Throughout his world travels, Galton had observed great differences in all kinds of human traits. He became convinced that these differences—physical, mental, and moral—were the result of genetic inheritance. In an attempt to verify this view, Galton traced the ancestry of various eminent people. He found that greatness runs in families. (Interestingly, Galton himself was considered a genius, and his cousin Charles Darwin was certainly a towering intellectual figure.) Galton published his findings in a book called *Hereditary Genius* (1869), which, as the title implies, set forth his argument that genius is a hereditary trait. We know today, of course, that this conclusion was premature. Galton ignored the alternative possibility that the tendency of genius to run in families might be the result of the exceptional environments and numerous social and economic advantages that close relatives also tend to share. Still, Galton's ideas captured the imagination of many other scholars of his time, and he pointed to a new direction that psychologists might take.

In order to investigate the genetic basis of human characteristics, Galton realized that he must find ways to accurately measure the traits that interested him. Remember that in Galton's day there was no such thing as an IQ or a personality test. So Galton set about inventing them. The measurement techniques he devised, although primitive, were the forebears of the modern personality and intelligence tests that every reader of this book has probably taken. But how could Galton compare the measurements he made and present them to others in a way that would be clear and meaningful? Again, the inventive Galton created the tools he needed, most notably a statistical measurement called the correlation coefficient. As you will see in Chapter 2, researchers in all branches of science still use the correlation coefficient to state the degree to which two variables are generally found together—that is, are correlated.

Although Galton began his work shortly before psychology emerged as an independent discipline, his theories and techniques quickly became central aspects of the new science. Clearly, many of his ideas, especially as later elaborated by test developers like Alfred Binet, collided head-on with behaviorism, which stated emphatically that the key to individual differences is not heredity but learning. The issue of whether human behavior is determined largely by heredity or by environment has flared into a heated controversy, especially in recent years. It lies at the center of such explosive topics as the reasons for differences between men and women. In general, people who have assigned a dominant role to heredity in determining characteristics like intelligence and personality have also tended to conclude that these traits are very resistant to change. Critics of this view claim that it provides an easy rationalization for maintaining discrimination. We will say much more about the heredity-environment controversy and the light psychologists have shed on it in Chapters 8 and 14.

The functionalists broaden the definition of psychology Another orientation strongly influenced by Darwin's theory of evolution was called **functionalism**. While Wundt and his followers had devoted most of their efforts to studying the structure of the mind, many psychologists in the United States were beginning to believe that understanding the mind's structure is not as important as understanding its activities or functions and the stream of consciousness that characterizes mental life. Since Darwin's theory maintained that there were not only similarities in bodily structure among all animals, including humans, but similarities in mental functioning as well, American psychologists became more interested in animal behavior than their European counterparts had been. At the turn of the century, many studies of animal behavior were in progress, including Thorndike's (1898) studies of cats in a puzzle box, and Watson's (1907) work on maze learning in the rat.

Funtionalism gained much prestige through the influence of William James (1842-1910), the brother of novelist Henry James. James studied medicine at Harvard, but the experience left him cynical about the practice of medicine. "With the exception of surgery, in which something positive is sometimes accomplished," he wrote in a letter to his cousin, "a doctor does more by the moral effect of his presence on the patient and family, than by anything else" (Miller, 1962). He decided to take a teaching job instead of going into practice, and was hired at Harvard in the 1870s to teach physiology. His earlier experiences in medicine had made him curious about the relationship between the mind and the body, however, and he decided to offer a course called "The Relations Between Physiology and Psychology". After teaching the course for three years, James became increasingly interested in psychology and agreed to write a text—the first textbook ever to be published in psychology—on this new and growing science. The book was filled with provocative insights about human behavior, and included such subjects as habits, emotions, consciousness, and the self. One of his most enduring contributions was his theory of emotion, which we will explore in more detail in Chapter 10. James was also an important figure in philosophy who made major contributions to our understanding of religious experience. His writings underscored the functionalist theme that the aim of mental life is to guide the organism in coping successfully with its environment.

The functionalist orientation resulted in the broadening of the definition and the methods of psychology. Studies of animals, the mentally retarded, the insane were all considered appropriate for exploring how the mind functioned.

Freud starts psychologists probing the unconscious No discussion of the history of psychological thought is complete without some mention of a remarkably imaginative Viennese physician named Sigmund Freud (1856-1939). Freud was impressed with the results that another Viennese doctor, Josef Breuer, had obtained in his treatment of a woman suffering from hysterical

Figure 1.3 Sigmund Freud (1856-1939).

Figure 1.4 William James (1842-1910).

paralysis. Breuer found that if he hypnotized this woman, she was able to discuss the psychological causes of her disorder quite freely, and after such discussion her condition tended to improve. Both Breuer and Freud became convinced that hysterical paralysis as well as other psychosomatic symptoms were the result of "unconscious" conflicts that, once brought to the patient's awareness, would lose their power to control that person's life. It was Freud, however, who developed this basic idea into an elaborate theory of personality development and structure.

The evolution of Freud's ideas grew out of his analysis of a large number of patients who came to him with symptoms that had no apparent physiological cause. Unlike Breuer, Freud rejected the use of hypnosis to bring a person's troubling thoughts into consciousness. Instead, he developed a method called **free association**, in which a patient said everything that came to mind, no matter how foolish or irrelevant it sounded. Freud also encouraged patients to talk about their dreams because he believed that dreams contained symbolic clues to the content of the unconscious mind. With this verbal information Freud helped his patients to interpret and understand their symptoms. The ultimate goal was for the patient to consciously recognize the psychological roots of his or her problem. This approach to treating neurotic symptoms Freud named **psychoanalysis**.

Freud took meticulous, extensive notes during all his treatment sessions. He found that when a patient's memory was probed for the critical events that had caused his or her symptoms to emerge, the most significant memories were usually those of some forbidden sexual experience during childhood. Based on this discovery Freud proposed that much of human behavior is driven by powerful biological urges, especially sexual ones, that often conflict with society's moral standards. It is these primitive impulses, Freud contended, that are buried in the recesses of the unconscious. When they break through our normal controls, they can give rise to neurotic anxiety.

Although Freud's modern-day followers have substantially modifed his original theories, Freud's ideas have had a powerful impact on psychology. We will explore the details of Freudian personality theory in Chapter 13. There you will learn that Freud saw the human psyche as composed of three constantly warring forces—the pleasure-seeking *id*, the pragmatic *ego*, and the idealistic *superego*. In Chapter 8 you will encounter Freud's ideas regarding psychological development from infancy to adolescence. Freud believed that every child passes through a series of stages in which the need for sexual gratification centers on a different part of the body. The idea that young children have sexual motivations deeply shocked the Victorian society in which Freud lived and worked. Yet Freud's controversial notions survived much vehement opposition to become a major influence on twentieth-century thought. Many contemporary researchers may strongly refute Freudian psychology, but almost no one can ignore it completely.

Building on the past As we have suggested in this brief overview of the history of psychological thought, many of the specific beliefs held by early investigators have since been rejected or modified. Yet their ideas have become the foundation for more modern and sophisticated points of view. Wundt's notions about the organization of consciousness, for instance, have long since been abandoned as untestable. But psychology still owes him a debt for giving the discipline the beginnings of a systematic, experimental approach. Though few psychologists today identify themselves as Gestaltists, that movement's recognition of the importance of context and the whole pattern of events formed the basis for the modern cognitive approaches to thinking and problem solving. Similarly, few psychologists today consider themselves to be strict behaviorists. Unlike the early behaviorists, most contemporary psychologists believe that what goes on within the mind of an organism is not only accessible to scientific inquiry but also of vital importance to understanding processes like thinking, remembering, and problem solving. Researchers like Pavlov and Watson were largely responsible for initiating the current definition of psychology as the study of behavior, even though that definition has now been expanded to include "mental behavior" as well as overt physical activities. And the behaviorist concept of learning by association has influenced nearly every field that psychologists investigate. Turning to the contribution of Galton we find a similar pattern. Even though his ideas were highly simplistic by today's standards, Galton helped initiate the modern-day version of the heredity-environment debate. He also started the development of measurement techniques on which contemporary psychologists still rely. The functionalist emphasis on the use of the mind drew attention to the importance of mental life in adapting to and coping with the environment. And this insight led, in turn, to the recognition of the importance of learning as a means of adapation. Finally, Freud, however much his original ideas have been refuted and modified, still gave psychology the very important concept that people are often influenced by powerful motivations hidden from conscious awareness. As you read and study more about psychology in subsequent chapters, you will repeatedly see how contemporary researchers have built on these fundamental ideas.

Contemporary fields of specialization

One hundred or even fifty years ago, a single diligent scholar could conceivably stay abreast of most developments in psychology. The discipline was young enough and narrowly enough focused to make such an undertaking possible. Today this has changed. With the diversity of subjects into which contemporary psychologists delve, and with some 80,000 active researchers in the United States alone, one person would be overwhelmed by the volumes of reading required to keep up with all the latest findings in every subfield of the discipline. Psychologists, by necessity, have become specialists, just like their colleagues in every other modern science. To get some idea of the diversity and specialization that exists in psychology today, consider some of the topics discussed at a recent meeting of the American Psychological Association. Psychologists explored subjects as varied as brain function in gifted children; visual analysis and memory among skilled readers; underlying causes of intense sensation seeking; food additives and hyperactivity; teacher diagnosis of learning disabilities; illicit alcohol use among elementary-school children; male-female differences in verbal assertiveness; programs for preventing and stopping smoking; approaches to treating depressed children; stress and coping in surgical patients; workplace design and worker behavior; amphetamine effects on the brain; the psychology of dieting, depression, and overeating; and the family life of pathological gamblers. Clearly such a range of topics is too broad for any one person to master.

Because of the enormous scope of psychology, we will not even attempt to describe all aspects of it here. Your understanding of the kinds of questions psychologists ask and how they go about answering them will grow as you study this discipline. At this point, we simply wish to provide a sample of some of the fascinating issues that researchers in different fields of specialization are raising. Our goal is both to acquaint you in very general terms with the different areas of psychology and to pique your interest in the subject matter of this diverse discipline.

Experimental and physiological psychology Everyone has had the frustrating experience of having a word on the tip of their tongue. The word is so close you can almost say it, and yet stubbornly it refuses to come. During these times you typically grope your way through a list of possible responses until the desired word eventually pops into mind. How did you manage to locate it? Did you search for the word by sound? By meaning? In some other way? The answers to such questions provide important clues to the way that information is "filed" in the brain. When you consider that a person stores and retrieves literally millions of facts over an average lifetime, you begin to realize how incredibly efficient this filing system must be. As you will see in Chapter 6, psychologists Roger Brown and David NcNeill (1966) devised a very clever way of creating the tip-of-the-tongue phenomenon in the laboratory in order to investigate the organization of memory. Their findings, and those of other researchers, have provided some intriguing insights into the way that the human information processing system works.

The organization of memory is just one of an enormous number of issues that **experimental psychologists** investigate. Unfortunately, the term *experimental psychology* is a bit of a misnomer. It implies that this field is defined strictly by the use of experimentation as a data-gathering technique. Experimental psychologists do rely largely on laboratory experiments to explore their topics of interest. But this fact alone is insufficient to distinguish them from their colleagues in other fields. Researchers in many other areas of psychology might also use a controlled experiment to help answer a question about behavior. So to define experimental psychology we must look as much to its subject matter as to its methods. The experimental psychologist focuses attention on one of several "basic" behavioral processes—basic in the sense that they are shared by a variety of animal species. These processes include sensation, perception, learning, memory, problem solving, communication, emotion, and motivation.

To understand what a broad and rich field of investigation this is, consider some recent discoveries that experimental psychologists have made.

In the area of perception, Blakemore and Cooper (1970) have helped to demonstrate the startling degree to which early life experiences shape how we see the world. They exposed newborn kittens to severely restricted visual stimuli, such as an environment with *only* horizontal patterns. Within a few weeks, these kittens were functionally blind to vertically oriented objects! Apparently, the development of normal visual capabilities depends in part on growing up in a visually normal world. We will discuss the link between perception and early life experiences in more detail in Chapter 4.

In the area of learning, John Garcia has found that when a rat learns to associate the taste of a particular food with illness, it develops a remarkably strong aversion to eating that food again (Garcia and Koelling, 1966). You may have acquired this kind of aversion yourself if you once ate a food that made you violently sick. Why are such associations learned so quickly and intensely? Garcia's answer is discussed in Chapter 5.

Figure 1.5 Experimental psychologists who work with animals try to find parallels between the behavior of their subjects and that of humans. This psychologist has found that rats, like many people, enjoy a cocktail after a hard day and that "rat drinking patterns often mimic those of harried executives."

In the area of motivation, a number of researchers have shown that obese animals, including humans, are extremely sensitive to external eating cues (Decke, 1971; Schachter, 1971a; Schachter, 1971b). They will gorge themselves on a good-tasting meal but shun food that is bland or slightly bitter. They will eat every last morsel of food that is placed within sight and easy reach, but if securing food involves any degree of effort the obese subject suddenly becomes indifferent. Why this finickiness in an organism inclined to overeat? Some possible causes will be explored in Chapter 11.

As you read more about experimental psychology, you will soon discover that biological explanations feature prominently in many of the issues raised. How can environmental stimuli permanently affect an organism's visual capabilities? The secret is found somewhere in the development of the animal's brain. Why are learned taste aversions so persistent? The answer probably lies in the structure of the nervous system among animals with diverse diets. Why would obese humans be such curiously choosy eaters? The ultimate control mechanisms once again are located somewhere in the brain. Researchers who study the underlying physical bases of behavior are called **physiological psychologists**. They focus on how the body's two principal communication networks—the nervous system and the endocrine glands—are related to virtually any response an organism might make.

Because most experimental and physiological psychologists are engaged in basic research, they tend to be affiliated with college and universities, as Table 1.1 indicates. However, a substantial minority—approximately 20 percent—have jobs outside of academia. Some of them work in clinical settings where they help to develop treatment programs of various kinds. An experimental psychologist, for example, might be involved in training people with chronic pain to lead more productive lives (Woods, 1976). Others are employed in private industry—for instance, pharmaceutical corporations hire such psychologists to assess the effects of newly developed drugs. In fact, as scientists learn more about the way the brain and nervous system function, **psychopharmacology** (the study of the relationship between drugs and behavior) is a very rapidly growing field.

TABLE 1.1 Doctorate Psychologists by Subfield and Employment Setting: 1972

Subfield	Schools	Junior colleges	Colleges	Univer-sities	Hospitals and clinics	Independent or group practice	Research or consulting organizations	Business and Industry	Government agencies	Other	No report	Total
Clinical	177	81	392	1,978	2,103	1,089	98	9	279	139	434	6,779
Counseling	70	102	290	1,056	200	84	39	9	94	40	96	2,080
Community	5	0	14	115	104	4	12	2	67	5	21	349
Developmental	13	22	130	567	23	6	24	1	31	5	61	883
Educational	95	33	211	797	24	12	86	18	45	18	82	1,421
Experimental/ comparative/physiological	5	18	406	1,423	76	3	113	28	86	21	71	2,250
General	3	23	75	109	5	5	7	1	7	3	14	252
Industrial/organizational	7	6	85	577	9	39	368	285	103	35	71	1,585
Personality	2	6	56	208	10	7	8	3	8	8	26	342
Psychometrics	2	2	12	103	7	3	27	20	15	4	8	203
School	444	10	45	184	20	11	6	4	7	2	64	797
Social	7	17	147	752	28	11	65	14	61	21	54	1,177
Other	9	5	34	215	29	14	39	13	26	14	42	440
No report	265	45	179	811	253	134	98	64	111	136	556	2,652
Total	1,104	370	2,076	8,895	2,891	1,422	990	471	940	451	1,600	21,210

Source: American Psychological Association. *1972 manpower survey.* Unpublished data, Washington, D.C., 1972.

Personality psychology If a person is independent, ambitious, self-reliant, and assertive (traits we usually consider "masculine"), what is the likelihood that he or she is also affectionate, gentle, compassionate, and sensitive (traits we usually consider "feminine")? Even in today's world of sex-role liberation, many people still maintain that these traits simply do not mix. They see masculinity and femininity as polar opposites, as two ends of a single continuum. Yet psychologist Sandra Bem has gathered impressive evidence that this common assumption is entirely wrong. Some men and women are truly androgynous: They successfully combine both masculine and feminine traits. (The term androgyny comes from the Greek words *andro*, which means male, and *gyne*, which means female.) Bem argues that such people are far more adaptable than those who portray strict masculine or feminine stereotypes. They can behave either assertively and independently or compassionately and affectionately depending on the demands of the situation (Bem, 1974, 1975).

Bem's research is an important example of the kinds of issues **personality psychologists** explore. Personality psychology is a field of investigation that focuses on measuring and explaining individual differences in behavior. To what extent is one person more aggressive than another, more manipulative, more outgoing, more obedient to authority? And how can we account for any differences in personality that researchers might observe? Is there something "inside" that makes us think, feel, and act in distinctive and characteristic ways? Are people driven by biological forces? Do we inherit personality traits? Or do "outside" factors—our experiences and personal histories, our culture, the times in which we live, the unique, immediate situation—largely shape the ways that we respond? How, in other words, does personality develop? And perhaps most important, can and does personality change over time? These are the central questions that personality psychologists ask. We will investigate them in detail in Chapters 8 and 13.

Social psychology Earlier we mentioned the innovative methods of psychologists John Darley and Bibb Latané in their study of bystander apathy. These researchers staged a series of bogus emergencies—fires, freak accidents, robberies, medical catastrophes—and watched to see whether unsuspecting witnesses would offer assistance. Their findings were somewhat disturbing: The willingness to help was *not* related to individual personality traits. A genuinely kind and sensitive person could ignore a stranger in apparent trouble as surely as a selfish person could. The factor that *did* influence how onlookers responded was the situation in which they found themselves. Bystanders were far more likely to seek or provide assistance in an emergency when they were alone than when in groups of two or more. Surprisingly, the presence of other people actually appears to inhibit the helping response. We will suggest some reasons for this phenomenon in Chapter 18.

You may be thinking that the powerful influence of other people revealed in Darley and Latané's research must be unique to emergency situations. If so, you are wrong. **Social psychologists** have shown repeatedly that our behavior is not just the result of our personalities and predispositions. Environmental factors, especially the presence and actions of others, greatly influence what we think, say, and do. This finding sheds light on many incidents that would otherwise be difficult to explain. How could a company of American soldiers have massacred nearly five hundred civilians, most of them women and children, at the Vietnamese village of My Lai? Social psychologist Stanley Milgram (1963) has demonstrated the incredible extent to which average people will inflict severe pain on their fellow human beings if an authority figure requires them to do so. How can intelligent, well-informed adults make decisions that are so terrible, so poorly thought out that any casual observer could point out their flaws? Social psychologist Irving Janis (1972) believes they may be victims of "groupthink." He argues that in a small, closely knit group the pressures for conformity and unanimity can become so great that members can no longer appraise alternatives realistically. In Chapters 17 and 18 we will explore these and many other examples of how human perceptions, beliefs, motivations, and behaviors are often influenced by situational factors, especially by the actions of other people. This is the unique and fascinating perspective of social psychology.

Industrial and organizational psychology Work. It is what most of us do at least half our waking hours for more than forty years. How can these thousands of hours on the job be made more pleasurable, more productive, more personally rewarding and satisfying? These are some of the questions of interest to **industrial psychologists** and **organizational psychologists**, those who focus on the relationship between individuals and their work.

The growing influence of psychology in the workplace is not a new phenomenon. It began many years ago with the use of intelligence and aptitude tests to help screen job applicants. But in recent decades the application of psychology to work-related problems has expanded enormously. One sizable challenge has been worker morale—curing the much-publicized "blue-collar blues" and "white-collar woes." To this end, some industrial psychologists have designed job-enrichment programs, especially at lower-level levels of employment where tasks are often repetitive and quickly become routine. Although job-enrichment programs vary in content, all involve efforts to improve the content of work by creating assignments that are more varied, by making the significance of tasks more salient, and by giving workers greater responsibility for outcomes. Some of the most innovative experiments with job enrichment have taken place in the Swedish automotive industry. In the early 1970s, for example, SAAB largely abolished its assembly line in favor of small, self-supervised work teams. Although job enrichment has not always been successful and is certainly no industrial panacea, many of these programs have been rated quite favorably both by employers and employees.

But creating and implementing job-enrichment programs is only one aspect of the work that industrial and organizational psychologists do. As Table 1.1 shows, more than 50 percent of the people in this field are employed outside of academia—in business and industry, in government agencies, in research or consulting firms, in independent or group practices. There they perform a great variety of tasks, including screening candidates for entry-level jobs and promotions and evaluating the performance of those who are selected (the domain of a subfield called **personnel psychology**), developing worker- and management-training programs, providing career counseling, and conducting market research on consumer attitudes and preferences.

An area closely related to industrial psychology is **engineering psychology**, the study of the relationship between human beings and machines. The major goal of engineering psychologists is to create machines that can be operated with maximum ease, efficiency, and safety. These technologists have contributed to the design of a wide range of twentieth-century inventions, including automobiles, jet airplanes, spacecraft, assembly lines, and computers.

Developmental psychology That people constantly change over time—physically, intellectually, emotionally, socially—is apparent to anyone who has ever watched a young child grow. What is less apparent, however, is the extent of these changes and how systematic and predictable most of them are. Consider the development of moral conceptions as studied by the Swiss psychologist Jean Piaget. When told the two stories in Figure 1.6 and asked which boy should be punished more severely, children under the age of seven typically insist that John, who broke fifteen cups, is by far the naughtier of the two. For children of this age the world is largely limited to concrete and observable facts. Hence, they measure misbehavior solely in terms of the objective damage done. Older children, in contrast, are able to infer a person's intentions and use these to assess wrongdoing. They understand that John did not "mean" to break anything and so is absolved from blame. Henry, on the other hand, although he broke only one cup, did so while in the act of doing something forbidden. According to this more sophisticated reasoning, in which intentions take precedence over consequences, Henry should be punished the most (Piaget, 1948).

Developmental psychology is the branch of the discipline that focuses on describing and explaining the systematic changes that occur in human beings throughout the life cycle, from conception to death. The development of moral

A little boy who is called John is in his room. He is called to dinner. He goes into the dining room. But behind the door there was a chair, and on the chair there was a tray with fifteen cups on it. John couldn't have known that there was all this behind the door. He goes in, the door knocks against the tray, bang go the fifteen cups and they all get broken!

Once there was a little boy whose name was Henry. One day when his mother was out he tried to get some jam out of the cupboard. He climbed up on a chair and stretched out his arm. But the jam was too high up and he couldn't reach it and have any. But while he was trying to get it he knocked over a cup. The cup fell down and broke.

Figure 1.6 In studying the moral development of children, Piaget selected a basic problem: What determines the seriousness of a crime? Each of these stories considers two relevant factors: the extent of the damage and the motive of the criminal. Younger children tend to take the first factor into consideration when assessing the seriousness of a crime, while older children pay more attention to the second (Piaget, 1948).

reasoning is just one of many topics that developmental psychologists study. In fact, virtually every field of psychology—from sensation and perception to learning and memory, thinking and problem solving, emotion and motivation, personality and social interaction—can be studied from a developmental perspective. How do newborn infants perceive the world? Do they see stable objects and hear identifiable sounds? Or are their surroundings a confusing perceptual blur? Why is it that most of us remember nothing about our first year of life? Are infants incapable of remembering? In what ways do children differ intellectually from adults? Why is it that a four-year-old will tell you that a lump of clay grows "bigger" as it is rolled into a snake, whereas an adult can easily see that the quantity of the clay does not change with a simple change in shape? What about intellectual skills during later life? Do memory, learning, and problem-solving abilities decline in old age? How did you develop your unique personality, your customary ways of interacting with other people? Are there any basic differences in personality between males and females, and if so, how can these differences be explained? The answers to these and many other questions are explored in Chapter 8.

Educational and school psychology The formal educational process is such an important part of twentieth-century life that it is not surprising to find psychologists who specialize in analyzing and improving it. The factors that contribute to good and bad teaching are not just a matter of common sense. To understand how true this statement is, consider a clever experiment performed by three psychologists studying the topic of teacher evaluation (Naftulin, Ware, and Donnelly, 1973). These researchers had a professional actor give a lecture to a rather perceptive student audience, which consisted of psychologists, psychiatrists, social workers, and educators. The actor was to deliver his discourse in a captivating style and with great enthusiasm—but the material he presented was totally without substance! The speech was filled with non sequiturs and invented words, circular reasoning and self-contradictions. Did students judge this lecturer to be terrible, as he certainly deserved to be judged? Not at all. All four groups in the audience rated this charming but double-talking teacher quite favorably. Apparently, student ratings of teacher effectiveness bear little or no relation to the knowledge and scholarly ability a teacher has. The highly rated teacher, some psychologists argue, is simply an exceptionally good talker (Kulik and McKeachie, 1975). Such findings clearly have important implications for the role of student evaluations in determining faculty salaries and promotions.

Research into the factors that contribute to a positive student evaluation is just one of a wide range of issues that **educational psychologists** investigate. Educational psychologists are concerned with all psychological aspects of the learning process. What factors affect a student's performance in the classroom? How important is motivation? IQ? Personality? The use of rewards and punishments? The size of the class? The expectations of the teacher? The manner in which the student and teacher interact? How can a student's performance best be evaluated? What are the strengths and weaknesses of various kinds of tests and other assessment techniques? What teaching approaches are most effective for students with various kinds of learning disabilities? As Table 1.1 shows, 73 percent of educational psychologists work in colleges and universities where they conduct basic or applied research and help train future educators and psychologists. Of the minority employed outside of academia, many are engaged in developing teaching materials and procedures for large school systems, government agencies, the military, and private business.

In contrast to educational psychology, **school psychology** is a strictly applied field. More than half the school psychologists in this country work in elementary and secondary schools. Their job is usually to assess children who have emotional or learning difficulties and to recommend to teachers and parents how these students might best be helped. Frequently a school psychologist will counsel children with mild behavioral problems. In addition, he or she is often required to administer a variety of standardized tests, such as tests of intelligence, achievement, and personality.

Clinical and counseling psychology Not too many years ago eight men and women presented themselves at the admitting offices of eight mental hospitals in five states. All were troubled by a similar symptom: They claimed to hear voices whispering gloomy messages like "hollow," "empty," and "thud." All were diagnosed as psychotic and admitted to the hospital wards. Then a curious thing happened. These patients reported no further symptoms. In fact, they behaved quite normally in every way; they were models of courtesy and cooperation. Within one to seven-and-a-half weeks their psychoses were proclaimed "in remission" (temporarily abated), and each was released from the hospital. Does this sound to you like a routine occurrence in the treatment of the psychologically disturbed? If so, you are certainly mistaken. In reality these eight patients were not psychotic at all. They were people from various walks of life who had agreed to take part in a psychological experiment. The experiment involved trying to get admitted to a mental hospital on the basis of a fictitious symptom and then seeing how the hospital staff would react to subsequent normal behavior. The startling finding was that not one staff member at any of the eight hospitals ever gave a hint that he or she suspected the fraud. Quite the contrary. They sometimes interpreted perfectly rational behavior as pathological because such interpretations "fit" the original diagnosis that these people were severely disturbed.

This provocative study conducted in the early 1970s (Rosenhan, 1973) rekindled a long-standing controversy among **clinical psychologists**, those who specialize in the diagnosis and treatment of behavior disorders. How accurate are professional diagnoses of abnormal behavior if eight sane people can be mistakenly labeled insane? And if diagnostic procedures are relatively unreliable, of what value are they? As you will see in Chapter 15, which begins a detailed discussion of clinical psychology, strong arguments have been raised on both sides of this important issue.

Clinical psychology, of course, involves much more than diagnosis alone. It also involves investigation into the causes of behavior disorders and into how such disorders can best be treated. Here, too, clinical psychologists frequently disagree. Are behavior disorders the result of unresolved conflicts and unconscious motivations, as Freud originally proposed? Or are behavior disorders learned responses that can be unlearned with proper training? Is there a biological basis to many psychopathologies, and if so, what might the underlying mechanisms be? As you will discover in Chapter 16, different answers to these questions have given rise to a wide variety of treatment programs for problems as diverse as phobias, depression, paranoia, and drug dependence.

Given the issues with which clinical psychologists are concerned, it is not surprising that nearly half are employed in hospitals, clinics, and private practice. There they often work closely with two other specialists in the mental-health field: the psychiatrist and the psychoanalyst. Unlike clinical psychologists, who have earned a Ph.D. and have completed specialized training in diagnosis and psychotherapy, **psychiatrists** first earn an M.D. and complete a medical internship, as other physicians do. Then, during a three-year residency program in psychiatry, nearly always in a hospital, they receive specific training in the treatment of mental disorders. As physicians, psychiatrists can prescribe drugs and use other medical procedures that clinical psychologists cannot. Some psychiatrists go on to become **psychoanalysts**, practictioners of the form of therapy originally developed by Freud. To become a psychoanalyst, psychiatrists must extensively study psychoanalytic theory, undergo psychoanalysis themselves, and analyze clients under the supervision of an experienced analyst. Psychoanalytic institutes that provide such training are found in a number of major cities.

Whereas clinical psychologists generally treat people with serious psychological disorders, **counseling psychologists** usually help those with much milder problems of social and emotional adjustment. Some counseling psychologists specialize in particular areas, such as marriage or family life. They may also help normally adjusted people to set vocational goals. As Table 1.1 suggests, most counseling psychologists provide their services to students in educational settings.

Emerging fields of specialization In addition to the areas we have discussed so far, psychologists are increasingly developing specialties in a number of less traditional fields. One of these is **environmental psychology**, the study of the relationship between human beings and all aspects of their environment. The growth of environmental psychology in recent years has been prompted by a general public concern that conditions of modern urban civilization have caused the quality of life to decline. Environmental psychologists help answer such questions as: How can the design of high density housing be made more amenable to human beings? What are the effects of excessive noise, heat, chemical pollutants, and overcrowding on human welfare, and how can these problems be alleviated? What can be done to encourage people to use mass transportation or to conserve energy? Because of their applied focus, environmental psychologists are often found outside traditional departments of psychology. For instance, they may be employed by a government agency like the Department of Transportation or the Department of Energy, serve as consultants to city planners in large metropolitan areas, or teach and conduct research at a school of architecture.

Another growing field is **forensic psychology**, the application of psychological principles to the problems of law enforcement and the courts. Today, forensic psychologists perform a variety of tasks. In urban police departments, for example, they evaluate officers who have emotional problems, help select psychologically stable recruits, analyze clues to construct personality profiles of those responsible for crimes, and help train police to handle crowd control, hostage crises, suicide threats, violent family quarrels, and any other situations that require an understanding of personality variables and reactions to stress. In addition, forensic psychologists are also found in correctional institutions

Figure 1.7 Forensic psychologists may work in prisons where they counsel inmates, using a variety of treatment techniques. Here a forensic psychologist and a case worker, using the family approach, meet with an inmate and his wife.

where, among their duties, they counsel and advise inmates and provide psychotherapy to those who have severe emotional problems. Another area for the skills of the forensic psychologist is the court system. Here they are often called on to determine the competency of a defendant to stand trial and to consult with judges and attorneys regarding the psychological aspects of a case. Because of the very specialized focus of forensic psychology, programs designed exclusively to train people in this field have now begun to appear.

Opportunities for psychologists are also expanding in the field of **health and health care**. For years scientists have known that emotional stress is related to certain illnesses like ulcers and heart disease. Now they are beginning to realize that the human psyche may play a role in many other physical disorders, from the common cold to cancer. In fact, some researchers suspect that psychological factors may be involved in the onset and progress of all diseases, as you will learn in Chapter 10. If this is so, then psychologists can obviously make a very important contribution to modern health care and disease prevention. For example, they can identify the psychological correlates of disease and devise ways to test individuals for susceptibility to illness. They can add to our current understanding of just how a psychological factor such as stress or depression can have a deleterious effect on the body. They can identify the psychological and social factors that motivate people to engage in behaviors that are hazardous to health, such as smoking and overeating, to ignore the signs of incipient disease until a condition is far advanced, or to neglect prescribed medical treatment once an illness has been diagnosed. They can help identify the most effective psychological strategies for coping with a serious disease or disability, for recent research suggests that a person's psychological response to catastrophe has a significant impact on his or her recovery. New programs to train psychological researchers and practitioners specifically in the health field will undoubtedly develop in the coming years.

A final emerging field of specialization in psychology is that of **program evaluation**. Logic suggests that not all government programs designed to alleviate social problems can be equally effective. Yet until quite recently, no systematic effort was made to determine which programs were working and which were not, and among those that appeared to be working which were most beneficial relative to their cost. Clearly such efforts were needed to avoid wasteful spending and accomplish our national aims. Thus the field of program evaluation came into being. Many observers feel that psychologists can make a unique contribution to program evaluation. With their intensive training in experimental methods, psychologists have the skills needed to rigorously measure and compare both the variables that go into a particular program and the results they bring about. Until now, participation of psychologists in program evaluation has been fairly modest and limited to certain areas such as education. But in the years ahead, more psychologists will undoubtedly be finding jobs in this important field and working on problems as diverse as health care, employment, transportation, energy conservation, and criminal rehabilitation.

PSYCHOLOGY AS A VOCATION AND A PERSPECTIVE

To prepare for a career in many of the fields discussed in the previous sections, a person must earn a doctoral degree. Traditionally, this has meant a Doctor of Philosophy (Ph.D.) in psychology. Candidates for a Ph.D. participate for four to six years in a university graduate program that involves broad exposure to the theories and findings of psychology, special focus on one subfield (such as developmental, personality, or social psychology), and extensive training in research methods. In addition, each Ph.D. candidate must complete an original research project under the direction of experienced researchers on the graduate faculty and submit their findings as a doctoral dissertation.

In the past a person who had just received a Ph.D. in psychology usually went to work at a college or university in a teaching and/or research position. Today, however, this traditional career pattern is changing as the ratio of psychology doctorates to positions in academia rapidly declines. Since 1970 the rate of growth of new doctorates in psychology has been more rapid than the rate of growth of doctorates in all other disciplines combined (Astin, 1976). At the same time undergraduate enrollments have started to level off and will continue to decline throughout the 1980s. Naturally, a decrease in the number of college students is bound to affect the number of faculty positions, even in an area like psychology, which is one of the most popular undergraduate majors. As a result of these combined factors, a growing number of people with psychology doctorates have been forced to seek employment outside of academia—in government agencies, industry, private practice, and nonprofit organizations, such as hospitals and clinics (Hynes, 1976). Fortunately, because there is substantial demand for psychologists in these nonacademic settings, employment opportunities for those with psychology Ph.D.'s are much better than they are for people with doctorates in many other disciplines (Astin, 1976).

As more psychologists seek employment outside academia, there is a growing concern that the traditional Ph.D. program is not adequately training students for nonacademic careers. So many graduate departments of psychology are beginning to add courses in such areas as environmental psychology, psychology and health, and program evaluation. In addition, some schools offer an alternative doctoral degree, called the Doctor of Psychology (Psy. D.), for those who are interested in applied vocations such as psychotherapy or forensic psychology. The major difference between the Ph.D. in psychology and the Psy.D. is that the latter places greater emphasis on practical experience than on research methodology. For example, the Psy.D. does not require a research-oriented dissertation as does the Ph.D. Instead, most Psy.D. candidates conduct a doctoral project related to their future profession.

Although a doctoral degree is a prerequisite for certain careers in psychology, a master's degree is adequate training for others. These include teaching at some two-year colleges, obtaining certain jobs in industrial, engineering, and environmental psychology, being a school psychologist, or being employed in various capacities in mental health and rehabilitation facilities. Earning a Master of Arts (M.A.) in psychology usually takes from one to two years of graduate work in a department of psychology plus successful completion of a master's thesis based on original research. But master's degrees with a focus on psychology can also be earned in other departments. For instance, a person can obtain a degree in educational psychology from a department of education or a degree in industrial psychology from a school of business.

What about the student who does not want or cannot afford graduate training? What benefit does the study of psychology offer him or her? Surveys show that there are many such students. Of those who earn a bachelor's degree with a major in psychology, approximately 50 percent have no immediate plans for further education (Cates, 1973). Some of these graduates will find employment directly related to psychology—as welfare case workers, for example, or in rehabilitation programs, correctional institutions, or community mental health centers—though not, of course, as therapists. Others will find that a major in psychology is indirectly related to many other careers. A person who finds a job in advertising, for instance, will probably consider courses in social psychology, human motivation, and human learning invaluable. Similarly, a person who enters the field of personnel management will make much use of information gained from courses on personality and individual differences and on assessment and testing.

But the value of psychology to the college student is not only vocational. Even if you take no psychology courses beyond this one, you will still learn much about yourself and others from this broad introduction to psychological findings and principles. Can anything be done to improve memory? What can I do to improve my study habits? How can I get my father to stop smoking? When people pressure me to do something I would rather not do, I often go along. Why? Whenever I babysit for my infant nephew he cries continually unless I hold him. What can I do to change his behavior? I get so tense when I sit down to take an exam that my mind goes completely blank. Have psychologists found a way to alleviate this problem? Answers to these and many other questions of great personal interest are contained in this book.

Finally, the study of psychology has the important benefit of giving you a perspective for evaluating new psychological findings reported in newspapers and magazines, on television, and in popular books. Consider, for example, a startling news item widely publicized several years ago. A team of medical researchers in England had found that chronic marijuana use was associated with cerebral atrophy, a wasting away of the brain (Campbell et al., 1971). This conclusion was based on brain x-rays of ten habitual marijuana users compared with brain x-rays of nonusers the same age. On the surface this evidence may strike you as very convincing. But consider some questions that a critical psychologist might ask. What evidence is there that the cerebral atrophy did not occur *before* the marijuana smokers started using the drug? And if there is good evidence to rule out this possibility, what is the likelihood that the observed brain damage was due to some other cause? As it turned out, the conclusion of the brain atrophy study became highly suspect when evaluated in this more rigorous way. Of the ten marijuana users with wasted brain tissue, all had also used the hallucinogen LSD (many over twenty times), eight had used amphetamines, another powerful drug, and several had frequently taken sedatives, barbiturates, heroin, or morphine. In addition, one young man had a medical history of convulsive seizures, and four had suffered substantial head injuries in the past (Kolodney, 1974). Thus, there was very good reason to believe that the cerebral atrophy revealed by the brain x-rays may have been caused by some factor other than marijuana.

This example nicely illustrates the perspective of the behavioral scientist. A good scientist is an incurable doubter. He or she is always asking: What is the evidence and how reliable is it? Was this study designed and carried out carefully enough? Were all other possible influences controlled before conclusions were drawn? Are alternative interpretations of the data possible, and if so what additional information is needed to rule them out? Exposure to the methods of psychology will help you develop this questioning approach yourself. By the end of this course you should share with the psychologist a healthy skepticism of the sweeping generalizations and psychological panaceas you read and hear so much about. This newly acquired outlook will obviously be of great personal value and will make you a more sophisticated consumer of information that can greatly affect your life.

SUMMARY

1. Psychology is, first of all, a science, and like all sciences, it relies on empirical data—information that has been systematically observed, measured, and recorded—to formally test its predictions. In psychology these predictions concern human behavior itself, for psychologists believe that there are patterns underlying human behavior, and that they can be understood.

2. The vast body of information psychology has amassed in its relatively short (one-hundred-year) history makes it not only a science but also an academic discipline. Psychological investigation covers all aspects of human behavior, and new knowledge is being acquired at a rapid rate.

3. The third dimension of psychology is its use as a means of promoting human welfare. Sometimes this application is a direct one, resulting from the deliberate use of research findings to solve a practical problem or to improve an aspect of human life. That kind of use is known as **applied science**. More often, it is the result of the application of knowledge acquired for its own sake, or **basic science**.

4. The founder of psychology is generally considered to be Wilhelm Wundt, who in the late nineteenth century created a laboratory to explore the workings of human consciousness. His movement came to be known as **structuralism**. Wundt's process of **introspection**, by which he concluded that conscious experience consists of three fundamental elements—sensations, images, and feelings—could not be subjected to proof because of personal differences in each person's explorations of his or her own consciousness.

5. In contrast to Wundt's emphasis on the isolated elements of mental life, the **Gestaltists** stressed the organized whole. They maintained that what emerges from perception of individual pieces of information is a whole that is greater than the sum of its parts. Every stimulus has meaning only within the context of surrounding events. This emphasis of context and pattern formed the basis for the modern study of perception.

6. The **behaviorist** researchers insisted that psychology rely only on data that can be empirically measured. Their concern with the study of how environmental stimuli can produce responses led to the pioneering work of Ivan Pavlov. In his famous experiment with dogs he initiated the concept of the conditioned reflex, a learned response to a previously neutral stimulus. In the United States, the ability to control responses by manipulating rewards and punishments was first delineated by John B. Watson and more recently refined by B. F. Skinner. The benefits of such molding have been hotly contested, but behavioral techniques have helped to shape the methods used in treating various psychological disorders.

7. Charles Darwin's ideas about evolution sparked psychologists' investigation into the genetic basis of human variation. One researcher, Sir Francis Galton, became convinced that all the differences he saw in human traits were the result of genetic inheritance, thus laying the groundwork for the heredity-environment controversy that continues today. He devised measurement techniques that were the forebears of modern personality and intelligence tests.

8. Darwin's theory, which saw similarities in body structure and mental functioning among animals, also influenced the movement called **functionalism**. The functionalists, whose leading exponent was William James, saw mental life as a stream of consciousness and the mind's activities as more important than its structure, as Wundt had believed. The aim of mental life was to help the organism adapt to and cope with its environment, and one of the major ways to achieve this end is through learning.

9. The Viennese physician Sigmund Freud emphasized the role of the unconscious in the development of personality. He felt that much of human behavior is driven by powerful biological urges, especially sexual ones, which often conflict with society's moral standards. His method of treatment, called **psychoanalysis**, involved the use of **free association**, in which patients suffering from neurotic symptoms attempted to bring unconscious conflicts to the surface by discussing everything that came to their minds, including dreams. While few psychologists would wholly accept Freud's ideas today, his influence on twentieth-century thought has been profound.

10. Psychology has branched into so many areas that its practitioners have been forced—like those of every other science—to become specialists. **Experimental psychology** relies largely on laboratory experiments to investigate the behavioral processes, such as sensation, perception, and learning, which are basic to many animal species. Researchers who study the underlying physical bases of behavior are called **physiological psychologists**.

11. Measuring and explaining individual differences in behavior is the focus of **personality psychology**.

12. Taking a different perspective, **social psychologists** look at the influence of the presence and actions of other people on what we think, say, and do.

13. Industrial and **organizational psychology** are growing specialties that focus on the relationship between individuals and their work. A closely related field, **engineering psychology**, examines the relationship between people and machines.

14. Developmental psychology is the branch of the discipline that focuses on describing and explaining the systematic changes that occur in human beings throughout the life cycle.

15. Psychologists who specialize in all the psychological aspects of the learning process are called **educational psychologists. School psychologists**, in contrast, work in the strictly applied field of assessing children with emotional or learning difficulties and making recommendations as to how these students might best be helped.

16. Clinical psychologists specialize in the diagnosis and treatment of behavior disorders. **Counseling psychologists** usually help those with much milder problems of social and emotional adjustment.

17. Besides the specialties we have listed, psychologists are beginning to explore new fields, such as **environmental psychology, forensic psychology, health and health care**, and **program evaluation**.

Suggested readings

American Psychological Association. *A career in psychology*. Washington, D.C.: American Psychological Association, 1976. You can obtain this booklet through the American Psychological Association, 1200 Seventeenth Street NW, Washington, D.C. 20036.

Boring, E. G. *A history of experimental psychology* (2nd ed.). New York: Appleton-Century-Crofts, 1950.

Hall, C. S., and Lindzey, G. *Theories of personality* (3rd ed.). New York: Wiley, 1978.

Murphy, G., and Kovach, J. *Historical introduction to modern psychology* (3rd ed.). New York: Harcourt Brace Jovanovich, 1972.

Nordby, V. J., and Hall, C. S. *A guide to psychologists and their concepts*. San Francisco: W. H. Freeman, 1974.

Schultz, D. *A history of modern psychology* (2nd ed.). New York: Academic Press, 1975.

Watson, R. I. *The great psychologists from Aristotle to Freud*. Philadelphia: Lippincott, 1978.

Wertheimer, M. *A brief history of psychology*. New York: Holt, Rinehart and Winston, 1970.

Wolman, B. B. *Handbook of general psychology*. Englewood Cliffs, N.J.: Prentice-Hall, 1973.

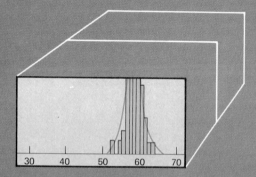

PREVIEW

1. Psychological research attempts to describe behavior, explain its causes, and predict the circumstances under which it might recur.

2. Many research methods are available, but their success depends on careful and accurate measurement of the variables under study.

3. Examining the methods that psychologists use affords us a better and more critical understanding of the conclusions that can be drawn from their research.

4. After data is collected, descriptive statistics communicate the results in abbreviated form. Inferential statistics are used to ensure that the results are not simply due to chance.

5. Before they are fully accepted in the field, the findings of a scientific study must be replicated by other researchers.

6. Psychologists must continually be aware of possible sources of error in their research. They must also consider the ethical implications of their work and conform to rules of conduct established by the American Psychological Association.

2 The methods of psychology

Most people are curious about human behavior. Some wonder whether certain emotional disorders are inherited. Others are interested in why some very capable people always perform poorly on exams. Still others want to know how they can most effectively persuade other people. And almost everyone is curious about why people fall in love. How would you go about answering such questions?

Undoubtedly, you would begin with everyday observations. If you were interested in techniques of persuasion, for example, you might start by observing that certain television commercials and magazine advertisements use fear appeals. Figure 2.1 shows an advertisement that was part of a recent antinuclear campaign. How effective are such tactics? On the basis of casual observation—how you and your acquaintances react to this and similar ads—you might venture the tentative generalization that fear appeals seem to work. But your investigation would probably not stop there. You might seek to confirm this generalization by conducting some simple tests. You might, for example, take a sample of antinuclear advertisements published by a local organization and

Can nuclear power
give you whiter teeth?

You
bet your life!

Everyone knows how dangerous,
expensive and unreliable nuclear power plants
are. But the utility companies say they're
worth the risk, because they allow us to keep using, and
wasting, more and more energy. With electric toothbrushes,
gas guzzling big cars and throw-away packaging.
That makes sense for the utility companies.
They make their money by selling electricity, not by saving it.
But it could be the death of us all.

Figure 2.1 Advertisements such as the one above often use scare tactics to persuade. Is fear likely to be an effective persuader? (Photograph courtesy of Public Media Center, San Francisco. Reprinted by permission.)

rank order them according to the amount of fear they aroused. You could then compare these rankings with the number of phone calls from concerned citizens that each ad prompted to see whether fear and public response were related. Or you might try a different approach. You might expose one group of smokers to a fear-arousing article about the serious health hazards of smoking and expose another group to a low-key antismoking appeal. You could then see which appeal had the greatest impact on the smokers' subsequent behavior. If either of these tests confirmed your suspicions that fear was an effective persuasive technique, you would be much more confident that your original generalization was correct.

The steps you have used in this amateur investigation are surprisingly similar to those used by professional psychologists or by their colleagues in any scientific field. The main difference lies in the rigor of the psychologist's approach. Like all scientists, psychologists gather a vast amount of data and subject their suppositions to carefully structured tests before they are willing to accept them as tentatively valid. Depending on the nature and the significance of the results, psychologists then summarize their findings in written form so that the data can be communicated to other researchers. Additional investigations are often conducted to determine whether the original finding can be replicated. Such testing and retesting can go on for many years. In fact, it never really ends. In science, no generalization is ever totally and unequivocally proved.

In the following sections we will describe many of the procedures that psychologists use to gather and analyze data. A knowledge of such procedures is of enormous value to the average person. Psychologists have a great deal to say about many important issues—from child care to education to mental health to race relations and sex roles. The more you know about the methods psychologists use to arrive at their conclusions, the better able you will be to understand and evaluate what they say.

But perhaps you feel that the details of scientific studies are much too complicated to be of interest to you. This is a very unfortunate and mistaken belief. As you become more familiar with the field of psychology, you will undoubtedly find that psychological investigation has all the fascination of unraveling a complex mystery. It begins with the same puzzling questions, proceeds to the same tentative conclusions, involves the same imaginative suppositions, logical reasoning, and carefully conducted tests as does detective work. And the eventual findings are always highly rewarding because they shed light on a person of great intrinsic interest—yourself.

GATHERING DATA

Imagine that you are a psychologist interested in determining people's attitudes toward smoking. You want to find out what percentage of smokers have stopped smoking or are planning to quit. How would you go about conducting your research? Now imagine that your interest shifts to knowing which particular method of quitting is more effective—cutting down or stopping "cold turkey." Would you use your previous approach to answer this new research question? Probably not. The research method that a psychologist uses to gather data depends in part on the nature of the question being asked. In general, a particular research project is intended to accomplish one or more of three basic goals: to *describe* behavior, to *explain* its causes, and to *predict* the circumstances under which that behavior might occur again. Each of the various methods of psychology has certain advantages and limitations that make it useful for achieving some of these aims but not all of them. Observation in a natural setting, for example, allows researchers to describe behavior and to generate possible explanations, but it does not allow them to test their hypotheses under a variety of conditions. Survey techniques also allow researchers to describe behavior, but they are not well suited for determining cause. An experiment allows explanations to be tested under controlled conditions and so helps to pinpoint cause, but it may not reveal the complexities of behavior as it occurs in the real world. Different research methods, then, often complement one another, and together they can enrich our understanding of many psychological issues.

Sampling

Before we describe the various research methods psychologists use, we should say a word about sampling. Few questions about human behavior permit every relevant person to be observed. The number of people that would have to be considered is usually far too large. As a result, psychologists almost always gather a **sample**, or selected segment, of the data available. The size of a sample is crucial, however. A poll intended to reflect the opinions of all the Democrats in the United States could not sample only six people, for given the millions of Americans who can be considered Democrats, such a small sample is very likely to produce bias. If, by chance, four of the six people came from Mississippi or Alabama, the findings would probably be weighted toward the views of southern Democrats, who frequently disagree with their northern counterparts.

The principal requirement of a sample, then, is that it adequately represent the population being considered. As we have seen, one way to achieve this is to ensure that the sample is sufficiently large. Another is to ensure that people are selected at random. A **random sample** is one in which every member of the total population has an equal chance of being included. Suppose you wanted to take a random sample of the student body at your university. You could obtain from the administration a list of all currently enrolled students and select, say, every fifth name. Depending on the total size of the student population, this technique would probably provide a sample that was representative along many dimensions. For example, the sample would probably closely reflect the total student body in terms of attitudes toward a campus issue such as lengthening mid-semester recess. If 60 percent of all students at the university supported this change, close to 60 percent of those in your sample probably would as well.

Sometimes, however, a psychologist wants to make certain that a sample includes the members of specific groups, such as black females under the age of thirty, or Spanish-speaking Americans living in large cities. In such instances, the psychologist would draw a **representative sample** in which people known to possess the specified characteristics are randomly selected in proportion to their numbers in the population as a whole. Public-opinion pollsters construct their samples in this way; they include certain proportions from each sex, from each ethnic minority, from each age group, from each geographic region, and so forth.

Typically, representative samples mirror the total populations they are meant to reflect more precisely than do random samples. Still, random samples are perfectly adequate for many kinds of studies. It all depends on the question the psychologist seeks to answer. The only universal requirement is that proper sampling procedures be followed. Haphazard sampling—that is, simply examining the most convenient or the first members of a population encountered—inevitably runs the risk of faulty results.

Although all psychologists recognize the importance of forming their generalizations on the basis of truly random samples, those conducting laboratory research are seldom able to follow strict sampling procedures. An example will illustrate why. Suppose you are a social psychologist interested in why people sometimes seek the companionship of others, and at other times prefer to be alone. To investigate this question you could design an experiment in which you created various conditions that you suspected might promote human affiliation and then observe how subjects reacted in each condition. But what are your chances of persuading hundreds of people from every part of the country and from all age brackets, ethnic groups, social strata, and the like to come to your laboratory just to participate in your research? Your chances, realistically, are slim. Although such a procedure would increase the representativeness of your sample, you will undoubtedly have to content yourself with a more homogeneous sample found closer to home. Like most experimental psychologists who study human beings, you will probably use students from your own university (often those taking introductory psychology) or perhaps residents from the surrounding community solicited via newspaper advertisements. True, this sample may not precisely mirror the human population as a whole. But in doing laboratory research one must weigh the ideal of random sampling against the difficulties of finding subjects. Does this sampling dilemma call into question the results of most experimental work with humans? No, it does not. It simply means that researchers must sometimes be cautious in generalizing from their findings to the behavior of all people everywhere.

Research methods

The experiment Many psychologists prefer to use an **experiment** whenever the question they are investigating allows. The main advantage of the experiment over other data-gathering methods is that it permits the researcher to control conditions and so rule out—to as large an extent as possible—all influences on subjects' behavior except the factors being examined. In this way the psychologist can more clearly infer cause-and-effect relationships from the results. The experimental method has one potentially important disadvantage, however. Eliminating all extraneous influences occasionally creates such an unnatural situation that one wonders if the results are applicable to behavior in real life.

The basic procedures in an experiment are best explained by describing a specific example. Consider the social psychological questions we raised earlier: Under what conditions is the human desire to affiliate with others likely to increase? Of the many experiments that have been conducted on this topic, we will focus on a classic one performed some twenty years ago by Stanley Schachter (1959). Schachter was one of the first psychologists to suggest that the desire to affiliate does not depend simply on individual personality traits. Affiliation, he proposed, also depends on the situations in which people find themselves, and among the situations most conducive to affiliation are those that arouse fear. This was Schachter's **hypothesis**, the proposition or belief that he set out to test.

Schachter's first step was to design an experiment in which subjects would experience fear. How could this goal be accomplished? The method Schachter eventually chose was devious but highly effective. He arranged for a number of students who had volunteered to participate in an experiment to be met at the laboratory door by a white-coated man who identified himself as Dr. Gregor Zilstein from the medical school's Department of Neurology and Psychiatry. Surrounded by an impressive array of electrical equipment, Dr. Zilstein told the students that they were part of a very important study on the physiological effects of electric shock. Each of them would undergo a series of shocks while their pulse rate, blood pressure, and other physical reactions were recorded. The shocks, the doctor warned in an ominous tone, would be extemely painful, for only intense shock could provide the information required. But, he added with a tight smile, they would cause no permanent tissue damage.

The students who encountered this diabolical doctor composed what is called the **experimental group**. An experimental group consists of those subjects who experience the experimental condition—in this case exposure to a fear-arousing situation. But all experiments must also have a **control group** to provide a source of comparison. Control subjects experience all the same conditions as experimental subjects do *except* the key factor the psychologist is evaluating. Thus, in Schachter's experiment the control subjects were also greeted at the door by a white-coated doctor who told them that they were about to participate in an experiment on the effects of electric shock. But this time, instead of grimly warning the subjects of impending pain, the doctor assured them in a kindly manner that the shocks would produce only a mild, not unpleasant, tingling sensation. Note that, as in all experiments, placement of subjects in either the experimental or the control group was done completely at random. This procedure ensures that any observed differences in the behavior of the two groups cannot be explained by systematic differences in the subjects assigned to each one.

Now that Schachter had created appropriate experimental and control conditions, one last step remained: He had to give his subjects the opportunity to affiliate with others in order to observe the effects, if any, of fear. So after Dr. Zilstein had finished describing the upcoming experiment, he announced that everyone must wait ten minutes while the experimental equipment was prepared. Each subject was given the choice of waiting alone in a private room or waiting in a classroom with other subjects. These choices, of course, provided the real experimental data. Once the subjects had expressed their preferences, the experiment ended and no shocks were ever given.

The results of Schachter's pioneering study are shown in Figure 2.2. They indicate that the tendency to affiliate does indeed seem to increase in fear-arousing circumstances. Subjects in the experimental condition (where the doctor's words were ominous and his smile sadistic) were much more likely to want to wait with others than were subjects in the control condition (where the doctor's words were reassuring and his manner kindly). Thus, Schachter's hypothesis that fear can promote affiliation was supported by his data. But note that these findings do not begin to answer all the important questions about the human motivation to affiliate. Are there other situations that can also encour-

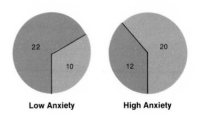

Low Anxiety   **High Anxiety**

● Subjects who chose to be alone or did not care
● Subjects who chose to affiliate

Figure 2.2 The results of Schachter's 1959 experiment testing the effects of anxiety on affiliation.

age affiliation? And exactly why, in Schachter's study, did fear induce a preference for waiting with other people? Did Schachter's fearful subjects simply want to be distracted? Did they want to express their anxious feelings to a sympathetic ear? Or might they be looking for a chance to compare their own emotions with those of others in the same predicament? Only additional research addressed specifically to such questions could help provide the necessary answers. Like a full understanding of any aspect of human behavior, a full understanding of human affiliation is something that can be gained only from a large number of studies that build and expand on one another.

But for our purposes in this chapter the important thing about Schachter's experiment is not the follow-up studies it generated but rather the fact that his basic procedures conformed to those required in all experimental work. An experiment is a controlled method of exploring the relationship between two **variables**—that is, between two factors capable of change. The factor that the experimenter deliberately manipulates is called the **independent variable**. In Schachter's study the independent variable was the degree to which the doctor's behavior was likely to induce fear. Note that in this case the doctor's warnings of severe pain were no guarantee that the subjects actually became frightened. But Schachter overcame this problem by measuring subjective fear directly. Before being asked which room they wished to wait in, each subject indicated on a five-point scale how anxious about the experiment he or she felt. Subjects exposed to the high-fear condition were significantly more worried about the impending shocks than were subjects exposed to the low-fear condition. This made Schachter reasonably sure that in manipulating his independent variable he was also manipulating the subjective experience of fear. Now consider the other factor in the relationship Schachter was investigating—the **dependent variable**. The dependent variable is what is expected to change when the independent variable is manipulated. In Schacter's experiment the dependent variable was the choice between waiting alone or waiting with other subjects.

It may help you to keep these terms straight if you remember that the words "independent" and "dependent" refer to the relationship between the variables. Changes in the independent variable are manipulated by the experimenter and are not controlled by changes in the dependent variable. Changes in the dependent variable, however, *depend* on changes in the independent variable if the experiment's hypothesis is correct. It is also helpful to know that an experimental hypothesis can always be phrased in an "if/then" statement. The variable that follows the word "if" is the independent variable; the variable that follows the word "then" is the dependent variable. For Schachter's experiment the "if/then" statement would be: "*If* a subject is exposed to a fear-arousing situation, *then* under these conditions the desire to affiliate with other subjects should increase over normal levels." Such a statement emphasizes that a cause-and-effect relationship occurs in only one direction. Change in the independent variable causes change in the dependent variable, and *not* vice versa. Because an experiment provides this means of establishing causality, it is the data-gathering method of choice for many psychologists.

Quasi-experimental designs and correlational research Some times researchers cannot study a cause-and-effect question by means of a true experiment. Some variables, such as sex, social class, or race, may have profound effects on behavior, but they cannot be experimentally manipulated. In other cases, manipulating the variable of interest would raise serious ethical problems. For example, a psychologist might suspect that overly harsh or overly lax parental discipline leads to juvenile delinquency, but he or she could hardly conduct an experiment to find out. To do so would entail convincing one group of parents to be extremely strict with their children from birth and another group to be extremely lenient. When the children grew to be teenagers, the experimenter could then count the instances of delinquent behavior. Obviously, few parents would agree to this procedure. In still other cases, an experiment is ruled out because the variable in question, for one reason or another, is beyond the researcher's personal control. For example, a psychologist may want to determine how people's dietary habits are affected by the recently publicized theory that no significant relationship exists between cholesterol intake and heart disease. But this theory has already been announced in the press, so how can the researcher manipulate it? Similarly, a researcher interested in how much the death penalty deters people from committing murder would certainly have difficulty arranging a true experiment.

How, then, can such questions be studied? One possibility is to conduct what has been called a **quasi-experimental design**—a design that approximates but does not meet, the requirements of a true experiment because subjects cannot be randomly assigned to conditions (Campbell, 1971). There are several types of quasi-experimental designs (Campbell and Stanley, 1963). In the **time-series design**, a researcher repeatedly observes or measures the dependent variable both before and after the independent variable changes. This design has been used to determine the effect of the death penalty on the homicide rate. In one study, the homicide rate in Sweden between 1754 and 1921, when the death penalty was in effect, was compared with the homicide rate between 1921 and 1942, when the death penalty was abolished (Schuessler, 1952). Since the number of murders fluctuated greatly each year, with little apparent change over time, the data suggested that the death penalty does not serve as a deterrent. The time-series design was also used to evaluate the effectiveness of a crackdown on speeding in the state of Connecticut after a record number of traffic fatalities in the year 1955. The initial statistics strongly suggested that the crackdown had worked. But caution had to be exercised in interpreting this quasi-experimental data. Because the fatality rate in 1955 was so unusually high, it is likely that traffic deaths would have dropped anyway, crackdown or not. Using complex statistical procedures to compensate for this problem, researchers were able to conclude that even taking a natural decline into account the crackdown was still effective.

Campbell (1971) has argued that because quasi-experimental designs do not permit the investigator to draw inferences that are as unambiguous as would be possible from a true experiment, they should be used only when true experiments are not feasible. Unfortunately, such designs are often employed when better alternatives are available, and individuals not aware of their shortcomings may draw invalid inferences. For example, suppose you are an aspiring lawyer and you see an advertisement for an expensive year-long program that will improve test scores on the LSAT exam. The advertisement states that students who have taken the course show an average gain of fifty points on their scores. On the basis of this evidence, should you sign up for the course? This type of quasi-experimental design, in which a group of individuals is

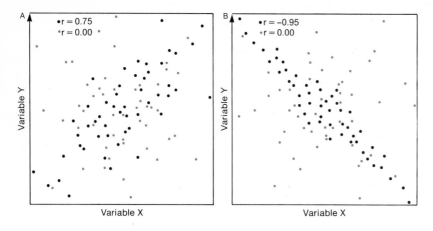

Figure 2.3 Data that are being examined for the existence of correlations are often plotted in the manner shown here. These "scatter plots" reveal visually the degree to which two variables are related. In both of these plots the set of lighter points shows a zero correlation. The darker-colored set of points in A represents a moderate positive correlation. The darker points in B represent a strong negative correlation.

tested, participates in treatment, and is retested, is fraught with problems. The students may do better on the second test not because of the special course, but because of what they learned in their college classes over the entire course of the year. Furthermore, students may do better on the second test because of "practice effects"—because they are more familiar with the test and therefore more relaxed. A better way to determine the effectiveness of the training program would be to conduct a true experiment, in which students are randomly assigned to the treatment or to the no-treatment control condition, and in which both groups are measured both prior to and after taking the course.

Another approach that can be used when a true experiment is not feasible is to conduct **correlational research**. For example, suppose an investigator wants to determine the extent to which two variables—parental discipline and juvenile delinquency—are related. The investigator might select a number of children at random and interview their parents to determine the severity of discipline in the home. The researcher might ask such questions as "How often do you spank your child?" or "What would you do if your child told a lie?" On the basis of his or her responses, each parent could then be assigned a severity-of-discipline score. The children's behavior could next be assessed, perhaps with the help of school or court records, to see which ones had committed delinquent acts, and if so how frequently. Finally, the researcher could calculate a numerical value called a **correlation coefficient**, which would indicate the strength and direction of the relationship between discipline and delinquency.

We will have more to say about the correlation coefficient later in this chapter. For now we can simply point out that the results of correlational studies vary widely. In some instances the relationship between the two variables under investigation turns out to be close and positive, meaning that a high rank on one is accompanied by a high rank on the other. For example, there is a strong **positive correlation** between IQ scores and academic performance: People who score high on IQ tests tend to get low grades. In other instances, the relationship between the two variables is close but negative, meaning that a high rank on one is accompanied by a low rank on the other. For example, there is a strong **negative correlation** between musical ability and tone deafness (inability to distinguish the pitch of musical notes). The more difficulty a person has perceiving pitch, the less likely that he or she will be able to play a musical instrument well. In still other instances, there is little or no relationship, positive or negative, between two variables. For example, there is no relationship between eye color and academic success or between hair color and tone deafness.

Correlations are especially useful because they allow psychologists to make predictions about behavior. If you know that a woman has a high IQ, you can predict that she is likely to get good grades. If you know that a man is tone deaf, you can predict that he is not likely to compose a piece of music that you would care to hear. Note that in either case your prediction, although probable, could ultimately prove wrong, for very few relationships are perfectly correlated.

It is very important to realize that although a correlational study can show that two variables have a strong tendency to be related in a certain way, it cannot establish that one factor *causes* the other. This is because a third factor, related to each of the other two, may also be involved. Consider a study of motorcycle accidents the army once conducted. They attempted to correlate the number of accidents a person had with other variables such as income and age. The best predictor of whether a person had been involved in a motorcycle accident turned out to be the number of tattoos that person had! Obviously tattoos do not cause motorcycle accidents nor does being in a motorcycle accident prompt a person to get tattooed. Instead, some third factor, perhaps a desire for risk or personal display, probably caused both tattooing and dangerous motorcycle driving.

Ruling out or demonstrating causality between two correlated facors, however, is not always this easy. People knew for years that a positive correlation existed between cigarette smoking and lung cancer, but the surgeon general (1974) was reluctant to announce that smoking *caused* cancer. Perhaps a third variable was related to both. Extreme nervousness, for example, might prompt both a tendency to smoke heavily and a tendency to produce some body chemical that irritated cells, increasing the likelihood of malignancy. Researchers conducted many tests to rule out all such logically possible third variables. In addition, they performed extensive laboratory experiments using animal subjects to confirm their suspicions that a causal link between smoking and cancer did exist. Only in this way could scientists confidently conclude that a causal relationship did underlie this particular correlation result. (Note that, in contrast to correlational research, a well-constructed quasi-experimental design does permit an investigator to draw causal inferences.)

The survey In all correlational studies the initial data about the variables under consideration must be collected by some means. Frequently, this means is a **survey**. A survey is an attempt to estimate the opinions, characteristics, or behaviors of a particular population by investigating a representative sample. Researchers conducting a survey gather the data of interest to them through interviews, questionnaires, or, sometimes, public records. Interviews have the advantage of letting the researchers see their subjects and of allowing them to modify their questions when clarification is needed. Questionnaires, on the other hand, take less time to administer and so are particularly useful when gathering information from a large number of people. In any case, if the researchers have carefully constructed their sample, they may consider the survey results to be representative of the entire population in question.

Although survey findings may later be used to seek correlations between factors, they are also of great interest in their own right. Probably the most famous survey in recent years is the one that resulted in the Kinsey reports, published in 1948 and 1953. Alfred Kinsey and his staff interviewed more than ten thousand men and women about their sexual behavior and attitudes—a radical thing to do at that time. Kinsey found, among other things, that behaviors often labeled abnormal, such as masturbation, homosexuality, and oral-genital sex, were much more common than most people supposed.

When conducting any survey, one of the most important concerns is that the sample used be truly representative of the group being studied. If it is not, the results may be invalid. In 1936, for example, a poll of more than two million people taken by *Literary Digest* magazine predicted an overwhelming victory for the Republican candidate Alf Landon over Democratic incumbent Franklin Roosevelt. Yet Roosevelt won by a landslide. The problems were that the magazine had polled people whose names appeared in telephone directories and on lists of automobile owners. In those days—this was during the Depression—people who had telephones and cars tended to be quite wealthy, and like the wealthy today, they were more likely to vote Republican. Thus, the population sampled in the survey, even though it was quite large, did not represent the population as a whole, and the survey results were consequently misleading. Interestingly, *Literary Digest* went out of business soon after publishing its faulty presidential prediction.

Another factor of vital importance to the success of a survey is the design of the questions themselves. Leading questions can completely bias the findings. Even very subtle changes in wording can alter a person's responses. Loftus (1975) found that subjects who were asked, "Do you get headaches frequently and if so how often?" reported an average of 2.2 headaches a week, whereas subjects asked "Do you get headaches occasionally and if so how often?" reported a weekly average of 0.7 headaches. Even when a question is neutrally worded, people can still give misinformation. Some people continually answer "yes" just to be agreeable; others seem to have a built-in tendency to say "no." If a survey contains questions that reflect on ability or character, people frequently describe themselves in a more favorable light than is warranted. They often claim, for example, to have held better jobs, to have voted more frequently, and to have donated more to charity than objective records show (Cannell and Kahn, 1968; Myers and Ridl, 1979). Similarly, if a survey covers a touchy area, such as sex or race relations, people are likely to claim that they *do* believe what they think they *ought* to believe.

A psychologist conducting a survey can often control for such problems by including several differently worded questions on the same topic and seeing how consistent a person's responses are. For example, in answer to one question a man might respond that he has no objection to homosexuality. Yet in answer to another question he might emphatically report that he has never engaged in homosexual acts and certainly never intends to. In such a case the psychologists would have reason to suspect that this man's true attitude toward homosexuality may be somewhat more negative than his first response implied.

Naturalistic observation As careful as researchers may be in gathering data through surveys or experiments, sometimes the very act of filling out a questionnaire or being in a laboratory changes the way a subject usually feels or behaves. Imagine investigating the effects of alcohol on social aggressiveness by means of an experiment. Even if you tried to design a laboratory to look like a bar, as at least one researcher has actually done (Marlatt and Nathan, 1978; Collins and Marlatt, in press), could you completely rule out the possibility that subjects were controlling their behavior because they knew they were being watched? Probably not. The only way around this problem would be to do your observing in a natural setting where the drinkers did not know they were being studied. The cardinal rule of such **naturalistic observation** is that the investigator stay out of the way.

Many questions lend themselves to naturalistic observation. A social psychologist might use this method to study leadership roles in a small group; a developmental psychologist might use it to study the way four-year-olds interact in a preschool class. Such observation is sometimes done through a one-way window so that the presence of the psychologist cannot interfere with routine behavior. Alternatively, psychologists sometimes use a form of naturalistic observation known as **participant observation**, in which they join an existing group in order to record thoughts and feelings accessible to only group members. In one such study three social psychologists joined a secretive group that predicted that a great flood would end the world on a certain day, at a certain time (Festinger, Riecken, and Schachter, 1956). By becoming members of this doomsday group the psychologists were able to be present when the fateful moment came and went, and to observe the way in which disconfirmation of the prophecy influenced behavior. Contrary to what might be expected, the group did not disband after the prediction was proved false. Instead, members became less secretive, diligently trying to publicize their views and to attract new believers.

In observational research it is very important to develop ways of recording data so as to avoid completely subjective interpretations. How do we know, for example, that the doomsday group became less secretive after disconfirmation of their prophecy? We know because the researchers kept careful records of what they saw and heard. Such records can take the form of written notes, tape recordings, or ratings on evaluation forms. In this way other researchers can detect biases and idiosyncratic interpretations.

Although naturalistic observation is extremely valuable for investigating many questions, it also has its limitations. The main problem is that a researcher has no way of controlling the situation and so cannot test cause-and-effect hypotheses. For example, if the psychologists in our hypothetical barroom study observed that customers get rowdier as they drink more, is it necessarily the alcohol that is inducing their behavior? What if, as the evening wears on, the bar becomes packed with people? Perhaps increased aggressiveness is due not so much to the amount of alcohol consumed as to the extent of crowding. As we saw earlier, the degree to which a particular factor is causally related to another can be established only through a controlled experiment.

The case study All the data-gathering methods we have discussed so far involve collecting information from a representative sample of people ideally chosen at random from a much larger population. But some phenomena of interest to psychologists occur too rarely to be studied in this way. Consider the psychological disorder commonly called a multiple personality, in which a single individual has two or more highly distinct personalities, at least one of which is typically unaware of the thoughts and actions of the others. Because only a very small number of multiple personalities have ever been reported, psychologists cannot study the nature and causes of the condition by means of, say, correlational research. Instead they must rely on intensive investigation of the few people known to have the disorder. Such in-depth analysis of a single individual is called a **case study**. In this instance, a case study would involve probing the past of the disturbed person to discover any factors that may possibly have contributed to the condition.

Case studies have been especially valuable for investigating the effects of damage to the human brain. For obvious ethical reasons, researchers cannot induce brain damage in human subjects simply for the sake of science. Instead, they must limit their investigations to injuries that occur through tragic accidents or through brain surgery to eliminate disease. Yet much has been learned about brain function through the case-study method. Brenda Milner (1966), for example, studied one young man whom she referred to by his initials, H. M. In an effort to relieve the severity of H. M.'s steadily worsening epileptic seizures, doctors removed a portion of his brain. The surgery helped the seizures, but it had a terrible side effect: H. M. could remember nothing new! As soon as he shifted his attention from a new piece of information, H. M. would lose all recollection of it. People he had just met would seem complete strangers to him five minutes later, and he could flip through the same magazines again and again without finding their contents familiar. Interestingly, however, H. M.'s recall of things learned *before* the operation was as good as ever. As we will see in Chapter 6, this and similar case studies provide strong evidence that human memory consists of a short-term and a long-term component and that what was surgically destroyed in H. M.'s brain was the mechanism for transferring information from one system to the other.

Case studies, then, provide a wealth of descriptive information about a particular psychological phenomenon, and they may also suggest important principles underlying that behavior. In the hands of a brilliant psychologist the case-study method can be a powerful tool indeed. Sigmund Freud's theory of personality, described in Chapter 13, was based on case studies of the patients who came to him for treatment. Similarly, Jean Piaget's theory of intellectual development in childhood, described in Chapter 8, began with intensive observation of his own three children as they were growing up. As insightful as they may be, however, case studies can never *prove* that suspected principles of behavior actually operate. Still, subsequent researchers can learn much by attempting to corroborate the patterns of behavior observed in case-study investigations.

Special measurement tools and approaches

How certain variables are measured The experiment, correlational research, the survey, naturalistic observation, and the case study are the five basic research methods that psychologists use. But we have not yet discussed specifically how psychologists go about measuring many of the variables of interest to them. One possibility is to use what psychologists call **behavioral measures**—objective, quantifiable measures of the respondent's behavior. For example, if you were interested in measuring social aggression in a barroom, you would probably try to count the number of aggressive verbal or physical acts that occurred in a given period of time. Similarly, if you were interested in whether a particular program in a rehabilitation center for paraplegics results in more activity, you could attach odometers to patients' wheelchairs.

An advantage of behavioral measures is that they are less likely than direct questioning to affect research results. If you questioned all the people in a bar about their aggressive feelings, you would almost certainly influence the phenomenon you were trying to measure. Furthermore, since behavioral measures are less likely to be influenced by subjects' attempts to give favorable impressions of themselves, they are often used to investigate sensitive topics. Webb and his colleagues (1966) have discussed many unobtrusive measures that may be used in such research (for example, inferring drinking behavior by counting the number of empty liquor bottles in trash cans).

But since so many factors can determine a person's behavior, behavioral measures are not always sensitive. For example, suppose an investigator is interested in assessing generosity or helping behavior. He or she may ask subjects to contribute to a fictitious cause as they prepare to leave an experiment. However, the amount of money a subject donates may be influenced by factors unrelated to the experimental variables, such as financial condition or the amount of change he or she happens to have. In addition, behavioral measures are often more troublesome to collect than are questionnaires or rating scales. Finally, some types of behavior, such as fantasies or sexual activity, are difficult to observe. It is interesting to note, however, that even our knowledge of sexual behavior has been greatly extended through direct behavioral measurement (Masters and Johnson, 1966). This form of research will be discussed more fully in Chapter 14.

Researchers have also devised ways of measuring various physiological changes that are known to be associated with particular psychological states, such as sleep or emotional arousal. Like behavioral measures, the great value of **physiological measures** is that they provide objective, quantitative data on phenomena that are difficult to assess precisely in other ways. For example, an electroencephalogram (EEG), which measures the electrical activity of the brain, allows sleep researchers to tell which of several stages of sleep a person is in. Similarly, psychologists studying emotion can usually learn more about the strength of an emotional response by measuring changes in heart rate, respiration, and galvanic skin response (GSR, a measure of the electrical conductivity of the skin, which increases when a person perspires), than they can by simply observing outward behavior or eliciting a subjective report. Like behavioral measures, physiological measures are especially useful in cases where the subject may not be willing to admit to particular feelings. For example, subjects may not tell an experimenter that they are upset because of something that has happened in the experiment. A problem with these measures, however, is that it is often difficult to interpret the direction of a subject's heightened emotionality. If a respondent shows increased heart rate or GSR, how is an experimenter to know whether he or she is afraid, excited, or sexually aroused?

Despite these problems, physiological data often provide a great deal of information that cannot be obtained from self-report data alone. In a study of fear in skydivers, for example, Fenz and Epstein (1967) asked novice and experienced divers to rate on a ten-point scale the intensity of their fear at various stages in the jump sequence. As Figure 2.4 shows, the novices reported that fear steadily increased until the "ready" signal, after which it dropped off. The experienced jumpers, in contrast, reported a very different pattern. They said that fear gradually decreased from a high point the morning of a jump to the moment the parachute opened, after which a sudden rush of fear occurred. Interestingly, the subjective ratings of the experienced divers did *not* correspond to their patterns of physiological arousal. Heart rate, respiration, and GSR tended to increase for novice and experienced jumpers alike right up to the moment of the jump. Fenz and Epstein speculated that perhaps the experienced jumpers had learned to inhibit the subjective experience of fear in response to the first signs of physiological arousal.

Because behavioral and physiological measures are more difficult to employ, more costly, and more time consuming than self-report measures, such as questionnaires and interviews, they are used much less frequently in psychological research. As we have noted earlier, however, people's responses to questionnaires can be changed considerably by the wording of the questions and by their desire to present themselves in a favorable light. Moreover, accurate responses to self-report data requires that subjects know how they would behave in a given situation, and this is not often the case. In 1963 Stanley Milgram conducted a study of obedience in which subjects were ordered to deliver increasingly painful shocks to a fellow subject as part of a bogus learning experiment. Milgram used a behavioral measure in his study—the number of shocks that the subject was willing to deliver—and found that a surprisingly large number of subjects delivered the maximum number of shocks to their fellow subject. Prior to conducting this study, Milgram asked people how they thought they would react in the experiment. Most people indicated that neither they nor anyone else would administer painful shocks to another person. In short, people were completely incapable of predicting how they would behave. This important study, and the controversy it has generated, are discussed more fully in Chapter 18.

Each of the measurement tools psychologists use has advantages and disadvantages. No single method is without bias (Webb et al., 1966). For this reason, psychologists are increasingly using all three kinds of measures in a single study. In studying the predictors of effective coping with permanent paralysis, for example, Wortman and her colleagues (1980) assess coping in a variety of ways. These include self-report measures, such as ratings of how well the respondents feel they are coping and how distressed they feel; behavioral mea-

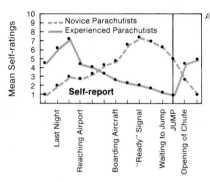

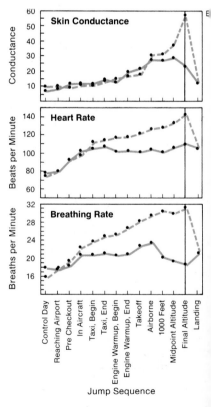

Figure 2.4 (A) When asked to assign numbers to their feelings of fear (with 1 meaning the time of least fear and 10 meaning the time of most fear), novice parachutists reported most fear at the "ready" signal just before the jump. Experienced parachutists said their fear was nearly at its lowest at this time. (B) Physiological measures indicated that both groups became more aroused right up to the time of the jump. Fenz and Epstein suggest that the experienced parachutists had learned to inhibit their experience of fear in response to the first signs of physiological arousal. (After Fenz and Epstein, 1967.)

sures, such as attendance at physical and occupational therapy sessions and the number of activities engaged in; and physiological measures, such as sleep disturbances and amount of pain medication requested.

How behavioral change over time is assessed Another special measurement problem psychologists sometimes face is that of assessing behavioral change over a relatively long period of time. Imagine, for example, that you are trying to find out whether dependent children grow up to be dependent adults. You might randomly select a group of adults, assess each person's degree of dependency, and then try to discover, by reconstructing their biographies, how dependent they were as children. But this approach would probably necessitate relying on people's memories to some extent, and memories for events that happened years ago are notoriously fuzzy. A more accurate way to answer the same question would be to conduct what is called a **longitudinal study**, a study in which the same group of people are examined over a number of years. Thus, you might select a group of children, assess their current level of dependency, and assess it again every few years as the children grow up.

In terms of reliability, longitudinal studies are the best method available for assessing long-term changes or consistencies in behavior. But longitudinal studies are also time consuming. An alternative approach that psychologists sometimes take is to study a population cross-sectionally by age. In a **cross-sectional study**, the population is divided into subgroups using certain criteria, the subgroups are randomly sampled, and the members of each sample are then surveyed, tested, or observed. If you were conducting a cross-sectional study of intelligence by age, for instance, you would administer an IQ test to people of various ages—some ten years old, some fifteen, some twenty, and so forth—and draw conclusions about intelligence through the life cycle on the basis of the results. Such studies usually show that the high point of intellectual development is somewhere around age thirty, after which intelligence consistently declines.

There is a serious problem with cross-sectional studies of intellectual development, however. The older people sampled have very different educations and life experiences from the younger ones, and these age-related differences in intellectual stimulation can easily influence the test results. In fact, longitudinal studies of intelligence over the life span have shown this factor to be highly significant. When psychologists examine the same people at different points in their lives, they generally find that intellectual performance either increases or stays the same until the age of fifty or sixty (Baltes, Reese, and Nesselroade, 1977). Thus, longitudinal studies have in some instances provided data quite different from that collected when a population is studied cross-sectionally by age.

This does not mean that the longitudinal approach is always preferred, however. Both longitudinal and cross-sectional studies have certain advantages and limitations that make each more or less useful in answering particular types of research questions. A combination of both methods is probably ideal. Cross-sectional research is less expensive, the data can be gathered in a much shorter period of time, and typically a greater number of subjects can be studied. When cross-sectional studies are used for preliminary investigations, they can often provide some direction for later, more extensive longitudinal research.

ANALYZING DATA

After a psychologist has collected data, how does he or she determine what the data mean? Usually a researcher gathers information in a form that can be analyzed by **statistics**—mathematical methods for assessing and presenting the data in summary form. There are two main kinds of statistics: descriptive and inferential.

Descriptive statistics

Descriptive statistics are used to reduce a mass of data to a form that is more manageable and understandable. Using descriptive statistics, investigators are able to say something meaningful about their findings using only a few words and a few figures.

Describing distributions of scores Suppose a congresswoman wants to know what upsets the people in her district, and whether blue-collar workers are more upset than white-collar workers. She asks two psychologists to conduct a survey to find out. They compose a questionnaire containing forty-five questions that can be answered yes or no—for example, "I am dissatisfied with the quality of education in my local schools" or "I am displeased with the job the police force is doing." The psychologists start by administering their questionnaire to fifty blue-collar workers in the congresswoman's district. They find that some are dissatisfied with many things, others are dissatisfied with only a few. No one, however, is unhappy about more than thirty-six items on the questionnaire, and no one complains about fewer than ten. The scores therefore spread between 10 and 36, and so are said to have a **range** of 26 (36 − 10 = 26). The researchers now construct a **histogram**—that is, a graph of the **frequency distribution**, in which the data are arranged so as to show the number of instances (the frequency) of each score. This is shown in Figure 2.5A. They then administer the questionnaire to fifty white-collar workers, tabulate their scores, and construct another histogram, shown in Figure 2.5B. This is the first step toward organizing the data in a meaningful way.

Measures of central tendency The next step is to choose some method of comparing blue-collar and white-collar responses. This usually involves comparing the central tendencies of the two distributions. A **central tendency** is a middle value of a set of scores. There are several middle values that psychologists might calculate, one of which is the **arithmetic mean**. To find the arithmetic mean, you merely add all the scores and then divide by the number of people who took the test. As Figures 2.5A and 2.5B show, the mean score for the blue-collar workers was about 21; for the white-collar workers it was about 32. The other two measures of central tendency indicated in Figures 2.5A and 2.5B are the median and the mode. The **median** is the score that falls in the exact middle of a distribution of numbers that are arranged from highest to lowest. For example, the median of the following set of numbers—84, 84, 78, 77, 70—which represent the height, in inches, of five players on a hypothetical basketball team, is 78. The **mode** is the score that is most frequently obtained in a distribution, in this case 84.

In the example shown in Figure 2.5A, the mean, the median, and the mode are equal. This indicates that the distribution is **symmetrical**, meaning that the

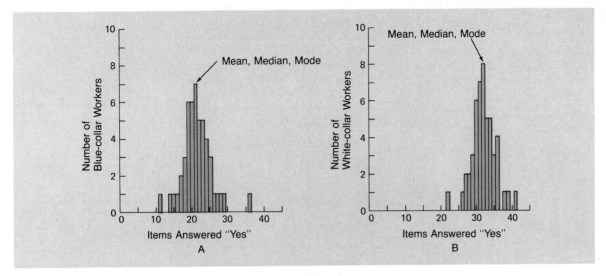

Figure 2.5 Two frequency distributions. In each figure, the vertical scale shows the frequency with which a score on the horizontal scale was observed. (A) The distribution of the scores from an imaginary group of blue-collar workers on an imaginary questionnaire. (B) The distribution of the scores of an imaginary group of white-collar workers on the same test. Note that these distributions are similar in range but different in their averages. Also note that mean, median, and mode—the three measures of central tendency—are the same in both of these normal, symmetrical distributions.

scores distribute similarly on both sides of the middle value. Equivalence of the mean, the median, and the mode is a defining characteristic of symmetrical distributions.

When plotted as a line graph instead of a histogram, some symmetrical distributions result in a curve with a "bell" shape, like the one in Figure 2.6. This is called a **normal curve**, and the distribution in this case is called a **normal distribution**. As Figure 2.6 shows, a normal curve gradually tapers off on either side of its central high point. This indicates that most of the scores are about average, or close to it, that some are a fair distance above or below average, and that very few are quite far above or below. Few curves, however, exactly match this shape. It is most nearly approximated when a very large number of scores is plotted, especially if those scores are primarily determined by chance.

Of course, the mean, median, and mode are not always equal. Some distributions, like the one in Figure 2.5B, are unsymmetrical, or skewed. In such cases, how does a psychologist decide what measure of central tendency to use? The answer depends in part on the exact way in which the scores are distributed.

Suppose someone told you that the mean income at a certain company was $18,000 a year. What would this suggest to you? Now look at Figure 2.7, the salary distribution for a hypothetical firm employing fifty people. The president of the company earns $70,000 a year; he pays three executives $40,000 and four executives $30,000; there are six managers who earn $20,000 and six salespeople who earn $15,000; and the remaining thirty manual and clerical workers all earn $12,666 or less. The mean of all fifty salaries is $18,000, but this is clearly not a fair representation of the actual distribution of incomes. It is far too high.

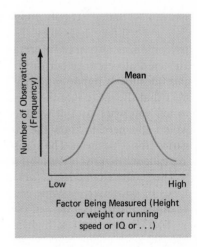

Figure 2.6 The "bell" shape of an ideal normal distribution of frequencies. The highest point of the normal curve represents the mean.

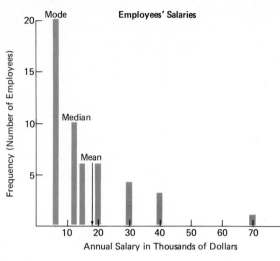

Figure 2.7 The distribution of incomes in an imaginary company. Note that the shape of this distribution is completely different from the shapes in Figure 2.5. Note also that the mean, median, and mode are not identical in this distribution. Frequency distributions of this kind—and of many other kinds—occur in psychology, but normal distributions are the most common.

In this case, a better measure of central tendency would be the median, the salary level at which the same number of people earn more than this amount as earn less than it. This level is $12,666. Because the mode, or most frequent salary, is only $6,333, it is as misleading an indicator of overall distribution as is the mean.

Why would anyone go to the trouble of calculating a measure of central tendency? Beyond the goal of organizing a mass of data into a meaningful and useful form, psychologists want to be able to describe their data using simple, quantitative statements. Being able to locate a point of central tendency helps accomplish this aim. For example, it is much easier to tell someone that the median salary earned at a particular company is $12,666 than it is to say "One person earns $70,000, three people earn $40,000, four people earn $30,000. . . ." Central tendencies, then, like other statistical tools, provide a kind of quantitative shorthand.

Measures of variability But a measure of central tendency like the mean, median, or mode actually supplies only a limited amount of information. It does not tell the whole story. To more fully describe a distribution of numbers, psychologists also need information about the **dispersion** of scores. Are scores clustered closely together or are they widely spread out? To understand why this question is important, imagine that you are visiting a foreign country and hear that the mean monthly rainfall there is five inches. Would this be enough to tell you what kind of weather to expect? The answer is clearly no, for you would also need to know the extent to which rainfall at different times of year varies from this mean. The statistical techniques for expressing this information are called measures of variability.

The range, mentioned earlier, is one measure of variability. But it can sometimes be deceptive. A single extreme score can dramatically alter a range. For example, the salary range at our hypothetical company was $63,667 ($70,000 − $6,333), but suppose high profits allowed the president to take a raise of $30,000 a year. The range would leap to $93,667, even though the amount of variation among the remaining forty-nine salaries stayed exactly the same. Clearly it would be helpful to have a more sensitive measure of variability—one that takes into account all the scores in a given set of data, not just the two outermost extremes.

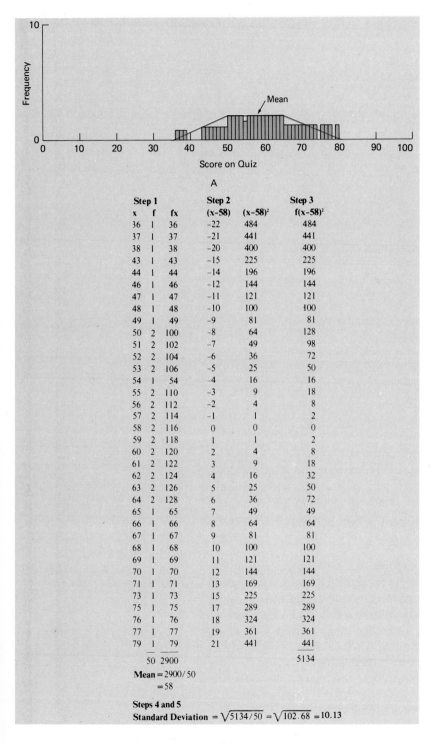

Figure 2.8A A frequency distribution with high variability, and the calculation of its mean and standard deviation. Compare this distribution with the distribution in Figure 2.8B. Note that the means of these distributions are exactly the same and that both distributions have the "bell" shape (indicated by the colored curves) of the theoretical normal distribution. In the calculations, the letter x stands for the values of various scores. The letter f stands for the frequency with which a score occurred.

The standard deviation is quite easy to calculate. Here are the steps to follow: (1) calculate the mean of all the scores you have obtained; (2) subtract this mean from each score and, in each case, square the difference; (3) add all the squares together; (4) divide the sum by the total number of scores; and (5) take the square root of that value.

The **standard deviation** is such a measure of variability. It indicates the average extent to which all the scores in a particular set vary from the mean. Consider the two distributions of psychology quiz scores shown in Figures 2.8A and 2.8B. The standard deviation for the scores in A is about 10, while the

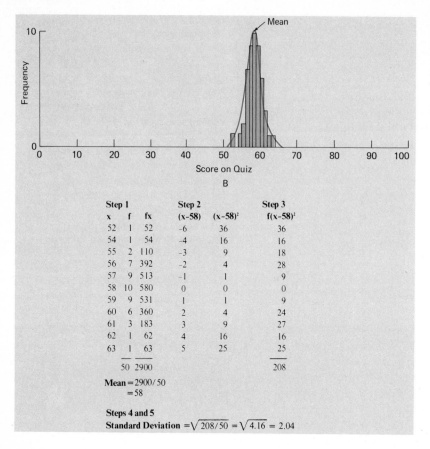

Figure 2.8B A frequency distribution with low variability, and the computation of its mean and standard deviation. Compare this distribution with the one in Figure 2.8A. Also compare the computations in each figure. The standard deviation is a measure of the degree to which individual scores differ from the central tendency of all the scores.

standard deviation for those in B is about 2. By knowing the standard deviation, then, you immediately know whether a set of scores vary widely or only narrowly from the mean. The greater the standard deviation, the wider the variation. The caption to Figure 2.8A explains how to calculate the standard deviation.

Correlation coefficients Earlier in this chapter, when we discussed correlational research, we said that psychologists assess the strength of a correlation (the degree of relatedness between two variables) by calculating what is called a **correlation coefficient**. Now we are ready to describe this statistical tool in more detail. A correlation coefficient is a number ranging from -1, which indicates a perfect negative correlation, through 0, which indicates no correlation, to $+1$, which indicates a perfect positive correlation. Thus the closer a correlation coefficient is to $+1$ or -1, the stronger the relationship—positive or negative—between the two variables.

It is important to remember that a correlation coefficent of, say, $-.65$ is just as strong as a correlation coefficient of $+.65$. This is because the strength of a correlation is determined not by the sign of its coefficient ($+$ or $-$), but by the coefficient's closeness to $+1$ or -1. To test your understandling of this potentially confusing point, suppose that researchers at a certain university find that grade-point average and number of traffic violations have a correlation of

— .42, while grade-point average and running speed have a correlation of + .26. Which relationship is stronger? In this fictitious example, a stronger correlation exists between traffic violations and grade-point average than between running ability and grade-point average; − .42 is closer to + 1 or − 1 than is + .26. The minus sign in front of the first of these two correlation coefficients simply indicates that the relationship is negative: as traffic violations *increase*, grade-point average *declines*, and vice versa.

To summarize, correlational studies are a way of discovering the extent to which two variables are related, and the correlation coefficient is a quantitative means of expressing this relationship. At one extreme, a correlation coefficient of 0 indicates that there is no relationship between the variables in question: they vary independently of one another. At the other extreme, a correlation coefficient of − 1 or + 1 indicates that a perfect relationship exists: If you know the quantitative change in one variable, you can precisely state the accompanying change in the other. Most of the relationships that psychologists study fall somewhere between these two extremes.

Inferential statistics

As you learned in reading about descriptive statistics, psychologists doing research typically collect large quantities of numerical information. Looking at this data in its initial, unorganized state can be a bewildering experience for a person with an untrained eye. But by using various procedures for presenting quantitative information, psychologists can summarize even vast amounts of data in forms that are meaningful, useful, and easy to convey. In many cases, however, the researchers' task is not over when they have finished "describing" their data. Often the goal of research is to explore hypotheses, and for this purpose psychologists must turn to what are called **inferential statistics**.

Inferential statistics provide ground rules or conventions for determining what conclusions can legitimately be drawn from data. Remember that researchers begin with a hypothesis—a conjecture that, under certain circumstances, people (or animals) will behave in a certain way. They collect data about how a sample of people do behave under those specific circumstances, data that are in a form that can be treated statistically (scores, ratings, and so on). They then summarize their data using descriptive statistics like those discussed in the preceding section. Now they must make use of inferential statistics to infer (draw a reasonable conclusion as to) whether the data clearly support their original hypothesis. Were the results due primarily to chance, or was there indeed a significant pattern or relationship?

Probability You undoubtedly know that the odds of getting heads on any given toss of an unbiased coin is fifty-fifty—that is, a head will most probably turn up half the time. Now suppose that out of one hundred tosses of a coin it lands heads up fifty-three times. Is the coin biased? What if it lands heads up seventy-nine times? Statisticians have determined the probability of obtaining any given result with any given number of tosses of an unbiased coin. Thus, they can tell you how often in, say, one hundred tosses one can expect to obtain twenty-eight, fifty-three, seventy-nine, or any other number of heads from zero to one hundred.

Probability is a complex area of mathematics that is frequently misunderstood. Our intuitions about "what the chances are" are not always correct. For example, assume that you have tossed a coin ten times and that it has landed heads up each time. You are about to toss it again. What do you predict will occur on this next toss? There are three possibilities: (1) another head will turn up; (2) a tail will turn up; or (3) the odds are still even (.50), so it is impossible to tell. If you predicted that a tail would turn up, you committed a common error known as the "gambler's fallacy." There is no reason to expect that the probability of a tail turning up is any better than even, regardless of how many heads have already appeared. Indeed, the prediction that another head will turn up probably has more merit than the prediction that a tail will turn up, for it appears that the coin you have been dealing with may, for some reason, be a biased one.

If the probability of getting a head on a single toss of a coin is one out of two, how do you determine the probability of getting several heads in a row? This is done by multiplying the odds for getting one event (one head) by the odds for getting each subsequent one. The probability of getting two heads in a row, therefore, is $\frac{1}{2} \times \frac{1}{2}$, or $\frac{1}{4}$. For four heads in a row, the odds would be $\frac{1}{16}$ ($\frac{1}{2} \times \frac{1}{2} \times \frac{1}{2} \times \frac{1}{2}$). The probability that a coin will come up heads ten times in a row is $\frac{1}{2}$ raised to the tenth power, which is $\frac{1}{1024}$. That is, odds against this event occurring by chance with a fair coin are 1,024 to 1, which is why you might begin to suspect in such a case that the coin is biased and that your coin-tossing results are not a matter of chance. What you are doing when you form this suspicion is making a judgment about the meaning of an event (ten heads in a row) based on the odds of it occurring purely by chance. Because the likelihood of a chance occurrence is so slim, you might favor some alternative explanation. This is exactly the kind of logic that psychologists employ when they use inferential statistics to judge the significance of their data.

Statistical significance The crux of the problem psychologists face is that the influence of chance can never be eliminated. Whenever a researcher conducts an experiment there will invariably be some difference, based strictly on chance, between the performance of one group and the performance of another. For instance, if you gave a vision test to one hundred people with brown hair and the same test to one hundred people with blond, you might find that the blonds, on average, had slightly better eyesight. Now vision undoubtedly has nothing to do with the color of a person's hair, so we can assume that this observed difference was caused entirely by chance. This means that if you ran the same test again with a different group of subjects you would be just as likely to get the opposite results. But how do you assess the influence of chance on a relationship that is far less implausible? Clearly what is needed is a statistical test to help decide when a given difference in performance is reliable—that is, when we can expect it to occur again and again under the same circumstances. Such a test is called a measure of **statistical significance**.

An example will help clarify the importance of being able to calculate statistical significance. Suppose that an experimental group of rats has been given an injection of caffeine, the stimulant in coffee. On the average, these rats learn to run a maze in thirty trials. A control group of animals is injected with a **placebo** (a substance that has no physiological effect) to ensure that the two groups will not perform differently merely because one has received an injection and the other has not. The control group learns to run the same maze in an average of thirty-eight trials. Is the difference between thirty and thirty-eight trials large enough for the experimenter to conclude that the caffeine increased the speed with which the experimental animals learned the maze, or might these results have occurred merely by chance?

Psychologists and other scientists have adopted an arbitrary convention for making such decisions. By various methods they calculate the probability that the outcome of the study could have occurred by chance alone. If this probability is quite low, say .05 (or 19 to 1 odds), they then have good reason to reject the "chance" explanation and to conclude instead that the variable under consideration caused the results. In this instance the researchers would report that the data had attained the .05 level of statistical significance. Some investigators choose more stringent levels, say .01 (or 99 to 1 odds). In each case, however, the investigator computes the probability that the results occurred solely by chance. Only if that probability is low does the researcher assert that the results support the hypothesis.

SELECTED METHODOLOGICAL PROBLEMS

In describing the methods and statistical techniques that psychologists commonly use, we have, for the sake of clarity, greatly simplified the process of conducting research. To give a more accurate picture, it is necessary to survey a few of the problems and pitfalls that can invalidate a study.

The self-fulfilling prophecy

The term **self-fulfilling prophecy** refers to the fact that the expectations of investigators can influence their findings. In psychology, as in other fields, people tend to find what they are looking for. More than that, they may even tend unwittingly to *create* what they seek. For example, if a researcher conducting an interview smiles faintly when a subject's response corroborates the theory under investigation, this inadvertent act can easily affect the subject's answers to subsequent questions. If this seems difficult to believe, consider the following real-life experiment.

Robert Rosenthal (1966) told a group of elementary-school teachers that certain pupils had obtained high scores on some special tests and so were sure to show unusual intellectual development during the school year. Actually, these pupils were no different from others who had not been labeled potential "late bloomers." Later in the year, the teachers rated the late bloomers as more interested, more curious, and happier than other students. And when all the children were given IQ tests at the end of the year, those who had been labeled late bloomers showed a significantly greater gain in IQ than did their classmates, as Figure 2.9 indicates. As you can see, this effect occurred primarily with first- and second-grade children, perhaps because their teachers had not yet had a chance to formulate contradictory opinions about these relative newcomers to the school. In this case, of course, it was the teachers, not the experimenter, who fulfilled the prophecy of academic success through their differential treatment of the supposed late bloomers. But an experimenter, even one

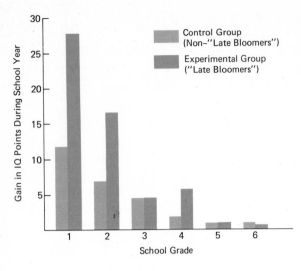

Figure 2.9 Teachers in each of the six grades of an elementary school were led to believe that certain of their pupils had been discovered to be "late bloomers" on the basis of a special test and would show great academic gains during the year. In fact, the pupils were selected at random. Intelligence tests were given both at the beginning and at the end of the school year. This histogram shows the relative IQ gains during the year of the control group (pupils not expected to be "late bloomers" by their teachers) and the experimental group (pupils who were expected to be late bloomers). Both groups gained in the lower grades, but the experimental group gained more. However, in the upper grades there was little effect, perhaps because the teachers already had strong expectations about the pupils based on their performances in earlier grades (After Rosenthal, 1966.)

who is fully aware that self-fulfilling prophecies can occur, can also sometimes inadvertently create the expected results.

One way for a researcher to avoid self-fulfilling prophecies is to employ a procedure called the **double-blind technique**, in which neither the experimenter nor the subjects know who has been assigned to the experimental group or who is acting as a control. (This procedure differs from the **single-blind technique**, in which the experimenter knows who is in which group but the subjects do not.) In an experiment testing the effects of a tranquilizing drug, for example, the experimental group would be given the tranquilizer and the control group would receive a placebo, perhaps in the form of a sugar pill. Only some outside party, such as the pharmacist who supplied the pills, would know which group received which kind of pill. The pharmacist would not give that information to the experimenter until after the effects of drug and placebo on the two groups of subjects had been recorded. In other types of studies similar techniques can be used. For example, psychologists looking for a possible positive correlation between IQ and psychological adjustment would assess psychological adjustment first, without knowing their subjects' IQ scores. In this way they could avoid seeing better adjustment in high-IQ subjects than was actually warranted.

Demand characteristics

Even if a researcher employs the double-blind technique, there is still a possibility that subjects will invalidate research findings by trying to behave like "good" subjects. Most students who volunteer for an experiment want to do well at the experimental task, so they come to the laboratory searching for clues as to what the experiment is about. The clues they uncover have been called **demand characteristics** because subjects feel these clues *demand* certain "correct" responses on their part (Orne, 1962). An example will illustrate the distorting effects demand characteristics can have.

Suppose you have volunteered for a psychological experiment. When you arrive at the laboratory a researcher tells you that the study involves memory for fast-moving events. She shows you a series of slides depicting successive stages in an automobile accident and then asks you twenty questions about them. One of the questions is: "Did another car pass the red Datsun while it was stopped at the stop sign?" This question puzzles you. The sign you remember seeing at the corner was a yield sign, not a stop sign. You conclude that the experimenter must be trying to trick you. But why? Later you believe you detect the experimenter's intentions. She shows you several pairs of very similar slides and asks which of each pair you saw previously. One pair shows the Datsun stopped at an intersection with either a stop sign or a yield sign at the corner. "Aha!" you say to yourself. "She expects me to choose the stop sign! Well, perhaps I should. After all, I'd hate to ruin her experiment." If you select the stop sign knowing full well it is the wrong sign, you have succumbed to demand characteristics. In doing so, you have obviously misled the experimenter and probably confused her interpretation of the results.

How can researchers counteract demand characteristics? One approach to this problem is to carefully question subjects after an experiment to see if demand characteristics were in fact influential. For instance, at the end of an experiment on memory similar to the one just described from a hypothetical subject's point of view, Loftus and her colleagues (1978) revealed their true purpose. They told subjects that they were trying to determine the effects of false information on eyewitness testimony by showing slides of an automobile accident and later asking questions about them. One of those questions, the researchers confessed, may have contained false information about the traffic sign located at the intersection. Would the subjects now please indicate which sign they *really* remember seeing. In this way, Loftus and her colleagues were able to get some idea of the extent to which demand characteristics had influenced their results. The answer: Hardly at all! We will explore some of the intriguing findings in the area of eyewitness testimony when we discuss memory in Chapter 6.

It should be kept in mind that even the most careful and sensitive questioning might not reveal the real reasons behind the subject's behavior. Moreover, as Carlsmith, Ellsworth, and Aronson (1976) have pointed out, "if the experimenter discovers at the close of the experiment that many subjects did behave in an artifactual way, the problem has not been solved" (p. 286). An alternative approach is to design the experiment in order to minimize the likelihood of experimenter demand. One possibility is to try to conceal the true purpose of the experiment through the use of deception. For example, in the study by Milgram (1963) described earlier, subjects were led to believe that the experiment concerned the effect of punishment on learning. The real hypothesis of interest was whether subjects would obey the experimenter and deliver painful shocks to a fellow subject. The use of deception in psychological research is highly controversial, however. We will discuss the ethical guidelines pertaining to it later in this chapter. Another way to reduce the effects of demand characteristics is to automate an experiment as much as possible in order to avoid personal sympathy or hostility toward the experimenter. A researcher, for example, might avoid face-to-face contact with subjects by using tape-recorded instructions and anonymous responses. But if carried to an extreme, this technique may make it difficult both to keep subjects involved in the experiment and to tailor procedures to suit their needs. In addition, automation can create an experimental situation so unnatural that the findings may have questionable application to the real world. A third approach is to increase the use of unobtrusive and/or behavioral measures. If subjects are not aware that a particular measure, such as activity, is being recorded, they are unlikely to distort it. Thus, white subjects may report that they are not prejudiced against blacks in order to please the experimenter or confirm the experimental hypothesis. But if their true attitudes toward blacks are negative, they would probably be unwilling to agree to spend a weekend escorting black students around campus (Marlowe, Frager, and Nuhall, 1965).

Problems of measurement

As we have mentioned earlier in this chapter, psychologists over the years have developed standard ways to measure certain phenomena. To measure intellectual ability, for instance, they use an IQ test. To measure the maze-running ability of a rat, they either time how long it takes the rat to run each successive trial or count how many trials are needed before the rat can run the maze flawlessly. For other phenomena, however, there are no set measurement procedures. So when faced with a choice of measurement approaches, psychologists can sometimes select a less than ideal one. Then, too, some phenomena are so elusive that even the cleverest psychologists may puzzle over how to measure them at all.

Measuring the independent variable: do the experimental and control conditions really differ? Sometimes faulty measurement invalidates an experiment almost before it begins: The technique for measuring the independent variable turns out to be seriously flawed. In such cases, the independent variable may remain the same for both the experimental and the control groups, but the researcher is unable to detect this. Needless to say, the results of such an experiment can be highly misleading.

Here is a case in point. You have probably heard about devices that supposedly allow you to "learn while you sleep." Such a device might consist of a tape recorder, several tapes on which to record material you want to memorize, and a small speaker to be placed under your pillow at night. The thought of such effortless learning is enticing indeed, but is it really possible? At first glance, designing a study to test whether sleep learning occurs appears fairly straightforward. You could present the same factual material to sleeping and wide-awake subjects and then see how much each group retains. Some studies that did just this seemed to show definite learning in the sleeping subjects.

The problem, however, is this: How do you know for sure that the subjects in the experimental group are asleep? In some early sleep-learning studies, the experimenters merely looked at the subjects, and if their eyes were closed, they assumed the subjects were sleeping. But having one's eyes closed, as you well know, does not necessarily indicate sleep. So it could be that in such studies no real difference existed between experimental and control subjects.

Subsequent studies have confirmed this criticism. In one experiment researchers presented subjects with ninety-six questions and answers concerning unfamiliar but easily learned material (Simon and Emmons, 1956). For example, one item was "Question: In what kind of store did Ulysses S. Grant work before the Civil War? Answer: A hardware store." The investigators gave the questions and answers to groups of subjects in different states of sleep, drowsiness, and wakefulness, as measured by EEG recordings of their brain waves. They then asked the questions again the next morning shortly after the subjects awakened. The results did not support the findings of the earlier studies or the claims of the manufacturers of sleep-learning machines. If the subjects were asleep, as indicated by the EEG recordings, they did not learn. The subjects who did learn were either dozing lightly or were awake, and the more awake they were, the more they learned. Thus, when appropriate measurements demonstrated that the experimental and control conditions really differed, it was found that sleep learning did not occur.

Measuring the dependent variable: is the measure sensitive enough? Even when a meaningful difference exists between experimental and control conditions, the method used to measure the dependent variable may not be sensitive enough to detect it. In such cases, no differences will be found between experimental and control groups, even though differences exist. Suppose two researchers are trying to determine if children between six months and one year old experience anxiety in the presence of strangers. They might expose babies of this age to strange and familiar adults and carefully observe their reactions. If the infants show no overt signs of distress in the presence of strangers, and if they smile at strangers as often as they smile at familiar faces, the researchers might conclude that the children did not experience stranger anxiety. But is this conclusion correct? More sensitive measures of anxiety suggest that it is not. Campos (1976), for example, has found that the heart rate of a nine-month-old infant tends to speed up when a stranger approaches, whereas the heart rate of a five-month-old infant slows down. Although we cannot yet say with certainty exactly what emotions these physiological changes indicate, it is clear that some difference in emotional reaction to strangers does exist between younger and older babies. Furthermore, fear is one of the human emotions generally associated with an accelerated heartbeat, so it is certainly possible that this was indeed the feeling that the nine-month-old infants in Campos's study were experiencing.

Additional evidence at least supports the hypothesis that a nine-month-old baby's response to strangers is negative. When babies of this age are given a choice, they show a strong preference to be away from strangers, even though they may not cry in a stranger's presence. This reaction is not displayed toward the people an infant knows. When nine-month-old babies have been taught to press a lever to get a glimpse of an adult, they press the lever more quickly to see their mothers than to see a female stranger. These various attempts to measure stranger anxiety in infants demonstrate how difficult it can sometimes be to measure a dependent variable accurately. Researchers must always be sure that their methods of measuring subjects' responses are sensitive enough to detect relatively subtle differences. Using several different measures simultaneously often helps achieve this goal.

Studying phenomena that defy direct, objective measurement At times psychologists encounter phenomena that defy direct, objective measurement. What do they do in such cases? Typically they develop indirect measures—and often highly ingenious ones.

Consider the problem of measuring what a hypnotized person experiences. Suppose a man in a deep hypnotic trance is told that he has lost his sense of hearing. How could you determine if he is deaf or not? You might try sounding a sudden loud noise to see if the man flinches. But even if he does not twitch a muscle, you still do not have proof of deafness. A startle reaction can, to some extent, be voluntarily controlled. A true test of hypnotic deafness, therefore, must be more subtle than this. Sutcliffe (1961) devised one such test, based on the knowledge that if a person hears his own voice played back about a fifth of a second after he has spoken, he cannot continue to speak normally. For obvious reasons such delayed auditory feedback has no effect on a deaf person. Sutcliffe found that even though hypnotized subjects show signs of being deaf, auditory-feedback tests indicated that they can in fact hear.

Similar problems of measurement exist in certain studies of human infants. How, for example, can researchers tell if an infant remembers something? How can they tell if a baby perceives the difference between two colors or two sounds? As you will see in Chapter 8, on human development, psychologists who study human infancy have devised many clever measurement techniques. One is a nipple that contains a device for measuring a baby's rate of sucking. Psychologists have found that sucking rate is a good measure of an infant's level of interest: the greater the interest, the more vigorous the sucking. By using this device, investigators can tell whether a baby finds a particular stimulus novel (and therefore interesting) or familiar (and therefore uninteresting). We will say much more about the measurement techniques developmental psychologists use in Chapter 8. The important point here is that with enough ingenuity, a method can be found to measure many psychological phenomena that initially appear to defy observation.

The replication requirement

During the course of their training, psychologists are taught to anticipate and overcome the kinds of methodological problems we have been describing. Despite all an investigator's efforts, however, errors sometimes occur. The need to bring these mistakes to light is one reason for the requirement that the findings of a scientific study be replicated—that is, duplicated by at least one other psychologist—before they are accepted by the profession.

Replicating a study does not necessarily mean repeating it in every detail. Sometimes a second psychologist attempts to reproduce all the conditions of the original study, but at other times the second investigator modifies some of the original conditions. For instance, he or she might use older adults as subjects instead of college students in order to assess the generality of the first psychologist's findings. When the results of either type of replication study do not agree with those of the original study, psychologists go back and try to figure out why.

In the process of replication psychologists often develop a fuller and more accurate understanding of the behavior being explored. Consider, for example, the following series of experiments. Several decades ago a pediatrician named Lee Salk proposed the interesting hypothesis that an unborn child, in the uterus, hears its mother's heart beating and comes to associate that sound with the security and comfort that unborn infants presumably experience in the womb (Salk, 1962). Consequently, Salk reasoned, newborn infants should find heartbeat sounds soothing; they should cry less, sleep more, and gain weight faster than infants who have no opportunity to hear the beating of a heart. Salk placed two groups of newborn infants in separate nurseries and played an amplified heartbeat in one. He found that the babies in the nursery with the heartbeat sound did cry less, sleep more, and gain weight faster than the babies in the other nursery. On the basis of these findings, he concluded that his hypothesis was correct.

Other researchers, however, were not satisfied. Just what characteristics of a heartbeat, they wanted to know, do newborns find so soothing? Is it the particular sound—the "lub-dub, lub-dub" that a beating heart makes—as Salk believed, or is it perhaps the rhythmic quality of the sound? Yvonne Brackbill and her colleagues (1966) tested the latter possibility by presenting groups of newborn infants with three different rhythmic sounds: a beating heart, a metronome, and a lullaby. As it turned out, all three sounds were equally effective in quieting the babies. This finding cast a certain amount of doubt on Salk's conclusions.

Furthermore, Brackbill thought, the crucial factor might not be the rhythmic quality of the sound at all. Beating hearts, metronomes, and lullabies are not only rhythmic but also constant and monotonous. Brackbill (1971) decided to find out the effect on newborns of other kinds of monotonous stimulation, such as constant light, increased heat, or the snug swaddling clothes in which babies in a number of cultures are dressed. Using different groups of infants, she assessed the effects of these stimuli singly and in various combinations. Her results were clear: The more types of constant stimulation the infants received, the quieter and more contented they seemed. And if a baby received only one kind of stimulation, the single most effective one was not the sound of a heartbeat but the sensation of being wrapped in swaddling clothes.

The sequence of events just described is a very common one in psychological research. A researcher conducts a study and obtains findings that are widely recognized as interesting, significant, and provocative. Other researchers study the first investigator's methods and conclusions and discover something about

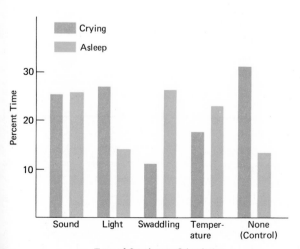

Figure 2.10 Percentage of time babies spent crying (while awake) and sleeping under various conditions of stimulation. The graph does not include time spent quietly awake or drowsy. (After Brackbill, 1971.)

them that raises questions. The other researchers then formulate and test hypotheses of their own, which differ in some way from those of the original experimenter. Ideally, these later investigations clarify, correct, and extend the findings of the first study, and so refine psychologists' understanding of that particular aspect of behavior.

ETHICAL PRINCIPLES IN PSYCHOLOGICAL RESEARCH

At several points in this chapter we have said that a certain research project could not be conducted because it would be "unethical." We noted, for example, that severely disciplining a group of children from birth in order to assess the relationship between harsh child rearing and juvenile delinquency would be completely out of the question. This procedure could obviously cause irreparable harm. But the propriety of other psychological studies is not always this clear-cut. Consider the following examples.

Suppose you are a clerk in a shoe store. At the busiest time of day a woman with a broken heel approaches you, wanting a new pair of shoes. You show her pair after pair but she curtly rejects each one. Would you feel annoyed or harassed to discover later that the woman was actually a psychologist who wanted to observe your reaction? Suppose this time that you are a homemaker. A man phones one morning claiming to represent a consumer group. He interviews you about the soap products you use, allegedly for a report in a public-service magazine. Several days later the same man calls again wanting to know if five or six other men could come to your home to "classify" all of the products you buy. If you found out later that this caller was a psychologist studying people's willingness to agree with such requests, would you feel that your privacy had been invaded? Suppose finally that you were riding on a New York subway and the passenger beside you collapsed at your feet, blood trickling from his mouth. This incident severely upset you. If you subsequently learned that the victim was a confederate in an experiment designed to investigate bystander apathy, would you feel that this deception was justified?

These are all actual experiments that psychologists have at some time performed (Schaps, 1972; Freedman and Fraser, 1966; Piliavin and Piliavin, 1972). As you can see, whether they are "right" or "wrong" is not easy to say. The crux of the problem is that psychologists have an obligation to find answers to important questions about human behavior, but they also have an obligation to protect the dignity and welfare of the people who participate in their research. These dual obligations can sometimes conflict. When they do, how, then, can a researcher decide whether or not to proceed with a particular investigation?

In 1973 the American Psychological Association issued ten principles to guide the conduct of research involving human subjects. These principles require, among other things, that an ethical researcher avoid all procedures that may in any way cause serious and lasting harm to participants. If the possibility of some physical or mental discomfort exists, the researcher should inform subjects of this fact and secure their consent before proceeding. A subject, of course, may choose to withdraw from a study because of some risk it poses; in such cases, the researcher must always respect the subject's decision. Finally, if a researcher finds it essential to employ deception at any time, he or she must later explain to subjects why this concealment was necessary.

In addition, there are federal regulations that require that all research sponsored by United States government grants be reviewed and approved by a panel of qualified people in light of these and similar standards of conduct. In fact, most universities today require that *all* research involving human subjects receive the approval of such a review board, and stringent standards also exist for the care and treatment of animal subjects.

The decision as to whether a particular study conforms to ethical principles is, of course, a complex one. In the 1960s and early 1970s, the decision was usually made by weighing possible risks to subjects against the value of the information to be gained. By the late 1970s, however, the ethical tide had turned, and researchers have become extremely sensitive to considerations. Some psychologists worry that the increasing regulations and concern about ethics may make it difficult for them to conduct meaningful research (Kimmel, 1979). But all agree that researchers have a responsibility to design their studies in ways that will safeguard the rights of participants.

SUMMARY

1. In order to answer the questions they ask, psychologists use a variety of research methods. Which method they use depends in part on the question being asked and in part on the goal of the research. Because it would be impossible to observe all the people relevant to any question about human behavior, psychologists almost always rely on a **sample**, or selected segment, of the data available. In a **random sample**, every member of the total population has an equal chance of being included. In a **representative sample**, people belonging to groups that contain specific characteristics are randomly selected in proportion to their numbers in the population as a whole.

2. The **experiment** is a method favored by many researchers because it permits them to control conditions and so rule out all influences on subjects' behavior except the factors being examined. The researcher works with two groups of subjects—the **experimental group**, which experiences the experimental condition, and the **control group**, which does not. All experimenters set out to test a **hypothesis**, or proposition. To do so they explore the relationship between two **variables**, or factors capable of change. The variable that the experimenter deliberately manipulates is called the **independent variable**; the **dependent variable** changes only when the independent variable changes.

3. When experiments are not possible, psychologists may use **quasi-experimental designs** or **correlational research** to determine the extent to which the variables they are concerned with are related to each other. A **positive correlation** means that a high rank on one variable is accompanied by a high rank on the other. In a **negative correlation**, a high rank on one is accompanied by a low rank on the other.

4. One way of collecting data for a correlational study is through a **survey**, an attempt to estimate the opinions, characteristics, or behaviors of a particular population by investigating a representative sample. Interviews, questionnaires, or public records may provide the data of interest.

5. In order to eliminate the effects that may occur from subjects' knowledge that they are being studied, psychologists sometimes use **naturalisitc observation**, observation in a natural setting where the subjects do not know they are being studied and the investigator stays out of the way. In **participant observation**, the setting is natural but the researcher joins an existing group to record thoughts and feelings accessible to only group members.

6. A **case study**, or in-depth analysis of an individual, can be used when there is not a population large enough from which to draw a sample.

7. Psychologists use a variety of tools for measuring individual differences. These include **behavioral measures** and **physiological measures**.

8. Even with all the tools available, it is still sometimes not enough to examine subjects at a single point in time. Then a **longitudinal study**—a study of the same group at intervals over a period of years—may be used.

9. To interpret the data they have collected, psychologists use **statistics**—mathematical methods for assessing and presenting the data in summary form. Statistics may be descriptive or inferential. **Descriptive statistics** enable investigators to present their findings with a few words and figures. In interpreting a survey, for example, the frequency of each score, or **frequency distribution**, is plotted on a graph called a **histogram**. In order to compare two histograms, researchers compare **central tendencies**, or middle values, of the two sets of scores. The **arithmetic mean**, the **median**, and the **mode** are all measures of central tendency.

10. Psychologists also need measures of variability, or ways of describing the variability in a set of data. The **range** gives the distance between the highest and lowest scores. The **dispersion** of scores tells whether they are clustered together or spread out. A more sensitive measure is the **standard deviation**, which indicates the average extent to which all the scores in a particular set vary from the mean. To find the strength of a correlation (the degree of relatedness between two variables) psychologists calculate a **correlation coefficient**.

11. Inferential statistics enable researchers to conclude whether the data clearly support their original hypothesis, or whether the results they have obtained could have been gotten by chance alone. They use measures of **probability** to supply the answer to that question. The researcher who finds that the data have attained the level of **statistical significance** concludes that the results are not due merely to chance and that they do indeed support the hypothesis.

12. The use of the research methods and statistical techniques we have described does not guarantee that researchers will not run into problems that can invalidate their studies. Among the possible pitfalls is the **self-fulfilling prophecy**, the fact that the expectations of investigators can influence their findings. To avoid this, psychologists may use the **double-blind technique**, in which neither the experimenter nor the subjects know who has been assigned to the experimental group or to the control group.

13. Another problem arises when subjects search for **demand characteristics**, or clues to the responses they think the researcher wants. Although demand characteristics and their biasing effect cannot be eliminated entirely, they can be minimized in a variety of ways.

14. Despite all a researcher's efforts to eliminate methodological problems, errors may still occur. For this reason, the findings of all scientific studies are subject to a replication requirement—the requirement that they be replicated, or duplicated, by at least one other psychologist before they are accepted by the profession.

15. In order to carry out research on human behavior without bringing harm to their subjects, psychologists have devised certain ethical guidelines that were formally issued as a set of ten principles in 1973 by the American Psychological Association. These include—besides avoiding all procedures that may cause harm to the participants—respecting a subject's decision to withdraw from a study and explaining why a certain deception or concealment was necessary if such was the case. The federal government and most universities require that all research meet similar standards.

Suggested readings

Anderson, B. F. *The psychology experiment* (2nd ed.). Belmont, Calif.: Brooks-Cole, 1971.

Christensen, L. B. *Experimental methodology* (2nd ed.). Boston: Allyn & Bacon, 1980.

Huff, D. *How to lie with statistics.* New York: Norton, 1954.

Neale, J. M., and Liebert, R. M. *Science and behavior* (2nd ed.). Englewood Cliffs, N.J.: Prentice-Hall, 1980.

Sternberg, R. J. *Writing the psychology paper.* Woodbury, N.Y.: Barron's Educational Series, 1977.

Wood, G. *Fundamentals of psychological research* (2nd ed.). Boston: Little, Brown, 1977.

BIOLOGICAL AND PERCEPTUAL PROCESSES

The biological and perceptual aspects of our functioning are discussed in Part 2. Chapter 3 describes communication within the nervous system, as the brain mediates behavior. Chapter 4 focuses on sensation and perception: how we perceive—and therefore experience—the world around us.

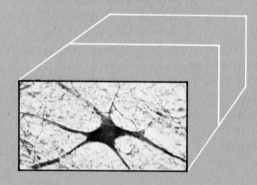

PREVIEW

1. In determining behavior, the brain is the most influential organ in the body. With the endocrine system, the brain and nervous system integrate and regulate all body signals and responses.

2. The neuron, or nerve cell, is the basic structural unit of the nervous system. Ultimately, we understand the role of the brain and nervous system in behavior only to the degree that we understand individual neurons.

3. Information is conveyed throughout the nervous system in electrochemical form.

4. Messages are also conveyed within the body by the endocrine system. Endocrine glands secrete hormones into the bloodstream, which regulate and influence our behavior.

5. The brain is studied by removing or stimulating sections of it or by monitoring its electrical activity.

6. Some specific behaviors are mediated by specific parts of the brain; others do not seem to be localized—and some parts of the brain are involved in the performance of many types of behavior.

3 Biological foundations of behavior

Questions about human behavior have always occupied scholars, but a great many centuries passed before the brain was identified as intimately involved in the answers. The Greek philosopher Aristotle, for example, believed that the heart controlled behavior. Others suggested that the various bodily fluids were responsible. Still others thought that all human thoughts, actions, and feelings were ultimately controlled by gods.

In the early nineteenth century the idea that behavior was somehow influenced by the brain gained special prominence. Franz Joseph Gall, a Viennese anatomist, compared the human brain with the brains of various animals. He also compared the head shapes of people who had many different traits and talents to see if he could detect any similarities among them. For example, after studying thieves and pickpockets in prisons throughout Europe, Gall came to the conclusion that most of them had a lump on their skulls above their ears. As a result of these studies, he arrived at a theory of the brain that he believed accounted for all behavioral similarities and differences, both among humans and between humans and other animals. Gall suggested that the human brain was composed of thirty-seven distinct organs, each related to a fundamental behavioral "trait," as shown in Figure 3.1. The more a person expressed a trait, the more the region of the brain related to that trait would swell up, much as our muscles develop with exercise. Thus, the size of a particular portion of the brain was believed to reflect the magnitude of a certain trait. For example, because the human frontal lobes are considerably larger than those of any

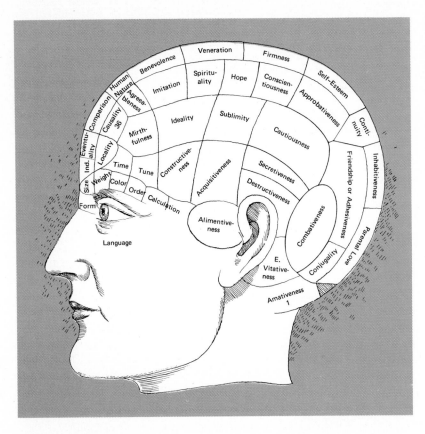

Figure 3.1 Franz Joseph Gall believed that the shape of the skull revealed the shape of the brain beneath it. Traits considered to be specifically "human" (such as logical thinking ability) were thought to be located in the front part of the brain, because this part was much larger in human beings than in other animals. Other, more "animal" traits such as amativeness (sexual behavior) were thought to be located toward the bottom and rear of the brain, since these areas appeared to be quite similar in many animals. According to Gall's "science" of phrenology, when the area of the skull presumably corresponding to the trait of, say, "causality" was very large in a particular individual, this meant the person was capable of deep and powerful reasoning. If this area was small, the individual was thought to be lacking in this trait.

other animal, Gall thought that certain traits, such as the abilities to calculate and reason, were located there. Those people with the largest frontal lobes, then, were believed to have more potential for these "higher-order" traits and so for becoming, say, poets, mathematicians, and statesmen. People with small frontal lobes were believed to be more "animal" in nature and to constitute the bulk of the criminal class. Gall's theory later came to be known as **phrenology**— the study of character by assessing the shape of the skull, which, Gall believed, closely conformed to the shape of the brain beneath (Fowler and Fowler, 1969).

As ludicrous as this theory may sound today, in the context of his own era, Gall's accomplishment was singularly creative and exciting. At that time solid scientific knowledge of brain function was virtually nonexistent. Even the most educated people knew far less about the workings of the brain than does a high school biology student today. Gall brought the brain into the limelight as the organ responsible for behavior, and he even suggested some testable hypotheses about how the brain was constructed.

In the century and a half since Gall proposed his theory, we have learned that the brain indeed has a rich and detailed relationship to all aspects of behavior. We know that damage to different parts of the brain can disrupt muscle movement and perception and produce a host of specific behavioral disturbances: inability to remember anything new, hypersexuality, overeating, inability to waken from sleep (or inability to go to sleep in the first place), and so on. Likewise, chemical or mild electrical stimulation of various parts of the brain may cause changes in eating, drinking, sleeping, mating, aggression, and other patterns of behavior. Because of the complex and intimate relationships between the brain and behavior, questions about brain function are a source of great fascination to all psychologists and especially to the large and active group of **physiological psychologists** who specialize in answering them.

In studying how the brain and behavior are related, psychologists examine the nervous system's anatomy and physiology—that is, its structure and function. They seek answers to three fundamental questions: (1) How does information from the environment, from either the world outside the body or the world within, become transformed into information that the brain can use? (2) How do the various components of the nervous system transform this information into thoughts, feelings, and actions? And (3) how does the brain activate the body's muscles and glands in response to environmental conditions? In this chapter we will look at what is known about the answers to these questions. We will begin by discussing some basic features of the body's two communication networks: the nervous system, of which the brain is a part, and the endocrine system, which consists of a number of hormone-secreting glands. Together these two systems are responsible for integrating and regulating all signals and responses in the body. We will then focus on the brain and how its different features are related to various aspects of behavior. In the process, we will explore the major techniques for studying brain function and some of the interesting findings they have revealed. And finally, we will look at the brain's role in complex behaviors like learning, memory, and problem solving. As you will see, how the brain performs these activities is still largely a mystery.

THE NERVOUS SYSTEM

Consisting of billions of interconnected cells that radiate throughout the body, the human nervous system is one of the most complex creations in the living world. Unfortunately, we cannot isolate the whole nervous system for study the way we might isolate the liver or the kidneys. Nevertheless, by examining its various component parts and by trying to determine how they are related, scientists have been able to unlock many of the secrets of how the nervous system functions.

The cells of the human nervous system are highly specialized. **Receptor cells**, embedded in the sense organs, are specialized for receiving various types of stimulation from the environment. **Effector cells** are specialized for contracting muscles and for stimulating glandular secretions. **Neurons**, or nerve cells, are specialized for conducting signals from one part of the body to another; they connect receptor cells to effector cells and integrate and coordinate their activities. During each waking second, a person's eyes, ears, and other sense receptors send approximately 100 million messages to the brain. To perform even a simple behavior like swinging a tennis racket, the brain must issue millions of commands to the muscles. In this section we will be most concerned with neurons, which form the major part of the nervous system. We begin with a description of the nervous system as a whole, and then turn to the structure and operation of its basic unit, the neuron.

Divisions of the nervous system

Most of the body's neurons are found in the brain and spinal cord, which lie within the bony casings of the skull and spinal column. These parts of the nervous system are called the **central nervous system (CNS)** because they provide the ultimate control center for all human behavior, from simple reflexes to abstract reasoning. Branching out from the central nervous system and leading to all parts of the body is the **peripheral nervous system (PNS)**. The peripheral nervous system conveys signals from the body's sensory receptors to the central nervous system and transmits messages back out to the muscles and glands. How the central and peripheral nervous systems interrelate is shown in Figure 3.2.

The peripheral nervous system can be further subdivided into the **somatic** and the **autonomic** divisions. In general, somatic activity is related to the external environment, and autonomic activity regulates the internal environment. More specifically, the somatic division controls the skeletal muscles—that is, the muscles that move the bones. When you raise an arm or wriggle a toe you are using your somatic nervous system. These are activities that we usually think of as being under voluntary control. The autonomic division, in contrast, controls the visceral muscles (blood vessels, heart, intestines) and the glands. Autonomic activity is usually classified as involuntary because it occurs more or less automatically. Most people do not consciously control the contraction of their digestive tract, for instance, or the beating of their heart. There is evidence, however, that people can *learn* to influence such "involuntary" autonomic activities when appropriate feedback is available. Thus, cardiac patients have sometimes learned to voluntarily lower their heart rate and reduce their blood pressure. Research on this procedure, called biofeedback, is discussed more fully in Chapter 12.

The autonomic nervous system itself has two divisions: the **sympathetic** and the **parasympathetic**. With a few exceptions, any given visceral muscle or gland in the body is innervated (supplied with nerves) by both these divisions. This is called *dual control*. In general, these two divisions can be viewed as working antagonistically; that is, they tend to have broadly opposite effects on the muscles and glands they innervate.

The sympathetic system is usually involved in mobilizing the body's resources. In an emergency or a stress situation, it responds by increasing blood sugar, raising heart rate and blood pressure, and inhibiting digestive processes. In contrast, the parasympathetic division dominates under conditions of relaxation and tends to conserve the body's energy. For example, after you eat a large meal, your parasympathetic system works to aid digestion, at the same time decreasing heart rate and blood flow to the skeletal muscles. The actions of the sympathetic and parasympathetic divisions, of course, do not always divide as neatly as these brief descriptions suggest. Often the effects of one influence the effects of the other. Thus, if you received distressing news while eating a meal, the sympathetic system would quickly exert itself, causing you to experience nausea and loss of appetite. Then, too, many behaviors require a combination of sympathetic and parasympathetic activity. For instance, sexual arousal is mediated by the parasympathetic division, but sexual orgasm is a sympathetic response. A schematic diagram showing how the various parts of the nervous system are related is presented in Figure 3.3.

Neurons and reflex arcs

Neurons are the building blocks or basic structural units of the nervous system. All the tissues we call **nerves** are simply bundles of many neurons. These cells

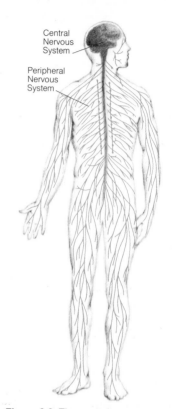

Central Nervous System

Peripheral Nervous System

Figure 3.2 The central nervous system (CNS) and the peripheral nervous system (PNS) in the human body. Both of these systems are made up of billions of nerve cells, or neurons, each of which is capable of transmitting a train of electrochemical signals in one direction. In the CNS, these neurons form an immensely complex network that organizes, stores, and redirects vast quantities of information. In the PNS, neurons in every pathway carry information either from receptors (such as the sense organs) toward the CNS or away from the CNS to effectors (in the muscles, for example). There is a close match between information going to the CNS and information coming from it. Every muscle, for example, not only receives from the CNS directions to contract or relax but also sends back information about its present state of contraction or relaxation.

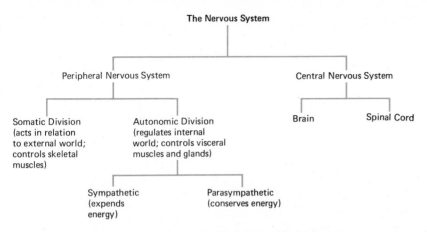

The Nervous System

Peripheral Nervous System

Central Nervous System

Somatic Division
(acts in relation
to external world;
controls skeletal
muscles)

Autonomic Division
(regulates internal
world; controls visceral
muscles and glands)

Brain   Spinal Cord

Sympathetic
(expends
energy)

Parasympathetic
(conserves energy)

Figure 3.3 Diagram of the relationship among the parts of the nervous system.

transmit messages in the form of electrochemical impulses from one part of the body to another. There are more than 12 billion neurons in the human body, and even the simplest action or behavior, such as blinking your eyes, involves many thousands of neurons all working together.

The vast majority of neurons are located in the brain, with the rest distributed throughout the spinal cord and the peripheral nervous system. Although all neurons appear to operate in much the same way, they vary greatly in size and shape depending on their locations in the nervous system. Still, most neurons have three major regions: the **cell body**, or **soma**, which contains the cell nucleus, and two types of fibers (**processes**) that branch out from the cell body—the numerous and relatively short **dendrites** and the long **axon**.

Neurons are categorized according to the structures between which they conduct messages (Figure 3.4). **Sensory neurons** (sometimes called **afferent neurons**) carry information from the sense organs to the brain and spinal cord;

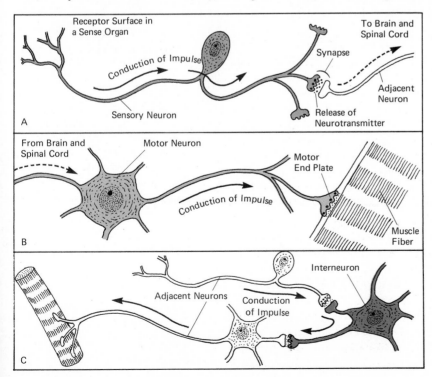

Figure 3.4 The three types of specialized neurons. (A) A sensory, or afferent, neuron. (B) A motor, or efferent, neuron. The motor end plate releases a neurotransmitter that can change the electrical state of the muscle it is connected to. (C) An interneuron. The interneurons either inhibit or excite the motor neurons that supply opposing muscles. Their action on the motor neurons is based on the input they receive from sensory neurons. For example, in order for the pain reflex to occur, the interneuron must receive information from a sensory neuron, which causes the interneuron to send inhibitory impulses to the connecting motor neuron. This motor neuron, in turn, inhibits the appropriate extensor muscle, thereby permitting withdrawal of the arm from a painful stimulus (adapted from Williams and Warwick, 1975).

motor neurons (sometimes called **efferent neurons**) carry signals from the brain and spinal cord to the muscles and glands. **Interneurons** connect neurons to other neurons and integrate the activities of the sensory and motor neurons. It is the relationships between interneurons that somehow become translated into what we subjectively describe as thoughts, feelings, perceptions, and memories. In humans, interneurons are much more numerous than sensory and motor neurons. For example, it has been estimated that for every motor neuron there are more than 4,000 interneurons.

Neurons share the central nervous system with cells called **glia**, which are usually smaller than neurons but about ten times more numerous. *Glia* means "glue," and the word precisely describes one of the functions that the glial cells serve: They surround the neurons and hold them in place. In addition, the glial cells also appear to carry nutrients to the neurons, to remove their waste products, to repair damaged neurons, and to provide a barrier that protects the neurons from certain substances in the bloodstream. They may also play a role in the propagation of impulses. The glia, then, are extremely important in enabling neurons to carry out their work. But it is the neurons themselves that play the major role in behavior.

The cell body is the metabolic center of the neuron and provides the energy for neural activity. The dendrites, which can be thought of as the "antennae" of the neuron, and sometimes parts of the cell body and axon, have specialized areas for receiving messages transmitted by other neurons. These messages usually travel in one direction: from the dendrites, to the cell body, and down the length of the axon, the "communication line," as illustrated in Figure 3.5. When the messages reach the end of the axon, they activate the muscle fibers, glandular cells, or other neurons with which the axon connects.

The simplest set of connections between neurons is the **reflex arc**, which links a sensory input to a motor response. Reflex arcs are located throughout the nervous system, but those that occur within the spinal cord, with no direct relay to the brain, have been the most systematically studied.

One well-known spinal reflex arc is the knee jerk, which is elicited by tapping the tendon below the kneecap. It involves only two kinds of neurons: the sensory neurons that convey information about stimulation of the tendon to the spinal cord, and the motor neurons that stimulate the muscle groups in the thigh attached to the tendon to contract, causing a kick. This two-neuron reflex arc is illustrated in part A of Figure 3.6. Most reflexes, however, are more complicated than the two-neuron knee jerk. For example, part B of Figure 3.6 diagrams a pain withdrawal reflex that involves three kinds of neurons, the extra neurons in this chain being interneurons, which connect the other two kinds. In the act of withdrawing a leg that is exposed to pain, the interneurons also pass information to the other leg, enabling body weight to be shifted when the withdrawal reflex occurs.

Although spinal reflexes can take place without control by the brain, this does not mean that the brain is uninvolved in them. For instance, the painful stimulation that triggers a withdrawal reflex must travel to the brain in order to be experienced as pain. This trip takes time, so the subjective feeling of pain often takes place after we have begun to perform the reflex response. You probably can recall an occasion when you touched a very hot object, withdrew your hand, and only then became aware of the pain. The neurons that travel the length of the spinal cord and lead to and from the brain also permit some

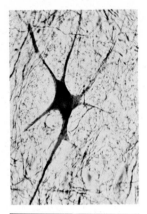

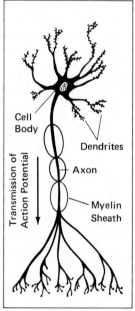

Figure 3.5 A photomicrograph and a diagram of the parts of a single neuron. The dendrites are the receiving end of the neuron; the axon is the sending end. An action potential is transmitted along the axon of a neuron when its dendrites have been sufficiently excited.

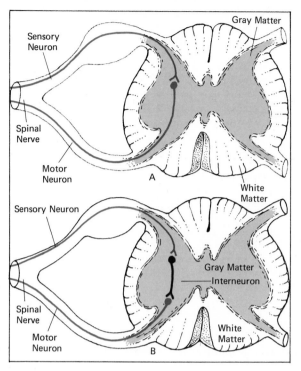

Figure 3.6 (A) A diagram of a two-neuron reflex arc, such as the one present in the knee-jerk reflex. This is the simplest form of reflex arc. (B) A diagram of a three-neuron reflex arc. The pain reflex, which causes a quick withdrawal from the painful stimulus, is an example of this type of reflex arc. It involves one set each of motor and sensory neurons (as in the two-neuron reflex arc), but in addition, an interneuron is present in the gray matter of the spinal cord. The extra neuron means that the information now crosses two synapses (Gardner, 1975).

voluntary control over reflexes. You can demonstrate this to yourself by having someone tap the tendon below your kneecap to elicit the knee-jerk reflex. Then have the person tap in the same place while you concentrate on preventing the response. The pathways that link the brain to the spinal cord should enable you to hold your leg steady.

The importance of these neural pathways can be appreciated by considering what happens to a paraplegic—a person whose spinal cord has been severed and hence cut off from control by the brain. Such individuals have no sensation in the lower part of their bodies, and they cannot move their legs voluntarily. Since the nerves in the spinal cord are not capable of regeneration, this loss of function is permanent. The reflexes controlled by the isolated spinal cord still operate, so a paraplegic will continue to show the knee-jerk reflex if his or her leg is tapped. Unlike people who have their spinal cord intact, however, paraplegics are not able to exert control over the knee-jerk reflex and thus prevent it. Nor can they feel the leg kick; in fact, they would not even know that their leg had moved unless they were watching it. A similar process occurs with sexual behavior, which can also be controlled reflexively by the spinal cord. If their genitals are directly stimulated, most male paraplegics are capable of erection and ejaculation. However, they experience none of the local sensations that normally accompany these responses.

We have discussed spinal reflex arcs in some detail because they provide a relatively simple model of reflex action. But reflex systems are by no means confined to the spinal cord. They are present throughout the nervous system and are involved in a large number of complex behaviors. Even a seemingly simple reflex, such as dilation of the pupil of the eye, can be linked to many neural pathways. At the most basic level, pupil dilation is a reflex reaction to a sudden reduction of light. The dimmed lighting is sensed by receptor cells in the eye, and the message is routed through sensory neurons, interneurons, and motor neurons until it reaches the appropriate muscles in the iris (the colored portion of the eye that surrounds the pupil). This you may have already known. But did you know that pupil dilation is also triggered by emotional arousal, and by the performance of various mental activities that seem to have no emotional overtones?

These facts were confirmed by psychologist Eckhard Hess, who studied pupil response extensively a number of years ago (Hess, 1965). In many of his earliest experiments, Hess had subjects peer into a box that had a projection screen at the rear. A motion-picture camera recorded the size of a subject's pupils while different slides were displayed. Hess found that pupils tend to dilate in response to pleasant or interesting visual stimuli (such as a nude of the opposite sex) and constrict in response to unpleasant ones (such as a picture of a crippled child). People in many Eastern cultures apparently have recognized this pattern for centuries. A Chinese jade merchant will usually observe the dilation of customers' pupils to judge their interest in a particular stone and to estimate the price they might be willing to pay. This is one reason why they may stand at a closer conversational distance than most Westerners find comfortable: Pupil response is difficult to scrutinize at a range much beyond two feet (Hall, 1979).

The pupils also dilate extensively when people taste a food they particularly like or listen to a piece of music they find especially pleasing. Moreover, pupil dilation occurs in situations seemingly unrelated to pleasure. If you were asked to solve a mental arithmetic problem, for instance, your pupils would steadily enlarge while you were computing the answer and then rapidly constrict once you announced the solution. Surprisingly, the maximum size your pupils reached would closely correlate with the problem's difficulty. Such findings clearly show how complex the circuitry of the human nervous system is and how even a seemingly simple reflex can be triggered by many nerve networks.

How neural signals are transmitted

Although we have talked about reflex arcs at some length, we have not yet explained how the neurons involved in such systems actually transmit their messages. For many years scientists recognized that nerve signals were electrical in nature, but the details of neural activity remained a mystery until researchers had the technology to measure the responses of a single nerve cell. These measurements revealed that neural impulses are conducted by means of an electrochemical process. The fluids in the body contain ions—electrically charged molecules or atoms. The nerve cell membrane selectively regulates the passage of particular ions into and out of the cell. In its resting state, the membrane allows potassium (K^+) and chloride (Cl^-) ions to enter the cell, but excludes sodium (Na^+) ions. As a result, the cell becomes **polarized**—negatively charged inside and positively charged outside. This electrical imbalance across the cell membrane is known as the **resting potential**. If a stimulus affects the cell with enough intensity, the membrane temporarily becomes permeable to a sudden inrush of sodium ions, which causes the cell's polarity to change at the point of stimulation: For an instant, the cell interior becomes positive and the exterior negative. This abrupt change, called the **action potential**, is conducted down the length of the axon much like a spark travels down a fuse. But the neuron, in contrast to a fuse, very quickly restores itself, thus enabling it to conduct a burst of many action potentials in rapid succession.

The velocity at which action potentials travel ranges from about one to four hundred meters per second—that is, from about two to nearly nine hundred miles an hour! The exact speed depends on the properties of the different axons. One important property is the presence of the **myelin sheath**, a fatty whitish substance that wraps around an axon. (Myelinated axons form the **white matter** of the nervous system; nonmyelinated axons, dendrites, and cell bodies form the **gray matter**.) The sheath serves as insulation and thereby increases the speed at which neural impulses can travel by as much as five times the velocity along nonmyelinated structures. Because the myelin sheaths perform such a key function, it is not surprising that extensive damage to them would severely hinder the workings of the nervous system. The disease called multiple sclerosis, for example, is caused by progressive destruction of myelin in the spinal cord and brain. The myelin is replaced with a hard, intermeshing plaque, and the axons that lie within it can no longer conduct nerve impulses. The results are the lack of coordination and progressive loss of muscular control associated with the disease. Scientists do not yet know what initiates multiple sclerosis, but they suspect that a virus may be involved and that the destruction of the myelin may be a tragic side effect of the body's efforts to combat this invader (Morell and Norton, 1980).

How is a neural message coded in action potentials? The *nature* of a message is determined in large part by the particular pathway along which it travels. Stimulation of the visual nerves, for example, produces a visual sensation. When you close your eyelids and rub your eyes, you often stimulate your visual nerves and perceive splashes of color. Similarly, stimulation of the nerves leading from your tongue, nasal membranes, and inner ears produce the sensations of taste, smell, and sound respectively. The *strength* of a message is primarily conveyed by the axon's rate of firing: The more intense a stimulus, the higher the firing rate. Some neurons can generate as many as one thousand action potentials per second. Also, as stimuli increase in intensity, many more neurons will fire.

We have said that when action potentials reach the end of an axon they stimulate the muscle fibers, glandular cells, or other neurons with which that axon connects. But we have not yet explained how this communication is possible, given that every axon is physically separated from adjacent cells by tiny gaps called **synapses**. The answer lies in chemical substances known as **neurotransmitters**, which are stored in vesicles at the terminals, or endings, of each axon. When action potentials reach an axon terminal, they stimulate the release of these neurotransmitters, which diffuse across the synapse and activate receptor sites on the adjacent cell. Figure 3.7 illustrates this general process, although it is unable to show several important details. First, a typical nerve cell has thousands of synapses rather than the few shown here. Second, the receptor sites are activated because the molecular structure of the neurotransmitter "fits" them, much as a key fits a lock. As Figure 3.7 suggests, a dendrite usually receives the neurotransmitter's message, but sometimes a cell body or an axon may receive it as well. In any case, depending on the chemistry of the neuro-

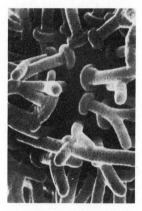

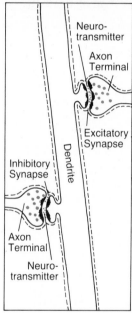

Figure 3.7 An electron micrograph and a diagram of the structures at the synapse. Note the correspondence between the axon terminals and the small protrusions on the dendrites in the diagram in Figure 3.5. When an action potential reaches the end of the axon of a neuron, small amounts of neurotransmitter are released from vesicles and diffuse across the synapse to activate the dendrites of another neuron. The substances from some neurons are excitatory in their effect, the substances from others are inhibitory.

transmitter and the nature of the receptor site, the message carried may be either *excitatory*, causing a reaction in the receiving cell, or *inhibitory*, decreasing or preventing a response.

You might think that the nervous system could make do with just two transmitters—one to excite and one to inhibit. But this is clearly not the case. In recent years scientists have isolated quite a number of neurotransmitters, and there are undoubtedly many more still to be discovered. Some experts think there may be several hundred (Snyder, 1980). Why so many chemical transmitters? No one knows for sure. At this point, researchers are primarily concerned with identifying these substances, mapping the locations of their receptor sites, and discovering in what behavioral processes they are involved. Consider acetylcholine, or ACh, one of the best understood of the neurotransmitters. It is found in various parts of the peripheral nervous system, in the spinal cord, and in specific regions of the brain. In the peripheral nervous system it activates receptor sites embedded in both muscles and glands. For instance, ACh carries messages across the synapses between motor neurons and skeletal muscles, where it has an excitatory effect. Thus it is instrumental in making skeletal muscles contract.

Identification of the roles that neurotransmitters play at various receptor sites has provided important insight into how certain drugs have their effects. Curare, the poison that South American Indians use on their arrows, appears to occupy the receptor sites that ACh molecules normally activate and so prevents ACh from functioning. The result is complete paralysis. The lethal poison botulin, which develops in improperly preserved food, also causes paralysis through its effects on ACh synapses, but these effects are quite different from those of curare. Botulin appears to block the release of ACh from the axon vesicles. Interestingly, the venom of the black widow spider seems to have the opposite effect: It causes a continuous flood of ACh into neuromuscular synapses. The result is violent and uncontrollable muscle contraction.

Scientists are now compiling an ever-growing list of neurotransmitters, each apparently associated with specific neural pathways, behavior functions, and psychological states. As we will see in Chapter 15, abnormalities in the activities of certain neurotransmitters have been implicated in many serious psychological disorders. For example, increasing the supply of the neurotransmitters norepinephrine and serotonin relieves depression, and reducing the activities of the neurotransmitter dopamine can dramatically ameliorate the symptoms of schizophrenia. (In fact, the drugs called phenothiazines, which are widely used to treat schizophrenia, are believed to inhibit the action of the brain's dopamine receptors.) Other recently discovered neurotransmitters, such as enkephalin and endorphin (neologism for "endogenous morphine," a morphine made in the body), seem to inhibit pain and produce a feeling of well-being. Morphine and other opiates are similar in molecular structure to these neurotransmitters and so mimic their effects (Snyder, 1980). Researchers now suspect that "psychological" pain relievers, such as placebos or perhaps acupuncture, may trigger the release of enkephalin and related chemicals in the nervous system (Fields, 1978). It has even been speculated that running stimulates the production of endorphins by causing the body pain. This may account for the feeling or euphoria that sometimes occurs after running and for the tendency of runners to develop a "positive addiction" to the sport. Precisely how these various transmitters actually carry out their work is not yet fully understood. But the more researchers learn about the role of neurotransmitters in human behavior, the more remarkably complex our nervous system appears.

THE ENDOCRINE SYSTEM

One impressive fact about the nervous system is the speed at which neural signals travel—a neural impulse can be transmitted through the body in roughly one-thousandth of a second. The nervous system plays such an important role in behaviors where speed is essential, such as withdrawing a hand from a flame or other painful stimulus. Not all behaviors necessitate such quick response, however. In those where speed is not crucial, such as sexual arousal, the endocrine system provides a more economical and comprehensive means of communicating with the millions of cells in the body's organs. Through the combined action of the nervous and endocrine systems, then, the brain has a highly efficient means of monitoring and controlling behavior.

The endocrine system is a chemical communication system: Its messengers are chemical substances called **hormones**, which are produced by the **endocrine glands** and secreted into the bloodstream. (The **exocrine glands**, in contast, secrete their products—such as saliva, tears, and sweat—through ducts to the body's surface or into body cavities.) When released, the hormones from the endocrine glands (Figure 3.8) have important effects on various aspects of behavior, including sexual function, physical growth, emotional responses, motivation, and the availability of energy. Although hormones circulate throughout the bloodstream, they have their effects only at certain **target organs**. Hormone action, in other words, is highly selective.

Probably the most influential gland in the human body is the **pituitary**, a structure only about half an inch (less than a centimeter) in diameter, which lies at the base of the brain just below a region called the hypothalamus. In spite of its small size, the pituitary controls a wide range of bodily functions. Consequently, it has often been called the "master gland."

The pituitary is divided into two distinct lobes, the anterior and the posterior. The posterior lobe, which is attached directly to the hypothalamus by a small stalk, secretes two hormones. One stimulates muscular contraction in the uterus (and so is involved in both female orgasm and childbirth) as well as the release of milk from the mammary glands. The other acts to decrease the amount of water that the kidneys excrete. The anterior pituitary lobe produces at least six hormones. Of particular importance is a *growth hormone*, which plays a key role in a child's physical development. If a severe deficit of growth hormone occurs during childhood, a person will become a midget. If, in contrast, overproduction of growth hormone take place at an early age, a child will become a giant. (Some pituitary giants have grown to heights of nearly nine feet!) When such glandular oversecretion begins in adulthood, a person does not suddenly resume growing; only a few adult tissues are sensitive to growth hormone—namely, the bones of the face, fingers, and toes. Adults with excessive output of growth hormone develop a condition called acromegaly, in which the hands, feet, and facial features become grossly enlarged and distorted. In addition to growth hormone and another hormone that stimulates the production of milk in female mammals, the anterior pituitary secretes four hormones that regulate the output of other endocrine glands: One affects the thyroid gland; another

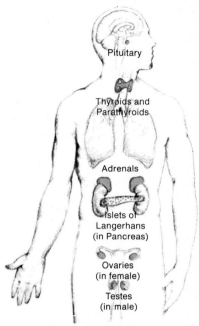

Figure 3.8 The endocrine glands. The glands whose activity is most important in the regulation of behavior are the pituitary, the thyroid, the adrenals, and the gonads (ovaries or testes).

affects the cortex of the adrenal glands; and two affect the output of the sex glands, or gonads.

The **thyroid gland** is located in the neck, on either side of the windpipe and esophagus (the tube that carries food to the stomach). Under the influence of the thyroid-stimulating hormone that the pituitary secretes, the thyroid produces several hormones of its own. One of these is *thyroxin*, which plays an important role in regulating the body's metabolism. Too much thyroxin speeds up metabolism and leads to a condition called hyperthyroidism. The victim suffers from weight loss, an elevated body temperature and profuse sweating, intense thirst, accelerated heart rate, general excitability, and often, difficulty sleeping. The opposite disorder—too little thyroxin, or hypothyroidism—slows down metabolism and creates a range of related symptoms including obesity, a slowed heartbeat, lowered body temperature and reduced sweat gland activity, physical lethargy, and lack of mental alertness. Hypothyroidism can have far more devastating effects in infants. If untreated in newborns it leads to a condition called cretinism, which is characterized by severely retarded mental and physical development.

The **adrenals** are a pair of glands that lie just above the kidneys. Each adrenal actually consists of two glands, an inner region called the medulla and an outer region called the cortex. The medulla produces the hormones *epinephrine* and *norepinephrine* (also called adrenalin and noradrenalin). They play a role in the body's reaction to stress. Suppose you are severely frightened or subjected to intense pain. The outpouring of epinephrine from your adrenal medulla would increase your heartbeat and blood pressure, release more sugar into your bloodstream, accelerate your rate of breathing, and increase the flow of blood to your skeletal muscles, among other things. (Norepinephrine has very similar effects.) These changes would help prepare you to deal with the threat you faced. You may have noticed that these responses closely parallel those produced by activation of the sympathetic nervous system. When the body's resources must be mobilized in emergency situations, the activities of the nervous system and the endocrine system greatly overlap.

The other portion of the adrenal glands, the adrenal cortex, is probably the most diversified hormone factory in the body. It produces at least fifty hormonelike chemicals, and perhaps many others that scientists have not yet identified. Some of these help regulate the supply of sugar in the blood; others help regulate the relative concentrations of minerals and water in the body; still others act as sex hormones, chiefly male ones called *androgens*. Gross overproduction of adrenal androgens in women can promote the growth of facial and chest hair, a deepening of the voice, and the development of muscular arms and legs.

The final set of endocrine glands we will consider are the sex glands, or **gonads**. These secrete hormones very similar in structure and function to the sex hormones that the adrenal cortex produces, although in much larger amounts. The female gonads, or ovaries, are located on either side of the uterus. They secrete the hormones *estrogen* and *progesterone*, which are involved in the development of female secondary sex characteristics at puberty as well as in the onset of the menstrual cycle. The male gonads, or testes, are located in the scrotal sac. The testes secrete the hormone *testosterone*, which is involved, among other things, in the development of male secondary sex characteristics, the regulation of sperm production, and the control of male sexual behavior.

Recent research suggests that the higher levels of testosterone and other androgens in males than in females may contribute to the generally higher level of aggression commonly displayed by males. When one group of researchers injected pregnant monkeys with testosterone, they found that the female off-spring were more inclined than normal young females to engage in aggressive, rough-and-tumble play (Young, Goy, and Phoenix, 1964). Similarly, a study of young girls who had been exposed to high levels of male sex hormones before birth (often due to abnormal functioning of their adrenal glands) revealed that they too exhibited more "masculine" behavior. They preferred active outdoor sports to quiet indoor activities, usually chose boys as playmates, and picked fights somewhat more freqently than hormonally normal girls (Ehrhardt and Baker, 1973). From these and similar findings, some researchers now believe that the sex hormones present before birth may have a significant effect on a person's readiness to respond aggressively to certain situations later in life (Maccoby and Jacklin, 1974). Much more will be said about both the biological and the environmental factors that contribute to behavioral differences be-tween the sexes in Chapter 8.

From our brief discussion of the endocrine system you probably have a sense of the delicate interaction that must exist between the activities of these glands and the activities of the nervous system. But how is this interaction actually conducted and controlled? The ultimate answer lies in the brain. The region of the brain called the hypothalamus is itself a source of hormones. The hormones of the posterior pituitary, for instance, are all produced in the hypothalamus; the posterior pituitary simply serves as a storehouse and distribution center for them. In addition, the hypothalamus secretes into the blood a number of sub-stances that trigger release of anterior pituitary hormones, which in turn regu-late the output of other endocrine glands. And the influence between the ner-vous and endocrine systems works in the opposite direction as well: The hormones that the endocrine glands secrete affect neural activity. Consider norepinephrine. It serves as a neurotransmitter as well as a hormone. Thus, the communication networks of the human body are intricately interconnected, with the brain having the ultimate responsibility for maintaining equilibrium. The brain, in short, is the body's master control center. We will spend the rest of this chapter exploring it.

MASTER CONTROL CENTER: THE BRAIN

Although it weighs only about three pounds in the average adult, the brain is the ultimate regulator of all human behavior. Your abilities to walk, talk, eat, sleep, think, plan, and remember all arise from the operation of your brain. The human brain is composed of numerous substructures whose functions are inter-related. However, the brain can generally be described as consisting of three overlapping regions—the central core, the limbic system, and the cerebral hemispheres—each region representing a consecutive stage in the brain's evolution.

The central core

The central core of the human brain is sometimes called the "old brain," be-cause in appearance and function it is highly similar to the brains of more primitive animals. In fact, the central core is similar in the brains of all verte-brates, or animals that have backbones. The central core includes several struc-tures that together carry out the functions most basic to survival, such as sleep-ing and waking, respiration, and feeding. The structures that make up the central core of the brain are shown in Figure 3.9.

The brain stem As the spinal cord enters the skull, it swells and forms a knobby extension known as the **brain stem**. The first structure of the brain stem is the **medulla**. The medulla plays a critical role in many autonomic activities such as circulation and breathing, and it controls chewing, salivation, and fa-cial movements. Above and extending forward from the medulla is the **pons** (meaning "bridge"), which connects the two halves of the cerebellum lying above it. The pons transmits motor information from the higher brain areas and the spinal cord to the cerebellum, and it is vital in integrating movements between the right and left sides of the body.

In the upper portion of the brain stem is a small structure called the **midbrain**. All neural information passing back and forth between the brain and the spinal cord must pass through the midbrain. The midbrain contains important centers for visual and auditory reflexes. For example, the "startle" reflex to sudden intense stimuli and the "orienting" reflexes, which allow you to locate and follow moving objects with your eyes or ears, are controlled by the midbrain. In species whose auditory and visual reflexes are essential to survival, these areas of the midbrain are relatively large. For instance, birds that sight, track, and capture prey in flight have very prominent and bulging visual areas in the midbrain. In contrast, bats, which use sound rather than sight to locate their

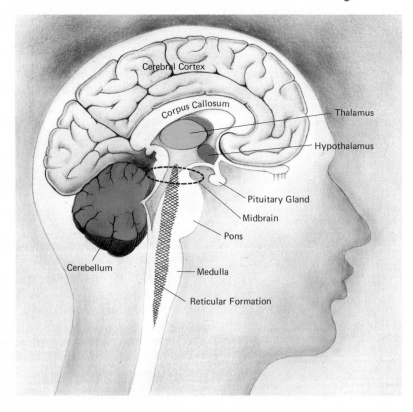

Figure 3.9 The structures composing the central core of the brain. (This il-lustration shows the left hemisphere of the brain as it would appear if it were sliced exactly in half from front to back.) The structures represented in this figure are the first to receive in-coming information, and they regulate the most fundamental processes of the body. The reticular formation, which controls the most general responses of the brain to sensory input, is located in the area that connects the brain to the spinal cord and to the rest of the ner-vous system. The thalamus has a cen-tral location in the brain, and the hy-pothalamus is attached to the pituitary gland, which controls the activity of the other endocrine glands. A few brain structures that evolved more re-cently than the central core are also shown here. Note particularly the cor-pus callosum, the large band of nerve fibers that connects the two hemi-spheres of the cerebral cortex.

prey, have small visual midbrain areas but very prominent auditory ones.

The **reticular formation** is a complex network of crisscrossing neural fibers and cells that extends from the spinal cord up through the core of the brain stem and into the thalamus. It appears to function as a sentry system, arousing the higher brain when information related to survival must be processed and permitting periods of sustained attention. The reticular formation also appears to help screen extraneous sensory input, especially during sleep. Damage to the reticular formation usually disrupts the natural sleep-waking cycle and can even result in an almost permanent, comalike state of sleep (Magoun, 1963).

The cerebellum To the rear of the brain stem and slightly above the medulla is the **cerebellum**. This name, which means "little brain," derives from the fact that the cerebellum is divided into two hemispheres and so looks like a miniature version of the higher brain. The cerebellum's chief function is to coordinate voluntary movement of the skeletal muscles and to regulate physical balance. Motor commands that originate in the higher brain are processed by the cerebellum before being transmitted to the muscles. At the same time, the cerebellum receives continuous information from the muscles about their tension and position. The cerebellum reconciles any differences in these messages to produce a smooth and balanced motor response (Eccles et al., 1967). Damage to the cerebellum may cause ataxia, a condition characterized by drunken movements, severe tremors, and a lack of balance. The person who has ataxia lacks the control needed for even simple reaching movements. For example, an ataxic person might accidentally hit a friend in the stomach while trying to reach out and shake the friend's hand.

The thalamus At the top of of the brain stem and deeply embedded within the central mass of the cerebral hemispheres is a pair of connected egg-shaped structures collectively called the thalamus—the word comes from the Greek word for inner chamber—forms part of the walls of a small central cavity in the brain. Early brain anatomists believed that all brain processes emanated from the clear fluid that fills this central inner chamber. Unfortunately, they mistakenly emphasized the cavity (or ventricle) rather than its walls (the thalamus) as being of special interest in understanding human behavior.

In terms of its influence on behavior, the thalamus is certainly not as significant a structure as the hypothalamus, which is located beneath it. However, the thalamus is a crucial link between the cerebral hemispheres and the sense organs. It acts partly as a relay station, sorting information from the sensory receptors and routing them to appropriate areas of the higher brain. In addition, the thalamus interrelates information coming from various areas of the cerebral hemispheres, processes that information, and sends it to the cerebellum and medulla. Thus, it performs a major integrative role in connecting one area of the brain to another.

The hypothalamus The **hypothalamus** is a small structure (about the size of the tip of your index finger) located just below the thalamus. As an important regulatory center for the body's internal environment, it monitors internal changes and initiates appropriate responses to maintain equilibrium. The hypothalamus performs these functions in two ways. First, it sends electrochemical signals to the entire autonomic nervous system, triggering the sympathetic or the parasympathetic division to respond to environmental changes. Second, through release of hormones it directly influences the pituitary gland, which in turn regulates the functioning of the endocrine system. The behaviors most profoundly influenced by the hypothalamus are those related to basic survival: for example, feeding, internal temperature regulation, emotional and physiological responses to stress, and sexual function.

An example of the hypothalamus's internal regulatory function is the control of body temperature. When a warm-blooded animal is exposed to cold, signals from the hypothalamus cause the blood vessels in the skin to contract, reducing heat loss from the surface of the body. Other hypothalamic signals instruct the pituitary gland to produce a thyroid-stimulating hormone, which activates the thyroid gland to produce the hormone thyroxin. Thyroxin, in turn, causes a general increase in body metabolism so that more heat is produced to compensate for the external cold. At higher levels, thyroxin induces the shivering response in the skeletal muscles, causing even more heat production. Conversely, when a warm-blooded animal is exposed to a hot environment, the hypothalamus mobilizes the body to cool itself by dilating the blood vessels in the skin, by sweating, and by reducing the metabolic rate. Thus, certain areas of the hypothalamus act as a kind of thermostat to maintain optimal body temperature. Other hypothalamic areas play similar roles in controlling many other bodily functions.

The limbic system

Above the central core lies the **limbic system**, so named because it forms the innermost border of the cerebral hemispheres (the term "limbic" means "bordering"). The limbic system contains a number of highly interrelated structures such as the **hippocampus**, the **amygdala**, and the **septal area**. These structures form a loop around the top of the central core and are closely connected with the hypothalamus and the inner surface of the cerebral cortex. Figure 3.10 shows the structure of the limbic system.

The limbic system has also been called the "nose brain" because its original function was presumably to analyze olfactory information and so allow an animal to identify food and potential mates and to avoid predators. It also appears to be closely involved with behaviors that satisfy certain motivational

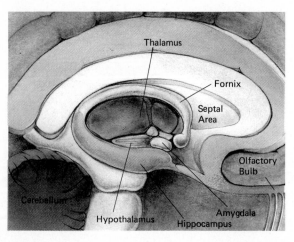

Figure 3.10 A schematic diagram of the limbic system. Structures within this system play a significant role in a variety of emotional behaviors. Damage to various regions of the limbic system may cause wild animals to become tame or tame animals to become vicious. Other limbic lesions may radically alter sexual and feeding behavior. The olfactory bulb (responsible for the sense of smell) is closely associated with other limbic structures, suggesting the importance of this sense to several limbic system functions.

and emotional needs, such as feeding, fighting, fleeing, and mating (MacLean, 1958). For example, damage to various parts of the limbic system can produce gross changes in aggressive behavior. Ordinarily intractable wild animals such as the lynx have become very tame following certain types of limbic system damage. Conversely, tame animals such as domestic cats have become quite savage after sustaining other kinds of limbic system injury. Disruption of the limbic system also produces marked changes in sexual and feeding behavior (Klüver and Bucy, 1939). Each of these classes of behavior has emotional components, and each involves making a decision about whether to approach or avoid things in the external environment. The limbic system seems to provide one basis for these approach–avoidance decisions.

In 1954 James Olds and Peter Milner quite accidentally discovered that rats will quickly learn to press a lever in order to receive mild electrical stimulation in certain parts of the limbic system. The apparent pleasure provided by stimulating these regions seems to be quite intense. A hungry rat hurrying to the feeding tray will stop in its tracks to receive such stimulation, and it will remain in that spot as long as the stimulation continues, even though food is only inches away. When allowed to stimulate their own limbic system pleasure centers by pressing a bar that connects the current, rats have been known to press frenetically thousands of times an hour, until they literally collapse in exhaustion. What could the nature of such intense pleasure be? Humans who have undergone pleasure-center stimulation (usually during treatment of some neurological disorder) report that they experience a rush of extremely "good" feelings, feelings that some have compared with the buildup to a sexual orgasm. Exactly how stimulation of these pleasure centers is related to behaviors like feeding and mating, which are also influenced by the limbic system, is still largely unknown.

The cerebral hemispheres

The cerebral hemispheres are the two large structures that lie above the brain's central core, one on the left side, the other on the right. Because of their prominence, most people think of them as "the brain." Human cerebral hemispheres constitute about 85 percent of the brain's total weight, and they are involved in the processes of learning, speech, reasoning, and memory, so important to human behavior. In addition to including much of the limbic system, which we have already discussed, the cerebral hemispheres are surrounded by a covering called the cortex.

The cerebral cortex Much of the "higher-order" processing that occurs in the cerebral hemispheres is carried out in the thin covering layer of gray matter, or **cortex** (the term means "bark" or "outer covering"). The cortex is the most recent evolutionary development of the nervous system. It is only about two millimeters (one-twelfth of an inch) thick, but it is highly convoluted, which allows it to accommodate more than 9 billion neurons. If the human cortex were flattened out, its area would be about 2.5 square feet.

The external surface of the cortex has certain characteristic "landmarks" that are used in studying the brain. The most prominent of these are the two deep fissures (Figure 3.11) that subdivide each hemisphere into its principal areas, or "lobes." The **central fissure** separates the frontal lobe from the parietal lobe; the

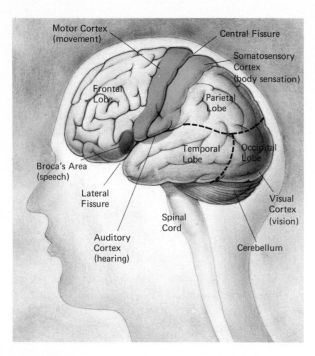

Figure 3.11 An external view of the left hemisphere of the cerebral cortex. The diagram shows the two major tissues, the four lobes, and several other cortical regions whose functions are relatively well known.

lateral fissure marks the top boundary of the temporal lobe. Demarcations between the occipital lobe and its neighboring lobes are much less distinct.

As the name implies, the **frontal lobe** is located at the front of each hemisphere. The area of this lobe next to the central fissure is primarily concerned with the regulation of voluntary movements and so is called the *motor cortex*. An area of the left frontal lobe is involved in the use of language. In 1861, a French physician named Paul Broca discovered that damage to this part of the left hemisphere affected the ability to use speech. Broca's discovery was the first indication that different parts of the brain might be involved in different types of behavior—that is, that the brain might show some *localization of function*. Some early brain anatomists, such as Gall, believed that the prefrontal area of the frontal lobe (the area to the left of the motor cortex in Figure 3.11) was the repository of intellectual ability. Most modern researchers reject this notion, however, for some people perform just as well on intelligence tests after massive amounts of frontal lobe tissue have been removed. The behavioral defects resulting from frontal lobe damage, it now appears, include the abilities to order stimuli, sort out information, and maintain attention to a particular task in the face of distraction, but not the kind of intellectual abilities measured by IQ tests (Milner, 1964).

The **parietal lobe** contains the so-called *somatosensory cortex*: the primary receiving area for the skin senses, as well as for the sense of body position. Damage to the somatosensory cortex generally impairs the sense of touch. Damage to parts of the parietal lobe on the right hemisphere disrupts spatial organization and may distort perception of personal body image.

The areas of auditory reception are located in the **temporal lobe** of each hemisphere, as are certain areas for the processing of visual information. In a series of studies with epileptic patients undergoing surgery, Canadian neurosurgeons Wilder Penfield and Theodore Rasmussen (1950) elicited some dramatic responses by applying electrical stimulation to certain points on the temporal lobe. At some locations stimulation caused complex auditory or visual hallucinations; at others it seemed to reactivate past sensations with such vividness that the patients felt as though they were reliving the experience rather than merely remembering it. One woman heard a familiar song so clearly that she thought a record was being played in the operating room. More will be said about Penfield's work later in this chapter.

The **occipital lobe**, located at the back of each hemisphere, is particularly concerned with the reception and analysis of visual information. Sensory receptors in the eye transmit their information to the occipital lobe via the optic nerve and thalamus. In humans, injury to this portion of the cortex can produce blind spots in the visual field.

This brief review of the functioning of the brain's principal lobes suggests that physiological psychologists have had the greatest success identifying cortical regions with motor and sensory functions. The motor cortex and the somatosensory cortex, for example, are extremely well defined, and their organizations have been quite precisely mapped (Figure 3.12). This mapping reveals that the amount of cortex concerned with movement or touch in a particular body part depends not on the size of that part but rather on its degree of motor control or sensitivity to stimulation. For example, the fingers, which can make very precise movements, have much larger representation in the motor cortex than does the trunk of the body. Similarly, the lips, which can also make fine movements and are extremely sensitive to touch, have a very large representation in the somatosensory cortex. It is interesting that these two areas are related to the two behavioral capacities that best distinguish humans from other animals—tool use and speech. In marked contrast to the precision with which researchers have defined the brain's motor and sensory areas, no locations have yet been found that are associated exclusively with learning, memory, and intelligence. About three-quarters of the cortex, however, is *not* devoted to a motor or sensory function. Undoubtedly these areas, called the *association cortex*, participate in more abstract mental processes. As we will see in the concluding section of this chapter, learning and remembering a complex task appear to involve cells in many parts of the cortex.

A   B

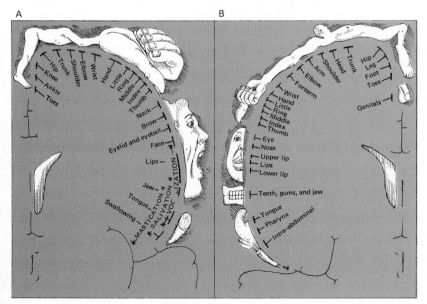

Figure 3.12 (A) A diagram representing the location and amount of cortical space devoted to the motor capacities of various body parts. Areas of the body capable of the most complex and precise movements take up the largest quantities of space in the motor cortex. For example, the eyelid and eyeball (capable of many precise movements), have a larger representation than the face. (B) A diagram representing the location and amount of cortical space devoted to the sensory capacities of various body parts. In the sensory realm, those organs capable of the highest sensitivity have the largest representations in the somatosensory cortex (Penfield and Rasmussen, 1950).

In depth

Exploring the two sides of the brain We have seen that the cerebral hemispheres and their outer covering, the cortex, are composed of two halves, the left and the right, each a rough mirror image of the other. In the early part of this century, most scientists assumed that the two hemispheres, although sometimes responsible for different functions, were nevertheless two sides of an inseparable whole. Research in the last several decades, however, has challenged this belief. When the cable of neural fibers that connects the cerebral hemispheres (the **corpus callosum**) is severed, the two hemispheres apparently operate as entirely separate brains sharing the same skull. This discovery and the research it has generated have raised such intriguing possibilities about the way a normal human brain functions that we will discuss them in depth.

About thirty years ago two scientists at the University of Chicago, Ronald E. Myers and Roger W. Sperry, were investigating the brains of laboratory cats (1953). They severed the corpus callosum, which links the cerebral hemispheres, and the optic chiasma, which transfers neural messages from the left eye to the right hemisphere and from the right eye to the left hemisphere, as shown in Figure 3.13. Their results were startling: The cats behaved as though they had two distinct brains, a left and a right, each one accessible through the eye on the same side of the body. For example, when the researchers covered a cat's left eye and taught it to solve a certain problem, the animal learned quickly, just as a normal cat would. However, when the researchers then covered the cat's right eye and presented the same problem through the previously covered left eye, the animal acted as though it had never encountered the problem before. It was forced to relearn the solution it had used just minutes earlier. Apparently, the left hemisphere, connected to the left eye, was operating independently from the right hemisphere, connected to the right eye.

Subsequent experiments have revealed that not only can the two cerebral hemispheres operate independently when the corpus callosum is severed, they can also operate simultaneously. For example, Gazzaniga and Young (Gazzaniga, 1967) placed split-brain and normal monkeys in the apparatus shown in Figure 3.14. Each monkey had to peer through special filters so that the left eye could see only the left side of the board in front of it and the right eye could see only the right side. For the split-brain monkeys (which had both a severed corpus callosum and a severed optic chiasma), this meant that each hemisphere had access *only* to what the eye on its own side of the body saw. Now the experimental procedure began. When a knob was pulled, a random eight of the sixteen panels lit up for a fraction of a second, four panels on each side of the board. The monkey's task was to duplicate the pattern it had seen by pressing the same eight panels. The normal monkeys remembered only about half the correct responses, but the split-brain monkeys recalled the entire pattern flawlessly. Apparently, by using each hemisphere independently but simultaneously, a split-brain monkey can process about twice as much visual information as a normal monkey can.

These findings naturally led to speculation about the effects of a severed corpus callosum on human beings. In the past, there had been cases in which doctors had severed the corpus callosum in people who suffered from epileptic seizures or convulsions that were violent and uncontrollable. Their reasoning was that by splitting the brain, the epileptic seizures could be confined to a

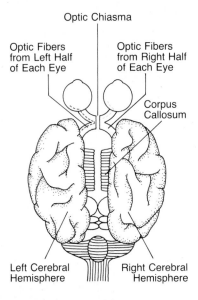

Figure 3.13 View of the brain from above, showing both the corpus callosum and the optic chiasma cut.

Optic Chiasma

Optic Fibers from Left Half of Each Eye

Optic Fibers from Right Half of Each Eye

Corpus Callosum

Left Cerebral Hemisphere

Right Cerebral Hemisphere

single hemisphere. The procedure proved quite successful in reducing seizures, but other aspects of the patients' behavior after the operation had not been systematically explored. Did such people actually have two distinct brains, each with no direct access to what the other was doing? Were the two hemispheres capable of experiencing different emotions simultaneously, or different but simultaneous trains of thought? These were intriguing questions, and answers to them were not long coming. Having evidence to suggest that a split brain did not seem to seriously impair a subject's daily activities, two doctors at the California College of Medicine became willing to try cutting the corpus callosum as a treatment of last resort for severe epilepsy. Their work provided psychologists Roger Sperry and Michael Gazzaniga with a number of split-brain subjects whose behavior might be observed.

When Sperry and Gazzaniga (Gazzaniga, 1967) studied these subjects, they found no change in personality or level of intelligence as a result of the operation. But special tests revealed more subtle changes in behavior. To understand how these tests were designed, you must first know a few more facts about the workings of a normal human brain. The brain's access to the environment and its control over behavior is largely *contralateral*; that is, the left hemisphere primarily receives input from and exerts control over the right side of the body, whereas the right hemisphere is primarily in contact with the left side of the body. One exception to this general rule is input from the eyes. The left hemisphere receives visual signals not from the right eye alone, but rather from the left half of each eye. Similarly, the right hemisphere receives visual signals from the right half of each eye. This pattern is shown in Figure 3.15. Note that because of it, input from the right visual field travels to the left hemisphere, and input from the left visual field travels to the right hemisphere. Knowing this, you can probably guess how Sperry and Gazzaniga managed to send visual information to one side of a subject's brain at a time. They flashed a picture or word to either the left or the right visual field while the subject's eyes were focused straight ahead. In this way, the stimulus was transmitted only to the opposite hemisphere. Because the stimulus was shown so briefly, the subjects did not have time to shift their eyes toward it and so allow the message to reach both sides of the brain simultaneously.

Now you are ready to consider a typical split-brain investigation. In this test, a male subject is sitting at a table with a small screen in front of him, as shown in Figure 3.16. After first making sure that the man's gaze is focused on a dot at the center of the screen, the experimenter begins to flash images to either the left or the right visual field. Suppose the researcher flashes a picture of a spoon onto the right side of the screen, so that the picture is relayed exclusively to the left hemisphere. When asked to report what he has seen, the subject says the word "spoon." So far the performance of this split-brain subject seems perfectly normal. But now observe what happens when the same picture is flashed onto the left side of the screen, so that the image is relayed exclusively to the right hemisphere. When asked again to report what he has seen, the subject answers that he saw nothing! Yet when asked to use his left hand (the hand controlled by the right hemisphere) to select the appropriate object from a group of objects hidden from view, the subject can retrieve the spoon effortlessly! What could account for this strange behavior?

Sperry and Gazzaniga concluded that the functional differences between the two sides of the brain must be greater than previously believed. Although both

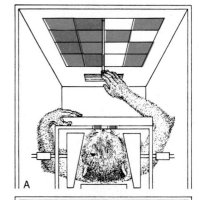

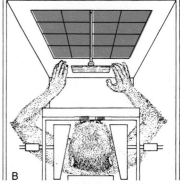

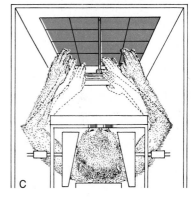

Figure 3.14 Split-brain animals have, in effect, two brains, each capable of mental functions of a high order. This implies that the two brains should have twice as large an attention span as a normal brain. Experiments with monkeys have confirmed this hypothesis. While normal monkeys are able to reproduce the pattern of lighted panels to only the third row from the bottom before forgetting which panels were lit, split-brain monkeys can reproduce the entire pattern (after Gazzaniga, 1969).

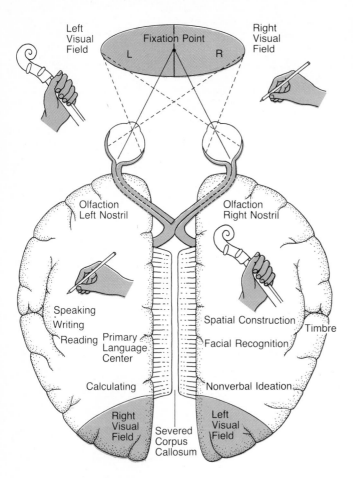

Figure 3.15 This schematic drawing of the brain from above shows the complementary dominance of the cerebral hemispheres for different tasks. For most people, the left hemisphere, which is specialized for writing, language, and analytical tasks, is dominant. The right hemisphere seems to be specialized for spatial, pattern, and musical recognition.

hemispheres play a role in most behaviors, and although each has the potential for performing some of the functions of the other, in most people the two sides of the brain tend to specialize. Language, mathematics, and analytical thinking are primarily left-hemisphere activities. Perception of spatial relationships, artistic abilities, and the ability to recognize faces are mainly right-hemisphere activities. Knowing this, the outcome of the experiment just described is much easier to understand. When the picture was projected to the left hemisphere, the subject could report the word *spoon* because the left hemisphere is proficient at speech. In contrast, when the same picture was flashed to the right hemisphere, the person verbally reported seeing nothing because the side of the brain that controls speech had in fact seen nothing. The right hemisphere, however, had recognized the spoon and could identify it if allowed to do so through touch rather than words—a mode of analysis at which it excels. In normal people, of course, this division in hemispheric function is not obvious, for the two halves of the brain constantly pass information back and forth across the corpus callosum.

What exist in split-brain subjects, then, are two cerebral hemispheres that cannot communicate directly, even though they lay side by side within the same skull. This loss of direct communication is not incapacitating, however, for most split-brain patients quickly find ways for their hemispheres to communicate indirectly. For instance, in one test Sperry and Gazzaniga devised (Gazzaniga, 1967), a split-brain subject is shown a light in the left visual field and

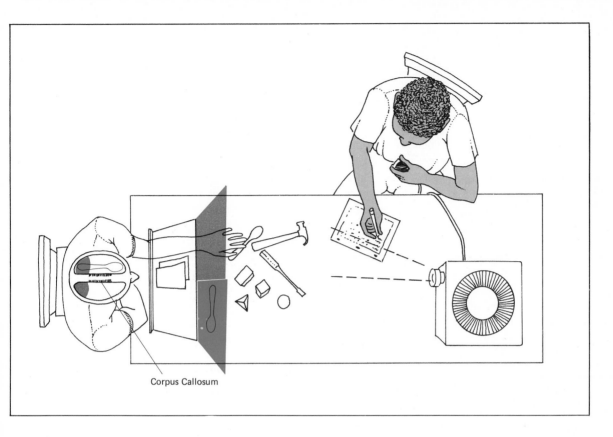

Corpus Callosum

Figure 3.16 Experimental apparatus used for testing split-brain patients. When a picture of an object is presented on a screen in one half of the visual field, this information is transmitted exclusively to the opposite hemisphere. In a person with an intact corpus callosum, this information is first received by the hemisphere opposite to the visual half-field in which the image was presented, and then this information is transmitted to the other hemisphere across the corpus callosum. In split-brain patients the hemispheres are disconnected, and therefore their independent functions can be studied. If a picture of a spoon were presented in the right half of the visual field (transmitted to the left hemisphere), and patients were asked to verbally identify the object they saw, they would readily say "spoon." If, however, the same picture was presented in the left half of the visual field (transmitted to the right hemisphere), patients would be unable to name the object. This is because speech mechanisms are found only in the left hemisphere in most people. Although the right hemisphere cannot name the object, it "knows" what the object is. The left hand, which sends its touch information primarily to the right hemisphere, is able to pick the spoon from several objects hidden behind a screen, as illustrated here (after Gazzaniga, 1972).

asked to verbally identify its color—either red or green. The image, as you know, is relayed to the right hemisphere, which has little capacity for speech even though it can usually understand the speech of others to some extent. The right hemisphere, therefore, remains mute. So the left hemisphere helps out by venturing a guess at the color the right hemisphere sees. Suppose the light is red and the left hemisphere mistakenly guesses green. What do you think might happen? The right hemisphere hears this response and recognizes that it is incorrect. Consequently, the right hemisphere initiates a frown and a negative shake of the head. The left hemisphere perceives these signals and quickly changes its answer: The person blurts out "No, no. I mean red!" A split-brain patient, then, can usually compensate rather well for the lost communication link provided by the corpus callosum. For this reason, the person's everyday behavior generally apperars quite normal.

Some have argued that because the right hemisphere is so inept at language it becomes little more than an automaton when the corpus callosum is severed. Researchers who have studied split-brain patients, however, strongly disagree with this view. They point out that when given a chance to express itself non-verbally, the right hemisphere's powers of visual perception are even better than those of the left hemisphere. Furthermore, there are certain other mental processes at which the right hemisphere far surpasses the left. Consider drawing ability. Figure 3.17 shows that the left hemisphere has great difficulty directing the right hand to copy a simple picture. The right hemisphere, in contrast, is much more proficient at guiding the left hand in this task, particularly when you consider that the patients who took these tests were not left-handed. Thus, even though it is the left hemisphere that possesses fluency at language, the right hemisphere is not as inferior a skull-mate as some people might assume.

What does the research on split-brain subjects suggest about the functioning of a normal human brain? There is little doubt that severing the corpus callosum leaves a person with essentially two separate minds—that is, two distinct spheres of consciousness (Sperry, 1964). But the question is, did the radical brain surgery *create* this duality, or did the surgery simply allow a preexisting duality to be clearly demonstrated? No one yet knows the answer to this question. Our own subjective impression is that the human mind is unitary, not dual. But it is possible that this perception of unity is just an illusion produced by constant and instantaneous communication across the corpus callosum. Robert Ornstein, a psychologist who has studied human consciousness extensively, essentially takes this second view. He maintains that coexisting within each of us are two distinct minds: the left logical and analytical, and the right

Example	Left Hand	Right Hand

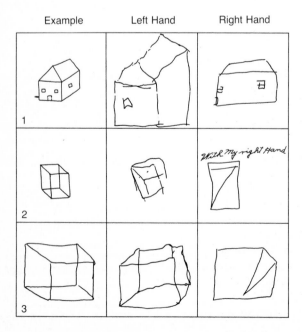

Figure 3.17 Visual tasks are handled better by the right hemisphere. The left hand, directed by the right hemisphere, can copy a three-dimensional drawing, while the right hand, directed by the left hemisphere, cannot reproduce the spatial aspects of the original design (after Gazzaniga, 1969).

intuitive and artistic (Ornstein, 1977). Perhaps, he and others have suggested, the general dominance of the left hemisphere in many people is simply a result of the great emphasis our science-oriented, highly computerized society places on analytical thought (Sperry, 1973; Bogen, 1977). If such speculations are correct, there may be more truth than metaphor in the assertion that each of us is composed of two distinct halves joined together at the middle line.

STUDYING BRAIN-BEHAVIOR RELATIONSHIPS

So far we have said a great deal about how different parts of the brain are involved in different kinds of behavior. But we have not yet explained in any detail how these facts were discovered. How have scientists gone about exploring a living, functioning brain? Over the years, researchers have developed a number of techniques for mapping the brain's pathways and control centers. Some involve observation of brain-damaged people or of people about to undergo neurosurgery. Others involve manipulation of the brains of laboratory animals so that the effects on behavior can be traced. And still others involve the use of highly sophisticated electronic equipment that allows researchers to eavesdrop on the brain's activity.

Clinical observations

The oldest method of mapping the brain involves careful observation of behavioral deficits in people with localized damage to the cerebral cortex due to head injuries, tumors, or strokes (the blockage or rupturing of blood vessels on the brain's surface, which cuts off the supply of oxygen and nutrients to that area). Early efforts of this kind provided many basic insights into the workings of the cerebral hemispheres. For instance, as we noted earlier, Broca found that speech difficulties usually resulted from damage to the left side of the brain. This was the first indication that one part of the brain was dominant in speech processes. Early medical practitioners also noted that damage to one side of the brain often produced paralysis or numbness on the opposite side of the body. Thus, scientists began to develop the notion of contralateral control of the body by the brain. At the same time observers found that damage to certain areas produced specific sensory deficits; for instance, damage to the back part of the brain often caused partial blindness. The hypotheses developed from these and other early observations have guided much of modern research on brain-behavior relationships.

But the usefulness of clinical observations has not ended. Brain-damaged patients continue to provide intriguing clues about the organization of mental activities such as reading, writing, and speaking, which are still only superficially understood (Gardner, 1975). For example, stroke victims sometimes suffer from a condition called pure alexia, in which the ability to read language is completely lost. But strangely enough, the patient is still able to write. Such findings suggest that reading and writing, activities that you might think would be linked in the brain, are in some way separate. Likewise, verbal and numerical symbols appear to be processed in different ways. The person with pure alexia is sometimes able to read numbers. Thus, he or she might be able to interpret the symbols MIX as meaning 1,009 in Roman numerals, yet be totally unable to see them as an English word. Even different grammatical structures may be processed independently. For instance, in cases where portions of the parietal and occipital lobes of the left hemisphere are damaged, the person may easily comprehend simple declarative sentences ("Here is the book") yet be baffled by sentences that contain prepositional phrases ("The book is on top of the table") or possessive contractions ("The book belongs to my brother's wife"). We will say more about the implications of these and other speech-related disorders in Chapter 9.

Brain stimulation

Because neural activity is electrochemical, it can be induced by applying tiny amounts of electrical stimulation to nerve tissue. Scientists have taken advantage of this fact in their efforts to explore the brain. Some of these efforts have been part of attempts to cure human neurological disorders. Neurosurgeon Wilder Penfield, for example, whose work we mentioned earlier (Penfield and Rasmussen, 1950), used electrical stimulation quite successfully to locate the sites of focal epilepsy. Focal epilepsy is a disease in which a small area of the brain periodically aggravates surrounding tissue until it prompts nerve cells to fire uncontrollably. The result is an epileptic seizure. In severe cases of focal epilepsy, doctors sometimes recommend surgical removal of the diseased area. But how can this area be found? Penfield's approach, innovative for its time, was to apply a weak electrical current to various portions of the brain and to ask the unanesthetized patient what sensations each produced. If the person experienced the precise feelings he or she always experienced just prior to a seizure, Penfield would know that he had probably located the focal region.

Over the course of many operations, Penfield kept careful records of the particular points on the brain that evoked particular responses. For example, stimulation of the part of the frontal lobe next to the central fissure produced muscle movements in the opposite side of the body, whereas stimulation of different areas in the left hemisphere either caused people to emit sounds or prevented them from speaking. Stimulation of the somatosensory cortex caused patients to claim that they had been touched somewhere on the body, the exact location corresponding to a specific location in the brain. The most intriguing aspect of Penfield's work was his claim that stimulation of certain points on the temporal lobe seemed to evoke remarkably vivid memories, sometimes apparently dredged from the very distant past. Whether the temporal lobe is indeed a storehouse of past events remains open to question, however. Penfield's patients were epileptics whose brains were in certain respects abnormal. This raises some doubt about the extent to which his findings can be generalized. In addition, Penfield never investigated each patient's history to check the accuracy of the memories he or she claimed to retrieve. We will say more about this criticism of Penfield's results in Chapter 6, which deals with memory.

Penfield's efforts to map the brain were largely incidental to his primary goal, locating diseased tissue. However, brain stimulation has also been used on laboratory animals for the sole purpose of identifying the brain's control centers. In the laboratory, researchers have used both electrical and chemical techniques. When chemicals are employed, the investigator implants a small hypodermic needle into an animal's brain so that the tip touches the area to be manipulated. Then he or she delivers a tiny amount of the chemical through the needle. This approach has generated many interesting findings. For example, different chemicals applied to the hypothalamus have been shown to affect feeding and drinking (Grossman, 1960), and sexual behavior can be stimulated or inhibited by applying minute amounts of specific hormones to hypothalamic regions (Fisher, 1956). Since the brains of the animals used in such research are organized very similarly to the human brain, information gleaned in this way is often directly relevant to human functioning.

In addition to their enormous value in charting the brain, electrical and chemical stimulation techniques are also providing new means of treating certain medical disorders. For example, an electrical current delivered through electrodes implanted in specific areas of the brain seems to provide temporary relief from pain. Consequently, electrical stimulation is now sometimes used to relieve the intolerable pain of patients who have terminal cancer and other serious illness. In some cases, electrodes implanted in the brain are activated by the patients themselves. This approach has been used to help control narcolepsy, a disorder in which a wide-awake person suddenly loses all muscular control and lapses into a period of sleep. Narcoleptic patients being treated in this way push a button of a self-stimulator attached to an appropriate area of the brain whenever they feel an attack coming on. Undoubtedly the most controversial application of brain stimulation is its use with mental patients. A number of psychiatrists have turned to brain stimulation to reduce violent aggression in patients for whom no other method of restraint has been successful. This application has raised substantial concern among those who fear the potential abuse of brain stimulation as a method of mind control (Valenstein, 1973).

Brain lesions

Like brain stimulation techniques, brain lesion techniques are used to determine which of an organism's behaviors a particular brain region controls. A **lesion** is produced in laboratory animals by surgically destroying or removing a small area of the brain. After the surgery, the researchers carefully assess changes or deficits in the animal's behavior. Brain stimulation and lesion procedures are often used together. In general, if electrical stimulation of a certain area *increases* a certain type of behavior, lesions in that same area will *decrease* the behavior; if stimulation tends to block a behavior when it is normally appropriate, lesions may cause the behavior to occur more vigorously.

Research on the hypothalamus provides a good example of how brain lesion and stimulation techniques have been used together to increase our understanding of how the brain controls eating behavior. Investigators have found that stimulation of the lateral part of the hypothalamus will cause an animal to eat voraciously, even if it has just consumed a full meal. In other words, the animal behaves as if it were hungry even though it has no immediate biological need for food (Miller, 1957). It would seem, then, that the lateral hypothalamus is in some way involved with an animal's ability to recognize when it is hungry, and brain lesion techniques have supported this idea. When an animal's lateral hypothalamus is selectively destroyed with a strong electrical current, it will not eat unless force-fed. Most animals, if well cared for, will eventually overcome this dysfunction and begin to eat again. This partial recovery may take months,

Figure 3.18 After destruction of the ventromedial area of the hypothalamus, the rat shown here has overeaten to such an extent that it weighs 1,080 grams. (The dial has gone beyond the 1,000–gram capacity of the scale and registers an additional 80 grams.) In contrast, a normal rat would weight about 320 grams.

however, and the animals will always be underweight and show a number of other permanent feeding problems (Epstein, 1971).

Lesions in the ventromedial (lower middle) area of the hypothalamus have an effect opposite to that caused by lateral hypothalamic lesions. That is, they prompt animals to overeat to the point of obesity (Hetherington and Ranson, 1940). A rat may eat enough to triple its normal weight, as shown in Figure 3.18. When this area in a normal animal is stimulated with a mild electrical current, the animal will stop eating even if it is starving. Thus it appears that this area of the hypothalamus is related to an animal's ability to recognize when it is full.

We will say a great deal more about the control of eating behavior in Chapter 11, on motivation. The important point here is that much of what we know about the brain's role in regulating hunger comes from the combined use of brain stimulation and lesion procedures. These same procedures have also been used to analyze many other kinds of brain-behavior relationships.

Evoked potentials

You may already know that scientists can trace the electrical signals of a human brain by taking what is called an electroencephalograph, or EEG. In a typical EEG procedure, electrodes are attached to different areas of the scalp, and the voltage emitted by the brain beneath causes a pen to record its patterns on rolling graph paper. A standard EEG, as you will learn later in this book, is useful for many types of psychological investigation. However, it poses serious limitations for a researcher who wants to determine how a particular stimulus—such as a flash of light or a mild shock to the fingers—affects electrical activity in the brain. The problem is that the brain emits a mass of electrical signals. How is the researcher to distinguish the specific electrical response evoked by the stimulus in question? One solution that researchers have found to this problem is actually quite simple. They present the stimulus many times and use a computer to average out the responses recorded from the brain. Over a large number of trials, electrical activity unrelated to the stimulus will sometimes be negative and sometimes positive and so will average to zero. What emerges, then, is the **evoked potential**—the pattern of electrical activity *caused* by the stimulus.

Evoked potential technology has helped scientists to chart many reactions in the brain. For example, when the notes of the musical scale are played to a subject, evoked potentials arise in a rather orderly fashion along the auditory cortex: Low notes produce potentials at one end of the region, high notes at the other end, and middle notes in between (Woolsey, 1961). Similar kinds of detailed arrangements have been found for other sensory areas.

One discovery made in recent years is that evoked potentials are not always produced by specific sensory stimuli. In the process of analyzing and coping with more general events in the environment, the brain routinely evokes its own potentials. For instance, if you were listening to a repetitive series of sounds and they suddenly and unpredictably stopped, your brain would register its surprise by emitting a large, positive electrical wave beginning three-tenths of a second after the sounds ceased (Restak, 1979). Alternatively, if you read a sentence that ended with a word that did not fit in the context, your brain would reveal its effort to make sense out of nonsense with a negative voltage beginning four-tenths of a second after you encountered the troublesome word. Researchers are now discovering that a wide variety of other mental processes are accompanied by their own characteristic patterns of electrical activity. It is not difficult to imagine the important diagnostic tools that such patterns could provide. Scientists working in this area have already developed tests for helping to spot learning disabilities in children, early signs of senility among the elderly, and various types of mental disorders—all by locating abnormalities in evoked potentials (Restak, 1979).

The evoked potentials we have discussed so far are measured by placing recording electrodes on the surface of the scalp or the brain. Consequently, they involve electrical activity in a *group* of neurons. But modern technology has also made it possible to record the electrical response of a *single* neuron, which at its widest has a diameter of only about one-thousandth of an inch. Single unit recording is accomplished with the use of a microelectrode that is placed into or very close to an individual nerve cell. The single-unit recording technique has provided some important insights into the functional organization of the brain. For example, when researchers inserted microelectrodes into the visual regions of a frog's brain, they discovered cells that increase firing *only* when dark spots move across the visual field—a useful adaptation for a creature whose major source of food is flying insects (Lettvin et al., 1959). The high degree of stimulus-response selectivity that many neurons exhibit is believed to provide a foundation for the very precise behavioral and perceptual capabilities that so many animals display.

THE BRAIN'S ROLE IN COMPLEX BEHAVIORS

Although the observations summarized in this chapter add to our picture of brain organization, the map is far from complete. The task of determining exactly how the brain controls behavior is obviously a very difficult one. At present, we can identify areas of the brain related to movement, to the senses, and to certain very general classes of behavior. However, we still do not understand how learning, memory, perception, and intellectual functioning are related to brain structure, and it is these behaviors that are of greatest interest to psychologists. These processes do not seem to be localized in any one area of the brain. In fact, almost everything that an animal does appears to involve activity in most or all of the brain. A famous physiological psychologist, Karl S. Lashley, called this the **principle of mass action**.

Mass action and learned behavior

Lashley attempted to locate specific areas of the cortex that were responsible for the learning and remembering of particular behaviors. In one set of experiments, rats were trained in mazes after lesions had been made in a number of different cortical areas of their brains. The locations of the lesions overlapped considerably, so that no area of the cortex was left unexplored. Lashley found that no lesion completely obliterated the rats' ability to learn a maze, although all of the lesions interfered with learning to some extent. In addition, he found that the degree to which learning was retarded by a lesion was directly related to the lesion's size—the larger the lesion, the greater the learning deficit. This was particularly true for learning the more complex mazes. On the basis of these findings Lashley came to an important conclusion: the learning of a specific task does not appear to be localized in any particular cortical area. Instead, the entire cortex seems to be involved in learning and memory (Lashley, 1929).

This view has been substantiated by more recent research. Consider psychologist E. Roy John's investigation of the brain's electrical activity during learning and performance. John presented a cat with a flashing light while recording the electrical waves from the animal's brain. Soon the waves in the visual region of the cat's cortex started to follow the same frequency pattern as the light. John called these waves "labeled rhythms" because in a very real sense they bore the light's imprint. Next John assigned meaning to the light. Whenever the cat saw the light flash, it had to jump a hurdle to avoid shock. What change, if any, did this produce in the brain's electrical activity? It caused the labeled rhythms to spread to other regions! Sometimes the rhythms would arise spontaneously when the light was turned off and the cat was only expecting it to flash. In such instances, the animal would often leap the hurdle several times, as though performing trial runs. John concluded that in observing these labeled rhythms he was observing the effects of memory formation. Significantly, these effects were spread throughout the brain (John, 1976).

The principle of multiple control

We have seen that the performance of any specific behavior is likely to involve most or all of the brain. The complementary principle also seems to be true—that is, a specific part of the brain is likely to be involved in the performance of many types of behavior. This is called the **principle of multiple control**. The cortex, for example, has been shown to influence behaviors ranging from complex intellectual activities to sexual and feeding behavior, sleeping and waking cycles, and simple spinal reflexes. This indicates that the cortex is involved not only in the "higher" behavioral functions but in other functions as well. Similarly, the lateral hypothalamus is involved in many behaviors other than feeding responses. For example, rats with lesions in the lateral hypothalamus show deficits in certain learning situations in addition to exhibiting impaired feeding behavior (Teitelbaum, 1971).

It is clear from these observations of mass action and multiple control that complex behavioral abilities, particularly intellectual performance, are not located exclusively in any specific area of the brain and that specific areas of the brain are each involved in many different behavioral functions. Although the brain is composed of billions of discrete neurons, it functions as a complete unit. Thus, our understanding of brain–behavior relationships must ultimately be based on research that examines both the activity of individual neurons and the organization of these neurons into the functioning brain of a behaving organism.

SUMMARY

1. It was not until the nineteenth century that scientists began to suspect that the brain might play a major role in behavior. One early theory, known as **phrenology**, divided the brain into distinct "organs," each related to a behavioral trait. The modern study of the relationship between the brain and behavior is called **physiological psychology.**

2. The human nervous system, an intricate communication network that radiates throughout the body and includes the brain, consists of billions of interconnected, highly specialized cells. **Receptor cells**, embedded in sense organs, receive various types of stimulation from the environment; **effector cells** cause muscles to contract and glands to secrete.

3. The **central nervous system** (CNS) consists of the brain and spinal cord and provides the ultimate control for all human behavior. Branching out from the CNS to all parts of the body to convey signals from the sensory receptors to the CNS, and to carry messages from the CNS to the muscles and glands, is the **peripheral nervous system** (PNS). Two divisions of the PNS, the **somatic** and **autonomic**, are related, in general, to external and internal environments respectively. The autonomic system can be further subdivided into **sympathetic** and **parasympathetic** components.

4. The basic structural units of the nervous system are **neurons**, or **nerve cells**, which conduct messages from one part of the body to another by means of electrochemical impulses. **Sensory**, or **afferent**, **neurons** carry information from the sense organs to the CNS, while **motor**, or **efferent**, **neurons** carry signals from the CNS to the muscles and glands. **Interneurons** connect and integrate the activities of the other types of neurons.

5. Most neurons have three structural components: the **cell body**, or **soma**, containing the nucleus; relatively short **dendrites**, along which impulses travel to the soma; and a long **axon**, along which impulses travel away from the soma to muscle fibers, glandular cells, or other neurons. The simplest set of neural connections is a **reflex arc**, in which a sensory input is linked to a motor response.

6. Nerve impulses are transmitted by means of an electrochemical process. The term **resting potential** refers to a **polarized** nerve cell—one that is negatively charged inside the cell membrane and positively charged outside. Upon a strong stimulus, the membrane becomes permeable to an inrush of positively charged sodium ions, which reverse the cell's polarity. This abrupt change in polarity, called the **action potential**, travels down the length of the axon.

7. Every axon is physically separated from adjacent cells by a gap called a **synapse**. **Neurotransmitters**, chemicals stored in vesicles at the axon's terminal, are released when the action potential reaches the terminal and diffuse across the synapse to activate receptor sites on the adjacent cell. Depending on the chemistry of the neurotransmitter and the nature of the receptor site activated, the message conveyed may be excitatory or inhibitory.

8. Where fast behavioral reactions are crucial, the nervous system plays an essential role. But not all behaviors require an instant response, and the endocrine system provides an economical but nonetheless comprehensive chemical communications network. **Hormones**, the endocrine system's messengers, are secreted by **endocrine glands** directly into the bloodstream. Hormones have important effects on sexual function, growth, metabolism, and other aspects of behavior. Their action is highly selective, for while they circulate throughout the bloodstream, they affect only specific **target organs**.

9. Weighing about three pounds in the average adult, the brain ultimately regulates all behavior. The brain can be described as consisting of three overlapping regions, each region representing a consecutive stage in the brain's evolution. The central core, or "old brain," whose important components include the **brain stem**, the **cerebellum**, the **thalamus**, and the **hypothalamus**, controls those functions most basic to survival, such as sleeping, waking, respiration, and feeding. Above the central core lies the **limbic system**. Containing a number of highly interrelated structures such as the **hippocampus**, the **amygdala**, and the **septal area**. The limbic system appears to be closely involved with behaviors that satisfy emotional and motivational needs such as feeding, fighting, fleeing, and mating. The third and final layer, constituting about 85 percent of the brain's weight, are the **cerebral hemispheres**. Consisting of two roughly mirror-image halves connected by a cable of nerve fibers called the **corpus callosum**, and surrounded by the **cortex**, the cerebral hemispheres are involved in the processes of learning, speech, reasoning, and memory.

10. Research on so-called split brain subjects—in whom the corpus callosum has been severed—suggests that each hemisphere is a separate respository of consciousness. Some researchers argue that language, mathematics, and analytical thinking are left-brain activities, while artistic ability and perception of spatial relationships are right-brain activities.

11. To map the brain's intricate structures and pathways, researchers use a variety of techniques. Clinical observations, for instance, have shed light on the relationship between localized damage to the cerebral cortex and the appearance of certain behavioral deficits, such as speech impairments or paralysis. The electrical or chemical stimulation of the brain (under highly controlled laboratory or surgical conditions) has helped clarify the involvement of certain areas of the brain with, for instance, memory and various kinds of physical sensation. Brain lesions, produced by surgically destroying or removing a small area of brain tissue, have also been used to link brain regions with specific behaviors. In general, brain lesions seem to produce an effect opposite to that of stimulation. A final technique for mapping the brain involves the measurement of **evoked potentials**, the pattern of electrical activity from brain regions caused by external stimuli.

12. Although scientists have been able to identify areas of the brain related to movement, to the senses, and to certain very general classes of behavior, the relationship between brain structure and memory, perception, and intellectual functioning remains a mystery, since these processes do not seem to be localized in any one area of the brain. For these processes the **principle of mass action** may apply: Rather than being localized in any particular cortical area, complex learning and memory seem to involve the entire cortex. The converse of this theory, the **principle of multiple control**, also seems to be true. That is, a specific part of the brain is likely to be involved in many kinds of behavior.

Suggested readings

Blakemore, C. *Mechanics of the mind.* New York: Cambridge University Press, 1977.

Chall, J. S., and Mirsky, A. F. (Eds.). *Education and the brain.* Chicago: University of Chicago Press, 1978.

Gazzaniga, M. S. *The bisected brain.* New York: Appleton-Century-Crofts, 1970.

Schneider, A. M., and Tarshis, B. *An introduction to physiological psychology* (2nd ed.). New York: Random House, 1979.

Schwartz, M. *Physiological psychology* (2nd ed.). Englewood Cliffs, N.J.: Prentice-Hall, 1978.

Sperry, R. W. Left brain, right brain. *Saturday Review*, 1975, *2*, 30-33.

Thompson, R. F. *Introduction to physiological psychology.* New York: Harper & Row, 1975.

Valenstein, E. S. *Brain control: A critical examination of brain stimulation and psychosurgery.* New York: Wiley, 1973.

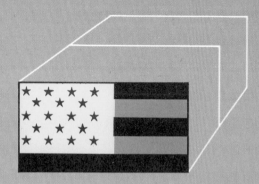

PREVIEW

1. We sense only part of the stimulus energy in our environment, using special organs called receptors that change, or transduce, physical stimuli such as light into sensations such as vision.

2. Light waves are transduced on the retina of the eye by specialized cells called rods and cones. Sound waves are transduced by the cochlea of the inner ear. Transducers in the skin sense touch, pressure, warmth, cold, and pain. Smell is transduced by the olfactory membranes in the nasal passage, and taste by the taste buds on the tongue.

3. Perception, or the interpretation of sensation by the brain, involves the organism's past experience and present condition as well as an immediate sensation. Perception can thus differ from sensation—creating an illusion.

4. Perceptual abilities vary among species, among individuals, and with circumstances.

5. Different cultures view illusions differently, illustrating the subjective nature of perception.

4 Sensation and perception

You live in the midst of a barrage of physical stimuli. Light waves from the sun and other sources bombard your eyes. Pulses of compressed and rarefied air molecules, called sound waves, impinge on your ears. Vaporized molecules from hundreds of substances assail the sensitive membranes of your nose. The human sensory organs are intricately designed to detect and discriminate these stimuli, thus giving you a window to the outside world. But how accurately do you perceive your surroundings? Are there certain stimuli you are unable to detect? Do you ever perceive things that are not really there or misperceive things that are? Are your perceptions in some respects different from those of other people? Psychologists who study perception seek to answer such questions, and equally important, they seek to explain just why we perceive things the ways we do.

One fact that has repeatedly emerged from the scientific investigation of perception is that each organism's view of the world is to some extent unique. This fact will be immediately clear if we compare our own perceptual capabilities with those of other species. Consider the ability to perceive sounds. Many animals can hear sounds far too high-pitched for humans to detect. A dog's range of hearing is more than twice that of ours and so is a cat's. Bats are virtuosos at high-pitched sound detection. In fact, they depend on such sounds for navigation. A bat sends out a shrill stream of ultrasonic cries, listens for the echoes bouncing off surrounding objects, and so locates those objects in space. But even though a flying bat is constantly emitting powerful noises, it seems virtually soundless to us because the human ear is tuned too low to detect most of its cries. Interestingly, from a bat's perspective we humans also appear mute, for the sounds we normally make are just below the pitch that a bat's ear can perceive.

Perceptual capabilities, then, clearly vary among different species, but do they also vary among members of the same species? The answer is a qualified yes. Although members of the same species usually experience the world in very similar ways, some perceptual differences do exist. Consider an example in taste perception. We all know that some people like their coffee black, and others insist on adding a great deal of sugar. Although a number of factors may contribute to these different taste preferences, one thing is certain: Most people who use lots of sugar in their coffee find the taste of black coffee extremely bitter. How, they wonder, could anyone drink such bitter-tasting stuff? One answer is that the black-coffee drinkers do not perceive coffee to be particularly bitter. And there are in fact genetic differences in taste receptors that make some people less sensitive to coffee's bitter flavor. We will return to this subject later when we discuss the physiology of taste. For now the important point to remember is that two people sitting side by side can, under certain circumstances, experience the world in significantly different ways.

A basic cause underlying all the perceptual differences we have mentioned so far is variation in the way that sensory systems are structured. The function of any physiological mechanism is inseparably linked to its structure. For example, the ability of your fingers to turn the pages of this book is largely governed by the structure of your hands. Because your thumb can rotate forward and touch any of your other four fingers, you are able to manipulate very small and delicate objects, such as a single sheet of paper a fraction of a millimeter thick. This link between structure and function will be seen again and again as we explore the workings of our major sensory organs and examine the role of the brain in perceptual processing. But first, let us briefly consider the general relationship between physical stimuli in the external world and the subjective sensations they create in us.

STIMULI AND SENSATIONS

If a tree falls in a forest where no one is present to hear, does it nevertheless make a sound? This question, frequently debated in the intellectual salons of eighteenth-century Europe, is perplexing at first glance because it clouds the distinction between a physical stimulus (sound waves produced by a falling tree) and a subjective sensation (hearing a crash). The two, of course, are not synonymous. A **stimulus** is any form of energy (sound waves, light waves, heat, pressure) to which an organism is capable of responding. A **sensation** is the response to that energy by a sensory organ. Stimuli and sensations, then, have a cause-and-effect relationship.

Most sensory organs respond to differences in both the quality and quantity of stimuli. The *quality* of a stimulus refers to the kind of sensation it produces. Color is a quality related to visual stimulation; musical pitch is a quality related to auditory stimulation. *Quantity*, in contrast, refers to the amount of stimulation present. Thus, brightness represents the quantity of light and loudness the quantity of sound.

Remember, though, that characteristics such as color, brightness, pitch, and loudness are simply ways in which an individual experiences a stimulus. They are not necessarily completely accurate reflections of the physical properties of the stimulus. In analyzing the relationship between what a person senses and what a stimulus is physically like, psychologists study three basic things: the quantity of a stimulus needed for a person to sense it in the first place; the ratio between the magnitude of the stimulus and the magnitude of the corresponding sensation; and the factors that reduce or increase sensory capacities. We will consider each in turn.

Absolute thresholds

How much light must be present before a person sees it? How much pressure must be applied to the skin before a person feels it? The answers to these questions involve the concept of **absolute threshold**: the minimum stimulus necessary to produce a specific sensation.

How do psychologists measure absolute thresholds? A person's absolute threshold for light might be measured in the following manner: The subject enters a completely dark room and, after being given time to adapt to the dark, watches for a light on the wall. The psychologist, using a specially calibrated instrument, begins by projecting a very dim beam and gradually increases the intensity until the person says, "I see it." Generally, this procedure will be repeated a number of times. An individual's absolute threshold is the lowest intensity light that the person is able to see 50 percent of the time.

Under ideal conditions our senses have very low absolute thresholds—that is, we experience sensations when exposed to very small amounts of stimulation. Human vision, for example, is keen enough to perceive the flame of a single candle from a distance of several miles on a clear, moonless night. Similarly, the human sense of smell is sensitive enough to detect the musky odor of mercaptan, the scent that makes skunks so unpopular, at concentrations as low as 1 part mercaptan to 50 trillion parts of air (Geldard, 1972). But in a natural setting ideal conditions seldom exist. Thus, if we want to determine how well our senses *normally* operate, we must consider them under less than ideal conditions.

Several factors regularly serve to limit our sensory capacities. One is the existence of irrelevant, competing stimuli, often referred to as background **noise**. You can probably think of many occasions when your ability to detect a particular sound was hampered by auditory noise—as when trying to hear what someone is saying at an especially loud party. But "noise" can affect other senses as well. An inexperienced person viewing a radar screen, for example, usually has great difficulty distinguishing the blips made by an airplane from those made by stormy weather, a form of visual noise. In much the same way, you would be hard pressed to smell the fragrance of a delicate flower in a smoke-filled room.

Lack of prior information about a stimulus also hinders the ability to detect it. A sound, for instance, is more difficult to hear when you do not know what its qualities will be or when to expect it (Swets and Sewall, 1961; Scharf, 1970), and a touch is more difficult to feel when you do not know where on your body it is going to occur (Meyer, Gross, and Teuber, 1963). The same is true of visual stimuli: A moving target is easier to see if you know what speed to expect and which direction to watch (Sekuler and Ball, 1977). Stimulus uncertainty, then, is a second factor that can reduce performance on sensory tasks.

A third factor is motivation. Sometimes people are strongly inclined to set rather stringent criteria for determining when a stimulus has occurred. People who fear illness, for instance, may ignore the sensations associated with physical disorder until a condition is far advanced. Such people are highly motivated *not* to perceive these stimuli. Similarly, there is evidence that the elderly, because they are usually more conservative than the young, are also more cautious in reporting stimulus detection. In one experiment, for example, subjects age sixty-five to seventy-seven were significantly more reluctant to say that they had heard a very faint sound (one just at the edge of their auditory thresholds) than were subjects age eighteen to twenty-one.

In summary, many factors can influence the ability to detect stimuli. Sensitivity to stimulation depends not only on how well a person's sensory systems operate, but also on the extent of interference from background noise, on the person's prior knowledge about what stimulus will occur and when and where to expect it, and on whether the person is motivated to ignore relatively weak stimuli. In recent years, psychologists have attempted to separate these various influences on sensation based on an approach known as *signal detection theory*. Their results clearly demonstrate that a person's absolute threshold for any given stimulus varies with the circumstances.

Sensory ratios

In addition to their interest in absolute thresholds and the factors that affect them, psychologists are interested in how people perceive changes in stimulus intensity. As you change the settings on a three-way light bulb from 50 to 100 to 150 watts, do you experience the same increase in brightness between 50 and 100 watts as you do between 100 and 150? Since the increase in the number of watts suggests that you would, psychologists' findings may surprise you.

Research in this area began in the mid-1800s when Ernst Weber discovered that although people can perceive small changes in a weak stimulus, they notice only large changes in a strong stimulus. You have undoubtedly experienced this phenomenon yourself. If you add one pound to the weight of two paperback books, the sensation of weight will greatly increase. But if you add one pound to a seventy-pound backpack, you will probably fail to sense any increase in weight at all.

After further study, Weber's brother-in-law, Gustav Fechner, specified the nature of this relationship more precisely (Fechner, 1860). Fechner noted that the amount by which a stimulus must be increased to produce a "just noticeable difference" in sensation is always a constant proportion of the initial stimulus intensity. In honor of his brother-in-law, Fechner called this rule **Weber's law**. Although the average person will notice a difference when a single pound is added to a backpack initially weighing fifty pounds, the just noticeable difference for a backpack initially weighing a hundred pounds is not one pound but two. For the sensation of weight, then, the proportional increase necessary to create a just noticeable difference is about one to fifty. Proportions for some other sensations are one to ten for auditory tones, one to seven for skin pressure, and one to five for the saltiness of a liquid. Although Weber's law does not hold under all circumstances, it is a useful approximation.

An important question still remained, however. Fechner had established the proportional increases in various stimuli needed to produce just noticeable differences, but what exactly was the relationship between any given increase in stimulation and the corresponding increase in sensation? S. S. Stevens (1957, 1962) helped provide the answer. According to **Stevens's power law**, the relationship between stimulus magnitude and magnitude of sensation differs for each of our senses, but when considering a single sensory system, the relationship is quite constant over a wide range of stimulus intensities. For example, when the volume of a sound is increased threefold, it usually sounds only twice as loud; and to increase the perceived brightness of a light by two, it must usually be increased eightfold. For both hearing and vision, then, the magnitude of a sensation increases more slowly than the magnitude of a stimulus. This is not true of all sensory judgments, however. When judging electric shocks, for instance, the magnitude of the sensation increases faster than the magnitude of the stimulus: Doubling the intensity of a shock to the fingers produces about a tenfold increase in perceived pain.

Sensory adaptation

All sensory systems display adaptation—that is, prolonged, constant stimulation reduces the ability of sensory systems to provide information. Some senses, like smell and touch, adapt quite quickly; others, like pain, adapt very slowly. All, however, do adapt.

The most obvious effect of adaptation is decreased sensitivity to a stimulus. For example, if you enter a room in which there is a distinctive odor, before long the odor appears to fade away. The sensory receptors in your nose, like those in other parts of your body, are designed to be maximally sensitive to *changes* in stimulation. Thus, if a given stimulus is applied to a typical receptor cell and is then held constant, the rate at which neural impulses are generated will steadily decline. This same adaptive process occurs in the visual receptors of the eyes; if you were truly able to stare at something, it would gradually disappear! You cannot, however, lock your gaze on a single point. Whenever you try to do so, your eyeball moves at a very fast rate (and so little that the movement is not observable to the unaided eye), spreading the light image over many visual receptor cells. This prevents any single group of cells from adapting to an unchanging light stimulus.

Because sensory adaptation affects sensitivity to stimuli, it can change the sensation produced by any stimulation. You can experience this with a simple experiment: Place one hand in ice-cold water and the other in bearably hot water. After your hands have adapted to these two temperatures, plunge them into a bucket of warm water. What temperature does this water feel? It feels both hot (to the hand that had been in cold water) and cold (to the hand that had been in hot water), even though you know it is neither!

This example of a perceptual distortion caused by sensory adaptation reinforces an important point raised at the beginning of this chapter: The way we view the world is not always an accurate reflection of the physical stimuli that exist there. Note, however, that distortions in perception are not necessarily caused by aberrations in sensory processing, as many people assume. They are frequently caused by the use of our normal sensory systems in unusual situations. We will say more about this later when we explain the reasons for certain visual illusions.

THE HUMAN SENSES

Our eyes, ears, nose, tongue, and skin are the organs that link us to the outside world via the familiar senses of sight, sound, smell, taste, and touch. But a human being possesses considerably more senses than just these basic five. The skin alone contains receptors for at least five sensations, and an organ in the inner ear gives us a sense of balance and equilibrium. In addition, sensory systems related to muscles and joints provide awareness of body position and movement, and many other internal receptors supply the brain with vital information about blood chemistry and temperature. Although the following discussion is restricted to the classic five senses, plus a number of other skin sensations, those omitted are no less important to normal human functioning.

Vision

Vision is the richest of the human senses. Our eyes receive light from surrounding objects and translate this light into neural impulses that carry information about shape, color, depth, texture, and movement to the brain. This translation of the energy in environmental stimuli into neural activity is called **transduction**. Transduction is common to all sensory systems, although each different kind of receptor in our bodies is sensitive to a different type of stimulus. Light, a form of electromagnetic radiation that travels in waves, is the basic stimulus for vision.

The nature of light The light energy to which our eyes respond is just one small part of the total electromagnetic spectrum. This spectrum, as Figure 4.1 shows, also includes longer wavelengths, such as radio and infrared waves, and shorter wavelengths, such as ultraviolet rays, x-rays, and gamma rays. It is no

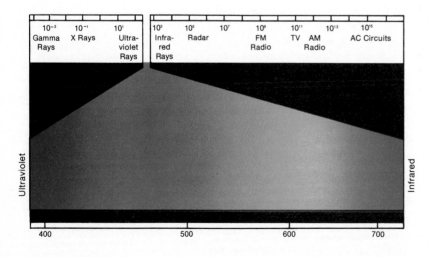

Figure 4.1 The spectrum of electromagnetic energy. The small portion of this spectrum to which the human eye is sensitive is shown expanded. The scale on the large spectrum is a logarithmic scale of wavelength: each step on the scale corresponds to a tenfold increase in the wavelength of the electromagnetic radiation.

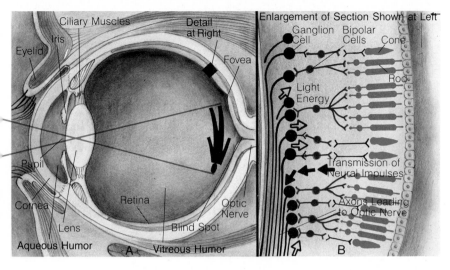

Figure 4.2 The structure of the eye and the transduction of light energy into an electrical signal. (A) A cross section of the human eye. Note that the lens transmits an inverted image onto the retina. (B) The detailed structure of a small portion of the retina close to the fovea. Note that cones are more common toward the fovea and that near the fovea each cone is connected to a single bipolar cell. Arrows on the figure indicate the passage of neural impulses from the receptor cells through bipolar cells and ganglion cells to the optic nerve on their way to the brain.

evolutionary accident that many living things use the same narrow band of electromagnetic radiation as we do to provide visual information about their environments. Basically, organisms use the radiation that is available to them, and a large portion of the sun's energy that strikes the surface of the earth is in the range we call "visible." However, if our eyes were structured just a little differently, it is possible that we could see some parts of the electromagnetic spectrum now invisible to us. People who have had cataractous lenses removed from their eyes, for instance, see slightly more ultraviolet light than normal people do because the eyes' lenses absorb a great deal of ultraviolet radiation.

Light has two characteristics that together determine if and how it will affect receptor cells in the eye. One is wavelength, the other intensity. Each influences a different aspect of vision. **Wavelength**, the distance between the crest of one light wave and the crest of the next, determines color; **intensity**, a measure of the quantity of light, is the major determinant of brightness. The intensity required for a light to be visible is different for different wavelengths.

Basic structure of the eye The structure of the human eye is shown in Figure 4.2A. Light enters the eye through the **cornea**, a tough, transparent window covering the front of the eyeball. Because the cornea is deeply curved, it bends the rays of incoming light and helps to focus them. Behind the cornea is a pouch of liquid (the aqueous humor) that helps maintain the cornea's rounded shape. To its rear lies the **iris**, a ring of pigmented tissue that gives the eye its color (brown-eyed people have pigmentation that blue-eyed people lack). Contraction of muscle fibers in the iris open and close the **pupil**, the opening in the center of the eye, which appears black. In this way the amount of light entering the eye is regulated. You can observe the action of your own iris by turning on a bright bulb in a dimly lit room and watching your pupil in a mirror. It will rapidly close to a very small hole, thus reducing the light that is able to pass through the pupil to the **lens** behind it. The lens is a transparent, elastic structure that allows the eye to adjust its focus depending on an object's distance. This is accomplished by ciliary muscles, which change the shape of the lens, flattening it to focus on more distant objects and allowing the lens to become more spherical to focus on near objects. The incoming light is then projected through the liquid that fills the center of the eyeball (the vitreous humor) and onto the **retina**, the eye's light-sensitive inner surface.

You can easily see how the structure and function of the eye are intimately related by considering some of the visual malfunctions caused by structural defects. For instance, with aging the lens of the eye typically loses much of its elasticity and so does not easily assume a convex shape when the ciliary muscles relax. As a result, elderly people have difficulty focusing on near objects. This is why they tend to hold books and newspapers at a much greater distance than younger people do, sometimes at a full arm's length. Such a loss of elasticity in the lens is known as presbyopia, or old-sightedness. Another structural defect of the lens usually associated with aging is the formation of cataracts. Because the cataractous lens is somewhat opaque, less light passes through it and visual images appear fuzzy and dimmed. When this condition becomes severe, the affected lens is often surgically removed. The patient then either wears special glasses to compensate for the lost lens or has an artificial lens implanted in the eyeball. An understanding of these and other structural pathologies has provided great insight into the normal functioning of a healthy human eye.

Transmission of visual information to the brain   So far, we have simply followed the movement of light into the eye and onto the light-sensitive surface called the retina. But how is the light then transformed into visual experiences registered by the brain? The answer lies in a network of millions of nerve cells. The outermost layer of each retina contains two types of **receptor cells**, the **rods** and the **cones**. When a receptor cell absorbs light energy, the cell generates a small electrical signal. The strength of this signal is proportional to the amount of light energy absorbed by the receptor. As shown in Figure 4.2B, the receptor cells then stimulate the neighboring *bipolar cells*, which in turn stimulate the neighboring *ganglion cells*. The ganglion cells form fibers of the **optic nerve**, which carries visual information from the eye to the brain for interpretation.

If we trace the path of each optic nerve to the brain, we find that the area of the retina through which the optic nerve leaves each eye contains no receptor cells. Consequently, this area is aptly named the **blind spot**. Using Figure 4.3, you can demonstrate to yourself that the image of an object that falls on the blind spot is completely invisible. Why, then, do we not see "holes" in our visual field? One reason is that the blind spot in each eye is off center, so one

Figure 4.3 Although you are never usually aware of it, the blind spot is literally blind. To demonstrate this fact to yourself, hold this figure at arm's length, cover your left eye, and focus on the center of the X. Slowly move the figure toward you, staring continuously at the X. At some point, you will no longer be able to see the red spot. This is the point at which the red spot's image has fallen on the blind spot in your right eye. The red spot will reappear if you move the figure even closer.

eye can usually see what the other does not. Also, because the eyes are constantly moving, the brain can readily fill in missing visual information.

Another feature of the optic nerve's pathway to the brain is the crossover point, called the **optic chiasma**, where the nerves from each retina meet and then split. Fibers from the left half of each eye go to the left hemisphere of the cerebral cortex, and fibers from the right half of each eye go to the right hemisphere. As a result, if damage occurs to the visual center of one hemisphere only one side of each eye is affected.

Abnormal pressure on the optic nerve is responsible for the disease called glaucoma, which primarily strikes people over forty. The buildup of pressure begins in the aqueous humor when fluid does not return to the bloodstream as quickly as it is produced. The fluid accumulates, exerting pressure on the lens and in turn on the vitreous humor and the retina. At first, this pressure shuts off messages in the nerve fibers that carry information about peripheral stimuli, thus causing what is called "tunnel vision." If the disease remains untreated, it will eventually cause total blindness. Glaucoma, in fact, is one of the most common causes of blindness among the elderly.

How the rods and cones function As the starting point in the neural transmission of visual information, the receptor cells in the retina play a vital role. So let us examine their structure and function in greater detail. Rods and cones are so named because of their characteristic shapes: rods are long thin cells; cones are more bulbous, tapering to a near point at one end. Each serves a different visual function: Simply stated, the rods mediate nighttime or low-intensity vision and the cones mediate daytime or high-intensity vision. The cones are also the primary mechanism for color vision (although some data suggest that rods can contribute to color vision as well) (McKee, McCann, and Benton, 1977). Thus, we see little color by moonlight because there is not enough light to stimulate the cones, but we can see shades of light and dark because moonlight *is* intense enough to stimulate the rods. Cones, however, provide a much sharper image than do rods. This is why objects lit by moonlight, although visible, may appear coarse and ill-defined.

Rods and cones are not evenly distributed over the surface of the retina. Cones are most highly concentrated in and near an area called the **fovea**, which lies at the center of the retina. In Latin the word *fovea* means "small pit," and this is exactly how the fovea of your eye appears—a tiny, pit-like depression about 1.5 millimeters in diameter. Thousands of cones are packed into the fovea. In fact, this area contains no rods at all. When you want to inspect something closely, you look at it with your foveal cones because these provide your sharpest, most detailed vision. One reason for the great visual acuity of the fovea is its high density of cones. Another is that the cones in the fovea are heavily exposed to light since the blood vessels and nerve cells that cover all rods and cones form only a thin layer over the fovea. Also, many cones in the fovea are connected to their own bipolar cells, which in turn are connected to their own ganglion cells. This gives each foveal cone, so to speak, its own private line to the brain. In contrast, many rods may be connected to a single bipolar cell, which in turn may be one of many such cells connected to a single ganglion. As a result, the signals from rods are usually blended.

Unlike the cones, which are densest at the center of the retina, the rods are densest at a point about 20 degrees away from the center of vision. This same region has very few cones, so it tends to be very insensitive to color. You can verify this by glancing at an object in a far part of your visual field without turning your head. Its color will probably appear much duller than when you look at it directly. The periphery of the retina, however, is very sensitive to movement and dim light. This is why if you have ever spotted a faint shooting star it was most likely out of the corner of your eye.

Regardless of their location, all photoreceptors, whether rods or cones, transduce light into electrical signals by means of chemical reactions. These reactions involve light-sensitive pigments. The pigment contained in the rods is called *rhodopsin*, or "visual purple," because of its purple color. When light strikes a rod, it changes the chemical structure of rhodopsin by bleaching it (Wald, 1968). This bleaching, in turn, generates neural activity that, after some transformations, travels to the brain. Similar processes take place in the cones, although different pigments are involved.

Because light breaks it down, rhodopsin must continually be regenerated for the rods to function. In very bright light, the speed of rhodopsin synthesis cannot keep pace with the speed of rhodopsin breakdown, and the pigment becomes depleted. This is illustrated in Figure 4.4, which shows the retina of a rabbit's eye after a period of exposure to intense light. You can see that the rhodopsin has been "bleached away." If the animal is placed in the dark the rhodopsin will replenish, but this process takes time. In humans, full recovery of the rods' rhodopsin supply can take up to about half an hour, depending on the intensity and duration of light to which the eye was previously exposed. This is why you have difficulty seeing when you first enter a dark room from bright sunlight: Your supply of rhodopsin has not yet had a chance to replenish.

Although most people's rods gradually become quite sensitive to dim illumination, some people have persistent difficulty adapting to the dark. This condition, known as night blindness, can be caused by several factors, but perhaps the most common is an inability to metabolize or store vitamin A, which is needed for rhodopsin production. For this reason an increase in vitamin A consumption is often prescribed for night blindness.

Compared with the mechanism of rod vision, the mechanism of cone vision is much less clearly understood. This is because of the greater complexity required in a system that provides color images. If you are presented with a certain wavelength in the visual spectrum, you will perceive it as a particular color. A stimulus with a wavelength of 450 nanometers, for example, will ap-

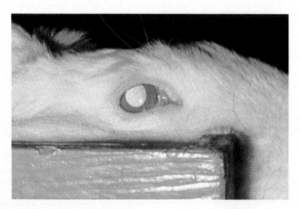

Figure 4.4 A rabbit's eye after it has been in bright light for some time. The pigment rhodopsin has been "bleached" away by the light (the same would be true of your eye after a few minutes on a sunlit beach, though it would not be as noticeable to an observer).

pear blue to you. But how do your cones translate different wavelengths of light into the experience of colors?

According to the most generally accepted explanation of color vision, called the **trichromatic theory**, there are three types of cones, each with a pigment that is maximally sensitive to different wavelengths. Some cones respond best to long-wavelength light (red band), others to medium-wavelength light (green band), and still others to short-wavelength light (blue band). The color that we see depends on the relative activation of the three kinds of cones. All the colors of the visible spectrum (about 150 discriminable colors when brightness factors are controlled) are synthesized from various combinations of the three kinds of cones (MacNichol, 1964). This "synthesis-of-sensing" notion is important in the study of sensory processes because it suggests an interesting economy in the way sensory systems are constructed. Instead of having separate receptors for each discriminable color, the pattern of activity in only three kinds of receptors yields the entire spectrum.

Beyond the cones, another part of the color vision system comes into play. These are the *color-opponent cells*, so named because they respond to stimulation of the eye by light in one wavelength region but are inhibited by light in another wavelength region (De Valois, 1965a, 1965b). Similar color-opponent cells exist at virtually every level of the visual system, from the retina to the cerebral cortex. To understand how color-opponent cells work, we must first understand what we mean by a color's opposite. Look at the color wheel in Figure 4.5. Colors on opposite sides of the wheel are *complementary*—that is, when they are combined they will be seen as achromatic (colorless), either gray

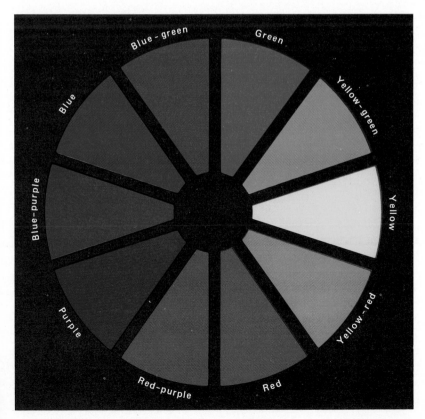

Figure 4.5 The color wheel. Any two colors that are opposite each other are complementaries; that is, combining them produces gray.

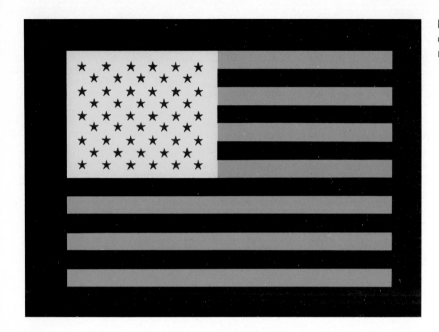

Figure 4.6 Reverse American flag that can be used to demonstrate the phenomenon of afterimages.

or white. According to the **opponent-process theory**, the three types of cones are linked to form three different opponent systems in the brain. One opponent system contains cells that are excited by red and are inhibited by its opposite, green. This system also contains cells that are excited by green and inhibited by red. The second opponent system responds in the same manner to yellow or blue. The third system is a broadly sensitive achromatic or brightness system, responding essentially to light or dark.

The easily observed phenomenon of afterimages provides evidence for the linkage of color opposites. An **afterimage** is a sensory impression that persists after removal of the stimulus that originally caused it. Rest your eyes for a few minutes and then stare intently at the lower right-hand star in the flag in Figure 4.6 for forty-five seconds. Now transfer your gaze to a white area, such as a blank sheet of paper. You should see an American flag in its correct colors, which are complementary to those shown in the figure. Similarly, a person usually reports seeing blue shortly after a brief flash of an intense yellow light, or red after a brief flash of green light. This strongly supports the idea that the perception of complementary colors is indeed linked.

We should not leave the subject of color vision and how it works without some mention of the abnormality called color blindness. Actually, there are several kinds of color blindness, each caused by a particular lack or defect in some part of the normal visual system. A person with normal color vision, as we said earlier, has three distinct visual pigments, each maximally sensitive to particular wavelengths of light. Such a person is called a normal *trichromat*. In contrast, a very few people are *monochromatic*, or totally color blind: They see the world in shades of gray, like the picture on a black and white television. For monochromats, visual information is transmitted only through the rods. Consequently, they must move their eyes rapidly back and forth so that everything registers where the rods are concentrated, away from the center of the retina.

More common is partial color blindness caused by a lack of one of the three visual pigments normally found in the cones. Such a person is called a *di-*

| A | B | C | D |

chromat. Most dichromats are red-green blind; although blue-yellow blindness also occurs, it is far less common. Finally, some people with defective color vision have three cone pigments, as people with normal vision have, but one of these pigments—typically one in the red-green range—is abnormally structured. In vision tests, these people require unusually large amounts of the affected color to produce a "mixed" hue such as yellow (formed by combining red and green). Thus, what he or she perceives as pure yellow is what a normal person perceives as a very reddish or a very greenish yellow, depending on which pigment is defective. Psychologists often refer to such a person as color "weak." Figure 4.7 illustrates how the world appears to people with various kinds of color vision abnormalities.

The perception of color is so basic to how we view the world that we tend to take it for granted. We assume that the way we as adults perceive colors must be the way we have always perceived them—that all aspects of color vision emerge fully formed at birth. But there is no reason why this common assumption is necessarily true. Since most people remember virtually nothing about their first few years of life, it could be that the way we saw colors as infants was significantly different from the way we see them now. This possibility is so intriguing, and the research it has generated so important, that we will explore it here in depth.

Figure 4.7 The same scene as perceived by a person with normal vision and by people with three kinds of color blindness. (A) The scene as people with normal vision see it. (B) The experience of a person who is red-green blind; he or she sees everything in shades of blue and yellow. (C) Someone who is blue-yellow blind sees the world in shades of red and green. (D) The scene as experienced by a monochromat.

Exploring the development of color perception

In depth

Do young children perceive colors in the same way as adults? Most people assume that they do. Yet in the early 1970s a number of studies began to raise some serious doubts. Several hundred children between the ages of three and ten were given a color-vision test in which they were required to arrange fifteen colored caps in a specific sequence of hues. Surprisingly, a full 28 percent made errors involving the color blue (Sassoon and Tolder, 1972; Sassoon, 1973. And the likelihood of making such an error decreased with age: More than 50 percent of the three-year olds made blue-related mistakes, whereas only 11 percent of the ten-year-olds did. These findings seemed to suggest that some kind of physiological change was causing the perception of blue to gradually improve with age. But what could this change possibly be? If it existed, it certainly challenged all theories of color vision and its development that had yet been proposed.

The answer, it turned out, became relatively simple when a second group of researchers noticed that in the color-vision tests that the earlier investigators had administered, the section dealing with blue had always come last. Apparently, what the earlier investigators had overlooked was the fact that children, especially very young ones, quickly grow bored with a repetitive task, lose their concentration, and begin to make mistakes. When this second group of researchers administered the same color-vision test backward—with the blue section coming at the beginning rather than at the end—their young subjects were no longer prone to blue-related errors. Instead, most of the errors continued to occur at the end of the test, regardless of the color presented there (Adams, Balliet, and McAdams, 1975). Carelessness due to boredom and fatigue, these researchers argued, accounted for the curious pattern that the earlier investigators had observed. Thus, when all irrelevant factors are controlled for, children appear to see the same colors as adults.

But even if we know that children can see all the colors adults can, another question about the development of color vision still remains unanswered. When you, as an adult, look at the visual spectrum, you automatically break it up into categories of color: hues of green, blue, red, and so forth. These categories, although they seem so natural, are not necessarily demanded by the wavelengths of light themselves. In physical terms the visual spectrum is a continuum, with each color merging into the adjacent one. So why is it, for instance, that you perceive wavelengths of light above about 490 nanometers as green and wavelengths of light below about 490 nanometers as blue? Is there something about your visual system that leads it to group wavelengths in this particular way? Or is this color classification scheme simply the one that as a child you were taught to use? This question is central to one of the most controversial issues in the field of color-vision research: the relationship between color perception and language. Are people born with a biologically based system for classifying colors into basic categories? Or do the color names used in a particular society determine the way in which its members categorize different hues?

At first glance this question seems almost impossible to answer, for it requires that we determine how babies perceive the color spectrum. How would one go about investigating such a topic? One clever way is to take advantage of the fact that babies grow bored with visual stimuli that appear familiar and so tend to look away from them. This is exactly what psychologist Marc Bornstein and his colleagues did (Bornstein, Kessen, and Weiskopf, 1976). They presented babies only four months old with a particular wavelength of light—say, a shade of blue—until the child grew accustomed to it and began to look at other things. Then they changed the wavelength. If the babies perceived the new wavelength as very similar to the original one, they should not be expected to look at it for very long. But if the babies perceived the new stimulus as novel, then they should be expected to gaze at it for a substantial length of time.

What the researchers found supported the idea that our system for classifying primary colors has a strong biological foundation. The babies generally showed renewed interest only when the new wavelength stimulus belonged to what adults consider a different color category from the first—when, for example, the original wavelength is perceived as blue and the second as green. In contrast, when the new stimulus was one that would appear to belong to the same color category as the first, the babies did not gaze at it very long, suggesting that they, like adults, perceived the two stimuli as being similar. This was the case even though each of the new wavelengths was always separated from the original one by the same physical distance on the color spectrum. For instance, when an original stimulus of 480-nanometer light (which adults perceive as blue) was followed by a stimulus of light of 450 nanometers (also seen by adults as blue), the babies paid little attention to the second stimulus. Yet when a stimulus of 480-nanometer light was followed by a stimulus of light of 510 nanometers (also a 30-nanometer distance from the original stimulus but perceived by adults as green), the babies showed a good deal of interest. The conclusion? Long before they are influenced by language, babies seem to perceive the visual spectrum as divided into the primary hue categories of blue, green, yellow and red. Apparently, biological factors present early in life, perhaps the existence of color-opponent cells in the brain, influence how we organize colors into categories.

If primary color categories reflect something basic to the structure of the human visual system, it would follow that color-naming systems throughout the world should be in many ways alike. As you will learn in Chapter 9 on language, to some extent they are. But there are also some interesting discrepancies. In one study, for instance, Bornstein (1973) analyzed the languages of 145 cultures and found that in 50 percent of the societies, the same word was used to describe both blue and green. If the perception of primary color categories is in large part biologically based, how can such a discrepancy be explained?

Bornstein suggests that people native to various parts of the world see the color spectrum in slightly different ways due to differences in physical traits and environmental conditions. For example, Bornstein noticed that societies whose languages do not have color terms for blue and green are often found at high altitudes or near the equator, regions where sunlight striking the earth contains a large amount of ultraviolet radiation. Significantly, people native to these regions tend to have darker pigmentation in both their skin and their eyes (Coon, 1966; Coon, Garn, and Birdsell, 1950; Silvar and Pollack, 1967). Presumably these denser pigments filter out harmful ultraviolet energy and so provide a kind of protective shield (Walls and Judd, 1933; Judd and Wyszecki, 1963). But coincidentally they also absorb significant amounts of light in the adjacent portion of the electromagnetic spectrum—that is, light in the range of 410 to 430 nanometers, or much of what we call "blue" (Thompson, 1951).

In this respect, people native to equatorial and high-altitude regions resemble those people who have a rare color-vision deficiency called tritanopia. Although the eyes of tritanopes receive normal amounts of short-wavelength (blue) light, tritanopes are insensitive to it and so have trouble distinguishing blue-green from green and tend to apply the same name to both (Pickford, 1951). Members of equatorial and high-altitude societies also have reduced sensitivity to short-wavelength light, but in their case the deficiency is due to eye pigmentation that screens that light out. The effect, however, is very much the same: confusion of blues and greens. This confusion, Bornstein argues, may underlie the fact that the languages of such societies often make no distinction between these two colors. Although this theory is still speculative, it is a fascinating argument in support of the idea that entire groups of people who share certain biological traits may tend to see the world in their own somewhat unique ways.

Hearing

Waves of sound Whereas visual receptors in the eyes transduce light waves into neural signals, auditory receptors in the ears transduce sound waves. Sound waves are caused when pressure changes in the atmosphere vibrate air molecules. To illustrate, when you turn on a radio, the amplifier makes the speaker vibrate. The vibrating speaker alternately pushes against the air in front of it, compressing it, and pulls away from the air, allowing it to become less dense, or rarefied. These waves of compressed and rarefied air molecules then strike the eardrum, pushing and pulling it in the same pattern as the vibrating speaker, although with much less intensity. Other sound-producing stimuli—a rustling piece of paper, a honking horn, a vibrating set of vocal cords—create sound waves in essentially the same way.

These sound waves behave in much the same way as waves of water moving through the ocean: The vibration of each molecule sets the next molecule in motion above or below its resting point, but the individual molecules do not advance with the waves. The molecules of water in an ocean wave ten yards from shore are not the same molecules that break against the beach; ocean waves are simply pulses of energy that travel through the medium of water. In the same way, sound waves are pulses of compression and rarefaction that usually travel through a medium of air. In a vacuum, where there is no air to transmit the waves, there can be no sound.

The number of compression-rarefaction cycles that occur per second determine a soundwave's **frequency**. (Sound waves are measured in units of cycles per second, or hertz, abbreviated Hz.) Frequency corresponds to the pitch we hear: The higher the frequency, the higher the pitch. The human ear is sensitive to frequencies from about 20 to 20,000 Hz. Since human voices range from 100 to 3,500 Hz, we can easily hear them. In fact, our ears are most sensitive to sounds in the frequency range of human speech. This is a good example of how two of our physiological systems—speech and hearing—have coevolved, thus facilitating communication. Frequencies outside our range, in contrast, are inaudible to us. You cannot hear the sound made by a dog whistle because it is above 20,000 Hz, but dogs can hear the sound because their auditory systems are sensitive to these higher frequencies.

The **intensity** of a sound wave, the amount of pressure it exerts, corresponds to its amplitude—that is, to the distance of its peaks and valleys from a baseline of zero. The greater the amplitude of a wave, the louder it sounds to a listener. Amplitude is usually expressed in a unit of measurement called a **decibel**. Normal conversation takes place at about 60 decibels, but humans can also hear sound of much lower amplitude. It has been calculated that a person can actually hear the sound of one air molecule striking the eardrum! This feat can only be accomplished under ideally quiet circumstances, however. Normally, background noise makes such acute hearing impossible. At the other extreme, sounds above 120 decibels are likely to be painful to the human ear, and people who are frequently exposed to such sounds can suffer permanent hearing loss through damage to delicate portions of the inner ear. Rock musicians, for example, sometimes become partially deaf, as do workers constantly exposed to the roar of heavy machinery.

Structure and function of the ear The human ear is a masterpiece of engineering. Into a space of about one cubic inch are packed all the amplifying mechanisms needed to make audible the buzz of a tiny mosquito or the splash of a single drop of falling water. To understand how the ear works, we must understand the structure and function of its three interrelated parts: the outer, the middle, and the inner ear.

Sound enters the outer ear through the **pinna**, the projection of skin-covered cartilage visible on the outside of the head. Some animals can move the pinna to help funnel sound into the ear, but we humans lost this ability somewhere in our evolutionary past. From the pinna, sound travels down the **auditory canal**, a passageway about an inch long sealed off at its inner end by a thin membrane called the **eardrum**. The surface of the auditory canal is covered with tiny hairs that keep out dust and insects, and it contains numerous wax glands that provide lubrication. Because of its long, narrow shape, the auditory canal resonates as sound passes through it, and so the sound is amplified. It has been calculated that for frequencies between 2,000 and 5,500 Hz, the pressure exerted at the eardrum is about twice that exerted at the entrance to the auditory canal.

The eardrum (also called the **tympanic membrane**) responds to changes in air pressure by moving in and out. Its movement, however, is extremely slight. When listening to a normal speaking voice, the eardrum vibrates only about 100 millionths of a centimeter! Nevertheless, this is enough to set into motion three tiny, interconnected bones on the inner side of the eardrum in the area known as the middle ear. These bones, called the **hammer**, the **anvil**, and the **stirrup** because of their distinctive shapes, are positioned and linked in such a way that movement of the eardrum moves the hammer, which in turn moves the anvil, which in turn moves the stirrup, which ultimately presses against the **oval window**, a membrane stretching across an opening to the inner ear. The hammer, the anvil, and the stirrup are collectively called the **ossicles**. They are the smallest bones in the human body, no bigger than the letters on this page.

But why are the ossicles needed at all? Why isn't the ear constructed so that sound energy passes directly from the eardrum to the inner ear? The answer lies in the fact that the inner ear is filled with liquid, and liquid is much more difficult to compress than air. Consequently, the pressure that sound waves typically exert on the eardrum must be substantially amplified if the liquid in the inner ear is to be set into motion. This is accomplished in two ways. First, the ossicles act as a series of levers, increasing the pressure ultimately exerted at the footplate of the stirrup by as much as threefold. In addition, the fact that the oval window is up to thirty times smaller than the eardrum means that the pressure per square millimeter it receives is likewise increased. The end result is

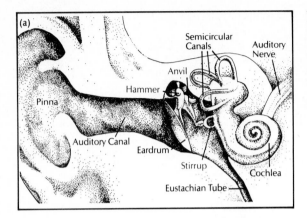

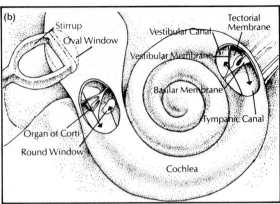

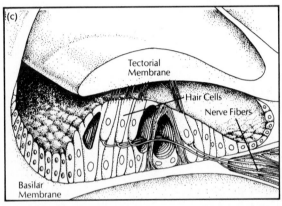

Figure 4.8 The hearing process. (A) Cross-section showing the outer, middle, and inner ear. Sound waves pass through the auditory canal and are transformed into mechanical vibration by the eardrum. The three small bones—hammer, anvil, and stirrup—amplify this motion and transmit it to the oval window of the cochlea, which is depicted in (B). The motion of the oval window sends pressure waves through the fluid in the cochlea in the directions shown by the arrows. (C) Closeup cross section of the organ of Corti, within the cochlea. Waves in the cochlear fluid cause the basilar membrane to vibrate, which in turn disturbs the hair cells, the receptor cells of hearing.

that the pressure that the stirrup exerts on the oval window can be up to ninety times greater than the pressure that the original sound wave exerted on the eardrum. Muscles attached to the ossicles contract in the presence of loud noises and reduce the amplification, thus protecting the ear.

This amplified pressure is then transmitted to the fluid in a spiral-shaped part of the inner ear called the **cochlea**. The cochlea is divided into several canals separated by membranes. Embedded in the central canal is the **organ of Corti**, our actual organ of hearing. It consists of a string of receptors, called **hair cells**, positioned between two membranes, the **basilar membrane** and the **tectorial membrane**. Movement of the fluid in the inner ear moves these membranes, which in turn bend and rub the hair cells between them. This action triggers neural impulses that travel via the adjacent auditory nerve to the brain, where the sensation of hearing occurs.

How the brain distinguishes among tones is not yet fully understood. One insight has come from the discovery that sound waves of different frequencies do not vibrate the basilar membrane uniformly. High-frequency waves have their maximum effect on the region near the oval window, while low-frequency waves have their maximum effect near the cochlea's inner tip. This finding has generated the *place theory* of pitch, which argues that the pitch we perceive depends on the part of the basilar membrane that a sound wave displaces the most. In support of this theory, researchers have demonstrated that mild electrical stimulation of small groups of neurons leading from different parts of the basilar membrane indeed results in the experience of different pitches (Simmons et al., 1965). Moreover, when damage occurs to selective portions of the basilar membrane, only certain tones are affected. For example, as people grow older they gradually lose their sensitivity to high-frequency tones, so that by the age of seventy most cannot hear frequencies greater than 6,000 Hz. Scientists now know that this high-tone hearing loss among the elderly, called presbycusis, or old-hearing, is caused by the deterioration of receptor cells close to the oval window.

In addition to place theory, which explains how we perceive frequency and therefore the pitch of sounds, the *volley principle* explains how we perceive intensity and therefore the loudness of sounds. Volley theory, proposed by Ernest Glenn Wever and Charles W. Bray (1930), suggests that the fibers of the auditory nerve fire in successive volleys, or rounds. As sounds become louder, the fibers fire more frequently.

As intriguing as these theories are, however, neither can explain all our powers of sound discrimination. The place theory does not satisfactorily explain how we can tell the difference between very similar low tones, since there is a great deal of overlap in the areas of the basilar membrane displaced at low frequencies. Nor does it adequately explain our ability to tell the difference between, say, a violin and a flute when both are playing the same note. Psychophysiologists are currently investigating these and other still unresolved questions about the workings of the human ear.

The skin senses

The skin contains receptors for at least five sensations: touch, pressure, warmth, cold, and pain. As Figure 4.9 shows, these receptors are variously structured, and they lie at different depths in the body tissue. All connect with neurons that transmit information to the brain.

We do not yet have a clear picture of the relationship between the different types of receptors that have been identified and the types of skin sensations that we experience. The receptors around the roots of hair cells seem to produce the sensation of touch on the skin's surface, as do the Meissner's corpuscles, which are abundant in hairless areas such as the fingertips, palms, and lips. Lying below these two surface receptors are the Pacinian corpuscles, which seem to

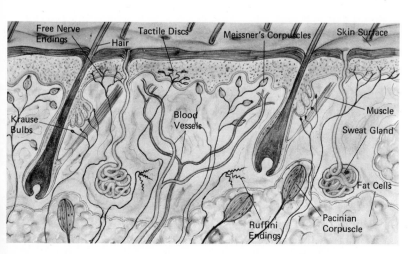

Figure 4.9 A cross-sectional diagram of human skin. A number of different kinds of receptors have been identified near the surface of the skin, but there is considerable uncertainty about their functions. Meissner's corpuscles are believed to be pressure sensitive. Pacinian corpuscles may be additional receptors for "deep" pressure. Free nerve endings may be important in the sensation of pain. It is speculated that Krause bulbs are responsive to cold and Ruffini endings responsive to warmth.

respond to pressure within muscles and internal organs. The receptors believed responsible for the sensations of warmth and cold are the Ruffini endings and the Krause bulbs, respectively. The sensation of "hot," quite interestingly, appears to be produced by the simultaneous activation of both warm and cold receptors (the "cold" receptors are those that respond to cold as well as to extreme heat). Scientists once believed that receptors in free nerve endings in the skin (in contrast to encapsulated nerve endings) were associated only with the sensation of pain. But the cornea of the eye, which almost exclusively contains free nerve endings, is responsive to pressure and temperature as well as pain. So there is still some confusion about the role of free nerve ending receptors (Geldard, 1972).

The chemical senses: smell and taste

The human senses of smell and taste are closely related. Both are chemical in nature—that is, both respond to the chemical composition of stimuli—and they are related through proximity. Because our receptors for smell and taste are located close together, we often confuse or blend their separate sensations. When describing how food "tastes," we usually include its odor, which circulates from the back of the mouth up into the nasal cavity. The intimate relationship that usually exists between taste and smell is most noticeable when the sense of smell is temporarily blocked. Try biting into an apple and then a raw potato while holding your nose. You will probably have difficulty distinguishing between the two tastes. And for the same reason food has a flat, uninteresting flavor when you have a bad head cold. Despite this close interaction, however, taste and smell are distinct senses, so we will consider each separately.

Smell The sense of smell, or **olfaction**, is commonly considered one of the "lower" senses, probably because it contributes less to reasoning and memory, our "higher" mental functions, than vision and hearing do. This lesser importance is reflected in the human brain: Relatively speaking, our olfactory centers are much smaller than those of lower animals, which depend more heavily on odors for information about their environments. Nevertheless, our sense of smell can be vital to survival. A primary function of smell for humans seems to be in warning us of potentially toxic substances that we might eat or inhale. In addition, the ability to detect odors is a major basis for one of life's greatest pleasures, eating, a pleasure that is backed by a multimillion dollar spice and condiment industry. As we will see later, loss or distortion of our sense of smell can be a very disturbing experience.

Smell requires that vaporized molecules of a substance enter the **nasal passages** and contact the **olfactory membranes** that line the roofs of these cavities. Within the olfactory membranes are millions of receptor cells, each with hair-like projections reaching out into the circulating air. These receptor cells transduce the airborne chemical stimuli into nerve impulses, which travel along the **olfactory nerves** directly to the brain.

Most odors to which human beings are sensitive are organic compounds, but little else is known about why people can smell some substances and not others or why certain groups of odors smell alike. A theory proposed by John Amoore suggests that the quality of an odor is related to the size and shape of the molecules that make up the odorous substance. In support of this "stereochemical" theory, two researchers (Amoore and Venstrum, 1967) have shown that people's judgments of the similarities among odors are correlated with measures of molecular similarity. Unfortunately, this relationship between chemical structure and type of odor does not hold for all substances, so we are still unable to describe exactly the physical basis of smell.

Taste Compared with our sense of smell, our sense of taste seems quite restricted. Although we can easily detect and identify odor sources from substantial distances, taste sources must be placed in the mouth to be perceived. In addition, we perceive fewer distinct tastes than odors. Most people can discriminate hundreds of odors, yet they appear to sense only four basic categories of taste: sweet, sour, salty and bitter. Other taste sensations are generally regarded as mixtures of these four or as some combination of taste and smell (Bartoshuk, 1971).

Figure 4.10 shows that different areas of the tongue are especially sensitive to one or more of the four basic taste qualities: The front of the tongue is particularly sensitive to sweet and salty; the sides to sour; the back to bitter. To a remarkable extent these various receptor sites operate independently. This is why, even though a food has a mixture of different taste qualities, we can still identify its component tastes.

The fact that we detect each of the four basic tastes somewhat independently also means that each can be selectively suppressed or distorted. Cocaine is one drug that temporarily suppresses all tastes, but it always eliminates them in a particular order: Bitter disappears first, then sweet, then salty, and finally sour (Moncrieff, 1967). Other chemical stimuli can completely change one of our normal taste sensations. For example, after chewing the leaves of a certain plant (*Gymnema sylvestre*), we no longer taste sugar as sweet because the plant suppresses sweetness detection. The sugar is as tasteless as sand. Eating an artichoke, in contrast, can make an ordinarily tasteless glass of water seem very sweet (Bartoshuk, 1974). This is why serving an artichoke as an appetizer can sometimes ruin the taste of a dry red wine.

In some instances a person's sense of taste may become permanently distorted. Consider the well-documented case of a restaurant owner named Rudy C. (see, for example, Roueché, 1977). After recovering from a brief bout of flu, Rudy found that everything tasted like rotting garbage. All he could manage to eat were bland foods, such as boiled potatoes and milk. His sense of smell was affected too, and this severely restricted his activities. He could not work because his restaurant kitchen stank of burning plastic; he could not relax in his back yard because his lawn had an overpowering odor of green grass; he could not even sleep because his pillow had a terrible stench of dirt. Rudy's affliction was finally diagnosed as *hypogeusia*, a condition that involves loss of taste discrimination, sometimes accompanied by distortions of smell. Doctors have found that hypogeusia can often be cured or substantially alleviated by administering heavy doses of zinc or copper, minerals that people with hypogeusia seem to lack. Apparently, these minerals play some role in maintaining the organs of taste, the **taste buds**, for under an electron microscope the taste buds of a person with hypogeusia appear worn and frayed.

How do the taste buds function in a normal person? The upper surface of a normal human tongue, where the taste buds are most concentrated, contains about ten thousand of these structures, mostly grouped in hill-like projections

A

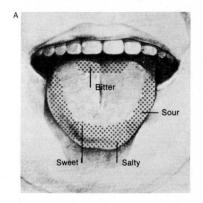

B

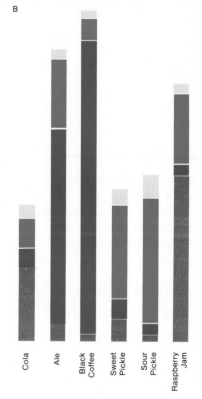

Figure 4.10 (A) A map of the human tongue showing the areas of maximum sensitivity to the four fundamental kinds of taste sensation. (B) The tastes of a number of foods analyzed into the four components of taste shown in A. The length of the colored bars indicates the amount of each component judged to be present in the taste of the food by a number of subjects in a psychophysical experiment (data from Beebe-Center, 1949).

known as *papillae*. It is the papillae that make the top of your tongue appear bumpy. With time, liquids washing over the tongue can gradually erode the papillae, thus decreasing the number of functioning taste buds. This is one reason why taste acuity tends to diminish in old age. The taste buds themselves are actually embedded beneath the surface of the papillae, with access to the outside through a tiny hole, or taste pore. Each taste bud contains receptor cells, which in turn are connected to nerve fibers carrying taste information to the brain. How these nerves function is not completely understood. In several animal species, the individual nerve fibers respond to more than one kind of taste stimulus. This suggests the possibility that the neural code for different tastes may be based on different patterns of activity in the thousands of nerve fibers leading from the tongue, in contrast to the alternative possibility that each nerve fiber carries a message regarding only one of the basic taste sensations.

The sense of taste is an excellent illustration of the fact that different people sometimes perceive the world in very different ways. You have undoubtedly known people whose taste preferences do not precisely match your own. Does the person who heaps four teaspoons of sugar into a cup of coffee taste what you would taste if you took a sip of this saccharine brew? There is a good possibility that he or she does not. This person may well be more sensitive to the bitter taste of coffee than other people are, thus requiring more sugar to compensate. The fact that such differences in taste sensitivity do exist has been demonstrated in the laboratory. For example, about a third of the human population is insensitive to a normally very bitter-tasting substance called phenylthiocarbamide, or PTC. The cause appears to be a genetically deter-mined absence of one of two tongue receptor sites for bitter taste. Interestingly, this same physical trait also seems to make those who cannot taste PTC insen-sitive to the bitter taste of the relatively small amount of caffeine in coffee (Bartoshuk, 1974). The sensations we experience, then, are always the products of our individual sensory systems, and these systems can in some ways differ from one person to the next.

PERCEIVING A COMPLEX WORLD

Until now we have emphasized the structure and function of the human sense organs. All the characteristic ways of perceiving the world we have discussed so far have derived quite directly from the nature of our eyes, ears, skin receptors, olfactory membranes, and taste buds. But we cannot ignore the fact that the information from these organs is ultimately analyzed by the brain. To fully understand how we process sensory data, therefore, we must turn to more complex aspects of perception—those primarily related to how the brain functions.

By organizing and giving meaning to the limited information our senses gather, the brain plays a vital role in perception. When the sensory data we receive from the environment is limited or incomplete, the brain appears to "fill in" the missing details. Consider the drawing in Figure 4.11. The shapes appear to have distinct contours, even though, on close examination, you will see that some of the lines defining them do not actually exist. This phenomenon is called a **subjective contour**—a line or shape that appears to be present but which

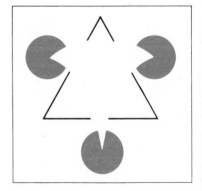

Figure 4.11 Subjective contours. The brain seeks to tie the components of an incomplete picture together by cre-ating the perception of contours that complete the picture (after Kanizsa, 1976).

is not physically there (Kanizsa, 1976). Subjective contours are the result of the brain's automatic attempts to complete the details of a partial image. Although you are seldom aware of it, the brain is constantly enhancing sensory data in this way.

In addition to filling in missing information, the brain compensates for sensory distortions. G. M. Stratton (1896) dramatically demonstrated this process by wearing spectacles that turned the retinal image upside down. At first, Stratton had great difficulty coordinating vision and movement, but after about a week he had adjusted enough to get around quite well. Although things did not look completely normal, they no longer appeared grossly distorted. Ivo Kohler (1962) studied this same compensatory process by using prism goggles that moderately distorted vision—making straight lines appear curved, for example. His subjects soon reported that their originally fluid perceptions had stabilized. Some even managed to perform difficult skills while wearing the goggles, such as skiing or riding a bicycle in traffic. Interestingly, when the goggles were finally removed after weeks or months of use, subjects had difficulty readjusting. Instead of seeing a "normal" world, they saw a world distorted in the opposite direction from what they had experienced with the goggles. For instance, if the goggles had produced line curvature to the left, the subjects now saw line curvature to the right. With time, however, these compensatory distortions disappeared, and the world appeared stable again.

Perhaps the most convincing evidence of the brain's role in perception comes from the observation that we sometimes perceive things in the absence of appropriate external stimuli. Dreams are one example of visual experiences not processed through our eyes. And as we will see in Chapter 11, subjects in sensory deprivation experiments, who are cut off from almost all external stimulation, nevertheless experience vivid and intense sensations that seem to come from the outside world (Bexton, Heron, and Scott, 1954). Finally, research described in Chapter 3 shows that electrical stimulation of the brain can cause people to perceive clearly nonexistent sights, sounds, and other sensations. Perception, then, does not depend exclusively on our sense organs. An essential part of the perceptual process is the manner in which the brain organizes the environmental stimuli our sense organs receive and gives those stimuli meaning.

Perceptual organization and the brain

The world we perceive, particularly our visual world, is enormously complex. Look for a minute out your window. You can probably see hundreds of discrete objects. A tree, a car, a telephone pole are not simply patterns of light waves striking your retinas; they are identifiable things, each with its own color, texture, size, and three-dimensional shape, each moving or stationary. How does the brain form these perceptions? How, for example, are we able to perceive a three-dimensional world when the images that our retinas receive are two-dimensional? Or how are we able to perceive stable objects when visual stimuli are constantly changing? In the following section we will provide some answers to these and other intriguing questions about the brain's role in perception.

Gestalt principles According to gestalt psychologists, we are constantly organizing bits and pieces of information into meaningful patterns. These patterns

Figure 4.12 A stable differentiation of the elements of this picture into figure and ground is difficult at first, and would probably be impossible if you had no previous knowledge of or experience with Dalmatian dogs. The knowledge that there is a Dalmatian dog in this picture, however, makes it possible to differentiate one set of spots as figure and the other spots as undifferentiated ground.

are called **gestalts**, after the German word for "pattern" or "whole." Because of the organization of the black patches in Figure 4.12, for example, we can perceive the form of a dog; a slight rearrangement of the patches would obscure the perception. The dog's form is a gestalt, a perceptual whole. Although we can see each of the elements in the pattern, we perceive more than just these elements—we recognize the whole form of the dog. The gestalt, therefore, is said to be greater than the sum of its parts.

Gestalt psychology originated in Germany early in the twentieth century with psychologists such as Max Wertheimer, Kurt Koffka, and Wolfgang Köhler, and its influence extends to present-day psychology. In their research the early gestalt psychologists presented people with various patterns—often consisting of dots or musical tones—and simply asked the people what they saw or heard. From their data they developed a number of principles to explain how the brain structures sensory stimuli so as to lead to the perception of gestalts. Two of the major concepts they formulated are grouping and figure-ground.

Grouping **Grouping** is the forming of associations among sensory data. Several of the organizing principles of grouping are illustrated in Figure 4.13. In part A dots of equal size are spaced equally across a field, and we perceive no stable distinguishing pattern. In part B the spacing between the dots has been changed so that we see them as forming four parallel lines. This demonstrates the principle of **proximity**: Stimuli that are close together will be seen as a group. In part C the dots in part B have been slightly rearranged so that we now perceive two curved lines. In this case, the principle of **continuity** overrules the influence of proximity: Dots that form a single, continuous grouping are seen as a gestalt. Another organizing principle, illustrated in part D, is **similarity**. Here we perceive a cross in the original pattern A because the dots making up the cross are similar in color.

These principles of grouping apply not only to vision but to other senses as well. Consider a musical composition. The notes of a melody are automatically grouped according to their proximity in time. However, in a composition that includes two melody lines played simultaneously—for example, a Bach fugue— the principle of continuity overrides proximity: Notes of the separate melodies are *not* perceived as a single gestalt.

Various psychologists have suggested that all these principles of grouping can be integrated under a single concept: **simplicity** (Attneave, 1954; Hochberg, 1964). Simple patterns are more easily perceived than complex ones, regardless of whether the simplicity is a result of proximity, continuity, similarity, or some other principle of perceptual organization. Thus, despite conflicting cues and possible interpretations, Figure 4.14 is seen as two interlocking circles, by far the simplest way to perceive it.

Figure and ground Another basic perceptual pattern, extensively studied by gestalt psychologists, is the division of stimuli into figure and ground. When we look at a scene with any detail, we automatically separate it into regions that represent objects, or **figure**, and regions that represent spaces between objects, or **ground**. This ability to distinguish objects from space does not seem to depend on past experience. When people who have been blind from birth are given sight through surgery, they are very quickly able to separate figure from ground, even though they have never had any experience with visual stimuli (von Senden, 1960). When stimuli are very ambiguous, however, experience does help us distinguish figure from ground. Your knowledge of what a Dalmatian looks like, for instance, is an enormous aid in perceiving the dog in Figure 4.12. In fact, without such knowledge, this perception would be almost impossible.

Figure and ground in Figure 4.12 are ambiguous because the blotches are vague and the contours ill-defined. In other cases figure-ground ambiguity is caused by the fact that the picture is essentially "reversible." Examine Figure 4.15. Is this a white vase against a black background, or two black facing profiles against a white background? Depending on your perspective it may be either, and most people can easily switch from one perception to the other.

Our tendency to distinguish figure from ground is not limited to vision. When we follow someone's voice at a noisy party, that voice becomes the figure and all other sounds become ground. If we shift our attention to another voice, the second voice replaces the first as figure. Similarly, if we walk into a kitchen filled with unfamiliar cooking odors and suddenly recognize the odor of brewing coffee, that odor becomes a figure, reducing the other odors to ground.

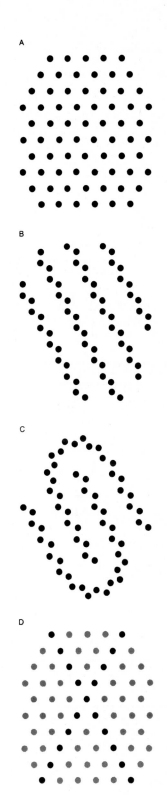

Figure 4.13 A demonstration of some of the gestalt principles of organization. The pattern of equally spaced identical dots in A is not easily organized. It is seen either as an undifferentiated field or as a set of unstable overlapping patterns. In B a stable perception of parallel lines emerges because of the *proximity* of some dots to others. When some of these lines are made *continuous* with one another in C, dots that are physically quite distant from one another are seen as belonging to a single curved line. In D a very stable organization emerges suddenly because some dots have been made *similar* to one another and different from the rest.

Perceptual constancy In addition to the principles of perceptual organization analyzed by gestalt psychologists, there are other ways that we routinely impose order on sensory information. One is our tendency to maintain perceptual constancy. When you walk toward a tree, for instance, the image that the tree casts on your retinas steadily enlarges, its color becomes more distinct, and the details of the branches and trunk sharpen. Yet you do not perceive the tree as suddenly growing bigger, changing its color, or acquiring details before your eyes. Even when large changes occur in the sensory information received from objects, we tend to ignore these moment-to-moment changes in favor of a view of the world that is constant and predictable. Thus, although the image of a departing car becomes progressively smaller, we do not perceive the car as actually shrinking, and when it turns a corner and we view it from the side instead of the rear, we do not think it has changed its shape. This tendency to perceive objects as having certain constant or stable properties is known as **perceptual constancy**.

The features of objects that we tend to perceive as stable include size, color, location, and shape. But how are such perceptual constancies actually maintained in a world of ever-changing stimuli? Let us consider size constancy as an example. We have said that an object's distance and its projected size are inversely related: The greater the distance, the smaller the projected image. This relationship, moreover, has a ratio of one to one: When an object's distance from the eye is doubled, for example, its projected size is halved. The brain takes these facts into account when judging true size. If a tree two hundred feet away looks about half the size of a tree one hundred feet away, a person will automatically perceive them as being nearly the same height.

This size analysis can operate effectively, however, only if distance cues are clear. If they are not, a person can easily be fooled about an object's real size. The reverse, of course, is also true: If an object is not the size you expect it to be, you can easily misjudge its distance from you. The Allies took advantage of this fact during their invasion of Normandy in World War II. In the early morning twilight they dropped two-foot-tall dummies of paratroopers onto fields away from the planned landing site on the coast. When the dummies hit the ground, the impact set off a series of small explosions, simulating rifle fire. In the poor light and general confusion, German observers thought the dummies were real paratroopers, attacking from a substantial distance. Only when the Germans mobilized and moved close enough to see the dummies did they realize that the dummies' small size had misled them about distance. In the meantime, the Allies had gained extra time for the landing.

Depth perception What the Allies had actually done in this case was to take advantage of the fact that relative size has an important influence on the perception of depth. **Depth perception** is simply the ability to tell how far away an object is. Because the images cast on the retina are in two dimensions, not three, depth perception cannot be explained by the eye's anatomical structure. Instead, depth perception, like perceptual constancy, must be an outcome of the way the brain organizes and gives meaning to sensory information. Let us examine some of the ways this process works.

First, depth perception is partly the result of the fact that the brain receives visual input from two eyes rather than one. Since the eyes are set apart from each other, each views the world from a slightly different angle, giving each

Figure 4.14 An illustration of the perceptual tendency toward simplicity. Despite conflicting cues, this figure is seen as two intersecting circles. The circle is among the simplest of perceived forms and provides by far the simplest means of interpreting this pattern.

Figure 4.15 This drawing is a classic demonstration of figure-ground ambiguity. What you perceive as figure and as ground depends on a number of factors, including your expectation.

retina a slightly different image. This difference in retinal image is called **binocular disparity**. You can demonstrate binocular disparity to yourself by holding a finger in front of you and looking at it with one eye at a time. The image registered by the right eye will be slightly left of center, while that registered by the left eye will be slightly right of center. Now line up your finger with some other object that is farther away, and look at both your finger and that object with one eye at a time. As you switch from eye to eye, your finger will seem to jump back and forth in relation to the more distant object because the binocular disparity of far objects is less than that of near ones. The brain uses such binocular disparity cues to help judge distances. In some way that is not yet completely understood, the information from our two eyes combines, probably in the visual cortex, to give a sense of depth.

It is not necessary to have two eyes to perceive depth, however. There are a number of *monocular cues*—that is, cues from one eye—that augment depth perception. One of these is **motion parallax**, the differences in the relative movement of retinal images that occur when we move or change position. An easy way to demonstrate motion parallax is to look toward two objects, one near you and the other some distance away. Close one eye so that binocular disparity is eliminated and move your head back and forth. The near object will seem to move more than the far object. Because of this disparity, when you look out the side window of a car as you drive along a highway, nearby trees seem to zip by while distant mountains may appear motionless. We use such differences in apparent movement between near and far objects to help perceive depth.

There are, of course, a number of other monocular depth cues that we often take into account. One, mentioned earlier, is **relative size**. When we think that objects are the same actual size, the one that casts the smaller retinal image is perceived to be farther away. Another monocular cue to depth is **linear perspective**, produced by the apparent convergence of parallel lines. **Texture gradient** also influences depth perception. In a highly textured scene, such as the one in Figure 4.16, the near stones appear coarser in texture and the more distant ones finer. Then, too, we judge distance by the **partial overlap** of objects. When one object appears to cover another, we perceive the object that is covered as farther away.

Figure 4.16 An example of texture gradient as a cue to depth perception.

Explaining illusions An **illusion** is a perception not in accord with the true characteristics of an object or event. Illusions are caused by one of two things: either a distortion in physical stimuli or a misapplication of our own perceptual processing. The mirages that sometimes appear on a desert horizon are well-known illusions caused by physical distortions of light. Similarly, the medieval Norse explorers believed that the earth was saucer-shaped, probably because they were exposed to the arctic mirage, an illusion that the distant horizon of the sea is higher than the observer. The arctic mirage is produced when relatively warm air contacts a very cold surface, such as the Arctic Ocean. This pronounced temperature inversion gives the air a refractive capacity (an ability to bend light waves) much like that of a prism. As a result, the air refracts images of distant land masses upward, making them visible to the eye when ordinarily they would be obscured by the earth's curvature (Sawatzky and Lehn, 1976).

As intriguing as illusions caused by physical distortions may be, psychologists are much more interested in illusions caused by our own perceptual processing.

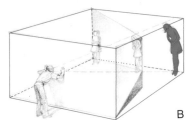

Figure 4.17 The Ames room. In A the actual construction of the room is compared with the way the room is perceived. The photograph in B shows the room as it is seen through the peephole. The illusion is produced by people's inexperience with any rooms except rectangular ones with flat floors. The brain infers that both women standing against the back wall are at the same distance from the eye and interprets the difference between the size of their images as a real difference in size.

Illusions of this second type provide important insights into how our sensory systems normally operate. At first glance this may appear to be a contradiction. How can illusions shed light on normal perceptual processing? To help answer this question, examine the room pictured in Figure 4.17, known as the Ames room. When you perceive the woman on the right as being gigantic in comparison to the woman on the left, it is not because your normal powers of perception have broken down. Instead, it is because you are applying the perceptual principles that successfully guide you every day to a stimulus specifically designed to produce errors, as the caption to this figure explains.

To understand this important point more fully, consider a number of other illusions apparently caused by a misapplication of the principles governing size constancy (Gregory, 1970). First, look at Figure 4.18A. Which line is longer, the left or the right? If you measure them with a ruler you will find that both lines are exactly the same length, even though the one on the left looks substantially longer. One explanation for this effect, called the Müller-Lyer illusion, is that we interpret the "arrows" at the top and bottom of each line as though they defined the edges of a three-dimensional corner. Thus, the line on the left suggests a recessed corner, while the line on the right resembles a projected one. This is illustrated in photograph B. Because both lines cast the same size image on the retinas, the line perceived as recessed (that is, as farther away from us) is interpreted as being larger in accordance with the principles governing size constancy. A very similar misinterpretation may explain the so-called Ponzo illusion, shown in drawing C. Here the converging lines look like railroad tracks or other parallel lines extending away from an observer, as illustrated in photograph D. The result is that the upper part of the drawing appears farther away. Once again, therefore, size constancy dictates that when two objects project the same size image on the retinas but one object is perceived as more distant than the other, the far object must be larger.

Illusions such as these are of more than simply theoretical interest. They can

be applied quite purposefully to create a desired effect. For example, a motorist driving at a constant speed over evenly spaced horizontal lines will become accustomed to the constant amount of time it takes to drive from one line to the next. If the lines are spaced progressively closer together, even though the motorist continues at the same constant speed, he or she will experience the illusion that the car is increasing in speed and will slow down to compensate (Denton, 1971). This technique has been used to force drivers to slow down when leaving high-speed roads and when approaching toll booths.

Some illusions demonstrate the way the brain fabricates much of our visual experience. For example, when moving, a highly repetitive pattern will frequently be perceived as though it covered the entire visual field, and we will "see" a complete pattern even if there are gaps in it. Such moving "phantoms" suggest that the visual system works by economizing on the amount of data it transmits, compressing stimuli, which are then reconstructed in the brain (Sekuler and Levinson, 1977). The process of extrapolation gets "caught out"—and we see illusions—only when the stimuli are unusual.

Virtually all readers of this book will perceive the illusions we have described so far, but not every illusion is this universal. For instance, if you follow the instructions for viewing Figure 4.19, you may think you see the spiral rotating—or you may not. In tests of more than one thousand people, Fraser and Wilcox (1979) found that about 60 percent of those exposed to this stimulus perceived the illusion of strong clockwise rotation. The other 40 percent perceived either counterclockwise motion or no motion at all. What accounts for such differences in the way people experience the world? Heredity may play an important part. Fraser and Wilcox discovered that 90 percent of all identical twins shown Figure 4.19 perceived it in the same way. In contrast, only 52 percent of fraternal twins and 54 percent of nontwin siblings did so. This is strong evidence that certain aspects of perception may be genetically based. As we will see in the following section, however, experience also plays a very important role in explaining perceptual similarities and differences.

Figure 4.18 Two famous illusions and possible explanations for how they work. The vertical lines of the figures in the Müller-Lyer illusion (A) are identical in length, but they do not appear to be. An explanation for this illusion, suggested in B, is that the arrow markings on the lines in A cause them to be perceived as three-dimensional objects that have corners. The corners seem to induce a size-constancy effect: The vertical line that appears to be distant is perceived as larger. The horizontal lines in the Ponzo illusion (C) are also identical in length. As the photograph in D suggests, this figure, too, could easily be perceived as three-dimensional, and again size constancy would cause the apparently more distant "object" to be scaled up in apparent size relative to the "nearer object" (after Gregory, 1970).

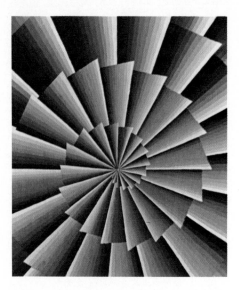

Figure 4.19 Under proper conditions, this painting by Alex Fraser produces an illusion of rotary motion in some people. To see if you perceive the illusion, stand about two feet from the drawing and gaze at a point about fifteen inches below the edge of the spiral. It may help to move your gaze slowly along a horizontal line. If you are like most people, you will see the spiral rotating clockwise.

Influence of experience on perception

Earlier we mentioned how experience enables a person to distinguish figure from ground in Figure 4.12 and so discern a picture of a Dalmatian dog. A moment's reflection will suggest similar examples of the impact of experience on perception. For instance, your ability to read the black squiggles printed on this page is based on past experience with letters and words. In both these cases experience has provided you with a store of accumulated knowledge that can be used to impose meaning on otherwise ambiguous stimuli. Experience also influences perception by molding our expectations about what we *ought* to perceive. Thus, if you expcct to see the word *expect*, you may not notice that it has been misspelled, and if you expect a word to be in a sentence, you may be unaware that it been left out.

Needs and motivations can also influence our perceptions by encouraging us to attend to associated stimuli. For instance, a hungry traveler usually becomes attuned to stimuli he or she might ordinarily ignore (golden arches, large red and white striped chicken buckets). In fact, hungry people may even perceive food-related stimuli where none actually exist. In one experiment, people deprived of food for varying amounts of time were asked to "identify" pictures that an experimenter said would be flashed very dimly onto a screen. In reality, no pictures were presented; the experimenter merely manipulated the projector as though he were projecting images. The subjects nevertheless reported seeing pictures, and the hungrier they were (that is, the longer they had gone without food), the greater the proportion of food-related pictures they perceived (McClelland and Atkinson, 1948).

In summary, the combined influences of accumulated knowledge, expectations, and psychological states *set* us to perceive the world in certain ways. **Perceptual set** refers to a readiness to ignore certain types of stimuli, and to be very sensitive to others. The perceptual sets described thus far are relatively short-lived. Others, however, can be virtually permanent, as we will see in the following sections.

Cultural experiences When you are shown a black and white photograph, you can easily translate this two-dimensional, sharply bordered, gray-shaded stimulus into a representation of the real world. Not all humans readily make this translation, however. For instance, one anthropologist reported that when an African Bushwoman was shown a photograph of her son, she had great difficulty perceiving the image because she, like other people in her culture, had no experience with photographs (Segall, Campbell, and Herskovitz, 1966). What she was accustomed to seeing, in other words, dramatically influenced what she in fact saw.

Your own perceptions are also shaped by cultural experiences. For example, you had no trouble seeing the Müller-Lyer illusion in Figure 4.18 partly because Western culture affords you numerous opportunities to view right angles, both in real life and on the printed page. People who have not had this experience, in contrast, are much less susceptible to the illusion. For instance, members of the Zulu tribe in Africa grow up in an environment characterized by roundness and lack of "carpentered" corners. As a result, while Westerners learn to use the angles in the Müller-Lyer illusion to infer distance, Zulus make no such automatic inference (Segall, Campbell, and Herskovitz, 1966).

Researchers have also reported cultural differences in the susceptibility to the Ponzo illusion, presumably because members of different cultures vary in the tendency to infer depth from two converging lines. One study (Leibowitz and Pick, 1972) compared responses made to this illusion by two groups of Ugandans: university students and rural villagers. Both groups were exposed to converging line-depth cues in their environment, in the form of roads, buildings, plowed fields, and so on. However, when the subjects were presented with stimuli like that pictured in Figure 4.18C and D, the Ugandan students were as likely as students in Pennsylvania to see the illusion, but the Ugandan villagers showed almost no perception of it. Educational experience appears to be the critical factor explaining this difference. University students in both Uganda and the United States are constantly exposed to books, photographs, newspapers, and so forth in which three-dimensional space is represented on a flat surface. Consequently, they are very sensitive to two-dimensional depth cues. Ugandan villagers, in contrast, are more sensitive to the flatness of a two-dimensional drawing and so are less likely to see the depth cues necessary to perceive the Ponzo illusion.

Studies such as these clearly demonstrate the crucial influence of cultural learning on perception. To some extent at least, people in the same culture tend to see things in similar ways. Yet even within a single culture there are many significant differences in the way that individuals process sensory information. The reasons for such differences are numerous and complex, but one important explanation seems to lie in early life experiences and their effect on neural development.

Sensory experiences in early life There is strong evidence that sensory experiences early in life, when the brain's circuitry is still being formed, have a critical impact on the development of perceptual capabilities. To understand the nature of this evidence, you must first understand something about how the cells in the visual region of the cerebral cortex operate. In virtually every species whose visual cortex has been probed with electrodes, scientists have found that most cells respond only to certain highly specific stimuli. In an adult cat, for example, some cells respond only to lines or edges oriented at a particular angle; others respond only to objects moving in a particular direction. Interestingly, however, the visual cortex cells of a very young kitten do not function in this manner; instead, they are equally sensitive to all visual stimuli. An intriguing question for psychologists, then, is to what extent the development of "feature-specific" cells in an adult visual cortex is influenced by early life experience and to what extent it is programmed genetically.

To find out, Blakemore and Cooper (1970) reared kittens in severely restricted visual environments. From the moment the animals first opened their eyes, they were kept in complete darkness except for several hours each day when they were exposed to either horizontal or vertical stripes, but never to both. After a number of weeks the kittens showed signs of extreme visual impairment. When placed in a normal room, those exposed to only horizontal stripes had no difficulty negotiating horizontal obstructions, but they seemed functionally blind to vertical objects. Conversely, kittens with only vertical-stripe experience had no trouble seeing vertically oriented things, but they bumped and stumbled over horizontal ones. Physiological examinations showed no deterioration of the retinas or optic nerves. Instead, what had happened was that the visual cortex cells in these animals had become permanently sensitive *only* to lines oriented in the direction to which they had been exposed.

Other researchers have confirmed these results and have demonstrated other ways that early sensory experiences permanently influence perception. Blake and Hirsch (1975), for example, denied kittens the simultaneous use of both eyes: On one day they covered the left eye with an opaque contact lens; on the next they covered the right eye, continuing in this manner over a period of several months. At the end of this period the kittens could not perceive depth. Why had this visual impairment occurred? The answer again lies in the visual cortex. The experimental treatment had prompted the development of two distinct sets of cells: one set activated by the left eye, the other by the right. This pattern is very different from that found in the visual cortex of a normal adult cat, where most cells receive impulses from *both* eyes. Such binocularly driven cells, it seems, are essential for depth perception. This is why Blake and Hirsch's kittens had become depth blind.

Perhaps you are thinking that these experimental manipulations, however fascinating, are rather remote from conditions encountered in real life. But this is decidedly not the case. Certain optical defects in humans produce restricted visual environments much like those we have just described. Consider, for example, astigmatism, a condition caused when the cornea is not perfectly spherical. Severe astigmatism results in very blurry vision along one axis (either the horizontal or the vertical), but not along the other axis. If this condition arises in infancy and remains uncorrected, the neural connections in the visual cortex will develop in much the same way as they did in Blakemore and Cooper's kittens—that is, the cells will become sensitive mainly to stimuli oriented in one direction. As a result, even when later given glasses that compensate for the misshaped cornea, the person will still have trouble perceiving objects that lie along the unfavored plane (Freeman, Mitchell, and Millodot, 1972; Freeman and Thibos, 1973).

Astigmatism, moreover, is not an isolated example of an optical defect that can cause abnormal brain development in children. When a child is born with misaligned eyes, a condition known as strabismus, the two eyes do not cooperate normally and the child gets little experience in using both eyes simultaneously. Thus, if strabismus is not corrected by the age of about five, few binocularly driven cortex cells will develop, in much the same way as they failed to develop in Blake and Hirsch's cats. The result, of course, is permanently impaired depth perception (Banks, Aslin, and Letson, 1975).

The research on sensory stimulation and neural development emphasizes an important theme of this chapter: Perceptual processing can differ from one individual to the next. Some of these differences seem to arise from differences in early life experience, others may be genetically based, and still others may be due to variations in learning, memory, or motivation. But whatever the cause, the end result is that each of us constructs a perceptual world that is in certain ways unique.

SUMMARY

1. Psychologists who study perception seek to understand how we perceive stimuli from the outside world. There are differences in perceptual capabilities not only among species, but among individuals. A **stimulus** is any form of energy to which an organism is capable of responding. A **sensation** is the response to that energy by a sensory organ. Sensations are not always completely accurate reflections of the physical properties of a stimulus. In studying the relationship between what a person senses and what a stimulus is physically like, psychologists analyze three things: **absolute threshold**, the minimum stimulus necessary to produce a specific sensation; **sensory ratios**, the amount by which a stimulus must be increased to produce a "just noticeable difference" in sensation; and factors that reduce or increase sensory capacities. Another reason our senses do not always give a completely accurate picture of the outside world is that after prolonged and constant stimulation, sensory systems **adapt**.

2. The sense of sight is the process by which the energy in light is translated—or **transduced**—into neural impulses that carry information about shape, color, depth, texture, and movement to the brain. The wavelength of light determines the color we perceive, while its **intensity** determines brightness. The main structures of the human eye are the **cornea, iris, pupil, lens,** and **retina**. Receptor cells in the retina stimulate neighboring bipolar cells, which in turn stimulate ganglion cells. The ganglion cells form fibers of the **optic nerve**, which carries visual information from the eye to the brain for interpretation.

3. The **receptor cells** in the eye are of two kinds, **rods** and **cones**. Rods mediate low-intensity vision, while cones mediate high-intensity and color vision. Both transduce light into electrical signals by means of chemical reactions involving the light-sensitive pigment rhodopsin. Cone vision is less clearly understood than rod vision. According to the most generally accepted explanation, the trichromatic theory, there are three types of cones. The color that we see depends on the relative activation of each type of cone. In addition, according to the opponent-process theory, the perception of complementary colors, those on opposite sides of the color wheel, is linked so as to form three opponent systems in the brain.

4. Hearing occurs when auditory receptors in the ears transduce sound waves, vibrating air molecules set in motion by pressure changes in the atmosphere. The **frequency** of a sound wave determines the pitch we hear, while its **intensity** determines loudness or softness. Sound enters the ear through the **pinna** and travels down the **auditory canal** to the **eardrum**, which responds to changes in air pressure by moving in and out. It sets into motion the **ossicles**—

three tiny bones called the **hammer, anvil,** and **stirrup**—which in turn press against the **oval window**, leading to the inner ear. Here, embedded in the spiral-shaped **cochlea**, is the **organ of Corti**, which contains the receptors, called **hair cells**, that send neural impulses through the auditory nerve to the brain.

5. The skin senses include touch, pressure, warmth, cold, and pain. Through receptors lying at different depths in the body tissue, all these sensations are transmitted to the brain.

6. The closely linked senses of smell and taste are called the chemical senses because they both respond to the chemical composition of stimuli. In smell, or **olfaction**, vaporized molecules of a substance enter the **nasal passages** and contact receptor cells in the **olfactory membranes** that send neural impulses along the **olfactory nerves** to the brain. We can perceive only four basic categories of taste: sweet, sour, salty, and bitter. Taste sources must be placed in the mouth to be perceived, and different areas of the tongue are especially sensitive to one or more of the four basic taste qualities. **Taste buds**, grouped on the upper surface of the tongue in hill-like projections called papillae, contain receptor cells connected to nerve fibers that carry taste information to the brain.

7. The brain plays a vital role in perception by organizing and giving meaning to the information our senses gather. The brain may fill in the details missing from sensory data through a **subjective contour**, for example. The brain also compensates for sensory distortion, and it accounts for perception in the absence of appropriate external stimuli. Dreams are one example of visual experience not processed through our eyes.

8. According to the Gestalt psychologists, the brain is constantly organizing pieces of information into meaningful patterns called **gestalts**. Two major ways it does this are through **grouping**, the associating together of sensory data, and through the division of stimuli into **figure** (objects) and **ground** (spaces between objects). Another way that we routinely impose order on sensory information is through **perceptual constancy**, the tendency to perceive objects as having certain constant or stable properties.

9. Visual depth is perceived binocularly as a result of **binocular disparity**. Depth is perceived monocularly with the help of a number of cues—**motion parallax, perspective, blocking,** and **texture gradients**.

10. Psychologists are interested in the study of **illusions** caused by our perceptual processing, because of the insights they give into how our sensory systems usually operate. While some illusions are almost universal, others may or may not be perceived by certain individuals, depending on various factors. One factor in determining how we perceive certain stimuli is heredity. Another is experience. Experience provides knowledge that can be used to impose meaning on otherwise ambiguous stimuli, and it also influences perception by molding our expectations about what we *ought* to perceive. Needs and motivations can also influence our perceptions by encouraging us to attend to particular stimuli. Knowledge, expectations, and psychological states together influence our **perceptual set**, or readiness to ignore certain types of stimuli, while being very sensitive to others. Finally, our perceptions are shaped by cultural experiences. To some extent, people in the same culture tend to see things in similar ways. Yet even within a single culture there are significant differences in the way individuals process sensory information. For example, there is strong evidence, confirmed by research, that sensory experiences early in life have a critical impact on the development of perceptual capabilities.

Suggested readings

Dember, W. N., and Warm, J. S. *Psychology of perception* (2nd ed.). New York: Holt, Rinehart and Winston, 1979.

Deregowski, J. B. Pictorial perception and culture. *Scientific American*, 1972, *227*, 82–88.

Gregory, R. L. *Eye and brain: The psychology of seeing* (2nd ed.). New York: McGraw-Hill, 1973.

Haber, R. N., and Hershenson, M. *The psychology of visual perception* (2nd ed.). New York: Holt, Rinehart and Winston, 1980.

Kaufman, L. *Perception: The world transformed.* New York: Oxford University Press, 1979.

Land, E. H. The retinex theory of color vision. *Scientific American*, 1977, *237*, 108–128.

PART 3

LEARNING AND INFORMATION PROCESSING

This section examines thinking. Chapter 5 focuses on learning, and the influences that can affect it. How is what we know stored—and how retrievable? Chapter 6 looks at the area of memory and forgetting. Cognition and problem solving are the subjects of Chapter 7: How does thinking proceed?

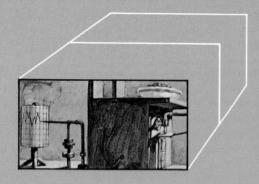

PREVIEW

1. An understanding of learning is necessary in order to explain human behavior. Learning is inferred from changes in performance.

2. Awareness of external stimuli is the simplest kind of learning. Classical and operant conditioning—learning that certain events interrelate—are more complex.

3. In classical conditioning, the onset of one stimulus predicts a second one. For example, if a warning light repeatedly precedes a shock, you learn to move in response to the light. In operant conditioning, the probability of a response is affected by its consequences. For example, if kindness were always financially rewarded, you would be kinder.

4. Extinction, or the gradual disappearance of learned responses, occurs when stimuli are no longer associated with each other or contingent on each other.

5. Cognitive psychologists maintain that important thought processes intervene between stimulus and response and that learning can occur without reinforcement.

5 Basic principles of learning

John B. Watson, the psychologist credited with founding the behaviorist movement in the United States, was one of the most colorful personalities ever to study how learning occurs. In his most famous experiment, Watson and one of his students, Rosalie Rayner, taught an eleven-month-old boy named Albert to fear a harmless laboratory rat (Watson and Rayner, 1920). Albert was a healthy, normal child who, at the beginning of the experiment, showed no fear of the furry, white animal. He seemed to enjoy watching the rat and even tried to play with it. That changed when Watson and Rayner began their experimental procedure. Every time they presented the rat to little Albert, one of them would strike an iron bar with a hammer just behind the child's ear. The terrible noise made Albert jump, wail, and attempt to bury his face in the mattress on which he sat. After several pairings of these two stimuli, Albert began to respond with fear to the sight of the rat alone, in the absence of the loud noise. And his fear generalized to other furry objects—a rabbit, a dog, a fur coat, even, it seemed, to a bearded Santa Claus mask.

To understand the process by which little Albert developed these unusual fears, we must understand the ways that human beings learn. The principles of learning provide insight into almost every phenomenon psychologists study. What causes you to perceive depth when you view two converging lines on a two-dimensional drawing? Why is it that women tend to be more emotionally expressive than men? What accounts for the fact that identical twins can develop quite different personalities? Why do people sometimes persist in behavior that seems to undermine their own well-being? What makes a person fall in love? All these and many other aspects of human behavior can be at least partially explained by learning.

THE NATURE OF LEARNING

Since learning is a mental activity and not something that can be seen, how do psychologists know when learning has occurred? The answer is that they infer learning by observing changes in *performance*. Unlike learning, performance is both observable and measurable. Therefore, a psychologist can set up various situations conducive to learning and measure a subject's performance in each one. To the extent that the situations are carefully controlled, changes in performance can be said to reflect differences in learning.

An example will help clarify exactly how psychologists infer that learning has occurred. Suppose an experimenter places some food in the goal box of a maze and then sets a hungry rat loose at the maze's starting point. The rat smells the food but does not know how to reach it, so it begins to run at random down the alleyways. After many wrong turns and retraced steps, the animal finally reaches the food and is allowed to eat for a short while. Then it is promptly returned to the starting point. With each subsequent run through the maze, the rat gradually makes fewer and fewer false turns, until eventually it can negotiate the maze without error. From this measurable change in performance, the experimenter is justified in concluding that the rat seems to have learned.

But inferring learning from changes in performance is not as simple as this brief description implies. Performance may be influenced by many factors other than learning. Physical maturation produces some changes in behavior, and behavior is also affected by emotion, motivation, health, and fatigue. Thus, if a football player performs better this week than last, we cannot infer that his improvement is necessarily due to the learning of some new skill. Instead, he may have had a cold the previous week, or a fight with the team manager, or this week's game may be especially important to him. Similarly, if performance changes for the worse, we cannot automatically conclude that something learned has been forgotten. If a rat wanders aimlessly through a maze that it previously ran flawlessly to obtain food, it may simply mean that the animal is no longer hungry. Performance, then, can vary even though learning remains constant. This makes the task of inferring learning from performance more difficult than at first glance it appears.

Given that learning can only be inferred from performance, yet performance is influenced by other things, how do psychologists define learning? A good definition of learning must make several points. First, it must specify that learning is not necessarily reflected in performance—that learning is merely a *potential* for performance. Second, it must differentiate learning from all the other factors that can possibly influence behavior. To distinguish learning from factors such as emotion or fatigue that affect us only temporarily, learning can be labeled a *relatively permanent* change in performance potential. And to distinguish learning from physically based factors such as maturation or disease, learning can be designated a change in performance potential that results from *experience*. Putting all these elements together, we have the following definition: **Learning** is a relatively permanent change in performance potential that arises from experience (Kimble, 1961).

Such a definition, of course, is quite general. It says nothing about how learning actually takes place, a subject we will explore in the remainder of this chapter. As you will see, there are actually several different types of learning, each involved in acquiring different kinds of information. *How* we learn, in other words, depends in large part on *what* we are learning.

Perhaps one of the simplest kinds of learning is acquiring the knowledge that stimuli in our environment exist and have distinguishing features. We accomplish this by examining novel stimuli with our senses. Most unfamiliar, unusually intense, or unexpected stimuli tend to produce what is called an **orienting reflex**, a response that involves a whole chain of activities—looking, listening, touching, sniffing—designed to ascertain what the new stimulus is about. But as we repeatedly encounter the same stimulus, the orienting reflex gradually disappears. The unfamiliar has become commonplace, and we tend to ignore it. Thus, when your car first develops a peculiar rattle you are likely to pay it close attention. But as time goes by you may seldom hear the noise, not because it has stopped but because you have become **habituated**, or accustomed, to it. This process of habituation is one sign that the existence of a stimulus has been learned.

But even very simple organisms are capable of learning far more than this about the stimuli around them. Animals also learn that certain events are associated with one another. Psychologists call this **associative learning**. Suppose your already rattling car suddenly acquires a new sputtering sound. Less than a minute after this noise begins, the engine inevitably stalls out and is very difficult to start again. If you experience a feeling of anxiety as soon as you hear your finicky engine cough, psychologists would say that you have learned an association between the sputter and the stall and that the anxiety you feel is a **classically conditioned response**. Classical conditioning is a very basic kind of learning, and with just a moment's thought you can probably think of many instances of it. Little Albert's fear of white rats was a classically conditioned one, acquired through the association of a rat with a terrifying noise. In much the same way, a dog will learn to cringe and whine whenever it hears the approaching footsteps of a person who regularly beats it. We will say much more about this pervasive form of learning in a subsequent section of this chapter.

There is another kind of associative learning that is equally pervasive. Organisms are continually discovering that their own actions have both positive and negative consequences, and these consequences in turn affect behavior. Thus, you may find that if you hit the accelerator every time your car emits its sputter, you can avoid the frustration of stalling in the middle of the road. Psychologists would say that the lurching style of driving you are sure to develop is an **operantly conditioned response**; it is due to a learned association between a particular action (quickly pressing the gas pedal) and a desirable consequence (keeping the engine running). Clearly, a great deal of our behavior is shaped in very similar ways. A child learns to be helpful around the house because that behavior brings him praise and affection. A student learns to study regularly because that behavior earns her good grades. After discussing classical conditioning, most of the remainder of this chapter will investigate how such operantly conditioned responses are formed and maintained.

Some psychologists have taken the extreme position that virtually all learning can be explained by classical and operant conditioning. But others argue that while these two forms of learning are important, much of human learning does not fall into either category. Various kinds of **cognitive learning**, they maintain, also play important roles in our lives. We conclude this chapter, therefore, with a look at learning from the cognitive psychologist's view.

CLASSICAL CONDITIONING

We have said that little Albert's fear of furry white rats was classically conditioned, but what exactly happens when a classically conditioned response is formed? Basically, a neutral stimulus (in this case a laboratory rat) is repeatedly paired with another stimulus (a loud noise) that evokes a reflex response (fear). Eventually, the rat alone elicits fear.

Note that this and all other instances of classical conditioning involve some **reflex behavior**. A reflex is a behavior produced involuntarily by a specific stimulus. A loud noise makes you jump and often induces fear; a sharp puff of air on your eye elicits a blink of your eyelid; the heat of a flame or the prick of a thorn causes you to pull back your hand or foot. These and other reflex behaviors are all capable of being classically conditioned to some neutral stimulus.

Perhaps the best known classically conditioned reflex is the salivation response studied by the great Russian physiologist Ivan Pavlov. Pavlov's international reputation grew out of his research on the physiology of digestion, which earned him one of the first Nobel Prizes in medicine. His work was characterized by both extraordinary ingenuity and total dedication. One story has it that Pavlov even refused extra food rations during the hard times of the Russian Revolution until additional food was also made available to his famous experimental dogs.

Like many great discoveries, Pavlov's discovery of classical conditioning was largely accidental. At the time, he was studying how the mouth prepares itself for food by secreting saliva, which contains digestive enzymes. In a series of experiments with dogs (1927), Pavlov found that the mouth also secretes saliva when food is merely seen or smelled. He called this salivation "psychic secretions" because it occurred in anticipation of food, *before* food was actually presented. Pavlov also found that when a dog first sees an unfamiliar food it does not salivate. Only when the animal learns that particular sights, odors, or other stimuli are associated with a desirable food will psychic secretions occur. These discoveries provided the foundation for Pavlov's subsequent investigations into **classical** (sometimes called Pavlovian) **conditioning**.

Establishing a classically conditioned response

Pavlov's experimental apparatus is illustrated in Figure 5.1. Before the experiment began, each dog underwent minor surgery: a tube was inserted in its cheek so that saliva would flow from the duct in the animal's salivary gland into a glass container. The mechanical device shown on the far left of the

Figure 5.1 The apparatus used in early studies of classical conditioning. Saliva dropping from a tube inserted into the dog's cheek strikes a lightly balanced arm, and the resulting motion is transmitted hydraulically to a pen that traces a record on a slowly revolving drum. Pavlov's discovery of conditioned salivation was an accidental byproduct of his researches into the activity of the digestive system.

drawing kept track of the number of drops secreted. In front of the dog was a food tray from which the animal could eat when food was made available. In his studies Pavlov presented a stimulus—say, a tone—and several seconds later dropped food into the dog's tray. The dog picked up its food and salivated as the food entered its mouth. As the pairing of the tone and the food continued, the previously neutral stimulus, the tone, began to elicit salivation. Eventually, the tone alone was enough to elicit this response. The outcome of a typical classical conditioning experiment is shown in Figure 5.2.

Let us summarize Pavlov's findings again. When a stimulus that has no effect on the salivary reflex, such as the sound of a tone, repeatedly occurs just before food is presented, the tone itself gradually comes to elicit salivation. In Pavlov's terms, the food in the mouth is the **unconditioned stimulus** (UCS), which elicits the **unconditioned response** (UCR) of salivation. The word *unconditioned* indicates that the connection between this particular stimulus and response does not have to be learned. In contrast, the new stimulus that comes to elicit salivation is called the **conditioned stimulus** (CS), and the animal's salivation response to it is called the **conditioned response** (CR). The word *conditioned* indicates that this new association is learned through a constant pairing of the food with a tone. Thus, the end result of a classical conditioning experiment is that a conditioned stimulus produces a response similar to the one produced by an unconditioned stimulus. This is shown in Figure 5.3.

Pavlov found that a large number of auditory, visual, or tactile sensations can serve as conditioned stimuli for salivation, including the sound of a metronome, the flash of a light, or a brush on the skin. He also found that, using procedures similar to those just described, he could condition reflexes other than salivation. Consider the eyeblink, for instance; this reflex is used in many classical conditioning experiments with humans, although it was not specifically studied by Pavlov. An eyeblink can easily be evoked by directing a quick puff of air at someone's eye. If a bell is rung immediately before each puff of air occurs, and if this pairing is repeated several times in succession, the subject will probably learn to blink at the sound of the bell alone, as though in anticipation of the puff. The eyeblink, in other words, will be elicited by a stimulus that does not normally evoke it. Blinking in response to the bell has been classically conditioned.

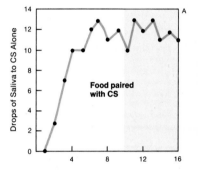

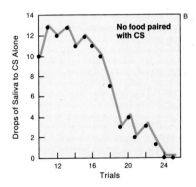

Figure 5.2 (A) Acquisition of a conditioned response. On early test trials—with the tone alone—there is little salivation. Later in the series the tone alone (CS) elicits considerable salivation. A conditioned response (CR) has been acquired. (B) Extinction of a conditioned response. When the tone–food pairings are eliminated, the amount of salivation (CR) to the light alone (CS) drops steadily until the relationship between the CS and the CR is destroyed.

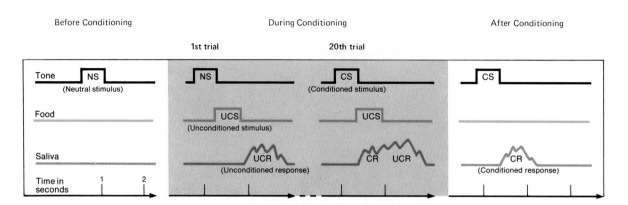

Figure 5.3 The relationship of events in classical conditioning (from left to right). *Before*—a stimulus such as a tone that elicits no salivary response can be described as a neutral stimulus (NS) with respect to salivation. This stimulus, the tone, is paired with an unconditioned stimulus (UCS), food, which elicits the unconditioned response (UCR) of salivation. *During conditioning*—Repeated pairing of the tone and the food begin to elicit salivation in response to the tone as well as to the food. Because the previously neutral tone is no longer neutral, but capable of calling forth salivation, the tone itself becomes a conditioned stimulus (CS), and the salivation it elicits now becomes a conditioned response (CR). *After*—Finally, a test with the tone alone is sufficient to elicit salivation.

This tendency to react to a previously neutral stimulus, now a CS, as though it were the UCS, Pavlov called **stimulus substitution.** In the examples given, Pavlov's dogs responded to a tone as though it were food and a person responded to the ringing of a bell as though it were a puff of air directed at the eye. In much the same way, a student may respond to the announcement that there will be a surprise test in two minutes (CS) with an accelerated heart rate, as though the actual test (UCS) were being presented immediately.

CS-UCS contingencies   A strong classically conditioned response can be established and maintained only if certain requirements are met. One is a perceived **contingency** between the presentation of the conditioned stimulus and the appearance of the unconditioned stimulus (Rescorla, 1967). By contingency we mean a relationship between the two variables such that the occurrence of one seems to depend on the occurrence of the other. For this reason, the CS in a typical conditioning experiment is presented slightly in advance of the UCS. Pavlov, for example, presented the tone (CS) five seconds before the food (UCS), and in some cases the tone continued until the food was given. If, in contrast, this order of presentation is reversed, and the food is given *before* the tone, the animal is less likely to learn to salivate at the sound of it because the tone does not signal that food is about to arrive. This presentation of the UCS before the CS is called **backward conditioning,** and it is a much less effective procedure for establishing a classically conditioned response.

A learned relationship between conditioned and unconditioned stimuli also will be weak or will not develop at all if these two events are presented randomly and independently in time—that is, if there is no consistent relationship between them. If the tone is presented five seconds before the food, then five seconds after the food, and then ten seconds before the food, and so on, the animal learns that the tone is not related to the food in any systematic fashion. In fact, this may make it difficult to establish a conditioned response to the same CS in later experiments, because the animal has already learned that this CS has not been related systematically to other events in the past (Rescorla, 1967).

Finally, in many classical conditioning situations, it is equally essential that the conditioned and the unconditioned stimuli occur reasonably close together in time, otherwise the subject may fail to perceive a relationship between them. In addition, the CS and the UCS must usually be paired several times in succession to establish a strong conditioned response. So basic are these requirements in most of the classical conditioning experiments psychologists have performed that many researchers once believed they constituted universal "rules" of conditioning. Findings in the last several decades, however, have uncovered some intriguing exceptions to these rules, as you will see in the following section.

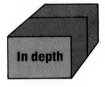

In depth

The Garcia effect The time is the mid 1950s. Just a decade earlier physicists working to develop an atomic bomb had succeeded in tapping the secrets of nuclear fission. But how serious were the hazards posed by nuclear wastes and fallout? Many concerned scientists were anxious to find out. Among them was a psychologist named John Garcia.

In the course of his investigation into the effects of radiation on living organisms, Garcia made a puzzling discovery (Garcia et al., 1956). Rats placed in a radiation chamber once a week and exposed to moderate levels of radiation for eight hours progressively lowered their intake of water, as though for some reason they were learning *not* to drink. Yet when returned to their home cages the rats drank as usual. It was only the water in the radiation chambers that they refused to touch. In fact, even when placed in the chamber with no radiation actually given, the rats still displayed this same avoidance of water. What could explain this strange behavior? Garcia suspected that it must reflect some kind of associative learning. But what specific stimuli were involved?

Later Garcia believed that he had deduced the answer. This behavior, he proposed, was essentially a case of classical conditioning. The water bottles in the radiation chambers were made of plastic, but the water bottles in the home cages were made of glass. Apparently, the plastic bottles imparted a peculiar taste to the water. It was this taste that served as the conditioned stimulus. The unconditioned stimulus was gastric dysfunction caused by exposure to radiation. Irradiating almost any animal, be it a rat, a monkey, or a human being, generally causes severe illness. Drinking the plastic-tasting water had been repeatedly paired with gastric dysfunction and the associated response of feeling ill. Soon, tasting the water alone was enough to evoke nausea and strong avoidance behavior.

Garcia's next step was to conduct a number of controlled experiments to test this hypothesis more thoroughly. He spiked water with various novel flavors and administered different kinds of illness-inducing agents. As predicted, rats did seem to acquire a classically conditioned taste aversion after the pairing of a new flavor with severe gastrointestinal upset. Furthermore, such learning seemed to occur with remarkable speed and persistence. In one of Garcia's experiments, for instance, a single pairing of salt-flavored water with illness was enough to cause rats to shun similar tasting water when they encountered it again more than a month later (Garcia, Hankins, and Rusiniak, 1974).

But why, Garcia wondered, had the rats developed an aversion specifically to the water? Why hadn't they developed an aversion to the sight of the experimental chamber as well? After all, it too had been associated with illness. Yet, subsequent experiments showed that it was extremely difficult to get a rat to avoid the *place* where it had become ill, even though that place was clearly distinguishable (Garcia, Kimeldorf, and Hunt, 1961). What could be going on here? Was there something special about the link between a certain cue and a certain consequence that made an association between them somehow easier or more difficult to learn? If so, this linkage contradicted one of the basic assumptions about classical conditioning prevalent at the time—the assumption, dating back to Pavlov, that a reflex response could become conditioned with equal ease to virtually *any* formerly neutral stimulus. Garcia's work suggested that this long-held belief might be false. The nervous system of an organism might be structured in such a way as to facilitate the learning of certain contingencies and hinder the learning of others.

To investigate this intriguing possibility, Garcia and his colleague Robert Koelling designed a clever experiment in which different kinds of stimuli were paired with different aversive outcomes (Garcia and Koelling, 1966). One group of rats was presented with saccharin-flavored water, and as soon as the animals drank it they either received a foot shock or were induced to become ill (by radiation poisoning or injection of a toxin). Another group of rats was presented with water that, when sipped through a drinking tube, set off an impressive display of flashing lights and loud noises. Drinking this "bright, noisy water" was again followed by either a foot shock or an induced illness.

The results of this experiment are shown in Table 5.1. As you can see, whether a rat subsequently avoided the water to which it had been exposed depended on the water's characteristics and what happened after the animal drank it. An aversion developed when saccharin-flavored water was paired with illness and when bright, noisy water was paired with shock. But no aversion resulted when these stimuli were paired in the opposite way—that is, saccharin water with shock and bright, noisy water with illness. Garcia concluded that the ease with which an animal learns a given association seems to depend on some intrinsic relationship between the cue (CS) and its consequence (UCS).

Why would this be the case? Garcia believes that the answer lies in the evolutionary history of the species. He argues that natural selection has favored a nervous system that allows rapid learning of contingencies that are common in an animal's environment and that are crucial to its survival. In Garcia and Koelling's experiment, taste–illness combinations produced rapid learning, while taste–pain combinations did not; audio-visual–pain combinations led to rapid learning, while audio-visual–illness combinations did not. Consider the dietary habits of a rat. These animals are opportunistic foragers: They eat virtually whatever they can find. Such a strategy has obvious advantages in

Table 5.1 Results of the Bright, Noisy Water Experiment

		Consequences	
		Illness	**Shock**
Cues	Taste	Avoid	—
	Audio-visual	—	Avoid

Source: From "Relation of cue to consequence in avoidance learning" by J. Garcia and R. A. Koelling, *Psychometric Science*, 1966, *4*, 123–214.

expanding the supply of available food. But it also runs some risks. It greatly increases the likelihood that a rat will become poisoned by eating something toxic. So any rat whose nervous system is "programmed" to remember foods previously associated with illness will clearly have a better chance of surviving to reproduce. In this way, a "built-in" facility for learning to avoid dangerous foods may have evolved.

This evolutionary perspective helps explain why learned taste aversions violate another traditional rule of classical conditioning—the rule that the UCS must follow the CS within a matter of seconds if learning is to occur. Even in his earliest experiments Garcia noticed that a fairly substantial delay could occur between tasting a novel flavor and becoming ill, yet the animal would still develop an aversion to that flavor. How prolonged could the separation between the CS and the UCS be? Subsequent research showed that it could be very long indeed. In one experiment Garcia found that if delays up to seventy-five minutes occurred between drinking saccharin-flavored water (CS) and falling ill due to injection of a toxic drug (UCS), a strong taste aversion to saccharin would still be learned (Garcia, Ervin, and Koelling, 1966). Other studies have shown that the lapse between the two can be even longer—anywhere from three to twelve hours, depending on the circumstances (Kalat and Rozin, 1971; Andrews and Braveman, 1975).Furthermore, in many cases tastes intervening between the CS and the UCS do not prevent a strong aversion to the CS from forming, provided that the flavor of the CS is novel and salient enough (Revusky and Bedharf, 1967). Such findings are understandable if you assume that organisms have biological predispositions to learn adaptive behaviors. In nature, substantial time gaps often occur between ingestion of a toxin and the subsequent feeling of illness, so any organism capable of learning in spite of such gaps would clearly have a survival advantage.

Do humans also have a built-in facility for learning tastes related to illness? Casual observation suggests that they may. Most of us know at least one person who claims to loathe the very sight of a certain food that was once associated with severe nausea. Unfortunately, however, psychologists have seldom investigated these responses in controlled experiments. One of the few such studies conducted to date has focused on learned taste aversions in children receiving chemotherapy for cancer. It is well known that cancer patients often suffer serious loss of appetite. Could it be that this symptom is due to a pairing of food with the gastrointestinal upset caused by many drugs used in cancer treatment?

Ilene Bernstein (1978) set out to explore this possibility. She took forty-one young cancer patients age two to sixteen and randomly assigned them to three groups. The patients in Group 1, the experimental group, were given a dish of Mapletoff, a novel-flavored ice cream, fifteen minutes to one hour before receiving treatment with a drug that would make them feel ill. The patients in Group 2 received no ice cream, but they too underwent illness-inducing chemotherapy. Finally, the patients in Group 3 ate the Mapletoff but did not subsequently become ill, either because they received no drug treatment or because the drug they were given did not cause nausea as a side effect. Four-and-a-half months later all the patients were offered two kinds of ice cream: Mapletoff and another unusual flavor called Hawaiian Delight. Only 25 percent of those in Group 1, for whom Mapletoff had previously been paired with illness, said that they preferred the Mapletoff. And as expected, these patients ate substantially less Mapletoff than Hawaiian Delight when given a choice of eating as much of either flavor as they wished. This was not true of control subjects in Groups 2 and 3. In these groups, 66 and 50 percent of the patients preferred the Mapletoff. Bernstein concluded that humans, like a number of other species, seem to readily acquire aversions to novel tastes paired with illness. She hopes that future research may suggest how such aversions can be minimized in patients who receive chemotherapies that cause gastrointestinal dysfunction.

Extinction of a classically conditioned response

Once a classically conditioned response has been established, can we expect it to be maintained indefinitely? That depends in part on the way that the conditioned stimulus and the unconditioned stimulus are related in the future. Pavlov found that a conditioned response will persist only if the conditioned and unconditioned stimuli continue to be paired at least occasionally. If this occasional pairing does not occur, the conditioned response will gradually disappear. For example, if a dog has been trained to salivate in response to a tone paired with food, and then the tone is repeatedly presented without the food, the number of drops of saliva will gradually decline toward zero, as shown in Figure 5.2. This slow weakening and eventual disappearance of the conditioned response is called **extinction** (Figure 5.4).

You have undoubtedly experienced the extinction of classically conditioned responses yourself. Think of something you feared as a very young child but no longer fear today. This change may well be an example of extinction. For instance, many small children come to fear the dark because of its association with strange sounds and eerie shadows. As they mature, however, and outgrow a belief in night goblins, the dark is no longer paired with frightening stimuli. As a result, this classically conditioned fear extinguishes.

The pervasiveness of classical conditioning

Pavlov's experiments on classical conditioning had an enormous impact on American psychology in general and on behaviorism in particular. John B. Watson was so impressed by Pavlov's work that he based most of his analysis of behavior on it. All learning, Watson argued, can be explained within the

Figure 5.4 The relationship of events in the extinction of a classically conditioned response. The CS is presented repeatedly without the UCS. As a result, the CR gradually diminishes until it is no stronger than it was before conditioning.

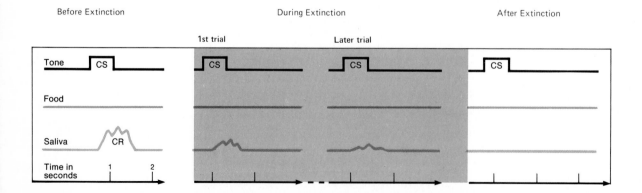

framework of classical conditioning. His famous experiment with little Albert was a provocative demonstration of the far-reaching impact classical conditioning can have.

Today, few behaviorists would agree with Watson's view that all learning can be explained through classical conditioning, but almost no one questions its importance in many types of learning. As we have seen, emotional responses are particularly prone to classical conditioning. Suppose in several consecutive arithmetic lessons a child is asked a question and does not know the answer. He feels acute anxiety each time this happens. Gradually the very thought of arithmetic may cause the child to feel nervous and upset. In this case the repeated pairing of a formerly neutral stimulus (arithmetic) with an unconditioned stimulus (failure to perform well) has led to a classically conditioned emotional response. This response, moreover, may be difficult to extinguish, for the very fact that the child feels anxious may cause him to perform poorly, thus maintaining an association between the conditioned and unconditioned stimuli.

Watson (1924) was one of the first psychologists to study how such difficult-to-extinguish fears can be reduced or eliminated. The following approach proved to be most successful. In a case like little Albert's, white rats would be paired with candy and special attention from adults instead of with a loud noise. Gradually a positive emotional response to furry animals would come to replace the former negative one.

This technique is quite similar to ones frequently used today to treat people with strong, persistent, and debilitating fears, called phobias. Imagine a young woman for whom riding in an elevator is a terrifying experience. The moment she sets foot inside one her heart pounds, her legs tremble, she feels queasy and has difficulty breathing. Such intense anxiety naturally imposes severe restrictions on her activities. She cannot live in a high-rise apartment nor can she visit friends who do; she cannot even accept a job with a firm whose offices are located in a tall building. One very effective technique for reducing such a phobia is called **systematic desensitization**. It involves teaching a person to relax totally in the presence of the fear-arousing stimulus, thus introducing a response incompatible with anxiety. If our woman with an elevator phobia underwent systematic desensitization, she would be trained to relax all the muscles of her body while imagining a series of increasingly anxiety-arousing situations—approaching an elevator, seeing the doors open, stepping inside, watching the doors close behind her, and so forth. If she mastered this, she might then attempt to remain relaxed during successive stages of an actual encounter with an elevator. By the end of the treatment, if it is successful, she should be able to lead a more normal life. Chapter 16 will say more about systematic desensitization and other therapies based on classical conditioning principles.

OPERANT CONDITIONING

Even before Pavlov's experiments on classical conditioning, the innovative and highly influential American psychologist Edward L. Thorndike was investigating another form of learning through association. Thorndike was interested in how the *consequences* of an organism's behavior can affect how it will behave in the future. In one famous experiment, published as part of his doctoral dissertation, he placed a hungry cat in one of his famous "puzzle boxes" (1932). The box was designed in such a way that if the cat made a certain combination of moves, the door to the box would fly open, allowing the animal to escape. Upon emerging, the cat would be given a piece of fish to eat. Thorndike found that the cat's initial behavior in the box was erratic; it would scramble about, and only accidentally would it make the correct response. But as the cat was returned to the same box again and again, the animal gradually became more proficient at escaping, until it was eventually able to open the door almost immediately. Thorndike concluded that the cat had learned to escape because the escape response was associated with a desirable consequence—food. This relationship he summarized in the **law of effect**. It states that responses that lead to satisfying consequences will be strengthened and are likely to be repeated, whereas responses that lead to unsatisfying consequences will be weakened and are unlikely to be repeated. In this way, Thorndike anticipated later studies of the effect of rewards and punishments on learning.

The central role of rewards and punishments

B. F. Skinner, the leading contemporary behaviorist, has been largely responsible for refining and extending Thorndike's observations. Skinner has proposed that Thorndike's law, which Skinner renamed the **principle of reinforcement**, is the basic mechanism for controlling human behavior. Our social environment, Skinner argues, is filled with positive and negative consequences that mold our behavior as surely as the piece of fish molded the behavior of Thorndike's cat. Our friends and families control us with their approval or disapproval. Our jobs control us by offering or withholding money. Our schools control us by passing or failing us, thus affecting our access to jobs. In short, in all areas of our lives, our actions are shaped by the occurrence of pleasant or unpleasant consequences.

Learning to either make or withhold a particular response because of its positive or negative consequences has come to be called **operant conditioning**. As we have already suggested, there are a number of important differences between classical and operant conditioning. One of the most basic is that classical conditioning applies to reflexes, whereas operant conditioning applies to voluntary behavior. Reflexes are sometimes called **respondent behavior**, to emphasize that they occur automatically in response to particular stimuli. **Operant behavior**, in contrast, is action that an organism emits spontaneously—that is, of its own accord. For instance, no particular stimulus is needed to induce a rat to sniff and move about its cage. Such behavior is as natural to a rat as flying is to a bird or swinging through the trees is to a monkey. Psychologists say that the rat is "operating" on its environment, not responding involuntarily to a particular stimulus in it.

Although operant behavior is not elicited by obvious, specific stimuli in the environment, it is *influenced* by environmental factors—in particular by its own consequences. Consequences can either increase or decrease the frequency of a response. A consequence that produces a repetition (increase in frequency) of the behavior that caused it is called **reinforcement** or **reward**. A consequence that results in the suppression (decrease in frequency) of the behavior that brought it about is called **punishment**. Note that whether a given consequence is rewarding or punishing can vary for different people. For example, some people find tennis extremely rewarding because the vigorous exercise makes them feel fit, but others regard the act of chasing a fuzzy ball around in the hot sun a severe form of punishment.

Psychologists classify rewards as positive or negative, but either way a rewarding consequence always strengthens a related response (Figure 5.5). In **positive reinforcement**, the frequency of a response increases because the response is followed by a positive (pleasant) stimulus. When a hungry rat presses a lever and receives a pellet of food, this behavior is being positively reinforced. In **negative reinforcement**, the frequency of a response increases because the response either removes some negative (painful or unpleasant) stimulus or enables the organism to avoid it. When a rat presses a lever that turns off an electric shock, this behavior is being negatively reinforced.

Because negative reinforcement and punishment both involve aversive stimuli, they can easily be confused. Note carefully how the two differ. When operant behavior *is followed by* aversive stimulus, punishment occurs. Punishment always tends to *decrease* the frequency of the response that provoked it. Thus, when a boy is severely scolded for taking his little sister's favorite toy, his action is being punished and he is less likely to steal the toy again. In contrast, when operant behavior *terminates* an aversive stimulus, negative reinforcement occurs. Negative reinforcement always tends to *increase* the frequency of the response that preceded it. Thus, when a boy gives his little sister back her favorite toy to stop her from hitting him over the head, his action is being negatively reinforced and he is more likely to return this toy when asked in the future.

In many cases there is a cause-and-effect relationship between a particular behavior and the outcome associated with it: The behavior specifically causes the consequences. But sometimes a behavior is strengthened or weakened because by mere chance it happens to precede reinforcement or punishment. Although the relationship between the behavior and the consequence in such instances is accidental (*not* contingent), the individual sometimes mistakenly assumes that the behavior *caused* the consequence and so repeats or inhibits the response. Behavior that arises in this way is called **superstitious behavior**.

Skinner (1948) produced superstitious behavior in pigeons by presenting them with a food reinforcer on a regular schedule, say every two minutes, regardless of what the pigeons were doing at the time. After a few hours every bird began to develop its own ritualistic, stereotyped behavior, such as bobbing

Figure 5.5 The relationship of events in operant conditioning (from left to right). Before conditioning, some particular response occurs infrequently. Then a food reinforcer is introduced as an immediate consequence of that response. The subsequent rate of responding increases markedly until the response occurs at a very high rate. If the food reinforcer is later stopped, responding will still continue, but only for a short period of time.

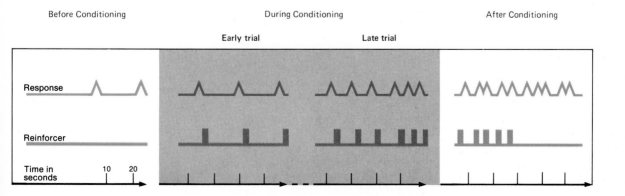

Before Conditioning   During Conditioning   After Conditioning

Early trial   Late trial

Response

Reinforcer

Time in seconds   10   20

its head, turning in circles, or hopping from side to side. Because this behavior had accidentally coincided with the presentation of a reward, the pigeon now performed it during the intervals between reinforcements, as though it thought there was some contingency between the behavior and the arrival of food.

Human intelligence does not protect us from acquiring similar superstitious behavior. Why does a gambler blow on the dice before every roll? Why does a football coach wear his "lucky" hat to every game? The reason probably is that sometime in the past these behaviors were accidentally linked with a winning streak. Because the behaviors were reinforced they tended to persist, even though the person "knows" that a cause-and-effect relationship is impossible.

Establishing an operantly conditioned response

We have said that operant behavior is voluntarily emitted by an organism rather than elicited by a specific stimulus. But the frequency of any operant behavior can be greatly influenced by its consequences. Thus, the general procedure for establishing an operantly conditioned response is to control the consequences of behavior by manipulating rewards and punishments.

The apparatus Psychologists have used many devices to carry out operant conditioning. One of the best known is the **maze**, in which a hungry or thirsty animal learns to find its way along a complex path that leads to food or water. Another widely used apparatus is the **Skinner box**, or **operant chamber**, developed by B. F. Skinner (1938). A Skinner box provides a controlled setting in which a rat or other animal may be trained to press a bar for a reward in much the same way as a person pulls a lever or knob to obtain food from a vending machine. The experimenter, of course, can vary the number of times the animal must press the bar to obtain the reward. The experimenter can also vary the type of reward offered—from positive reinforcers, such as food or water, to negative reinforcers, such as the cessation of shock. Figure 5.6 shows the basic features of a Skinner box.

The conditioning device called a **jump stand** was invented many years ago by Karl Lashley. Lashley, you may recall from Chapter 3, was an eminent neuropsychologist who devoted most of his career in the first half of this century to a search for the location of learning and memory in the brain. He taught experimental animals various kinds of tasks and then produced lesions in different areas of their brains to see if memory of the newly acquired skill would be impaired. The jump stand proved to be one way of teaching an animal a fairly complex visual discrimination (Lashley, 1960). Air blown through a tube on the platform forces a rat to jump through one of two doors. Behind the "correct" door, in this case the one with vertical bars, the rat finds food or some other reinforcement. The other door, marked with horizontal bars, is locked, so that when the rat jumps incorrectly, it is punished by bumping its nose and falling down into a net. To avoid the possibility that the rat is learning a position preference—right or left—rather than learning to discriminate between the vertical and horizontal stimuli, the experimenter randomly switches the two stimuli from side to side.

Shaping In order to establish an operantly conditioned response, an experimenter must systematically reward or punish a particular behavior. But how

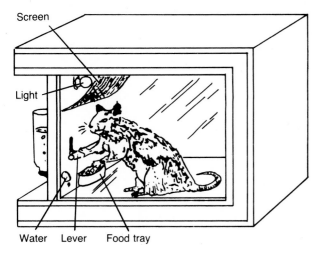

Figure 5.6 The operant chamber, or Skinner box. When a rat or other animal presses the bar, a pellet of food drops into the tray.

Screen

Light

Water   Lever   Food tray

does he or she manage to persuade an experimental animal to perform that behavior in the first place? Usually the experimenter selects a behavior that requires no inducement. Pigeons, for example, will peck at virtually everything. So when placed in a small box the average pigeon soon hits on the button the experimenter wants it to press.

But suppose an animal is slow at performing the particular behavior a psychologist wants to reinforce. Physically forcing the desired behavior would be an ineffective technique because the animal would be too frightened to learn. Must the psychologist, therefore, wait for a fortuitous accident? To overcome the potential frustration of waiting for an animal to stumble on the correct response, B. F. Skinner developed a technique called **shaping**, in which an animal is reinforced for displaying closer and closer approximations of the desired behavior. This procedure, of course, will be effective only if the animal is hungry or thirsty or otherwise motivated to work for reinforcement.

To understand how shaping works, suppose you are trying to get a reluctant rat to press a bar. You would begin by reinforcing the first response that shows the rat is on the right track—in this case, approaching the bar. After a few reinforcements, the rat will interrupt its other activities to walk toward the bar. Now you would withhold reinforcement until the rat not only approaches the bar but also rises slightly off the floor in front of it. At first, you might reward

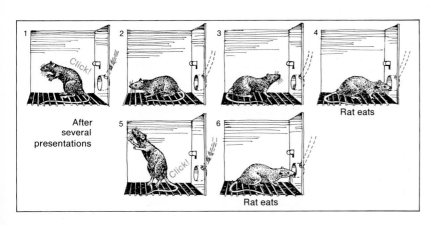

After several presentations

Rat eats

Rat eats

Figure 5.7 Shaping the bar-press response. A clicking noise first cues the rat to orient itself toward the food box and the bar. The rat is rewarded at first for any movements in the general vicinity of the bar, later only if it rises on its hind legs; and finally only when it places its forepaws on the bar. The weight of the paws activates an electric circuit that automatically dispenses food (reinforcer). The shaping process is now complete.

the rat for merely lifting one paw, but gradually you would reinforce it only if both paws were lifted high enough to reach the bar. Finally, you would make the reward contingent on actually pressing the bar. When the animal learns this contingency, the desired behavior would be shaped. Shaping, then, is a form of operant conditioning based on reinforcement of ever-closer approximations. Each successive approximation, however, must be only a small step beyond what the subject was previously doing; otherwise, the procedure will fail.

Shaping has been used to train performing animals to do complicated tricks. Dolphins, for example, can be taught to leap from the water on cue, and elephants can be taught to dance. Shaping procedures can also be used to modify human behavior. For instance, the focus of the popular book *Toilet Training in Less Than a Day* (Azrin and Foxx, 1974) is the use of shaping to produce the desired response. Likewise, shaping procedures provide an important foundation for modern behavioral therapy and have proven to be highly effective in treating a number of modern behavior disorders in adults (Lanyon and Lanyon, 1978), as we will see in Chapter 16.

Maintaining an operantly conditioned response

Once an operant response—say, bar pressing—has been established, how does the experimenter ensure that the subject will continue to perform this behavior? The key to maintaining operant behavior is reinforcement. By altering the relationship between behavior and reinforcement, the experimenter can influence many aspects of a subject's response.

Schedules of reinforcement A man who hires himself out to plow fields can generally be paid in one of three ways: by the hour, by the number of acres plowed, or by a percentage of the farm's profits. Clearly, the method of payment could exert a powerful influence on how this man works. For instance, if he is paid by the hour, he may work relatively slowly, especially if there is only a limited amount of work available. If paid by the acre, he may set his plow shallowly so that he can work faster, and he may space his furrows farther apart. If paid a percentage of the profits, he may take care to cultivate the land as effectively as possible, perhaps by plowing the soil deeply to produce plants with a higher yield. In psychological terminology, each method of payment represents a different **schedule of reinforcement**, and the plowman alters his behavior accordingly to produce the greatest reward. The same is true of people in other situations. At school, on the job, or in the laboratory, the prevailing schedule of reinforcement considerably controls behavior.

Psychologists have found that different schedules of reinforcement are most effective for establishing and maintaining an operantly conditioned response. New operant behavior is usually firmly established by providing reinforcement each time the response occurs, as when a rat is given a food pellet every time it presses a bar. This is called a **continuous reinforcement schedule**. Once the behavior has been established, however, the best way to maintain it is to use a **partial reinforcement schedule**. Paradoxically, withholding the reward some of the time results in more behavior per unit of reward than if the reward is given every time the behavior occurs.

One schedule of partial reinforcement is called a **fixed-ratio schedule**. On this schedule the subject is rewarded each time it makes a specified number of responses. For example, a rat would be reinforced with a food pellet for every twenty bar presses. This is analogous to the plowman being paid by the number of acres plowed. The rat performing on a fixed-ratio schedule tends to press the bar at a more rapid rate than if it were rewarded continuously. The relationship between the work and the reward is direct and explicit: The faster the rat works, the more it eats.

Another schedule of partial reinforcement is called a **fixed-interval schedule**. In this situation, the rat is rewarded for a bar press at the end of a fixed interval of time, say one minute, regardless of how many presses it made during the interim. Thus, the first correct response the rat makes after the fixed period triggers reinforcement. This schedule is somewhat analogous to an hourly wage, and the rat, like the plowman, may learn to work the minimum amount necessary to obtain reinforcement. Immediately following a reward, the rat will tend to ignore the bar for a while and then will gradually increase its bar pressing as the time when the next reward will be available approaches. A fixed-interval schedule, then, may yield a relatively low frequency of response because the total amount of work performed is unrelated to delivery of the reward.

In contrast to fixed-ratio and fixed-interval schedules, that establish regular and predictable relationships between behavior and reward, some partial reinforcement schedules are irregular and unpredictable. For example, a reward might be given *on average* once every ten responses, with reinforcement sometimes arriving after every response and other times after twenty or thirty responses. This is called a **variable-ratio schedule**. Similarly, reinforcement might be given *on average* once every ten minutes, with the actual times ranging randomly from once every ten seconds to once every quarter hour. This is called a **variable-interval schedule**. How do you think such reinforcement patterns would affect the frequency of behavior? Because variable-ratio and variable-interval schedules are somewhat unpredictable, they encourage a subject to constantly test for a reward. As a result, they tend to produce very high rates of response—higher than those associated with fixed reward schedules.

Variable-ratio schedules also result in behavior that is very resistant to extinction. To understand why, imagine yourself at a slot machine. Now slot machines are designed to make money, not lose it, and most people are aware that in the long run the player is bound to lose. Yet, because the amount and schedule of reinforcement are so highly varied, slot machines have a compelling effect on behavior. People continue to harbor the hope that the next pull of the handle will bring the big jackpot. Consequently, they keep right on playing coin after coin. This would certainly not be the case if a slot machine paid off, say, on a fixed-interval schedule, where the first response after a fixed period of time triggers a reward. Then people would only have to wait around for the fixed period to elapse, insert a coin, and then collect the money. If no reward appeared, they would quickly conclude that the machine was broken and quit.

Because irregular schedules of reinforcement are so powerful, they can easily maintain undesirable responses unintentionally. For example, when new parents rush to soothe their crying infant, they may simply be reinforcing "crying behavior" with adult attention. The child soon learns that crying is a sure way to bring a parent running. Realizing this, some parents try to avoid reinforcing "unnecessary" crying by ignoring it. The child, in an effort to regain their attention, may intensify crying. When this happens, the parents may reach the point where they cannot stand it any longer and attend to the infant, thus reinforcing the even louder crying. Eventually, the infant's crying behavior may be maintained by frustrated parents, who are unwittingly providing rewards on a very effective partial-reinforcement schedule. The only way to halt such behavior is to consistently refuse to reward attention-getting crying, forcing the baby to learn that only under certain conditions is crying reinforced. However, the parents must first learn to distinguish between crying for "legitimate" reasons, such as hunger or wet diapers, and crying for attention.

Stimulus control Besides controlling the vigor and pattern of operant responses, reinforcement has another important effect. It relates a particular behavior to stimuli associated with the learning situation. Suppose that a rat has been conditioned to press a bar for a reward whenever a bulb in a Skinner box lights up. In this case, the stimuli of a Skinner box and a lighted bulb have become associated with reinforcement and the behavior of bar pressing. Thus, whenever these stimuli are present, the rat is likely to press the bar. This is called **stimulus control**: The stimuli prevailing at the time of reinforcement have come to control the organism's response.

A human example may help clarify the concept of stimulus control. Suppose you live in a university dormitory with poor plumbing. Because the cold-water pressure is low, flushing the toilet invariably reduces the amount of cold water being fed to the shower. So if you are unfortunate enough to be taking a shower when the toilet is used, the sound of the flush will probably send you fleeing from the shower stall to avoid the sudden scalding water. What has happened psychologically in this situation? First, you have acquired an operantly conditioned response: running from the stall to avoid a painful burn. Second, this behavior is under the control of a specific stimulus: the sound of the toilet being flushed. You flee only when you hear this cue.

This example also illustrates how classical and operant conditioning can be combined in a single learning situation. Your flight from the shower to avoid pain is an operantly conditioned response. But what about your reaction of fear to the sound of the flush? This has probably been learned through classical conditioning. A previously neutral stimulus (the flushing toilet) has been repeatedly paired with a fear-arousing unconditioned stimulus (scalding water) until the flush alone comes to elicit fear. Thus, it is not always easy to tell which aspects of a particular response have been operantly conditioned and which have been classically conditioned.

Extinction of an operantly conditioned response

When an operantly conditioned response is no longer reinforced, its frequency gradually decreases, and eventually the response disappears. This extinction process is illustrated in Figure 5.8. For the crying child, the withdrawal of parental attention may eventually result in a decrease in crying. For the rat in a Skinner box, bar pressing will die out when food pellets are no longer presented. But these learned behaviors are not extinguished easily. Although a behavior that is no longer reinforced may occur less frequently, during the initial phases of extinction it tends to be executed more forcefully and in a wider variety of ways. For example, if a pigeon that has been reinforced for

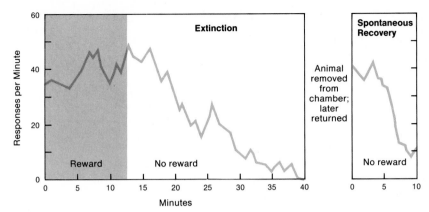

Figure 5.8 Extinction of an operantly conditioned response. Initially the animal's responding is reinforced. After 12½ minutes reinforcement is withheld, and responding steadily declines. After 40 minutes the animal is removed from the chamber. When it is returned, its response begins again at nearly the original rate, even though there is *no* reinforcement. This spontaneous recovery may result from an association between the chamber and being rewarded.

pecking at a light has this reinforcement withdrawn, the bird becomes agitated and upset and tends to exaggerate the response that formerly brought rewards. Similarly, the child whose cries are ignored will probably cry even louder before this response is finally extinguished.

If you think about this exaggeration of previously reinforced behavior when the reward is withdrawn, you can probably find parallels in your own behavior. For example, suppose your front door, which usually works well, does not open one day. In psychological terms, the previously reinforced response of grasping the knob and turning it is no longer rewarded by entrance into the house. Before giving up on the door, however, your efforts to open it will probably become more variable and forceful—you may rattle the door, pound it, and give it a good solid kick before finally going to another door.

Now suppose you have been away from home for several days. When you return, would you be likely to try the front door again? Most people would. In the same way, if an animal is removed from an experimental chamber for a while after a response has been extinguished and then is put back in, the response will reappear. This phenomenon is called **spontaneous recovery**. During the period when the animal is away from the experimental apparatus, its behavior seems to recover spontaneously from the effects of extinction, at least to some extent. It may be that the behavior reappears because the animal is responding once more to the stimuli associated with the chamber. In the past it was reinforced for a certain behavior when placed in the chamber. Why not this time?

Applications of operant conditioning principles

In the last twenty years operant conditioning has gradually found its way out of the laboratory, with its experimental rats and pigeons, and into virtually every center of human life. Behavioral learning principles have invaded our schools, our hospitals, our prisons, our rehabilitation centers, our offices and factories, even our own homes. Two of the most important outcomes of this trend have been the educational method called programmed instruction and the therapeutic approach called behavior modification.

Programmed instruction However it is presented, whether by means of textbooks, teaching machines, or even computers, **programmed instruction** always emphasizes reinforcement in the learning situation. This is done by providing the student with immediate feedback for every response. Information is presented sequentially in small segments, and a student does not proceed to a new unit until after he or she has demonstrated comprehension of the present one. Thus, each student's progress through a program is paced according to his or her individual abilities. In this way, slow and fast learners alike receive a great deal of positive reinforcement. The aim is to encourage a sense of competency and to minimize the frustration and defeat that inevitably accompany frequent failure.

Programmed instruction also incorporates the principle of active repetition. Usually a program presents information with numerous examples. It also requires the student to answer several questions about new material or to restate it in various ways before proceeding to the next segment. The student, of course, is positively reinforced for each correct answer. In this manner, the correct response is strengthened, just as any response is strengthened by repeating the contingency between behavior and reinforcement.

There are several methods for presenting programmed instruction. Perhaps the most common is the programmed textbook. Another is the teaching machine, developed by B. F. Skinner in the 1950s. The most sophisticated method of programmed teaching is computer-assisted instruction (CAI). This method has several advantages over earlier techniques. Instead of proceeding in a linear fashion from step A to step B, the computer can branch off into remedial or supplementary lessons if the student's responses indicate that this will improve comprehension. The computer can also be programmed to jump back to the beginning of a sequence that is causing difficulty or to jump forward to a new sequence for the fast learner. Finally, the computer can maintain a record of each student's progress and use this information to structure subsequent work.

Programmed instruction has many advantages over traditional teaching, not the least of which is that it is easy to use with large groups of students. But it also has some drawbacks. Students may dislike working with machines for long periods of time and may miss certain stimulating aspects of classroom instruction—the human interaction, the exchange of ideas, even the competition. For these reasons, it seems most sensible to use programmed instruction as a supplement to regular classroom teaching rather than as a substitute for it. Then, too, the expense of installing and maintaining a computerized system will probably limit the availability of this type of instruction, at least in the immediate future.

Behavior modification The scene is an elementary classroom. One boy, who is about ten, takes out a large watch, places it in front of him, and selects some learning material from a nearby table. The material consists of a series of problems in addition. He works on the problems slowly, and when he has finished he notes the time and summons the teacher. She corrects the material, smiles, and says, "Very good. You get ten tokens for this." The boy takes his tokens and crosses the hall to another room where he trades them for a large candy bar. Smiling happily he skips back to his ward in this hospital for the mentally retarded. The boy's IQ when he came to the institution was extraordinarily low. Now he can perform tasks that no one then thought him ever capable of learning.

This is an example of **behavior modification**, the conscious use of operant conditioning principles to change human behavior. The boy in this case has been reinforced for performing a relatively complex task—solving some arithmetic problems. His reward is a handful of tokens that can later be exchanged for more basic reinforcers such as food. Some of the earliest behavior modification programs involved the creation of such **token economies** at mental hospitals and other institutions for people with severe behavioral problems. A more detailed discussion of token economies, their uses, and their limitations, is presented in Chapter 16.

Since the earliest behavior modification programs, learning principles have gradually been applied to the full range of everyday human problems. Behavioral therapists address themselves to matters as diverse as smoking, overeating, truancy, stuttering, shyness, poor study habits, volatile tempers, and lack of self-assertion. Operant conditioning techniques have even been used by employers to raise worker productivity and by government officials to stop littering in public parks. In all cases the procedure is much the same: trying to eliminate inadvertent rewards for the problem behavior and at the same time instituting a program to reinforce a more desirable, alternative response. Thus, a teacher trying to engage a shy boy in group activities would be careful not to give him attention when he withdraws from the class but instead would encourage and praise him whenever he interacts with others. A full discussion of behavior modification, including the controversy it has raised, will be reserved for Chapter 16.

BEHAVIOR CONTROL

So far we have focused on a number of differences between classical and operant conditioning, differences that are important enough so that most psychologists consider these separate and distinct models of learning. There are, however, similarities between classical and operant conditioning. Consider the role of reinforcement. Reinforcement is clearly essential in establishing and maintaining operantly learned behavior. But it plays a part in classical conditioning as well. In Pavlov's experiments, for example, a hungry dog came to salivate at the sound of a tone, after which it received food. This food can be said to have served as a reinforcer because it increased the likelihood that the dog would salivate again when it heard the tone. And when the food was no longer presented, the conditioned response of salivation gradually extinguished, just as an operantly conditioned response would extinguish after removal of the reinforcer. Another similarity between classical and operant conditioning lies in the fact that both involve stimulus control. In the classical conditioning model, the organism's behavior comes under the control of the conditioned stimulus (in Pavlov's experiments, the tone). In operant conditioning, the controlling stimuli are the salient cues associated with the learning situation (a lever, a light, a Skinner box, a maze, or what have you). Given these basic similarities, then, it is not surprising that some of the same principles of behavior control apply to both classical and operant conditioning.

Stimulus generalization and discrimination

Suppose that we have successfully trained a dog to salivate at the sound of a bell. Can we also expect this animal to salivate if it hears a gong, a ringing telephone, or a high-pitched voice? Conversely, can we train this dog to salivate only when it hears a *particular* bell and to ignore all other bell stimuli? The first process is called **stimulus generalization**—the expression of a learned response in the presence of a number of similar stimuli. The second process is called **stimulus discrimination**—learning to make a particular response to only a particular stimulus. Both processes are important aspects of behavior control.

Stimulus generalization is common in everyday life. Watson's famous baby Albert generalized his conditioned fear of white rats to other white, furry animals and objects. This is an example of stimulus generalization in classical conditioning, but the same phenomenon also occurs with our operantly learned responses. For example, an adult who has installed a smoke detector at home may bolt for the front door when an alarm clock accidentally sounds in the middle of the night. Generalization can even help to account for complex social phenomena, such as racial prejudice. A black person who has a hostile interaction with a white southerner may generalize these negative feelings to all white southerners, or even to all whites. In general, the more similar subsequent stimuli are to the original stimulus, the more likely it is that generalization will occur. Generalization is important because it explains how experience acquired in one situation can be utilized in other settings. If such transfer did not occur, people would profit little from past experience.

The example of the possible development of racial prejudice indicates that generalization is not always appropriate. Through discrimination, we can learn to make certain responses in some situations but not in others. In animal research, a procedure called **discrimination training** can be used to limit the extent of stimulus generalization. Suppose an experimenter has trained a pigeon to peck at a yellow key in order to receive a food reward. How do you think the bird will respond if the experimenter suddenly presents it with a green key? As you may have guessed, the pigeon will probably peck at the green key as well, although not as frequently as it pecks at the yellow key. To reduce the response to the green key still further, the experimenter could present the yellow key alternately with the green one but reward the pigeon only for pecking at the yellow. Provided the bird has the sensory capacity to discriminate the reinforced stimulus, it would soon learn to peck exclusively at the yellow key. Note that both reinforcement and extinction have been used together to bring behavior under the control of a specific stimulus—in this case, a yellow key. A parallel procedure could easily be used in classical conditioning. If a particular bell was always followed by food and another bell was never followed by food, a dog would soon learn to salivate only at the sound of the first bell. In these examples, the yellow key and the distinctive-sounding bell are **discriminative stimuli**; they control the learned behavior because they provide specific information about when reinforcement will occur.

Psychologists can test the effectiveness of discrimination training by comparing the behavior of two animals—one that has learned to respond to only the discriminative stimulus and one that has not. For instance, a pigeon trained to discriminate yellow from several other colors and another bird conditioned simply to peck at a yellow key might be given a test consisting of different colored stimuli. The psychologist would then measure the number of responses each pigeon made to the various colors before key-pecking behavior was extinguished. Figure 5.10 shows the results of a typical experiment of this kind. The number of responses are plotted along the vertical axis, and the resulting curve is called a **generalization gradient**. The peak of the generalization gradients for

Figure 5.9 Through discrimination training—reinforcing only the appropriate response—the pigeon has learned to peck at a key of a certain color.

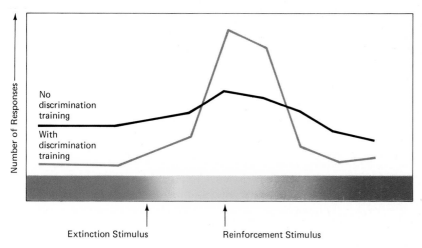

Figure 5.10 Graph showing generalization gradients for two pigeons in a test of color generalization. One pigeon had previously received discrimination training; the other had been rewarded for pecking at a yellow light but had seen no other colored lights before the generalization test. Discrimination training results in a much more sharply peaked generalization gradient. That is, the pigeon that had received discrimination training treats the colors as more distinct than does the pigeon without this training. Color difference exerts more control over its behavior.

both pigeons is for the yellow key—that is, the less similar the stimulus is to yellow, the less either bird responds. However, the pigeon that did not receive discrimination training produces a wider and flatter generalization gradient than does the bird that was so trained. In other words, the one without discrimination training responds more to colors other than yellow. This points up an important and well-documented finding: The effect of discrimination training is to sharpen and strengthen stimulus control.

An organism is said to be under stimulus control when it responds consistently in the presence of the discriminative stimulus and not in its absence. As we will see in Chapter 16, this concept is very important in helping people to control problem behaviors, such as overeating or smoking. Once such behavior is brought under stimulus control, a person can reduce the frequency of particular responses by minimizing exposure to the stimulus. Suppose an overweight woman is interested in decreasing the frequency of eating behavior. She might be told to confine all eating behavior to one specific location and not to combine it with other activities, such as watching television, studying, or socializing. If followed, this program would gradually eliminate all other cues for eating and thereby eliminate impulsive and random eating behavior.

Conditioned reinforcers

Stimulus generalization means that an animal performs a learned behavior even though the controlling stimulus is not precisely the one to which the animal was originally trained. By the same token, an animal may perform a learned behavior even though the reinforcer it receives is different from the one that initially established the response. Thus, in most of the learning experiments we have discussed so far, the reinforcer that established and maintained the conditioned response was a **primary reinforcer**, such as food or water, that satisfied some basic biological need. But the effects of a primary reinforcer can also generalize to **secondary**, or **conditioned, reinforcers**. A conditioned reinforcer is a stimulus that signals that the primary reinforcer is on its way. For example, the clicking sound of food being released into a food cup signals to a hungry rat that the primary reinforcer, the food, will be present. If this signal

Figure 5.11 A powerful conditioned reinforcer in human life is money. Wolfe (1936) showed in a series of experiments that chimpanzees, too, can learn to use "money." Chimps were conditioned to pull down a heavily weighted handle in order to obtain tokens (poker chips), which they could then use to buy peanuts or bananas from a Chimp-O-Mat. The value of the tokens to the chimps was evident from the fact that they would work for them and save them—and would sometimes try to steal them from one another.

consistently precedes the arrival of food, it may itself acquire the power to reinforce a learned response.

In the world outside the laboratory, it is rare for a learned behavior to be immediately followed by a primary reinforcer. Usually, the gap between response and reinforcement is bridged by a signal that reinforcement is forthcoming. For example, most people are paid for their work with money, a secondary reinforcer that can later be exchanged for primary reinforcers. If a currency should lose its value, however, it will also lose its power to maintain behavior. This is precisely what happened in Europe during the economic depression of the 1930s. When currency became worthless, people quickly stopped working for money and insisted on being paid directly in essential goods and services.

The power of conditioned reinforcers was demonstrated in an early series of experiments with chimpanzees (Wolfe, 1936). The chimps readily learned to perform tasks in order to obtain tokens that they could later use to buy food from a vending machine called a Chimp-O-Mat (Figure 5.11). The most important conclusion stemming from research with the Chimp-O-Mat was that conditioned reinforcers—the tokens—will bridge very long delays between the performance of a task and the arrival of a primary reinforcer, such as food. Without the tokens even small delays between responding and receiving food made the chimpanzees reluctant to continue performing the task. This aspect of conditioned reinforcement is put to very effective use in the form of a type of behavior modification that was mentioned earlier, the token economy.

Although the effectiveness of conditioned reinforcement is most obvious in the operant conditioning model, it can also be used to control behavior acquired through classical conditioning. For example, suppose a dog has been trained to salivate at the sound of a bell (CS), which is always followed by food (UCS, or primary reinforcer). Pavlov called this **first-order conditioning**. If the sound of the bell is then repeatedly paired with, say, a flashing light, in time the dog will salivate in response to the light alone. This Pavlov called **second-order conditioning**. Because the bell signals that the primary reinforcer is about to arrive, it is able to serve as a conditioned reinforcer. In the same way, if Watson had repeatedly paired presentation of his white rat with, say, the sound of someone singing, little Albert would probably have developed a second-order conditioned fear of lullabies.

The previous examples illustrate that conditioned reinforcers can be used to establish new responses. When several such responses are established in succession, long sequences of behavior can be effectively maintained by a series of conditioned reinforcers. It is easy to find examples of this in everyday life. Although people derive many kinds of satisfaction from their jobs, the behavior of working is maintained in part by the conditioned reinforcer of receiving a paycheck. The behavior of going to the bank and cashing that paycheck is maintained by the conditioned reinforcer of obtaining paper money. The behavior of spending that money in the grocery store is maintained by the conditioned reinforcer of taking home a bagful of food. And finally, the behavior of cooking and serving a meal is maintained by the primary reinforcer of eating. Learning a sequence of operant behaviors such as this one, which eventually ends in a primary reward, is often called **chaining**. Each link in the chain is presumably maintained by its own conditioned reinforcer.

Punishment and its side effects

Virtually all the learning situations we have discussed so far have involved some form of reinforcement, either positive or negative. When an animal does something that allows it to receive food, for example, or to avoid shock, it is likely to repeat that behavior in the future. Thus, delivery of food and avoidance of shock are both reinforcing. But everyone knows that the consequences of behavior are not always rewarding. A child's misbehavior often leads to a spanking; a student's lack of effort usually results in poor grades; a bank robber's holdup can end in imprisonment. These are all examples of punishment, a controversial mechanism of behavior control that psychologists have debated for years.

Learning theory tells us that whenever a behavior results in some negative consequence, the frequency of that behavior should tend to decrease. This principle has been used therapeutically to eliminate a variety of undesirable responses. For example, punishment has been used to cure the disorder called writer's cramp, in which the hand of a person who writes frequently is afflicted with uncontrollable spasms. Sylvester and Liversedge (1960) designed writing equipment that delivered an electric shock each time a hand tremor occurred. Of the thirty-nine people they treated in this way, twenty-four improved enough to return to work. Similarly, therapists have used other forms of punishment to treat more severe behavior disorders, as we will discuss in Chapter 16.

Although punishment has been successful in helping to suppress maladaptive behaviors, as a method of behavior control it has important limitations. For one thing, punishment may only temporarily discourage the behavior it is intended to eradicate. When the punisher is no longer present, or when the motivation to commit the act is extremely strong, the suppressed behavior can reappear. In addition, when punishment is harshly or capriciously administered, it can sometimes create emotional disturbances. Then, too, punishment can readily result in the punisher becoming an "aversive stimulus," to be escaped from or avoided. This can clearly cause a dilemma for parents, who naturally want their children to love, not fear, them. It can also result in a "backfire" effect, as when a child punished at school for truancy comes to dislike school even more. Finally, punishment may only indicate to a person what he or she is *not* to do; it does not, in itself, establish a positive response. Consequently, when one undesirable behavior is suppressed through punishment, another may appear in its place. Thus, if a little boy is punished for biting his sister, he may simply take to hitting her instead.

It appears, then, that punishment will probably be most effective when used in conjunction with positive forms of behavior control. Punishment's greatest benefit is in preventing, even temporarily, some extremely undesirable behavior, so that a more acceptable response can then be rewarded and strengthened. In many instances, moreover, a negative behavior can be completely eliminated without resorting to punishment. For example, a psychologist can determine which reinforcer is maintaining some undesirable behavior; then by eliminating the reinforcer, he or she can extinguish the response. Another technique that avoids punishment is to use positive reinforcement to condition behavior that is incompatible with the unwanted behavior. Thus, instead of attempting to eliminate a child's selfishness by using punishment, a parent or teacher can reinforce sharing and cooperation with others. Still another method is to try to avoid the need to punish incorrect behavior by ensuring from the start that only correct behavior occurs. This technique, however, usually requires careful initial shap-

Figure 5.12 The relationship of events in positive reinforcement, negative reinforcement, and punishment. Reinforcement always means that some response is *strengthened*, or increased in rate. In positive reinforcement the consequence that strengthens a response is the *onset* of some pleasant event. In negative reinforcement the consequence that strengthens a response is the *removal* of some unpleasant event. In punishment the effect on responding is the opposite; responding decreases because the response produces the onset of an unpleasant event.

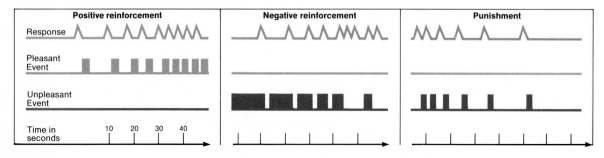

ing of behavior and elimination of opportunities to carry out an undesirable response. Outside the laboratory, such highly controlled conditions seldom occur.

LEARNING AND COGNITION

The early behaviorists, such as Thorndike and Watson, explained the process of learning in a very mechanistic way. They argued that when an organism makes a response to a certain stimulus, and that response is reinforced, a stimulus-response (or S-R) connection forms in the brain. Subsequent reinforcement of the same response strengthens this neutral connection until eventually the behavior will almost always occur in the presence of the controlling stimulus. Thus, the pigeon that pecks at a button as soon as it lights up, the dog that sits by the table just when dinner is served, and the person who answers the telephone whenever it happens to ring are simply exhibiting automatic stimulus-response patterns that in the past have been reinforced.

Many contemporary psychologists, however, strongly object to this interpretation because it ignores the mental activity going on inside the organism. They maintain that in almost any learned association important thought processes intervene between the stimulus and the response. This view has come to be called the **cognitive** (or "thinking") **approach** to learning. One of its earliest proponents was Edward Tolman, an American psychologist who worked at a time when the discipline in this country was largely dominated by strict behaviorists. Tolman argued in favor of the then unorthodox view that most animals capable of learning are adaptive, intelligent, creative organisms and that any explanation of learning must take these qualities into account. Tolman's professional career was spent at the University of California at Berkeley, and the mass of research that came from his laboratory there made Berkeley the center of cognitive psychology for a number of years. Today, the cognitive approach is highly influential in all areas of learning.

Explaining associative learning: The cognitive view

Central to the cognitive interpretation of associative learning is a concern for the thought processes that presumably occur when conditioning takes place. For example, many cognitive psychologists now stress that what an organism learns during classical conditioning is an *expectation* that a previously neutral event, say, the ticking of a metronome, will be followed by an unconditioned stimulus, such as food. It is this expectation that brings about the conditioned response. The cognitive view of classical conditioning is suggested by an interesting anecdote about one of Pavlov's experimental dogs that had been conditioned to respond to the ticking of a metronome. When the metronome was turned off, the dog planted himself in front of it, whining and begging. If this story is true, more may be going on here mentally than the development of a mechanistic stimulus-response association.

Similarly, cognitive psychologists argue that what a rat acquires when it learns to run a maze is not necessarily a series of automatic movements controlled by specific stimuli, but rather a "cognitive map" of the maze's spatial layout. This was suggested in an ingenious experiment by one of Tolman's students (Macfarlane, 1930). He filled the maze with several inches of water and trained rats to swim to a goal box where they could hoist themselves out and obtain food. He then drained the maze and tested to see if the rats could still find their way to the goal. Now if what the rats had learned was simply a set of S-R associations, this change should severely disrupt the animals' performance. After all, the controlling stimulus was no longer the same (a body of water had been replaced with a dry chamber), and swimming and running do not involve anything like the same set of responses. But the rats negotiated the dry maze flawlessly. What they appeared to have acquired during their previous training was a mental image of the maze, which could be used to locate the goal regardless of change in surrounding stimuli or in required muscular movements. Such findings seriously question the view that associative learning is strictly mechanistic.

Learning without reinforcement

Bolstering the cognitive view of learning is the demonstration in recent years that learning can apparently occur in the absence of reinforcement. Such learning presents some difficulty for a strict S-R model, according to which an association will not be established unless it is reinforced. Yet cognitive psychologists maintain that much of human learning takes place without overt rewards or punishments being meted out. Two types of learning that fall into this category are latent learning and social learning through observation.

Latent learning When an organism learns a new behavior but does not demonstrate this knowledge until an incentive to do so arises, the learning is called **latent.** In an early demonstration of latent learning, Tolman and Honzik (1930) permitted one group of rats to explore a maze in the absence of any reward; meanwhile, another group of rats were presented with food whenever they reached the goal box. As expected, the rewarded rats soon learned to run the maze quickly and without error. The unrewarded rats, in contrast, seemed to wander the maze aimlessly. However, when a food reward was subsequently given to the rats that had not previously been reinforced, their running time and error rate fell quickly to the same level as that of the first group. In fact, the second group seemed to learn the maze more quickly than the first.

Tolman and Honzik concluded that the initially unrewarded group of rats had profited by their early exploration trials, but their learning remained latent until after a reward for reaching the goal box was introduced. This experiment provided support for Tolman's notion that learning is cognitive in nature, rather than being a series of S-R connections stamped in by reinforcement. This viewpoint corresponds to much of our own experience. People, for example, can find their way without error from one part of a strange city to another simply on the basis of having once been given verbal instructions. Reinforcement and repeated practice are not essential for learning the specific route. Instead, the verbal instructions are stored in memory until the time comes to put them to use. Reinforcement, in effect, is not needed for learning to occur.

Social learning through observation The work on latent learning suggests that organisms acquire a great deal of information about their environments with-

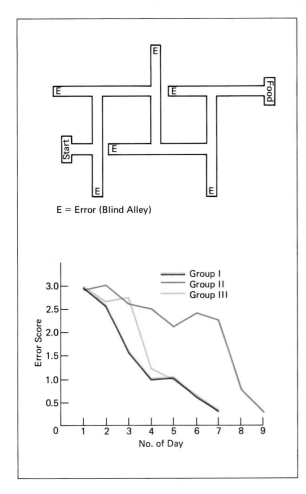

E = Error (Blind Alley)

Figure 5.13 Latent learning. Tolman and his colleagues argued that learning was a result of cognition—a thinking process that involves more than just the association of stimuli and responses through reinforcement. Support for this idea came from a series of experiments like the one shown here (Blodgett, 1929). Rats in Group I were put in the complex maze once a day for nine consecutive days; they always found food at the maze's end. Group II rats were also put in the maze, but they were not rewarded on their first six trials; reward was introduced on the seventh day. Group III found their first reward on day 3. Rats in II and III began by making many errors, but these dropped profoundly on the day *after* reward was first introduced. Thus, during *nonrewarded* trials the rats had been learning more than they had exhibited; reward improved performance, but did not determine it.

out being directly reinforced for it, even though they may not exhibit that knowledge until they want to achieve a specific goal. Such information is largely amassed through casual observation—looking, listening, touching, and the like. But a very important part of the human environment consists of other people. Is our knowledge of how to interact with others primarily shaped through rewards and punishments, as conditioning theories suggest? Once again, cognitive psychologists believe not. They argue that a great deal of such learning is accomplished simply by observing the behavior of others, often in the absence of reinforcement. This view is central to what has come to be called **social learning theory.** And the process of learning how we should act by watching the behavior of others is variously called **observational learning, imitative learning,** or **modeling.**

Note that the social learning theorists are *not* saying that rewards and punishments are unimportant to learning social behavior. They are simply saying that reinforcement is not essential for such learning to occur. According to Albert Bandura (1977), one of the leading proponents of this view, reinforcement is much more important in getting people to exhibit a newly learned behavior than it is in teaching that behavior in the first place. Thus, a little girl who observes her older brother building a playhouse enters this behavior into her repertoire of possible responses regardless of what the outcome of her brother's actions may be. But if she also observes that her brother is warmly praised for his accomplishment, she will probably be even more inclined to imitate his performance in the future.

As you will discover in subsequent chapters, Bandura and other psychologists have conducted a variety of experiments that show that imitative learning can certainly take place without reinforcement. In a typical study different groups of children observe a model who responds to a situation in some unusual way. Then the experimenter puts the children in a similar situation and notes the number of imitative responses they make. Such studies clearly demonstrate that children often imitate a novel behavior with no external inducement at all. Bandura's classic experiment, in which very young children learned a series of highly aggressive acts by observing an adult model, is discussed in Chapter 18.

Modeling, then, appears to be a very pervasive form of human learning. The following descriptions in a well-known experimental paper provide some instances of modeling that should be familiar to most readers, especially those with younger brothers or sisters or with children of their own:

Most of Viki's imitation occurs in play. At about 16 months of age, she began to imitate such bits of household routine as dusting furniture and washing clothes and dishes. Before she was two years old, . . . some of her play was . . . complex and precise. For instance, she appropriated a lipstick, stood on the wash-basin, looked in the mirror, and applied the cosmetic—not at random, but to her mouth. She then pressed her lips together and smoothed the color with her finger, just as she had seen the act performed (Hayes and Hayes, 1952, p. 415).

What is particularly interesting about the above observations is that they are not descriptions of the behavior of an active human child. Viki is a chimpanzee! The researchers raised her like a child in order to study the intellectual and social development of this most humanlike animal under such conditions. They concluded that the three-year-old chimpanzee reared in a human environment displayed imitative behavior very similar to that displayed by a three-year-old child. Although many animals besides humans are able to learn through modeling, humans can acquire certain things through imitation that other species generally cannot. Through observation, we learn more than just a variety of overt behaviors. We learn a full range of emotions, social styles, and attitudes as well.

So powerful a mode of human learning does modeling seem to be that some psychologists have developed psychotherapies based primarily on it. Consider the treatment of phobias. Modeling approaches to this disorder rest on the assumption that if people with phobias can observe someone else performing the activity that they so greatly dread, they will be likely to develop confidence that they too can perform the behavior without adverse results (Bandura, 1977). The most effective of the modeling procedures appear to be those in which the clients are gradually encouraged to engage in the feared activity themselves rather than simply watching others do so. In one study of people with snake phobias, for instance, subjects who stood by while the therapist approached and handled snakes and then performed the same behaviors themselves in progressively bolder steps were much more successful in overcoming their phobias than were subjects who simply watched a film of people handling snakes or who imagined themselves interacting with snakes while trying to remain relaxed (Bandura, Blanchard, and Ritter, 1969). We will say much more about these and other learning approaches to treating behavior disorders in Chapter 16.

At this point, it seems clear that observational learning is very widespread and that cognitive forms of learning have great relevance to both human and animal behavior. Cognition is an obvious part of human experience, and learning theories that do not consider the role of mental activity and knowledge seem to ignore a crucial facet of human life. Cognitive theories of learning contribute to many areas of psychology, including personality and social development, psychopathology, and psychotherapy. This theoretical approach to human behavior will reappear in many of the following chapters. It provides the major foundation for the next chapter, which deals with memory.

SUMMARY

1. Learning is a relatively permanent change in performance potential that arises from experience. Psychologists infer learning by observing changes in performance. The simplest kind of learning is an **orienting reflex**, a response to any novel stimulus. **Habituation** occurs when the subject becomes accustomed to the stimulus and ceases to respond to it. **Associative learning** is more complex, involving the association of events. Two kinds of associative learning are **classical conditioning**, which involves reflexive behavior, and **operant conditioning**, which involves voluntary behavior. A different learning theory emphasizes **cognitive learning**—thinking and reasoning.

2. Classical conditioning involves **reflex behavior**—behavior produced involuntarily by a specific stimulus. Pavlov, while studying the physiology of digestion, found that the **unconditioned stimulus** (UCS) of food in a dog's mouth elicited the **unconditioned response** (UCR) of salivation. When the UCS (the food) is repeatedly preceded by a **conditioned stimulus** (CS), for example, a bell, the dog's eventual salivation in response to the CS is called the **conditioned response** (CR). This tendency to react to the CS as though it were the UCS is called **stimulus substitution**. To establish and maintain a classically conditioned response, there must be a predictable relationship between the conditioned stimulus and the unconditioned stimulus, and the CS and the UCS must continue to be paired at least occasionally. The weakening and eventual disappearance of the conditioned response is called **extinction**. Classical conditioning is important in many types of learning and is used to extinguish fears and phobias through such techniques as **systematic desensitization**.

3. Operant conditioning involves voluntary behavior rather than reflexes. According to Thorndike's **law of effect**, responses that result in satisfying consequences will be strengthened, while responses that lead to unsatisfying consequences are unlikely to be repeated. Skinner went on to propose that the principle of reinforcement is the basic mechanism for controlling human behavior. A factor that increases the frequency of a behavior is called a **reward** or **reinforcement**; a factor that decreases the frequency of a behavior is called **punishment**. In **positive reinforcement** the frequency of a response increases because the response is followed by a positive stimulus; in **negative reinforcement** the frequency of a response increases because the response removes some negative stimulus. **Superstitious behavior** occurs when behavior is strengthened or weakened because it happens by chance to precede reinforcement or punishment.

4. Operant responses have been established experimentally by manipulating rewards and punishments in such devices as the Skinner box, a maze, and a jump stand. **Shaping**—a technique in which a subject is reinforced for displaying closer and closer approximations of the desired behavior—has been used to modify both animal and human behavior.

5. Once established, an operantly conditioned response is maintained through reinforcement. The **schedule of reinforcement** controls behavior to a great extent. A **continuous reinforcement schedule**—reinforcement each time the response occurs—is used to establish new behavior; a **partial reinforcement schedule**—withholding the reward some of the time—is most effective for maintaining the behavior. Schedules of partial reinforcement include a **fixed-ratio schedule**, in which the subject is rewarded each time it makes a specified number of responses, and a **fixed-interval schedule**, in which the subject is rewarded at the end of a fixed interval of time, regardless of the number of responses. Two schedules that result in high rates of response that are resistant to extinction are the **variable-ratio schedule**, which randomly provides reinforcement after an average number of responses, and the **variable-interval schedule**, which randomly rewards responses that occur after an average amount of time has elapsed. An operantly conditioned response gradually decreases and disappears when it is no longer reinforced. The reappearance of the response after it has been extinguished is called **spontaneous recovery**. Operant conditioning principles have been used in a number of ways including **programmed instruction** and **behavior modification**.

6. Many factors may influence performance of a learned behavior. **Stimulus generalization**—the expression of a learned response in the presence of a number of similar stimuli—may be limited by **discrimination training** to bring behavior under the control of the discriminative stimulus. A subject may perform a learned behavior even though the reinforcer it receives is different from the one that established the response. The effects of a **primary reinforcer**—one that satisfies a biological need—can be generalized to secondary, or conditioned, reinforcers. Conditioned reinforcement can also be used to control behavior acquired through classical conditioning. **First-order conditioning** involves a conditioned stimulus paired with a primary reinforcer; **second-order conditioning** involves pairing the conditioned stimulus with another stimulus, which signals the primary reinforcer. **Chaining** is the learning of a sequence of operant behaviors that ends in a primary reward.

7. Because of severe limitations, punishment has been found to be most effective in suppressing maladaptive behaviors when used with more positive forms of behavior control.

8. According to the cognitive approach to learning, in associative learning there are important thought processes that intervene between the stimulus and the response. Cognitive psychologists believe that in classical conditioning a subject has the expectation that a previously neutral event will be followed by an unconditioned stimulus. They also maintain that much human learning takes place without subsequent overt rewards or punishments. Two such types are **latent learning**—behavior that is learned but not demonstrated until there is an incentive—and **observational learning**, also called **modeling** and **imitative learning**, which results from observing the behavior of others.

Suggested readings

Hilgard, E. R., and Bower, G. H. *Theories of learning* (4th ed.). Englewood Cliffs, N.J.: Prentice-Hall, 1975.

Horton, D. L., and Turnage, T. W. *Human learning.* Englewood Cliffs, N.J: Prentice-Hall, 1976.

Hulse, S. H., Deese, J., and Egeth, H. *The psychology of learning.* New York: McGraw-Hill, 1975.

Pavlov, I. P. *Conditioned reflexes.* New York: Oxford University Press, 1927.

Skinner, B. F. *The behavior of organisms.* New York: Appleton-Century-Crofts, 1938.

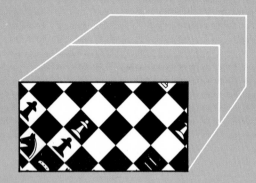

PREVIEW

1. Psychologists describe three types of memory: sensory memory, a mere clearing house for incoming information; short-term memory, where information is stored for about twenty seconds; and long-term memory, an enduring store for information that might be needed again.

2. Retrieving specific information from long-term memory can be difficult because its capacity is enormous. Unconsciously we may create details if we cannot remember them—a problem in eyewitness testimony. Techniques do exist, however, for improving long-term memory retrieval.

3. In place of the theories of short-term and long-term memory, some critics attribute differences in recall to the way we process or store memories.

4. Transferring information from short-term to long-term memory may involve a change in the way neurons connect in the brain.

5. Forgetting may mean either an inability to retrieve information—or that some memories are permanently altered or lost.

6 Memory and forgetting

Not long ago a San Francisco newspaper (San Francisco *Examiner*, June 25, 1978) carried a story of an information junkie named Michael Barone. Barone collected facts about America. He could tell you the results of just about every presidential election in the twentieth century. He could describe in detail the boundaries of the 435 national congressional districts. He could rattle off the populations of most major cities, and for different years. What was the population of St. Louis in 1960? "Uh, 750,026." He claimed to do it by "instinct."

As incredible as Michael Barone's feats of recall may seem, they are well within the bounds of normal human memory. We are all endowed with a remarkable capacity for processing information, even though we seldom devote the time and energy to factual memorization that Barone has done. Who were your closest friends in high school? When was the American Revolution? In which state is Chicago located? What is the melody of the "Star Spangled Banner"? How does the air smell after it rains? You immediately know the answers to these and hundreds of thousands of other questions. Clearly, the capacity of human memory far exceeds that of the most sophisticated computer.

Psychologists usually divide memory into three distinct types: sensory, short-term, and long-term. **Sensory memory** is the momentary lingering of sensory information we experience after a stimulus has been removed. We can store a

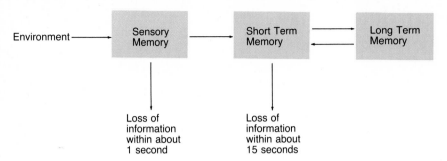

Figure 6.1 A diagram of the human memory system, showing the relationship among sensory memory, short-term memory, and long-term memory.

great deal of information in this memory system, but only for the briefest instant. **Short-term memory** involves the conscious retention of things we have just encountered. This storage system holds only a small amount of information, and the contents fade in less than half a minute if not renewed. **Long-term memory**, in contrast, stores information indefinitely to be used over and over again. The capacity of long-term memory is thought to be essentially limitless. One theory of the relationship between sensory, short-term, and long-term memory is illustrated in Figure 6.1.

Much of this chapter is devoted to a discussion of these three memory systems. We will be answering many questions you may already have about memory. Why is it usually so difficult to remember a long string of numbers but so easy to remember a sentence with the same number of words? Why do some people seem to have remarkable powers of recall while others appear to be constantly forgetting? Is there such a thing as a photographic memory? How can you improve your own memory? Next, we will turn to the biological side of memory. How, we ask, does the human brain manage to form memory traces? Exciting recent findings in this area may provide a whole new dimension to our understanding of how memory works. And finally, we will explore one of the most frustrating realities of daily life—the experience of forgetting. How much do we really forget? Is it possible that everything we have ever learned is still stored somewhere in memory if only we knew how to retrieve it? These are just some of the many issues we will raise in this chapter.

SENSORY MEMORY

Glance very briefly at the pattern of letters and numbers in Figure 6.2. Then close your eyes and try to list out loud as many as you can. You will probably find that your powers of recall are rather disappointing. In fact, the results of many carefully controlled experiments indicate that most people can remember only about four or five of twelve unrelated items that are flashed to them for just an instant. Yet such findings seem to contradict much of everyday experience. When we glance at a scene and then look away, most of us are left with the impression of a fairly complete and accurate image, however fleeting that image may be. The fact that so many people have the distinct impression that sensory memory is very rich puzzled psychologists for a long time. If sensory memory was indeed rich, why in laboratory tests did it appear so poor?

This puzzle greatly intrigued a young psychology graduate student named George Sperling. Perhaps, Sperling reasoned, previous researchers had been testing sensory memory in the wrong way. So he set about devising a new test (Sperling, 1960). He flashed a twelve-item pattern like the one in Figure 6.2,

Figure 6.2 When exposed to this array of unrelated items for a brief period, people typically recall no more than four or five of them. But if subjects are signaled immediately after the exposure to recall just one of the lines, they can almost always recall all four items correctly. This evidence suggests that people "read" the information from some sort of complete sensory image of the stimulus, which fades in the time it takes to say the names of a few of the letters and numbers in the image.

but he did *not* ask subjects to specify all the letters and numbers they had seen. Instead, on removing the pattern, he immediately sounded a high, medium, or low tone to indicate which line subjects should report. Under these conditions, subjects could correctly report almost all of the four items in *any* of the three rows. Sperling's research demonstrated that the ability to process information through the senses is indeed better than verbal reports suggest. The instant after we scan a multi-item pattern we usually retain a fairly complete image. This visual memory is fleeting, however; it lasts for only about a second. Consequently, during the time it takes to report four or five items, the remaining images fade from memory.

This momentary storage of visual material is just one example of sensory memory. Actually, people may have five separate sensory memories, corresponding to each of their five senses—sight, hearing, smell, taste, and touch. In all cases, incoming information is stored within the receiving sensory system, not in some central region of the brain. So subsequent information entering the same sensory pathway always disrupts what is currently being held there. If, for example, you view a set of twelve X's immediately after seeing Figure 6.2, you will lose your sensory memory of the initial pattern. However, if the second stimulus is a sound or an odor rather than a visual display, it will not interfere with your image of Figure 6.2 because the two different kinds of information are stored in separate sensory systems.

We are seldom aware of the instantaneous decay of information entering sensory memory because new information is constantly following old. Only special circumstances can make us aware of how fragile sensory storage is. Old-time movies provide one demonstration. In today's movies the action seems smooth and realistic because the time lapse between frames is extremely brief—brief enough to be within the limits of visual sensory storage. The result is a blending of successive images that gives the illusion of continuous motion. In contrast, when movies made early in this century are shown with a modern projector, the action seems jerky and unnatural. The reason is that too much time is left between frames, permitting the image of one frame to begin to fade from sensory storage before the next frame appears.

SHORT-TERM MEMORY

If sensory memories are so fleeting, what purpose do they serve? Apparently, they provide a second or so during which a person can select information that warrants further processing. After all, if we tried to scrutinize intently all the many sights, sounds, odors, tastes, and tactile sensations that bombard us from all sides we would surely be overwhelmed. Some kind of selectivity is clearly essential. But how, with so many stimuli impinging on us, do we manage to screen out those that are peripheral and attend mainly to those that are important? The answer lies in two cognitive processes that are crucial to getting information into short-term memory—sensory gating and selective attention.

Instatement into short-term memory

Sensory gating The mind monitors all incoming sensory information to some extent, directing attention to one type of input while putting a damper on information entering through other channels. When reading a very interesting book, for example, you may be only vaguely aware of surrounding sounds and odors. This selective turning up of one kind of sensory input while turning down others is called **sensory gating**. By cutting down extraneous "noise" in the environment, sensory gating permits you to focus attention on the most important sensory channel at any given time. Information from the damped-down senses is not completely eliminated, however. If you suddenly detect a strange sound, or even an unexpected silence, your attention will probably shift from what you are seeing to what you are hearing. This indicates that you are still processing information from your turned-down senses to some extent; otherwise, you would not know when to shift your attention.

Actually, it should come as no surprise that we can focus our attention on information entering one sensory channel while still processing at least some input through the others. We all do this every day. When driving a car, for example, we routinely watch the road, listen to the radio, and perhaps even enjoy the taste of food at the same time. In the past many psychologists have argued that people can perform activities simultaneously only when some of them are "automatic"—that is, when they require little if any central processing by the brain. But this view has recently been challenged. Neisser and his colleagues (Hirst, Neisser, and Spelke, 1978) have trained subjects to read difficult encyclopedia articles at a normal speed and level of comprehension while simultaneously hearing, transcribing, and understanding the meaning of dictated sentences unrelated to those articles! These results indicate that people can indeed learn to process highly complex material through several sensory channels at once. Still, this skill is not acquired without many hours of practice. Under normal circumstances, people do tend to turn down extraneous sensory channels when performing a task that requires substantial concentration.

Selective attention In addition to damping down information entering peripheral sensory channels, we may also damp down some of the information entering the *same* sensory channel. This process is called **selective attention**. When you are carrying on a conversation at a crowded cocktail party, for example, your ears receive a great deal of extraneous information. Not only do you hear the person you are speaking with, you also hear the din of other voices, the clink of glasses, and perhaps the sound of music. Despite this confusion of sounds, however, you somehow manage to follow your partner's conversation. You may think this is accomplished by completely ignoring all the many other sounds, but in fact you actually give them an elementary form of attention. In the same way that sensory gating does not completely eliminate information from your other senses, selective attention allows some processing of peripheral information entering a single sensory channel.

Psychologists have extensively studied this "cocktail party phenomenon." Cherry (1953) used a **dichotic listening** technique in which subjects wearing earphones simultaneously heard one message played into the left ear and a different message played into the right ear. Cherry instructed his subjects to "shadow" one of the messages—that is, to repeat it aloud as they heard it. (The subject's voice, like a shadow, trails along immediately behind the recorded message.) Later, he tested to see if subjects could recognize or recall material from the nonshadowed message, the one coming into the other ear. If the subjects had completely ignored the nonshadowed message, they would have been unable to remember anything about it. But this was not the case. Under most conditions, people detected the physical characteristics of the nonshadowed message, but generally not the meaning. Thus, they could correctly report whether a voice was present and whether it changed midway from male to female. About a third of the time they could also detect the sound of their own names. Generally, however, the subjects could not identify the content of the nonshadowed message or even the language in which it was spoken. They did not even notice the difference between speech and nonsense syllables. Thus, selective screening of auditory information seems to be fairly complete.

How is selective attention possible? How do we manage to "filter out" some but not all of the information that enters a particular sensory channel? One clue comes from the fact that a person can selectively attend to a stimulus only when it is physically or conceptually distinct from other stimuli around it. As stimuli become more similar in all their potentially differentiating features, they also become increasingly difficult to segregate (Glass et al., 1979). This insight has led researchers to propose several explanations for selective attention. One theory is that we discriminate among the physical aspects of different stimuli entering the same sensory channel, and it is these physical differences that guide our attention (Broadbent, 1958). For example, when you attend to something heard in one ear at the expense of something heard in the other, you have become attuned to the difference in location between the two messages (right versus left). In much the same way, physical differences among voices (pitch, volume, accent, and other qualities) allow you is attend to a single speaker even at a crowded party. But although this explanation seems logical, experiments have shown that it is probably incomplete. Speakers who are asked to direct their attention *only* to what is played into one ear find themselves switching momentarily to the other ear in order to follow a message's meaning (Triesman, 1960). Selective attention, then, is probably based on both physical and conceptual unity. At first we may attend to the physical characteristics of a message where it comes from, what the voice qualities are), but this strategy may then yield to the message's meaning when we have gathered enough information to make sense of what is being said (Treisman, 1964).

Short-term storage

Once information has been attended to, it must be stored long enough to be useful. This means longer than the duration of our fragile sensory memories. After you look up a telephone number in a directory, for example, you must certainly retain it longer than a second, otherwise you would not be able to dial. However, you probably dial quickly, knowing that you will not remember the number very long without some special effort. Often, you repeat the number several times—either aloud or mentally—while reaching for the phone. If you get distracted for a few seconds and interrupt this repetition, you will probably be forced to consult the directory again. This example illustrates a basic feature of short-term memory; information entering short-term memory is lost rather rapidly unless a person regards it as important enough to renew it by **rehearsal**.

The rehearsal process usually involves some kind of speech—either overt, as when you repeat a telephone number aloud, or implicit, as when you repeat a number mentally. Rehearsal seems to maintain information in short-term memory in the following way: a person says the information aloud or silently, hears what is being said, and then re-stores it. Rehearsal, in other words, often maintains items in memory *acoustically*—it is the *sounds* of the items that are repeated and stored. Although rehearsal can also be visual, acoustic rehearsal (especially the silent, mental kind) seems to be more efficient (Weber and Castleman, 1970). Yet it can easily be disrupted either by external distractions (the sound of someone talking, for instance) or by internal events (such as thinking about your own telephone number while trying to remember a new one).

Exactly how long does an item stay in short-term memory without rehearsal? Studies yield figures under twenty seconds. For example, when researchers ask subjects to remember a short series of letters—say, CPQ—and then instruct them to count backward by threes from, say, 270 (267, 264, 261, and so on), the subjects are likely to forget the letters within about fifteen seconds. The backward counting is an interfering task, a device psychologists use to prevent rehearsal. If the interfering task is ineffective and subjects manage to secretly rehearse CPQ while appearing to take a deep breath between counts, their memory of the letters will probably last longer. The exact duration depends on the amount of rehearsal they are able to squeeze in. In addition, duration depends on the information to be remembered and on the nature of any interfering task (Peterson and Peterson, 1959).

How much information does short-term memory hold? In 1956 George Miller published a paper entitled "The Magical Number Seven, Plus or Minus Two." In it he summarized the results of many experiments, all of which indicated that the majority of people can hold only between five and nine items in short-term memory. Most psychologists agree that the capacity of short-term memory is very near this range. If anything, Miller's estimate may be a bit too high.

At first, researchers were puzzled by the ability of humans, despite the limited capacity of their short-term memories, to process large amounts of information. How, they wondered, can we read and comprehend even a very brief sentence if we are unable to handle more than seven letters at once? George Miller had an answer: We expand our relatively limited capacity by "chunking" information. We see groups of letters as words (small chunks), groups of words as phrases (larger chunks), and finally series of phrases as sentences. In this manner, we greatly increase the amount of information we can process at any one time.

Interestingly, the process of chunking uses information already stored in long-term memory to categorize new information entering short-term memory. For example, the number 1,492 is easier to recall than the number 2,568 if you remember that 1492 is the year Columbus landed in America. What you have done is to use this "old" information to reduce your memory load to a single date instead of four separate digits. Conceivably, you could recall a string of twenty-eight numbers if they could be chunked into seven familiar dates.

Information can also be chunked by using a rule that organizes it. Consider the following sequence of numbers, 149162536496481100121. Impossible to remember? Not if you must only recall a single rule instead of twenty-one digits. The rule is simply to square, in succession, the numbers 1 through 11 ($1^2 = 1$, $2^2 = 4$, $3^2 = 9$, $4^2 = 16$, and so on). Such chunking allows us to bypass the "bottleneck" created by the limited capacity of short-term memory.

Chunks, of course, need not be verbal. Success at the following task requires visual chunking. First study the chessboard shown in Figure 6.4A for about five

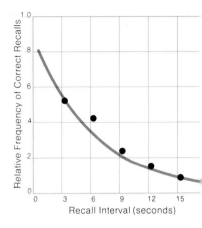

Figure 6.3 The results of Peterson and Peterson's (1959) experiment to measure the length of time that short-term memory lasts without the aid of rehearsal. Subjects were shown a three-consonant combination (CPQ, for example) that they were to remember; immediately after they saw it, they began to count backward by threes from some number supplied by the experimenter. The longer the experimenter let them count before asking them to recall the combination, the less likely the subjects were to recall it correctly.

seconds, then turn the page and see how many pieces you can draw correctly on the empty board. If you are unfamiliar with the game of chess, your limit will probably be close to the magical number seven. In fact, you may recall far fewer than seven pieces because storing each one requires several chunks of information. What the piece looks like, the row in which it is located, and also its column. It may surprise you to know that master chess players can reproduce the entire arrangement after just a five-second look. Does this mean that chess masters have remarkably good memories? Research suggests not (De Groot, 1965; Simon and Gilmartin, 1973). When pieces are arranged on a chessboard in a random pattern, the chess master's memory is no better than anyone else's. But when pieces are arranged in a way that might possibly occur in a game between good players, the master can easily encode the pattern as a number of large chunks, making the entire arrangement well within the limits of normal short-term memory. With how many visual chunks are chess masters familiar? Research shows that they can identify between 25,000 and 100,000 distinct groupings. Although this sounds like an astronomical number, it does not seem so unreasonable when you consider that an educated speaker of English has a vocabulary of about the same size.

Figure 6.4A Study this arrangement of chess pieces for five seconds. Then turn to the empty chess board on the next page and try to reproduce the arrangement. The amount you are able to recall correctly represents approximately seven of the chunks you have developed for processing information about chess games.

LONG-TERM MEMORY

A few pages back we discussed the process of looking up a telephone number and holding it in short-term memory. This information remains available only as long as we repeat it to ourselves. If we are distracted even for just a few seconds, the number is likely to evaporate. If this were the entire capacity of human memory, we would be forced to spend our days continually repeating our own names just to remember who we were! Obviously, there is much more to memory than this short-term "holding pattern."

Learning and intelligence are made possible through what is called long-term memory. Because of long-term memory, our experiences are not lost the moment we cease to think about them. Instead, we are able to retain the past and use it to shape the present. As the repository of all our accumulated knowledge, long-term memory must contain an extraordinary amount of information. Consider the hundreds, even thousands, of facts you store away daily over a lifetime of some seventy years. Viewed in this light, the capacity of long-term memory seems almost beyond comprehension.

Long-term storage and retrieval

How information is transferred from short-term to long-term memory is not completely understood. Studies show that transfer depends in part on the amount of time we rehearse information: the longer the rehearsal the more likely the transfer. But the *type* of rehearsal is equally important (Craik and Lockhart, 1972). When people simply repeat something to themselves without giving it any thought, as they tend to do when rehearsing a telephone number, they may maintain that information in short-term memory indefinitely, but they may not transfer it to long-term memory. In contrast, when people take a new piece of information and mentally do something with it—image it, apply it, relate it to other things—it is more likely to be deposited in long-term storage.

Once information is transferred to long-term memory we must have some way of retrieving it when needed if it is ever to be useful again. In some ways, our ability to retrieve items from long-term memory is even more impressive than our ability to store them. Consider, for example, the fact that most people can read at a steady rate of 300 to 600 words per minute—five to ten words per second. Clearly, this skill requires an amazingly efficient system for retrieving the meaning of words.

Retrieval from long-term memory is measured in two basic ways: recognition and recall. In **recognition**, you are presented with a particular stimulus and asked if you have ever encountered it before. Identifying a suspect from a police line-up is an example of recognition. **Recall**, in contrast, entails retrieving specific pieces of information, usually guided by retrieval cues. Asking a witness to a robbery "What did the thief look like? Do you remember what he was wearing?" demands that the person recall. He or she must search through memory and come up with an appropriate description. Thus, recognition and recall are different kinds of memory tasks. Nevertheless, the mental processes involved in them overlap substantially. Let us see how.

Figure 6.4B Turn to Figure 6.4A on the preceding page, if you have not already looked at it, and study it for five seconds. Then try to reproduce the arrangement shown there on this empty chess board. Your success in doing so will depend heavily on your experience with the game of chess.

Recognition is essentially a matching process: we consider a given stimulus and decide whether it "matches" something already stored in memory. In doing so, we tend not to evaluate the object as a whole but instead to analyze its various components. If all the components match, the object is quickly recognized. If, however, some of the components match while others do not, we are left with a feeling of only vague familiarity. Such "partial matches" can easily occur on meeting a person again after many years. Some of the old acquaintance's features immediately match—the eyes and smile, for example—but others do not—body weight perhaps (some fifteen pounds heavier), or amount of hair (decidedly thinner). The result is the uncomfortable feeling: "Do I know you?" This same process of partial recognition may account for the phenomenon called **déjà vu**—the distinct feeling that something is familiar even though we have never encountered it before. In this case we may be partially matching a novel experience with a very similar but unidentifiable past event.

In contrast to recognition, recall, according to many psychologists, involves two processes. First, we must search through memory to find the appropriate information. Second, we must determine, as in recognition, whether the information we come up with "matches" the correct response. If we think it does we give the answer; if we think it does not we search again.

Retrieval cues are especially important to the success of the search component of recall. In one experiment (Tulving and Pearlstone, 1966) subjects read lists of words that included both categories (animals, fruits, furniture, for example) as well as one or more instances of each category (dog, plum, chair). The subjects were asked to remember only the instances, not the categories. When the time came to recall the words, half the subjects were given the category words as retrieval cues. These subjects remembered about 50 percent more words out of a list of forty-eight than subjects who were not given the categories to help them recall. Without adequate retrieval cues, therefore, things that are stored in memory may be difficult to find.

This fact should come as no surprise. We have all had the frustrating experi-

A

B

C

ence of knowing that something is stored somewhere in memory but of being unable to locate it quickly. We say that such information is on the tip of our tongues, which is why psychologists call this the **tip-of-the-tongue phenomenon**. How do people pry these uncooperative facts loose? Usually they employ a variety of retrieval cues based on the bits of information about the target word they are unable to recall. Suppose you were asked to remember the word for "a small Chinese boat propelled by a single oar over the stern and with the deck usually covered by a roof." You might grope your way through a string of similar-sounding words—"Cheyenne" . . . "Siam" . . . "Saipan"—until you eventually arrived at the correct response, "sampan" (Brown and McNeill, 1966). Similarly, when shown a picture of Elliott Gould and asked to remember his name, you might first recall his profession and then his recent films: "Movie actor . . . Starred in Bob, Carol, Ted, and Alice . . . Elliott Gould!" (Yarmey, 1973). When we store information in long-term memory, therefore, we also seem to create a number of retrieval pathways to it. These typically involve both sounds (particularly the first letter) and associated facts and events. (Try to recall the names of people shown in Figure 6.5 and see what retrieval pathways you use.)

Since recall always involves a search through memory to find the correct response, is recall necessarily more difficult than recognition? Frequently yes. As a student you have probably deduced this yourself. Most students find that multiple-choice or true-false questions (recognition tests) are substantially easier than fill-in-the-blanks (recall tests). Studies confirm that under ideal circumstances our ability to recognize familiar stimuli can be impressive indeed. Haber and Standing (1969), for example, showed stalwart subjects more than 2,500 photographs of various scenes. The next day the subjects were able to recognize between 85 and 95 percent of these pictures. Our capacity to discriminate among different stimuli is far from limitless, however. Much depends on the similarity between the initial stimulus and subsequent ones. If you were shown a scene of a crowded railroad station, for instance, and later shown an almost identical scene with one or two details changed, you would be very apt to say that the second picture was the same one you saw originally. The same holds true for recognizing other types of stimuli. Circumstances always determine the accuracy of memory.

Figure 6.5 Do you know who these people are? Try to recall their names and follow the pathways you use.

(A) Tracy Austin. (B) Ed Asner. (C) Jimmy Walker.

Improving long-term memory

Most of us complain about our memories. We consider them at best unreliable and in some instances downright poor. Often, however, it is not memory itself that is deficient but rather our knowledge of how best to use the memory capacities we have. A number of simple techniques can greatly improve virtually anyone's performance on recall tasks. These techniques are frequently called **mnemonic devices**, from the Greek word *mneme*, which means "memory."

Many mnemonic devices simply involve clever ways of organizing material when it is stored in long-term memory. Consider how the ancient Greek poet Simonides managed to aid the families of victims in a tragic accident. As Cicero tells the story, Simonides was called away from a banquet to speak with two visitors. While he was gone, the roof of the banquet hall collapsed, killing all the guests. The bodies were mutilated beyond recognition. How could relatives identify them? Simonides found that he could help. By picturing the banquet in his mind, he easily remembered where each guest had been sitting. The bodies were then claimed according to their location in the hall.

This technique is called the **method of loci**. It involves assimilating items to be remembered with a series of places, or loci, that are already firmly fixed in memory. You can easily use this device yourself. Suppose you had to learn, in chronological order, the names of all the presidents of the United States in the twentieth century. You would simply visualize a familiar place, say the house in which you live, and imagine each president in a particular location. Teddy Roosevelt, carrying a big stick, might greet you at the front door. Stout William Howard Taft might be found talking to a thin, bespectacled Woodrow Wilson in the entrance hall. On you would go, through the living room, up the stairs, until you finally came to the attic window through which you would spot a smiling Ronald Reagan sunning himself on the roof.

A somewhat similar mnemonic device is called the **key word system**. This

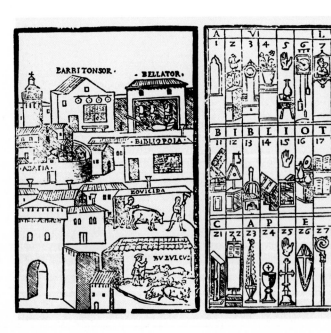

Figure 6.6 Technical aids to memory have a long history, beginning with the use of the method of loci by Greek and Roman orators. These woodcuts are from a text explaining the method of loci that was written in the sixteenth century by a Dominican monk for the benefit of such professionals as jurists, confessors, and ambassadors. At the left is a set of loci, an abbey and its associated buildings. At the right are objects that can be placed in these loci and so remembered. Note that each row on the right corresponds to one of the abbey buildings (top row, the courtyard; middle row, the library; bottom row, the chapel). Note also that every fifth place in each row is marked by a hand and every tenth by a cross. As the memorizer mentally moves through the abbey, he or she can "tick off" the items that are being recalled on the fingers of each hand.

method requires you to memorize a list of simple words or sentences such as:

One is a bun.	Six is sticks.
Two is a shoe.	Seven is Heaven.
Three is a tree.	Eight is a gate.
Four is a door.	Nine is a line.
Five is a hive.	Ten is a hen.

The key words (in this case the predicate nouns) must be concrete and easily visualized. If you now have to learn a series of digits or words in a certain order, all you have to do is mentally associate each one with the appropriate key word. As a simple example, suppose you wish to remember the number 4,391. You would say to yourself: "Four, three, nine, one, door, tree, line, bun. I open the *door* and see a *tree*, and from the tree runs a *line* leading to a *bun*." Though this may sound silly, it works. If you want to remember a list of objects rather than numbers, you might imagine the first one inside a bun, the second in shoes, the third up a tree, and so on.

Although the method of loci and the key word system are primarily based on organization, they also employ imagery. Research shows that people can remember verbal material better if they relate the words to be learned to visual images of some kind (Bower and Clark, 1969; Paivio, 1971). For example, you would probably have an easier time remembering that the French word *escargot* means "snail" if you pictured a giant snail carrying a cargo of S's on its back. This would leave you with the paired images "S-cargo" and "snail."

Imagery helps verbal memory most when the words to be remembered are concrete. Try to imagine the word combinations "steamship-canary" and "dissonance-republic." The first pair immediately suggests specific images because it consists of two concrete nouns. The second pair, in contrast, is very difficult to picture because the words are too abstract to bring images quickly to mind. If you finally did manage to come up with a mental picture for either of these words, say an image of the American flag for the word "republic," you might later recall the wrong word, because "republic" and "American flag" are not uniquely tied to each other.

Imagery is even more effective as a memory aid when the things to be remembered are pictured in some interacting way. Bower and his colleagues (1972) trained some subjects to form interactive images for each of twenty pairs of concrete nouns. (Figure 6.7 shows the kind of image that might be formed

Figure 6.7 A visualization that might aid a person to remember the word pair "locomotive-towel."

for the noun pair "locomotive-towel.") Control subjects were left to their own devices to memorize the pairs. All subjects were then given the first word in each pair as a retrieval cue and were asked to recall the second word. Those who had linked the words through interactive imagery recalled on the average about one and half times as much as control subjects did.

Why is imagery such a powerful memory tool? No one knows for sure. Possibly, we are more likely to remember words plus images than words alone for the same reason that it is better to have two reminder notes for ourselves— one at home and one in a pocket. According to this line of reasoning, having two different kinds of notes—verbal and visual—makes it twice as likely that we will remember. Recent research, however, suggests that this explanation may not be enough. Imagery has been found to improve memory even for subjects who have been totally blind since birth (Jonides, Kahn, and Rozin, 1975). These people cannot be said to store visual "reminder notes" in the normal sense of the word. Perhaps, then, the simple act of trying to imagine an object in some way leads to deeper cognitive processing and so to memories that are richer, more detailed, or unique.

We should not leave the subject of imagery without some mention of what is often called a "photographic" memory. You may have heard of people who, like human cameras, can retain exact images of almost anything they see. Does such an ability really exist? Something very close to it is found in a tiny percentage of the human population (Haber, 1969). These people, most of whom are young children, can form **eidetic images**—that is, visual images of incredible accuracy and clarity of detail. After looking for only a few seconds at a picture of, say, a long picket fence, a person capable of eidetic imagery can tell you the exact number of pickets shown, and perhaps even the number of nails holding on each one! They apparently do this by "reading" the information off their visual images. Psychologists do not yet know how eidetic images are formed. Research indicates, however, that various factors can disrupt them. For example, if eidetic children are asked to describe a picture while in the act of viewing it, they retain no visual images. It seems that verbal processes interfere with eidetic ability. Interesting, too, eidetic children are no more skilled than other children in storing verbal information.

Although few of us have photographic memories, we do have at our disposal many other very valuable memory aids. Reconstructing the context in which information was learned is one commonly used technique. If you were asked to recall the names of your high-school classmates, how would you go about it? Research show that you would probably reconstruct various scenes from your high-school days—hockey practice, for example, or an after-school hangout— and then try to name all of the people you picture present. Using this device, people can often remember the names of a large number of classmates even after a period of many years (Williams, 1976).

Even information that seems totally impossible to retrieve may suddenly emerge through reconstruction. Suppose you were asked to recall what you were doing at 1:30 in the afternoon on April 27 two years ago. Your initial response to this question might be "Ridiculous!" But try breaking the problem down into smaller subproblems. What day of the week was it? Were you in school at the time? What courses were you taking? At what hour did each class meet? In this way, you could probably reconstruct that particular afternoon.

Retrieval, then, can often be viewed as a problem-solving task in which the right answer comes from asking the right question (Lindsay and Norman, 1977). You may want to try out your problem-solving ability on some of the questions in Figure 6.8.

Memory distortions

Reconstructing an experience bit by bit may be a helpful memory device, but it is far from foolproof. People commonly confuse what happened one time with what happened another. When memories are vague people fill in the gaps with what they *believe* to be true. In short, the process of piecing together the past is often prone to distortion. This tendency to distort is one of the most fascinating aspects of the way we humans remember.

Preconceptions and inferences What causes memory distortions? Interestingly, they are not the aberrations many people believe them to be. The tendency to edit and embellish what we learn and recall seems to be a natural outcome of the way the human memory works. Consider the story in Figure 6.9A, a North American Indian tribal legend. After reading it through at a normal pace, retell the story as completely as you can without referring back to the original. You will undoubtedly find many differences between your version and the one in Figure 6.9A. Are there any predictable patterns in the kinds of changes you made?

Psychologist Frederick C. Bartlett set out to answer this question some fifty years ago (Bartlett, 1932). In one series of experiments Bartlett had subjects play a version of the "telephone game" popular among children. He gave the story in Figure 6.9A to one subject who read it and then told it to another subject, who in turn told it to another, and so on. After many subjects and many renditions the story became substantially changed. But Bartlett found that the changes were not haphazard. Several important patterns emerged. First, subjects tended to "flatten" details that did not fit within their existing scheme of things. If you look at Figure 6.9B, a version produced by the tenth subject in one of Bartlett's experiments, you will find that all references to ghosts have been eliminated. The story is simply about an Indian out seal hunting who joins some other Indians in a battle. Bartlett argued that because the mystical references to ghosts were not easily assimilated into most subjects' existing concepts of life, warfare, and death, they tended to be dropped. For a somewhat similar reason other details tended to be "sharpened." Note in Figure 6.9B that the second Indian turns down the offer to join the warriors because his elderly mother is dependent on him. This is obviously an expansion of the reference to concerned relatives in the original text—an expansion that fits our preexisting concept of filial responsibility. Finally, subjects also introduced distortions that conformed to their expectations based on past experience. For example, many subjects added a "moral" to the story, because this kind of ending is typical of the folktales they were accustomed to.

The influence of expectations on memory storage and retrieval has since been demonstrated many times. In one experiment two psychologists showed subjects the scene from a subway car reproduced in Figure 6.10 (Allport and Postman, 1947). Among other things, it shows a black man apparently talking

In the rooms you live in, how many windows are there?

What were you doing on Monday afternoon in the third week of September two years ago?

Can pigeons fly airplanes?

Figure 6.8 Retrieval problems that demonstrate the reconstructive nature of memory. If, at first glance, any of these questions seems impossible to answer, try anyway. You may be surprised at what you can recall if you put your mind to it. (After Lindsay and Norman, 1977.)

A

One night two young men from Egulac went down to the river to hunt seals, and while they were there it became foggy and calm. Then they heard war-cries, and they thought: "Maybe this is a war party." They escaped to the shore, and hid behind a log. Now canoes came up, and they heard the noise of paddles, and saw one canoe coming up to them. There were five men in the canoe, and they said:

"What do you think? We wish to take you along. We are going up the river to make war on the people."

One of the young men said: "I have no arrows."

"Arrows are in the canoe," they said.

"I will not go along. I might be killed. My relatives do not know where I have gone. But you," he said, turning to the other, "may go with them."

So one of the young men went, but the other returned home.

And the warriors went on up the river to a town on the other side of Kalama. The people came down to the water, and they began to fight, and many were killed. But presently the young man heard one of the warriors say: "Quick, let us go home: that Indian has been hit." Now he thought: "Oh, they are ghosts." He did not feel sick, but they said he had been shot.

So the canoes went back to Egulac, and the young man went ashore to his house, and made a fire. And he told everybody and said: "Behold I accompanied the ghosts, and we went to fight. Many of our fellows were killed, and many of those who attacked us were killed. They said I was hit, and I did not feel sick."

He told it all, and then he became quiet. When the sun rose he fell down. Something black came out of his mouth. His face became contorted. The people jumped up and cried.

He was dead.

B

Two Indians were out fishing for seals in the Bay of Manpapan, when along came five other Indians in a war-canoe. They were going fighting.

"Come with us," said the five to the two, "and fight."

"I cannot come," was the answer of the one, "for I have an old mother at home who is dependent upon me." The other also said he could not come, because he had no arms. "That is no difficulty," the others replied, "for we have plenty in the canoe with us"; so he got into the canoe and went with them.

In a fight soon afterwards this Indian received a mortal wound. Finding that his hour was coming, he cried out that he was about to die. "Nonsense," said one of the others, "you will not die." But he did.

Figure 6.9 The original version of Bartlett's "War of the Ghosts" appears in A. The story as reproduced by the tenth subject appears in B. (From Bartlett's War of Ghosts, 1932. Courtesy of Cambridge University Press.)

to a white man who is carrying a razor. The researchers asked one subject to describe the picture to a second subject, and so on until the description had passed through many people. Significantly, the razor tended to migrate from the white hand to the black hand. The common stereotype that blacks are more violent than whites influenced what subjects saw and recalled.

Bartlett was one of the first psychologists to propose that such distortions provide important clues to the way that human memory works. Apparently, people try to assimilate new information within the framework of existing knowledge and beliefs. If we learn that an Indian goes to battle, for example, we try to fit this fact into our established notion of what Indian warfare is like. Information that does not conform to our expectations we may recast or simply drop. Thus, the process of storing information in memory is one of active construction. So is the process of retrieving it. During retrieval we may actively construct fairly detailed accounts on the basis of schematic representations. Here too we are guided by our existing concepts. If we know that a black man,

Figure 6.10 The original figure used in the Allport and Postman experiment (1947).

a white man, and a razor appeared in a certain picture, and if we believe that blacks are generally more violent than whites, a logical inference is to place the razor in the black man's grasp.

The tendency of people to make many inferences on the basis of preconceptions can be illustrated in other ways. Look very briefly, for example, at the top drawing in Figure 6.11A. Then turn away and try to reproduce from memory this sketch of a pair of eyeglasses. If you are like most people, your drawing will look very similar to the one at the top of the left-hand column in Figure 6.11B. Although the original sketch consisted of two circles joined together by a short, straight stick, people who are told that this is a representation of eyeglasses tend to connect two circles with a slightly curved and elevated line—much as we think eyeglasses should look. In contrast, people who are told that the same initial stimulus is a picture of a dumbbell tend to reproduce the drawing as shown in the right-hand column of Figure 6.11B. Memory for visual material, in other words, is easily distorted by what we are *told* we see (Carmichael, Hogan, and Walter, 1932).

Findings such as these have enormously important implications for the success of our legal system. A person who witnesses an accident or a crime will almost always be questioned before a trial takes place. Could it be that something said during this initial interrogation could alter the witness's later recollection of events? And if so, under what conditions are distortions most likely to occur? Recent research on the accuracy of eyewitness testimony provides some interesting answers (Loftus, 1979).

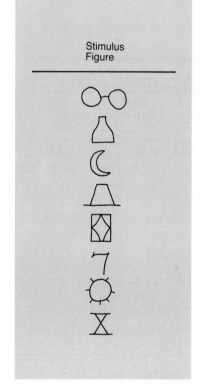

Stimulus
Figure

Figure 6.11A Carmichael, Hogan, and Walter (1932) designed an experiment to study the influence of set on perception. Subjects were shown these line patterns, which were described as drawings of various objects. When the subjects were asked to reproduce the patterns they had seen, they made the drawings shown in Figure 6.11B.

In depth

Studying eyewitness testimony Much of the recent work in the area of eyewitness testimony has been conducted by Elizabeth Loftus, one of the authors of this book. Loftus began her investigation of this important topic with several questions in mind. Prior research had clearly suggested that human memory is a process of active construction, in both the storage and the retrieval stages. Yet the stimuli that subjects in these past experiments had been asked to re-

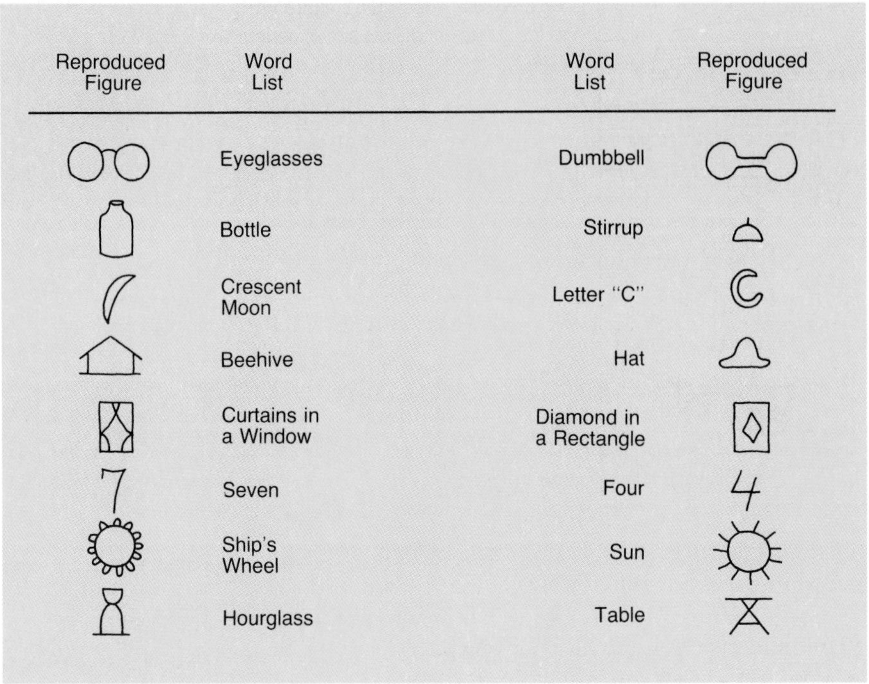

Reproduced Figure	Word List	Word List	Reproduced Figure
⊂⊃	Eyeglasses	Dumbbell	⌾—⌾
⬭	Bottle	Stirrup	△
⌒	Crescent Moon	Letter "C"	ℂ
⌂	Beehive	Hat	⌒
⧅	Curtains in a Window	Diamond in a Rectangle	◇
7	Seven	Four	4
⚙	Ship's Wheel	Sun	☀
⧖	Hourglass	Table	⧓

Figure 6.11B You can see how the naming of the patterns influenced the subjects' drawings. (After Carmichael, Hogan, and Walter, 1932.)

member were unlike much of the information learned in everyday life. Many were verbal stimuli—word lists, sentences, or at times brief stories. And those that were visual were almost always static, like a simple picture of two circles connected by a stick. Loftus felt that such stimuli were not highly representative of the memories we most commonly form. In the world outside the laboratory, we are constantly processing information that is not only largely visual, but also fast-moving and complex. Did the past findings regarding memory apply to such events as well? In addition, Bartlett and other psychologists had stressed that new information instated into memory is somehow assimilated within the framework of prior knowledge and beliefs. This was fine as far as it went. But what about the relationship between memory for a given experience and information acquired *after* that event? Is *subsequent* information also integrated into a person's existing memory representation?

This second question may sound abstract to you, but it is critical to the subject of eyewitness testimony. To understand why, imagine yourself in the following situation. It is nine o'clock on a rainy Christmas Eve, and you are hurrying home from some last-minute shopping. The streets are practically deserted, but ahead you spot a man with an armful of packages stepping off the curb into the crosswalk. Halfway across the street he drops a small box and bends to pick it up. Suddenly you see a car headed toward the stooped figure. The next instant the car strikes the man, throwing him some twenty feet to the side of the road. You have witnessed a serious automobile accident.

Within a few minutes police and ambulance are at the scene and a young officer begins to ask you a series of questions. Where was the man standing when he was hit? From what direction did the car come? How fast was the car going when it ran the stop light at the crosswalk? Although you may not have noticed it, this last question presupposes a piece of information you did not actually witness—a red traffic light. Do you think this subsequent information introduced by the police officer would alter your representation of the accident already held in memory? Research suggests that it very well might.

Loftus (1975) showed subjects a brief videotape of an automobile accident and then asked them questions about it. For half the subjects, one of the questions was: "How fast was the white sports car going while traveling along the country road?" For the other half, a similar question was: "How fast was the white sports car going when it passed the barn while traveling along the country road?" In fact, there was no barn in the film. Yet when questioned again about the accident a week later, more than 17 percent of those exposed to the false information about a barn answered yes to the question: "Did you see a barn?" In contrast, only about 3 percent of the remaining subjects answered yes to the same question. Apparently, the assumption of a barn during the initial questioning caused many subjects to incorporate the nonexistent barn into their recollections of the event. Moreover, a subsequent experiment showed that simply asking people whether they had or had not seen a barn—a question to which they usually answered no—was enough to increase the likelihood that they would later instate a barn into their memories of an accident.

What is happening in both these cases is that the initial memory of an event is being *supplemented* with additional, false information. On a previously empty country landscape, subjects now imagine a barn. In a sense, their recollection of the facts is not so much altered as amplified—albeit incorrectly. An important question therefore remains. Can something said to a witness immediately after an incident actually *transform* that person's original memory of what occurred? Suppose in our hypothetical Christmas Eve accident you thought you remembered the car's proceeding through a green light. Could the police officer's mention of a red light cause you later to recall the light as being red instead of green? Studies indicate yes.

Loftus, Miller, and Burns (1978) showed subjects thirty color slides of successive stages in an automobile accident involving a red Datsun. The critical slide was of the Datsun stopped at an intersection before it eventually turned right and hit a pedestrian. Half the subjects saw a slide with a stop sign at the corner; half saw a slide with a yield sign. (Figure 6.12 shows these two, almost identical

Figure 6.12 The critical slides used by Loftus, Miller, and Burns (1978) to test the accuracy of recollection. Half the subjects saw the picture with the stop sign at the corner and half the picture with the yield sign.

pictures.) Immediately after viewing the slide series, the subjects answered a number of questions about them. One of the questions presupposed the existence of either a stop sign or a yield sign. For half the subjects the presupposed sign was consistent with what they had actually seen; for half it was inconsistent. The subjects then performed a distracting task for twenty minutes, after which a final recognition test began. The researchers showed the subjects fifteen pairs of slides and asked them to choose the one slide out of each pair that they had seen before. How do you think the subjects responded when shown two views of the intersection—one with a stop sign and one with a yield sign? When the critical question asked earlier had presupposed a traffic sign *consistent* with what the subjects had actually seen, they chose the correct sign 75 percent of the time. In contrast, when the earlier question presupposed an *in*consistent traffic sign, the subjects chose the correct slide only 41 percent of the time. Thus, presuppositions do indeed seem capable of *transforming* a witness's memory. The rate at which such transformations occur, moreover, can be substantially increased by changing the timing of misinformation. If exposed to inaccurate information a week after witnessing an accident, when the true details have begun to fade, subjects are susceptible to the misinformation 80 percent of the time (Loftus, Miller, and Burns, 1978).

To what extent can a witness's memory be shaped by suggestion? Further than you would probably think. Even rather implausible false information can often be injected into memory. Loftus (1979) managed to induce subjects to accept suggestions as unlikely as a telephone booth in a farmyard! In all cases, however, people's susceptibility to implausible suggestions was substantially less than their susceptibility to plausible ones.

There appears to be a limit, then, as to how far our recollections can be swayed. Information to which we have committed ourselves is particularly resistant to change. If we publicly state that we remember a particular detail to be one way, it is unlikely that subsequent suggestions will cause us to change our minds (Loftus, 1977). In addition, we tend to resist information that blatantly contradicts a clearly perceived detail. In one experiment, for example, subjects viewed a series of slides showing the theft of a large, bright red wallet from a woman's handbag. Few accepted the blatantly false suggestion that the wallet had in fact been brown (Loftus, 1979). This clumsy lie, moreover, made most subjects suspicious of subsequent false information to which they might ordinarily fall prey. Thus, although our memories may be malleable, they are not infinitely so.

Besides helping reveal how memory works, research on eyewitness testimony is important for other reasons. In criminal and civil trials, jurors tend to believe the testimony of eyewitnesses, and yet such testimony can be faulty, sometimes leading to mistaken identity. No one is immune from the possibility of being mistakenly identified—whether he or she is a criminal or a priest. In fact, in August 1979, a Roman Catholic priest stood trial for a series of armed robberies in Delaware. He had been identified by seven witnesses as the "gentleman bandit," so called because of the polite manners of the well-dressed robber. At the priest's trial, this parade of witnesses positively identified the accused priest. Then, in a move that could have come from a television melodrama, the trial was abruptly halted when another man confessed to the robberies. Police became convinced that this man had committed the crimes when he told them details that only the robber himself could have known. The prosecutor dropped the charges against the priest, and his tragedy was finally over. The priest was lucky in one respect: others who have been convicted of crimes on the basis of misidentification have not been released until they have spent a year, sometimes five, occasionally more than ten in prison.

THE RELATIONSHIP BETWEEN SHORT-TERM AND LONG-TERM MEMORY

We have talked in some detail about the nature of long-term memory, how the information in it is stored and retrieved, and how it can sometimes be transformed. But we have not yet discussed the relationship between long-term and short-term memory. Are these separate and distinct systems? Certainly there are several significant differences between them. Consider short-term memory. Its duration is brief—under twenty seconds if information is not renewed by rehearsal. The capacity of short-term memory is also very limited—it can hold no more than nine items and perhaps as few as five. Long-term memory, in contrast, endures for many years. Some of our long-term memories never fade. Moreover, the capacity of long-term memory is virtually limitless. Even if a person lives to be a hundred, he or she can continue to store new information in long-term memory. These differences suggest that short-term and long-term memory are in fact separate systems. A number of laboratory and clinical findings strongly support this view.

Evidence for a dual memory

Studies involving what is known as **free recall** lend substantial support to the **dual memory view**. In a typical experiment, subjects are presented with a list of words, one at a time, and then asked to recall as many as they can in whatever order. The results are represented in Figure 6.13. This graph is called a **serial**

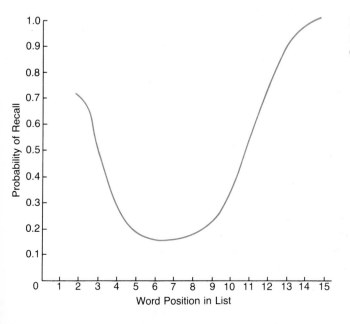

Figure 6.13 Results of a free-recall experiment: a serial-position curve (after Loftus and Loftus, 1976).

position curve, because it shows the percentage of words, averaged over many trials, that subjects recall at each of the positions on the list. As you can see, memory for words at the end of the list is excellent, memory for words at the beginning is also good, and memory of words in the middle is weakest of all. Those who believe that short-term and long-term memory are two distinct systems explain this pattern in the following way: The nearer a word is to the end of the list, they argue, the greater the likelihood that it is still in short-term memory. Such words would naturally be recalled very well. The words at the beginning of the list are also recalled quite well, but for a very different reason: Because subjects have had more time to rehearse and think about them, these items are more likely to be fixed in long-term memory. In short, the shape of the curve reflects the existence of two separate memory "storage compartments."

A variation of the free-recall experiment just described provides further evidence in support of this view. As usual, subjects are presented with a list of words. This time, however, before they are given a chance to recall, they are asked to perform a distracting mental task, such as counting backward by threes from 100. If memory is a single system, this task should interfere equally with recall of *all* the words on the list—that is, the resulting curve should be virtually the same shape as the one in Figure 6.13, only lower on the graph. But this is definitely not the case. Generally speaking, such a task interferes with memory *only* for words at the end of the list, as shown in Figure 6.14. For those who adopt a dual memory view, this result is not the least bit surprising. The distracting mental task, they argue, enters short-term memory and so dislodges the words that were formerly held there. Words at the beginning of the list, on the other hand, should hardly be affected at all because they are stored in long-term memory, not short-term.

As persuasive as this support for a dual memory system is, the condition known as **anterograde amnesia** provides even more compelling evidence. This form of amnesia affects memory only for new events. Things that were learned before the condition started are recalled perfectly. Neuropsychologist Brenda

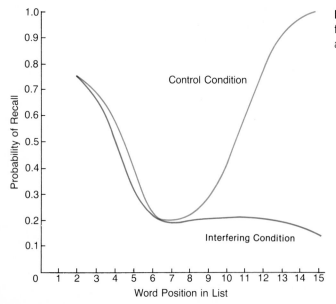

Figure 6.14 Results of a modified free-recall experiment. (After Loftus and Loftus, 1976.)

Milner (1966) studied a number of people with anterograde amnesia and has described in detail the case of one young man whom she referred to as H. M. This man developed his tragic condition after radical brain surgery to relieve severe epileptic seizures. Although H. M. was actually twenty-nine at the time Milner interviewed him, he believed that he was twenty-seven—his age at the time of the operation. He could remember new experiences only as long as he paid attention to them; as soon as he shifted his attention the memories would be lost. As a result, he faced enormous problems in his daily life. When his family moved, for example, he was completely unable to remember the new address. Over and over he would return to the old house. For those who seek evidence for a dual memory system, a very plausible explanation for H. M.'s condition is this: The operation somehow destroyed this man's ability to transfer information from short-term to long-term memory. There must, they argue, be two types of memory, which are separate and distinct systems.

The depth of processing view

The dual memory view has received widespread support, but it is not without its critics. Some psychologists have argued that the observed differences between short-term and long-term memory might be attributed not to separate memory systems but to differences in the way that information is processed. If, on the one hand, we process information "shallowly," then instatement into memory will be weak, and forgetting will quickly occur. If, on the other hand, we process information "deeply," then we are likely to remember it much longer. This argument is called the **depth of processing view**.

But what exactly is meant by shallow and deep processing? Intuitively, it seems reasonable to surmise that some kind of semantic processing (probing the meaning of a word) would be deeper and therefore result in better retention, than visual or auditiory processing (focusing on the look or sound of a word). Craik and Tulving (1975) designed a series of experiments to test this hypothesis. In one study they asked subjects one of several types of questions about each word on a list. Sometimes the question related to the *look* of the word—for example, "Is it written in capital letters?" Other times the question pertained to the *sound* of the word—for instance, "Does it rhyme with weight?" And still other times the question had to do with the *meaning* of the word—"Would it fit in the following sentence?" Thus, the questions induced processing at one of three different levels: visual, auditory, or semantic. The researchers then distributed another list of words and asked the subjects to check off all items that had appeared on the previous list. As expected, memory of a given word increased as processing went from visual to auditory to semantic. The greater the depth of processing, then, the better the retention.

The depth of processing view of memory is still relatively new, so its validity as a general theory remains to be demonstrated. Ultimately, however, it seems likely that physiological research will provide the final answer to the question of whether human memory is a dual or a unitary system. As you will see in the following section, the findings in this area to date seem to support the notion of a dual memory. Certainly the results of depth of processing experiments like those by Craik and Tulving are not incompatible with this view. Shallow or deep processing of information held in short-term memory might determine what and how much gets transferred to long-term storage.

THE PHYSIOLOGY OF MEMORY

A central mystery of memory is how, physiologically, we manage to record information. The answer lies somewhere in the billions of interconnected neurons that make up a human brain. Some of the earliest clues to the biological basis of memory came from clinical findings. When a person suffers a severe blow to the head, as might happen in an automobile crash, he or she may lose all recollection of events leading up to and during the accident. (Such a condition is called **retrograde amnesia** because the memory deficit involves only a specific segment of the past, not recollection of new events.) These symptoms imply that information stored in short-term memory at the time a head injury occurs is held far more fragilely than information stored in long-term memory. This, in turn, suggests that long-term and short-term memory may employ two separate physiological mechanisms.

What could the fragile, short-term mechanism be? The answer is far from clear. But many neurophysiologists believe that it somehow involves a temporary circulation of electrical impulses around complex loops of interconnected neurons. This theory is supported both directly and indirectly. Some indirect evidence is provided by the fact that any event that either suppresses neural activity (such as a blow to the head, carbon monoxide poisoning, or heavy anesthesia), or causes neurons to fire incoherently (such as electroconvulsive shock) can apparently "erase" information held in short-term memory. (As we will later see, these same factors also appear to interfere with the transfer of information from short-term to long-term memory.) More direct evidence comes from studies in which researchers have probed the brains of experimental animals with electrodes and found that different circulating patterns of electrical activity are indeed associated with attention to different stimuli (Vereano et al., 1970). Exactly how such activity relates to short-term memory, however, still remains a mystery.

Whatever the basis of short-term memory is, the brain must ultimately have some means of transferring information from short-term to long-term storage. One thing that is certain is that this transfer process takes time. In a classic experiment, Duncan (1949) trained rats to run from a darkened compartment on the flash of a light in order to avoid an electric shock to their feet. After each training session, the rats were given electroconvulsive shock (ECS) administered through the ears. (Electroconvulsive shock means that enough electrical current passes through the brain to induce convulsions and unconsciousness.) The timing of the ECS varied for each rat. Some were shocked as soon as twenty seconds after training; others were shocked after intervals of as long as fourteen hours. As you might expect, the rats that received the ECS shortly after training showed almost no recollection of what they had previously experienced about darkened rooms and flashing lights. But significantly, the rats that had received ECS up to an hour after training *also* showed memory deficits. Thus, it seemed to take a period of nearly an hour for an experience to become firmly fixed in a long-term memory. The idea that a series of solidifying events occurs when a memory is acquired is termed the **consolidation hypothesis**. If ECS is given *after* consolidation is complete—that is, after information is instated into long-term memory—no memory loss occurs.

Because most long-term memories are so impervious to artificially induced

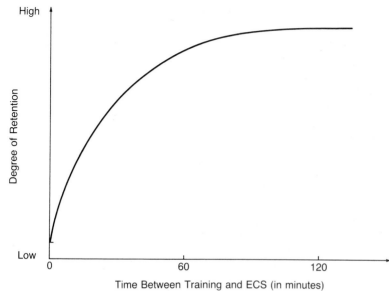

Figure 6.15 Typical gradient of retrograde amnesia. The degree of retention increases as the amount of time between the training (for instance, avoiding an electric shock) and the posttraining treatment (for instance, electroconvulsive shock) is lengthened.

change, neurophysiologists assume they must reflect relatively permanent alterations in the ways that neurons interconnect. Remember from Chapter 3 that electrochemical messages are transmitted from neuron to neuron across tiny junction gaps called synapses. Synapses, then, are the means by which neurons "communicate." Consequently, scientists believe that long-term memory must involve some sort of synaptic change. Such change could be either structural or chemical—or perhaps both. By structural change scientists mean changes in the size or the number of neural synapses. By chemical change they mean changes in the amount or the composition of the transmitter substances that carry neural impulses across synapses. It may be that the neural activity associated with short-term memory is itself capable of initiating the physical changes that create long-term memory traces. Alternatively, neural activity may initiate only the first stage of consolidation into long-term memory.

In spite of the logic of these assumptions, specific neurological changes due to learning and memory stubbornly elude researchers. Perhaps their measurement techniques are not yet sensitive enough. Perhaps in the near future more sophisticated methods of probing the brain will allow the detection of subtle changes in neural tissue associated with memory formation. At this point we at least know that environmental stimuli are capable of effecting gross changes in the anatomy and physiology of the brain. Consider, for example, a fascinating series of experiments with young rats. Baby rats from the same litter were placed in two radically different environments. One was an "enriched" environment that consisted of wheels, ladders, slides, and a variety of other "toys" that the rats could explore and manipulate. The researchers changed the toys frequently so as to ensure a continual barrage of new learning experiences. The remaining rats were placed in an "impoverished" environment that consisted of an empty cage located in an isolated room. After nearly three months in their respective worlds the young rats were killed and their brains compared. The differences were dramatic. The cerebral cortices of rats that had spent their days in the enriched setting were thicker and heavier, endowed with more blood vessels, and contained more of an enzyme related to the neurotransmitter acetylcholine than did the cortices of the animals relegated to the impoverished environment (Rosenzweig, Bennett, and Diamond, 1972). What's more, subsequent research revealed that rats raised in an enriched environment had a significantly greater number of dendrite spines on their cortical neurons, dendrite spines being the structures on a neuron where other neurons connect to form synapses (Globus et al., 1973). Such experiments clearly demonstrate that various kinds of neural changes do result from different kinds of experience. But whether and how such changes might be related to the formation of memory traces remains unknown. No alteration in brain tissue has yet been found to be the mechanism of long-term memory.

Although scientists are still a very long way from understanding the biological processes underlying memory, it is clear that the permanent structural and/or chemical changes associated with memory formation must somehow involve changes in the way an organism's genes are expressed. Those who are unfamiliar with the subject of genetics should note that the genes contained in the nucleus of each of the body's cells provide the blueprints for all of the body's biochemical and anatomical features. The instructions coded in the genes are transported from the cell nucleus via various "messenger" molecules composed of ribonucleic acid (RNA). It seems likely, therefore, that if permanent changes take place in the brain when memory traces are formed, the quantity or the composition of RNA in those cells should also change.

Hydén and Egyhazi (1962) first found this to be true, and other researchers have since confirmed their findings. For example, Victor Shashoua at the Harvard University Medical School devised an imaginative technique for studying learning and RNA synthesis in goldfish (Shashoua, 1970). He attached a small piece of styrofoam to a fish's underbelly, causing the animal to float upside down. With great effort, the goldfish eventually learned to right itself and swim normally. Then it was killed and dissected. Analysis of the goldfish's brain showed significant changes in RNA compared with the RNA in the brain of a control fish spared this arduous learning experience. There is an important problem with such studies, however. They do not demonstrate conclusively that the observed changes in RNA are related to memory formation rather than to some other factor, such as stress or muscular activity, associated with the learning task.

The logical link between RNA synthesis and the development of long-term memory traces has intrigued many researchers. Some have even wondered if memory might not be transferred from one organism to another simply by injecting the RNA from the brain of a "trained" individual into the brain of a "naive" one. McConnell and his colleagues (1966) attempted to find out. They conditioned planarians (flatworms) to contract their bodies on the flash of a light by repeatedly pairing the light with an electric shock. (Planarians naturally contract when shocked but not usually when stimulated by light.) They then extracted RNA from the trained planarians and injected it into the untrained ones. The naive planarians contracted in response to light more often than control planarians did. McConnell speculated that specific memories might in fact be chemically transferrable, and this idea became widely publicized. Perhaps, science-fiction writers proposed, we might one day learn the theory of relativity simply by consuming some RNA from the brain of a theoretical physicist!

Memory transfer studies have many serious problems, however. One is the enormous difficulty in replicating them. At times even the same researchers have been unable to reproduce their own findings. In addition, because large molecules like RNA cannot cross a cell membrane, it is difficult to imagine how they might penetrate the brain cells of another organism. It is much more likely that the results obtained in certain memory transfer studies are caused instead by a chemical other than RNA (Ungar, 1970). Significantly, many of the RNA extracts used in such studies have also contained other substances. This chemical might be a hormone or another substance that has a general arousing or tranquilizing effect. If so, then the substance is not so much a "memory molecule" as a chemical that somehow facilitates learning or simply enhances performance (McGaugh, 1966). In any case, most scientists now agree that injecting RNA from the brain of one organism into the brain of another cannot in itself transfer specific memories. A memory can be formed only if the appropriate structural and/or chemical changes occur in an animal's neural synapses, and externally produced RNA cannot induce these changes.

The scientific investigation of memory and the brain has only begun. Even after the mechanisms of short-term and long-term storage are better understood, there are many other mysteries to unravel. Consider retrieval, for example. The average adult can quite quickly recall any one of many thousands of facts and experiences stored away in the brain. How is such remarkably efficient retrieval accomplished? Why do we not have to laboriously sort through an enormous number of episodes just to arrive at the memory of a single event? No one yet knows. Undoubtedly in the years ahead many fascinating discoveries will be made in this and other frontier areas of neurophysiology.

FORGETTING

Until now we have concentrated primarily on the successful side of human memory. We have seen that people can instate, store, and retrieve information from long-term memory with a reasonable degree of speed and accuracy, even if some distortions of memory occur. But what about the all-too-familiar process called forgetting? It too is of interest to psychologists.

Psychologist Marigold Linton (1978), frustrated by the undependability of her own memory, set out in the early 1970s to investigate the phenomenon of forgetting personal experiences. Following the lead of the nineteenth-century memory researcher Hermann Ebbinghaus (1885), Linton chose herself as the most willing and reliable subject available. For six years she recorded on file cards two or more discrete events that happened to her each day. The entries varied from mundane occurrences such as eating dinner at a Chinese restaurant to rather unusual happenings like an important job interview. Every month she tested her recall of some 150 events selected at random from the card file. The results were not encouraging. By the end of 1978, Linton had slowly but steadily forgotten almost a third of the events she had considered memorable six years earlier.

Theories of forgetting

What are the reasons for this persistent pattern of forgetting? Psychologists have suggested three major causes: decay, interference, and motivated forgetting. Although these explanations conflict with one another in several important ways, they are not entirely incompatible. A full account of forgetting should probably include all three.

Decay of memory traces Perhaps the oldest theory of forgetting is that memories simply fade away, or **decay**, with the passage of time if they are not renewed through periodic use. This notion has a certain poetic appeal and tends to fit well with some of our personal experiences. The memory of a movie seen last week, for example, is usually stronger and more detailed than that of a movie seen last year. Nevertheless, some of the things we know about human memory appear to contradict decay theory. For one thing, not all long-term memories seem to dissipate with time. Motor skills, for instance, are particularly resistant to decay. An adult who has not ridden a bicycle in twenty years usually has no trouble demonstrating the skill for a child. Second, if long-term memories do in fact fade over the years, then the structural or chemical changes in the brain that originally encoded those memories must also break down in some way. As yet, however, we do not know why such a breakdown would regularly and spontaneously occur. The concept of decay, then, may be useful in explaining loss from fragile short-term memory, but its application to long-term memory is open to question.

Interference The phenomenon of **interference** is another reason for forgetting. According to this view, memory of a year-old movie fades due to the unavoidable confusion that results when people subsequently encounter very similar experiences (such as other movies or television shows). Although interference probably does not explain all forgetting, it does account for some interesting experimental findings. Suppose you were asked to memorize list A below and then to memorize list B.

A	B
happy	gay
big	large
hard	solid
funny	humorous
thin	slender
calming	soothing
neat	tidy

If sometime later you were asked to recall list A, you might very well add some of the words from list B. This confusion of similar items is said to result from interference. When information learned later interferes with information learned earlier, psychologists say that **retroactive interference** has taken place. (*Retro* means "backward in time.") In contrast, when material learned earlier interferes with recall of material learned later, **proactive interference** has occurred. (*Pro* means "forward in time.")

Sleep seems to be one of the best safeguards against interference. Research has shown that people forget substantially less if they sleep for several hours after learning than if they continue their waking activities. In one experiment subjects who stayed awake for eight hours recalled only about 10 percent of material they had previously learned, whereas subjects who slept for eight hours remembered about 60 percent of the same material (Jenkins and Dallenbach, 1924). Presumably, those who went to sleep were not subject to interference. These findings can be applied to your own study habits. Getting a good night's sleep after studying for an exam will probably increase your powers of recall in the morning.

Motivated forgetting It is not hard to believe that we sometimes forget because we *want* to. Such **motivated forgetting** is, in fact, the foundation of Freud's psychoanalytic theory. According to Freud, people often push unacceptable, anxiety-provoking thoughts and impulses into their unconscious so as to avoid confronting them directly. This psychological defense mechanism is called **repression**. Thus, a young woman who is sexually attracted to her father may try to repress her disturbing incestuous desires. But her behavior may indicate that these feelings are not completely forgotten. The woman may pause or fumble for words when discussing certain things about her father, and she may show other signs of anxiety such as sweating or blushing.

Not all motivated forgetting is a defense mechanism against severe anxiety, however. Research shows that people generally tend to forget unpleasant experiences more readily than pleasant ones, even when the unpleasant events are not especially threatening. In one early experiment students returning to college after Christmas vacation tended to remember more pleasant than unpleasant experiences about the holiday. Moreover, when unexpectedly interviewed again six week later, the same students remembered even fewer unpleasant holiday experiences relative to pleasant ones (Meltzer, 1930). Negative memories, it appears, are banished more readily than positive ones.

Part of this tendency to remember the past as better than it actually was may be motivated by a desire to enhance our own self-esteem. Research shows that people often remember themselves as having held more responsible, better-paying jobs than they actually had. They also recall donating more to charity, voting more frequently, and raising more intelligent children than objective records indicate (Cannell and Kahn, 1968). We tend, in other words, to edit our personal memories so as to cast ourselves in a more favorable light (Myers and Ridl, 1979). From this point of view forgetting is partly self-serving.

How much do we really forget?

The theories of interference and motivated forgetting suggest an interesting possibility. Perhaps many of the things we fail to remember are not really completely lost. Perhaps they lie somewhere in the recesses of the brain, awaiting the right retrieval cue to coax them to the surface. The notion that forgetting reflects a retrieval failure and not a permanent memory loss has widespread appeal. In an informal survey of people across the country, including many professional psychologists, 75 percent agreed with this point of view (Loftus and Loftus, 1980).

What is the basis of this conviction that memories are essentially indelible, even if many are difficult to retrieve? The evidence is quite intriguing. As mentioned in Chapter 3, brain surgeon Wilder Penfield has found that people sometimes report vivid memories of apparently long-forgotten events when parts of the cerebral cortex are electrically stimulated (Penfield, 1969). For example, when a mild electrical current was passed through a region of one patient's brain, he claimed to hear an old tune being played. Another patient "relived" the birth of her child through brain stimulation. Yet another "revisited" the midway of a traveling circus. In these and other instances, Penfield reports, it is as though a former stream of consciousness is made to flow again with all the clarity of the original experience.

Although Penfield's findings are especially convincing, other evidence also supports the belief that whatever enters long-term storage may well remain there for life. For instance, we have all experienced sudden recall of some long-forgotten detail from the past. You might be walking by the building where you attended grade school and unexpectedly remember an event that happened to you in the playground as a very young child. Similarly, many psychologists have been impressed with the apparent ability of people in a hypnotic trance to give detailed reports of events that occurred long ago. The hypnotist might ask a subject to describe his sixth birthday, and the subject complies with a detailed account of a child's party complete with cake, decorations, presents, and guests. People undergoing psychoanalysis also seem to dredge up deeply repressed happenings from the distant past. Surely these are strong indications that virtually everything we learn stays permanently locked away in memory. All we seem to need is the proper key.

As compelling as these findings may seem, however, they can all be explained in other ways. For example, of the small percentage of Penfield's patients who actually experienced lifelike memories from brain stimulation, some reported events as though observing them from the sidelines, much as we often do in a dream. Others recalled being in places where in all probability they had never really been. There is a good possibility, therefore, that many of Penfield's cases of memory "retrieval" did not involve accurate retrieval at all. Instead of "reliving" the past these people may simply have been reconstructing it. Similarly, although hypnotized subjects are usually convinced that what they report is true, objective evidence often contradicts them. It can frequently be shown that the subject has committed an error called **confabulation**: When unable to retrieve a certain item from memory, he or she manufactures something else that seems inappropriate. Thus, the man asked to remember his sixth birthday combines his recollections of several childhood parties and invents the missing details. The same may be true of many people who appear to recover memories through psychoanalysis.

The evidence for memory permanence, then, is not as strong as it appears at first glance. But this fact alone does not demonstrate that some memories are completely and irrevocably lost. Unfortunately, permanent forgetting is a phenomenon that can never really be proved. Simply because we fail to retrieve a memory is not absolute proof that the memory trace no longer exists. Still, if we can show that rigorous efforts to dislodge the information are unsuccessful, we at least have a strong indication that complete memory loss *may* occur.

Loftus performed such rigorous tests in variations of the eyewitness testimony studies discussed earlier. First, she subtly suggested to subjects that they had viewed a traffic sign other than the one they had actually seen. Most of the subjects incorporated the false information into their recollections of the picture in question. But was the correct information still stored somewhere in memory? Loftus tried to find out. She provided subjects with powerful incentives for correct responses—up to twenty-five dollars in cash—and still most clung to the misinformation (Loftus, 1979). She offered subjects a second chance to give the correct response (out of three possible choices), but their performance on the second try was no better than sheer guessing (Loftus, 1979). Such results imply that the true information may have been entirely and permanently dismissed.

The fact that memories may be impermanent, however, should not be cause for dismay. Consider what life would be like if we *never* forgot. For thirty years the Russian psychologist Aleksandr Luria studied a man with a so-called "perfect" memory (Luria, 1968). This man remembered everything in astonishing detail. Images of each experience haunted him for hours. Whatever he had seen, done, read, or heard—pleasant and unpleasant, trivial and important, from his earliest childhood to his old age—stayed in his memory, shifting, combining, piling up. He was left with a junk heap of impressions. Often he got confused and frustrated. The mere thought of such complete and total recall is probably enough to make most of us grateful to have an ordinary memory— one that lets us remember almost everything we want or need to and forget almost everything else.

SUMMARY

1. Sensory memory is the momentary lingering of sensory information after a stimulus has been removed. This information is held within the receiving sensory system, not in some central region of the brain. A person can store a great deal of information in sensory memory, but its duration is very brief—only about a second.

2. Short-term memory is often considered "working" memory. Whatever you are actively thinking about at a given moment is held in this system.

3. Instatement of information into short-term memory must somehow be limited, otherwise we would surely be overwhelmed by sensory stimuli. One process that contributes to this screening of information is **sensory gating**. It involves a turning of one kind of sensory channel while simultaneously turning down others. Another process crucial to preventing short-term memory overload is **selective attention**, a damping down of some of the information entering a given sensory channel while directing attention to other information entering the same channel.

4. Once information is instated into short-term memory, it will fade in less than half a minute if not renewed by **rehearsal**. The rehearsal process usually involves some kind of speech—either overt (saying the information aloud) or implicit (repeating it mentally).

5. In addition to being of rather short duration, short-term memory is also rather limited in capacity: it seems to hold only between five and nine items. But through "chunking" (perceiving groups of related items as larger units) we can greatly increase the amount of information processed in short-term memory at any one time.

6. In contrast to short-term memory, **long-term memory** stores information indefinitely, and its capacity is essentially limitless. Successful transfer of information from short-term to long-term storage depends on both the amount and the type of rehearsal.

7. Retrieval from long-term memory is measured in two basic ways: **recognition** and **recall**. Recognition seems to involve a kind of matching process. We consider a given stimulus and decide whether it matches something already stored in memory. Recall appears to be somewhat more complex. It demands that we first search through memory and locate appropriate information before we test for a "match." This search is largely directed by retrieval cues. So when retrieval cues are weak and we may have difficulty recalling and experience the **tip-of-the-tongue phenomenon.**

8. Fortunately, a number of simple techniques, called **mnemonic devices**, can greatly improve virtually anyone's performance on recall tasks. Some involve clever ways of organizing information when it is stored in memory. Others make effective use of imagery. Still others are based on reconstructing the context in which information was learned.

9. One fascinating aspect of long-term memory is the extent to which it appears to involve a process of active construction. New information is assimilated within the framework of existing knowledge and beliefs, making us prone to recast or dismiss facts that do not fit our expectations. At the same time, information acquired after an event has taken place can transform our memory of that experience. This process is especially important to keep in mind when evaluating the accuracy of eyewitness testimony.

10. Many psychologists believe that long-term and short-term memory are two separate systems, a view that is supported by a number of laboratory and clinical findings. However, other psychologists argue that the apparent differences between long-term and short-term memory might instead be attributed to differences in the "depth" with which people process information. Although there is also strong evidence to support this **depth of processing view**, it is not incompatible with the idea of a **dual memory system**.

11. The ultimate answer to the question of whether human memory involves two separate systems may come from the study of the brain. Scientists still know very little about how, physiologically, our brains manage to store information. The current thinking is that short-term memory somehow involves a temporary circulation of electrical impulses around complex loops of neurons. Long-term memory, in constrast, is thought to involve some kind of permanent change—either structural or chemical or both—in the way that neurons interconnect. What these changes are, however, remains a mystery.

12. Although psychologists have concentrated on the study of memory, they have also investigated the process of forgetting. Three major causes of forgetting have been proposed. **Decay theory** suggests that memories simply fade away, or decay, with the passage of time if they are not renewed through periodic use. The concept of **interference** holds that forgetting is basically due to the confusion that results when we encounter very similar stimuli. Finally, forgetting may also be **motivated**—we may forget because we want to forget. A complete account of forgetting should probably include all three of these explanations.

13. Psychologists are not yet certain how much of what we learn over a lifetime is retained and how much is forgotten. Some have argued that we permanently retain almost everything we learn, but we often lack the retrieval cues needed to bring these momories to the surface. Others believe that at least a portion of the information we acquire is permanently altered or lost. Unfortunately, permanent forgetting may be a phenomenon that can never really be proved.

Suggested readings

Baddeley, A. D. *The psychology of memory*. New York: Basic Books, 1976.

Crowder, R. G. *Principles of learning and memory*. Hillsdale, N.J.: Erlbaum, 1976.

Haber, R. N. Eidetic images. *Scientific American*, 1969, *220*, 36–44.

Klatzky, R. *Human memory: Structures and processes*. San Francisco: Freeman, 1979.

Loftus, E. F. *Memory*. Reading, Mass.: Addison-Wesley, 1980.

Loftus, G. R., and Loftus, E. F. *Human memory: The processing of information*. Hillsdale, N.J.: Erlbaum, 1976.

PREVIEW

1. Thought, which is more than learning or memory alone, involves the purposeful organization of information in a novel way.

2. Classifying similar objects and events into concepts allows us to formulate the rules and principles necessary for complex thinking.

3. Problem solving requires familiarity with relevant concepts and their interrelationships. It proceeds sequentially: interpretation of problem, search for solutions, selection of solution.

4. To make a logical decision, it is necessary to consider both the value of each potential outcome and its probability.

5. Our decisions are not always logical, especially if they are complex or made under stress. They can be improved, however, by examining the systematic biases that lead to faulty decision making.

7 Cognition and problem solving

A bear, starting from point P, walks one mile due south, turns left and walks one mile due east, turns left again and walks one mile due north. It is now precisely at point P, where it began. What color is the bear? At first glance this problem may seem ridiculous, but don't give up. Where on the earth's surface could a bear possibly walk three miles in the manner described and return to its starting point? Clearly, the only place is the North Pole, which means that the animal must be a white polar bear.

The very fact that you can solve such a problem demonstrates that there is much more to human cognitive capabilities than learning and memory alone. Although you held in memory all the separate facts needed to arrive at the answer, you had to combine these facts in a novel way to yield the correct response. This process of organizing information in our minds to help accomplish some desired end is the essence of what we call thought. In our ability to engage in complex thinking—to ponder, to reason logically, to draw conclusions, to have sudden bursts of creative insight—we humans are unparalleled in the living world.

Yet mental activities are highly subjective and thus not easy to explore. If you were a researcher how might you go about studying the workings of the human mind? In the early part of this century many psychologists used a method called **introspection**. A subject was typically given a question or problem and asked to describe in detail the thought processes leading to an answer. The accumulated results were believed to reveal much about the way the human mind operates. But other psychologists were critical of the introspection method. Behaviorists at the time were very skeptical that such a technique could ever provide accurate and meaningful data. As a result, early behaviorists took the radical view that the study of human thought processes had no place in the scientific investigation of behavior. Psychology, they argued, should be confined to activities that can be directly observed and measured. Contemporary psychologists agree that research must be objective and scientific, but they also believe that the mental activities that intervene between an external stimulus and an organism's response are far too important to be ignored. This is why interest in cognitive processes has steadily grown in recent decades until today it is a major field of investigation.

The difficulty of studying human thought, however, still remains. When people are simply asked to explain what factors influenced a particular response, their replies often contradict the observable facts. Consider the results of a classic experiment conducted by Norman Maier (1931). He hung two long strings from the ceiling of his laboratory, positioning them far enough apart so that a person could not hold the end of one and reach the other. Subjects were asked to figure out ways of tying the two strings together. They were allowed to use any object found in the laboratory, including pliers, clamps, extension cords, ringstands, and poles. Every time a subject came up with a solution, such as tying an extension cord to one string and pulling it toward the other, Maier would say "Now do it another way." One solution was particularly elusive. This was the pendulum technique. By tying a pair of pliers or some other weight onto the end of one of the strings, that string could be set swinging and grasped as it approached the other string. Although few subjects thought of this solution on their own, most were susceptible to a hint. When Maier saw that a subject was clearly stumped for another approach, he would walk by one of the strings and casually set it in motion. Within less than a minute the hint usually "took," and the subject was busy constructing a pendulum. But here is the curious part. When asked what caused the pendulum idea to occur to them, very few subjects mentioned Maier's hint. Most gave vague answers like "It just dawned on me" or "It was the only thing left." Yet the hint had undeniably been influential. The unavoidable conclusion, then, was that thought processes were going on in these people's minds of which they were totally unaware!

Subsequent research has shown that this is not an isolated case. In a lengthy series of studies Nisbett and Wilson (1977) found that subjects can easily make mistakes in assessing the impact of a stimulus on their behavior, especially when that impact differs from what one would normally expect. Under these circumstances, people often maintain that a truly influential factor has no effect on them, or they insist that a noninfluential one was indeed important. Nisbett and Wilson argue that people tend to assess a factor as influential if logic or cultural norms suggest that it *should* be influential. In short, our estimates of the causes of our own behavior may be little more than plausibility judgments. Although we are certainly aware of the content of our thoughts at any given moment, we apparently have very limited access to what affects our thinking. If this view is correct, then introspection would not be a very reliable method of exploring cognitive processes. This is one reason why many psychologists who study cognition prefer to focus on mental activities that have results they can observe and measure.

In this chapter we will examine some of the results of these investigations. Because cognition is such a broad topic, including all the numerous activities of the mind, our focus must be limited. We will concentrate on three areas that psychologists have examined in depth: concept formation and structure, problem solving, and decision making. In the process we hope to reveal some important generalizations about human thought. One of them is a curious paradox: Although the human brain is truly remarkable in the amount of information it can store and retrieve, and although the average human can solve problems of enormous complexity, the amount of information that can actually be processed at any one time is significantly restricted by the limited capacities of our short-term memories. You will see the impact of this restriction at many points in this chapter.

USING CONCEPTS

If asked what you saw in front of you at this moment, you would undoubtedly answer with a series of single-word names: a book, a pen, a coffee mug, a lamp, a desk, a wall. The nature of these responses illustrates an important point about human cognition. Although the world consists of a multitude of objects and events, each in many ways unique, we tend to simplify and order our surroundings by classifying together those things that have common features. The mental constructs that enable us to make such classifications are called **concepts** (Anglin, 1977). A moment's reflection will reveal that your world is very neatly structured through hierarchies of concepts (Collins and Quillian, 1969). The object in your hand, for example, may be an instance of the concept *felt-tip pen*, which in turn is an instance of the more general concept *pen*, which in turn is an instance of the even broader concept *writing instrument*. In a similar manner, we classify and subclassify an enormous variety of other objects, qualities, and behaviors that possess shared characteristics.

It is difficult to overestimate the importance of concepts to cognitive processing. In a very real sense, concepts are the building blocks of thought. They enable us to move beyond a welter of unrelated stimuli to impose structure and predictability on the world. With concepts we can take advantage of regularities: We need not treat everything encountered as though it were completely novel and unique. It is an understanding of the concepts *stove* and *hot*, for example, that enables a child once burned by a stove to learn to avoid similar objects. It is your understanding of the concepts *student* and *professor* that guides your behavior in a college classroom. Through concepts, then, we formulate general rules that can be applied to particular situations. Such generalizations make complex thought possible.

Theories of concept formation

Whenever we ask the question "What is that?" we are usually searching for a concept in which to place an unfamiliar stimulus. What does this search process entail? Many psychologists believe that it involves feature comparisons. We compare the salient features of the new stimulus with the features of a concept previously learned. If the two sets of features seem to match, at least along key dimensions, we label the stimulus an instance of the concept.

But how do we arrive at the defining features of a concept in the first place?

Most theories of concept formation suggest that we systematically test a series of hypotheses, guided by some overall strategy. For example, you might begin with what is called a *global hypothesis*: when you first encounter a stimulus said to be an instance of an unfamiliar concept, you assume that all its salient features are defining characteristics until proven otherwise. To give a specific illustration, suppose you are told that a housefly is an example of the concept *arthropod*, but you have no idea what attributes qualify it as such. So you begin by hypothesizing that the concept "arthropod" includes any creature with all the basic features that a housefly possesses: external skeleton, segmented body, membranous wings, six legs, and two antennae. According to this definition, houseflies would be classified as arthropods, as would mosquitoes, wasps, and other flying insects. But now someone tells you that an ant is also an arthropod. Your understanding of the concept must consequently change. Wings cannot be defining features. Through more and more experience with other examples of arthropods you would gradually learn to eliminate from your definition all those features that can be varied and still yield an instance of the concept. This approach to concept formation is called a *focusing strategy* because you begin with a composite hypothesis and gradually focus in on the relevant characteristics.

Alternatively, you might arrive at an understanding of a concept by beginning with a much more limited hypothesis. To continue with our example of learning the concept *arthropod*, you might begin with the tentative assumption that all six-legged creatures belong in this category. Then, as you discover that spiders, centipedes, and lobsters are also arthropods, you would revise your hypothesis until you hit upon those attributes that together differentiate arthropods from other animals: an external skeleton, segmented body, and jointed legs. This approach is called a *scanning strategy* because you systematically scan stimuli for potentially relevant features.

Early research suggested that people generally use some variation of either a focusing or a scanning strategy when attempting to abstract the defining features of an unfamiliar concept (Bruner, Goodnow, and Austin, 1956). There are, however, age-related differences (Gholson, Levine, and Phillips, 1972). Young children tend to be scanners, which is why they often overextend concepts. When a toddler learns that *dog* is the word for the family pet, he or she may apply it not only to dogs but to all other furry creatures as well. Adults, in contrast, often adopt a global focusing strategy, at least when forming new concepts in the laboratory. With this approach errors of underextension are more common. Of course, children also occasionally commit errors of underextension. After learning that the concept telephone refers to a boxlike object with dial and receiver that sits on a table or desk, a child may fail to recognize as an instance of this concept a phone of unusual design.

Psychologists interested in concept formation are currently attempting to formulate a comprehensive theory of this important process. Many issues are still unsettled, but one widely accepted viewpoint is that people begin to form a new concept by selecting a plausible hypothesis from a "pool" of potential hypotheses. In applying this hypothesis to various stimuli, they follow the rule "win-stay, lose-shift." That is, if they receive feedback that they have used the concept correctly, they stick with their current definition; however, if they learn that they have used the concept incorrectly, they return to the hypothesis pool and select another possibility. As this process of hypothesis-testing proceeds, the pool of potentially correct hypotheses is continually narrowed, until eventually the person establishes the meaning of the concept (Levine, 1975). Note that this pattern applies mainly to adults. Although children also test hypotheses, in general they are less cognitively sophisticated in their approaches to concept formation (Gholson, Levine, and Phillips, 1972).

The structure of concepts

In recent years much of the past research on concepts has been severely criticized for failing to take into account the structure of many **natural concepts**—that is, categories we use every day. The problem is that in the laboratory many investigators have found it useful to focus on concepts with totally unambiguous attributes. In a typical experiment, for example, a researcher might arbitrarily decide that all red triangles constitute a concept that subjects are required to discover. Then, by showing the subjects various geometric shapes of different colors and asking them to determine whether each is or is not an instance of the unknown concept, the researcher can deduce the strategies people use to identify a concept's defining features. But how similar, critics ask, are arbitrary concepts like red triangles to the concepts we use in daily life? Do most natural concepts have defining features that are this clear-cut? Psychologist Eleanor Rosch (1975), among others, believes not. Granted some concepts, such as *arthropod*, do have a set of well-defined physical features that apply fairly unambiguously to all instances of the class. But try to list the defining features of such concepts as *furniture, candy,* or *fruit.* You will probably find this rather difficult. Although it is possible with careful thought to perform a feature analysis on these and many other natural concepts, we are unaccustomed to thinking of them in quite this way.

Rosch proposes that we do not encode most natural concepts into memory in terms of a list of defining features. Instead, we encode them in terms of a prototype—that is, an example that best illustrates the concept—plus an implicit understanding of the degree to which stimuli can vary and still be regarded as instances. Rosch points out that this theory explains why some stimuli are considered better instances of a natural concept than others. For example, you would probably agree that a robin or a sparrow is a better instance of the concept *bird* than a penguin or an ostrich. According to Rosch, this is because robins and sparrows are very close to our prototypical bird, whereas penguins and ostriches are not. If natural concepts were learned only in terms of a list of defining features, Rosch asks, why then isn't one example as good as another?

It may be that Rosch is taking too rigid a view of the feature approach to concept formation. For example, Smith and his colleagues (1974) have argued that people may divide the attributes of a concept into "defining" features, which are essential for category membership, and "characteristic" features, which many but not all instances of the concept possess. Thus, a penguin is not considered as good an example of a bird as a robin because, although a penguin has all the defining features of a bird (a two-legged, egg-laying vertebrate with bill, wings, and feathers), it lacks many of the characteristic features of a bird (the ability to fly, for example) (Smith, Shoben, and Rips, 1974). The feature approach, then, may not be as incompatible with the prototype approach as a number of critics currently believe. But whether these two views of the structure of concepts will eventually be reconciled still remains to be seen.

SOLVING PROBLEMS

A knowledge of concepts and relationships among them make problem solving possible. To understand why, observe the role that concepts play in solving the following puzzle. Take six matches all the same size and assemble them so that they form four equilateral triangles with every side equal to the length of a match. Most people find this task quite difficult. If you see the solution it is undoubtedly because of your knowledge of the concepts *triangle* and *pyramid* and how they relate to each other. Only by building a three-dimensional structure, as shown in Figure 7.1, can you perform the task described.

The problems we face every day vary greatly in complexity. They may demand reproductive or creative thinking. **Reproductive thinking** involves the direct application of previous knowledge to a new situation. For example, if you had been asked to form only two equilateral triangles using six matches, you could easily have done so by reproducing two of the familiar three-sided shapes you have drawn many times before. Such a straightforward solution is not possible in situations that require **creative thinking**, for here previously learned rules, for one reason or another, do not apply. Consequently, you must use whatever information you have to generate a solution that is novel in your experience. The pyramid solution to the six-match problem is one example of creative thinking. Another is the solution that the merchant's daughter found to the problem in Figure 7.2. Because it involves insights and innovations, problem solving that requires creative thinking is the most intriguing kind to psychologists and will be the main focus of our discussion.

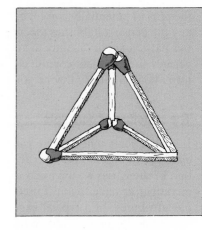

Figure 7.1 The match problem is solved by building a three-dimensional pyramid; most people assume that the matches must lie flat, as they were first perceived.

An old money-lender offered to cancel a merchant's debt and keep him from going to prison if the merchant would give the money-lender his lovely daughter. Horrified yet desperate, the merchant and his daughter agreed to let Providence decide. The money-lender said he would put a black pebble and a white pebble in a bag and the girl would draw one. The white pebble would cancel the debt and leave her free. The black one would make her the money-lender's, although the debt would be canceled. If she refused to pick, her father would go to prison. From the pebble-strewn path they were standing on, the money-lender picked two pebbles and quickly put them in the bag, but the girl saw he had picked up two black ones. What would you have done if you were the girl?

Figure 7.2 Psychologist Edward de Bono uses the terms *vertical* and *lateral thinking* to distinguish between what we have broadly labeled *reproductive* and *creative thinking*, respectively. The problem shown in this figure requires a more flexible, generative, lateral type of thinking. Try to solve the dilemma yourself, and then check your solution with that described in Figure 7.17. (The problem is taken from *New Think*, written by Edward de Bono, the originator of the concept of lateral thinking. © 1967, 1968 Edward de Bono, Basic Books, Inc., Publishers, New York.)

Stages in problem solving

For purposes of analysis, psychologists sometimes divide problem solving into three stages: initially interpreting the problem, searching for solutions, and deciding when a satisfactory answer has been found. The demands of individual problems, of course, vary greatly, so it is doubtful that precisely the same steps are involved in all the problems we solve. Nevertheless, these three basic stages remain a useful way to organize a general discussion of problem solving (Posner, 1973).

Initially interpreting the problem No single aspect of problem solving has a greater impact on the speed and likelihood of a correct solution than how the problem is initially interpreted. Consider Figure 7.3. It shows a circle with a radius of five inches; in it is drawn a right-angled triangle, *xdl*. What is the length of side *l*, that is, of the triangle's hypotenuse? If you are searching your memory for the formula to calculate the length of a hypotenuse, stop. Instead of viewing figure *xdl* as a triangle, view it instead as half a rectangle. Now the solution is obvious. Line *l* is one diagonal of a rectangle, the other diagonal being the radius of the circle. Since you know that the radius is five inches, *l* too must be five inches long. Thus, what at first glance appears to be a fairly difficult problem may suddenly become much easier when interpreted in a different way.

Ironically, then, when you interpret a problem quickly and decisively, you may actually be hindering your ability to solve it. Once you have committed yourself to defining a problem in a certain way you automatically structure available information accordingly, which in turn reduces your chances of seeing better alternatives. This is why psychologists who study problem solving often suggest that people avoid settling on a solution strategy as soon as they encounter a seemingly difficult problem. Instead, they should view the question from various angles, searching for different ways to perceive its requirements. Making notes about the problem, or drawing a simple sketch of it, can help accomplish this end when a problem is presented verbally.

Of course, changing your perspective on a problem is not always easy, especially when the alternative view is in some way unusual. Look at Figure 7.4A, a square consisting of nine dots. Can you connect all the dots with four continuous straight lines without lifting your pencil from the paper? If you are having trouble with this problem it is probably because you have defined its requirements too narrowly. Most people perceive the nine dots as a square and assume that the pencil lines must be drawn within it (Scheerer, 1963). Actually, the only way to solve the problem is to draw lines that extend beyond the perceptual boundaries of the square (Figure 7.4B). The tendency to cling to a commonplace interpretation of a problem, despite the fact that it is not helpful in a particular situation, is called **fixation**. Fixations of all kinds can powerfully inhibit successful problem solving. If you had difficulty solving the six-match problem presented earlier, it was probably because of a strong spatial fixation somewhat similar to the one imposed by the nine dots.

A different type of fixation, which can also severely hinder problem solving,

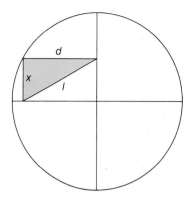

Figure 7.3 Problem illustrating the importance of the initial representation.

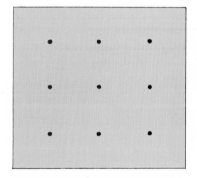

Figure 7.4A Nine dots are arranged in a square. The problem is to connect them by drawing four continuous straight lines without lifting pencil from paper (after Scheerer, 1963).

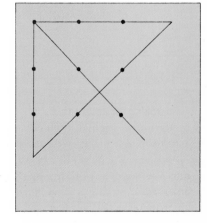

Figure 7.4B The principal impediment in the dot problem is perceptual fixation. It is solved by extending the lines beyond the dots; most people assume that they must stay within the perceived square structure.

Figure 7.5 A problem used by Duncker (1945) to demonstrate functional fixedness: He gave subjects the materials shown and asked them to mount a candle on a wall so that it could be used to give light. Try to solve the problem yourself. (The use of the term "functional fixedness" gives you a clue to the solution of the problem that Duncker's subjects did not have.) The solution is given in Figure 7.17.

is the tendency to view an object as being used only for its customary function. This tendency is called **functional fixedness**. Functional fixedness may help explain why the pendulum solution is so elusive to people faced with Maier's problem of tying together two strings positioned farther apart than the human arm span. A pair of pliers or some other object apt to be found in a laboratory is not ordinarily used as a pendulum weight. Consequently, this alternative function is not likely to occur to people. Another example of a problem where functional fixedness can be an obstacle is illustrated in Figure 7.5 (Duncker, 1945). How would you use these materials to mount a single lighted candle on a vertical wooden wall? Because the candles and the matches are presented in their boxes, you may be encouraged to fixate on the familiar function of a box as a container. But a box can also serve as a platform on which to stand a candle, as illustrated in Figure 7.17. If you were flexible in your view of how a box can be used, you probably arrived at this same solution.

Situational factors can often intensify functional fixedness. For example, if a person's attention is drawn to the customary function of an object just prior to a problem in which the object must be used in a novel way, functional fixedness is more likely to occur. This was demonstrated in a variation of Maier's two-string problem (Birch and Rabinowitz, 1951). Subjects who had just finished wiring a switch or a relay into an electrical circuit were much less likely than control subjects to use a switch or a relay as a pendulum weight. In addition, functional fixedness may also increase when people are required to refer to an object by its usual name, rather than by a nonsense label. This is because an object's name is often strongly associated with its customary function (Glucksburg and Danks, 1968). Perhaps, then, one way to "break" functional fixedness might be to analyze available tools visually, without referring to each by name. Another aid might be to examine thoroughly the separate parts of all objects instead of perceiving them strictly as wholes.

Searching for solutions So far, we have focused on problems that, once interpreted in the right way, yield immediately to solution: The answers seem to leap to mind in a single burst of insight. Not all problems are simply a matter of proper interpretation, however. Sometimes the initial information given must be supplemented or manipulated in some way before the final answer emerges. In such cases, we must search our memories and/or the surrounding environment for the facts and procedures we need to obtain a solution. The interesting aspect of these searches is that they are seldom hit-or-miss. Instead, they are usually guided by an overall strategy that seems capable of getting us where we want to go. Psychologists interested in problem solving have spent a great deal of time investigating these search strategies. They have found that the strategy we select varies primarily with the type of problem we are confronting.

Some problems can best be solved by a strategy called an **algorithm**: a precisely stated set of rules that usually works for solving problems of a particular type. For example, the rules for subtraction of whole numbers, given in Figure

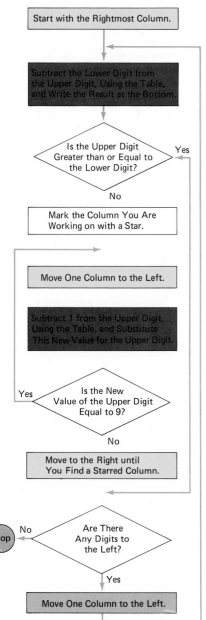

Figure 7.6 An algorithm for subtraction of whole numbers. An infinite number of subtraction problems can be correctly solved by following this precise set of rules. To use the algorithm to solve the sample problem, begin at step 1 and continue down the chart, as directed. Try making up your own subtraction problem and using the algorithm to get the answer (adapted from Lewis and Papadimitriou, 1978).

7.6, form an algorithm that works for all subtraction problems regardless of the specific numbers involved. Similarly, the formula πr^2 is an algorithm for finding the area of a circle, given its radius, regardless of whether the radius is measured in millimeters or miles. As you might guess, the major advantage of an algorithm is that it guarantees success if applied in the right circumstances and followed correctly.

The use of algorithms is not always practical, however. Consider the task of rearranging the letters *koknc* to form an English word. An algorithmic solution would be to systematically arrange the letters in all possible ways until a meaningful combination appeared. Obviously, this procedure could be enormously time-consuming, for five letters can be combined in a total of 120 ways! Most people, therefore, would follow a short-cut strategy: They would focus on letter combinations likely to appear in the English language, such as *kn* at the beginning of a word or *ck* at the end. Using this approach, they would probably discover the work *knock* quite quickly (Bourne, Dominowski, and Loftus, 1979). A rule of thumb problem-solving strategy like this one is called a **heuristic**. Although heuristics do not guarantee success they frequently pay off with very speedy solutions. This is why we tend to use them so often. In the "Adventure of the Dancing Men," Sherlock Holmes, the consummate expert in deductive problem solving, employed a heuristic strategy to decode the puzzling set of hieroglyphics shown in Figure 7.7. Knowing that each man represents a letter, what heuristics would you use to decipher this cryptic five-part message?

The heuristics used for solving anagrams (scrambled word problems) or coded messages are very specific to these particular tasks, but there are also a number of very general heuristics that people commonly use in problem solving of all kinds (Newell and Simon, 1972). One is **subgoal analysis**. Consider a chess

Figure 7.7 Match your skill against that consummate expert in deductive problem solving, Sherlock Homes. The case of Hilton and Elsie Cubitt began when client Hilton handed Sherlock the first hieroglyphic fragment. Several days later Sherlock received three more samples; shortly afterward the last example came. Sherlock rushed into action after seeing the last fragments and realizing that they were addressed to Elsie. Why? What message did these last figures contain? How would you solve this puzzle of the "dancing men"? What heuristics, or rules of thumb, might be helpful? Check your solution with the one explained in the caption of Figure 7.17.

player. A person beginning a game of chess could never consider all the 10^{120} play sequences that are theoretically possible. Even if the person could evaluate one play every micromillisecond (one millionth of one thousandth of a second), it would still take billions upon billions of centuries to consider all the alternatives. Clearly a chess player must have some way of limiting his or her focus. The strategy seems to be to break down the problem of winning the game into a series of smaller problems, or subgoals, each of which is manageable in scope. For example, the person might first determine if the king is in danger of attack, and if so concentrate on moves that protect the king. If, however, the king is safe, the person might proceed to the next most important subgoal: ensuring that all other major pieces are safe. If the other pieces do not need defending, the person might then work through a series of offensive subgoals. In this way the demands on the person's limited information processing capabilities are substantially reduced, even though there is no guarantee that the player will spot the best move.

In one early investigation Karl Duncker (1945) summarized how subgoal analysis often directs memory search in a problem-solving situation. Duncker presented subjects with the following problem:

A person has an inoperable stomach tumor. He can be treated with radiation, but radiation of sufficient intensity will destroy healthy tissue as well as the tumor. How can radiation be used to eliminate the tumor without destroying the healthy tissue surrounding it?

Duncker then asked subjects to "think out loud" while trying to reach a solution. Figure 7.8 is a diagram of the search strategy used by one person who generated an unusually large number of ideas. Early in the problem-solving process, this subject conceptualized the problem in terms of three possible sub-

Figure 7.8 A diagram of the attempts made by one subject to solve the tumor problem posed by Duncker. Note that the subject's thoughts (spoken aloud, as Duncker requested) can be interpreted in terms of a hierarchy—from extremely general syntheses at the top to highly specific analyses at the bottom. The technique of requiring a subject to "think out loud" has since been used repeatedly in studies of problem solving. It is a method that you can use with yourself as subject, with the aid of a tape recorder or pencil and paper (after Duncker, 1945).

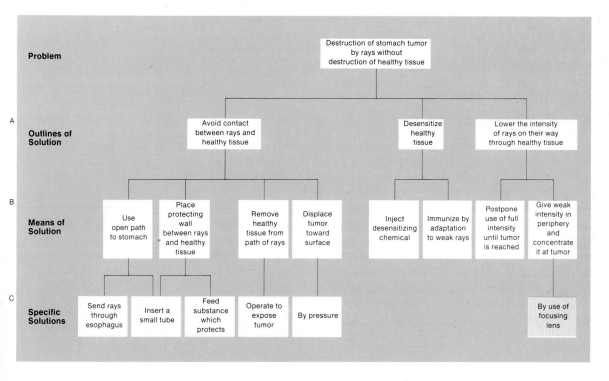

goals: avoiding contact between the radiation and the healthy tissue, desensitizing the healthy tissue, or lowering the intensity of the radiation on its way through the healthy tissue. Each of these subgoals then guided a search for general means that could accomplish that end. In turn, these general means guided the search for specific solutions to the problem. The specific solution that the subject deemed "best" is shown at the lower right-hand corner of the diagram.

Subgoal analysis, of course, is not the only problem-solving strategy people use. Another general heuristic, often applied to problems with very specific goals, is **means-end analysis**. It involves comparing one's current position with a desired end position and then trying to find a means of closing the gap between the two. To take a very simple example, if you had to get to work on a morning when your car broke down, means-end analysis would tell you that you had a distance of, say, five miles between you and your destination. This you might cover by walking, riding a bicycle, or catching a bus that would leave you two miles from the office. Note, however, that means-end analysis has a built-in bias: It encourages you to focus on reducing the *existing* distance between where you are and where you want to be. If, alternatively, a problem can best be solved by first *increasing* the gap between your current state and your desired goal, means-end analysis might actually divert you from the optimum solution. Thus, if you employed a strict means-end analysis on the morning your car broke down, you would be unlikely to consider walking a mile in the *opposite* direction to catch a ride with a friend. Keep the bias of means-end analysis in mind, because it may impede your efforts to solve a problem later in this chapter.

Our brief discussion of means-end analysis points up a central dilemma in problem solving. Human information processing is substantially constrained by the limited capacity of active (short-term) memory, described in Chapter 6. As a result we must find ways of solving problems that avoid cognitive overload. One way is to employ a heuristic that guides our search along selected pathways. In using a heuristic, however, there is always a risk that our attention will be drawn to inferior solutions or to no solutions at all.

The tendency of people to use previously successful heuristics even when they no longer work was demonstrated in a classic experiment by Abraham Luchins (1946). If you had been a subject in one of Luchins's experiments you would have been given a series of six problems like the ones in Figure 7.9. Each problem requires that you imagine three jars, labeled A, B, and C, with the capacities listed from left to right in each row of the table. Your task is to use these jars to measure out the amount of water shown at the far right. For example, in problem 1 you are to use jars with capacities of 21, 127, and 3 quarts to measure out 100 quarts. A moment's thought will probably give you the solution: You fill jar B (127 quarts), pour off enough to fill jar A (21 quarts), and then pour off enough to fill jar C (3 quarts) twice. This will leave you with 100 quarts of water in jar B (127 quarts − 21 quarts − 2 × 3 quarts = 100 quarts). Now proceed to solve the remaining five problems.

If you breezed through problems 2 through 5 but were stumped by problem 6, you probably encountered the same obstacle that two-thirds of Luchins's subjects did. You became so accoustomed to using the strategy jar B − jar A − 2 jar C that you failed to explore other possibilities. Actually, problem 6 is extremely easy: You simply fill jar A and subtract jar C. Luchins found that

Figure 7.9 Luchins's (1946) classic demonstration of set in problem solving. In each of the problems in this series you must work out how you could measure out the quantities of liquid indicated on the right by using jars with the capacities shown on the left. Try the series yourself before reading on. After solving the first five problems, nearly two-thirds of Luchins's subjects were unable to solve the sixth. The sixth problem actually requires a simpler strategy than the first five, and it would be easily solved were it not for the set established by the first five.

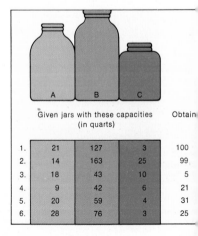

	Given jars with these capacities (in quarts)			Obtain
	A	B	C	
1.	21	127	3	100
2.	14	163	25	99
3.	18	43	10	5
4.	9	42	6	21
5.	20	59	4	31
6.	28	76	3	25

almost anyone could solve this problem if he or she had not already learned the strategy for solving the other five problems. But if a subject had acquired the B = A − 2C rule, that person was very likely either to give up on problem 6 or to insist staunchly that the previously successful formula still worked—that 76 − 28 − 2(3) did in fact equal 25!

Psychologists call the common inclination to repeat a solution that has worked in the past a **mental set**. It can clearly have both positive and negative results. On the one hand, transfer of a previously successful strategy to similar problems offers speedy solution with little cognitive strain, as it did with problems 2 through 5 in Luchins's experiment. On the other hand, application of a past solution to problems that are only superficially similar to previous ones can actually prevent these new problems from ever being solved.

Luchins's experiment emphasizes the importance of flexibility in the search phase of problem solving. A person must be able to counteract the tendency to stick with a familiar strategy even though it is proving unproductive. A number of psychologists have suggested ways of encouraging this flexibility. One is to get away from the problem for a while, that is, to seek a period of **incubation**. Does research confirm that incubation facilitates problem solving? The limited evidence available suggests that under certain circumstances it may.

Consider the following problem:

A man had four chains, each three links long. He wanted to join the four chains into a single closed chain. Having a link opened cost 2¢ and having a link closed cost 3¢. The man had his chains joined into a closed chain for 15¢. How did he do it? (Silveira, 1971)

See if you can solve this problem in a reasonable amount of time. Most people find it extremely difficult, perhaps because they rigidly employ a means-end analysis. If the problem is to join four chains into a single circular chain, disassembling one of the chains completely seems to be working in the wrong direction. Yet, as illustrated in Figure 7.17, this is the only way to produce the desired result by opening and closing only three links.

Silveira (1971) presented this problem to subjects, allowing them work and incubation periods of varying lengths. She found that if a subject worked on the problem steadily for some time, taking a temporary break from it greatly increased the likelihood that he or she would later find the solution. What occurred during incubation that facilitated problem solving? One possibility is that subjects were simply given a rest and so were more energetic and persistent in later efforts to solve the problem. Then, too, a period of interruption may have enabled subjects to break free of inappropriate mental sets that were blocking more productive approaches. In short, they may have returned to the problem with a fresh eye. These two factors are enough to explain Silveira's results, but another factor might also have been at work. It could have been that subjects continued to search for the solution on an unconscious level, even though they were engaged in other cognitive tasks. The extent to which such unconscious processes are actually responsible for creative insights is not yet known, but the possibility is a highly intriguing one (Posner, 1973). We will say more about unconscious processes later in this chapter when we look at how some of the accomplishments of highly creative people have come about.

Deciding when a solution is satisfactory For some problems the task of deciding when a solution is satisfactory poses no difficulty at all. Problems like the four-chain puzzle just described have very clearly defined goals that can be achieved in only one way. When that goal is reached, the problem is solved. No questions or doubts remain. Often the solution to such a problem occurs in a moment of what psychologists call **insight**—a rather sudden perception of the critical relationships. A less formal name for insight is the "Eureka!" or "Aha!" experience.

The gestalt psychologist Wolfgang Köhler conducted some of the earliest studies of insight. In one famous investigation using chimpanzees as subjects, Köhler (1925) suspended a banana from the ceiling of a chimp's cage, out of the animal's reach. The cage also contained a number of boxes that the chimp could move and stack. Usually a chimp would try to reach the banana by jumping, climbing the bars of the cage, or using some other futile approach. When all these efforts failed, the animal often paused for a long while, as though studying the situation. Then suddenly it appeared to see the value of the boxes as a means of obtaining the fruit. Hurriedly the chimp would pile the boxes beneath the banana and climb them to reach the goal. From then on, the animal had little difficulty solving similar problems. Köhler used his findings as evidence that animals do not always solve problems through simple trial and error, as behaviorists at the time maintained. A cognitive restructuring of information is often at work, even when the problem solver is a chimp.

In describing the human experience of insight, Köhler stressed the enormous feeling of satisfaction it brings. A puzzle that moments earlier seemed impossibly difficult is suddenly seen in a new light and its solution is completely clear. Note that just solving a problem is not necessarily accompanied by insight. The solution must be understood in its entirety with no doubts or questions remaining. Thus, if you do the set of subtractions in Figure 7.11 you will soon realize that the answer is always the next highest odd number. But unless you understand precisely *why* this pattern occurs, you will not experience the insight phenomenon.

Unfortunately, the solutions to many problems are not as final as those associated with insight. How, for example, would you determine when you had reached the "best" solution to Duncker's tumor problem? Or when you had made the "best" move in a game of chess? It is clearly very difficult to say. But one thing that psychologists have learned about the termination of such problems is that people are often willing to settle for a less than optimum solution if finding the ideal solution places too great a demand on cognitive capacity (Posner, 1973). This concession makes sense. To function effectively people must avoid cognitive overload, and one way to do so is to accept a solution that may not be perfect, but is good enough. This is why a person sometimes returns

Figure 7.10 Wolfgang Köhler's (1925) classic work with chimpanzees. In this instance, the chimp seemed to have an "Aha!" experience when it realized the value of using objects as tools to achieve a goal. In this photo Grande builds a four-story structure out of boxes in order to obtain food that is hung out of immediate reach.

Figure 7.11 This subtraction problem illustrates the importance of insight in problem solving. Subtracting each successive square number from the next larger one produces the series of odd digits.

1	4	9	16	25	36	49	64
0	1	4	9	16	25	36	49
1	3	5	7	9			

to a previously rejected solution after devoting a great deal more time to a problem. Locating a better solution no longer seems worth the effort. We will say much more about the effects that our cognitive limitations have on decision making in the final section of this chapter.

Highly creative problem solvers

We have been talking about the stages through which most people proceed when trying to solve problems. But what about highly creative people? Does their approach to problem solving differ from that of the average person? Psychologists do not yet have all the answers to this question, but based on personal accounts by famous artists, writers, scientists, and the like, it appears that the problem-solving experiences of the highly creative are much like those of other people, only in some respects more intense.

Consider how the German chemist Friedrich August Kekulé discovered the molecular structure of benzene, a highly volatile and flammable liquid often used as a solvent. Until the mid-nineteenth century, chemists could not figure out why benzene had the chemical properties it did. The answer had to lie in the way that benzene's six carbon atoms and six hydrogen atoms were structured. But what that structure was remained a perplexing mystery. Then one evening Kekulé was busy writing a textbook when his thoughts began to wander from his work. As he tells the story:

I turned my chair to the fire and dozed. Again the atoms were gambolling before my eyes. This time the smaller groups kept modestly in the background. My mental eye . . . could now distinguish larger structures . . . all twining and twisting in snake-like motion. But look! What was that? One of the snakes had seized hold of its own tail, and the form whirled mockingly before my eyes. As if by a flash of lightning I awoke.

Kekulé had found the answer. The carbon atoms of benzene formed a closed ring, with a hydrogen atom attached to each one.

One striking aspect of Kekulé's experience is the suddenness and unpredictability with which the solution occurred. Apparently, this is characteristic of many great creative insights, whether they are made by composers, writers, mathematicians, philosophers, or scientists like Kekulé. Here is how the poet A. E. Housman described the creation of some of his best work during long afternoon walks:

As I went along, thinking of nothing in particular, . . . there would flow into my mind, with sudden and unaccountable emotion, sometimes a line or two of verse, sometimes a whole stanza at once, accompanied, not preceded, by a vague notion of the poem which they were destined to form a part of. . . . When I got home I wrote them down, leaving gaps, and hoping that further inspiration might be forthcoming another day. Sometimes it was . . . but sometimes the poem had to be taken in hand and completed by the brain, which was apt to be a matter of trouble and anxiety, involving trial and disappointment, and sometimes ending in failure.

Thus, creative insight often comes when the artist is not actively engaged in his or her work. In fact, deliberate effort, as Housman describes, sometimes even thwarts success. This repeated finding has led some psychologists to suggest that many creative inspirations seem largely the products of unconscious thought (Ghiselin, 1952).

Figure 7.12 Figure preference test that required subjects to express a preference, or no preference, for line drawings. Subjects chosen at random seem to prefer symmetrical designs, like those on the left, while creative subjects prefer drawings like those on the right.

A small boy and his mother hurrying along on a dark windy day, trying to get home before it rains

In addition to probing the nature of the creative process, psychologists are interested in discovering what highly creative people are like. What personality traits, besides creativity, do such individuals share? Although there is no single set of traits that describes all creative people, some interesting general patterns do exist. For one thing, the creative person tends to show a marked independence in judgment. If his or her views differ from those of other people, the creative person is often willing to stand alone as a minority of one. The less creative person, in contrast, is typically much more influenced by group pressure to conform (Barron, 1958). The creative person also tends to show a rather unusual preference for the asymmetrical and complex. For instance, when asked to express their opinions of various abstract drawings, the highly creative person is likely to prefer those to the right in Figure 7.12, whereas the less creative person is likely to prefer those to the left. This difference in preference may be related to a talent highly creative people have for seeing a comprehensive, synthesizing order in what other people see as a confusing chaos. Consider the interpretations that two very creative people gave to the inkblots shown in Figure 7.13. They are certainly notable for the total order they manage to impose on what to others may look simply like meaningless blotches. Thus, the creative response to disorder, according to one researcher in this field, "is to find an elegant new order more satisfying than any that could be evoked by a simpler configuration" (Barron, 1958).

Mexican in sombrero running up a long hill to escape from rain clouds

Figure 7.13 Examples of Rorschach inkblots devised by Frank Barron (1958), with the "uncommon responses" given by creative subjects.

MAKING DECISIONS

Although creativity is a great asset in many kinds of problem solving, it does not necessarily help people make sound judgments in the hundreds of decisions they face every day. Granted, most of these are simple, mundane choices—deciding whether to carry an umbrella on a cloudy morning or which of several routes to take when driving to work. But some of our decisions are far more complex and have a much greater impact on our lives. Such decisions as whether to get married, have children, go to graduate school, or change careers can greatly alter one's future. And political decisions made by voters and government officials can affect a nation, the world, even the course of history. The far-reaching importance that many decisions have has helped fuel great interest in the processes by which human beings make choices. Recent bibliographies list well over a thousand references to books and articles on decision making (Barron, 1974; Kleiter, Gachowetz, and Huber, 1976). In the following sections we will explore some of the highlights of this research.

How rational is decision making?

Suppose you are faced with the following decision: Your friends are planning a weekend ski trip, but you have an exam scheduled for Monday morning. Although you have already studied, you are not certain how difficult the exam will be. And because it is early in the ski season, conditions on the slopes may be only fair. Should you go with your friends or not?

According to psychologists two sets of variables will probably enter into your decision. One is the value you place on potential outcomes. How much pleasure will you derive from a weekend of fun and relaxation? How much distress will you suffer if you do poorly on this particular exam? Your answers to these and other questions indicate the relative *utility* you assign to each of your possible choices. But estimates of utility are not enough. In addition, you must also estimate the *probability* that each potential outcome will actually take place. What are the chances that insufficient snow will ruin the skiing? What are the odds that this particular instructor will give a difficult exam? Your decision, then, involves a combined evaluation of both utility and probability. This is true of most decisions regarding one's own behavior.

If you were a completely rational creature, you might tackle this problem as a mathematician would. You would start by assigning a utility value to each potential outcome of spending the weekend skiing, using a scale of, say, -10 to $+10$. You would then multiply these figures by your estimated probability that each outcome is likely to occur. Tallying up these results would give you a plus or minus number—minus telling you to stay at home, plus telling you to go skiing.

How closely does this very rational approach match the way people actually make such decisions? In some cases we may approximate this strategy, although we seldom calculate the variables in a strictly mathematical way. Beach and his colleagues, for example, recently asked married couples who were contemplating having a child to assign relative utilities to a number of outcomes associated with parenthood. These outcomes included such things as opportunities for personal growth and maturity, changes in vocational or educational plans, changes in family finances, approval or disapproval from relatives and

	Positive Anticipations	**Negative Anticipations**
Tangible gains and losses for *self*	1. Satisfactory pay. 2. Plenty of opportunities to use my skills and competencies. 3. For the present, my status in the organization is okay (but it won't be for long if I am not promoted in the next year).	1. Long hours. 2. Constant time pressures—deadlines too short. 3. Unpleasant paper work. 4. Poor prospects for advancement to a higher-level position. 5. Repeated reorganizations make my work chaotic. 6. Constant disruption from high turnover of other executives I deal with.
Tangible gains and losses for *others*	1. Adequate income for family. 2. Wife and children get special privileges because of my position in the firm.	1. Not enough time free to spend with my family. 2. Wife often has to put up with my irritability when I come home after bad days at work.
Self-approval or self-disapproval	1. This position allows me to make full use of my potentialities. 2. Proud of my achievements. 3. Proud of the competent team I have shaped up. 4. Sense of meaningful accomplishment when I see the products for which we are responsible.	1. Sometimes feel I'm a fool to continue putting up with the unreasonable deadlines and other stupid demands made by the top managers.
Social approval or disapproval	1. Approval of men on my team, who look up to me as their leader and who are good friends. 2. Approval of my superior who is a friend and wants me to stay.	1. Very slight skeptical reaction of my wife—she asks me if I might be better off in a different firm. 2. A friend in another firm who has been wanting to wangle something for me will be disappointed.

Based on information from Irving Janis and Leon Mann, *Decision making*, N.Y.: Free Press, Division of Macmillan, 1979
Table from Irving Janis and Dan Wheeler, Thinking clearly about career choices, *Psychology Today*, May 1978, pp. 67–76, 121. Table on p. 75.

friends, change in the quality of one's marriage, and so forth. The couples then estimated the probability that each outcome would actually take place if they decided to have a child. From this data the researchers calculated an overall score that could be used to predict the likelihood of that particular couple having a child within the next two years. This score proved reasonably accurate: It correctly predicted the decision to have or not to have a child more than 70 percent of the time (Beach, Campbell, and Townes, 1979). Thus, at least in this decision, both utility and probability seem to have been taken into account in much the way that a rational model would predict.

There is also evidence that, with proper guidance, people can learn to become more rational decision makers. One technique for making more rational decisions is to fill out a simple balance sheet for each major alternative one faces. Figure 7.14 shows a balance sheet drawn up by a production manager who was trying to decide whether to remain in his present job. As you can see, the positive and negative consequences he anticipates from this particular alternative are divided into several categories: (1) tangible gains and losses for self; (2) tangible gains and losses for significant others; (3) self-approval or self-disapproval; (4) social approval or disapproval. Psychologists Irving Janis and Dan Wheeler, who recommend the balance sheet as a decision-making aid, believe it helps people consider *all* the consequences related to a particular choice. As a result, they are less likely to encounter unpleasant surprises and are more likely to develop contingency plans in case negative outcomes do arise. Does such an approach really work? Research suggests that it may. In

Figure 7.14 A production manager at a manufacturing plant who was trying to decide whether to remain in his present position drew up this grid, which lays out the pros and cons of his alternatives. A grid such as this can be used for working out the alternatives in any important decision-making situation (after Janis and Mann, 1979).

several large-scale studies of people making decisions of various sorts (high-school seniors deciding where to go to college, adults deciding whether to start a diet and attend an exercise class), those who constructed a balance sheet before making a final choice expressed significantly fewer regrets later on (Janis and Wheeler, 1978).

Yet the very fact that such a technique is needed suggests that the decisions people make are not always sound. Studies show that people often ignore important information pertaining to a decision even though it is readily available. For instance, research on consumer behavior indicates that shoppers motivated to buy the most economical product may still choose relatively expensive items despite the fact that unit prices are posted on grocery shelves (Russo, Krieser, and Miyashita, 1975). Even matters of personal survival are not exempt from poor decision making. Residents of flood-plain areas, for example, tend to ignore the hazards of living where they do: They refuse to purchase flood insurance, and they rebuild houses destroyed by a flood in exactly the same locations (Slovic, Kunreuther, and White, 1974). The question, of course, is why.

Part of the answer may lie in a person's emotional reaction to very difficult choices. When decisions must be made under unusual stress, critical faculties may be impaired. This is one reason why some people whose careers have been going poorly and whose jobs are in serious jeopardy fail to make the very rational decision that they must improve their performance or look for other work. Instead, they engage in wishful thinking that allows them to deny the severity of the threat. Janis and Wheeler (1978) call this defensive avoidance. Its most common symptoms are rationalization ("I've been under a lot of pressure lately"), procrastination ("I'll do something about it after next month's sales meeting"), and buck passing ("He deserves more blame than I do for missing that deadline").

Yet despite the undeniable impact that stress can have on sound decision making, much recent research shows that it is not the only factor that can lead people's judgments astray. Another is the persistent human tendency to restrict cognitive focus due to our rather limited capacity for processing and weighing information. Especially when a decision is fairly complex, we tend to reduce our choices to simpler ones by concentrating on a few of the relevant facts and largely ignoring the others. Often this approach serves us quite well. In a study of how highly skilled radiologists assess the malignancy of an ulcer, six relevant factors were available for assessment, but the radiologists tended to focus on only one or at most two of these. If they used the other factors at all, it was only to make small adjustments in their diagnoses (Hoffman, Slovic, and Rorer, 1968). Still, their assessments were correct most of the time.

Narrowing the range of relevant information is not always this successful, however. Sometimes it leads to choices that are less than optimal. Figure 7.15 allows you to demonstrate this to yourself. On which factors did you focus when trying to decide between these two bets? Did this strategy prompt you to select the bet that offered the greatest chance of wining, calculated mathematically? Probably not. In this case, then, narrowing the cognitive focus led to decision making that from a strictly logical point of view makes little sense. Nevertheless, from the point of view of your limited time, attention, and memory, this strategy is understandable.

As you undoubtedly learned from Figure 7.15, one factor that can greatly

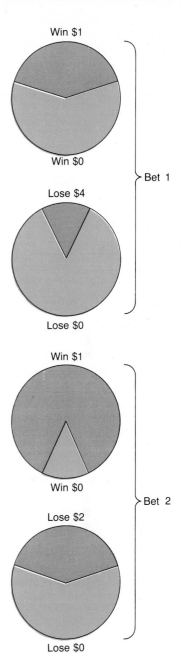

Figure 7.15 Psychologists who study decision making often look to gambling as an exemplary situation. If you were offered a choice between these two bets, how would you make your choice, taking into consideration the four attributes of the gambles: the probability of winning, the amount to win, the probability of losing, and the amount to lose (after Slovic and Lichtenstein, 1968)?

influence the information to which we attend when making a decision is the size of the risk or payoff involved. When the potential gain or loss is extremely great, we tend to focus on utility and discount probability. This is why so many people buy tickets for million-dollar sweepstakes even though their odds of winning are minuscule. It is also why so many wage earners with dependent families purchase life insurance even though their chances of dying young are slim.

So far we have looked at circumstances that prompt us to focus on utility and largely disregard probability, but this is far from the only cognitive bias we experience when making decisions. When estimating the odds of uncertain events, for example, we are also prone to serious errors due to the strategies we use to limit cognitive focus. Because errors in probability judgments have generated much interest in recent years, we will consider them here in depth.

Judging uncertain odds

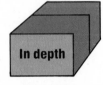

In depth

Most of the decisions we make require some intuitive estimate of probability. Should I have my car serviced or wait another month? What are the chances something will go wrong if I neglect it? Should I study this evening or go to a movie? What are the chances my instructor is planning a surprise quiz? Should I get married or stay single? What are the chances either choice will affect my career? Psychologists have found that in making such probability estimates, people do not approach the problem as a statistician would. Instead, they rely on one of a number of heuristics to simplify the judgmental task. Two very common heuristics are representativeness and availability. As you will see, when people overlook their limitations, both can lead to serious errors.

Representativeness Read the following description of a young man named Steve, who was picked at random from the population as a whole:

Steve is very shy and withdrawn, invariably helpful, but with little interest in people, or in the world of reality. A meek and tidy soul, he has a need for order and structure, and a passion for detail (Tversky and Kahneman, 1973, p. 1124).

Given this brief personality profile, what would you estimate the chances in percentage terms to be that Steve is engaged in each of the following occupations: salesman, airline pilot, librarian, physician? Write your answers on a sheet of paper before reading further.

How did you arrive at your probability estimate of Steve's line of work? If you are like most people, you relied on a heuristic called **representativeness**. You compared what you knew about Steve's personality with your understanding of what an "average" or "representative" salesman, pilot, librarian, or physician is like. The extent to which Steve matched these stereotypes determined your estimated probability that he was indeed employed in that particular occupation. The job to which you gave the highest probability was undoubtedly librarian. Salesman, on the other hand, probably scored close to zero.

There is no doubt that the representative heuristic is a useful device—as long as it does not blind you to other relevant information. The problem is that it sometimes does. Take the task of predicting Steve's occupation. What other factors, besides similarity to occupational stereotypes, might enter into your estimates of what he does for a living? A moment's thought will probably suggest that the relative proportion of salesmen, pilots, librarians, and doctors in the population as a whole should also influence your judgment. Did you consider this factor previously? Probably not. When asked a question of this type, most people employ the representative heuristic and completely ignore what statisticians call prior probabilities.

Interestingly, this remains so even when prior probabilities are specifically given. In one experiment (Kahneman and Tversky, 1973), subjects were given a series of personality profiles allegedly drawn from a group of one hundred lawyers and engineers, the proportion of each being clearly stated. Logically these proportions should have influenced the subjects' estimates that a given profile belonged either to a lawyer or to an engineer. But they did not. The subjects based their evaluations solely on the similarity between each profile and the personality stereotypes of people in these two occupations. Thus, a particular profile was just as likely to be judged an engineer when the group consisted of only 30 percent engineers as when it consisted of 70 percent engineers. Prior probabilities were simply ignored in favor of the representativeness heuristic.

Psychologists believe that the same judgmental bias may frequently influence decisions outside the laboratory. For instance, most admissions boards of medical schools assign a great deal of importance to personal interviews with candidates. They are convinced that a variety of personality traits are representative of a "good" aspiring doctor. Yet there is no statistical evidence that a favorable admissions interview is any indication of subsequent success in medical school. Here, then, is a case where prior probabilities, as measured by quite reliable yardsticks such as past academic performance and scores on entrance exams, are given less weight than they deserve in favor of a very intuitive assessment of representativeness (Nisbett and Ross, 1980).

And prior probability is not the only factor that the representativeness heuristic can prompt us to overlook. Consider the following problem:

A certain town is served by two hospitals. In the larger hospital about 45 babies are born each day, and in the smaller hospital about 15 babies are born each day. As you know, about 50 percent of all babies are boys. However, the exact percentage varies from day to day. Sometimes it may be higher than 50 percent, sometimes lower. For a period of one year, each hospital recorded the days on which more than 60 percent of the babies born were boys. Which hospital recorded more such days?
-The larger hospital.
-The smaller hospital.
-About the same—that is, within 5 percent of each other (Tversky and Kahneman, 1974).

Most people asked this question select the third response: both hospitals, they say, recorded approximately the same number of days. You may therefore he surprised to learn that this answer is incorrect. If you assumed that each hospital is equally representative of the population as a whole and so has an equal chance of obtaining more than 60 percent male births in a day, you overlooked an important fact learned in Chapter 2. The smaller the size of a sample, the greater the likelihood that it will stray from the expected average. Thus, the smaller hospital is more likely than the larger hospital to have a day in which predominantly boys are born. If you answered otherwise, it was probably because the representativeness heuristic dominated your thinking.

You can probably think of instances of this same oversight occurring in everyday life. Here is just one example. Members of the United States Congress have been known to discount EPA mileage estimates, which are based on a sample of ten or more cars, when a fellow legislator reports a different mileage figure for his or her own car (La Breque, 1980). Clearly, information derived from a sizable sample should be considered more representative of a car's true performance than data obtained from a single person's experience. Yet in this case sample size is ignored completely and judgments are based instead on intuitive feelings about representativeness.

Availability Although we use the representativeness heuristic in making many probability judgments, there are numerous situations where this approach does not apply. For example, if you travel about ten thousand miles a year by car, how would you estimate the probability that you will some day be involved in an automobile accident? In order to make such a judgment you would probably try to reconstruct the frequency of automobile accidents from past experience. Have you or anyone you know ever been involved in a collision? Have you ever witnessed a car accident? How often do you hear about traffic accidents in the news? What you are doing by raising such questions is assessing the probability of an uncertain event according to the ease with which instances come to mind. Events that are easy to remember are perceived as more frequent and therefore more probable than events that are difficult to remember. This approach is called the **availability** heuristic, and it makes a good deal of sense. In general, the present probability of an event is directly related to its frequency in the past, and the more frequently an event has been experienced in the past the easier it is to recall. But note the qualification "in general." Like any rule-of-thumb device, the availability heuristic has significant limitations that people frequently ignore.

The basic problem is that some things come more readily to mind than others for reasons that have nothing to do with the frequency of past instances. A person who has just seen a highway accident is far more likely to remember it than a person who saw one ten years ago, for recency affects availability. So does the salience of an object or event. A five-car collision witnessed first hand is far more likely to be remembered than one merely described in a newspaper. The impact of salience on availability was demonstrated in an experiment using lists of very famous and not-so-famous people. When the very famous people on a particular list were all women and the not-so-famous people on the same list were all men, an overwhelming majority of subjects mistakenly judged the list to be composed primarily of women, even though the number of men and women were in fact equal. The fame of the women made them easier to remember and so distorted perceptions concerning their relative frequency (Tversky and Kahneman, 1973). For other demonstrations of how salience affects availability, try the two problems in Figure 7.16.

The availability heuristic is often used in making everyday judgments. Consider how we estimate the risks we face from diseases, accidents, natural disasters, and exposure to various toxins. The availability heuristic undoubtedly plays a part. This was illustrated in a set of studies in which researchers asked subjects to estimate the likelihood of dying from an assortment of potential hazards (Slovic, Fischhoff, and Lichtenstein, 1976, 1980). The subjects greatly *over*estimated the risks from dangers that were both highly publicized and very dramatic—tornadoes, nuclear accidents, and homicides, for example. At the

Figure 7.16 Two problems that demonstrate the availability heuristic (after Tversky and Kahneman, 1973).

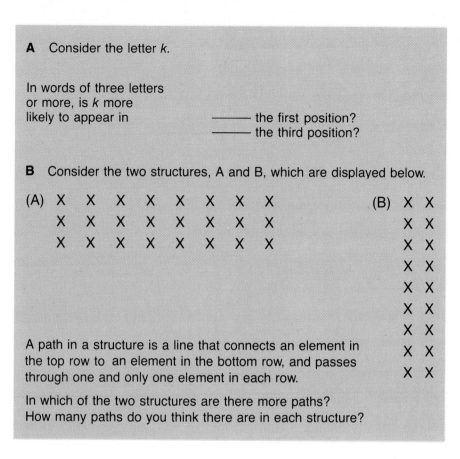

A Consider the letter *k*.

In words of three letters or more, is *k* more likely to appear in
—— the first position?
—— the third position?

B Consider the two structures, A and B, which are displayed below.

(A) X X X X X X X X   (B) X X
    X X X X X X X X   X X
    X X X X X X X X   X X
                                        X X
                                        X X
                                        X X
                                        X X
A path in a structure is a line that connects an element in   X X
the top row to an element in the bottom row, and passes
through one and only one element in each row.   X X

In which of the two structures are there more paths?
How many paths do you think there are in each structure?

same time, they greatly *under*estimated the risks from such diseases as diabetes, tuberculosis, and asthma, which are often found in nonfatal form and which are only rarely reported as causes of death in the news. Thus, because our recollection of death from various hazards is affected by factors (sensationalism, media coverage) that are unrelated to actual mortality rates, reliance on the availability heuristic can cause serious misperceptions regarding risk.

Another important outcome of reliance on the availability heuristic is that it can reinforce erroneous stereotypes. The following experiment shows how this works (Chapman and Chapman, 1967). Researchers obtained forty-five drawings of people made by patients at a state mental hospital. Each drawing was randomly paired with a symptom (suspiciousness of others, impotence, extreme dependence, and so forth) that supposedly described the patient who produced that drawing. The drawing–symptom combinations were then shown to a group of introductory psychology students, who were allowed to look at them for half a minute each. Afterward the students were asked if any special features in the drawings were frequently associated with a particular symptom. The students reported frequent associations between symptoms and features that fit common stereotypes. Suspicious patients, they said, tended to draw people with peculiar eyes; impotent patients tended to draw figures with broad shoulders and muscular bodies; overly dependent patients tended to produce feminine or childlike drawings, and so forth. Of course, these perceived correlations were strictly illusory: The symptoms and the drawings had been randomly paired. But the random associations that stuck in the students' minds were those that preconceptions told them *should* go together. These associations were readily available to memory, and as a result the students misjudged them as unusually frequent. It is not difficult to imagine that the same process could reinforce other common stereotypes.

It is clear that the intuitive ways in which people judge the likelihood or frequency of uncertain events makes them prone to systematic errors. And these errors are difficult to avoid. Even when people are offered rewards for correct judgments, they still continue to make the same mistakes. Nor are our errors due strictly to lack of knowledge or skill. Experienced research psychologists, extensively trained in statistics, are also prone to errors when they intuitively judge probabilities (Tversky and Kahneman, 1971). The factors that they, like everyone else, tend to overlook are simply not part of a person's normal repertoire of intuitions. However, a knowledge of human decision-making strategies can at least alert us to common biases and so help us to compensate for them.

Answers to problems   (Figure 7.17)

(A) The answer to the problem shown in Figure 7.7:

"Having recognized . . . that the symbols stood for letters, and having applied the rules which guide us in all forms of writing, the solution was easy enough. The first message was so short that it was impossible to do more than say that the symbol — stood for E. As you are aware, E is the most common letter in the English alphabet . . . [so] it was reasonable to set this down as E . . . in some cases, [this] figure was bearing a flag, but it was probable, from the way in which distributed, that they were used to break the sentence up into words. I accepted this as a hypothesis. . . . I waited for fresh material. . . . [Now] I got the two E's coming second and fourth in a word of five letters. It might be 'sever' or 'level' or 'never'. . . . The latter as a reply to an appeal is far the most probable. . . . Accepting it as correct, we are now able to say that the symbols ——— stand respectively for N, V and R." And so on. The last fragment was a threat of murder against Mrs. Cubitt: "ELSIE. PREPARE TO MEET THY GOD." (A. Conan Doyle. *The Return of Sherlock Holmes*, "The Adventure of the Dancing Men." New York: Ballantine Books, © 1975.)

(B) The answer to the problem shown in Figure 7.2 (left). (C) The answer to the problem shown in Figure 7.5 (right). (D) The answer to the four-chain prob-

hen the girl put her hand into the bag to draw out the fateful pebble, she fumbled and dropped it, where it was immediately lost among the others. "Oh," she said, "well, you can tell which one I picked by looking at the one that's left." The girl's lateral thinking saved her father and herself.

lem. Take one chain completely apart (for 6¢) and use its links to join the remaining three chains (for 9¢).

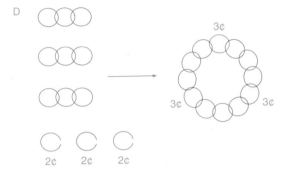

SUMMARY

1. Cognition, or thought, has become in recent decades a major field of psychological investigation. It is the study of how we organize information in our minds to help accomplish some desired end, such as the solution of a problem. Human thought is difficult to study because **introspection**, the subjective description of one's own thought processes, is often faulty. Thus psychologists tend to focus on mental activities with observable and measurable results. Important among these are concept formation and structure, problem solving, and decision making.

2. Our ability to form **concepts**—the mental constructs that allow us to classify those things that have common features—enables us to make generalizations and thus to engage in complex thinking. To form a new concept, psychologists suggest, we test hypotheses, guided by a strategy. With a *global hypothesis*, we assume that all the salient features of a new stimulus are defining characteristics of a concept. Then we apply a *focusing strategy*, by which subsequent instances of the concept show us which features can be eliminated from the original concept. Alternatively, by using a more limited hypothesis, we pick out only one or two features as the defining characteristics. Then a subsequent *scanning strategy* enables us to scan other stimuli for relevant features and eliminate those that do not appear to form part of the concept.

3. Eleanor Rosch, among others, has proposed another perspective on concept formation—the prototype approach—in which we formulate a concept in terms of an example that best illustrates the concept, and which would help account for the structure of **natural concepts**, those categories we use everyday.

4. A knowledge of concepts and relationships among concepts make problem solving possible. Psychologists focus not so much on **reproductive thinking**—the direct application of previous knowledge to a new situation—as on **creative thinking**. To analyze creative thinking, they sometimes divide it into three stages: initially interpreting the problem, searching for solutions, and deciding when a satisfactory answer has been found.

5. Usually the best way to interpret a difficult problem is to look at it from all angles before arriving at a solution strategy. **Fixations** that can interfere with seeing the best way to solve a problem include the tendency to cling to a commonplace interpretation of a problem, even though it is not helpful in a particular situation. The tendency to view an object as being used only for its customary function is called **functional fixedness**.

6. When the proper interpretation alone will not yield the solution to a problem, we employ search strategies to help us find a solution. Some problems can best be solved by a strategy called an **algorithm**, a precisely stated set of rules that works for solving all problems of a particular type. Where the systematic approach of an algorithm is not practical, however, we use **heuristic**, or rule-of-thumb, strategies. One kind of heuristic is **subgoal analysis**, in which a large problem is broken down into small problems of manageable size. Another is **means-end analysis**, which involves comparing one's current position with a desired end position and then trying to find a means of closing the gap between the two. Heuristics enable us to avoid overloading the limited capacity of our short-term memory, but the tendency to use previously successful solutions—called a **mental set**—can limit the capacity to solve certain problems. One way to achieve flexibility in the search phase of problem solving is to seek a period of **incubation**, or getting away from the problem for a while, which can help make it possible to find a solution later on. While the solution to some problems is clear-cut, it is not always easy to determine when one has found the best solution. People are often willing to settle for a less than perfect solution if finding the ideal solution places too great a demand on cognitive capacity.

7. The problem-solving experiences of the highly creative seem to be much like those of ordinary people, except more intense. Solutions come suddenly and unpredictably, often when the person is not actively engaged in finding a solution.

8. Psychologists have studied a number of the processes involved in decision making. Among the more rational processes we use in making a decision is the weighing of two sets of variables: the *utility*, or potential value, of each possible choice, and the *probability*, or chance, that each potential outcome will actually take place. Such rational approaches, however, are restricted by our persistent tendency to limit cognitive focus. When a decision is fairly complex and requires that we process and weigh substantial amounts of information, we tend to reduce our choices to simpler ones by concentrating on a few of the relevant facts and largely ignoring the others. When the potential gain or loss of a particular outcome is very great, we tend to focus on utility and to discount the actual probability of the event's taking place. We tend also to overlook certain probabilities when we use two heuristics—**representativeness** and **availability**—in making decisions. Representativeness involves, for example, predicting the probable occupation of a person from a set of given personality characteristics. This can lead to the discounting of prior probabilities, such as the number of people in that occupation in the total population. Availability is the approach by which we assess the probability of an event according to the ease with which instances of its occurrence come to mind. This approach is limited by the fact that things may come to mind for reasons that have nothing to do with the frequency of past instances, such as the recency or salience of the events we remember. When people make probability judgments, then, they often use intuitive estimates and are prone to systematic errors.

Suggested readings

Adams, J. L. *Conceptual block-busting*. San Francisco: Freeman, 1974.

Davis, G. A. *Psychology of problem solving: Theory and practice*. New York: Basic Books, 1973.

Lindsay. P. H., and Norman, D. A. *Human information processing: An introduction to psychology* (2nd ed.). New York: Academic Press, 1977.

Newell, A., and Simon, H. A. *Human problem solving*. Englewood Cliffs, N.J.: Prentice-Hall, 1972.

Posner, M. *Cognition: An introduction*. Glenview, Ill.: Scott, Foresman, 1973.

THE PROCESS OF DEVELOPMENT

Human development is explored in Part 4: the unfolding of personality throughout the life span in Chapter 8, and the development of language—verbal and nonverbal—in Chapter 9.

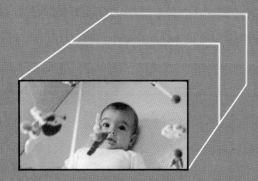

PREVIEW

1. The patterns of growth and change are examined in developmental psychology, which investigates why people change and why the changes occur as they do.

2. Development, which is sequential and predictable, is the result of an interplay between inherited and environmental factors.

3. Despite the appearance of helplessness, newborns are well equipped to respond to their environments. In these interactions, their cognitive abilities expand, and they learn rapidly.

4. By the age of two or three, most children can represent objects and events symbolically, a vast improvement over the thinking abilities of infants. By adolescence, children think hypothetically and in abstract terms, much as adults. Cognitive changes continue through adulthood, though less dramatically.

5. Personality evolves similarly, enhanced in infancy by a loving caretaker and sensory stimulation. Later, children learn and practice social values such as sex-appropriate behavior and a moral code. Adolescents begin to establish identities and face adult challenges.

8 Life-span development

The development of a human being is a remarkable process. In only nine months, two microscopic cells transform themselves into a fully formed human infant. Six years later, this newborn has grown into an accomplished first grader, as proficient in language as many adults and ready to begin mastering such complex skills as reading and arithmetic. From here it is a relatively short step to social and sexual maturation in adolescence, and then to such adult roles as worker, wife or husband, and parent. During the fifty or more years of adulthood remaining, a person continues to develop. Development, in fact, is a continuous process from conception until death. The branch of psychology that seeks to explain the regular patterns of growth and change that occur during the life cycle is called developmental psychology.

THE PROCESS OF DEVELOPMENT

In investigating the process of human development, psychologists generally ask two closely related questions: How do people change—physically, intellectually, emotionally, socially—as they grow older? And why do these changes occur in the ways that they do? These questions, the how and the why of human development, are the subject of this chapter.

Developmental sequences

Anyone who has ever watched young children grow knows that there is an orderly sequence to the emergence of basic motor skills, cognitive capabilities, and social behaviors. Nor are such developmental sequences limited to childhood. Throughout young and middle adulthood and on into old age, sequential patterns of development and change can be observed in all human beings.

Perhaps the most familiar example of a developmental sequence is the emergence of various motor skills during infancy. When babies are about one month old, they can raise their chin while lying on their stomach, and at about two months they can raise their head and chest. Between the fourth and seventh months, their hand-eye coordination has improved so much that they can reach out and grasp almost any object within range. By seven months, infants usually can sit up without support, and a few months later they can stand while holding on to furniture. At age ten months, most babies are accomplished creepers, scooting around on their hands and knees. And finally, usually around the first birthday, infants take their first solo step.

It is important to note that this description of an infant's motor development, like all such descriptions, consists of averages or norms established by observing a large number of babies. It does not tell us what the *ideal* behavior is, but merely what the "average" baby does. In fact, there are wide variations in the age at which normal infants master motor skills. Some babies, for example, never creep, but go directly from sitting and standing to taking their first steps. Some babies walk as early as eight months; others as late as twenty. Such individual variations can be seen in all other developmental sequences. Still, the concept of developmental sequences is useful because it emphasizes the important fact that human growth and change is not random: The normal progression through various developmental events is generally an orderly process that makes accurate predictions possible.

The interaction of heredity and environment

In addition to describing how people change over the life cycle, psychologists are interested in explaining why these particular changes take place, and why there are always individual variations from any statistically calculated average sequence of development. The answers to these questions lie in two sets of factors: heredity and environment. But exactly how the two interact to yield a given developmental pattern is never easy to say. Any developmental event is always the product of both acting together.

Perhaps the best way to get a clear picture of how heredity and environment interact is to begin at the moment of conception, when a male germ cell, or sperm, penetrates a female germ cell, or ovum. Each germ cell contains twenty-three **chromosomes**, structures within the cell nucleus that carry the organism's **genes**, its units of hereditary information. All other cells in the human body contain twenty-three *pairs* of chromosomes, or forty-six in all. The germ cells are different because toward the end of their development they undergo a form of cell division called **meiosis**. During meiosis the twenty-three chromosome pairs of the maturing germ cell are split, rearranged, and distributed to two "daughter" cells, each having twenty-three single chromosomes. The need for such a reduction process is easy to understand. At the time of fertilization, the twenty-three chromosomes from the father's germ cell pair with the twenty-three from the mother's to form a complete set of genetic instructions for a new human being. And because meiosis involves a shuffling of genes and chromosomes, it also guarantees variety in future generations.

How exactly do chromosomes and the genes they carry influence development? It is only within the last several decades that scientists have begun to answer this question. Chromosomes are essentially long, spiral-shaped molecules of a complex substance called **DNA (deoxyribonucleic acid)**. A gene is a small portion of a DNA molecule that either contains the code for producing one of the many proteins from which the body is built or specifies the plan for combining proteins to form the organ systems and general physical properties of the body. Genes, in other words, are the chemical "instructions" for the development and maintenance of a living organism.

Like all sets of instructions, however, those contained within a gene may or may not be carried out, or they may be modified in any number of ways. It depends on the biochemical environment in which the gene operates. For instance, if a developing fetus does not receive adequate amounts of certain nutrients—particularly the vitamins B, C, and D and the minerals calcium, phosphorus, and iodine—the genetic plan may go awry and malformations will result. Various drugs can also adversely affect fetal development. The thalidomide tragedies of the 1960s, when some pregnant women took the sedative thalidomide and produced babies with grossly deformed arms and legs, clearly illustrates the critical impact that the biochemical environment has on gene expression.

Once a person is born, moreover, new opportunities for influencing the body's chemistry arise. People affect their internal environments through the food they eat, the water they drink, even the air they breathe. In addition, sensory information is constantly being stored in memory, a process that affects the physiology of the brain. And the stimuli that people encounter can provoke a wide range of emotions, which are often associated with intense responses in various nerves and glands. All these forces can and do influence the ways in which genes are expressed.

Consider, for example, the effects of emotional deprivation on physical growth. When a baby is raised by an indifferent caregiver, the child may be sickly and slow to mature. It is thought that emotional barrenness is somehow linked to reduced secretions of the pituitary gland, including its growth hormone (Gardner, 1972). Thus, a child with genes for normal body stature may end up stunted and frail if he or she grows up in a deprived environment.

Conversely, a child with a genetic defect can sometimes escape the defect's deleterious effects through environmental intervention. An excellent example is the genetic abnormality called phenylketonuria, or PKU. PKU is caused by a defect in the gene that normally codes for an enzyme that converts the amino acid phenylalanine, primarily found in milk and egg white, into another substance that is usable by the body. In a child with PKU this conversion is impossible; unless the child receives treatment the phenylalanine and its by-products will build up, eventually damaging the central nervous system and causing severe mental retardation. Today, most American newborns are routinely screened for PKU, and babies found to have the defect are immediately placed on a diet low in phenylalanine. If this diet is maintained for the first six years of life (while critical features of the brain are forming), the child will

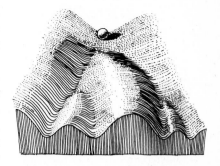

Figure 8.1 Geneticist Conrad Waddington's graphic analogy for the interaction of heredity and environment in development. The landscape represents the possibilities determined by genetic factors, and the path of the rolling ball represents the actual course of development. Such forces on the ball as cross-winds represent environmental factors. The ball can roll down different valleys, depending on the forces that are brought to bear on it, but it cannot easily change from one valley to another once it has started (after Waddington, 1957).

develop normal intelligence. Thus, adjusting the infant's internal environment can prevent the devastating effects of a faulty gene.

Unfortunately, the expression of many other genetic defects cannot be blocked completely by a simple change in the environment. Yet almost all genetic traits, to some extent at least, are susceptible to environmental influences. Consider recent research with children who have Down's syndrome, a condition caused by a chromosome abnormality. Children with Down's syndrome are usually retarded and show slow motor development. In one study, a group of two-year-olds with Down's syndrome were given eighteen months of intensive practice in a number of sensorimotor tasks. By age three and a half, these children performed as well on these tasks as normal children the same age (Rynders, 1975). The Down's syndrome children had not become normal; their improvement was limited to performance of specific sensorimotor tasks. Nevertheless, this research shows that even the effects of a chromosomal abnormality like Down's syndrome, once thought impervious to environmental manipulation, can be modified to some degree through experience and learning. Thus, one can never look at genetic makeup in isolation from the environment. Heredity and environment constantly interact.

The competency of the human newborn

Interaction between a baby and the outside world begins immediately after birth. This fact may come as a surprise to many people because babies appear so helpless. The infant's physical limitations are deceptive, however. The motor reflexes and sensory capacities of the newborn present an entirely different picture.

Figure 8.2 A baby begins to explore the environment with his or her eyes.

Human newborns come equipped with a set of motor reflexes to help them survive in their new surroundings. One of the most basic is the *rooting reflex*, the baby's tendency to turn its head toward any object that gently stimulates a cheek. This reflex is obviously very adaptive for feeding: It helps infants locate a nipple with their mouths. A newborn baby also has a strong *grasping reflex*. If you place a one-week-old baby on its back and touch a finger to one of its hands, the baby is likely to grasp the finger firmly. Sometimes a grasping newborn can literally hang by one arm! The purpose of this reflex is not entirely clear. One theory is that it may be a vestige from our evolutionary past. If our early ancestors carried their young on their backs or undersides, as many apes and monkeys do, the ability to cling tightly to the mother would have obvious survival value (Prechtl, 1965).

In addition to their well-developed motor reflexes, human newborns also have some very sophisticated perceptual capabilities. What the newborn sees and hears is not just a blur of meaningless shapes and noises. But how exactly does one explore the sensory world of a newborn child, who can neither speak nor understand the questions of curious psychologists? The answer is to take advantage of what babies *can* do. They can suck, turn their heads, look at things, cry, smile, and show signs of surprise or fright. By measuring such behaviors while stimulating the baby in different ways, it is possible to infer how the infant perceives the world.

Consider investigations into the auditory capabilities of newborns. Can a newborn baby tell, for instance, where a sound is coming from? To an adult this seems like a simple task, but in fact it is more complex than one might think.The human ear has no specific mechanism for locating the direction of a sound. Instead, we locate sounds mainly by noting which ear the sound hits first. A sound coming from the left, for example, is heard by the left ear a fraction of a second before it is heard by the right. Can newborns make this split-second discrimination? One interesting experiment suggests that they can (Wertheimer, 1961). The subject in this study was a baby girl only a few minutes old. The researcher made a soft clicking sound with a toy cricket, first near the baby's right ear and then near her left. On the very first click, the baby stopped crying, opened her eyes, and looked to the right. Then, when the sound moved to the left, she turned and looked in that direction. Not only was this newborn able to locate sounds, but she also coordinated two of her senses. On hearing a noise with her ears, she turned her head as though to locate the source with her eyes. Although such coordination can be considered reflexive, it is nevertheless impressive in a baby less than ten minutes old.

Young babies also seem quite adept at sound discrimination. In one experiment with three-week-old infants, the children were placed behind a screen, out of sight of the other participants in the experiment, and given a pacifier wired to measure their sucking responses (Mills and Melhuish, 1974). Hearing the sound of a voice—either their mother's voice or that of a female stranger—was contingent on vigorous sucking. The babies sucked much harder to hear the familiar sound of their mother than they did to hear the sound of the stranger. Thus, even before they are a month old, infants can differentiate between familiar and unfamiliar voices.

The visual capabilities of an infant are equally impressive. Although a baby does not develop 20/20 vision until somewhere between the ages of six and twelve months (Cohen, De Loache, and Stauss, 1978), young infants are capable of surprising visual feats. Remember that the world is represented in only two dimensions on the retina of the eye. Yet even very young babies seem capable of perceiving depth. How do psychologists know this? One ingenious experimental apparatus is called the "visual cliff." As shown in Figure 8.3, it consists of a center board resting on a large glass table with a checkerboard pattern beneath. On one side of the board the pattern is directly against the glass, but on the other side it is several feet below, giving the impression of a cliff. When babies only a month-and-a-half old are placed in the middle of the table's "deep" side, their heart rates increase significantly, suggesting that they perceive the cliff (Campos, Langer, and Karowitz, 1970). And experiments with infants ranging in age from six to fourteen months found that a child would crawl to its mother across the glass with the pattern touching it, but refused to crawl onto the glass over the visual cliff.

Of course, it is possible that even by the age of a month-and-a-half a baby has had enough experience with distant objects to gradually learn to perceive depth. The ability to perceive depth, in other words, may not be innate. But even if depth perception is a learned skill, there is no denying that it develops at a very early age. Even newborns show signs that they see the world in three dimensions. For instance, when a newborn is held upright and an object is moved toward its face, the infant protects itself by raising its hands and pulling back its head (Bower, Broughton, and Moore, 1971). Moreover, newborns seem capable of making the fine distinction between an approaching object that is likely to hit them and one that will sail harmlessly by (Ball and Tronick, 1971). These findings suggest that what the baby perceives in this situation is not

Figure 8.3 The visual cliff apparatus. An infant who can crawl may cross the glass surface over the ''shallow'' side but is unlikely to venture out over an edge that appears to be a sudden drop or to cross the surface over the ''deep'' side.

simply a flat image that grows larger, but rather a concrete, oncoming object in three-dimensional space.

When we explore the perceptual capabilities of a newborn, then, we find surprisingly mature and well-integrated systems. Because of these systems a baby can interact with people and objects from the very first moments after birth. As we shall see, this interaction has a profound effect on both cognitive and social development.

COGNITIVE DEVELOPMENT

The amount of information people acquire in a lifetime is staggering. By the time most children enter school, they have mastered many of the intricacies of language. They can count, recite the alphabet, narrate the plots of their favorite stories, and explain the rules of many games. They can also operate mechanical equipment such as a television set, a telephone, or perhaps even a hand-held calculator. Upon graduation from high school twelve years later, they have probably learned more science and mathematics than their great-grandparents learned in a lifetime. As adults, they will find their way in a complex society that depends on sophisticated machines. They may choose an occupation that requires highly technical skills, such as programming a computer, performing brain surgery, or perhaps even piloting spacecraft.

How does a person's intellectual ability develop from the rudimentary capacities present at birth to the sophisticated skills exhibited in adulthood? Many psychologists view cognitive development as a series of *qualitatively* different stages. At each progressive stage, they argue, the child's characteristic ways of thinking about and approaching the world become more mature. The most influential stage theory of cognitive development yet proposed is that of the Swiss psychologist Jean Piaget (1896–1980) (Piaget, 1952, 1954, 1971; Inhelder and Piaget, 1958). Over the course of his long and productive career, Piaget made detailed observations of many children, including his own three (Piaget, 1926). From these observations have emerged important insights that have shaped the work of many other developmental psychologists. Piaget believed that intellectual development proceeds through four main stages: the **sensorimotor period**, which encompasses the first two years of life; the **preoperational period**, which occurs during the preschool years; the **concrete-operational period**, which begins to appear between the fifth and seventh years and continues to develop during the elementary-school years; and the **formal-operational period**, which begins around adolescence and may continue to develop throughout adulthood (Piaget and Inhelder, 1969).

Not all psychologists agree with a stage approach to cognitive development, however. Some believe that many of the qualitative differences in cognitive ability that seem to exist between an older and a younger child may be largely explained by *quantitative* differences in the knowledge that the two have acquired. For example, the fact that an older child has discovered certain effective strategies for remembering information may account for that child's superior performance on memory tasks as compared with the performance of a younger, less experienced child. Undoubtedly, both the qualitative and the quantitative views of cognitive development have some validity. We will consider evidence supporting each of them as we explore intellectual growth from infancy through adulthood.

Cognitive development in infancy

If you have ever met a child at age six months and then met the same child again only two years later, you may have been astounded at the transformation that had occurred. And this transformation was not simply physical. The cognitive changes that take place in a person during the first several years after birth are perhaps the most remarkable of all. A two-and-a-half-year-old, although immature, can use language, interact socially in a rather adultlike fashion, and understand the meaning of most events in the environment. A six-month-old infant, in contrast, can do none of these things. How does such an enormous growth in cognitive skills occur in such a short period of time?

The infant's capacity for learning and memory Part of the answer lies in the fact that babies are capable of learning from the moment of birth—and probably even before. It was not until fairly recently, however, that researchers discovered just how well developed the learning capacity of infants actually is. Consider the results of one operant conditioning experiment with newborns (Sique-land and Lipsitt, 1966). Babies only two to four days old were presented with different sounds as their right cheeks were gently stroked. A tone signaled that a head turn to the right would be rewarded with a mouthful of sugar solution. A buzz indicated that no reward would be given, regardless of whether the babies turned their heads. The infants quickly learned this pattern of reinforcement. They turned their heads far more when they heard the tone than when they heard the buzz. Furthermore, their learning ability proved quite flexible. When the meanings of the two signals were reversed, so that the buzz meant "reward" and the tone meant "no reward," the infants adapted to the new cues in just a few trials.

Babies will learn rapidly even when the "reward" for doing so is simply the flash of a light bulb or some other seemingly ordinary event (Papoušek, 1969). It is as though the babies learn for the sheer fun of it. Suppose a baby boy of about nine months is placed in a crib with a mobile above his head. A string is attached to each of the baby's wrists and to each of his ankles. Only the string tied to the right ankle makes the mobile move. What does the baby do in this situation? Usually he starts to wave his arms and kick his legs, just as babies of this age normally do. But suddenly he notices that the mobile is moving. The baby stops and observes the bobbing objects. Slowly he moves arms and legs until he discovers the relationship between his own movements and those of the mobile. The baby then gurgles with apparent delight, kicking his right leg and watching the mobile flutter. If the contingency is then changed, so that, say, the right arm now operates the mobile, the baby will again search for the solution and coo vigorously when he discovers it (Monnier, Boehmer, and Scholer, 1976). John S. Watson, who was one of the first researchers to notice this infant response to learning, suggested that babies derive a form of intellectual pleasure from solving a problem in much the same way that older children and adults do (Watson, 1972).

The fact that infants have this capacity for learning implies that they must also be able to remember. But what is the span of an infant's memory? This is not an easy question to answer, for a baby cannot simply be asked if he or she remembers something. How, then, do psychologists go about studying memory in children who cannot yet speak? One approach is to watch for signs of interest or inattention when a stimulus is presented. Interest suggests that the baby finds the stimulus novel, whereas inattention suggests that the baby finds the stimulus familiar (provided, of course, that the baby is not tired or distracted by other things). In one study that used this technique, four- to six-month-old infants showed signs that they recognized a photograph of a human face two weeks after they had first seen it (Olson, 1976). Such findings support the conclusion that infants can remember for fairly long periods of time, even during the earliest months of life.

Sensorimotor intelligence and the development of the object concept There is little doubt, then, that even very young babies can and do learn a great deal. But what exactly do they learn about? As we have just seen, much of what babies learn about is the existence of simple relationships between objects in the world around them and between their own behavior and those objects. Such learning is part of what Piaget calls *sensorimotor intelligence.* As this term implies, infants learn to act in the world. But they do not appear to contem-

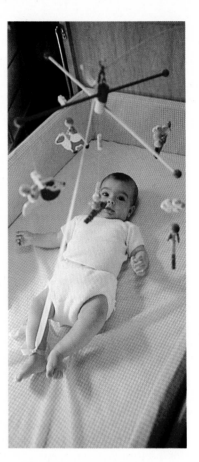

Figure 8.4 Babies can make their own fun. If a mobile is attached to an infant in such a way that the infant's movements activate the mobile, the infant soon discovers the relationship and seems to delight in making the appropriate kick to set the mobile in motion.

plate their own behavior—to think about what they are doing and why they are doing it. They simply act.

Key to the development of sensorimotor intelligence is the emergence of what Piaget called the **object concept**, or the **concept of object permanence**. According to Piaget, a very young infant does not seem to recognize that objects have a permanent existence outside his or her own interaction with them—that they continue to be, to move, and to be acted on by others when he or she is not present. The ability to conceive of objects as having an existence of their own emerges gradually during the first two years of life.

Early in infancy, from birth to perhaps four months of age, babies will naturally look at a toy, follow it with their eyes, and try to grasp it if it is within their reach. But as soon as the object is moved out of sight, the babies act as though it ceased to exist. They do not search for it either with their eyes or with their hands, nor do they show any other sign that they are aware of its continued existence.

According to Piaget, the baby begins to develop the object concept at around four months (or even much earlier, in the view of some other researchers). If part of a familiar object is visible, babies of this age may reach for it, suggesting that they realize the rest of it is attached to the part that is showing. Babies of this age also seem to be learning that a "disappearing" object may still exist. Infants between four and eight months not only turn their heads to follow a moving object, but continue to look along its path even after it has vanished. But oddly enough, if the object is placed behind a piece of paper or under a pillow, babies at this stage will not search for it with their hands, even though they can reach it. Nor will they retrieve the "hidden" object even when they are already grasping it. If a pillow is quickly placed over an object that a baby is holding, he or she will gaze aimlessly around or will let go of the object and withdraw the empty hand. Clearly, the infant's object concept at this age is still rudimentary.

At the next stage in the development of the object concept, from about eight to twelve months of age, infants for the first time search manually for an object that disappears from sight (Piaget, 1952, 1954). An infant at this stage, seeing a toy put under a pillow, will toss the pillow aside and grasp the toy. But if the toy is then placed under a second pillow—in full sight of the child—he or she will still look for the toy under the *first* pillow. In short, the baby repeats the action that produced the toy earlier, rather than looking for it where it was last seen.

When children reach the last purely sensorimotor stage in the development of the object concept, they can follow all the visible movements of an object and

Figure 8.5 This infant of about six months has not yet developed the concept of object permanence. She looks intently at a toy elephant that is in front of her, but when the toy is blocked from her view, she gives no indication that she understands that the toy is still present.

Figure 8.6 This older infant realizes that the disappearance of an object does not necessarily mean that it is no longer present. When the object he sees is shielded from his view by a towel, he searches for it by crawling under the towel.

therefore find it in the last place it was hidden. The only remaining limit to the baby's understanding of actions carried out on objects is that he or she still cannot cope with unseen transformations. Suppose that an object is hidden in a matchbox, and the matchbox is placed under a pillow. Then, while the infant is not looking, the object is secretly removed from the box and left under the pillow. The empty matchbox is put in front of the child, who quickly searches it for the object. The baby, however, does not search under the pillow. He or she cannot yet take into account the possibility that something unseen might have happened. The final recognition of object permanence comes when children understand that an object can be moved from place to place even when they do not see it being moved. This development marks the end of the sensorimotor period.

Cognitive development in the preschool years

Between the ages of two and three, children leave the cognitive world of infancy far behind. With the discovery that objects and events can be represented by symbols, they have begun to acquire language. This is a tremendously important accomplishment. With words, children's powers of thought and communication are greatly expanded, and they continue to expand as intellectual skills mature.

One of the most important cognitive skills underlying preschool children's intelligence is the ability to engage in what is called *representational thought*. The development of the object concept marks the beginning of this new, important capacity. Children can now think about objects that are not directly in front of them. They can imagine, and by doing so, they expand their world far beyond the limits of their immediate perceptions. One sign that children can think representationally is their ability to imitate someone else's actions a long time after they have seen them. Significantly, preschool children begin to play "make-believe," pretending, for example, that they are astronauts and that a large cardboard box they have found is a spaceship. And, of course, preschool children also begin to use language, an intellectual accomplishment quite distinct from the communication skills learned during infancy.

But although preschool children's cognitive development is impressive, their intellectual capacities are still immature. For one thing, their thought is often egocentric. This does not mean that children of this age are deliberately selfish. Rather, it means that they do not always understand that different people have different perspectives and that their own is merely one among many. In one experimental demonstration of this egocentrism conducted by Piaget and Inhelder (1969), a child was shown a model of a mountain range composed of three mountains in a triangular arrangement (Figure 8.7). The model was large, so the child had to walk around it to look at all its sides. After he or she was familiar with the landscape, the child sat in a chair facing one of the mountains. The experimenter sat in a chair facing another side of the model and asked the child which of several pictures showed what the experimenter saw. The child repeatedly chose the picture showing his or her own view of the landscape.

From this experiment Piaget concluded that young children were too egocentric to understand another person's perspective. However, other researchers

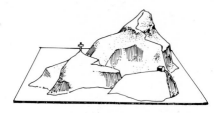

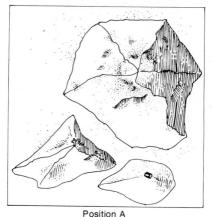

Position A

Figure 8.7 A model used to demonstrate egocentrism. Piaget and Inhelder first had children walk all around the model and look at it from all sides. Then they seated children of various ages at position A and asked them how the scene would appear to observers at other positions. Preoperational children regularly indicated that the scene would appear as it did from position A, no matter where the observer was located. Their thinking did not allow them to mentally reconstruct the scene from a point of view other than their own (after Piaget and Inhelder, 1956).

have suggested that Piaget's conclusion may have been too hasty and too absolute. For example, in one study, children around the age of four were able to describe how the *Sesame Street* character Grover would view a rural scene from different positions (Borke, 1975). Thus, Piaget's three-mountain experiment may have been too difficult. Given an easier task, young children can sometimes see another's viewpoint.

Cognitive development in later childhood

Although some of the thinking of older children is similar to the thought of preschoolers, older children can think in logical ways that younger children cannot. For one thing, children between the ages of five and seven begin to understand what Piaget called **concrete operations**—logical operations that involve reversible transformations of concrete objects and events. It takes an additional five years or more, however, for this capacity to become fully developed. An excellent example of the gradual development of concrete operations is the emergence of what are called **concepts of conservation**.

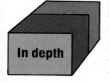

In depth

Studying how concepts of conservation develop Suppose you show a four-year-old two identical short, wide beakers filled with water and ask the child to say whether beaker 1 or beaker 2 contains more water. Most likely, the child will correctly report that both beakers contain equal amounts. Now suppose you pour the water from beaker 2 into a third beaker, which is tall and thin. If you now ask the child which beaker contains more water, beaker 1 or beaker 3, the

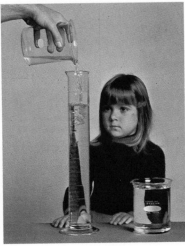

child is very apt to say that beaker 3, the tall thin one, has more. Piaget and others concluded that children of this age fail to understand that the amount of liquid does not change simply because it is poured into a container of a different shape. Preschoolers, in other words, have not yet grasped the concept of conservation of liquid volume.

Nor have they grasped other concepts of conservation. For instance, if you show a preschooler two parallel rows of six identical-sized marbles, with the marbles in each row lined up so that they are touching one another, the child will correctly report that both rows have an equal number. But if you then spread out the marbles in one row, as shown in the bottom panel of Figure 8.9, the child will now say that the lengthened row has more, even though the number of marbles has not changed. Psychologists say that this child does not yet understand conservation of number. He or she believes that number can vary with an irrelevant transformation, such as a change in spacing. Two other conservation problems beyond the grasp of the preschooler, conservation of mass and conservation of length, are also shown in Figure 8.9.

Older children gradually come to understand concepts of conservation. A girl of eight, for example, will probably pay close attention to the transformation that occurs as the liquid is poured from one container to the other. She will also be able to coordinate her thoughts about this transformation with her thoughts about the height and width of each container. As a result, she will answer correctly that the amount of water in both containers is the same. Yet, an eight-year-old does not understand *all* types of conservation. This broader understanding may take many years to acquire. Conservation of number is usually understood first at around age six or seven, then conservation of liquid, still later conservation of weight, and so on. Thus, although older children grasp a growing number of specific concrete operations, they cannot yet understand the similarities among them.

Do the age differences in performance on conservation tasks suggest that preschoolers and older children are in qualitatively different stages of cognitive development? It is difficult to say. Part of the problem is that the tests psychologists use to examine such intellectual differences probably measure more than one cognitive skill. This means that some preschoolers may be failing these tests for reasons unrelated to an understanding of conservation. Consider the stan-

Figure 8.8 The girl taking part in this demonstration has not yet acquired the ability to understand the concept of conservation of liquid. She agrees that there is an equal amount of water in the two shorter beakers, but when the water from one of them is poured into the taller beaker, she incorrectly asserts that there is more water in the taller beaker than in the shorter. To develop an understanding of the principle of conservation, the child must be able to coordinate her thoughts about the length and width of the first container, the length and width of the second container, and the change or transformation brought about by pouring the liquid from the shorter beaker into the taller.

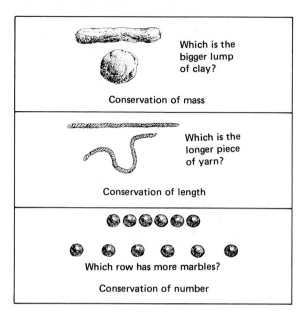

Figure 8.9 Examples of problems for which a child must acquire the concept of conservation. Concrete-operational children interiorize the possibility of making and unmaking the transformations for each task shown here. Thus, they come to see the lengths and quantities as unchanged in each case. Preoperational children, who are not able to imagine the transformations required, respond to perceptually striking but irrelevant aspects of the objects in attempting to answer the questions. For example, preoperational children will answer that there are more marbles in the bottom row than in the top one.

dard conservation-of-number test described earlier and illustrated in Figure 8.9. Might some preschoolers say that there are more marbles in the longer row simply because they mistakenly assume that *more* is a synonym for *longer*? Alternatively, might the attention of some children be misdirected when they are instructed to watch as the experimenter spreads out the marbles in one of the rows? So later, when the experimenter again asks "Which row has more?" the child might conclude that this is a question about length. Both these explanations of the preschoolers' poor performance on traditional conservation-of-number tests are certainly possible. The problem is, how can you design an experiment that will rule them out?

One approach is to do what psychologist Rochel Gelman (1972) did. She presented children ages three to six-and-a-half with two plates. On one plate was a row of three toy mice fastened to a strip of Velcro. On the other plate was a row of two toy mice similarly fastened. The children were told that they were about to play a game in which they had to identify the "winning" plate. Gelman pointed to the plate with three mice and said that it would always be the winner. But she never described the plate in any way. The children had to decide for themselves which attributes—the number of mice the plate contained, the length of its row, the spacing between the mice—made the plate the winner. This was Gelman's way to avoid using the words *more* or *less* to identify the two rows.

Now Gelman began her experiment. She covered each plate with a large lid and shuffled the plates. The child was then asked to pick the lid under which the "winning" plate lay. Whenever the child picked the three-mouse plate and correctly identified it as the "winner," he or she was given a prize. After several rounds of shuffling and picking, Gelman made the critical transformation. She surreptitiously changed the three-mouse display, either by moving the mice closer together or farther apart or by removing one mouse entirely. The fact that these transformations were made covertly was Gelman's way of making sure that she did not call attention specifically to the change and so bias the child's thinking.

Gelman's findings clearly showed that most of the children, even the youngest ones, considered number the relevant attribute differentiating the two plates, rather than the length of its row or the spacing between the mice. Almost no child claimed that a change in the length of the three-mouse row disqualified it as a "winner." In fact, many children failed even to notice such a change. In contrast, almost all subjects noticed removal of a mouse from the previously "winning" plate. Many showed great surprise that one of the mice had disappeared, exclaiming, "Where is it?", "Where'd it go?", or "Where'd ya put the threes?" Others searched for the vanished toy—under the lids, beneath the table, all around the room. Even more important, the overwhelming majority of children doubted whether a three-mouse plate with one of its mice missing could still be considered a "winner." Over two-thirds emphatically said that the plate had now been transformed to a "loser." The only way to fix things, many said, would be to add another mouse. Clearly these children seemed to understand that number can be changed only by addition or subtraction. Yet this directly contradicts the results of traditional conservation of number experiments, in which preschoolers appear to believe that number can also be affected by physical movement (shortening or lengthening of a row). How can these different findings be reconciled?

The two tests must somehow make different cognitive demands on the child. But what is the nature of these differences? Could it be, for example, that the number of items used in a traditional conservation of number test (often six or so per row) is beyond the estimating power of a preschooler, whereas the number of items in Gelman's experiment (only two or three per row) was not? This is a very plausible possibility, but the control study Gelman conducted appears to rule it out. She gave preschoolers a traditional conservation of number test using only three poker chips per row. Few of the children showed any grasp of conservation. Virtually all the three-year-olds and most of the four-year-olds believed that lengthening a row produced "more" chips. Apparently, some other characteristic of Gelman's disappearing mouse experiment made it easier for preschoolers to display a basic understanding of number invariance rules.

It may be that the answer lies in one or both of the factors that Gelman's mouse procedure was deliberately designed to eliminate—differences in language comprehension between older and younger children and perceptual biases created by having the child watch as one row is spread out. Or it may be that the older child is better able to use his or her understanding of numbers in combination with other cognitive skills. In any case, Gelman's work clearly shows how difficult it is to design a test that measures only one cognitive capacity. Psychologists must therefore be cautious in drawing sweeping conclusions about the qualitative differences between a preschooler's intelligence and that of an older child.

The development of memory capabilities You have seen that as children mature their thinking takes on many of the characteristics of adult thought. They master a number of concrete operations, of which conservation is just one. They also become more adultlike in their memory capabilities. On most standard recall tests, young children perform significantly poorer than adults. But why is this the case?

Part of the answer is apparently found in the efficiency with which younger and older subjects store and retrieve information. Children of six use far fewer memory cues and strategies than adults (Flavell and Wellman, 1977). In one experiment (Kobasigawa, 1974), six-, eight-, and eleven-year-olds viewed pictures of three related objects along with a card that could serve as a memory cue. One group of pictures, for example, showed a bear, a monkey, and a camel, while the cue card showed a zoo with three empty cages. The experimenter explicitly related the card to the pictures by pointing out that the zoo is the place where these animals live. Later, some of the children were given the stack of cue cards and asked to recall the three pictures associated with each one. They were told that they could look at the cards if that would help them remember.

Two-thirds of the six-year-olds virtually ignored the cards. They seemed not to grasp the relationship between the cues they held and their ability to retrieve information from memory. The eleven-year-olds, in contrast, used the cues quite effectively, often recalling all three items associated with a card before moving on to the next one. The eight-year-olds were somewhere in between. They sometimes used the cue cards, but their strategy was not as effective as that of the eleven-year-olds. But when all the children were *required* to use the cue cards, age differences in recall disappeared! These results suggest that at least some of the performance differences originally observed were caused not by differences in memory capacity, but rather by differences in knowledge of a particular retrieval strategy and its effective use.

A second factor that may help give older children and adults an edge on most memory tasks is their greater familiarity with the items to be recalled. In general, the less familiar material is, the more difficult it is to remember. You would probably have more difficulty memorizing medical terms, for instance, than a doctor would. Since children are less familiar than adults with most kinds of stimuli, this may partly account for their poorer recall performance. But how can one measure the impact of stimulus unfamiliarity on a child's memory? One way is to reverse the knowledge differential that usually exists between adults and children, as psychologist Michelene Chi did (Chi, 1978). She assembled a group of subjects in which the children were substantially more knowledgeable about the game of chess than were the adults. The children turned out to be significantly better than the adults at remembering various arrangements of pieces on the board, suggesting that differential knowledge does indeed contribute to developmental differences in memory performance.

The development of metacognition If you gave a preschool boy a set of pictures to study until he was sure he could remember the sequence in which they all appeared, you would probably discover that the child will greatly overestimate his ability to recall the pictures. When asked to list them, he will probably hesitate, fumble, and make many mistakes. An older child, in contrast, is much more apt to *know* when he or she has fully memorized a list. This ability to monitor one's own thoughts—whether on a memory test, a problem-solving task, or any other cognitive activity—is called **metacognition**. It is another important intellectual capability that develops in later childhood.

To understand the extent to which differences in metacognition influence the thinking of older and younger children, consider a recent experiment on comprehension of instructions (Markman, 1977). First, second, and third graders were asked, among other things, to evaluate a set of oral instructions about how to play a card game. The instructions omitted such a vital piece of information that no one could possibly understand them. Yet most of the first graders were convinced that the instructions were perfectly clear; only when they tried to play the game did they finally realize the problem. In contrast, the majority of the third graders spotted the blatant gap in the instructions far sooner. Perhaps the younger children were unaware of their faulty comprehension because they did not process the instructions deeply enough (by trying to imagine them being executed, for example). In any case, the fact that the older children were much better than the younger children at gauging their own lack of understanding points to a significant difference in how children at different ages think.

What explains such differences in metacognitive skills? One answer may be young children's limited exposure to metacognitive techniques such as self-testing, in which potential responses are mentally "checked" for accuracy and effectiveness. Yet it is unlikely that differences in experience alone provide a full explanation. When very young children are deliberately taught metacognitive strategies, they often quickly forget them or fail to see their applicability to subsequent memory tasks. So there may also be age constraints on the development of metacognition.

Cognitive development in adolescence

Around the beginning of adolescence a new set of cognitive capabilities, which Piaget (1952) called *formal-operational intelligence*, starts to emerge. Children are able to carry out systematic tests to prove or disprove possible explanations, and they are able to think hypothetically and in abstract terms. As a result, they can solve new kinds of problems that would have been beyond their reach only a few years ago.

One of the most important new skills of adolescents is the ability to consider all the possible combinations of factors that may have caused an event and, through a process of careful reasoning, to eliminate the irrelevant ones. In other words, they can carry out systematic experiments. One task Piaget (Piaget and Inhelder, 1969) created to investigate this skill involves the following materials: four beakers of colorless, odorless liquids labeled 1, 2, 3, and 4, plus a smaller bottle, labeled *g*, also containing a colorless, odorless liquid. The children are given some empty glasses and asked to find the liquid or combinations of liquid that will turn yellow when a few drops from bottle *g* are added to it (Figure 8.10). The combination that produces the yellow color is 1 plus 3 plus *g*. The liquid in 2 is plain water and has no effect on the reaction, and the liquid in 4 prevents the yellow from appearing. Because the children must find out by trial and error what each liquid does, they must try all possible combinations. Otherwise, they cannot be sure of their conclusions. If they succeed, they are questioned about the function of each of the four liquids.

When presented with this task, elementary-school children often begin by systematically trying out all the single possibilities. They may test 4 plus *g*, then 2 plus *g*, then 1 plus *g*, then 3 plus *g*. When none of these combinations produces yellow, they are likely to say, "I tried them all and none of them works." With a little coaching from the experimenter, they may realize that more than

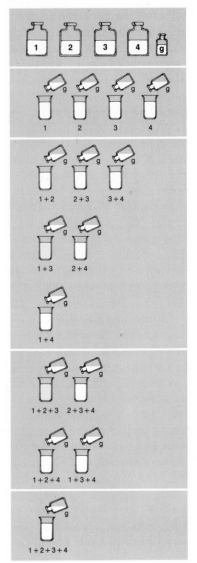

Figure 8.10 A problem that requires the systematic examination of hypotheses for its solution. The chemicals selected by Piaget and Inhelder for this problem have unexpected interactions. It is virtually impossible to determine how the color yellow is produced without trying every possible combination of the liquids, as shown here, and keeping track of the results. Not until children reach the formal-operational period can they conceive of such a procedure (after Piaget and Inhelder, 1969).

one liquid can be combined with g, but they mix the liquids haphazardly. Adolescents, in contrast, can systematically consider all possible combinations of the four liquids. Some may need a paper and pencil to keep track of the combinations that they have made, but they nevertheless understand how to generate the full set.

Simply because adolescents have reached the stage of formal operations, however, does not mean that they will be able to apply their reasoning ability successfully to all appropriate situations. They may misunderstand the demands of a particular task or find a certain problem too difficult. Moreover, research has shown that even well-educated adults commit all sorts of errors on problems of formal reasoning (Henle, 1962; Wason and Johnson-Laird, 1972). Piaget himself felt that most adults may be capable of using formal thinking only in their own areas of experience and expertise.

Cognitive development in adulthood

As anyone reading this book knows, cognitive development does not stop with adolescence. Although individuals vary, most people proceed through a similar cycle of intellectual growth and productivity from early to middle to later adulthood.

Early adulthood, from age twenty to roughly age forty, is a time of peak intellectual accomplishment. On any kind of learning or memory task, young adults usually perform better than they ever have before. And if success at a task depends on how fast one does it, they probably do at least a little better than they ever will again. Early adulthood is also likely to be the time when people are most intellectually flexible. They can usually accept new ideas quite easily, and they can readily shift their strategies for solving problems.

Provided a person remains healthy, verbal skills and reasoning ability are likely to get even better during middle adulthood—roughly the years between age forty and age sixty. A thirty-eight-year study of intellectual performance revealed that IQ generally increased into the middle years (Bradway, 1944; Kangas and Bradway, 1971). And since middle-aged adults continue to learn and store new information just as they always have, they are often more knowledgeable than they were in their younger years. In addition, the ability to think flexibly, to shift the set of one's mind to solve a problem, is likely to be as good as it was in early adulthood. Only when people are asked to do a task that involves coordinated hand-eye movements do they tend to do less well than they used to, because motor skills often decline in middle age (Baltes and Schaie, 1974). In all other ways, however, adults in their middle years are in their intellectual prime.

What about cognitive skills after the age of sixty? Do they decline in later adulthood as so many people assume? The most recent answers to this question are extremely encouraging. Research shows that although a few cognitive skills decline with advancing age, in many older people these losses are not great enough to cause any serious impairment. Some cognitive skills, in fact, hardly diminish at all with advancing years.

Consider memory capability, an intellectual capacity widely assumed to drop off precipitously in old age. Most researchers now agree that differences between younger and older adults in short-term, or "working," memory are negligible (Craik, 1977). Many studies of short-term memory show no significant changes throughout adulthood. And when short-term memory decrements among the elderly are detected, they are usually extremely slight.

A somewhat different picture emerges when we consider long-term memory, however. Suppose you gave an elderly person a list of unrelated items to remember. He or she would probably recall fewer items from the beginning and middle of the list than would a younger adult. As you may remember from Chapter 6, these are the items believed to be stored in long-term memory. Consequently, psychologists conclude that older people experience at least some decline in long-term memory capability. And this decline holds true for memory of visual material as well. In one study in which people of different ages were asked to recognize twenty line drawings they had examined one month earlier, the older subjects recognized somewhat fewer drawings than did the younger ones (Harwood and Naylor, 1969).

What about an older person's memory for even more remote experiences? One popular belief is that elderly people, although poor at recalling things that happened just yesterday or last week, have very vivid recollection of events from their youth. This common assumption, it turns out, is a myth. Like everyone else, older people have the greatest difficulty remembering information from the distant past, while their recall is best for events that happened most recently. This has been demonstrated in a study in which subjects of different ages were questioned for their retention of major news events that had happened from one month to two years earlier. For all age groups, the amount of information recalled declined with the number of months that had elapsed since the event occurred. And, in keeping with the findings of other long-term memory investigations, this decline was somewhat greater for the older than for the younger subjects (Warrington and Sanders, 1971). Perhaps, psychologists suggest, the reason that older people seem to recall the past so vividly is that they have relived it so many times through thought and words. Thus, the elderly man's recollection of his exploits during World War I is not entirely from sixty-odd years ago but partly from the last time he recalled them.

Certain cognitive changes, then, do tend to be associated with aging. Yet, in the average person, none of these are enormous. Most researchers who have studied long-term memory in the elderly have been impressed with the high levels of retention they normally demonstrate (Craik, 1977). In addition, research shows that none of the cognitive changes that tend to accompany aging are inevitable. Some elderly people suffer no decline in cognitive functioning whatsoever. If there is one indisputable fact about aging, it is that its effects are widely varied. Psychologists, of course, are eager to learn why.

Biology certainly contributes to intellectual performance in later adult life. Identical twins are more alike in their cognitive functioning some forty or more years after completing school than unrelated individuals or even fraternal twins (Jarvik, 1975). Of course, these similarities do not necessarily mean that one's timetable for aging is genetically programmed. It may be that what identical twins share is a predisposition toward, or resistance to, certain degenerative diseases, which in turn affect cognitive functioning. But whatever the causal link, some of the wide variation in cognitive decline among the elderly may well be biologically based.

Equally important, however, are environmental factors. Among these are the techniques one has learned for storing and retrieving information. Research shows that if older adults are trained in strategies for organizing information to be lodged in long-term memory and for providing themselves with good re-

Figure 8.11 Among healthy adults, intellectual skills do not decline; older peoples' minds and memories work as well as they ever did, though not as quickly.

trieval cues, age differences in memory performance can be greatly reduced (Craik, 1977). Then, too, the amount of intellectual stimulation in one's environment also appears to be critical to cognitive performance in later life (DeCarlo, 1971; Spirduso, 1975). If older people keep active and involved in interesting and challenging activities—if, in short, they continue to *use* their minds—then there is a strong likelihood that their intellectual powers will not be blunted at all.

SOCIAL AND PERSONALITY DEVELOPMENT

We have seen how the cognitive capabilities of a human being change from birth to old age. But change in intellectual skills is clearly not all there is to human psychological development. Equally important is the emergence of characteristic ways of behaving in various situations and of interacting with others. These patterns are part of an individual's personality and social development.

When casually comparing people's personalities, we are apt to emphasize the many differences that exist: one person is outgoing and aggressive, another introspective and shy. Yet despite such obvious variations in personality and social behavior, there are also striking similarities in the ways that people develop, at least in the sequences of developmental events through which they pass. Developmental psychologists try to understand these common sequences while still accounting for the wide diversity among people.

Social and personality development in infancy

Usually a baby begins to interact with other humans almost immediately after birth. Adults hold and cuddle the infant, smile and talk to him or her, and provide food, warmth, and other necessities. By the time the child is only six weeks old, a smiling adult face is likely to elicit a smile in return. Several months later, the infant shows signs of having formed a strong emotional bond to his or her principal caregiver, typically the mother. The baby smiles, gurgles, and coos when mother approaches and cries loudly when she departs. When the child is old enough to crawl, he or she usually tries to follow wherever mother goes. Since the baby does not behave in this way toward strangers, psychologists infer that the child has formed a very specific **attachment**.

What underlies the attachment of the infant to the principal caregiver? Social-learning theorists have argued that attachment is a positive response to the person who satisfies the baby's needs for food, warmth, comfort, and so forth. But which specific needs are most important? Does an infant form an attachment to the person who generally provides food? To the person who most frequently holds and fondles the baby? Or to the person who does both these things as well as others? This is essentially the question Harry Harlow and his colleagues set out to answer some twenty years ago.

Harlow's experimental design was quite ingenious. He separated newborn monkeys from their natural mothers and provided them with "surrogate mothers" of various kinds. In a series of studies, Harlow (1958; Harlow and Harlow, 1966, 1969) raised infant monkeys in cages that contained two surrogate mothers, one made of stiff, bare wire and the other covered with soft terrycloth. Even when the wire mother was equipped with a milk dispenser, the babies still preferred the terrycloth mother. They spent a great deal of time clinging to its soft, inanimate body, just as baby monkeys cling to their real mothers. And it was always the terrycloth mother to which the infant monkeys would run when alarmed. The little monkeys seemed truly attached to the cloth mother: Even after a year's separation, a young monkey would often rush to embrace the surrogate's soft, familiar form.

Thus it appears that the tactile sensations provided by a mother have something to do with attachment formation in infant monkeys. Harlow, however, did not stop with this discovery alone. Through variations on his basic experiment he found that a number of other factors can influence attachment as well. For instance, when baby monkeys had two cloth-covered mothers, one that dispensed milk and one that did not, they consistently preferred the nourishing one. Feeding, then, also seems to promote attachment, although it is apparently of less importance than tactile comfort. In addition, Harlow's monkeys more readily became attached to a warm mother (one equipped with heating coils) than to a cool mother (one with ice water circulating inside it). And they preferred a surrogate mother that provided a rocking motion to one that remained stationary (Harlow and Suomi, 1970).

Given the propensity of infant monkeys to become attached even to surrogate mothers, it seems likely that attachment in general must be important to a developing monkey. To find out just how important, Harlow and his colleagues separated baby monkeys from real mothers to whom they had already become attached (Seay, Hansen, and Harlow, 1962; Seay and Harlow, 1965). The babies showed signs of acute anxiety. Some initially expressed their protest by running about the cage, chattering and screeching. Soon, however, they became withdrawn and apathetic, refusing to play with their peers.

Fortunately, when these monkeys were reunited with their mothers, they returned to a normal emotional state. The effects of complete attachment deprivation, in contrast, are usually far more devastating and far more difficult to

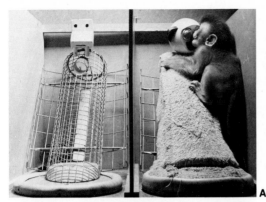

Figure 8.12 (A) One of Harlow's monkeys clings to its terry cloth surrogate mother. (B) A monkey stays in contact with the terry cloth mother even as it nurses from the wire mother. (C) Typical posture of a monkey raised in isolation.

cure. Monkeys raised in total isolation from other monkeys have shown profound behavioral abnormalities (Harlow, Harlow, and Suomi, 1971). Early in life they spend a great deal of time clutching themselves and rocking back and forth. Then they either become apathetic and inactive or display behavior similar to that of some human schizophrenics. When they finally reach maturity and are placed in the company of other monkeys, they are social misfits, incapable of normal sexual behavior and often prone to outbursts of violence. Can these social misfits ever recover from the effects of isolation? Harlow and Suomi (1971) tried to find out. First they tried rewarding appropriate behaviors and punishing inappropriate behaviors, but this did not work. Then they tried putting the maladjusted monkeys together with normal monkeys, but this also failed. Finally, they tried putting a disturbed monkey with a younger, normal monkey—and this worked. The normal monkey clung to the isolate, the two eventually formed an attachment, and the disturbed monkey recovered from the earlier deprivation. This technique could be used to rehabilitate the social misfit even after periods of isolation as long as a year (Novak and Harlow, 1975).

Recent neurological research suggests that part of the reason for the unusual behavior of a monkey reared in isolation may lie in abnormal development of both the cerebellum (involved in physical movement and the sense of balance) and the limbic system (closely tied to behaviors, such as fighting and mating, that satisfy certain motivational and emotional needs). It may be that these abnormalities are initiated by early deprivation of the touching and rocking that a mother normally provides (Prescott, 1979).

As we have seen, much of the research on the factors affecting attachment in infancy and the results of attachment deprivation has been carried out with monkeys. For obvious ethical reasons, experiments of the type Harlow performed cannot be conducted with human beings. Much of our information about the effects of attachment deprivation on humans comes from observation of babies raised in poorly managed orphanages. Such institutions provide adequate food and physical care but little sensory and cognitive stimulation and virtually no opportunity to establish close emotional bonds. In a foundling home in Lebanon, for example, where children spent most of their first year lying on their backs in bare cribs, ignored by adults except for routine feeding, bathing, and changing, the children's physical and cognitive skills were profoundly retarded. Emotionally, the children were as apathetic and distant as their well-meaning but inadequate caretakers (Dennis and Sayegh, 1965). The problem with this study, however, is the difficulty of pinpointing exactly what caused the infants' responses. Was it lack of a one-to-one relationship with a loving adult caregiver? Or was it lack of playthings, opportunities for exploration, and sensory stimulation in general?

The negative effects of continuous institutionalization during childhood, with no possibility to form an attachment to a caring adult, have raised important questions about the consequences of early day care on a child's personality and social development. The most common approach researchers have taken to studying this problem is to watch the reaction of day-care and home-raised children when temporarily separated from their mothers. The child's response after the mother departs, as well as his or her behavior when the mother finally returns, is believed to provide an indication of the quality of the mother–child relationship. The findings of such studies have been somewhat contradictory, but one of the best controlled investigations of this kind to date revealed little difference between day-care children's attachment to their mothers versus the attachment of children reared exclusively at home (Kagan, Kearsley, and Zelazo, 1976). Nor does it appear that day-care children form attachments to their day-time caretakers that supersede attachment to their mothers (Belsky and Steinberg, 1978). Much of the research on day care, however, has been conducted in high-quality, university-affiliated centers with carefully designed programs. Because this type of day care is unavailable to many working mothers, important questions still remain about the effects of average-quality day care on the developing child.

We have discussed the formation of attachment during infancy in some detail because it has such a marked effect on social and personality development. But attachment is not the only socially significant event that occurs in the first two years of life. In the course of interacting with the environment, especially with other people, an infant begins to develop a sense of self. How do researchers know that a young child, who as yet has only rudimentary language skills, is gradually acquiring a self concept? Primarily they observe how children respond to images of themselves. For instance, when a spot of rouge is surreptitiously dabbed on the tip of a child's nose and the child is placed in front of a mirror, about 25 percent of those age fifteen to eighteen months and 75 percent of those age twenty-one to twenty-four months will touch the nose and examine it intently in the glass (Lewis and Brooks, 1978). Such behavior suggests that these children recognize the image in the mirror as themselves. Thus it appears that by the end of the second year at least, most children have developed a concept of self. With this awareness that their own thoughts and actions are distinct from those of others, two-year-olds begin to strive for greater autonomy. That striving helps mark their entry into the social world of childhood.

Social and personality development in childhood

The role of the parents in a child's life gradually changes as the end of infancy approaches. To the baby the parents are primarily caregivers—nurturing, loving figures. But as the child matures and becomes more active and more autonomous, the parents provide less physical care and more discipline. Their tasks now include teaching the child to act in ways consistent with society's notions of good and bad, acceptable and unacceptable. This process of instilling society's values in the child is called **socialization**. It is one of the major learning experiences of childhood and has a profound effect on social and personality development. The basic goal of socialization is **internalization**—incorporation of society's values into the self or personality to such an extent that violation of these standards produces a sense of guilt. In this section we will discuss two areas of childhood development in which socialization plays an important part: the development of gender roles and the development of moral behavior.

Acquiring gender roles At a very early age most children begin to acquire the patterns of behavior generally associated with masculinity and femininity. For instance, one-year-old boys tend to play more vigorously than girls of the same age (Maccoby and Jacklin, 1974), and they tend to prefer toys that require gross motor activity (Goldberg and Lewis, 1969). The average toddler girl, on the other hand, has greater linguistic competence than her male counterpart (Clarke-Stewart, 1973), and she also tends to be less physically aggressive (McIntyre, 1972). Psychologists say that such patterns are signs of incipient **gender roles**. The important question is why such gender-based differences in behavior arise.

The impact of biology It is not easy to assess the precise impact of biology on what we consider masculine and feminine behavior. But psychologists have been able to identify some behavioral differences that exist between males and females very early in life, before the social environment has a chance to exert much of an influence. They have found that newborn boys are generally more active than newborn girls (Phillips, 1978), and as young infants males also tend to cry more and sleep less than females (Moss, 1967). What this means in terms of future personality and social development is difficult to say, for almost immediately after birth, biological tendencies begin to interact with experiences. For instance, initial differences in level of activity may cause male and female babies to experience different kinds of care from parents and different patterns of social interaction. A very active, squirming infant, for example, may be played with more energetically, but hugged and cuddled less. Similarly, a high level of activity could prompt a baby to explore the physical environment more extensively, and this, in turn, could encourage certain patterns of cognitive and personality development. In short, innate differences between boys and girls in activity level alone could interact with environmental factors to gradually produce a variety of behavioral differences.

Yet some psychologists now believe that there may be more of a biological factor in male-female differences in behavior than simply innate differences in activity level. As we mentioned in Chapter 3, the relative quantities of male and female sex hormones present in the body either before or after birth seem to affect the inclination to react aggressively in relevant situations. Of course, learning experiences also have an influence on aggressive tendencies, helping to create wide variations in the amount of aggression different men and women display. But in general, it appears that males may have a somewhat greater biologically based readiness to respond aggressively in certain circumstances than do females (Maccoby and Jacklin, 1974), although there may be instances in which women are not less aggressive (Frodi, Macaulay, and Thome, 1977).

Although biological factors may produce some gender-related differences in behavior, however, it is extremely doubtful that biology alone is responsible for all the behavioral differences that generally exist between boys and girls. If such differences were primarily genetic in origin, then males and females everywhere would exhibit the same gender-role patterns. But this is definitely not the case. Anthropologists have observed marked differences among the world's cultures in the behavioral and personality characteristics ascribed to men and women (see, for example, Mead, 1935). Learning, therefore, seems to play a very important part in the acquisition of gender roles. The exact nature of this learning has been a subject of much debate.

The Freudian view According to Freud, gender role identification and the adoption of sex-typed behaviors are the result of the **Oedipus conflict**, which presumably occurs between the ages of three and five or six. This is the time when most children discover the genital differences between the sexes, and this discovery, according to Freudian theory, prompts children to see themselves as rivals of their same-sex parent for the affection of the parent of the opposite sex. Freud believed that a great deal of anxiety develops as a result of these desires. Eventually, however, the child gradually comes to realize that the longing for the opposite-sex parent is unlikely ever to be fulfilled. So the child compromises: He or she tries to be like, or identify with, the parent of the same sex, adopting that parent's values, behaviors, and so on. This process of **identification**, according to Freud, is crucial to the child's normal development. In identifying with the parent of the same sex, the child constructs a concept of an ideal self that includes the same-sex parent's gender role. Freud argued that if the Oedipus conflict is not satisfactorily resolved, the child may never develop appropriate gender-role behavior.

A number of researchers have tried to test Freud's notion that identification with the same-sex parent is precipitated by the Oedipus conflict. Their findings have usually been inconclusive (Sears, Rau, and Alpert, 1965) or have not supported the theory. For instance, Bronislaw Malinowski (1929), a noted anthropologist, observed that the Oedipus conflict does not occur among the inhabitants of the Trobriand Islands in the South Pacific. There the relationship between father and son is casual and protective throughout childhood. Still, identification with the same-sex parent is common among the Trobrianders, just as it is in many other cultures throughout the world. So whether or

 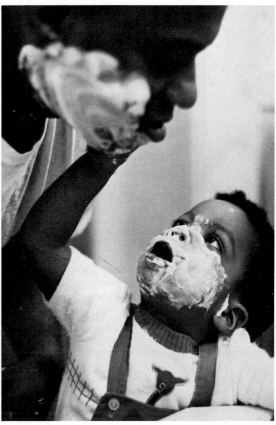

not identification occurs in exactly the way Freud described, psychologists widely regard it as an important part of gender-role acquisition and of personality development in general.

The social learning perspective Unlike Freud and his followers, social-learning theorists believe that the acquisition of gender-related behavior is not initiated by a single anxiety-laden event in a child's life, but rather is a gradual process of learning that begins in infancy. Parents and other adults, they say, shape the child's behavior to conform with established gender roles by reinforcing "appropriate" responses and discouraging "inappropriate" ones. In addition, adults, as well as older brothers and sisters, provide numerous gender-role models for the child to imitate. The result, according to the social-learning view, is that the behavior expected of a boy or girl has begun to emerge even by the age of one or two.

There has been some controversy, however, over whether parents do in fact shape a child's behavior in accordance with traditional sex roles. One review of nearly two hundred published studies concluded that parents do not seem to behave much differently toward their sons than toward their daughters (Maccoby and Jacklin, 1974). Most of the studies found little or no evidence that parents encourage aggression in boys more than in girls, or that they tolerate dependence more in daughters than in sons. But other researchers believe that this conclusion may be premature (see Block, 1975, for example). When asked to assess their own behavior, most parents say that they emphasize achievement, competition, independence, and emotional control more in boys than in

Figure 8.13 Learning sex-role behavior begins almost at birth. The ways adults respond to children, the toys they are given, and the models they see contribute to this learning process.

girls. They also feel that they punish their sons more firmly than they do their daughters. In contrast, parents think that they treat their daughters with greater warmth and physical closeness. Of course, these findings are based on interviews with parents, not on observation of parent-child relationships, and what parents say they do may differ from what they actually do.

Yet additional research shows that parents' judgments about the different ways they treat their sons and daughters may be at least partly accurate. For one thing, some recent observational studies have shown that adults do seem to be more nurturant toward girls and more inclined to encourage activity in boys (Frisch, 1977), and that they emphasize achievement as desirable for boys and social skills as desirable for girls (Block, Block, and Harrington, 1974). Furthermore, it is reasonable to suspect that parents may treat sons and daughters differently because many adults tend to interpret a child's behavior in terms of sex-role stereotypes.

To understand what we mean by this, consider the following study (Condry and Condry, 1976). Young adult subjects were asked to evaluate a baby's emotional responses to four stimuli—a teddy bear, a jack-in-the-box, a doll, and a loud buzzer. Half the subjects were told they were watching a boy, while half were told they were watching a girl. In reality, they were all watching the same nine-month-old child who had previously been filmed on videotape. When the infant cried after being presented with the jack-in-the-box several times, the subjects who believed they were observing a boy attributed the reaction to anger, whereas those who believed they were observing a girl attributed the same response to fear. In an ambiguous situation, in other words, the common stereotype that females are more fearful than males tended to influence the subjects' thinking. It is easy to imagine that as parents these same subjects might respond in very different ways to a crying daughter and a crying son— not because they think boys and girls merit different treatment, but because they perceive each child to be expressing a different emotion.

The cognitive developmental view Psychologists interested in the cognitive aspects of early childhood development have contributed yet another insight to the question of how sex roles are acquired. They argue that it may not matter whether a child is actively reinforced for behavior deemed appropriate for his or her sex, for the child has a "built-in" motivation to imitate such behavior. According to this view, once children have the cognitive ability to understand the concepts of male and female and to recognize that one of these concepts applies to themselves, they will automatically want to adopt behaviors consistent with their newly discovered status (Kohlberg, 1969). Children, cognitive developmental theorists say, strive to be competent at all things—including the actions and attitudes associated with being a boy or a girl.

Note that according to the cognitive developmental view, a child should begin to show a preference for imitating the behavior of same-sex adults only *after* he or she has mastered the concept of gender identity (knowing one's own sex). Moreover, this preference should gradually grow stronger as the child comes to grasp the notions of gender stability over time (knowing that one has always been the same sex) and gender constancy given different situations and desires (knowing that one cannot change sex simply by changing hairstyle or by wanting to be the opposite sex). A number of psychologists have tried to test these predictions. In one study, for example, researchers showed children a movie in which a man and a woman performed the same tasks at the same time

(Slaby and Frey, 1975). If the cognitive developmental view is correct, the children with the best grasp of gender concepts should have perceived the same-sex actor as more similar to themselves, and therefore spent more time watching and learning from that person—and this is exactly what happened. Thus, some awareness of gender identity does seem to be necessary for gender role learning through imitation to take place.

Although the cognitive developmental explanation of sex role learning has thus received some support, it also has an important limitation. Children are unable to identify themselves as male or female until the age of two-and-a-half or older (Thompson, 1975), yet gender-related differences in behavior begin to appear during infancy. It thus seems likely that either biology or parental reinforcement influences the earliest development of gender roles. Indeed, many psychologists argue that any full explanation of sex-role acquisition must probably incorporate elements of more than one theoretical approach (Mussen, 1969).

Moral development Undoubtedly, several theoretical approaches are also needed to fully explain how children gradually acquire concepts of morality— that is, rules of proper conduct by which they judge their own and others' behavior. Remember that an infant enters the world as an amoral creature, bent on nothing more than the satisfaction of immediate needs and desires. How is this totally self-centered baby transformed over the years into a person keenly sensitive to the values, needs, and opinions of others? Three of the perspectives we discussed in exploring gender-role acquisition—the Freudian, the social learning, and the cognitive developmental—also provide some an-swers to this important question.

The Freudian view According to Freud, a child internalizes the moral code of the same-sex parent during resolution of the Oedipus conflict. This process results in a dramatic change in the child's moral orientation: A strong sense of right and wrong emerges where previously there was none. The child, in other words, quite rapidly develops a conscience.

Research has not provided a great deal of support for Freud's view of moral development, however. Although case studies of children undergoing psycho-therapy have provided some evidence for Freud's theory of identification with the same-sex parent, other research has shown that moral development is a very gradual process. The child does not seem to acquire a conscience as the result of a distinct developmental crisis, as the Freudian view implies. Instead, moral development appears to begin in the preschool years and to continue into adulthood (Kohlberg, 1969; Hoffman, 1976).

The social learning perspective Unlike the Freudian view, the social learning perspective can accommodate the gradual nature of moral development. Social learning theorists claim that children behave morally because over the years they are reinforced for "good" behavior and punished for "bad" behavior, and they are also provided with moral models to imitate. Experimental studies have furnished some support for these ideas, finding that children frequently (but not always) imitate the immoral or moral behaviors they observe. For example, children will often behave generously after observing an unselfish adult (Bryan, 1975), and they will behave aggressively after observing an aggressive model (Bandura, Ross, and Ross, 1961).

Research has also shown that the way parents socialize their children is important to the establishment of self-regulated moral conduct. An excessive use of power-assertive techniques of punishment (spankings, withdrawal of privileges, or the threat of either) tends to be associated with low levels of moral development (Hoffman, 1976). In contrast, reasoning with children about their behavior—explaining why a certain act is right or wrong, pointing out how their behavior affects others—appears to be associated with high levels of moral development, including consideration for others, capacity for moral reasoning, and feelings of guilt over wrongdoing (Hoffman and Saltzstein, 1967; Aronfreed, 1969; Hoffman, 1976).

The cognitive developmental view The social-learning view of moral development implicitly assumes that a child's acquisition of conscience depends more on the amount and type of training he or she receives than it does on the child's age and level of maturation. In contrast, the cognitive developmental view reverses the importance of these two sets of factors. Its proponents argue that a child progresses through a number of distinct stages of moral judgment, and that these stages reflect changes in the child's cognitive capabilities that are broadly related to age (for example, Piaget, 1948).

The psychologist most closely associated with the cognitive developmental view of moral learning is Lawrence Kohlberg (1963, 1969). Kohlberg, who was greatly influenced by Piaget's concept of stages, maintains that the stages of moral development occur in an invariable sequence, each one developing out of its predecessor and each one cognitively more complex than the one before. Kohlberg and his colleagues assess a person's level of moral development by presenting him or her with a series of moral dilemmas and asking what should be done in each situation and why. Consider, for example, the dilemma of Heinz:

In Europe, a woman was near death from cancer. One drug might save her, a form of radium that a druggist in the same town had recently discovered. The druggist was charging $2,000, ten times what the drug cost him to make. The sick woman's husband, Heinz, went to everyone he knew to borrow the money, but he could only get together about half of what it cost. He told the druggist that his wife was dying and asked him to sell it cheaper or let him pay later. But the druggist said, "No." The husband got desperate and broke into the man's store to steal the drug for his wife. Should the husband have done that? Why? (Kohlberg, 1969, p. 379.)

Note that a person at any stage of moral development could conclude that Heinz should or should not have stolen the drug. What matters to Kohlberg is not the particular decision a subject makes, but the explanations for that choice. Table 8.1 presents typical reasons for stealing or not stealing the drug at each of the three major developmental levels, each of which has two stages. At the first major level, the **preconventional**, a child adheres to the rules of society because he or she fears the consequences of breaking them. The child, in other words, acts "good" to avoid punishment. At the second major level, the **conventional**, the child is concerned about winning the approval of others and meeting their standards and expectations. He or she is often inclined to follow the dictates of established authority. The final major level of moral reasoning, the **postconventional**, is not reached during childhood. In fact, it is attained by only a few adults. A person at this level recognizes that universal ethical principles can transcend the specific laws of a society. Failure to adhere to these principles brings self-condemnation and loss of self-respect.

As Figure 8.14 shows, a person's level of moral reasoning is related to his or her age. Older children tend to be more advanced in their thinking than youn-

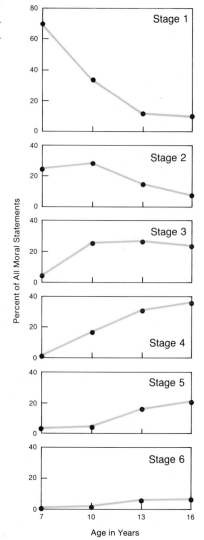

Figure 8.14 Evidence that children progress through moral stages in an invariant sequence. Kohlberg asked children to respond to moral dilemmas such as the Heinz story presented in the text. He classified their statements according to stage of moral development. Each graph here shows the average percentage of all the statements made by children of a given age at each of Kohlberg's six stages. For example, the top graph shows that about 70 percent of the statements made by seven-year-olds were classified as stage 1 thinking (after Kohlberg, 1963).

TABLE 8.1 Motives for Stealing or Not Stealing the Drug at Various Levels of Moral Development

	For stealing drug	Against stealing drug
Preconventional level		
Stage 1: obedience, or reward, orientation		
Action motivated by avoidance of punishment, and "conscience" is irrational fear of punishment.	If you let your wife die, you will get in trouble. You'll be blamed for not spending the money to save her and there'll be an investigation of you and the druggist for your wife's death.	You shouldn't steal the drug because you'll be caught and sent to jail if you do. If you do get away, your conscience would bother you thinking how the police would catch up with you at any minute.
Stage 2: instrumental exchange, or marketplace, orientation		
Action motivated by desire for reward or benefit. Possible guilt reactions are ignored and punishment is viewed in a pragmatic manner.	If you do happen to get caught, you could give the drug back and you wouldn't get much of a sentence. It wouldn't bother you much to serve a little jail term, if you have your wife when you get out.	He may not get much of a jail term if he steals the drug, but his wife will probably die before he gets out so it won't do him much good. If his wife dies, he shouldn't blame himself, it wasn't his fault she has cancer.
Conventional level		
Stage 3: conformist, or "good boy, good girl," orientation		
Action motivated by anticipation of disapproval by others, actual or imagined.	No one will think you're bad if you steal the drug, but your family will think you're an inhuman husband if you don't. If you let your wife die, you'll never be able to look anybody in the face again.	It isn't just the druggist who will think you're a criminal; everyone else will too. After you steal it, you'll feel bad thinking how you've brought dishonor on your family and yourself; you won't be able to face anyone again.
Stage 4: "law and order" orientation		
Action motivated by anticipation of dishonor—that is, institutionalized blame for failure of duty—and by guilt over concrete harm done to others.	If you have any sense of honor, you won't let your wife die because you're afraid to do the only thing that will save her. You'll always feel guilty that you caused her death if you don't do your duty to her.	You're desperate and you may not know you're doing wrong when you steal the drug. But you'll know you did wrong after you're sent to jail. You'll always feel guilty for your dishonesty and lawbreaking.
Postconventional level		
Stage 5: social-contract, legalistic orientation		
Concern about maintaining respect of equals and of the community (assuming their respect is based on reason rather than emotions). Concern about own self-respect—that is, about avoiding judging self as irrational, inconsistent, nonpurposive.	You'd lose other people's respect, not gain it, if you don't steal. If you let your wife die, it would be out of fear, not out of reasoning it out. So you'd just lose self-respect and probably the respect of others too.	You would lose your standing and respect in the community and violate the law. You'd lose respect for yourself if you're carried away by emotion and forget the long-range point of view.
Stage 6: universal ethical principle orientation		
Concern about self-condemnation for violating one's own principles.	If you don't steal the drug and let your wife die, you'd always condemn yourself for it afterward. You wouldn't be blamed and you would have lived up to the outside rule of the law but you wouldn't have lived up to your own standards of conscience.	If you stole the drug, you wouldn't be blamed by other people but you'd condemn yourself because you wouldn't have lived up to your own conscience and standards of honesty.

Source: Adapted from Lawrence Kohlberg. Stage and sequence. The cognitive-developmental approach to socialization. In David A. Goslin (Ed.), *Handbook of socialization theory and research*. Chicago: Rand-McNally, 1969.

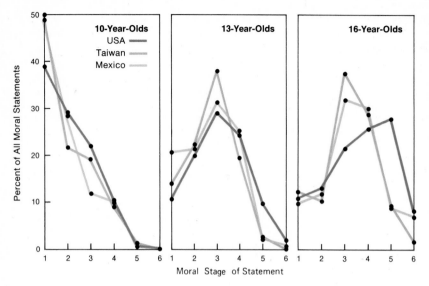

Figure 8.15 On the basis of these data and others like them Kohlberg maintains that moral development is not culturally relative but shows a similar pattern in a variety of cultures. Responses to moral dilemmas made by ten-, thirteen-, and sixteen-year-olds from three countries were classified according to moral stage. In all three countries, most ten-year-olds were at stage 1 and most thirteen-year-olds, at stage 3. The steady progression of moral stage with age suggests not only that moral development occurs in an invariant sequence, but also that this sequence is the same for different cultures (after Kohlberg, 1963).

ger children, even though there is wide variation in the speed at which a given individual moves through the stages and the point at which that person ceases to advance. In addition, a child's level of moral reasoning is also related to his or her level of cognitive development, as measured by the ability to perform various logical tasks (Selman, 1976; Kuhn et al., 1977). Not surprisingly, therefore, several cross-cultural studies have shown that children in all parts of the world tend to proceed through the same stages in the same order (Kohlberg, 1963). The results of one such study are shown in Figure 8.15.

Kohlberg's cognitive theory of moral development has received some criticism, however (Kurtines and Greif, 1974; Holstein, 1976). His methods of collecting and analyzing data have been questioned, as have his assertions that the stages of moral reasoning are universal and unvarying in sequence. Nevertheless, many psychologists continue to believe that Kohlberg's theory is one of the best available approaches to understanding the progression from a young child's sense of morality based on the consequences of his or her acts to the abstract moral codes adhered to by many adults (Hoffman, 1977).

Social and personality development in adolescence

The word *adolescence* comes from the Latin word *adolescere*, meaning "to grow into maturity." And so the beginning of adolescence is marked by the onset of **puberty**, the period of sexual maturation. This biological event transforms a child into a physical adult, and carries with it important psychological and social consequences. The need to establish an independent identity, to gain a sense of one's self as a separate, autonomous person, becomes a major concern during this period.

According to psychologist Erik Erikson (1950), who introduced the concepts of identity and the identity crisis, the physical, sexual, and social demands on the adolescent often produce internal conflict. To resolve this conflict successfully, adolescents must develop an inner sense of continuity between what they were in the past and what they will become. This they often attempt to do by temporarily trying out different roles. Thus, one adolescent may try her hand at acting, throw herself into the study of philosophy, and become involved in politics. By experimenting with a variety of possible choices, adolescents acquire some idea of the life style associated with various roles, yet do not commit themselves irrevocably to any one. Erikson notes that these experiments with different identities are much more possible in some societies than others. While an American teenager has a prolonged period of adolescence during which to experiment, young people in societies that have either no period between socially defined childhood and adulthood, or only a very short one, are forced into permanent adult roles soon after puberty.

How stormy is the search for identity during adolescence? The term "identity crisis" has become so common in our society that many people assume it is normal for all adolescents to go through a difficult time achieving this important goal. However, it is important to note that conflict and open rebellion against parents are not inevitable hallmarks of adolescent development. Many high-school and college students cope quite well with the developmental tasks of adolescence and make the passage through these years without major turmoil (King, 1973).

Social and personality development in adulthood

Many people assume that social and personality development slows and eventually ceases once a person has entered adulthood. In fact, Freud argued that basic personality traits are essentially fixed in childhood and that adult identity is established around the end of adolescence. As you will see in Chapter 13, however, there is much debate over this notion of a stable, largely invariable adult self. Certainly, people do face different challenges, have different concerns, and find different sources of satisfaction at various stages in their adult lives. And recent research indicates that these differences in life experiences make the attitudes and outlook of a man or woman of twenty-five significantly different from those of the same person twenty or forty years later.

If adolescence is a time of searching inward for personal identity, autonomy, and values, early adulthood is a time of looking outward to the external tasks of launching a career, a marriage, and perhaps a family. In one study of the feelings, concerns, and activities of more than five hundred men and women, those between the ages of twenty-two and twenty-eight were found to be busy making commitments, taking on responsibilities, and focusing their energies on the attainment of goals (Gould, 1972, 1978). Thus, rather than being a period of deep introspection, the early and mid-twenties are usually a period of action.

The decade from age twenty to age thirty poses a special challenge to women. A young woman today is faced with a much wider range of choices concerning her life's work than was her grandmother or probably even her mother. Like generations of women before them, many women in their twenties still see marriage and motherhood as major life goals. But a growing number are rejecting or postponing childbearing in favor of establishing a career. In addition, many other options are available between the two extremes of full-time wife and mother on the one hand, and full-time member of the labor force on the other. As Gail Sheehy has pointed out in her best-selling book *Passages* (1976), women today are frequently choosing to marry and have both a family and a career, the relative balance between the two being adjusted again and again throughout early and middle adulthood.

The attitudes and concerns of adults in their twenties gradually start to change as the thirtieth birthday approaches. Many of those between the ages of twenty-eight and thirty-four begin to question the commitments they have made in the past decade, the values they have chosen, and the goals they have worked so hard to achieve. In short, this is a time of life when many people stop and ask: "What is life all about now that I have done what I am supposed to do?" (Gould, 1972, 1978). Such misgivings, of course, can often lead to difficult and very painful reversals. Marriages may end, careers may be abandoned, and entire life styles may be changed. People in their early thirties sometimes feel that any unsatisfactory aspect of their lives must be rectified immediately because soon it will be too late. This period of life has been called the age-thirty crisis (Levinson, 1978).

As the questioning and changes that accompany the age-thirty crisis subside, a person enters a new period of adulthood. For working men and women, the years between thirty-five and forty can be especially productive ones. In one recent study of both professional and working-class men, this was a time of "making it"—of establishing oneself in the adult world and of actively carving out a niche (Levinson, 1978). Usually this means moving up the ladder of prestige and achievement in the person's chosen career.

At about the age of forty the period of early adulthood comes to an end and a mid-life transition begins. For the woman who has devoted her adult life to the role of wife and mother, a crisis may occur when her children begin to leave home. To adjust to these changes, the woman in mid-life transition may search for satisfying work outside the home, returning to an interrupted career or perhaps starting a new one.

For men the mid-life transition usually centers around questions about both personal life and career. Like women at this stage they may wonder: "What have I done with my life?" "What have I accomplished?" "What do I still wish to do?" Of the sample of men recently studied by Daniel Levinson and his colleagues (1978), fully 80 percent experienced the mid-life transition as a moderate to severe crisis, characterized by a questioning of virtually every aspect of their lives.

Once a person emerges from the critical mid-life transition, he or she is firmly entrenched in the middle adult years. For many people, this is a period of greater stability than they have ever known. Income is typically higher than at any time in the past. People usually have confidence in whatever skills they possess, and their productivity is often at its peak. But with middle age comes a new sense of time. People are increasingly aware that life is finite, and so they begin to think more in terms of priorities. Personal relationships may also become more important. Many people report greater satisfaction with their husband or wife, warmer ties with their children, and an increased value placed on friends. In many people these values and outlooks continue into later adult life (Gould, 1972, 1978).

We have seen that making the transition from one phase of adulthood to another is not always easy. But many people cope with major transitions—marriage, divorce, the birth of a baby, the departure of children from home, retirement, the death of a spouse, and the approach of one's own death—without undue stress (Neugarten, 1976). Apparently, these events are not necessarily traumatic. They become so only when they are not anticipated or when they occur at an unexpected time in the life cycle. Thus, the death of a child is much more stressful than the death of a parent, and divorce when a woman

Figure 8.16 The relationship of young and old symbolize the continuity of human development.

is forty is much more difficult for her to accept than widowhood when she is sixty-five. A study of men who had retired from their life's work (Barfield and Morgan, 1970) found that nearly 70 percent of those who retired as planned were content with their new status, whereas less than 20 percent of those who retired unexpectedly due to layoffs or poor health were. Similarly, a study of elderly people showed that those who were living in familiar and stable surroundings were less afraid of dying than those who were about to be admitted to a home for the aged (Lieberman and Coplan, 1970). The prospect of dying in unknown circumstances creates stress. But as long as the expected rhythm of the life cycle is not disrupted, most adults cope successfully with life, even in its final stages.

SUMMARY

1. The branch of psychology that seeks to explain the regular patterns of growth and change that occur during the life cycle is called **developmental psychology**. In investigating the process of human development, psychologists generally ask two closely related questions: How do people change as they grow older, and why do these changes occur in the ways they do? They have found that throughout life, change does not occur at random, but tends to follow sequential patterns—although individual variations can be seen in all developmental sequences.

2. To explain *why* particular changes take place—and why there are always individual variations—psychologists look to heredity and environment, since any developmental event is always the product of an interaction of the two.

3. The human newborn begins life with some surprisingly mature and well-integrated systems that make possible interaction with people and objects from the very first moments after birth. These systems include a set of motor reflexes and impressive auditory and visual capabilities.

4. The development of intellectual ability—**cognitive development**—is viewed in two ways by psychologists. Some see it as a series of *qualitatively* different stages during each of which the child's characteristic ways of thinking become more mature. Others believe that *quantitative* differences in the knowledge that children of different ages have acquired account for what appear to be qualitative differences in cognitive ability.

5. The cognitive changes that take place during the first few years of life are perhaps the most remarkable of all those we undergo. Factors in this striking development include the infant's capacity for learning and memory. It has been shown that babies are capable of learning from the moment of birth—and probably even before—and that they can remember for fairly long periods of time, even during the earliest months of life.

6. The most influential stage theory yet proposed is that of Jean Piaget, who saw four main periods or stages: the **sensorimotor** (in which the child discovers the concept of object permanence), the **preoperational** (in which the child begins to use language and other symbols), the **concrete operational** (in which the child begins to use concepts of conservation), and the **formal operational** (in which the child is able to carry out systematic tests of hypotheses and to think in abstract terms).

7. Older children also become more adultlike in their memory capabilities, partly because they store and retrieve information more efficiently than younger children, and partly because they are more familiar with the items to be recalled. In addition, the older child develops a capacity for **metacognition**, the ability to monitor his or her own thoughts.

8. Cognitive development continues throughout early, middle, and late adulthood. Early adulthood, from about ages twenty to forty, is a time when learning or memory tasks are usually performed better than they ever have been before and when people are most intellectually flexible. In middle adulthood—approximately ages forty to sixty—motor skills may decline, but verbal and intellectual ability are likely to get even better. In late adulthood—after age sixty—some cognitive skills such as long-term memory may decline, but these changes are not inevitable, and both biological and environmental factors can influence the extent to which the changes associated with aging take place.

9. In addition to cognitive development, psychologists study **personality and social development**, the emergence of the characteristic ways in which we behave in various situations, and how we interact with others.

10. Human interactions begin immediately after birth, and the baby who is a few months old has usually formed a very specific **attachment** to the mother or principal caregiver. In addition to attachment, most human infants by the end of the second year have developed a sense of self that enables them to begin to strive for greater autonomy.

11. When children leave infancy, parents begin the process of **socialization**—instilling society's values in the child. The basic goal of socialization is **internal-**

ization—incorporation of society's values into the self to such an extent that violation of these standards produces guilt.

12. One are where socialization plays an important role is in the acquisition of **gender roles**, the patterns of behavior generally associated with masculinity and femininity, which most children begin to acquire at a very early age. Although biology contributes to the behavioral differences that exist between boys and girls, learning appears to play a very important part in the acquisition of gender roles.

13. The acquisition of **morality**—rules of proper conduct by which children judge their own and others' behavior—has been approached from several points of view. According to Freud, a child internalizes the moral code of the same-sex parent during resolution of the Oedipus conflict. Social learning theorists claim that children acquire morality gradually by being reinforced for good behavior and punished for bad. The cognitive-developmental view argues that a child progresses through a number of distinct stages of moral judgment that reflect the child's cognitive capabilities.

14. Adolescence brings with it important psychological and social consequences, because it marks the transition from childhood to adulthood. Erik Erikson proposed that adolescents go through an **identity crisis**, which they may try to resolve by temporarily trying out different roles.

15. Adults of different ages continue to change and develop. The early and mid-twenties are usually a period of action, involving for women especially a growing number of choices that may involve continual readjustment throughout early and middle adulthood. Slightly older adults may go through an "age-thirty crisis," in which they evaluate, and may reverse, the choices they have so far made. For working people, the period from ages thiry-five to forty appears to be an especially productive time. Both men and women around age forty may go through a mid-life transition. The middle adult years, from about forty to sixty and even later, are for some a period of greater stability than they have ever known.

16. Major life transitions seem to be traumatic only when they are not anticipated or when they occur at an unexpected time in the life cycle. Otherwise, it appears, they can be handled without undue stress.

Suggested readings

Bee, H. *The developing child* (2nd ed.). New York: Harper & Row, 1978.

Conger, J. J. *Adolescence and youth: Psychological development in a changing world* (2nd ed.). New York: Harper & Row, 1977.

Flavell, J. H. *Cognitive development*. Englewood Cliffs, N.J.: Prentice-Hall, 1977.

Harlow, H. F., Harlow, M. K., and Suomi, S. J. From thought to therapy: Lessons from a primate laboratory. *American Scientist*, 1971, *59*, 538–549.

Papelia, D. E., and Olds, S. W. A. *A child's world: Infancy through adolescence* (2nd ed.). New York: McGraw-Hill, 1979.

Parke, R. D., and Sawin, D. B. Fathering: It's a major role. *Psychology Today*, 1977, *11*, 109–112.

Woodruff, D. S., and Birren, J. E. *Aging: Scientific perspectives and social issues.* New York: Van Nostrand Reinhold, 1975.

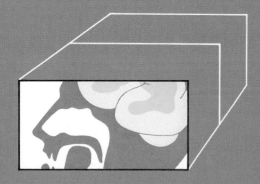

PREVIEW

1. Language is our principal means of communication, facilitating most of the activities we consider uniquely human.

2. Chimpanzees can learn sign language, reflecting either an ability to communicate symbolically, conditioning, or a combination of both.

3. A region in the human brain may be specialized for the acquisition of language, and there may be an optimal time for language learning in our development.

4. Language develops rapidly and sequentially. In early stages, this development is characterized by primitive grammatical rules, not simply imitation and reinforcement.

5. Some psychologists believe language determines the form of thought; others, that thought processes determine language use.

6. Nonverbal communication—intonation, posture, gesture, and body movement—is subtle and harder to control than language.

7. Nonverbal behavior, which is somewhat consistent and somewhat varied among cultures, is probably partly inherited and partly learned.

9 Language and its development

If you have ever tried to learn a foreign language, you know how complex and painstaking a task it can be. Now try to remember learning your native language. Do you recall mastering how to phrase a question? Or struggling with the verb forms for past, present, and future? Probably not. For one thing, these milestones in language acquisition occurred when you were very young, usually before your fifth birthday. For another, we cannot say that people learn their native language in the same arduous way that adults learn a foreign language. For children, language acquisition is much more a process of creative experimentation, motivated by a desire to communicate their thoughts and feelings to others. Anyone who has ever observed a young child develop language is usually impressed with how effortless the child's progress seems to be. Yet proficiency at language is probably one of the most difficult skills the average person ever acquires. It certainly rivals all others in importance.

That language is central to human existence becomes clear the moment you try to imagine a world without language of any kind. Even the most ordinary activities would be extremely difficult, if not impossible. How could you give directions, explain your feelings, make a promise, or ask a favor without language? Would you even be able to think without language? How could you deduce another person's motives, plan for the future, or puzzle over the meaning of life if language did not exist? Clearly the ability we call language enables us to perform most of the activities that we consider uniquely human.

In this chapter we will explore many fascinating issues about language. We will begin with a discussion of what language is—how it functions, how it is structured, and how it is used. Next we will turn to the topic of human language and animal communication. The subject of language acquisition is also of central concern to psychologists. In this regard, we will follow young children through the milestones in language development—speaking their first words and first sentences and eventually acquiring complex grammatical rules. From here we will investigate the relationship between language and thought. Finally, we will conclude with the subject of nonverbal communication. You will learn how people communicate many of their feelings through facial expressions, gestures, and tones of voice. And you will also examine the important question of how these modes of communication arise.

THE NATURE OF LANGUAGE

We are so accustomed to using language in every aspect of our lives that we seldom stop to consider all that speaking and listening involve. If we did, we would soon realize that language is incredibly complex. Those who study it generally agree that language can best be described in three ways: by its function, by its structure, and by the mental processes that underlie its use.

How language functions

Language functions as our principal means of communication. This statement is simple enough. But unfortunately it does not begin to convey how rich a communication system human language is. There is almost nothing you might want to express that you cannot say with language. What makes language such a remarkably flexible and efficient system?

One reason is that language is *symbolic*—it involves the use of sounds to represent objects, events, and ideas. As a result, language is tied neither to the concrete nor to the present. You can talk about things that are immediately before you as well as things removed in time and space. When you utter the string of sounds that make up the word *book*, for example, you are symbolically referring to the collection of bound, printed pages in front of you or to any other book ever produced. Note that your use of these particular sounds to represent this object is completely arbitrary. A German conveys the same meaning with the word *Buch*, as does an Italian with the word *libro*. Language is simply a set of conventions that speakers agree to share.

Another reason why language is so versatile is that it is built up from numerous components (sounds, prefixes, suffixes, root words) that can be combined in an enormous variety of ways. Language, in other words, is based on a principle of combination, and this principle makes the possibilities for speech production virtually unlimited. This is why precise sentence duplication is so rare in any language. Except for the occasional conventional form, such as "How are you?," the vast majority of English sentences you hear or speak each day are in some way novel. To prove this to yourself, select any sentence in this book and then try to find another one just like it. Your chances of success are very low.

The number of possible ways that the hundreds of thousands of words in the English language can be combined is staggering, making exact repetition highly unlikely. It has been estimated that it would take 10,000 billion years, nearly 2,000 times the estimated age of the earth, merely to utter all the possible twenty-word sentences in English!

Linguistic structure

Our brief discussion of how language functions so flexibly makes it clear that an understanding of the function of language cannot be divorced from an understanding of its structure. In this respect, language is like any other tool humans might invent. The way in which a wrench is structured, for instance, largely determines the purposes for which it can be used, just as the functions a wrench is to serve largely govern its structure. In much the same way linguistic function and structure are intimately linked. Linguists have consequently spent much time dissecting human languages into their component parts and trying to specify the rules for combining these parts into meaningful utterances. They have found that the structure of language can be analyzed at three basic levels: in terms of the sounds that make up the language (**phonology**); in terms of the rules by which these sounds are combined to form basic units of speech and these basic units of speech are combined to form complex words (**morphology**); and in terms of the rules by which words are combined into grammatical phrases and sentences (**syntax**).

Phonology Out of the great number of vocal sounds a human being can make, each language uses certain ones as its fundamental building blocks. Linguists divide these sounds into categories called **phonemes**. A phoneme is a class of slightly varying sounds that speakers of a language perceive as linguistically similar. Consider the sounds of the /t/s in the word *total*. If you hold your palm several inches in front of your mouth while you say this word out loud, you will quickly discover that the two /t/s are not identical. The first is aspirated (it concludes with a short puff of breath); the second is not. Yet speakers of English ignore this difference because, linguistically, it is not significant to us. An aspirated and an unaspirated /t/ can be used interchangeably in an English word without altering the word's meaning. This is another way of saying that in English these two sounds belong to the same phoneme. Not all languages classify sounds in the same way that English does. In Chinese, an aspirated and an unaspirated /t/ belong to different phonemes: To interchange them can alter the meaning of a word. Consequently, speakers of Chinese are very sensitive to the differences between these two sounds.

Most languages use some sounds that are completely meaningless in English. In the African language Xhosa, for example, a clicking sound made with the tongue is linguistically significant; so is a guttural /ch/ in German, as in the word *Achtung!* English, in turn, uses some sounds that other languages do not. The sound of the /j/ in the English word *jump*, for instance, is not used in Spanish. Because of their distinctive ways of selecting and classifying sounds, different languages have different kinds and numbers of phonemes. English, for example, has about forty phonemes, the exact number depending on the regional dialect spoken. (These correspond to all our vowel and consonant sounds, plus indivisible sounds made by such combinations of letters as /ch/,

Figure 9.1 Speakers of English agree that the sound of /e/ is linguistically meaningful, and speakers of French agree that the sound of /è/ is also linguistically meaningful in a different way—as this work by Saul Steinberg, entitled *The Dream of E*, wittily implies.

/sh/, and /th/.) As languages go, English is neither frugal nor abundant in its number of phonemes. Some Polynesian languages get away with as few as fifteen phonemes; other languages use as many as eighty-five. All, however, are equally effective in expressing their speakers' thoughts.

Morphology   In order to convey ideas, the sounds of a language must be combined into meaningful utterances. These combinations are not haphazard. Every language has its own set of rules regarding which groupings of sounds are acceptable and which are not. You know immediately, for instance, that the sequence of sounds *mfiydnu* cannot be an English word. It violates too many of our rules of proper sound ordering. The sequence of sounds *mundify*, however, is a different matter. Although you may not know for sure whether this is an actual English word without consulting a dictionary, it is certainly a plausible possibility.

The smallest combinations of speech sounds that have meaning in a given language are called **morphemes**. English has more than 100,000 morphemes, including *free morphemes* (words that can stand alone, such as *big*, *boat*, and *believe*) and *bound morphemes* (units like the prefixes *un-* and *anti-* or the suffixes *-ly* and *-ed*, which must be combined with another morpheme to convey meaning). Thus, many of the nearly 1 million words in the English language are made up of several morphemes. The word *unbelievable*, for instance, has three morphemes: the prefix *un-* meaning "not," the root word *believe*, and the suffix-*able* meaning "capable of being." All languages have rules specifying how such prefixes, suffixes, and root words can be combined. These rules are central to the language's morphology.

Syntax Finally, languages also have rules specifying how words should be combined to produce meaningful phrases and sentences. These rules constitute each language's syntax. The sentence "The old goat ate the rusty can" is a perfectly grammatical English statement because it adheres to our syntactic rules. In contrast, "The goat old ate the can rusty" violates our rule for the placement of adjectives and so sounds jumbled to us. In a language like English, which uses many free morphemes, word order is particularly important to conveying a speaker's thoughts correctly. The sentence "Jane hit Jerry," for example, expresses a very different meaning from the simple rearrangement "Jerry hit Jane." Thus, a single change in word order can drastically alter the meaning of an English sentence.

The syntactic rules of any language are numerous and complex. Yet at a very early age speakers of that language implicitly grasp and follow them. In fact, most speakers find the syntax of their native language so "natural" that they think it odd that speakers of other languages adhere to different rules. In Spanish, for example, adjectives usually *follow* the noun they modify, not precede it as in English. So in Spanish the sentence "El cabrón viejo comió la lata mohosa" ("The goat old ate the can rusty") is perfectly correct. Like all aspects of language, then, rules of syntax are simply arbitrary conventions. What is grammatical in one language may be ungrammatical in another.

The process of using language

Our implicit understanding of the **grammar** of a language (its morphology plus its syntax) gives rise to what is called **linguistic competence** (Chomsky, 1965). Linguistic competence is a person's intuitive grasp of the rules for constructing grammatical sentences. But there is obviously much more to human language than implicit knowledge of structural rules alone. These rules must somehow be put to use whenever we speak or interpret what other people say. The application of our implicit knowledge of grammar during speaking or listening is known as **linguistic performance**.

Psychologists are just beginning to understand the complex mental processes that underlie linguistic performance. One very important insight has come from comparison of a sentence's **surface structure** (the words spoken and their organization) with its **underlying representation** (essentially its meaning). For example, the surface structure of the sentence "Hamlet bought Ophelia an anchovy pizza" can be described according to its grammatical elements. *Hamlet* is the subject of the sentence and *bought* the verb; *Ophelia* is the indirect object, *pizza* the direct object, and *an* and *anchovy* are modifiers of *pizza*. But although such an analysis is useful in specifying how the sentence is constructed, it does not help us explore what the sentence means. This underlying representation can best be summarized by units of meaning called **propositions**. The propositions contained in our sample sentence are expressed in Figure 9.2. As you can see, each proposition is a unitary idea, and when these ideas are combined in a certain way, the meaning of our sentence emerges. Yet the propositions are not

Hamlet bought Ophelia an anchovy pizza.

a. Hamlet bought a pizza.

b. The pizza is for Ophelia.

c. The pizza is topped with anchovies.

Figure 9.2 The propositions, or units of meaning, of the sample sentence in the text.

directly present in the surface structure. Instead, the surface structure transforms these three separate propositions into two phrases and a clause.

The processes of speaking and listening, then, can be simply viewed as different kinds of transformations. Speaking involves the transformation of an underlying representation (held in the speaker's mind) into the surface structure of a grammatical sentence. Listening is essentially the opposite. It involves the transformation of a sentence's surface structure into its underlying representation (the propositions it expresses) so that its meaning can be understood.

If you pause to think about these activities you will quickly see just how complex they really are. First, consider the sentences "I have no money" and "I don't have any money." Clearly, they mean essentially the same thing—their underlying representations are virtually identical. Yet their surface structures are quite different. Because the same underlying representation can be expressed by a variety of surface structures, the process of speaking must certainly be one of constant planning and decision making. Now consider the sentence "Visiting relatives can be tiresome." Here you have an instance of a single surface structure with two possible underlying representations (roughly equivalent to "Relatives who visit can be tiresome" and "Going to visit relatives can be tiresome"). Ambiguous sentences like this one are common in language. They suggest that the task of listening must be one of constant interpretation, often a rather difficult process.

As important as these clues to the nature of speaking and listening may be, they still do not tell us exactly what mental operations go on inside a person's head in the process of communicating through language. When you ask the question "Do you know what time the movie starts?" how did you go about planning this sentence? How did you determine what words you would use and in what order you would say them? And when a friend answers "I think it starts about eight," how did you go about interpreting what this sequence of sounds means? These are central questions that psychologists interested in language raise, and in recent decades they have begun to propose some fascinating answers. Because of space limitations, we can take a closer look at only a few of these answers. So let us focus on the process of speech comprehension.

Most psycholinguists believe that as a person listens to the surface structure of a sentence, he or she automatically divides it into phrases and subphrases called **constituents**. A constituent is a group of words that has a conceptual unity. Thus, the sentence "My eccentric neighbor has twenty cats" naturally divides into two major constituents: the noun phrase "My eccentric neighbor" and the verb phrase "has twenty cats." These, in turn, further divide into smaller constituents, as Figure 9.3 shows. It is from such constituents that listeners extract the underlying propositions, or units of meaning, that a sentence contains. And it is these propositions, not the sentence verbatim, that people somehow represent in long-term memory.

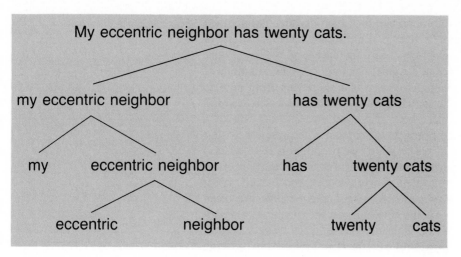

Figure 9.3 Tree diagram—so called because it resembles an upside-down tree—of the sample sentence in the text.

How do psychologists know that listeners analyze sentences according to constituents? The evidence comes from several sources. For one thing, if a reader is shown a passage printed so that each line contains a separate constituent, he or she will comprehend the passage better than if the lines break mid-constituent (Graf and Torrey, 1966). It appears that dividing a sentence in the middle of its constituents disrupts our usual mode of thought. Similarly, if a person listening to a sentence played into one ear hears a single unexpected click played into the other ear, he or she will tend to perceive the click as occurring near the boundary of a constituent, even though the click actually occurred mid-constituent (Fodor and Bever, 1965). It is as though the brain tries to preserve the integrity of each constituent by resisting interruptions to it.

Psychologists are not yet certain how listeners go about isolating and identifying constituents, how they build underlying propositions from them, and in what order these processes occur. One line of reasoning holds that listeners rely heavily on syntactic clues when they segment and interpret sentences. Consider the opening lines from Lewis Carroll's poem "Jabberwocky":

'Twas brillig, and the slithy toves
   Did gyre and gimble in the wabe:
All mimsy were the borogoves,
   And the mome raths outgrabe.

The words are without question nonsensical, yet somehow we feel they convey meaning. Why? We are probably using function words (articles, conjunctions, prepositions, and the like) plus prefixes and suffixes and an occasional English verb to divide this string of words into constituents and to identify the role that each constituent plays in the sentence. Seeing the word *'Twas* ("It was"), for example, we immediately know that an adjective modifying *It* must follow and complete an initial constituent. So we assign this role to the word *brillig*. Similarly, when we encounter the coordinating conjunction *and*, we expect a major new constituent to start. This expectation is immediately confirmed by the appearance of the word *the*, which we know must begin a noun phrase. Searching for the noun that heads this phrase, we find the words *slithy* and *toves*. The suffixes of these words, *-y* and *-s* respectively, tell us that *slithy* must be an adjective and *toves* a plural noun. You can conduct a similar analysis yourself for the next three lines. The point is that in English we have a battery of syntactic clues to the constituent structure of any sentence, and we readily use these clues to segment each sentence and to identify implicitly the functions of its parts. According to this *syntactic approach*, it is a short step from here to extracting the intended meaning of a sentence when the content words are ones we know.

One problem with the syntactic approach to sentence interpretation is that the function words, prefixes, and suffixes on which we presumably rely so heavily to divide a sentence into its constituents are the very words that are most likely to be spoken quickly and enunciated poorly (Pollack and Pickett, 1964; Woods and Makhoul, 1973). Out of context, in fact, these words are often unintelligible. How, then, can they be the sole clues to the meaning of a sentence? The answer is that they are not. Consider the sentence "The vase that the maid that the agency hired dropped broke on the floor" (Stolz, 1967). Using a purely syntactic approach, this sentence is very difficult to interpret, for one relative clause ("that the agency hired") is confusingly embedded within another ("that the maid dropped"). Yet you can probably guess the intended meaning of this sentence just from hearing the major content words alone: *vase, maid, agency, hired, dropped, broke, floor.* According to the *semantic approach* to sentence interpretation, listeners make such skillful guesses all the time. We know from experience that certain nouns and verbs can relate to one another only in certain ways. So just by hearing key content words within a given context we can form very plausible hypotheses about the underlying propositions a speaker is intending to convey. In actual conversations, of course, listeners undoubtedly make use of both the syntactic and the semantic approaches to sentence comprehension.

Investigation into the process of speech comprehension is still in its infancy, although this brief survey only skims the surface of what psycholinguists already know. Equally challenging is investigation into the process of speech production—of how we take our various thoughts and transform them into grammatical sentences. This process seems so effortless, yet we know that it must be extremely complex. Think of all the planning and organization that must take place to express even a simple idea. Think how quickly these decisions must be made if speech is to sound reasonably smooth and articulate. Again, psycholinguists still know relatively little about the mental activities that underlie speaking. But in the years ahead researchers will undoubtedly discover much more about these important processes.

HUMAN LANGUAGE AND ANIMAL COMMUNICATION

We have seen how complex the use of language is, from the standpoint of both production and comprehension. For many years researchers believed that this very sophisticated form of communication was unique to human beings. Is this assumption valid? All the evidence is not yet in, but recent studies with other primates, especially chimpanzees, suggest that our closest relatives in the animal kingdom may be capable of learning a communication system that has many of the basic features of human language.

Chimp talk

In the 1940s two psychologists, Keith and Cathy Hayes, undertook a project quite innovative at the time: They attempted to teach a young chimpanzee named Viki to speak English words. The task was arduous. The Hayeses had to shape Viki's mouth and lips in the correct positions to get her to say simple words like *mama*, *papa*, and *cup*. After six years of painstaking training, Viki was able to make sounds that roughly approximated four words—hardly an impressive vocabulary (Hayes and Hayes, 1951).

Why was Viki so inept at language? Do chimps lack the cognitive capabilities to use sounds symbolically? This conclusion seemed questionable, for in the wild, monkeys and apes use a variety of calls, hoots, and grunts to communicate with one another and to express emotions. But chimpanzees cannot learn spoken language because they lack the necessary vocal apparatus. As Figure 9.4 illustrates, the human tongue, palate, lips, teeth, and facial muscles are well designed for producing a great variety of speech sounds. Chimpanzees and other nonhuman primates lack these adaptations.

This realization led to an interesting question. Granted that chimpanzees cannot learn spoken language, might they be able to learn some visual form of language instead? A number of researchers were eager to find out. Psychologists Beatrice and R. Allen Gardner (1969, 1972), for example, experimented with American Sign Language (or Ameslan), the language used by many deaf people in North America. Ameslan is based on a system of gestures, each one corresponding to a word. Many, though by no means all, signs visually represent aspects of the word's meaning. Ameslan also has devices for signaling verb tenses and other grammatical meanings and is fully able to express anything that can be said in words. Because chimpanzees, like all primates, are extremely nimble-fingered and spontaneously use gestures to communicate, it seemed likely that a chimpanzee might prove to be a rather skillful signer.

The Gardners began their research with a young female chimp named Washoe, whom they raised almost as though she were a human child. Washoe's training in Ameslan began when she was about one year old. The Gardners and their associates signed to Washoe and to one another just as deaf parents might. Whenever Washoe made a correct sign, she was rewarded. Sometimes her natural gestures were close enough to the correct signs to permit shaping. Other times the Gardners taught her signs by placing her fingers in the correct position. Because Washoe was raised among her caretakers, she had rich opportunities to learn signs while interacting with her companions. After four years of training, Washoe had acquired about 160 signs.

The Gardners saw many parallels between Washoe's progress and that of a young child learning spoken language. Once she had learned a particular sign, Washoe generalized its use to appropriate activities or objects. For example, after learning the sign *more* to request more tickling, she used the same gesture to request more swinging and a second helping of food. Many of her mistakes seemed to resemble those children commonly make, as when she applied the sign for flower to all kinds of smells—an apparent case of overgeneralization. Furthermore, as soon as she had learned her first eight or ten signs, Washoe spontaneously began to use some of them in combination, forming statements like "more sweet" and "Roger come." Later she combined three or more signs: "hurry gimme toothbrush" and "you me go there in." The Gardners felt that

○ Areas of the brain associated with speech

⬭ Larynx

"oo" "aw" "ee"

Figure 9.4 The human speech apparatus, including the larynx (which houses the vocal cords), areas of the brain associated with speech, and other such essential physical structures as the tongue and lips. Below are the configurations of these structures necessary for the production of three sounds.

Figure 9.5 Hand signs used by the Gardners' chimpanzee Washoe within twenty-two months of the beginning of training. Signs are presented in order of their original appearance in her repertoire. Washoe not only used signs independently but combined them in sequences that suggest some capacity to employ a meaningful syntax. The most common combinations involved combining signals the Gardners called emphasizers (signals for "please," "come-gimme," "hurry," and "more"), with one other signal. She also used sequences of more than two signs involving names or pronouns, such as "you go gimme," "Roger you tickle," or "please Roger come."

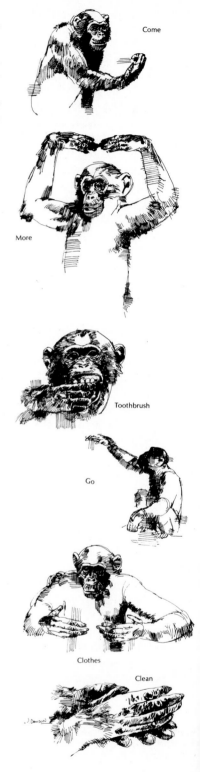

by the age of five Washoe's command of language was roughly equivalent to that of a three-year-old child.

Washoe's accomplishments were not unique. In another research project, psychologist David Premack (1971a, 1971b) taught a chimpanzee named Sarah a language based on small arbitrary plastic symbols of varying colors and shapes, like those shown in Figure 9.6. Each piece of plastic stands for a word. Sarah has learned to construct simple sentences by arranging the symbols on a magnetized board. Premack's system is easier for the chimpanzee than Ameslan; because the symbols are in front of her, Sarah does not have to remember them. A major drawback, however, is that Sarah is "mute" when she does not have her symbols.

In yet another approach, Duane Rumbaugh, Timothy Gill, and E. C. von Glasersfeld (1963) have taught a chimp named Lana to operate a special typewriter controlled by a computer. The machine has fifty keys, each displaying a geometric configuration that represents a word in a specially devised language called Yerkish (after the primatologist Robert M. Yerkes). When Lana types a configuration, it appears on a screen in front of her. She has learned to correct herself by checking the sequence of configurations as it appears. Not only does Lana respond to humans who converse with her via her computer, she also initiates some of the conversations. And when confronted with an object for which she has not been taught a word, Lana has been observed to create one. For example, when she was shown a ring for the first time, Lana identified it, using terms that she already knew, as a "finger bracelet."

Can chimpanzees be said to use language in the human sense of the word? There is still some debate over this question. Chimpanzees certainly use symbols meaningfully and accurately. And like humans, they are able to refer to things removed in time and space. This is an achievement that the chimpanzees' own call system, used in the wild, does not allow. Finally, there is some evidence that chimps can create novel and appropriate word combinations, such as Lana's "finger bracelet," based on simple grammatical rules. Such word combinations have led some primate researchers to conclude that chimps have at least some capacity for understanding elementary syntax.

But other researchers are not so certain. David Premack (1976) has wondered if the linguistic creativity of chimpanzees may not be limited to word substitutions using restricted sentence structures—transforming "Mary eat apple" to "Mary wash apple," for example. Psychologist Herbert Terrace, who spent nearly four years teaching sign language to a young male chimp named Nim Chimpsky, has recently voiced much the same reservation (Terrace, 1979).

While working with Nim, Terrace became convinced that his chimp was indeed combining words into grammatical utterances comparable to a child's first sentences. But on analyzing all the data he had collected, Terrace began to doubt that Nim's accomplishments were really as sophisticated as a human child's. For one thing, a child's sentences quickly grow in both length and complexity, incorporating the correct rules of syntax. Nim did not progress in this way. Although he sometimes signaled fairly lengthy sequences, he gave no indication of an expanding grasp of syntax. Furthermore, analysis of video-tapes showing conversations with Nim revealed that many of the things he uttered were a partial imitation of something a teacher had just said. This finding led Terrace to believe that subtle prompting by human trainers, cou-pled with the delivery of rewards, may play a primary role in a chimp's use of language.

Terrace believes that chimps may have the *potential* to create grammatical sentences, but the ultimate evidence that they in fact do this has not yet been obtained. The important question is not whether chimps are capable of using language, for nonhuman primates *are* capable of using symbolic systems that have many of the basic features of language, but whether there are limits to a nonhuman primate's ability to communicate symbolically. Psychologists are hopeful that one of the research projects currently under way will help provide some answers.

The human adaptation for language

Our discussion of recent efforts to teach language to chimpanzees makes it clear that a young chimp's linguistic progress is certainly not identical to that of a human child. A child's acquisition of language seems amazingly effortless, given the great complexity of the task. In contrast, it takes years of careful training to provide a chimp with a vocabulary of something over a hundred words. Most psychologists agree that the cognitive differences between chimps and people impose on the chimp linguistic constraints that do not exist for humans. To understand the nature of these differences, we must turn to an exploration of the brain.

Brain lateralization Compared with the brain of a chimpanzee, the brain of a human is larger and heavier, the cerebral cortex is more convoluted, and a larger proportion of the cortex is devoted to functions other than the control of sensory-motor activities. These are certainly significant differences, and they no doubt contribute to the greater intellectual capacity of humans. But probably more important from the standpoint of language is the fact that a human brain, unlike the brain of an ape or monkey, is **lateralized**. By this we mean that different behavioral functions are controlled by different sides of the brain.

Hemispheric lateralization of the human brain was discussed at length in Chapter 3. There you learned that language, mathematics, and analytical thinking are primarily left-hemisphere activities, whereas the perception of spa-tial relationships, artistic abilities, and the ability to recognize faces are mainly right-hemisphere activities. Observations made of patients anesthetized to un-dergo neurosurgery nicely illustrate this asymmetrical functioning. In most people, including most left-handed ones, anesthetizing the left hemisphere dis-rupts the ability to sing the words of a familiar song but does not interfere with the ability to carry the melody. Anesthetizing the right hemisphere generally

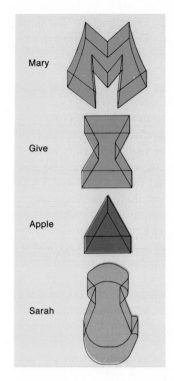

Mary

Give

Apple

Sarah

Figure 9.6 A sentence formed with the plastic symbols that David Pre-mack and his associates (1971a, 1971b) used in their training regimen with the chimpanzee Sarah.

has the reverse effect: The patient loses the melody but is still able to recite the words (Gorden and Bogen, 1974).

Many researchers believe that the unique lateralization of the brain in humans is the biological foundation of our capacity for language. Some see this foundation as a very general one. The left hemisphere, they say, is specialized for analytical thought, and it is this specialization that makes our linguistic ability possible. Others believe that parts of the human brain are specialized *specifically* for language use. But how can the brain be specialized specifically for the use of language when different languages (English, Russian, and Japanese, for example) vary so greatly? Is it possible that the human brain is specialized for learning *any* language? The well-known linguist Noam Chomsky believes that it is. According to Chomsky (1972), the languages of the world have more in common structurally than is apparent at first glance. All languages have rules for combining sounds into words (morphology) and for combining words into sentences (syntax). These rules are similar in certain very general respects. Chomsky maintains that these similarities reflect underlying cognitive abilities built into every human brain. Thus, in mastering the grammar of their native languages, children, Chomsky argues, are aided by specific structural characteristics of their brains.

Exactly how the left hemisphere is organized to make language possible is still far from fully understood. Much of our current information comes from studies of people with left-hemisphere injuries due to tumors, accidents, or strokes. When a front (or anterior) portion of the left hemisphere is significantly damaged, the result is serious difficulty both in producing and in comprehending speech. This condition is known as *anterior aphasia, aphasia* being a general term referring to any language disorder caused by brain damage. If you met a person with this affliction you would immediately spot the symptoms. The speech is slow and labored, filled with stammers and hesitations and frequent missing words. Particularly troublesome for the anterior aphasiac are function words: conjunctions, prepositions, pronouns, articles, auxiliary verbs, and the like. For example, when asked to repeat the sentence "Tom must be in class by ten," he or she might reproduce "Tom . . . be . . . class . . . ten." Comprehension of function words is likewise impaired, making it difficult for many victims of anterior aphasia to do much more than merely guess at the meaning of a sentence on the basis of its nouns and verbs. Thus, an anterior aphasiac might correctly interpret the sentence "The bicycle that the boy is holding is broken" from comprehending the four content words—*bicycle, boy, holding, broken*. But he or she would be at a complete loss to understand the sentence "The lion that the tiger is chasing is fat," for which an understanding of the function words is essential to grasping the sentence's meaning (Caramazza and Zurif, 1976).

Recovered anterior aphasiacs often say that listening to language when one has this disorder is like listening to words that sound very familiar, but that somehow cannot be understood. This common description clearly implies that aphasia affects more than the use of function words alone. Verbs and concrete nouns can also present painful problems to the anterior aphasiac. For example, if shown a saucer and asked to name it, such a person might pause, appear confused, and then incorrectly venture the word *cup*. Comprehension is similarly affected. If an anterior aphasiac is instructed, say, to touch his or her elbow, the person may hesitate and then touch a shoulder instead (Goodglass and Geschwind, 1976). Interestingly, the difficulties the anterior aphasiac has in producing and comprehending speech are not that different in nature from the lapses we all occasionally experience. The difference is that for the aphasiac these problems are grossly exaggerated. Even simple vocabulary words, over which a normal person would hardly ever stumble, can be stubbornly recalcitrant for the aphasiac.

Critical period for language learning The fact that a child has a far better chance of fully recovering from aphasia than does an adult suggests that humans may be adapted for using language in yet another way. There may be a **critical period** early in life during which a human being has a special facility for learning a language. The classic example of a critical period in lower animals was first described by ethologist Konrad Lorenz (1965). Lorenz found that a newly hatched duckling or gosling will form an attachment, or **imprint**, to the first moving object it encounters. As a result, it will follow that object faithfully wherever the object goes. In the wild, of course, the first object a baby bird spots is almost always its mother, so this attachment is adaptive. In the laboratory, however, a newly hatched bird can be exposed to some stimulus other than its mother and so become inappropriately imprinted. It can, for example, be made to follow a bird of a different species, a box on wheels, or even a human being, as the accompanying photo of Lorenz illustrates. The length of the critical period during which such imprinting can occur is always fairly restricted. A slightly older duckling or gosling, sometimes only a few hours older, will not form these attachments.

Some psychologists believe that a somewhat similar critical period is involved in the acquisition of human language. This period is said to begin at roughly the age of two and to extend until just before puberty. What is the evidence that such a period exists? If there is indeed a critical period for language learning, then several predictions should hold true. First, children who lose their speech as a result of brain damage should be more likely to recover it than adults, for presumably they are still within the critical period. As we have already mentioned, this is in fact the case. Second, if there is a critical period in language development, then it should be difficult or even impossible to learn a first language (one's native language) after this period. Since almost everyone learns a first language well before puberty, it is difficult for psychologists to test this prediction. The study of people born deaf, however, does provide some evidence in favor of a critical period, while therapeutic work with so called closet children speaks against a critical period. Deaf people readily acquire language when given the opportunity to do so during childhood. But if this opportunity is lacking, language learning later in life is quite difficult for the deaf. Cases of closet children—children brought up under conditions of severe isolation—illustrate the possibility of recovery from early language deprivation (Mason, 1942; Curtiss, 1977). One child spent her first thirteen years in a small room with a minimum of human contact. When discovered, she was at the developmental level of a one-year-old. But after five years of intensive treatment, the child was speaking at an advanced level (Curtiss, 1977), though she did not even begin to learn to speak until well beyond what is usually considered the critical period for language acquisition.

There does seem to be a measurable difference in the ease of acquiring a *second* language before and after puberty. Reviewing a number of pertinent studies, one researcher (Krashen, 1975) found that a child tends to acquire a

Figure 9.7 Imprinting. A few hours after they were hatched (during a critical period), these goslings saw Konrad Lorenz instead of their mother. Thereafter they followed him around as though he were their real mother.

second language more effortlessly than an adult. He or she may even do so without formal instruction. Moreover, a child often acquires a command of a foreign language (its phonology and grammar) that eludes many older people. Yet the differences in the capacity for acquiring a second language before and after puberty are not quite as dramatic as we might expect if a true critical period existed. Thus, whether there is in fact a critical period for language development is still open to question.

If a critical period does exist, what is its biological basis? What is it about the human brain at a time when most cognitive processes are relatively unsophisticated that makes it capable of acquiring the complex grammar of a language? Lenneberg (1967) has argued that a critical period for language may be related to lateralization of the brain. He believes that this lateralization takes place gradually between birth and adolescence, the same age period when the ability to learn a language is presumably at its peak. Other researchers, however, question Lenneberg's view. They believe that brain lateralization is completed long before puberty. Why do some psychologists suspect this? Their evidence is rather cleverly obtained. In one study, for example, researchers placed earphones on three-month-old babies and played different speech sounds (say, *ba* and *da*) into each ear. When a baby's rate of sucking on an electronically wired pacifier indicated that he or she was accustomed to the two sounds, one of them was changed. An infant was more likely to respond with vigorous sucking to a new sound played into the right ear (controlled by the left hemisphere) than to one played into the left ear (controlled by the right hemisphere). Thus, even in the earliest months of life, a baby's left hemisphere appears to be already specialized to some extent for processing language (Glanville, Best, and Levenson, 1977). Such findings raise some doubt as to whether brain lateralization alone can be the basis of a critical period for language learning extending over ten to twelve years.

HOW CHILDREN ACQUIRE LANGUAGE

Although the human capacity for language may begin to develop soon after birth, infants come into the world totally speechless. In fact, the very word *infant* comes from the Latin word *infans*, which means "without language." Yet by the age of four or five all children of normal intelligence are highly skilled speakers and listeners. This fact is truly remarkable when you stop to think how complex the grammar of a language can be. In this section you will follow an infant's progress from meaningless babbling, to one- and two-word utterances, and finally to longer, more complicated sentences. You will also explore psychologists' views about why language learning takes place.

The stages of language acquisition

Although children grow up in different cultures, they seem to go through a similar sequence in learning to speak their native language (Brown and Fraser, 1963; Bloom, 1970; Brown and Hanlon, 1970; Brown, 1973). One child may reach a particular stage at an earlier age than another, but both reach that stage. One child may express himself or herself more fluently than another, but all normal children learn the basic features of their language.

Prespeech communication From the earliest weeks of life, the sounds that babies make serve to attract the attention of others and to communicate with them. Newborns quickly develop three patterns of crying: the basic rhythmical pattern (often erroneously called the hunger cry); the anger cry; and the pain cry. By playing a tape recording of a baby's cries on different occasions when the mother was out of the room, psychologist Peter Wolff (1969) discovered that a mother recognizes the differences in the cries of her own baby and responds appropriately. Whenever Wolff played the pain cry, for example, the baby's mother immediately rushed into the room with a worried expression on her face.

As babies grow older, they begin to produce more varied sounds. By three months they can coo. By six or seven months they can babble—that is, chant various syllabic sounds in a rhythmic fashion. Infants' early babbling, a type of motor play and experimentation, is not limited to the sounds used in their parents' language. Instead, infants seem to make sounds from many languages. For the first six months of life, deaf babies cry and babble like children who can hear, a further indication that early vocalizations are spontaneous and relatively independent of what the child hears. Eventually, children develop the capacity to imitate the sounds made by others and to control the sounds that they themselves make.

Although older prespeech babies communicate many things through actions and gestures, they also express themselves through intonation. The pattern of pitch in the sounds they make to convey such things as frustration, satisfaction, a question, or a command correspond closely to typical adult patterns (Tonkova-Yampol'skaya, 1973). For example, babies at seven to ten months of age express commands with the same sharply rising then falling pitch that adults use: "Stop that!" Some months later, they begin to use the intonation that signifies a question, which is distinguished by the sharp rise in pitch at the end: "Are you going?" Because pitch and emphasis can profoundly affect the meaning of an utterance, sometimes even reversing it, this early learning of intonation is a very important part of language development.

First words By the end of the first year, children know the names of a few people or objects, and they begin to produce their first words. To reach this stage, the child must understand that sound can be used to express meaning. Generally, the first wordlike sounds accompany gestures—as, for example, saying "bye-bye" when waving at someone. Although prespeech babies may make these sounds in appropriate circumstances following prompting from adults, most do not understand the rather abstract meaning that the sounds convey. Instead, a child's first true words refer to the immediately tangible and visible. These words label objects (*doggie*), express moods (*good*), and issue simple commands (*cookie*). What they have in common is that they all focus on the here and now.

During this stage, infants often rely on intonation to give meaning to a single word. For example, depending on intonation, the one-word utterance *door* can be a declaration: "That's a door"; a question: "Is that a door?"; or a demand: "Open the door!" (Menyuk and Bernholtz, 1969). In most cases, these utterances can be understood only in context. Thus early, one-word sentences succeed largely because other people are able to interpret the child's intentions from the gestures, intonation, and context that accompany the word.

This is also the stage when children tend to overextend the meaning of a word. For example, children who have learned the word *bow-wow* as a label for dogs may apply it to any four-legged creature that moves. When they learn a new animal word, say, *moo* for cows, they may begin to use *bow-wow* for small animals, *moo* for large ones. The new word has called their attention to another feature of animals, namely their varying size. Each new animal name they learn inclines them to attend to new features. Their concepts of *bow-wow* and *moo* become narrower, and eventually they zero in on the correct applications (Clark, 1973). The link between new labels and attention to new details works in the other direction as well: A child's increasing ability to perceive distinctions among things helps to set the stage for learning new words (K. Nelson, 1974).

First sentences Once children have acquired a basic vocabulary, they are ready for the momentous step of combining words into longer utterances. But just as the first step on their own two feet must await a certain level of motor control, so the emergence of grammar must await a certain level of neurological maturation. This maturation is achieved around the age of two. At first children's sentences are very primitive compared with those of adults. Early sentences are short, and their components are largely limited to concrete nouns and action verbs. Nonessential words, such as articles and conjunctions, are omitted. Prefixes and suffixes are also omitted (Brown, Cazden, and Bellugi-Klima, 1968). People who know the child can usually understand what he or she means, and they often respond by expanding the child's utterances into well-formed adult sentences. Here are examples of a young child's *telegraphic speech* and his mother's interpretation (Brown and Bellugi, 1964):

Child	Mother
Baby highchair	Baby is in the highchair.
Eve lunch	Eve is having lunch.
Throw Daddy	Throw it to Daddy.
Pick glove	Pick the glove up.

Even at this early stage the child's speech is highly structured. Children do not merely combine words in haphazard order. For example, a two-year-old might say "Eat cake" while devouring a slice of birthday cake. Although children fail to include all the proper function words and inflections, they do correctly put *cake* after *eat*, which tells the listener that the cake is the object being eaten rather than the agent doing the eating. Of course, not all children's sentences are simply reduced versions of adult sentences. The sentence "All-gone sticky" (after washing hands) is just one example of the kinds of utterances unique to children. But even though such sentences are not predictable from adult rules, they are predictable from the child's rules. In fact, psycholinguists have been able to specify rules that describe what is acceptable in a young child's linguistic system and what is not.

The range of meanings children express with two-word utterances is impressive. The basic categories of meanings shown in Table 9.1 are based on data about children around the world. It seems that around their second birthday children start to put two words together to express the same universal range of concepts. These basic concepts form the core of all human language. Indeed, a

Table 9.1 Categories of Meanings Expressed in theTwo-Word Stage

Category of Meaning	Description
Identification	Utterances such as "See doggy" and "That car" are elaborations on pointing, which emerged in the preverbal stage, and naming, which began in the one-word stage.
Location	In addition to pointing, children may use words such as *here* and *there* to signal location—as in "Doggy here" or "Teddy down." To say that something is in, on, or under something else, children juxtapose words, omitting the preposition—as in "Ball [under] chair" or "Lady [at] home."
Recurrence	One of the first things that children do with words is call attention to, and request, repetition—as in "More cookie" or "Tickle again."
Nonexistence	Children who pay attention to the repetition of experiences also notice when an activity ceases or an object disappears. Utterances such as "Ball all gone" and "No more milk" are common at this stage.
Negation	At about age two, children discover that they can use words to contradict adults (pointing to a picture of a cow and saying, "Not horsie") and to reject adults' plans (saying, "No milk" when offered milk to drink).
Possession	In the one-word stage children may point to an object and name the owner; in the two-word stage they can signal possession by juxtaposing words—as in "Baby chair" or "Daddy coat."
Agent, Object, Action	Two-word sentences indicate that children know that agents act on objects. But children at this stage cannot express three-term relationships. Thus, "Daddy throw ball" may be expressed as "Daddy throw" (agent-action), "Throw ball" (action-object), or "Daddy ball" (agent-object). Children may also talk of the recipient of an action by using similar constructions—saying, "Cookie me" or simply "Give me" instead of "Give me a cookie."
Attribution	Children begin to modify nouns by stating their attributes, as in "Red ball" or "Little dog." Some two-word sentences indicate that children know the functions as well as the attributes of some objects—for example, "Go car."
Question	Children can turn types of sentences described here into questions by speaking them with a rising intonation. They may also know question words, such as *where*, to combine with others—as in "Where kitty?" or "What that?"

Source: Adapted from Roger Brown, *A first language: The early stages.* Cambridge, Mass.: Harvard University Press, 1973.

large part of later language development is simply a matter of elaborating and refining basic ideas that are already present at this early stage.

Acquiring complex rules Two-word sentences are usually difficult to interpret out of context. For example, "Baby chair" could mean "This is the baby's chair" or "The baby is in the chair" or "Put the baby in the chair" or even "This is a little chair." An adult must be present when the sentence is spoken to know which meaning is intended. The grammatical information contained in longer adult sentences reduces this dependence on context to convey meaning. The sentence "The baby is in the chair" is unambiguous because of the addition of the verb *is* and the locational preposition *in*. Thus, the mastering of complex grammatical rules expands the child's ability to communicate beyond the immediate situation.

This stage in the acquisition of language occurs largely between the ages of two and five. By the time they enter school, most children have a good grasp of the grammar of their native language. This is not to say that children memorize a set of textbook rules. They do not. Indeed, many adults have trouble stating grammatical rules, although they are able to apply them correctly. What children acquire during this period, then, is an implicit sense of how to organize words into increasingly complex sentences.

Children seem to acquire grammatical rules in a fairly stable order. There is some variation from child to child, but not as much as might be expected. Certain rules are apparently acquired in steps. A good example is the use of the negative (Bellugi, 1964). Two-year-olds have a very simple rule for forming negative sentences: They simply add *no* to a positive statement: "No get dirty." This rule seems to be adequate as long as the child's sentences are quite simple; but as sentences grow in complexity, more complex rules of negation become necessary. So the child learns to place *no* or *not* just before the verb: "I not get it dirty." The last step is to add the required auxiliary verb: "I won't get it dirty."

Additional evidence supports the idea that children acquire grammatical rules in steps. For example, psychologist Thomas Bever (1970) had two-, three-, and four-year olds act out the following sentences, using a toy horse and a toy cow.

1 The *cow kisses* the horse.

2 It's the *cow that kisses* the horse.

3 It's the horse that the *cow kisses*.

4 The horse is kissed by the cow.

The two-year-olds nearly always acted out the first three sentences correctly, although their performance on the fourth sentence was random. The three- and four-year-olds tended to reverse the interpretation of sentence 4, making the horse the actor. And the oldest children, the four-year-olds, also tended to misinterpret sentence 3, again making the horse the actor. Why did the younger children perform better? Bever suggested that two-year-olds have a simple rule or strategy for interpreting sentences: If the noun and verb occur in sequence, the noun is the actor of the verb's action. If several words interrupt that sequence, as happens in sentence 4, two-year-olds get confused and make a random guess. Apparently, four-year-olds have gone beyond the simple noun-verb strategy and have developed a rule that the first noun in the sentence is the actor. That is why they consistently misinterpret sentences such as 3 and 4. It seems that children do not progress directly toward adult grammar. Instead, they construct and discard a variety of temporary grammars as they go along.

One reason the acquisition of grammar is so difficult is that there are exceptions to many grammatical rules. Consequently, young children tend to commit errors of **overregularization**—that is, they overextend a grammatical rule to instances in which it should not apply (Bellugi, 1970; Slobin, 1972). Overregularizations, which are very common in the speech of three- and four-year-olds, are "smart mistakes," because they show that children are trying to use general rules and that their speech is systematic.

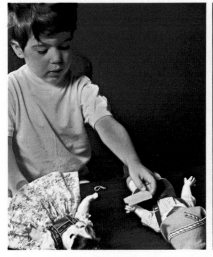 

Figure 9.8 How can a researcher know for sure how a young child is interpreting adult sentences? One way is to have the child act the sentences out. This boy has been handed two dolls and a washcloth and asked by an experimenter to "Show me 'The boy is washed by the girl.' " The boy treats this sentence as though it were "The boy washes the girl." The grammatical rules that he has acquired so far are inadequate to process correctly a sentence in the passive voice.

A good example of overregularization is the way in which children learn forms of the past tense in English. At first, they correctly use certain irregular past-tense verbs such as *fell* and *came*, verbs that are very common in adult English. Each word probably enters a child's repertoire as a separate vocabulary item. But then children learn the general rule for forming the regular past tense by adding a *d* or *t* sound to the base, as in *hugged* or *walked*. Once they have acquired this rule, they try to apply it to the irregular verbs as well, and such incorrect sentences as "He goed to the store" and "I falled down" begin to creep into their conversation.

Such behavior cannot be explained as imitation: Most children who psycholinguists study come from homes in which incorrect verb forms are rarely used. Nor can it be explained as a lack of reinforcement, because most children practice, are reinforced for, and correctly use the irregular tenses before replacing them with the incorrect forms. The only explanation, then, is a predisposition among children to look for regularities in language and to impose these regularities on everything they say.

Explaining language acquisition

Most parents believe that they actively teach their children to speak by praising them for correct grammar and by expressing disapproval when they make mistakes. In other words, they believe that they use reinforcement to shape language development. Yet our discussion of how children acquire irregular verbs suggests that, in this case at least, reinforcement is not particularly important. Does reinforcement play a central role in other aspects of language development? Or are parents' perceptions of its influence largely incorrect?

When one team of researchers studied tapes of actual parent-child interactions, they concluded that adults greatly overestimate the roles of praise and criticism in acquiring linguistic rules (Brown, Cazden, and Bellugi-Klima, 1968). Parents do correct gross mistakes in a young child's choice of words; they occasionally correct errors in pronunciation. But in most cases it is intelligibility, not correct grammar, that elicits a parent's approval. Parents praise a young child for successfully communicating his or her request to open a door or get a cookie, regardless of the child's grammar. When a child who was trying to say that her mother was a female came up with the sentence, "He's a girl," the mother responded, "That's right." However, when another child produced the grammatically perfect sentence, "There's the animal in the farmhouse" the mother corrected her because the building was, in fact, a lighthouse. Most parents pay little attention to grammar as long as they can understand what the child is trying to say and as long as the child's utterances conform to reality. Thus, reinforcement alone cannot explain language development.

Neither can imitation. All children produce sentences they have never heard before. Children who say "All-gone sticky" or "I seed two mouses" are not mimicking adults. Adults do not speak this way. Even when asked to reproduce exactly what an adult says, a child may make "mistakes." Consider, for example, the following dialogue between a little girl and her mother:

CHILD: Nobody don't like me.
MOTHER: No, say "Nobody likes me."
CHILD: Nobody don't like me.
(*Eight repetitions of this dialogue*)

MOTHER: No, now listen carefully; say "*Nobody likes me.*"
CHILD: Oh! Nobody don't *likes* me. (McNeill, 1966)

Clearly, the little girl is not directly imitating her mother. She is filtering what she hears through her own system of rules.

This is not to say that reinforcement and imitation have no impact on language development. Certainly they do. When children learn to say something that other people can understand, this in itself is reinforcing because it provides the child with a way of communicating needs and desires. Grammatically correct constructions tend to be repeated, not because they are praised by adults, but because they get results.

Similarly, although children do not imitate what adults say exactly, adult modeling does influence the development of grammar. One researcher (K. E. Nelson, 1977) was able to accelerate two-year-olds' acquisition of certain grammatical forms through modeling. For example, when a child asked, "Where it go?" the experimenter modeled the use of future-tense verbs by responding to the child's question in slightly more complex form: "It will go there" and "We will find it." Soon the children began using the new forms in their own sentences—for example, picking up an object and saying "I will get up, hide it." To some extent, then, imitation is involved in learning linguistic rules. But this imitation is not mechanical. One thing that is certain is that the process by which a child comes to acquire language is a very creative one.

LANGUAGE AND THOUGHT

There is little doubt that language contributes to cognitive development, enabling children to express increasingly complex ideas. But some psychologists have argued that the impact of language on the developing child is even greater than this. According to this view, language restricts *how* a person thinks about objects and events, as well as *what* he or she is able to think about. "The limits of my language," wrote philosopher Ludwig Wittgenstein, "mean the limits of my world" (1963). Yet a moment's reflection quickly suggests that the relationship between language and thought cannot be strictly one-sided. If language is able to influence thought, thought must also be able to influence language. At the very least, human cognitive capabilities must impose some limit on how language can be structured and used. Then, too, because language is a means of communication, a way of conveying information about objects and events, it seems likely that certain aspects of language will be influenced by what people experience and learn. In the following sections we will trace these two important threads: the influence of language on thought, and the influence of thought on language.

How language influences thought

In the twentieth century, the strongest proponent of the idea that language shapes thought was the linguist Benjamin Lee Whorf (1897–1941). Whorf argued that the way people perceive the world is largely decreed by the unique vocabulary and structural rules of their native language (Whorf, 1956). For example, English has a single word *snow*, while Eskimo has more than twenty terms for various types of snow—fluffy, drifting, packed, and so forth. This difference has important implications, according to Whorf. He argued that when Eskimos gaze out across a winter landscape, their language forces them to perceive certain qualities of snow that the typical speaker of English is inclined to ignore. This tendency is often called *forced observation*. Whorf believed that the grammatical conventions of a language affect thought in a similar way. Consider one of the differences he noticed between English grammar and the grammar of the Hopi Indian language. Whorf called Hopi a "timeless" language because, although it recognizes duration, it does not force a speaker to distinguish between the present, past, and future of an event. English, in contrast, always does so. Speakers must either inflect their verbs to show tense ("He talks," "He talked") or otherwise designate timing through their choice of words ("Tomorrow I talk"). Following Whorf's line of reasoning, this grammatical convention might be said to account in part for the careful track Americans keep of time, their tendency to think of time in quantifiable terms, and their obsession with speed and efficiency. In other words, when an American child acquires language, he or she, according to Whorf, also acquires a particular "world view." This notion that language heavily influences thought is called the **linguistic relativity hypothesis**. Its far-reaching implications are spelled out in George Orwell's chilling novel *1984*, in which a tyrannical government sets out to control all thought by removing certain words from the language, coining some new ones, and redefining others.

Does language actually influence thought to the extent that Whorf believed? Recent evidence suggests not. For instance, just because a language lacks a specific term for a particular object or event does not mean that a speaker of the language necessarily ignores the features that differentiate that stimulus from all others. Consider the perception of color. Although people tend to think of their own way of naming colors as the natural way, other languages have quite different systems. In fact, the number of *basic color terms* in a language (those terms that consist of one word and are not subsumed under another color) vary from two to eleven. Do people whose language has only a few basic color terms perceive the same distinctions in hue that people whose language has more basic terms perceive? (According to Whorf's linguistic relativity hypothesis, they should not.) To answer this question, Brent Berlin and Paul Kay (1969) prepared a chart with 320 small squares of color, virtually all the colors that the human eye is capable of distinguishing. Then they asked native speakers of dozens of languages to point out the best example of each of the basic color terms in their language. With the exception of languages that have only two basic color terms, the choices were virtually identical from one language to the next. The Navaho *lichi* is the same as the Japanese *aka*, the Eskimo *anpaluktak*, and the English *red*. What varies is where the boundaries of basic color categories lie. Whether pink is included in red, for example, or is given a separate label depends on the number of basic color terms that a language has.

Berlin and Kay concluded that all people find certain basic colors more salient than others. These they called *focal colors*. Even when a language does not have a basic term for every focal color, speakers of that language can easily learn invented terms for the missing ones. Indeed, as you saw in Chapter 4, infants seem able to perceive differences among focal colors long before they learn labels for them (Bornstein, Kessen, and Weiskopf, 1976). Thus, although languages may categorize stimuli in very different manners, people everywhere seem to perceive their physical surroundings in much the same way.

How thought influences language

Evidence like that obtained by Berlin and Kay has led most psychologists to conclude that Whorf greatly overstated the control of language over thought. The extent to which language actually limits thought appears to be small. There is no thought that you as a speaker of English can have that a speaker of any other language cannot also experience under appropriate circumstances. Consequently, interest has now shifted to the opposite side of the relationship between language and thought—that is, the extent to which thought influences language.

One effort this shift has prompted is a search for **linguistic universals**—features found in *all* languages as a result of shared characteristics of thought. Color terms again provide a good example. Due to the structure of the human visual system, most people see the color spectrum in much the same way. (For

Figure 9.9 Some of Berlin and Kay's evidence that there is a universal cognitive basis for the naming of colors. The large color chart (D) shows most of the color chips Berlin and Kay presented to members of various cultures. (They also presented a black chip, a white chip, and several shades of gray chips.) The three small diagrams correspond to the large color chart, with the bands at the top and bottom of each diagram corresponding to the black and white not shown in the large chart. (Grays are not shown at all.) Each diagram shows the names that members of a particular culture applied to various chips. A name inside an outlined area indicates that it was applied to all the chips that correspond to that area in the large chart. The surrounding gray areas indicate chips to which that name was applied with less certainty. Thus, English speakers (C) designate as "green" a small set of chips that are included in a somewhat larger set of chips called "awawa" by speakers of Ibibio, a language of South Nigeria (B). These chips in turn are among an even larger set of chips for which the people of New Guinea who speak Jalé (A) have no name at all (after Berlin and Kay, 1969).

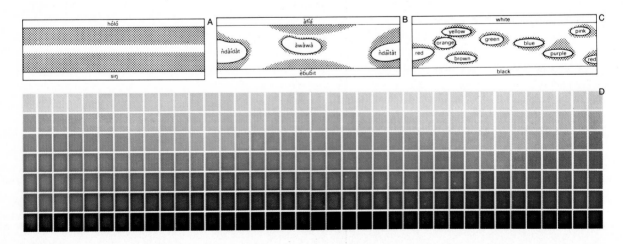

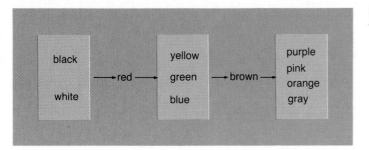

a fuller discussion and some exceptions to the rule, see Chapter 4.) Studies show that this universal neural organization leads to a rather startling regularity among cultures in their selection of basic color terms (Berlin and Kay, 1969). Regardless of the number of basic color terms a given language has, those terms always have their focal points from among the colors that speakers of English call black, white, red, yellow, green, blue, brown, purple, pink, orange, and gray. Furthermore, color terms are generally incorporated into a language in a fairly set order. If a language has only two such terms, it always chooses the colors black and white (often more appropriately translated dark and light). If a language has a third color term, that term will invariably be red. If a fourth color term exists, the choice is usually made from among the colors yellow, green, or blue. The complete sequence is illustrated in Figure 9.10. Thus, there is a universal pattern to the ways that different languages select their basic color terms, a pattern that is due to perceptual processes that all humans share. In much the same way, other universal aspects of human perception and thought appear to generate other linguistic universals.*

It is not only universal thought processes that influence language, however. The knowledge that an individual has stored and can retrieve from long-term memory also has a marked effect on language use. Remember from Chapter 6 that human beings always filter new information through the framework of what they already know and believe. What does not seem to fit within the context of existing knowledge they may elaborate, recast, or simply drop. To understand the powerful effect that prior knowledge has on language comprehension, consider the following paragraph:

If the balloons popped the sound wouldn't be able to carry since everything would be too far away from the correct floor. A closed window would also prevent the sound from carrying, since most buildings tend to be well insulated. Since the whole operation depends on the steady flow of electricity, a break in the middle of the wire would also cause problems. Of course, the fellow could shout, but the human voice is not loud enough to carry that far. An additional problem is that the string could break on the instrument. Then there would be no accompaniment to the message. It is clear that the best situation would involve less distance. Then there would be fewer potential problems. With face to face contact, the least number of things could go wrong.

It would be extraordinary if you found this paragraph comprehensible, even though the words are familiar and the sentences grammatically correct. The reason is that you are reading it completely out of context. You have no frame

---

*This is not to say, of course, that different cultures always express things in a similar way. As we will see later in the chapter, a nonverbal expression used in one culture means something very different in another culture.

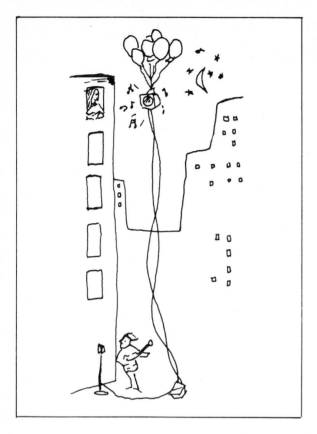

Figure 9.11 This picture supplied the context and helped subjects remember the material in a difficult and seemingly incoherent passage in the Bransford and Johnson experiment (1972).

of reference through which to extract the passage's overall meaning. Now look at Figure 9.11 at the top of this page, a cartoon entitled "the electronic serenade." Suddenly the meaning of the once baffling description becomes perfectly clear. In an experiment using these same materials Bransford and Johnson (1972) found that subjects who were allowed to see the picture first found the description far more comprehensible and remembered much more about it

Figure 9.12 People who live together can often read each other's nonverbal cues about their emotional states with lightning rapidity.

than did subjects given the paragraph cold. Clearly, the ability to understand language is highly dependent on our ability to retrieve general knowledge from long-term memory and to place what we hear within its appropriate context.

LANGUAGE WITHOUT WORDS

Consider the picture in Figure 9.12. Not a word is being exchanged between this couple. Does this mean that they are not communicating their emotions? Obviously not. The man's folded arms, the tilt of his head, his averted eyes all suggest a stubborn form of anger. The woman, in contrast, conveys resignation and despair by her bowed head, her stooped shoulders, and the way she has buried her face in her hand. We would be incredulous if someone tried to tell us that this domestic scene involved a casual conversation about a neighbor's new car. Powerful emotions are clearly being expressed here.

Words, then, are only one means of conveying our thoughts and feelings to others. Spoken language is almost always accompanied by a diversity of non-verbal cues—facial expressions, movements of the body, pitch and tone of voice—that may reinforce, modify, or even reverse the meaning of what we express with words. In this concluding section we will investigate the subject of nonverbal communication. We begin with an in-depth look at some of the research on how nonverbal messages are sent and received. We then turn to the intriguing question of why humans express themselves nonverbally in the ways that they do.

Studying nonverbal communication

In depth

No one doubts the power of nonverbal messages. As we mentioned in Chapter 2, Robert Rosenthal found that just by virtue of encouraging gestures, expressions, or tones of voice, teachers can apparently raise the IQs of randomly se-lected students (Rosenthal, 1966). Like many other psychologists, Rosenthal became intrigued with the ability of humans to communicate in this subtle yet highly effective way. What, he wondered, is the "vocabulary" of body lan-guage? Clearly a certain gesture or expression does not always mean the same thing. A frown can convey annoyance or confusion. A stare can express seduc-tion or command. The intended meaning often depends on the context. Thus, the task of deciphering nonverbal messages is complex indeed. And as with any difficult task it seems likely that some people will be more skilled performers than others. But how can individual ability to decode nonverbal messages be measured? This is one of the central questions that Rosenthal and his col-leagues asked.

To answer it they devised a fascinating test called the Profile of Nonverbal Sensitivity, or PONS. It consists of a forty-five-minute film in which a young woman very briefly acts out a variety of situations, such as expressing jealous anger, asking for forgiveness, or demonstrating deep affection. In some cases, only visual cues are given: The viewer sees only the woman's face, only her body, or both. In other cases, nonverbal information is exclusively auditory: The test taker can hear the pitch or intonation of the performer's voice, but her words are completely inaudible. In still other instances, both visual and auditory cues are available. After each scene, which lasts only a few seconds, the subject must decide what message the woman is trying to convey.

By administering the PONS to hundreds of subjects, Rosenthal and his colleagues have discovered interesting patterns to the variations in nonverbal sensitivity that different people display (Rosenthal et al., 1974). For instance, in accordance with popular belief, women tend to be more sensitive to nonverbal messages than men. Even girls in the third grade tend to be better at detecting nonverbal cues than their male classmates. The only general exceptions to this rule are men in occupations that we think of as "expressive" or that demand sensitivity to others. Thus, male artists, designers, actors, psychiatrists, clinical psychologists, and teachers tend to score higher than most men on the PONS. How such differences in nonverbal deciphering skills are acquired—to what extent they are biologically based and to what extent they are learned—is a subject that is still being explored. Many researchers suspect that learning may play a very important part. One basis for this hypothesis is that, in general, adults are more adept at interpreting nonverbal messages than are children, a pattern that suggests that the skills the PONS measures are gradually developed with experience and practice (Rosenthal et al., 1974).

Regardless of how accurate a given person may be at decoding nonverbal messages, we all tend to give special weight to the gestures, facial expressions, and voice qualities we detect. People, in other words, tend to trust nonverbal messages (Mehrabian, 1972; Ekman and Friesen, 1969). When verbal and nonverbal information is contradictory—when, for example, a person denies that she is angry while repeatedly clenching and unclenching her fist—we generally conclude that the nonverbal message is the true one. This is because most people believe that body language is extremely difficult to control. We feel that nonverbal channels of communication, unlike words, cannot easily be used to deceive (Ellsworth, in press).

Psychologists have shown that there may be a basis for this common assumption; nonverbal channels of communication *do* appear to be much more difficult to control than words. Movement of the body is particularly difficult to disguise, more so than facial expressions. In one experiment designed to test our control over nonverbal cues (Ekman and Friesen, 1969, 1974), subjects watched a gory film showing amputations and burn victims. They then tried to conceal the true nature of the film from others. When observers could see only a speaker's head and face, they could not distinguish the liars from people who were truthfully describing a pleasant film. But when given the opportunity to view the rest of a speaker's body, observers could perceive deception. Apparently, the liars managed to mask their feelings with a pleasant smile, but their anxiety showed through in the movement of their bodies.

Thus, even when we attempt to suppress nonverbal communication, our true emotions can "leak out" without our conscious awareness, and we may convey nonverbal messages we do not consciously intend. For example, psychologist Ernest Beier and his colleagues (Beier, 1974) asked subjects to express nonverbally six very different emotions: happiness, sorrow, indifference, seductiveness, anger, and fear. The subjects' performances were videotaped and played to other people to see if the viewers could decipher what moods the actors were trying to convey. The results were unexpected. Most senders successfully expressed only *two* of the six emotions. Faulty nonverbal communication occurred a full two-thirds of the time! Although some of the problem may have been due to relatively insensitive observers, it is unlikely that this explanation accounted for the entire effect. At least some of the subjects seemed to be sending messages that in no way said what they intended. Particularly noteworthy were two young women who invariably were seen as expressing the same emotions regardless of what feeling they were actually trying to convey. One was judged perpetually seductive, the other perpetually annoyed.

It is not difficult to imagine what problems in interpersonal communication such faulty nonverbal cues can cause. Unintended messages can adversely affect many important relationships, such as those between doctors and patients, teachers and students, employers and employees, and husbands and wives. A better understanding of the ways in which we "speak" without words is clearly a vital step in improving our interactions with others. Some psychologists have even argued that our social environments are largely created by the nonverbal messages we consciously and unconsciously send (Beier, 1974). If this is true, it is essential to examine our own behavior to explain the impact we have on others.

What is the basis of nonverbal expression?

The ability to express nonverbal messages appears to be based on a combination of biological and learned factors. People from widely diverse cultures show a great deal of similarity in the postures, gestures, and facial expressions they use to convey a variety of emotions, and this suggests a common biological foundation. However, there are also differences in nonverbal modes of expression among various cultural groups. Otto Klineberg (1938) pointed out, for example, that in Chinese literature the expression "He scratched his ears and cheeks" was supposed to let the reader know that a person was happy. In Western culture this might be interpreted as indicating that a person was anxious, even distraught. Thus, learning, as well as biology, appears to play an important role in shaping how people express their feelings nonverbally.

Biological factors In his book *The Expression of the Emotions in Man and Animals* (1872), Charles Darwin asserted that many of our patterns of nonverbal expression are inherited—that they evolved because they had survival value. When we are enraged, for example, we commonly grimace and bare our teeth. Other animals also bare their teeth as a threat or when preparing to fight, thus warning their enemies that an attack is impending and perhaps preventing a violent encounter. According to Darwin, the baring of teeth served a similar communication function for our early ancestors. Although human aggression today seldom involves biting, this way of expressing a threat still remains as a characteristic of our species.

One of the most frequently cited pieces of evidence supporting the proposition that nonverbal expression has biological underpinnings is a study of a ten-year-old girl who had been deaf and blind from birth (Goodenough, 1932). Obviously the little girl could not have learned nonverbal cues by observation, so her behavior was presumed to reflect primarily her innate tendencies. When the girl displayed pleasure upon succeeding in finding a doll hidden in her clothing, she "threw herself back in her chair. . . . Both the hand containing the doll and the empty hand were raised in an attitude of delight, which was further attested by peals of hearty laughter. . . . Her laughter was clear and musical, in no way distinguishable from that of a normal child." The girl also showed anger in very characteristic ways. "Mild forms of resentment are shown by turning away her head, pouting the lips, or frowning. . . . More intense forms are shown by throwing back the head and shaking it from side to side, during which the lips are retracted, exposing the teeth which are sometimes clenched." Thus, despite some differences, the way this child expressed common emotions was remarkably similar to the patterns of emotional expression in most normal ten-year-olds. Later studies of disabled children have produced similar findings (Eibl-Eibesfeldt, 1970). A blind child will smile with pleasure without ever having seen a smiling face.

Finally, evidence that biological factors play a significant role in nonverbal expression of emotion also comes from cross-cultural research. In one study, people in different societies were asked to identify the emotions expressed in a series of photographs of faces, some of which are shown in Figure 9.13. Anger, fear, disgust, surprise, and happiness were consistently recognizable, regardless of the culture from which a subject came (Ekman and Friesen, 1971). Even members of New Guinea tribes, who had little previous contact with Westerners and their characteristic patterns of expression, had little trouble labeling these basic emotions. Such evidence argues in favor of a strong biological component underlying certain aspects of nonverbal communication.

The role of learning People from different cultures do vary, however, in their use of certain other nonverbal cues to convey emotion. Such differences have been suggested by the fact that people from different countries tend to vary rather consistently in the scores they receive on the PONS. After administering the PONS to more than two thousand subjects from twenty nations, one group of researchers found that people from cultures similar to that of the United States (where the test was developed) performed best. Although all subjects did better on the test than would occur by chance, the differences obtained strongly suggest that some aspects of nonverbal expression are culturally learned (Hall et al., 1978).

Additional evidence for the role of learning in nonverbal expression is provided by the fact that men and women differ in their nonverbal display of emotion. When researcher Ross Buck (1976) showed the same series of emotion-arousing pictures to a group of men and women, observers could guess the content of the pictures much more easily from the faces of the women than they could from the faces of the men. Even though the men often reacted with increased heartbeat and sweating palms, they kept their faces "masked." Significantly, this sex-based difference in emotional expressiveness does not exist in preschool children. Although young children vary in their responses to emotion-arousing pictures, their varied reactions are a function of personality, not of gender. In the process of growing up, men apparently learn to control certain aspects of emotional expression. Thus, how we respond to emotion-arousing situations is not biologically programmed.

Finally, studies of nonhuman primates also support the conclusion that the

Photograph Judged						
Judgment	Happiness	Disgust	Surprise	Sadness	Anger	Fear
Culture			**Percent Who Agreed with Judgment**			
99 Americans	97	92	95	84	67	85
40 Brazilians	95	97	87	59	90	67
119 Chileans	95	92	93	88	94	68
168 Argentinians	98	92	95	78	90	54
29 Japanese	100	90	100	62	90	66

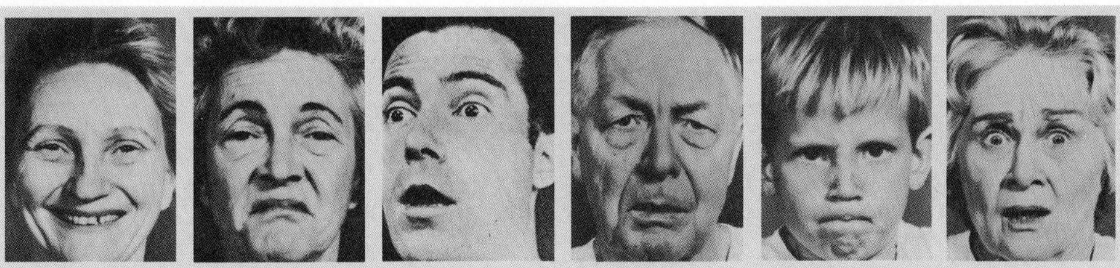

nonverbal expression of emotion is to some extent learned. Experiments have shown that under normal circumstances monkeys and apes use facial expressions and body language to communicate emotion, just as humans do. In one study, rhesus monkeys knew when to save a fellow monkey from an electric shock by watching the emotion of fear conveyed on the other monkey's face (Miller, Caul, and Mirsky, 1967). But monkeys raised in social isolation were significantly retarded in nonverbal skills. They usually lacked both the ability to display an appropriate facial expression when shock was impending and the ability to interpret the nonverbal signs of fear expressed by other monkeys. In rhesus monkeys, then, early social contact appears to be critical for the proper development of emotional expression. Some researchers believe that this may be true of humans as well. It has been suggested that the damaging effects of early isolation from human contact may occur in part because the isolated child fails to develop basic nonverbal communication skills (Mason, 1961).

Figure 9.13 As this table indicates, there is a great deal of agreement among the members of different cultures about the meaning of facial expressions. This suggests that we are biologically programmed to recognize and produce the emotions conveyed by certain facial expressions (after Ekman, Friesen, and Ellsworth, 1972).

SUMMARY

1. To understand and define language, those who study it look at its function, structure, and the mental processes that underlie its use. Language functions efficiently as our principal means of communication first because it is made up of a set of arbitrary symbols that enable the speakers of a particular language to refer to things and events removed in time and space; and second because it is based on the principle of combination—its components can be combined in an almost endless variety of ways.

2. Language can be divided into three basic levels of sturcture. **Phonology**

refers to the sounds that make up a language. In every language the relatively fixed number of fundamental sounds used to create words are called **phonemes**. The rules by which these sounds are combined to form words are called **morphology**. **Morphemes** are the smallest combinations of speech sounds that have meaning in a given language. The **syntax** of a language consists of the rules specifying how words are combined to produce grammatical phrases and sentences.

3. In the process of using language we exhibit both **linguistic competence**—our understanding of the **grammar** (morphology and syntax) of the language—and **linguistic performance**—the ability to apply this knowledge during speaking and listening. One useful way of analyzing sentences is to divide them into their **surface structure** (the words spoken and their organization) and their **underlying representation** (meaning), which can be further divided into units of meaning called **propositions**. Propositions in the underlying representation are transformed through a set of rules into the surface structure.

4. Most psychologists believe that we understand sentences by dividing them automatically into phrases and subphrases called **constituents**. The syntactic approach focuses on the syntactic clues we use to understand sentences, while the semantic approach stresses our ability to guess the meaning from a knowledge of the major content words alone.

5. Experiments with teaching language to primates, especially chimpanzees, have shown that they may be capable of learning a communication system that has many of the basic features of human language. Although the animals cannot learn to speak, they are able to use other forms of language to some extent. It is still not clear whether chimps can create grammatical sentences; psychologists continue to investigate the limits of nonhuman primates' ability to communicate symbolically.

6. Humans appear to be especially well equipped for the acquisition of language because their brains are **lateralized**—that is, different behavioral functions are controlled by different sides of the brain. Language is primarily a left-hemisphere activity. Although many researchers believe that the lateralization of our brain is the biological foundation of our capacity for language, some see this foundation as a very general one, based on the fact that the left hemisphere is specialized for all types of analytical thought, while others believe that parts of the brain are specialized specifically for language use.

7. Psychologists disagree over whether there is a **critical period** early in life—from approximately age two until puberty—during which a human being has a special facility for learning language. Of those who feel there is such a period, some argue that it corresponds to the time when the lateralization of the brain is taking place. Others doubt that brain lateralization alone can account for a critical period of such long duration.

8. Children from all cultures appear to go through similar stages in acquiring language. Prespeech communication consists of different patterns of crying in newborns, and cooing, followed by babbling, in older babies. Older prespeech babies also learn to express themselves through intonation. By age one, most children produce their first words, and at this stage, they are apt to overextend the meaning of a word. Around age two, children begin to use what is known as telegraphic speech—short sentences whose components are largely limited to nouns and action verbs. The ability to organize words into increasingly complex sentences develops between ages two and five. Children seem to acquire an implicit knowledge of grammatical rules in a fairly stable order. Once children have mastered the rules of their language, they tend to commit errors of **overregulation**, misapplying these rules to words that are exceptions. Neither reinforcement by, nor imitation of, adults can account for all of language development. Instead, development seems to proceed according to certain established patterns in a highly creative way.

9. One of the aspects of language that interests psychologists is how language and thought influence each other. In the 1950s, linguist Benjamin Lee Whorf argued that the vocabulary and rules of their native language strongly influence how people perceive the world through a phenomenon called forced observation—the tendency to focus on certain aspects of the environment and ignore others. This notion—the **linguistic relativity hypothesis**—has largely been discredited by recent evidence, including research on color perception, that indicates that all people seem to perceive their physical surroundings in much the same way.

10. Researchers have also studied the opposite phenomenon—how thought influences language. In their search for **linguistic universals** (features found in all languages), they have again turned to color perception, and found that there is indeed a universal pattern to the ways that different languages select their basic color terms. Besides universal thought processes, the knowledge stored in our memories and the ability to place what we hear within context also aid our capacity for understanding language.

11. Nonverbal communication—facial expressions, body movements, and pitch and tone of voice—is a powerful force in human interaction. Individuals vary in their ability to decode nonverbal messages, as evidenced by results of the *Profile of Nonverbal Sensitivity* (PONS). Researchers have also found that learning plays a role in our ability to perceive nonverbal clues.

12. The ability to communicate nonverbally appears to be both inherited and learned. Darwin and other scientists have shown that many of our patterns of nonverbal expression, such as the display of anger, are hereditary. Some aspects of nonverbal expression, for example, the differences between the nonverbal communication of men and women, are, however, culturally learned. Studies of nonhuman primates also support the conclusion that the nonverbal expression of emotion is to some extent learned.

Suggested readings

Brown, R. *A first language: The early stages.* Cambridge, Mass.: Harvard University Press, 1973.

Clark, H. H., and Clark, E. V. *Psychology and language: An introduction to psycholinguistics.* New York: Harcourt Brace Jovanovich, 1977.

Dale, P. S. *Language development: Structure and function* (2nd ed.). New York: Holt, Rinehart and Winston, 1976.

Davis, F. *Eloquent animals: A study in animal communication.* New York: Coward, McCann & Geoghegan, 1978.

Foss, D. J., and Hakes, D. T. *Psycholinguistics: An introduction to the psychology of language.* Englewood Cliffs, N.J.: Prentice-Hall, 1978.

Moskowitz, B. A. The acquisition of language. *Scientific American*, 1978, *239*, 92-108.

EMOTION, MOTIVATION, AND CONSCIOUSNESS

Part 5 covers three aspects of internal experience. Emotions, the subject of Chapter 10, are difficult to study, yet they hold the attention of psychologists nevertheless, as they give our experience its unique feeling and tone. What makes us behave? What makes our behavior characteristic of us? Motivation is considered in Chapter 11. Chapter 12 examines the nature of consciousness—its various states and the circumstances under which it is altered.

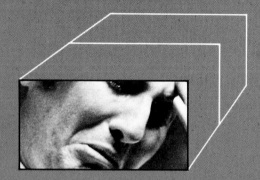

PREVIEW

1. Emotions are states of feeling that can affect behavior. They are frequently accompanied by physiological changes and cognitive components.

2. Several theories have attempted to explain the relationship among physiological arousal, situational cues, and the experience of an emotion.

3. Though many people believe that there are universal emotional reactions to crisis, research shows that people actually respond to crisis with a good deal of variability.

4. Increased levels of emotional stress have been linked to increased incidences of illness, although there is much individual variation in this relationship.

5. Several theories have been proposed to account for the positive, enduring state of happiness. Factors such as satisfying social relationships apparently correlate with happiness more strongly than factors such as money, age, or a happy childhood.

10 Perspectives on emotion

He could not help but observe in his mother's actions a concealed nervousness, an irresolution as if under the strain of waiting. Unlike the fluent, methodical way in which she habitually moved about the kitchen, her manner now was disjointed, uncertain. In the midst of doing something or of saying something, she would suddenly utter a curious, suppressed exclamation like a sudden groan of dismay, or lift her hand in an obscure and hopeless gesture, or open her eyes as though staring at perplexity and brush back her hair. Everything she did seemed insecure and unfinished. She went from the sink to the window and left the water running and then remembering it with an odd overhastiness, turned, missed the handkerchief she was pegging to the clothesline and let it fall into the yard.

HENRY ROTH, *Call It Sleep*

The world now looks remote, strange, sinister, uncanny. Its color is gone, its breath is cold, there is no speculation in the eyes it glares with. "It is as if I lived in another century," said another, "things are not as they were, and I am changed."—"I see," said a third, "I touch, but the things do not come near me, a thick veil alters the hue and look of everything."—"persons move like shadows, and sounds seem to come from a distant world."—"there is no longer any past for me; people appear so strange; it is as if I could not see any reality, as if I were in a theatre; as if people were actors, and everything were scenery; I can no longer find myself; I walk, but

why? Everything floats before my eyes, but leave no impression. . . . the things I see are not real things."
WILLIAM JAMES, *The Varieties of Religious Experience*

Emotions are so much a part of our daily existence that it is difficult to imagine life without them. Try to imagine yourself standing in line for two hours without experiencing annoyance, winning a $100,000 lottery without elation, learning of a loved one's death without grief. Such lack of emotion is almost inconceivable. Emotions set the tone of our experiences and give life its vitality. Without the ability to feel rage, grief, joy, and love, we would hardly recognize ourselves as human.

Yet as familiar as emotions are to us, it is not easy to frame a general definition. Consider the passages at the beginning of this chapter. They clearly express anxiety and depression, but what do these two states have in common? What attributes do all emotions share?

Clearly, emotions involve a variety of feelings, feelings that are often aroused by external circumstances and over which we exert relatively little control. The speakers in the second passage, for example, are so overcome by their feelings of despondency that they are engulfed in totally colorless, dreamlike worlds. Typically, emotions also entail physiological changes. Although not specifically described in the first passage, we can imagine the increased heartbeat, flushed face, and slight hand tremors that often accompany acute anxiety. Finally, emotions may also affect behavior. The actions of the woman in the first passage, for instance—her odd, disjointed movements and apparent confusion of thought—are all the result of her emotional state. Thus, although no definition can ever capture the depth of many human emotions, we can define emotions in the following way: **emotions** are states of feeling that can affect behavior; they often arise in response to social relationships and other external stimuli, and they are frequently accompanied by physiological changes as well as by various cognitions.

Given the subjective nature of emotions you can readily see why they are so difficult to identify, measure, and study. Our private experiences cannot be directly scrutinized by others, so psychologists must explore emotions by soliciting verbal reports, measuring physiological changes, and observing overt behavior. These approaches pose difficulties, however. To understand why, consider how you might go about studying the emotional reactions of young people who have been seriously injured while engaging in athletic activities (Bulman and Wortman, 1977). First, you might note physiological responses, such as heartbeat and rate of breathing. But although such responses may suggest that some emotion is being felt, they do not indicate the precise nature of that emotion. Accelerated heartbeat and respiration may be associated with fear, but they may also be associated with anger. As a result, you would probably want to consider the patients' verbal reports—or what they say they are feeling. The problem here, of course, is that verbal reports are not necessarily accurate or complete. A person may be extremely anxious and frightened and yet reluctant to admit these emotions to others. So for additional clues you might make systematic observations of the patients' behavior—tone of voice, facial expressions, gestures, willingness to cooperate with treatment, and so forth. These too, however, can sometimes be misleading: How a person acts is not always an indication of how he or she really feels. Thus you can see that each means of determining emotion has its own limitations. These restrictions have hampered research on emotions and have led to considerable disagreement about which indicators of emotion are most revealing.

But despite the problems in studying them, emotions are a central part of human existence and an important area of psychological investigation. Research on emotion has focused on a number of critical issues. What role do physiological changes play in emotional experience? If you are simply injected with a drug that creates physiological arousal, will you become emotional? Can a person with a severed spinal cord, who no longer experiences physiological change, still feel emotion? What types of emotional reactions accompany life crises such as rape or the death of a loved one, and how long do such reactions usually last? To what extent can intense or prolonged emotions lead to serious illness or even death? Why are some people able to take stress in stride, while others react by becoming seriously ill? Are some people more likely to experience happiness than others? Are people who have more money, more friends, or more pleasurable childhoods generally more happy than people who do not? These are some of the topics we will explore in this chapter.

THE PHYSIOLOGY OF EMOTION

The role that physiological factors play in human emotion has intrigued psychologists for nearly a century. Is physiological arousal the primary cause of emotion? Does arousal vary for different emotions? Although many answers to these questions have been proposed and a great deal of controversy has been generated, all psychologists agree on one point: Strong emotion is in fact associated with changes in the autonomic nervous system.

Emotion and the autonomic nervous system

As discussed in Chapter 3, the autonomic nervous system regulates the body's internal environment and usually functions without our moment-to-moment awareness or conscious control. It is composed of two divisions, the sympathetic and the parasympathetic. Both divisions innervate almost every visceral muscle and gland, but the two have broadly opposite effects. Generally speaking, the sympathetic division dominates during emergency or stress and promotes energy expenditure. It encourages the increased blood sugar, heart rate, and blood pressure needed for sustained physical activity, and at the same time it inhibits digestion. The parasympathetic division, in contrast, dominates during relaxation and promotes energy conservation. It works to decrease heart rate and blood flow to the skeletal muscles, while also enhancing digestion. Not surprisingly, most of the physiological changes associated with strong emotion, such as intense anger or fear, are caused by activation of the sympathetic division.

What exacty happens when the sympathetic nervous system is activated? Suppose it is 2:00 A.M. and you are walking to your car, which is parked on a deserted city street. Suddenly a man emerges from a dark alley. What physiological changes would occur in this fear-arousing situation?

1. The blood vessels leading to your stomach and intestines would constrict, and digestive action would virtually stop. At the same time, the vessels leading to your

larger skeletal muscles would expand, diverting the oxygen and nutrients carried in your blood to where they may be needed for fight or flight.

2. Your pancreas would secrete the hormone glucagon, which would stimulate your liver to release stored sugar into the bloodstream, sugar that could supply extra energy to your skeletal muscles should they need it. In addition, your adrenal glands would secrete the hormone epinephrine, which would help sustain many of the other physiological changes brought about by activation of the sympathetic nervous system.

3. Your breathing would become deeper and more rapid, and your broncioles (the small air passages leading to your lungs) would expand. These changes would increase the supply of oxygen to your blood, oxygen that is needed to burn the sugar being sent to your skeletal muscles.

4. Your heartbeat would increase, perhaps more than doubling, thus speeding the circulation of your blood and hastening the delivery of oxygen and nutrients to your skeletal muscles.

5. The pupils of your eyes would dilate, and your visual sensitivity would increase.

6. Your salivary glands might stop working, causing your mouth to become dry. The activity of your sweat glands, however, might increase, since sweating is one way to dissipate the heat generated by increased energy expenditure.

7. The muscles just beneath the surface of your skin would contract, causing hairs to stand on end. For our furry forebears the erection of body hair may have been part of a threat display, but we relatively hairless humans simply break out in "goose bumps" (Lang, Rice, and Sternback, 1972).

These various changes prepare the body to deal with a potential threat—either by confronting it or by escaping. In fact, in unusual circumstances the activation of the sympathetic nervous system has made possible feats of great strength or endurance. Cases have been reported in which a woman manages to lift a car to free her child trapped beneath a wheel or a man somehow swims against a powerful current in order to reach safety. This is not to say that arousal suddenly embues a person with superhuman powers. It is more accurate to say that physiological arousal enables a person to use the body's muscles more effectively and for a more prolonged period of time than would ordinarily be the case. Yet the effects of intense activation of the sympathetic nervous system may not be all positive. As you will see later in this chapter, the physiological stress caused by intense and sustained emotional arousal can sometimes contribute to serious illness.

Once a threatening situation is over, diverse physiological changes again take place. Suppose that your would-be attacker turns out to be a police officer on patrol. Almost immediately the opposing effects of the parasympathetic nervous system would begin to reassert themselves. Your heartbeat, respiration, glandular secretions, blood flow, and muscular tension would all return to normal, and the bodily sensations associated with fear would subside. This general cycle of physiological arousal—caused by assertion of the sympathetic nervous system over muscles and glands, followed by reassertion of the parasympathetic division—is the cycle associated with most strong emotions.

Physiological changes and the brain

Although it is the autonomic nervous system that triggers the physiological changes associated with emotions, this system in turn is coordinated by the brain. In particular, the hypothalamus and certain areas of the limbic system (see Chapter 3) are involved in a number of emotional reactions, including anger, aggression, and fear. This has been demonstrated by research on experimental animals in which different parts of these brain regions are mildly stimulated or surgically removed. For example, research with cats has shown that stimulation of particular areas of the hypothalamus can induce intense activation of the sympathetic nervous system and an emotional display that can only be interpreted as feline rage. The cat's pupils dilate, the fur on its back and tail stands erect; the cat flattens its ears, arches its back, unsheathes its claws, and hisses and snarls intensely (Flynn et al., 1970). In contrast, surgical lesions in areas of the amygdala (part of the limbic system) produce extremely docile behavior. For this reason, some of the "wild" animals that circus performers use have had part of the amygdala surgically removed.

Some researchers have found cases in which exaggerated emotional behavior in humans has accompanied damage to certain areas of the limbic system. Such damage can take place before, during, or after birth, and it can arise from a variety of causes, including diseases that affect the brain, drug abuse, and trauma due to auto accidents, athletic injuries, or gunshot wounds. A widely publicized case that occurred in 1966 involved a young man at the University of Texas. For a number of months Charles Whitman had unsuccessfully sought psychiatric help for the irrational thoughts and violent impulses that periodically overcame him. A letter he wrote the evening before his death showed a deep concern about these sudden changes in his behavior, which he suspected might be due to a physical disorder. That night Whitman killed his wife and mother, and the next morning he climbed to the top of a campus tower carrying a high-powered rifle with a telescopic sight. From there he proceeded to fire at every moving object he could see. An hour and a half later, when Whitman was finally killed by police, he had shot thirty-eight people, killing fourteen of them. An autopsy revealed a malignant tumor on the amygdala (Sweet, Ervin, and Mark, 1969).

Documentation of other cases in which damage to the limbic system has been associated with uncontrollable violence has led some researchers to suggest that extremely volatile individuals may often be suffering from brain disease or injury of some sort (Mark and Ervin, 1970). This possibility has generated renewed interest in psychosurgery as a form of treatment. **Psychosurgery** is the removal or destruction of parts of the brain for the purpose of altering behavior. In the case of people who experience episodes of unprovoked violence, psychosurgery usually involves the destruction or removal of part of the amygdala. But such a procedure, in addition to controlling violence, can also alter an individual's personality in highly adverse ways. This is just one reason why the use of psychosurgery is highly controversial and so is relatively rare. Much more will be said about it in Chapter 16, which deals with the treatment of psychological disorders.

THEORIES OF EMOTION

Whenever you encounter an emotion-provoking stimulus, such as the menacing figure in a dark alley imagined earlier, two things are likely to happen: (1) your brain triggers your sympathetic nervous system into action, causing physiological arousal, and (2) you subjectively experience a certain feeling known as fear, which is related to your awareness of potential danger. One of the oldest de-bates about human emotion concerns the sequence of these two events. Do you experience the feeling of fear because your heart is pounding and your hands are trembling? Or does your mind's appraisal of a particular situation induce the feeling you call fear, which is then followed by a set of physiological changes preparing you for fight or flight? Over the years psychologists have proposed theories suggesting different answers to this debate. These theories, and the experiments conducted to test them, have greatly increased our under-standing of why people experience emotion.

The importance of physiological arousal

Our language suggests that the physiological changes accompanying each emo-tion are in some ways quite distinct. When we are frightened, for example, we say we feel a "knot" in the stomach; when we are nervous we say we experience "butterflies." During intense anger we sometimes refer to a "pounding" in the temples; when we are embarrassed we often describe what we feel as a "blush." Is it possible that the diverse emotions we experience are simply the result of different sets of bodily changes? And if not, what role *do* physiological changes play in the experience of emotion?

The James-Lange theory William James was one of the first psychologists to propose that the ability to identify and label our own emotional states might be based on our ability to interpret the bodily changes associated with them. This proposal directly contradicted many of the theories of emotion popular in James's day. Most other writers in the late nineteenth century argued, quite logically, that events in the environment trigger a psychological state—the emotion—which in turn gives rise to physiological responses. But James disagreed:

My theory, on the contrary, is that *the bodily changes follow directly the perception of the exciting fact, and that our feeling of the same changes as they occur IS the emotion.* Common-sense says, we lose our fortune, are sorry and weep; we meet a bear, are frightened and run; we are insulted by a rival, are angry and strike. The hypothesis

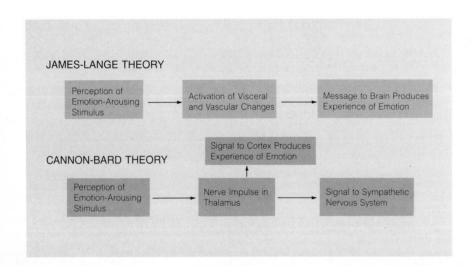

Figure 10.1 Comparison of the se-quence of events outlined in the James-Lange and the Cannon-Bard theories of emotion.

here to be be defended says that this order of sequence is incorrect . . . and that the more rational statement is that we feel sorry *because* we cry, angry *because* we strike, afraid *because* we tremble. . . . Without the bodily states following on the perception, the latter would be purely cognitive in form, pale, colorless, destitute of emotional warmth. We might then see the bear, and judge it best to run, receive the insult and deem it right to strike, but we should not actually feel afraid or angry (James, 1890).

According to James, then, our perception of a certain stimulus in the environment triggers a pattern of changes in the body. These changes prompt sensory messages to be sent to the brain and produce the actual experience of emotion. Each emotional state is signaled by a unique physiological pattern. James emphasized patterns of response in the viscera, or abdominal organs, but another psychologist, Carl Lange, proposed a similar theory that emphasized vascular changes (changes in blood pressure). Because the work of James and Lange coincided in time, the view that the perception of bodily changes *is* the emotion came to be called the **James-Lange theory** (Lange and James, 1922).

The Cannon-Bard theory The James-Lange theory stimulated a great deal of research on emotions, much of it designed to disprove that theory's claims. In 1927 Walter B. Cannon published a powerful critique based on several arguments. First, if the James-Lange theory was correct, and we come to feel our emotions by interpreting our bodily sensations, then each emotion must be characterized by a somewhat different set of physiological changes. Following the publication of James's theory, other psychologists tried to identify unique physiological responses for each emotional state, but their results were consistently negative, as Cannon pointed out. The evidence showed that many of the

Figure 10.2 Although common sense may tell us that *first* we feel grief, and *then* we cry, the James-Lange theory maintains that *first* we cry, and *then* we feel grief—in other words, that feelings *follow* behavior.

same bodily changes occur in conjunction with very different emotions.

Second, the idea that bodily reactions *cause* the experience of emotion is questionable on the basis of timing. Often we feel emotions quite rapidly. We see a bridge collapsing beneath us and feel immediate panic; we spot an old friend and feel instantaneous joy. Changes in the viscera occur rather slowly, since the internal organs are insensitive and are not very well supplied with nerves. How, then, can the viscera be the source of sudden emotion, as James suggested?

Third, if James was right in assuming that physiological arousal causes emotion, then artificially inducing the physiological changes associated with emotion—by an injection of a drug, for example—should give rise to an emotional reaction of some kind. But as Cannon noted, physiological arousal alone is not sufficient to induce emotion. As evidence, Cannon cited a study by Gregorio Marañon (1924). Marañon injected 210 subjects with the hormone and neurotransmitter epinephrine and asked them to report the effects. About 71 percent said that they experienced only physical symptoms—a rapid heartbeat, a tightness in the throat—with no emotional overtones at all. The remainder reported emotional responses of some kind, but most described what Marañon called "as if" emotions. These subjects said, "I feel *as if* I were afraid" or "I feel *as if* I were happy." Their feelings, then, were similar to emotions but clearly not identical to them.

After critiquing James's theory, Cannon (1927) offered his own account of the relationship between physiological arousal and the subjective experience of emotion. He argued that the thalamus plays a central role in emotional experience. This idea was later elaborated by Philip Bard and has become known as the **Cannon-Bard theory** (Cannon, 1929). It maintains that the perception of an emotion-arousing stimulus triggers a nerve impulse in the thalamus that then splits, with one signal traveling to the cerebral cortex and causing the subjective experience of emotion (fear, anger, joy, love), and another signal arousing the sympathetic nervous system. Thus, according to the Cannon-Bard theory, physiological arousal and the subjective experience of emotion are produced simultaneously, initiated by the same nerve impulse. Although more recent findings have shown that some of the details of the theory are incorrect (the brain areas that control emotions are the hypothalamus and the limbic system, not the thalamus), the idea that physiological arousal alone does not *cause* emotion has had an important influence on subsequent research.

Subsequent findings Subsequent investigation into the question of whether each emotion is characterized by a unique physiological state has suggested that Cannon's very negative conclusion may have been too strong. There is now evidence that *some* physiological responses do differ during different emotions. For example, Wolf and Wolff (1947) located a subject with a gastric fistula—an opening in the stomach wall that made it possible to observe the stomach lining. They found that stomach movement, gastric secretion, and dilation of the blood vessels increased during anger and decreased during fear. Although they studied their subject for many months through a great variety of emotions, they were able to distinguish only two general patterns.

Albert Ax (1953) wondered if these findings might not be due to the unique response patterns of this particular individual. So he designed an experiment in which he could measure the physiological correlates of anger and fear in a large

Figure 10.3 According to Walter Cannon, feelings such as joy are instantaneous and thus cannot be caused by visceral reactions, as was suggested by James, because they are relatively slow.

number of subjects. By today's standards Ax's procedure might raise ethical questions. He connected his subjects to a polygraph under the pretext of recording their physiological responses during a period of relaxation. Then, at different points during the recording session, he provoked in his subjects both intense anger (by having the polygraph operator rudely insult them) and intense fear (by leading them to believe that the polygraph was short-circuited and might electrocute them). Ax found that certain responses, such as breathing rate and sweating, increased more during fear, and certain other responses, such as blood pressure, increased more during anger.

Research on the physiological correlates of abnormal behavior also suggests that different emotional states may have different physiological underpinnings. Depressed states are characterized by reduced levels of norepinephrine, and drugs that deplete norepinephrine produce depression (Schildkraut and Kety, 1967; Schildkraut and Freyhan, 1972). Conversely, antidepressant drugs usually stimulate norepinephrine secretion, and induction of anger (associated with high levels of norepinephrine) is often used therapeutically to counteract depression (Dienstbier, 1979). Such patterns are very general, of course. They are a long way from demonstrating that each emotion is associated with unique physiological changes. But keep in mind the difficulty of studying this topic. It is only very recently that advances in technology have allowed scientists to trace hormones and neurotransmitters with any precision.

Yet despite the fact that we have much more to learn about the physiology of emotion, most researchers now agree that physiological arousal is not simply incidental to emotional experience. If it were, then people with damage to the sympathetic nervous system would still feel normal emotions, but research shows that they do not. For example, psychologist George W. Hohmann (1966), himself a paraplegic, interviewed twenty-five army veterans who had severed spinal cords. He found significant changes in the nature and intensity of certain emotions, especially anger and fear. Generally speaking, the higher on the spinal cord that the lesion occurred, the more extensive the disruption of sympathetic arousal and the greater the change in emotional experience. This is not to say that these men failed to perceive the significance of emotion-arousing situations, or even that they failed to display much of the behavior associated with strong emotion. But the quality of their emotional experiences was often altered. As one man remarked about his feelings of anger: "Sometimes I get angry when I see some injustice. I yell and cuss and raise hell, because if you don't do it sometimes I've learned people will take advantage of you. But it just doesn't have the heat to it that it used to. It's a mental kind of anger." It seems that the physical correlates of anger—pounding heart, trembling hands, the sensation of being "heated up"—contribute to the full experience of the emotion.

The role of cognition

Hohmann's study suggests that physiological arousal is necessary to a complete experience of emotion. Yet, the work by Marañon, discussed earlier, shows that physiological arousal alone is not enough. When subjects were artificially aroused by a shot of epinephrine they did not feel emotional; something was missing from the experience that prevented it from being a true emotion. That something, according to Stanley Schachter, is an appropriate cognition that enables us to comprehend our stirred-up physiological state in emotional terms and so to label it joy, anger, jealousy, fear, or any one of a number of other emotions. To Schachter, then, emotion involves two closely interacting factors: a state of physiological arousal *plus* a cognitive interpretation of that arousal. Which comes first is not important to Schachter. What is important is that the cognitive interpretation enables us to label a *general* state of physiological arousal as a *specific* emotion.

Schachter's two-factor theory It is difficult to isolate the role that cognition plays in labeling arousal as emotion, because in most cases arousal and a related cognition are closely interlinked. What is so intriguing about Schachter's approach, therefore, is that he invites us to consider an unusual situation—one in which the state of arousal and the explanatory cognition are to some extent independent. What would you do, he asks, if you felt the bodily sensations of emotion but could perceive no obvious reason for them? Schachter's answer is that you would experience a need to explain your feelings in some way and so would search your surroundings for a reasonable cause. As a result, you could label the very same state of arousal as joy, love, jealousy, or hate, depending on the cognitions available to you.

In trying to design an experiment to test this hypothesis, Schachter and his colleague Jerome E. Singer (1962) faced several problems. First, they had to find some nonemotional way to induce physiological arousal. This they solved by giving subjects an injection of epinephrine, under the pretext that they wanted to study the effects of "vitamin injections" on vision. Subjects were randomly assigned to one of four conditions. In the *informed condition*, the experimenters announced that the injection would produce certain side effects, such as hand tremors and heart palpitations, that are real effects of epinephrine. In the *misinformed condition*, subjects were led to expect side effects unrelated to epinephrine, such as headache and itching. In the *ignorant condition*, subjects were incorrectly told that the injection would have no side effects at all. And finally, in the *placebo condition*, which served as a control, subjects received an injection of saline solution, which produced no side effects. Schachter and Singer predicted that, lacking an adequate explanation for their aroused state, subjects in both the misinformed and the ignorant conditions would be likely to search their environments for information that could help explain how they felt.

But what might subjects find in their environments that could help them account for physiological arousal? Schachter and Singer solved this second problem by providing emotional cues. They had each subject wait for the "vision test" in a room with another person, who was actually a confederate in the experiment. In some cases this accomplice acted very happy and frivolous, throwing paper airplanes, laughing, and playing with a hula hoop. In other cases the accomplice acted increasingly incensed over a long and rather insulting questionnaire he and the subject had been asked to fill out, finally tearing up the questionnaire and storming out of the room. This was Schachter and Singer's way of creating two very different emotion-related cognitions: one of euphoria, the other of anger. They predicted that the subjects who had no explanation for their physiological arousal would label their feeling either euphoria or anger depending on the emotion expressed by the confederate to whom they were exposed. In short, Schachter and Singer believed that the same state of arousal would be labeled very different things depending on environmental cues.

The results of the experiment gave qualified support to Schachter and Singer's theory. Subjects who did not expect the injection to produce arousal, and so presumably had no way to explain their physiological state, did tend to show behavioral signs that they had adopted the mood of the confederate. They too threw paper airplanes in the euphoric condition and criticized the questionnaire in the angry one. In contrast, subjects who were told to expect the side effects of epinephrine were less likely to behave as the confederate did. Furthermore, subjects in both the misinformed and ignorant conditions who were exposed to the euphoric confederate tended to describe their own feelings as somewhat more "good or happy" than subjects in the informed condition. Unfortunately, the emotional self-ratings of subjects exposed to the angry confederate were not completely consistent with the experimenters' predictions, for those in the ignorant condition described their overall mood as slightly happy rather than substantially annoyed. And, contrary to Schachter's prediction that there would be significant differences between the ignorant and misinformed subjects and the placebo (control) subjects, the analyses revealed no significant differences in self-reported emotion between the two unexplained arousal groups and the placebo group.

In summary, then, Schachter's two-factor theory proposes an interaction between physiological arousal and emotionally toned cognitions. Arousal signals to a person that an explanation of some kind is needed. According to Schachter's theory, however, it does not indicate what that explanation is. Schachter maintained that to place a label on one's physical sensations, a person looks to environmental cues. If an emotional explanation is the most plausible one available, the person is likely to conclude that the arousal is due to euphoria, anger, fear, embarrassment, or whatever other emotion the situation seems to

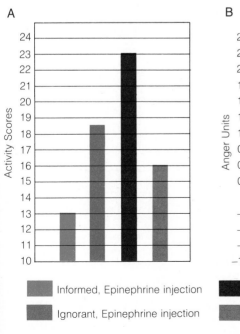

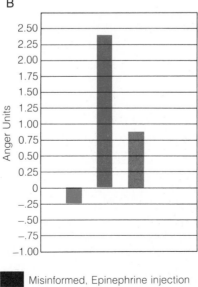

Figure 10.4 Comparison of the activities of the subjects in the euphoria and the anger conditions of the Schachter and Singer experiment. (A) Euphoria condition. (B) Anger condition. (The numbers on the vertical axis refer to scores on tests; they are only important in showing the relationship among the subjects' activities.) (Schachter and Singer, 1962)

suggest. It is easy to see how Schachter's theory might be used to account for a wide variety of misattributed feelings. For example, some psychologists have argued that if we are aroused for any one of a number of reasons—sexual excitement, frustration, or even fear—and we find ourselves in the company of a potential lover, we may mislabel our arousal as love (Walster and Walster, 1978). You can undoubtedly think of other situations in which a specific emotional label might be incorrectly attached to a general state of physiological arousal.

Extending Schachter's research Although the results did not entirely support Schachter's theory, the Schachter and Singer experiment nonetheless generated a great deal of subsequent research. Much of it was aimed at refining the original theory and examining how far people's appraisals of their own emotions could be manipulated. What would happen, for instance, if information about physiological arousal were not real? What if we only *believed* we were aroused? Would we still be motivated to explain this bogus arousal in the way that Schachter suggests?

In an ingenious experiment designed to answer this question, Stuart Valins (1966) showed male subjects ten pictures of nude women from *Playboy* magazine while the subjects supposedly listened to the amplified beating of their own hearts. In fact, however, the sound they heard was prerecorded. When displaying five of the pictures, Valins altered the fake heartbeat so as to lead subjects to believe that they were sexually aroused. Later the subjects tended to rate the five women whose pictures had been accompanied by a change in "heart rate" as more appealing than the other nudes. Apparently, each time they heard the artificial heartbeat change, the subjects searched the current picture for especially attractive attributes that might have prompted this response. Then, on finding such attributes, they judged the picture more positively.

This study suggests that it is not real arousal but simply the belief that one is aroused that is important in the labeling of an emotion. Other investigators, however, have challenged Valins's conclusion. One criticism is that false physiological feedback, such as a bogus heartbeat, can cause a "mimic effect," driving actual arousal in the direction of the false feedback. Recent studies have provided some support for this phenomenon (Harris and Katkin, 1975). If it occurred in Valins's experiment, his subjects may have been searching for an explanation of real, not imaginary, arousal. In either case, however, Valins's results still support Schachter's theory: The subjects are using environmental cues to interpret the meaning of bodily sensations, whether those sensations are authentic or not.

Since it suggests that the way we assign causality for our arousal influences our emotional experiences, Schachter's analysis raised other interesting questions. For example, if a person is exposed to an emotion arousing stimulus (electric shocks) and led to attribute arousal to a false cause (the effects of a drug), will the emotional reaction to the shocks be reduced? To test this hypothesis, Nisbett and Schachter (1966) gave subjects a placebo pill and told half that the pill would cause physiological arousal (hand tremors, heart palpitations, butterflies in the stomach) and half that the pill would cause itching, numbness of the feet, and other irrelevant symptoms. Then they asked the subjects to report how much pain they experienced from a series of electric shocks. Naturally, the act of being shocked aroused the subjects, but to what should they attribute this arousal? When subjects had been told that the shocks would be mild and harmless (the low-fear condition), attributing the arousal to the shocks did not make much sense. A more plausible explanation available to half the subjects was to blame their physical symptoms on the "arousal-producing" pill. And this is apparently what they did, for subjects who were led to believe that the pill would cause arousal were willing to tolerate shocks four times as severe as the other subjects were. Thus it appears that genuine emotions can sometimes be suppressed when people are given alternative explanations for their arousal.

Other researchers have suggested that this finding might be applied to people with certain emotional disorders. Davison and Valins (1972) have argued that a variety of problems, including extreme shyness, stuttering, and even impotence, are characterized by a vicious cycle: Symptoms occur, the person becomes upset about these symptoms, and the symptoms consequently increase. They suggest that if a therapist can induce a person to misattribute his or her emotional arousal to some other cause, the cycle might be broken and the person's distress reduced.

Criticisms of Schachter's approach   The idea that the same state of physiological arousal can be attributed to different emotions depending on available cognitions has been tremendously influential in social psychology. But it is not without its critics. Many reservations revolve around problems with the original Schachter and Singer experiment. As we noted earlier, the results of the study were relatively weak: Many of the differences that Schachter and Singer expected were in the predicted direction, but were small in magnitude and not statistically significant. A number of methodological shortcomings may have contributed to this weak pattern of results (Plutchik and Ax, 1967; Zimbardo, Ebbeson, and Maslach, 1977). For example, consider the fact that ignorant subjects in the angry condition did not report feeling angry, although they showed some behavioral signs of anger when they were alone with the confederate. As Schachter and Singer themselves have pointed out, the subjects in this condition may have experienced anger but may have been reluctant to admit it to the experimenter. The subjects, who had volunteered to participate in the study for extra points on an exam, may have "simply refused to endanger these points by publicly blowing up [or] admitting their irritation to the experimenter's face." In Chapter 2, we discussed how such **demand characteristics** can make experimental results difficult to interpret. It is unfortunate that the study was not designed to eliminate these demand characteristics—for example, by having a second experimenter, with no control over the subjects' grades, request mood ratings from them.

Another methodological shortcoming of the study was that except for a single before–after measure of pulse rate, Schachter and Singer failed to monitor the subjects' physiological responses during the experiment. Thus it is not clear what percentage of subjects were actually aroused when they met the confederates. Because reactions to epinephrine are highly variable and sometimes very short-lived, such information would have been highly desirable. In fact, data regarding subjects' physiological responses would have been helpful in assessing the validity of Schachter and Singer's theoretical notions. According to Schachter's theory, people show different emotional responses not because of different physiological reactions, but because of generalized arousal and an appropriate cognition from the environment. But because no physiological measures were taken, it is by no means clear that subjects who became angry remained in the same physiological state as subjects in the euphoria condition.

Critics have also charged that even those results that are consonant with Schachter's theory cannot be given much credence because there are plausible alternative explanations for them. For example, Schachter and Singer maintained that subjects in the ignorant and misinformed conditions expressed the same emotion as the confederate because, unlike the informed subjects, they had no label or explanation for their arousal. As other researchers have pointed out, however, these subjects differed not only in whether they had a label for their feelings, but also in how they were treated by the experimenter and in what judgments they probably formed of him (Kemper, 1978). Consider the "ignorant" subjects. They had just been given an injection that was said to have no side effects, yet immediately afterward they began to feel aroused. Might not such subjects be justifiably angry at an experimenter who appears either incompetent or untruthful? And might not these feelings be aggravated in the anger condition, where the subject must fill out a tedious and insulting questionnaire presumably written by the same experimenter? Similarly, in the euphoria condition, might not joining the confederate in his frivolous activities be a way of expressing one's disrespect and hostility toward this questionable research? In fact, it may make subjects feel good to discharge hostility against the experimenters, and this may be why they subsequently indicated positive feelings on the mood questionnaire they were asked to complete.

In addition to these and other methodological criticisms of Schachter and Singer's experiment, questions have been raised about the experimenters' theoretical assumptions. For example, Maslach (1979) accepts Schachter's notion of a cognitive search for an explanation of unexplained arousal, but points out that people may not only search the situation, but may also search their memory for past events that might provide an explanation for the current state of arousal (for example, "I've never liked getting stuck with needles by doctors, so that's why this injection bothers me," p. 955). If the person can find such an explanation by reviewing past experiences, his or her emotional reactions may be less influenced by events taking place in the environment. Maslach has also challenged Schachter's theoretical ideas concerning the kinds of explanations that people are likely to adopt when trying to account for their feelings. Maslach believes that when unexplained arousal is experienced, subjects find this not only "an unusual experience but a disturbing and even frightening one" (p. 955). For this reason, a search for a cognitive label for unexplained arousal may be biased toward negative factors rather than positive ones. Recent research by Maslach (1979) supports this view.

It is important to realize that some of the criticisms leveled against the Schachter and Singer study can mean different things depending on one's point of view. On the one hand, those who question the basic hypothesis underlying Schachter and Singer's work argue that the problems with the study raise the possibility that the findings are misleading, or even false. This may be one reason, critics say, why other researchers have not always been able to replicate Schachter and Singer's results (Maslach, 1979; Marshall and Zimbardo, 1979). On the other hand, supporters of Schachter and Singer's view admit that their original study had methodological problems. But they contend that some of these problems may have worked *against* Schachter and Singer, thus making it even more difficult for them to obtain significant results. Schachter and Singer themselves argue that they never intended this one experiment to be the sole basis for their theory of emotions. Other studies, they say, bolster their theoretical position. And of those that have failed to replicate the original findings, most have had methodological problems of their own (Schachter and Singer, 1979).

Thus, perhaps the most serious criticisms of Schachter and Singer's position are ones that are not tied strictly to problems with their original experiment. Although some of Schachter's critics have acknowledged that his experiment and its theoretical underpinnings were very important in "redirecting the field of social psychology toward a more cognitive orientation" (Marshall and Zimbardo, 1979), they still argue that Schachter's theory carries the cognitive interpretation of emotions too far. It makes the implicit assumption that emotional states are differentiated *only* by cognitive factors. The physiology of emotion, Schachter suggests, is virtually the same from one emotion to the next. Granted, researchers in the 1960s, when Schachter first published his work, had been unable to find large physiological differences among emotions. But this does not prove that such differences do not exist. Indeed, research in the last decade has suggested that they might. Using very advanced technology, scientists have found significant differences in hormone responses to such stress-producing factors as physical exertion, fasting, and exposure to intense heat and cold, among others (Mason, 1975; Mason et al., 1976). These investigators are still in the process of measuring hormone secretions during different emotions. However, they believe that specific hormone patterns for specific emotions will eventually be found (Lazarus et al., 1980). Thus, it is probably correct to say, as Schachter does, that emotion involves an interaction between cognitive factors and physiological arousal. But at this time it seems likely that a more important role will eventually be assigned to physiological patterns as a means of identifying specific emotional states and differentiating them from nonemotional stimuli (Dienstbier, 1979).

EMOTIONAL REACTIONS TO CRISIS

At some point in our lives most of us will encounter tragedy of some kind. We or someone we love may be the victim of violent crime, a disabling accident, or a serious, sometimes terminal, illness. How do people respond emotionally to such experiences? Do they progress through discrete stages in attempting to cope with misfortune? Do they eventually recover, or at least learn to live with their adversity? These are very important questions that some psychologists have recently begun to answer.

One thing that has become increasingly clear is that popular conceptions about the ways people cope with crisis—conceptions often shared by those in the medical and helping professions—may be largely incorrect (Silver and Wortman, 1980). For example, it is commonly believed that when tragedy strikes, people react with clear displays of emotion. But research shows that it is probably a misconception. People actually respond to crisis with a good deal of variability. Some become highly emotional, while others remain relatively composed. In a study of mothers who had experienced the death of a terminally ill child, for example, some reacted "hysterically," but others responded with "calm sorrow and relief" (Natterson and Knudson, 1960). The same variability is seen in reactions to violent crime. Within a few hours after being raped, half the women in one study expressed intense emotions (crying, sobbing, displaying severe tension and restlessness), but half appeared outwardly quite controlled (Burgess and Holmstrom, 1974). Interestingly, recent research has shown that a rape victim who appears controlled immediately after the attack may be judged more negatively by others, and even viewed as less credible, than a victim who is more emotional (Calhoun et al., in press).

The idea that emotional response to crisis follows a predictable sequence of stages is also widespread, but it too may be unwarranted. One of the best known proponents of a stage model of coping is Elisabeth Kübler-Ross (1969). She has proposed that the terminally ill person passes through five discrete stages. The first stage is denial, the second anger, the third bargaining (for example, promising to become a better person if given more time), the fourth depression, and the fifth peaceful acceptance of one's fate. Is there any evidence to support such a model? Unfortunately, most of the people who have proposed stage models have based them on anecdotal evidence or on their own subjective impressions. The few pertinent empirical studies that have been conducted do not seem to support a stage model. In a study of people who were permanently paralyzed from spinal cord injuries, Lawson (1976) attempted to determine whether subjects experienced a stage of depression. Multiple measures of depression were obtained 5 times per week for an average of 119 days per patient. Surprisingly, there was no clear period of at least one week in which any patient's measures were consistently in the depressive range. Such findings raise considerable doubt as to whether a stage model of response to crisis is valid.

Yet despite the scarcity of evidence for a stage model, most people continue to believe in one, including most people in the health-care and helping professions. As a result, people who experience life crises are often told by well-meaning professionals how they *should* react. Worse still, when a person does not conform to these expectations, he or she may be treated with little patience. One researcher has reported that because of a widely held belief in Kübler-Ross's five stages of dying, terminally ill patients "who did not follow these stages were labeled 'deviant,' 'neurotic,' or 'pathological' diers. Clinical personnel became angry at patients who did not move from one stage to the next" (Pattison, 1977, p. 304). Similarly, if patients' emotional reactions are dismissed as "just a stage," legitimate complaints may be ignored. For example, when one hospitalized cancer patient complained because she was given the wrong tests, a nurse was overheard telling a co-worker: "Don't worry about Mrs. A.; she's just going through the anger stage" (Wortman and Dunkel-Schetter, 1979). Clearly, such responses from others may only serve to compound the sufferer's problems.

What about the prognosis for successfully overcoming a life crisis? Does "time heal all wounds," as many people believe? Again, this common assumption may be untrue for many people. There is considerable evidence that those who manage to recover from trauma do so less quickly and less completely than they or others expect. A large minority of people are still extremely upset long after their tragedy has occurred. In one study of women who had undergone mastectomies to remove malignant breast tumors, 39 percent experienced serious anxiety, depression, and/or sexual difficulties a year after the operation

(Maguire et al., 1978). Another study (Parkes, 1975) found that fully 44 percent of bereaved persons were still severely anxious two to four years following their loss. In a study of rape victims, 26 percent did not feel they had completely recovered even four to six years after the assault (Burgess and Holmstrom, 1978). And even among those who have apparently accepted their new life circumstances, many periodically experience renewed distress (on the anniversary of the crisis, for example) (Bornstein and Clayton, 1972; Wiener et al., 1975; Parkes, 1970).

Nevertheless, health-care professionals often expect emotional recovery to be quite rapid. In one survey, 52 percent of physicians anticipated that a widow or widower would have "experiences of pleasure" within a few weeks after the husband or wife's death (Schoenberg et al., 1969). In contrast, only 19 percent of widows and widowers were this optimistic (Schoenberg et al., 1975). And it is not only professionals who expect speedy recovery. Friends and relatives may be even less aware of the adjustment problems that life crises may pose. They often expect people to "get back on their feet" once the immediate crisis is over. For example, parents who had experienced the death of a newborn infant were expected not to grieve and to "put the death behind them"; they were also reminded that they could have another child (Helmrath and Steinitz, 1978). Those who are unable to recover quickly are often labeled self-pitying. Such demands may only add to the sufferer's adjustment problems, for in addition to feeling continued distress, he or she must cope with the belief that this reaction is somehow inappropriate. These expectations about recovery may even prevent people from seeking help from others in times of crisis. Kaltreider, Wallace, and Horowitz (1979) found that although one-third of the young women they studied were still extremely distressed one year after undergoing a nonelective hysterectomy, they "were hesitant to seek medical or psychological help because they thought that they should be able to cope with this normal crisis" (p. 1503).

In short, although researchers have traditionally emphasized the impressive ability of many people to deal with adversity, this emphasis may deflect attention from the sizable minority of those who exhibit distress much longer than is commonly expected. Outsiders should be sensitive to the fact that for many people, a life crisis is never really forgotten, and the experience may be carried with them for the rest of their lives (Silver and Wortman, 1980).

Much more needs to be learned about emotional reactions to life crises. Hopefully, the more information researchers obtain, the better able they will be to help people cope successfully with distress. Of course, it is important to examine any physical symptoms that may accompany stress as well as emotional reactions. As you will see in the following section, a person's reaction to stress can have a marked effect on his or her physical well-being, sometimes contributing to the onset of serious illness.

EMOTIONAL STRESS AND ILLNESS

Emotions—love, anger, joy, frustration—give texture and meaning to our lives. But emotional stress, if severe or prolonged, can take a harsh toll on the body. And stress is everywhere; it can scarcely be avoided. Contrary to the popular notion of stress as induced by negative life events, the body can respond with stress to pleasure as well as to pain. As Hans Selye, the dean of stress researchers, explains:

Stress is the body's nonspecific response to *any* demand placed on it, whether that demand is pleasant or not. Sitting in a dentist's chair is stressful, but so is enjoying a passionate kiss with a lover—after all, your pulse races, your breathing quickens, your heartbeat soars. And yet who in the world would forego such a pleasurable pastime simply because of the stress involved (Selye and Cherry, 1978, p. 60)?

According to Selye, then, all unusual demands on the body tend to evoke a similar set of physiological responses. Selye calls these responses the **general adaptation syndrome**.

Reacting to stress: Selye's general adaptation syndrome

According to Selye (1956), the general adaptation syndrome involves three stages: alarm, resistance, and exhaustion. The alarm stage begins with activation of the sympathetic nervous system. The organism is made ready for action: Glucose level rises, heartbeat and breathing accelerate, in short the body pulses with energy. But this stage does not last indefinitely. If stress continues, the body soon responds with what Selye calls resistance. During the resistance stage the organism appears to be physiologically normal because heartbeat and breathing rate are no longer elevated. This appearance, however, is only superficial. Analysis of the blood shows that the body is under the influence of an increase in the pituitary hormone ACTH, as well as in the hormones of the adrenal cortex that ACTH stimulates. These elevated hormone levels, in turn, keep the level of blood glucose unusually high. Interestingly, the overabundance of ACTH and its related hormones also makes the organism more susceptible to infection because it weakens the body's defenses against invading microorganisms. This is one possible reason why many students are prone to infectious diseases—from colds and flu to mononucleosis—during the stress of final exams. Like the alarm stage, of course, the resistance stage cannot last forever. The pituitary and the adrenal cortex gradually lose their ability to produce elevated amounts of the hormones needed to sustain energy. Selye's final stage, called exhaustion, begins to set in. Now the body's capacity to combat stress is steadily declining as all physiological processes start to break down. If the stress persists under these weakened conditions, the inevitable outcome is death.

Selye's general adaptation syndrome is based on his observation of different kinds of experimental animals under a variety of stressful circumstances. Can we therefore conclude that this same pattern also occurs in humans? The answer to this question is still incomplete. Recent work by other scientists suggests that the human response to stress may in some ways be more complex than that of other organisms. In particular, stress researcher John Lacey has found that the reaction of the human sympathetic nervous system varies with the individual: Each human being's physiological responses to stress appear in some respects to be unique. Furthermore, sympathetic reactions also seem to vary with the type of stress to which a person is exposed. Some stressors, for instance, cause a person's heart to race; others actually decrease heartbeat (Lacey and Lacey, 1962; Lacey, 1967). Then, too, there is evidence that physiological reactions may vary somewhat depending on a person's cognitive appraisal of a stressful situation (Lazarus, 1966, 1974; Mason, 1971, 1974, 1975). Such findings call into question Seyle's view that physiological response to stress is the same in all stressful circumstances. But regardless of the apparent variability with which the human body reacts to stress, there is little doubt that stressful conditions, especially prolonged and repeated ones, can contribute to the onset of human disease.

Stress-related disease and death

There is now abundant evidence that stress is related to certain serious diseases. The evidence that stress is associated with heart disease is particularly strong (Friedman and Rosenman, 1959, 1974). People who persistently exhibit excessive competitive drive, aggressiveness, impatience, and a chronic sense of time urgency—collectively labeled Type A personalities—typically suffer twice as much heart disease and twice as many heart-related deaths as Type B personalities, who exhibit calmer, more relaxed styles of behavior (Rosenman et al., 1975). In an important study of more than 3,500 men (Western Collaborative Group Study, 1970), twenty-two of twenty-five deaths from heart disease in a five-year period were of Type As. Moreover, when all deaths, regardless of cause, were looked at, post-mortem examinations showed that atherosclerosis was six times more prevalent in Type As than in Type Bs. In another large-scale investigation, Type A behavior was found to be associated with a twofold risk of coronary heart disease for both men and women (Haynes, Feinleib, and Kannel, 1980). In addition, there is evidence that stress is implicated both in the onset and course of bronchial asthma (Groen, 1971), where frustration may produce breathing changes, and in diabetes (Minuchin, 1978; Bradley and Cox, 1978). And there is even an indication that stress may be related to the onset of cancer, although the evidence is still only suggestive (Cohen, 1979). There is growing evidence that among people who have been diagnosed as having cancer, emotional expressiveness (which may help reduce stress) is predictive of longer survival rates (Rogentine et al., 1979; Derogatis et al., 1979).

Measuring life stress The first systematic attempt to quantify the degree of stress experienced in life and to demonstrate the effects of stressful events was undertaken in 1967 when psychologists Thomas Holmes and Richard Rahe devised a Social Readjustment Rating Scale (SRRS). The SRRS consists of forty-three possible life events and their corresponding weights—that is, their relative impact on life and the degree of readjustment involved in coping with them. In this scheme it does not matter whether an experience is positive or negative; for example, the birth of a much-wanted child could be equally as stressful if not more stressful than the foreclosure of a mortgage or a fight with one's in-laws. Table 10.1 shows that on the Holmes and Rahe scale, death of a spouse ranks highest with 100 life change units; minor legal violations rank lowest with 11. Totals exceeding 150 units in any one year are said to indicate "life crises," and are frequently associated with increased incidence of illness—not only such predictable illnesses as heart disease (Rahe and Lind, 1971; Edwards, 1971) but also, more surprisingly, bone fractures (Tollefson, 1972) and the onset of leukemia in children (Wold, 1968).

TABLE 10.1 Social Readjustment Rating Scale

Rank	Life event	Mean value
1	Death of spouse	100
2	Divorce	73
3	Marital separation	65
4	Jail term	63
5	Death of close family member	63
6	Personal injury or illness	53
7	Marriage	50
8	Fired at work	47
9	Marital reconciliation	45
10	Retirement	45
11	Change in health of family member	44
12	Pregnancy	40
13	Sex difficulties	39
14	Gain of new family member	39
15	Business readjustment	39
16	Change in financial state	38
17	Death of close friend	37
18	Change to different line of work	36
19	Change in number of arguments with spouse	35
20	Mortgage over $10,000	31
21	Foreclosure of mortgage or loan	30
22	Change in responsibilities at work	29
23	Son or daughter leaving home	29
24	Trouble with in-laws	29
25	Outstanding personal achievement	28
26	Wife begin or stop work	26
27	Begin or end school	26
28	Change in living conditions	25
29	Revision of personal habits	24
30	Trouble with boss	23
31	Change in work hours or conditions	20
32	Change in residence	20
33	Change in schools	20
34	Change in recreation	19
35	Change in church activities	19
36	Change in social activities	18
37	Mortgage or loan less than $10,000	17
38	Change in sleeping habits	16
39	Change in number of family get-togethers	15
40	Change in eating habits	15
41	Vacation	13
42	Christmas	12
43	Minor violations of the law	11

The amount of life stress a person has experienced in a given period of time, say one year, is measured by the total number of life change units (LCUs). These units result from the addition of the values (shown in the right column) associated with events that the person has experienced during the target time period.

Source: Thomas H. Holmes and Richard H. Rahe. The social readjustment rating scale. *Journal of Psychosomatic Research*, 1967, *2*, 213–218.

The impact of Holmes and Rahe's work was enormous, and warnings about the effects of stress have proliferated in the media and within the health-care system. Some health-maintenance organizations, for example, have announced plans to counsel patients who have already undergone many life changes to limit additional changes in an attempt to prevent illness (Cohen, 1979). But several issues need clarification before such programs are adopted. Are positive life changes really as potentially stressful as negative ones? Do all people with many negative life changes run equal risks of illness, or is greater illness correlated with those people who have the most difficulty adjusting? And finally, in some cases where significant life changes are expected, might *no* change—not getting a promotion, not going to college—also induce stress (Gersten et al., 1974; Graham, 1974)? Thus, there is a clear need for more precise definition of the kinds of life events that promote stress, and under what circumstances.

In addition, there is a need for clarification about the meaning of many studies that have used the Holmes-Rahe scale to demonstrate that high life stress is indeed related to illness. One problem is that most such studies have been retrospective—that is, the scale is administered *after* the onset of illness. It is easy to see that such a procedure might cause biases. People who are ill and looking back over their lives may be more pessimistic and more inclined to remember stressful events than people who are in good health. Another problem is that some of the events listed on the SRRS could actually be early signs of incipient illness (events like changes in eating or sleeping habits, for example). If so, they would artificially inflate the association between "life changes" and illness (Hudgens, 1974). For these and other reasons, some researchers now believe that it may be most important to study the methods of coping that allow some people to handle life changes well, without becoming ill, rather than focusing on specific life events (Cohen, 1979).

Factors mediating the stress-illness connection The prediction of stress-related illness is difficult because of the great differences in the ways individuals react to stressful situations. One person who is fired from a job may cheerfully set out to find a new one; another may regard being fired as an opportunity to take a long-postponed vacation. A third person, however, may begin to experience

Figure 10.5 We are increasingly aware of the intimate relationship between our emotions and our health. This woman, being comforted by a friend, mourns the death of her husband. Her grief may affect her physical as well as mental health.

agonizing migraine headaches. What enables some people to take stressful events in stride, while others react by becoming seriously ill?

One explanation may involve a person's social support. Although this explanation has not yet been firmly established, a clear link has been found between receiving encouragement and understanding from other people and having the ability to cope with a variety of tragic events, including death of a loved one, paralysis, blindness, severe burns, cancer, and criminal assaults. In a study of rape victims, for example, nearly half of the women whose relatives and friends were supportive recovered within a few months. In contrast, none of the women who lacked social support recovered in this short a time. Even four to six years later, 53 percent of the women without support from others were still psychologically scarred by the rape (Burgess and Holmstrom, 1978). And social support promotes not just psychological recovery but also physical well-being. One nine-year investigation showed that people who lacked close social ties were three to three hundred times more likely to die in the period studied than were people who enjoyed such ties (Berkman and Syme, 1979).

Another reason why some people are more likely than others to cope successfully with stress may have to do with their orientation toward life. Consider a study of two groups of male executives at a public utility company: those who had experienced both high stress and a high incidence of illness, and those who had experienced equally high stress with few adverse physical effects (Kobasa, 1979). Subsequent personality tests revealed that the stress-ridden executives who had avoided illness differed from their less healthy counterparts in what Kobasa described as psychological "hardiness." The hardy executive would view the stress of a sudden job transfer to an unfamiliar city as a challenging new opportunity. He would throw himself into the new job, using whatever capabilities he had to shape the course that the new assignment took. In contrast, the executive low in hardiness would view the transfer as an imposition. Because he felt he had no choice, he would acquiesce to it but would resent the change a meaningless interruption of his career. The major conclusion of this study was that these marked differences in orientation put the less hardy men at a disadvantage in coping with stress.

A third, particularly provocative, possibility is that some of those who remain healthy simply care less about achieving life goals, have shallow attachments to other people, lack involvement in life affairs, and are more concerned with their own well-being, compared with those who suffer frequent illness (Hinkle, 1974). Clearly, such people would tend to be quite well "insulated" from many upsetting emotions. But much more research will have to be done to determine to what extent this theory is correct.

The factors we have discussed so far all seem to be related to the ability to keep stress and its associated arousal from reaching acute levels and so precipitating illness. But not all successful coping strategies necessarily reduce arousal. For instance, many researchers have observed that being engaged in activity, rather than remaining passive, can be effective in reducing threat and influencing the bodily precursors of disease. Although active coping strategies increase physiological arousal, especially of the adrenal cortex hormones (Gal and Lazarus, 1975), they are associated with lower psychological perception of anxiety and distress (Miller et al., 1970). Similarly, researchers have found that people who respond with anger to serious illness often have a better prognosis for recovery than those who respond with depression (Weisman and Worden, 1975). Angry patients are certainly not reducing their levels of physiological arousal, and yet their survival rates are relatively good. What could explain this relationship?

One possibility is that people who respond to stress with depression and apathy may neglect self-care. They may fail to eat properly, or they may not bother to take medication. This possibility may help explain why depressed patients have lower survival rates than angry patients, who are far less likely to neglect themselves. It also suggests another beneficial effect of social support: Supportive friends and relatives can ensure that a patient does not abandon prescribed medical regimes (Cobb, 1976). Another possibility is that psychological states may be linked to physical symptoms through a direct, hormonal route. If each emotion is indeed associated with a different pattern of hormone response, as recent work suggests, then the state of depression may be hormonally more lethal than other psychological states (Lazarus et al., 1980).

We can hope that future research will shed more light on these important questions. The benefits of untangling this complex web of cause-and-effect relationships is clearly enormous. Once social scientists understand more about why certain psychological reactions increase or decrease the deleterious physical effects of stress, they can suggest better ways of dealing with stressful circumstances. For example, people who suffer some major setback might be encouraged to become angry rather than to accept their condition with passive resignation. Such approaches will undoubtedly be more effective than simply cautioning people to avoid or reduce stress, for in a complex, industrial society like ours, exposure to stress is virtually a way of life.

STUDYING THE NATURE OF HAPPINESS

In depth

So far we have focused on several important topics related to *all* emotions—the physiological changes associated with emotion, the relative importance of internal and external factors in explaining our subjective feelings, and the fact that severe emotional stress can sometimes give rise to illness and even death. It seems appropriate, therefore, to conclude this chapter with an in-depth look at one particular emotional state. We have selected happiness, not only because it is the emotion that most people devote a large proportion of their time pursuing, but also because "nowhere is the relevance of psychology to human concern more evident than in studies of happiness or subjective well-being" (Costa and McCrae, 1980, p. 668).

When asked to define *happiness*, different people emphasize different aspects of this elusive state (Freedman, 1978). Some see happiness as mainly passive contentment—the inner peace and tranquillity that come from deep satisfaction with one's environment, one's relationships with others, and one's self. Others see happiness as primarily deriving from active pleasures—stimulation, excitement, challenge, accomplishment, and moments of exhilaration and joy. These differences in definition, however, are simply differences in emphasis.

Most people agree that both these sides of happiness should be included in any definition of the term. **Happiness**, then, can generally be described as "a positive, enduring state that consists of positive feelings about the self and the world and that includes both peace of mind and active pleasures and joy" (Freedman, 1978, pp. 34-35). Note that this definition refers to happiness as a fairly enduring state, as distinguished from the transient kind of happiness (the brief elevation of mood) we may experience at a given moment. It is this more long-term kind of happiness that we will be emphasizing in this section.

Theories of happiness

One of the central questions in the study of happiness concerns the conditions that make a person happy. What brings us happiness? Psychologists have proposed a number of provocative answers. One is that happiness is primarily a matter of comparison. If our present situation compares favorably with that of others who are similar to us in an important comparative sense, we feel happy; if it compares unfavorably and we learn that they are obtaining more rewards than ourselves, we feel discontent. Based on this notion some have argued that a utopian society in which people receive everything they want would not foster happiness (Brickman, 1978). How in such a society of perpetual fulfillment could people ever judge themselves to be fortunate?

Empirical research has often supported the comparative theory of happiness. One of the first pieces of evidence in its favor came from a survey of soldiers during the 1940s (Merton and Kitt, 1950). The survey revealed a number of puzzling paradoxes. For example, soldiers who lacked a high-school diploma were much less likely to be promoted than were soldiers with a high-school education or better. Yet the men with *less* education were generally *more* satisfied with the army's promotion policies than were their better-educated counterparts! The reason apparently had to do with each group's sources of comparison. Relative to advancement possibilities in the civilian world, the more educated soldiers were doing quite poorly, but the less educated soldiers were doing quite well. As a result, the former were very dissatisfied, while the latter were reasonably content. More recently, other researchers have devised experiments to test the "happiness is relative" hypothesis directly. In one study, Milwaukee residents who read vivid descriptions of how terrible life in their city was at the turn of the century reported more satisfaction with their current circumstances than did subjects who read a glowing description of Milwaukee's earlier years (Dermer, Cohen, and Anderson, 1978). This finding clearly demonstrates that perceived happiness can be consciously manipulated, and both business and government sometimes take advantage of this fact. Advertisers, for instance, undoubtedly increase our displeasure with our current possessions by showing us pictures of people with possessions far more elegant than our own (Brickman, 1978). Similarly, it has also been argued that Cuban president Fidel Castro may have raised the satisfaction level of his people simply by eliminating the rich American tourists who used to flock to Cuba each year (Brickman and Campbell, 1971).

The comparison theory of happiness has limitations, however. One problem is its failure to adequately explain why a person who is extremely fortunate relative to other people can still be unhappy and why a person who is extremely unfortunate relative to other people can still be content. Such cases have been clearly documented. For example, one study showed that winners of a million-dollar state lottery were reportedly no more satisfied with life than less financially fortunate people (Brickman, Coates, and Janoff-Bulman, 1978). Conversely, people who have suffered some terrible misfortune—who are blind, retarded, or malformed—are no less happy, on average, than people without these afflictions (Cameron et al., 1973). These findings certainly challenge the predictions that would be made by comparison theory alone. How, then, might they be explained?

Adaptation theory provides one answer (Helson, 1964). It argues that over time such people have become accustomed to their unusually positive or negative circumstances and so no longer use them to determine whether they are happy or not (Brickman, 1978). Million-dollar lottery winners, for example, are initially delighted with their windfall gain. But soon they begin to take their new financial status for granted. Just as people become adapted to bright sunlight or monotonous background noise, the lottery winners become adapted to their new-found wealth. Although they still regard their windfall as an exceedingly positive event, they are no happier than people who have never won a lottery, and they tend to take less pleasure than nonwinners in mundane activities like eating breakfast or watching television. These findings can be viewed either pessimistically or optimistically. On the one hand, they can suggest that the pursuit of happiness is a kind of hedonic (pleasure-seeking) treadmill, whereby today's happiness becomes tomorrow's norm. In this view, happiness will never be permanent unless our circumstances are constantly improving. On the other hand, these same findings can be used to show that, although we all believe we would be happier if we had more money, more prestige, more beauty, or more of any number of other traits, in fact these circumstances have a very limited impact on our subjective estimates of well-being. Habituation makes the extremes of both fortune and misfortune appear more normal to the person who possesses them.

But if objective circumstances really play so small a role in our subjective impressions of happiness, what accounts for the large differences in happiness observed among people? One answer is that a person's level of happiness is an outcome of fairly stable personality traits that tend to contribute to either negative or positive feelings. For instance, it has been suggested that extroverted traits such as sociability, warmth, and involvement with people contribute to satisfaction in life, although they do not necessarily reduce the unpleasantness of negative life circumstances. In contrast, neurotic traits such as feelings of guilt or anxiety tend to make a person more aware of misfortune, but they do not necessarily lessen his or her pleasures. This means that the introvert low in neurotic qualities and the extrovert high in them may have a similar overall level of happiness, but they reach this level in very different ways. The former is inclined to very moderate emotional upswings and downturns, while the latter is inclined to great emotional highs and lows (Costa and McCrae, 1980).

Another possible way of explaining why some people are happier than others invites us to define happiness in a rather unusual way. According to this definition, true happiness is found in the ability to abandon all concern about whether one is happy or not (Brickman and Campbell, 1971). Granted, this state of mind is difficult to accomplish. But it is sometimes attained through total absorption in a challenging task that demands undivided attention. Dancers, composers, chess players, mountain climbers, and surgeons often report this kind of submergence in their profession or sport (Csikszentmihalyi, 1975). When it occurs, the person is completely unaware of all other stimuli except the task at hand. Most important, the person's self-consciousness fades and with it all questions about happiness. Thus, according to this view of happiness, the truly happy person is not aware of emotional states at all.

As yet, psychologists have made few attempts to test these various theories of happiness in order to determine under which circumstances each is most likely to apply. For example, if those you compare yourself to differ from you in background or personality, are you still likely to derive satisfaction from a favorable comparison? Is there any limit to the human ability to adapt to situations? Might we adapt less readily to intangible assets like love and self-esteem than we do to material possessions? Are opportunities for the pleasures of total absorption available to people in ordinary walks of life? These and many other interesting questions about the theories of happiness remain for future research to explore.

Factors associated with happiness

In addition to developing theories of happiness, psychologists have tried to discover what life circumstances are generally associated with happiness. Jonathan Freedman recently conducted a survey of 100,000 people regarding their life situations and their feelings of happiness or discontent (Freedman, 1978). The survey showed that a satisfying intimate relationship is one of the factors most consistently related to happiness. Especially from the viewpoint of people who do not have it, love contributes a great deal to happiness. Sex, too, contributes, but it is apparently the quality of one's sexual relations, not their quantity, that counts. The fact that married couples are on average somewhat happier than single men and women is probably related to their attainment of both love and enjoyable sex, although marriage is no guarantee of either. Interestingly, couples who are living together seem to fall between married and single people in their attainment of happiness. Other studies have confirmed the importance of social relationships to happiness (Wessman and Ricks, 1966; Bradburn, 1969). Apparently, the happiest people are those who, among other things, are very actively involved in the world around them, especially with other people.

The Freedman survey has also revealed that certain factors are *not* related to happiness. These findings may give you some surprises, for they contradict a number of common assumptions. As the lottery studies show, money does not usually provide happiness. As long as you have enough money to live on, you would probably not be very much happier if your income was substantially increased. Age, too, is unrelated to happiness. People on average are equally happy at all stages of the life cycle, even though different age groups derive their satisfaction from different things. The only qualification regarding age and happiness concerns the elderly. As individuals, elderly people are either extremely happy or extremely unhappy. Other factors that are rather unexpectedly *not* related to happiness include a happy childhood (many happy children become unhappy adults and vice versa), religious commitment (religion does not necessarily bring peace of mind), and place of residence (city dwellers in general are just as happy as rural residents).

Two cautions about these findings, however. First, although the sample size was extremely large, the respondents may have been unrepresentative—they were answering a survey in *Psychology Today* magazine. Second, it should be remembered that such data are simply correlations. Having many or even all of the factors generally associated with happiness does not guarantee that you will be satisfied with your life. Conversely, even if you are lacking any number of these conditions, you may still be very content (Freedman, 1978). Further research in this area will probably shed more light on the age-old question of how happiness can best be achieved.

SUMMARY

1. All human beings experience **emotions**, states of feeling that can affect behavior, which often arise in response to social relationships and other external stimuli and are frequently accompanied by physiological changes.

2. The role of physiological arousal in emotion has long intrigued psychologists. Strong emotion, such as anger or fear, is often associated with a number of changes in the sympathetic nervous system, including increased heartbeat and rapid breathing.

3. The brain coordinates the activities of the autonomic nervous system, and parts of the brain—the hypothalamus and the limbic system, in particular—are involved in a number of emotions. Stimulation of or damage to these parts has been accompanied by exaggerated emotional behavior.

4. Most theories of emotion have centered on the relationship between the two main indicators of emotion: (1) physiological arousal, and (2) the subjective feelings we call fear, anger, and so on. William James and Carl Lange, in the 1920s, proposed that our perception of our bodily changes is *itself* the emotion, and that each emotional state is signaled by a unique physiological pattern. This view came to be known as the **James-Lange theory**.

5. Other researchers, primarily Walter Cannon, found fault with this theory. According to the **Cannon-Bard theory**, physiological arousal alone does not cause emotion, but rather is initiated simultaneously with the subjective experience of emotion by the same nerve impulse.

6. Many subsequent researchers have found that there may be some physiological changes that can be identified in a general way with different emotions, but that each particular emotion does not bring with it unique physiological changes.

7. Psychologists have also investigated the issue from another angle: Is physiological arousal even necessary for the feeling of emotion? George Hohmann, in an experiment with army veterans with severed spinal cords, concluded that while emotional responses to events still occurred, their quality was altered.

8. Stanley Schachter has proposed that emotion involves two closely interacting factors: a state of physiological arousal plus a cognitive interpretation of that arousal. He attributes our capacity to comprehend our emotional arousal to our ability to label *general* sensations as *specific* emotions. Schachter and others found that arousal simply signals to a person that an explanation of some kind is needed, and that a person looks solely to environmental cues to place a label on these physical sensations. Criticism of the Schachter approach has centered on his assumption that emotional states are differentiated *only* by cognitive factors, and some researchers working since Schachter's theories first appeared in the early 1960s have concluded that there may indeed be unique hormone patterns associated with specific emotional states.

9. Three assumptions about emotional reactions to crisis characterize the beliefs of laymen and health-care professionals: that there are universal reactions that occur in response to crisis; that people go through stages as they cope with crisis; and that the crisis is ultimately resolved. Though widely held, these assumptions have not been experimentally supported.

10. Both painful and pleasurable stimuli can produce emotional stress, and this stress in turn can take a toll on the body's health. Researcher Hans Selye has concluded from animal studies that the body responds to all types of emotional stress with a similar three-stage pattern—alarm, resistance, and exhaustion—which he calls the **general adaptation syndrome**. Other researchers believe the human response to stress may be more varied and complex than that outlined by Selye, particularly since different types of stress appear to cause different sympathetic reactions.

11. Many scientists are convinced that the onset of many, and perhaps all, diseases involves emotional factors. Psychologists Thomas Holmes and Richard Rahe developed the Social Readjustment Rating Scale (SRRS) to measure the quantity of stress a person is undergoing by assigning a fixed number to different stressful events. They have found that high numbers for an individual within a given period are associated with a significant increase in illness, though many of the events in the scale could be signs of oncoming illness.

12. The prediction of stress-related illness is complicated by the differences in individuals' reactions to stress. An individual's personality and degree of social support are both influential in helping him or her cope successfully with negative events. It is not yet clear exactly how such feelings are translated into physical symptoms, but neglect of self-care and the hormonal response associated with depression are among the explanations that have been offered.

13. Happiness is an emotion that combines positive feelings with both peace of mind and active pleasures. Psychologists who have looked for the foundations of happiness have proposed several theories. One, the comparative theory, says that we are happy if we think our situation compares favorably with that of other people. Another, adaptation theory, argues that we continually adapt to our circumstances and thus always need improvements in the status quo to keep us happy. A third holds that true happiness comes from ignoring one's comparative situation and becoming instead totally absorbed in a task at hand.

Suggested readings

Cofer, C. N. *Motivation and emotion.* Glenview, Ill.: Scott Foresman, 1972.

Darwin, C. *The expression of the emotions in man and animals.* Chicago: University of Chicago Press, 1965. (Originally published, 1872.)

James, W. The emotions. In *The principles of psychology* (Vol. II). New York: Holt, 1890.

Schachter, S. *Emotion, obesity, and crime.* New York: Academic Press, 1971.

Selye, H. *Stress without distress.* Philadelphia: Lippincott, 1974.

Weisman, A. *Coping with cancer.* New York: McGraw-Hill, 1979.

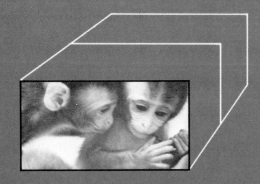

11 The dynamics of motivation

Questions about human motivation probably began long before there was written language to record them. Whenever people wonder what gives impetus and direction to behavior, they are usually wondering about motivation. Why, for instance, in the early 1950s did two men expose themselves to weeks of bitter wind and cold, scarcity of oxygen, and treacherous icy terrain in order to be the first humans to set foot on the summit of Mount Everest? Why, a decade earlier, did the Nazi regime in Germany systematically kill more than 6 million Jews in a manner so brutal it defies comprehension? Why in Nazi concentration camps did some prisoners risk their own lives to steal food for a friend near death from starvation? The answers to all such questions are bound up in the complex web of human motivations.

Motivation is thought to encompass those variables that arouse, sustain, and direct behavior toward attainment of some goal (Madsen, 1959). According to this definition, motivational factors are numerous indeed. They include a range of physiological changes that encourage goal-directed activity, plus a diversity of external stimuli that an organism seeks to approach or avoid. Not all psychologists agree with such a broad definition, however. Over the years narrower concepts of motivation have also been proposed. Examining some of these concepts is a good way to understand why, even today, the definition of motivation is still controversial.

THE DEVELOPMENT OF MOTIVATIONAL CONCEPTS

With the growing popularity of Charles Darwin's theory of evolution, humans began to see themselves as part of the biological world, related through distant ancestry to every living creature. This was a radically new self-concept, and it prompted new perspectives on behavior. If the behavior of lower animals is controlled primarily by instincts, and if we humans are indeed kin to all other living things, might not our behavior also be influenced by innate tendencies? Such speculation launched a widespread effort to identify human "instincts." One of the most influential of the instinct theorists was psychologist William McDougall, who in 1908 proposed a list of instincts that included the following: flight, repulsion, curiosity, pugnacity, self-abasement, self-assertion, reproduction, gregariousness, acquisition, and parental care. Other investigators proposed different lists of instincts, and the number of instincts continued to multiply as researchers tried to account for more and more behaviors. One survey conducted in 1924 (Bernard) found that nearly 850 human instincts has so far been proposed!

While these lists of instincts provided intriguing descriptions of behavior, they did very little to explain why particular behaviors occur. To say that people act pugnaciously because of a pugnacious instinct is not very informative. Why are some people more pugnacious than others? Under what circumstances is pugnacious behavior especially likely to occur? For these reasons, instinct theories fell out of favor with psychologists, and later theorists have tried to provide more precise and coherent views of human motivation.

Freud and unconscious motivation

One alternative was offered by the Viennese physician Sigmund Freud, whose theories will be discussed in detail in Chapter 13. Freud sought to reduce the many human instincts that McDougall and others had proposed to a few basic ones. Accordingly, he maintained that all human drives can be subsumed under two broad categories. One is the urge toward life, procreation, and self-preservation, which includes the drives for food, water, warmth, and above all sex. Freud called this fundamental impulse *Eros*, after the Greek god of love. In addition, Freud believed that all people also possess an urge toward death and self-destruction—a return to the inanimate matter of which all living organisms are composed. This urge he called *Thanatos*, after the Greek personification of death. Because self-destruction is diametrically opposed to self-preservation, Freud regarded Eros and Thanatos as conflicting forces. He speculated that this conflict is often resolved by turning the energy of Thanatos outward against others. Hence the human tendencies to compete, to conquer, and to kill.

Because satisfaction of sexual and aggressive drives is often unacceptable to our moral standards (particularly the strict moral codes of Victorian Europe, in which Freud lived and worked), Freud believed that people push "forbidden" impulses deep into the unconscious, where they cause less anxiety. In Freudian terms, these impulses are **repressed**. But often a repressed urge, still alive in the unconscious, directs a person to engage in some substitute, more socially acceptable behavior, thus giving the impulse an outlet of some kind. This process is called **sublimation**. For example, Freud hypothesized that many of the beautiful male and female nudes that Renaissance artists created on canvas and in marble were the products of sublimated sexual impulses. Similarly, we may unconsciously express anger toward our parents by losing or accidentally breaking one of their cherished possessions or by showing up late for a special holiday dinner. The possibility that our behavior may be controlled by unconscious motives—motives that we are not aware of—is one of Freud's most important contributions.

Learning approaches to motivation

As provocative as Freud's notions of unconscious motivation are, many of his ideas are difficult to test experimentally. Many investigators in the United States, including the behaviorist John Watson, believed that psychologists must take a more scientific approach to motivation. These investigators rejected the mysterious realm of instinct and the unconscious and came to view variations in human behavior in terms of conditioning or learning. An individual behaves aggressively not because of a "pugnacious instinct" but because he or she has been rewarded or reinforced for such behavior in the past. The behaviorists have had an enduring influence on psychology, as we will see when we study learning approaches to personality, abnormal psychology, and treatment in later chapters. But as research accumulated, some problems emerged for those behaviorists who believed that all variations in goal-directed behaviors could be explained by learning. For example, investigators found it difficult to condition the behavior of a dog who had recently been fed. In other words, if the animal is not motivated by a biological need, little learning will occur. For these reasons, psychologists began to focus on the role of physiological drives.

Drives and motives

In 1918, psychologist Robert Woodworth used the term *drive* to describe the internal energy force that propels an organism toward the satisfaction of a particular need. According to drive-reduction theories of motivation, when a drive is aroused, an animal is impelled (motivated) to engage in whatever behavior has in the past been associated with reducing that drive. Thus, the food-deprived animal is motivated to reduce its hunger drive by eating and the sexually aroused animal to reduce its sex drive by mating (Hull, 1952). Closely related to the notions of drive and drive reduction was the concept of **homeostasis**—the body's automatic tendency to maintain its internal equilibrium regardless of changing external conditions (Cannon, 1934).

Drives to satisfy unlearned biological needs, such as hunger, thirst, and sex, have been called **primary drives**. Of course, it is obvious that humans engage in many activities besides those related to satisfaction of their biological needs. Acquired or learned drives, such as those related to achievement, affiliation, or power, have been called **secondary drives**. However, the distinction between primary and secondary drives is not clear-cut. Learning plays an important role even in the expression of primary drives like eating and sexual behavior.

Today, the terms *drive* and *motive* are often used interchangeably. There has been a great deal of research on both biologically based and learned motives. A large number of learned motives have been proposed, including a social-con-

tact motive (Harlow and Harlow, 1966), a power motive (Adler, 1962), a possession, or acquisition, motive (Murray, 1938), and an achievement motive
(McClelland et al., 1953). Some psychologists have become concerned that as
more and more motives are identified, the concept may come to lose its usefulness and be abandoned, much as the study of instincts was eventually abandoned. Unlike the early instinct theorists, however, the psychologists who have
proposed theories of motivation have focused on how motives develop and
under what conditions they are activated.

There have also been some important attempts to organize and integrate
human motives. One of the most intriguing of such systems for classifying
human motives has been proposed by Abraham Maslow (1954, 1971), a leader
in the development of humanistic psychology. Maslow argued that individuals
are motivated to satisfy different types, or levels, of needs: physiological needs,
safety needs, belongingness needs, esteem needs, and self-actualization—a term
he applied to the process of becoming the most productive, creative person that
you can. According to Maslow, these needs are related in a hierarchy. If we are
unable to satisfy basic needs, we will be distracted and thus unable to fulfill our
potential. Maslow's theory will be discussed more fully in Chapter 13.

Beyond drives and drive reduction

As persuasive as drive reduction initially seemed as a comprehensive theory of
motivation, it was not long before problems began to emerge. For example,
conceptions of motivation based on drives assume that the goal of behavior is
to reduce tension or stimulation. As evidence accumulated, however, researchers began to question this assumption. Why does a rat offered a choice between
a short, direct path to food, and a longer, indirect path frequently prefer the
more difficult, but perhaps more interesting, route? Why are animals willing to
work for the opportunity to begin, but not complete, the act of copulation?
Why do people go to amusement parks or participate in dangerous sports? In
order to account for such behaviors, psychologist Donald Hebb (1955) hypothesized that organisms are motivated to maintain an optimal level of arousal.
When physiological motivation, or drive, increases, the organism can be viewed
as overaroused and thus motivated to reduce the drive by satisfying the biological need. When the arousal level is too low, the organism seeks stimulation.
This theory, and the implications that it raises, will be discussed later in this
chapter.

A second problem with drive-reduction theory is that being in a drive state is
not always enough to provoke goal-directed behavior. If a very hungry animal
is given food with a slightly unpleasant flavor, it may refuse to eat, or eat very
little. In fact, goal-directed behavior has been found to occur when an animal is
not in a drive state at all. For example, a completely satiated animal will often
eat eagerly if the food it is offered is especially tasty. Such findings suggest that
what is essential for goal-directed behavior to occur is not a physiological drive,
but rather the expectation of receiving a reward. Psychologists call these expectations **incentives**. There is evidence that a person's cognitions and expectations
about receiving particular rewards play a major role in sustaining behavior, as
we will see in the subsequent discussion of achievement motivation.

Because motivation is a subject that spans so many areas of psychology, the
topics covered in this chapter will necessarily be diverse, ranging from behav-

iors that are greatly influenced by innate physiological mechanisms to motivations that are entirely learned. First, we will discuss two motivations with strong biological components—hunger and sexual behavior. We next examine sensory-seeking drives, such as the need to explore one's environment and the need for optimal stimulation. Finally, we will discuss the more complex, learned human motives, with special emphasis on achievement motivation.

EATING AND WEIGHT CONTROL

A remarkable aspect of the motivational systems that control eating is their ability to balance energy intake (food) against energy expenditure so precisely as to maintain a relatively constant body weight. An adult animal with widely fluctuating weight is relatively rare in any species. This stability is all the more impressive when you consider that an excess food intake of only one hundred calories a day can add nearly one hundred pounds to a person's weight in just ten years! To understand how most of us avoid such excessive weight gain, we must first look at the physiological factors that regulate hunger.

Physiological factors regulating hunger

What, physiologically speaking, makes a person feel hungry? How does a person determine when he or she has had enough to eat? Early researchers suspected that the answers might lie in the bodily sensations most commonly associated with hunger and satiation: the stomach contractions we call hunger pangs and the feeling of a full stomach. To investigate this mechanism, psychologist Walter B. Cannon persuaded his assistant to swallow a balloon, which he then inflated and used to measure stomach contractions. As expected, the contractions were highly correlated with subjective feelings of hunger (Cannon and Washburn, 1912). Later findings suggested that distension of the stomach plays a role in cessation of eating. When one team of researchers loaded a large bulk of nonnutritive material directly into a dog's stomach (via a surgical incision) the animal ate less than normal or did not eat at all (Janowitz and Grossman, 1949, 1951). However, the most recent evidence indicates that cues from the stomach are of secondary importance in regulating hunger and eating. Rats whose stomachs have been surgically removed still learn mazes in order to obtain food, and the fact that they remain active at feeding time suggests that they still experience hunger (Penick et al., 1963). Similarly, humans who have had the stomach removed because of ulcers or other diseases continue to report hunger pangs (Janowitz, 1967).

Other investigators have suggested that eating may also be regulated by changes in the sensation of taste. As Figure 11.1 shows, the hungrier a person is, the more likely that person is to judge a sweet-tasting food as "pleasant." Once full, the person will rate the same food as "unpleasant" (Cabanac, 1971). Thus, the first bite of a food may taste better than the last, regulating intake accordingly. The decline in the palatability of a particular food as consumption increases appears to be counteracted if a new food is introduced. Research has shown that simply by giving a rat a diet that includes four distinct tastes, rather than one, the animal may overeat by as much as 270 percent—or nearly four times its normal intake (LeMagnen, 1971). As each new taste is introduced, the

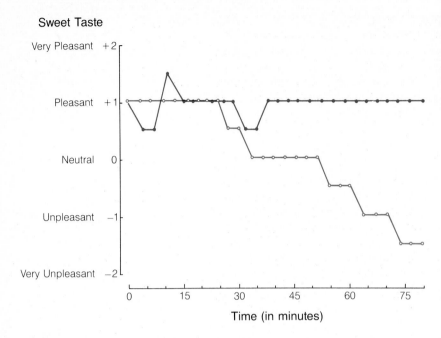

Sweet Taste

Figure 11.1 Graph of Cabanac's (1971) findings in his experiment on changes in the palatibility of a sweet solution. The closed circles represent the response of a subject who sampled the solution without swallowing it. The open circles represent the response of a subject who swallowed the solution.

rat begins to eat with gusto once again. You may recognize the same tendency in yourself. When you eat a meal of several courses, with the tastiest courses coming last, you may unwittingly counteract the effects of declining palatability and, therefore, eat more than you should.

Like stomach cues, however, taste cues do not appear to play a central role in the regulation of eating. If they did, animals with no access to taste should have difficulty controlling their food intake, and experiments show that they do not. When humans or other animals must press a lever to receive an injection of liquid food through a tube into the stomach, they are able to control their body weight quite well despite the fact that they never taste their food at all (Epstein and Teitelbaum, 1962; Jordan, 1969). In fact, an animal fed this way can maintain a stable weight even when the experimenter varies the amount of food delivered with each press of the bar. Clearly some control system other than taste is at work.

The message in this other system seems to be carried in the blood. When the blood from a rat that has eaten from forty-five minutes to two hours earlier is transferred to the veins of a food-deprived rat, the latter no longer appears hungry. It nibbles indifferently at food it would otherwise devour (Davis et al., 1969). This finding clearly implies that something in the blood of the well-fed rat signals satiation. But what, exactly, is the nature of this signal? And how is the signal "read"? To answer these questions it is best to look first at the part of the brain that seems to play a special role in the regulation of eating. This is the hypothalamus.

Electrical or chemical stimulation of the lateral portion of the hypothalamus can cause a previously satiated animal to eat voraciously (Brugger, 1943; Epstein, 1960). Conversely, when the same area of the hypothalamus is surgically destroyed, a rat will completely refuse food. Because the animal spits out any food that is placed in its mouth and thoroughly removes stray morsels that cling to its fur, it appears that the rat finds eating highly aversive. In fact, a rat with lesions in the lateral hypothalamus will die of starvation unless force fed (Anand and Brobeck, 1951). Such findings imply that the lateral hypothalamus serves as a kind of feeding center that both initiates the hunger drive and helps sustain eating.

Another area of the hypothalamus—the ventromedial region—seems to have roughly opposite effects. When the ventromedial hypothalamus is artificially stimulated, a formerly hungry animal will refuse to eat (Hoebel and Teitelbaum, 1962). Conversely, surgical destruction of this area causes an animal to eat prodigious amounts of food and grow to incredible obesity (Hetherington and Ranson, 1940). Thus, the ventromedial hypothalamus seems to serve as a kind of satiety center. As such, its effects tend to counter those of the lateral hypothalamus: An increase in the firing rate of cells in the ventromedial hypothalamus tends to decrease the firing rate of cells in the lateral hypothalamus and vice versa (Oomura et al., 1967; Van Atta and Sutin, 1971.)

Although we have said that the lateral hypothalamus serves as a feeding center and the ventromedial hypothalamus as a satiety center, the term *center* is used here in a very broad sense. Remember from Chapter 3 that control over a certain kind of behavior is never localized in one area of the brain. Almost everything that an animal does appears to involve activity in most or all of the brain. This is the principle of mass action. At the same time, a specific part of the brain is likely to be involved in the performance of many types of behavior. This is the principle of multiple control. Eating behavior and the hypothalamus are no exceptions to these rules. The lateral and ventromedial regions of the hypothalamus do not maintain exclusive control over eating and satiety respectively. Instead, they are important parts of much larger neural networks that radiate through many areas of the brain (Grossman, 1975). In addition, a number of other neural pathways, related to other motivational states, also seem to traverse the hypothalamus. This is demonstrated by the fact that an animal with a lesioned ventromedial hypothalamus is not only a voracious eater but is also "irascible, emotional, and generally bitchy" (Schachter, 1971a), implying that an intact ventromedial hypothalamus is involved in the regulation of emotional responsiveness as well as eating.

The discovery that the hypothalamus is involved in the regulation of eating is important. But how does this area of the brain receive information about the body's need for food, so that eating can be initiated or terminated? The research by Davis and his colleagues (1969) suggests that the blood must be the vehicle for the signal to the hypothalamus. But precisely what signal is carried by the blood? Some investigators have hypothesized that the glucose (sugar) in the blood plays a key role. When glucose is injected into the hepatic portal vein of a hungry rat (the hepatic portal vein supplies blood to the liver), the animal shows no interest in food (Russek, 1971). This finding suggests not only that the level of sugar in the blood is an important signal in the control of eating, but also that the liver may play a critical role in "reading" this signal and relaying it to the brain.

As persuasive as this evidence is, however, researchers suspect that the glucose signal is not the only one involved in the regulation of hunger. The level of fat in the body also appears to be involved in adjusting food intake over the long run. Consider the behavior of a rat with a lesion in the ventromedial hypothalamus. As you know, such an animal will eat itself to obesity, but this voracious eating does not last forever. After a number of weeks, it begins to eat only enough to maintain its new grossly large size. It is almost as though the rat's behavior is directed toward achieving some new "optimum" weight set by the lesioned hypothalamus. In keeping with this theory, if obese rats are forced to eat more food than needed to maintain their newly stabilized hefty weight, they will subsequently refrain from eating until their former obese weight is reestablished (Teitelbaum, 1955). Conversely, if large portions of the rat's fat tissue are surgically removed, it will eat its way to precisely the same level of obesity as before (Liebelt, Bordelon, and Liebelt, 1973). Of course, the hypothalamus cannot really act as a scale measuring how many pounds of fat an animal has loaded on its frame. Instead, the hypothalamus must be responding to something associated with increases or decreases in the body's fat content.

In summary, it appears that eating is regulated by several physiological mechanisms that work together. Knowledge of the physiological factors that regulate hunger have very practical implications. Approximately 40 percent of the population of this country are considered to be obese, or 20 percent over normal body weight. An overweight person has significantly greater chances of being stricken with heart disease, hypertension, and diabetes than a person of average weight. Thus, the question of what causes obesity and how it can be controlled is a very important one—important enough to consider in depth.

Studying the causes of obesity

In depth

Although a few researchers have argued that extremely overweight humans may have the equivalent of a lesioned ventromedial hypothalamus, most are convinced that this is an unlikely explanation for most cases of obesity. Nevertheless, there are many similarities between the behavior of an obese person and that of an animal with surgical damage to the ventromedial hypothalamus: Both eat more than subjects of normal weight, and they also eat more rapidly. But they are both particularly choosy eaters. If a small amount of quinine is added to food, making it slightly bitter, a lesioned rat will eat substantially *less* than a normal rat will. Similarly, if offered a bitter-tasting food, such as ice cream laced with quinine, an overweight person will eat far less than an underweight one will. In fact, when obese patients in a nutrition clinic and normal-weight volunteers were allowed to eat as much as they wanted of a bland liquid diet, the overweight subjects reduced their calorie consumption by as much as 80 percent, whereas the normal-weight subjects maintained their usual calorie intake (Hashim and Van Itallie, 1965). A particularly delicious food, however, will usually prompt the overweight person to feast (Nisbett, 1968; Decke, 1971).

Another of many interesting parallels between animals with lesions in the ventromedial hypothalamus and obese humans is that both are very reluctant to work for their meals, especially when the ultimate food reward is not particularly salient. For instance, if a hypothalamic-lesioned rat is taught that it can press a lever to receive a pellet of food, it will press less and less often as the number of presses required to obtain the food increases (Teitelbaum, 1957). Again, compare this behavior with that of obese humans. In one study in which subjects were given the opportunity to eat from a bag of nuts while filling out some questionnaires, only one out of twenty obese subjects bothered to indulge when the nuts had to be shelled, but nineteen out of twenty ate the nuts eagerly when the shells had been removed. For normal-weight subjects, in contrast, nut consumption was unrelated to the obstacle of a shell (Schachter and Friedman, 1974).

Psychologist Stanley Schachter and his colleagues have tried to find a common element that could explain the behavioral similarities between the rat with ventromedial hypothalamic damage and the obese human. He has arrived at the very intriguing conclusion that both are extremely sensitive to external eating cues. This, Schachter argues, is why the overweight person is so affected by relatively modest changes in the availability, quality, or appearance of food—changes that the average person might not even notice. In one study, for instance, the lighting on a bowl of nuts was enough to influence the eating behavior of obese subjects (Ross, 1974). When lights were focused on a dish of cashews, overweight people ate about twice as many of the nuts as they did when cashews were less conspicuously displayed under dimmed lights. Research has shown that this responsiveness to external cues is present quite early in life (Costanzo and Woody, 1979). Overweight infants just a few days old will suck more rapidly than normal weight babies if given a sweet solution, suggesting that they are already extremely sensitive to taste cues (Nisbett and Gurwitz, 1970). For this reason, Schachter believes that such heightened sensitivity to food-related stimuli has its orgins in the structure of the brain.

But is the externality of the obese person limited to only food-related stimuli? Schachter and his former student Judith Rodin suspected not, so they designed a number of experiments to test this suspicion (Schachter and Rodin, 1974). In one study, subjects were asked to work at a proofreading task that required substantial concentration. The performance of obese subjects fell off rapidly when distracting stimuli were introduced (Rodin, 1973). In contrast, the performance of normal-weight subjects did not show this pattern. Based on these and similar findings, Schachter has proposed that any stimulus above a certain intensity level, be it food-related or not, is more likely to evoke a response from an obese person than from a normal-weight one (Schachter, 1971a). On the basis of this research, Rodin has suggested that this heightened sensitivity to external cues is the major cause of overeating (Rodin and Slochower, 1976). According to this view, the person who overresponds to external stimuli in general will also overrespond to the sight, smell, and taste of delicious food. That person will consequently eat too much and so become obese.

Psychologist Richart Nisbett (1972) has a different view of the finding that the obese are more sensitive to taste cues and more easily distracted than the nonobese. According to Nisbett, the obese exhibit these behaviors because they are in a constant state of hunger. Nisbett arrived at this conclusion after noticing a striking similarity between the behavioral characteristics of the obese and the behavior of normal-weight individuals who undergo a starvation diet for any length of time. Starving people are also highly sensitive to external food cues. In addition, both the obese and starving individuals are more prone to emotional upset, are more easily frustrated, are more inactive, and are less interested in sex than nonstarving or normal-weight individuals.

If the starving and the obese person have this much in common behaviorally, it seems logical to expect that the obese might show signs that they are in a perpetual state of hunger. One physiological indication of hunger is the level of free fatty acids in the blood, for during periods of fasting, fat is broken down into free fatty acids to meet energy requirements. Significantly, the obese have a higher level of free fatty acids than normal-weight people do. This led Nisbett to conclude that the obese are in a state of chronic energy deficit. According to Nisbett, then, a state of physiological hunger causes both a tendency to overeat and so become obese *and* a tendency to be overresponsive to external cues and prone to emotional upset.

But how can an obese person be hungry when he or she eats more than enough to maintain a normal body weight? Nisbett's answer is that what is a biologically "normal" weight varies from one person to the next. Some people have a base line, or "set point" for fat tissue (determined by both heredity and early nutrition) that is well above the average. These people, in other words, are programmed to be fat. As Nisbett has put it, it is "as if their hunger switch were stuck in the 'on' position" (1972, p. 53). What mediates this biological tendency toward obesity is not yet fully understood. Naturally obese people may produce an excessive amount of insulin, a hormone that, among other things, causes the body to store energy as fat (Bray and Gallager, 1975). Alternatively, the naturally obese person may possess an unusually large number of fat cells (Knittle and Hirsch, 1968). Research suggests that the total number of fat cells in the body may be set very early in life, even at birth. Subsequent overeating or undereating can increase or decrease the size of these cells, but it may not be able to affect their number to any appreciable extent (Hirsch and Knittle, 1970). In any case, Nisbett argues, the obese cannot become slender without feeling continually starved.

But obese people do not want to be fat. Obesity in our society is considered unattractive, so the obese person is under great pressure to lose weight. Thus people who are biologically prone to obesity find themselves in perpetual conflict. Their bodies are telling them that they are hungry and should eat more, while society is telling them that they are fat and need to drastically restrict their diets. As a result, many obese people end up eating less than required to meet their physiological demands but not enough to be truly slender.

Some intriguing evidence supports Nisbett's theory that the obese are often hungry people vainly trying to become slim. Consider the fact that the *grossly* obese usually do not display the behavioral symptoms of hunger. Presumably these people have given up any effort to remain slender and so eat as much as they want. Significantly, it is the person who is only moderately obese and who is constantly watching his or her weight who is likely to display the emotionalism, inactivity, and heightened responsiveness to external cues that tend to be associated with obesity (Hibscher and Herman, 1977).

In an intriguing extension of Nisbett's theory, C. Peter Herman and his associates have argued that obesity per se is not the critical factor determining whether a person will display the behavioral traits of the obese. The critical factor is the extent to which that person is constantly dieting. Presumably such people, whether they are currently thin, grossly obese, or somewhere in between, would gain a great deal more weight if they were to "let themselves go." These people are appropriately called *restrained eaters* (Herman and Polivy, 1975). Herman and his colleagues have developed the scale in Table 11.1 to measure a person's degree of eating restraint. You can easily use it to assess your own eating behavior. If you score high on this test—averaging a fourteen or more—you are likely to be constantly struggling to restrict what you eat. And when your restraint for some reason is broken, you may not just eat, you may gorge.

This tendency of restrained eaters to periodically go on eating binges ex-

TABLE 11.1 Eating Restraint Scale

1. How often are you dieting? Never; rarely; sometimes; often; always. (Scored 0–4)

2. What is the maximum amount of weight (in pounds) that you have ever lost within one month? 0–4; 5–9; 10–14; 15–19; 20+. (Scored 0–4)

3. What is your maximum weight gain within a week? 0–1; 1.1–2; 2.1–3; 3.1–5; 5.1+. (Scored 0–4)

4. In a typical week, how much does your weight fluctuate? 0–1; 1.1–2; 2.1–3; 3.1–5; 5.1+. (Scored 0–4)

5. Would a weight fluctuation of 5 pounds affect the way you live your life? Not at all; slightly; moderately; very much. (Scored 0–3)

6. Do you eat sensibly in front of others and splurge alone? Never; rarely; often; always. (Scored 0–3)

7. Do you give too much time and thought to food? Never; rarely; often; always. (Scored 0–3)

8. Do you have feelings of guilt after overeating? Never; rarely; often; always. (Scored 0–3)

9. How conscious are you of what you are eating? Not at all; slightly, moderately; extremely. (Scored 0–3)

10. How many pounds over your desired weight were you at your maximum weight? 0–1; 1–5; 6–10; 11–20; 21+. (Scored 0–4)

plains some rather curious experimental findings (Herman and Mack, 1975). Immediately following lunch or dinner, subjects either were given nothing to eat or were asked to consume one or two good-sized milkshakes as parts of a bogus "taste test." Then each subject was left alone to taste and rate the flavor of three kinds of ice cream. Subjects were told that after rating the flavors they could eat as much of the ice cream as they wanted. Enough ice cream was supplied so that a subject could eat a gluttonous amount without making an embarrassing dent. The researchers expected that the *unrestrained eaters* (those who reported rarely giving a thought to dieting) would compensate for having previously consumed a milkshake or two by eating relatively little ice cream. As shown in Figure 11.2, this is exactly what they did. But what about the re-

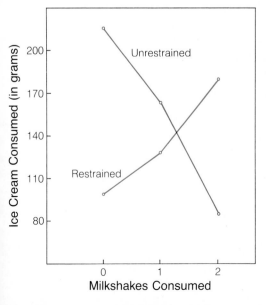

Figure 11.2 Unrestrained eaters, having consumed one or two milkshakes, show appropriate compensation when asked to taste and rate the flavors of three kinds of ice cream. Restrained eaters, however, eat more ice cream the more milkshakes they have already consumed. Herman and Polivy (1975) hypothesize that the suspension of their self-imposed restraint (in this case, in the form of the milkshakes) causes dieters to capitulate to internal (hunger) and external (taste) cues.

strained eaters? As Figure 11.2 shows, the restrained eaters ate very little ice cream when they had previously consumed no milkshakes, but they ate a very hefty portion when they had previously consumed two milkshakes! Why did overeating tend to breed more overeating? Apparently, after having already been required to indulge in the milkshakes, the restrained eaters reasoned that all hope of dieting for that day was lost. The consequence? A total collapse of self-restraint and a sizable eating binge. Many subsequent studies have replicated this tendency for restrained eaters to show marked overeating once they are induced to go off their diet (Herman and Polivy, 1980).

The fact that the restrained eater is battling such a powerful tendency to overindulge, one that Nisbett and others believe is biologically based, makes it very difficult for such a person to maintain a slender shape. The person may have to live in a rather persistent state of hunger, and such a state may cause physiological stress. Furthermore, when people who have been fat since childhood lose substantial amounts of weight, they often experience anxiety, depression, and lethargy even after they return to a weight-maintenance diet (Gluckman et al., 1968; Grinker, 1973). Such findings have led a number of researchers to conclude that it may be more biologically appropriate for some people who have been obese all their lives to continue to be overweight by societal standards rather than to reduce drastically (Herman, 1975).

Of course, the overwhelming majority of obese people—probably some 70 percent—do not become fat as children, but gain weight as they reach middle age and begin to lead more sedentary lives. Many widely publicized diets are primarily directed toward this kind of obesity. Unfortunately, many also promise miracles they cannot deliver. How much fat you gain or lose depends entirely on the *number* of calories you consume. The body does not distinguish between calories derived from chocolate cream pie and those derived from sirloin steak. The only way to lose a pound of fat is to consume roughly 3,500 fewer calories than you burn off. Thus, unless you exercise long and strenuously, about a half a pound a day (a 1,750-calorie deficit) is near the upper limit of shed fat even for fairly heroic dieting.

Prominent researchers in the area of obesity agree that if a popular diet works at all, it is by subtly getting people to eat less (Cohen, 1979). For instance, in eliminating carbohydrates from the diet, a dieter effectively eliminates many foods that are high in calories. Even carbohydrates that are not rich in calories (bread and potatoes, for instance) are often smothered in butter, cream, or other fattening sauces. In addition, cutting out carbohydrates eliminates a great deal of snacking and binging. Similarly, diets that restrict a person to certain food categories, such as proteins or rice, can also subtly influence the amount consumed. Because these foods quickly become tiresome, the dieter tends to eat less.

Although popular diets may help you lose weight in the short run, many have serious shortcomings. A few, if used without medical supervision, can actually cause severe harm by eliminating essential nutrients. For instance, the liquid protein diet, very popular several years ago, was linked to fifty-eight deaths. And even if fad diets cause no measurable harm, there is no evidence that they are effective in promoting long-term weight control. The biggest problem with such diets is recidivism: About 95 percent of the "successful" dieters regain their lost weight.

Psychologists now believe that one of the most successful approaches to long-term weight control is behavior modification, the conscious use of basic learning principles to change human behavior. As discussed in Chapter 5, the goal of behavior modification is to eliminate inadvertent rewards for a problem behavior while reinforcing more desirable alternative responses. Most behavior-modification programs directed toward weight control begin by having the client record when, what, and how much he or she eats in a typical week. The results usually reveal some significant patterns. Suppose, for instance, you find that you are a recreational eater and that particular stimuli have become powerful signals to eat. One way to break such a habit is to try to avoid the stimuli that control your compulsive eating. For instance, if you find that you begin to munch as soon as you turn on the television, try planning some other form of entertainment. In addition, you might try reducing the reward associated with snacking by making yourself keep a log of how many and what size snacks you eat. The very act of having to keep a record can be aversive enough to lessen your eating. Another technique is to replace the habit of snacking with another pleasurable activity.

Some researchers believe that obese individuals will find it easier to modify their eating habits if they are made aware of their own extreme sensitivity to external eating cues. As Schachter (1971b) has pointed out, an overweight person will "stroll by a pastry shop, find the window irresistible, and, whether or not he has already eaten, buy something." The research by Schachter and his associates suggests that the obese may be able to control their food intake if they store food out of sight, plan meals that require difficult preparation, and order or serve only small portions.

Drawing from Herman's finding that restrained eaters tend to overeat when they go off their diets, some researchers have emphasized that people should set dietary restrictions that are realistic and achievable, thus lessening the likelihood of failure and consequent overeating (Mahoney and Mahoney, 1976). And perhaps by recognizing that "binging" is common once a person feels that his or her diet is broken, the dieter will be able to control this behavior more successfully.

Researchers still have much to learn about the causes and cures of obesity. Some investigators are trying to determine how a person's base line for fat tissue is set. With this knowledge, doctors might be able to alter an obese person's base line so he or she would not feel hungry at a normal weight. One interesting clue to the factors that might be involved here comes from observation of grossly obese patients who have undergone bypass surgery. (With bypass surgery a tube diverts food from the stomach to a lower section of the small intestine, thus bypassing a substantial part of the area where food is absorbed into the blood.) The interesting thing about these patients is that they not only lose weight because their bodies are receiving fewer calories, many also report that they actually *desire* to eat less. In short, they no longer feel hungry on a reduced-calorie diet (Stunkard, 1980). Exactly why this operation would cause a reduction in hunger is a puzzle yet to be solved.

Another important aspect of weight control still only superficially understood concerns variation in body metabolism. It has always intrigued researchers that some people can eat as much as 30 percent more than others of the same age, weight, height, occupation, and so forth and yet not gain a single pound (Garrow, 1978). Such people seem to have metabolisms set at a level much higher than normal. Conversely, obese people sometimes appear to have unusually "thrifty" metabolisms: Their bodies seem to keep going on very few calories a day. Why such differences exist and how they might be safely modified is one of the many questions scientists hope to answer in the future.

SEXUAL BEHAVIOR

As complex as the factors that regulate eating are, those that regulate human sexual behavior are probably even more complex. In addition to being influenced by drives and incentives, human sexuality is also greatly influenced by a whole range of cultural, religious, and moral prescriptions. Of course, how we satisfy our desire for food is likewise shaped by what our culture considers acceptable. But when it comes to sexual behavior, even the way we are first aroused—the very motivation itself—is substantially influenced by social learning. You will see this influence more clearly as we review the various factors that promote and inhibit sexual response.

Factors regulating sexual activity

In lower animals sexual behavior is heavily controlled by hormones. A female rat is sexually responsive *only* during ovulation, when the ovaries secrete high levels of the female hormone estrogen. It is therefore not surprising that when the ovaries of a female rat are removed, she becomes totally unreceptive to a male. Significantly, injections of estrogen can completely restore her normal sexual responsiveness. A somewhat similar pattern is seen in the male rat. When its testes are removed, sexual activity often gradually declines, and only injections of the male sex hormone testosterone can restore normal sexual behavior.

In contrast, sex hormones may help initiate sexual activity in humans, but they certainly do not control it. Human females are sexually responsive throughout the normal monthly cycle of rising and falling estrogen levels. Even complete removal of the ovaries has only a negligible effect on a woman's sexual responsiveness. In fact, the sex hormones secreted by the adrenal glands may have more of an effect on female arousal than those secreted by the ovaries. When diseased adrenals are surgically removed, a woman's sexual urge drops appreciably. As you would expect, sexual drive in such patients can be fully restored with injections of adrenal hormones. In the human male the hormone testosterone appears to be involved in normal sexual response. Its role, however, is not absolutely essential. If the testes are surgically removed in adulthood, only a very gradual decline in sexual activity occurs. Castration before puberty, however, does have a marked effect: It inhibits both normal development of secondary sex characteristics and normal sexual responsiveness. This is why, in some Eastern cultures, males who had been castrated before adolescence were used to guard harems.

Hormones, of course, do not operate independently of the central nervous system. As we saw in Chapter 3, the nervous system and the endocrine system closely interact. In sexual behavior the hypothalamus, in particular, stimulates the anterior pituitary gland to release hormones that in turn stimulate the gonads (the ovaries and testes) and the adrenal glands to secrete sex hormones. These sex hormones then travel in the bloodstream back to the hypothalamus, where they activate neural circuits involved in sexual arousal.

One area of the hypothalamus that seems to play a key role in integrating normal patterns of sexual responsiveness is the preoptic region. In male rats, lesions in this area either completely eradicate or drastically reduce sexual activity (Giantonio et al., 1970). Conversely, electrical or chemical stimulation of the preoptic region greatly increases mating behavior in both male and female rats (Malsbury, 1971; Fisher, 1956, 1967). Males so stimulated will mount other males if females are not available, and they can ejaculate at the impressive rate of once every twenty-seven seconds. Interestingly, the nature of the neural circuit that traverses the hypothalamus in the preoptic region is probably more important in determining sexual response than the nature of the hormone that chemically stimulates it. When the female hormone estrogen is injected into adult male animals, they show vigorous male, not female, sexual behavior (Fisher, 1956). Apparently, once the neural pathway governing sexual behavior is formed, injection of any sex hormone in relatively large amounts tends to activate it.

Hormones reaching the hypothalamus serve only to prime the neural pathways involved in sexual arousal. Appropriate external stimuli are also needed to translate that initial arousal into full-fledged sexual behavior. In lower animals the visual, auditory, olfactory, and tactile stimuli that serve as sexual cues tend to be both very specific and very powerful. For instance, the male silkworm moth is strongly attracted to the female by a chemical scent that she exudes. So dominant is this olfactory stimulus that a male moth will attempt to mate with surgically removed scent glands in preference to a scentless but otherwise normal female (Kellogg, 1907). We humans, of course, are freed from such rigid control of specific sensory stimuli. For us, many different sights, sounds, smells, and touches can be sexually arousing. These have their effect by stimulating neural circuits that are channeled through the hypothalamus. In this way hormonal and sensory influences on sexual arousal are closely integrated.

One very general external factor that affects sexual responsiveness in many species is variety. Suppose a male rat is allowed to copulate with the same female until it reaches utter exhaustion and shows absolutely no further interest in its partner. If a new female partner is then introduced, the male undergoes a spontaneous recovery. In fact, if that partner is replaced with another partner, and yet another, and so forth, the male will continue copulating far longer than it will when only one female is available (Fisher, 1956). This phenomenon has been called the "Coolidge effect" in honor of an anecdote about President Calvin Coolidge and his wife during their tour of a farm. "Observing the vigor with which one particularly prominent rooster covered hen after hen, Mrs. Coolidge asked the guide to make certain that the President took note of the rooster's behavior. When President Coolidge got to the hen yard, the rooster was pointed out and his exploits recounted by the guide, who added that Mrs. Coolidge had requested that the President be made aware of the rooster's prowess. The President reflected for a moment and replied, 'Tell Mrs. Coolidge that there is more than one hen' " (Walster and Walster, 1978). Whether or not the Coolidge effect applies to humans has yet to be put to a scientific test.

As we have seen, the interaction of external stimuli, secretion of sex hormones, and activation of sexually related neural circuits traversing the hypothalamus plays a central role in initiating, sustaining, and directing sexual arousal. But sexual behavior is still more complex than this illustration suggests; the cerebral cortex also has a role, which even in lower animals can be quite significant. When the temporal lobes of a male cat's cerebral cortex are surgically removed, the animal lacks all discrimination in its choice of sexual partners. It will attempt to mate with cats, dogs, furniture, the experimenter— virtually anything it can conceivably mount (Schreiner and Kling, 1956). Such findings suggest that, in the cat at least, the cerebral cortex may help direct sexual behavior toward appropriate goals.

As we move up the evolutionary ladder, the involvement of the cortex in sexual behavior becomes increasingly important. In humans the cortex can clearly excite or inhibit the sexual responses mediated by lower brain structures. The fact that we do not attempt to mate with every man or woman who sexually arouses us is evidence of the strong control that social learning exerts via the cortex. Similarly, the fact that both men and women can become highly aroused simply by sexual fantasies also testifies to the powerful role of the cortex in human sexuality. In two studies of male sexual arousal subjects were able to both increase and decrease the vigor of their erections by means of various fantasies (Rubin and Henson, 1975; Laws and Rubin, 1969). And in a survey of suburban housewives, as many as 65 percent reported that they sometimes had erotic fantasies while engaging in sexual intercourse with their husbands. Fantasies about imaginary lovers and submission to a dominating male were most common. Interviews with these women indicated that they used such fantasies to enhance their sexual responsiveness (Hariton and Singer, 1974).

Studying human sexual response

As you have probably already noted, much of what scientists know about the factors that regulate sexual activity has come from studies of laboratory animals. Until the middle of this century, data about human sexual response where scarce indeed. Most came from the self-reports of people undergoing psychoanalysis or from patients with various glandular or neurological problems. Clearly this left an enormous gap in the scientific understanding of human sexuality. By the 1940s and early 1950s a number of researchers were determined to fill that gap.

One of the pioneers in the study of human sexual response was Alfred Kinsey. A biologist by training, Kinsey spent most of his early career studying the gall wasp. In 1930 he was asked to teach a course on sex education, and unable to find reliable information on human sexual behavior, he decided to collect it himself (Pomeroy, 1966). Kinsey and his associates spent the next eighteen years talking to people of different ages, backgrounds, and marital statuses about their sex lives. The results of confidential interviews with 5,300 American men, *Sexual Behavior in the Human Male* (1948), and with 5,940 women, *Sexual Behavior in the Human Female* (1953), made history—and headlines. Kinsey's most controversial findings concerned premarital and extramarital sex (most men and many women reported such experiences) and homosexual activity (it was far more common than anyone at that time believed).

Although Kinsey's work was widely acclaimed for its comprehensiveness and value, it left many questions about human sexuality unanswered. In particular, Kinsey's surveys obtained information only about what white, well-educated American men and women in the 1940s said they did or did not do sexually. But what people *say* they do is not always what they actually do. Furthermore, Kinsey's methodology did not allow study of the physiological side of human sexuality. To overcome these limitations, carefully conducted observational research was clearly needed.

This need was finally met by two other pioneers in the field—William Masters, a research-oriented gynecologist, and Virginia Johnson, a psychologist. One of the first problems was how to measure human sexual response fully and accurately without inhibiting the behavior under investigation. This problem was solved through a variety of relatively unobtrusive techniques, including automatic monitoring of physiological changes such as heart rate and respiration, and films of all phases of the sexual cycle. Over a period of twelve years, Masters and Johnson observed some 10,000 sexual episodes engaged in by nearly 700 male and female volunteers.

Because Masters and Johnson's data were collected in a rather unnatural setting, and because the people who volunteer for such research may be in some ways unusual, some scientists were cautious in generalizing from Masters and Johnson's (1966) results. But Masters and Johnson were convinced that their physiological findings were representative of sexual behavior in most human beings, although they recognized that no two people ever react to stimulation in precisely the same way. Briefly stated, they found that sexual response in both men and women can be divided into four phases: excitement, plateau, orgasm, and resolution.

During the **excitement phase**, the heart begins to beat faster and the breathing rate increases. Blood flows into the genitals (see Figure 11.3) and causes the penis to become erect and the clitoris to swell. Drops of fluid form on the

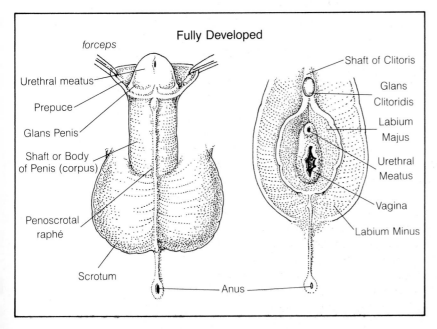

Figure 11.3 The male and female genitals (after McCary, 1978).

vaginal walls. Women's (and some men's) nipples may become erect, and women may develop a "sex flush" (a reddening, usually beginning on the chest, caused by the dilation of small blood vessels in the skin).

In the **plateau phase**, the genitals become fully engorged with blood. The clitoris retracts into its hood, though it remains highly sensitive. The glans of the penis enlarges and deepens in color, and some fluid (which can contain live sperm) may seep out the opening of the penis. As excitement reaches a peak, a feeling of approaching orgasm sweeps over the person. This feeling appears to be very much the same for both men and women.

During **orgasm**, involuntary muscular contractions force the blood that has been collecting in the genitals back into the bloodstream. The muscles around the vagina push the vaginal walls in and out, and the uterus pulsates. The muscles in and around the penis contract rhythmically, causing ejaculation—the discharge of semen, which is the fluid containing the sperm. For both men and women, the first few orgasmic contractions are the strongest and most pleasurable.

The body gradually returns to its normal, unstimulated physiological state during the **resolution phase**. Most women are capable of having another orgasm if effectively aroused again during resolution. In contrast, most men experience a refractory period—a period of time (ranging from minutes to hours) that must pass after an orgasm before they can respond to sexual restimulation.

Sexual dysfunction and therapy

Although Masters and Johnson were originally interested in normal sexual responses, they and other sex researchers soon turned their attention to sexual dysfunction. **Sexual dysfunction** refers to any problem that prevents a person from successfully engaging in sexual relations or from reaching orgasm during sex. Of course, everyone occasionally has trouble becoming sexually aroused or is unable to be sexually satisfied. A person may be tired, preoccupied, drunk, angry at his or her partner, or simply uninterested in sex at the time. But for the sexually dysfunctional person, such episodes are chronic and therefore highly distressing.

Among men, the most common sexual problems are impotence (inability to maintain an erection long enough to achieve orgasm), premature ejaculation (ejaculating before the man or his partner would like), and nonemissive erection (failure to ejaculate during sex with a partner). Among women, the most frequent sexual complaint is inability to achieve orgasm during intercourse. Some sex researchers, however, have questioned whether this condition is necessarily dysfunctional. The goal of achieving orgasm through vaginal stimulation alone may be unrealistic for many, perhaps even most, women, since the walls of the vagina are not well supplied with nerve endings (Kaplan, 1974). Another female sexual complaint, one that can cause severe worry and embarrassment, is vaginismus—involuntary muscle spasms that tightly shut the vagina, making penetration by the penis either impossible or extremely painful.

What causes sexual dysfunction? Masters and Johnson (1970) and many others believe that only rarely does a sexual problem have a physiological basis. Usually some psychological reason exists. Often couples are simply misinformed about sex, or they fail to communicate their sexual needs to each other. Others are overly concerned about the adequacy of their sexual performance. Still others were raised with rigid religious, moral, or social standards concerning sex. Then there are those who have been the unfortunate victims of some form of sexual trauma, such as rape, incest, or simply utter and humiliating failure during their first sexual encounters. Finally, there are cases in which people with sexual problems have received well-meaning but grossly misinformed advice from clergymen, physicians, marriage counselors, and yes, even psychologists. Sexually dysfunctional men have reported being given such counsel as "Once a grown man has homosexual experience he always ends up impotent" or "Any man masturbating after the age of thirty can expect to become impotent" (Masters and Johnson, 1970). Not surprisingly, such advice only tends to make an incipient problem worse.

Masters and Johnson (1970) have reported much success with a treatment program that encourages couples to discuss their sexual problems openly and frankly and that leads couples through more and more intimate sexual encounters. They calculate an overall failure rate (initial failures plus relapses within a five-year period after treatment) of only 20 percent—far lower than the failure rates for most kinds of psychotherapy. In fact, it is extremely impressive. Yet many other sex therapists have been unable to achieve comparable rates. As a result, some have begun to question Masters and Johnson's evaluative techniques (Zilbergeld and Evans, 1980). Precisely what criteria do Masters and Johnson use to determine treatment failure and success? Are their criteria less stringent than those of other researchers? And why do Masters and Johnson report failure instead of success rates? Does this imply that all their "nonfailures" have achieved an equal amount of success? Clearly, all the evidence on the success of current sex therapy is not yet in. Undoubtedly, in the years ahead, sex therapists will be working to produce as accurate and specific data as possible concerning the success of various treatment approaches, how long such treatment can be expected to take, what the likelihood of relapse is, and what, if any, additional problems might be created by treatment failures.

STIMULUS-SEEKING AND AROUSAL

Having explored much of the latest research on hunger and sexual arousal, it is now time to step back and look once again at psychologists' efforts to devise general theories of motivation—efforts that we touched on at the beginning of this chapter. The early drive-reduction theorists believed that organisms act to reduce states of tension inevitably caused by certain physiological changes. These changes arise through such conditions as deprivation of food or water, exposure to painful or sexually arousing stimuli, or through exposure to anything that has come to be associated with one of these more basic biological states. So compelling was the drive-reduction view when first proposed that it came to dominate psychological thinking on motivation in the early twentieth century.

It soon became apparent that drive-reduction theory had serious trouble explaining many motivated behaviors. For instance, if you give a monkey a mechanical puzzle, such as a metal clasp used to fasten a door, it will manipulate the object with great curiosity, searching diligently for the solution even though it is not physiologically deprived in any way (Harlow, Harlow, and Meyer, 1950). Similarly, think of the human penchant for puzzles and games of various sorts. What makes a person stay up all night to finish a mystery novel? Why do people spend hours on end playing bridge or chess? Such behaviors

Figure 11.4 Young monkeys become engrossed in a problem-solving situation.

simply do not fit the classic concepts of primary and secondary drive reduction.

One obvious solution to this problem is to propose the existence of still other innate drives—drives for solving problems, manipulating novel objects, exploring unfamiliar environments, and so forth. Many psychologists have done just that. But one might go on hypothesizing new drives indefinitely. At some point, what would seem to be needed would be an overall theory of motivation that could encompass activities as diverse as reading a book or watching television, doing a crossword puzzle, or working long hours for little or no pay. Such attempts began to be made in the early 1950s.

The optimum level of arousal concept

By the middle of this century psychologists had collected a wealth of information related to motivation. Included in these data was a fascinating set of findings concerning arousal and the brain. In particular, scientists had learned that when sensory stimuli impinge on an organism they activate not one but two pathways in the brain. First, there is the well-known pathway whereby sensory information travels from receptor cells, through sensory nerves, to the thalamus, and then to appropriate sensory areas of the cerebral cortex. But in addition, sensory input activates an area of the brain stem called the reticular formation, and from there the neural impulses travel upward, producing a very diffuse arousal of the entire cortex.

Most important for an understanding of motivation, this general state of cortical arousal seems essential for sensory signals otherwise reaching the cortex to activate a goal-directed response. When there is very little diffuse cortical arousal induced by the reticular formation, the chains of neurons associated with goal-directed behaviors may be unable to fire effectively. Not surprisingly, therefore, very low activation of the reticular formation is associated with coma or deep sleep. Conversely, when there is a great deal of diffuse cortical arousal induced by the reticular formation, the neural circuits associated with goal-directed behaviors may be effectively blocked (perhaps because the neurons are overstimulated and cease to fire at all, or perhaps because inappropriate com-

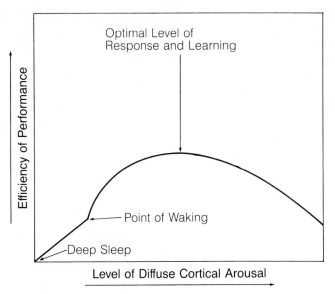

Figure 11.5 As the level of cortical arousal increases, performance increases to an optimal level and then decreases. Thus higher animals may be attracted by risk taking, or mild fear, and by problem solving, or mild frustration, since both serve to increase arousal (after Hebb, 1955).

peting responses tend to intervene). As a result, the organism that is over-aroused by the reticular formation may become temporarily paralyzed or respond in irrational ways. No wonder, then, that at the height of a battle only an estimated 15 to 25 percent of soldiers ever fire their guns (cited in Hebb, 1955)! The rest are immobilized with fear. Figure 11.5 shows the general relationship between diffuse cortical arousal and efficiency of performance. As you can see, the relationship is U-shaped: As arousal increases, performance first improves and then declines.

Psychologist Donald Hebb, among others, has elaborated these findings into a general theory of motivation (Hebb, 1955; Lindsley, 1951; Duffy, 1957). According to Hebb, motivated behavior begins with the occurrence of some appropriate sensory event. An organism may spot something sexually arousing, feel a painful stimulus, or experience hunger or thirst in the presence of food or water. These sensory inputs then travel to appropriate regions of the cortex, where they serve to direct behavior. Simultaneously, the same sensory signals activate the reticular formation, which bombards the cortex with diffuse neural impulses. If this diffuse cortical arousal is within a certain range, appropriate goal-directed behaviors will result. Thus, there is an *optimal level of arousal* for effective behavior. And this optimal level tends to be automatically maintained. When activation of the reticular formation is low, any response that produces increased stimulation and greater arousal will be facilitated and therefore is likely to be repeated. Conversely, when activation of the reticular formation is high, any behavior that produces decreased stimulation and reduced arousal will likewise be facilitated and therefore tends to be maintained. In humans, of course, with their high levels of self-awareness, an optimal level of arousal is often consciously and actively sought.

Theories like Hebb's were quite provocative because they could explain a number of motivated behaviors that had seemed rather puzzling. Consider, for example, the intriguing results of an experiment conducted just a few years before Hebb published his theory. In this study, male college students were paid $20 a day to remain in an environment with very low levels of sensory stimulation (Bexton, Heron, and Scott, 1954). Each of the subjects lay on a bed in a small room, as illustrated in Figure 11.6. A hollowed pillow enveloped their ears, muffling the only sound that was audible—the low, monotonous hum of an electric fan. Their eyes were covered with translucent goggles that diffused light, so the few objects around them appeared blurred and indistinct. Because they were wearing loose-fitting pajamas, the students did not even feel the pressure of a belt or a shoe. Cardboard tubes encased their arms from elbow to fingertips, cutting off the sense of touch. On demand, the subjects received food or water and were allowed to use the bathroom. Otherwise, they heard almost nothing, saw almost nothing, and felt almost nothing. How do you think they responded to such conditions?

A drive-reduction theory of motivation would predict that they should remain happily quiescent. After all, their biological needs for food, water, relief from pain, and so forth were being admirably met. But this is not what happened. Many of the subjects quit the experiment after only a few days. Why this negative reaction? Part of the explanation probably had to do with the stress of social isolation (Suedfeld, 1975), but sensory isolation undoubtedly played a role. For one thing, the subjects seemed to develop a strong desire for sensory stimulation of almost any kind. When given the chance to listen to very boring recordings, such as the same monotonous stock-market report or the same lecture on the dangers of alcohol written at a six-year-old level, they repeatedly requested them (Bexton, 1953). Such behavior is in keeping with an optimum arousal theory of motivation, in which very low levels of stimulation prompt a need for increased levels. Also in keeping with an optimum arousal theory of motivation was the fact that subjects' performance on many cognitive tasks often decreased after a day or so of sensory deprivation.

This study thus suggested that extremely low levels of sensory stimulation and arousal can have a detrimental effect on performance. But what about very high levels of arousal? Can these too inhibit performance? The answer seems to be yes. In one study of people's responses to life-threatening emergencies like fires and flash floods, at least 75 percent of the victims showed definite impairment of their ability to react rationally (Tyhurst, 1951). Many behaved in ways that simply did not make sense, such as wandering aimlessly rather than seeking a viable escape route. A full 12 to 25 percent were hopelessly disoriented: They screamed and cried hysterically or remained frozen to one spot. Similarly, in a study of nearly one hundred owners of small businesses damaged by hurricane floods, those reporting moderate levels of distress immediately after the disaster had, eight months later, made significantly more progress toward rebuilding than those reporting either very high or very low levels of distress (Anderson, 1976).

Such findings naturally lead to the question: What is the optimum level of arousal for effective performance? As you might expect, there is no single answer. For one thing, the optimum level of arousal varies with the complexity of the task. Remember from Figure 11.5 that the relationship between arousal and performance is U-shaped: As arousal increases, performance first improves and then deteriorates. But the improvement appears to begin later and the deterioration to set in earlier when a cognitive task is especially complex (Suedfeld, 1975). As a result, for a difficult task like taking an exam, both extremely low and extremely high levels of motivation and arousal will usually produce less than optimal results. This is rather unfortunate, for arousal is often greatest when we face a very difficult challenge.

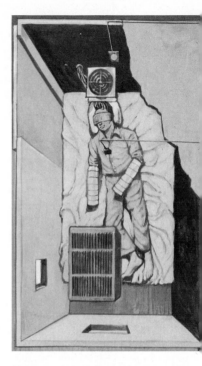

Figure 11.6 In a classic series of experiments on sensory deprivation conducted in the 1950s, subjects were isolated in sound-resistant cubicles. Gloves and cotton cuffs prevented input to their hands and fingers, a plastic visor diffused the light coming into their eyes; a foam pillow and the continuous hum of the air conditioner and fan made input to the ears low and monotonous. Except for eating and using the bathroom, the subjects did nothing but lie on the bed. Few chose to remain longer than three days (after Heron, 1957).

In addition to varying with the complexity of the task, the optimum level of arousal also seems to vary with the individual. This idea was first proposed by psychologist Hans Eysenck (1967), who argue that people differ greatly in their need for stimulation due to differences in how their brains function. These differences, Eysenck maintain, underlie the contrast between introverts (people who are generally withdrawn) and extroverts (those who are generally sociable and lively). The reticular formation of an introvert, according to Eysenck, is activated to a relatively high degree by sensory inputs. Consequently, the introvert has a high "natural" level of cortical arousal. This means that such a person needs very little external stimulation to achieve an optimum arousal level, giving the introvert a preference for quiet, solitary activities. The extrovert, in contrast, has a reticular formation that is activated to a relatively low degree by sensory inputs, and so a naturally low level of cortical arousal. As a result, the extrovert requires a great deal of external stimulation to boost arousal to an optimum level. Hence the extrovert's preference for noise, excitement, and constant companionship.

If introverts and extroverts have different natural levels of arousal, they should perform quite differently under conditions of varying external stimulation. Introverts, with their normally high state of arousal, should be less tolerant than extroverts of high levels of stimulation and so not perform as well under these conditions. A striking experiment (Revelle, Amaral, and Turriff, 1976) confirmed this hypothesis. Researchers asked college students to complete a section of the Graduate Record Examination under one of three conditions: relaxed, with time pressure, or with both time pressure and caffeine. Since both time pressure and caffeine are arousing, the investigators predicted that these conditions would raise extroverts from their natural low level of arousal to a more optimal level, and that the same conditions would raise introverts to a level of arousal too high for good performance. The results strongly supported this prediction. Compared with performance under relaxed conditions, the extroverts did much better when stimulated by time pressure and caffeine, and the introverts did much worse.

Conversely, under conditions of reduced arousal, the introverts should outperform the extroverts. This, too, has been demonstrated experimentally. When deprived of sleep (an arousal-reducing condition), extroverts perform worse on a complex motor task, while introverts perform better (Corcoran, 1972). Presumably, the lack of sleep reduces the naturally low arousal of the extroverts to a level of underarousal, but it reduces the naturally high arousal of the introverts to a more optimal level.

In summary, then, the performance of an underaroused person will generally improve with increased stimulation. Yet at some point, depending on the nature of the task and the individual's personality, additional stimulation will only serve to hinder performance. Psychologists are not yet certain why stimulation is beneficial at some levels and detrimental at others. In searching for a reason, Revelle and Humphreys have begun to explore the effects of arousal on both attention and short-term memory. It may be, they argue, that increased stimulation will improve the attention of an underaroused person and so improve performance. However, further increases in stimulation may adversely affect short-term memory, thus leading to performance decrements (Humphreys, Revelle, Simon, and Gilliland, in press). Only additional research will reveal whether this or some other hypothesis best explains the intriguing relationships between arousal and performance.

Why people take risks

Although optimal level theories are helpful in explaining an organism's general tendency to seek stimulation, they cannot explain why some people risk their lives in high-arousal activities. What is it that draws the race-car driver back to the track and the sky diver back to the sky?

The opponent process model One theory that provides some insight has been proposed by Solomon and Corbit (1974). Beginning with the assumption that organisms are designed to maintain a certain biological and psychological balance, Solomon and Corbit argue that when a strong emotional response disrupts this balance an "opponent process" is activated. By opponent process they simply mean an opposite response. If the initial emotional response is negative, the opponent process will be positive, and vice versa. Usually the opponent process reduces and eventually cancels out the original emotion, thus returning the organism to a normal, emotionally neutral state. However, if the stimulus that caused the initial emotion is suddenly removed, the opponent reaction can temporarily overwhelm the organism.

Applied to a high-arousal sport, such as sky diving, the opponent process theory says that on the sky diver's first leap from a plane he or she is likely to feel a moment of utter terror. Almost immediately, however, an opponent process begins to counteract this intense fear, and soon the jumper feels highly anxious but no longer terrified. Once the diver lands safely on the ground, the stimulus that caused the original arousal is suddenly removed, thus eliminating the anxiety. But the opponent process remains active, and so it takes over. As a result, the novice sky diver is likely to feel relieved and happy.

It is this pleasurable sensation that coaxes the person back for another try. But this is not all. According to Solomon and Corbit, additional dives only serve to *intensify* the positive experience because the opponent process is strengthened every time it is elicited. Consequently, if a sky diver continues to jump, the opponent process that is activated becomes more and more powerful until eventually a jump provokes only mild anxiety. Furthermore, when the person now lands, he or she experiences exhiliaration that can sometimes last for hours. It is this euphoria that presumably draws even the previously injured diver back jump after jump.

The opponent process model has been used to account for a wide variety of experiences that might otherwise be difficult to explain. (Solomon, 1980) For example, people generally find that running becomes less agonizing after a certain distance, and very experienced runners report feelings of euphoria after a good run. Similarly, the pleasure of certain psychoactive drugs may decrease with increased use, although subsequent withdrawal symptoms may become increasingly aversive (Siegel et al., 1978). In addition, the opponent process model has received support in a number of experiments with laboratory animals (Overmier et al., 1979). Yet the theory is not without its problems. Some critics find it hard to believe that every emotion necessarily induces an equal and opposite response. If this were true, then how could we explain cases in which an emotion, such as grief, endures for a prolonged period of time? Clearly, more research is needed to determine the limits of Solomon and Corbit's theory and to shed more light on the physiological mechanisms that might underlie it.

TABLE 11.2 Sensation-Seeking Scale

1. A. I would like a job that requires a lot of traveling.
   B. I would prefer a job in one location.
2. A. I am invigorated by a brisk, cold day.
   B. I can't wait to get indoors on a cold day.
3. A. I get bored seeing the same old faces.
   B. I like the comfortable familiarity of everyday friends.
4. A. I would prefer living in an ideal society in which everyone is safe, secure, and happy.
   B. I would have preferred living in the unsettled days of our history.
5. A. I sometimes like to do things that are a little frightening.
   B. A sensible person avoids activities that are dangerous.
6. A. I would not like to be hypnotized.
   B. I would like to have the experience of being hypnotized.
7. A. The most important goal of life is to live it to the fullest and experience as much as possible.
   B. The most important goal of life is to find peace and happiness.
8. A. I would like to try parachute-jumping.
   B. I would never want to try jumping out of a plane, with or without a parachute.
9. A. I enter cold water gradually, giving myself time to get used to it.
   B. I like to dive or jump right into the ocean or a cold pool.
10. A. When I go on a vacation, I prefer the comfort of a good room and bed.
    B. When I go on a vacation, I prefer the change of camping out.
11. A. I prefer people who are emotionally expressive even if they are a bit unstable.
    B. I prefer people who are calm and even-tempered.
12. A. A good painting should shock or jolt the senses.
    B. A good painting should give one a feeling of peace and security.
13. A. People who ride motorcycles must have some kind of unconscious need to hurt themselves.
    B. I would like to drive or ride a motorcycle.

Scoring

Count one point for each of the following items that you have circled: 1A, 2A, 3A, 4B, 5A, 6B, 7A, 8A, 9B, 10B, 11A, 12A, 13B. Add up your total and compare it with the norms below.

1–3 Very low on sensation-seeking   6–9 Average   12–13 Very high
4–5 Low   10–11 High

Individual differences in sensation seeking Solomon and Corbit's model provides one rationale for the drawing power of dangerous sports, but it does not explain why some people are more attracted to risks than others. One answer to this second question relates back to Eysenck's theory about "natural" levels of cortical arousal. High-sensation seekers may simply be Eysenck's extroverts—those people who need a great deal of external stimulation to attain an optimum arousal level. Accordingly, psychologist Marvin Zuckerman has tried to assess the needs of high- and low-sensation seekers for other kinds of stimulation. He has developed a personality scale that includes items ranging from preferences for exotic vacations and spicy foods to the desires to try risky sports or hallucinogenic drugs. (A brief version of Zuckerman's Sensation-Seeking Scale is shown in Table 11.2.) More than ten thousand people have taken this test, and the results show that the drive for excitement and diversity is seldom confined to one area of life, just as Eysenck's theory would predict. "The high sensation-seekers," Zuckerman writes, "are likely to have not just one but a number of adventurous tastes, from an eagerness to try risky sports such as sky-diving to a desire for variety in sexual partners" (Zuckerman, 1978, p. 40).

What are the implications of these findings for adjustment to life and to other people? Zuckerman suggests that high-sensation seekers may react badly if they feel trapped in unstimulating situations. They often do poorly in academic settings that lack creative interchange. And when tied down to dull, routine kinds of work they may, according to Zuckerman, turn to excessive use of alcohol or drugs. Moreover, even when high-sensation seekers are able to select schools, jobs, and hobbies that provide outlets for their needs, they may still be misunderstood by low-sensation seekers who consider some of their actions "reprehensible, foolish, and even crazy. The 'highs,' for their part, consider the caution of the 'lows' prudish, stuffy, timid, or inhibited. High and low sensation-seekers do not understand one another, and this can be an unfortunate state of affairs if they are a therapist and patient, or a husband and wife" (Zuckerman, 1978, p. 99).

LEARNED MOTIVATIONS: THE CASE OF ACHIEVEMENT

Most psychologists would admit that the arousal of the cerebral cortex we have been discussing sheds more light on some human behaviors than others. Why are we willing to go out of our way to do a favor for a friend? Why does a student work weekends and abandon other interests to get accepted into medical school? Why does a politician spend an entire lifetime and a personal fortune trying to become president of the United States? For answers to these and similar questions we must look to the motivations people learn through their interactions with others in the course of growing up. Among these are the desires for achievement, affiliation, power, and social approval. Rather than trying to discuss all the learned motivations psychologists have identified, we will concentrate on one of them, achievement, in order to provide a thorough exploration of how such motives develop and affect behavior, and how knowledge gained from their study can be applied for human benefit.

Individual differences in achievement motivation

To measure individual differences in achievement motivation, researchers typically use pictures from the Thematic Apperception Test (TAT), discussed in detail in Chapter 14 (McClelland et al., 1953; Atkinson, 1958). In this test subjects are presented with ambiguous pictures (such as a man standing by a machine or a boy apparently daydreaming) and are asked to write a brief story about each one. Through these invented stories the subjects presumably express their own motivations. Stories that receive high scores for achievement motivation are those in which the major character performs at a high level or accomplishes something unique, is concerned with standards of excellence or pursuit of a long-term goal, expresses pride in success or shame in failure, or displays other achievement-related feelings and behaviors.

People who test high and low in achievement motivation differ from one another in several important ways. Those with high need for achievement persist longer and show better performance on exams than those with low need for achievement (Atkinson and Raynor, 1974). They also tend to select occupations that require individual initiative, such as owning a business, selling, or dealing in real estate. People with low achievement motivation, in contrast, tend to be attracted to such jobs as routine office work, which demand little sustained individual effort (McClelland, 1955).

Interestingly, people with high need for achievement also tend to set challenging but realistic goals; those with low need for achievement tend not to. In one study researchers measured how far each subject chose to stand from the target when playing a ring-toss game. Those who scored high in achievement motivation stood at an intermediate distance, making the game challenging but not impossible. Those who scored low in achievement motivation, in contrast, usually stood either very close to the target or very far from it (Atkinson and Litwin, 1960). Similarly, some psychologists have found that students with a high need for achievement tend to seek challenge in their majors and future careers but also to be realistic in those choices. Students with a low need for achievement, on the other hand, tend to choose either very easy or extremely difficult majors (Isaacson, 1964). Note, however, that the behavior of people with low achievement motivation may be biased in one direction: A number of studies have shown that most such people tend to overaspire rather than underaspire (Mahone, 1960; Hamilton, 1974).

Part of the behavior of people with low need for achievement can be explained by the compounding effect of a high fear of failure. Subjects who stand either close to or far from the target in a ring-toss game, for example, also tend to score high in the fear of failure. So do students who select very easy or extremely difficult majors. Knowing this sheds additional light on the reasons for their choices. Those who select the very easy options assure their own success, and those who select the very difficult options provide a very good explanation for failure. Anxiety about failure, then, is an important determinant of behavior in achievement settings. People will actually seek challenge and accomplishment only if their motivation to achieve success is stronger than their motivation to avoid failure (Atkinson, 1964).

The fear of failure is related to another trait that people with low need for achievement exhibit: the tendency to attribute failure to a personal lack of ability. Those with high achievement motivation do not think this way. Instead, they tend to attribute failure to insufficient effort. People with high and low need for achievement also differ in the explanations they give for success. Those with low achievement motivation tend to attribute success to external factors such as ease of the task or simple good luck; those with high achievement motivation tend to view success as a reflection of their own ability and effort (Weiner, 1972).

Thus we see a complex relationship among the causes people attribute to success and failure, their emotional responses to them, and their tendency to seek or avoid challenge. Those who attribute success to their own ability and effort tend to take pride in accomplishment and so may be strongly motivated to achieve. Moreover, such people may persist even in the face of failure because they believe that increased effort will almost always yield success. In contrast, people who attribute success to external causes and failure to themselves do not generally find accomplishment very rewarding, but they do find failure highly threatening. Consequently, their motivation to achieve can be expected to be quite low. And because they believe that inability causes their lack of success, there is little reason for them to persist when failure threatens. Ironically, therefore, people with low achievement motivation often give up in a challenging situation, thereby ensuring the failure they so greatly fear (Heck-hausen, 1977).

Instilling achievement motivation

Clearly, a person's level of achievement motivation can have an enormous impact on his or her success in life. As we said earlier, the need for achievement seems to be heavily shaped in the course of growing up, especially by the child-rearing practices of one's parents. Is it possible, then, to change achievement orientation in adulthood? Psychologist David McClelland and others believe so. In one study McClelland and Winter (1969) encouraged and guided college students in the creation of success fantasies, and the students subsequently improved their grades and academic performance.

In a far more ambitious project the same researchers tried to raise the achievement motivation of businessmen in an entire village in India. This program, called the Kakinada project, consisted of encouraging the businessmen to have high-achievement fantasies, to make plans that would help them realize the goals of a successful entrepreneur, and to communicate with one another about their goals and their methods of reaching them. McClelland approached the project pragmatically. His aim was to raise the achievement-motivation level among the businessmen, rather than to identify the best techniques for doing so. For that reason, he does not know exactly why his program succeeded—whether one technique worked and the others did not or whether all of them helped—but succeed it did. The businessmen became more productive as entrepreneurs, starting several large industries, enlarging their businesses, and hiring more than five thousand of their neighbors (McClelland and Winter, 1969). Moreover, unlike many other economic development projects, which succeed only in the short run, the Kakinada project appears to have had continuing impact for more than a decade. In a ten-year reassessment of the program, McClelland (1978) speculated on the reasons for its success. He argued persuasively that while other development projects are based on the popular assumption that people will do things if they are simply taught how, the Kakinada project was based on the scientific finding that motivation, not knowledge alone, is essential to altering people's behavior.

Achievement motivation among women

In the many studies of achievement motivation that have been conducted, some of which we discussed earlier, researchers found a peculiar but persistent pattern: Achievement motivation did not predict the behavior of females as well as it predicted the behavior of males. For example, women who scored high in the need for achievement did not always set themselves challenging goals nor did they always persist in achievement-oriented tasks. In fact, the performance of some such women actually declined in certain competitive situations. Psychologists wondered why. An answer that has generated a great deal of controversy, still being resolved today, was proposed by Matina Horner.

To explain the differences in behavior between men and women with high achievement motivation, Horner (1968) argued that achievement-oriented

Anne has a boyfriend Carl in the same class and they are quite serious. Anne met Carl at college and they started dating around their sophomore years in under-graduate school. Anne is rather upset and so is Carl. She wants him to be higher scholastically than she is. Anne will deliber-ately lower her academic stand-ing the next term, while she does all she subtly can to help Carl . . . . His grades come up and Anne soon drops out of med school. They marry and he goes on in school while she raises their family. Aggressive, unmarried, wearing Oxford shoes and hair pulled back in a bun, she wears glasses and is terribly bright. Anne is really happy she's on top, though Tom is higher than she—though that's as it should be . . . Anne doesn't mind Tom winning.

Congrats to her! Anne is quite a lady—not only is she tops aca-demically, but she is liked and admired by her fellow students. Quite a trick in a man-dominated field. She is brilliant—but she is also a lady. A lot of hard work. She is pleased—yet humble and her fellow students (with the ex-ception of a couple of sour puss-es) are equally pleased. That's the kind of girl she is—you are always pleased when she is—never envious. She will continue to be at or near the top. She will be as fine practicing her field as she is studying it. And—always a lady.

John is a conscientious young man who worked hard. He is pleased with himself. John has always wanted to go into medi-cine and is very dedicated. His hard work has paid off. He is thinking that he must not let up now, but must work even harder than he did before. His good marks have encouraged him. (He may even consider going into research now.) While others with good first term marks sluff off, John continues working hard and eventually graduates at the top of his class. (Specializing in neurology.)

John is very pleased with him-self and he realizes that all his efforts have been rewarded, he has finally made the top of his class. John has worked very hard, and his long hours of study have paid off. He spent hour after hour in preparation for fi-nals. He is thinking about his girl Cheri whom he will marry at the end of med school. He realizes he can give her all the things she desires after he becomes estab-lished. He will go on in med school making good grades and be successful in the long run.

women are propelled in opposite directions by two very powerful forces. They are pushed toward achievement by their desire to obtain the psychological satisfactions associated with accomplishment. But at the same time, they have learned from childhood that success for a woman is both "unfeminine" and socially disapproved, especially by men. Consequently, they are also motivated to avoid success.

Horner devised an interesting way to measure this "fear of success," as it came to be called. She gave male and female college students an opening sentence and then asked them to complete the "story." For the ninety women in the study, the opening sentence was, "After first-term finals, Anne finds herself at the top of her medical school class." For the eighty-eight men in the study, the sentence was the same except that the name "John" was substituted for the name "Anne." Horner reasoned that if a subject was fearful of success, that fear should be reflected in the story he or she wrote about a highly success-ful medical student of the same sex. Specifically, if a story contained references to social rejection, anxiety, or a negative self-image as a result of success, if it linked success to abandonment of a medical career, or if it outright denied that such success was possible, the story was said to include fear-of-success imagery. Samples of stories with fear of success imagery are given in Figure 11.7.

The results of this study confirmed Horner's predictions. The women showed significantly more evidence of a fear of success than the men. But the most

Figure 11.7 Stories written by sub-jects in Horner's (1970) research on the motive to avoid success. The first three stories, written by women, show the motive theorized by Horner. The rest of the stories, only one of which was written by a woman, do not.

striking feature of Horner's results was the sheer magnitude of the differences between the kinds of responses men and women made. More than 65 percent of the women wrote stories containing fear-of-success imagery, but fewer than 10 percent of the men did.

Horner's research and her provocative conclusions made headlines in the popular press, prompting many women to wonder if their slow climb in the business world might not be due to a deep-seated fear of success. This widespread interest in the theory helped to generate a wave of subsequent research. Later findings, however, far from substantiated Horner's original conclusions. Although something psychologically important is going on when women link negative consequences to another woman's success, that something may not be a fear of success at all.

An enormous blow to Horner's theory came when researchers discovered that they could not always replicate her findings. In sixty-one studies in which subjects were asked to write stories in response to an achievement cue (such as Anne at the top of her medical school class), the proportion of women expressing fear of success ranged from 11 to 88 percent, while the proportion of men expressing such fear ranged from 14 to 86 percent. Fear of success, in other words, was not always dramatically greater in women. In fact, in seventeen out of thiry-six studies that included males, the men expressed *more* fear of success than the women (Tresemer, 1974). If fear of success is a stable personality trait found primarily in women, how could these results be explained?

Important clues began to emerge when researchers looked for patterns in the circumstances surrounding fear-of-success imagery. For instance, some psychologists "completed" Horner's experimental design by having males write about Anne's success and females write about John's. Under these circumstances, the men envisioned many negative outcomes related to achievement, whereas the women envisioned relatively few (Monahan, Kuhn, and Shaver, 1974). In addition, the amount of negative or positive imagery a subject expressed could be increased or decreased simply by changing the achievement situation. For example, women wrote much less fear-of-success imagery about Anne when told that half of Anne's classmates were women (Katz, 1973), or when told that Anne was at the top of her *nursing* school class (Alper, 1974). Similarly, men wrote far more fear-of-success imagery when discussing John's success in nursing school (Cherry and Deaux, 1975).

On the basis of these and similar findings many researchers have concluded that Horner's original experiment may not have been measuring a fear of success at all. Instead, what she may have been measuring was subjects' assessment of the negative consequences associated with deviation from traditional sex roles. A fear that the woman who deviates from sex-role standards will be rejected by men may be particularly strong among women. And this fear may not be groundless. One recent study found that some men do indeed fear being "outdone" by their girl friends and so prefer to work alone rather than with their girl friends on achievement tasks. The message to the girl friends is clear: If you outperform me, I will be threatened and avoid you. Such negative consequences may be what women are responding to when they react ambivalently to Anne's success in a male-dominated field. Even today the successful woman may pay a price for her achievement. Thus, "women who describe such negative consequences as male rejection and punishment in their 'fear of success' stories may only be showing a clear perception of reality, for men in reality do seem to punish successful women" (Condry and Dyer, 1976, p. 74).

The need for achievement is just one of many learned motivations that psychologists have studied. In Chapter 13 you will see that some personality theorists have devoted a great deal of effort trying to identify and measure a diversity of human needs, from the need for achievement to the needs for affiliation, aggression, autonomy, dominance, nurturance, and so forth. They have also attempted to organize such needs into hierarchies, based on the assumption that for every individual some motivations are more fundamental than others.

SUMMARY

1. Motivation gives direction to our behavior by arousing, sustaining, and directing it toward the attainment of some goal.

2. Early in this century Sigmund Freud proposed a theory of motivation according to which people are directed by two largely unconscious basic drives—one the urge toward life, procreation, and self-preservation (*Eros*), and the other the urge toward death and self-destruction (*Thanatos*). Because satisfaction of some of these drives, pratically the sexual and aggressive ones, may be unacceptable to one's moral standards, these impulses are often **repressed** and **sublimated** into more socially acceptable forms of behavior.

3. In the 1920s, psychologists in the United States developed a theory of motivation more centered on physiological drives—**drive-reduction theory**. When a tension is created in the body by a **primary drive**—for example, hunger, thirst, or sexual arousal—an animal is impelled (motivated) to eat, drink, mate, or to engage in whatever behavior has in the past been associated with reducing that drive. A **secondary drive** is not innately biological but is learned, frequently by association with a stimulus that induces a primary drive.

4. In addition to drives, our behavior is motivated by **incentives**, expectations of receiving a reward. Drives and incentives often interact in bringing about goal-directed behavior.

5. Psychologists have done much research into hunger and the motivations behind eating. They have found that cues from the stomach, and taste sensations, do not play a central role in the regulation of eating. Rather, organisms appear to regulate their food intake, and thus maintain a relatively constant body weight, through messages originating in the hypothalamus. The lateral hypothalamus appears to initiate the hunger drive and help sustain eating, while the ventromedial hypothalamus serves to indicate satiety. Levels of sugar in the blood and of fat in the body also appear to give needed information to the brain about the body's need for food.

6. Among the proposed causes of obesity in humans are a heightened sensitivity to food-related stimuli and a perpetual state of hunger that may be caused by an unusually large number of fat cells in the body. Restrained eaters are those with a tendency toward obesity who would gain a great deal of weight if they did not watch their food intake. The large majority of overweight people, however, become so not through biological causes but from overeating and lack of exercise. For them, psychologists now believe that one of the most successful approaches to long-run weight control is behavior modification, the conscious use of basic learning principles to change human behavior.

7. The factors that regulate human sexual behavior are probably even more complex than those that regulate eating. They include external stimuli such as sights and sounds, which can be sexually arousing. In addition, hormones secreted by the ovaries, testes, and the adrenal glands help to initiate sexual activity. These sex hormones then travel in the bloodstream to the hypothalamus, where they activate neural circuits involved in sexual arousal. Finally, the cerebral cortex can act as a stimulator or an inhibitor of sexual responses.

8. Sexual response in both men and women can be divided into four phases. *Excitement* is characterized by rapid heartbeat and breathing and a flow of blood into the genitals. In the *plateau phase*, the genitals become fully engorged with blood. During *orgasm*, involuntary muscle contractions force the blood that has been collecting in the genitals back into the bloodstream. The body gradually returns to its normal, unstimulated physiological state during the *resolution phase*.

9. In their continuing search for a theory of motivation, researchers have noted that when sensory stimuli impinge on an organism they activate two pathways in the brain, one of which stimulates an area of the brain called the reticular formation, causing a diffuse cortical arousal. If this arousal is within a certain range, appropriate goal-directed behavior results. Psychologist Donald Hebb, among others, has postulated that there is an *optimal level of arousal* for effective behavior that is automatically maintained by lower animals and often consciously sought by humans. Optimal levels vary with the complexity of the task to be performed and with the individual performing it. Psychologist Hans Eysenck has proposed that differences in the need for stimulation—due to differences in level of cortical arousal—underlie the contrast between introverts, who need little external stimulation to achieve an optimum arousal level, and extroverts, who need a great deal.

10. One intriguing area of motivation research is why people take risks. One theory is based on the **opponent process model**, according to which a strong emotional response activates an opposite response, so that the anxiety associated with a high-risk activity triggers an exhilaration that draws the person back to the activity again and again. Another theory holds that individual differences in risk taking may be related to level of cortical arousal, so that extroverts appear to look for excitement and diversity in all areas of life.

11. All motivations are not regulated by the brain and other physiological mechanisms. Many are learned, among them desires for achievement, affiliation, power, and social approval. To measure individual differences in achievement motivation, researchers typically use pictures from the Thematic Apperception Test (TAT). People who measure high in achievement motivation persist longer and do better on exams, tend to select occupations that require individual initiative, and are apt to set challenging but realistic goals. People with low need for achievement may have a high fear of failure and a tendency to attribute failure to lack of personal ability.

12. Studies of achievement motivation have not been able to predict women's behavior as well as men's. Matina Horner has argued that women who are achievement oriented may be motivated at the same time to avoid success. The "fear of success" that she postulated for women has not been substantiated in later research. According to more recent findings, women's fear may be less of success than of deviation from traditional sex roles.

Suggested readings

Bolles, R. C. *Theory of motivation* (2nd ed.). New York: Harper & Row, 1975.

Cofer, C. N., and Appley, M. H. *Motivation: Theory and research.* New York: Wiley, 1964.

Freud, S. *Beyond the pleasure principle.* New York: Norton, 1975. (Originally published, 1920.)

Kinsey, A. C., Pomeroy, W. B., Martin, C. W., and Gebhard, P. H. *Sexual behavior in the human female.* Philadelphia: Saunders, 1953.

Morrison, E. (Ed.). *Human sexuality* (2nd ed.). Palo Alto, Calif.: Mayfield, 1977.

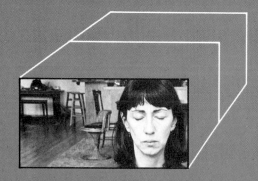

PREVIEW

1. Consciousness comprises the thoughts, images, sensations, and emotions that flow through the mind. The brain constantly processes information in our awareness as well as information of which we are unaware.

2. Many states of consciousness can be experienced, some very different from everyday modes.

3. Sleep, one mode of consciousness, is composed of several cyclical ninety-minute stages, each with a characteristic brain wave pattern. Dreams occur during the REM (rapid eye movement) stage. Though we clearly need REM sleep, the function of dreaming has not yet been established.

4. Hypnosis bears little similarity to either wakefulness or sleep. Psychologists are divided in their attempts to explain hypnosis.

5. By focusing the attention, meditation and biofeedback allow consciousness to be regulated, with physical and emotional benefits.

6. Alcohol, marijuana, stimulants, and hallucinogens also alter consciousness, but the nature of their impact is yet unclear.

12 The nature of consciousness

Humans have pondered the meaning of consciousness since civilization began. Loosely defined, **consciousness** is an awareness of the many thoughts, images, sensations, and emotions that flow through one's mind at any given moment (Marsh, 1977). As such, consciousness is highly subjective—a private world, accessible mainly through introspection.

Various psychologists have at times attempted to dismiss as meaningless questions about the nature of consciousness and with them the study of changes in consciousness, such as those produced by hypnosis, drugs, meditation, and even dreaming. Behaviorism originally grew out of the assertion that mind, consciousness, awareness, and similar concepts cannot be analyzed scientifically and therefore should be banished from psychology. But many psychologists, including some contemporary behaviorists, have not accepted this view. With the help of modern research tools, such as equipment for recording brain waves and other physiological activities, they have provided a number of important insights into the workings of consciousness.

DEFINING CONSCIOUSNESS

There is no completely satisfactory definition or explanation of consciousness, although many psychologists have tried to produce one. Perhaps the only points on which most would agree are, first, that consciousness is limited; second, that it is related to brain activity; and, third, that it has various modes.

Consciousness is limited

Consciousness is limited in the sense that we are unaware of much of what is going on both inside and outside our bodies. One reason for this is the relatively narrow range of our perceptual capacities. The human eye is sensitive to only a small portion of the electromagnetic-wave spectrum; the human ear responds to only a limited range of sound frequencies; the human receptors for light touch are located only near the surface of the skin, not deep inside the body. Our subjective worlds would undoubtedly be quite different if we could see x-rays, hear the high-frequency sounds that porpoises and bats can hear, or feel the detailed workings of our internal organs. Our channels of awareness are limited to a few sensory dimensions. Consciousness is likewise limited.

Consciousness is also limited in that we cannot attend to all the information available to our senses at any one time. If we tried to pay attention to all the sensations, feelings, thoughts, and memories that are accessible to us at any given moment, we would certainly be overwhelmed and probably immobilized. By necessity, therefore, much of the information available to consciousness is automatically screened out. In attending to some things, we become unaware of others—like the baseball player at bat who is unaware of the noise of the crowd.

Finally, consciousness seems to be limited primarily to the content of thought. The *process* of our thinking—exactly how we make connections between one fact and another—is often inaccessible to us. This curious limitation was discussed in Chapter 7, but it deserves mention again here. Studies show that when a given stimulus is not an especially salient or likely cause of a particular response, people will often label it noninfluential even though it did in fact have a significant influence on their behavior. For instance, researchers interested in consumer behavior often find a marked "position effect": A buyer will prefer an item that is located in a certain position relative to competing goods even though it is virtually the same as all the others. Nisbett and Wilson (1977) observed the position effect in consumers' evaluation of four identical pairs of nylon stockings. The pair on the far right was heavily overchosen as being the best in terms of quality. Yet when asked why they had made this choice, not one person mentioned position. In fact, when the experimenter offered the position effect as a possible explanation, the subjects looked at him as if he were mad. The unavoidable conclusion, then, is this: people often judge the factors that give rise to their own behavior simply on the basis of plausibility! If this is true, it appears that many aspects of our thinking must be unavailable to consciousness.

Consciousness, then, is limited in three ways. First it is limited by the restricted range of our sensory organs. Second, it is limited by the fact that our attention is necessarily selective: We can attend to only a small number of stimuli at any one time. And third, consciousness is limited by the restricted access of humans to many of their own cognitive processes.

Consciousness is related to brain activity

People have thought for centuries that the subjective awareness we call consciousness must be closely related to the activities of the brain. Modern research confirms this belief. Neurosurgeon Wilder Penfield (1969), for example, whose work we discussed in Chapter 3, demonstrated that stimulating certain parts of the cerebral cortex activates specific conscious experiences. Some of these are so vivid that people are convinced that they are hearing a sound, seeing a scene, or feeling a touch, none of which is actually there.

Clearly, subjective awareness and brain activity are indeed closely related. But because scientists still understand relatively little about the workings of the brain, the exact nature of the relationship between consciousness and brain activity remains largely unknown. One puzzling factor is that the relationship appears to be interactional: Brain activity is necessary for consciousness to emerge, yet consciousness seems to have a role in directing brain activity. Precisely how such a complex system might work is, according to psychobiologist Roger Sperry, "one of the most truly mystifying unknowns remaining in the whole of science" (Sperry, 1976, p. 9).

Consciousness has various modes

"We all recognize as different great classes of our conscious states. Now we are seeing, now hearing; now reasoning, now willing; now recollecting, now expecting; now loving, now hating; and in a hundred other ways we know our minds to be alternately engaged." These words, written almost a hundred years ago by psychologist William James (1890), vividly describe what is perhaps the most familiar aspect of human consciousness—its variability. We have all experienced the diverse states James mentions and many others. Some states, in fact, are quite dramatically different from what we consider "ordinary" consciousness. Dreaming, for example, is a state of consciousness radically different from our usual waking state. So too are the states of consciousness induced by certain drugs, such as alcohol or marijuana. Psychologists call any qualitative alteration in overall mental functioning, such that a person feels that his or her consciousness is distinctively different from the way it ordinarily functions, an **altered state of consciousness** (Tart, 1969). Such states are the topic of the rest of this chapter. We begin with sleep and dreams.

SLEEP AND DREAMS

Most people think of sleep as a period when mental activity virtually stops, except during intermittent dreams. And for those people who claim they never dream, the entire time spent sleeping seems to be a mental void. In the past thirty years, however, psychologists have made discoveries about sleep that show these common assumptions to be wrong. Some mental activity goes on during all or most of sleep, and everyone dreams, although most people have trouble recalling their dreams after they awaken (Dement, 1976).

Brain activity from wakefulness to deep sleep

The most revealing data concerning sleep have been obtained using the electroencephalograph, a device for recording the brain's electrical activity. The graph of tracings of brain waves that an electroencephalograph produces is called an **electroencephalogram**, or **EEG.** In a typical sleep experiment, a volunteer subject is hooked up to the electroencephalograph by means of several electrodes attached to the scalp and face. The subject then returns to a nearby laboratory

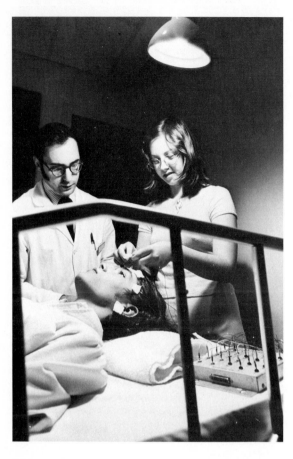

Figure 12.1 Measuring brain waves.

bed to spend the night (Figure 12.1). As Figure 12.2 shows, the pattern of brain waves changes consistently as the subject drops from wakefulness into light sleep and then into deep sleep.

Each stage in the process of falling asleep is dominated by certain brain wave frequencies, measured in cycles per second. Beta waves are the fastest, at fourteen or more cycles per second; alpha waves fall in the range from eight to thirteen per second; theta are between five and seven; and the slowest waves, delta, are four or under. The EEG of a person who is fully awake and alert, eyes open, usually displays a predominance of beta waves. A person who is awake, but relaxed with eyes closed, typically displays an EEG with a predominance of alpha waves. As a person begins to fall asleep (stage 1, Figure 12.2), the brain still shows a large proportion of alpha waves, but mixed in with them are some theta waves, with occasional bursts of high-frequency beta waves. As sleep becomes progressively deeper the alpha pattern disappears (stage 2), and delta waves begin to dominate the record (stage 3).

In the stage of deep sleep (stage 4), the very slow delta waves occupy more than 50 percent of the EEG record. During this stage a person's muscles are relaxed, the heart rate and breathing slow and regular. The nature of consciousness during stage 4 is somewhat of a puzzle. It is difficult to awaken someone from deep sleep: It seems almost as though the person were in a coma. By the time the person is finally forced into wakefulness, the researcher cannot simply ask what he or she was thinking about while asleep, because it is

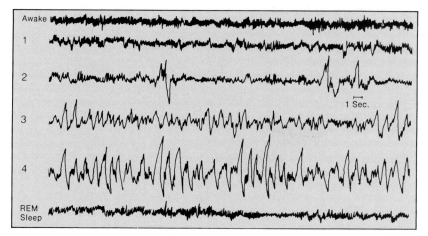

Figure 12.2 Records of the electrical activity of the brain (EEG) in a person in various stages of sleep and in the relaxed waking state known as "alpha." Note that in the deeper stages of sleep the high-frequency, small-amplitude waves give way to lower-frequency, large-amplitude waves. This change is thought to reflect the fact that the neurons in the brain are all firing at about the same level and in about the same pattern. Note also that the EEG pattern in REM sleep is very similar to the waking pattern.

now uncertain whether what is recalled actually occurred during stage 4 or during the process of awakening. Yet some sort of mental activity clearly occurs during stage 4, since most episodes of sleepwalking, sleeptalking, and intense nightmares happen during this stage as well as during the neighboring stage 3.

REM sleep

During a night's sleep you do not merely fall into progressively deeper sleep and then gradually wake up. Instead, your brain waves show a regular cyclical pattern that recurs about every ninety minutes, as shown in Figure 12.3. First you fall into deeper and deeper sleep, but then you gradually return to a stage 1, or "waking," pattern. At this point, though, you do not wake up, as might be expected. Instead, you remain sound asleep and your eyes move rapidly back and forth under your closed eyelids. This stage is known as **REM** (rapid eye movement) **sleep**. The average person has about four or five episodes of REM sleep each night, totaling about 25 percent of sleep time, or from one and a half to two hours. Since the discovery of REM sleep some twenty-five years ago, psychologists have come to recognize that the sharpest and most important distinction between the various stages of sleep is that between REM and all the other stages, collectively called non-REM sleep (Aserinsky and Kleitman, 1953; Kleitman, 1963; Dement, 1976).

REM sleep and dreaming When researchers first observed REM sleep, they suspected that the stage might be related to dreaming. To investigate this pos-

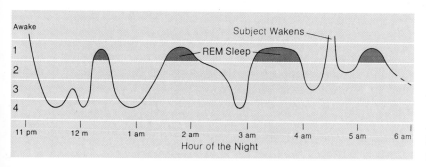

Figure 12.3 A typical night's sleep described in terms of the stages mentioned in the text and Figure 12.2. Note that the depth of sleep increases and decreases in cycles and that sleep becomes shallower and REM sleep periods longer as the night wears on.

sibility, they woke subjects during the different stages of sleep and found that during REM periods dreams with vivid visual imagery were reported about 80 percent of the time. During non-REM periods, in contrast, the storylike episodes that we usually consider dreams occurred far less frequently, the exact percentage depending on how *dream* was defined. Apparently, much of non-REM mental activity is more like drifting, unstructured thinking than like dreaming.

With the discovery that rapid eye movements accompany dreams, it was natural to speculate that these movements may be due to the dreamer's "watching" the activity unfolding in the dream. This theory, called the **scanning hypothesis**, was first proposed by sleep researcher William Dement (1976) on the basis of data collected in his laboratory. For example, when Dement awakened one subject who showed only horizontal eye movements during a particular REM priod, the subject reported that he had been dreaming about a Ping-Pong match. The problem with the scanning hypothesis, however, is that the relationship between rapid eye movements and dream content is usually far less clear-cut. A complicated mixture of eye movements, with very few highly distinct patterns, occur during most dreams.

This does not mean that the scanning hypothesis should be completely discarded, however, for even in the waking state a person's eye movements are not perfectly correlated with reported visual attention (Dement, 1976). An additional source of evidence in favor of the scanning hypothesis has come from the observation of blind sleepers. A one-night study of the jazz pianist George Shearing, who has been blind from birth, found he had no eye movements during any of the stages of sleep. He reported only hearing things during his dreams, not seeing them (Offenkranz and Wolpert, cited in Dement, 1976). Further research on blind people has shown that those who are blind from birth have no rapid eye movements and, like Shearing, do not see anything during dreams. But individuals who have become blind later in life have both rapid eye movements and visual images during dreams (Oswald, cited in Dement, 1976). At this point, then, the scanning hypothesis is an interesting one, but the practical problems of putting it to a definitive test are too difficult to overcome with available methods.

The paradoxes of REM sleep One curious fact about REM sleep is that in some respects it seems similar to being awake. The EEG pattern during REM sleep looks very much like that of a wide-awake person, as do other physiological patterns: Heartbeat, breathing rate, and blood pressure are irregular and varied, and there is evidence of sexual arousal. Usually these patterns would be observed in a person who is not only awake but also excited. It may therefore come as no surprise that certain medical catastrophes seem to occur during REM sleep, including heart attacks and acute worsening of duodenal ulcers and emphysema (Snyder, 1965; Armstrong et al., 1965; Trask and Cree, 1962).

Yet, quite paradoxically, other measures indicate that REM is a *deeper* stage of sleep than the other stages. It is very difficult to awaken people from REM sleep. They do not respond to touch or sound as readily as during stages 2 and 3. In addition, while all the erratic physiological activity mentioned above is going on, virtually all the major body muscles lose their tone and become flaccid (limp). This loss of muscle tone is associated with temporary paralysis: A person in REM sleep, unlike a person in stage 4 sleep, is totally unable to move. For these reasons REM is sometimes called "paradoxical sleep": People seem to be awake and yet deeply asleep at the same time.

Apparently, activation of a specific area of the brain is responsible for the loss of muscle tone and motor control associated wich REM sleep. When this small region was removed from the brain of a cat, REM sleep still occurred, but during it the animal no longer lay still. Instead, it jumped up and moved about—asleep all the while (Jouvet, 1967). The cat's behavior in this experiment suggests a curious possibility: If our muscles were not paralyzed during REM sleep, our bodies might act out our dreams!

Do we need REM sleep? Suspecting that dreams might in some way be essential to our psychological well-being, Dement (1960) deprived people of REM sleep over a series of nights. Whenever he saw the beginning of a REM period, he would awaken the sleeper. He found that it became harder and harder to arouse the sleeper with the onset of each subsequent REM stage, and that the longer he denied REM, the more frequent its appearance became. By the third night he was running in and out of subjects' bedrooms so fast that he could hardly keep up the pace. Finally, on the fifth night he let the sleepers go into REM without interruption. What resulted was a *REM rebound* effect: The total time spent in REM doubled over each person's normal level. (A similar rebound effect occurs with stage 4 sleep.)

Although we apparently have a need for REM sleep, judging from the fact that our bodies automatically compensate for a loss of it, what REM sleep actually does for us is not clear. Any deprivation of sleep—whether of REM or other sleep stages—may make a person tired and perhaps somewhat irritable. But loss of our dream time seems to be no more capable of inducing these effects than loss of other kinds of sleep. Still, REM sleep may have some special value that is not so easy to detect. What could this special value be?

There are currently several theories. Some evidence suggests that REM sleep may be a time when the brain adapts to disturbing or unusual life experiences. In one study, for example, some medical students wore goggles with distorting lenses for several days. The students slept at night in the laboratory. While they were adapting to the weird lenses, they showed a greater than usual amount of REM sleep; but once they had become accustomed to the lenses, REM sleep dropped back to normal (Luce, 1971). In addition, there is also evidence that REM sleep may play some role in the consolidation of information into long-term memory. Consider a study in which pairs of subjects heard a tape-recorded string of nonsense phrases before going to bed. During the night one of each pair was REM-deprived and the other was awakened at the same time whether or not the person was in a REM period. The REM-deprived subject had significantly poorer recall of the nonsense phrases the next morning (Empson and Clarke, 1970).

Yet another clue to the special functions of REM sleep comes from developmental research. As shown in Figure 12.4, REM time steadily lessens as people grow older. Newborns spend about half their sleep time in REM; infants under two years, 30 to 40 percent; adolescents and adults, about 20 to 25 percent; and old people, less than 5 percent. Some researchers have proposed that dreams may offer the brain an internal source of mental stimulation, which enhances the growth and maintenance of neural tissue (Anders and Roffwarg, 1973). Such stimulation may allow key sensory and motor areas to prepare to handle

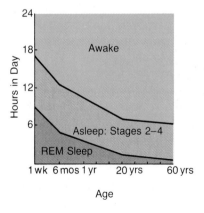

Figure 12.4 The amount of time the average person spends each day in three states: awake, non-REM sleep, and REM (dreaming) sleep, as it changes over the years. In order to show the changes more clearly, the time intervals shown here are wider for younger people than for older people. As people get older, they tend to need less sleep (adapted from Hartman, 1967).

the enormous rush of stimulation from the outside environment during waking hours. Logically, the need for such "rehearsal" time would be greatest in the newborn and decrease with age, just as REM time does (Roffwarg, Muzio, and Dement, 1966).

The content of dreams

One researcher estimates that by age seventy the average person will have had about 150,000 dreams (Snyder, 1970). Does this mean 150,000 fascinating adventures? Not at all. We have selective recall for our dreams, remembering the more dramatic ones and forgetting the rest. When people are awakened randomly during REM sleep and asked what they have just been dreaming, the reports generally are commonplace, even dull (Hall and Van de Castle, 1966). The dreams we remember and talk about "are more coherent, sexier, and generally more interesting" than those collected in systematic research (Webb, 1975, p. 140). Even so, psychologists (especially psychoanalysts) find great symbolic meaning in the most prosaic of dreams. From where does the stuff of dreams come?

Dreams and external stimuli The realization that the bell persistently ringing in your dream is really your alarm clock is a fairly common occurrence. Some of the content of a dream is simply incorporated from what is happening near the sleeping person—events such as sounds, temperature changes, or touches. Dement and Wolpert (1958) sprayed water on the faces of some sleepers in the laboratory and left a control group of sleepers undisturbed. Those who were sprayed reported more dreams about water than did those who were left dry.

This incorporation of environmental stimuli into dreams may serve to "protect" sleep to some extent. For example, volunteers in a British sleep laboratory were awakened during REM sleep by a gradually increasing noise. When they awoke they reported what they had just been dreaming. Those whose dreams somehow incorporated the noise were able to stay asleep longer while the noise increased to higher intensities (Bradley and Meddis, 1974). A sleeper who incorporates external stimuli into a dream, then, may be harder to awaken. However, such incorporation does not protect a sleeper from waking up at some point. And external stimuli are certainly not the fundamental *cause* of dreaming, as some psychologists at the turn of the century believed.

Dreams and waking life A papyrus in the British Museum dating from 1350 B.C. is about interpreting dreams—an indication that one of the most ancient beliefs about dreams is that they are portents, containing hidden truths about our lives. As we will discuss in more detail in Chapter 13, Sigmund Freud made famous the view that dreams express the hidden needs and desires of the unconscious (Freud, 1900). If dreams could be properly analyzed, he argued, these hidden feelings could be brought into consciousness. Accordingly, Freud optimistically proclaimed dreams to be "the royal road to the unconscious."

But how could the true meaning of our nighttime fantasies be tapped? In *The Interpretation of Dreams* Freud (1900), distinguished between the manifest and the latent content of a dream. The **manifest content** is the readily perceived "story line"—the actors, the setting, the chain of events that takes place. The

Figure 12.5 The interiors of our dreams are often furnished with a mixture of the "real" and the "unreal." The "storylike" character of dreams is reflected in much of modern art such as Saul Steinberg's *Eighth Street.*

latent content, in contrast, is the deeper meaning of the dream—the underlying, largely unconscious wishes it reflects. These hidden desires and motives, according to Freud, arise primarily from early but still unresolved psychosexual conflicts. Through "dream work," the manifest content presumably veils the unconscious wishes in symbolic images that are more acceptable to the dreamer. Over the years, psychoanalysts have modified Freud's theory of dreams; only his most ardent followers still adhere strictly to Freud's methods of dream interpretation. Still, Freud did much to draw the attention of psychologists to the important emotional information often contained in dreams.

Today, some therapists (Ullman, 1962; Foulkes, 1964) have largely abandoned the search for latent content in favor of direct meaning. They say that the student who dreams about writing an exam in disappearing ink is not trying to resolve an infantile sexual conflict, but is simply worried about his or her upcoming final. The dream is not saying one thing and meaning another; it is merely a reflection of the dreamer's current concerns. From this perspective, dreams deal with the full range of events in the dreamer's life, not just with his or her sexual conflicts. Thus, a recent study's finding that manifest dream content is seldom overtly sexual (Barrett, 1979) would be interpreted by these psychologists to mean that sexuality is not most people's principal concern.

Most psychologists interested in dream interpretation assume that the waking person has little control over what he or she dreams during sleep. Substantial differences in the content of nocturnal dreams and daydreams suggest that this may be true. People can consciously select their daydreams, so not surprisingly our waking reveries are overwhelmingly filled with themes of happiness and friendship. In sharp contrast, our nighttime dreams are much higher in negative themes like hostility and fear (Barrett, 1979). Does this mean that conscious control over nocturnal dreams is impossible?

Perhaps. But other cultures, most notably the Senoi of the Malay Peninsula, have tried to develop techniques for actively controlling dreams (Stewart,

1972). The management of dream content is part of every Senoi child's education. At the first meal of the day the elders of a house talk to the children about their dreams. Suppose a child has had a terrifying dream about a tiger, or about falling from a great height. The adult will instruct the frightened child to relax and transform this dream into something pleasant. A dream about falling might be transformed into a dream about being able to fly. A dream about a tiger might be transformed into a dream about being a brave and successful hunter.

Some psychologists have tried to test whether such self-control of dreams is actually possible. In one study, for example, subjects identified a personality trait they particularly disliked in themselves (Cartwright, 1979). Then, as they were falling asleep, they repeated a wish to change that trait. Over and over they would say to themselves, "I wish I were not so sarcastic," "I wish I were not so hostile," or whatever. Some of the subjects did dream about the target trait more than would be predicted by chance. However, only a few showed signs of acting out a wish to rid themselves of the undesirable characteristic. For many, displaying the negative trait in their dreams seemed to give them pleasure! Thus, the question of whether we can successfully control the content of our dreams still remains unanswered. Some psychologists, however, are currently trying to develop dream-management techniques as therapy for situationally caused anxiety and depression. The theory is that if the troubled person can incorporate more constructive conclusions into dreams related to his or her present life crisis (divorce, loss of a job, failure at school, or whatever), that person's self-image and outlook may significantly improve (Cartwright, 1978).

HYPNOSIS

The scene is a college classroom, with thirty students sitting in straight-back chairs. A professor is speaking to them in a soft, reassuring tone: "I want you to relax your body, become comfortable as I talk. Just relax and become limp. You will find yourself becoming warm, at ease, more comfortable. Now you will become drowsy and sleepy, drowsy and sleepy. . . ." One by one the students close their eyes and lower their heads. When everyone is still, the professor tells them: "Now clasp your hands together tightly, as though they were locked together by a steel band. Try as you might, you can't get them apart. Try to open them. You can't!" The students strain to pry apart their hands, but their fingers remain interlocked. Finally, the professor breaks the tension: "Stop trying and relax. Your hands are no longer locked together. You can take them apart now." The straining stops, and all hands easily separate. The entire class relaxes. Some students test their fingers to see if they function properly.

Such demonstrations of hypnosis create the popular conception that a hypnotized person is in a state like a sleepwalker—seemingly awake yet out of touch with his or her normal waking awareness and self-control. There are, however, substantial differences between the sleepwalker and the hypnotized person. First, their EEGs are very dissimilar. The sleepwalker has the slow brain waves typical of stage 3 or stage 4 sleep; the hypnotic subject's brain waves are no different from those of a person in a normal waking state. Second, the sleepwalker, unlike the hypnotized person, pays no attention to other people and does not take instructions. Finally, the sleepwalker does not remember sleepwalking, whereas the hypnotic subject remembers everything that went on under hypnosis, as long as he or she is not given specific instructions to forget (Barber, 1975).

Clearly, sleep and hypnosis are in many ways quite different states. But what exactly is hypnosis if not a variant of sleep? After years of experimentation with hypnotism, psychologists still do not have a firm answer to this question. In fact, the difficulty of defining hypnosis except by describing the behavior of hypnotized people has caused many to doubt whether it represents a unique state of consciousness at all. Although hypnosis has been successfully put to a range of medical and therapeutic uses, from anesthetizing patients during surgery to curing psychosomatic allergies, migraine headaches, and insomnia, there is little clear agreement as to how hypnotism works.

Hypnotic susceptibility

According to one estimate, about nineteen out of twenty people can be hypnotized to some degree if they want to be and if they trust the hypnotist. But some people can be more easily and more deeply hypnotized than others. Psychologists measure the trait of hypnotic susceptibility through various standardized tests. The Stanford Hypnotic Susceptibility Scale, for instance, requires that the hypnotist attempt to bring a subject under hypnosis and then make a series of suggestions such as: "Your left arm will become rigid," or "You will be unable to say your name when asked." If the subject is unable to bend his or her arm more than two inches in ten seconds, or to speak his or her name for ten seconds after being asked, this response indicates susceptibility. The subject who responds similarly to the rest of a dozen suggestions, which include hallucinating that he or she sees a fly and being unable to remember part of the proceedings afterward, is rated highly susceptible to hypnosis. In a test of 533 college students, about 10 percent were identified by the Stanford scale as highly susceptible (E. Hilgard, 1965). There are several such scales for assessing hypnotic susceptibility, and their results tend to be correlated.

What are the people who score high in hypnotic susceptibility like? Many often become spontaneously absorbed in such experiences as reading a novel, listening to music, or appreciating the beauty of nature. Many also occasionally experience trancelike states in which they feel somehow separated from their usual way of experiencing things (K. Bowers, 1976). One researcher suggests that this ability to become deeply absorbed develops early in life. Her research shows that people who are highly susceptible to hypnoisis are more likely as children to have had a history of daydreaming and imaginary companions (J. Hilgard, 1970, 1974). It seems that people who are easily hypnotized have developed in childhood the fantasy skills that make them more open to hypnotic suggestion as adults. Interestingly, these same fantasy skills may also make the easily hypnotized person very creative at certain tasks, for the ability to lose oneself in fanciful possibilities sometimes leads to imaginative problem solving (P. Bowers, 1979).

The hypnotic state

As we mentioned earlier, the question of whether hypnosis is a discrete state of consciousness has not yet been settled. To date, no single objective measure has been found to correlate with hypnotic trance. There is no specific set of physiological changes that are sure signs a person is hypnotized. Some researchers, such as Ernest Hilgard, say this simply means we have yet to find the appropriate measures. He points out that only recently did researchers discover that rapid eye movements were a sign of dreaming. Until then, there was no "hard" evidence that dreaming was a discrete state of consciousness, although everyone, on the basis of personal experience, could acknowledge its uniqueness. In the same way, contends Hilgard (1975), hypnosis is a state that we can recognize subjectively but cannot yet monitor objectively.

Other psychologists disagree. They argue that the behavioral changes associated with hypnosis are insufficient to suggest a special state of consciousness. Theodore Barber is a leading proponent of this view. He claims that brief instructions, exhortations to try one's hardest, and assurances that the tasks one is being asked to perform are easy, have the net effect of allowing nonhypnotized subjects to accomplish the same "feats" as hypnotic subjects (Barber, 1965). Nonhypnotized subjects can, for example, hold a heavy weight at arm's length for several minutes; they can lie with a chair under their shoulders and a chair under their feet but nothing else between to support them; they can even stick needles through their hands. In short, Barber contends that everything done under hypnosis can also be done without hypnosis. If this is so, the question arises, "Is hypnosis real?"

A case of hypnotic blindness A particularly dramatic case that underlines this question was reported by Frank Pattie (1935). Pattie wondered if he could make a hypnotized person blind in one eye. He chose for his investigation five subjects who were known to enter a deep trance readily. One woman, whom he called E., did seem to become blind in one eye under hypnosis. Throughout most of a long series of tests, E. consistently appeared to have no awareness of sensory impulses from that eye, although there were some signs that she might be cheating. For this reason Pattie devised an extremely subtle test for blindness, one on which it was virtually impossible to cheat. With this test he showed that E. was not blind at all.

Pattie had E. look at the top line of Figure 12.6 with a red filter over her seeing eye and a green filter over her "blind" eye. The effect of the filters was to block out parts of the top line, as shown. If E. had truly been blind in the green-filtered eye, she would have seen only what appeared through the red filter. But this was not what she reported seeing. Strangely enough, even when she failed this test, E. insisted that she had not cheated and that she was, in fact, blind in

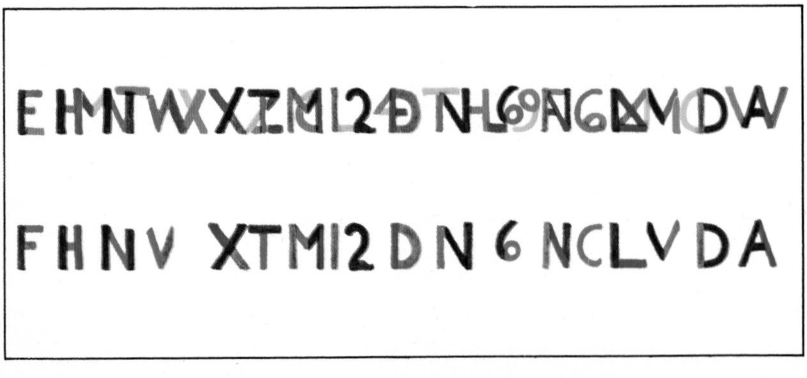

Figure 12.6 The technique used by Pattie to expose a suspected cheater in an experiment on hypnotically induced blindness. The subject was required to look at a line (top) of mixed colored letters and numbers with a red filter over her "seeing" eye and a green filter over her "blind" eye. The effect of the red filter is shown in the bottom line. If the subject had really been blind, she would have seen only a line of distinct letters and numbers (after Pattie, 1935).

one eye. According to every indication, she really believed that she had not cheated.

What can account for E.'s adamant denial? One school of thought contends that she was indeed unaware of what her "blind" eye was seeing, even though it displayed normal physiological reactivity. But another school claims that the unusual relationship between the hypnotist and his subject somehow elicited from E. an unusually good job of acting out the role of a "hynotized" person. The first of these explanations is called neodissociation theory; the second, role enactment theory.

The neodissociation view In studies done at Stanford University by Ernest Hilgard (Hilgard and Hilgard, 1975; Hilgard, 1978), subjects under hypnosis plunge one hand into a bucket of extremely cold ice water with the instruction that they will feel no pain. When asked what they feel, the subjects verbally report no pain, yet at the same time their free hand reports a very different message. Covered by a box, and out of the subject's sight, the free hand writes that the experience is indeed painful, just what you would expect a person in a normal state of consciousness to say. According to Hilgard (1973, 1977) what occurs is a **dissociation**—that is, a split in consciousness whereby certain thoughts, feelings, and behaviors operate independently from others.

"Automatic writing" that contradicts a verbal report is a very dramatic example of this split-consciousness phenomenon. But Hilgard and others contend it is far from unique. You may have experienced an instance of dissociation yourself. In everyday life it is not uncommon to be able to respond correctly to a message that you thought you did not hear. Similarly, people with severe phobias often insist they have no idea what incident caused the phobia to arise, yet their emotional reaction to the feared object is that of a person who remembers the traumatic event quite well. Dissociations involving memories can also be induced through hypnosis. A hypnotist can instruct a subject to forget all that happened in the hypnotic state until a cue to remember is given. The subject, upon coming out of the hypnotic trance, will adamantly maintain that he or she remembers nothing. Then suddenly, on cue, the person recalls everything.

Are the subjects in such cases just faking—going along to please the hypnotist as sometimes happens in psychological experiments? Researchers such as Hilgard believe not. Although it is usually very difficult to distinguish between a truly hypnotized subject and one who is merely pretending, subtle differences in behavior sometimes exist. In one experiment, for example, subjects under hypnosis were given the answers to a list of esoteric questions ("What color does an amethyst turn when it is heated?" "What was the primary profession of the author Lewis Carroll?") and were then told to forget everything that had happened. Upon returning to normal consciousness, the subjects claimed to remember nothing about events while under hypnosis. Yet when asked the same list of esoteric questions, about a third of them immediately gave the correct responses even though they claimed to have no idea how they knew such things. This phenomenon is called **source amnesia** because the person remembers certain facts but fails to remember the context in which they were learned. Significantly, subjects who are asked to fake hypnosis and try to fool the hypnotist never display source amnesia when told to forget all that happened. Such a mistake is far too "dumb" for a person who is only playacting to make (Evans, 1979).

Based on the evidence regarding dissociations, Hilgard has proposed a neo-dissociation theory of hypnosis. He argues that consciousness depends on many neural systems, all coordinated with one another. During hypnosis, control over these various systems may shift, "so that what is normally voluntary may become involuntary, what is normally remembered may be forgotten, and (under some circumstances) what is normally unavailable to recall may be recalled" (1973, p. 406). In terms of neodissociation theory, therefore, E.'s insistence that she was indeed blind in one eye—despite evidence to the contrary—was the result of a split in consciousness between her visual system and the part of her awareness that testified she was blind.

The role enactment view Proponents of **role enactment theory** take a very different view. They see hypnosis not as a special state of consciousness, but as a special case of role playing. The hypnotized person is simply acting *as though* he or she were hypnotized, just as an actor plays a role. The hypnotist prepares the subject for playing the part of a hypnotized person by establishing expectations: The subject is given specific instructions about what is to happen, and the hypnotist reinforces these expectations by playing the role of competent hypnotist. Role expectations become more explicit during the induction of hypnosis, through instructions such as, "You can enter a state of hypnosis by concentrating on my voice. . . . You will become relaxed." In this way the hypnotist defines and refines the subject's understanding of the role to be played. The transition to the role of hypnotized person is complete when the subject continues to meet the hypnotist's role demands as they change. The subject's reported experiences, then, are determined by what he or she believes is appropriate and proper to report (Sarbin and Coe, 1972).

For the role enactment theorist, therefore, E.'s insistence that she was blind in one eye was typical of someone acting as though she had been hypnotized. So is insistence that one feels no pain or cannot remember what happened. As for the fact that people under hypnosis sometimes behave differently from people just pretending to be hypnotized, advocates of role enactment theory remain unconvinced. They argue that these differences are simply the result of two slightly different roles being enacted: the role of a truly hypnotized person and the role of a person merely faking hypnosis.

Although we are unable to reconcile here these two interpretations of hypnosis, we should note that, either way, the phenomenon of hypnosis is remarkable. That psychological instructions can "set" some people to tolerate severe pain, for example, demands an explanation of some sort. But the question of whether the explanation will ultimately be expressed in terms of role enactment theory or of neodissociation theory, or in some other terms, should not diminish our interest in hypnosis and its proven and potential usefulness.

THE SELF-REGULATION OF CONSCIOUSNESS

A yogi sits in a laboratory in India with legs crossed and eyes closed, deep in meditation. From his head a forest of EEG electrodes lead to a portable monitoring device. A team of psychologists watch intently as the arms of the monitor trace the yogi's brain waves on paper. When the graph shows that the yogi's brain is emitting a steady flow of slow, rhythmic alpha waves, the experiment begins. A psychologist strikes a tuning fork and holds it next to the yogi's ear. The alpha waves steam on, unbroken—a sign that the yogi is not aware of the sound at all. The test is repeated with a hand clap and even with a hot test tube applied to the yogi's arm, all with the same result: His brain, deep in meditation, registers no reaction to these disturbances. The yogi is in *samadhi*, a state in which his awareness appears to be separated from his senses through intense concentration on a single thought or object (Anand, Chhina, and Singh, 1961).

This investigation was one of the first attempts to study the ways people might regulate their own consciousness. Like hypnosis, self-regulating techniques such as meditation have found a wide range of clinical uses, from the control of pain and psychosomatic disorders to psychotherapy. Furthermore, each technique is forcing us to revise our ideas about the degree of control people can exert over their own minds and bodies.

Techniques of self-regulation vary both in the altered states of consciousness they can (and cannot) produce and in the changes in bodily function they create. Nevertheless, they all share one basic characteristic—self-regulation—which distinguishes them from the other altered states discussed so far. For example, the changes in consciousness that take place during sleep are largely beyond our control; self-regulation techniques, in contrast, allow certain changes to occur at will, provided we master special exercises. Similarly, hypnosis stresses the control of the hypnotist over the subject through the power of suggestion, whereas in self-regulation it is the subject who is in control of the changes he or she undergoes. In the following sections we will explore two popular methods of self-regulation: meditation and biofeedback.

Meditation

Meditation is the most ancient and widespread of all self-regulation techniques. In one form or another, it is part of the spiritual practice of every major religion, including Judaism and Christianity. But despite the vast differences in the beliefs and trappings that surround the many kinds of meditation, they all share the same definition: **Meditation** is a retraining of attention that induces an altered state of consciousness (Goleman, 1977).

Learning to meditate Although there are hundreds of meditation techniques, most Americans have heard of only three: transcendental meditation (TM), yoga, and Zen. TM was developed by the Maharishi Mahesh Yogi from classical Indian techniques; it is basically a method for the passive focusing of attention. What is popularly called yoga is actually not a form of meditation, but a series of stretching and bending exercises that were devised thousands of years ago in India as a relaxing prelude to meditation. Zen is the name of a Buddhist sect in Japan whose members practice *zazen*, a set of meditation techniques designed to make the meditator more fully aware of each moment.

Most forms of meditation involve sitting quietly with eyes closed, focusing attention on one thing. In TM that object of attention is a *mantra*, a sound from the Sanskrit language that the meditator chants over and over. (The best-known mantra is the sound *Om.*) In one form of zazen the meditator simply notices the normal flow of his or her breathing, without trying to control it in any way. Other common objects used in meditation are short prayers (early Christians used *Kyrie eleison*, Greek for "Lord have mercy"), a sacred picture,

Figure 12.7 In today's high-pressure society, many people find that meditation helps them to relax.

a candle flame, a spot in the lower abdomen, various bodily sensations, or a mandala, which is designed so that the gaze always returns to the center (Figure 12.8). Whatever the object of meditation, the task is always the same: to let go of normal thoughts and feelings that intrude on one's attention.

Physiological changes during meditation The body of the meditator may undergo a number of changes that reflect a slowing of metabolism during deep relaxation. Two researchers (Wallace and Benson, 1972) recorded these changes in subjects practicing TM. Oxygen consumption fell markedly, breathing and heart rates slowed, skin resistance to electrical conduction rose abruptly, and blood pressure dropped. Comparing these bodily indicators with those found during sleep and hypnosis, these researchers concluded that meditation produces a unique state.

Although the meditator undergoes physiological changes like those of relaxation (Woolfolk, 1975), the state meditation produces is unlike that of simple relaxation. The difference can be seen in the meditator's more pronounced changes in brain wave patterns. The relaxed person shows only modest changes in brain wave activity compared with activity during a normal waking state; the meditator's brain waves can change markedly. The brain wave activity of the meditator depends to a large extent on the kind of meditation being done. One study of Zen meditators (Kasamatsu and Hirai, 1966) found that monks practicing zazen had alpha waves in their EEGs as soon as they started meditating, even though their eyes were wide open. Alpha is normally found in large amounts only in people whose eyes are closed. As the meditation session pro-

Figure 12.8 To meditate, it is necessary to empty the mind of distracting thoughts by focusing on a simple pattern or thought that will not lead to distractions. In some forms of meditation the meditator concentrates on a visual pattern such as the mandala shown here, which continually returns the gaze to its center.

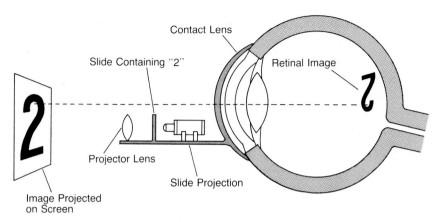

Contact Lens

Slide Containing "2"

Retinal Image

Projector Lens

Slide Projection

Image Projected
on Screen

Figure 12.9 Diagram of the eye fitted out with the lens miniprojector. Each movement of the eyeball causes the lens and the projector to move with the eye; thus the image projected onto the retina remains the same, the photoreceptor cells are not stimulated, and the image disappears. Subjects' reports of the disappearance of the image correlate with the appearance of alpha waves in the subjects' brains.

gressed, the monks' alpha waves changed progressively to the slower theta waves—very unusual in a person with open eyes.

How could a person with eyes open display such brain wave patterns? The answer is still very incomplete, but studies on the effects of restricted awareness have provided a fascinating insight. Remember from Chapter 4 that whenever you try to fix your gaze steadily on a single point your eyes involuntarily move. This movement, you will recall, prevents your photoreceptor cells from adapting to constant stimulation and ceasing to respond to stimulation. Ingenious researchers have managed to demonstrate the startling effect on visual perception that a truly steady gaze would have. One of their techniques involves a tiny projector attached to a contact lens (Figure 12.9). As the subject's eye moves the contact lens moves with it, and so does the miniprojector. The result is that the projector steadily casts its image on one part of the retina. Subjects who have volunteered to wear this strange device report that the picture they see gradually disappears! And when it does, the person's visual cortex suddenly emits the preponderance of alpha waves generally found only when the eyes are closed (Lehmann, Beeler, and Fender, 1967). Meditation, then, may involve a similar loss of awareness of the outside world, for it too is brought about through restricted focus on one unchanging stimulus (Ornstein, 1977).

Biofeedback

A primary reason why scientists are interested in meditation is that experienced meditators seem able to control certain bodily processes, such as blood pressure and heart rate, that were previously thought involuntary. Indian and Tibetan yogis, for example, have been known to slow their respiration to such an extent that they can survive in airtight cubicles containing far too little oxygen to keep an average person alive for long. Similarly, on bitterly cold nights high up in the Himalayas they have been observed to raise their body temperature high enough to melt surrounding ice (David-Neel, 1971). Such feats raise an intriguing question. Using modern electronic devices to monitor physiological responses, can Westerners unskilled in meditation also learn to control their internal processes? The technique of self-regulation called biofeedback has proved they can. **Biofeedback** is the use of monitoring instruments to give a person a continuous flow of information about his or her own biological state (hence the combination term "bio-feedback"). Using this data the person can experiment with various ways of altering physiological function and can find out immediately which ways are successful. By trial and error, then, the person may gradually learn to control target responses at will.

Some researchers have reported that biofeedback has been very successful in helping people regulate a variety of physiological processes, including heart rhythms, body temperature, and muscle tension. In a therapeutic application involving, say, the control of cardiac arrhythmia (irregular heartbeat), the patient is connected to a machine that monitors heart rate. When the heart beats too slowly, a green light goes on; when it beats too quickly, a red light flashes. An amber light signals when the heart is beating in the right range. Slowly, by attending to subtle body cues associated with increases or decreases in heart rate, the patient may learn how to keep the amber light on, and in doing so develop some ability to keep his or her heart rate within the healthy range (Marcus and Levin, 1977). The same general procedure—using biofeedback to learn to control a specific physiological response, then controlling it without electronic feedback—has been tried successfully with a number of other disorders. For instance, biofeedback appears to be quite effective in helping people relax the tightened muscles of the forehead associated with tension headaches (Budzynski, 1979). It is also commonly used to help alleviate Raynaud's syndrome, a condition in which the blood vessels of the hands or feet constrict, especially during stress, and so cause the extremities to turn exceedingly cold (Blanchard, 1979).

It is important to note, however, that the potential of biofeedback is still being tested. Although some popular writers give the impression that biofeedback is a simple answer to many stress-related illnesses, this is certainly very far from true. Unless biofeedback training is supervised by a competent professional with access to good equipment, the results may be at best totally useless. And even when properly supervised, some people have much more difficulty than others learning to regulate a given physiological response. It is particularly difficult to learn to control a target response consistently over the long run. As a result, in most clinical applications biofeedback is used in conjunction with other forms of therapy. Still, many researchers in this field hope that biofeedback will some day offer a reliable alternative to drug treatment for a diversity of medical disorders such as gastrointestinal ailments and high blood pressure. In the more distant future, biofeedback may even be put to interesting nonmedical uses. It might, for example, find a role in education to help students maintain full concentration when learning difficult material (Ornstein, 1977).

Figure 12.10 The escape artist Houdini learned how to control certain bodily processes in order to perform his feats. In one of his tricks, he was handcuffed and put into a trunk, which was then put under water. How, then, could he escape?

Houdini had swallowed the key, which opened both the handcuffs and the trunk, before his performance, and, having learned how to control his digestive system, he regurgitated the key and opened the locks.

No one yet knows how many of these and other ambitious goals for biofeedback will ultimately be achieved (Gatchell and Price, 1979).

One reason why some psychologists are very cautious in accepting far-reaching claims for biofeedback is that some of the earliest claims for it have failed to hold up—most notably the claims concerning biofeedback's use in controlling alpha waves (Miller, 1974). It was once thought that biofeedback training could markedly enhance the production of alpha waves and that this was accompanied by an "alpha experience"—a state of calm, blissful euphoria (see, for example, Brown, 1974). But subsequent research has shown that such an experience does not reliably accompany alpha activity (Plotkin and Cohen, 1976). Moreover, there is evidence that biofeedback cannot teach people to generate more alpha waves than they would simply by relaxing and closing their eyes (Lynch, Paskewitz, and Orne, 1974).

This conclusion has been confirmed by a recent study (Lindholm and Lowry, 1978) in which control groups received computer-generated false feedback for their alpha rhythms while an experimental group received accurate, genuine biofeedback. The biofeedback subjects did no better at controlling their brain waves than the control subjects did. Apparently, the increases in alpha wave production found in earlier studies simply reflected the subjects' gradual relaxation as they became accustomed to the biofeedback situation over the course of the experiment. Thus, there is currently much doubt as to whether biofeedback can be used to produce an altered state of consciousness similar to that apparently created through meditation. In general, biofeedback is a much more specific procedure than meditation: It is used most effectively to regulate a particular physiological function.

DRUG-ALTERED CONSCIOUSNESS

If a **drug** is any substance that can alter the functioning of a biological system, there is hardly a person alive who is not a drug user. Many substances fall within this broad definition, ranging from aspirin and antibiotics to vitamin C. The drugs of interest for the study of consciousness, however, are those that interact with the central nervous system to alter a person's mood, perception, and behavior. Such **psychoactive drugs** range from the caffeine in coffee and cola drinks to powerful consciousness-altering substances like marijuana, alcohol, amphetamines, and LSD.

Many psychoactive drugs are taken for medical reasons, to treat physical or psychological disorders. Others, because they are highly addictive for virtually everyone who uses them, create medical problems. Here we will consider drugs that are taken mainly to alter consciousness and that induce a range of changes in mood and thought.

The effects of certain drugs on consciousness

Alcohol The most widely used mind-altering drug in this country is undoubtedly alcohol. Americans consume about 500 million gallons of alcoholic beverages annually. Alchohol, administered slowly and in small doses, is often regarded as a social wonder drug. It relaxes inhibitions and makes many people gregarious. Under the influence of a moderate amount of alcohol, "The tongue-tied become eloquent, the shy grow bold, the awkward become graceful" (De

Ropp, 1976, p. 122). How does alcohol have these social lubricating effects?

Judging from its ability to transform a collection of ill-at-ease strangers into a laughing, boisterous group of friends, many people assume that alcohol must be a stimulant. It is not. In fact, alcohol is a **depressant**, a chemical that suppresses nerve impulses. The reason alcohol appears to "stimulate" is that, among other things, it slows down and eventually turns off centers in the brain that control normal social inhibitions. As a result, people with as little as .05 percent alcohol in their bloodstream often say and do things they would never ordinarily do. As a person consumes more alcohol, a steady deterioration of all bodily functions occurs. Perception becomes distorted, speech begins to slur, and the drinker has trouble controlling simple movements of the arms and legs. How soon these and related symptoms arise depends on how rapidly alcohol enters the bloodstream and on how much alcohol is consumed relative to body weight. When blood alcohol reaches a level of .3 or .4 percent, a person may lapse into a coma. At a blood alcohol level of about .5 percent, heartbeat and breathing stop and the drinker dies a painless death (Combs, Hale, and Williams, 1980).

One fact often apparent to the drinker the morning after a heavy drinking session is that alcohol can dramatically affect memory. This influence, however, is rather selective. Alcohol consumption leaves short-term memory relatively intact (Jones and Jones, 1977), which is why drinking seldom affects a person's ability to follow a simple conversation. Nor does drinking have much impact on retrieval of information already stored in long-term memory (Birnbaum, Parker, Hartley, and Noble, 1978). An intoxicated person is perfectly capable of boring you with the details of his or her life story. What alcohol does affect, however, is the *transfer* of information from short-term to long-term storage (Parker, Birnbaum, and Noble, 1976). For the person who has been drinking heavily, new information may seem to evaporate as soon as attention shifts. This is one reason why drinkers may have great difficulty remembering the names of those they meet while under the influence of alcohol. It also helps explain the phenomenon called *alcoholic blackout*: fragmentary or even total memory loss for events that occurred while drinking. Apparently, many of the things that the drinker experiences simply do not find their way into long-term storage.

Another factor may also play a role in alcohol-related memory lapses. In some instances, information that a person manages to store while under the influence of alcohol may be more difficult to retrieve when he or she is sober than when drunk (Weingartner et al., 1976). It is almost as though going from drunk to sober produces a form of memory dissociation. This is called **state-dependent memory** because successful retrieval of particular information depends on a person's being in the same state as when that information was originally stored. A comic example of state-dependent memory is depicted in the Charlie Chaplin film *City Lights*. Chaplin plays a tramp befriended by an alcoholic millionaire who invites him to live in his mansion. On the rare occasions when the millionaire is sober, he has no recollection of Chaplin and unceremoniously throws him out. But as soon as the millionaire gets drunk again, Chaplin once more becomes an honored guest. Of course, actual cases of state-dependent memory are seldom this extreme. The differences in retrieval success from one state to the other are more typically a matter of degree.

Exactly why alcohol and certain other drugs sometimes induce state-dependent memory is not yet completely understood. One theory is that the inebriated state re-creates the learning context and so serves as a kind of internal retrieval cue.

Given alcohol's adverse effects on memory, people sometimes wonder if alcohol can permanently affect the brain. For the person who drinks constantly, such dangers are very real. About 10 percent of those who seek help for alcoholism are discovered to have chronic brain damage and accompanying memory deficits. In severe cases the patient can remember almost nothing about events occurring since the disorder set in. This acute condition is called *Korsakoff's psychosis*, and it is often considered irreversible. For the more fortunate alcoholics who escape permanent brain damage, the prognosis for recovering normal memory is far more encouraging. One recent study showed that alcoholics tested four to five weeks after giving up drinking performed remarkably well on a number of memory tests (Parsons and Prigatano, 1977).

What about those who are merely "social drinkers"? Need they worry about the long-term effect of alcohol on memory? Probably not. Research shows that many gallons of alcohol consumed over a lifetime have little, if any, effect on cognitive capabilities—as long as the drinker does not regularly indulge in bouts of heavy drinking. Social drinkers who incur the greatest risk are those who may go for days without drinking, but who then consume large quantities of alcohol in a single session. In terms of the impact on cognitive efficiency in the sober state, it is apparently better to consume one drink every day for an entire week than to wait until Saturday night and splurge with seven drinks. Even though the amount of alcohol ingested is the same, the effects on the brain and memory are quite different (Parker and Noble, 1977).

Marijuana   Marijuana has been used as an intoxicant among Eastern cultures for centuries; in some societies it is legally and morally acceptable whereas alcohol is not. Before 1960 marijuana use in the United States was common only among members of certain subcultures, such as jazz musicians and artists in big cities. By 1960, however, college students had discovered marijuana, and since then its rate of use has increased by a factor of perhaps ten thousand. According to government figures, at least 50 million Americans, and perhaps many more, have tried marijuana, (Zinberg, 1976), and more than 13 million consider themselves regular users. This suggests that marijuana, along with alcohol and the nicotine in tobacco, is one of America's top three recreational drugs. In addition, doctors are beginning to discover several important therapeutic uses for marijuana. The United States government has approved its use, under experimental conditions, to treat glaucoma, a leading cause of blindness; marijuana seems to have the effect of relieving the abnormal pressure on the optic nerve. And the government may soon make available to cancer patients pills containing a derivative of the drug. It has been found that the active ingredient in marijuana helps reduce the severe nausea and vomiting caused by chemotherapy (Cohen and Stillman, 1976).

The active ingredient in marijuana is a complex molecule called tetrahydrocannabinol (THC), which occurs naturally in the common weed *Cannabis sativa*, or Indian hemp. Marijuana is made by drying the plant; hashish is a gummy powder made from the resin exuded by the flowering tops of the female plant. Both marijuana and hashish are usually smoked, but they can also be cooked in food and eaten.

Subjective effects of marijuana Although the subjective effects of marijuana vary somewhat from person to person and also seem to depend on the setting in which it is taken, there is considerable consensus among regular users on how marijuana affects them (Tart, 1970). Most sensory experiences seem greatly enhanced or augmented—music sounds fuller, colors are brighter, smells are richer, foods taste better, and sexual and other sensations are more intense. Users become elated, the world seems somehow more meaningful, and even the most ordinary events may take on a kind of extraordinary profundity. For example, people may become so entranced with a common everyday object that they sit and stare at it for many minutes, marveling at its newly discovered traits. The sense of time is also greatly distorted. A short sequence of events may seem to last for hours. A musical phrase of a few seconds' duration may seem to stretch out in time until it becomes isolated from the rest of the composition and the hearer perceives it as never before.

As many users of marijuana have found, however, the drug can sometimes heighten unpleasant as well as pleasant experiences. If a person is in a frightened or depressed mood, the chances are excellent that taking the drug will blow the negative feelings out of proportion, so that the user's world, temporarily at least, becomes very upsetting. Cases have been reported in which marijuana appears to have helped bring on psychological disturbances in people who were already unstable before they used it.

Despite the obvious need for careful research on marijuana, the first well-controlled scientific studies of its effects on human beings did not appear until the late 1960s. One of the first of these studies was conducted with college students; some of the subjects had had experience with the drug, and others had not. All of the experienced users but only one of the inexperienced subjects reported getting high. Yet on tests of both intellectual and motor skills, the inexperienced subjects displayed impairment whereas the experienced users did not (Weil, Zinberg, and Nelsen, 1968). Likewise, in a laboratory study of motor skills using a simulated driving situation, inexperienced subjects showed greater impairment than experienced subjects (Rafaelsen et al., 1973). Other studies, however, have found that experienced and inexperienced subjects suffer roughly similar impairment in certain kinds of intellectual tasks. How can these seemingly inconsistent results be reconciled?

Taken together, the findings to date suggest that marijuana does induce certain short-term cognitive and motor deficits, but regular users often learn to compensate for many of these. The degree of impairment marijuana produces in a given individual, then, depends in part on how much prior experience that person has had with the drug. Some aspects of behavior are easier to control than others, however. This is why experienced and inexperienced users show equal impairment on certain tasks. For example, research has shown that marijuana interferes with memory processes in both novice and habitual users. Even long-time pot smokers have trouble compensating for this effect as it is typically measured in the laboratory. But exactly which aspects of memory does the drug impair? Some of the experiments designed to answer this question are such fascinating examples of psychological detective work that we will examine them in depth.

In depth

Studying marijuana and memory In the early 1970s researchers at a California veterans hospital recruited a group of volunteers willing to expose their marijuana highs to scientific scrutiny (Darley et al., 1973). Upon arriving at the laboratory, half the volunteers were assigned to the experimental group, which was to be given marijuana, and half were assigned to the control group, which was to be given a placebo. Then all the subjects were given a memory test consisting of ten lists of words. The task was simple. After each list was presented, the subjects were to recall as many of the words as possible in whatever order. As Figure 12.11A shows, there were no significant differences in performance between subjects who were soon to receive marijuana and subjects who were soon to serve as controls. Both groups remembered virtually the same number of words, and the words they remembered most frequently were those at the beginning and the end of each list. This pattern of recall is typical of such tests. Remember from Chapter 6 that subjects have more time to rehearse the words at the beginning of a free recall list. Consequently, these items are likely to become fixed in long-term memory and so remembered quite well. Words at the end of the list are usually still in short-term memory when the recall part of the experiment begins. Hence, they too have a high likelihood of being remembered.

Having determined that no differences in memory ability preexisted between experimental and control subjects, the researchers brought out two trays of brownies. The brownies on one tray were generously laced with THC; the brownies on the other tray looked and tasted identical but contained no THC. Each subject was then given either a THC or a non-THC brownie, depending on whether that person belonged to the experimental or the control group. An hour later, when the experimental subjects were substantially stoned, the researchers requested that everyone attempt to recall the words included on the previous memory tests. It may surprise you to learn that once again the two groups performed almost identically, as shown in Figure 12.11B. The marijuana, it seemed, had virtually no measurable effect on retrieval of information stored in long-term memory.

But what about memory for new information? Would marijuana disrupt it? The researchers wanted to find out. So about two hours after the subjects had eaten their brownies, and while the experimental subjects were still quite high, they presented both groups with a new series of word lists. The percentage of words each group correctly recalled is shown in Figure 12.11C. As you can see, although recall of the last few words was equal, the drugged subjects forgot considerably more words from the beginning and middle of each list than the

Figure 12.11 Comparison of the memories of volunteers who ate either placebo or marijuana-laced brownies. The serial position curve of the experimental subjects is shown in blue; that of the control subjects is shown in red. (A) Before eating the brownies, both groups were equally good at remembering lists of words. (B) An hour later, both groups were still equally good; marijuana did not affect their ability to remember the words they learned before eating the brownies. (C) But when tested for words learned while high, the experimental subjects did worse than the placebo subjects (after Darley et al., 1973).

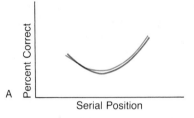

A   *Percent Correct* / Serial Position

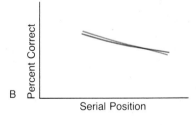

B   *Percent Correct* / Serial Position

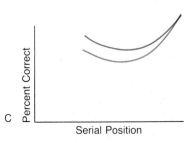

C   *Percent Correct* / Serial Position

nondrugged subjects did. These, of course, are items that would normally be recalled from long-term memory; therefore, the marijuana must be affecting long-term memory in some way. But what could this way be? Certainly retrieval from long-term memory was not being disrupted, for the previous test had ruled this possibility out. Thus, the researchers concluded that the drug must be interfering with the *transfer* of information from short-term to long-term storage. In this respect marijuana acts much like alcohol. And also like alcohol, marijuana appeared to leave short-term memory (represented by words at the very end of a free recall list) largely intact.

For several years many psychologists accepted these findings as gospel: Marijuana disrupts the transfer of information to long-term storage but does not interfere with short-term memory. But then a puzzling contradiction emerged. Across the country a group of researchers at the University of Kentucky Medical Center were also investigating the effects of marijuana on memory (Miller et al., 1977, 1978). As in the earlier California studies, these researchers randomly assigned subjects to drug and placebo conditions and asked them to recall lists of words. The problem was that the serial position curves they obtained did not look like those obtained earlier by the California group. As expected, marijuana impaired recall of words at the beginning and middle of the lists—those that had to be transferred to long-term memory. But interestingly marijuana also impaired recall of words at the *end* of the lists—those presumably held in short-term memory. How could this apparent contradiction be explained? Did marijuana affect short-term memory or didn't it?

The Kentucky researchers returned to the available data and compared the conflicting studies step-by-step. It was not long before they discovered a critical difference. The California subjects had eaten their marijuana in brownies, whereas the Kentucky subjects had smoked theirs. When you smoke marijuana it works more rapidly than when you eat the drug in food, so the Kentucky subjects were undoubtedly more stoned at the time of the memory test than were their California counterparts. One possible answer to the mystery, then, was this: Low doses of marijuana do not usually impair short-term memory, but high doses of the drug generally do. Thus, the results of both the California and Kentucky studies were probably correct; it was just that their circumstances were different. Further experimentation is of course needed to verify this answer.

In any case, there is little doubt that marijuana does have an adverse effect on memory. But to what extent can highly experienced users compensate for this impairment? Psychologists are not yet certain. There is evidence, however, that some people who have smoked marijuana regularly for a substantial period of time do manage to overcome part of its negative impact. For instance, when groups of regular marijuana users are created in the laboratory by administering the drug once a day for a month or more, performance on recall tests while under the drug's influence often gradually improves. The implication is that the subjects in these experiments are learning to compensate for the memory deficits caused by marijuana.

Of course, smoking marijuana once a day for one or two months is a far cry from smoking it many times a day year after year. What are the effects of marijuana on the habitual, lifetime user? This is a difficult question to answer, for there is not much sound data on the long-term effects of marijuana on American users. Studies from other countries, however, may provide some insights. One study of working-class Costa Ricans who had smoked marijuana regularly for many years (Carr, 1978) showed that the *heaviest* users generally had the highest incomes, the least unemployment, and the most stable job histories of all those surveyed! But before you jump to the conclusion that prolonged and regular marijuana use need not impair daily performance, remember that this is only one study of working-class subjects in a country far less industrialized than the United States. Remember too that these results say nothing about other variables that may be influencing both marijuana use and steady employment.

Stimulants *Stimulants* are a class of drug that produces physiological and mental arousal. Specifically, they can decrease fatigue, increase talkativeness and physical activity, enhance endurance, diminish appetite, produce a state of alertness, and for a time elevate mood—often to the point of euphoria. Stimulants vary widely in their potency. Some, such as caffeine and nicotine, are relatively mild; others are extremely powerful. It is on two of the more powerful stimulants—cocaine and amphetamines—that we will focus here.

Cocaine, a product of the leaves of certain coca plants, used to be one of the ingredients in Coca-Cola, which was originally sold as an invigorating tonic. Today, although cocaine is both illegal and expensive, its popularity is growing among middle-class professional people. Cocaine is usually taken in the form of a fine white powder inhaled, or "snorted," into the nostrils and absorbed into the bloodstream through the mucous membranes. It may also be injected intravenously.

Although there has been little laboratory research on the effects of cocaine, some researchers have studied its effects by interviewing users (Grinspoon and Bakalar, 1976). A moderate dose of cocaine produces a euphoric state that can last for thirty minutes to an hour (Resnick et al., 1977). Users claim that it improves attention, reaction time, and speed in simple mental tasks, and so can be helpful for work that requires wakefulness, a free flow of associations, or the suppression of boredom and fatigue. However, the euphoria cocaine brings can make users overestimate their own capacities or the quality of their work. Like other stimulants, cocaine provides a short-term burst of energy, but since it does not replenish energy stores, users will pay the price in physical exhaustion after the drug wears off and the body "comes down," or "crashes."

Long-term use or large doses of cocaine can have much harsher effects. Repeated use can irreversibly damage the mucous membranes of the nasal septum, which separates the nostrils. Chronic use can also result in a general poisoning of the system, characterized by mental deterioration, weight loss, agitation, and paranoia. Cocaine taken in large doses can produce hallucinations, one of the most horrifying of which is formication, a condition in which the person feels there are bugs crawling under his or her skin. This hallucination may be caused by drug-induced hyperactivity of the nerves in the skin. In excessive doses, especially by injection, cocaine can produce headache, hyperventilation, nausea, convulsions, coma, and sometimes even death.

The amphetamines, commonly called "speed," "uppers," or "bennies," are also powerful stimulants. Before all the risks of amphetamines were known, they were sold without prescription under such trade names as Dexadrine and Benzedrine. Many people—truckers on long hauls, students studying for exams—used them to stay awake. Others, particularly women, used them to suppress appetite and help "burn off" fat. But in addition to these more practical effects, amphetamines significantly alter consciousness. Along with a boost in energy, arousal, and alertness comes a marked increase in confidence. People get the feeling they can take on the world, solve any problem, achieve any goal. Are people really more capable under the influence of amphetamines? Not on intellectual tasks. Studies show that amphetamines do not improve problem-solving ability or performance or any other complex cognitive task (Tinklenberg, 1971).

As long as they are taken irregularly and in low doses, amphetamines do not appear to cause any measurable harm. But the problem is that people develop a tolerance for amphetamines, which means that they must take higher and higher doses to achieve the same effect. If intake of the drug becomes chronic and excessive, the user begins to develop ungrounded suspicions. He or she may imagine that people are staring in a peculiar fashion or talking behind one's back. The user may also imagine objects on the skin and get caught up in meaningless meandering trains of thought. As the drug wears off, the person typically sinks into a period of depression and apathy that may last for days and sometimes be severe enough to provoke attempted suicide. At its very worst, amphetamine abuse can also cause serious brain damage.

Hallucinogens Hallucinogens—so-called because one of their main effects is to produce hallucinations—are found in plants that grow throughout the world and have been used for their effects on consciousness since earliest human history (Schultes, 1976). These drugs are also called *psychedelic* ("mind-manifesting") because they are seen as demonstrating the diverse ways in which the mind can potentially function. Among the more common hallucinogenic plants are henbane, mandrake, datura (Jimson weed), one species of morning glory, peyote cactus, many kinds of mushrooms, and also marijuana, which we have already discussed. While we still do not know the exact chemical effects of hallucinogens on the brain, some contain chemical compounds that seem to mimic the activity of certain neurotransmitters, the chemical messengers that regulate brain cell activity.

LSD (lysergic acid diethylamide), the best-known and most extensively studied of the hallucinogens, is also the most potent; in fact, it is one of the most powerful drugs known. LSD, which is a synthetic substance, is one hundred times stronger than psilocybin, which comes from certain mushrooms, and four thousand times stronger than mescaline, which comes from the peyote cactus. A dose of a few millionths of a gram has a noticeable effect; an average dose of 100 to 200 micrograms affects the brain within thirty to sixty minutes and produces a "trip" that lasts from ten to twelve hours (Combs, Hales, and Williams, 1980).

Perceptual hallucinations are very common with LSD. A typical hallucinatory progression begins with simple geometric forms, progresses to complex images, and then to dreamlike scenes (Siegel, 1977). The user may encounter such distortions in form that familiar objects become almost unrecognizable. A wall, for example, may seem to pulsate or breathe. One's senses, too, seem to intermingle: Sounds may be "seen" and visual stimuli may be "heard." A person may experience a dissociation of the self into one being who observes and another who feels. Distortions of time, either an acceleration or a slowing down, are also common. A single stimulus may become the focus of attention for hours, perceived as ever-changing or newly beautiful and fascinating.

Thinking, as measured by the ability to perform simple tasks, is also impaired by LSD, even though the user may feel that he or she is thinking more clearly and logically than ever before. Lifelong problems may suddenly seem resolved, or the need to solve them may seem absurd. The person often experiences the "great truth" phenomenon—that is, he or she feels that previously hidden and ultimate inner truths have been revealed. When the trip is over, the magnitude of these discoveries shrinks, and the solutions reached may turn out to be untenable. After three to five hours the experience begins to become less intense. After ten hours or so the hallucinations and illusions disappear—if no complications occur.

During an LSD trip a person can experience any number of mood states, often quite intense and rapidly changing. The person's "set"—one's mood, expectations, beliefs—and the circumstances under which he or she takes LSD can affect the experience, making it euphoric or terrifying.

Panic reactions are the most common of LSD's unpleasant side effects. Those who experience panic and later describe it often say that they felt trapped in the experience and feared they would never escape or would be driven mad. Panic usually arises when a person tries to ignore, change, or otherwise get rid of the effects of the drug—rather than yielding to the sensations it generates—then realizes he or she cannot. The best treatment, if the panic is not too severe, seems to be the comfort offered by friends and the security of pleasant, familiar settings. Medical attention is sometimes necessary for very intense reactions.

LSD is proving valuable in the study of certain biochemical and physiological functions of the brain. Serotonin, a neurotransmitter that may play an important role in the regulation of sleep and emotion, is chemically similar to part of the LSD molecule. Apparently, LSD blocks the effects of serotonin on brain tissue, which may account for some of its effects on human behavior. But the exact mechanism by which LSD works has yet to be discovered.

Drugs and creativity

Many contemporary poets, novelists, and artists attribute creative insights to their use of drugs. Novelist Ken Kesey used peyote and LSD while he wrote parts of *One Flew Over the Cuckoo's Nest* (1962); poet Allen Ginsberg used LSD in writing *Kaddish and Other Poems* (1960); the book *Psychedelic Art* (Masters and Houston, 1968) is a collection of paintings inspired by experience with hallucinogens. Do drugs really enhance creativity? The evidence is by no means clear. On the one hand, the altered states that drugs induce seem conducive to the creative process. For example, under the influence of certain drugs some people find free association easy, are relaxed and open, have heightened sensory awareness, and can fantasize freely.

On the other hand, aspects of the drug state can hinder creative production:

Figure 12.12 Drawings done by a man under the influence of LSD. (A) Twenty minutes after the first dose, the drug had not yet taken effect. (B) Twenty-five minutes after the second dose was administered, the subject experienced the first alterations in perception. He saw the model correctly but could not control the sweeping movements of his hand. (D) Two hours and forty-five minutes after the first dose, the subject experienced the most intense effects of the drug. (E) Five hours and forty-five minutes after the first dose, the effects of the drug began to wear off. (F) Eight hours after the first dose, the effects were almost completely gone.

Some users experience a diminished capacity for logical thought, reduced ability to direct concentration or to control sequences that they imagine, and a tendency to become absorbed in the altered state of consciousness itself. Another problem is that during drug states a person's capacity for self-criticism is often blunted. William James, for example, had several mystical illuminations during experiments with nitrous oxide (laughing gas), but he was never able to record these revelations before he blacked out from the drug. One night, though, he managed to write down his monumental thoughts before losing consciousness. On returning to his normal state, James rushed to find out what he had written. It was this:

Hogamous, Higamous   Higamous, Hogamous
Man is polygamous   Woman monogamous.

There are, as yet, very few well-controlled studies of the effects of drugs on creativity. The best evidence to date suggests that while drugs can open new perspectives for almost anyone, it takes an already highly skilled person to translate these new ideas into a finished artistic product (Leavitt, 1974).

SUMMARY

1. Consciousness—the awareness of the thoughts, images, sensations, and emotions flowing through one's mind at any given moment—has never been satisfactorily defined. Few psychologists would disagree, however, that consciousness is limited by the narrow range of our perceptual capabilities, by the fact that we cannot attend to all the information available to our senses at any one time, and by the impossibility of identifying the process by which consciousness is created.

2. Consciousness takes many forms: sleeping, dreaming, states induced by various drugs are some examples.

3. Each stage in the process of falling asleep is characterized by a particular brain wave frequency. During REM (rapid eye movement), **sleep**, which accounts for about 25 percent of sleep time, a person's eyes move rapidly back and forth under the eyelids. In fact, the most important distinction between the various stages of sleep is that between REM sleep and all other stages, called non-REM. One reason is that most vivid, visual, storylike dreaming occurs during the REM stage, with non-REM stages being characterized by drifting, unstructured mental activity.

4. The benefit or importance of REM sleep remains unclear, but several theories suggest that it is necessary for psychological well-being. Some evidence suggests that during REM sleep the brain adapts to disturbing or unusual life experiences. There is also some reason to believe that REM sleep may play some role in the consolidation of information into long-term memory, or that dreams provide the brain with an internal source of stimulation, leading to the growth and maintenance of neural tissue. Some dream content is simply incorporated from the external environment. Some theorists, following Freud, have argued that dreams express the hidden needs and desires of the subconscious mind. Others argue that there are no hidden meanings in dreams—just a reflection of current concerns.

5. Although sleep and hypnosis clearly differ, the exact difference remains unclear. No specific set of physiological changes has yet been correlated with the onset of hypnotic trance. Nor is there any significant agreement over the question of how hypnosis works, even though it has been put successfully to a wide variety of medical and therapeutic uses. Psychologists have, however, devised various ways to measure a person's susceptibility to hypnosis, and by one estimate, as many as nineteen out of twenty people can be hypnotized to some degree if only they are willing, and trust the hypnotist.

6. Some investigations of hypnotic states have led to the view that when a subject is hypnotized, what occurs is a **dissociation**, or split in consciousness, such that certain thoughts, feelings, and behaviors operate independently from others. Proponents of the role enactment theory of hypnosis, by contrast, contend that hypnosis is not a special state of consciousness, but rather a special case of role playing in which the subject, following increasingly specific cues provided by the hypnotist, simply acts *as though* he or she were hypnotized.

7. The ability of practitioners of yoga to bring about an apparent separation between their awareness through intense concentration raises the possibility that people might be able to regulate their own states of consciousness. The various techniques of self-regulation of consciousness challenge traditional concepts of how much control people can exert over their own minds and bodies. The most ancient and widespread of these techniques is **meditation**, a retraining of attention that induces an altered state of consciousness. During meditation, a person's metabolism may undergo a dramatic and measurable slowing, and brain wave patterns change. How or why this happens cannot yet be explained.

8. The technique of self-regulation called **biofeedback** involves the use of monitoring instruments to give a person a continuous flow of information about his or her own biological state. By experimenting with various ways of altering physiological function, the person can gradually learn to control target responses at will.

9. Altered states of consciousness involving changes of mood and thought can be induced by certain kinds of **psychoactive drugs**, including the depressant alcohol; marijuana; the stimulants caffeine, nicotine, cocaine, and the amphetamines; and the hallucinogens LSD, peyote, and certain mushrooms.

10. The altered states that drugs induce seem conducive to the creative process, but such drugs can reduce or hinder creative production. The best evidence to date suggests that drugs can open new perspectives—good or bad—for anyone, but that for these to become finished artistic products presupposes a person already highly skilled.

Suggested readings

Dement, W. C. *Some must watch while some must sleep: Exploring the world of sleep.* New York: Norton, 1976.

Goleman, D. *The varieties of the meditative experience.* New York: Dutton, 1977.

Hilgard, E. R. *Divided consciousness: Multiple controls in human thought and action.* New York: Wiley, 1977.

Jones, B. M., and Parsons, O. A. Alcohol and consciousness: Getting high, coming down. *Psychology Today*, 1975, *9*, 53-58.

Ornstein, R. D. *The psychology of consciousness* (2nd ed.). New York: Harcourt Brace Jovanovich, 1977.

Schwartz, G. E. Biofeedback, self-regulation, and the patterning of physiological processes. *American Scientist*, 1975, *63*, 314-324.

Webb, W. B. *Sleep: The gentle tyrant.* Englewood Cliffs, N.J.: Prentice-Hall, 1975.

Yates, A. J. *Biofeedback and the modification of behavior.* New York: Plenum, 1980.

Zinberg, N. E. The war over marijuana. *Psychology Today*, 1976, *10*, 45ff.

PART 6

PERSONALITY AND INDIVIDUALITY

To many people, the chief concern of psychology *is* the study of personality: What makes us each unique? What forms the stable, enduring constellation of qualities we each recognize as *me*? Chapter 13 surveys the four main approaches taken to the study of personality. Chapter 14 explores the area of testing: How are our strengths and abilities ascertained? How are we measured?

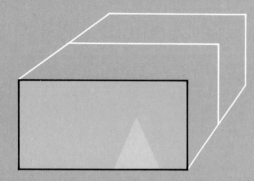

PREVIEW

1. Personality comprises the characteristics and tendencies that determine our responses to environmental circumstances. Several theories attempt to illuminate the structure and functioning of personality.

2. Sigmund Freud, founder and leader of the psychoanalytic approach, indentified unconscious sexual conflicts as the fundamental motivating force in human behavior.

3. Behaviorists view personality as the product of past learning experiences; they believe that the study of personality should rely on objective and measurable observations.

4. Trait theorists understand personality as a collection of traits. A trait is any enduring way in which individuals differ.

5. Phenomenological approaches emphasize the individual's unique perception of the world and the inherent potential in each of us to contribute to our surroundings.

13 Personality theories and research

The concept of personality is one with which we are all familiar. It is as commonplace as the observation that people behave differently. One person blushes and stammers in almost every social situation; another is nearly always the life of the party. One person responds to the slightest problem with confusion and distress; another seems to remain cool in the worst of situations. The concept of personality also refers to the ways of behaving that tend to be relatively stable and enduring in an individual. The person who is acutely shy in one social setting tends to be shy in many others. The person who becomes violently agitated just from misplacing the car keys hardly ever seems to have a calm moment. These two factors—individual differences in thought, feeling, and action and their relative stability over time—form the core of any definition of personality. Thus, **personality** can be defined as a fairly stable set of characteristics and tendencies that determine an individual's responses to a variety of environmental circumstances (Maddi, 1976).

This definition suggests that all personality theorists address two key questions. First, when several people encounter the same situation, why do they not all behave the same? And second, what accounts for the relative consistency of a person's behavior from one situation to the next? In answering these questions, psychologists must keep in mind the interplay of several factors that shape personality: our biological make-up; our unique experiences, especially within the family; and the values, beliefs, and customs we learn from our culture. As you will see, each personality theorist stresses some of these factors more than others, and each approaches them from a somewhat different angle. In addition, each psychologist who studies personality tends to focus on only certain aspects of this broad and complex phenomenon. Some have been primarily concerned with a number of measurable traits, such as dominance or dependency. Other have chosen to focus on the broad integrative qualities, such as the concept of the self. Still others have turned their major attention to internal feelings such as anxiety and conflict. This diversity is what makes the field of personality so challenging—and so frustrating. Introductory students often feel that just when they are convinced that one theory is "correct," they encounter another that seems equally persuasive! The best way to cope with this state of affairs is to consider the theories you are about to meet as complementary rather than competing. Each sheds valuable light on certain, but not all, aspects of personality. Consequently, each by itself fails to give a complete account of the reasons for human behavior. Together, however, they paint a rich portrait of how people behave and why.

In this chapter we will discuss four broad perspectives on personality. The first is a group of theories known as **psychoanalytic approaches**, which began with Sigmund Freud. Psychoanalytic approaches emphasize childhood experiences as critically important in shaping adult personality. They also stress the role of the unconscious in motivating human actions. In contrast, **behavioristic** and **social learning approaches** are those based mainly on principles of learning and reinforcement, discussed in Chapter 5. Behaviorism views the development and functioning of the personality as a set of learned responses, not as the result of psychic drives or the promptings of the unconscious. **Trait theories** say simply that human behavior can be organized according to characteristics that are called traits—for example, aggression, friendliness, and honesty. People differ from one another in the extent to which they exhibit particular traits. Finally, **phenomenological approaches** emphasize the potential of human beings for growth, creativity, and spontaneity. They reject both the Freudian emphasis on irrational and destructive instincts and the behaviorist idea that people respond only to reward and punishment. As we shall see, despite their varying emphases, each of these broad perspectives offers valuable insights into human behavior.

PSYCHOANALYTIC THEORIES

Although Sigmund Freud was the founder and most well-known proponent of the psychoanalytic approach to personality, there is more to psychoanalytic theory than Freud's ideas alone. A number of other psychologists have expanded on Freudian concepts, often modifying them substantially. In fact, modern psychoanalytic thought differs greatly in many respects from the original beliefs of Freud. All psychoanalytic theorists, however, have certain things in common. First, they are all concerned with powerful but largely unconscious motivations believed to exist in every human being. Second, most agree that the following concepts are central to explaining human personality: conflict between opposing motives, anxiety over unacceptable motives, and defense mechanisms to prevent anxiety from becoming too great. Freud, of course, provided the foundation for all later psychoanalytic writers. In fact, he is generally regarded the single most important theorist in the field of personality. Many of Freud's concepts (Freudian slips, penis envy) are widely used in everyday language, even if the average person has only a superficial understanding of them. Because of Freud's enormous importance in the history of twentieth-century thought, and because of the heated controversy his ideas have generated, we will discuss his work in some detail.

Basic concepts of Freudian theory

Sigmund Freud was born in Moravia in 1856, the son of a Jewish wool merchant whose business failures prompted him to move his family to Vienna when Sigmund was still a very young boy. In this important cultural and intellectual capital of Europe the young Freud grew to maturity and spent nearly all of his long and productive adult life. At the age of seventeen, Freud entered medical school at the University of Vienna with the goal of becoming a professor of neurology. But opportunities for Jews in the Viennese academic world were extremely limited, so upon graduation Freud was reluctantly forced to set up private practice as a physician specializing in nervous disorders. The practice of medicine never greatly appealed to Freud; but for him it was a financial necessity. Fortunately, however, his chosen field brought him many patients who were suffering not from neurological disease but from psychosomatic illnesses. Freud's study of these patients and his innovative efforts to treat them marked the beginning of his far-ranging theories about the structure and function of the human psyche.

As we mentioned in Chapter 1, Freud's approach to treating "hysterical" patients (as people suffering from psychosomatic illnesses were then called) was greatly influenced by the work of other medical practitioners of his time. Freud spent a year in Paris studying with the great French psychiatrist Jean Charcot, who was using hypnosis as a means of treating hysteria. He was also influenced by Josef Breuer, a fellow Viennese physician who was experimenting with a "talking cure." Breuer encouraged hysterical patients to talk about their emotional problems under hypnosis until their physical symptoms disappeared. But it was Freud who developed the "talking cure" into a more elaborate procedure called **free association**. In free association the unhypnotized patient is asked to lie down on a couch and say out loud whatever comes to mind. When a topic arises about which the person appears to be resisting the spontaneous flow of ideas, this subject is presumed to be related to the patient's emotional problem and so becomes a focus of further inquiry. Through this persistent probing, the patient is gradually made to recognize the nature of his or her conflicts.

Freud found that the roots of many patients' problems could be traced back to childhood experiences, especially those related to sexuality. Yet these early experiences were not usually available to consciousness. Only through great effort could they be coaxed into active memory. Freud concluded from this discovery that the cause of neurotic anxiety, hysteria, and other psychological disorders often lay in sexual conflicts that had been pushed deep into unconscious recesses of the mind but that were capable of surfacing in disguised form. Thus, hysterical paralysis of the hand, for instance, was explained as a compromise between a desire to engage in a forbidden act—perhaps masturbation—and the requirement that sexuality be expressed only in socially acceptable ways. Freud coined the term **psychoanalysis** to describe the process by which he attempted to bring thoughts and feelings from the unconscious into the conscious so that the patient could examine them rationally and break their power to control.

The concept of the unconscious is undoubtedly one of Freud's major contributions to the understanding of human behavior and personality. Before Freud's time, psychologists were concerned only with the conscious thoughts and feelings of people. Now Freud proposed something radically different: that there are aspects of our functioning of which we are not fully aware or able to verbalize. He likened the mind to an enormous iceberg, of which consciousness was only the small, exposed tip; the massive structure of the iceberg that lies beneath the surface is the vast region of the unconscious. To Freud the unconscious was both a reservoir of instinctual drives and a storehouse for all the thoughts, wishes, and urges we want to conceal from conscious awareness because they cause us internal conflict. In fact, Freud maintained that the unconscious is *the* major motivating force behind all human behavior. Much of what we say and do is presumably an effort either to find some socially acceptable way of expressing unconscious impulses or to manage to keep those impulses under control. This is why Freud believed that a psychology limited to the study of consciousness was inadequate.

Closely related to Freud's view of the unconscious and its powerful control over behavior is his belief that few words or actions, however trivial they may seem, are without deep significance. Slips of the tongue, accidents, forgetting an appointment or losing something, even mispronouncing a name or telling a joke were to Freud all signs of unconscious drives, wishes, and conflicts. In his writings he cites many examples. For instance, the president of the Austrian parliament once opened a new session with the words: "Gentlemen, I declare a quorum present and herewith declare the session *closed*," an indication, according to Freud, that he really wished the troublesome session was over. Even the most seemingly purposeless acts—doodling, twirling a button or lock of hair, humming a tune to yourself—all had deeper meaning to Freud. All presumably afford glimpses into important mental processes going on in the subterranean world of the unconscious.

Part of the fascination of reading Freud's work derives from the fact that he was a highly skilled and engaging writer, with a keen eye for human behavior and a broad background in literature and history as well as medical science. But these very positive traits did not make Freud's climb to international prominence an easy one. Freud's first great work, *The Interpretation of Dreams* (1900), sold a mere six hundred copies in its first eight years in print! Why such staggering rejection of a man as brilliant as Freud? Much of the problem was that Freud's ideas collided sharply with turn-of-the-century morality. People were deeply shocked at Freud's focus on powerful and persistent sexuality. Many prospective patients simply refused to see him for fear that their sex lives would be probed. As a result, Freud's very livelihood was threatened by his unconventional theories. But still he persevered. Finally, around 1906, Freud began to attract a sizable following. Over the ensuing years, as he expanded and refined his theories, a full-fledged psychoanalytic school developed with Freud at its head. To understand the concepts around which this movement developed it is helpful to first explore Freud's revolutionary ideas about the structure of the human psyche.

Structure of the human psyche Based on his work with troubled patients, Freud developed a comprehensive theory of the human mind that he believed applied to all people regardless of how psychologically healthy or neurotic they might be. Freud divided the human psyche into three separate but interacting elements: the **id**, the **ego**, and the **superego**. As you read about these elements in the discussion that follows, do not make the mistake of viewing them as three distinct people, locked in perennial combat. True, Freud himself often suggested this very image in order to dramatize his points. But he did not intend to be taken literally. The id, the ego, and the superego are not entities, not physical divisions of the brain. Instead they are names given to strong motivational forces, the existence of which is inferred from the ways that people behave.

Freud described the id as a reservoir of psychic energy, the pool of biological drives that arises from our basic physiological needs for food, water, warmth, sexual gratification, avoidance of pain, and so forth. These drives Freud called instincts, and he believed that they powered and directed all of human behavior. The id in Freud's scheme is an unconscious force. It has no link with objective reality, only with subjective experience. Consequently, the id seeks one thing only: the discharge of tension that accompanies satisfaction of bodily needs. This tendency of the id to devote itself exclusively to the immediate reduction of tension—without regard for logic or reason, reality or morality—is called the **pleasure principle**. The id is therefore like a demanding, impulsive, selfish child. It seeks only its own pleasure and cannot abide frustration or deprivation of any kind. In Freud's native German the word for id is *es*, which means "it," thus implying an alien force, something in a person that is not recognized as part of the self.

Although the id seeks satisfaction of biological needs, it has no way of determining which means of tension reduction are safe and which are dangerous. This task falls to a second structure of the human psyche, the ego. The ego, according to Freud, begins to develop soon after birth, but it does not become apparent until the age of about six months. The ego's role is to serve as a mediator between the id and reality (Freud, 1920, 1923). Unlike the id, much of the ego is conscious. In German the word for ego is *Ich*, which means "I," signifying the part of the personality recognized and accepted as the self. By remembering prior experience with reality and reasoning on the basis of it, the ego tries to satisfy the desires of the id, to anticipate the consequences of a particular means of gratification, and sometimes to delay gratification in order to achieve long-range goals. Thus, in contrast to the pleasure principle of the id, the ego operates on what is called the **reality principle**, the foundation of which is the concern for safety. It is through this basic ego function of finding realistic means to satisfy the id that the mind develops and refines all its higher cognitive functions: perception, learning, memory, problem solving, judgment, and planning.

As if the job of the ego is not difficult enough, given the irrational, insistent nature of the id, there is yet another psychic component the ego must contend with. This is the superego, the part of the personality that represents the moral standards of society as conveyed to a person by his or her parents. The superego is approximately equivalent to what we call "conscience." This is why the German word for superego is *überich*, which means "over the I." Like the id, the superego is oblivious to reality. Instead of considering what is realistic or possible, it constantly commands all sexual and aggressive impulses be stifled in favor of lofty moral goals. The superego, then, is the great naysayer. Its function is to prohibit any thoughts and actions that express our instinctual drives. As such, the superego puts the ego in a very difficult position. On the one hand, the ego must find a way to satisfy the id. But on the other, it must do so without giving pain, experienced as remorse or guilt, to the superego.

Thus, the ego must serve three harsh and intolerant masters: the pleasure-seeking id, the moralistic superego, and an unforgiving reality. Here is how Freud (1933) described the ego's plight:

> We are warned by a proverb against serving two masters at the same time. The poor ego has things even worse: it serves three severe masters and does what it can to bring their claims and demands into harmony with one another. . . . In its attempt to mediate between the id and reality, the ego is often obliged to cloak the commands of the id in its own rationalizations, to conceal the id's conflicts with reality, to profess, with diplomatic disingenuousness, to be taking notice of reality even when the id has remained rigid and unyielding. On the other hand it is observed at every step it takes by the strict superego, which lays down definite standards for its conduct, . . . and which, if those standards are not obeyed, punishes it with tense feelings of inferiority and of guilt. Thus . . . we can understand how it is that so often we cannot suppress a cry: "Life is not easy!"

"Not easy" is probably an understatement. Given the natures of the id, the superego, and reality, harmony among them must at times be almost impossible. So how is this difficult balance accomplished? This important question brings us to a second aspect of Freud's theory—his ideas about anxiety and defense mechanisms.

Anxiety and defense mechanisms According to Freud, the signal that the ego is losing its struggle to reconcile the divergent demands of the id, the superego, and reality comes in the form of **anxiety**, a state of psychic distress. Freud distinguished three types of anxiety. He viewed these as dependent on which of the ego's three masters is the primary cause of the threat. In reality anxiety, a person is threatened by something in the outside world. For instance, when a person faces social ostracism for behaving in a highly selfish way, he or she experiences reality anxiety. In morality anxiety the source of the danger is the superego, which threatens to overwhelm the person with guilt or shame over something that he or she has done or merely thought of doing. Finally, in neurotic anxiety the danger comes from id impulses that threaten to burst through ego controls. Since the danger is internal, the ego cannot flee as it could from external danger. Of these three forms of anxiety, neurotic anxiety was the most fundamental to Freud and the one against which he believed that most of our psychological defense mechanisms are directed.

Defense mechanisms, according to Freudian theory, are a whole range of mental strategies that the ego uses to reduce its own anxiety. The most basic of the defense mechanisms is **repression**, a pushing back of unacceptable id impulses into the unconscious. As such, repression is both a defense mechanism in its own right and the aim of all other defense mechanisms. For no matter what our specific strategy for coping with neurotic anxiety, our ultimate goal is to make sure that the "forbidden" thoughts and feelings no longer intrude into consciousness. Throughout his writings Freud mentioned many different defense mechanisms, the psychosomatic illness that plagued many of his patients being just one. But it was Freud's daughter Anna, herself a psychoanalyst, who finally discussed the ego's defenses in detail (A. Freud, 1946). Among the most important ones she described are regression, reaction formation, projection, displacement, and sublimation.

Regression occurs when a person made anxious by threatening thoughts and feelings behaves in ways characteristic of an earlier stage in life, before the present conflicts began. For example, a middle-aged man who is having difficulties with his wife may resort to taking long afternoon naps on weekends, just as he did as a small child.

Reaction formation is the replacement of an anxiety-producing impulse or feeling with its direct opposite. For instance, a person who is strongly attracted to pornography may vehemently insist that all sexually explicit material is filthy and disgusting. Or a parent who feels an impulse to abuse his or her child may instead shower the child with expressions of love. To "protest too much" may therefore be a sign of reaction formation.

Projection occurs when a person unknowingly attributes his or her own objectionable impulses to other people. For example, a man who has had many extramarital affairs may begin to accuse his wife of being unfaithful, thereby transferring his own shortcomings to her. And people who constantly complain about the sexual promiscuity of the younger generation may be projecting fears of their own sexual urges onto others.

Displacement is the transfer of unacceptable feelings from their appropriate target to a much "safer" object. A familiar example is the man who is constantly belittled by his boss and so vents his anger on his secretary, the elevator operator, a store clerk, or anyone else unlikely to retaliate. Thus, cases of wife beating and child abuse may sometimes be forms of displaced aggression.

Sublimation is a kind of displacement in which forbidden impulses are diverted toward socially desirable goals. In *Civilization and Its Discontents* (1930), Freud argued that civilization itself came about through such a rechanneling of primitive drives. For example, he suggested that Leonardo da Vinci's urge to paint Madonnas was a sublimated expression of his longing for reunion with his mother, from whom he had been separated at an early age.

It is important to note that sublimation is not the only defense mechanism that can have quite positive outcomes. When used in moderation almost any defense mechanism that does not injure others can help us get through life's more disagreeable times. Thus, displacing hostility from your boss onto a tennis ball can be a wise thing to do if you want to keep your job. But extreme reliance on defense mechanisms, to the point where they dominate a person's life or prevent healthy relationships with others, can cause far more problems than they solve.

How personality develops   Because Freud learned from his work with troubled patients that psychological conflicts often begin in childhood, he developed an extensive theory about how adult personality is shaped by early life experiences. Freud argued that at different stages in a child's life, the drive for pleasure centers around a particular area of the body: first the mouth, then the anus, and finally the genitals. All these id urges he loosely labeled "sexual" to emphasize that the earlier strivings for sensual pleasure emanate from the same reservoir of psychic energy as does the striving for genital sex. Freud believed that adult personality is shaped by the way in which the conflicts between these early sexual urges and the restrictions imposed by society (weaning, toilet training, prohibitions against masturbation, and so forth) are resolved. Failure to resolve any of these conflicts can result in **fixation**, in which the person becomes perpetually "locked" in that particular psychological battle, forever expressing the conflict in symbolic ways. To understand these ideas more fully, let us consider each of Freud's five stages of psychosexual development.

The stages of psychosexual development Freud believed that during the first year of life—the **oral stage**—a child's sexual pleasure focuses on the mouth. Since sucking is the only means for a baby to obtain food, it is not surprising that this activity would be an important aspect of the child's life. But Freud argued that to a baby the significance of sucking goes far beyond the basic satisfaction of hunger. Sucking is a source of intense pleasure in its own right, pleasure akin to that which genital sex holds for adults. According to Freud this is why babies suck, lick, bite, and chew virtually anything they can get into the mouth. Fixation at the oral stage can occur for a variety of reasons. For example, when a baby repeatedly experiences anxiety over whether food will be given or withheld, the child may come to learn that he or she is totally dependent on others. This usually leads to a passive, overly dependent, unenterprising adult.

The next stage of development in Freud's scheme is the **anal stage**. It occurs during the second year of life when the child begins to develop more voluntary control over bowel movements. As a result, he or she comes to derive great sensual pleasure from holding in and expelling feces. But no sooner are these pleasures established than the demands of toilet training are imposed. Toilet training, according to Freudians, is a crucial event because it is the first large-scale conflict between the child's id impulses and society's rules. If this conflict is not satisfactorily resolved, fixation will again occur. For instance, the child faced with severe regulation may repress the urge to defecate in a free and enjoyable manner. Repeated repression of this urge may result in the development of personality traits that are very much the opposite of uninhibited defecation, such as fastidious neatness or orderliness.

Freud's third stage of development, the **phallic stage**, spans the ages from about three to five or six. During this time the child's erotic pleasure focuses on masturbation—that is, on self-manipulation of the genitals. The phallic stage is said to be particularly important to a person's psychological development because this is the period when the Oedipus conflict presumably occurs. As we already discussed in Chapter 8, this conflict involves intense desire to take the place of the same-sex parent in the affections of the parent of the opposite sex. Freud regarded this conflict as explicitly sexual: "When the little boy shows the most open sexual curiosity about his mother, wants to sleep with her at night, or even attempts physical acts of seduction, the erotic nature of this attachment to her is established without a doubt"(Freud, 1935, p. 342). This conflict is eventually resolved when the child gradually comes to realize that these incestuous longings will never be fulfilled. So the child does the next best thing: He or she tries to be like the parent of the same sex by adopting that parent's attitudes, behavior, moral values, and so forth. This identification with the same-sex parent is believed to be crucial to the development of the child's conscience, or superego.

After the phallic stage, children move into the fourth stage of psychosexual development, a period of **latency**. From the age of five or six until puberty, a child's sexual impulses appear to remain in the background while he or she is busy learning a whole range of social and cognitive skills. Finally, during adolescence, sexual feelings reemerge and the **genital stage** begins. The focus in this last stage of psychosexual development is on the pleasures of sexual intercourse. Feelings of dependency and Oedipal strivings that were not resolved earlier may resurface during this time. In fact, Freud maintained that the turmoil of adolescence may be partly attributable to such conflicts. With successful resolution of these conflicts, a person is capable of forming deep and mature love relationships and of taking his or her place in the world as a fully independent adult.

Freud's ideas about psychosexual development were the aspect of his theory that his contemporaries found most shocking. How perverse, they charged, to attribute such grossly sexual thoughts and actions to innocent little children! But these critics were largely missing Freud's point. Freud was not seeking to uncover the "sins" of childhood, but simply trying to emphasize that we are all born with biological drives, among them erotic ones. Human sexuality cannot suddenly emerge out of nowhere when a person reaches puberty, Freud reasoned. It is much more logical to think that erotic impulses are present all the time, although they take different forms at different ages. And if people persist in seeing children as completely asexual, despite all the evidence to the contrary, it is only because that is what they wish children to be and have tried to make them.

Freud on the development of women As if Freud's theory of psychological development was not controversial enough, his ideas about the development of women have stirred up an even greater clamor, especially in the last decade. Freud has been accused of degrading women, and it is not difficult to see why. His writings are liberally sprinkled with passing references to female inferiority. The basis of this inferiority, and of female psychology in general, is the simple absence of a penis. According to Freud, when little girls finally notice that they lack this fine piece of anatomical equipment, they "feel themselves heavily handicapped by the absence of a large visible penis and envy the boy's possession of it"(1925, p. 327). And this is the beginning of their long slide into inferiority. Freud reasoned that because a girl lacks a penis she cannot undergo the same Oedipus conflict as a boy. For a boy this conflict involves more than just a desire to possess his mother. It also involves a fear that his father will punish these incestuous longings by castrating him. This terrible fear Freud called *castration anxiety*.

Since Freud believed that successful resolution of both the Oedipus conflict and castration anxiety was vital to the formation of the superego, he concluded that women's superegos were naturally stunted. As Freud wrote,

I cannot evade the notion (though I hesitate to give it expression) that for women the level of what is ethically normal is different from what it is in men. Their superego is never so inexorable, so impersonal, so independent of its emotional origins as we require it to be in men. Character-traits which critics of every epoch have brought up against women—that they show less sense of justice than men, that they are less ready to submit to the great exigencies of life, that they are more often influenced in their judgments by feelings of affection or hostility—all these would be amply accounted for by the modification in the formation of their superego. . . . (1925, p. 258).

Thus, according to Freud, women are morally inferior. As a result, they are culturally inferior as well. Freud believed that the ability to contribute to the advance of civilization depends on the mechanism of sublimation, which in turn depends on a strong, mature superego—the very thing a woman lacks. According to Freud, women have made only one contribution to civilization, the art of weaving, a practice unconsciously motivated by woman's desire to conceal her "genital deficiency."

The opposition to Freud's penis-envy theory was first articulated in 1926 by the psychologist Karen Horney, who retorted that Freud was in a poor position to know what little girls think. According to Horney (1967), it is not little girls who perceive themselves as genitally deficient. Rather, it is little boys—and the men they eventually become—who see their penisless counterparts as woefully castrated and who thus have created the self-fulfilling prophecy that has doomed womankind to inferiority. More recent feminist writers have taken this argument several steps further, claiming that Freud's theory was merely the reflection of an age-old cultural bias against women and that it is nothing more than a devious attempt to justify male supremacy. We will say much more about prejudice and discrimination against women in Chapter 17, where we discuss the psychology of sexism.

Other psychoanalytic theorists

As we mentioned earlier, Freud's ideas about human personality eventually attracted many followers, and a psychoanalytic movement was born. From all over Europe and the United States, young people came to Vienna to study with Freud. Like Freud himself, some of these students were highly creative thinkers in their own right. So it is not surprising that a number of them began to expand on and modify Freud's original theories.

Although it is difficult to briefly summarize all the different directions that later psychoanalytic thinking has taken, two paths in particular stand out. First, post-Freudian theorists have tended to give an increased importance to the ego and a decreased importance to the id. In Freud's view, the ego was simply the id's dutiful servant, trying as best it could to satisfy id instincts without neglecting reality or causing the superego remorse. Most later psychoanalytic thinkers, in contrast, have abandoned the idea that sexual and aggressive drives are all-powerful and all-consuming. Instead, they have seen the ego as an important force in its own right, capable of much creativity, rational planning, and the formation of self-fulfilling goals. Second, psychoanalytic thinkers after Freud have also emphasized the importance of social interaction in explaining how human personality develops. Instead of seeing a person's nature as solely the outcome of conflicts over id impulses, they have seen personality development as much more the product of a child's relationships with significant others in his or her life.

The deviations from orthodox Freudian theory that were most personally distressing to Freud were those instigated by his two closest colleagues, Carl Jung (1875-1961), and Alfred Adler (1870-1937), both former students of Freud. Jung strongly disagreed with Freud on several important issues (Jung, 1953). One was the nature of the unconscious. Jung believed that the unconscious was not simply a dark reservoir of "forbidden" urges and repressed memories; it was also the center of many positive thoughts and forces. Accordingly, Jung's view of human nature was broader and more positive than that of Freud. While Freud argued that human personality is fully determined in the course of psychosexual development, Jung emphasized continual growth and change. Thus, future aims were just as important in Jung's view as experiences from a person's past.

Adler also stressed the importance of self-generated goals in the development of human personality. He believed that the great motivation in human life is a striving upward toward "superiority" (Adler, 1930). By this he did not mean social distinction or prominence, but rather an inner quest for self-perfection. Adler proposed that all children are born with a deep sense of inferiority because of their small size, physical weakness, and lack of knowledge in the world of adults—in fact, it was Adler (1931) who coined the widely used term *inferiority complex*. How parents interact with their children, Adler argued, has a crucial effect on the children's ability to overcome feelings of inferiority and so achieve competency and meet challenges later in life. Thus, Adler saw human personality as heavily shaped by the quality of early social relationships.

Other psychoanalytic thinkers since Adler's time have elaborated this view of the self as a product of social relationships. The writings of the psychoanalyst Karen Horney (1885-1952) provide a good example. Horney was born in Germany, trained in Europe by one of Freud's students, and emigrated to the United States shortly before World War II. Like Freud, Horney saw adult personality as shaped largely by childhood experiences. But unlike Freud she believed that personality development was a product of social relationships (especially with parents) rather than an expression of innate sexual and aggressive drives (Horney, 1945). In particular, Horney argued that when parents' behavior toward a child is indifferent, disparaging, and erratic, the child feels helpless and insecure. Horney called this *basic anxiety*. Accompanying basic anxiety, according to Horney, is a feeling of deep resentment toward the parents, or *basic hostility*. This hostility cannot be expressed directly, because the child needs and fears the parents and strongly wants their love. So the hostility is repressed, leading to increased feelings of unworthiness and anxiety. The conflict between basic anxiety and basic hostility leads the child, and later the neurotic adult, to adopt one of three modes of social interaction: moving *toward* others, moving *against* others, or moving *away* from others. Someone who moves toward other people becomes compliant, always anxious to please in order to gain affection and approval. The person who moves against others is attempting to find security through domination. The goal of the person who moves away from others is to find security by becoming aloof and withdrawn, never allowing close relationships. Clearly all of these self-protective strategies give rise to many interpersonal problems.

Evaluating the psychoanalytic approaches

Like all controversial viewpoints, psychoanalytic approaches to personality face a number of forceful and persuasive criticisms. First is the charge that the data supporting them have not been collected and analyzed in rigorously scientific ways. Freud, for instance, never attempted to quantify his findings, nor did he ever use standardized tests to assess his patients' behavior. Instead, he relied exclusively on his own subjective appraisals. Such lack of quantification and objective measurements suggests that Freud may have inadvertently biased his own observations by focusing on those aspects of behavior that tended to confirm his hypotheses and overlooking those that did not.

Contemporary researchers have tried to resolve some of these issues by putting some of Freud's notions to scientific tests. Recently, two psychologists have reviewed the many hundreds of such tests conducted over the years, with the goal of evaluating Freudian theory as a whole (Fisher and Greenberg, 1977). They found that the available scientific evidence gives fairly good support to some of Freud's notions. For instance, people who experience unusual anxiety over anal subjects do tend to show the "anal" traits of orderliness, frugality, and obstinacy. In addition, there is evidence that arousal of erotic feelings may produce some anxiety in men and increase their concern about harm or attack to their bodies. This finding is in keeping with Freud's Oedipus theory and his concept of castration anxiety. In other cases, however, the available scientific evidence does not support Freud's views. For instance, there is absolutely no evidence that women regard their bodies as inferior to men's because they lack penises. If anything, females are more accepting of and more comfortable with their bodies than are males. Nor is there much evidence that dreams are simply disguised expressions of unconscious wishes, as Freud strongly believed. Thus, the scientific verdict regarding the validity of Freudian theory appears at this point to be mixed.

In addition to criticisms about Freud's lack of scientific rigor, many psychologists have complained that a large number of Freud's concepts are too ambiguous or too metaphorical to be pinpointed and measured. For example, in precisely what behaviors must a little boy engage to be considered embroiled in the Oedipus conflict? Is any sign of strong attachment to the mother an indication of a desire to "possess" her? Or must the little boy's words and actions have explicitly sexual overtones? Freud never really specified. Moreover, some of Freud's ideas are conceptualized in a way that allows virtually *any* behavior to be used as evidence in their support. If a person acts in a blatantly sexual or aggressive manner, he or she is said to be expressing an unbridled id instinct. But if the person acts the *opposite,* he or she may also be said to be driven by the very same impulse, only this time the impulse is surfacing as a reaction formation. In fact, many different actions could be interpreted as forms of compromise between a particular id impulse and the demands of conscience and reality. This looseness of Freudian theory prohibits its adherents from accurately *predicting* behavior. Instead, the theory can only be used to explain behavior after the fact, and this is a serious weakness.

A final criticism leveled against Freud and other psychoanalytic thinkers is that their ideas are applicable only to members of the Western societies in which those psychoanalysts lived and worked. This charge is particularly strong against Freud. Because his patients were primarily upper-middle-class women who lived in a sexually rigid and puritanical society, it is likely that Freud attributed greater importance to erotic impulses, morality, and guilt than is appropriate for people in general.

Despite these strong criticisms of Freud, his influence on twentieth-century thought has nevertheless been profound. Freudian concepts like *anxiety, repression,* and *defense mechanisms* are used by psychologists and lay people alike. The fact that we often analyze an individual's personality in terms of childhood experiences or worry about the way in which we toilet train our children is all a legacy of Freud. Although Freud may not have been a rigorous scientist, he was certainly a keen and meticulous observer of human behavior. The enormous originality of his thinking, his perseverence in the face of severe criticism, and the sheer comprehensiveness of his theories have earned him great distinction in the history of psychological thought.

BEHAVIORAL AND LEARNING APPROACHES

At approximately the same time that Freud was developing his theories of personality in Vienna, psychologists in the United States were formulating and expounding the doctrine of behaviorism, discussed in Chapters 1 and 5. Unlike Freud, the behaviorists maintained that psychology must be limited solely to what can be observed and measured. As a result, they set about investigating how observable stimuli in the environment can, through learning, produce observable responses. The brilliant young psychologist John B. Watson took the extreme position that all behavior is simply a matter of learned associations. Another innovative young American scholar, Edward L. Thorndike, was revealing to the scientific world the power of rewards and punishments. In this intellectual climate a number of personality theories began to emerge. Although differing from one another in important respects, all tried to explain behavior not in terms of unconscious motives as a psychoanalyst would, but in terms of what a person has learned.

Dollard and Miller's psychodynamic behavior theory

When Freud's ideas became known in America, some learning theorists were eager to assimilate his work into their own. The most ambitious of these attempts came in the 1940s when Yale psychologists John Dollard and Neal Miller used learning principles to explain many of Freud's concepts. Consequently, their approach is often called **psychodynamic behavior theory**.

Dollard and Miller (1950) argued that behavior is motivated by a variety of drives, which they saw as roughly equivalent to Freud's instincts. Like instincts, drives are states of arousal that demand reduction through an appropriate response. Hunger, for instance, is a drive that is reduced by the response of eating. Central to Dollard and Miller's model is the notion that conflict often occurs in the attempt to reduce drives. Conflict, of course, is also central to Freudian theory. But whereas Freud's ideas about conflict grew out of inferences based on observation of troubled patients, Dollard and Miller's ideas were the product of carefully controlled experiments. In one experiment Miller (1944) allowed a hungry rat to run down an alley and reach a feeding tray. While the animal was eating, it received a very painful electric shock. Later, when the still hungry rat was again placed at the head of the alley, it ran only halfway down toward the food before it stopped and vacillated, as though torn between the desire to eat and the desire to avoid pain. Such **approach-avoidance conflicts** parallel Freud's notions about clashes between the divergent goals of the pleasure-seeking id and the reality-conscious ego. But Dollard and Miller explained this conflict in a very concrete way. They showed that approach-avoidance conflict is learned through exposure to a situation in which a pleasurable drive-reducing response is associated with a highly negative consequence. When approach and avoidance tendencies are equally strong, conflict results.

Dollard and Miller agreed with Freud that in humans most conflicts arise when reality or conscience imposes restrictions on the expression of biological drives. They also agreed with Freud that unresolved conflicts cause anxiety and that defense mechanisms are strategies devised to reduce anxiety. But once again Dollard and Miller placed the concept of defense mechanisms within a learning framework. Defense mechanisms, they argued, are learned responses that are reinforced because to some extent they work: They *do* reduce some of the anxiety the conflict-ridden person feels. Consequently, defense mechanisms are often repeated, thus becoming neurotic habits. To take just one example, suppose a young woman who feels anxious whenever she thinks about having sexual intercourse finds that her anxiety will be lessened if she shifts her thoughts to some less threatening subject. As a result, not thinking about her conflict is strongly reinforced because it is associated with relief from anxiety. Note that the end result is something very similar to Freudian repression, but Dollard and Miller have accounted for this behavior in terms of learning theory. This is why they chose to refer to repression as "learned not-thinking" (Miller, 1948, 1959).

Many psychologists have criticized Dollard and Miller for basing their ideas about human behavior and personality too much on animal research. Dreams and other symbolic processes, these critics argue, are not likely to be illuminated by the study of rats and pigeons. Yet Dollard and Miller's psychodynamic behavior theory accomplished several important things. First, it showed that psychoanalytic concepts need not be inaccessible to American researchers with a behavioral point of view. When restated in the language of learning theory, many Freudian concepts became quite congenial to a number of American psychologists. The result has been a great deal of experimental research in such areas as childhood socialization and human conflict and anxiety. Second, Dollard and Miller's approach helped pave the way for behavior therapy—a set of procedures, based on learning principles, designed to change neurotic and psychotic behavior. We will say more about behavior therapy in Chapter 16.

Skinner's radical behaviorism

About the time that Dollard and Miller were developing their psychodynamic behavior theory, psychologist B. F. Skinner was launching the brand of stimulus-response psychology for which he eventually became famous. Skinner's approach is called **radical behaviorism** because it totally rejects the claim that humans possess free will. Instead, Skinner believes that all our actions are shaped and controlled by events in the environment, particularly by rewards and punishments. Once these controlling factors are understood, behavior itself presumably becomes largely predictable. In Skinner's view, it makes no sense to talk of inner drives capable of motivating behavior. The causes of behavior, Skinner contends, lie outside the organism.

Research has shown that the basic premise underlying radical behaviorism is at least partly valid. As we saw in Chapter 5, an organism's behavior can indeed be changed by altering the conditions associated with it. For instance, when a mother praises her child for acting independently, she certainly increases the likelihood that the child will repeat such behavior. Similarly, if a husband showers his wife with concern and affection whenever she acts helpless and frail, he will certainly increase the likelihood that she will act this way in the future. Thus, Skinner suggests that if you want to change behavior, you must eliminate the external rewards inadvertently maintaining it. And his advice has often worked. He and his followers have had success in modifying a wide range of behaviors, including smoking, overeating, alcoholism, stuttering, nail-biting, marital discord, classroom disciplinary problems, even littering in public parks. The use of behavioral techniques to treat neurotic and psychotic disorders will be discussed in detail in Chapter 16.

Although behavioral principles have been widely accepted, few psychologists consider themselves to be strict behaviorists. Skinner's radical form of behaviorism remains quite controversial because of his insistence that the way people act is totally a product of the surrounding circumstances. In his book *Beyond Freedom and Dignity* (1971), Skinner proclaimed that freedom of choice is nothing more than an illusion. External reward and punishment shape the way people act, not some inner motivation. The lifelong thief, in Skinner's view, is just as capable of performing acts of great charity and kindness when the reward structure is right. But Skinner believes that today's society often rewards people for behaving immorally. The slumlord, for example, earns more profit if he lets his property run down than he would if he spent money to maintain it. Skinner argues that if we wish to change this situation we should not try to appeal to the slumlord's inherent goodness—unless, of course, our approval would be a reinforcer for him. Instead, we should arrange for rewards to be associated with slum renovation, perhaps by providing tax incentives. The passage in Figure 13.1, taken from Skinner's novel *Walden Two* (1948), suggests how such behavioral principles might be used to create a "utopian" society.

The idea of controlling people with systematic rewards and punishments is a frightening concept to many people, reminiscent of Aldous Huxley's *Brave New World* (1932). Who would decide what values would be imposed in such a society? Other of Skinner's critics seriously doubt whether such total manipulation of human behavior would ever really be possible. As you will see later in this chapter, some prominent personality theorists strongly endorse the notion that human beings are not at the mercy of external forces—that they are self-directed and free.

Social learning theory

As we have just seen, Skinner's radical behaviorism answers the question "Why do people behave as they do?" by focusing exclusively on how events in the environment shape and control responses. What goes on *inside* the organism is not important to Skinner. This does not mean that Skinner denies that subjective thoughts, feelings, and perceptions exist. He simply believes that cognitive processes are incidental to learning and behavior. Not all psychologists agree with him, however. In recent years many researchers have begun to argue that cognition does in fact play a key role in determining how we act. They believe that people's actions are responses to external stimuli, but they see those stimuli as mentally interpreted in light of existing memories, beliefs, and expectations before they are acted on. Differences in such mental processing can help explain why people can behave so differently in the same external situation.

Consistent with this emphasis on cognition is the view that people do not need to have new behaviors gradually "stamped in" through repeated reinforcement, as strict behaviorism suggests. Remember from Chapter 5 that the way Skinner and his followers get an animal to emit a novel response is through

"After all, it's a simple and sensible program. . . . We set up a system of gradually increasing annoyances and frustrations against a background of complete serenity. An easy environment is made more and more difficult as the children acquire the capacity to adjust."

"But why? . . . What do [the children] get out of it?"

"What do they get out of it! . . . what they get is escape from the petty emotions which eat the heart out of the unprepared. They get the satisfaction of pleasant and profitable social relations . . . . They get new horizons, for they are spared the emotions characteristic of frustration and failure."

Figure 13.1 Can destructive or antisocial emotions be eliminated, or will such emotions always haunt us? In this dialogue from *Walden Two*, B. F. Skinner's novel about a utopian society, traits and emotions are seen not as inherent biological qualities or essences, but as learned and therefore *controllable* or *extinguishable* behaviors. Through principles of operant conditioning and reinforcement, Skinner argues, we can engineer a perfect society. Do you agree? (Skinner, 1948.)

shaping—that is, through systematically rewarding the animal for successive approximations of the desired action. But imagine how grossly inefficient learning would be if all our acquisition of new skills proceeded in this laborious fashion. Imagine, for instance, trying to teach children to swim or teenagers to drive simply by waiting for them to stumble on a partially correct response, which could then be promptly rewarded. As psychologist Albert Bandura (1966) has pointed out, few people would survive socialization if this were our sole training method. Clearly, we often accelerate the learning process by providing models of the appropriate response. In fact, some kinds of learning would probably be impossible in the absence of modeling. "It is highly doubtful," Bandura writes, "that an experimenter could get a mynah bird to sing a chorus of 'Sweet Adeline' during his lifetime by differential reinforcement of the bird's squeaks and squawks" (Bandura, 1966). In contrast, using modeling procedures opens up whole new possibilities. Bandura reports that a gifted mynah bird appearing on television sang a very credible rendition of this sentimental ballad. The secret of the bird's success? Mimicking the voice of its dedicated trainer, of course. Because such learning involves conscious observation and imitation of others' behavior, it has become a keystone of what is called **social learning theory**. Not surprisingly, social learning theorists focus primarily on observational learning and its effects on personality among human beings.

It is not that social learning theorists deny the importance of reward and punishment in influencing how people act. They decidedly do not. But they feel that reinforcement is more important in getting a person to perform some response than it is in getting him or her to learn that response in the first place. For instance, a little girl may learn the basic technique of hitting a tennis ball by watching her older sister play. But she will probably be more inclined to start swinging a racket herself if she observes that her sister is heartily praised for her performance on the court and so anticipates a similar reward herself. In short, reinforcement often strengthens and maintains responses that have already been learned. But it is through modeling that most human learning occurs.

Social learning theorists argue that learning through imitation is more widespread than most people realize. Every parent knows that children frequently imitate the behavior of others, especially of those they admire or respect. But observational learning, according to social learning theorists, goes far beyond these overt actions. Consider what is being learned through modeling in the following incident:

Jim, age five, found a dead rat, picked it up by the tail, and brought it over to Rita, also age five, waving it in front of her, and evidently hoping to frighten her. Rita showed interest in the rat and wanted to touch it, much to Jim's apparent disappointment. He then took the rat to Dorothy, age seven, who reacted with apparent disgust and fear and ran away from Jim and toward Rita, screaming. When Jim pursued Dorothy, Rita also ran away from Jim and the rat and began to scream. Later, when Jim showed up with his rat, Rita ran and showed fear even though Dorothy was not around any more (Corsini, 1979, pp. 422-423).

Note that Rita has not only learned an overt act—running and screaming at the sight of a dead rat—through her observation of Dorothy, but she has also learned a strong emotion (fear of dead animals) and a number of related cognitions (dead animals are dirty, disgusting, and so forth). Psychologists have even demonstrated that people can learn highly abstract principles simply by watching people perform behaviors that embody those principles. As we saw in Chapter 9, young children can acquire abstract grammatical rules just by listening to adult models using those rules correctly (K. E. Nelson, 1977).

Learning by imitation plays an important role in the development of personality. In Chapter 18 we will discuss Bandura's studies of how very young children learn aggression through observation. He has found that youngsters are much more likely to behave aggressively if they see adult models doing so. And in Chapter 16 we will discuss how modeling procedures have been used therapeutically to help people overcome a variety of maladaptive traits, from snake phobias to acute shyness. The important thing to remember here is that people often learn how to act by following the models available to them.

TRAIT THEORIES

At the beginning of this chapter, we mentioned some of the enduring personal qualities that make people different from one another: shyness, gregariousness, calmness, excitability, and so on. Psychologists call any "relatively enduring way in which one individual differs from another" a **trait** (Guilford, 1959). Trait theorists are not so much interested in single behaviors as they are in the patterns of behavior that, taken together, add up to dominance, self-sufficiency, generosity, or any other trait capable of being measured. More than any other personality theorists, trait theorists emphasize and try to explain the *consistency* of human behavior. They believe that the traits a person possesses are part of that person's psychological makeup—the result of either inheritance or learning. As such, these traits predispose the person to act in characteristic ways across many different situations.

Trait theorists assume that most traits are not qualities that a person either has or does not have. Instead, traits are dimensions of personality along which any person can be assessed. In other words, everyone can be classified as more or less dependent, more or less friendly, more or less timid, or whatever. In addition, most (but not all) trait theorists believe that there are a few basic traits that can explain other, more superficial traits. The basic trait of self-confidence, for example, might explain other traits such as friendliness, independence, and adventurousness. Psychologists who take this approach try to identify the few crucial traits that seem to be the keys to all others.

The trait approach to personality presents an interesting contrast with the Freudian approach. Freud recognized that different people have different traits, but his main concern was to explain those traits in terms of his theory. (Stinginess, for example, was to Freud a displaced form of anal retentiveness, the infant's pleasure in retaining feces.) Trait theorists, in contrast, do not start by seeking the origins of stinginess, as Freud did. Instead, they try to determine whether a person's degree of stinginess is in fact a consistent quality. That is, they try to find out whether people who are extremely stingy in one kind of situation are also extremely stingy in others. Then they might ask whether stinginess is a sign of a more basic trait—for example, possessiveness. Is the stingy person also very possessive in relationships? Thus, an important question for trait theorists is: Which behaviors seem to go together? Which, in other words, are correlated?

Essentially, then, trait theory is more a descriptive approach to personality than an explanatory one. When people try to use traits to *explain* behavior, their reasoning often becomes circular. Why does Frank get so little done? Because he is lazy. How do you know he is lazy? Because he gets so little done. Some trait theorists, however, have attempted to go beyond description and propose underlying causes of traits. We will say more about this later.

Allport's classification of traits

Gordon W. Allport was a leading trait theorist for almost forty years, during which time he continually developed and refined his ideas (Allport, 1937, 1961, 1966). Allport believed that personality traits have a very real existence: They are somehow embedded in the structure of each individual's nervous system. If a woman has a trait of aggressiveness, for example, her nervous system is organized in such a way that she is likely to interpret many circumstances as calling for aggressive behavior. Thus, in Allport's view traits can easily account for the broad consistency of a person's reactions, even to situations that on the surface appear quite different.

One of the first steps Allport took in his investigation of traits was to go through an unabridged dictionary noting all the terms that could be used to describe people (Allport and Odbert, 1936). There turned out to be almost eighteen thousand! Even after omitting words that simply evaluate another person's character (words such as *worthy* or *insignificant*), as well as words that could describe transient states (*joyous* or *flustered*), there were still between four thousand and five thousand items. Surely, Allport thought, an individual personality could be reduced to a much smaller number of traits.

Allport ultimately argued that any given personality could be defined according to three types of traits, which formed a kind of hierarchy. A **cardinal trait** is one that directs a major portion of a person's behavior. Someone consumed by ambition or by greed would be described as dominated by a cardinal trait. Famous historical and mythical figures have given their names to cardinal traits: for example, Machiavellian, narcissistic. Actually, Allport believed that cardinal traits are quite rare. Most people, he felt, do not have one predominant trait but develop a few **central traits** as the result of life experiences. Central traits are characteristic ways of dealing with the world; they can be captured by such adjectives as *honest, loving, gregarious,* and so on. Thus, a person's traits cannot be fully understood by administering personality tests and comparing the responses to group norms. Instead, Allport recommended that people be studied intensively on an individual basis. For example, he might conduct an interview in which people are asked to describe two extremes: the "very best" or "ideal" way of life as well as the "worst possible" way of life they could imagine for themselves. Then they might be asked how their actual life compared with these extremes two, five, and ten years earlier.

Factor analysis: Cattell and Eysenck

More recent trait theorists have relied more heavily than Allport did on comparisons among individuals. And they have tried to do so in very precise and scientific ways. Their primary tool in this task has been a sophisticated mathematical technique called **factor analysis**. Basically, factor analysis is a way of looking for underlying sources of consistency (Helmstadter, 1970). Suppose you examined people's test scores in a number of academic subjects and found that scores in calculus predicted scores in chemistry quite well (although not perfectly, of course), and scores in chemistry were fairly good predictors of scores in physics. You also found that scores in English predicted scores in both Latin and French with a high degree of accuracy. It would not be surprising if you concluded that two underlying factors explain these results: mathematical ability on the one hand, and verbal ability on the other. What you have done is to extract an underlying element that is common to those subjects that have a high degree of intercorrelation. Mathematical ability, in other words, is common to success in calculus, chemistry, and physics; verbal skill is common to success in English, Latin, and French. Factor analysis is a high-powered correlational procedure for identifying just such underlying elements. Figure 13.2 gives an example of how factor analysis might be applied to various behavioral tendencies.

Psychologist Raymond B. Cattell (1965) has used factor analysis extensively to extract the key dimensions of personality. Cattell began by identifying what he calls **surface traits**. These are clusters of behaviors that tend to go together. As such, our language usually categorizes them with a single-word label. Nervousness, for instance, is a surface trait. It involves a variety of related behaviors, like trembling, stammering, forgetting simple things, and so forth. The different surface traits a given person possesses can often be assessed by simple observation. Typically, however, Cattell has measured them by using three data-gathering techniques: self-reports (answering questions like those in Figure 13.2), objective tests, and life records (which include everything from information gleaned from family and friends to school report cards and records of automobile accidents).

Cattell has used surface trait data to isolate what he calls **source traits**, and for this he employs factor analysis. Source traits in Cattell's scheme are the fundamental elements of personality. They underlie all surface traits and give

Figure 13.2 An example of the technique of factor analysis. Imagine that the five items on the left have been presented to a number of different people, and, from the resulting data, correlations between the various items have been computed. These correlations are shown in the matrix on the right. As you can see, they reveal that items 1 and 5, for example, are closely related; people tend to answer these two items in the same way. Items 1 and 2 appear not to be related; the way a person responds to one has little to do with how he or she responds to the other. By rearranging the order of the items in the matrix as shown here, it is possible to see that two distinct and independent personality factors are being measured. Items 1, 3, and 5 seem to have something to do with confidence in working ability, and items 2 and 4 seem to describe sociability.

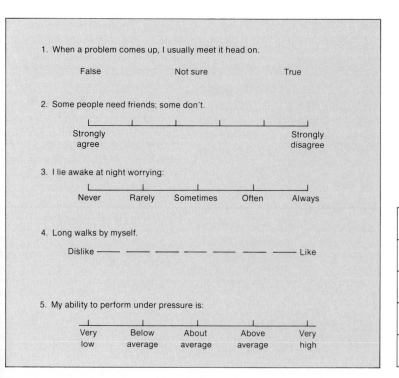

	Problems	Awake at Night	Performance Under Pressure	Need Friends	Long Walks
	1	3	5	2	4
1	—	-.73	.94	-.05	.03
3		—	-.80	.10	.01
5			—	-.06	.03
2				—	-.68
4					—

1. When a problem comes up, I usually meet it head on.

    False   Not sure   True

2. Some people need friends; some don't.

    Strongly   Strongly
    agree   disagree

3. I lie awake at night worrying:

    Never   Rarely   Sometimes   Often   Always

4. Long walks by myself.

    Dislike ———————— Like

5. My ability to perform under pressure is:

    Very   Below   About   Above   Very
    low   average   average   average   high

rise to their expression. For instance, degree of emotional stability is said to be a source trait that influences such surface traits as nervousness, displays of temper, displays of hypochondria, and so forth. Cattell has identified sixteen such source traits and has developed a test of personality that measures the relative strength of each one. A sample personality profile using Cattell's system is shown in Figure 13.3.

But Cattell's scheme is not the only one to use factor analysis. Employing mathematical techniques similar to Cattell's, psychologist Hans Eysenck (1970) has concluded that personality structure can be reduced to two major dimensions. One is neuroticism versus emotional stability, the degree to which people have control over their feelings. The other is extroversion versus introversion, the degree to which people are outgoing, sociable, and excitement-seeking on the one hand versus quiet, reserved, and cautious on the other.

Eysenck believes there is a biological basis for where people fall along these two dimensions. For example, as we saw in Chapter 11, he suggests that people who are extroverted have a naturally low level of arousal in the cortex of the brain. As a result, they seek high levels of external stimulation to raise cortical arousal to an optimum level. In contrast, the introvert already has a naturally high level of cortical arousal and so seeks out situations that minimize external stimulation. Many different observations have supported this basic idea. Introverts, for instance, take longer to fall asleep and are more sensitive to pain than extroverts, suggesting that their brains are somehow more alert. And alcohol, which lowers cortical arousal, makes introverts more extroverted. Conversely, when extroverts take amphetamines, which increase cortical arousal, they become more introverted. Whether Eysenck's theory will ultimately be proved

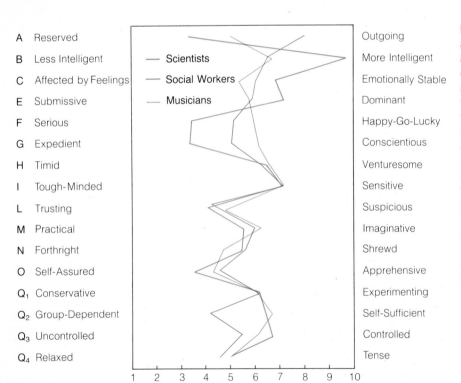

Figure 13.3 The traits listed to the left and the right of the graph are personality factors obtained by factor analysis of many ratings. The traits are paired and describe the ends of the scales that comprise the dimension. Traits A through O were obtained from analyses of ratings of one person by another; factors Q_1 through Q_4 are self-ratings. This graph shows the scores on personality tests composed of these sixteen factors that were administered to different professional groups. The red profile shows the average scores for a group of musicians; the blue shows the average scores for a group of social workers; and the green for a group of scientists (working in all scientific professions).

correct still remains to be seen. Nevertheless, it is an intriguing attempt to provide physiological explanations for what are essentially descriptive traits.

How consistent is behavior?

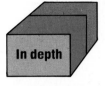

In depth

The trait approach to studying personality makes an important assumption about the nature of human behavior: It assumes that people are relatively consistent in the way they act. Granted, situational pressures can encourage or discourage the expression of any given trait. A boisterous person is certainly more apt to be boisterous at a party than at a funeral, and an aggressive person is more likely to display that aggression on a tennis court than in church. But in general, a person's central traits, according to trait theorists, incline him or her to behave similarly in many different contexts.

This view of relative consistency in human behavior conforms to most people's intuitive perceptions, and a large number of psychologists accepted it for many years. But then, in the late 1960s, social learning theorist Walter Mischel made a very startling assertion in his book *Personality and Assessment* (1968). Reviewing study after study, Mischel showed that there was actually very little correlation among behaviors typically thought of as reflecting the same trait. In one study, for instance, children were given a variety of opportunities to be dishonest, including lying to save face, cheating on a test, and stealing money (Hartshorne and May, 1928). Furthermore, these opportunities were presented in different settings. The researchers found that only rarely did a child's degree of honesty when faced with one temptation in one setting correspond with his or her degree of honesty when faced with another temptation in another setting. In other words, a child might lie to save face when interacting with peers but refuse to steal money that belonged to the experimenter. Similarly, a child might steal money that belonged to a brother or sister but refuse to cheat on a school exam. Many other studies yielded similar results. Mischel also argued that there is often a low correlation between a person's score for a certain trait, as measured by a questionnaire, and that person's behavior in other settings. Usually, for example, people who score high on a scale measuring generosity are only slightly more willing than other people to give money to charity, to donate blood, or to perform other actions typically considered indicative of a generous nature. This means that our ability to predict behavior based on a typical personality questionnaire is almost negligible. If a person's behavior is so variable, Mischel concluded, attempts to measure individual traits may be of little practical value.

If behavior is not very consistent from one situation to the next, why do most of us (including many psychologists) firmly believe that it is? Why are we all convinced that fairly stable personality traits do indeed exist? The answer, Mischel and others have argued, is that the traits a particular person possesses lie as much in the eye of the beholder as they do in the psyche of the beheld. In short, people may be inclined to see great consistency in personality where there in fact is little because of biases in the information available to them and in the way the human mind works.

One common tendency that encourages the perception of consistency in other people's behavior is the so-called primacy effect. This is the inclination to maintain our first impression of a person even if he or she acts quite differently later on. Thus, if your first impression of a particular woman is that she is selfish and cruel, it will be difficult for you to view her otherwise even after you see her perform several acts of kindness. Part of the reason for this tendency may be a strong human inclination to seek consistency in our beliefs and perceptions. As a result, we may simply discount any contradictory information (assume it is a freak aberration), or we may distort what we see to fit our preconceptions. We will say more about this perceptual bias, and how it affects our relations with others, in Chapter 17.

Another reason why we may see more consistency in behavior than actually exists is that we tend to see most people in only one role. Consequently, we may confuse the behavioral role demands with underlying personality traits. For instance, if you see the head librarian only when she is sitting quietly at her desk, you may assume that she is indeed a very reticent person. Similarly, if your only encounter with a handyman is when he hastens to do what you have asked, you may assume that he is by nature submissive. Neither assumption, of course, is valid, for both the librarian and the handyman are simply performing their jobs, which require certain behavioral patterns. In other contexts they may very well behave quite differently. The problem is that you will never have a chance to see them do so.

Ironically, our own behavior may also conspire to produce the appearance of relatively consistent personality traits in others. If you believe that a person is hostile, you may, by subtle cues of speech and body language, elicit the very acts of hostility you expect to see. This fact simply reiterates a point we made in Chapter 9: People often unconsciously create the reactions they see in others. To the extent that our behavior toward another person consistently elicits the same responses, we may attribute to that person very stable traits that in reality are not so stable.

Mischel and others have pointed to a number of other informational and perceptual biases—all supported by experimental data—that could cause us to see behavior as more consistent than it actually is. So persuasive were their arguments at the time they were proposed that many psychologists came to accept them. The view that situations generally exert a far more powerful influence on human behavior than do stable inner dispositions became widely favored. Note that this does not mean that psychologists were adopting the radical behaviorist position that people are totally shaped and molded by forces beyond their control. Mischel's view is a social learning one in which human behavior is always the result of cognitive processing and interpretation. Still, there is little doubt that from Mischel's perspective people are extremely flexible: They frequently bend and modify their behavior according to the conditions of the moment.

Other psychologists, however, viewed Mischel's perspective as a broadside attack on the concept of personality itself. How can personality have any real meaning, they asked, if inner dispositions are so weak? Not surprisingly, a number of researchers soon began to counter Mischel's claims. Daryl Bem and Andrea Allen (1974), although recognizing the validity of much of what Mischel said, cautioned that the concept of traits should not be discarded. Our intuition about the consistency of people's behavior, they argued, is not entirely wrong. Although no one is consistent in all areas of behavior, most people are relatively consistent in at least some areas. To demonstrate this fact, Bem and Allen asked students to rate their own consistency regarding "friendliness" and "conscientiousness." As predicted, those who described themselves as being quite consistent on one or the other of these traits did tend to show a high degree of consistency in behaviors related to that trait. Bem and Allen concluded that most of us do have some traits on which we are relatively consistent, but those traits differ for different people. As a result, when researchers study a large group of randomly selected subjects regarding an arbitrarily chosen trait, the behavior *on average* is bound to appear only slightly consistent.

Studies that support Mischel's view have also been criticized for not observing the subjects in enough situations. How fair is it, this second group of critics asks, for a researcher to give a subject the chance to contribute spare change to a worthy cause and to donate blood to a blood bank and then, if the two responses are dissimilar, conclude that there is little evidence for a stable trait of generosity? Yet this is essentially what some psychologists have done: They have based their conclusions on a very small sample of behaviors. When other researchers have observed behavior across many events, much greater consistency has been found. Epstein (1980) administered the Eysenck scale of extroversion to a group of subjects. These subjects were also asked to keep a daily record of behaviors related to the trait of extroversion (for example, the number of social contacts initiated) for a fourteen-day period. When a subject's extroversion scale was compared with behavior on any one day, the relationship between the two was negligible—just as Mischel had claimed. But when subjects' behavior was averaged over the fourteen-day period, strong and significant correlations emerged between extroversion scores and behavior. Other researchers have produced similar results comparing data over even longer periods of time (Block, 1971; Matas, Arend, and Sroufe, 1978).

When all the research on the consistency of personality is taken together, it is clear that neither traits nor the situation can be ignored. The fact is that inner dispositions and external situations constantly interact. In recent years a number of psychologists have begun to illustrate just how complex the interaction of traits and situations is. People not only respond to situations in light of their predispositions and beliefs, but also may actively seek out certain situations. For example, some people may repeatedly seek out relationships that are safe and in which there is little chance of being rejected. Bowers (1973) has emphasized that by examining the types of situations that people choose for themselves, we can learn a lot about their personalities. In fact, Bowers points out that the typical psychology experiments are inherently limited because they present all subjects with a standard situation. Instead, Bowers recommends studying people in the context of the situations they have created themselves.

Bowers (1977) has also stressed how the behavior of individuals interacting in a given situation is interdependent. He suggests that by behaving in certain ways, people help to shape the situation by provoking particular kinds of responses (Bowers, 1973). A startling example comes from investigation into the causes of child abuse, a problem usually studied by focusing primarily on the parent. Interestingly, it has been found that a sizable minority of battered children have traits that adults find annoying—hyperactivity, constant fussing, a particularly grating cry, and so forth (Gil, 1970). Obviously, this is insufficient reason for a normal adult to beat a child. But when these traits are presented to a parent who is emotionally unstable to begin with, the result can be uncontrolled aggression. The child in turn, because of his or her own disposition, may intensify the original abrasive behavior in response to this abuse. So the parent responds with more abuse, and so on in a monotonous and tragic interplay of traits and situations. Many psychologists believe that much future research in personality is likely to focus on just such interactions between traits and situations.

PHENOMENOLOGICAL APPROACHES

The current emphasis on interaction between situations and traits is not the only negative reaction psychologists have had to the idea that people are controlled by external forces. Around the middle of this century a number of psychologists began to shape a new vision of human personality—new at least in terms of the conceptions of personality that predominated at the time. Although these thinkers differ substantially in the specific theories they propose, all broadly share a similar set of assumptions. First, all stress the individual's unique perception of the world, what is called his or her *phenomenology* (hence the name phenomenological approaches). This stress gives rise to a strong belief that an individual's personality can be understood only by seeing the world through that person's eyes. Second, these psychologists also share a belief in human potential. All say that people are free to become what they want to be, to fulfill themselves, and to carve their own destinies. This view contrasts sharply with psychoanalysis and behaviorism, both of which hold that behavior is largely determined by forces beyond our control. Phenomenological approaches, in fact, were partly a reaction against both these earlier views. Two highly influential thinkers whose ideas are representative of phenomenological perspectives are Carl Rogers and Abraham Maslow.

The self theory of Rogers

Carl Rogers, a clinical psychologist, developed his theory of personality from observations made while practicing psychotherapy. He noticed that his clients (a term he prefers to "patients" because it does not imply illness) repeatedly expressed an organized set of perceptions, feelings, and attitudes about themselves. They made statements like: "I haven't been acting like myself; it doesn't seem like me" or "I don't have any emotional response to situations; I'm worried about myself." Such statements led Rogers to conclude that the *self*—the body of perceptions we think of as "I" or "me"—is a vital part of human experience. Furthermore, most people are engaged in a continuous struggle to become their "real" selves. In short, Rogers believed that the overriding human motivation is a desire to become all that one truly is—to fulfill all one's capabilities and to achieve all one's potential. This lifelong striving Rogers (1970, 1971) referred to as **self-actualization**.

But Rogers also discovered from his clients that self-actualization is often thwarted by an existing self-concept that is narrow and restricting. His clients seemed to have trouble accepting their true feelings and experiences as part of themselves. They seemed to have learned during childhood that in order to obtain the regard of others, they had to feel and act in ways that distorted or submerged what they were really like. In short, they had to deny certain feelings and inclinations in order to be accepted by parents, relatives, or peers.

Rogers explained this denial or distortion of feelings by arguing that almost every child is the victim of *conditional positive regard*. That is, love and praise are withheld until the child conforms to parental or social standards. For instance, if a little boy dislikes rough-and-tumble play, he may be admonished not to be such a "sissy." Or if he enjoys long walks in the woods by himself, he may be cautioned that it is not good to be such a "loner." On the other hand, contact sports and group activities are usually rewarded with smiles and compliments. This initiates a process whereby the child, and later the adult, learns to act and feel in ways that earn approval from others who are important to him or her rather than in ways that may be more intrinsically satisfying. Children incorporate into the self what Rogers calls *conditions of worth*—strong ideas about which thoughts and behaviors will bring positive regard and so are desirable and "good." In contrast, they suppress, distort, or deny those feelings and experiences that will prevent positive regard, even though they are genuine and would be intrinsically satisfying.

Rogers sees two possible outcomes from one's early life experiences. When the conditions of worth a person learns are few and reasonable, the self will usually be flexible enough to allow a wide range of feelings and experiences. Rogers describes such people as *fully functioning*. They are open, undefensive, realistic, creative, self-determining, and have an underlying confidence in themselves. If, however, the conditions of worth are severely restrictive, prohibiting many thoughts and actions in which the person would otherwise engage, self-actualization is blocked. The person is anxious, fearful, defensive, conforming, unrealistic in self-demands, and feels manipulated rather than free.

To help such people find their way back toward self-actualization, Rogers (1951) has developed what he calls **client-centered therapy**. In this approach the therapist's role is not to judge the client. Instead, the therapist tries to see the world from the client's point of view and to mirror whatever feelings he or she expresses. Most important, the therapist offers the client *unconditional positive regard*: The therapist supports the client regardless of what the client says or does. In this warm, sympathetic, and accepting environment, the client is presumably released from the need to defend unrealistic conditions of worth. As a result, he or she can at last confront formerly suppressed feelings and experiences that are part of the true self. Rogers believes that as people become more fully functioning, they "live more intimately with their feelings of pain, but also more vividly with their feelings of ecstasy; anger is more clearly felt, but so also is love; fear is an experience they know more deeply, but so is courage" (Rogers, 1961, p. 195).

It may be asked whether a child who receives unconditional positive regard may not become selfish, cruel, and destructive. After all, it is to prevent this kind of behavior that children are punished and police forces are maintained. Rogers answers that in all his years as a therapist he has seen little evidence that people are endowed with aggressive, destructive instincts, such as those Freud proposed. Instead, he has inferred that human beings naturally seek growth and positive relations with others. Consequently, if raised in a warm and accepting atmosphere—where the need to follow social rules is based on reason, not on fear of loss of love—the child will grow into a happy, productive, self-actualizing adult.

One study conducted by psychologist Stanley Coopersmith (1967) lends some support to this view. Coopersmith scored a large number of children for their degree of self-esteem. Children with high self-esteem were found to be significantly more creative, independent, assertive, flexible, and original in their ideas than those with low self-esteem. In other words, the children with high self-esteem were much closer to Rogers's ideal of the fully functioning, self-actualizing person. What kind of home life was related to the development of these traits? Coopersmith found several important factors. First, the amount of love, interest, and acceptance a child received from the parents was closely related to the development of self-esteem. Children of mothers who were warm, affectionate, and attentive had a more positive image of themselves than did other children. Although the parents of children with high self-esteem could not be called permissive, they were careful not to punish undesired behavior by withholding love, thus making the child feel ashamed and unworthy. In another study of child-rearing practices, however, the support for Rogers's theories has been more mixed (Mussen and Eisenberg, 1977). These researchers found that among parents who follow Rogers's advice in raising their sons and daughters, some produced cooperative children who were concerned with the rights of others, but others produced selfish children. The difference in this case seemed to lie in the kinds of examples the parents set.

Maslow's self-actualized person

Like Carl Rogers, psychologist Abraham Maslow (1908–1970) began with the assumption that people are basically good and that the most important motive in their lives is the drive to achieve self-actualization. A self-actualized person, as defined by Maslow, finds fulfillment in doing the best of which he or she is capable, not in competition with others, but in being "the best me I can be" (1971a, 1971b). Maslow criticized psychoanalysts and behaviorists for their pessimistic, negative, and limited conceptions of human beings. Where is the psychology, he asked, that takes account of gaiety, exuberance, love, and expressive art to the same extent that it deals with misery, conflict, shame, hostility, and habit (1966, 1968)? Accordingly, Maslow deliberately set out to create what he called a "third force" in psychology, one that offers a strong alternative

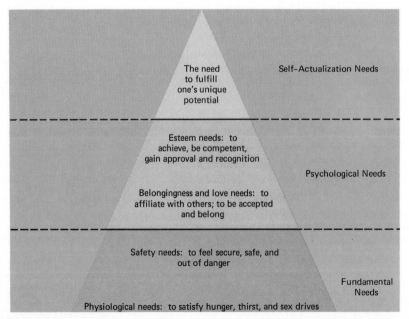

The need to fulfill one's unique potential

Self-Actualization Needs

Esteem needs: to achieve, be competent, gain approval and recognition

Belongingness and love needs: to affiliate with others; to be accepted and belong

Psychological Needs

Safety needs: to feel secure, safe, and out of danger

Fundamental Needs

Physiological needs: to satisfy hunger, thirst, and sex drives

Figure 13.4 This pyramid represents Maslow's hierarchy of needs. According to Maslow, fundamental needs must be satisfied before a person is free to progress to psychological needs, and these in turn must be satisfied before a person can turn to self-actualization needs. More recently, Maslow (1970) has added a need for transcendence that is even higher than the need for self-actualization (after Maslow, 1971).

to psychoanalysis and behaviorism.

One of Maslow's key concepts is what he called the **hierarchy of needs**, illustrated in Figure 13.4. Maslow believed that all humans face a series of needs in life, and that needs at the lower levels must be met before the person can go on to fulfill those at the next highest level. At the bottom of Maslow's hierarchy are the *fundamental needs*: those associated with such physiological requirements as eating and drinking, and those associated with a desire for a safe and a secure environment. Next Maslow identified a set of *psychological needs*. These include both the need to develop a sense of belonging and of being loved and the need to achieve competence, recognition, and positive self-esteem. Finally, once all fundamental and psychological needs are met, a person can begin fulfilling the need for self-actualization—that is, the need to realize his or her unique potential.

Unlike Rogers, Maslow tried to base his theory of personality development on studies of healthy, creative, self-actualizing people who make full use of their talents and capabilities. As such, he analyzed a group of historical figures whom he considered to be self-actualized—among them Abraham Lincoln, Henry David Thoreau, Ludwig von Beethoven, Eleanor Roosevelt, and Albert Einstein—and also some of his own friends (Maslow, 1954). Their distinguishing personality characteristics are listed in Table 13.1. Critics of Maslow have pointed out that some people who are apparently "self-actualized" do not seem to have scaled the hierarchy of needs in the way Maslow said is necessary. Many writers and artists, for example, have created their masterpieces in spite of miserable childhoods, insecurity, personality problems, and poverty. To Maslow, however, these are the exceptions that prove the rule.

Evaluating Maslow and Rogers

As we have noted, both Maslow and Rogers have been criticized. Maslow's list of self-actualized people has been called arbitrary, and his hierarchy of needs impressionistic and unscientific. Rogers's claims about the need for unconditional positive regard have also been disputed. Moreover, the ideas of both

---

TABLE 13.1 Characteristics of Self-Actualized Persons

They are realistically oriented.

They accept themselves, other people, and the natural world for what they are.

They have a great deal of spontaneity.

They are problem-centered rather than self-centered.

They have an air of detachment and a need for privacy.

They are autonomous and independent.

Their appreciation of people and things is fresh rather than stereotyped.

Most of them have had profound mystical or spiritual experiences, although not necessarily religious in character.

They identify with mankind.

Their intimate relationships with a few specially loved people tend to be profound and deeply emotional rather than superficial.

Their values and attitudes are democratic.

They do not confuse means with ends.

Their sense of humor is philosophical rather than hostile.

They have a great fund of creativeness.

They resist conformity to the culture.

They transcend the environment rather than just cope with it.

Source: Abraham Maslow, *Motivation and personality* (New York: Harper & Row, 1954).

these theorists have been labeled vague and difficult to verify by any scientific tests. Rogers, for example, has said that we cannot define what a fully functioning person is in hard and fast terms. Instead, we must always consider the particular client. "Progress and maturity for one person," writes Rogers, "means developing sufficient autonomy to divorce himself from an unsuitable marriage partner; in another it means living more constructively with the partner he has. For one student it means working hard to obtain better grades; for another it means a lessened compulsiveness and a willingness to accept poorer grades" (Rogers, 1963, p. 9). Although this may in fact be true in a clinical context, it renders Rogers's theory of personality too slippery to either prove or disprove.

Nevertheless, Rogers considered himself a scientist, and much of his behavior justifies this view. For instance, Rogers was the first clinical psychologist to carefully record all the communications occurring in therapy sessions in order to make this data available for research and teaching purposes. Both the therapist's and the client's words and actions could then be classified, and the effects of different types of exchanges could be systematically studied. Rogers himself conducted many such investigations. In fact, his very concept of the self, which lies at the heart of his theory, emerged from a thorough and quantitative analysis of the content of therapy interviews. In addition, Rogers's efforts prompted similar research by many other psychologists. In this respect, his data-gathering methods stand in marked contrast to those of Freud (Krasner, 1978).

However one evaluates the specific theories of Maslow and Rogers, there is little doubt that the basic questions they raised were important ones for the study of personality. For example, both theorists attacked the Freudian notion that adaptation to the imperatives of society is necessary for the proper development of personality. From the more humanistic viewpoint of Maslow and Rogers, excessive adaptation produces conforming, unimaginative, inhibited, and unfulfilled people. Although recognizing that some degree of adaptation is clearly necessary, Maslow and Rogers stressed the importance of transcending—going beyond—society's demands. Maturity, both pointed out, must entail a certain willingness to defy social conventions and at times to take risks. Studies of creative people have shown that their lives are often somewhat unconventional. For instance, a study that compared creative architects (so judged by their peers) with randomly selected architects found that the creative group socialized less, cared little for others' opinions, held unconventional beliefs, and had idiosyncratic work habits (MacKinnon, 1962, 1965). Thus, perfect adaptation or "adjustment" may not always be compatible with creative endeavor. Humanists like Maslow and Rogers have done psychology a service in urging us to study such positive aspects of personality.

COMPARING APPROACHES TO PERSONALITY

Throughout this chapter we have discussed a range of personality theorists, often showing how the ideas of one either expanded on the ideas of another or arose in reaction to them. Now it is time to step back and take a broader look at personality theorizing. When we do, we can identify several important themes that tend to cut across different theoretical viewpoints.

One such theme is *conflict*, first introduced to the discipline of psychology by Sigmund Freud. To Freud conflict was inherent in the human psyche. The best we could hope for was an uneasy balance among competing forces. Although not usually as pessimistic as Freud in their views of the inevitability and persistence of conflict, other psychoanalytic thinkers also incorporated the conflict theme into their work. In addition, John Dollard and Neal Miller brought conflict within the framework of learning theory with their study of approach-avoidance tendencies and how people cope with them. Finally, Carl Rogers also introduced a conflict theme when he argued that clashes between a person's true inclinations and the values of others can cause suppression and distortion of reality.

A second recurring theme in personality research is the importance of *external influences* on thought and behavior. You can see this theme in the work of the psychoanalytic thinkers Alfred Adler and Karen Horney, who stressed that the early social environment has a crucial impact on our lives. Rogers also recognized the importance of social influences when he argued that a person's self-concept is partly shaped by the conditions of worth imposed by others. Radical behaviorism takes the view of external forces to an extreme, claiming that what goes on inside a person—fears, hopes, conflicts, ambitions—is not at all important. In response, the social learning theorists have tried to return the "person" to the behaviorist position by stressing our cognitive processing of external stimuli.

Continuity and consistency is a third theme we find in the work of personality theorists. It was certainly emphasized by Freud, who took the extreme view that personality is totally formed by resolution of childhood conflicts and thus is very resistant to change in adulthood. The trait theorists also stress continuity and consistency, hence their efforts to identify and measure relatively enduring dispositions. Unlike Freud, however, most trait theorists believe that personality change over time is possible.

Finally, we come to the theme of *self-fulfillment*. It can be seen in the writings of Adler, who saw life as a kind of striving for self-perfection. The fulfillment theme is most fully developed in the phenomenological approaches of Rogers and Abraham Maslow. Here the striving to realize one's own potential becomes the overriding human motivation.

In summary, then, personality theorists often differ sharply in their viewpoints, sometimes engaging in heated, seemingly irreconcilable debates. Yet a broader look shows that all seem to be touching in different ways on many of the same themes. This is not surprising, for all are investigating the same subjects: those complex animals called human beings. Regardless of how one conceptualizes or explains them, conflict, external influences, continuity, and self-fulfillment are all part of the human condition.

SUMMARY

1. Personality can be defined as a fairly stable set of characteristics and tendencies that determine the individuality of a person's responses to a variety of environmental circumstances.

2. Psychoanalytic approaches to personality stress the importance of childhood experience in shaping adult personality and focus on the role of the unconscious in motivating human actions. Central to all psychoanalytic theories are the concepts of conflict between opposing motives, anxiety over unacceptable motives, and defense mechanisms to prevent anxiety from becoming too great.

3. The founder of the psychoanalytic approach, and the single most important theorist in the field of personality, was Sigmund Freud. As a physician in Vienna at the turn of the century, he developed the treatment known as **psychoanalysis**, during which, through a technique of **free association**, patients are able to bring thoughts and feelings from the unconscious into the conscious and thus gain control over them.

4. Freud originated the concept of the unconscious and considered it the motivating force behind all human behavior. He saw the human psyche as divided into three separate but interacting elements: the **id**, the **ego**, and the **superego**. The unconscious id operates on the **pleasure principle**, seeking the resolution of bodily needs. The ego, whose role is to serve as a mediator between the id and reality, operates according to the **reality principle**. The superego represents the moral standards of society, or "conscience."

5. When the demands of these three conflicting forces cannot be met, we experience **anxiety** and use **defense mechanisms** to try to reduce it. The most basic defense mechanism is **repression**, pushing unacceptable id impulses into the unconscious. Others are **regression, reaction formation, projection, displacement**, and **sublimation**.

6. According to Freud, the child goes through five stages of psychosexual development—the **oral, anal, phallic, latency**, and **genital**—which are characterized by conflicts between the id and society. It is their resolution that shapes the adult personality. A person who fails to resolve one or another of these conflicts may become **fixated**, or locked into a psychological conflict that is expressed symbolically throughout life.

7. Post-Freudian psychoanalysts have tended to give decreased importance to the id and increased importance to the ego, which they see as capable of creativity, planning, and the formation of self-fulfilling goals. They have also come to see personality development as less a result of conflicts over id impulses than as a product of a child's relationships with significant others. Important psychoanalytical theorists besides Freud were his contemporaries Carl Jung and Alfred Adler, both of whom broke with him, and Karen Horney.

8. Psychoanalytic approaches have been criticized for lack of scientific rigor in collecting and analyzing data, for a looseness of theory that makes accurate predictions impossible, and for being culture-bound.

9. By contrast, **behavioral** personality theory focuses on how observable stimuli in the environment can, through learning, produce observable responses. In the 1940s psychologists John Dollard and Neal Miller incorporated Freud's ideas into their **psychodynamic behavior theory**, placing such Freudian concepts as instincts, conflict, and defense mechanisms within a learning framework. At about the same time, psychologist B. F. Skinner developed what is known as **radical behaviorism**, the theory that all our actions are shaped and controlled by events in the environment, particularly by rewards and punishments. In order to change behavior, according to Skinner, you must eliminate the external rewards inadvertently maintaining it.

10. In recent years psychologists have begun to argue that one's responses to external stimuli are influenced not only by the environment but also by cognitive processes—memories, beliefs, and expectations. Moreover, **social learning theorists** believe that we learn not merely by repeated reinforcement but mainly by observing and imitating models. Their research focuses primarily on such observational learning and its effects on personality.

11. Another approach to personality is called **trait theory**. Psychologists define a **trait** as any relatively enduring way in which one individual differs from another, and trait theorists focus on isolating the most crucial traits in order to explain consistency in human behavior. Trait theorist Gordon W. Allport identified a hierarchy of three types of traits—**cardinal traits, central traits**, and **secondary traits**—according to which he argued that any given personality could be defined. More recent trait theorists, including Raymond Cattell and Hans Eysenck, have used the mathematical technique of **factor analysis** to look for fundamental elements of personality and to measure the strength or weakness of these elements in individuals.

12. Psychologists since the late 1960s have tried to determine how much consistency there is in human behavior. Social learning theorist Walter Mischel has asserted that our ability to predict future behavior based on past behavior is almost negligible, because people frequently modify their behavior according to the conditions of the moment. Other psychologists have argued that while no one is inconsistent in all areas of behavior, most people are at least relatively consistent in some areas. Many psychologists would now agree that the interaction of traits and situations makes it impossible to separate one from the other, and that it is the study of this interaction that will prove most fruitful in the future.

13. A final approach to personality is the **phenomenological** perspective, which stresses the individual's unique perception of the world and a belief in human potential. Psychologist Carl Rogers has evolved a theory of the self according to which each person is engaged in a lifelong striving for **self-actualization**—the process of achieving one's potential. Psychologist Abraham Maslow also believed in the self-actualized person, and he postulated that one must fulfill a **hierarchy of needs** before reaching the goal of realizing one's own unique potential. One important donation of Rogers and Maslow to personality theory was their stress on the importance of transcending society's demands, as well as adapting to them.

14. While personality theorists take many approaches to their study, all have in common a concern with four basic themes: conflict, external influences, continuity and consistency, and self-fulfillment.

Suggested readings

Allport, G. W. *Pattern and growth in personality*. New York: Holt, Rinehart and Winston, 1961.

Bandura, A. L. *Social learning theory*. Englewood Cliffs, N.J.: Prentice-Hall, 1977.

Goble, F. *The third force: The psychology of Abraham Maslow*. New York: Pocket Books, 1970.

Hall, C. S., and Lindzey, G. *Theories of personality* (3rd ed.). New York: Wiley, 1978.

Lundin, R. W. *Personality: A behavioral analysis* (2nd ed.). New York: Macmillan, 1974.

Maddi, S. R. (Ed.). *Personality theories: A comparative analysis* (3rd ed.). Homewood, Ill.: Dorsey, 1976.

Maddi, S. R., and Costa, P. *Humanism in personology*. Chicago: Aldine, 1972.

Magnusson, D., and Endler, N. (Eds.). *Personality at the crossroads: Current issues in interactional psychology*. New York: Halsted Press, 1977.

Mischel, W. *Introduction to personality* (2nd ed.). New York: Holt, Rinehart and Winston, 1976.

Monte, C. F. *Beneath the mask: An introduction to theories of personality*. New York: Praeger, 1977.

Wollheim, R. *Sigmund Freud*. New York: Viking, 1971.

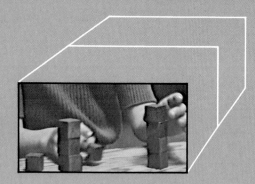

PREVIEW

1. Reliability and validity characterize a good test. Reliability requires that a test yield the same results again and again, given the same conditions. Validity requires that it measure what it is supposed to measure.

2. Intelligence tests, used in groups and individually, attempt to measure general intellectual potential. Much public concern stems from their use, especially over the issue of racial differences in IQ.

3. Intelligence is probably determined by both hereditary and environmental factors.

4. Personality tests attempt to measure one's individual characteristics. Interest tests serve to clarify one's interests, which is helpful when one needs to make choices about the future.

5. The usefulness of a test depends on its being used for its intended purpose. Misuse and misinterpretation of tests can be harmful and should be prevented.

14 Assessment and individual differences

In the spring of 1975 the Department of Mathematics of Johns Hopkins University conducted a talent contest; eleventh-grade math teachers in the area were invited to nominate the most promising students in their classes. On hearing of the contest, Julian C. Stanley, director of the Study of Mathematically Precocious Youth at Johns Hopkins, requested and received permission to nominate ten students. He needed special permission since his was a special situation—the candidates he had in mind were not in any of his classes; he was not, in any case, an eleventh-grade math teacher. In fact, some of the students had not even been nominated by their own math teachers. His connection with these students was that two or three years earlier, when they were thirteen-year-old eighth-graders, he had administered to them the mathematical part of the College Entrance Examination Board's Scholastic Aptitude Test (SAT-M).

The results of the talent contest—which consisted of testing by the university math department—were astounding.

Among the fifty-one persons who entered the contest, the ten chosen by SAT-M ranked 1, 2, 3, 5.5 [that is, tied for fifth place], 7, 8, 12, 16.5, 19, and 23.5. Points earned by the top three were 140, 112, and 91. The highest-scoring person nominated only by a teacher scored 83. Just three of ten (ranks 2, 5.5, and 19) had also been nominated by their teacher (Stanley, 1976, p. 313).

In other words, teachers, even after almost the whole school year had passed, were less able to predict which of their students would do well on a math test than a standardized objective test of mathematical aptitude given several years earlier.

This example is certainly a striking one. But before we conclude that tests possess some extraordinary powers—powers far beyond those of the usual eleventh-grade math teacher—let us ponder the results. SAT-M did accurately identify those students who would do well in a talent contest—but the "contest" was another test. Some critics of testing argue that the talent identified by tests like SAT-M is the talent to take mathematics tests. Although most people would agree that something more than that is involved, it has not always been easy to identify the "something more."

In this chapter we will examine tests such as SAT-M, or what are known as aptitude tests. We will also consider intelligence tests, those closely related tests that presume to measure our mental ability precisely enough to reduce it to a number, the Intelligence Quotient, or IQ, and evaluate in depth the arguments that have been raised both for and against IQ testing. Finally, we will consider tests that assess personality and tests used in vocational counseling and selection.

As we examine each category of test, we should keep in mind the rationale for their existence. Tests of one kind or another have existed through much of human history (in fact, the ancient Chinese administered civil-service tests) and have often proved useful. They can tell us—and our teachers—whether we have mastered a body of material. They can tell school administrators whether the students in their schools are progressing as well as those in other systems. They can help diagnose a specific problem—for example, identify a "problem child" who is so far ahead of the rest of the class that he or she misbehaves to relieve the boredom. A proper test can also help a teacher devise an appropriate instructional plan for such a child, or for any child who is having problems in school. And finally, tests can help select those individuals—as the SAT-M did—whose superior academic abilities warrant special attention.

For every one of these positive functions of tests, however, there are also negative features. When some people are selected, others are rejected. When some people are diagnosed, they may be stigmatized. Testing inevitably reveals inequalities of ability and achievement, and for this reason it is likely to remain extremely controversial in our society. Tests are unlikely to disappear, however; it is vital for us to be able to recognize their valuable uses, while constantly keeping in mind their potential for misuse.

REQUIREMENTS OF A TEST

In essence, a psychological test is an objective, standardized measure of a sample of a person's behavior. The value of a test depends on the extent to which it serves as an indicator of some significant area of behavior. For example, a job applicant may be asked to work a series of mechanical puzzles as a test of problem-solving ability on the job. The applicant's score on these puzzles, in and of itself, is not of much interest or importance. But if it is possible to demonstrate that there is a close correspondence between the applicant's score and subsequent job performance, then the test is serving as an indicator of an important aspect of behavior.

Suppose a child gets a score of 88 on a test of general intelligence. How good is this test? Is it good enough to justify assigning the student to a "slow" track in school? In order to answer these questions, we would have to obtain information about the **reliability** and the **validity** of the test in question. We would also want information about whether the test had been **standardized**—that is, whether norms have been developed indicating how other students have performed. These three concepts—reliability, validity, and standardization—are discussed in detail in the following sections.

Reliability

An assessment technique or a test is reliable if it consistently yields the same results. If a child received a score of 115 on an intelligence test administered on Monday and a score of 88 on one administered on Tuesday, we would have cause for concern about the test's reliability. The top portion of Figure 14.1 shows a pattern of scores for a highly reliable test, while the bottom portion shows a pattern of scores for an unreliable test.

Before a test or an assessment technique is adopted it is important for the developers of the test to demonstrate its reliability. Several kinds of reliability might be assessed. One is test-retest reliability, which can be determined by administering the same test to the same person on more than one occasion. If a child takes the same intelligence test on two consecutive days, we would expect the scores to be similar if the test is reliable. If test-retest reliability is high, we gain confidence that the test scores are not highly susceptible to fluctuating conditions of the subject (such as fatigue or nervousness), or to the testing environment.

One problem with test-retest reliability is that even though a given person's retest yields a score highly similar to the score on the original test, this similarity does not necessarily mean that the test is reliable. If the interval between tests is fairly short, the student may simply recall many of his or her former answers; the test may thus appear more reliable than it really is. For this reason, psychologists have devised other methods to assess reliability. One such method is the use of alternative forms of a test. Ideally, the tests should include different items, but otherwise be comparable in length, difficulty, and so on. A person can be tested with one form on one occasion and with a comparable form on the second occasion. For example, suppose we are interested in the effects of a new orientation program on the self-esteem of college freshmen. Alternative forms of a self-esteem test, assuming that the test is reliable, can be used to assess the impact of our program. Subjects can be given one form of the test prior to and a second form after the orientation.

It takes a great deal of effort and pilot testing to create alternative forms of a test that are truly equivalent. For this reason, alternative forms have not been developed for many assessment procedures. Another problem with alternative forms, as well as with test-retest reliability, is that it is not always possible to administer a second test. Suppose we are interested in assessing the emotional reactions of hospitalized patients prior to surgery—by administering a mood scale with twenty items on anger, twenty on depression, and twenty on anxiety—and correlating the reactions with later recovery. Hospital personnel may insist that patients be interviewed only once prior to surgery. A type of reliability that can be calculated in this setting is called *split-half reliability*. The items

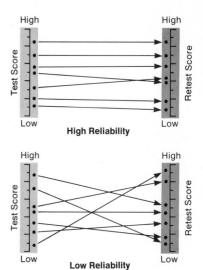

Figure 14.1 The concept of test reliability. On the left in each diagram the test scores obtained by seven individuals are ordered on a scale. On the right the corresponding scores on a second version of the same test, or on the same test given at a later time, are ordered. In the upper diagram the two sets of scores correspond very closely. This pattern of scores means that the test is highly reliable. In the lower diagram, there is little relationship between the two sets of scores. This scrambled pattern means that the test has a low reliability: Two different administrations of the same test gave quite different results.

making up a particular scale (for example, that of anger) can be randomly divided in half, and the subject's score on one set of items can be related to his or her score on the second set. This measure of reliability is sometimes called *internal consistency*. A test is internally consistent if a given subject responds in the same way to items that are supposed to be measuring the same thing. Of course, many tests are designed to measure more than one thing. If the SAT were internally consistent, we would expect a subject's verbal score on half of the items to be similar to his or her score on the other half. We would *not* expect the score on the verbal items to be highly similar to the score on the math items, since the two parts of the SAT are designed to measure different abilities.

As we will see in the sections that follow, some assessment techniques are completed by the subject and are objectively scored, while in others, the subject's behavior or test responses are interpreted by other people. For example, on the assessment tool called the Rorschach, subjects are required to comment on a series of inkblots, and trained clinicians interpret the subject's responses. In tests that involve judgments of this type, *interjudge reliability* is important. We would want to have evidence that two people who had been trained in interpreting the Rorschach would independently make similar judgments if asked to interpret the same responses.

While it is important for an investigator to demonstrate that a test is reliable, the type of reliability that is most appropriate depends on the type of test and on the stability of the trait or attribute being measured. If we are measuring intelligence, for example, we would expect this construct to remain stable over time, and so could examine test-retest reliability or alternative forms reliability. But if we are interested in assessing mood, test-retest reliability would not be very informative because we would expect mood to fluctuate over time. Thus, we might use a split-half technique in assessing the reliability of a mood scale.

Validity

The reliability of a test merely assures us that we have established a consistently accurate procedure for measuring. Now we must establish the *meaning* of these measurements: Are they indeed valid indicators of what we are measuring? There are several kinds of validity, each of which is discussed below.

Suppose you see that a course on solar energy is being offered at your university, and you decide to enroll. But when you attempt to register, you learn that the instructor has decided to limit the course to people who understand basic physics. Therefore, you are asked to complete a short physics test. In order for this test to serve the purpose for which the instructor intends, it must have *content validity*—it must cover a representative sample of the material that is taught in elementary physics. Developers of tests commonly used in educational settings, such as achievement tests, usually determine content validity by consulting with experts in the field covered by the test to ensure that the test items are representative of the content of the field.

Content validity is very important for some tests—particularly those employed in educational settings. But it is not a particularly appropriate criterion for other kinds of tests, such as aptitude tests or personality tests. Over the years, it has been established that a test can sometimes be a valid predictor of

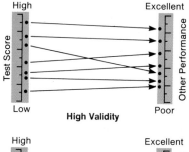

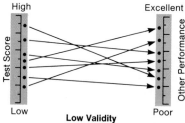

Figure 14.2 The concept of test validity. A comparison of this figure with Figure 14.1 shows that reliability and validity are assessed in exactly the same way. The difference is that while assessment of reliability requires that a test be checked against itself, assessment of validity requires that the test scores be compared with some other measure of behavior.

performance or personality even if the items do not seem to be closely related to the ability or trait being measured. For this reason, a type of validity called *criterion-related validity* is usually employed to evaluate these kinds of tests. Criterion validity refers to the relationship between a person's test score and some outside criterion—that is, an independent measure of the construct that the test is designed to tap. For example, we may validate a paper-and-pencil test of depression by comparing the scores with the judgments of trained clinicians. Or we may validate a written test of job performance by comparing the responses with *actual* job performance.

As the above examples illustrate, two kinds of criteria can be used to validate a test. If a test has been validated by demonstrating a relationship with scores that are available at the same time, it is said to have *concurrent validity*. For example, a brief paper-and-pencil test of depression would have concurrent validity if scores on the test correlate highly with other available measures of depression, such as the judgments of trained clinicians. But if other criteria are available, why develop such a test? One reason is that a short paper-and-pencil test is convenient and economical. If administrators in mental health facilities have such a test available, they can save hours of valuable staff time. Second, once a test has been validated, it can be used in settings where alternative criteria are *not* available. A researcher may want to study people who are depressed, for example, but may lack the resources to have each person interviewed by one or more clinicians.

In some cases, an investigator is not so much interested in a person's *current* standing on a certain trait or ability as in predicting his or her future standing. What type of students are likely to be successful in a given college program? Which job applicants are likely to make an important contribution in the company's future? A test is said to have *predictive validity* if a relationship has been demonstrated between test scores and criteria that become available in the future. It takes many years of research to demonstrate predictive validity, but this type of validity is extremely useful, especially on tests used in the selection of personnel. And once the predictive validity of a test has been established, it can be used in other similar settings. The distributors of the SAT, for example, claim that their tests have predictive validity since they predict subsequent grades in college.

Of course, it is important to select criteria very carefully in order to establish this type of validity. If SAT scores predict grades in college, but grades in college show little relationship to subsequent success, then there will be strong grounds for criticizing the validity of the test. As we will see below, just this criticism has been raised against the developers of the SAT.

Psychological tests have been developed for many purposes, ranging from job prediction to personality assessment. In many cases, the traits being assessed are hypothetical *constructs*, such as anxiety, introversion, or neuroticism, for which there is no single, clear, objective criterion available. Anxiety is a construct that plays an important role in many theories. In developing a scale to measure anxiety, the investigators would draw from these theories in an effort to produce a series of concrete items to reflect anxiety. For example, one item may involve becoming emotionally aroused during exams; another may involve feeling tense in new situations. If the test has *construct validity*, we would expect all the subjects to show a similar response to all the items thought to represent a given construct. We would also expect that subjects' responses to items thought to measure anxiety were different from their responses to items thought to represent other constructs, such as depression.

Standardization

It is important in evaluating the usefulness of a test to determine whether the test has been standardized. One important step in standardization concerns the development of procedures by which the test is administered and scored. Suppose one group of students took the SAT tests under an administrator who permitted questions during the test, while another group took the test under an administrator who did not permit questions. It would be unfair to compare the scores of students tested under such disparate conditions. To avoid such problems, the test constructor usually provides detailed directions for administering a particular test, including information about time limits, oral instructions, and ways of handling questions from subjects.

A second important step in the standardization of a test is the development of norms. Suppose a nineteen-year-old student scores 90 on an intelligence test. This fact alone is not particularly informative. To interpret this score, we have to know the range of scores obtained on that test. Testers develop such normative distributions, or **norms**, before a test is put into general use by giving it to a large **standardization group**. The arithmetical average of the standardization group's score is used as a reference to interpret other scores. Since it is important to ensure that the standardization group is representative of the population that will be tested, many tests are developed with norms appropriate for people of different ages, races, and social classes.

THE MEASUREMENT OF MENTAL ABILITY

The most frequently administered test measuring mental characteristics is the intelligence test. Alfred Binet (1857–1911), a gifted and versatile French psychologist, was the first to develop a reliable test of intelligence. Binet's research on the measurement of children's intelligence, the work for which he is best known today, came at the end of a career that included degrees in law and medicine and the publication of plays, psychological treatises, and books on hypnotism, zoology, and chess (Miller, 1962). Binet's work is particularly significant because of its departure from earlier methods of measuring intelligence. Before Binet, psychologists tested people's ability to estimate the passage of time, the efficiency of their hand–eye coordination, their speed of finger tapping, and their memory. Near the end of the nineteenth century Binet began testing children's vocabulary, their recognition of familiar objects, their understanding of commands, and the like; he was trying to determine which abilities changed with age. Binet reasoned that if older children did better on the tests than younger children, then children who performed better than others of their own age must be mentally older—more intelligent—than their agemates.

In 1905 the Minister of Public Instruction for the Paris schools asked Binet to develop a test that could identify mentally defective children, who could then be taught separately. In collaboration with Theodore Simon, a psychiatrist, Binet devised a thirty-item test, arranging the items or tasks in order of increasing difficulty. Binet originally defined as retarded those children whose scores were two years or more below the average scores for children of their chronological age. One problem with this definition was that children aged fourteen who were two years behind their age group were considered to be as retarded as children of six who were also two years behind their age group. A German psychologist, William Stern (1914), suggested that instead of using the *difference* between mental age (defined as the average age of children who obtain a particular score on an intelligence test) and chronological age, examiners should use the *ratio* of mental age to chronological age. His idea resulted in the **intelligence quotient (IQ)**, which is computed by dividing mental age by chronological age and multiplying by 100 (to get rid of the decimals). For example, if a child has a mental age of 12 and a chronological age of 16, his or her IQ would be $^{12}/_{16} \times 100$, or 75.

There are many ways of measuring intelligence. Some tests are designed to be administered to individuals, others to groups. Still other tests measure aptitude or achievement rather than IQ. There has been considerable debate about whether IQ tests should be regarded as measures of intelligence. In the sections that follow, we will consider examples of the various kinds of tests that have been developed, as well as the controversy that has arisen over the use of these tests.

Individual intelligence tests

Individual intelligence tests are administered by one examiner to one subject. Two individual intelligence tests in wide use today are the current version of Binet's test and the intelligence scales developed by David Wechsler.

The Stanford-Binet test Binet's test of intelligence has been revised many times since he developed it. The Stanford University revision was developed under the direction of Lewis Terman and is known as the **Stanford-Binet test** (Terman, 1916). This test is widely employed in the United States today. It contains a number of subtests—some of verbal ability and some of performance—that are grouped by age. Performance subtests include such activities as picture completion, block design, picture arrangement, and object assembly (Figure 14.3). They are arranged in an order designed to hold the interest of the person being tested. To ensure that the scores do not reflect factors other than ability, the examiner is trained to carry out the standardized instructions exactly, but at the same time to try to put the subject at ease and keep him or her motivated.

The examiner first asks the subject some questions—often from the vocabulary test—to locate the proper level at which to start. For example, if a nine-year-old who seems reasonably bright is being tested, the examiner will probably begin with the tests for an eight-year-old. If the child misses some of the questions, the examiner drops back to tests for year seven. After locating the basal age—the highest age at which the child can pass all items—the examiner proceeds with tests at later year levels. When the child reaches the level at which he or she can pass no items, the testing session ends.

In the final scoring, the mental age indicates the level of development the child has reached. For example, if it has been determined that most twelve-year-olds can pass a given item, this item is placed in the test at the twelve-

Figure 14.3 Two tests on the Stanford-Binet Intelligence Scale being administered to a little boy. Both are ones that he would easily pass unless he were severely retarded. (Above) The examiner has built a tower of four blocks and has told the child, "You make one like this." The average two-year-old is able to build the tower. Three-year-olds are asked to copy a three-block bridge. (Below) The examiner shows the child the card with six small objects attached to it and says, "See all these things? Show me the dog," and so on. The average two-year-old can point to the correct objects as they are named.

year-old level. If a child passes all items at this level, he or she is said to have a mental age of 12. If the child's chronological age is also twelve, the IQ is 100. If the chronological age of the child is lower (for example, ten), his or her IQ is higher than 100 (120 in this case). If the chronological age is more than twelve (for example, fifteen), his or her IQ is lower than 100 (80 in this case). The IQ indicates how that level of development compares with the level reached by other children of the same chronological age. In addition, the examiner generally picks up a good deal of qualitative information about how the child's mind works, information that can be useful to teachers or psychotherapists who work with the child. The original Binet tests were designed for school-age children, but successive revisions of the Stanford-Binet tests have extended the scale to both preschool and adult levels.

In the 1960 revision the method of reporting scores was changed. A person's score is no longer expressed as the quotient of mental age to chronological age. Instead, it is the standard score that he or she would be assigned in the appropriate norm group, with a mean of 100 and a standard deviation of 15. These are still called IQ scores, but they are more accurately called "deviation IQs" because they show how far a person's score deviates from the mean of the appropriate norm group (Terman and Merrill, 1973).

The WAIS and the WISC The other most frequently used individual intelligence tests are the **Wechsler Adult Intelligence Scale (WAIS)** and the **Wechsler Intelligence Scale for Children (WISC)** (Wechsler, 1955, 1958). Like the Stanford-Binet, these tests are made up of both verbal and performance subtests.

The Wechsler tests differ from the Stanford-Binet in several ways. For one thing, the Wechsler tests have more performance tasks and are therefore less biased toward verbal skills. For another, the Wechsler tests do not have different items for different ages; the WISC items (similar to those shown in Figure

Figure 14.4 Items like these make up the performance subtests of the Wechsler Intelligence Scale for Children. Picture arrangement requires that the panels be properly sequenced; picture completion requires that the missing detail be supplied. Object assembly, like putting together a jigsaw puzzle, requires the construction of a whole object from its pieces. Coding requires the proper matching of digit and symbol when only the digit is given. In all these tasks—especially the coding—speed and accuracy are at a premium. It should be noted that maximum performance on these subtests does require familiarity with the general objects and situations depicted, and this familiarity is highly influenced by such factors as cultural, educational, and socioeconomic background.

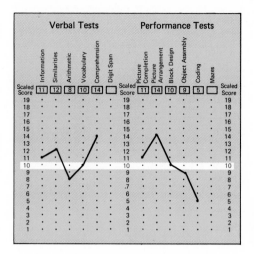

Figure 14.5 A simplified version of a WISC profile for a thirteen-year-old male. (The optional digit span and mazes subscales were not administered.) Scores from each of the subscales within the verbal and performance groupings are first converted into special scaled scores and plotted accordingly on the chart. Then individual subtest scores are added together, yielding a total verbal and a total performance score. In turn, these scores are summed to reflect the full-scale score. Finally, the full-scale score is converted into the full-scale IQ score—in this case 103, or about average. The separability of scores on the subscales is sometimes useful in determining specific talents or deficits that might not have been apparent if only the overall IQ score were reported (adapted from WISC-R record form, © 1971, 1974, The Psychological Corporation).

	Scaled Score	IQ
Verbal Score	55	106
Performance Score	49	98
Full Scale Score	104	103

14.4) are the same for children of all ages, and the WAIS items are the same for all adults. Finally, there is one major overall difference between the two tests: The Stanford-Binet yields a single IQ score; the Wechsler tests give separate scores for each subtest—vocabulary, information, arithmetic, picture arrangement, block design, and so on. The subtest scores are in turn combined into separate IQ scores for verbal and performance abilities. This method of scoring helps the examiner make a qualitative sketch of how an individual reacts to different kinds of items. Most important, it encourages the treatment of intelligence as a number of different abilities rather than as one generalized ability. For an example of this method of scoring, see Figure 14.5.

Group tests

Group tests are strictly paper-and-pencil measures; there is no person-to-person interchange, as with individual tests. The convenience and economy of group tests have led to their use in schools, employment offices, and many other mass testing situations. One of the primary purposes of group tests is to screen or classify large numbers of people. The Army Alpha and Army Beta tests, for example, were developed and used during World War I to classify soldiers. Group tests greatly simplify the role of the examiner. Despite their economy, group tests have disadvantages. It is usually difficult for the examiner to establish rapport or to maintain the interest of the people being tested. The examiner is also unlikely to detect illness, fatigue, anxiety, or other factors that may interfere with test performance. In short, group tests provide little opportunity for the examiner to identify the causes of very good or very poor performance. So most experts recommend that "when important decisions about individuals are to be made, it is desirable to supplement group tests either with individual examination of doubtful cases, or with additional information from other sources" (Anastasi, 1976, p. 302).

The Scholastic Aptitude Test Group tests have been developed to measure intelligence as well as other specific abilities. One group test that almost all college students have taken is the College Entrance Board's **Scholastic Aptitude Test**, which measures abilities that are similar to those frequently included on

IQ tests. This test, designed to measure "aptitude for college studies," is used primarily for the admission, placement, and counseling of college students. It is a direct descendant of the Army Alpha test; it was first administered in 1926 and has since been meticulously revised and updated. Currently it yields two scores, SAT-V for verbal aptitude and SAT-M for mathematical aptitude. The reliability of both scores is very high: .89 for SAT-V and .88 for SAT-M (Wallace, 1972)—quite close to a perfect correlation, which, as we saw in Chapter 2, would be 1.00. The validity for predicting college grades is .39 for SAT-V and .33 for SAT-M. High school records, which show a validity of .55, are more valid than the two SAT scores as a predictor of college grades. But when all three measures are combined into one index, the correlation with college grades is .62 (DuBois, 1972). These validities are high enough to make the SAT useful in predicting college performance, but low enough to make it clear that other factors, such as motivation, are also important determinants of academic success.

In recent years, the appearance of a number of private "coaching" services that purport to raise enrollees' SAT scores up to one hundred points (out of eight hundred) has led to a controversy over whether coaching is in fact effective. A study by the Federal Trade Commission's Bureau of Consumer Protection concluded that coaching can raise scores an average of twenty-five points. The Educational Testing Service, which administers the SAT, has countered with its own research, which shows only a ten-point difference after intensive coaching. The controversy is likely to continue; in the meantime, the FTC has allowed the various coaching organizations—which constitute a $10 million business nationwide—to continue to operate (Rice, 1979).

Variations in intelligence

A score of 100 on an intelligence test is commonly called "average"; actually, however, the range of normal intelligence covers a fairly wide band. About 68 percent of the population scores between 85 and 115—the "normal" range. Although a few people can be found at the outermost extremes of the intelligence distribution, more than 95 percent of the population scores between 70 and 130, and more than 99.7 percent scores between 55 and 145. It is to the exceptional fraction—those either unusually low or unusually high in intelligence—that we now turn.

The mentally retarded   **Mental retardation** has been defined as "significantly subaverage general intellectual functioning existing concurrently with deficits in adaptive behavior, and manifested during the developmental period" (Grossman, 1977, p. 11). Levels of retardation have traditionally been associated with particular ranges of scores on standard IQ tests: For example, on the Stanford-Binet test, a score from 67 to 52 has been said to indicate "mild" retardation; from 51 to 36, "moderate" retardation: from 35 to 20, "severe" retardation; and less than 19, "profound" retardation. However, these figures should not be taken as indicating clear-cut categories, since the level of adaptive behavior must also be considered. Thus, a child whose score suggests moderate retardation, but who shows some evidence of adaptive skills (speech, social skills, self-care), would more appropriately be considered mildly retarded.

Mental retardation affects from 2 to 3 percent of the population, or about 6

TABLE 14.1 Characteristics of Mentally Retarded Children

Area of functioning	Mild	Moderate	Severe and profound
Self-help Skills	Feeds and dresses self and cares for own toilet needs.	Has difficulties and requires training but can learn adequate self-help skills.	No skills to partial, but some can care for personal needs on a limited basis.
Speech and Communication	Receptive and expressive are adequate. Understands communication.	Receptive and expressive language are adequate. Has speech problems.	Receptive language is limited to good. Expressive language is limited to poor.
Academics	Optimal learning environment—third to sixth grade.	Very few academic skills. First or second grade.	No academic skills.
Social Skills	Has friends, can learn to adjust adequately.	Capable of friends but has difficulties in many social situations.	Not capable of having "real" friends. No social interaction.
Vocational Adjustment	Can hold a job. Competitive to semi-competitive. Primarily unskilled work.	Sheltered work environment. Usually needs constant supervision.	No employment for the most part. May be in an activity center. Usually needs constant care.
Adult Living	Usually marries, has children. Needs help during stress.	Usually does not marry or have children. Dependent.	Always dependent on others. No marriage or children.

Chart from William R. Van Osdol and Don G. Shane, *An Introduction to Exceptional Children* Dubuque, Iowa: William C. Brown, 1977), p. 68.

million persons in the United States (Gearheart, 1980). The causes of retardation are varied, including prenatal infections or injury, metabolic disorders, chromosomal abnormalities, prematurity, and environmental deprivation. In some cases, mental retardation can be identified very early—sometimes even before birth through a procedure known as amniocentesis. In amniocentesis a small amount of the mother's amniotic fluid is withdrawn and analyzed; this can reveal the presence of several abnormalities, including Down's syndrome (formerly called "mongolism"), early in pregnancy. Some kinds of retardation are evident at birth, and infants whose retardation is not serious can sometimes be helped by special programs of enrichment and stimulation. If not obvious at birth, most serious retardation reveals itself to parents or the child's physician in the first few years of life. Some children, despite their slow development, are not identified as retarded until they enter school.

The stigmatizing effects of labeling children "retarded" as they begin their schooling have led educators to plead for greater care in evaluating children for evidence of retardation. In the past, children from non-English-speaking families, emotionally disturbed children, and those with hearing and other perceptual defects were sometimes erroneously classed as retarded on the basis of a single intelligence test that was inappropriately chosen and administered. Proper evaluation should include tests of hearing and vision, consideration of the child's general health and linguistic and cultural background, and examination of his or her adaptive behavior. Only if the child exhibits both a low IQ and deficits in adaptive behavior, and only if these cannot be explained by a sociocultural, emotional, or health problem, can the child be considered retarded.

The mentally gifted William James Sidis, born in 1898 to Russian immigrant parents who were both medical doctors, entered Harvard College at the age of eleven. His intellectual brilliance had been recognized early: He learned to read before he was three and could read Russian, French, and German by the age of five. At the age of eight, he passed the entrance examination for the Massachusetts Institute of Technology. He quickly passed through the classes offered by the public schools, and his parents continued his education at home. He eventually graduated from Harvard at the age of sixteen.

Unfortunately, Sidis's life after college was not a happy one. After brief periods spent in graduate study and teaching, he spent the rest of his life in obscurity, working at low-paying clerical jobs. More than anything else, he sought to avoid the press, which had hounded him since childhood with sensational stories of his genius. When he died, at the age of forty-six, he was living alone in a rooming house (Montour, 1977).

Tragic stories such as Sidis's have given rise to a number of myths about gifted children: principally, that their early brilliance generally fades, leaving them failures in later life. Other common misconceptions are that gifted children tend to be unhealthy, mentally unstable, and socially inept.

In 1921, the psychologist Lewis B. Terman initiated an ambitious long-term study of gifted children that aimed at disproving these myths (Terman, 1916). Terman selected 1,528 subjects aged three to nineteen whose IQs exceeded 135. Over the years, he followed the development of this group to see how they fared in later life. His results were striking (Terman and Oden, 1947; Oden, 1968): Not only were the gifted children superior in health, adjustment, and achievement as youngsters, but their superiority continued as they moved through adulthood. Terman's group far exceeded persons with average IQs in education, occupational level, and income. In addition, their health and emotional adjustment were far above average: The group showed relatively few premature deaths, few cases of alcoholism, delinquency, or criminality, and few divorces.

Some have seized on Terman's findings as evidence that high intelligence somehow assures personal superiority. Arthur Jensen, for example, has stated that "findings such as these establish beyond a doubt that IQ tests measure characteristics that are obviously of considerable importance in our present technological society" (1972, p. 9). Others, however, have disputed Jensen's conclusion. As David McClelland has written, "Terman's studies do *not* demonstrate unequivocally that it is the kind of ability measured by the intelligence tests that is responsible for . . . the greater success of the high-IQ children" (1973, p. 5). McClelland based his criticisms on methodological flaws in Terman's experiment—principally the unrepresentativeness of the study population. Terman's sample was heavily drawn from middle- and upper-class populations, nearly all white; hence, what the study may in fact show is that (as McClelland put it) "the rich and powerful have more opportunities and therefore do better in life" (1973, p. 5). Furthermore, when Terman divided his group into "more successful" and "less successful" subgroups, it was clear that family environment was an important factor in success: Far more members of the leading subgroup grew up in especially stimulating intellectual environments and had fathers who had graduated from college. Thus, intelligence could hardly be the sole cause of greater success, since both subgroups had approximately the same IQs.

Regardless of the methodological flaws in Terman's research, we can accept it as evidence that gifted children do not usually conform to the "child prodigy" stereotype of physical frailty and social ineptitude. What, then, are the problems of the gifted? One is that they often suffer in conventional school programs, easily becoming bored and frustrated with assignments that seem to them little more than busywork. Without the sympathy and understanding of parents and teachers, they may "turn off" and refuse to do schoolwork or even to attend school. Their obvious differences from other children may lead to their being rejected or taunted by their peers. Worse yet, their abilities may simply never be developed, particularly if their home or school offers an impoverished intellectual environment (Hershey, 1976).

In an effort to overcome some of these problems, school systems are increasingly offering special classes and enrichment programs for their gifted students. Some schools offer courses in advanced subjects, such as chemistry, astronomy, and computer programming, in the elementary grades. Other schools offer "real world" activities, such as internships in businesses and television stations, to pique the interest of older students. Still other schools provide advanced courses in the performing arts, allowing students with special creative abilities to choreograph their own ballets or make their own films (Rice, 1980).

Creativity and intelligence—is there a difference?

It is interesting to note that although many of Terman's highly intelligent children became successful businesspersons, doctors, lawyers, university professors, and so on, few produced any notable creative work. Intelligence, it would seem, is not the same as creativity. To be sure, many creative persons are highly intelligent, and a certain level of intelligence is necessary for creative achievement. Yet, as one prominent researcher in the field has written, "intelligence alone does not guarantee creativity" (MacKinnon, 1962, p. 62).

If not all intelligent persons are creative, what characterizes the creative personality? This question has been studied by analyzing creative persons' biographical histories or antecedent experiences (Roe, 1952), and by administering personality tests to creative writers or architects and to their less creative counterparts in order to determine the traits that differentiate the two groups (Barron, 1968; MacKinnon, 1962, 1965). This research has revealed a number of traits shared by creative individuals. Creative people are self-confident, intensely motivated to succeed, and committed to their creative work. In her study of eminent American scientists, for example, Roe concluded that "the one thing that all of these sixty-four scientists have in common is their driving absorption in their work. They have worked long hours for many years, frequently with no vacations to speak of, because they would rather be doing their work than anything else" (1952). Creative persons also tend to approach life enthusiastically, to be open to experience, and to follow their own bent even when they must overcome obstacles or indulge in unconventional behavior to do so. Creative people are highly independent and do not place much value in pleasing others. For example, Barron (1968) found that creative writers scored lower on a test measuring the desire to make a good impression than their less creative counterparts. Creative persons have strongly intuitive natures and are often introverted. Because they are usually frank and fluent in describing them-selves—and thus often ready to own up to their conflicts and emotional prob-lems—they are often stereotyped as being "crazier" than the rest of us, or as the common description runs, "living close to the edge of insanity" (Taylor, 1975). Of the various characteristics that creative persons have been found to share, their self-confidence and persistence are notable: Creative accomplishment re-quires not only a feeling that one's new idea is right, but the determination to keep trying to prove it even in the face of contradictory evidence.

Since creativity is different from intelligence, it is not surprising that stan-dard intelligence tests often fail to identify creative people. Among artists such as painters, sculptors, and designers, the correlation between rated quality of work and measured intelligence is usually negligible (Barron, 1968). In the past few decades, psychologists have begun constructing tests designed to identify creativity. Most such tests are still in the experimental stage, and none has been accepted as standard (Anastasi, 1976). Typically, such tests ask open-ended questions. The subject might be given the name of an object and asked to list as many uses as possible—for example, tin can: "A vase for flowers; A cookie-cutter." Or he or she might be asked to produce as many sentences as possible in which each word begins with a given letter—for example, K-U-Y-I: "Keep up your interest; Kill useless yellow insects" (Guilford and Hoepfner, 1971). In another test, the subject is asked to paste a brightly colored shape on a blank sheet of construction paper and use the shape as a starting point for drawing an unusual picture that tells an interesting story (Torrance, 1965). Measures of creativity such as these are likely to find increasing use in the future, especially as tools for assigning students to classes for the gifted. Many such classes aim at developing not only students' intellectual powers but also their creative abilities.

IQ scores: nature or nurture?

Many people have tried to use intelligence tests to obtain definitive answers to the age-old question of whether there are innate intellectual differences among groups, but it has proved to be almost impossible to come to reliable conclu-sions. People whose childhood environment has differed widely from that of the majority of American and European children tend to score lower on tests de-veloped in the United States and Europe. IQ tests, however, have no way of directly measuring genetic endowment. By the time a child is old enough to take such a test, he or she necessarily has developed (or failed to develop) that endowment in a particular way depending on environmental influences. A child's score reflects not only his or her genetic potential for intellectual devel-opment (nature) but also what he or she has learned from experience (nurture). Despite the always-thorny problem of trying to isolate the influence of genetic inheritance from that of environment, debate has continued through the years over which factor is responsible for the differences among groups—a contro-versy we shall now explore in depth.

Racial differences in IQ—the debate

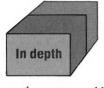

In depth

In 1969, Arthur Jensen, an educational psychologist, published an article in the *Harvard Educational Review*. In it he asserted that genetic factors might prove to be "strongly implicated" in the fact that the IQ scores of black people are, on the average, 11 to 15 points lower than the scores of white people. Jensen's thesis, that IQ is highly heritable and that therefore racial differences in IQ are due largely to differences in the gene distributions of the populations studied, caused an uproar that has not yet died down.

In order to understand the arguments for and against Jensen's view, it is necessary first to understand the concept of heritability. **Heritability** is the extent to which an observed individual variation of a trait (such as IQ) can be attributed to genetic differences among members of a particular population in a particular environment. To say that a trait has high heritability is not to say that genes "cause" it. Heritability is a measure that is specific to a given population in a given environment; it is not a constant property of the trait per se.

Another concept crucial for understanding genetic influences is that of the **reaction range**. The genetic makeup of each person has a unique range of possible responses to the environment he or she encounters. Consider the physical characteristic of height, for example. Good nutrition will make each of us taller than poor nutrition will, but under both conditions genetic makeup will dictate that some of us will be taller than others. Genes do not specify a particular height for anyone. What they do specify is a *pattern* of growth that varies in response to nutrition and other environmental factors. Thus, the height a person reaches is a result of both heredity and environment.

The development of the intellectual skills measured by IQ tests also has a reaction range. No matter how stimulating their environments, few people become Albert Einsteins or Leonardo da Vincis. And in other than extremely deprived circumstances, most people do not become mentally retarded. Each person who is not subjected to severe deprivation (which would make almost anyone mentally retarded) has a range of perhaps 20 to 25 points in which his or her IQ score can vary, depending on that person's environment (Scarr-Salapatek, 1971a).

Jensen's position Jensen claimed that individual differences in IQ were largely traceable to heredity. In his work he used data from a series of studies by the English psychologist Sir Cyril Burt (1966, 1972) that compared the IQs of identical and fraternal twins. Burt's studies showed, for example, that when identical twins—necessarily having the same genetic makeup—were separated early in life and brought up in quite different environments, their IQs as adults turned out to be similar. This suggested that environmental differences played a minor role. If individual differences in intelligence *within* given populations—such as racial groups—had a high heritability, Jensen reasoned, it was also possible that average differences *between* such groups were also the result of genetic differences. As he put it in the 1969 article, it is "a not unreasonable hypothesis that genetic factors are strongly implicated in the average Negro-white intelligence difference."

Reactions and implications The ink was barely dry on Jensen's published article before the news media began to purvey a highly simplified and sometimes inaccurate version of his ideas. Given the national political climate in 1969, it was inevitable that Jensen would be attacked from all corners as a racist seeking to promote the idea that blacks were genetically inferior. An article in *Newsweek* (March 31, 1969), for example, entitled "Born Dumb?" summed up Jensen's theory as the idea that black intelligence was fixed at birth at a level far below that of whites—with the implication that no amount of compensatory schooling could have any effect on black intelligence. Although the vagueness of some of Jensen's claims had left them open to such interpretations, he had actually made no such statements. Nevertheless, nearly every popular article on Jensen drew such a conclusion (Cronbach, 1975).

At the same time that Jensen was being virulently attacked by the media and his fellow academics, his ideas were welcomed by the conservative policy makers of the Nixon administration in Washington (Blum, 1978). If Jensen were right, they were justified in dismantling a variety of social programs, such as Head Start, that were aimed at helping disadvantaged children—largely blacks—catch up to the level of the more privileged. At one point, William Shockley, another Jensen sympathizer, even proposed a program of voluntary sterilization for those who were apparently "born dumb"—at least those who were poor. Under his plan, which he detailed in a speech to the American Psychological Association, the government would pay welfare clients with IQs under 100 one thousand dollars per IQ point below 100 if they would undergo sterilization (Chorover, 1979).

The Burt data: further controversy As if Jensen's article in itself had not stirred up enough controversy, in 1976 another feud erupted. This time, researchers who had gone beyond Jensen's arguments to the data on which they were based suggested that these data were at best questionable and possibly even fraudulent. An American psychologist, Leon Kamin (1974, 1976), and a reporter for the London *Sunday Times*, Oliver Gillie, after carefully examining Burt's data and doing a bit of detective work, discovered irregularities in some of Burt's figures. For one thing, correlations between twins' IQs kept showing up as the same—to three decimal places—despite changes in the number of twins studied. The odds against such an outcome occurring even once are many millions to one, yet in twenty different places in Burt's data, the same correlations appeared (Gillie, 1977). More suspicions were raised when it was discovered that Burt's supposed collaborators in the research—Margaret Howard and J. Conway—may never have existed, for Gillie's research turned up no records of them. This is significant, since both of these "associates" of Burt's were responsible for a good deal of the raw research used in his study. Moreover, both had supposedly written several articles praising Burt's work—which were published in the journal Burt edited. In reply to these criticisms of Burt, Jensen argued that the errors were "of a rather trivial nature. . . . even if all of Burt's findings were thrown out entirely, the picture regarding the heritability of IQ would not be materially changed" (Jensen, 1977, p. 471). Moreover, Jensen suggested, if Burt were alive today, he would be able to win a libel judgment against his detractors.

Growing opposition to Jensen Even before the Burt research was called into question, Jensen's critics had elaborated a number of arguments against him.

These have generally attacked his methodology or pointed out environmental factors he failed to take into account. Arguments in rebuttal to Jensen's include the following:

1. Blacks and whites differ in numerous ways besides genetic ones, such as their living conditions and the degree to which they experience discrimination. Blacks and whites supposedly in the same socioeconomic class actually differ considerably in income, education, and quality of housing.

2. Jensen's assertion that black-white IQ differences are not explainable by the few environmental factors investigated does not rule out a possible explanation due to other, as yet unspecified, environmental factors. For example, lead is present in the old paint on the walls of many slum dwellings. Young children sometimes eat paint chips; the lead in the paint they eat can cause brain damage, which results in sharp decreases in intelligence (Needleman, 1973, 1974). Many such environmental factors that apply disproportionately to black people have not yet been fully studied. For example, one researcher has pointed to a study in which children whose mothers had received dietary supplements during pregnancy averaged eight IQ points above a control group. "With effects like that," he commented, "why are we discussing anything else?" (Lederberg, 1969).

3. IQ tests are affected by such nonintellectual influences as motivation, anxiety, and test-taking skills. These nonintellectual influences lessen the value of the IQ score as a reliable measure of the differences in intelligence among racial groups.

4. Jensen's critics say that he seems to imply that heredity "fixes" intelligence-test scores within limits and that he does not take account of the facts of reaction range. Data from adoption studies (Skodak and Skeels, 1949) suggest that when children are adopted by a family belonging to a higher social class than the one into which they were born, this can produce a significantly higher IQ than would be expected if the same children had been reared by their natural parents.

As Sandra Scarr-Salapatek (1971a), in a review of Jensen's article, has pointed out, "While we may tentatively conclude that there are some genetic IQ differences between social-class groups, we can make only wild speculations about racial groups. . . . [R]acial groups are not random samples from the same population, nor are members reared in uniform conditions within each race." There is, in fact, a common misunderstanding of the concept of heritability in relation to IQ: If heritability "is high, this reasoning goes, then intelligence is genetically fixed and unchangeable. . . . This misconception ignores the fact that it [heritability] is a population statistic, bound to a given set of environmental conditions at a given point in time. Neither intelligence nor [heritability] estimates are fixed."

Scarr-Salapatek insists that not enough proof exists to support either the arguments of those who say there are racial differences in IQ or the arguments of those who say all such differences can be accounted for by environmental influences. Rather, she has suggested, hereditary and environmental factors may operate together, combining in different ways under different circumstances (Figure 14.6). For example, adverse environmental conditions limit intellectual achievement and make accurate observations of heritable IQ difficult; in people who grow up in favorable surroundings, genetic differences show up more. From her study of 992 sets of twins (1971b), Scarr-Salapatek concludes that adverse environments affect expression of the reaction range, so

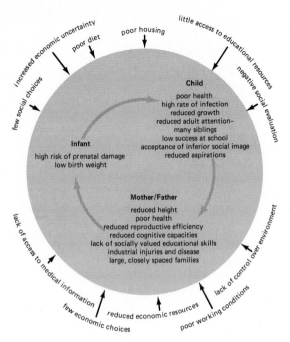

Figure 14.6 While environmental differences do not account for all differences in IQ, one's economic, social, and educational opportunities do play a major role. As this diagram suggests, a vicious circle may be created in which the factors of nature and nurture cannot be easily separated because each, in fact, implies the other (Richards, Richardson, and Spears, 1972).

that the differences between races are due at least in part to environmental differences.

A recent study (Scarr and Weinberg, 1976) has confirmed that IQ has a fairly broad reaction range and can be dramatically affected by changes in the environment. These researchers measured the IQ scores of black children who had been adopted by white couples of higher than average socioeconomic status and of above average intelligence. The children were found to have an average IQ of 106, well above the average for the population and about 15 points above the average IQ of black children reared in their own homes in the part of the country in which the study was conducted. In addition, the researchers were able to determine that the biological parents of the adopted black children had been of about average intelligence, lending added support to the assertion that the reaction range of IQ scores is at least as broad as the average differences between racial groups.

The debate over IQ differences among races seems destined to continue for some time, for it seems impossible to gather definitive data. In a careful review of the evidence, John C. Loehlin, Gardner Lindzey, and James N. Spuhler (1975) have concluded that on intellectual-ability tests the average differences in the scores of members of different American racial and ethnic groups reflect in part inadequacies and biases in the tests, in part environmental differences among the groups, and in part genetic differences among the groups. In fact, all three factors interact, and "differences among individuals *within* racial-ethnic and socioeconomic groups greatly exceed in magnitude the average differences between such groups" (p. 239). Moreover, as N. J. Block and Gerald Dworkin have noted in their book *The IQ Controversy*, "Between United States blacks and whites, there are systematic cultural differences and differences in psychological environment, both of which influence the development of cognitive skills in complex ways over long periods of time. Since we have no way of estimating how much these differences affect performance on IQ tests, we can say nothing about genetic differences between the two groups" (1976, p. 202). Thus, although the debate on the role of heredity in determining IQ may continue, it is unlikely that a definitive answer will ever emerge.

Public concerns about intelligence tests

The controversy that followed the publication of Jensen's famous article about race and IQ sparked a good deal of discussion about the use of intelligence tests as well as considerable criticism of the tests themselves. One group of critics charged that the tests reflected the language and culture of the middle-class (and predominantly white) test developers so thoroughly that they were inappropriate for measuring the intelligence of children from other backgrounds, especially the urban ghetto. For example, of all the kinds of items on intelligence tests, vocabulary provides the best single estimate of IQ scores; yet one's vocabulary clearly depends on one's cultural background. A person who has never heard words like *sonata* or *ingenuous* will perform poorly on verbal intelligence tests. And a person who has grown up in a community where the primary language is not English will be handicapped even further. But cultural bias is not limited to verbal tests; George W. Albee has cited this example:

One psychologist, Wayne Dennis, tested children in 56 different societies around the world with a simple test called "Draw-a-Man."(This task is a good measure of the child's I.Q. in that it correlates highly with scores on verbal I.Q. tests among American middle-class children.) But on this nonverbal test Bedouin children averaged 58 I.Q. and Hopi and Zuñi Indian children averaged about 125.

Are the Indian children really superior to middle-class school children? Are Bedouin children really so retarded? Further investigation revealed that the Arab children lived in a culture that forbade drawing or the making of images. On the other hand, the Indian children lived in a culture that emphasized and rewarded drawings and decoration. Even this nonverbal I.Q. test was highly sensitive to practice and experience (Albee, 1978).

The problem of developing a culture-free intelligence test, then, is a difficult one. Nevertheless, efforts in this direction are continuing. One way in which researchers have sought to eliminate unfairness has been to develop tests that offer some kind of "adjustment" for children from minority cultural backgrounds. The best known of these is the System of Multicultural Pluralistic Assessment, or SOMPA, developed by sociologist Jane Mercer (Rice, 1979). SOMPA includes three kinds of evaluation: a standard IQ test, which gives an estimate of the child's mental ability measured against the standard school culture; a one-hour interview with the child's parents, aimed at identifying the family's sociocultural background and the child's level of nonacademic performance at home; and a complete medical examination, aimed at identifying any physical impairments the child might have. SOMPA has been called by some the first nondiscriminatory test of a child's intellectual development. Some critics, however, oppose its reliance, even in part, on a standard IQ test. It is likely that further efforts to develop culture-free tests such as SOMPA will continue.

A second major criticism of intelligence tests has been that they fail to measure anything of importance. Although they have been shown to be good pre-

---

The Dove Counterbalance Intelligence Test
by Adrian Dove

If they throw the dice and "7" is showing on the top, what is facing down?
(a) "Seven"   (b) "Snake eyes"
(c) "Boxcars"   (d) "Little Joes"
(e) "Eleven".

Jazz pianist Ahmad Jamal took an Arabic name after becoming really famous. Previously he had some fame with what he called his "slave name." What was his previous name?
(a) Willie Lee Jackson
(b) LeRoi Jones
(c) Wilbur McDougal
(d) Fritz Jones   (e) Andy Johnson

In "C. C. Rider," what does "C. C." stand for?
(a) Civil Service
(b) Church Council
(c) County Circuit, preacher of an old-time rambler
(d) Country Club
(e) "Cheating Charley" (the "Boxcar Gunsel")

Cheap "chitlings" (not the kind you purchase at the frozen-food counter) will taste rubbery unless they are cooked long enough. How soon can you quit cooking them to eat and enjoy them?
(a) 15 minutes   (b) 2 hours
(c) 24 hours
(d) 1 week (on a low flame)
(e) 1 hour

If a judge finds you guilty of "holding weed" (in California), what's the most he can give you?
(a) Indeterminate (life)   (b) A nickel
(c) A dime   (d) A year in county
(e) $100.00.

A "Handkerchief Head" is
(a) A cool cat   (b) A porter
(c) An "Uncle Tom"   (d) A hoddi
(e) A "preacher"

Figure 14.7 The Dove Counterbalance Intelligence Test, devised by Adrian Dove, a black, to be culturally biased against whites, is an extreme example of how an intelligence test may depend on knowledge specific to one culture. A population of urban blacks would score high on this test, and a population of suburban whites would score low. Even when a test's items do not show this kind of obvious culture loading, a test may have validity problems. For example, many subcultures within Western society place great emphasis on competence in test taking. In a subculture where such emphasis is lacking, the validity of almost any test is likely to suffer.

dictors of a person's grades in school and college, there is almost no evidence that good grades lead to any particular kind of achievement in life (Blum, 1978). Although grade level attained has been shown to have an influence on a person's future occupation and income, the person's grades themselves have little relation to his or her ultimate success. In fact, intelligence tests often seem blind to some other factors that determine success, such as strongly held interests, motivation, and creativity. As David McClelland has noted, "no consistent relationships exist between scholastic aptitude scores in college students and their *actual accomplishments* in social leadership, the arts, science, music, writing, and speech and drama" (1973, p. 3).

A related problem is that intelligence tests are sometimes used to "weed out" applicants for certain kinds of jobs, even when the duties of the job have no apparent connection with the skills measured by the test. McClelland offers a telling example:

. . . suppose you are a ghetto resident in the Roxbury section of Boston. To qualify for being a policeman, you have to take a three-hour-long general intelligence test in which you must know the meaning of words like "quell," "pyromaniac," and "lexicon." If you do not know enough of these words or cannot play analogy games with them, you do not qualify and must be satisfied with some such job as being a janitor for which an "intelligence" test is not required by the Massachusetts Civil Service Commission. You, not unreasonably, feel angry, upset, and unsuccessful. Because you do not know those words, you are considered to have low intelligence, and since you consequently have to take a low-status job and are unhappy, you contribute to the celebrated correlations of low intelligence with low occupational status and poor adjustment. Psychologists should be ashamed of themselves for promoting a view of general intelligence that has encouraged such a testing program, particularly when there is no solid evidence that significantly relates performance on this type of intelligence test with performance as a policeman (1973, p. 4).

As a consequence of these kinds of criticisms and others, intelligence tests have come under something of a cloud. Some school systems have dropped the use of IQ tests altogether, and others have begun to avoid their use as a simple device to "track" students into accelerated, average, and slow classes—a practice once followed extensively. An important factor in this change was PL 94-142, a federal law passed in 1977 that deals primarily with the rights of retarded and other disabled children. One of its most important provisions is that children no longer can be assigned to a "special education" class—that is, a class for mentally retarded children—solely on the basis of an IQ score. Among the provisions of the law are the following:

Tests and other evaluation materials . . . are provided and administered in the child's native language. . . . Tests and other evaluation materials include those tailored to assess specific areas of educational need and not merely those which are designed to provide a single general intelligence quotient. . . . No single procedure is used as the sole criterion for determining an appropriate program for a child, and . . . The child is assessed in all areas related to the suspected disability, including where appropriate, health, vision, hearing, social and emotional status, general intelligence, academic performance, communicative status and moter abilities (Federal Register, August 23, 1977, pp. 42,496–42,497).

Although criticisms of IQ tests have been valuable in reducing their misuse in school systems, some psychologists and educators have argued that it is a mistake to throw them out altogether. One ostensible reason IQ tests were originally developed for use in school systems was to help identify academically talented children from underprivileged environments or cultural backgrounds that differ from the norm. If the tests are eliminated, this argument goes, these bright children may go through school without the help and encouragement they need.

Probably the most compelling argument for using group IQ tests . . . for routine testing of all pupils at the elementary level is in screening the school population to discover academic talent in children from disadvantaged backgrounds. Academic talent in such children is more apt to go unnoticed by parents and teachers and needs early fostering to develop its fullest realization in the more advanced levels of scholastic achievement that are prerequisite for a college education (Jensen, 1980, p. 738).

Finally, criticisms of existing tests have inspired extensive research into possible new and better measures of intelligence. One direction the new tests may take is to include measures of "social intelligence," or the subject's ability to interact with others in given ways. For example, a test for entrance to medical school might ask the subject to simulate an interview with a patient (Rice, 1979). Another promising trend is toward measuring subjects' "learning potential": The subject is presented with a certain body of information and subsequently asked to apply it. The subject is given several trials to master the material, and the speed at which he or she works yields an estimate of mental ability. Techniques such as these may one day change the way we assess intelligence, even as they change our definition of the term itself.

THE MEASUREMENT OF PERSONALITY

In the preceding section, we have discussed several issues concerning the assessment of intelligence and other abilities. But understanding a person involves much more than knowing his or her abilities. Is the person motivated to perform at his or her potential? Is the person self-confident or shy? Emotional or unemotional? Does he or she relate well to others? In other words, we would be interested in the qualities that are characteristic, or representative, of a person's behavioral repertoire or personality. Personality assessment is the process of objectively measuring the features or characteristics of a person's personality.

Personality assessment serves a number of important functions. Clinical psychologists, psychiatrists, and social workers are interested in assessment because knowledge about a client's depression, anxiety, or low self-esteem can be very helpful in diagnosis and treatment. But personality assessment is also important to school psychologists, industrial psychologists, and vocational counselors. Information about personality can be instrumental in helping a person select a career or be placed in a satisfying and rewarding job. In addition, researchers are interested in personality assessment because it helps to illuminate many of the conceptual issues that we discussed in Chapter 13, such as the stability of behavior over time and the influence of the environment or situation on behavior.

In the rest of this chapter, we will discuss several methods for assessing personality. It is important to keep in mind that the particular assessment technique that a psychologist selects often depends on his or her theoretical approach. As we discussed in Chapter 13, some theorists regard personality as a constellation of stable, enduring traits or characteristics, such as introversion or dominance. Such psychologists would administer personality inventories that have been developed to measure particular traits. In contrast, psychologists who follow a behaviorist orientation regard personality as more variable. They believe that an individual's behavior is influenced by factors in the environment. If confronted by a parent with an aggressive child, for example, the behaviorist would try to determine what concrete stimuli in the environment were eliciting and maintaining the aggressive episodes. The main tools for obtaining this type of information include interviews, direct observation, and self-monitoring diaries, in which clients are asked to keep a record of problem behaviors and the situations in which they occur. In contrast to behavior theorists, psychodynamic theorists see behavior as controlled by intrapsychic factors, such as childhood conflicts or psychosexual history. When psychologists with a psychodynamic orientation attempt to assess an individual's personality, they try to provide the subject with a free atmosphere in which unconscious conflicts can emerge. For this reason, psychodynamic theorists may use projective techniques—ambiguous stimuli like ink blots or pictures to which the subject is asked to respond. Ideally, the subject should fall back on his or her imagination and thus project onto the image whatever is lurking in the unconscious. A variety of assessment techniques are discussed in more detail in the following sections.

Projective tests

In projective tests personality characteristics are revealed by the way a subject responds to and interprets ambiguous material. The subject is presented with a stimulus—most often a picture—and is asked to describe or explain it. The test is relatively unstructured: The subject is allowed to respond in any way, using whatever words or ideas come to mind. These tests have been heavily influenced by Freudian concepts of the unconscious and of projection as a defense mechanism. The idea behind such a procedure is that the subject's responses will yield information about the workings of his or her personality. Important feelings and conflicts, the theory goes, will be *projected* onto the test materials in some way. For example, a subject who repeatedly "sees" peering eyes and threatening figures in abstract blobs of color may be revealing the exaggerated suspiciousness typical of paranoia. As the example suggests, projective tests are most often used in clinical settings, where they originated as ways of "getting into" the minds of troubled patients.

The Rorschach Inkblot Test Perhaps the best-known projective diagnostic technique is the one developed in 1921 by Hermann Rorschach, a Swiss psychiatrist (Rorschach, 1942). In the **Rorschach Inkblot Test** the subject is handed a series of ten inkblots, one at a time, and asked to report what he or she sees in the blot. The examiner carefully notes not only what the subject says about the inkblot, but also how he or she responds—how quickly, with what kind of emotional expression, and so on. After the subject has seen all ten inkblot cards, the examiner presents the cards a second time and questions the subject about his or her initial responses. If the subject saw two elephant heads, for

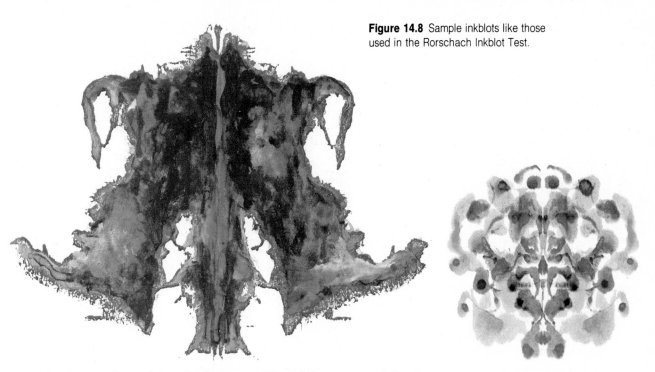

Figure 14.8 Sample inkblots like those used in the Rorschach Inkblot Test.

example, the examiner might ask what part of the inkblot suggested that interpretation—the overall shape or the protrusions that brought to mind tusks or
trunks?

There are several systems of scoring Rorschach responses, but three are most
common. The first is *location*: What part of the blot does the subject respond
to? The entire shape of the blot, the white space around it, or a particular
detail? The second category is *determinants*: Does the subject react to the form,
color, or shading of the blot? (Several of the blots are brightly colored; some
are in shades of gray and black.) Does the subject perceive the blot as showing
some kind of movement? (For example, "It's a man riding away on a motorcycle, and he's got his legs stretched out to keep from getting splashed as he goes
through a puddle.") The third system is *content*: What does the subject see—
human figures (such as our motorcycle rider), animals, plants, or other things?

The examiner analyzes the subject's responses according to these three categories and in addition looks for any patterns that may be apparent in the
subject's reactions. Traditionally, certain patterns of Rorschach responses have
been thought to point out some facet of the subject's personality: For example,
many or pronounced responses to color are thought to be associated with emotionality; many descriptions of human movement supposedly indicate an active
imagination and fantasy life (Anastasi, 1976). Although many such guidelines
have been developed to help the examiner interpret the subject's responses,
inevitably much of the "meaning" found in the test results depends on the
examiner's skill in finding it. As one commentator has noted:

One of the advantages often attributed to the Rorschach, a capacity exemplified in
the likening of the test to a psychological x-ray, is that since the subject is ignorant of
the nature and purposes of the test, he cannot censor his responses or defend himself
in any way. Moreover, the standardization and objectivity of the Rorschach
procedure, perhaps along with the professional standing of the people who use it,

were supposed to be quite a sufficient safeguard against any biases of the examiner himself. Unfortunately, but quite predictably, both the above suppositions have proven wrong (Sechrest, 1968, p. 578).

Not only can the results of the test depend on who administers and interprets it, but the subject's responses can also differ depending on the test situation—whether he or she is nervous or calm, sees the test as a measure of intelligence or pathology, or feels comfortable with the examiner. Some people are defensive and wary in the test situation and give short and "careful" answers; others answer freely and in great detail. Although the skilled clinician can to some extent correct for such differences, that such correction is needed only points out the necessity for a highly experienced examiner if the test is to have any usefulness. While its validity has not been scientifically documented, the Rorschach is nonetheless one of the most frequently used tests for the assessment of personality in clinical psychology (Aronson, Reznikoff, and Rauchway, 1979).

The Thematic Apperception Test The **Thematic Apperception Test (TAT)**, developed by Henry Murray in 1935, consists of a series of cards depicting ambiguous scenes that include one or two people. Usually, the subject is shown twenty or fewer of these cards, chosen for their appropriateness to his or her age and sex. The subject is asked to tell a coherent story about each picture, including what led up to the situation, what the characters are thinking and feeling, and how the situation will end (Figure 14.9).

The stories are usually analyzed on an individual basis; that is, one person's stories are not compared with another's. Originally, Murray suggested that the TAT be interpreted in terms of a person's "internal needs" and "environmental

Figure 14.9 One of the stimulus cards used in the Thematic Apperception Test (after Murray, 1943).

presses"—concepts in Murray's own theory of personality (Murray, 1938). Needs that Murray thought the TAT might identify included the need for achievement, the need for affiliation, and others. "Presses" he considered to be forces in the environment that might either frustrate or help satisfy the needs. The relative importance of needs and presses, Murray thought, would be shown by the frequency with which these elements showed up in the subject's stories. Today, interpretation of the TAT involves not only an analysis of needs and presses, but an examination of other aspects of the subject's responses, somewhat in the manner of Rorschach interpretation.

The TAT has gained wide acceptance as a personality test, and it is extensively used both in clinical settings and in research. (In research projects the TAT is sometimes administered as a group test, with subjects writing down their stories rather than giving them orally.) Despite the test's acceptance, however, it has been subject to some of the same criticisms as the Rorschach: Its interpretation often depends on the skill of the examiner, and subjects' responses may depend not only on their psychological makeup but also on their physical and emotional condition.

Self-report tests

Like intelligence tests, self-report personality tests assume that subjects have varying amounts of the trait being measured. Just as on an intelligence test, many items are used in order to obtain the most reliable measurement, because no single item is a useful measure of the trait.

One type of self-report personality test is akin to intelligence tests in that such tests are constructed by a factor-analytic method. As we saw in Chapter 13, factor analysis is the process of finding the smallest number of factors that can account for all the correlations among a set of variables.

Just as a person of a certain level of intelligence will be able to answer a certain item on an intelligence test correctly and someone of a lower level will not, a person with a certain degree of, say, nurturance will usually agree strongly with a statement on a personality test such as "It is important to help others," and those possessing a small amount of nurturance will not. Consequently, items that are believed to be related to a specific trait are grouped together on the test. The test is then administered experimentally several times until the pool of items is reduced to those that have the highest amount of internal consistency and the highest relationship to the trait being measured.

Another type of personality test is constructed and developed very differently: according to the empirical method. In such a test a large number of items are selected without regard to their relationship to a certain trait. The items are then administered to an experimental group of people who are known to have various psychological disorders and to another group of people who are known to be "normal," or free of the disorder being measured. Those items that differentiate between the two groups—that is, the items receiving one answer from most of the disturbed subjects and a different answer from most of the normal subjects—are identified and retained; the others are discarded. This refinement and selection process is repeated several times until a test has been constructed that is as reliable and valid as possible. The Minnesota Multiphasic Personality Inventory, discussed next, is an example of a test developed according to this empirical method.

It must be noted that the validity of both kinds of tests can be questioned. The type of test that assumes an item has a high relationship to a trait usually has little against which it can be validated. We cannot tell, for example, if an item tests for nurturance unless we have some other independent measure of nurturance, which itself must be validated. Those tests that are developed empirically depend on the reliability of the diagnosis by which people are divided into groups of the normal and the disturbed. If the experimental groups on which the test depends are not well differentiated, the test will not generate data that can make subsequent diagnosis possible.

The empirically developed test is valuable for diagnostic purposes—provided, of course, that the diagnostic groups on which it is based are reliable. Such a test should be able to identify other persons who have similar psychological characteristics. Tests developed by the factor-analytic method are frequently useful tools for research on the structure of personality.

The Minnesota Multiphasic Personality Inventory The most widely used personality inventory is the **Minnesota Multiphasic Personality Inventory (MMPI)**. This test was originally developed to aid in the diagnosis of psychiatric patients by finding out whether their statements about themselves were similar to those of patients whose conditions had already been diagnosed. The developers of the test (Hathaway and McKinley, 1940) gathered a number of diverse true-false statements, some of which were clearly related to mental disturbance and others of which were more general statements about attitudes, habits, physical health, interests, and so on. (Some examples of these statements are given in Figure 14.10A.) These test items were tried out on groups of patients suffering from various psychological disturbances—schizophrenia, depression, hypochondria, and so on. The same items were also given to groups of normal individuals. The responses of the various subjects were analyzed, and the state-

133 I have never indulged in unusual sex practices.
151 Someone has been trying to poison me.
182 I am afraid of losing my mind.
234 I get mad easily and then I get over it soon.
244 My way of doing things is apt to be misunderstood by others.
288 I am troubled by attacks of nausea and vomiting.
A

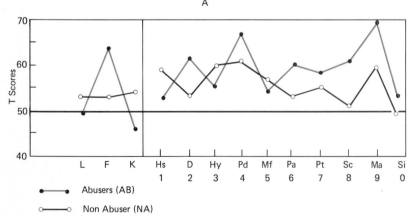
B

Figure 14.10 (A) Sample MMPI items. (B) MMPI profiles for abusive and nonabusive fathers. The letters along the bottom of the graph correspond to the scales described in Table 14.2. Note that the two groups obtained different profiles: Fathers who abused their children scored much higher than nonabusive fathers on the depression (D), psychopathic deviate (Pd) and mania (Ma) scales. Although it appears that the MMPI can differentiate between abusive and nonabusive parents, further study would be necessary before a more conclusive profile of an abusive parent could be drawn. This research does offer some tentative hypotheses about important personality differences between abusers and nonabusers (adapted from Paulson et al., 1974).

ments that discriminated among the various groups were retained. For example, from the initial collection of items, fifty-three were found to discriminate sharply between depressed people and normal people. Later, a few items were added to sharpen the differentiation between patients with severe depressive conditions and those with other psychiatric diagnoses. The result was the D, or depression, scale, which has been found to be a highly sensitive indicator not only of psychotic depression but also of less severe forms of depression, of varying mood states, and even of reactions to various methods of psychological treatment.

The MMPI eventually came to contain 550 statements that yielded a rating on each of ten clinical scales (Figure 14.10B). Three other scales were built into the MMPI to test the validity of the subject's responses: These are the L, F, and K scales. The L, or lie, scale is designed to identify those subjects who are faking their responses in order to appear in a better light. For example, a subject who replies "true" to the statement "I have never even thought of exceeding the speed limit" is probably lying, and many such responses will earn him or her a high L score. This tells the examiner that other responses must be interpreted with caution. The F, or infrequency, scale is a measure of how often the subject chooses responses only very rarely chosen by most people who take the test. A high score on this scale can indicate that the subject is answering carelessly—even randomly. It may also suggest that he or she is highly deviant or is trying to appear that way. The K, or correction, scale yields a measure of the subject's frankness or evasiveness in responding to the test items. This scale is used as a check by the psychologist as he or she interprets the ten clinical scales, described in Table 14.2.

The MMPI is best used for its original purposes, the identification and diagnosis of psychopathology (Dahlstrom and Welsh, 1960). It is a useful tool when employed by a skilled clinician who has been trained to interpret the profile of the clinical scores. Some of the clinical scores have proved useful in determining the effectiveness of various forms of psychotherapy. The depression scale, for example, has been used in studies that evaluate different therapies. But the MMPI is not as useful for the measurement of normal personality or as a selection or employment screening device, because it was not developed for these purposes.

TESTING FOR VOCATIONAL SELECTION AND COUNSELING

A variety of tests are used in vocational and counseling settings, including several of the kinds of tests we have discussed thus far. Intelligence tests and personality measures, for example, may be used by a corporation to screen prospective employees. In addition, vocational interest tests are useful counseling tools, and special performance tests of various kinds have extensive uses both as selection and evaluation devices.

Interest tests

Interest tests find their most important use in educational counseling. By the time a person is old enough to begin considering the choice of a vocation, he or she has developed a certain pattern of interests. Measuring these interests can

TABLE 14.2 Scales of the MMPI

Validity scales

Lie Scale (L)	Items that reflect socially desirable but unlikely behavior and are therefore likely to be marked true by a naive faker.
Infrequency Scale (F)	Items that are rarely marked true except by people who either are deliberately trying to give an exaggerated impression of their problems or are in fact highly deviant.
Correction Scale (K)	Items that reflect how defensive or how frank the person is being. The scale is sensitive to attitudes more subtle than those that affect the Lie Scale.

Clinical scales

1. Hypochondriasis (Hs)	Items selected to discriminate people who persist in worrying about their bodily functions despite strong evidence that they have no physical illness.
2. Depression (D)	Items selected to discriminate people who are pessimistic about the future, feel hopeless or worthless, are slow in thought and action, and think a lot about death and suicide.
3. Hysteria (Hy)	Items selected to discriminate people who use physical symptoms to solve difficult problems or avoid mature responsibilities, particularly under severe psychological stress.
4. Psychopathic Deviate (Pd)	Items selected to discriminate people who show a pronounced disregard for social customs and mores, an inability to profit from punishing experiences, and emotional shallowness with others, particularly in sex and love.
5. Masculinity-Femininity (Mf)	Items selected to discriminate men who prefer homosexual relations to heterosexual ones, either overtly, or covertly because of inhibitions or conflicts. Women tend to score low on this scale, but the scale cannot be interpreted simply "upside-down" for women.
6. Paranoia (Pa)	Items selected to discriminate people who have delusions about how influential and how victimized they are or how much attention is paid them by other people.
7. Psychasthenia (Pt)	Items selected to discriminate people with obsessive thoughts, compulsive actions, extreme fear or guilt feelings, insecurity, and high anxiety.
8. Schizophrenia (Sc)	Items selected to discriminate people who are constrained, cold, aloof, apathetic, inaccessible to others, and who may have delusions or hallucinations.
9. Hypomania (Ma)	Items selected to discriminate people who are physically overactive, emotionally excited, and have rapid flights of disconnected, fragmentary ideas; these activities may lead to accomplishment but more frequently are inefficient and unproductive.
10. Social introversion (Si)	Items selected to discriminate people who are withdrawn from social contacts and responsibilities and display little real interest in people.

Source: Based on W. G. Dahlstrom, G.S. Welsh, and L. E. Dahlstrom, *An MMPI Handbook*, Vol. 1 (Minneapolis: University of Minnesota Press, 1972).

be as important in its own way as measuring intelligence, since both intelligence and interest contribute to job satisfaction and achievement. Oddly, individuals are sometimes not conscious of their interests at this time of life, or (more commonly) they have little idea of how their interests relate to the actual tasks involved in a particular occupation. For example, a young woman with scientific talent might respond, if asked, that she is interested in medicine. She may, however, have very little interest in dealing with other people's problems and complaints all day long, which is an important part of a physician's work. Interest tests attempt to identify a person's interest in the actual activities of a given vocation, making possible a good match between a person's interests and the actual day-to-day duties of a particular type of work.

The Strong-Campbell Interest Inventory The Strong-Campbell Interest Inventory, originally developed in the 1920s by E. K. Strong, Jr., and known as the Strong Vocational Interest Blank, has been revised several times over the years. It has been known as the **Strong-Campbell Interest Inventory (SCII)** since 1974. This test is made up of 325 items, most of which describe various activities; the subject is asked to mark each item as "like," "indifferent," or "dislike." The items list actual occupational activities, school subjects, amusements, and contact with various kinds of people. One item, for example, asks, would you like repairing a car? Solving a series of math problems? Reading for pleasure? Working with children? The subject's answers are fed into a computer and rated according to six occupational scales: realistic, investigative, artistic, social, enterprising, and conventional. In addition, two other scales are used. One, an academic orientation scale, predicts the likelihood that the subject will continue with advanced education. The other, an introversion–extroversion scale, indicates whether the subject would work better alone or with other people. The six occupational scales of the SCII are further divided into twenty-three basic interest scales, which further pinpoint the subject's interests.

Other tests used in vocational selection

As we noted earlier, intelligence tests are sometimes used in the process of vocational selection. However, since intelligence tests predict school achievement far better than vocational achievement, they are of limited usefulness. Some companies, recognizing this, prefer to administer special aptitude tests to measure applicants' abilities to perform the specific kinds of tasks their jobs would require. Factories seeking workers to assemble tiny electronic components, for example, often give applicants a small parts dexterity test. Aptitude tests have also been developed to identify an ability to work with computers, various types of machinery, and so on. Another kind of test often used to screen prospective employees is a performance test. In such tests, the subject must show how well he or she can actually perform a given type of work. For example, a typist may be asked to type a few pages or a proofreader to correct an actual proof. Finally, some corporations use personality tests to identify candidates for special kinds of jobs. To enter an executive training program, for example, an applicant might have to rank high in assertiveness and tolerance to stress, and moderately high in conformity.

In addition to formal tests, of course, employers assess job candidates by many other means. Application blanks, for example, supply a certain amount of biographical data and a summary of the applicant's schooling and employment history. The interview, another assessment technique, is used almost universally. The interview does have certain advantages over other methods of assessment, allowing the skillful intereviewer to get a good "feel" for the kind of person he or she is evaluating; however, it is interesting to note that it is not necessarily a valid assessment device. One study (Landy, 1976) examined the predictive validities of decisions made by a committee in charge of screening police candidates and found them to be only low to moderate. From the point of view of the employer, the best selection policy would seem to be to use a variety of assessment practices and to validate those practices that are chosen.

THE ETHICS OF TESTING

We have seen that tests can be very effective tools for differentiation and diagnosis when properly used. However, like any other tool, tests are not always used properly. Their results are not always accurate, and they can be used unfairly to change the course of people's lives. Yet the number of tests and the situations in which they are used have been steadily increasing—a development that lends urgency to many questions, some of which we have already touched on.

So many variables affect the score on an examination—the personality of the examiner, the mood of the test taker, and the middle-class orientation of the questions, to name a few—that even if we could all agree on what the scores mean, their validity as a measuring tool would still be questionable. Then there is the problem of interpreting the results: Just what has been measured? If a student scores high on an examination in English and math, can we really conclude that he or she will be successful in medical school?

The results of such tests can and do change people's lives. Whereas a high score on a mathematics examination may result in placement in an accelerated math program for one student, a low score on the same exam may mean the denial of admission to college for another. Even if a test score were a true indicator of aptitude or intelligence, why should certain educational experiences be reserved for the very talented? Why not also admit the most highly motivated students? Or the most creative? Or those with the most leadership ability?

Some basic ethical issues lie behind all these questions. One issue concerns what is appropriate in the interpretation of tests results. Many people succumb to the temptation to draw sweeping conclusions from personality and intelligence test scores, forgetting that these tests often measure much less than we think they do and that they never supply absolutely certain information. The results of all tests are always a matter of probability—at best, they provide only a good estimate of what they are designed to measure. We must therefore be sure that a given test is valid *for the specific purpose for which it is being used*. An intelligence test will probably give us some idea how an eighteen-year-old will do in college; it may tell us nothing at all about his or her performance in work—or life.

Another ethical issue concerns the proper use of test information. Even if the test results are valid, should test scores be made available to the subjects themselves? To their employers? To college admissions boards? Should a psychologist tell a child that he or she has obtained a poor IQ score when it may have the effect of decreasing the child's motivation to learn? Should people's private fantasies and fundamental beliefs be made available to companies or organizations for which they work or to which they are applying for work? Are there times when we would be better off *not* administering a test at all?

Personality and intelligence tests may be used for desirable or undesirable ends. Personality assessment and intelligence testing can be useful in helping individuals lead more productive lives. Realistic information about one's capabilities and dispositions can help a person make appropriate social and occupational choices. We must remember, however, that knowledge about people entails power over their lives. Psychological tests, then, can be used either to help or to hurt. Careful attention to the ethical issues raised by the use of tests is a continuing necessity if tests are to be used for the benefit of the individual and of society.

SUMMARY

1. The value of a test is determined by its **reliability** and **validity**. A test is reliable if it yields the same results over and over again. High reliability depends on three factors: internal consistency, test-retest reliability, and interjudge reliability. In addition, the quality or characteristic being measured must be relatively stable.

2. A test is valid if it measures what it is supposed to measure. A given test may be evaluated for three kinds of validity: It has concurrent validity if its results correlate with other tests measuring the same characteristics; it has content validity if its content actually measures what it is meant to measure; and it has predictive validity to the extent to which it predicts a subject's subsequent performance on tasks related to the characteristic being measured. To yield meaningful results, a test must rate high in both reliability and validity.

3. Standardization of a test is also necessary for determining the significance of an individual's score. Before a test is put into general use it is given to a **standardization group**. The arithmetical average of the group's scores is used to determine normative distributions (**norms**), against which subsequent scores on the test will be measured.

4. Many types of tests are used today for measuring intelligence. Usually they contain both verbal and nonverbal (performance) skills. Individual intelligence tests are administered by one examiner to one subject. The **Stanford-Binet Test** is the current form of the test first developed by Alfred Binet to measure **intelligence quotient** (IQ), the ratio of one's mental age to one's chronological age. The other most frequently used individual intelligence tests are the **Wechsler Adult Intelligence Scale** (WAIS) and the **Wechsler Intelligence Scale for Children** (WISC). These differ from the Stanford-Binet in giving separate scores for each subtest.

5. Although group tests do not generally predict school performance as well as individual tests, many are widely used. The **Scholastic Aptitude Test** (SAT), which is used by many colleges as one criterion for admission, is a useful predictor—though by no means the only one—of college performance.

6. Normal intelligence covers a wide range; at one of its outermost extremes are the **mentally retarded**, who show, during the developmental period, below average intellectual functioning together with deficits in adaptive behavior. Because of the stigmatizing effects of labeling children "retarded," educators have become more careful in their evaluation of intelligence and do not label a child retarded unless he or she has both a low IQ and deficits in adaptive behavior, and only if these cannot be explained by sociocultural, emotional, or health problems. At the other extreme of the intelligence scale are the **mentally gifted**, who have been shown to be superior in health, adjustment, and accomplishment to less intelligent people. In response to the needs of the gifted, many school systems offer special classes and enrichment programs.

7. Intelligence is not the same thing as creativity; creative people are typically independent, self-confident, and persistent. Since intelligence tests often fail to identify creative people, new tests—none of which has yet been accepted as standard—are being developed to indicate creative abilities.

8. IQ scores reflect not only one's genetic potential for intellectual development (nature) but also one's environment and experience (nurture). Debate has continued over the years as to which factor is responsible for the differences among groups. Educational psychologist Arthur Jensen has proposed that genetic factors might be implicated in the fact that the IQ scores of blacks are lower than those of whites. The publication of his findings caused an uproar, and both his methodology and the data on which his work was based were called into question.

9. The Jensen controversy sparked considerable criticism of IQ tests themselves. Some argued that the tests reflect the language and culture of the predominantly white middle class too thoroughly to be valid for children from other backgrounds. Subsequent attempts were made to create a culture-free intelligence test. The best known of these is the System of Multicultural Pluralistic Assessment (SOMPA), which includes an interview with the child's parents and a complete medical examination in addition to a standard IQ test. IQ tests have also been criticized as being poor predictors of actual accomplishments in many fields. In addition, they are sometimes used to weed out applicants for jobs, even when the duties of the job have no apparent connection with the skills measured by the test. In response to many of the criticisms leveled against the tests, a federal law now prohibits children from being assigned to classes for the mentally retarded on the basis of an IQ test alone. And efforts continue to devise new and better measures of intelligence.

10. Tests to measure personality have evolved from research in two fields. Those that developed from differential psychology—the study of differences among individuals—are used primarily to measure personality traits among the normal population. Those that developed from abnormal psychology—the study of psychological disorders and the practice of psychotherapy—were intended for diagnostic use of the insane or abnormal.

11. Many diagnostic tests in use today are projective tests, in which personality characteristics are revealed in the way a subject responds to and interprets ambiguous material. The tests are also subjective in nature, because there is no standard score against which to measure an individual's performance. Such tests include the **Rorschach Inkblot Test** and the **Thematic Apperception Test** (TAT). Because the subject's responses can differ depending on the test situation, and because much of the "meaning" found in the test results depends on the examiner's skill in finding it, these tests are of little use unless given by a highly experienced examiner.

12. Other personality tests are objective in nature. The most widely used of such tests is the **Minnesota Multiphasic Personality Inventory** (MMPI), which contains 550 true-false statements that yield a rating on each of ten clinical scales. It is best used for the identification and diagnosis of psychopathology.

13. A variety of tests are used for vocational selection and educational counseling. Interest tests, which attempt to identify a person's interest in the actual activities of a given vocation, include the **Strong-Campbell Interest Inventory** (SCII). Some companies administer aptitude tests to measure applicants' abilities to perform the tasks their jobs would require. They may also give performance tests to determine how well one can actually perform a given type of work. The application blank and the job interview are also among the various assessment techniques companies use in trying to decide whom to hire.

14. The increased used of testing has raised a number of ethical issues, one of which is the appropriate interpretation of test results. It should be remembered that personality and intelligence tests are not perfect measures but instead provide a good estimate of what they are designed to measure. Moreover, test results should be used for only the specific situations in which they are valid. Another issue concerns the proper use of test information, and the decision about who should and should not know the results of particular tests. If tests are to be beneficial to individuals and society, careful attention must be paid to the ethical issues they raise.

Suggested readings

American Psychological Association. *Standards for educational and psychological tests.* Washington, D.C.: American Psychological Association, 1974.

Anastasi, A. *Psychological testing* (4th ed.). New York: Macmillan, 1976.

Cronbach, L. J. *Essentials of psychological testing* (3rd ed.). New York: Harper & Row, 1970.

Hearnshaw, L. S. *Cyril Burt, psychologist.* London: Hodder and Stoughton, 1979.

Loehlin, J. C., Lindzey, G., and Spuhler, J. *Race differences in intelligence.* San Francisco: W. H. Freeman, 1975.

Sundberg, N. *Assessment of persons.* Englewood Cliffs, N.J.: Prentice-Hall, 1977.

Torrance, E. *Gifted children in the classroom.* New York: Macmillan, 1965.

Wechsler, D. *The measurement and appraisal of adult intelligence* (14th ed.). Baltimore: Williams and Wilkins, 1958.

PART 7

PSYCHOLOGICAL DISORDERS

Part 7 is concerned with the clinical practice of psychology: How does mental illness manifest itself, and what strategies exist to improve it? Chapter 13 surveys abnormal behavior and Chapter 14, its treatment.

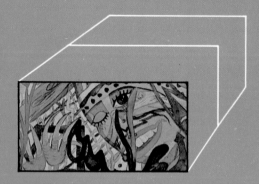

PREVIEW

1. Abnormal behavior is defined by several criteria and described by various theories, each with a characteristic perspective on causes, consequences, and treatment.

2. In all theories of abnormal behavior, psychological disorders are classified according to the symptoms involved.

3. The anxiety or "neurotic" disorders involve problems in coping with some aspect of life.

4. The affective disorders—such as mania (extreme elation) and depression (severe and lasting sadness and inactivity—are characterized by disturbances in mood.

5. Schizophrenia, or disturbances in thought, perception, affect, and motor behavior, is the most severe psychological disorder.

5. Personality disorders are maladaptive behaviors that cause distress to those affected—but little or no guilt or anxiety for the antisocial personality who engages in them.

15 Exploring abnormal behavior

How do we distinguish between "normal" and "abnormal" behavior? Consider the behavior of the following people:

A twenty-four-year-old man, armed with a .44-caliber revolver, cruises a New York neighborhood late at night, looking for "pretty girls" to shoot. When he is finally captured by police after a yearlong search, he has killed six people and wounded seven others. He says that "demons" drove him to the crimes.

A middle-aged businessman, fed up with his stressful job, his hourlong commute, and the demands of his suburban life style, packs a small bag of clothing and flees to the mountains, where he settles in an abandoned cabin, determined to live a life of isolation.

A young women who showed great academic promise in high school begins having difficulty with her studies in college. She believes that she is constantly behind in her work and will not be able to catch up, no matter how hard she tries. She feels lonely and becomes increasingly depressed and withdrawn.

A widely acclaimed young pianist, winner of many awards, begins to experience inexplicable attacks of "nerves." These feelings of anxiety become more intense and develop into waves of panic. Eventually, the thought of performing in public becomes so terrifying that the pianist's career is jeopardized.

To what extent are these individuals behaving "abnormally"? Is it accurate to label such diverse actions "psychopathological"? Are all these people in need of treatment? If they sought therapeutic help, what diagnosis would be made and what treatment prescribed?

In this chapter, we will examine "abnormal" behavior. We begin by considering what constitutes abnormality—a subject that remains controversial, as we shall see. We will then discuss some theories that have been advanced to identify the nature of abnormality and its causes. Finally, we will describe the principal types of abnormal behavior. This entire discussion—the nature of abnormality, the theories that have sought to explain it, and the ways of classifying it—should shed some light on the problems of the four individuals described above.

WHAT IS ABNORMAL BEHAVIOR?

Some patterns of behavior, for example the murderer who hears voices urging him to kill, can clearly be labeled abnormal. But would we be justified in applying the same label to our hypothetical harried businessman or the depressed college student? A number of standards are applied to evaluate the normality or abnormality of any given behavior. These include deviation from statistical norms, conformity with social or cultural values, and comparison with an absolute standard.

The simplest standard is a statistical criterion: Normality is what most people do, and abnormality is any substantial deviation from the average. Consider, for example, a person who experienced anxiety after starting a new job. Because most people feel some anxiety in a stressful situation, a therapist applying this standard would consider mild anxiety "normal" behavior. But extreme anxiety in such a situation—or even none at all—might be considered abnormal.

Another common standard of evaluation would compare a client's behavior with social or cultural norms. A woman who started dressing peculiarly and walking around her neighborhood screaming insults at strangers would, by this criterion, be considered to be behaving abnormally: She would be violating the social rules governing dress and deportment. Behavior that deviates substantially from social norms is usually considered abnormal. It is also likely to be statistically infrequent: These two criteria reinforce each other.

These two related standards, while useful in identifying abnormality, are not always sufficient. In some instances we may hesitate to apply the label "normal" to statistically frequent behaviors. For example, several studies have suggested that many college freshmen have serious problems with loneliness and depression. Yet sensitive administrators do not brush this problem off by calling it "normal"; they take steps to help students deal with the problem, such as offering counseling. Moreover, it is sometimes difficult to tell whether a given behavioral response is in fact statistically frequent. Even therapists are sometimes unaware of the frequency of particular behaviors and mistakenly conclude that they are abnormal. Consider this example: A recently widowed woman told her therapist that she had heard her dead husband speaking to her. The therapist, assuming that such behavior was "abnormal"—that is, statistically infrequent—might conclude that the woman was losing touch with reality. In fact, the number of bereaved people who experience such hallucinations is estimated to range between 50 and 90 percent (Coates and Wortman, 1980).

But perhaps the most serious problem with applying cultural or statistical norms is that neither approach distinguishes between desirable and undesirable deviations. Much of a society's vitality comes from people who venture beyond the norms, striking out in innovative directions. If we were to rigidly apply the "norm" approach, we might well discourage socially valuable abnormalities and support mediocrity.

The problems associated with the first two approaches to defining abnormality can be avoided by comparing a given behavior not with a cultural or statistical norm but with some absolute criterion. This approach assumes the existence of a certain universal or absolute standard of mental health. In practice, such a standard is elusive; the one held up as ideal is necessarily based on the evaluator's orientation and values. Some see freedom from emotional distress as the most important criterion, but even this ideal poses a problem. Under some circumstances emotional distress would seem to be the appropriate—and highly normal—reaction. The mother who experiences no emotional distress at the death of her child would hardly seem normal. In fact, some theorists argue that we cannot grow and reach our full human potential without taking risks and making decisions that may cause us pain and distress.

There is still another problem with this standard: Some people whose behavior is clearly abnormal show no apparent emotional distress. A psychologically disturbed killer, for example, may only smile vaguely when his crimes are recounted in court; although he is free from emotional distress, his behavior cannot be defined as normal.

No one of these three approaches to defining abnormality gives us an infallible standard. In practice we are influenced by all of them. As a result, not all agree on what is normal or abnormal. Abnormality might best be seen as a continuum. Most people have fears, anxieties, conflicts, and feelings of depression. They do not always conform to societal norms. Their reactions and behaviors are judged as abnormal only when they are prolonged and interfere with daily functioning.

APPROACHES TO ABNORMALITY

Centuries ago, some people theorized that the mentally ill were possessed by demons. With this theory they attempted to suggest a cause for the disturbance—the presence of a demon—which implied a treatment—cast the demon out. Even in so primitive a theory, we see two elements: a hypothesis about cause, and implications about treatment.

Over the years, a great many theories have been advanced to explain mental disturbance. Some theories have ascribed mental illness to physical sources, others have attributed it to psychological causes; and all have suggested ways to relieve the suffering of the mentally disturbed. In this chapter we will briefly describe six of today's major theories. Each has articulate advocates and claims of treatment successes. Some theories are more all-embracing than others, but all contribute to our understanding of abnormal behavior. And since what we have come to think of as abnormality includes such a wide range of behaviors, no one theory is ever likely to explain everything.

Figure 15.1 In previous centuries, abnormal behavior was sometimes considered to be the result of demonic possession. This sixteenth-century woodcut shows the devil carrying off a woman.

The medical model

Probably the single most influential theoretical perspective on abnormal behavior is the medical model. It views psychological disorders as similar to physical illnesses. Each disorder is thought to have a specific organic cause, which produces a specific set of symptoms (called a **syndrome**). In the medical model the causes of mental disorder are sought in such physical problems as dysfunction of the brain and faulty metabolic or endocrine functioning. Such problems can be brought on by a virus or germ (as in general paralysis, caused by syphilis), a physical trauma (such as a blow to the head), faulty heredity (such as an inborn malfunction in a gland), or similar physical causes. More recently, certain experiences have been found to alter the integrity of the body. Repeated exposure to stressful stimuli, for example, may lower brain norepinephrine, thereby bringing on depression. Whatever the process involved, according to the medical model a single cause leads to a single pattern of changes in the body, which in turn leads to a single cluster of symptoms.

The influence of the medical model can be seen in the common acceptance of the term "mental *illness*." From the time modern study of mental disturbance began, this model has predominated. The important early figures in the field were all physicians, and this mode of thought, with its reliance on such terms as *symptoms* and *treatment*, came naturally to them. It still comes naturally to us today. The influence of the medical model is also apparent in the *Diagnostic and Statistical Manual of Mental Disorders* (*DSM*) published by the American Psychiatric Association. This book is generally accepted as the official reference book of mental disorder. It lists hundreds of specific disorders in great detail, and lists characteristic symptoms in exactly the manner that other medical references list the symptoms of physical illnesses.

Like any theory, the medical model often influences the selection of treatment. Consider, for example, the case of a patient with depression. A therapist of this persuasion would be likely to ask whether any close relatives have suffered from the problem. Learning that the patient's mother had committed suicide, the therapist might suspect a genetic predisposition to mood disorders and hypothesize that the disorder is caused by endocrine dysfunction or biochemical imbalances. The therapist might then prescribe some kind of antidepressant medication (a type of treatment that will be considered in detail in the next chapter).

Broadly accepted as the medical approach to mental disturbance is, its implications are in some ways troubling. Consider what happens when a disturbed person becomes a "mental patient." His or her behavior is reduced to a set of "symptoms," characteristic of a particular illness, the person is considered a candidate for hospitalization and/or drug therapy, and it is assumed that treatment should be provided by medical personnel. One of the most vocal critics of the medical model, Thomas Szasz (himself a psychiatrist), has argued that casting a disturbed person into a "sick" role may be the worst thing we can do. When we call people "sick" and "treat" them accordingly, they often learn to act in just that way. Szasz, in *The Myth of Mental Illness* (1961) and his other books, has urged that we not think of "abnormal" behavior as an illness or a disease, but rather as a departure from social norms. People who are troubled by psychological disturbances, he says, are not ill; they suffer from "problems in living" that they will never be able to solve if they are not allowed to accept responsibility for their own behavior. Although Szasz's position is logically argued, it remains a minority view: most professionals in the field accept the existence of mental "disease."

The psychoanalytic perspective

The psychoanalytic approach, pioneered by Sigmund Freud, focuses on the critical role of the first few years of life. Psychological problems in later life, this theory holds, can be traced back to childhood conflicts, which, if not resolved, may interrupt the child's psychological development. In Freudian terms, the conflict causes a fixation (in a sense, a psychological stunting of growth) at the stage of development where it occurs.

Freud believed that a fixation at any stage will hamper full development of the adult's personality, but that the kind and severity of the adult's problem is determined by the stage at which the fixation occurs. If the fixation occurs in early childhood, before the ego is properly developed, the adult would experience drastic breakdown in functioning known as **psychosis**. If the fixation occurs later in life, while the superego is developing, the individual's problem would be less severe, a **neurosis**. In neuroses, conflicts between the id, ego, and superego produce **anxiety**, which the individual either experiences directly as discomfort, nervousness, or dread, or attempts to control through defense mechanisms. Although normal people commonly use defense mechanisms to gain relief from anxiety, neurotics use defense mechanisms excessively and in exaggerated form, tying up useful energy to a degree that interferes with normal functioning.

That Freud's ideas have pervaded our cultural life is evidenced by the terms that have become a part of our everyday vocabulary—*repression, Oedipus complex, castration anxiety*, and *ego*, to mention just a few. The perspective has made many contributions to our understanding of the sources of our behavior, not the least of which is the attention it has directed to the richness of our inner, subjective lives—our dreams, fantasies, and hidden motivations.

Freud's model, however, has been controversial from the beginning. Moreover, much of it is subjective and relies on the therapist's ability to infer causes and hidden motives from behavior. As a result, strict scientific validation of the model can be elusive. If a man calls his fiancee by his former girl friend's name, can we say he made a "Freudian slip," indicating preoccupation with an earlier romance? Or is there a more innocent explanation? Is psychoanalytic theory too subjective to evaluate scientifically? As we noted in Chapter 13, a recent review of the research bearing on Freud's model (Fisher and Greenberg, 1977) indicated that many parts have been scientifically evaluated and supported by empirical research. Studies have found that children do go through a period of erotic interest in the parent of the opposite sex (as Freud's Oedipus complex proposes) and that people who are especially sensitive to oral imagery do tend to show the "oral" traits of dependency and passivity. Clearly, this is not to say that all psychoanalytic theory has been proven, but merely that many of its aspects can be tested.

Psychoanalytic theory and the medical model, though two quite distinct models, are in certain ways compatible. In both, the patient's problems are considered symptoms of some underlying disorder—an organic dysfunction in the medical model and a conflict within the psyche in the psychoanalytic perspective. The two are also related in practice; many psychoanalysts are medical doctors, and American medical schools have traditionally offered psychiatric training based on Freud's theories.

The learning-theory perspective

The learning-theory perspective takes a different approach to abnormality. It stresses that psychological "disturbance" is maladaptive behavior that we have *learned* exactly as we learn anything else. Most abnormality, learning theorists argue, is the result neither of organic dysfunction nor of unresolved psychic conflicts. Instead, those who behave abnormally do so either because they have learned inappropriate behaviors or because they have failed to learn adaptive ones. True, many of us learned our maladaptive behaviors in childhood, but we could as well have learned them last month. To the learning theorist, nothing is sacred about the lessons learned in the "formative" years of childhood. Learning theory does share with psychoanalytic theory a belief that abnormality is rooted in past experience. But whereas psychoanalytic theory sees the experiences of infancy and early childhood as giving definite and lasting shape to the personality, learning theory argues that our experiences continue to shape us throughout our lives.

Learning theorists assume that people learn maladaptive behavior through the same principles of modeling, classical conditioning, and instrumental learning that apply to the learning of normal behavior (Chapter 5). Thus, a person may learn to be fearful and anxious by observing the anxiety of others (Rosenthal and Bandura, 1978), and children often learn to fear the same things their parents fear. Alternatively, a person may learn fears through classical conditioning, developing anxiety and phobias following a natural disaster or accident. All but one of the thirty-five survivors of a gasoline tanker explosion on the Delaware River reported severe symptoms of nervousness, depression, and phobic reactions four years after the accident (Leopold and Dillon, 1963).

We may also develop maladaptive behaviors through instrumental learning. A child who hates going to school may learn to get a stomach ache every morning or learn to behave so disruptively in class that he is repeatedly suspended. With either behavior, the child is rewarded with attention from parents or teachers and also allowed to avoid the unpleasantness of attending school.

Unlike medical or psychoanalytical thinkers, learning theorists do not see

Figure 15.2 According to the learning theorists, we learn abnormal behavior by the same mechanisms as we learn normal behavior. As children, for example, we may learn that bad behavior is our only means of gaining attention from our parents.

maladaptive behavior as symptomatic of some illness or "deeper" problem. They believe the behavior itself is the problem, and when the mechanisms that maintain the behavior can be identified, the problem can be solved. Consider, for example, phobias, a relatively common maladaptive behavior. Many phobias are maintained by avoidance—a dog-phobic person avoids all dogs, and thus never learns that some dogs are harmless. Therapy for such a person would be aimed at breaking the pattern of avoidance: The person would be helped to approach dogs (perhaps in a series of steps, from looking at pictures of dogs to touching a real dog), learning that dogs need not be dreaded.

Historically, the learning-theory approach has confined itself to identifying abnormal *behaviors* and the mechanisms that underlie them. A recent trend has been to focus as well on certain patterns of thought, or **cognitions**, that seem to contribute to maladaptive behavior. This cognitive approach emphasizes that how we interpret events may be almost as important as the events themselves. Our explanations to ourselves inevitably affect both our state of mind and our future behavior. One student, after failing an especially difficult exam, might take the failure in stride and decide to study harder and pass the next exam. Another student, however, might interpret the failing grade as an indication that she is incapable of doing college work—and become so depressed that she considers dropping out of school. These two cognitions ("I'll have to study harder" versus "I don't have the brains for college") show how our pattern of thought influences how we feel and how we will behave in the future. The cognitive approach has pointed out that we go through life constantly interpreting and drawing conclusions from what happens to us, and the quality of our internal dialogue—whether we accept ourselves or berate ourselves, build ourselves up or tear ourselves down—has profound consequences for our mental health.

Learning theory, with its emphasis on observable and understandable causes for maladaptive behavior, has contributed much to our understanding of abnormality. If abnormal behaviors are learned, then we can study their causes and treat their manifestations without inquiring into the mysteries of body chemistry or attempting to dip into the unconscious mind. Some argue, however, that learning theory is too simple, and that it does not do justice to the complex motives, needs, and internal conflicts that characterize human beings. In addition, some theorists argue that learning theory relieves people of responsibility for their actions—that if people have been taught maladaptive behavior by their environment, they cannot help being the way they are. In this, however, learning theory differs little from the medical and psychoanalytical approaches, both of which are also deterministic.

The family, or systems, approach

The three approaches discussed thus far focus on the troubled individual—the man, woman, or child who is behaving abnormally. In contrast, the family, or systems, approach sees mental disorders as necessarily involving the network of relationships binding the individual. The abnormality of the individual, in this view, can only be understood in the context of the family in which it arises.

This point of view developed largely from the experiences of psychotherapists who treated children. These professionals were unable to ignore the role of the family environment in producing the children's problems and began to expand their perspective beyond the child-patient to the roles of the parents and the other siblings. They concluded that the family is a system in which the interrelationships among family members are important forces in producing and maintaining maladaptive behavior.

Some family theorists (see, for example, Minuchin, 1974) examine the family as a set of interlocking roles. In their view, a family may have a disciplinarian, a scapegoat, a baby, and still other roles, and while these roles may not be good for the family members, they allow the system to maintain a degree of equilibrium. In this context, one member of the family might become an "identified patient" because the family role system requires a sick member. The sick person's recovery can force other members to abandon their roles, and thus cause turmoil in the family.

Other family theorists focus on the communications among family members (see, for example, Watzlawick, Beavin, and Jackson, 1967). According to this view, the contradictory messages that family members receive from one another cause distress and bizarre behavior. One simple example is seen when a parent encourages a child to speak his mind and then punishes him severely for "talking back." As will be discussed in a section to follow, family communication theorists have suggested that placing a child in such "double-bind" situations can lead to the development of schizophrenia. However, studying communication patterns within the families of disturbed individuals presents methodological and ethical problems, and as yet these theories have not received strong empirical support (Haley, 1980).

The sociocultural perspective

The sociocultural perspective, like the family approach, looks beyond the individual for the causes of abnormal behavior. However, it argues that mental disorders are caused by social ills such as poverty, poor nutrition, overcrowding, and discrimination against minority groups, women, and the aged. The primary evidence in support of this proposition has been the higher proportion of serious mental disorder, such as schizophrenia, found among the lowest socioeconomic classes, where the stresses of society are likely to be greatest (Hollingshead and Redlich, 1958; Kolb, Bernard, and Dorenwend, 1969). But these findings are open to other interpretations. Some theorists have suggested that severely disturbed middle-class people drift downward on the socioeconomic ladder (Dunham, 1965; Wender et al., 1973), so that by the time they are diagnosed and treated they reside in lower-class communities. An alternative possibility is that disturbed behavior is *labeled* as a more serious disorder if the person comes from the lower classes than if the person comes from the middle or upper classes (Scheff, 1975). Possibly many diagnosticians, themselves from the higher social classes, find the characteristic style of deviant behavior of the upper and middle classes less bizarre than the types of deviance common among the lower classes.

Nevertheless, the sociocultural perspective is important in calling attention to factors outside the individual that may cause mental disorders. Other psychological theories, with their emphasis on the individual, neglect the obvious fact that exposure to some environments and social institutions may cause "mental illness" in almost anyone.

The humanistic-existential perspective

The humanistic-existential perspective is a fairly recent school of thought within psychology. In contrast to all the approaches discussed previously, this perspective does not see abnormal behavior as the result of anything that has "happened" to us, whether through organic dysfunction, childhood trauma, inappropriate learning, or stresses in the family or the environment. Rather, it views human beings as born with an innate drive to "actualize" themselves— that is, to make the most of their unique talents and enjoy good relationships with others. Abnormal behavior, then, is a failure to achieve the self-actualization we are capable of. Often, our problems can be traced to our own poor choices; we choose safety over growth in our lives and unwittingly fail to achieve our full potential. The humanistic-existential perspective is optimistic, placing great faith in our ability to learn to make new choices that will liberate our unique human qualities.

With its emphasis on the importance of each individual's experience of the world, this perspective necessarily lacks a precise, universal theory and rejects the idea that a single set of psychological formulas can be applied to all people. Instead, the humanistic-existential therapist tries to attend closely and respond sympathetically to each person's problems and, if possible, to see the world from the client's point of view. (One type of humanistic therapy is appropriately called "client-centered.") The therapist places relatively little emphasis on delving into the person's past and instead concentrates on identifying how the person's innate tendencies toward self-actualization or "growth" can be liberated. This perspective emphasizes the positive rather than the negative—the person's capacity to change and to make new choices rather than the immediate problems he or she is experiencing.

The humanistic-existential model differs from the others in the importance it assigns to individual responsibility. In other therapies, a person may blame his or her problems on some external cause and sit back expecting the therapist to effect a cure. Humanistic-existential therapy insists that each person assume responsibility for his or her life. In this view, for example, if you are depressed, dislike your job, and find your marriage stifling, you have to some extent chosen depression instead of confronting the difficult choices of quitting the job or ending the marriage. Obviously, this kind of therapy is often not easy, and some humanistic and existentialist writers have suggested that a certain amount of pain and anxiety are necessary parts of "growth."

The writings of several of this movement's articulate spokesmen, such as Carl Rogers (1970) and Rollo May (1969), have given its ideas considerable prominence. It is this broad philosophy, especially its emphasis on human potential, that has inspired many of the diverse group therapies that have developed in the past decade.

Evaluating the perspectives

No one of the perspectives discussed can account for every kind of abnormal behavior, let alone provide us with a certain approach to treatment. Each perspective offers us a way of looking at mental disorder: in some respects these viewpoints are completely incompatible and in others they overlap. Some are broad enough to encompass most kinds of mental disturbance; others are more limited in scope.

Because each perspective proposes different causes for abnormal behavior, therapists who subscribe to a particular perspective will ask their clients different questions and offer very different kinds of treatment. Consider the case of a woman who experiences severe and prolonged depression after the death of her elderly father. A psychoanalyst might question the woman closely about her childhood and her feelings about her parents, hoping to find a clue to an unconscious process of the mind that had turned normal grief into serious depression. A learning theorist might look for factors in the woman's immediate environment that might be reinforcing her symptoms of depression. An existentialist therapist, after acknowledging the woman's need to mourn her father, might help her accept the fact that everyone is ultimately alone. Each theory with its accompanying therapy attacks the same problem in a different way. As we consider the various disorders in the sections that follow, we will examine the particular contributions of the different perspectives.

CLASSIFYING PSYCHOLOGICAL DISORDERS

Whatever model they may apply to abnormal behavior, psychologists and psychiatrists must have some means of identifying which individuals have a disorder and determining what kind of disorder it is. Usually, this is done by observing a person's behavior, or symptoms. As in medicine, the symptoms are expected to suggest a diagnosis. But in order to reach a diagnosis, some system of classification is needed. In all sciences, classification is an essential underpinning to the growth of knowledge. It gives mental health professionals a common vocabulary for disseminating information and communicating effectively within their field. It enables researchers and clinicians to group similar cases together and to suggest appropriate treatment for a whole class of disorders.

The guide to naming and classifying mental disorders relied on by virtually all psychologists and psychiatrists is the *Diagnostic and Statistical Manual of*

Mental Disorders, commonly referred to as the *DSM*. This manual, published by the American Psychiatric Association, includes a detailed list of the major mental disorders and their characteristic symptoms.

Criticisms of classification

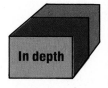

Essential as some system of classifying mental and emotional disorders would seem, the idea has its critics. Most argue that clearly defined categories, such as the *DSM* diagnoses, are unreliable, invalid, and even destructive. These so-called diagnoses, this argument contends, are simply labels that have been devised for the convenience of psychologists and psychiatrists—labels that may obscure the real condition of the patient and at the same time reduce him or her to subhuman status.

The best-known elaboration of this anticlassification argument came in the form of a paper by D. L. Rosenhan, published in 1973, called "On Being Sane in Insane Places." In Rosenhan's study, eight people who had never suffered symptoms of serious psychiatric disorder were sent to psychiatric hospitals, where they requested admission as patients. The group included three psychologists, a psychiatrist, a graduate student in psychology, a pediatrician, a painter, and a housewife. In the admission interview, they gave their personal histories truthfully, concealing only their identity. They faked only one symptom: hearing voices, which seemed to be saying "empty," "hollow," and "thud." After being admitted to the hospital, all the pseudopatients stopped simulating any symptoms of abnormality. Instead, they behaved normally and took notes on what they observed on the wards.

The pseudopatients stayed in the hospital from seven to fifty-two days, with an average stay of nineteen days. None were recognized as normal by the professional staff, although several real patients suspected that they were normal. Seven of the eight participants were diagnosed as schizophrenic and were discharged with the diagnoisis of "schizophrenia in remission."

In view of what happened to his pseudopatients, Rosenhan argued that psychiatric diagnosis is not valid; as he said, "we cannot distinguish the sane from the insane in psychiatric hospitals." Once the label of schizophrenic was applied, he argued, "the pseudopatients' normal behaviors were overlooked entirely or profoundly misinterpreted." Even note taking was seen as a symptom: "Patient engages in writing behavior" was one nurse's comment in the hospital record. Rosenhan argued further that the label is even more insidious:

A psychiatric label has a life and an influence of its own. Once the impression has been formed that the patient is schizophrenic, he will continue to be schizophrenic. When a sufficient amount of time has passed, during which the patient has done nothing bizarre, he is considered to be in remission and available for discharge. But the label endures beyond discharge, with the unconfirmed expectation that he will behave as a schizophrenic again (1973, p. 253).

One consequence of labeling patients, Rosenhan argued, is that their humanity is diminished; they become "lepers," stigmatized by their disorder. The pseudopatients' observations confirmed this contention. Staff members avoided contact with patients, addressed them with obscenities, struck them for petty offenses, and ignored their questions and requests for help. Rosenhan further contended that the label can follow real patients out of the hospital and influence the behavior not only of family and friends, but of the patient as well: "Eventually, the patient himself accepts the diagnosis, with all of its surplus meanings and expectations, and behaves accordingly" (1973, p. 254). The diagnosis, then, eventually becomes a self-fulfilling prophecy.

Not surprisingly, the publication of Rosenhan's study generated considerable controversy. In detailed critiques, Robert L. Spitzer (1975, 1976) accused Rosenhan of "logic in remission" (1975, p. 442). Spitzer argued that the fact that pseudopatients were able to lie their way into the hospital does not invalidate the diagnostic system. To suggest a parallel, if a person swallows a cup of blood, goes to an emergency room, spits it up, and is then diagnosed as having a bleeding ulcer, does this invalidate the diagnostic criteria for a bleeding ulcer?

Spitzer also pointed out that the hospitals responded very quickly to the absence of symptoms. An average hospitalization of nineteen days is quite brief for someone initially complaining of a serious symptom—and according to the diagnostic manual, hearing voices is a serious symptom, one of the classic symptoms of schizophrenia. Further, the hospitals were justified in keeping the patients even though their behavior seemed to return to normal, because diagnosis must consider both past and present behavior. The pseudopatients had reported a serious symptom, and the absence of such symptoms once they were hospitalized does not mean that they had no psychiatric abnormalities. Some truly schizophrenic patients have lucid intervals during which they seem normal. Further, Spitzer observed that "schizophrenia in remission," a diagnosis which is rarely used, indicates that the hospital staff did detect that these patients were symptom free.

Finally, Spitzer noted that Rosenhan's study contains very little actual data. For example, Rosenhan states that subjects' normal behavior was often seen as pathological by staff members. However, Spitzer says, "The only datum presented to support this claim is that the daily nursing comment on one pseudopatient was, 'Patient engages in writing behavior'" (1975, p. 445). He goes on to say that Rosenhan erred in not providing additional information about how the pseudopatients actually behaved in the hospital. "What did the pseudopatients say [in their admission interviews] . . . when asked, as they must have been, what effect the hallucinations were having on their lives and why they were seeking admission into a hospital?" Spitzer asks (1975, p. 447). Without a verbatim report of such interviews, we have no way of knowing exactly how the pseudopatients described their problems and thus how "sick" they seemed to the hospital staff.

In response to some of these criticisms, Rosenhan (1975) stressed that what was finally important about his study was that it illustrated the important role of context in the identification and diagnosis of mental disorders. Context, he contended, often leads diagnosis astray. In the case of the pseudopatients, their presence in the hospital itself acted almost to guarantee that their behavior would be considered pathological: Writing (a normal behavior in other contexts) became "writing behavior," presumably a symptom of some kind of disturbance. Once the pseudopatients were hospitalized, their claims to be normal and not in need of further hospitalization would be interpreted in the same way. One real patient advised a pseudopatient on how to negotiate this problem: " 'Don't tell them you're well. They won't believe you. Tell them you're sick, but getting better. That's called insight, and they'll discharge you!'" (Rosenhan, 1975, p. 472).

In view of all these problems, Rosenhan argues, we would be better off without diagnosis: ". . . at present, my own preference runs to omitting diagnoses entirely, for it is far better from a scientific and treatment point of view to acknowledge ignorance than to mystify it with diagnoses that are unreliable, overly broad, and pejoratively connotative" (1975, p. 467).

To this, supporters of psychiatric diagnosis respond that diagnosis is essential in order to advance knowledge. "Should we eliminate the diagnoses of antisocial personality, drug abuse, and alcoholism until we have treatments for these conditions whose benefits exceed the potential liabilities associated with the diagnosis? How do we study the effectiveness of treatments for these conditions if we are enjoined from using the diagnostic categories until we have effective treatments for them?" (Spitzer, 1975, p. 469).

Advocates such as Spitzer recognize that the reliability of diagnosis is often much lower than we would like. In fact, the new revision of the *DSM* attempts to improve the reliability of diagnosis by making the criteria much more specific. However, no matter how reliable the diagnostic system, there will be critics who point out the evils of diagnostic labeling and argue that diagnosis does more harm than good.

The APA classification system

Despite criticisms, the American Psychiatric Association's (APA) diagnostic manual, the *DSM*, in its three editions has been the preeminent system of classifying disorders. As such, it supplies a useful shorthand to professionals, who in a single word (such as *schizophrenia*) can communicate to others the existence of a whole group of related symptoms. In addition, the diagnostic category carries with it information about the seriousness of the disorder, how long it can be expected to last, and the likelihood that it will respond to treatment.

The *DSM* is an exhaustive list of the diagnoses professionals give to all types of mental disorders. Under each diagnosis is a detailed summary of the symptoms that must be present for the diagnosis to be appropriate, as well as estimates of the incidence of the disorder, whether it tends to occur in men more than women (or vice versa), whether it tends to "run in families," and so on. The diagnoses in the manual are based on judgments of mental health professionals, and they reflect the fact that these judgments change over time. In the first two editions of the *DSM*, for example, homosexuality was listed as a disorder. In 1973, however, the APA voted to strike homosexuality from the manual. The third *DSM* (1980) includes a category called "ego-dystonic homosexuality," which is applicable to only those homosexuals who are disturbed by their condition. It is interesting to note that the APA decided to drop homosexuality from the diagnostic manual by *voting* on the question. This illustrates the difference between the diagnosis of a physical illness and of a mental disorder (the American Medical Association would be unlikely to vote that influenza or arthritis was no longer a disorder).

The APA has been sensitive to criticisms of its manual, and the new *DSM* has been greatly revised in an attempt to meet those criticisms. The second edition of the manual, *DSM-II*, had been faulted for leaving diagnostic categories so broad as to be virtually meaningless. Several studies had shown that clinicians familiar with *DSM-II* categories often disagreed on the diagnosis of particular patients, and this disagreement seemed to be caused in large part by the vagueness of the diagnostic categories (Ward et al., 1962; Spitzer and Fleiss, 1974). In the new manual, *DSM-III*, the relatively brief descriptions of the *DSM-II* are replaced with lists of symptoms that often run to several pages. With the descriptions of the various disorders pinned down more precisely, the APA hopes that the new volume will be far more useful and reliable than the previous two editions.

In the sections that follow, we will examine some of the major disorders described by *DSM-III*—the anxiety disorders, somatoform and dissociative disorders, affective disorders, schizophrenia, personality disorders, and organic disorders. In addition we will see how the perspectives already discussed contribute to our understanding of these disorders.

"NEUROTIC" DISORDERS

Most people have difficulty in coping with some area of their life. One person may worry about getting cancer whenever he or she has a sore throat; another may be afraid to make decisions; a third may become tongue-tied in social situations. For most of us, such personality quirks do not severely limit our activities or interfere with our daily lives. They may cause us some inconvenience, but life is still liveable.

For some people, however, such difficulties become a major source of anxiety, taking up more and more of their attention until it seriously impairs their daily functioning. **Anxiety** is a feeling of dread, apprehension, or fear, often coupled with feelings of confusion and physiological symptoms, such as increased heartbeat, perspiration, muscle tension, and rapid breathing. Until recently, a number of different disorders characterized by anxiety were classified as *neuroses*. These are now considered separate disorders. They include anxiety disorders, somatoform disorders, and dissociative disorders. Although these disorders differ considerably from one another, they all tend to be relatively mild, and the afflicted person can continue to function in everyday life.

Anxiety disorders

Anxiety disorders are classified as generalized anxiety and panic disorders, phobic disorders, and obsessive-compulsive disorders. All three types are fairly common, affecting 2 to 4 percent of the population at any time (*DSM-III*, 1980).

Generalized anxiety disorder and panic *Generalized anxiety disorders* are characterized by diffuse and generalized fears that are impossible to manage through avoidance. The person is jumpy, irritable, and frequently upset. He or she expresses a great many fears and worries, yet is unable to specify what is generating these fears—a condition that Freud called *free-floating anxiety*.

Those suffering from anxiety disorders may have nightmares in which things close in on them or in which they are lost or abandoned. Furthermore, their daily coping is severely impaired. They are so preoccupied with their worries that they cannot concentrate on their work, and they may be forgetful and disorganized.

Various physical symptoms often accompany anxiety disorder. Victims may complain of stiff, aching muscles, the result of sustained muscle tension. Their appetite tends to be poor, and they may be troubled by indigestion and by a frequent need to urinate. Their sleeping patterns are also disturbed; they may have insomnia, or they may begin awakening suddenly in the night. In the morning they feel tired rather than refreshed. The following case illustrates a number of these symptoms:

Mr. Wright, a man of 35, was referred to hospital because of a "dizzy turn" which he had experienced during his work as a laborer. He had had similar attacks in the past but, with each one, the associated feelings of panic became more acute. . . .

As the attacks developed, he began to sleep badly. He had difficulty in getting off to sleep because of worrisome thoughts that raced through his mind; frequently his dreams had a menacing content and more and more they were only resolved by his awakening in a cold sweat, accompanied by frequent headaches. . . .

[Later] he began to complain of pressure in the front of his head and uncontrollable trembling and palpitations. He became more and more dependent on his wife and would go nowhere without her. . . . This meant of course that he had to give up work. . . . The worries about his failure to support his family caused his anxiety to "spiral" (McCulloch and Prins, 1975, p. 54).

People who suffer from anxiety disorders may also experience *panic attacks*, episodes in which the already heightened state of tension mounts to an acute and overwhelming level. During an attack the victim may experience difficulty in breathing, choking sensations, chest pain, heart palpitations, dizziness, faintness, hot or cold flashes, or fear of dying or going crazy. These terrifying sensations seem to come from nowhere. They may last for a minute or two or (more rarely) persist for an hour or more. When the attack subsides, the victim may feel exhausted.

Phobia When a person's anxiety focuses irrationally on a particular object or situation, it is called a **phobia**. Unlike those with generalized anxiety, people with phobias believe they know what triggers their intolerable anxiety, even though their fears may seem as irrational to them as they do to others. The case below is in many ways typical:

The client was a 30-year-old male who reported intense fear of crossing bridges and of heights. The fear had begun 3 years earlier when he was driving over a large suspension bridge while feeling anxious due to marital and career conflicts. Looking over the side he had experienced intense waves of fear. From that time onward his fear of bridges had become progressively more severe. At first, only bridges similar to the original were involved, but slowly the fear generalized to all bridges. Concurrently, he developed a fear of heights. Just before he came for treatment, he had been forced to dine with his employer in a restaurant atop a 52-story building. He had developed nausea and diarrhea and been unable to eat. This had decided him to seek treatment (Hurley, 1976, p. 295).

A phobia, then, can be extremely disruptive in a person's life. Ironically, the person may recognize that the fear is irrational; still, he or she usually cannot be reasoned out of the phobia. Only avoidance of the feared object relieves the anxiety.

Mild phobias are fairly common, and the stimulus is often something that it seems natural to fear—animals such as snakes, bees, and spiders, or natural phenomena such as lightning and darkness. Learning theorists have hypothesized that some phobias develop because of classically conditioned fears: A child stung by a bee thereafter fears bees and avoids going where bees are present. But how can we explain phobias that seem to develop without direct contact with the feared object? If a person has never been on an airplane, how could we account for his developing a phobic fear of all airplanes, as sometimes happens? Learning theorists have suggested that such phobias are learned from others (Bootzin and Max, in press). If we have heard other people express a fear of flying, we may learn to fear it ourselves, even before we ever get near a plane. Freudians, in contrast, have argued that phobias develop as a defense against dangerous or unacceptable impulses. Our despondent man with a bridge phobia, for example, might be protecting himself from an impulse to commit suicide by driving off the bridge.

Obsessions and compulsions An **obsession** is a recurring irrational thought, one that the victim recognizes as senseless and tries to suppress. A **compulsion** is an act of irrational behavior, again recognized as irrational, that the person seems unable to control. Obsessions and compulsions are closely related: Obsessive thinking often leads to compulsive behavior. A common example is the person who is obsessed with the idea of germs and feels compelled to repeatedly wash her hands to get rid of them. Below is a somewhat more extreme example:

Mr. B was unmarried, aged 45, and had a 30-year history of obsessive-compulsive problems. . . . [His] basic problem was a compulsion to be slow, meticulous, and ritualistic, especially when dressing, washing, shaving, cleaning his teeth and combing his hair. . . . For instance, cleaning his teeth involved 192 slow meticulous brush strokes for each application of toothpaste and for each rinse. . . . Bathing would take him up to three hours with half an hour spent in rinsing the bath before filling it and half an hour rinsing the bath afterwards. Every action was performed in a slow meticulous manner reminiscent of the care taken by a bomb disposal expert (Hodgson and Rachman, 1976, p. 29).

Obsessions without compulsions are experienced as ideas that cannot be dismissed from the mind. McCulloch and Prins (1975) reported the case of a man who became unable to carry on his normal life, so troubled was he by the recurring thought that Christ was a homosexual. The person with an obsession often dwells on some thought continually, ruminating on its pros and cons in a pattern of doubt and uncertainty, as illustrated by the following case:

Eliot H., a college student, went to a telephone booth to call up a wealthy girl whom he had recently met, to ask her for a date. He spent an hour there, anxious and indecisive, unable to put the coin in the slot and unable to give up and go home. Each time his hand approached the telephone he anxiously withdrew it because he felt that telephoning her might ruin his chances with her. Each time he withdrew his hand he seemed to be throwing away a golden opportunity. . . .

His whole future seemed to Eliot to hang on the outcome of this little act. . . . He was helplessly caught in an obsessive dilemma, as he had been caught before hundreds of times (Cameron, 1963, p. 396).

Such behavior, disabling though it is, can be seen as an exaggeration of the normal doubt and indecisiveness we all experience from time to time. But many obsessions and compulsions are much more bizarre. People have been obsessed with the idea that they would kill a family member or disrobe on a busy street. Compulsive hand washers have been known to continue their repetitious scrubbing until their hands were raw. Other victims of compulsions have been unable to sleep at night, compelled to repeatedly get out of bed to see that the doors were locked.

If you asked those who suffer from compulsions why they do these things, most would say that they feel uneasy unless they do them. Performing the compulsive behaviors seems to avert anxiety. Unfortunately, compulsions may have serious consequences for the victim. When every step must be counted or every doorknob touched twelve times before it can be turned, normal life becomes impossible.

Somatoform disorders

The distinguishing characteristic of a **somatoform disorder** is some physical, or somatic, malfunction caused by psychological distress. There are several different types of somatoform disorders, but we will discuss just one: conversion disorder.

Conversion disorder This disorder was so named because anxiety was thought to be "converted" into what appears to be a physical dysfunction. A person suddenly becomes blind, deaf, paralyzed, or loses sensation in some part of the body, usually following some traumatic event. However, no organic basis can be found for the condition and it violates neurophysiological laws. For example, a person's hand might become completely numb—even insensitive to the stab of a pin—but quite illogically, the person might feel normal sensations in an area directly above the wrist (Figure 15.3). This is called glove anesthesia because the loss of sensation occurs in an area that would be covered by a glove rather than in an area that corresponds to actual neurological pathways.

A conversion disorder often takes a form that makes it impossible for the victim to engage in some anxiety-provoking activity. The student who has failed a crucial exam becomes blind and can no longer study; the soldier who has had a brush with death on the battlefield develops a paralyzed arm and can no longer fire a gun. We should emphasize that these persons are not faking or malingering; their blindness and paralysis are real. However, they are caused not by physical processes but by psychological ones. The role the symptoms play in reducing anxiety is revealed by the calm way in which the victim sometimes seems to accept even a severe disability.

Conversion symptoms often appear and disappear suddenly. The blind student wakes up one morning able to see normally. Many so-called miracle cures in which the paralyzed suddenly leave their wheelchairs and walk or the blind suddenly see may be cases in which the disability was actually a conversion symptom.

Several theories have been put forth to explain these disorders. Freud argued that conversion disorders develop as defenses against forbidden impulses. Guilt

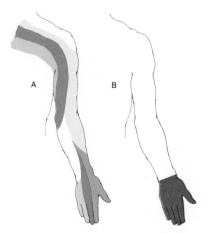

Figure 15.3 A person who complained of numbness in the hand might be diagnosed as suffering either from damage to the nervous system or from conversion disorder, depending on the exact pattern of the numbness. The skin areas served by different nerves in the arm are shown in A. The "glove anesthesia" shown in B could not result from damage to these nerves.

over masturbation or an urge to strike one's parents might result in paralysis of the arm. Learning theorists, in contrast, tend to see conversion symptoms as means of escaping anxiety and responsibility and of gaining the care and attention of others. Finally, family theorists might attempt to discover whether the conversion was serving some useful role in the family relationship. Haley (1973) tells of a woman who developed conversion blindness when her husband retired. Her condition served to help him cope with the difficult transition from his demanding job to an inactive role at home. Caring for her and running the household made him feel useful. When she began to recover, he became depressed, and he began to feel better only after she suffered a relapse.

Dissociative disorders

In the **dissociative disorders**, psychological rather than physical functioning is affected. A part of the personality is split off, or dissociated, so that the person's memory or identity is disturbed. These disorders include amnesia, fugue, and multiple personality.

Amnesia Amnesia is the partial or total forgetting of past experiences after a stressful experience, such as an automobile accident or a battle. Unlike organic amnesia, dissociative amnesia appears suddenly in proximity to stress, the pattern of forgetting is selective and the forgotten material can be recovered under hypnosis. Interestingly, such persons always retain some memories of their former lives, even if their identity has vanished. A woman might not recognize her family, for example, but she might remember how to knit.

Fugue In a **fugue** ("flight"), people walk away from their home and their identity. They may be absent for hours, days, months, or years, and in rare cases may take up a totally new life. Typically, they recall nothing of what happened in the fugue state. The following case is in many ways typical:

A young married woman, chronically unhappy and in conflict over her marriage, occasionally wandered from her home in the daytime and got lost, much as unhappy little children do. She would suddenly "come to" far from home, and with no memory of having left it (Cameron, 1963, p. 339).

Multiple personality In a more extreme form of dissociation, called **multiple personality**, a person's personality structure divides into two or more complete identities, each well defined and distinct from the others. Two recent cases of this rare disorder have been widely publicized in the films *The Three Faces of Eve* and *Sybil*. Often the personalities contrast strongly with one another; Eve, for example, included the "good girl" personality of Eve White and the naughty, uninhibited Eve Black. Usually, the personalities emerge or disappear suddenly and are generally unaware of one another.

AFFECTIVE DISORDERS

Affective disorders are characterized by disturbances of mood. All of us undergo frequent changes in mood, and some of us are more "moody" than others (Wessman and Ricks, 1966). In most cases, our emotional reactions are influenced by some change in our lives. Naturally we are elated if we win the lottery and dejected if the person we love rejects us. Sometimes we feel marvelous—or miserable—for no apparent reason. Such variations in mood are normal. Elation or depression becomes abnormal only when it is so prolonged as to interfere with daily functioning and so pronounced as to distort the person's whole outlook on life. In extreme cases victims may completely lose touch with reality. The sections that follow will examine depression, mania, and manic-depressive disorder.

Depression

We are all familiar with the normal feelings of sadness or what we might call the blues. We feel unhappy and perhaps guilty, lethargic, and slowed down. Initiating any activity—even an enjoyable one—becomes too much trouble; food and sexual activity lose their appeal. The symptoms of **clinical depression** are similar, but they are more severe and prolonged; the depressed person may lack the energy even to get out of bed, and utterly dejected, may abandon work, family, hobbies, and social activities. Typically, the victims lose their appetites and consequently lose weight; their sleep is disturbed. Here is how one patient described her experience of depression:

I began not to be able to manage as far as doing the kinds of things that I really had always been able to do easily, such as cook, wash, take care of the children, play games, that kind of thing. . . . I think one of the most frightening aspects at the beginning was that time went so slowly. It would seem sometimes that at least an hour had gone by and I would look at my watch and it would only have been three minutes. And I began not to be able to concentrate. Another thing that was very frightening to me was that I couldn't read any more. And if awakened early . . . earlier than I needed to, I sometimes would lie in bed two hours trying to make myself get up because I just couldn't put my feet on the floor. Then when I did, I just felt that I couldn't get dressed. And then, whatever the next step was, I felt I couldn't do that.*

In more extreme cases of depression, the sufferer may weep uncontrollably or become suicidal. The person may dwell on his or her inadequacies, becoming preoccupied with past "sins" or "crimes." In the most severe depression, called *psychotic depression* (a term that indicates so serious a disorder as to cause a break with reality), the person has hallucinations or delusions (and sometimes both). A *hallucination* is a sensory perception unrelated to an external stimulus; the person hears, or more rarely sees, something that is not there. A severely depressed man may hear voices that threaten hellfire or that call him names. The hallucination usually reflects the person's feelings of guilt or self-hatred. A woman who is depressed about her inability to meet the constant demands of her family, for example, might hear voices accusing her of being a bad mother. A *delusion* is an irrational belief held in spite of evidence that it has no basis in reality. A deeply depressed man might be convinced that he caused his father's death, for example, or that he himself is slowly dying of cancer. Or he might think that he has committed a terrible crime or even is the Devil himself.

Depression tends to be a persistent disorder, often coming and going in spells that may last weeks or months. People who have had one episode face a 50

Figure 15.4 Severe depression carries with it the danger of suicide. Overwhelmed with hopelessness, the sufferer may see suicide as "the only way out." (Woodcut by Käthe Kollwitz; Courtesy of the National Gallery of Art, Washington, D.C., Rosenwald Collection.)

*From "Depression: The Shadowed Valley," from the series *The Thin Edge*, © 1975 by the Educational Broadcasting Corporation.

percent chance of having another. A distinction can be drawn between reactive depression, or depression that seems to be caused by some external event (such as the loss of one's job), and endogenous depression, which seems unrelated to any external event. In practice, however, the distinction is seldom clear-cut; it is often difficult to pinpoint the cause of a particular depressive episode. Although all the symptoms of depression (even hallucinations) are common in people who lose a spouse or other loved one, their depression is generally not considered to be the same as clinical depression. *DSM-III* recognizes this distinction by calling this phenomenon "uncomplicated bereavement" and setting it apart from actual disorders.

Mania

At the opposite end of the affective spectrum is **mania**, a state of elation and feverish activity. Mania is far more extreme than normal elation, and it is often uncontrollable and prolonged—lasting for days, weeks, or even months. The manic person may feel brilliant and superior, ready and able to do anything. He or she may discharge surplus energy in constant chatter, in elaborate schemes to make money, or in shopping sprees to spend it. Whatever activities the person engages in, he or she is unlikely to persist at any one for very long: The manic person may energetically pursue an activity for an hour or a day, only to abandon it unfinished for another and yet another. This distractibility is likely to be evident in the person's speech, which is often characterized by unfinished sentences and leaps from subject to subject. As in severe depression, in mania a person may experience hallucinations and delusions. Voices may tell him he is a king or the smartest person in the country. The person may be deluded into thinking that she is about to become a multimillionaire or receive the Nobel Peace Prize.

Under the two broad headings of mania and depression, there are many patterns that affective disorders may follow. Some people suffer only mania or depression; others experience both. Some people have recurrent mood swings; others have just a single episode, recover, and are never troubled again.

Manic-depressive disorder

Manic-depressive disorder is characterized by the episodic nature of extremes of mood. The periods of disturbed affect are usually fairly short, often with some interval of normality between them. In rare instances, the two extreme moods may appear at alternating intervals over a long period of time. Or the person may have several episodes of depression interspersed with only a few periods of mania (or vice versa). But both extremes—severe depression and manic excitement—eventually are present.

Depression: current theories and research

Because depression is such a common disorder—affecting millions of people in this country every year—and because it can be so disabling, researchers have sought diligently to discover its causes. Approaching the problem from one of the several perspectives discussed earlier in the chapter, investigators have put forth several intriguing theories. We will briefly examine the most important of these.

The psychoanalytic perspective The psychoanalytic view of depression, first expressed by one of Sigmund Freud's students, Karl Abraham (1911, 1916) and then elaborated by Freud (1917), contends that depression stems from the loss of a loved one toward whom one has ambivalent (that is, both positive and negative) feelings. When the loved one dies or otherwise "abandons" the individual, the negative feelings turn to rage. The individual, however, does not experience this rage consciously, for he or she is afraid to express anger toward a departed loved one. Instead the person turns this powerful feeling inward and experiences it as self-reproach and self-loathing, which leads to depression. Some research suggests that Freud's insight in connecting the loss of a loved one to depression was accurate; for example, many depressed people suffered the death of a parent when they were children (Heinicke, 1973). Whether some deeply felt loss lies at the root of most cases of depression is as yet unproven, but theorists of many schools have noted the connection between depression and unexpressed anger.

The learning-theory perspective The learning-theory perspective offers several intriguing theories about the causes of depression. We shall examine three such theories, concentrating on the research of Peter M. Lewinsohn, Aaron Beck, and M. E. P. Seligman.

Lewinsohn: social skills and self-perception Lewinsohn's research on depression has focused on the role an individual's social relations play in producing and maintaining depression. He has argued (1974) that depression is maintained by a low rate of positive reinforcement. In other words, depressed people remain depressed because, being passive and inactive, they no longer obtain pleasurable reinforcement from life. They stay home and avoid social activities or when they do participate, they lack the social skills to enjoy themselves.

Lewinsohn and his colleagues conducted a recent study (1980) to determine whether depressed people have difficulty interacting with others. They asked a group of depressed people and two control groups to rate their "social competence" (friendliness, ability to converse with others, and so forth) after participating in a discussion group. The three groups were simultaneously rated by a group of trained observers. The observers found that the depressed people did indeed lack social skills. Moreover, they recognized their deficit and rated themselves realistically. Their low self-ratings corresponded with the low ratings given them by the observers. Both control groups (normal persons and nondepressed psychiatric patients), in contrast, overrated their social skills: They rated themselves as significantly *more* socially competent than the observers rated them. As the depressed people received therapy they continued their participation in the experiment. Both their self-ratings and the observers' ratings of their social skills rose. In fact, as the depressed people recovered they began to see themselves more positively than the observers had—exactly as the control groups did. The experimenters suggest that an important ingredient in *not* being depressed may thus be "illusory self-enhancement." They concluded that "a key to avoiding depression is to see oneself less stringently and more favorably than others see one" (Lewinsohn et al., 1980, p. 212).

Beck: the cognitive theory The cognitive theory sees the roots of depression not in what people do but in what they think. This theory, elaborated by Aaron Beck (1967, 1974), suggests that errors in thinking lead depressed people to put a consistently negative interpretation on virtually everything. If a man is fired from his job, he concludes that he is hopelessly incompetent, when in fact his boss may need to trim the staff and do so by dismissing the most junior employee. Depressed people twist their own experiences in their minds, giving a pessimistic—and self-critical—interpretation to every event.

According to cognitive theorists, encouraging depressed people to become more active or to socialize more—as learning theorists recommend—will not, of itself, improve their condition. Their new experiences will simply provide them with new occasions to criticize themselves. Several studies have offered support for this contention, suggesting that depressed people tend to "look on the dark side" or dwell on the negative in any given situation (Lloyd and Lishman, 1975).

Seligman: the "learned helplessness" theory In a series of experiments with dogs, M. E. P. Seligman and his colleagues made an interesting discovery (Seligman, Maier, and Geer, 1968). Seligman first strapped dogs into a harness and exposed them to electric shocks from which they could not escape. He then placed the dogs in another experimental chamber and again administered shocks. But this time the dogs could learn to escape the shocks by jumping from one side of the compartment to the other. The dogs that had previously received uncontrollable shocks failed to initiate any attempts to escape the shocks in this new situation and passively endured as many shocks as the experimenter chose to give. After the experiment, the dogs exhibited symptoms much like those seen in depressed people: lethargy, inactivity, and decreased appetite. In contrast, dogs that had not received any uncontrollable shocks prior to being placed in the second chamber were able to learn very quickly to escape from and avoid the shocks.

How can the passivity of the first group of dogs be explained? According to Seligman, the dogs had learned that termination of the shocks was independent of their behavior. In other words, they learned that they were helpless to control the shocks, and they continued to act on this belief in the second phase of the experiment, during which the shocks *were* controllable. On the basis of this data, Seligman proposed a general theory of learned helplessness: When people are unable to alter or influence something important to them, they may not only stop trying in the present setting but may become depressed and show little initiative in new settings where success might be achieved.

Seligman's original research and his theory have generated considerable controversy. Some investigators have argued that Seligman's dogs may have become passive and failed to avoid the shocks because they *habituated* to the shocks and no longer found them aversive (Jackson, Maier, and Coon, 1979). But most investigators have criticized the theory itself rather than the experimental data. For example, the theory does not account for the fact that symptoms of depression, as well as its intensity, can vary considerably. Why do some people experience intense feelings of self-blame or guilt when they are depressed, while others do not? And when does exposure to an uncontrollable outcome result in a depression that is severe and prolonged, as opposed to a more minor or fleeting depressive episode?

As a result of these and other criticisms, Seligman and his associates have modified their theory (Abramson, Seligman, and Teasdale, 1978). The reformulated model maintains that it is not uncontrollable outcomes themselves, but a person's causal explanations for these outcomes, that determine the nature and magnitude of depression. People who attribute an undesirable outcome to their own inadequacies will experience guilt and self-blame. Those who attribute an undesirable outcome to external factors may feel equally depressed, but will not feel self-blame. And those who attribute an outcome to something stable and unchangeable or to something operating in different settings should have the most prolonged and debilitating depressions. For example, a person who attributes his or her business failure to personal incompetence should be more severely depressed, and more reluctant to initiate behavior in other areas, than a person who ascribes the failure to insufficient effort, bad luck, or temporary unfavorable economic conditions.

Since this reformulated model addresses many of the problems of the original model, a number of researchers have become enthusiastic about it, though it has been criticized. Perhaps the most serious criticism is that the model does not indicate the conditions under which a person is likely to make a certain type of attribution. Why does one person attribute his or her low grade to the teacher or to unfair tests, while another reacts with feelings of inadequacy (Wortman and Dintzer, 1978)?

Biological and physiological theories In research similar to Seligman's experiments with dogs, Jay Weiss and his colleagues (Weiss, Stone, and Harrell, 1968, 1970) have found that an electric shock (or any of several other stressful experiences, such as a dip in cold water) causes rats to become inactive, accepting additional shocks even when they could avoid them. But instead of ascribing these results to "learned helplessness," Weiss points out that the shocks have a biological effect: They reduce the substance norepinephrine in the brain. In fact, Weiss suggests (Weiss, Glazer, and Pohorecky, 1974a, 1974b) that depression may have a biological cause: low levels of norepinephrine, brought about by stress.

Seligman (1975) has critized this biological interpretation, noting that if the animals are allowed to rest for several hours to several days and are then reexposed to shocks, they still show "helpless" behavior. Seligman has argued that during this rest period, the level of norepinephrine should return to normal, so the animals' behavior must be the result of learning rather than of a neurochemical deficit. But some data collected by Anisman and Sklar (1979) cast doubt on Seligman's interpretation. They found that if animals are exposed to inescapable shocks and then allowed to rest, reexposure to shocks on the next day results in a rapid decline in norepinephrine. Their research suggests that once an animal has been exposed to a stressor that results in neurochemical depletions, it becomes conditioned and therefore reacts to subsequent shock exposure with pronounced neurochemical changes. At present, neither the learning nor the biological theory is universally accepted, and research into the role of norepinephrine continues.

Several other biological factors have been considered as possible contributors to depression. Some research (Depue and Evans, 1976) has suggested that depressed persons retain excess sodium in their bodies. Since sodium ions are involved in the transmission of nerve impulses in the brain, excess sodium might act to produce the "slowing down" typical of depression. However, since the blood sodium level is also affected by bodily activity, depressed persons may have higher levels of sodium because they are inactive. As yet, the exact nature of the connection is unclear. Other research (Berger, 1978) has linked depression to a deficiency in certain brain neurotransmitters, either norepinephrine (mentioned above), or serotonin, or both. Still other evidence suggests that hormones may be involved or that a combination of hormone and neurotransmitter deficiencies is to blame. Although investigations into the biological causes of depression have produced some interesting findings, still further research is needed to determine exactly what role body chemistry plays in producing depression.

Family, or systems, theories The family, or systems, approach, as we noted earlier, seeks the causes of abnormal behavior in disturbed interactions among family members. James Coyne (1976a) has elaborated an "interactional" theory of depression that attempts to describe how this process works. According to his theory, when a person begins to complain of the symptoms of depression (sadness, tiredness, sleeplessness, and so on), he or she gets what might be called negative feedback from family members. As Coyne states:

Members of the social environment attempt to reduce the aversive behavior of depressed persons and alleviate guilt by manipulating them with nongenuine reassurance and support. At the same time, these same persons reject and avoid the depressed persons. As discrepancies between the reassurance of others and their actual behavior becomes apparent, the depressed persons are confirmed in their suspicions that they are not accepted. . . . To maintain their increasingly uncertain security and to control the behavior of others, depressed persons display more symptoms and convey more distress, thereby further stimulating the depressive social process (1976b, p. 187).

In an interesting experiment designed to test the theory that those around the depressed person often respond with hostility, forty-five normal subjects spoke by telephone to either a depressed or a nondepressed subject. Those who spoke to a depressed subject were themselves found to be significantly more depressed, anxious, hostile, and rejecting after the phone conversation (Coyne, 1976b).

Coyne's ideas contrast most sharply with the learning theorists' contention that depression is maintained by the *positive* responses of others (sympathy, concern, and so on). It also differs from the "cognitive" hypothesis, which suggests that depressed persons negatively distort information from the environment. Coyne's evidence suggests that no distortion may be involved: The depressed person may actually be getting very negative information from family members. Finally, if Coyne is correct, depression does not stem solely from a lack or deficit in the personality of the victim. Instead a "depressive social process" within the family environment is also to blame.

An integrative hypothesis In view of the number of competing theories that have been proposed, we might be left to wonder which is "right." Research has been fragmentary in many areas, and we can hope that further study will shed more light. In the meantime, some investigators have proposed that several of the theories can be unified (Akiskal and McKinney, 1973, 1975). Their view stresses the complex interaction between biological activity and psychological responses to external events in causing and maintaining depression. The initial depressive symptoms, they argue, may be caused by a biological defect and maintained by learning or family interaction. Or alternatively, if the symptoms are caused by trauma, unfortunate events, or a person's reaction to his or her life experiences, the depressed behaviors—such as inactivity—may in turn trigger a physiological reaction that reinforces the symptoms—such as a drop in brain neurotransmitter levels, retention of sodium in the blood, or changed hormonal functioning. This integrative theory recognizes the close relationship between mind and body and at the same time reminds us of their complexity.

SCHIZOPHRENIA

Schizophrenia, perhaps the most severe disorder recognized by our nomenclature, is the disorder suffered by most of those who occupy our mental hospitals. It is resistant to treatment and is seldom completely cured. The victim of schizophrenia experiences a profound disorder of thought and is unable to function in normal life. The following case illustrates the disruption of personality that is associated with this disorder:

Six months before his admission Arnold began to scream while at work, with no apparent provocation, turned off all the machinery, and continually interfered with the work of others. When his supervisor reprimanded him, Arnold told him to go to hell, and was fired. He claimed that he could see his mother's body floating in the air. . . . Four months before his admission he broke in the door of his home with an ax and threatened the members of his family. He was arrested for this, but released soon thereafter. On the day before his admission he threatened to burn the house, and then broke into his father's room and said, "You have got to kill me or I will kill you. Tonight the time is up." Faced with this choice his father had Arnold arrested again. The next morning Arnold told the police, "I see a whole bunch of dead people sitting there now. They run about my cell at night like crazy men, pulling me around. I hear them whispering to me." He was then committed to the local state hospital.

On admission he was quiet, and indifferent to his commitment. His conversation and behavior were childish and marked by foolish and inappropriate laughter. At first he though it was "awful to be among so many crazy people" but shortly thereafter he realized that it was quite a joke, and laughed heartily about his fate. He felt that the attendants were going to kill him, but laughed foolishly while telling of his fears. He was very childishly changeable in his behavior and affect. . . . He felt that people always made fun of him and declared, "I won't stand it, they take me for a raven." He experienced a series of vivid hallucinations, including feeling a man's claws on his throat, although he did not see or hear the man, feeling electricity jar him, seeing ghosts haunting him, seeing blue shadows going around and red shadows going up and down through the air, and seeing wingless female spirits flying through the air (Zax and Stricker, 1963, pp. 101–102).

Symptoms of schizophrenia

Although Arnold's violent behavior is somewhat atypical of this disorder, his other symptoms are characteristic: disordered thought, including delusions; hallucinations; nonsensical speech; and expressions of emotion that seem inappropriate to the situation. The name for this disorder comes from the Swiss psychiatrist Eugen Bleuler (1911), who coined the term from the Greek words *schizein*, meaning "to split," and *phren*, meaning "mind." Bleuler referred not to the splitting of personality into multiple or alternating parts—this, as we have seen, is characteristic of a dissociative disorder, multiple personality. Instead, Bleuler was attempting to describe a psychic split, the breaking of connections among various psychic functions within a single personality. Emotions, for example, may be split from perception and thus be inappropriate to the situation, as they were in Arnold's case. To use Bleuler's words, "the personality loses its unity" (1911, p. 9).

Clinicians have distinguished several subtypes of schizophrenia according to their predominant symptoms. Table 15.1 lists four classifications. All schizophrenics, however, show certain characteristic disorders of thought, perception, affect, and motor behavior.

TABLE 15.1 Four Subtypes of Schizophrenia

Disorganized (hebephrenic) schizophrenia	Most severe disintegration of personality. Most common symptoms are frequent or constant incoherent speech and odd affect, such as laughing or crying at inappropriate times. Disorganized hallucinations and delusions are present.
Catatonic schizophrenia	Characterized either by excessive, sometimes violent, motor activity or by a mute, unmoving, stuporous state. Some catatonic schizophrenics alternate between these two extremes, but often one or the other behavior pattern predominates.
Paranoid schizophrenia	Characterized by delusions of persecution, grandeur, or both. Paranoid schizophrenics trust no one and are constantly watchful, convinced that others are plotting against them. They may seek to retaliate against supposed tormentors.
Undifferentiated schizophrenia	Characterized by hallucinations, delusions, and incoherence without meeting the criteria for the other types or showing symptoms characteristic of more than one type.

Disorders of thought Most schizophrenics demonstrate a split, or lack of association, among various ideas or between ideas and emotions. Normal people mentally link concepts and symbols and establish logical connections with a main idea that they wish to express. They might think, for example, that they are hungry and would like to eat a steak. The concept of hunger is joined to the concept of steak, and a relationship is set up between the two—namely, steak satisfies hunger. The incoherence of dissociation in the thought processes of the schizophrenic, however, interrupts such relationships. The schizophrenic thus may shift from one frame of reference to another, following a verbal tangent:

I have just looked up "simplicity" and the dictionary says "sim - one, plicare - to fold, one fold." I told Dr. H—that I dreamed he returned to me the story I sent him which he had folded six times then I had folded it once making it double. Jesus said that the sheep he called would make one fold. I thought at the time that the Latin for six is sex, and that the number of the Beast is 666. Is sex then beastly? I think I will leave you to puzzle out the difference between 6 and 666 and 6 fold in substitution of one fold; for the number of the Beast is a mystery (Mayer-Gross, Slater, and Roth, 1969, p. 267).

Here the speaker has moved from a fold in a piece of paper to a sheep fold and from six to the Latin word for six (sex) to the nature of sex itself.

Besides showing interruptions in the logical connections of words, schizophrenic thought is often characterized by a tendency to lose track of the subject at hand and pursue other lines of thought. This phenomenon is well illustrated by the following letter, written by one of Bleuler's patients:

Dear Mother,
I am writing on paper. The pen which I am using is from a factory called "Perry & Co." This factory is in England. I assume this. Behind the name of Perry Co. the city of London is inscribed; but not the city. The city of London is in England. I know

this from my school days. Then, I always liked geography. My last teacher in that subject was Professor August A. He was a man with black eyes. I also like black eyes. There are also blue and gray eyes and other sorts, too. I have heard it said that snakes have green eyes. All people have eyes. There are some, too, who are blind. These blind people are led about by a boy. It must be very terrible not to be able to see. There are people who can't see and, in addition can't hear. I know some who hear too much. One can hear too much (Bleuler, 1911, p. 17).

This kind of communication actually "communicates" nothing: Although many words were used, little was said. This empty quality, often observed in schizophrenic speech, is called *poverty of content*.

In addition to these aberrations in the style of thought and speech, the content of schizophrenic thought also is disturbed. Schizophrenics suffer from delusions, which, as we noted earlier, are irrational beliefs held in spite of overwhelming evidence to the contrary. Delusions take several forms. In delusions of grandeur, an individual believes that he or she is some famous person like Napoleon or Jesus Christ. In delusions of persecution, the individual believes that others, often extraterrestrial beings or secret agents, are plotting against him or her, controlling his or her thoughts and actions. Schizophrenics will often report that their thoughts are being stolen or broadcast aloud, or that "foreign" thoughts are being inserted into their heads.

Disorders of perception One of the major distinguishing characteristics of schizophrenics is their distorted view of reality. Although this is accounted for in part by disturbed thought processes such as those we described, it is directly related to the fact that schizophrenics seem to perceive the external world in a different manner from ordinary people. They consistently report distortions in sensory perception—auditory, visual, olfactory, and occasionally tactile hallucinations. Most commonly, schizophrenics report auditory hallucinations: Voices keep up a running commentary on their actions, repeat their thoughts aloud, or tell them to do things.

Disorders of affect Like other aspects of functioning, the emotional response, or affect, of schizophrenics is often disturbed. Schizophrenic emotional responses are usually either inappropriate or somewhat "flattened"—that is, little emotion is expressed. A schizophrenic might laugh when told of the death of a favorite relative, get angry when given a present, or show no emotion at all on either occasion. Again, the external situation or stimulus fails to trigger the appropriate response.

Disorders of motor behavior The schizophrenic may display physical behavior that is bizarre, such as head banging, or more often that is simply inappropriate to the situation and repetitive beyond the norm. One patient might spend hours rubbing his forehead or slapping his leg; another might sit all day on a couch tracing the pattern of the fabric with her finger. In some cases, there is no physical activity at all; the patient is said to be in a catatonic stupor, remaining in one position for hours at a time, responding to neither persons nor things.

Schizophrenia: current theories and research

The condition we now know as schizophrenia had been puzzling researchers even before Bleuler gave it a name. The most disabling of the common mental

Figure 15.5 Paintings done by a schizophrenic man with paranoid tendencies. Both works are characterized by the consistent symbolism of watchful eyes, grasping hands, and the self as subject. The top painting, which reflects a subdued emotional state, shows a strong emphasis on the eyes, with a figure watching over the shoulder. The central figure is surrounded by hands, and the figure in the background is reaching out. The bottom painting, elaborately composed and vividly colored, reflects a more active emotional state. Again there is an emphasis on eyes and hands, represented by tentacles and claws.

disorders, it has also been one of the most mysterious. Researchers from several different theoretical perspectives have offered theories about its causes. We will now examine the most prominent hypotheses.

Sociocultural theories As we mentioned in our discussion of the sociocultural perspective, studies have consistently shown that schizophrenia is more common among members of the lower social classes than among the more prosperous. Sociocultural theorists have suggested two possible explanations for this. One is the effect of labeling: There may appear to be more schizophrenics in the lower classes only because people from these classes are more likely to be labeled schizophrenic (Scheff, 1975).

The second explanation involves the impact of environmental stress on psychological well-being. In an extension of this theory, Kohn (1968) suggests that certain factors make the lower classes more vulnerable to stress-induced mental illness, and in particular to schizophrenia. One factor may be genetic predisposition. Since there are more schizophrenics in the lower classes than in others, their offspring may have a higher likelihood of being genetically predisposed to being unable to handle stress. Another factor is an attitude of fatalism and helplessness that has been identified as characteristic of the "culture of poverty." This feeling of being at the mercy of forces beyond one's control, Kohn argues, makes those who live in poverty particularly likely to collapse under stress.

Learning approaches Learning theorists such as Ullmann and Krasner (1975) have argued that many of the bizarre behaviors schizophrenics exhibit are the products of their learning histories: Schizophrenics find some kind of reward in acting "crazy" and no longer find a reward in responding appropriately to normal social cues. Learning theorists also point out that once hospitalized, the patient's more bizarre behaviors are repeatedly reinforced. Indeed, the stranger the behavior, the more likely that schizophrenic patients will gain the attention of the staff. Normal behaviors, on the other hand, because they are ignored, eventually tend to disappear. Clinicians sometimes notice that "crazy" behavior seems more pronounced when other people are around, suggesting that attention does indeed act to reinforce it. Moreover, a patient's schizophrenic behaviors often seem to decrease when they are ignored and when normal behaviors are reinforced with attention (Agras, 1967). Although none of this evidence proves that faulty learning *causes* schizophrenia, learning theory has contributed to our understanding of how our reactions to schizophrenic patients serve to maintain their behavior.

Family or systems approaches The family or systems approach seeks the causes of schizophrenia in disturbed family interactions. One group of investigators, headed by Theodore Lidz (Lidz et al., 1957; Lidz, 1973), maintained contact with schizophrenics and their families for several years. They held weekly interviews with family members, observed how the families interacted among themselves and with hospital staff members, visited the subjects' homes, and conducted diagnostic and other testing. From the findings of their first sixteen cases, the researchers suggested that families of schizophrenics can be classified as one of two types: the "schismatic family," in which parental strife has divided the family; and the "skewed family," in which strife is avoided by the total submission of one spouse to the unbalanced behavior of the other. In either kind of family, the child grows up feeling confused, rejected, and uncertain about the feelings of his or her parents. Such a situation, these researchers argue, contributes to an eventual schizophrenic breakdown.

Another group of investigators, headed by Gregory Bateson and Don Jackson, examined the family environments of schizophrenics and developed the *double-bind hypothesis* (Bateson et al., 1956). The basic idea can be seen in the following brief case reported by Bateson and his associates:

A young man who had fairly well recovered from an acute schizophrenic episode was visited in the hospital by his mother. He was glad to see her and impulsively put his arm around her shoulders, whereupon she stiffened. He withdrew his arm and she asked, "Don't you love me any more?" He then blushed, and she said, "Dear, you must not be so easily embarrassed and afraid of your feelings." The patient was able to stay with her only a few minutes more and following her departure he assaulted an aide (p. 251).

A child who perceives such a discrepancy between a parent's overt actions and covert feelings repeatedly receives two contradictory messages. The child, therefore, never learns to understand and make distinctions among the meanings expressed in normal language and behavior. He or she develops the bizarre language and social ineptness characteristic of schizophrenics. Although families of schizophrenics often show deviant communication patterns, it is difficult to evaluate whether the deviant communication caused the schizophrenia. Another possibility is that the presence of a disturbed child within a family produces abnormal communications among family members (Gunderson, Autry, and Mosher, 1974; Liem, 1974).

The humanistic-existential approach One influential theorist of the existential point of view has been the British psychiatrist R. D. Laing. Laing began by studying family interaction and its relation to schizophrenia (Laing and Esterson, 1971), but eventually he developed a more radical position: that emotional disturbance is inherent in contemporary Western society and that schizophrenics are victims not only of their families but also of the perverse values of society itself. Schizophrenia, then, is "a special sort of strategy that a person invents in order to live in an unlivable situation" (Laing, 1964, p. 187). In this view, the schizophrenic may be less disturbed than society itself, and Laing sees a person's passage into schizophrenia as a search for a reality less "crazy" than our own. Laingian therapy, therefore, does not aim at reeducating the patient, but in helping him or her find a new authentic identity to replace the false identity imposed by society.

Laing's approach has been vehemently rejected by clinicians from other perspectives, most of whom deny his basic assertion that society is sicker than the schizophrenic. Nevertheless, the humanistic-existential approach has provided a service by emphasizing the importance of each person's subjective experience, even that of the schizophrenic.

Biological approaches Studies of schizophrenics and their families have shown that relatives of schizophrenics are more likely to develop the disorder than people from families free of schizophrenia (see, for example, Kallmann, 1953). The problem with interpreting such studies, however, is the difficulty of

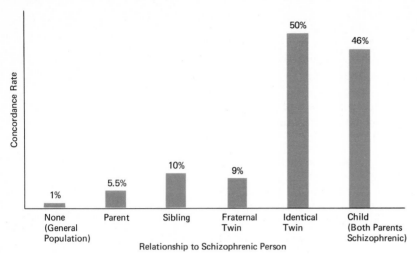

Figure 15.6 The concordance rates that accompany various degrees of relationship to a schizophrenic person. A concordance rate of 100 percent would mean that if one member of the related pair is schizophrenic, the other person will be, too. Note that if a fraternal twin is schizophrenic, the concordance rate is about the same as that for any other sibling, but that if an identical twin is schizophrenic, the concordance rate is far higher (after Gottesman and Shields, 1972).

separating the role of heredity from that of environment: Families share not only the same genes but usually a similar environment as well. In an attempt to separate genetic and environmental influences, researchers have devised several kinds of family studies. We will look briefly at two such studies.

If a tendency to develop schizophrenia is inherited, then presumably people who share the same genetic makeup would be equally likely to develop the disorder. If we find that schizophrenia more often affects both members of a pair of identical twins (who have the same genetic makeup) than it does both members of a pair of fraternal twins (who are not genetically identical), then our hypothesis would be supported. It has indeed been found that when one identical twin develops schizophrenia, the other is five times as likely to succumb than is the other twin in a similar pair of fraternal twins (Ban, 1973). However, even this evidence does not exclude the possibility of environmental influence. Identical twins often share an almost identical environment: They are always the same sex, are dressed alike, and share the same family.

A second type of study involves children who have been adopted away from their biological families at birth. These children have the genes of one family and the social environment of another. Would such children, born to schizophrenic mothers but adopted and reared by normal parents, subsequently develop schizophrenia at a higher rate than adopted children of nonschizophrenic mothers? If so, then a hereditary component to schizophrenia would be strongly suggested. In one study, 33 percent of the children born to schizophrenic parents but subsequently adopted by normal parents manifested some symptoms of schizophrenia. In a control group of adopted children whose parents were not schizophrenic, only 15 percent showed symptoms (Rosenthal et al., 1971).

Although these studies suggest that heredity is a factor in schizophrenia, they do not conclusively rule out environmental influences. If schizophrenia were entirely a matter of heredity, the percentage of identical twins who both have schizophrenia would be 100 percent instead of only 40 to 50 percent. Environmental factors, therefore, seem to have some bearing on the development of the disorder.

The discovery that schizophrenia might to some extent be an inherited disorder suggested that biochemical factors might be involved, that those who developed schizophrenia might have inherited some kind of abnormality in their body chemistry. Over the years researchers who have studied schizophrenics have made several "discoveries" that seemed to promise a biochemical key to the disorder, only to learn that their experimental findings were in error. Given the complexity of human biochemistry, this is hardly surprising. Such invest-igations are confounded by the fact that hospitalized schizophrenics—the usual research population—are physically different from control populations. Most hospitalized patients, for example, eat an institutional diet, smoke heav-ily, get little exercise, and have long histories of drug therapy. Any of these factors can alter a person's biochemistry. Moreover, as Seymour Kety (1969) has pointed out, the extreme emotional and physical stresses associated with having a mental disorder can also cause changes in biochemical functioning. When researchers find that the body chemistry of disturbed persons differs from that of nondisturbed people, they must find ways of determining whether these differences are related to the causes or to the effects of the disorder.

Despite these problems, researchers have identified some substances that seem closely related to the disorder. One such biochemical agent, dopamine, has recently come under intense investigation (reported in Valenstein, 1978). The findings are very complex and can be summarized only briefly here. Cer-tain drugs, called phenothiazines, that are highly effective in reducing the pri-mary symptoms of schizophrenia (thought disorder, blunted emotional re-sponses, withdrawal, and disturbed motor behavior) are known to block the absorption of dopamine by the dopamine receptors in the brain (Creese, Burt, and Snyder, 1975). One hypothesis suggests that an excess of dopamine in the brain overstimulates the receptors, producing schizophrenic symptoms (Meltzer and Stahl, 1976). It is thought that blocking the receptors with the phenothi-azines reduces the impact of the excess dopamine and thus diminishes the symptoms of schizophrenia (Paul, 1977). However, some recent research, based on post-mortem examinations of the brains of schizophrenic and nonschizo-phrenic subjects, suggests that the brains of schizophrenic people have more dopamine receptors in certain critical locations (Lee and Seeman, 1977). Thus, the schizophrenic symptoms would be produced by hyperactivity at these sites, not by an excess of dopamine itself. The action of the phenothiazine drugs can be explained as a blocking of the absorption of dopamine through reduction of the number of active receptors. These results must be interpreted with caution because of the differences in histories of drug usage between the nonschizo-phrenic subjects and the schizophrenic ones.

A second line of research involves the neurotransmitters called **endorphins**, which are morphinelike substances naturally present in the brain. Although research into the role of the endorphins is just beginning, it has already been shown that when schizophrenics are given a substance that interferes with the action of the endorphins, their hallucinations and confusion are relieved (Gunne, Lindström, and Terenius, 1977). And when endorphins are injected into rats, the rats become rigid, as in a catatonic posture (Bloom et al., 1976). Further research into the role of the endorphins is continuing.

An even more interesting bit of research has indirectly pointed to another biochemical factor in schizophrenia. When Robert Cade, a kidney specialist, treated a young schizophrenic woman on the dialysis machine (for relief of her high blood pressure), he found that not only was her blood pressure lowered but her schizophrenic symptoms also disappeared (Wagemaker and Cade,

1977). When dialysis was tried on four other schizophrenic patients, three of the four improved enough to return to work or school (the fourth dropped out of the program). A further trial of dialysis was conducted with ten schizophrenics. After sixteen dialysis treatments seven no longer showed obvious symptoms, and the other three showed considerable improvement. Wagemaker and Cade theorize that the dialysis removes some substance from the blood that, when it builds up, acts to produce the schizophrenic symptoms. What this substance might be we do not know, but research into this fascinating finding is continuing.

The vulnerability theory All of the theories discussed so far point to factors that seem to increase the *risk* of developing schizophrenia: inheriting a genetic predisposition, growing up in an environment of poverty, and having a family that communicates in conflicting ways, to name just three. The vulnerability theory (Zubin and Spring, 1977) proposes that each of us is more or less vulnerable to schizophrenia depending on the accumulation of such factors. For example, people whose genes, family, and social surroundings are all working against them may develop the disorder despite relatively little environmental stress. Less vulnerable people would have to be subjected to much greater stress before they would succumb. Since episodes of stress, such as family conflicts, can push the vulnerable individual over the brink, this theory proposes "improving the coping abilities and competence of the vulnerable," thus making them more resistant to stress (Zubin and Spring, 1977, p. 122).

PERSONALITY DISORDERS

Although **personality disorders** may greatly disturb the lives of those who suffer from them, they do not cause the gross breakdown of functioning and separation from reality that we saw in schizophrenia. These disorders are milder. They can be thought of as deep-seated maladaptive patterns of relating to others that cause distress either to the victim, those around the victim, or both. Unlike the anxiety disorders—which are also maladaptive—personality disorders usually do not produce high levels of guilt and anxiety. The personality-disordered individual often does not recognize that he or she has a disorder. The problem behaviors are so deeply ingrained in the core personality that they are accepted as familiar character traits. Often adopted at an early age to cope with specific stress in the environment, the pattern of deviant behavior is difficult to change. Frequently these individuals have little motivation to change their behavior, since it generally causes more discomfort to others than to themselves. Although *DSM-III* lists twelve such disorders, we shall be concerned here with only one—the one most studied, most reliably diagnosed, and probably most serious: the antisocial personality.

The antisocial personality

The **antisocial personality**, or **sociopath**, follows his or her impulses without consideration for the rights or feelings of others and without guilt. Such people appear to be blind to moral considerations, to have no conscience, and to be untouched by a whole range of emotions shared by the "normal" population, even though their intellectual faculties are intact and their abilities to reason and to perform tasks are unimpaired.

Impulsiveness characterizes much of the antisocial personality's destructive behavior. Unlike criminals who plan their crimes carefully and take measures not to be caught, the antisocial personality will engage in random vandalism or other apparently purposeless crime. Such a person may steal a car for a joy ride or shoplift articles he or she has no use for. The antisocial personality seems to drift through life with no apparent purpose except to gratify whatever impulses come to mind.

When confronted with their offenses, antisocial personalities rarely show guilt. Instead, they may remain unperturbed and try to lie their way out of the situation. Even if shown that they have injured someone, they will display no concern. In fact, a striking characteristic of this disorder is the virtual absence of emotion. Antisocial individuals are typically incapable of a normal friendship or love relationship; they view other people as existing primarily to be used. The remarks of one sociopath reported by E. B. McNeil (1967) are typical. Dan F. felt nothing at all when his best friend died of leukemia. Thinking it over that night in bed, Dan decided that he wouldn't miss his mother and father if they died and "wasn't too nuts about my brothers and sisters for that matter."

Although a few successful sociopaths have bullied their way to the top of their fields (Harrington, 1972), most come into conflict with society early in life. They are often in trouble with the police before they are out of their teens, for this disorder is always evident by adolescence. And once arrested or imprisoned, antisocial personalities typically become "repeaters." Lacking the ability to plan ahead or foresee the likely consequences of their actions, they are usually caught before they can become "successful" criminals. Typically, their careers consist of repeated petty thefts, embezzlement, or passing bad checks. They may repeat the same crime again and again, even if they are caught and punished each time; in this respect they seem unable to learn from experience.

Theorists of many persuasions have speculated about the cause of this disorder. Psychoanalytic thinkers suggest that sociopaths are products of rejecting parents: If there is no love between parent and child, the child is unlikely to adopt parental values in the form of a conscience. The goal of therapeutic techniques based on psychodynamic principles is to create trust between the antisocial individual and the therapist as a replacement for the relationship that failed to develop between parent and child. In this way the therapist hopes to win the sociopath over to more responsible, humane values.

Learning theorists stress the importance of the child's learning history in the development of this disorder. The child may learn aggressive behavior from parents, peers, and the media. Or parents may fail to reinforce the child's prosocial behavior or even resort to punishment regardless of the nature of the child's behavior. Children with extremely punitive parents may learn that they will be punished at any time for any behavior; thus, they have no incentive to be good and fail to learn normal moral standards. Finally, some learning theorists point out that antisocial behavior may produce the reinforcement of attention for the child who finds no other way to obtain it. Treatment based on learning theory usually aims at placing the individual in an environment—such as a residential community—in which prosocial behavior will be consistently reinforced and antisocial behavior extinguished.

Figure 15.7 Normal individuals are capable of strong emotional ties. The antisocial personality, in contrast, usually does not form strong bonds to others; to such a person, others exist largely to be used.

Biological theorists take a quite different approach. They propose that antisocial individuals suffer from underarousal of the autonomic nervous system, which is highly involved in emotional response (Hare, 1970). This might explain some of the antisocial personality's puzzling behavior, such as the need to gratify impulses or commit crimes for thrills—all presumably to compensate for autonomic underarousal. It might also explain why sociopaths seem unnaturally calm and unperturbed about the consequences of their actions.

Whatever form therapy for the sociopath takes, this disorder is often highly resistant to treatment. Without much insight and apparently without feelings or the desire to improve, the antisocial personality can be a difficult and uncooperative client for the therapist. Unfortunately, many antisocial individuals end up in reformatories or prisons where they are unlikely to receive much therapeutic help.

SUMMARY

1. A number of standards can be used to evaluate the normality or abnormality of any given behavior. Among these are deviation from statistical norms, conformity with social or cultural values, and comparison with an absolute standard.

2. Theories of psychological disorder are important because they suggest effective treatments—and treatments in turn may yield evidence about the causes of a disorder.

3. The medical model, probably the most influential perspective in mental illness, sees psychological disorders as similar to physical illness. In this view, mental disturbance is the result of physical dysfunction.

4. The psychoanalytic perspective, pioneered by Sigmund Freud, sees psychological disturbances as the result of conflicts in the individual's childhood, resulting in fixation. If the fixation occurs early in childhood, the individual will develop a drastic breakdown of functioning called **psychosis**; if the fixation occurs later, the result will be the milder condition known as **neurosis**.

5. According to the learning-theory perspective, we learn abnormal behaviors much as we learn normal ones—through modeling, classical conditioning, instrumental learning, and so on. A recent extension of learning theory has gone beyond the focus on observable behavior to consider the role that patterns of thought—**cognitions**—play in abnormal behavior.

6. The family (or systems) approach sees psychological problems as necessarily involving the network of relationships in an individual's life. In this view, problems can only be understood in the context of the family.

7. The sociocultural perspective sees the roots of mental illness in social ills such as poverty and discrimination; it looks beyond the individual and the family to focus attention on the role of environment and social institutions.

8. The humanistic-existential perspective sees abnormal behavior as a failure to achieve self-actualization. This perspective stresses an individual's ability to grow and change, to make positive choices that will liberate his or her inherent potential.

9. The standard system of classifying mental disorder is the *Diagnostic and Statistical Manual of Mental Disorder* (DSM) of the American Psychiatric Association. Although diagnosis has its critics, it is hard to imagine treatment of the mentally ill without it.

10. The *anxiety disorders* include generalized anxiety and panic disorders, phobic disorders, and obsessive-compulsive disorders. In *generalized anxiety disorder*, the individual complains of such symptoms as nervousness, aching muscles, sweating, headaches, lack of appetite, and insomnia. The sufferer may also experience *panic attacks*, often accompanied by chest pain, dizziness, difficulty breathing or swallowing, and intense fear and agitation. In a *phobia*, the anxiety is aroused only by one particular stimulus, such as dogs or high places. *Obsessions* are troubling recurrent irrational thoughts, and *compulsions* are acts of irrational behavior; these often occur together, obsessive thinking leading to compulsive behavior.

11. In *somatoform disorders*, a physical malfunction is caused by psychological factors. One such condition is *conversion disorder*, in which a person loses a sensory or motor function—becoming blind or unable to walk, for example—without organic impairment.

12. *Dissociative disorders* involve a splitting off (dissociation) of a part of the individual's personality, so that memory or identity is disturbed. In *amnesia*, the person forgets all or part of his or her identity and personal past. In a *fugue*, a person flees his or her normal life or identity. In *multiple personality*, the individual develops two or more distinct personalities, which may contrast strongly with one another.

13. *Affective disorders* are characterized by disturbances in mood. In *depression*, the person feels sad, guilty, slowed down, and in severe cases, suicidal. *Mania* is a condition of extreme elation and feverish activity. In *manic-depressive disorder*, the individual experiences both extremes, often with an interval of time in between.

14. *Schizophrenia* is characterized by disordered thought, including delusions and hallucinations, nonsensical speech, inappropriate emotional reactions, and disturbed motor behavior. There are several different subtypes of schizophrenia, but all share these symptoms. Schizophrenia is a severe disorder, rendering the individual unable to cope with most of the demands of ordinary life.

15. *Personality disorders* are deeply ingrained maladaptive patterns of behavior that distress either the victim or those around the victim. The most serious of these is *antisocial personality disorder*. The antisocial personality is characterized by impulsively destructive behavior, by a lack of insight, emotion, and concern for others, and by a tendency not to learn from experience.

Suggested readings

Axline, V. M. *Dibs: In search of self.* Boston: Houghton Mifflin, 1965.

Freud, S. *New introductory lectures on psychoanalysis.* New York: Norton, 1933.

Freud, S. *Therapy and technique.* New York: Basic Books, 1977.

Goffman, E. *Asylums: Essays on the social situation of mental patients and other inmates.* Hawthorne, N.Y.: Aldine, 1961.

Green, H. *I never promised you a rose garden.* New York: Holt, Rinehart and Winston, 1964.

Kesey, K. *One flew over the cuckoo's nest.* New York: Viking, 1962.

Kisker, G. W. *The disorganized personality.* New York: McGraw-Hill, 1964.

Schreiber, F. R. *Sybil.* Port Washington, N.Y.: Regency, 1973.

Szasz, T. S. *The myth of mental illness: Foundations of a theory of personal conduct.* New York: Harper & Row, 1961.

PREVIEW

1. Freudian psychoanalysis, behavior therapy, family systems therapy, and humanistic-existential therapy all use different techniques to aid a patient to regain a normal way of life.

2. Group therapies, which borrow from all these traditions, involve the treatment of several people at once.

3. Research on the effectiveness of the various therapies suggests no clear "winner," but it does indicate that therapy facilitates improvement in patients.

4. Drug therapy has become very common since the 1950s. Before then, electroconvulsive therapy and psychosurgery were the primary methods of controlling violent behavior.

5. Psychotherapy has recently become involved in the community health movement, which attempts to bring psychological help to the underprivileged and to establish moral and legal guidelines in the field of mental health.

16 Approaches to treatment

Each age has dealt with the manifestations of mental disorder according to the prevailing notions of the time. When people were thought to be possessed by evil spirits, the spirits were let out by cutting holes in the skull or, later, driven out by exorcism. For many centuries the church was the agency of treatment. During other periods, families kept strangely behaving individuals at home, sometimes hiding them away in attics. In this century, community institutions and mental health professionals have assumed many of the advisory and regulatory functions once provided by family and church, and psychotherapy has become the primary method of treatment.

Psychotherapy may be defined as a systematic series of interactions between a therapist trained to aid in solving psychological problems and a person who is troubled or is troubling others. In contrast to the advice of family and clergy, psychotherapy is a more formal arrangement in which the therapist is a paid professional. In recent years, psychotherapy has expanded and diversified rapidly. In the process, it has also become far more widely accepted, losing most of the stigma once attached to it. Freudian psychoanalysis and related therapies, once predominant in the field, have been challenged in the past few decades by newer schools—the behavior therapies, humanistic-existential therapies, and family therapies—and each of these has spawned a host of therapeutic approaches. Today more than one hundred schools of psychotherapy can be identified, each with its own ideas about the appropriate treatment of various disorders.

These many therapies and those who offer them differ widely in theory and technique. Practitioners of psychotherapy may have one of several kinds of professional training. The **psychiatrist** is a physician (an M.D.) who specializes in the diagnosis and treatment of mental illness. Usually, but not always, he or she has completed three years of residency training in psychiatry. The **psychoanalyst** is usually a psychiatrist (although sometimes a lay person or psychologist) who has had advanced training in psychoanalysis and who has been psychoanalyzed as part of that training. The **clinical psychologist** has earned a doctorate in clinical psychology and has completed a one-year internship. The **psychiatric social worker** has earned a master's degree in social work and has specialized in psychiatric social work. The **psychiatric nurse** is a registered nurse who has specialized in psychiatric nursing during training and is usually employed in a mental hospital.

Therapists differ not only in their training, but also in their theoretical approaches. This means that therapists make different assumptions about the causes and treatments of the various disorders. Psychoanalytic therapists, for example, focus on the client's past, asking him or her to talk freely about childhood experiences. Humanistic-existential therapists are likely to be more interested in the client's present, in how he or she might make more "self-actualizing" choices. Behavior therapists look for the reinforcements in the client's life that serve to maintain the maladaptive behavior.

In this chapter, we will discuss a number of broad theoretical approaches to treatment, among them psychoanalysis, behavior therapies, family therapy, humanistic-existential therapies, and group therapies. In practice, however, most therapists do not adhere inflexibly to one particular theory. Instead, most are at least to some extent "eclectic" therapists, borrowing insights from other theoretical schools to supplement their own perspective. Some family therapists, for example, also practice individual therapy; some humanistic therapists are sympathetic to certain of Freud's ideas. This overlap should be kept in mind as we consider the various therapies. In addition to discussing the five broad theoretical approaches to therapy, we will discuss biological treatments, and finally, some attempts at prevention.

PSYCHODYNAMIC THERAPIES

The psychodynamic therapies, particularly psychoanalysis, are closely identified with Sigmund Freud. **Psychoanalysis** is at once a general theory of personality, a theory of psychopathology, and a form of psychotherapy. The influence of Freud's ideas has been profound: All therapies that focus on a dynamic interplay of conscious and unconscious elements are derived from psychoanalysis. For a variety of reasons, however, few practitioners today use traditional Freudian psychoanalysis (Korchin, 1976). Although it can be effective, it is a very long and expensive process.

Freudian psychoanalysis

Freud's experience with his patients led him to conclude that the source of most disorders was the anxiety experienced when unacceptable unconscious impulses threatened to break through the constraints established by the ego. To deal with this threat, the patient would resort to defense mechanisms, the most important of which was repression—the pushing of shameful thoughts and impulses into the unconscious mind. But while the impulse could be hidden for a while, it remained alive in the unconscious. During this time it would drain strength from the ego, which expended energy in keeping it hidden. Freud believed that the proper treatment was to coax the unconscious impulse out into consciousness so that the patient could confront it. These thoughts could then be "worked through," or explored to facilitate change and understanding. According to Freud, this process should gradually reduce anxiety and should free psychic energy for more constructive endeavors.

The basis of psychoanalysis is the uncovering of these long-buried impulses, putting a person in touch with his or her unconscious, where past traumas and childhood conflicts still live. Various techniques are employed to restore these events to consciousness. The client lies on a couch, a relaxing position that helps to loosen the restraints on the unconscious. The client **free associates**, verbalizing whatever thoughts come to mind in whatever order, without self-censorship, logical structure, or interruption from the therapist, whose remarks are kept to a minimum and who sits out of the patient's view.

The therapist and the patient look for clues to the present anxiety in dreams, in which the usual restraints on the unconscious are loosened. However, according to Freud, even in sleep the unconscious is censored, and forbidden material appears only in symbolic form. Thus every dream has its **manifest content**, its plot or story line, and its **latent content**, the symbolic meaning of the dream, which exposes unconscious conflicts. For example, a woman who has just had a baby might dream that she had given birth to two boys and that one had died (manifest content). The symbolic meaning (latent content) of the dream may indicate the new mother's feelings of ambivalence toward the child, whom she both does and does not want.

Naturally, the conscious confrontation and recognition of such thoughts are not pleasant. Often at this stage in therapy clients begin to show signs of **resistance**, or attempts to block treatment. They may avoid talking about certain subjects, pause frequently, or report that their minds are blank. They may dwell on one subject to avoid discussing others that are more painful. They may even lapse into lengthy monologues about politics or world problems if the therapist does not interrupt. The therapist's interpretation of resistance is an important part of treatment, for all patients resist the painful process of uncovering unconscious conflicts.

As the psychoanalysis progresses, the client may transfer to the analyst, who has now shared the client's deepest secrets, feelings of love and hostility that were originally directed toward his or her parents or other authority figures. Through this process of **transference**, which involves reenacting childhood conflicts with the analyst, the client can bring out repressed emotions, unsatisfied needs, and misconceptions and can begin to deal with them realistically. The analysis of transference is considered the key to successful psychoanalysis. Only

Figure 16.1 During psychoanalysis, patients must resolve childhood conflicts that originated in their relationship with their parents.

in this way can the client's unconscious conflicts be resolved, freeing him or her to respond to interpersonal interactions more realistically.

Psychoanalytically oriented therapists often use the technique of **dream interpretation**, which Freud pioneered. Through the process of free association, the hidden meaning of the dream can be brought to light, and unconscious wishes, fantasies, and conflicts can be explored. In the following psychoanalytic dialogue the patient reports the manifest content of a dream, and then the therapist guides her toward discovery of the latent content.

"Well," she said, "this is what I dreamed. . . . I was in what appeared to be a ballroom or a dance hall, but I knew it was really a hospital. A man came up to me and told me to undress, take all my clothes off. He was going to give me a gynecological examination. I did as I was told but I was very frightened. While I was undressing, I noticed that he was doing something to a woman at the other end of the room. She was sitting or lying in a funny kind of contraption with all kinds of levers and gears and pulleys attached to it. I knew that I was supposed to be next, that I would have to sit in that thing while he examined me. Suddenly he called my name and I found myself running to him. The chair or table—whatever it was—was now empty, and he told me to get on it. I refused and began to cry. It started to rain—great big drops of rain. He pushed me to the floor and spread my legs for the examination. I turned over on my stomach and began to scream. I woke myself up screaming."

Following the recital Laura lay quietly on the couch, her eyes closed, her arms crossed over her bosom.

"Well," she said after a brief, expectant silence, "what does it mean?"

"Laura," I admonished, "you know better than that. Associate, and we'll find out."

"The first thing I think of is Ben," she began. "He's an intern at University, you know. I guess that's the doctor in the dream—or maybe it was you. Anyhow, whoever it was, I wouldn't let them examine me."

"Why not?"

"I've always been afraid of doctors . . . afraid they might hurt me."

"How will they hurt you?"

"I don't know. By jabbing me with a needle, I guess. That's funny. I never thought of it before. When I go to the dentist I don't mind getting a needle; but with a doctor it's different. . . ." Here I noticed how the fingers of both hands clutched her arms at the elbows while her thumbs nervously smoothed the inner surface of the joints. "I shudder when I think of having my veins punctured. I'm always afraid that's what a doctor will do to me." . . .

"What about gynecological examinations?"

"I've never had one. I can't even bear to think of someone poking around inside me." Again silence; then, "Oh," she said, "I see it now. It's sex I'm afraid of. The doctor in the dream *is* Ben. He wants me to have intercourse, but it scares me and I turn away from him. That's true. . . ."

"But why, Laura?"

"I don't know," she cried, "I don't know. Tell me."

"I think the dream tells you," I said.

"The dream I just told you?"

"Yes. . . . There's a part of it you haven't considered. What comes to your mind when you think of the other woman in the dream, the woman the doctor was examining before you?"

"The contraption she was sitting in," Laura exclaimed. "It was like a—like a wheel chair—my mother's wheel chair! Is that right?"

"Very likely," I said.

"But why would he be examining her? What would that mean?"

"Well, think of what that examination signifies for you."

"Sex," she said. "Intercourse—that's what it means. So that's what it is—that's what it means! Intercourse put my mother in the wheel chair. It paralyzed her. And I'm afraid that's what it will do to me. So I avoid it—because I'm scared it will do the same thing to me. . . ." (Lindner, 1954, pp. 93-95).

In fact, the mother's paralysis was totally unrelated to sex. However, the patient had unconsciously connected her mother's condition with the muffled cries and moans that, as a child, she had heard through the walls during her parents' love making.

The client in psychoanalysis attends one-hour sessions three, four, or five times a week for several years. In successful psychoanalysis the client eventually breaks through resistance, confronts unconscious conflicts, and resolves the transference neurosis, thereby eliminating anxiety and self-defeating responses to it.

Psychoanalysis has many proponents, among them many "graduates" of analysis whose lives have been changed by the process. However, psychoanalysis is invariably a long and costly procedure, often requiring years of analytic sessions and an investment of thousands of dollars. In addition, since psychoanalysis is based on talk and insight, it tends to work best for those who are articulate and well-educated (Luborsky and Spence, 1978). Thus, although psychoanalysis may be of great help to those who can afford it, it is rather limited as a general treatment strategy.

Other psychodynamic therapies

Some of Freud's earliest associates, such as Carl Jung and Alfred Adler, began to modify psychoanalytic theory even as Freud was still formulating it. These neo-Freudians developed variations on Freud's techniques of therapy as a re-

HE HAD PROBLEMS WITH HIS PARENTS — SO WE TALKED ABOUT IT.

HE HAD PROBLEMS WITH HIS WIFE, — SO WE TALKED ABOUT IT.

HE HAD PROBLEMS WITH HIS KIDS — WE TALKED ABOUT THAT TOO.

HE HAD PROBLEMS PAYING ME FOR TREATMENT, WE'RE NOT TALKING ANYMORE! © GIL SPATZER '78

sult of their theoretical disagreements. Somewhat later Karen Horney, Harry Stack Sullivan, Erich Fromm, Erik Erikson, and others formed a loosely knit group called ego psychologists. Freud maintained that all energy originates in the id and is borrowed by the ego, which merely serves as mediator between reality and the sexual and aggressive desires of the id. In contrast, the ego psychologists argued that the ego has substantial energy of its own and controls such important functions as memory, judgment, perception, and planning. **Ego analysis** emphasizes the strengthening of the ego to enable the client to control his or her environment and social relationships so as to achieve the greatest satisfaction.

The many therapies that rely to some degree on the ideas of Freud and his followers have been called, collectively, psychoanalytically oriented psychotherapy (Korchin, 1976). While therapists with such an orientation believe that training in psychoanalytic theory and techniques enhances their effectiveness, today only a small percentage of them rigorously follow Freud's techniques. Many retain the general psychoanalytic framework, uncovering unconscious motivation, breaking down defenses, and dealing with resistance, but in practice their therapy differs significantly from psychoanalysis. The couch is generally dispensed with, and clients sit up and face their therapists. The therapists take a more active role, advising, interpreting, and directing. Moreover, these modern psychotherapists tend to place more emphasis on situations in the present, especially personal relationships, than on events from the distant past. Therapy is briefer and less intensive and usually aims for less than complete restructuring of the client's personality.

Figure 16.2 Although some forms of therapy, such as psychoanalysis, are often expensive, other kinds of treatment, such as group therapy and services offered by clinics, are relatively inexpensive, and sometimes free.

BEHAVIOR THERAPIES

Behavior therapy is the attempt to apply learning and other experimentally derived psychological principles to problem behavior (Begelman, 1975; Bootzin, 1975). Basic to the approach of behavior therapy is the belief that the same principles govern all behaviors, normal or deviant. Behavior therapists regard psychological problems as learned responses. For these therapists, problem behaviors are not symptoms of unconscious conflicts that must be uncovered—as in psychoanalysis—but are themselves the primary and legitimate targets of therapy.

Behavior therapists also believe that the environment plays a crucial role in determining behavior and that problem behaviors are specific to given types of situations. Consequently, behavioral assessment requires accurate descriptions of observable behaviors and the environmental events that accompany them. Behavior therapy also differs from psychoanalysis in its treatment of the person's inner life. Behavior therapists consider internal events relatively accessible; they take thoughts and feelings at face value rather than as symbols of unconscious conflicts. To them, a person's emotional reactions and thoughts are subject to the same principles as overt behaviors and therefore equally open to change (for example, Wolpe, 1978). Behavior therapists also participate more actively in the psychotherapeutic process. Instead of spending long hours listening to clients recall their childhood experiences, describe their dreams, and free associate, they often ask direct questions, give explicit advice and instructions, and in general actively engage the client (Sloane et al., 1975).

Behavior therapy is not a unified set of procedures, but a collection of techniques developed to change problem behavior. We will describe some of the therapies that have been developed from classical conditioning, operant conditioning, and the recently developed cognitive-behavioral approach.

Therapies based on classical conditioning

Many emotional responses are elicited by environmental stimuli through classical conditioning. That is, we learn to connect certain events or objects with pleasant or unpleasant experience. Behavior therapy is often directed at helping the client unlearn the connection between a particular stimulus and some kind of maladaptive behavior—between boarding an airplane and becoming anxious, for example. After therapy, a more adaptive response takes the place of the conditioned response. In other cases, a client will be helped to decrease a behavior that produces pleasure but is maladaptive (such as smoking or drinking) by classical conditioning involving repeated pairings of the maladaptive behavior and an aversive stimulus. We will briefly examine two therapies based on classical conditioning: systematic desensitization and aversive conditioning.

Systematic desensitization *Systematic desensitization*, developed by Joseph Wolpe (1958, 1973, 1976) is based on the principle that it is impossible to be relaxed and anxious at the same time. Suppose a client's anxiety centers on a particular stimulus, such as flying in airplanes, taking examinations, or speaking in public. The therapist asks the client to describe what part of an encounter with the stimulus is most frightening, what is slightly less frightening, what merely begins to arouse fear, and so on. The therapist then arranges these elements into a hierarchy. For a person who fears flying, the hierarchy might read (from the most frightening to the least) like this:

1 Feeling the plane touch the runway as it lands

2 Experiencing midair turbulence

3 Taking off

4 Taxiing down the runway

5 Boarding the plane

6 Waiting to get on the plane

7 Riding to the airport in a car

8 Buying an airline ticket

The client is next taught a technique of deep muscle relaxation. When he or she is thoroughly relaxed, the therapist presents the least frightening scene in the hierarchy and asks the client to imagine it while remaining relaxed. When this has been accomplished the procedure is repeated with each item on the list. Eventually the client is able to imagine the most frightening scene without becoming afraid. Having learned to remain relaxed while progressively confronting the feared situation, the client ceases to fear it.

Systematic desensitization has undergone extensive evaluation and has been found to be effective with such diverse problems as phobias, recurrent nightmares, chronic alcoholism, and complex interpersonal problems such as fears of intimacy and fears of rejection (Kazdin and Wilson, 1978; Rimm and Masters, 1979).

Aversive conditioning The clearest example of a therapeutic technique based on the Pavlovian model is that of *aversive conditioning*. This technique aims at reducing the frequency of a maladaptive response, such as excessive smoking, alcoholism, or bedwetting, by associating it with an aversive stimulus like mild electric shock, nausea, or loud noise.

As an example, consider how this method is applied to the treatment of alcoholism (Nathan, 1976). The presentation of alcohol (conditioned stimulus), including its taste and smell, is paired with a drug that causes vomiting (unconditioned stimulus)—a stimulus that is tied innately to a discomfort reaction (unconditioned response). Usually, the drug is given immediately before the drink, or it is mixed with the drink. After a sufficient number of pairings, alcohol takes on a stimulus function similar to that of the drug; the client comes to react with discomfort and nausea to the sight, smell, and taste of alcohol (conditioned response).

Joseph Cautela (1966, 1967) has developed an alternative to aversive conditioning known as covert sensitization. Here the aversive stimulus is an imagined unpleasant event. For example, a therapist may instruct a smoker to close her eyes, relax, and picture herself taking out a cigarette. As she imagines lighting up and taking a puff, she is told to imagine that she feels nauseated, starts gagging, and vomits all over the floor, the cigarettes, and finally herself. The details of this scene are conjured up with excruciating vividness. The client also rehearses an alternative, "relief" scene, in which the decision not to smoke is accompanied by pleasurable sensations. This technique, requiring no special equipment or medication, has obvious advantages, not least of which is that clients can carry out conditioning sessions on their own.

Therapies based on aversive conditioning have been highly effective in the treatment of bedwetting (Sherman and Levin, 1979) and somewhat effective in the treatment of alcoholism (Mills, Sobell, and Schaefer, 1971; Schaefer, 1972) and sexual deviations such as transvestism (Marks and Gelder, 1967). However, there has as yet been little carefully controlled research into the compara-

Ratings	Hierarchy Items
0	Beginning a new course
5	
10	
15	Hearing an instructor announce a small quiz two weeks hence
20	Having a professor urge you personally to do well on an exam
25	
30	
35	Trying to decide how to study for an exam
40	Reviewing the material I know should be studied—listing study to do
45	
50	
55	
60	Hearing an instructor announce a major exam in three weeks and its importance
	Hearing an instructor remind the class of a quiz one week hence
65	
70	
75	Hearing an instructor announce a major exam in one week
	Standing alone in the hall before an exam
80	Getting an exam back in class
	Anticipating getting back a graded exam later that day
	Talking to several students about an exam right before taking it
85	Thinking about being scared and anxious regarding a specific exam
	Studying with fellow students several days before an exam
	Hearing some "pearls" from another student which you doubt you'll remember, while studying in a group
90	Cramming while alone in the library right before an exam
	Thinking about not keeping up in other subjects while preparing for an exam
95	Thinking about being anxious over schoolwork in general
	Talking with several students about an exam immediately after
	Thinking about being generally inadequately prepared
100	Thinking about not being adequately prepared for a particular exam
	Studying the night before a big exam

Figure 16.3 A graduated hierarchy of situations that elicited different amounts of anxiety from a client being systematically desensitized to tests and examinations. A rating of 100 means "as tense as you ever are"; a rating of zero means "totally relaxed." The behavior identified as the target behavior, however, was incorrectly chosen. The student's anxieties turned out to be caused by a fear of disappointing his family; he was not anxious about test taking in itself. He was then desensitized to his real fear, and his test anxiety decreased dramatically (after Kanfer and Phillips, 1970).

tive effectiveness of various aversive techniques. More study is needed to determine whether self-administered aversive stimuli, for example, are more effective than unpleasant fantasies. These therapies have also shown a high relapse rate, and research is needed to identify how this problem can be remedied. Some therapists have suggested that relapse may be less likely if the client is taught adaptive behaviors that can be substituted for the problem behaviors decreased by the therapy. In part because of the possibility of relapse, neither aversive conditioning nor covert sensitization is typically used as the exclusive treatment for a client. Aversive techniques are generally but one part of a comprehensive treatment program (Mahoney and Arnkoff, 1978). A client undergoing aversive conditioning for alcoholism, for example, may also be provided with instruction in appropriate drinking behavior, explicit guidelines on how to refuse a drink, and videotaped feedback on how he or she behaves when drunk (Mills, Sobell, and Schaefer, 1971; Strickler et al., 1976).

Therapies based on operant conditioning

In therapies based on operant conditioning, desirable behaviors are increased by reinforcement; undesirable behaviors decreased by extinction or punishment. This approach is often effective in institutional settings. Severely retarded children have been taught to dress and feed themselves by rewarding them for successful attempts at tying their shoes, using a fork, and so on, thus encouraging them to repeat the desired behavior (Thompson and Grabowski,1977). Autistic children can be taught to stop engaging in self-destructive behavior such as head banging if they are given a mild electric shock after each instance of the undesired behavior (Bucher and Lovaas, 1968). But the use of operant conditioning is not limited to serious behavior problems. It can help people with such commonplace concerns as overeating and insomnia (Stuart, 1967; Bootzin and Nicassio, 1978); couples undergoing marital difficulties can also benefit, with husband and wife learning to reinforce each other's behavior (Liberman et al., 1976).

Token economies The success of operant-conditioning techniques in changing behavior has led to attempts to structure environments so that appropriate behavior is reinforced and inappropriate behavior extinguished. When tangible conditioned reinforcers, or tokens, are used to reward desirable behavior, these structured environments are called *token economies*. In institutional settings, for example, patients receive tokens in the form of poker chips or slips of paper for each instance of appropriate self-care, work skills, and social interaction. They can trade the tokens for candy or books, or for access to preferred activities such as watching television or participating in games.

Token economies have been used successfully in many settings: in classrooms, in residential programs for juvenile offenders, and with retarded persons, to name a few (Fixsen, Phillips, and Wolf, 1976; Kazdin, 1977). A major study recently found that a token economy, combined with individual behavior therapy, resulted in greater improvement in a group of chronic mental patients than did either of two alternative therapies (Paul and Lentz, 1977).

Although token economies work well while they are in operation, some therapists are concerned that the gains made will not be maintained when clients leave the controlled environment (Condry, 1977). To minimize the chance of such regression, a number of strategies are employed. First, therapists select target behaviors that will themselves be reinforcing—more effective social interaction, for example—or that will be reinforced by others in the person's environment—such as improved personal hygiene (Ayllon and Azrin, 1968). Second, as the person acquires new behaviors, he or she is shifted from tangible reinforcers (tokens) to social approval (praise from a staff member or instructor), bringing the treatment environment closer to the environment to which the person will return. Third, arrangements are often made to continue some

aspects of the treatment program, either through transitional programs such as halfway houses or by training family members to reinforce target behaviors. And fourth, the person may be taught to provide his or her own reinforcement (for example, treating himself or herself to a movie as a reward for cleaning up the apartment or looking for a job) rather than relying on receiving it from others (Kazdin, 1977).

Therapies based on modeling and cognitions

Modeling In **modeling** a person learns a new behavior by observing another person perform that behavior. The more similar the model is to the person and the more the person wants the model's approval, the more readily he or she will engage in the desired behavior. Once therapists have won the client's attention and regard, they can begin teaching adaptive behaviors by demonstrating these behaviors themselves. Modeling principles have been particularly useful in the treatment of phobias. In one study Rosenthal and Bandura (1978) reported a very high success rate in ridding subjects of snake phobias through modeling. In another study, children's dog phobias disappeared after they observed another child happily playing with a dog (Bandura, Grusec, and Menlove, 1967).

Recently, there has been considerable interest in *participant modeling*. The therapist models the feared activity, and then guides the client through a series of steps culminating in the same activity. In one study (Bandura, Blanchard, and Ritter, 1969), therapists led snake phobics through a series of gradual steps (thinking of snakes, seeing a snake in a cage, coming close to it, touching the cage, and actually handling the snake) that eventually led to the extinction of their snake phobias. In this experiment, participant modeling was found more effective than either *symbolic modeling* (showing subjects a film of models interacting with a snake) or systematic desensitization. Other research has produced similar findings (Rimm and Mahoney, 1969; Thase and Moss, 1976).

Why participant modeling should be so effective is not yet completely known. Bandura (1977) speculates that when subjects not only watch others engaging in a daring or frightening activity, but join in it themselves, they gain a sense of "self-efficacy," or mastery over the situation, which results in further behavior change. The treatment includes many different components: live modeling by the therapist, practice by the subjects, social feedback and reinforcement, and so on. As A. Robert Sherman has written, "It remains for future research to isolate the essential components of participant modeling and to identify its limitations" (1979, p. 49). He notes, however, that unfortunately it cannot be applied in all anxiety-provoking situations—for example, the therapist cannot guide the subject through taking an exam or speaking in public.

Cognitive approaches As we saw in Chapter 15, the cognitive model of abnormality stresses the role of distorted cognition, or extremely negative thinking, in causing mental disorder. The therapy called *cognitive restructuring* focuses on identifying the client's negative patterns of thought and changing them. It is aimed at showing the client the irrationality of his or her beliefs. Several different treatments are all variations of cognitive restructuring. Perhaps the oldest is *rational-emotive therapy* (RET), developed by Albert Ellis (1962). Ellis argues that thousands of people lead unhappy lives because of irrational beliefs. For example, they tell themselves, "I must be loved and approved of by everyone whose love and approval I seek," or "I must be utterly competent in everything I do." As clients begin to recognize the irrational nature of these long-unexamined beliefs, they are helped to construct a more realistic set of assumptions.

Similar in theory if not in tone is Aaron Beck's (1976) *cognitive therapy*. Like Ellis, Beck holds that emotional disorders are caused primarily by irrational thoughts. Beck's view has been particularly influential in the treatment of depression (Beck et al., 1979). According to Beck, depressed people view themselves and the external world in erroneous ways. They interpret trivial setbacks as substantial, read disparagement into innocuous statements by others, and constantly devalue themselves.

To change such cognitions, Beck uses a Socratic approach, questioning patients in such a way that they themselves discover the irrationality of their thoughts. As Beck has written, "By pointed, but friendly questioning, the therapist can make the patient aware of the incongruity of some of his assumptions. Recognition of the incongruity helps to shake his faulty belief system" (1976, p. 289). By way of example, Beck offers the following dialogue:

Therapist: Why do you want to end your life?

Patient: Without Raymond, I am nothing . . . I can't be happy without Raymond . . . But I can't save our marriage.

Therapist: What has your marriage been like?

Patient: It has been miserable from the very beginning . . . Raymond has always been unfaithful . . . I have hardly seen him in the past five years.

Therapist: You say that you can't be happy without Raymond . . . Have you found yourself happy when you are with Raymond?

Patient: No, we fight all the time and I feel worse.

Therapist: You say you are nothing without Raymond. Before you met Raymond, did you feel you were nothing?

Patient: No, I felt I was somebody.

Therapist: If you were somebody before you knew Raymond, why do you need him to be somebody now?

Patient: [Puzzled] Hmmm. . . .

Therapist: If you were free of the marriage, do you think that men might be interested in you—knowing that you were available?

Patient: I guess that maybe they would be.

Therapist: Is it possible that you might find a man who would be more constant than Raymond?

Patient: I don't know . . . I guess it's possible. . . .

Therapist: Then what have you actually lost if you break up the marriage?

Patient: I don't know.

Therapist: Is it possible that you'll get along better if you end the marriage?

Patient: There is no guarantee of that.

Therapist: Do you have a *real marriage?*

Patient: I guess not.

Therapist: If you don't have a real marriage, what do you actually lose if you decide to end the marriage?

Patient: [Long pause] Nothing, I guess. (1976, pp. 289-291)

Research (for example, Rush et al., 1977) has shown that this kind of therapy can be extremely effective, particularly in the treatment of depression.

Donald Meichenbaum (1977) takes a more active approach in helping patients defeat old, negative patterns of thought. Meichenbaum's version of cognitive therapy is *self-instructional training*. Clients can apply this therapy themselves by simply making a conscious effort to think rational and positive thoughts in stressful situations instead of plunging into negative, self-defeating patterns. For example, a student who regularly becomes anxious when taking examinations might be thinking like this:

I'm so nervous, I'm afraid I'll forget the most important parts of the material . . . the teacher will read this test and lose all respect for me . . . if I get a D on this test, I'll have to get a B on the final just to get a C for the course. . . . I *know* everybody here studied more than I did, which will shoot the curve way up. . . . If I don't get an A in this course, I may as well forget about grad school . . .

Of course, this pattern of thought makes the student even more nervous and less likely to do well on the exam. Meichenbaum tries to teach clients to replace such internal monologues with more rational thoughts, such as:

I'm going to take slow, deep breaths and keep myself calm. . . . All I have to do is be calm and take my time . . . just consider the questions one by one . . . I spent a fair amount of time studying for this test and I'm going to take each question in turn and be calm while I'm thinking about the answer. . . . I'm an intelligent, competent person, and that fact is not mitigated by whatever grade I get on this test.

This kind of therapy can be practiced by the client in a variety of stressful situations, including job interviews, achievement settings, and social events like dating. Because research is accumulating that supports this approach (Meichenbaum, Henshaw, and Himmel, in press; Dweck and Wortman, in press), it is gaining increased acceptance.

FAMILY, OR SYSTEMS, APPROACHES

As we saw in Chapter 15, the **family**, or **systems, approach** to abnormality stresses the importance of disturbed relations within the family in causing the maladaptive behavior of a family member. The family therapist focuses on the patterns of interaction within the family: No therapeutic progress can be made unless the interpersonal relationships within the family change (McPeak, 1979). In practice, this means that the family therapist's work is often somewhat different from that of the conventional therapist, who treats only one individual at a time:

The family therapist is right there in the front lines, heaving and hauling his way through the clutter of disturbed transactions. He has to be actively involved, for it is only the force of his influence that can oppose the weight of the system. The family therapist can't wait around for a "family unconscious" to rise toward him; he has to introduce new energy into a system that will otherwise roll right along on the path it has carved for itself (Kovel, 1976, pp. 188–189).

One technique often used by family therapists is the "double bind." To illustrate how this technique works, imagine a family that comes for treatment, ostensibly because of the delinquent behavior of a teenage daughter (Haley, 1980). In therapy sessions, the daughter becomes so disruptive that no interaction is possible. The family therapist might instruct the daughter to go ahead and disrupt the sessions thus putting her in a position where her behavior no longer has the effect she desires. If she continues to be disruptive, she is cooperating with the therapist. If she stops, she is also helping, since therapy can proceed.

Family-systems theorists often regard a symptom, or problem behavior, as an attempt to influence others. By prescribing the symptom, the therapist can take away its usefulness and pave the way for change. If a boy compulsively soils himself despite the disgust and consternation of his parents, the therapist may "order" him to soil himself and bring the product to the next session (Kovel, 1976). This usually brings the "symptom" to an end.

In contrast with other therapists, family therapists usually believe that providing "insight," or explaining to people why they do a certain thing, does not lead to change. In fact, family therapists would argue that problem behaviors are frequently maintained by an individual's own or others' attempts to change them. Suppose, for example, that a person has anxiety attacks. He or she may attempt to deal with this problem simply by trying *not* to have them, perhaps with the "help" of other family members. But worrying about having the attacks, watching for signs that one might be on the way, or avoiding circumstances where attacks have occurred in the past can actually contribute to bringing them on. In contrast, when the client is "ordered" to have anxiety attacks, he or she may find it impossible (Solyom, Garza-Perez, and Ledwidge, 1972).

Another technique used by family therapists is to change the ways family members react to the "symptomatic" individual, sometimes even when the family's behavior seems positive and sympathetic. Paul Watzlawick and James C. Coyne (1980) reported the case of a "Mr. B.," a middle-aged man who, following a stroke, lapsed into a depression so severe that, according to his family, he became a "vegetable." Mrs. B. and the other family members made every effort to help Mr. B. They emphasized the positive and all he had to live for, and repeatedly tried to involve him in family activities. But the more they encouraged him, the more depressed he appeared. The therapist advised the family to change their behavior, telling them "You must encourage him by discouraging him." In other words, family members were instructed to agree with Mr. B.'s negative outlook. They were to urge him to spend more time in bed and not to bed and not to exert himself by becoming involved in household activities. At the same time, Mrs. B. began to "stage" minor household emergencies and to pretend that she could not cope with running the household. Mr. B., a proud and stubborn man, began to feel that he was needed. He also became determined to show his family that he could accomplish more than they thought. He began taking part in family activities once again, and the depression began to lift.

Although some critics have called these paradoxical tactics unethical and manipulative, family therapists disagree. Family members already "manipulate" one another, they argue, and these approaches allow them to do so in a beneficial rather than a harmful way.

In recent years, interest in family therapy has been increasing, as has research designed to evaluate its effectiveness (McPeak, 1979). There is some evidence that this approach may be particularly useful in the treatment of disturbed adolescents, whose problems frequently center around maladaptive interactions with their parents (Haley, 1980). Ro-Trock, Wellisch, and Schoolar (1977) found that after a three-month follow-up, adolescents receiving family therapy showed more rapid return to community functioning and lower rehospitalization rates than those receiving individual therapy.

HUMANISTIC-EXISTENTIAL APPROACHES

Humanistic-existential therapists believe that psychological treatment should lead to personal growth, enabling the client to leave old, unfulfilling patterns of behavior behind and instead choose new more fulfilling ones. This perspective has had a number of advocates, and not surprisingly it includes several therapies, each with a slightly different approach.

Client-centered therapy

The best-known of the humanistic therapies is Carl Rogers's system of **client-centered therapy**, also referred to as nondirective counseling. Rogers (1951) believes that clients are innately motivated to fulfill their own individual potentials; the therapist's role is to help them clarify their feelings and come to value their own experience of the world. The therapist sets up a warm and accepting dialogue, helping clients to express their problems and needs. The therapist expresses neither approval nor disapproval and avoids offering any advice, interpretation, or guidance. Instead, the therapist communicates empathy and what Rogers calls "unconditional positive regard." He or she also attempts to "mirror" the clients' feelings so that the clients will become more aware of them. With this heightened awareness, according to Rogers, clients will then make constructive choices that fit in with their goals. The following excerpt from a psychotherapeutic session illustrates this technique (the client is a college student plagued by feelings of inferiority):

Client: Well, it happened again yesterday. I got back that exam in American Lit.

Therapist: I see.

Client: Just like before. I got an A all right—me and eight others. But on the third question the instructor wrote a comment that I could have been a little clearer or else could have given more detail. The same old crap. I got an A all right, but it's pretty damn clear that I'm like a machine that can generate correct answers without ever understanding. That's it. I memorize, but there's no spark, no creativity. Boy! . . .

Therapist: Even though you got an A you are not satisfied.

Client: That's right. Never satisfied. I could get 42 A-pluses and never feel good. I hate myself . . . I know I should be satisfied with an A. Other guys would be. They'd be glad to get an A. . . . A lot of times I've tried to forget my lack of potential. Just go on and plug along.

Therapist: Yeah. I guess you really felt people put you down because of this lack of potential?

Client: Boy, did they! Especially my folks. They never really said so, but I could tell from the way they acted. . . .

Therapist: And this made you feel sort of worthless? . . .

Client: That's right (Phares, 1979).

As this example shows, the therapist accepted and "mirrored" the client's feelings, thereby gaining his trust and increasing his understanding of himself. Rogers and his followers have placed a major emphasis on evaluting the effectiveness of client-centered therapy. Rogers was among the first to publish transcripts of his therapy sessions, not only to illustrate how his therapy works, but also to encourage analysis of the therapeutic process. He has also conducted research showing that client-centered therapy improves self-image and also helps people to have more realistic expectations for themselves. In addition, research has generally supported Rogers's belief that the most progress is made when the therapist is perceived as warm, empathic, and sincere (Mitchell, Bozarth, and Krauft, 1977).

Gestalt therapy

Frederick (Fritz) S. Perls, who developed Gestalt therapy, drew heavily on Freudian ideas of motivation and defense, but his therapeutic technique and philosophical orientation differ considerably from Freud's philosophy and approach to treatment. *Gestalt* (meaning "whole") *therapy* attempts to make the person whole by helping him or her get rid of defenses, unfold potential, increase awareness, and release pent-up feelings. The emphasis throughout the therapeutic dialogue is on the present, on being in touch with one's immediate feelings and expressing them as they are felt. The client is discouraged from looking to the past or speculating about the future. As Perls wrote: "The past is no more and the future not yet. Only the *now* exists" (1970, p. 14).

In the therapeutic session, the Gestalt therapist seeks to stimulate the client to express his or her feelings honestly and to take responsibility for them. The client is expected to use the first person singular—"I, me, mine"—and the active voice—"I am, I do, I feel"—to show that he or she takes responsibility for his or her actions and feelings. The client says, for example, "I am angry," rather than "don't you think I have a right to be annoyed?" (Levitsky and Perls, 1970). Some Gestalt exercises are designed to heighten the client's awareness of conflicts. The client may be asked to role-play different aspects of his or her personality, shifting from one role to another to experience the conflicting needs and demands. Or the therapist might take the role of the client's father or mother to encourage the client to act out long-buried feelings. Other exercises help clients become aware of their own movements, tones of voice, and feelings. Clients may be asked to repeat some statement over and over, louder each time. Or they may be asked to add the phrase "and I take responsibility for that" after describing their feelings: "I feel miserable . . . and I take responsibility for that!" (Phares, 1979). The following excerpt from a therapy session illustrates how this can work:

Therapist: Tom, what are you experiencing now?

Patient: Anger.

Therapist: Where do you feel this anger?

Patient: (indicating chest) Here, and (indicating hands) here.

Therapist: Just stay with the feeling, and let it increase. And you may get more in touch with it if you breathe deeply, in your abdomen, and let a sound come out when you exhale. . . .

Patient: (Breathing abdominally) Ooooh! ooooh! ooooh!

Therapist: What is that experience?

Patient: Anger, resentment.

Therapist: Will you address that resentment to somebody?

Patient: Mother, I resent you . . . everything about you.

Therapist: Specify your resentment.

Patient: I . . . I resent you for making me dependent on you.

Therapist: Tom, how is your voice?

Patient: It's . . . it's a whine.

Therapist: Will you own your voice? Take responsibility?

Patient: I . . . I'm whining . . . I'm whining.

Therapist: Do that. Whine to your mother, and experience yourself doing that.

Patient: (Whining voice; reaching out with hands) Mother . . . Please . . . please let me go . . . please turn me loose (Phares, 1979, p. 374).

This approach, with its emphasis on the expression of pent-up feelings, has had considerable influence on other therapies, particularly group therapies. It has also attracted many adherents, possibly because modern society discourages the expression of feelings in most contexts. Despite the influence of Gestalt therapy, however, its validity has not been supported by an accumulation of research data.

GROUP APPROACHES

The group-therapy movement gained impetus after World War II, when it became necessary to treat large numbers of people, both veterans and civilians, who had suffered from the social, political, and economic upheavals of the period. Group therapy lessens the economic problem that other therapies pose by allowing more patients to be treated at lower fees. But its chief advantage is that it concentrates on and promotes better interpersonal relationships. Moreover, certain problems that are extremely resistant to individual therapy seem to respond to the emotional support of the group.

Each approach to psychotherapy discussed thus far has given rise to a form of group psychotherapy. There are psychoanalytic therapy groups, behavior therapy groups, and humanistic (especially Gestalt) therapy groups. And many groups borrow from several theoretical schools. In this section, we will consider three prominent group approaches: transactional analysis, encounter groups, and self-help groups.

Transactional analysis

Transactional analysis, or TA, was developed in the 1950s and 1960s by Eric Berne, who popularized it in his book, *Games People Play* (1964). It is based on the idea that our relationships with one another can be seen as transactions between the more and less mature aspects of our personalities. According to Berne, each of us possesses within us a Child, a Parent, and an Adult. The Child is that part of our personality shaped by our relationship with our parents: The Child in us feels small and inferior and is oriented toward the satisfaction of impulses. The Parent represents the extent to which we have adopted our own parents' rules and standards: The Parent usually acts to tell us what to do or not to do. The Adult is that rational, mature part of us that can see both sides of an issue, exercise empathy toward others, and otherwise behave in a mature, responsive way. The relative strengths of Child, Parent, and Adult in us are shown in our transactions with others. The goal of TA is to enable us to identify the pattern of our transactions, helping us recognize our tendencies to behave as Parent or Child. Are we sometimes pompous or authoritative, issuing arbitrary orders to others? This is the Parent in us speaking, and it can cause us problems with our spouse and coworkers. Are we overly dependent on others, ready to interpret their slightest negative reaction as rejection or criticism? Then we are acting the Child. TA aims at building up the Adult within us, breaking these negative patterns of behavior.

TA has become extremely popular in recent years, in part because of the zeal of its proponents. Besides Berne's best-selling book, Thomas Harris's *I'm OK— You're OK* (1969) brought many followers to TA. Perhaps the simplicity of the approach—we easily recognize ourselves and our life predicaments—is one reason for its success. Despite the glowing testimonials from the many people who feel TA has helped them, it is difficult to estimate the effectiveness of the therapy or its applicability to the various kinds of disorders; little sound, empirical research has been conducted to date.

Figure 16.5 Three examples of what Eric Berne describes as "crossed transactions." Drawing an analogy between human relations and economic transactions, Berne refers to interactions among people as transactions. He considers each personality to be capable of expressing itself as a Child (C), an Adult (A), or a Parent (P) (compare Freud's id, ego, and superego). Berne maintains that normal, or healthy, transactions can be represented in diagrams like these with arrows that run horizontally; Adult to Adult, Parent to Parent, Child to Child. It is not difficult to see that the transactions illustrated here, with their diagonal lines, are the ones that lead to trouble (after Berne, 1964).

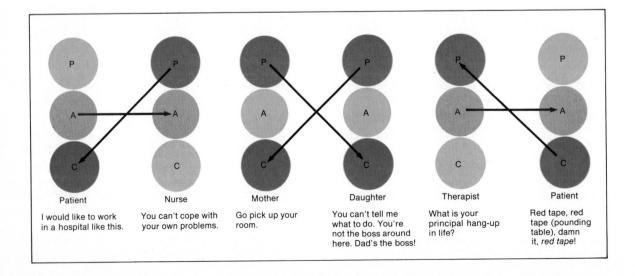

Patient	Nurse	Mother	Daughter	Therapist	Patient
I would like to work in a hospital like this.	You can't cope with your own problems.	Go pick up your room.	You can't tell me what to do. You're not the boss around here. Dad's the boss!	What is your principal hang-up in life?	Red tape, red tape (pounding table), damn it, *red tape!*

Encounter groups

Unlike most group therapies, the goal of an *encounter group* is usually not to help a person overcome a particular psychological problem, but rather to help people "grow," to lead them to experience more joy, warmth, and spontaneity in their lives—a generally positive if somewhat vague goal. They do this in a variety of ways. Sometimes exercises involve touching, yelling, or even weeping—all aimed at letting down the defensive barriers we build around ourselves. Nearly always, group members are encouraged to express emotions honestly at all times, even to the point of criticizing one another and the group itself in the bluntest terms. How effective such groups are depends largely on the effectiveness of the group leader and on his or her ability to guide the group and interpret its activities. When they work as they are intended to, encounter groups live up to their ideals of increasing spontaneity and releasing positive feelings. Such successes have produced vivid testimonials, such as this one, from a man who participated in a "marathon" encounter group, that is, one that lasted for a number of consecutive hours:

At first I felt terrible after the marathon. I seemed unable to achieve the kind of warmth and closeness of the rest of the group and I felt so left out. Then slowly I began to see how I keep other people away, which is what Dr. B. [his therapist] has been trying to point out to me for months, but I never saw it before. I'm working on it and I am really understanding myself better. . . .

The marathon was almost a year ago and I'm still dating my life from Before and After Marathon. I just never knew people could be so decent and so nice and real. Of course they're not that way all of the time, not all of them, but I'm so much more willing to meet them half-way and take a chance (Mintz, 1974, p. 123).

But unfortunately encounter groups have also produced casualties. One study (Lieberman, Yalom, and Miks, 1973) reported that 9 percent of those who had participated in such groups appeared to suffer psychological damage from the experience. These researchers found that many who were unable to go along with the uninhibited emoting of the group were ridiculed and attacked:

I tried to overcome my defenses as best I could but I couldn't do it. The leader kept pressuring me to express my feelings but I didn't know what I felt. When I said this I was attacked as a phony. This reinforced my defenses so later in the sessions I just withdrew and watched. (Lieberman, Yalom, and Miks, 1973, p. 186)

The potential for such negative reactions—some of which can be severe and long-lasting (Yalom and Lieberman, 1971)—should not be discounted. It is ironic that a therapy that aims at a distinct positive effect can damage some of its participants. Although encounter groups may pose no problems for the psychologically healthy, people who are less secure or stable may be better off elsewhere.

Self-help groups

A fast-growing phenomenon of recent years has been the *self-help* groups—groups of people who share a particular problem and meet to discuss it among themselves, without the active involvement of professional therapists. The most familiar, and to some extent the inspiration for all these groups, is Alcoholics Anonymous. But many problems lend themselves to this kind of therapy, and

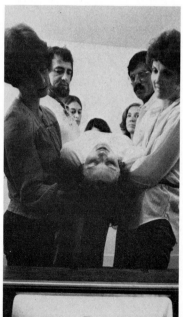

Figure 16.6 An encounter group at the Institute for Human Potential in Houston. This group is participating in a "trust exercise." The videotape is being made to provide the group with feedback.

groups have been formed by single parents, former drug addicts, displaced homemakers, mastectomy patients, overeaters, smokers, child-abusing parents, and former mental patients. Following the lead of AA, these groups organize themselves so that members can appeal directly to one another for help. A father tempted to explode at his child, for example, can telephone another member of his abusing-parents group for help in controlling his rage.

Some groups form to help their members control a particular problem behavior, such as smoking or overeating. Others give their members an opportunity to share their feelings with those who have undergone similar experiences and understand the difficulties of, for example, single parenthood or mastectomy (Wortman and Dunkel-Schetter, 1979). Self-help groups provide their members with valuable emotional support. Moreover, there is evidence that some such groups do their members as much good as more orthodox, professional help (Silverman, 1980).

Evaluating the group therapies

The various group therapies—and we have mentioned only a few—are among the most popular forms of treatment in use today. But they are also among the least researched. We simply do not have much evidence that they work. This, of course, is understandable; conducting sound research on groups and group therapy is extremely difficult. Until research establishes that these groups actually help their participants, those considering group thereapy would be wise to choose their group and check the credentials of the leader carefully.

THE EFFECTIVENESS OF PSYCHOTHERAPY

Has psychotherapy proven itself? Can we say unequivocally that therapy "works"? We have described several types of psychotherapy. Have some been shown to be more effective than others? Investigators have addressed themselves to such questions, but their answers must be evaluated carefully.

In 1952 Hans Eysenck published a review of five studies of the effectiveness of psychoanalytic treatment and nineteen studies of the effectiveness of "eclectic" psychotherapy—that is, treatment that combines different therapeutic approaches. Eysenck concluded, to the astonishment of therapists, that psychotherapy was no more effective than no treatment at all. According to Eysenck's interpretation of these twenty-four studies, only 44 percent of the patients receiving psychoanalytic treatment improved, and 64 percent of those given eclectic psychotherapy were "cured" or had improved. Moreover, Eysenck argued that even this 64 percent improvement rate did not demonstrate the effectiveness of psychotherapy, pointing to a study that showed 72 percent of a group of hospitalized neurotics improved *without* treatment (Landis, 1937). If no treatment leads to as much or more improvement as psychotherapy, the obvious conclusion is that psychotherapy is not effective, a controversial position that Eysenck (1966) vigorously defended. Needless to say, his contentions generated many responses and still more studies of the effectiveness of psychotherapy.

One of the most thoughtful and carefully reasoned reviews was written by Allen Bergin (1971). Bergin pointed out that Eysenck's treatment and control groups were not precisely comparable: They differed in education, socioeco-

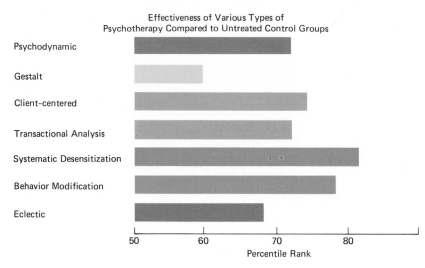

Effectiveness of Various Types of
Psychotherapy Compared to Untreated Control Groups

Psychodynamic

Gestalt

Client-centered

Transactional Analysis

Systematic Desensitization

Behavior Modification

Eclectic

50   60   70   80

Percentile Rank

Figure 16.7 Is psychotherapy effective? Researchers Smith and Glass think the answer is yes. Clients receiving each of the types of psychotherapy shown in this graph were compared with untreated control groups. The bars indicate the percentile rank that the average treated client attained on outcome measures when compared with control subjects for each type of therapy. Thus the average client receiving psychodynamic therapy scored more favorably on outcome measure than 72 percent of the untreated controls (adapted from Smith and Glass, 1977).

nomic status, motivation to improve, and other factors. Moreover, many members of the control population (those who received no "treatment") were in fact treated by general practitioners, who listened sympathetically and calmed their patients with sedative medications. This constituted therapy of a sort. Finally, Bergin argued that the criteria used to assess improvement in the psychotherapy groups differed from those applied to the control group. According to Bergin, more lenient standards were used in assessing the improvement of control subjects. On reexamining Eysenck's data, he concluded that the rate of improvement without treatment was actually about 30 percent, not 72 percent (Bergin and Lambert, 1978).

Bergin's review cast doubt on the validity of Eysenck's original study; other researchers argued that Eysenck was simply wrong. Reviews of controlled studies by Luborsky, Singer, and Luborsky (1975) and by Perloff and his colleagues (1978) have concluded that psychotherapy is generally effective. An even more ambitious investigation reviewed more than four hundred studies and came to the same conclusion (Smith and Glass, 1977; Smith, Glass, and Miller, in press). "On the average," they state, "the typical therapy client is better off than 75 percent of untreated individuals" (1977, p. 752). These investigators found little evidence for harmful effects of therapy. Interestingly, their study also found little difference in effectiveness among different types of therapy—psychoanalytic, behavior, or humanistic.

However, methodological problems have been found in many of the studies reviewed. For example, most therapy studies accept the therapist's opinion of whether the patient improved, and the therapist bases his or her opinion, in large part, on the patient's reports. Both patients and therapists might inadvertently bias their reports to make their therapy look better. Another problem is that the patient's expectations of improvement may be more important than the actual therapy (Goldstein, 1962). This is called a placebo effect, from drug research in which a subject experiences a therapeutic effect from a sugar pill. In studies of psychotherapy outcome, the placebo effect can be controlled by administering a treatment that elicits therapeutic expectations but does not provide active treatment. For example, the patient may receive attention from a therapist but no therapeutically meaningful discussion and no specific techniques (McCardel and Murray, 1974).

Finally—and obviously—effectiveness of psychotherapy depends on how we define "effectiveness." A common approach is to say that therapy is effective if it helps the client feel better. But a woman might say she feels better, yet continue to drink too much and neglect her children. Could we say therapy has been effective in her case? Or conversely, a man may complain of still feeling anxious, but he may be getting along better with his family and on the job. Has therapy failed in his case? Then too, the goals and expectations of both therapist and client affect their judgments of effectiveness. A client entering therapy for treatment of a phobia may overcome the phobia but still remain anxious, withdrawn, and dependent. Yet, because the phobia was conquered, the treatment might be labeled a success. Evaluating the outcome of psychotherapy is clearly not a simple matter, and therefore, sophisticated studies usually measure the outcome in several ways.

One study of therapy outcomes took special pains to measure improvement in several ways. In this study, done at the Temple University Outpatient Clinic (Sloane et al., 1975), ninety-four outpatients with moderate ("neurotic") disturbances were assigned to one of three groups: behavior therapy, psychoanalytically oriented therapy, or a waiting list. After four months, subjects were measured by interviews, reports from their close associates, and several psychological tests. (The interviews, it should be noted, were conducted by blind-independent raters. These raters were psychologists who, because they did not know which group the subjects had been assigned to, could be presumed free of bias.) The results? Those receiving therapy improved more than those on the waiting list (80 percent of both therapy groups improved; 48 percent of those on the waiting list improved). The subjects were retested after one year and showed no evidence of relapse. In general, all patients continued to improve—and patients on the waiting lists eventually tended to approach or equal those in the therapy groups. Over time, then, the group that received no treatment became more similar to the groups who had had treatment, suggesting that therapy may not so much produce change as accelerate it.

Nevertheless, the Temple study offers evidence that undergoing therapy is better than doing without it. As the authors of the study concluded:

This is rather clear evidence that therapy in general "works," that the improvement of patients in therapy is not entirely due either to "spontaneous recovery" or to the placebo effect of the nonspecific aspects of therapy, such as arousal of hope, expectation of help, and an initial cathartic interview. Our control patients were exposed to all these nonspecific aspects and yet improved significantly less than treated patients (1975, p. 224).

Overall, the researchers noted, behavior therapy had been slightly more successful than psychoanalytic therapy; behavior therapists did somewhat better, for example, with more seriously disturbed patients. This suggests that behavior therapy works better with a broader range of patients than does psychoanalytic therapy, or as the researchers put it, "behavior therapy is clearly a *generally* useful treatment."

Comparative studies such as the Temple study are becoming more and more common. Kazdin and Wilson (1978), reviewing a number of methodologically strong comparative studies of effectiveness, found that nine showed better results for behavior therapy, seven showed no difference between behavior therapy and other treatments, and none showed an alternative treatment to be more effective than behavior therapy.

Of course, the most important issue is not which therapy is most effective in general, but which techniques work best for particular problems. In the future, we can expect more research that attempts to pinpoint the specific problems that are most effectively treated by a given therapeutic approach.

BIOLOGICAL APPROACHES TO THERAPY

The therapies discussed thus far can be seen as emphasizing talking or learning—gaining insight or changing behavior. They require the active involvement and cooperation of the person undergoing treatment. Biological therapies, in contrast, effect treatment by altering the underlying physiology, primarily but not exclusively with psychotherapeutic drugs. **Psychopharmacology** has become an important science in its own right: Drugs have been developed to treat anxiety, schizophrenia, depression, mania, and other disorders. Most of these drugs have been introduced in the past few decades, and their development constitutes an enormous advance in treatment. Drug therapy is available to all patients, not just those with time and money for extended treatment or those who are educated and articulate. Drugs also have proved useful in some cases where few other therapies have worked. After exploring the available evidence on drugs, this section will also consider two other physiologically-based treatments: electroconvulsive therapy and psychosurgery.

Antianxiety drugs

Commonly known as "minor" tranquilizers, antianxiety drugs reduce excitability and cause drowsiness. Since most people experience anxiety and insomnia at one time or another, these drugs are widely used. The most popular antianxiety drugs are Miltown (meprobamate), Librium (chlordiazepoxide hydrochloride), and Valium (diazepam). In fact, tranquilizers have become so popular that Valium is now the most widely prescribed drug in the world (Ray, 1978).

The major effect of Valium, Librium, and Miltown is to depress the activity of the central nervous system. These drugs are sometimes prescribed by family physicians for people who, while not undergoing psychological treatment, are having trouble coping with difficult periods in their lives (Uhlenhuth, Balter, and Lipman, 1978). Antianxiety drugs are also used, often in combination with other forms of treatment, for anxiety disorders, stress-related physical disorders, and withdrawal from alcohol (Mellinger et al., 1978). Side effects include fatigue and drowsiness, prolonged use may lead to dependency, and heavy doses taken along with alcohol can result in death.

Although antianxiety drugs can be useful on a short-term basis, many questions about their ultimate impact are as yet unanswered. Does taking pills to relieve anxiety help a person cope more effectively with the underlying stress? We do not know. We do know that anxiety can be a signal to a person that something needs correcting (Schwartz, 1977), and that antianxiety pills may merely suppress the signal without correcting the problem.

Antipsychotic drugs

Antipsychotic drugs are major tranquilizers used to alleviate extreme symptoms of agitation and hyperactivity in psychotic patients (Davis, 1975). The most popular of these drugs are the phenothiazines, including Thorazine (chlorpromazine) and Stelazine (trifluoperazine hydrochloride), which are widely used in the treatment of schizophrenia. When they were introduced about twenty-five years ago, these drugs were viewed as major breakthroughs in the treatment of serious mental disorders (MacDonald and Tobias, 1976). Compared with other biological therapies of the time—psychosurgery and electroconvulsive therapy—they had many advantages: They were more humane, more effective, and more easily administered.

The actions of these drugs—like those of electroconvulsive therapy—were not well understood when they were first put into use. They were welcomed because, by reducing the disruptive behaviors of severely disturbed patients, they changed the nature of institutional care. Patients who had once required such physical restraints as straitjackets were able to walk around freely; patients whose waking hours had been completely devoted to bizarre motor behaviors (rocking, posing, or pacing the floor) became much calmer and were better able to function. The wide acceptance of these drugs testifies to their usefulness. Today, it has been estimated that 87 percent of all psychiatric inpatients are receiving some such medication (MacDonald and Tobias, 1976). Theories about how the drugs worked came later. The observation that the drugs produced good results with schizophrenic patients led to speculation that schizophrenia might be caused by some kind of chemical imbalance in the brain. Investigations of the drugs' effect on the brain led directly to the dopamine hypothesis, currently a promising theory about the causes of schizophrenia.

The major tranquilizers, however, are not without drawbacks. Although the drugs produce calm, they often produce fatigue and apathy as well. As one patient reported:

On Thorazine everything's a bore. Not a bore, exactly. Boredom implies impatience. You can read comic books and *Reader's Digest* forever. You can tolerate talking to jerks forever. Babble, babble, babble. The weather is dull, the flowers are dull, nothing's very impressive. Muzak, Bach, Beatles, Lolly and the Yum-Yums, Rolling Stones. It doesn't make any difference. . . . What the drug is supposed to do is keep away hallucinations. What I think it does is just fog up your mind so badly you don't notice the hallucinations or much else. (Vonnegut, 1975, pp. 196-197)

More troubling is the fact that some hospitals have been known to use the drugs' calming effect in "patient management," giving stupor-inducing doses to troublesome patients.

The major tranquilizers also have harmful side effects, and some are irreversible. The drugs often produce what is known as "pseudoparkinsonianism," or a cluster of symptoms similar to those shown by patients suffering from Parkinson's disease. These include trembling, stiffening of muscles, and drooling, symptoms that sometimes continue for as long as a year after drug therapy ceases (Parkes, 1976). Some patients also experience dizziness, fainting, restlessness, nausea, diarrhea, blurred vision, sensitivity to sunlight, and other side effects.

More serious still is an apparently irreversible condition called *tardive diskinesia* that develops in some patients, especially those who take the drugs for

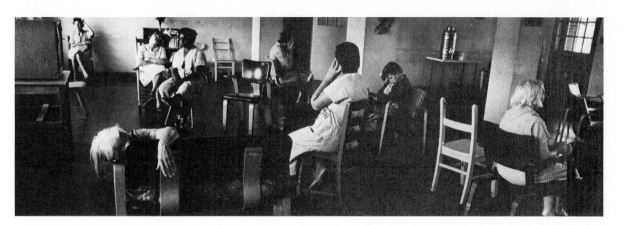

prolonged periods or in high doses. Tardive dyskinesia comes on gradually and persists even when the drug is discontinued. It is painful and its victims have difficulty chewing and swallowing. Its symptoms include grotesque movements of the face—grimaces, lip smacking, and protrusions of the tongue—and some patients, acutely embarrassed by these symptoms, avoid all contact with people, becoming social isolates (Widroe and Heisler, 1976). Permanent brain damage also appears to be associated with this condition (MacDonald, Lidsky, and Kern, 1979). Estimates of the incidence of tardive dyskinesia range from 10 percent to 56 percent of those taking the drug (Jus et al., 1976), with elderly patients apparently most prone to the disorder.

Growing awareness of the harmful side effects of the antipsychotic drugs has led to controversy over their use. Although advocates of these drugs have argued that they are immediately effective in calming psychotic patients and that they prevent relapses into serious disturbance, these claims have been disputed (MacDonald, Lidsky, and Kern, 1979). One study found the drugs no more effective than a placebo in calming agitated patients (Hamill and Fontana, 1975). Although many studies appear to support the contention that patients on maintenance doses of these drugs are less likely to relapse, a number of methodological flaws have been found in these studies (Sulzbacher, 1973). A careful review of all these findings (MacDonald, Lidsky, and Kern, 1979) has concluded that "psychoactive drug treatment, once thought to be the hope for the future, seems to have become the myth of the present" (p. 437). In view of the conflicting evidence on the effectiveness of the major tranquilizers and the possibility that their use may produce serious—or even permanent—side effects, the final verdict must await further definitive research.

Figure 16.8 Antipsychotic drugs may not only calm patients but leave them in a constant state of drowsiness and fatigue. Scenes like this—patients nodding in front of a television set—are common in today's mental hospitals.

Antidepressant drugs

The antidepressant drugs were discovered by accident in 1952. Irving Selikof and his colleagues were treating tuberculosis patients with a drug called Iproniazid when they noticed that it produced a mood elevation. Further investigation of mood regulators led to the development of effective antidepressants such as Tofranil and Elavil. These drugs are known as the tricyclics, so named from their three-ringed molecular structure. They seem to work by increasing the level of certain neurotransmitters in the brain, among them norepinephrine and serotonin. The tricyclics seem to work well against certain types of depression (Gelenberg, 1979). However, like the antipsychotic drugs, they have unpleasant side effects, including restlessness, faintness, trembling, blurred vision, constipation, and dry mouth (Rosenbaum, Maruta, and Richelson, 1979).

Lithium, a simple metallic substance relatively new to the psychiatric community in the United States, has been widely used in Europe for the past twenty years to treat manic-depressive psychosis. It is effective in returning patients to a state of emotional equilibrium without extreme swings of mood. Lithium can also have side effects, including restlessness, nausea, weight gain, and increased urination. It can even be fatal if its level in the bloodstream becomes too high. For this reason, patients taking the drug must have their dosage monitored by a physician through regular blood tests (Branchey, Charles, and Simpson, 1976).

Electroconvulsive therapy

"Shock treatment," as **electroconvulsive therapy** (ECT) is commonly called, has proven extremely effective in the treatment of severe depression, though no one understands exactly how it works. A series of brief electrical shocks of approximately 70 to 130 volts are administered over several weeks, inducing convulsions similar to epileptic seizures. It is the convulsion, rather than the electricity, that produces the therapeutic result; the purpose of the shock is merely to bring on the convulsion. Although it sounds extreme, ECT as it is now applied entails very little discomfort. The patient is given a sedative and injected with a muscle relaxant before treatment to alleviate involuntary muscular contractions and prevent physical injury. Shortly after the shock is administered, the patient awakens with no memory of the treatment. It is well established that ECT can be useful in the treatment of endogenous depression, though apparently not in that of other disorders (Scovern and Kilmann, 1980). Since its effects begin to be apparent almost immediately it is sometimes preferable to the tricyclic drugs, which are much slower to work—an important consideration if a patient is suicidal (Avery and Winokur, 1977). However, ECT is a drastic treatment that should be used with great caution. One common side effect is temporary memory loss, which in rare cases may persist for several years.

Psychosurgery

Psychosurgery is the most extreme of all biological treatments. It is a high-risk surgical procedure with irreversible effects. In 1935, Egas Moniz and Almeida Lima developed a procedure known as prefrontal lobotomy, in which a surgical cut is made between the brain's frontal lobes and the thalamus. They expected the interruption in communication between these two areas of the brain to help reduce the impact of disturbing stimuli on patients who were agitated or violent. Over the next twenty years other methods of psychosurgery evolved, and thousands of operations were performed. Some severely disturbed patients were helped by these procedures, but many were left in childlike and lethargic states, and others died on the operating table. In the 1950s the discovery of drugs that calmed the severely disturbed brought a halt to most psychosurgery.

Today the surgical techniques of the 1940s and 1950s have been abandoned in favor of "fractional operations," which destroy very small amounts of brain tissue in precise locations (Valenstein, 1973). Such operations are performed on about four hundred patients a year in the United States, and only after all other modes of treatment have been exhausted. The National Commission for the Protection of Human Subjects in Biomedical and Behavioral Research released a report in 1976 that concluded that these new procedures have been beneficial in cases of depression and depression associated with intractable pain. Furthermore, the serious side effects and risks associated with lobotomy appear not to occur with the new techniques. The commission encouraged further research, but recommended that, for now, psychosurgery be considered an experimental procedure to be employed only under the most stringent safeguards of the rights and welfare of the patient.

COMMUNITY MENTAL HEALTH

Over the past several decades, it has become increasingly apparent that therapy is often not available to those who need it most—the poor and ill-educated. As we have seen, these are the people most likely to experience serious mental disorder, yet least likely to have the time or money necessary for psychotherapy. The community mental health movement has attempted to speak to this special need: to identify the psychological problems of the less advantaged and to attempt to alleviate them. This movement has pointed out the need for prevention, the failure of large institutions as primary sources of treatment, and the inappropriateness of middle-class therapy for the poor. Suppose an unemployed woman, left by her husband with several children to support, appears in the therapist's office complaining of depression. It would seem ridiculous not to consider her problem as at least as much the result of her life situation as of traumas in her childhood development or some other "internal" cause. The community psychology movement has also been important in providing support to those reentering society after hospitalization.

Community mental health centers

The Community Mental Health Centers Act of 1963 was designed to provide comprehensive mental health services throughout the country on a decentralized basis. This legislation mandated one mental health center for every 50,000 people. The centers would supply treatment without sending people to large institutions outside their own communities. Other purposes of those centers were to educate community workers in the principles of preventive mental health, to train paraprofessionals, and to carry out research. A nationwide system of mental health centers has not yet been achieved, and funding for existing centers has been cut back in many cities. However, those centers that are in operation supply important services—outpatient, inpatient, and emergency services and community consultation.

Outpatients can walk into a clinic and receive therapy once, twice, or several times a week, without leaving school, job, or family, and without feeling stigmatized as institutionalized mental patients. The centers also serve as a bridge between hospitalization and complete independence by giving aftercare and supplementary services to patients released from hospitals.

For the more severely disturbed, hospitalization is provided within the community. Friends and family have easy access to patients, who feel less isolated and more accepted. Many centers have arrangements for day hospitals, in which patients take advantage of the support systems and therapy offered by a hospital during the day and go home at night. Night hospitals work in a similar manner: Patients work or go to school during the day and spend the night at the hospital.

Many community mental health centers also maintain storefront clinics that are open around the clock to deal with such emergencies as acute anxiety attacks, suicide attempts, and bad drug trips. Here the troubled person can discuss his or her problem with a paraprofessional, a member of the community trained to deal with just such events. (The paraprofessional can be particularly useful in this kind of setting, since professional therapists, who often come from a higher social class than their clients, can be intimidating to some.) The centers may also have teams of trained personnel on call to go to city hospital emergency rooms to deal with psychological traumas.

Mental health centers provide qualified personnel to serve as consultants to teachers, police, and clergy, advising them on how to handle psychological problems in the classroom and within the community. Sensitivity workshops give instruction on such matters as how to intervene in potentially violent family quarrels, how to talk potential suicides out of self-destructive behaviors, and how to keep truants from dropping out of school.

Halfway houses

Halfway houses, so named because they are an intermediate step between the hospital and the community, are houses in which individuals with common problems live together, providing support for one another and receiving whatever supplementary services are necessary until they are able to function entirely on their own. These houses have proliferated in recent years—despite some community opposition—and have provided a useful transition between hospital care and community life. Such halfway houses have been successful in the rehabilitiation of drug addicts, newly released mental patients, exconvicts, and alcoholics. Reports indicate that such individuals are less likely to require rehospitalization than those who have been returned to the community with no supplementary support system (Fairweather et al., 1969).

In large urban centers, however, a very small percentage of discharged mental patients reside in true halfway houses. Large numbers of former mental patients live in large converted hotels that are little more than mental hospital back wards located within the community (Jones, 1975). In such settings, patients often receive little or no therapy except for their daily doses of drugs; they do not get the help that would allow them to resume truly independent living. Neglect can exist in the community as well as in the mental hospital.

Crisis intervention: the hot line

Community services such as those available at community mental health centers are costly and complicated to set up. The crisis hot line, in contrast, provides an instant, economical, and effective way to deal with emergency situations. People in trouble can pick up a telephone and receive immediate counseling, sympathy, and comfort. The best known of these systems is the Los Angeles Suicide Prevention Center, established in 1958. Similar hot lines have been set up for alcoholics, rape victims, battered women, runaway children, gamblers, and people who just need a shoulder to cry on. In addition to providing sympathy, hot-line volunteers provide information on the community services available to handle each kind of problem.

Prevention

The basic goals of the community mental health movement are to prevent the development of mental disorder (primary prevention), to prevent the worsening of disorder (secondary prevention), and to prevent the severe effects of major disorder on the victim and on society (tertiary prevention). Primary prevention of mental disorder is very desirable but extremely difficult to achieve. It requires changing those aspects of society and the environment that lead to psychological disturbance, and we have seen in Chapter 15 how complex the causes of disorder can be. Nevertheless, nutritional counseling, genetic counseling, and the design of less stressful school environments are all potentially important methods of reducing the incidence of disorder.

Secondary prevention, the early detection and treatment of problems before they become severe, is somewhat less complex but still no easy task. Outpatient clinics, emergency services, hot lines, and some paraprofessional programs are examples of secondary prevention. Early detection of problems usually requires a trained professional, but consultation programs with schools and law enforcement agencies are a means of expanding secondary prevention.

Tertiary prevention programs include day hospitals, night hospitals, and halfway houses. These facilities are designed to help those who have suffered a serious disorder to resume useful roles in society, and to prevent the recurrence of disorder.

The prevention of disorder is the goal of the community mental health movement, but some psychologists maintain that this has led to a preoccupation with the delivery of individual services, whereas the major goal should be the improvement of social conditions. Encouraging the development of effective human beings in communities that have the resources to provide their residents with satisfying lives is the goal of the newly emerging specialty of community psychology. Leonard Goodstein and Irwin Sandler (1978) maintain that community psychologists should focus on the design of social systems that foster health and growth. If that goal could be achieved, the incidence of psychological disorder would probably be significantly reduced. In a careful review of efforts at prevention, however, H. Richard Lamb and Jack Zusman (1979) have argued that unless programs have a precise goal (not just the improvement of social conditions), they are unlikely to have much effect on mental health. Primary prevention remains an elusive goal.

THERAPY AND BEHAVIOR CONTROL

In depth

The therapeutic treatments reviewed thus far have enormous potential to benefit individuals, groups, and entire wards of patients. However, a potential for misuse also exists. Drugs can be used to make patients dull and drowsy—and thus easy to manage. Behavior techniques can be used to make children obedient and conforming. Psychosurgery and electroconvulsive treatments may even be held over patients as threats to make them behave, or they may be administered to patients "for their own good" even when they refuse consent. In this section, we shall consider some important questions of control. Who decides which people need treatment? Who decides on the nature of treatment? And what considerations should be weighed in such decisions?

Control in psychotherapy

To some extent, the values of the therapist are bound to influence interactions with the patient. But to what extent should the therapist's values dictate the treatment given to clients? Suppose, for example, a professor comes to ask a therapist for help in reducing the guilt he feels over an affair with one of his students. How should the therapist respond? If the client's behavior conflicts with the therapist's values, will this affect therapy? Or imagine a woman who seeks help in breaking away from her husband and children to pursue her own identity. Will the therapist accept her goal as legitimate or seek to remind her of her responsibility to her family?

If therapists are aware that their values conflict with those of a client, they can attempt to put their own values aside in the therapeutic relationship. However, this is not always easy. In addition, therapists may not always be aware of the values that guide their efforts at treatment. One study (Broverman et al., 1970) found that when therapists were asked to describe "healthy" males and females, they responded in extremely stereotyped terms: healthy women were more submissive, emotional, and dependent; healthy men, more aggressive and competitive. The implications of such value judgments for treatment are obvious: Women who are independent and competitive will be seen as "unhealthy" and in need of therapy to correct their "maladjustment." Similarly, women who are unhappy with their dependent role (such as the "housewife" in a conventional marriage) will be encouraged to adapt to their situation, not to change it. As one therapist has written:

Many wives . . . discontented with the narrow pattern of suburban life, have been stabilized for years by intensive analysis. Instead of encouraging them to take action that would lead to a richer and more complex life, the therapy prevents that change by imposing the idea that the problem is within their psyche rather than in their situation (Haley, 1973, p. 43).

It should be noted, however, that not all research has supported the idea that therapists think in such stereotypes. One thorough review of the research on the subject concluded that although biases based on social class, race, and sex do exist, they may not be extreme ones (Abramowitz and Dokecki, 1977).

Control in institutional settings

Under the laws of most states, a person can be committed to a mental institution involuntarily if it is decided that he or she is mentally ill and either needs treatment or is dangerous. Involuntary commitment is fairly common: Of all hospitalized patients, the ratio of voluntary to involuntary patients is about three to two. Formal commitment proceedings involve a court hearing, during which a person has the right to object to the commitment and to present evidence against it. Many patients, however, are committed without this court process. Such patients have usually entered the hospital voluntarily or been brought to the hospital by police after some episode of "crazy" behavior; they are subsequently judged by the hospital staff to be in need of treatment. Once in the hospital, a patient can be kept involuntarily if two physicians simply sign statements certifying that he or she is ill and needs treatment (and in some states, is dangerous).

The problems with involuntary commitment are many. Without question, the procedure can be abused—for example, by a family wanting to be relieved of the responsibility for a demanding elderly parent or a misbehaving child. Recognizing the need to protect citizens from such abuses, the Supreme Court in *Addington* v. *Texas* (1979) ruled that a person cannot be involuntarily committed without "clear and convincing" evidence that he or she is mentally ill and otherwise meets the legal requirements that may justify commitment. This ruling, however, leaves open the question of "dangerousness": If a state can commit a person who is dangerous to himself, herself, or others, how is the state to determine who is dangerous? Unfortunately, mental health professionals have a poor record of predicting in advance who will be dangerous (Kozol, Boucher, and Garofolo, 1972).

Not only may commitment procedures be misused to deprive a patient of his or her rights, but the potential for abuse becomes much greater once the patient is institutionalized. Some token economies at one time were set up so that patients could obtain their meals only by presenting tokens earned for appropriate behavior. The patient who failed to perform the designated behaviors (self-care, work skills, or social interaction) would be forced to go without a meal. The courts, however, have begun to enumerate the rights guaranteed to institutionalized patients. After reviewing the case of *Wyatt* v. *Stickney* (1972), the Supreme Court addressed itself to patients' rights to treatment and to a humane environment. In this case, the state of Alabama was accused of grossly violating the rights of patients by confining them in filthy, dark, chaotically managed facilities with inadequate food and virtually no treatment. The court ruled that every institutionalized patient must be given not only adequate meals but also a comfortable bed and the opportunities to have visitors, be outdoors regularly, and have access to recreational facilities. These protections are certainly appropriate. Ironically, however, they may mean that many severely disturbed patients cannot be treated with some behavior therapies: debilitated patients will often respond only to basic reinforcers (such as food). As one proponent of behavior therapies has written:

Here there is a direct conflict between the right to treatment and the right to enjoy basic privileges. By depriving some patients of an effective treatment, we may be condemning them to a lifetime of institutionalization (Bootzin, 1975, p. 56).

Although the law in this area is still evolving, a strong trend toward guaranteeing patients certain basic rights has emerged. These include the right to a humane environment, the right to treatment, and even the right to refuse treatment (Bootzin and Acocella, 1980). The right to refuse treatments that are likely to have irreversible harmful effects or are "experimental" is being recognized in many states. For example, there is greater recognition of the "right to refuse" psychosurgery and ECT than of the right to refuse less intrusive treatments (Ennis and Emery, 1978). However, even the less intrusive treatments are coming under more regulation. Since even these treatments sometimes produce very harmful side effects (as in the antipsychotic drugs' producing tardive dyskinesia), the right to refuse treatment is important.

On the other hand, the right to refuse treatment is a complicated issue. Should the right extend to a person who is not capable of making a rational decision? If a young woman is profoundly depressed and seems bent on suicide, should she be given ECT despite her objections? Does the paranoid man, convinced that the doctors are trying to poison him, have a right to refuse to take any drug that might calm his delusions? Are there ever circumstances in which people should be treated "for their own good" against their wishes?

In response to such questions, institutions have established review boards and ombudsmen to ensure that patients' complaints receive due consideration. One such body is the Committee on Scientific and Professional Ethics and Conduct of the American Psychological Association. This committee receives and reviews charges against professional psychologists and can discipline members found to have violated professional ethics.

SUMMARY

1. Through the centuries society has attempted to deal with mental disturbance in many ways. Today, psychotherapy of many kinds has come to replace more informal kinds of "help." **Psychotherapy** may be defined as a systematic series of interactions between a therapist trained to aid in solving psychological problems and a person who is troubled or is troubling others.

2. In Freudian **psychoanalysis**, the goal is to restore unconscious conflicts to consciousness so that they can be resolved. Various techniques are used in psychoanalysis, among them free association and dream analysis. Many other therapies have envolved as variants of Freud's technique.

3. Behavior therapy is the attempt to apply learning and other experimentally derived psychological principles to problem behavior. Behavior therapists use techniques based on classical conditioning (such as systematic desensitization and aversive conditioning), operant conditioning (such as the token economy), and modeling and cognitions (such as participant modeling and cognitive restructuring). Behavioral treatments have been applied to a great many problem behaviors, including phobias, alcoholism, bedwetting, self-destructive behavior, and depression.

4. Family, or systems, therapy stresses the importance of altering the roles and patterns of communication that maintain maladaptive behavior within the family. Family therapists often meet both with the whole family and with individual family members.

5. Humanistic-existential therapies are a diverse group of techniques that aim at helping clients "grow." Client-centered therapy aims at providing the client with warmth and empathic understanding of his or her individual problems. Gestalt therapy emphasizes the necessity to release pent-up emotions.

6. The group-therapy movement has grown rapidly since World War II. Prominent group therapies today include transactional analysis, encounter groups, and self-help groups. Although group therapies are popular, there is yet little research as to their effectiveness.

7. Although the effectiveness of psychotherapy has been disputed, research indicates that treatment does help patients to improve. However, it is not yet clear whether any one kind of treatment is more successful than any other.

8. Drug therapy is now very common for many disorders. Antianxiety drugs are widely used by people without severe disturbances. Antipsychotic drugs are often prescribed for more seriously disturbed patients, such as those in institutions. Although the antipsychotics seem to calm the severely ill, their effetiveness has been disputed, and they have serious side effects. Antidepressant drugs work well against endogenous depression, and Lithium is useful in the treatment of manic-depressive conditions.

9. Electroconvulsive therapy induces a brief convulsion similar to an epileptic seizure, which for reasons unknown relieves severe depression. ECT has not been found useful in the treatment of other conditions.

10. Psychosurgery is the most extreme of the biological treatments. It involves destruction of small amounts of brain tissue. Since it is a radical procedure with permanent effects, it is only used today as a treatment of last resort.

11. The community mental health movement is aimed at bringing psychological help to the poor, with prevention of disorder as the ultimate goal. Although many communities now have public clinics, they are by no means universal. Halfway houses are another way in which treatment has been integrated into the community.

12. Psychotherapeutic treatments bring up many moral and political issues. These include the role of the therapist whose values conflict with those of the client, the appropriateness of involuntary commitment, and the rights of institutionalized patients.

Suggested readings

Garfield, S. L., and Bergin, A. E. (Eds.). *Handbook of psychotherapy and behavior change: An empirical analysis.* New York: Wiley, 1978.

Gurman, A. S., and Razin, A. M. (Eds.). *Effective psychotherapy: A handbook of research.* Elmsford, N.Y.: Pergamon, 1977.

Korchin, S. J. *Modern clinical psychology.* New York: Basic Books, 1976.

Lanyon, R. I., and Lanyon, B. P. *Behavior therapy: A clinical introduction.* Reading, Mass.: Addison-Wesley, 1978.

Menninger, K., and Holtzman, P. S. *Theory of psychoanalytic technique* (2nd ed.). New York: Basic Books, 1973.

O'Leary, K. D., and Wilson, G. T. *Behavior therapy: Application and outcome.* Englewood Cliffs, N.J.: Prentice-Hall, 1975.

Rogers, C. R. *On becoming a person: A therapist's view of psychotherapy.* Boston: Houghton Mifflin, 1970.

Szasz, T. S. *The manufacture of madness.* New York: Harper & Row, 1977.

Yalom, I. D. *The theory and practice of group psychotherapy* (2nd ed.). New York: Basic Books, 1975.

SOCIAL PSYCHOLOGY

Social psychology studies human behavior in its daily context—in constant
interaction with others. The factors that affect our interpersonal relations
are the subject of Part 8. How we evaluate people is examined in Chapter
17, while Chapter 18 explores the quality of our relationships.

PREVIEW

1. Attitudes—with their thinking, feeling, and behavior components—are learned tendencies to respond favorably or unfavorably.

2. Attitudes can be changed in two ways: by persuasive argument or by reducing the inconsistency between conflicting views.

3. First impressions can substantially determine our subsequent attitudes. For example, physical attractiveness often affects our perceptions of people.

4. When we analyze people's characters, we generally make attributions about their personality on the basis of their behavior—but we attribute their behavior to different causes than we would use were we explaining our own.

5. Friendship and love, which are special cases of attribution, are the subject of much current research and theory.

6. Prejudice, such as sexism and racism, also involves attribution—negative attribution. Prejudice can be reduced in situations in which, for their common welfare, participants *must* cooperate.

17 Attitudes and social perception

In 1969, social psychologist Philip Zimbardo and his colleagues (1972, 1973) began a two-week simulation of the effects that prisons have on people's behavior. Student volunteers were recruited through newspaper ads. They were given extensive personality tests, and those judged to be emotionally stable were invited to participate. By a flip of the coin, half were randomly assigned to the role of prisoner and half were assigned to the role of guard. After only six days, Zimbardo was forced to abandon the study because it had become frighteningly real: the subjects assigned the role of guard began to use their power harshly; those assigned the role of prisoner developed severe symptoms of anxiety or were reduced to servility. As Zimbardo reported: "It was remarkable how readily we all slipped into our roles, temporarily gave up our identities, and allowed these assigned roles and social forces in the situation to guide, shape and eventually to control our freedom of thought and action" (Zimbardo et al., 1972, p. 12).

The extraordinary behavior of participants in this study, which will be discussed in more detail in Chapter 18, dramatically illustrates the social psychological perspective discussed very briefly in Chapter 1. How people act is not simply the result of their personalities and predispositions. Every student who was randomly assigned to the role of guard exhibited abusive, authoritarian behavior during the course of the study. In similar although less dramatic ways than the subjects in Zimbardo's experiment we are all influenced by the social situations in which we find ourselves. The powerful social forces that shape our behavior are what social psychologists investigate. They seek to understand and explain how the thoughts, feelings, and actions of people are influenced by the presence and behavior—either actual, imagined, or implied—of other people (Allport, 1968).

The subject of social psychology is so broad that we will devote two chapters to it. In this chapter we will focus on how people form judgments about their social environments and on how those judgments influence their behavior. In doing so, we cover such topics as attitudes, first impressions, attraction to others and falling in love, inferring the causes of other people's behavior, and the psychology of prejudice and discrimination. Then in Chapter 18 we return to the issues raised by Zimbardo's prison study. We will discuss many areas of research suggesting that behavior is often strongly influenced by powerful social forces outside the individual. These include pressure to conform to group norms, to obey those in authority, to adhere to social roles, to seek group unanimity and cohesiveness, and to follow the behavior of others in a variety of circumstances. At this point, however, we will examine attitudes, a subject that social psychologists have spent much time investigating.

ATTITUDES

Each of us has attitudes on an enormous number of topics—Ronald Reagan, nuclear energy, abortion, New York City, jogging. But as easy as it is to compile a list of *attitude objects*, the concept of *attitude* itself is rather difficult to define. Many psychologists have offered definitions. Not all of them agree. One way to summarize their efforts is to say that an **attitude** is a learned, relatively enduring predisposition to respond to a given object in a consistently favorable or unfavorable way (Fishbein and Ajzen, 1975). This definition emphasizes four important attributes. First, an attitude is learned, not innate. Second, it persists over a relatively long period of time. Third, it motivates us to act, helping us to shape and direct our behavior. And fourth, it is evaluative—it represents our likes and dislikes.

It is important to keep in mind the complexity and multidimensionality of attitudes. Attitudes are generally thought to reflect three components: (1) cognitions or beliefs about an object; (2) an affective, or emotional, reaction; and (3) a tendency or intention to behave in a particular way (Insko and Schopler, 1967). Unfortunately, these different components of an attitude are not always consistent with one another. For example, a person may hold cognitions that smoking is deleterious to his or her health but nonetheless smoke regularly and enjoy it. The complexity of attitudes raises two issues. First, how should attitudes be measured? Second, do attitudes predict a person's behavior? And if not, why study them?

Probably the most common method of assessing attitudes is to administer a carefully constructed questionnaire that in a variety of ways asks subjects to indicate both the direction and strength of their feelings toward a particular person, idea, event, or thing. What people say they feel, however, is not always what they actually feel, so researchers have looked for additional ways to measure attitudes. Some have tried to assess the emotional component of attitudes by taking physiological measurements of heart rate (Katz et al., 1965), galvanic

skin response (Rankin and Campbell, 1955), and even pupil dilation (Hess, 1965; Hess and Polt, 1960, 1964) while a person encounters an attitude object. Others have inferred attitudes from direct measurements of behavior, particularly behavior that the subject does not know is being observed. Such measures can be highly unobtrusive. In one study, for instance, people's attitudes toward a museum exhibit were inferred from the amount of wear on the surrounding floor (Webb et al., 1966). In Chapter 2 we discussed the advantages of each of these ways of measuring attitudes.

In assessing behavioral measures of attitudes, one is assuming that the way a person acts is largely consistent with her or his attitudes. Can attitudes actually be used to predict behavior?

Figure 17.1 The process by which attitudes toward such topics as abortion are formed is seldom a clear-cut, completely rational one. Our attitudes are influenced by our emotions, our expectations of rewards and punishments, our desire for approval, our need for consistency between beliefs and actions, and many other factors.

Attitudes and behavior

In Chapter 1 we discussed the results of a classic study designed to shed light on just this question. Psychologist Richard LaPiere (1934) traveled around the United States with a Chinese couple at a time when anti-Oriental feeling was relatively common. In 10,000 miles of travel, the group was refused service only once. Did this mean that most Americans were not prejudiced toward Chinese? Apparently not. When LaPiere subsequently wrote to the establishments he had visited and asked the proprietors if they would provide food or lodging to Orientals, more than 90 percent of those responding answered with a flat no.

The fact that studies attempting to demonstrate a relationship between attitudes and behavior sometimes have had mixed results has prompted some psychologists to suggest that the study of attitudes be abandoned. If attitudes cannot predict behavior, they argue, of what scientific use are they? But others contend that it is unrealistic to expect a perfect correspondence between attitudes and behavior. Behavior, they point out, is seldom if ever the product of one influence acting alone. So in making predictions about behavior we must take into account not just attitudes, but a number of other important factors as well.

What are the implications of our discussion for the measurement of attitudes? Many investigators feel that because attitudes are so multifaceted, it is important to assess them in more than one way. In a program designed to alter teenagers' attitudes toward smoking, for example, the investigator may use both paper-and-pencil measures and a saliva test to determine the presence of nicotine in the body (Evans, 1980).

Explaining attitude change

The question of how a person's attitudes can be changed has enormous practical significance. Every day we are flooded with appeals for attitude change—from politicians, advertisers, teachers, doctors, parents, friends, even auto mechanics and department store clerks. And hardly a day goes by that we ourselves do not, in some way, try to influence the opinions of others. The topic of attitude change has consequently generated a great deal of psychological research. Much of this research has been guided by one or two basic approaches—the persuasive communication approach and the cognitive approach. Although each has suggested different reasons for attitude change and different tactics for inducing it, both have contributed much to our understanding of this important process.

Persuasive communication and attitude change One influential approach to attitude change began during World War II when the War Department asked psychologist Carl Hovland and his colleagues to help solve certain problems of troop training and morale. After the war Hovland continued his work at Yale University. There he tried to identify the characteristics of **persuasive communications**—messages consciously intended to persuade—that promote attitude change. In particular, he was concerned with those characteristics of source and content that get people to attend to, comprehend, and remember a message and with the rewards that induce them to accept the message's content. Hovland and his coworkers explored many topics and inspired a number of other psychologists to undertake similar research.

How message content can influence attitude change has been extensively investigated. One important question that psychologists have attempted to answer is whether a one-sided or a two-sided argument is more persuasive. That is, does it strengthen or weaken a case to also present the opposing viewpoint? One early study found that although one-sided and two-sided messages produced substantially the same net change in attitudes, when the subjects' initial opinions and levels of education were taken into account, important differences emerged. The one-sided argument was most effective with people who initially favored the communicator's position and who were rather poorly educated, whereas the two-sided argument was most effective with those who initially opposed the communicator's viewpoint and who were fairly well educated (Hovland, Lumsdaine, and Sheffield, 1949).

Another aspect of message content, and one that has aroused considerable controversy, is the effectiveness of fear-inducing appeals. Imagine that your dentist is trying to influence your attitude toward oral hygiene. He begins by telling you that failure to floss your teeth daily may lead to serious gum infections. But he does not stop there. To dramatize his message, he produces graphic, full-color photos of advanced mouth diseases. How do you think you would react? Would you brush and floss your teeth with renewed diligence to prevent these terrible outcomes? Learning theory suggests you would. As we saw in Chapter 5, an organism generally increases the frequency of a response that enables it to avoid a painful or unpleasant stimulus.

Yet in a classic study of the impact of fear appeals, this prediction was not borne out (Janis and Feshbach, 1953). The researchers showed subjects one of three presentations on oral hygiene. The low-fear appeal simply stated that

"We're 2,000 miles apart now, but still just as close."

Before I could tell time, I knew when my dad would be home from work. I'd be waiting at the window, watching for him to turn the corner.

When I was old enough, I'd run to the bus stop to wait for him. And we'd race each other to the porch, then sit on the steps and talk about everything from football to cowboys.

That part of the day was ours. Now, we're 2,000 miles apart, but I still get a kick out of sharing my day with him.

Long Distance is the next best thing to being there.

Figure 17.2 The purpose of this advertisement, like all other advertisements and persuasive communications, is to persuade people to do something they might not otherwise have thought of doing.

failure to brush can lead to tooth decay and gum disease; the moderate-fear appeal illustrated the nature of these problems with pictures of mild infection and decay; and the high-fear appeal showed hideous color slides of rotting teeth and diseased gums, infections that, the experimenters warned, could spread throughout the body, causing "paralysis, kidney damage, or total blindness." Contrary to what the researchers expected, the appeal that aroused the *most* fear was the *least* effective in changing behavior. Although subjects who viewed the high-fear appeal generally claimed immediately afterward that it had made a greater impact on them, only 8 percent subsequently improved their oral hygiene. In contrast, 22 percent of those who viewed the moderate-fear appeal and 36 percent who viewed the low-fear later improved their dental habits.

To make matters more puzzling, subsequent research yielded quite different results. One series of experiments consistently demonstrated that arousal of fear tends to promote change in both attitudes and behavior (Leventhal, Jones, and Trembly, 1966; Leventhal and Singer, 1966; Leventhal, Singer, and Jones, 1965; Leventhal, Watts, and Pagano, 1967). Similarly, a review of these and other studies on the effects of fear appeals, dealing with issues ranging from smoking to the use of seat belts to the importance of regular chest x-rays, likewise concluded that the majority of fear-arousing communications have a positive effect (Higbee, 1969).

How can these conflicting findings be reconciled? One possible explanation is that fear promotes attitude change, but only to a point. When fear reaches an extremely high level, people may attempt to reduce their anxiety by ignoring or discounting the message (McGuire, 1968). According to this view, the gory pictures of gum diseases may have been so frightening that most subjects tried either not to think about them or to convince themselves that such hideous outcomes were extremely rare. Alternatively, people who become highly frightened by a persuasive appeal may feel so overpowered by the perceived threat that they react with complete helplessness and give up all effort to cope (Leventhal, Meyer, and Nerenz, 1980).

In addition, other factors can decrease the likelihood that people will take appropriate action after exposure to a fear-arousing message. When people are not told how to avoid the feared consequences, when they feel incapable of taking the necessary steps, or when they believe that their behavior will be ineffectual, they may fail to take remedial action. For example, big-city office workers, urged to stave off serious energy shortages by turning out lights, may well disregard the message because such individual efforts seem so minuscule. Conversely, when an audience *is* told specifically how to avoid something undesirable and *does* believe that preventive action is possible and effective, even relatively high levels of fear will usually promote both attitude and behavioral change. Generally speaking, the more specific the recommendations for action, the greater the response will be (Leventhal, Singer, and Jones, 1965).

There is accumulating evidence to suggest that providing very specific instructions might be the most effective way to cope with the fear that often accompanies medical procedures. In one study of people undergoing a stomach examination that required them to swallow a cumbersome tube, those who received precise information about the sensations to expect reacted with a much lower increase in heart rate, much less gagging, and a greater ability to swallow the tube quickly than did those who were not comparably prepared (Johnson and Leventhal, 1974). Similar techniques have been very successfully used to ease a number of other medical procedures, including childbirth and postsurgical recovery (Shacham et al., 1978; Johnson et al., 1978).

As we have seen, researchers who have studied persuasive communication have generally tried to identify variables that enhance the effectiveness of such messages. This approach has been very influential in generating important research, and it has provided much practical information about how persuasive appeals—from television commercials to political speeches—might best be structured. But because investigators have not been able to specify how these variables relate to one another, the persuasive communication approach does not provide a general theory of attitude change. Nor does the theory take into account the recent findings that some messages, no matter how effectively they are structured, have little impact on behavior. As psychologist Richard Evans has pointed out, "The fact that 85 percent of . . . self-identified eighth-grade smokers indicated beliefs in the unhealthiness of smoking demonstrates the inadequacy of using merely informational messages" (1980, p. 295). Evans's research suggests that providing teenagers with specific strategies to cope with peer pressure to smoke, as well as information about the dangerous consequences of smoking, is highly effective in reducing smoking among teens.

Cognitive consistency and attitude change Another important approach to attitude change revolves around the concept of **cognitive consistency**. Several psychologists have proposed cognitive consistency theories, each of which differs from others in a number of important respects. All, however, are based on the assumption that any perceived incompatibility among our various thoughts and actions—any cognitive *in*consistency—makes us feel uncomfortable. In a sense, such perceptions place us in a state of psychological tension, which we are motivated to reduce. But how exactly should we go about reestablishing cognitive consistency? Which of our incompatible cognitions should we change? One answer is that the attitude or belief that is *less* firmly held will be the one that we change (Osgood and Tannenbaum, 1955).

The theory of cognitive dissonance The most influential of all the cognitive consistency theories is the theory of **cognitive dissonance**, proposed more than twenty years ago by psychologist Leon Festinger (1957). Dissonance theory focuses primarily on discrepancies between attitudes and overt behavior. Such discrepancies, according to Festinger, produce a state of psychological distress. Take the case of a man who is president of a company that manufactures and sells cigarettes. He will probably experience dissonance if he believes himself to be a moral person and also believes that cigarettes cause cancer. His two inconsistent cognitions are: "I am a kind, well-intentioned person, yet through manufacturing cigarettes I am contributing to the premature death of thousands of people." To reduce this dissonance, the man is not likely to convince himself that he is uncaring and ruthless. Instead, he will probably modify his cognitions concerning the dangers of cigarettes or the effects of his manufacturing them. He could minimize the link between smoking and lung cancer ("Most of those studies were done when cigarettes contained more cancer-causing properties than they do now"). Or he could add positive cognitions to counterbalance his negative ones ("Cigarettes may create health problems, but these are more than compensated for by the fact that smoking contributes to mental well-being by reducing stress and making life more enjoyable"). Or he could simply minimize the importance of the dissonance-arousing behavior ("It doesn't really matter whether I manufacture cigarettes or not because if smokers didn't buy my cigarettes, they'd just buy someone else's").

In this example cognitive dissonance arose because a person engaged in an activity that violated his standards of right and wrong. But this is only one of many possible applications of dissonance theory. Dissonance theorists have also explored the effect of various inducements to behave in an attitude-discrepant way. Suppose one person is paid a great deal of money to say something he or she does not believe, while another person is paid very little to do the same thing. Which one would you expect to experience cognitive dissonance? How would this dissonance affect the person's attitudes? See if your answers agree with the findings in the following classic experiment conducted by Festinger and Carlsmith (1959).

Subjects were asked to perform an exceedingly boring task: either turning the pegs in a pegboard a quarter turn each and then repeating the procedure many times, or lining up spools in a tray, dumping them out, and lining them up again and again. When each subject finally finished, the experimenter confided that he was actually investigating the effects of preconceptions on performance. Would the subject help out by telling the next subject that the study had been fun and exciting? The researcher offered some of the subjects one dollar and some of them twenty dollars for telling this lie. (A third group, the control, merely did the task and was not asked to do any persuading.) All the experimental subjects voluntarily complied with this request. Then each subject was asked to evaluate the experimental task. Those who had been paid twenty dollars for telling the lie and those who had not done any persuading rated the job as boring—which by objective standards it certainly was. But those who had been paid only one dollar for telling the same lie disagreed. They reported that the experimental task had in fact been fairly enjoyable.

Why did the one-dollar subjects rate an intrinsically boring task quite favorably? According to dissonance theory, saying something you do not believe causes psychological discomfort *unless* you have adequate justification—such as a large, twenty-dollar fee. Thus, unlike the subjects offered twenty dollars, those offered only one dollar had insufficient means to justify the lie to themselves. As a result, they experienced dissonance and responded by convincing themselves that the task had not been so boring after all.

These results have practical implications. They suggest that the *greater* the reward for engaging in a disliked behavior, the *less* likely that attitudes will change to justify that act. Thus, when a girl who hates school work is offered five dollars to bring home a good report card, she may decide that she is working for the money and continue to dislike studying. But a girl who is offered fifty cents for the same behavior may be induced to feel that studying is actually fun. The same logic can be applied to the use of punishment. If you want to convince a small child that it is wrong to play with the knobs on the stereo set, threatening severe punishment is probably the wrong approach. It may temporarily produce the desired behavior out of fear, but it may not produce lasting attitude change. A better tactic is to induce the desired behavior using only a mild threat. Then the child will have less external justification for avoiding the stereo and so is more apt to change his or her attitude toward the stereo as a desirable plaything.

The suggestion to parents, then, is never threaten more than you have to. The validity of this advice has been demonstrated experimentally (Aronson and Carlsmith, 1963). Researchers showed preschool children a very desirable toy but forbade them to play with it, threatening either severe or mild punishment. When left alone with the toy, none of the children played with it. However, when the children's attitudes toward the toy were reevaluated, many of those who had been threatened with mild punishment decided that they did not like the toy very much after all. Presumably, they had experienced cognitive dissonance ("I didn't play with the nice toy even though I wouldn't have been punished much") and therefore changed their attitudes. Such change, moreover, appears to be quite long-lasting. When children who participated in such an experiment were given complete freedom to play with the attractive toy several weeks later, many of those previously exposed to the "mild punishment" condition continued to avoid playing with the toy (Freedman, 1965). Apparently, their feelings about playing with the toy underwent a fairly enduring change.

In spite of the extensive evidence researchers have gathered in support of cognitive dissonance, the theory is not without its critics. Some have argued that certain of the early cognitive dissonance experiments had serious methodological flaws (Chapanis and Chapanis, 1964; Rosenberg, 1965). If subjects are offered twenty dollars simply for telling a lie, might not suspicion about the psychologist's motives affect their feelings toward the experimental task? Such criticisms have prompted better and more sophisticated studies. In fact, social psychologists have conducted hundreds of cognitive dissonance experiments since the theory was first introduced. Many of the findings continue to support the theory. However, researchers now realize that simply holding two inconsistent cognitions is not necessarily enough to provoke dissonance. Certain other conditions must also be met. For instance, cognitive dissonance tends to arise only when a person's behavior is voluntary (Linder, Cooper, and Jones, 1967); when the consequences of an act are aversive for the person who performs it or for someone else (Cooper and Worchel, 1970); and when those consequences are both foreseeable and perceived as one's own responsibility (Collins and Hoyt, 1972; Goethals and Cooper, 1975).

Such findings are a good example of how a theory such as cognitive dissonance is gradually refined and the conditions that give rise to it more precisely specified. Like all social psychological phenomena, cognitive dissonance is highly dependent on the situation. Nevertheless, there is now little doubt that attitude change does indeed occur under certain circumstances in which behavior and existing opinions conflict.

Reassessing dissonance: Bem's self-perception theory Is it possible that the results of cognitive dissonance experiments could be explained in some other way? Psychologist Daryl Bem (1967) believes they can. Bem begins by asking how we come to know the attitudes of other people. The answer is often through inference. We observe people's behavior, interpret it in light of the situation in which it occurs, and attribute attitudes accordingly. For instance, if we observe shoppers in a grocery store all buying the same brand of coffee and we note that the brand is not on sale, we are likely to conclude that these people must like the way it tastes. If, however, we observe shoppers in a television commercial eagerly purchasing the same product, we are not likely to make the same inferences about their true attitudes, for these actors and actresses have an ulterior motive (money) that ordinary shoppers do not. Thus, both overt behavior and the situational context are important in inferring other people's opinions.

So far there is nothing unusual about what Bem suggests. But what if he argued that we use the very same inference strategy to assess our *own* attitudes? This is exactly what Bem maintains. At times, he says, people's internal cues about their own attitudes are "weak, ambiguous, or uninterpretable" (Bem and McConnell, 1970, p. 23). Consequently, they must look to their own behavior and the circumstances surrounding it to "know" their attitudes. For example, a person might observe: "I ate a large serving of lamb stew in spite of the fact that I was not especially hungry. I guess I must like lamb more than I thought." In the same way, Bem argues that the subjects in the Festinger and Carlsmith experiment who favorably rated a boring task implicitly asked themselves: "What must my attitude toward this task be if for only one dollar I was willing to tell another subject it was fun? I guess my feelings must be fairly positive after all."

Bem's self-perception theory and the theory of cognitive dissonance make similar predictions about attitude change. Both say that the attitudes of the subjects paid only one dollar will become more favorable toward the endorsed view, whereas the attitudes of those paid twenty dollars will not. But also note that the *explanations* proposed by these two theories are quite different. Dissonance theory argues that the low-paid subjects change their opinions because they experience an uncomfortable motivational state due to conflict between an existing attitude and a behavior. Self-perception theory, in contrast, argues that no such psychological discomfort occurs. Instead, people faced with an ambiguous situation simply infer their attitudes by examining their behavior and the surrounding circumstances in the same manner as they would assess the behavior of others.

Because dissonance theory and self-perception theory usually make similar predictions, it has been difficult to determine which is correct. A number of researchers have tried to demonstrate that in situations in which attitudes conflict with behavior, people do experience an uncomfortable state of arousal, as dissonance theory suggests. Their general success in these efforts have lent support to the dissonance interpretation (Waterman, 1969; Zanna, Higgins, and Taves, 1976; Kiesler and Pallak, 1976). In addition, there is evidence that in many cases people are not as unaware of their own attitudes as self-perception theory assumes. For instance, when people are given false feedback about their feelings, they often note a discrepancy (Eagly and Himmelfarb, 1978).

There are some phenomena, however, that self-perception theory can account for that dissonance theory cannot. For instance, although the findings have been somewhat conflicting, there is accumulating evidence that when people are offered a reward to do something they already like, their interest in the activity may decrease (Deci, 1971; Lepper, Greene, and Nisbett, 1973; Bates, 1979). Bem would argue that such a person may be reasoning: "If I am being rewarded to do X, perhaps I am only doing it for the reward. Perhaps I do not really like X that much after all." Dissonance theory, in contrast, cannot explain such an outcome, for doing something one likes, no matter how much one is paid, is not dissonance-arousing.

Because his analysis can be applied to behavior that people like or enjoy, Bem has stimulated a great deal of research on how to maximize intrinsic motivation to pursue a task (Lepper and Greene, 1978). This research has intriguing implications, since it suggests that we may undermine the inherent satisfaction that people receive from enjoyable tasks if we compensate them too much.

Resistance to attitude change

We have seen that when people are induced to behave in ways that are inconsistent with their existing beliefs, attitude change is likely to occur. Such change is not inevitable, however. People often resist attitude change. The reasons are many and complex, but one important fact is **psychological reactance**. This phenomenon results when a person, faced with choices, finds that one of them is eliminated or threatened with elimination. As a result, he or she feels an increased motivation to engage in the blocked behavior (Brehm, 1966). If you have ever valued an activity more highly after it was forbidden, you have experienced psychological reactance.

Suppose, for example, that two similar groups of people read a speech arguing in favor of equal treatment for the American Communist party. The content of both speeches is virtually the same, except that in one the wording includes numerous phrases such as "You have no choice but to believe this" and "You cannot believe otherwise." How do you think the two groups would react? Worchel and Brehm (1970) performed this experiment and found that those who encountered remarks that threatened their freedom of choice were much less likely to agree with the endorsed point of view. Moreover, a full 40 percent of the subjects presented with the exhortations actually changed their attitudes *away* from those advocated in the speech. In contrast, only 15 percent of subjects in the "no-threat" condition showed this "boomerang effect."

The results of this and similar studies have ironic implications. It is when we are trying hardest to change a person's attitudes that our efforts may be *least* effective. For example, when parents strenuously oppose the person a son or daughter is dating, their heated arguments may be viewed as a threat to freedom of choice and be stubbornly resisted. In fact, such an approach can have an effect completely opposite to what the parents intend. Research shows that parental interference in a love relationship may only serve to intensify the couple's feeling of mutual attraction (Driscoll, Davis, and Lipetz, 1972). This phenomenon is called the Romeo and Juliet effect, because it parallels the plot of Shakespeare's famous tragedy.

PERSON PERCEPTION AND ATTRIBUTION

The attitudes we hold toward other people are undoubtedly among the most important of any we form. What factors help shape our perceptions of others? Imagine it is the first day of a new semester and you are seated in an American history class. The bell rings, announcing the start of the period. Eveyone watches the classroom door expectantly. Five minutes pass. Ten minutes. Fifteen. Some of the students gather up their books and prepare to leave. Suddenly, the door opens and a young man saunters in. He is wearing faded jeans, sandals, and a crumpled work shirt with the top three buttons open. Although the sign above the blackboard reads "No Smoking," he draws heavily on a cigarette, flicking the ashes on the floor. Unhurriedly, he places his books on the instructor's desk, seats himself on top of it, legs dangling, and announces, "Hi. I'm Ed Walters, your instructor for this course."

At this point, about half the students conclude that this is going to be the easiest course they have ever taken, one in which there certainly will be no penalties for late papers, cut classes, or missed homework assignments. Here, they think, is a teacher they can relate to without the usual stiffness and formality. But an equal number of students immediately decide to change sections. This man, they think, is just too casual about everything. His course will obviously end in chaos.

As you can see, opinions about the new instructor were formed rather quickly and on the basis of fairly scant information. Is this unusual? Not at all. We constantly size up complete strangers on far less "evidence" than this. In the first of the following sections we will explore some of the factors that influence such first impressions. Then, in the second section, we will turn to the subject of how people make more enduring judgments about others. In particular, we ask how people use observed behavior to infer underlying personality traits. If Ed Walters continues to smoke each day despite a ban on smoking in classrooms, what should you conclude? Should you infer that he is so nervous that he simply *has* to smoke, or that he is indifferent to authority? As many psychologists have noted, the causes we assign to others' behavior can be important in our future dealings with them. If you conclude, for example, that your instructor is indifferent to rules, you can risk missing an assignment or coming late to class. This is one reason why researchers have spent so much time investigating how people assign causes to behavior and so draw inferences about themselves, others, and the environment.

Figure 17.3 Suppose you were seeing Mikhail Baryshnikov dance for the first time. You would probably have some very strong impressions about what he is really like as a person. Such first impressions do not, as we generally assume, pass quickly away. Rather, they influence what we subsequently feel about a person.

First impressions

Like inferences about the causes of behavior, first impressions can have a marked impact on our subsequent dealing with a person. Whether we continue to interact with that person, whether we are willing to invest the effort to search for more information about him or her, even how we interpret the additional information we do obtain is all influenced by first impressions. Let us explore some of the factors that shape these important perceptions.

The primacy effect The order in which we perceive traits has a definite impact on the opinions we form of others. Traits that we perceive first seem to count the most. If someone is introduced to you as a member of the university wrestling team, it may be difficult to view him as a sensitive musician when you later learn that he plays oboe in the chamber orchestra. This **primacy effect** has been demonstrated in many experiments. In one classic study (Luchins, 1957), subjects were presented with the two paragraphs in Figure 17.4, which describe a young man named Jim. Those who read only paragraph A saw Jim as extroverted and friendly; those who read only paragraph B saw him as introverted and shy. How do you think subjects viewed Jim when asked to read both paragraphs? Generally the order of presentation governed their impressions. Most of those who read the "extroverted" paragraph first perceived Jim as basically outgoing, and most of those who read the "introverted" paragraph first perceived him as essentially a loner. The reasons for the primacy effect are not completely clear. Perhaps once we have formed an impression of someone, we are less attentive to subsequent information about him or her (Hendrick and Constantini, 1970). Or perhaps we discount or reinterpret things we learn later.

A Jim left the house to get some stationery. He walked out into the sun-filled street with two of his friends, basking in the sun as he walked. Jim entered the stationery store, which was full of people. Jim talked with an acquaintance while he waited for the clerk to catch his eye. On his way out, he stopped to chat with a school friend who was just coming into the store. Leaving the store, he walked toward school. On his way out he met the girl to whom he had been introduced the night before. They talked for a short while, and then Jim left for school.

B After school Jim left the classroom alone. Leaving the school, he started on his long walk home. The street was brilliantly filled with sunshine. Jim walked down the street on the shady side. Coming down the street toward him, he saw the pretty girl whom he had met on the previous evening. Jim crossed the street and entered a candy store. The store was crowded with students, and he noticed a few familiar faces. Jim waited quietly until the counterman caught his eye and then gave his order. Taking his drink, he sat down at a side table. When he had finished his drink he went home.

Source: A. S. Luchins, Primacy-recency in impression formation. In C. I. Hovland (ed.), *The order of presentation in persuasion*. New Haven, Conn.: Yale University Press, 1957, pp. 34–35.

Figure 17.4 How do first impressions strike us? Quite powerfully, suggests the Luchins experiment. How do you picture Jim after reading paragraph A, then paragraph B? Do you see him differently after reading the paragraphs in reverse order?

For example, if we have come to believe that Jim is basically friendly, we may assume that he is not feeling well when he avoids social contact. (Anderson, 1968).

Expectations based on physical attractiveness In real life, of course, we are not always given prior information about people we meet for the first time. What clues do we then use to form our impressions of them? Is physical attractiveness important? Most people maintain that it is not. We are fond of saying that beauty is only skin deep. In fact, however, physical attractiveness is a critical component in our evaluations of others. Elaine Walster and her colleagues (1966) demonstrated this in a well-known experiment. The researchers assessed physical attractiveness, intelligence, and personality traits of more than seven hundred college freshmen who signed up to attend a computer-dating dance. But rather than using a computer to match men and women according to shared interests (as the dance advertised), the researchers randomly paired participants into couples. Later in the evening subjects were asked to evaluate their partner's desirability as a date. Neither intelligence nor personality had much impact on whether a date was rated favorably or not. The only factor that consistently influenced how well a date was rated by his or her partner was the date's physical attractiveness.

What is it about beautiful people that so attracts us to them? Apparently, beauty creates the illusion of a whole set of desirable traits. When researchers showed subjects pictures of men and women of varying physical attractiveness and asked them to evaluate their personalities, the subjects consistently viewed the physically attractive people more positively. They rated them more sensitive, kind, interesting, strong, poised, modest, and sociable, as well as more sexually responsive (Dion, Berscheid, and Walster, 1972). In addition, people are inclined to perceive a beautiful person as reasonably competent, even in the face of objective evidence to the contrary. When given a very poorly written essay to read, male college students evaluated the author's ability much more leniently when led to believe that she was beautiful than when led to believe that she was homely (Landy and Sigall, 1974).

The biases related to physical attractiveness also extend to children. Teachers who are led to believe that an attractive and a homely child received identical report cards still tend to judge the attractive student as more intelligent and more apt to go to college (Clifford and Walster, 1973). Furthermore, an act of misbehavior is often rated as less naughty when committed by an attractive child than when committed by an unattractive one (Dion, 1972). Even youngsters themselves seem to take attractiveness into account in making judgments about their peers. Children as young as three years of age have been found to prefer physically attractive children as playmates (Dion, 1973).

Not only do we attribute a wealth of desirable characteristics to beautiful people, we also attribute similar traits to those who merely associate with the beautiful. For instance, a man is admired if he is romantically attached to an attractive woman (Sigall and Landy, 1973). Apparently, people conclude that if a beautiful woman, who can easily attract many men, has chosen to become romantically involved with this particular man, he must be special indeed. One reason for our pursuit of beautiful people, then, may be our implicit knowledge that association with the beautiful will enhance our social standing.

First impressions and self-fulfilling prophecies When forming first impressions, it is clear that people often make unjustified inferences. This in itself is unfortunate, for a genuinely warm and considerate person can easily be mislabeled. But consider the further effects of incorrect first impressions. When you judge a person to be unfriendly, for example, you are likely to be somewhat standoffish. Your demeanor, in turn, increases the likelihood that he or she will respond in ways that confirm your original evaluation. Through your own behavior, in other words, you have encouraged the very unfriendliness you initially expected. Your once erroneous belief has become a reality—a self-fulfilling prophecy.

That first impressions can become self-fulfilling prophecies has been demonstrated in a number of provocative experiments (for example, Rosenthal, 1966). In one recent study, researchers asked previously unacquainted college men and women to "get to know one another" through a ten-minute telephone conversation (Snyder, Tanke, and Berscheid, 1977). Beforehand, each man was given a snapshot of a woman said to be his future "phone-mate." In fact, however, the photo was of an entirely different woman—either a very attractive or a very unattractive one. As predicted, the men held many stereotypes based on physical appearance. If they received a snapshot of a beautiful woman they imagined her to be outgoing, poised, humorous, and socially adept. If they received a snapshot of a homely woman, they assumed her to be exactly the opposite. How do you think these expectations influenced the men's behavior during their subsequent phone conversations? Not surprisingly, those who thought they were talking with an attractive partner were judged by unbiased listeners to be more friendly, interesting, sexual, humorous, and socially adroit than were those who thought they were talking with an unattractive partner. And the women responded in kind. Those presumed to be attractive by their phone-mates acted in a friendly and sociable way; those presumed to be unattractive acted aloof and withdrawn. Apparently, each took her cue from her partner's behavior. She became the person he expected her to be.

Causal attribution

We have seen the importance of first impressions in shaping social relationships. But in many cases we are not satisfied by these hastily made judgments. Especially when first impressions are relatively positive, we want to learn more about the people we have just met. We want to understand the meaning of their actions, not only to shed light on specific incidents but also so that we can infer their underlying personality traits. How do we go about this? Generally, we start by attributing causes to behavior. Fritz Heider (1944, 1958), the first psychologist to study causal attribution, pointed out that behavior can be explained in one of two ways: Either it can be attributed to a person's disposition ("She must have donated all that money to charity because she is a very generous person"), or it can be attributed to some situational factor ("She must have donated all that money to charity because it gave her such a big tax write-off"). Only when we can confidently attribute behavior to a person's disposition do we then infer a stable underlying personality trait.

An example in the area of international relations indicates the importance of causal attribution. In December 1979 thousands of Soviet troops suddenly invaded Afghanistan. The Russians claimed that Afghanistan's president had invited them in to quell a rebellion—a tale somewhat difficult to believe, since the Russians promptly deposed and executed him. Other nations speculated about the reasons for the Soviets' action. Was it part of a continuing and aggressive plan to extend Soviet power and weaken both the Western nations and China? Or was it a limited and defensive move to keep the Moslem Afghan rebels from instigating insurrection among the Moslems of the Soviet Union? The nature and severity of the American response would depend, at least in part, on what the United States believed were the causes of the Soviet behavior. In the language of attribution theory, the action (the Soviet invasion) could be attributed either to an underlying disposition (hostility toward the United States) or to a factor in the environment (fear of a rebellion).

But the problem with many such efforts to infer the causes of behavior is that causes are often ambiguous. Frequently we must decide among several very plausible explanations. When a student tells a professor how much he likes her organic chemistry course, does he really mean what he is saying or is he simply trying to wheedle a favorable recommendation for medical school? It may be difficult to say. As we saw earlier when discussing attitudes, similar ambiguity may even surround our own behavior viewed in our own eyes. Psychologist Daryl Bem has argued that in such situations we are forced to piece together clues about our own feelings. We analyze our actions and the contexts in which they occur to determine the causes of our behavior, and we make dispositional inferences accordingly. It was Bem's work, in fact, that helped focus social psychologists' attention on the importance of causal attribution.

In studying causal attribution, researchers have raised two primary questions: First, what processes do people use to guide them in making causal inferences? If a man takes a woman out and, at the end of the evening, promises to call her the next day but fails to do so, the woman could reach a number of conclusions. She could attribute causality to her date ("He's forgetful or even inconsiderate"), to herself ("I must not be very attractive to him. What's wrong with me?"), or to situational factors ("Maybe he had a personal emergency and couldn't call"). Second, what kinds of errors or biases do people typically make in assigning causality for their own behavior or that of others, and what is the ultimate impact of these biases? Suppose the woman decides that her date failed to call back because he is highly inconsiderate, whereas the real reason was that he found her self-centered and immature. As long as the woman continues to misattribute such actions to external factors, she may fail to make changes in her own behavior that would improve her interpersonal relationships. In the following sections we will explore these issues in some detail.

Attribution processes Different psychologists have looked at slightly different aspects of the attribution process and so have formulated somewhat different views. One model is that of Jones and Davis (1965), who have focused on the kinds of behaviors to which people attend when making causal attributions. Not all behavior is equally informative, Jones and Davis argue. Some behaviors are so common, so socially expected, that they reveal very little about a person. If, for example, a hotel bellhop smiles and treats you cordially, do you immediately assume that this is a genuinely warm and friendly person? Probably not, because courtesy is part of a bellhop's job and the basis for earning tips. According to Jones and Davis, then, behavior that is in some way unexpected provides the greatest insight into a person's nature. This theory has been tested experimentally (Jones, Davis, and Gergen, 1961). Each subject listened to a tape recording of a man interviewing for a job that required very specific personality traits. When later asked to assess what the job applicant was *really* like as a person, most subjects were willing to make confident judgments only when the applicant unexpectedly portrayed himself as the exact opposite of what the job demanded. Their apparent reasoning was that underlying personality traits must be extremely strong if they can counteract such sizable external pressures. In other words, behavior *inconsistent* with external pressures is used as a powerful indicator of personality. Conversely, when a person tends to do something *consistent* with external pressures, we tend to discount that behavior as a clue to personality. The behavior, we reason, could just as well be explained by external factors as by internal, dispositional ones.

We often use precisely the same reasoning to assess the behavior of people who are close to us (Kelley, 1979). For example, if a woman constantly complains that her husband does not love her because he never tells her so, is she likely to conclude from a few "I love you's" that the husband has had a change of heart? Probably not, because there is simply too much external pressure that could also be compelling his response.

Does this mean that behavior that could plausibly be explained by both external and internal factors is seldom used as a clue to personality? Jones and Davis suggest that this is the case. But psychologist Harold Kelley (1967, 1971) disagrees. Kelley argues that we can sometimes attribute meaning even to initially ambiguous behavior if we have time to compare it with other instances of behavior. Suppose you observe a classmate named Anne arguing angrily with a cashier in the bookstore. Is Anne by nature argumentative and ill-tempered, or did an understandable set of circumstances provoke this outburst? Kelley suggests that you might find out by using the following strategy. First, consider the factor of *consistency*. Does Anne repeatedly lose her temper in check-out lines? If not, you are likely to attribute this particular fit of anger to some unusual provocation, not to a stable personality trait. If consistency is high, however, you might proceed to a consideration of *distinctiveness*. Does Anne explode at other people or only at cashiers? If you have seen her raging at professors, librarians, and fellow students alike, then the distinctiveness of this behavior is low, and you would be led to believe that she possesses a perennial short temper. Finally, you might confirm your suspicions by considering the factor of *consensus*. Do other students frequently argue with this particular cashier? If not, then consensus is low, and you have strong evidence that Anne's disposition is indeed feisty. Like Jones and Davis's views concerning how people make causal attributions, Kelley's ideas have been confirmed experimentally.

An important difference between the two views of attribution we have discussed here is that Kelley's assumes comparisons over time, whereas Jones and Davis's does not. Thus, by using Kelley's strategy, people can make inferences based on accumulated observations that by themselves might be too ambiguous to be useful. This makes Kelley's model somewhat broader than Jones and Davis's. Still, the two theories have very similar views of how people approach the problem of attribution. Both assume that people infer the causes of behavior in highly logical ways. We screen available evidence carefully, eliminate that which is questionable, and conduct further tests to prove or disprove hypotheses. In this respect, we behave much like amateur scientists.

Attribution biases   As amateurs, however, we are prone to letting cognitive and motivational biases color our perceptions. Thus, in spite of our frequent successes at attribution, we also make attributional errors. And we appear to make these errors in highly systematic ways (Ross, 1977; Nisbett and Ross, 1980).

Probably the most widespread attribution error is the tendency to give too much weight to personality factors and not enough to situational ones. For example, if you see a person behaving in a rude, abrupt manner, you are much more inclined to infer that he or she is rude by nature than you are to attribute the cause of this behavior to unusual circumstances. This tendency to assume that behavior is mainly a reflection of personality can be so strong that it causes us to underestimate the role of even very obvious situational pressures. In one study, for instance, subjects read an essay that either praised or criticized Castro's leadership of Cuba (Jones and Harris, 1967). Most subjects strongly inferred that the essay reflected the author's true, underlying attitude, even when specifically told that the author had simply been instructed to adopt that position. Because of its pervasiveness, this tendency to overestimate the role of dispositional factors has been called the **fundamental attribution error** (Ross, 1977).

What prompts us to so readily ascribe behavior to a person's disposition? Perceptual tendencies seem to play an important part. Research shows that when trying to generate the solution to a problem, people tend to focus on the most salient cue available (Kahneman and Tversky, 1973.) The same may be true when making causal inferences. After all, the person who performs a behavior is a dynamic, intrinsically interesting stimulus that easily attracts attention. Perhaps, then, we assign dispositional causes to behavior because the actor is the most salient of all the various factors we observe.

Experiments have verified that salience does indeed affect causal attributions (Taylor and Fiske, 1978). In one study (Taylor and Fiske, 1975) subjects perceived a participant in a discussion as being more influential when that person was visually prominent. In this research, visual prominence has been influenced by such seemingly trivial factors as the participant's position in the room, whether the person is moving or stationary, and how well he or she is illuminated (McArthur and Post, 1977). Even being an "odd man out" can establish a person's salience. For instance, a "solo" black in a group of whites or a "solo" female in a group of males is generally perceived as exerting greater influence in a group discussion (Taylor et al., 1979).

The effect of salience on attribution has interesting implications when we are assigning cause to our own behavior. Remember that as we act we do not usually see ourselves performing. Instead, our attention is usually drawn away from ourselves and toward the environmental factors to which we are responding. This perceptual bias naturally inclines us to pay more attention to the surrounding situation than to ourselves. As a result, we tend to attribute our own behavior to environmental causes, whereas observers tend to attribute it to some enduring personality trait (Jones and Nisbett, 1971). This common difference in attributions is called the **actor-observer bias**.

Bolstering the actor-observer bias is the fact that we have far greater knowledge of our own past behavior than does an observer. Thus, if we act very rudely in a given situation but we know that we have seldom behaved this way before, it makes sense to look to environmental causes to explain this particular action. An observer, however, has seen us acting in far fewer circumstances than we have ourselves and consequently is more likely to conclude that this particular instance is highly representative of the way we always behave. In short, an observer, because of limited information, is likely to attribute a person's actions to his or her underlying personality traits.

The actor-observer bias has important implications for interpersonal relationships (Kelley, 1979). Clearly conflict can easily arise between people when they attribute behavior to different causes. Parents, for example, might attribute a son's poor grades to sheer laziness on his part. The son, on the other hand, might attribute his performance to the demands of a heavy course load. Such conflicts are due to differences in perspective. In each case, the observer blames the disposition of the actor, and the actor blames the situation. Perhaps an awareness of the actor-observer bias could help make the parties to such disagreements more sensitive to the other person's point of view.

As common as the actor-observer bias is, it is interesting that its presence often varies with the circumstances. The bias is usually most pronounced when the effects of behavior are negative and least pronounced when the effects of the behavior are positive. In fact, when the outcomes of an action are especially favorable, the attributions predicted by the actor-observer bias can completely reverse. In such instances, observers assign environmental causes to an actor's behavior, and the actor claims responsibility for his or her actions.

The fact that people tend to take credit for their good deeds and to find situational excuses for their bad ones has been called the **self-serving bias**. A number of studies have confirmed this tendency (Bradley, 1978). For example, in experiments in which subjects are asked to play competitive games, winners usually attribute the results to skill, and losers usually attribute them to bad luck (Stephan, Rosenfield, and Stephan, 1976). Researchers have also found that the self-serving bias is most likely to occur when the person is highly involved in the activity, when he or she has a choice about engaging in it, and when the person's performance is public (Bradley, 1978).

The reason for the self-serving bias is still controversial. Many psychologists have argued that it arises from a strong desire to protect our self-esteem. Recently, however, some researchers have challenged this motivational view (Miller and Ross, 1975; Nisbett and Ross, 1980). Might not a strategy of avoiding disagreeable truths about oneself backfire in the long run? they ask. If people actively try to attribute all positive outcomes to themselves, won't they eventually find it impossible to live up to their overblown self-images? And if people actively try to attribute all negative outcomes to extenuating circumstances and so deny any reason to make changes in themselves, won't they be destined to very painful, disappointing lives? According to these critics, a purely motivational explanation of the self-serving bias simply does not make much sense.

An alternative explanation, proposed by Nisbett and Ross (1980), is that the self-serving bias may be due more to cognitive than to motivational factors. People, they say, may unwittingly surround themselves with information that makes it difficult for them to evaluate their own behavior accurately. Suppose a newly appointed sales manager's first year on the job is blessed with high sales—all of it attributable to highly fortuitous circumstances and none of it attributable to him. In fact, as a manager, the man is quite incompetent. What information might this person have to help him focus attention on the situational causes of the company's success rather than on himself? Realistically, he may have very little. The people who work for him are not likely to tell him of his ineptitude, even though they may discuss it among themselves. Instead, some are probably motivated, for reasons of self-advancement, to inflate the sales manager's self-esteem. Then too, the manager's friends undoubtedly view him in a very favorable light, which is part of the reason why he originally chose them as friends. Their flattering views only help to convince him that attributing positive outcomes to himself is valid. In short, this man is unwittingly being exposed to very one-sided evidence of his own talents. No wonder he should feel responsible for the company's impressive sales.

Psychologists do not yet know whether a motivational or a cognitive explanation of the self-serving bias is most accurate. Very likely the two forces often interact. If so, then our wishful thinking about ourselves seldom flies in the face of reality. Instead, it is "usually supported, even encouraged, by the available evidence" (Nisbett and Ross, 1980, p. 236).

ATTRACTION, FRIENDSHIP, AND LOVE

The processes of forming first impressions and attributing causes to behavior are extremely widespread. They apply to almost everyone with whom we interact. But not everyone becomes what we would call a close friend. And fewer still are accorded that special, very intense feeling known as romantic love.

Social psychologists are interested in why these two phenomena—forming friendships and falling in love—occur. In this section we will examine some of their findings.

Interpersonal attraction and friendship

If asked why you were attracted to your three closest friends, you would probably begin by listing all the things you have in common with them. One of the last things you would mention, if you mentioned it at all, would be the fact that your friends live or work in close proximity to you. It may therefore surprise you to learn that physical proximity, far from being incidental, is actually the single most important factor in friendship formation.

In a classic investigation of the effects of physical proximity on friendship, researchers surveyed married couples in a student housing complex at Massachusetts Institute of Technology (Festinger, Schachter, and Back, 1950). All the residents were asked to name the three closest friends they had made in the complex since they moved in. The results were quite clear-cut: The closer a person lived to another person, the more likely they were to identify each other as a close friend. People who lived next door to each other were much more likely to have become friends than were people who lived two doors apart. Furthermore, people who were assigned an apartment near a heavily trafficked area—at the head or foot of the stairs, for example, or near the mail boxes—were much more likely to have a very active social life than were those assigned an apartment in a relatively secluded corner. In short, if a person's proximity to others is altered even in some seemingly trivial way, it can dramatically affect his or her popularity.

The finding that repeated exposure to a particular stimulus often breeds liking is undoubtedly related to the effects of proximity on friendship. In one study designed to demonstrate this (Saegert, Swap, and Zajonc, 1973), researchers told subjects that they were participating in a study on taste. The subjects were shuttled in and out of several small cubicles, where they tasted and rated different liquids and in the process encountered a number of other people. The researchers arranged for each subject to see one person ten times, a second person five times, a third person twice, a fourth person once, and a fifth not at all. No talking or interaction was permitted during these encounters. After the bogus taste-testing was finished, all subjects were asked to fill out a lengthy questionnaire that included their reactions to other people. Subjects

Figure 17.5 The results of the study by Festinger, Schachter, and Back at MIT housing in Cambridge. The investigators studied the relationship between proximity and choice of friends in a housing development. (A) The illustration of one of the seventeen apartment buildings shows how proximity was measured: in roughly equal units of physical distance with a special S unit indicating a flight of stairs. (B) The subjects' statements of where their three closest friends lived is given as a percentage of all the possible people who could have been chosen at a given distance. By far the largest proportion of friends were next-door neighbors (after Festinger, Schachter, and Back, 1950).

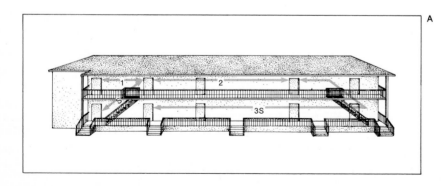

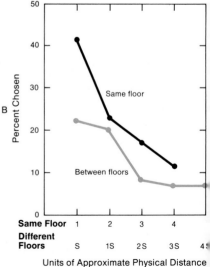

generally expressed the greatest liking for those they had encountered the most.

Why do people tend to like people they are repeatedly exposed to? One possibility is that as you become more familiar with another person's ways, he or she becomes less threatening and more predictable. Thus, although you may never come to love another person solely through repeated exposure, you may at least come to feel comfortable in his or her presence. This feeling of comfortable familiarity is one basis for friendship.

Interpersonal attraction and love

In the early 1970s Senator William Proxmire made headlines with vociferous complaints about the so-called wastefulness of many government-funded studies. Among his prime targets were several psychological investigations into the nature and causes of romantic love. The thrust of Proxmire's criticisms were mentioned in Chapter 1. He argued that falling in love is a mystery that no scientist can possibly unravel; consequently, American tax dollars should not be spent trying to scrutinize the inscrutable. Love, according to Proxmire, is a subject that should be left strictly to poets and song writers. Psychologists, of course, vehemently disagree. They believe that all human behavior, including love and intimate relationships, are valid topics of scientific inquiry. In this section we will review some of the findings they have made in the relatively few years since research on love began.

The experience of falling in love Twentieth-century Americans are repeatedly exposed to the notion of falling in love. So important is romance in our popular culture that by the time children reach adolescence, they have come to believe that falling in love is an inevitable part of growing up. We also tend to think of love as something that comes suddenly, unavoidably, and without our conscious control. Is this a realistic view of how love develops?

Psychoanalyst Carl Jung so believed that love sometimes occurs in just such an explosive fashion that he devised a theory to explain the phenomenon called love at first sight. According to Jung, every male possesses an unconscious representation of the feminine side to his nature, and every woman possesses an unconscious image of the masculine side to her self. When a man or a woman meets a person who closely resembles this ideal representation, the result is instantaneous attraction. As much as Jung's theory may appeal to our romantic notions, there is no empirical evidence to support it. Instead, men and women seem to find, become attracted to, and fall in love with each other in much more mundane ways. In one survey of more than two hundred engaged college students, only 8 percent of the men and 5 percent of the women reported feeling strong physical attraction for their partner within the first day or two after they met—a far cry from what could be called widespread love at first sight. When researchers interviewed these couples, they found that with most of them mutual attraction developed gradually over several months (Rubin, 1973).

Nevertheless, psychologists have found measurable differences between the feeling of liking another person and the feeling of loving him or her. In one study (Rubin, 1970, 1973), several hundred students were given a long series of statements that expressed a variety of feelings one might have toward a lover or

Liking

1. *Favorable evaluation.* I think that _____ (my boyfriend or girlfriend) is unusually well-adjusted.

   It seems to me that it is very easy for _____ to gain admiration.

2. *Respect and confidence.* I have great confidence in _____ 's good judgment.

   I would vote for _____ in a class or group election.

3. *Perceived similarity.* I think that _____ and I are quite similar to each other.

   When I am with _____ , we are almost always in the same mood.

Loving

1. *Attachment.* If I could never be with _____ , I would feel miserable.

   It would be hard for me to get along without _____ .

2. *Caring.* If _____ were feeling badly, my first duty would be to cheer him (her) up.

   I would do almost anything for _____ .

3. *Intimacy.* I feel that I can confide in _____ about almost anything.

   When I am with _____ , I spend a good deal of time just looking at him (her).

Source: Z. Rubin, Measurement of romantic love. *Journal of Personality and Social Psychology*, 1970, 16, 265–273.

Figure 17.6 Rubin's love scale items, some of which are shown here, were developed to distinguish between liking and loving in young opposite-sex student couples, but it is interesting to extend the analysis that these scale items make possible to same-sex relationships, relationships between very old people, and relationships between people of different ages. People form strong likes *and* loves outside the romantic context as well as within it.

toward a friend. The students were then asked to indicate which statements expressed their own feelings toward their current boyfriend or girl friend. The results showed that the students' feelings could be grouped into two categories, one corresponding reasonably well to what people typically mean by *liking* and the other corresponding to what they mean by *loving*. Some items from the "liking and loving" scales developed from this analysis are presented in Figure 17.6.

In addition to attempts to characterize romantic feelings, efforts to define love have also focused on observable behavior. For instance, the notion that lovers spend a great deal of time gazing into each other's eyes is part of our folklore, and it appears to be true. Couples who received high scores on the "loving" scale just described spent more time looking into each other's eyes than did couples who received lower scores on the scale (Rubin, 1973). Sociologist Erving Goffman (1963) has suggested that eye contact serves as a mutually understood signal that the communication channel between two people is open. (Strangers in an elevator take pains to avoid eye contact because communication between them is closed.) Thus, the sustained eye contact of lovers supports the idea that love is characterized by strong feelings of attachment and intimate communication. In addition, several more subtle behavioral indicators of strong mutual attraction have been found. Consider posture. Research shows we have a strong tendency to lean toward a person we like and away from a person we dislike (Mehrabian, 1968). We also adjust our physical distance according to our feelings. The more two people are attracted to each other, the closer together they stand (Byrne, Ervin, and Lamberth, 1970).

Finally, physiological psychologists have also begun to probe the biological correlates of romantic love. Some of their findings are quite intriguing. For instance, psychologists Michael Liebowitz and Donald Klein (1979) have suggested that being in love may be associated with an abundance in the brain of a chemical called phenylethylamine. This substance is related to the artificial stimulant amphetamine. Both produce a boost in energy, arousal, and alertness, and a feeling that one can take on the world. Liebowitz and Klein have maintained that some individuals have a chronic disorder that is characterized by problems in romantic relationships: "The hallmark of this disorder is an extreme intolerance of personal rejection, with a particular vulnerability to loss of romantic attachment" (1979, p. 555). People with this disorder usually spend much of their time seeking approval, especially of a romantic nature. They respond to romantic interest with elevation of mood and energy. However, romantic attachments are usually short-lived, since these individuals' constant need for praise and attention often drives the partner away. When feeling rejected, they experience a "depressive, painful, crashlike reaction" (Liebowitz and Klein, 1979, p. 556). Liebowitz and Klein have suggested that this disorder is caused by a biological defect in the ability to regulate phenylethylamine in the brain. Preliminary evidence indicates that such individuals may be helped by drugs that restore the chemical balance. Interestingly, these researchers have found that people with this disorder often go on chocolate-eating binges each time a love relationship ends. It is significant that chocolate is rich in phenylethylamine and so may serve as a kind of "self-medication" for these lovelorn people.

Why do people fall in love? In addition to trying to define what the experience of love involves, psychologists also seek to explain why people fall in love in the first place. One provocative explanation is based on Stanley Schachter's theory of emotion, discussed in Chapter 10. As you may recall, Schachter has proposed that the subjective experience of an emotion depends on a person's cognitive appraisal of the situation at the time he or she becomes aware of a racing heart, trembling hands, flushed face, and other bodily sensations of physiological arousal. In situations where the true cause of physiological arousal is not immediately obvious, a person may easily misattribute his or her inner upheaval to some other plausible factor in the environment. Applied to the phenomenon of falling in love, Schachter's theory suggests that if a person is physiologically aroused for whatever reason but is unsure why that arousal has occurred, that person may search the surroundings to find a cause for these feelings, spot an attractive acquaintance or stranger, and decide that the feelings must be due to incipient love.

There is some experimental support for this misattribution explanation of love. Researchers arranged for male subjects to be approached by an attractive female (a confederate in the experiment) as they crossed one of two bridges. One bridge was a narrow, rickety structure that swayed in the wind several hundred feet above a rocky canyon. The other was a solid structure only a few feet above a shallow stream. The attractive confederate explained that she was doing a class project, and asked them to compose a short story based on a picture she showed them. The subjects who met her after crossing the rickety bridge expressed more sexual imagery in their stories than did those who met her on the solid bridge. The rickety bridge subjects were also more likely to telephone the woman later, supposedly to get more information about the study. The researchers explained these results by arguing that the men were physiologically aroused by the frightening bridge, and when approached by the attractive confederate they relabeled their feelings as sexual attraction (Dutton and Aron, 1974). According to this theory, then, when the circumstances are right, almost any strong emotion can be misinterpreted as love.

This "adrenaline makes the heart grow fonder" explanation of love has been challenged, however (Kenrick and Cialdini, 1977). Schachter's theory of emotional misattribution applies to situations in which the true cause of physiological arousal is ambiguous. And it is difficult to believe that the cause of arousal is ambiguous when one is suspended several hundred feet above a canyon on a swaying, rickety bridge! An alternative explanation for the same experimental findings is that the subjects may have been attracted to the woman because she was associated with a reduction in fear. She was present when the subjects reached the far side of the bridge safely and so was paired with a feeling of relief. According to this explanation, based on the principle of reinforcement, any stimulus associated with the reduction of a negative state becomes more attractive. Hence, a person associated with a reduction of fear might, under the right circumstances, become an object of love.

Once a romantic relationship has formed, several factors seem to be fairly good indicators of whether that relationship will grow or decay (Hill, Rubin, and Peplau, 1976). One is how well matched the couple are in age, intelligence, educational plans, physical attractiveness, and so forth. Another is whether the partners are equally involved in the relationship. Finally, contrary to what might be expected, neither having sexual intercourse nor living together seems to "cement" a relationship. Couples who have never had sex, much less lived together, are just as likely to stay together or to break up as their more sexually liberal peers. Apparently, these behaviors depend as much on a couple's social attitudes as they do on the depth of their commitment.

Clearly, psychologists still have much to learn about why people fall and stay in love. But critics like Proxmire who say that love is beyond our comprehension are taking an extremely limited view of the human capacity for self-understanding. Moreover, the argument that love is better left a mystery for fear of being spoiled by too much scientific probing also has serious shortcomings. Knowledge about a particular behavior, feeling, or event does not destroy one's emotional appreciation of it.

THE PSYCHOLOGY OF PREJUDICE

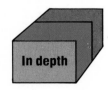

In depth

We know that people are capable of forming strong positive attachments to one another, attachments of liking, friendship, and love. But humans are also capable of deep and intractable prejudice. Consider the following dialogue:

Mr. X: The trouble with Jews is that they only take care of their own group.
Mr. Y: But the record of the Community Chest campaign shows that they give more generously . . . to the general charities of the community than do non-Jews.
Mr. X: That shows that they are always trying to buy favor and intrude into

Christian affairs. They think of nothing but money; that is why there are so many Jewish bankers.

Mr. Y: But a recent study shows that the percentage of Jews in the banking business is negligible. . . .

Mr. X: That's just it; they don't go in for respectable businesses; they are only in the movie business or run night clubs (Allport, 1954).

That humans are capable of such illogical reasoning and such total denial of hard facts—all to defend their negative attitudes toward members of a minority group—is a phenomenon important enough to consider in depth.

The nature of prejudice

Psychologists define **prejudice** as a negative and inflexible attitude based on erroneous or incomplete information. Prejudice is usually directed toward an entire group of people, and so also toward particular individuals who just happen to be members of that group. As such, prejudice unjustly places its targets in a highly unfavorable light (Allport, 1954). Note that this definition stresses three things. First, prejudice involves hostile and negative attitudes. Second, these attitudes are inaccurate; they are formed on faulty or partial information. And third, prejudiced attitudes are peculiarly resistant to change even in the face of strong contradictory evidence. These three characteristics of prejudice are well illustrated in the brief conversation you just read between Mr. Y and the highly prejudiced Mr. X.

Underlying prejudice toward any given group is the existence of a negative **stereotype**—that is, a cluster of preconceived beliefs and expectations about the way members of that group think and act. To some extent forming stereotypes is a natural outgrowth of our tendency to impose order on the world by classifying stimuli into categories based on shared features. But stereotyping, unfortunately, goes far beyond this. Stereotyping leads us to assume without question that anyone possessing a particular key trait (femaleness, for example) necessarily possesses a whole range of other traits (docility, emotionalism, lack of managerial skills) believed to be associated with the first. As a result, stereotypes blind us to individual differences; even positive stereotypes are unjust because they too ignore a person's uniqueness. Furthermore, stereotypes can easily become abusive when used to justify *discrimination* (the behavioral expression of prejudice). The stereotype that blacks are less intelligent than whites, for instance, can easily be used to justify depriving them of equal opportunities.

But how can stereotypes be maintained in the face of so much evidence that they are erroneous overgeneralizations? The answer lies partly in the way that human memory works. Remember from Chapter 6 that people filter new information through a screen of existing knowledge and beliefs. Anything that does not fit our preconceived notions we may recast or simply ignore. And anything that *does* conform to our expectations is likely to make a strong impression on us. As a result we are often victims of illusory correlations: We think that certain stereotyped associations are far more frequent than they actually are. For instance, there is no truth to the common assumption that women are unreliable employees because they inevitably leave to get married or to have children. Yet many people believe this myth. Why? Part of the reason is that they tend to notice and remember instances of high turnover among female workers (instances that fit this stereotype) more than they notice comparable turnover among males (Nisbett and Ross, 1980).

Of course, some pieces of contradictory information are too salient for even the most prejudiced person to successfully ignore (the woman who stays with a company for many years and rises to a position of status and power, the black man who eventually becomes a Supreme Court justice). Unfortunately, it is all too easy to dismiss such instances with "yes-but" reasoning. In one study, for example, male police officers who had been sent out on patrol with a female partner were asked to evaluate that partner's performance (Milton, 1972). Although most of the men believed that their own partner had done a good job, they were still unwilling to endorse the addition of many more women to the police force. Their reasoning went this way: "*Yes* my female partner is O.K., *but* she's the exception." The same reasoning helps maintain many other stereotypes.

As we will see in the sections that follow, there is no doubt that prejudice and discrimination are very common. Two widespread examples are *racism* (prejudice directed toward racial minorities) and *sexism* (prejudice directed toward members of one sex, almost always toward women). Interestingly, sexism and racism have many similarities (Myrdal, 1944). In fact, the women's movement got its start in the United States when female abolitionists fighting against slavery became aware of their own oppression. But there are also many differences between sexual and racial prejudices. Consequently, we will explore them separately.

Sexism

The view of women as weak and inferior has existed throughout recorded history. Both the Bible and the Koran (the sacred book of the Moslems) are filled with references to man's moral and intellectual preeminence over women. The Greek philosopher Aristotle maintained that women are afflicted with a "natural defectiveness." Even thinkers of the eighteenth-century Enlightenment, who advocated sweeping social, political, and educational reform, were reluctant to admit women into the new order on an equal footing with men. Females, wrote Rousseau in *The Social Contract*, "must be trained to bear the yoke from the first, so that they may not feel it, to master their own caprices and to submit themselves to the will of others."

Unfortunately, even in the United States, where many forms of economic discrimination against women have been outlawed, unequal treatment of women still persists. For instance, when laws were passed requiring employers to give equal pay for equal work, many firms simply redefined men's jobs to justify paying them more. And although sex discrimination in hiring practices is now illegal, many recruiters for large corporations still tend to prefer men over equally qualified women (Dipboye, Fromkin, and Wiback, 1975). The result is that, overall, women still earn only 58 percent the salaries of men, even when male and female workers of the same age, education, skill, experience, and job tenure are compared (Levitin, Quinn, and Staines, 1973; Treiman and Terrell, 1975). In many other countries the economic status of women is far worse. Although women comprise one-half the world's population, they contribute two-thirds of the total working hours, earn one-tenth of world income, and own only one-hundredth of all property (U.N. Conference on Women, 1980).

Despite the fact that the actual differences in behavior between the sexes are not very great (Maccoby and Jacklin, 1974), most people believe that they are. When asked to describe the personality of the "average" male, for instance, people tend to view him as active, aggressive, independent, dominant, competitive, ambitious, and a good decision maker, all traits we associate with competency. In addition, the so-called "average" male is not a very warm or demonstrative person. Like the John Wayne image, he is seen as rather blunt and outspoken, not very quick to perceive the feelings of others, and not inclined to express emotional tenderness. The "average" woman is usually described as very much the opposite. She is seen as unaggressive, uncompetitive, dependent, passive, submissive, unambitious, and a generally poor decision maker. Emotionally, however, she is viewed as a caring and giving person—tactful, quiet, sensitive to others, nurturant, and tender, although her need for security is thought to run high (Broverman et al., 1972). What is startling about these stereotypes is how widely held they are. Surveys of children, college students, older adults, even of clinical psychologists, all yield essentially the same male and female stereotypes (Abramowitz et al., 1973). Moreover, these stereotypes are held by both men and women.

How do these stereotypes develop? The process probably begins at the moment of birth, when a baby is proclaimed a boy or a girl. Even though there are no systematic differences between male and female newborns in size, muscle tone, facial features, and so forth, most parents and other adults perceive differences. In one study, for instance, the parents of newborn baby girls described their infant as smaller, softer, weaker, more delicate, and more finely featured than did the parents of newborn boys (Rubin, Provenzano, and Luria, 1974). To what extent parents act on these stereotypes is still not completely clear. As you learned in Chapter 8, some studies have produced little or no evidence that parents treat their sons and daughters differently, but other studies have.

One possible reason for these apparently conflicting findings may be that subtle forms of differential treatment are sometimes overlooked. For instance, in one study of teacher–child interaction at nursery schools, the teachers did not directly reward dependency in girls and independency in boys (Serbin and O'Leary, 1975). But they did tend to do certain things for girls that they helped boys do for themselves. Such subtle inequalities in treatment may provide a repeated message that girls are somehow less competent than boys.

Reinforcing these early learning experiences are the images of males and females portrayed in the mass media. In television commercials, for instance, men are more likely than women to be the "expert" on the advertised product, whereas women are more likely to play the role of easily persuaded consumer (McArthur and Resko, 1979). Psychologists Sandra Bem and Daryl Bem (1970) believe that such messages are so pervasive in our society that many people are unable to conceive of the behavior of the sexes in any other way. As a result, even when they try to create a more egalitarian division of labor and responsibility between the sexes, people often continue to impose the same biases. To test this unconscious acceptance of sex-role stereotypes in yourself, read the man's description of his marriage in Figure 17.7. If it sounds quite equal to you, reread the same description, this time imagining that a woman, not a man, is speaking.

Both my wife and I earned Ph.D. degrees in our respective disciplines. I turned down a superior academic post in Oregon and accepted a slightly less desirable position in New York where my wife could obtain a part-time teaching job and do research at one of the several other colleges in the area. Although I would have preferred to live in a suburb, we purchased a home near my wife's college so that she could have an office at home where she would be when the children returned from school. Because my wife earns a good salary, she can easily afford to pay a maid to do her major household chores. My wife and I share all other tasks around the house equally. For example, she cooks the meals, but I do the laundry for her and help her with many of her other household tasks.

Source: Bem, S. L., and Bem, D. J. Case study of a nonconscious ideology: Training the woman to know her place. In D. J. Bem, *Beliefs, attitudes, and human affairs*. Monterey, Calif.: Brooks/Cole, 1970.

Figure 17.7 Role stereotypes can so pervade a society that many people are unable to recognize biases in their thinking and behavior. This man sees himself as free from traditional sex role stereotypes and his marriage as a truly equalitarian relationship. Yet the husband's unconscious biases become immediately obvious if you reword the paragraph, changing *wife* to *husband* and using masculine pronouns where there are now feminine ones.

A striking peculiarity about the impact of sex-role stereotypes is their acceptance by a large majority of women as well as men. In fact, there are some circumstances in which women appear to be more prejudiced against other women than men are. In one study, college students were asked to evaluate a course syllabus for one of several seminars to be offered (Linsenmeier and Wortman, 1979). The seminar leader was described to some students as an expert in the area and to others as very interested but not an expert. In addition, some students were informed that the syllabus was prepared by a male, while others were told by a female. Otherwise, the syllabi were identical. When the leader was supposedly an expert, there were no differences in evaluations of the syllabi. But when the leader's expertise was not established, females rated the syllabus prepared by a female less favorably than the identical one prepared by a male, and showed less willingness to enroll in the seminar. This result held regardless of whether the seminar topic was male-oriented (e.g., on sports) or female–oriented (e.g., on childbirth).

If women see themselves and other women as innately less competent than men, they may be reluctant to seek out challenging opportunities. This may explain what happened several years ago when the Bell Telephone Company made all its jobs available to both sexes. Surprisingly, there was much less of an influx of women into the traditionally male job of telephone installer than there was an influx of men into the traditionally female job of operator (Boehm, 1974). Why? Many women apparently felt that they were somehow unsuited for this previously male chore. When women come to accept that they are less qualified for certain jobs than men and so avoid careers in traditionally male-dominated fields, they only serve to reinforce current sex-role stereotypes.

Racism

Evidence of prejudice against racial and ethnic minorities dates back nearly as far as evidence of prejudice against women. In the United States, some degree of prejudice and discrimination has existed against virtually every non-Anglo-Saxon Protestant group. The cost of such prejudice to those who suffer it has of course been enormous. It can be measured in the dramatically lower life chances among members of the discriminated groups—menial jobs, low incomes, poor housing, inferior education, poor nutrition and health care, high mortality rates. It can also be measured in reduced self-esteem. For instance, little more than a decade ago one study found that North American Indians agreed with non-Indians on the adjectives that best described themselves: They selected such words as *lazy, drunkards, superstitious,* and *quiet* (Trimble, 1968).

Psychologists have tried to discover the causes of such deeply held prejudices. One theory is that dominant groups use bigotry to justify their claim to the majority of limited jobs, income, and property. There is some historical evidence that prejudice does increase when job markets become tight. For example, when the Chinese immigrants first came to the United States to help build the western railroads, construction jobs were plentiful and the Chinese were looked upon as hard-working and industrious. However, after the Civil War when large numbers of ex-soldiers headed West and jobs became scarce, anti-Oriental sentiment grew dramatically (Aronson, 1980). Of course, it is difficult to say from such real-life incidents whether it was greater economic competition or some other factor that caused bigotry to increase. Isolating the role that competition plays in promoting prejudice requires a controlled experiment. One such experiment was designed by psychologists Muzafer and Carolyn Sherif (Sherif and Sherif, 1953). They assigned twelve-year-old boys attending summer camp to one of two groups, the Red Devils or the Bulldogs. After fostering a period of friendly cooperation, the Sherifs began to pit the groups against each other in a series of intensely competitive activities. The result was a great deal of intergroup hostility. The Sherifs concluded from this study that fierce competition can indeed initiate and escalate prejudice.

But the fact that prejudice tends to increase during times of economic hardship can also be explained in noncompetitive terms. Some psychologists have argued that when people are frustrated by adverse conditions yet are powerless to make things better, they often vent their anger and aggression on the most readily available scapegoat. This tendency has been demonstrated experimentally (Miller and Bugelski, 1948). Researchers measured subjects' attitudes toward various minority groups and then placed them in a frustrating situation: They denied them the chance to see an interesting film, requiring instead that they complete a long series of difficult tests. When asked again to express their attitudes toward the same minorities, most subjects showed significant increases in prejudice. No such increases were found among control subjects, who had not undergone the frustrating experience.

People may not all have an equally strong tendency to displace frustration and aggression onto minority groups, however. A third theory of prejudice holds that people with a so-called **authoritarian personality** are often more inclined toward prejudice and hatred than others (Adorno et al., 1950). The authoritarian personality is measured by a test called the Potentiality for Fascism, or F scale. It measures the extent to which a person agrees or disagrees with items such as:

1 Sex crimes such as rape and attacks on children deserve more than mere imprisonment; such criminals ought to be publicly whipped, or worse.

2 Most people don't realize how much our lives are controlled by plots hatched in secret places.

3 Obedience and respect for authority are the most important virtues children should learn.

(A)

(B)

Figure 17.8 Examples of racial prejudice. (A) Anti-Chinese riots in Denver, Colorado, in 1880. (B) Neo-Nazi groups in the United States stress white supremacy.

Those who score high on the F scale show rigid adherence to conventional values about authority and morality, as well as a preference for strong, anti-democratic leaders. High scores on the F scale also correlate closely with high scores on tests of prejudice. In fact, people with authoritarian personalities often hate and fear almost everyone different from themselves. How does such a bigoted personality develop? One finding is that authoritarian people often come from families with a domineering, status-oriented father and a punitive mother. Both parents tend to impose severe discipline through a combination of threats and physical coercion. And parental love is almost always contingent on "good" or "appropriate" behavior. As a result of these early life experiences, children presumably grow up to be fearful yet hostile toward all authority figures and also to be highly insecure. These traits incline them to displace any frustration outward onto others less powerful than themselves.

The problem with the authoritarian personality as a general explanation of prejudice is that it cannot explain why bigotry is stronger and more prevalent in certain geographic areas than in others, even though high scores on the F scale are quite evenly distributed throughout a population. In some instances prejudice cannot be explained by economic competition either, for it is sometimes high even when jobs are plentiful. One disarmingly simple explanation for prejudice in such cases is that it is merely a reflection of conformity to social norms. There is some evidence to support this theory. For example, people sometimes become more prejudiced when they move to an area where bigotry is common (Watson, 1950). Conversely, prejudiced people often become more tolerant when they find themselves surrounded by others who do not share their views (Pettigrew, 1961). According to this perspective, then, some expressions of prejudice may not be very deeply engrained at all. People may simply be going along with what the majority of others say and do.

Regardless of how prejudice develops—whether through competition, unusual frustrations, deep-seated personality needs, or conformity to social norms—the question of how to reduce it is of primary concern. Trying to change negative stereotypes simply by disseminating accurate information is seldom an effective technique. As we noted earlier people are inclined to ignore or distort new information when it conflicts with their existing beliefs. At the very least, contradictory evidence can often be rationalized away with simple "yes-but" reasoning. How, then, can prejudice be reduced?

One promising approach is to encourage interaction among the races in ways that foster mutual understanding and respect. For this purpose, not just any form of interaction will do. Before the civil rights movement, generations of blacks and whites interacted with each other on a daily basis, yet little reduction in prejudice occurred. Psychologist Stuart Cook (1978) has identified five conditions of interracial contact that facilitate favorable attitude change. One is equal status among the interactants. If whites encounter blacks only in the low-status roles of porter, janitor, domestic servant, and the like, traditional stereotypes will probably endure. A second favorable condition is the chance for people of different races to get to know one another as individuals. Simply living next door to a minority family will not often reduce prejudice unless mutual involvement is encouraged. Such involvement can sometimes be prompted by a third important condition: the existence of norms prescribing friendliness and courtesy. For instance, if the belief that neighbors should act "neighborly" overrides all other considerations (such as skin color or national-ity), a setting conducive to favorable attitude change will exist. Fourth, prejudice is also likely to diminish when the minority group members with whom the majority interacts do not conform to traditional stereotypes. In fact, it is extremely helpful for all interactants to be quite similar in interests, backgrounds, values, and personality traits.

Finally, and most importantly, situations that encourage interdependence rather than competition are highly conducive to favorable attitude change. This is how the Sherifs eventually managed to reduce hostility between two groups of young campers. They created incidents that required the boys to cooperate closely. Soon they were making friends across groups. A similar tactic was used by psychologists Elliot Aronson and his colleagues in an effort to reduce interracial strife in newly integrated fifth- and sixth-grade classrooms. Aronson set up special study groups in which each group member contributed part of the lesson. All group members therefore had to cooperate if they wanted to pass their exams. The results of Aronson's experiment were quite dramatic. Within about a week, most children had abandoned old racial put-downs and insults in favor of much more positive interaction (Aronson and Osherow, 1980). This is not to suggest that overcoming racial prejudice is easy. It is simply to point out that psychologists have proposed some programs that do seem capable, in the right circumstances, of reducing hostile interracial feelings.

SUMMARY

1. Social psychologists seek to understand how the presence and behavior of others influence the way we act.

2. One area they investigate is **attitudes**. Some psychologists define attitudes as learned, relatively enduring predispositions to respond to given objects in a consistently favorable or unfavorable way. Other psychologists suggest that an attitude can best be understood by dividing it into three components: the cognitive, the affective, and the behavioral. The most common method of assessing attitudes has been through questionnaires, but researchers are experimenting with other methods that are not so susceptible to willful distortion.

3. How attitudes can be changed is a topic that has generated much psychological research. One of the two main approaches to attitude change, is to study the content of **persuasive communications**—messages consciously intended to persuade—that promote attitude change. The second main approach to attitude change is based on the concept of **cognitive consistency**, the assumption that any perceived incompatibility among our various thoughts and actions creates a discomfort that we then try to reduce. The most influential of these theories, proposed by Leon Festinger, focuses primarily on the attitude change that occurs when we experience a conflict between existing attitudes and overt behavior. Daryl Bem has proposed, by contrast, a **self-perception theory**, which holds that we infer our attitudes from our behavior and the circumstances surrounding it. Since these two theories generally make similar predictions, it seems useful to consider them complementary theories that best apply to different situations.

4. People often resist attitude change. One important factor in this resistance is **psychological reactance**, whereby a person who finds a particular line of action blocked feels increased motivation to engage in the blocked behavior.

5. How we perceive other people and the qualities we attribute to them have attracted the interest of psychologists for some time. First impressions are strong enough to influence our subsequent dealings with people. One reason for this is the **primacy effect**, whereby the traits we perceive first seem to count the most. Another is the fact that physical attractiveness is a critical component in our evaluations of others. We attribute to attractive people a whole set of desirable traits.

6. Once we get beyond first impressions of people, we begin attributing causes to their behavior. According to Fritz Heider, the first to study **causal attribution**, behavior can be attributed either to a person's disposition or to a situational factor. Jones and Davis argue that behavior that is in some way unexpected provides the greatest insight into a person's nature. Psychologist Harold Kelley proposes that we can sometimes attribute meaning even to initially ambiguous behavior if we have time to consider the *consistency, distinctiveness,* and *consensus* of such behavior.

7. There are many common errors of attribution that we frequently make. One, the **fundamental attribution error**, is the tendency to give too much weight to personality factors and not enough to situational ones. When it comes to assessing our own behavior, though, we are apt to attribute it to environmental causes. This common difference in attributions is called the **actor–oberver bias**. One exception to this tendency is the **self-serving bias**: We tend to take credit for our good deeds and find situational excuses for our bad ones.

8. Love has only recently begun to be an area of psychological research. Although love has been shown not to happen "at first sight," as psychoanalyst Carl Jung believed, but to develop gradually, psychologists have found that there are differences in feeling between liking and loving another person. In addition, there may be biological correlates, such as an abundance of certain chemicals in the brain or other parts of the body, to the condition of being in love.

9. One theory of why people fall in love is Stanley Schachter's **misattribution explanation**, whereby physiological arousal due to another cause is mistaken for feelings of love. Other researchers suggest that the feelings of love Schachter observed reflect not the resolution of an ambiguous arousal but relief at the termination of a negative or fearful state.

10. At the opposite pole from attachment to another person is **prejudice**, a negative and inflexible attitude based on erroneous or incomplete information. Prejudice, which is usually directed toward an entire group of people, is reinforced by an underlying negative **stereotype**—a cluster of preconceived beliefs and expectations about the way members of that group think and act. Stereotypes are often used to justify **discrimination**, the behavioral expression of prejudice. Stereotypes are maintained in the face of much contradictory evidence partly because our memory causes us to be impressed by what conforms to our expectations and to disregard what does not.

11. One widespread form of prejudice is **sexism**, directed toward members of one sex, almost always women. Influenced by very early learning experiences that are then reinforced by images in the mass media, most people—including women—greatly exaggerate the actual known differences in behavior between males and females and come to accept the sex-role stereotypes.

12. Racism is the prejudice against racial and ethnic minorities. Some psychologists have theorized that dominant groups use bigotry to justify their claim to the majority of limited jobs, income, and property. Others have argued that frustration causes people in adverse conditions to vent their anger on a scapegoat. A third theory holds that people with an **authoritarian personality** are more inclined toward prejudice than others. A final view sees prejudice as a reflection of conformity to social norms.

13. One means of reducing prejudice that has shown some success is the encouragement of interaction between the races where five conditions, as identified by psychologist Stuart Cook, exist: the participants have equal status, similar interests, and the opportunity to get to know one another as individuals; and the situation is a noncompetitive one in which norms prescribing friendliness and courtesy prevail.

Suggested readings

Aronson, E. *The social animal* (3rd ed.). San Francisco: W. H. Freeman, 1980.

Bem, D. J. *Beliefs, attitudes, and human affairs*. Belmont, Calif.: Brooks/Cole, 1970.

Bersheid, E., and Walster, E. *Interpersonal attraction* (2nd ed.). Reading, Mass.: Addison-Wesley, 1978.

Festinger, L. *A theory of cognitive dissonance*. Stanford, Calif.: Stanford University Press, 1957.

Harvey, J. H., Ickes, W., and Kidd, R. (Eds.). *New directions in attribution research* (2 vols.). Hillsdale, N.J.: Lawrence Erlbaum, 1976, 1978.

Rubin, Z. *Liking and loving*. New York: Holt, Rinehart and Winston, 1973.

Shaver, K. *An introduction to attribution processes*. Cambridge, Mass.: Winthrop, 1975.

Walster, E., and Walster, W. *A new look at love*. Reading, Mass.: Addison-Wesley, 1978.

Zimbardo, P. G., Ebbesen, E. B., and Maslach, C. *Influencing attitudes and changing behavior* (2nd ed.). Reading, Mass.: Addison-Wesley, 1977.

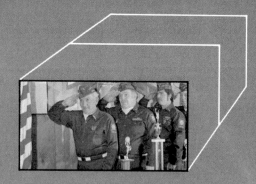

PREVIEW

1. Social conditions affect our behavior in many ways. In instances of conformity, for example, social pressure produces a tendency to shift one's opinions or actions to correspond with those of others.

2. Membership or participation in a group has important effects on our behavior—which, in turn, can affect the quality of decisions reached by groups.

3. Many factors influence human aggression, including biological influences, social learning influences, and frustration.

4. Altruism, or helping behavior, is also affected by several factors, including the number of bystanders present, the demands of the situation, and the costs and rewards of helping.

18 Conflict and cooperation

On March 16, 1968, three platoons of American soldiers, collectively known as Charlie Company, swept into the South Vietnamese village of My Lai and proceeded to kill several hundred unarmed civilians—women, children, and old men. When reports of the massacre reached the United States, most citizens reacted with outrage and shock. How could these men, reportedly normal, decent "all-American boys," have committed such an atrocity? In the investigation that followed the tragedy, it was revealed that the soldiers of Charlie Company, although only in Vietnam for one month, had already sustained heavy casualties. Frightened by the dangers of entering My Lai, which was thought to be an enemy stronghold, upset by the loss of their comrades, and eager for revenge, the soldiers seemingly began to shoot without thinking. Although the civilians offered no resistance, the soldiers set fire to huts, drove the villagers into open areas, and began to shoot everyone. Some of the men reported that they had been following the orders of their leader, Lieutenant William Calley; others said they had simply followed the example of others, who had begun to shoot the peasants who were trying to flee. Most of the soldiers joined in the shooting, even firing at children at close range. Of those who did not fire their rifles, not one attempted to stop the slaughter. They stood by without protest as bodies piled up in ditches and the village was burned to the ground.

The My Lai massacre was one of America's darkest moments in the long and controversial Vietnam War. Although what happened at My Lai is an extreme example of the human potential for inhumanity, many of the factors that underlie the incident also underlie less destructive behaviors in everyday life. This chapter explores some of these powerful social forces.

We will begin by discussing two subjects of major concern to social psychologists: conformity and obedience. Provocative findings in both these areas explain much about the events at My Lai. We then turn to the topic of human groups, exploring how group norms and roles influence attitudes and behavior, and how groups affect performance and make decisions. Next we examine the diverse causes of two powerful human inclinations: aggression and altruism. We then present a discussion of environmental psychology, and we conclude by examining emerging trends in the behavioral sciences.

SOCIAL INFLUENCE AND INDIVIDUAL BEHAVIOR

Most Americans insist that they would never have supported Adolf Hitler's fanatical policy of exterminating Jews if they had lived in Germany during World War II. Yet thousands of Germans did, and these people were not unusual in any significant respect—not particularly weak or especially open to suggestion. Most of them were relatively ordinary people responding to extraordinary circumstances.

Social psychologists have devoted a great deal of attention to such social influences. They have extensively studied how social pressure can induce a person to conform to a prevailing attitude or perception and how people in positions of authority can induce others to obey commands—even when those commands may violate the person's basic moral standards. We will discuss these two topics in the following sections.

Conformity to prevailing norms

Conformity is the tendency to shift one's opinions or actions to correspond with those of other people because of implicit or explicit social pressure (Kiesler and Kiesler, 1969). An extreme example of conformity occurred under the stress of war at My Lai. Some of the men in Charlie Company were simply copying the behavior of their fellow soldiers when they joined in the massacre of Vietnamese civilians. As one soldier put it, "I looked around and saw everyone shooting. I didn't know what to do, so I started shooting" (*Time*, December 5, 1969). Although the consequences of conformity are seldom this devastating, essentially the same psychological process underlies many of the choices we make every day. When you find yourself ridiculing a man who considers you a friend because others whom you admire are denigrating him, you are conforming to group opinion. Note that when you conform you are not necessarily convinced that what you are saying or doing is right. You may simply take a particular public stance because you believe that others prefer or even demand that you do so.

Social psychologist Solomon Asch (1951) revealed the power of conformity in a classic series of experiments. Asch designed an ingenious, if rather devious, way of studying conformity in the laboratory. If you had been a subject in Asch's research some thirty years ago, this is what you would have experienced. You and seven other students report to a classroom for an experiment on visual judgment. The experimenter displays two large white cards like the ones shown in Figure 18.1. On one card is a single vertical line, which is to serve as a standard; on the other card are three vertical lines of different lengths. You are simply to determine which of the three lines is of the same length as the standard line. The experiment opens uneventfully. The subjects give their answers in the order in which they are seated in the room, you being next to last. On the first comparison, everyone chooses the same line. The second set of cards is shown, and once again the choice is unanimous. The discriminations seem very easy, and you settle in for what you expect will be a rather boring experiment.

On the third trial, however, something strange happens. The first person declares that line 1 matches the standard. This puzzles you, because you are virtually certain that the correct response is line 2. The second person agrees with great certainty that line 1 is the right answer, and so do the third, fourth, fifth, and sixth subjects. Now it is your turn, and you are faced with a disturbing dilemma. Your own eyes unmistakenly tell you that line 2 is the correct choice, but six other people have unanimously and confidently selected line 1. What should you do? Stand alone as a minority of one, or go along with the unanimous majority? If you think you would have stuck to your initial judgment you may well be wrong. About a third of Asch's subjects agreed with the clearly inaccurate choice of the other participants (actually confederates in the experiment) at least half the time. It should be noted that Asch's experiment included situational factors that one would expect to *lower* the pressure to conform. The confederates were complete strangers to the subject (thus having little claim to personal loyalty) and were peers in status and intelligence (not superiors whose opinions might carry special weight). For these and other reasons, some psychologists have concluded that Asch's work may have revealed only the tip of the conformity iceberg.

What accounts for such frequent conformity? Part of the answer may lie in situational factors built into the experimental design. For one thing, the judgments of the confederates were unanimous; not one gave even a hint that another answer might be possible. In variations of his original experiment, Asch found that the extent of group consensus was indeed an important factor. When just one confederate out of six gave the correct answer, the proportion of subjects who agreed with the incorrect majority view dropped dramatically from 32 percent to 5 percent (Asch, 1956). In addition, the fact that Asch's subjects had to interact with the confederates face to face apparently made it more difficult for them to deviate from group norms. Later research has shown that when people are allowed to respond anonymously—when, for example, they sit in a private compartment and indicate their answer by pressing a button—they conform significantly less (Deutsch and Gerard, 1955).

From the comments made by Asch's subjects in postexperiment interviews, it is clear that they were concerned not only with being correct, but also with what others might think of them if they violated group expectations. One subject who acquiesced in eleven out of twelve trials opened the interview by saying: "If I'd been first I probably would have responded differently." This

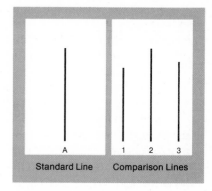

Figure 18.1 The stimuli in a single trial in Asch's experiment. The subject must state which of the comparison lines he or she judges to be the same length as the standard. The discrimination is easy to make: Control subjects (those who made the judgments without any group pressure) chose line 2 as correct more than 99 percent of the time (after Asch, 1951).

was his way of saying that he had known perfectly well what the correct answers were, but that he was still unable to contradict the group. This finding has relevance to the My Lai experience. In its wake a number of Americans suggested that the massacre would not have taken place if the Charlie Company soldiers had been properly trained to know the difference between right and wrong. But, as Asch's subjects demonstrated, conformity is not lessened or eliminated just because the group response is clearly wrong.

The importance of group approval is indicated by other studies. An individual is more likely to conform to a group when he or she is lower in status than other group members (Raven and French, 1958). Also more likely to conform are those who are attracted to the group but do not feel completely accepted by it (Dittes and Kelley, 1956), and those who expect to interact with the group in the future (Kiesler, Zanna, and DeSalvo, 1966). It has also been found that persons with low self-esteem are far more likely to yield to group pressure than are those with high self-esteem (Aronson, 1980).

Although group pressure may induce people to conform, some may conform half-heartedly or temporarily. Kelman (1958, 1961) has pointed out that several kinds of conformity can be distinguished. In **compliance**, a person yields outwardly to pressure but retains his or her own opinion and belief. For example, a teenage boy might continue to attend church with his family every Sunday even though he does not privately accept the church's teachings. In **internalization**, the individual actually comes to accept the opinion or action of another as correct—as, for example, when a reluctant churchgoer becomes convinced that there is some merit in the church's teachings. In **identification**, a person conforms with the expectation of another in order to maintain a valued relationship. For example, a man might go to church with a woman friend if doing so were necessary to maintain the relationship. These distinctions among types of conformity are significant because they allow us to predict a person's behavior, at least to some extent. Since compliance and identification are maintained by external factors (coercion in the first instance and the desire to please another person in the second), these types of conformity are likely to cease if the external factors change. Only the person who has internalized the values of another person or of a group can be expected to continue to conform.

Just how great is the pressure to conform? Research suggests that the nonconformer is ostracized in subtle and not-so-subtle ways. He or she is frequently treated negatively or ignored. For example, when conventionally and unconventionally dressed college students asked shoppers in a supermarket to change a dime for two nickels, the unconventional-looking students were much more likely to be shunned (Raymond and Unger, 1972).

Some social critics have argued that in modern society, with its large organizations that require extensive reliance on other people, pressures to conform have increased (Riesman, 1950; Whyte, 1956). This trend, they maintain, is predominantly negative because it reduces individuality, personal initiative, and independence. Others, however, are not so quick to denigrate conformity. Conformity, after all, can encourage people to perform socially valued acts, and it can also fulfill such important personal needs as the desire to be liked and accepted. As one social psychologist has remarked, "The person who refused to accept anyone's word of advice on any topic whatsoever would probably make just as big a botch of life . . . as the person who always conformed" (Collins, 1970, p. 21).

Research on obedience

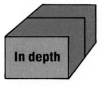

In depth

After the My Lai massacre had been made public, the men of Charlie Company were asked to explain their brutal assault. A response familiar from the Nuremberg trials of Nazi war criminals some twenty years earlier was heard again and again: "I was simply following orders." As one young man remarked, "Well, hell, I was just following the orders of my officer like any good soldier—what's the good of having officers if they've nobody to obey them?" (*Time*, December 5, 1969). To many observers, such explanations are completely unacceptable. How, they ask, could anyone with a conscience have obeyed such a blatantly inhuman demand?

One social psychologist who has done extensive research on why people follow orders is Stanley Milgram. Milgram's research (1963, 1965) has shown that many "average" people, people who would probably find participating in the My Lai massacre unthinkable, might themselves inflict severe pain on their fellow human beings if an authority figure required them to do so. To grasp the meaning of Milgram's research, we must first examine the phenomenon of obedience.

In the previous section we defined conformity as the tendency to change one's behavior or beliefs in response to group pressure. Conformity is more voluntary than **obedience**, which is compliance with the explicit commands of a person in authority. In Asch's experiments, as we have seen, peer-group pressure induced subjects to *conform*. In Milgram's experiments, the pressure to *obey*—to follow clearly defined orders—came from an authority figure. In some social settings, obedience can serve constructive purposes. Children are protected from harm by many of their parents' demands for obedience. Society itself could not function if most people decided to use their own judgment

Figure 18.2 Individuals tend to obey figures of authority more quickly than they do other people, especially when the authority figure is wearing a uniform.

about when to pay taxes or stop at traffic lights. Sometimes, however, obedience calls for actions that violate moral standards, as happened in My Lai. Such *destructive obedience* was the subject of Milgram's research.

Milgram's initial experiment Milgram's subjects (Milgram, 1963) were men of different ages and occupations, but all had one thing in common: They had answered a request for participants in a study on learning at Yale University. Upon arriving at the laboratory, each man was introduced to his supposed cosubject, a mild-mannered likable man of about fifty who was actually a confederate in the experiment. The two were asked to draw lots to determine who would be the "teacher" and who the "learner." The drawing, of course, was rigged. The real subject always became the teacher.

The experimenter, a rather stern man in a gray laboratory coat, then explained the study's purpose and procedure. The experiment was designed to find out more about the effects of punishment on learning. First the teacher was to read a list of word pairs to the learner. Then, when the teacher gave the first word as a cue, the learner had to recall the second one in each pair. Every time the learner made a mistake, the teacher was to punish him by administering an electric shock from an authentic-looking shock generator. The generator had thirty clearly marked voltage switches, ranging from 15 to 450 volts. Beneath the switches, verbal labels indicated the intensity of the shock, beginning with slight shock and progressing through moderate, strong, very strong, intense, extremely intense and severe, also marked "Danger," to most severe, ominously labeled "XXX." With each additional mistake the learner made, the teacher was to increase the voltage by one level.

Everyone then proceeded to an adjacent room, and the teacher watched while the learner was securely strapped into a large chair and an electrode (presumably connected to the shock generator) was fastened to his wrist. The learner mentioned that he had a heart condition. He was told by the experimenter that the shocks may be painful but not dangerous. The experimenter and teacher then returned to the generator room, and the learning trials were ready to begin. The experimental plan called for the learner to make frequent mistakes, requiring the teacher to administer increasingly severe shocks. The victim protested as the shocks became more intense. (All protests were tape-recorded so that different subjects would hear the same sounds.) The protests included a grunt at 75 volts; a "Hey, that really hurts," at 125 volts; an "I can't stand the pain—don't do that!" at 180 volts; complaints of heart trouble at 195 volts; a high-pitched scream at 285 volts; a pounding on the wall in protest at 300 volts; a refusal to answer at 315 volts; and only ominous silence thereafter. The experimenter would then tell the subject to treat the absence of a response as a wrong response and continue raising the voltage. If at any point the subject asked to stop the procedure, the experimenter would instruct him to continue with a number of standardized commands ranging from a stern "Please go on" to an emphatic "You have no other choice, you *must* go on." If the subject still refused to obey, the experiment would immediately end.

How long do you think most subjects continued to deliver what they believed to be painful and increasingly dangerous electric shocks to a defenseless victim? When Milgram posed this same question to several psychology majors, they confidently predicted that few, if any, subjects would go beyond the "very

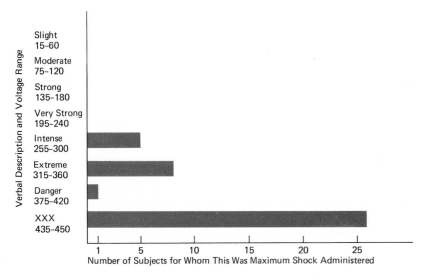

Figure 18.3 Results of Stanley Milgram's classic experiment on obedience. Subjects were told to administer increasing amounts of shock to a "learner" on the pretext that scientists were studying the effects of punishment on learning. Of forty experimental subjects, all administered shocks scaled "intense" or higher, and only fourteen refused to go all the way to the most severe, "XXX" shock level (after Milgram, 1963).

strong shock" level—that is, they would not even get to the point where the learner had to pound on the wall for release. Forty psychiatrists who were also asked for their opinions predicted that most subjects would quit when the learner first asked to be freed, at 150 volts. Only 4 percent of the subjects, the psychiatrists predicted, would continue to shock the learner when he failed to respond—at 315 volts—and less than 1 percent would administer the highest shock. But this is far from what actually happened. Out of a total of forty subjects, twenty-six, or 65 percent, obeyed the experimenter all the way to the very highest voltage level on the generator!

These men were not sadists. In fact, most showed signs of severe emotional strain and psychological conflict during the session. They trembled, stuttered, groaned, perspired heavily, bit their lips, laughed nervously, and dug their fingernails into the palms of their hands. They frequently asked the experimenter if they might please stop. Yet they continued. As Milgram related:

I observed a mature and initially poised businessman enter the laboratory smiling and confident. Within 20 minutes he was reduced to a twitching, stuttering wreck, who was rapidly approaching a point of nervous collapse. He constantly pulled on his earlobe and twisted his hands. At one point he pushed his fist into his forehead and muttered: "Oh God, let's stop it." And yet he continued to respond to every word of the experimenter and obeyed to the end (1963, p. 377).

Follow-up research: what factors influence obedience? What could have prompted such an extraordinary degree of obedience? Milgram (1965, 1974) designed a series of follow-up studies to identify the factors that made a subject most likely to comply. In a pilot study (Milgram, 1961) he had noticed that when the experiment was varied to permit the teacher to glimpse a vague outline of the learner through an opaque glass partition, the teacher always averted his eyes. Could it be that the remoteness of the learner in the original experiment had made it easier for subjects to obey? Milgram investigated this possibility by setting up three new conditions. In one, the learner was again in a separate room from the subject, but this time the subject could hear groans escalating to screams as he increased the shocks. In another arrangement, the

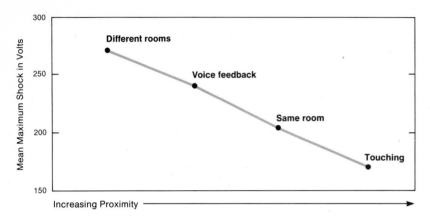

Figure 18.4 This graph of the results of some of Milgram's studies on obedience shows that the closer the subject was to the victim, the less the amount of shock he was willing to administer, despite the experimenter's demands that he continue. With increased proximity, there was a decrease in compliance (after Milgram, 1974).

victim was moved to the same room as the subject and seated only eighteen inches from him. And in the final condition, the subject not only sat close to the victim but was also required to force the victim's hand onto a shock plate to administer the punishment. As Figure 18.4 shows, the maximum shock that subjects delivered decreased steadily as contact with the victim—auditory, visual, and physical—increased. Still, even in the final condition, a full 30 percent of the subjects delivered the highest possible voltage.

If the subject's proximity to the victim influences his willingness to obey, might not his proximity to the experimenter also have an effect? Milgram wondered about this possibility too. To explore it, he varied the experimenter's physical closeness to the subject as well as his degree of surveillance over the experimental proceedings. Obedience dropped sharply when the experimenter, after giving his initial instructions, left the room and gave his subsequent orders by telephone. Whereas 65 percent of the subjects obeyed to the end when the experimenter was sitting just a few feet away, only 22 percent obeyed throughout when the experimenter was not physically present. Apparently, it is easier for people to disobey an authority they do not have to confront face to face.

Another factor that might have increased obedience, Milgram thought, was the prestige of Yale University. Perhaps subjects would be more resistant to authority in a less distinguished setting. Milgram therefore replicated this original study in a rather run-down office building in the industrial city of Bridgeport, Connecticut (Milgram, 1970). This time the experimenter claimed no ties to Yale. Instead, he said he was doing research for private industry. Milgram found that in spite of these marginally respectable circumstances, 48 percent of his subjects still delivered the maximum shock.

The controversy over Milgram's research Milgram's experiments have produced an explosive controversy over the ethics of his procedures. His critics charge that without forewarning and prior permission he exposed his subjects to enormous stress. The experimental subjects were not screened for psychological or health problems that might have been worsened by the stress of the experiment. And once it was clear that the experiment was so stressful, critics have argued, Milgram should have discontinued it. More than this, opponents maintain, many of the nearly 1,000 people who participated in Milgram's research may have suffered long-term psychological harm (Baumrind, 1964). Undeniably, a subject who followed the experimenter's commands to the end learned a disturbing fact about himself: He was willing to obey an authority figure even if it meant performing a callous and inhumane act. Might not some subjects find this self-revelation difficult to live with? At the very least, might it not injure their self-concept? According to Bem's (1967) self-perception theory, discussed in Chapter 17, people who have observed themselves acting cruelly are more likely to do so in the future; their perceptions of themselves are changed. Finally, might not participation in the experiments reduce the subjects' ability to trust legitimate authorities in the future, since they were entrapped into committing potentially harmful acts by people they had reason to trust?

Milgram (1964, 1968, 1974) flatly rejects the idea that his procedures caused any lasting harm. He points out that all his experimental sessions ended with a thorough "dehoaxing" in which the experimenter explained that shocks had never really been given and took care to reassure obedient subjects that their behavior had been entirely normal. What Milgram calls a "friendly reconciliation" (1963, p. 374) was arranged between subject and victim. As a result of these measures, Milgram contends, no subject left the laboratory in a continuing state of anxiety. Moreover, follow-up questionnaires indicated that most (84 percent) of the subjects were glad to have participated in Milgram's research because they learned something important about human behavior. And as for damaging subjects' ability to trust legitimate authorities, Milgram argues that skepticism toward authorities who require us to act harshly toward other human beings is a very valuable quality.

The two sides of this debate illustrate the conflict that can sometimes arise in psychological research, a conflict we discussed briefly in Chapter 2. On the one hand, the subjects in Milgram's experiments clearly suffered psychological strain, even if only temporarily, and those who obeyed throughout certainly observed a negative potential in themselves, even if that potential was shared by many other people. On the other hand, Milgram's studies revealed startling information about the extent to which average adults will obey commands to harm their fellow human beings. The central question therefore is: Does the significance of this knowledge justify the means used to obtain it?

Milgram's critics contend that it does not. They have raised serious doubts that his results could be generalized to the world outside his laboratory. For example, subjects who had volunteered to participate in a laboratory experiment might have been especially inclined to obey someone who seemed to be a legitimate researcher (Orne and Holland, 1968). Moreover, subjects were repeatedly prodded to continue with the experiment if they hesitated. In real life, Milgram's critics argue, we seldom find ourselves in this type of position.

Milgram argues that the protests against his work arose more from the disturbing results of his experiments than from the procedures he used. As he has written, "I'm convinced that much of the criticism, whether people know it or not, stems from the results of the experiment. If everyone had broken off at slight shock or moderate shock, this would be a very reassuring finding and who would protest?" (Milgram, 1977, p. 98).

The fact that strong arguments have been raised on both sides of the controversy makes a key point: In psychological research, conflict between the need to answer important questions and the obligation to avoid causing subjects distress is not always easy to resolve. However, since the 1960s, when Milgram conducted his experiments, ethical standards governing human experimentation have become stricter (Chapter 2). New ethical guidelines require that subjects must be informed about any stresses they will encounter in the course of the experiment. If performed today, Milgram's experiment would have to be modified to protect the participants—with the result, perhaps, that different findings would be obtained.

THE SOCIAL SIGNIFICANCE OF GROUPS

In the mid-1970s, a young woman we shall call Joan was a well-known political activist on her campus. As she put it, "I was into the radical feminist group at school; I was a political radical; I was trying to overthrow the system." Shortly thereafter, she became a member of a religious cult. Much to the surprise of her family and friends, who had always considered her an extremely strong-willed person, she began to grow meek and obedient. "In three months, they recycled me and I was obeying everybody. . . . Any guy who asks me anything, I feel I should sacrifice for them; that's how I did for four years in the group" (Singer, 1979, p. 79).

In 1957 the Ford Motor Company proudly announced its development of the Edsel, a new automobile in which the company had invested a record-breaking quarter of a billion dollars. The Edsel was designed by a specially created committee at Ford. It turned out to be one of the ugliest cars yet to appear in an automotive era dominated by ornate chrome decorations and high-sweeping tail fins. Within two years Ford had lost some $350 million on the venture, and it summarily discontinued Edsel production.

Although these two events are very different, they share one important feature: They illustrate the profound influence that groups are capable of exerting. In the first example membership in a religious cult seemed to change a young woman's personality completely. In the second instance a committee of automotive experts, backed by millions of dollars and reams of market research, made one of the most disastrous decisions in marketing history. What processes underlie such far-reaching group effects?

Before answering this question, it is important to define what social psychologists mean by **group**. In everyday language we often use the term to describe any collection of people who happen to be in the same place at the same time. In social psychology, however, the definition is more precise (DeLamater, 1974; Hare, 1976; Shaw, 1976). First, members of a group must regularly interact with one another in fairly structured and predictable ways. Second, a group is always oriented toward one or more specific goals, which satisfy certain needs of its members. And finally, the members have a feeling of group identity, solidarity, and interdependence. The members of a group tend to feel themselves part of a collective whole, sharing to some degree a collective fate apart from that of nonmembers.

Since this chapter could never attempt to cover all the influences groups can have on human behavior, we will focus on just two of many important and interesting ones. First, we shall see how groups affect individual attitudes. Second, we shall see how groups can influence problem solving and decision making.

Group effects on individual attitudes and behavior

As we have seen in Asch's studies of conformity, the judgments of those around us can have a powerful effect on our own opinions. In various ways, membership in a group can change our attitudes. This change may be accomplished subtly, as were the types of attitude change discussed in Chapter 17, or blatantly, as in the case of brainwashing.

The concept of group norms One powerful way in which groups influence our thinking is by presenting us with **norms**, a set of shared guidelines and standards. Group norms are important because they define the nature of social reality. For example, the norms of a street gang define the social situation as an ongoing war between "us" and "them"; violence is seen as necessary and inevitable.

The group that first presents us with a particular set of norms is our family: As we grow up, our parents generally expect us to adopt their standards of appropriate behavior. When we begin to develop friendships outside the family, we may reject our family's norms and adopt those of our friends. Or we may come to accept the norms of teachers, coworkers, or others we admire or respect. Social psychologists call the people to whom we look for guidance in formulating values, beliefs, and attitudes our **reference groups**. A *positive reference group* is one whose outlook we tend to adopt; a *negative reference group* is one whose views we tend to reject.

How strong is the influence of reference groups other than the family? Consider, for example, how political beliefs are formed. Have your views changed since your high-school days? If so, how—and why? In a classic five-year study of students attending Bennington College during the 1930s, Theodore Newcomb (1943) investigated the dual impact of parents and the college community on attitude formation.

Many of the students at Bennington (then an expensive all-women's college) were born into wealthy, conservative families where labor unions were believed

Figure 18.5 For each member of this VFW post, the other members serve as "reference others." In attempting to validate our beliefs, we generally turn to those individuals whose judgments we respect.

dangerous, Franklin Roosevelt considered a radical, and the welfare state feared as an ever-encroaching threat. For these young women, the Bennington campus was a whole new world. Most of the faculty members were liberals who believed it their duty to inform an overprotected student body about the effects of the Great Depression and the implications of impending war. How did the Bennington women adapt to these new ideas? The majority gradually fell into step with the college community, becoming more liberal in their outlook toward public affairs. For example, during the 1936 presidential election, 62 percent of the freshmen supported the conservative Republican candidate Alf Landon, while only 14 percent of the juniors and seniors did.

Newcomb argued that the degree to which a particular student changed her attitudes was strongly related to her reference groups. For the majority whose attitudes became more liberal, the college community as a whole or a close circle of liberal friends were important positive reference groups. Freshman students were influenced by upperclass women, among whom liberals tended to be more outgoing and popular. "I was so anxious to be accepted," said one student, "that I accepted the political complexion of the community here." Similarly, the minority of students who did not become more liberal turned to family or conservative friends as positive reference groups. Explained one: "Every time I've tried to rebel against my family I've found how terribly wrong I am, and I've very naturally kept to my parents' attitudes."

Twenty-five years later Newcomb and several colleagues reinterviewed some of the women who had participated in the original Bennington study (Newcomb et al., 1967). They found that most of those who had been liberal in college had remained liberal, and that most of those who had been conservative in college had remained conservative. Apparently, most of those who had conformed to the liberal views of the college had internalized those views (Kelman, 1958, 1961). The attitudes shaped by their college experience led them to select friends, husbands, and careers that reinforced liberal opinions. The same was true of the women who had stayed conservative in college. For instance, in the 1960 presidential election, the husbands of 67 percent of the college conservatives preferred Nixon to Kennedy. Thus, the political preferences of the Bennington women were shown to be highly enduring.

Brainwashing The example of the young woman whose personality changed after her conversion to a religious cult shows the profound influence such groups can have on attitudes. Since it has been alleged that some religious groups effect conversions not by persuasion but by brainwashing, it is important that we gain some understanding of this phenomenon.

The term **brainwashing** was coined by Edward Hunter, a journalist who published a book in 1951 detailing the techniques used by the Communist Chinese to bring the Nationalist Chinese to accept their point of view. One of the most extensive studies of brainwashing was that done by Edgar H. Schein (1956, 1961), who described the procedures used by the North Koreans and Chinese to "reform" the thinking of United Nations prisoners of war in Korea. Schein studied this process by conducting intensive interviews with a number of ex-POWs. He concluded that brainwashing is not as mysterious as many people believe. Essentially, it is an extremely intense, determined effort to persuade people to change their opinions, backed by various types of pressure: social isolation, physical hardship, and verbal attacks on their values. A person who is lonely, afraid, poorly housed and fed, and subjected to constant pressure to change his or her opinions is a good candidate for brainwashing.

The cult phenomenon Brainwashing, ordinarily thought of in a wartime context, has become a subject of considerable interest recently as a result of charges that certain religious groups use brainwashing techniques to obtain converts. Some of the groups that have been implicated include the Unification Church of the Reverend Sun Myung Moon, the Hare Krishna sect, the Children of God, and the ill-fated Peoples' Temple of the Reverend Jim Jones. Of course, religious cults—with the possible exception of the Peoples' Temple— rarely hold people against their will or threaten them with violence or death. Nevertheless, the cults' ways of inducing people to convert and join the group are quite similar to the technique of brainwashing, which may account in part for the cults' spectacular growth—cults now claim as many as 3 million members in the United States (Singer, 1979). Commonly, recruits are invited to rural retreats or seminars lasting a weekend or longer. They have little or no contact with the outside world, their activities are carefully scheduled from morning to night, and they are allowed little time for introspection or for conversing with the other recruits. Instead, the program consists mainly of lectures, singing, meditation, and sometimes games and sports. As Schein has noted, such control of the subject's social environment is an important step in controlling his or her attitudes and beliefs:

If the only contacts a person is permitted are with persons who *unanimously* have beliefs different from his own, it is very likely that he will find at least some among them with whom, because of growing emotional bonds, he will identify and whose beliefs he will subsequently adopt (1956, p. 171).

In one systematic study (Galanter et al., 1979), a representative sample of over 200 members of the Unification Church were asked to complete a measure of psychological well-being. Their responses were compared with those of 300 young people matched for age and sex but who were not in a cult. Church members were also asked to describe their feelings and behavior prior to commitment and at present. We might expect some distortion of people's recall of earlier psychological states as well as their evaluation of their current psychological state. And, of course, the survey included only those who agreed with the teachings of the Moon cult; those who had left the cult or decided not to join were not studied. Despite these limitations, the study revealed some interesting findings. "Moonies" reported a significant decline in feelings of psychological distress, such as nervousness and depression, since their conversion. However, these young people had experienced greater than usual psychological difficulty before joining the church. A sizeable minority reported serious emotional problems and drug use prior to joining the cult. And even though they became less distressed over the course of membership, their self-reported happiness, satisfaction, and emotional stability were significantly lower than those of the matched comparison group.

Although many people do seem to find that the cults give to their lives a meaning that was absent before, some eventually drop out. Of these, many show long-term effects from the experience (Singer, 1979). Once cut off from their friends within the cult community and the regular regime of work and worship, many feel lost and depressed. They feel uneasy about returning to conventional life and often face difficulties in going back to school or work. Their relations with their families and with the opposite sex may be disturbed. Further, they may drift indecisively, unable to cope with a life in which all actions are not prescribed and ordered. Some former cultists, especially ones who had become accustomed to long periods of meditation or chanting, even experience "flashbacks"—brief lapses into trancelike states. Friends and family members may report that the person seems a bit slowed and mentally passive. The person may find independent thought and careful reasoning difficult. Finally, some former cultists fear harassment by the cult for their defection (Singer, 1979).

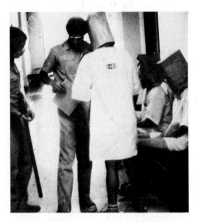

The power of group roles Casual observation tells us that an individual's personality often fits his or her role within a group. The clergyman, for instance, is frequently paternal, the drill sergeant demanding, the bureaucrat inflexible. Do people bring such stereotyped traits to the roles they fill, or do the roles instead largely shape the person's characteristic ways of behaving? This is one of the questions psychologist Philip Zimbardo and his colleagues (1972, 1973) set out to answer when they designed a study, briefly described in Chapter 17, to examine two of the most compelling of all group roles—those of inmate and guard in a maximum security prison.

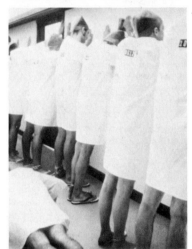

Studying a real prison would have presented difficulties, not only because of the strict rules established by prison authorities, but also because variables (such as differences in individual background) would have made it difficult to separate the participants from their roles. Zimbardo therefore constructed a very realistic "mock" prison in the basement of the Stanford University psychology building during summer session. More than seventy-five young men, mostly college students on vacation, volunteered to participate in a paid two-week functional simulation of prison life. (It was a *functional* simulation because it aimed not at simulating a prison in precise physical detail, but in creating many of the psychological aspects of a prison—the power structure, the helplessness experienced by the prisoners, the emphasis on order and rule-following, and so on.) Of the seventy-five volunteers, Zimbardo selected twenty-one for their emotional stability and maturity. Ten were randomly assigned the role of prisoner, eleven the role of guard. The guards were given no instructions other than the general need to maintain "law and order." How do you think the guards and prisoners behaved in this situation? Zimbardo's findings were both surprising and disturbing.

Figure 18.6 Life inside "Stanford County Prison."

To make the simulation as authentic as possible, prisoners were "arrested" at their homes and then taken to the so-called Stanford County Prison. There they were issued uniforms and ushered into sparsely furnished cells. The first day of the experiment passed without incident, but on the second day the prisoners staged a surprise revolt. This episode marked a critical turning point in the participants' behavior. After quelling the rebellion by striking or threatening the prisoners with billy clubs and fire extinguishers, the guards began to use their power harshly and arbitrarily. They created petty rules and demanded that prisoners follow them to the letter. They made the inmates perform meaningless, exhausting, and degrading chores and repeatedly ridiculed and demeaned them. The reaction of the prisoners was equally disturbing. Five of them developed such severe anxiety symptoms that they had to be released from the experiment; the other five were reduced to servile robots. After only six days, Zimbardo was forced to abandon the study because it had become too frighteningly real.

How can one explain such extraordinary behavior? Because participants had been screened for emotional stability, we know they were not psychologically disturbed before the experiment began. In addition, each person was randomly assigned the role of guard or prisoner, thus eliminating the possibility that systematic personality differences preexisted between the two groups. Zimbardo concluded that the experimental results must have been caused by the power of prison roles. The demands of being an inmate or a guard so dominated the subjects' lives, he argued, that their personalities were temporarily changed. As one prisoner remarked: "I began to feel that I was losing my identity. The person I call——— (subject's real name), . . . was distant from me, was remote, until finally I wasn't that. I was #416—I was really my number." If a normal, well-adjusted young man can be this transformed by the part he is playing in a psychological experiment, it is likely that certain roles in real life can also exert an enormous influence on behavior.

Zimbardo has acknowledged that his study, because of its effects on its subjects, presents an ethical dilemma, similar to the one brought up by Milgram's study of obedience. He has argued, however (Zimbardo et al., 1972), that the knowledge gained from the experiment has been important. For example, the study has been extremely useful in illustrating the socially destructive nature of the prison environment, apart from the supposed personality problems of either prisoners or guards. Zimbardo also attempted to help his subjects recover: He "debriefed" them extensively, encouraging them to vent their feelings at the end of the experiment. His follow-up efforts, which included questionnaires, interviews, and group reunions, suggested that the subjects recovered reasonably well from the experience (Zimbardo et al., 1972).

Group effects on problem solving and performance

It is clear that groups operate through norms and roles to shape individual attitudes. What is their effect on performance?

Social facilitation One of the earliest experiments in social psychology showed that cyclists who competed with one another rode faster than those who merely raced the clock (Triplett, 1897). In later studies, Floyd Allport (1920, 1924) found that subjects working at such tasks as solving multiplication problems and generating word associations performed better in the presence of four or five other people, even though the subjects worked individually. Allport called this phenomenon, in which the presence of others seems to improve people's performance, **social facilitation**. A similar effect has been noted among animals. For example, Chen (1937), after observing ants digging tunnels, noted that individual ants worked harder (moved more dirt) when they worked in groups of two or three than when they worked alone.

But there was also contradictory evidence. Subjects trying to learn complex finger mazes did better when alone (Husband, 1931). In animal experiments, the performance of certain kinds of tasks by parakeets and finches was inhibited by the presence of other birds (Allee and Masure, 1936; Klopfer, 1958).

A way out of the dilemma was proposed by Robert Zajonc (1965, 1966, 1972). Zajonc first distinguished between the learning phase and the performance phase of task performance. He then went on to argue that the crucial factor in task performance is drive, or motivation. It had been shown (Hull and Spence, 1966) that high drive increases the chances of an individual's responding with a well-known and dominant behavior (that is, the response a person is most likely to give in a particular situation). Zajonc suggested that the presence of others increases drive, and that this in turn will facilitate some tasks but inhibit others. The performance of easy tasks (such as simple arithmetic), which have already been learned, would be facilitated by increased drive, since the dominant response is the correct one. The opposite would be true for the performance of complex tasks (such as learning a maze), which require the subject to learn a new behavior and in which the dominant response would thus be incorrect.

Zajonc's model has some very practical applications. Performers who have a good grasp of their material—skilled musicians or actors, for example—are likely to do better in front of an audience than alone. But when we are beginning pianists or fledgling actors, we will probably be rattled by the presence of others and make mistakes.

Decision making: groupthink But what about the effects of others on performances of a highly creative task like complex decision making, where there is seldom a single "right" response? We seem to assume that a group of people can produce better results than an individual operating alone. Is this assumption correct? Are two heads always better than one?

Decision making in groups has several obvious advantages. If a decision requires specialized information, the members of a group are more likely than a single individual to have the necessary expertise. Furthermore, individuals inevitably have certain biases, blind spots, and other weaknesses that the collective insights of a group can help to overcome. Despite these benefits, however, decision making in groups also poses certain risks. Airing a large number of views can be a slow and cumbersome process, a significant drawback when a quick decision is required. Then, too, groups impose strong pressures for conformity, pressures that can override reason and have tragic results—as we saw in the My Lai example. Such pressures are especially powerful in small, close-knit groups (Blake and Mouton, 1979). When a group becomes so concerned with maintaining unanimity that it can no longer appraise alternatives realistically, it has fallen victim to a mode of decision making that social psychologist Irving Janis (1972) calls *groupthink*. The results can be disastrous, as the following example illustrates.

In the early months of 1961, a confident and tightly knit group, including men of outstanding intelligence, made what has come to be regarded as one of the worst decisions in recent history. The group, President John F. Kennedy's inner circle of foreign-policy advisers, met over the course of three months and reached the unanimous decision to invade Fidel Castro's Cuba, using an invasion force of Cuban exiles who had been trained by the Central Intelligence Agency. Some 1,400 exiles took part in the attack at Cuba's Bay of Pigs, aided by the United States Navy and Air Force and the CIA. Within three days, Cuban forces had sunk the ships that carried ammunition and supplies and had captured about 1,200 of the invaders, killing the rest. Subsequent reflections about the Bay of Pigs blunder by President Kennedy and his staff revealed that the group had ignored many obvious and vital factors. It had failed to take into account available data on the size and strength of Castro's forces, the loyalty of his troops, and the deteriorating morale of the invaders. It had also failed to consider worldwide reaction to such a morally questionable military venture. "How," President Kennedy asked after the fiasco was over, "could we have been so stupid?"

Janis believes that the poor decision making was the result of several forces, all characteristic of groupthink. One was the group's "illusion of invulnerability"—its belief that, no matter what the odds, it would always succeed. As one member of the inner circle recalled: "It seemed that, with John Kennedy leading us and with all the talent he had assembled, nothing could stop us" (Janis, 1972, p. 36). The other men around Kennedy shared this conviction, and it prompted them to underestimate many potential obstacles. Castro was deemed unpopular and ineffectual; his forces were dismissed as too weak to resist attack. Such highly simplistic assumptions were obviously incorrect.

Other symptoms of groupthink also undermined the administration's judgment. In extremely cohesive groups like Kennedy's, Janis argues, members feel a strong inner compulsion to avoid disrupting group unity and the positive feelings it creates. As a result, they tend to convince themselves that all the group's decisions are sound. Victims of groupthink tend to suppress any objections they might have and to minimize the importance of their doubts. As Kennedy adviser Arthur Schlesinger, Jr., wrote, "I can only explain my failure to do more than raise a few timid questions by reporting that one's impulse to blow the whistle on this nonsense was simply undone by the circumstances of the discussions" (Janis, 1972, p. 40). Such self-imposed censorship, in turn, has another important result. It fosters an "illusion of unanimity." Members of the Kennedy team mistakenly assumed that anyone who remained silent during policy talks must be in complete accord. This, of course, was not true. But once an illusion of unanimity was established, it reinforced the members' conviction that their existing plan *must* be right.

How can optimistic, cohesive groups avoid the dangers of groupthink? Janis has offered several suggestions (Janis, 1972; Janis and Mann, 1977). First, the group leader should encourage members to express their doubts without fear of disapproval. If the leader has already formed an opinion, he or she should adopt an impartial stance while others are airing their views. Group members should also be encouraged to discuss deliberations with other colleagues whose opinions they value, and outside experts with differing views should be invited to address the group. In addition, at least one member at every group meeting should adopt the role of devil's advocate, challenging majority preferences. Finally, when the group has reached a preliminary decision, it should hold a "second chance" meeting in which everyone voices residual misgivings as forcefully as possible before making a final choice.

AGGRESSION AND ALTRUISM

In January 1978 a man in Phoenix, Arizona, walked up to a derelict sleeping outdoors in the city's skid row, doused him with gasoline, and set him on fire. Two other men met similar fates before the attacker was finally arrested. As far as authorities could tell, the victims had done nothing whatever to provoke the incidents. In the same month, also in Phoenix, concerned citizens showered gifts and money on a desperately poor family, the father of which had been arrested for a minor offense. None of the donors knew the family personally. They had simply read about its plight in the local newspaper and responded with an outpouring of generosity.

These starkly contrasting stories underline one of the central paradoxes of human nature: People can be aggressive and cruel, but they can also be generous and kind. What explains these opposing tendencies? In the next section of this chapter we shall examine some of the most important factors underlying each.

Factors affecting aggression

In the single year of 1968, more people were beaten or murdered on the streets of America than were killed or wounded in the seven and a half years of the Vietnam War (Mark and Ervin, 1970). And 1968 was not an exceptional year in this respect. Annually, about 1 million Americans are victims of reported violent crime (FBI Uniform Crime Reports, 1977). It is estimated that between 1820 and 1945, worldwide, 58 million people died at the hands of their fellow human beings. Murder, rape, and assault are extreme examples of *interpersonal aggression*—behavior directed toward the goal of injuring another human being who is motivated to avoid such harm (Baron, 1977). What accounts for the disturbingly high level of such aggression?

Biological influences The fundamental idea that human aggression is biologically based has taken various forms. One basic idea of Freud's theory of personality, for example, is that aggression is a part of human nature. As he wrote, "The tendency to aggression is an innate, independent, instinctual disposition in man" (1930, p. 102). Aggressive drives, he thought, originate within each person and constantly demand some form of release; we are driven to discharge aggressive energy, and we may do so in various ways—by engaging in arguments, running in marathons, working to elect our favorite political candidate, holding up banks, or, unfortunately, killing our neighbor.

One prominent analyst of our tendency toward aggression, the Nobel Prize-winning ethologist Konrad Lorenz, also sees our aggressive tendencies as innate. Lorenz believes that all animals have a "fighting instinct" directed toward members of their own species (Lorenz, 1974). This instinct, he maintains, nor-

Figure 18.7 War has always been a means of legitimizing human aggression.

mally plays an important role in survival and evolution. An animal's urge to protect its territory disperses populations over wider areas and so increases each individual's chances of living and reproducing. In addition, aggressive contests over mates ensure that the strongest males will father the most offspring, thus improving the species as a whole.

Lorenz proposes that violence has become a problem for humans because human aggression differs from aggression in other species in two important respects. First, because our ancestors were relatively harmless creatures, they never evolved the innate inhibition against killing members of their kind that virtually all carnivorous species possess. According to Lorenz, fighting among members of the same species rarely becomes lethal—*except* among human beings. However, Lorenz's contention that *only* human beings murder their own kind has been refuted by recent evidence that lions, hyenas, macaques, langurs, and other species do at times kill one another wantonly (E. Wilson, 1975).

Lorenz argues that our lack of inhibition against killing others of our own kind is compounded by a second human trait: Human beings are the only species in which the fighting instinct is constantly suppressed. Lorenz suggests that if expression of the fighting instinct in any animal is constantly prohibited, aggressive impulses build up and may eventually be discharged in a particularly vicious way. Such blocking of aggression is common in human societies. Consequently, we are prone to periodic outbreaks of extreme violence.

However intriguing Lorenz's theories may be, they are open to serious criticism. First, even though there may be some biological factors involved in causing aggression, to argue that all people have an aggressive instinct does not explain the obvious variations that exist in human aggressiveness. Anthropological research shows that the level of aggression differs greatly from culture to culture. Some Brazilian Indian tribes, for example, engage in almost constant warfare (Chagnon, 1967, 1968), whereas the members of other societies (Eskimos, for instance) avoid even verbal quarrels (Gorer, 1968). And within any one society, some individuals are more aggressive than others. Instinct theories shed no light on these important differences. Second, to argue that human aggression is solely instinctive ignores the important role of learning in all human behavior. In fact, one classic study has shown that even in lower animals, many responses once thought to be purely "instinctive"—for instance, cats hunting rats—are actually learned (Kuo, 1930). If instinct alone cannot explain the aggressive behavior of animals, it certainly cannot explain the aggressive behavior of humans, who are even more influenced by learning. This is why social learning theories of aggression have generated such interest among psychologists.

Social learning influences According to the social learning perspective, people learn how to injure other people through exposure to violent models and through reinforcement (Bandura, 1976). The power of models to elicit aggressive behavior was demonstrated in a classic experiment (Bandura, Ross, and Ross, 1961). Nursery-school children observed one of two adult models: either an adult who ignored a five-foot inflated "Bobo" doll while playing quietly with a Tinker Toy set, or an adult who physically and verbally abused the Bobo doll. The violent model's attack was unlike anything that normal preschoolers would do spontaneously. Pinning the doll to the floor, the model repeatedly punched it in the face, yelling "Sock him in the nose!" He or she also beat the Bobo over the head with a mallet, tossed it angrily in the air, and kicked it about the room, punctuating these assaults with cries of "Throw him in the air!" . . . "Kick him!" . . . "Pow!" The researchers found that when the children were later given access to a Bobo doll under mildly frustrating conditions, those exposed to the violent model behaved much more aggressively than those exposed to the subdued model or to no model at all. Furthermore, the children who had witnessed the violent model tended to imitate that person's behavior quite closely. They punched, hammered, tossed, and yelled right down to the final kick and last emphatic "Pow!" Exposure to aggressive models, then, appears both to reduce general inhibitions against aggression and to suggest specific aggressive acts.

What factors affect the degree to which a person is likely to imitate aggression? One important influence is the presence of rewards or punishments. In a follow-up study to the one just described, Bandura (1965) found that children are much less likely to imitate a model who is punished for aggression than a model who is rewarded for the same behavior. The inhibiting effect of punishment, however, has its limitations. As soon as the threat of negative consequences is removed, a person may reenact observed aggression, especially if the potential rewards for doing so are great. And research shows that most aggression *is* extremely rewarding. In one study of children (Patterson, Littman, and Bricker, 1967), close to 80 percent of physical and verbal assaults on others produced highly positive results for the aggressor, whether those results were tangible (such as obtaining a desirable toy), social (such as winning the admiration of peers), or internal (such as boosting the child's sense of power).

One of the most controversial issues related to the social learning of aggression is the effect of widespread television violence on audience behavior. Approximately 75 percent of the programs currently shown on television depict some form of aggression. By the time the average child reaches the age of sixteen, he or she has witnessed more than 13,000 dramatized murders and an even greater number of nonfatal assaults (Waters and Malamud, 1975). In some widely publicized incidents, acts of extreme violence in real life have paralleled behavior recently shown on television.

Defenders of television programming argue that, for the most part, exposure to television violence has a positive, cathartic effect: It offers viewers a harmless release of much of their pent-up hostility. But other observers are not convinced that television violence is this benign. They maintain that television provides children with heroes who are constantly rewarded for aggression. As a result, children are very likely to imitate them. They also argue that it provides models for destructive behavior.

Although research on the impact of media violence is still incomplete, most of the studies to date support television's critics. Witnessing violence on television does seem capable of instigating more violence (Liebert, Neal, and Davidson, 1973; Baron, 1977). In one study, boys who were shown violent movies five nights in a row displayed significantly more verbal and physical aggression than boys who watched only neutral movies (Parke et al., 1977). There is some evidence too that the impact of media violence may be quite enduring. Boys who reportedly watched a great deal of television at the age of eight have been show to be more aggressive at the age of eighteen than peers who had watched very little television as youngsters (Eron et al., 1972). Findings such as these have led most psychologists to agree that a constant barrage of television violence can breed imitative aggression.

This answer may eventually prove a bit simplistic, however. As research continues, more ideas are likely to be introduced into this debate. For example, one recent study (Fenigstein, 1979) found that male subjects who fantasized about violence or who actually engaged in aggressive acts subsequently preferred to watch films with violent themes. Thus, as this study concludes, "aggressive behaviors are not only a *result* of viewing violence . . ., but may also be a *cause* of the viewing of violence" (Fenigstein, 1979, p. 2315). Other researchers have suggested that merely seeing violence on television is not so important as the *kind* of violence one sees. According to Goranson (1970), imitative aggression is less likely to occur when viewers are exposed to the maiming, blood, and suffering that accompany real violence. By contrast, most television shows present what he calls "clean violence"—bloodless stabbings, shootings without pain—which, paradoxically, may encourage imitative aggression. We can hope that further research will shed more light on the specific effects of various kinds of televised violence.

The influences of frustration Although social learning theories provide great insight into how people acquire a repertoire of aggressive acts and how performance of those acts is shaped by rewards and punishments, they say nothing about the relationship between aggression and a person's underlying emotional state. For example, many highly aggressive acts seem to be a direct result of intense or prolonged frustration. Is frustration systematically related to aggression? John Dollard and his colleagues (1939) proposed that it is. In fact, they took the extreme position that "aggression is *always* a consequence of frustration," and, conversely, that "frustration *always* leads to some form of aggression" (Dollard et al., 1939, p.1). By **frustration** they meant interference with any goal-directed behavior. Thus, when people are thwarted in their attempts to obtain food or shelter, sex or sleep, love or recognition, they become aggressive. This is not to say that they immediately lash out at the cause of their frustration. An aggressive response, Dollard argued, can be delayed, disguised, transferred to other people and objects (displaced), or otherwise deflected from its immediate and logical goal. But it is never destroyed.

In a classic test of this **frustration–aggression hypothesis**, a team of researchers (Barker, Dembo, and Lewin, 1941) deliberately frustrated a group of children. They were taken to a room, shown a collection of attractive toys, and told that they could look but not touch. Later, when the children were allowed to play with the toys, they treated them with great hostility, smashing them against the walls and floor. Another group of children, who had not been frustrated, played happily and peacefully with identical toys. Thus, frustration did seem to induce aggression.

Critics, however, were quick to point out that the frustration-aggression hypothesis had flaws. Frustration, they said, may lead to aggression in certain instances, but this link is not inevitable. Some people withdraw when their efforts are thwarted; others simply work harder to achieve their goal. Aggression, then, is only one of many possible reactions to frustration. In answer to this criticism, Miller (1941) modified the frustration-aggression hypothesis by saying that frustration produces a number of responses, one of which is aggression. But this modification created problems of its own. Under what circumstances would frustration lead to aggression, and under what circumstances would it promote some other response? And how, for that matter, could one tell if a seemingly passive response to frustration was not simply a disguised form of aggression?

Such questions were very difficult to answer experimentally, and the frustration-aggression hypothesis was almost abandoned as a result. But then Leonard Berkowitz proposed a new version of the theory, which could be empirically tested (Berkowitz, 1962, 1965, 1969). He argued that the immediate outcome of frustration is the emotional reaction of anger, not aggression. Anger, however, can easily instigate aggression if suitable aggressive cues exist. If no such cues are present, then anger may give rise to other forms of behavior, such as withdrawal or renewed effort. Berkowitz tested his ideas by exposing frustrated subjects to aggressive stimuli like guns and violent films, and, as predicted, such cues did increase the likelihood that frustration would promote aggression (Berkowitz and Geen, 1966; Berkowitz and LePage, 1967).

Factors affecting altruism

Although they seldom make front-page headlines, acts of human altruism occur every day. At great risk to their own lives, bystanders have been known to rush into burning buildings to rescue children trapped inside. People give millions of dollars to charitable organizations, donate blood, and volunteer their time to help others. What accounts for such behavior?

The idea that human beings are genetically programmed to help one another—that we have altruistic instincts—has received a good deal of attention

Figure 18.8 A tender moment between a young man and his helpless grandfather. Often we are in conflict between the desire to help others and the desire to think of ourselves first.

recently (Dawkins, 1975; E. Wilson, 1975). However, most social scientists reject this proposition for the same reason that they reject the instinct theory of human aggression: a genetic factor alone cannot explain variations in the incidence of altruism, and it ignores the role that learning plays in human interaction. Instead, social psychologists ask which situational and emotional factors—or combinations of factors—tend to encourage the helping response and which ones tend to inhibit it.

Influences on bystander intervention in emergencies At about 3:00 A.M. in a middle-class area of Queens, a borough of New York City, a young woman named Kitty Genovese was savagely attacked outside her apartment building as she arrived home from work. As the victim screamed for help, at least thirty-eight neighbors came to their windows, but no one offered assistance. No one even called the police. The attack continued for more than thirty minutes before Kitty Genovese died of multiple stab wounds.

The Genovese murder caused a sensation in the press. How could people be so apathetic, so indifferent to the fate of another human being? Many saw it as a classic illustration of urban callousness, of city dwellers' reluctance to "get involved." Yet investigation revealed that the witnesses to Kitty Genovese's murder had been far from indifferent. Her neighbors did not just close their blinds and go back to bed. They stood and watched transfixed, "unable to act but unwilling to turn away" (Latané and Darley, 1976, pp. 309–310). What prevented them from acting? Research on bystander intervention, inspired in part by the Genovese murder, indicates that a number of powerful social forces operate in any emergency situation, and some of them strongly inhibit the helping response.

John Darley and Bibb Latané, who have studied bystander intervention extensively, argue that the act of aiding the victim in an emergency is the result of many events and choices, all of which are *less* likely to occur in the presence of other people (Darley and Latané, 1968). First, the bystander must notice that something unusual has occurred; the external event must somehow intrude on his or her private thoughts. But most people consider it bad manners to watch the actions of others too closely. Practicing what the sociologist Erving Goffman (1963) has called "civil inattention," we tend to tune out sights and sounds and stare straight ahead when we are in a crowd of people. Thus we are less likely, as individuals in a group, even to see the signs of a possible emergency. Many victims are not so much ignored as unnoticed.

Simply noticing the indications of an emergency is not enough, however. A bystander must also determine whether this particular event is serious enough to warrant intervention. This decision is often far from easy, for most of the signs that suggest an emergency are ambiguous. Cries for help from the next apartment might be genuine, or they might be coming from your neighbor's television set. When other people are present, most of us think twice before rushing to the rescue because we are concerned about appearing foolish if no emergency exists. So we adopt an air of calm indifference while looking around to see how other people are acting. The problem is that everyone else may be trying to appear indifferent too. The result is that each bystander is taken in by the others' nonchalance and led—or misled—to define the situation as a nonemergency.

Latané and Darley (1968) demonstrated the presence of both these social processes in an interesting experiment. Male college students, who had volunteered to be interviewed about the problems of life at an urban university, were directed to a waiting room to fill out a preliminary questionnaire. Some of the students were alone in the room; others were in groups of three. In either case, shortly after the subjects had started writing, the experimenters began to pump in smoke through a small vent in the wall. They observed the subjects' reactions through one-way mirrors. The object was to see how long it would take each subject to notice, evaluate, and report this potential emergency. Latané and Darley found that two-thirds of the subjects in the "alone" condition spotted the smoke immediately, whereas only one-quarter of the subjects in the "group" condition noticed it as quickly. Clearly, when others are present, people are much slower to perceive unusual events.

When people do perceive events, those in groups are much more inclined to label them nonthreatening than are people alone. In Latané and Darley's experiment, eighteen of the twenty-four subjects in the "alone" condition were concerned enough about the smoke to report it before the experimental period ended. In contrast, only three of the twenty-four subjects in the "group" condition reported the smoke. Instead, the typical subject in a group "would look at the other people, see them doing nothing, shrug his shoulders, and then go back to his questionnaire, casting covert glances first at the smoke and then at the others." What did he think was causing the smoke that made it safe to ignore? Steam or air-conditioning vapors were named by most subjects in postexperimental interviews, but some responses were much more imaginative. A few subjects concluded that the smoke was artificial smog intended to simulate an urban environment, and two actually suggested that it was "truth gas" to induce accurate responses on the questionnaires! Note that all these answers, no matter how implausible, ruled out the possibility that the smoke indicated danger. In this way, those who failed to report the incident justified the appropriateness of their behavior.

But even if a bystander notices an event and correctly labels it an emergency, the presence of others may dilute that person's feeling of responsibility for action and so decrease the chance that he or she will intervene. This diffusion of responsibility may have occurred among witnesses to the Kitty Genovese murder. Onlookers may have thought that other people were also watching, so that they were not the only persons available to act. In such a situation people can fail to act without feeling personally accountable. After all, they reason, someone else has probably already summoned help. As a result, no one acts until it is too late.

To test this hypothesis, Darley and Latané (1968) staged another emergency. College students who had volunteered for an experiment were ushered into private rooms containing earphones and a microphone. The study was said to involve a group discussion about the personal problems caused by life in a high-pressure urban environment. Subjects were told that the talk would take place over an intercom system, to preserve anonymity, and that the experimenter would not be listening in. Each subject was led to believe that one, two, or five other people were participating in the discussion, but in fact all voices except the true subject's were prerecorded.

The first speaker led off by saying that he was having difficulty adjusting to New York City and to his professors' academic demands. Then, very hesitantly and with some embarrassment, he added that he had even suffered nervous seizures, similar to epileptic attacks, when under severe stress. This young man was soon to be the victim. When it was again his turn to speak, he began to stutter and fumble for words, simulating very realistically the onset of a seizure. Within a few minutes he was choking and pleading for help. How do you think the subject who overheard this performance reacted? As predicted by Darley and Latané, the larger the perceived group, and therefore the greater the potential diffusion of responsibility, the less likely a subject was to summon help. Whereas 85 percent of those who thought they alone were speaking with the victim reported his plight sometime during the faked attack, only 62 percent of those who thought there was one other bystander did so, and only 31 percent of those who thought there were four other bystanders. Thus, the responsiblity-diluting effect of other people appears to be quite marked.

Darley and Latané conclude that the explanation of so-called bystander apathy may involve more than the person's indifference to human suffering. In the experiment just described, subjects who failed to report the seizure were anything but indifferent. Many showed symptoms of extreme anxiety as they considered what to do. Their failure to intervene appeared to be not so much a decision against responding as a state of indecision. A bystander in an emergency appears to be, in Darley and Latané's words, "an anguished individual in genuine doubt, concerned to do the right thing but compelled to make complex decisions under pressure of stress and fear. His reactions are shaped by the actions of others—and all too frequently by their inaction" (Darley and Latané, 1968, p. 300).

Darley and Latané's findings are quite pessimistic about the prospects of receiving help when many bystanders are present. But do the social processes they have described always operate to deter intervention when more than one person witnesses an emergency? Fortunately, the answer appears to be no. When the signs of an emergency are unambiguous and there is no doubt that a life-threatening event is taking place, and when it is also clear that no one else has stepped forward to help, a victim may be more likely to receive aid in the presence of a sizable group. This was demonstrated in an emergency staged on a New York City subway (Piliavin, Rodin, and Piliavin, 1969). In 70 percent of the trials, bystanders immediately came to the aid of a young man who collapsed on the floor of the train. And the helping response was quicker when seven or more people were in the car than when there were only one, two, or three people. Note that in this case the emergency was unambiguous: The

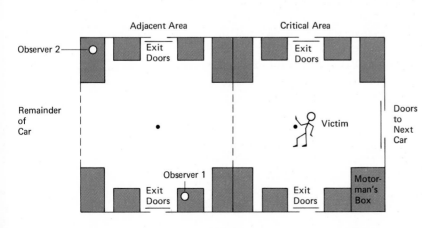

Figure 18.9 This diagram shows the positions of the "victim" and the two observers in the New York City subway car used in Piliavin's experiment on bystander intervention (after Piliavin, Rodin, and Piliavin, 1969).

victim was sprawled on the floor directly in front of the bystanders, and they could not diffuse responsibility by telling themselves that someone else was taking care of the situation.

Other influences on helping behavior In addition to studying factors affecting bystander intervention in emergencies, social psychologists have studied factors affecting other forms of prosocial behavior, such as giving to charities or doing favors for people. Their research has shown that many factors intrinsic to the pace of modern life can promote or inhibit the helping response. Consider time pressures, for instance.

Could it be, asked John Darley and Daniel Batson (1973), that time pressures affect our willingness to help others? They explored this hypothesis in an experiment with students at a theological seminary who were led to believe that they were either early, moderately late, or very late for a speaking engagement. On the way, each student passed a poorly dressed man slumped in a doorway. The tendency to help the victim varied directly with the time pressure. Whereas 63 percent of the students in the "low hurry" condition offered assistance, only 10 percent of those in the "high hurry" condition did so. Nor did it matter that half the students were on their way to speak about the Biblical parable of the good Samaritan; some of these literally stepped over the slumped victim as they hurried on their way!

There are several possible explanations for these results. One is that a person in a hurry may not even notice someone in distress. Although this explanation may apply in some instances, it does not account for the behavior of most of Darley and Batson's seminary students. Postexperimental interviews showed that almost all these subjects had seen the victim but still failed to stop. An alternative possibility is that time pressure raises the cost of the intervention and so makes us less likely to act. Then, too, time pressure may also create a difficult conflict between the desire to help a stranger and the desire to be thoughtful toward those who are awaiting our prompt arrival. Darley and Batson feel that such conflict may have existed in the minds of many of the students in their good Samaritan experiment.

Time pressure, in any case, seems to exert a powerful inhibition on the helping response. Researchers have also sought to identify other factors that might help explain the city dweller's tendency to bypass strangers in need. Psychologist Stanley Milgram has suggested that cities, with their high densities of people, impose a sort of cognitive "overload" to which urban residents must adapt. This they do by paying less attention to what is going on around them, by developing blasé attitudes toward deviant, even bizarre, behavior, and by being highly selective in their responses to human demands. Milgram argues that without these very rational adaptations to crowded and stressful surroundings, city dwellers could hardly carry on their lives (Milgram, 1970).

The dynamics of helping

What of the person who *does* stop to help the person slumped on the sidewalk—of what use is his or her help? Most researchers who investigate the reasons for and frequency of altruistic behavior do not concern themselves with its effectiveness. But the question of whether help does any good may well be as important as a knowledge of the conditions under which it is given. Ideally, of course, both motives and consequences must be examined together, as Brickman and his colleagues emphasize in a provocative paper (1979).

Why helping fails Research indicates that many of our helping efforts are unsuccessul, if not actually counterproductive. Pessimistic indeed are the views of those who have studied prisoner rehabilitation (J. Wilson, 1975; Yochelson and Samenow, 1976); educational programs for the disadvantaged (Jensen, 1969; Bentler and Woodward, 1978; Stebbins et al., 1978); and various helping efforts for people in stressful life situations (Lieberman and Mullen, 1978). Why the poor results? Brickman and his associates (1979) discuss several factors, a few of which we shall mention here.

One problem with help is that it is often given on the assumption that the recipient is incompetent. The helping that is offered can leave recipients worse off than before by preventing them from acting, and thus from learning. B. F. Skinner points out: "We watch a child tying a shoelace and grow jittery, and to escape from our jitteriness we 'help' the child tie the lace. In doing so we destroy one chance to learn to tie shoes" (Skinner, 1978). Indications are that the ill health, unresponsiveness, and poor memory of nursing-home residents are due in part to the fact that so much is done for these elderly persons, albeit poorly or grudgingly (Langer, 1980).

Another, related, difficulty is that givers and recipients alike may see any improvements as resulting solely from the helpers' efforts. Such a perception could obviously hinder improved performance on the part of recipients. According to one observer, this is a flaw of affirmative action programs (Sowell, 1976). Blacks, for example, made perceptible economic and educational progress during the 1960s—before such programs were instituted—but it was obscured by the conferring of benefits later on, which made the achievements look like gifts.

Given assumptions like these, it is no wonder that recipients of help often respond by becoming passive—a stance that may make total institutions easier to run, but that is hardly conducive to meaningful change, let alone autonomy. One observer of social workers notes: "When staff complain about clients 'who cannot stand on their own two feet,' . . . they often fail to recognize that the source of these difficulties is the clients' passivity and dependence which the staff members themselves have done much to encourage" (Maslach, 1978, p. 119).

The helping role: burnout The inseparability of consequences from motives in helping becomes even more apparent when we examine the role of the professional helper. Jobs in such fields as social work and health care have traditionally been regarded as providing enough emotional and psychological gratification to compensate for their low monetary returns. But recent evidence indicates that helping is not, in effect, its own reward. Indeed, a good many service professionals seem to suffer from what has been termed **burnout**, a syndrome characterized by the following symptoms, among others: loss of concern for clients; a tendency to treat clients in a detached and even dehumanizing way; rationalizing failure by attributing it to clients; a decline in motivation and self-esteem; irritability and anger; and resistance to change (Maslach, 1976).

What causes burnout? Apparently, it serves as an important defense mechanism. A social worker with a caseload of two hundred and only limited community resources may try to avoid feelings of guilt and frustration by distancing herself from clients, who become little more than statistics in a file (Cherniss, Egnatios, and Wacker, 1976). Another factor is the very mystique of the helping professions: that they offer interesting work among compassionate colleagues, work that benefits cooperative and grateful clients. Such unrealistic expectations lead to early disillusionment (Cherniss et al., in press). Thus it is the most dedicated professionals who suffer burnout first.

Clearly, the dehumanizing and victim-blaming components of burnout have a negative psychological effect on the people who need help. Not only that, but an entire program may suffer from the professionals' absenteeism, inefficiency, or apathy (Cherniss, 1978; Maslach, 1976). And burnout is self-reinforcing for its professional victims: Discouragement and subsequent withdrawal from clients lead to more failure in the future.

Since burnout results in part from exaggerated expectations, service professionals can reduce it if not eliminate it altogether by cultivating more realistic attitudes about their jobs. They may also find that restructuring the work situation is useful. For example, the outlook of child-care workers improved after a simple reorganization made individual responsibilities less diffuse and more personal (Pines and Maslach, 1978). Research shows too that burnout is less likely among professionals who can discuss their problems candidly with one another and who can minimize interactions with clients at their own discretion when the stress becomes too great (Maslach, 1976; Wortman and Dunkel-Schetter, 1979).

ENVIRONMENTAL PSYCHOLOGY

The relatively new field of **environmental psychology** is an excellent illustration of the direction that psychology has been taking in recent years. Apparently inspired by the general concern for environmental quality that developed among the public in the late 1960s and early 1970s (Stokols, 1978), environmental psychology focuses on the interrelationships between people and their physical and social surroundings. Environmental psychologists have begun their investigations on a variety of fronts, asking questions such as: Does the density of urban life tend to increase stress and produce crime? Are high-rise apartment buildings as suitable as smaller-scale housing for people to live in? Does constant exposure to noise from low-flying airplanes harm the people who live near airports?

These questions point up two trends that are emerging in psychology as a whole and that are especially evident in this subdiscipline. One is the tendency for psychologists to broaden their focus and to share information with professionals in other disciplines. Environmental psychology is by its nature an interdisciplinary field; its subject matter is potentially of interest to sociologists, engineers, urban planners, physicians, and architects as well as to psychologists. The second is the increasing concern of psychologists with the application of their studies to the world outside the laboratory.

In a field that encompasses so much, we cannnot do justice to all the recent research; therefore, we will concern ourselves here with only two areas of interest within environmental psychology, the effects of noise and the effects of crowding.

Noise

It has long been known that noise produces physiological arousal in human beings and thus can be a source of stress. Laboratory studies have shown that noise can interfere with subjects' abilities to perform tasks (Broadbent, 1978). In addition, noise has been shown to affect our sensitivity to others: According to Mathews and Canon (1975), we are less apt to offer to help others in a noisy environment than we are in a quiet one. Our reactions to noise, however, are not determined solely by the physical properties of noise itself. To some extent, the impact of the noise on our behavior depends on whether we can control it (shut it off). This point was established in an interesting program of research by Glass and Singer (1972).

Glass and Singer asked subjects to solve simple problems in arithmetic and verbal reasoning. While working on the problems, one group heard loud bursts of noise regularly for a few seconds of each minute. Another group heard the same amount of noise, but the bursts were delivered for varying lengths of time at unpredictable intervals. A third group worked on the problems with no background noise. Glass and Singer found that subjects were able to adapt to the noise and work effectively on the problems, regardless of their experimental condition. In the second part of the experiment, the experimenter turned off the noise. He then asked subjects to proofread a manuscript and to work on some puzzles. Some interesting findings emerged: Subjects who had been exposed to the unpredictable noise made more proofreading errors and gave up on the puzzles more quickly than subjects exposed either to predictable noise or to no noise.

What is it about unpredictable noise that causes these adverse effects? Glass and Singer hypothesized that unpredictable noise is particularly detrimental because it heightens people's perception that a situation is beyond their control. Because they cannot anticipate or prepare for the noise in any way, they may feel more helpless. In order to test this explanation, Glass and Singer added a new experimental condition in which subjects were again exposed to loud, unpredictable noise. They were told that while the experimenter would prefer that they listen to all the noise bursts, they could press a button to terminate the noise. Actually, very few subjects took advantage of this button, but their perception of control over the noise had an important influence on their proofreading and puzzle performance. Subjects who believed they could control the noise performed as well as subjects who heard no noise. This research program has important implications, since many of the noises we are exposed to outside the laboratory are uncontrollable. Any means of making such noise seem controllable may ameliorate the adverse effects of the noise.

Laboratory studies such as these, however, can give us only limited information about what noise does to us in a real-life situation. For example, exposing subjects to noise during the brief time span of an experiment may not tell us much about what noise does to people who are exposed to it over long periods of time. Researchers have therefore begun to attempt to measure the effects of noise in naturalistic settings (Cohen, Glass, and Phillips, 1979). Such studies present problems, however, because it is often difficult to isolate the effects of noise from that of other variables. Workers in a noisy factory, for example, may also be more or less affected by the stresses of their tasks, noxious fumes emitted from substances they work with, and many other factors. Thus in naturalistic studies it is important that extraneous variables be controlled.

One recent study that did control carefully for extraneous influences was done by Sheldon Cohen and his colleagues (Cohen et al., 1980). These researchers studied 271 elementary-school pupils in the Los Angeles area, some of whom attended noisy schools near the city's busiest airport and some of whom attended schools in quiet neighborhoods. The two groups of children were carefully matched by age, ethnicity, race, and social class, and those with hearing difficulties were excluded. The researchers even measured the air quality in the two areas to make sure that heavier air pollution in one neighborhood was not a factor. Cohen and his colleagues found that the children who attended the noisy schools had higher blood pressure than those who attended the quiet schools. In addition, the children from the noisy schools were more easily distracted. Like the subjects in the Glass and Singer study, they more readily gave up on solving rigged puzzles than did the other children. Moreover, the children showed no evidence of having adapted to the noise; in fact, the longer the children had been exposed to the noise, the more distractible they were. Cohen and his colleagues did a follow-up study (Cohen et al., in press) of these children one year after their original work. In the interim, 43 percent of the classrooms in the noisy schools were modified to exclude some noise. The researchers found that the children now in the less noisy classrooms showed no significant improvement from the noise abatement; they were still more distractible than children from the quiet schools. This suggests that the ill effects of noise may be long-lasting. Ongoing study by these researchers and others may eventually show that prolonged exposure to noise results in permanent cognitive damage to children.

Crowding

Many students of animal behavior have observed the importance to various species of a certain amount of space, or territory—an observation that laboratory studies have confirmed. In an extensive study of rats, Calhoun (1962) found that when colonies of rats were closely confined in pens, the animals' behavior became extremely maladaptive. The rats failed to build their nests, they were incapable of normal mating, they failed to care properly for their young, and they began to fight among themselves. Provocative as such studies are, the more important question is whether studies of rats—or other animals— tell us anything about the importance of space to human beings.

Demographic research has been one way investigators have sought to discover the effects of crowding on people. Researchers look for correlations between crowding and various kinds of social ills—disease, crime, family disorganization, and so on. Early demographic studies (for example, Schmitt, 1957, 1966) seemed to support the idea that where the population was dense, more pathology could indeed be expected. However, most studies did not isolate crowding from other variables associated with ill health and disturbed behavior, such as poverty and race. And in any case, the findings of demographic studies have been contradictory (for example, Winsborough, 1955; Schmitt, 1963).

To clarify the exact effects of crowding itself, free of the contamination of other variables, researchers began to conduct controlled experiments in the laboratory. In most such experiments, participants were subjected to various

Figure 18.10 City dwellers must cope with crowding, which poses a threat to physical and psychological well-being, as an aspect of daily life.

degrees of crowding and their reactions assessed in several ways—primarily by performance tests and self-reports as to the degree of stress they experienced. A number of such studies (Evans, 1975; Stokols et al., 1973; Hutt and Vaizey, 1966) found that high stress and poor performance did seem to be related to crowding. Other studies, however, disputed this conclusion (Sundstrom, 1978; Freedman and Staff, 1975). Moreover, as we saw in the case of noise, laboratory studies of such a complex phenomenon as crowding are necessarily somewhat artificial and may not yield any reliable generalizations about the effects of crowding in the real world.

Recently, investigators have attempted to overcome the limitations of laboratory studies by combining them with studies of the same subjects under conditions of crowding in the real world. For example, Baum and his associates (Baum and Valins, 1977; Baum, Aiello, and Calesnick, 1978) compared the behavior of freshmen living in different kinds of dormitories, to which they had been randomly assigned. Some were assigned to dorms with long corridors, in which thirty-two to forty residents shared public areas (lounge, bathrooms, and hallways). Others were assigned to dorms with short corridors, in which only six to twenty residents shared public areas. Each freshman was asked to complete a survey about his or her experiences in the dorm. Students living on long corridors were less satisfied with their college and dormitory experience, and felt that their dorms were more crowded, than were short-corridor residents. Students in the long-corridor dorms encountered their neighbors more often and more unpredictably than did students in the short-corridor dorms. They reported having more difficulty in avoiding people when they did not want to see them and more problems in regulating their social interactions. They seemed to find these problems stressful. As a result, long-corridor residents became passive and withdrew from social interactions. The surveys indicated, for example, that they had fewer friends and belonged to fewer social groups in the dormitory than did residents of short-corridor dorms.

Students who lived in long-corridor dorms were also likely to feel that it was useless to try to change conditions in the dorm. In short, these students seemed to react to the crowding they perceived and to their inability to control the situation with some degree of learned helplessness. In addition, the students' helpless behavior was found to generalize to settings other than the dormitory. When they were brought into the laboratory to play a game with another student, residents who had been living on long corridors were more passive and withdrawn and less cooperative than residents living on short corridors (Baum, Aiello, and Calesnick, 1978; Baum and Gatchel, in press).

Researchers have suggested a number of explanations for why crowding sometimes produces deleterious effects on people. A common theory is that people find the close presence of so many others overstimulating (Altman, 1975): Too much contact with others "overloads" us with stress. Some researchers, as we saw in the study of dormitory residents, suggest that crowding is most stressful when we feel we cannot avoid it and thus have no control over the frequency of our encounters with others (Sherrod, 1974). Studies such as these may eventually help us reduce the stress placed on people when, of necessity, they must coexist in close quarters. People moving into a hospital or army barracks, for example, might be allowed as much choice as possible as to room and roommates, so as to feel some control over their situation.

The future of environmental psychology

Although environmental psychology is a new discipline, it is not likely to prove a fad. We are only beginning to recognize the crucial effects that the physical environment can have on our behavior. And this is no idle or "academic" field of inquiry. What we discover from studies of crowding, for example, could save many millions of dollars of public funds that might otherwise be spent on poorly designed public housing. Psychologists pursuing research in this field could potentially make highly practical contributions to the architects, engineers, and planners responsible for the design and construction of our physical environment. It may be that we build noisy schools and overly dense housing projects at great social cost.

PSYCHOLOGY AND THE FUTURE

Our brief discussion of environmental psychology points up a prominent trend in psychology, and one that is likely to continue. Psychologists today are less satisfied with the limitations of laboratory settings. As we saw in our brief look at research on noise and crowding, they are increasingly combining laboratory research with "real-world" investigations (Wortman et al., 1980; Cialdini, 1980). Admittedly, working in such settings is often difficult; the everyday world lacks the neatness and control possible in the laboratory. But many social psychologists believe that theories are enriched by attempts to test their validity in naturalistic settings (McGuire, 1967a, 1967b). An increasing number of research programs represent an interplay between the laboratory and the "real world." For example, initial natural observation might suggest hypotheses for controlled laboratory investigations. This was the case for Darley and Latané (1970): Bystander intervention was inspired, in part, by learning of the brutal murder of Kitty Genovese. Or a finding originally obtained in the laboratory can be given external validation through further naturalistic research. This is true of Glass and Singer's (1972) research on the effects of unpredictable noise, which was extended by Cohen and his colleagues (1980; in press) in their studies of the impact of aircraft noise on schoolchildren.

One bonus of this trend of conducting research in applied settings is that such research often has important implications for public policy. What we discover from studies of crowding, for example, could save many millions of dollars of public funds that might otherwise be spent on poorly designed public housing. Social psychological research has a history of influencing social policy. A prime example is the landmark Supreme Court decision in *Brown* v. *Board of Education* (1954), which was influenced, in part, by social-science research. In this decision, the Supreme Court maintained that segregation deprived minority group children of their rights to equal educational opportunities. The Court argued that separate but equal educational facilities generate "a feeling of inferiority as to their status in the community that may affect their hearts and minds in a way unlikely ever to be undone. . . . We conclude that in the field of public education the doctrine 'separate but equal' has no place. Separate educational facilities are inherently unequal" (1954).

Social scientists contributed to the *Brown* decision both by testifying in court and by filing a brief with the Court that summarized the body of social psychological knowledge at the time. One program of research that played an important role was that of Clark and Clark (1947), who had concluded from projective tests given to black children that discrimination and segregation harmed black children's self-esteem. Their results suggested that black children as young as three years old were already convinced of black inferiority, rejecting black dolls in favor of white ones, which they judged to be prettier and generally superior.

Many social psychologists have become enthusiastic about the prospect of using psychological research to formulate enlightened social policy. But what factors determine whether a particular study or program will be embraced by policy makers? One might think that this would depend on such factors as the quality of the research or the consistency of the results of several studies. Unfortunately, the picture may not be as optimistic as that. There is some evidence to suggest that a person's evaluation of a study is strongly influenced by whether the study is consistent with his or her beliefs or values. In an intriguing study by Lord, Ross, and Lepper (1979), college students who either strongly supported or strongly opposed capital punishment were asked to read two supposedly authentic research studies on the deterrent effects of capital punishment. The studies used different experimental designs: One compared the murder rates for states before and after adoption of capital punishment; the second compared murder rates during the same time period for states with or without capital punishment. Which of these studies do you think is methodologically superior? The study was counterbalanced so that half of the students were told that one type of study supported their position and the other opposed it, and the remaining subjects were told the reverse. Interestingly, subjects found whatever type of study supported their own position to be significantly "more convincing" and "better conducted" than the study that opposed their position. As Nisbett and Ross (1980) have indicated in summarizing the results of this and similar research: "supportive evidence was handled with kid gloves; opposing evidence was mauled" (p. 179). Unfortunately, this phenomenon may not be limited to college students' evaluations of research in a laboratory setting. Caplan, Morrison, and Stambaugh (1975) conducted 204 interviews on social-science research utilization and policy formation with people holding important positions in many governmental departments and agencies. The results revealed that policy makers routinely rejected policy-relevant information when the results contradicted what they considered to be true. Caplan and his associates concluded that those interested in the utilization of social-science research must find ways to increase the acceptability of counter-intuitive or unpopular findings. We must also find ways to enhance peoples' *awareness* of how their own values can shape their evaluation of research findings.

SUMMARY

1. Social pressure often induces us to **conform**, or to shift our opinions and actions to correspond to those of others. There are degrees of conformity, however; sometimes we merely comply, and at other times we actually embrace new values.

2. Research on **obedience**, defined as compliance with the commands of a person in authority, has shown that many of us are willing to obey orders even when our actions apparently harm other people. Although research on this subject remains controversial, Milgram's basic conclusion that we are often prone to destructive obedience has not been refuted.

3. Groups often come to change our attitudes by teaching us a new set of **norms**, a set of shared guidelines and standards. In the extreme instance, we may learn new values by being **brainwashed**, or subjected to intense efforts at persuasion, generally involving the threat of force. Brainwashing techniques seem to account for some of the power that certain religious cults have over their converts.

4. The roles we take within groups can be extremely powerful in changing our behavior, as Zimbardo's frightening mock-prison experiment demonstrated.

5. Being among others may enhance our ability to perform in some contexts, a phenomenon known as **social facilitation**. However, when small, cohesive groups collaborate on decisions, the result may be groupthink, which is characterized by distorted logic and denial of reality.

6. Aggression is a fundamental problem in human behavior. Freud and Lorenz have argued that our aggressive drives are innate, but social-learning theorists have demonstrated that aggression can also be learned through modeling.

7. Whether we act altruistically depends on our perception of events: the nature of the event, whether a few or many other people are present, the environment in which the event occurs, and so on.

8. Many helping efforts have been found to be unsuccessful. The work of the professional helper, especially, may lead to passivity on the part of the recipient, who may then be blamed for his or her misfortune. This has been identified as one factor in the "burnout" that professionals in the social services sometimes develop.

9. Environmental psychology focuses on the interrelationship of people and their surroundings; environmental psychologists have studied such stresses of modern life as noise and crowding.

10. Two new trends in psychology generally are a reliance on combining laboratory and naturalistic experiments and a tendency to draw insights from other disciplines.

Suggested readings

Aronson, E. *The social animal* (3rd ed.). San Francisco: W. H. Freeman, 1980.

Baron, R. *Human aggression*. New York: Plenum Press, 1977.

Bar-Tal, D. *Prosocial behavior: Theory and research*. Washington D.C.: Hemisphere, 1976.

Brown, R. *Social psychology*. New York: Free Press, 1965.

Darley, J., and Latané, B. *The unresponsive bystander: Why doesn't he help?* New York: Appleton-Century-Crofts, 1970.

Hollander, E., and Hunt, R. *Current perspectives in social psychology* (4th ed.). New York: Oxford University Press, 1976.

Kaufmann, H. *Aggression and altruism, A psychological analysis*. New York: Holt, Rinehart and Winston, 1970.

Lorenz, K. *On aggression*. New York: Harcourt Brace Jovanovich, 1966.

MacCauley, J., and Berkowitz, L. (Eds.). *Altruism and helping behavior: Social psychological studies of some antecedents and consequences*. New York: Academic Press, 1970.

Glossary

The boldface number after each entry refers to the page number(s) on which the term is defined in the text.

absolute threshold The minimum stimulus necessary to produce a specific sensation. **107**

action potential An abrupt change in a cell's polarity which temporarily makes the cell interior positive and the cell exterior negative. **78**

actor-observer bias A common difference in attributions in which we tend to attribute our own behavior to environmental causes, whereas observers tend to attribute it to some enduring personality trait. **562**

adrenals A pair of endocrine glands located above the kidneys that affect the body's reaction to stress as well as producing sex hormones and numerous other hormonelike chemicals. **82**

affective disorders Psychological disorders characterized by disturbances of mood, such as depression. **490**

afterimage A sensory impression that lasts after removal of the stimulus that caused it. **116**

algorithm A precisely stated set of rules that usually works for solving problems of a particular type. **217**

altered state of consciousness Any qualitative alteration in mental functioning, such that a person feels that his or her consciousness is distinctively different from the way it ordinarily functions. **375**

amnesia The partial or total forgetting of past experience after a stressful experience such as an automobile accident or a battle. **490**

amygdala One of three interrelated structures of the limbic system; the others are the hippocampus and the septal area. **86**

anal stage According to Freud, the second psychosexual stage (occurring from about one and one-half to three years of age) during which bowel control is accomplished and pleasure is focused on the function of elimination. **412**

anterograde amnesia A form of amnesia that affects memory only for new events; things that were learned before the condition started are recalled perfectly. **196**

antianxiety drugs Commonly known as "minor" tranquilizers, these drugs reduce excitability and cause drowsiness. **531**

antidepressant drugs Mood regulating drugs effective in treating certain types of depression; known as the tricyclics because of their three-ringed molecular structure. **533**

antipsychotic drugs Major tranquilizers, used to alleviate extreme symptoms of agitation and hyperactivity in psychotic patients. **532**

antisocial personality (sociopath) A self-interested person who behaves in a manner which shows little regard for rights or feelings of others, and who does so without guilt. **504**

anvil One of a set of three tiny, interconnected bones in the middle ear that transmit sound from the eardrum to the cochlea. **121**

anxiety A feeling of dread, apprehension, or fear, often coupled with feelings of confusion and physiological symptoms; according to Freud, a state which occurs when the ego loses its struggle to reconcile the divergent demands of the id, the superego, and reality. **486**

anxiety disorders The group of mental disorders that includes generalized anxiety and panic disorders, phobic disorders, and obsessive-compulsive disorders. **486**

applied science The deliberate use of research findings to solve some practical problem, or to improve the quality of human life. **10**

approach–avoidance conflicts According to Dollard and Miller, a conflict resulting from a situation where both attraction to and avoidance of a stimulus is experienced by an organism. This often occurs when a desirable response is associated with negative consequences. **417**

arithmetic mean The measure of central tendency derived by adding the scores and then dividing by the number of people who took the test. **50**

associative learning Learning that certain events are associated with one another. **145**

attachment The emotional bond of an infant to the mother or other caregiver. **258**

attitude A learned, enduring predisposition to respond to a given object in a consistently favorable or unfavorable way. **546**

auditory canal The tubular passage that extends from the opening of the outer ear to the eardrum. **121**

authoritarian personality The personality of an individual who shows rigid adherence to conventional values about authority and morality, as well as a preference for strong, antidemocratic leaders. **573**

autonomic nervous system The division of the peripheral nervous system that controls the visceral muscles (blood vessels, heart, intestines) and the glands. **74**

availability A heuristic involving the assessment of the probability of an event by the ease with which instances come to mind. **230**

aversive conditioning A therapeutic technique which attempts to reduce the frequency of a maladaptive response by pairing an aversive stimulus, such as a loud noise, with the natural stimulus that precedes the response, thereby making the natural stimulus itself become aversive. **516**

axons The long extensions of a neuron that transmit impulses away from the cell body. **75**

backward conditioning The reversal of the order in which the unconditioned stimulus is presented before the conditioned stimulus. **148**

basic science A quest for knowledge purely for its own sake. **10**

basilar membrane A membrane in the cochlea whose motion stimulates the auditory nerve. **122**

behavioral measures Objective, quantifiable measures of a subject's behavior. **46**

behavioristic and social learning approaches The methods of understanding personality that view the development and functioning of the personality as a set of learned responses, not as the result of psychic drives or the promptings of the unconscious. **406**

behaviorists Psychologists who stress the study of observable behavior and account for such behavior in terms of an association that the organism has learned in the past. **14**

behavior modification The conscious use of operant conditioning principles to change human behavior. **162**

behavior therapy The attempt to apply learning and other experimentally derived psychological principles to problem behavior. Basic to this therapy is the belief that the same principles govern all behaviors, normal or deviant. **514**

binocular disparity The difference between the retinal images of the two eyes. **131**

biofeedback The use of monitoring instruments to give a person a continuous flow of information about his or her own biological state. **389**

blind spot The area of the retina where the optic nerve leaves the eye and that is devoid of rods and cones. It is insensitive to light. **112**

brain lesion The void left by surgical destruction or removal of brain tissue. **97**

brain stem The knobby extension that the spinal cord forms at the point where it enters the skull. **84**

brainwashing An intense and determined effort, backed by pressure, to persuade people to change their opinions. **590**

burnout A syndrome among some service professionals characterized by loss of concern for clients, rationalizing failure by attributing it to clients, irritability and anger, and resistance to change. **605**

Cannon-Bard theory The theory that physiological arousal alone does not cause emotion, but is produced simultaneously with the subjective experience of emotion. **316**

cardinal trait According to G. Allport, a trait that directs a major portion of a person's behavior. **422**

case study Intensive investigation and in-depth analysis of a single individual. **46**

cell body (soma) The metabolic center of the neuron that provides the energy for neural activity. **75**

central fissure The separation between the frontal lobe and the parietal lobe of the brain. **87**

central nervous system (CNS) The ultimate control center of all human behavior, consisting of the brain and the spinal cord. **73–74**

central tendency A middle value of a set of scores. **50**

central traits According to G. Allport, an individual's characteristic ways of dealing with the world. **422**

cerebellum Located to the rear of the brain stem, it coordinates voluntary movement of the skeletal muscles and regulates physical balance. **85**

chaining Learning a sequence of operant behaviors which eventually ends in a primary reward. **167**

chromosomes Thread-shaped structures within the cell nucleus that carry the organism's genes. **240**

classical conditioning Also called Pavlovian conditioning, the repeated pairing of a neutral stimulus with a stimulus that evokes a reflex response until the previously neutral stimulus alone evokes the response. **146**

classically conditioned response Behavior that results when a neutral stimulus is repeatedly paired with another stimulus that evokes a reflex response, such as fear. **145**

client-centered therapy Carl Rogers' system of psychotherapy, based on the belief that the client is responsible for his or her own potential and self-actualization and which creates an atmosphere of acceptance and feedback to aid the client. **429**

clinical depression A severe and prolonged form of depression in which one lacks energy, loses one's appetite, sleeps poorly, and may abandon work and social activities. **491**

clinical psychologists Those with doctorates in clinical psychology who specialize in the diagnosis and treatment of behavior disorders. **510**

cochlea The coiled organ in the inner ear containing the receptors for hearing. **122**

cognitions In learning theory, patterns of thought that seem to contribute to maladaptive behavior. **479**

cognitive approach The psychological theory that in almost any learned association, important thought processes intervene between the stimulus and the response. **169**

cognitive consistency The reduction of the psychological discomfort caused by having two blatantly contradictory cognitions by modifying one of the beliefs. **550**

cognitive dissonance The theory advanced by L. Festinger that people are motivated by the need to achieve consistency between their attitudes and their behavior. **551**

cognitive restructuring A therapeutic technique in which a therapist identifies a patient's negative patterns of thought and tries to change them by revealing the irrationality of the beliefs. **520**

cognitive therapy A variation of cognitive restructuring therapy developed by Aaron Beck in which patients are questioned in such a way that they themselves discover the irrationality of their thoughts. **520**

compliance Seeming to outwardly yield to pressure while actually maintaining one's own opinions and beliefs. **582**

compulsion An act of irrational behavior that the person seems unable to control. **488**

concepts Mental constructs that enable a person to classify objects by the characteristics they share with other objects. **211**

concepts of conservation The understanding that materials stay the same even though their shape or spatial arrangement is altered. **249**

concrete-operational period The third of Piaget's periods of intellectual development (which usually comprises the elementary-school years), during which a child begins to deal with specific systems of operations but cannot think abstractly. **245**

concrete operations Logical operations that involve reversible transformations of concrete objects and events. **249**

conditioned response (CR) The response elicited by the conditioned stimulus after the process of conditioning. **147**

conditioned stimulus (CS) The stimulus which elicits a new response as a result of the conditioning process. **147**

cones Cells in the retina that are sensitive to color and that are used primarily for daytime vision. **112**

confabulation The manufacture of an item to replace one that cannot be retrieved from memory. **204**

conformity The tendency to shift one's opinions or actions to correspond with those of other people because of implicit or explicit social pressure. **580**

consciousness An awareness of the many thoughts, images, sensations, and emotions that flow through one's mind at any given moment. **373**

constituent A group of words that has a conceptual unity. **280**

contingency A perceived relationship between two stimuli such that the occurrence of one seems to depend on the occurrence of the other. **148**

continuity A Gestalt principle of organization proposing that items will be perceived as belonging together if they appear to form a single, uninterrupted pattern. **128**

continuous reinforcement schedule The providing of reinforcement each time the organism exhibits the desired behavior. **158**

control group In an experiment, subjects who experience all the same conditions as experimental subjects except the key factor the psychologist is evaluating. **39**

conventional stage According to Kohlberg, the stage in moral development during which a child adheres to rules to win the approval of others, and is inclined to follow the dictates of established authority. **266**

conversion disorders The loss of a sensory or motor function without organic impairment, usually following some traumatic event. **489**

cornea The tough, transparent outer covering of the lens and iris that admits light into the interior of the eye. **111**

corpus callosum The cable of nerve fibers that connects the two cerebral hemispheres and transmits information between them. **90**

correlational research A process used to find out the extent to which two variables are related when a true experiment is not feasible. **42**

correlation coefficient A numerical value calculated to indicate the strength and direction of the relationship between two variables. **42**

cortex The covering of gray matter of the cerebral hemispheres, in which much of the "higher-order" processing that occurs in the cerebral hemispheres is carried out. **87**

counseling psychologists Those who help individuals deal with mild problems of social and emotional adjustment. **27**

covert sensitization A behavior therapy technique that uses imagined unpleasant events as an aversive stimulus designed to make a natural stimulus of a maladaptive response also aversive. **516**

creative thinking Using the available information to generate a solution that is novel in one's experience. **214**

critical period A relatively restricted period of development in which an animal is especially susceptible to particular influences that may bring about enduring behavior changes or effects; in relation to language learning, a period early in life during which a human being has a special facility for language learning. **287**

cross-sectional study A study in which the population is divided into subgroups using certain criteria, the subgroups are randomly sampled, and the members of each sample are then tested, surveyed, or observed. **49**

decay theory The view that memories simply fade away with the passage of time if they are not renewed through periodic use. **202**

decibel A unit of acoustical intensity. **120**

defense mechanisms According to Freudian theory, a range of mental strategies that the ego uses to reduce anxiety. **410**

déjà vu The distinct feeling that something is familiar even though we have never encountered it before. **184**

demand characteristics In an experiment, clues felt by the subject to demand certain "correct" responses. **58**

dendrites The short, branched extensions of a neuron that carry neural impulses toward the cell body. **75**

dependent variable A factor that may or may not change when the independent variable is manipulated. **40**

depressant A chemical that suppresses nerve impulses. **392**

depth of processing view The theory that we have only one memory system and that the observed differences between short-term and long-term memory are due to how shallowly or deeply we process information. **197**

depth perception The ability to judge how far away an object is. **130**

descriptive statistics Statistical methods used to reduce a mass of data to a form that is more manageable and understandable. **50**

developmental psychology The study and explanation of the systematic changes that occur in human beings throughout the life cycle, from conception to death. **24**

dichotic listening A technique developed by E. C. Cherry, involving the simultaneous input of different information into each ear. **180**

discrimination training A procedure used to teach an animal to respond to only a specific stimulus by presenting similar stimuli which will not elicit a reward. **164**

discriminative stimuli The stimuli which elicit rewards in discrimination training. **164**

dispersion The degree of scatter among the individual scores of a set of scores. **52**

displacement According to psychoanalytic theory, a defense mechanism that involves the transfer of unacceptable feelings from their appropriate target to a "safer" object. **411**

dissociation A split in consciousness whereby certain thoughts, feelings, and behaviors operate independently from others. **385**

dissociative disorders Psychological disorders that involve the splitting off of a part of the personality so that the victim's memory or identity is disturbed. **490**

DNA (deoxyribonucleic acid) An organic molecule composed of subunits of chemical structures whose sequence determines the genetic information carried by the chromosome. **241**

double bind A state of confusion that occurs when an individual is exposed to contradictory communications simultaneously. **480**

double-blind technique A procedure in which neither the experimenter nor the subjects know who has been assigned to the experimental group or who is acting as a control. **58**

dream interpretation A technique used in psychoanalytically oriented therapy in which the hidden meaning of a dream can be brought to light, and unconscious wishes, fantasies, and conflicts can be explored. **512**

drug Any substance that can alter the functioning of a biological system. **391**

dual memory view The theory that there exists a separate long-term and short-term memory. **195**

eardrum (tympanic membrane) A membrane between the outer and inner ear that responds to changes in air pressure by moving in and out. **121**

educational psychologists Researchers who study all psychological aspects of the learning process. **25**

effector cells Cells specialized for contracting muscles and for stimulating glandular secretions. **73**

ego According to Freud, the part of the psyche that handles transactions between the external environment and the demands of the id and the superego based on the reality principle. **409**

ego analysis In psychoanalysis, the strengthening of the ego to enable the patient to control his or her environment and social relationships. **514**

eidetic images Visual images of incredible accuracy and clarity of detail. **188**

electroconvulsive therapy (ECT) A form of biological therapy used to treat mania, depression, and schizophrenia, in which an electric current is passed through the brain, causing a convulsion which is therapeutic. **534**

electroencephalogram (EEG) A device that records the electrical activity of the brain by electrodes placed on the skull. **375**

emotions States of feeling that can affect behavior and that are often accompanied by physiological changes. **310**

encounter group A form of group therapy emphasizing personal growth and improved interpersonal interactions through intensive experience in a small group that encourages openness and sensitivity. **527**

endocrine glands Those glands that produce hormones and secrete them into the bloodstream. **81**

endorphins Morphinelike neurotransmitters whose role in schizophrenia is being studied. **503**

engineering psychology The study of the relationship between human beings and machines. **24**

environmental psychology The study of the relationship between human beings and their physical and social surroundings. **27**

evoked potential The pattern of electrical activity in the brain caused by a stimulus. **99**

excitement phase The first phase of sexual response, involving accelerated heartbeat and respiration, blood flow into the genitals, erection of the penis or swelling of the clitoris, and erection of the nipples in both men and women. **355**

exocrine glands Those glands which secrete their products, such as saliva, tears, and sweat, through ducts to the body's surface or into body cavities. **81**

experiment A situation in which the researcher can control conditions and variables and so rule out all influences on people's behavior except the factors being examined. **38**

experimental group In an experiment, subjects who experience the experimental condition. **39**

experimental psychologists Psychologists who use experimentation to gather data on those behavioral processes shared by many animal species. **20**

extinction The slow weakening and eventual disappearance of a conditioned response. **152**

factor analysis The process of identifying underlying sources of consistency, which is useful in the study of personality. **422**

family-systems therapy Psychotherapy which stresses the importance of altering family roles and patterns of communication that maintain maladaptive behavior. **521**

figure The section of the perceptual field which represents objects. **129**

first-order conditioning Classical conditioning in which a conditioned stimulus is followed by a primary reinforcer. **167**

fixation The tendency to cling to a commonplace interpretation of a problem, despite the fact that it is not helpful in a particular situation; in psychoanalysis, a state of arrested development where an individual remains "locked" in a particular psychological battle and expresses this conflict symbolically. **215**

fixed-interval schedule A partial reinforcement schedule in which a reward is given for the first correct response after a certain time interval. **159**

fixed-ratio schedule A partial reinforcement schedule in which a reward is given after a specified number of responses. **158**

forensic psychology The application of psychological principles to problems of law enforcement and the courts. **27**

formal-operational period The last of Piaget's periods of intellectual development (from adolescence through adulthood), during which a person learns to think simultaneously about many systems of operations and to think hypothetically. **245**

fovea A small depression near the center of the retina, containing cones but no rods, that is the point of highest visual acuity. **113**

free association A psychoanalytic technique for exploring the unconscious through a patient's unrestrained expression of thoughts that occur spontaneously. **407**

free recall The recounting of memorized material in no particular order. **195**

frequency The number of compression-rarefaction cycles that occur per second. The frequency of a soundwave corresponds to the pitch we hear. **120**

frequency distribution The number of instances of each score. **50**

frontal lobe The portion of each cerebral hemisphere that is concerned with motor activities and speech. **88**

frustration Interference with any goal-directed behavior. **599**

frustration-aggression hypothesis John Dollard's theory that aggression is always a consequence of frustration, and frustration always leads to some form of aggression. **599**

fugue A total abdication of one's home and identity. People suffering from this disorder may be absent from their home for hours or years, and recall nothing of what happened in the fugue state. **490**

functional fixedness The tendency to view an object as being used only for its customary function. **215–6**

functionalism The view, influenced by Darwin's theories and expounded chiefly by William James, that mental life is a stream of consciousness and the mind's activities are more important than its structure. **17**

fundamental attribution error The tendency to overestimate the role of dispositional rather than situational factors in behavior. **561**

gender roles The patterns of behavior that one's society teaches as appropriate for masculinity and femininity. **261**

general adaptation syndrome As outlined by Hans Selye, the set of physiological responses that is evoked by unusually demanding stress. **326**

generalization gradient The curve appearing in the graph of responses from a discrimination training exercise, showing the number of responses per each stimulus. **164**

genes Ultramicroscopic particles within the cell nucleus that are the basic units for the transmission of hereditary characteristics. **240**

genital stage According to Freud, the fifth psychosexual stage (occurring from puberty on), during which the sexual focus shifts from autoeroticism to sexual intercourse. **413**

Gestalt psychology The approach to psychology that maintains that what emerges from perception of individual pieces of information is a whole that is greater than the sum of its parts. **14**

gestalts Meaningful, unified perceptual wholes. **127**

Gestalt therapy Psychotherapy that emphasizes the present and attempts to make a client whole by ridding him or her of defenses, increasing awareness, and releasing pent-up feelings. **524**

glia Cells that hold neurons in place, carry nutrients to them, repair and protect them, and aid in the propagation of impulses. **76**

gonads Glands that secrete sex hormones. The female gonads are the ovaries, which secrete estrogen and progesterone. The male gonads are the testes, which secrete testosterone. **82**

grammar The structural rules that speakers of a language share. **279**

gray matter The nonmyelinated axons, dendrites, and cell bodies of the nervous system. **79**

ground The part of the perceptual field that represents space between objects. **129**

group A collection of people who regularly interact with one another in a structured way, are oriented toward specific goals, and who have a feeling of group identity and interdependence. **588**

grouping The associating together of sensory data; a Gestalt principle. **128**

habituated Accustomed to a stimulus, so that it no longer produces an orienting reflex. **145**

hair cell A cell, containing hairlike projections, that is a receptor for hearing in the organ of Corti. **122**

hallucinogens (psychedelic drugs) Drugs that produce unusual and exaggerated mental effects, especially in cognition and perception. **398**

hammer One of a set of three tiny, interconnected bones in the middle ear that transmit sound from the eardrum to the cochlea. **121**

happiness A positive, enduring state that consists of positive feelings about the self and the world and that includes both peace of mind and active pleasure. **332**

health and health care A field in which psychologists' roles are expanding due to the increased recognition of psychological factors in illness. **28**

heritability The extent to which an observed individual variation of a trait can be attributed to genetic differences among members of a particular population in a particular environment. **451**

heuristic In problem solving, a strategy that points to a particular solution without testing all possible operations. **218**

hierarchy of needs Maslow's concept that all humans face a series of needs in life, and that needs at the lower levels must be met before the person can go on to fulfill those at the next highest level. **431**

hippocampus One of three interrelated structures of the limbic system; the others are the septal area and the amygdala. **86**

histogram A graph arranged so as to show frequency distribution, the number of instances of each score. **50**

homeostasis The body's automatic tendency to maintain its internal equilibrium regardless of changing external conditions. **341**

hormones Chemical substances produced by the endocrine system which travel through the bloodstream and regulate physiological activities. **81**

humanistic-existential therapies Those therapies that view psychological treatment as an experience that should lead to personal growth, enabling a client to drop unfulfilling patterns of behavior and to choose new ones instead. **523**

hypothalamus Located below the thalamus, it regulates the body's internal environment, and acts to maintain homeostasis. **85**

hypothesis A proposition or belief that one sets out to test. **39**

id According to Freud, the impulsive and unconscious part of the psyche which operates via the pleasure principle towards the gratification of instinctual drives. **409**

identification According to Freud, a method of reducing the anxiety produced by the Oedipus and Electra conflicts by categorizing oneself as psychologically similar to the parent of one's own sex, and therefore adopting the parent's gender role as one's own. **262**

illusion A perception not in accord with the true characteristics of an object or event. **131**

imprinting The process by which birds form attachments to other organisms or objects during an early critical period. This attachment is somewhat resistant to later modification. **287**

incentives Expectations of receiving a reward that stimulate or maintain goal-directed behavior. **342**

incubation A period of rest from problem solving, which encourages mental flexibility. **221**

independent variable A factor that the experimenter deliberately manipulates. **40**

industrial psychologists Psychologists who study work and personnel problems in business and industry. **23**

inferential statistics Statistical methods used to conclude whether the data clearly support one's original hypothesis. **55**

insight A sudden understanding of the critical relationships of a problem. **222**

intelligence quotient (IQ) A measure of an individual's mental development obtained by dividing a person's mental age (the average age of children who obtain a particular score on an intelligence test) by a person's chronological age and multiplying the quotient by 100. **443**

intensity The measure of amount of energy or sensory input. In light, the intensity is the major determinant of brightness. In hearing, intensity corresponds to loudness. **111**

interference The fading of memory due to the inevitable confusion caused by the subsequent encountering of similiar events. **202**

internalization Incorporation of society's values into the self or personality to such an extent that violation of these standards produces a sense of guilt. **261**

interneurons The neurons that connect neurons to each other, and integrate the activities of the sensory and motor neurons. **76**

introspection Wilhelm Wundt's technique of looking beyond the immediate content of one's own thoughts, and focusing instead on the constituent elements of consciousness. **13**

iris A ring of pigmented tissue that gives the eye its color and expands and contracts to control the amount of light that enters the retina. **111**

James-Lange theory The view of William James and Carl Lange that the perception of bodily changes produces the actual experience of emotion. **314**

jump stand A conditioning device invented by Karl Lashley in which a rat is forced (by a puff of air) to jump through one of two doors. **156**

key word system A mnemonic device involving the memorization of a list of simple words that can be visualized easily. **186-7**

latent content In psychoanalysis, the symbolic meanings of dreams that expose unconscious conflicts. **381**

latency stage According to Freud, the fourth stage of psychosexual development (occurring from age five until the start of puberty), during which sexual impulses are repressed while the child learns social and cognitive skills. **412**

latent learning Learning in which knowledge of a new behavior is not demonstrated until an incentive to do so arises. **170**

lateral fissure The top boundary of the temporal lobe of the brain. **88**

lateralized The term used to describe the human brain, in which different sides control different behavioral functions. **285**

law of effect Thorndike's theory that responses that lead to satisfying consequences will be strengthened and are therefore likely to be repeated, whereas responses that lead to unsatisfactory consequences will be weakened and are unlikely to be repeated. **154**

learning A relatively permanent change in performance potential that arises from experience. **145**

lens In vision, a transparent structure that covers the iris and the pupil and changes its shape in order to focus images on the retina. **111**

limbic system A set of neural structures bordering the cerebral cortex that are important in emotion, motivation, and some visceral functions. **86**

linear perspective The impression of depth created by the convergence of parallel lines. **131**

linguistic competence A person's intuitive grasp of the rules for constructing grammatical sentences. **279**

linguistic performance The application of implicit knowledge of grammar during speaking or listening. **279**

linguistic relativity hypothesis Whorf's notion that language heavily influences thought. **295**

linguistic universals Features found in all languages as a result of shared characteristics of thought. **296**

longitudinal study A study in which the same group of people are examined over a number of years. **49**

long-term memory The storage of information for an indefinite period of time to be used over and over again. **178**

mania A prolonged state of elation and feverish activity. **492**

manic-depressive disorder A psychological disorder characterized by the episodic nature of extremes of mood. **492**

manifest content In psychoanalysis, dream material that is recalled and reported by the dreamer; the surface content of the dream. **380**

maze A complex path leading to food or water; used to carry out operant conditioning in animals. **156**

means-end analysis A heuristic by which means are sought that will move the problem solver closer to the goal. **220**

median The score that falls in the exact middle of a distribution of numbers arranged from highest to lowest. **50**

medical model The theoretical perspective on abnormal behavior that considers psychological disorders to be similar to physical illnesses; each disorder is thought to have a specific organic cause, producing a set of symptoms. **476**

meditation A retraining of attention that induces an altered state of consciousness. **387**

medulla The part of the brain stem that controls autonomic activities and facial movements. **84**

meiosis The process of germ cell division resulting in germ cells with half the number of chromosomes present in normal body cells. **240**

mental retardation As defined by Grossman in 1977, it is significantly subaverage general intellectual functioning existing concurrently with deficits in adaptive behavior, and manifested during the developmental period. **446**

mental set The inclination to repeat a solution that has worked in the past. **221**

metacognition The ability to monitor one's own thoughts. **253**

method of loci A mnemonic device involving the association of items to be remembered with a series of places, or loci, that are already firmly fixed in memory. **186**

midbrain A small structure of the brain stem that contains centers for visual and auditory reflexes. **84**

Minnesota Multiphasic Personality Inventory (MMPI) An objective personality test, designed to provide a detailed list of a subject's personality traits based on his or her answers to a series of over 500 statements. **462**

mnemonic devices Various techniques that improve recall ability, including method of loci, key word system, and eidetic images. **186**

mode The score that is most frequently obtained in a distribution. **50**

modeling The process by which someone learns a new behavior by observing other people perform that behavior. **519**

morphemes The smallest combination of speech sounds that have meaning in a given language. **278**

morphology The study and description of how sounds form basic units of speech, and how these basic units form complex words. **277**

motion parallax The apparent movement of stationary objects that occurs when the position of the observer changes. Near objects seem to move in wider arcs than far objects. **131**

motivated forgetting The forgetting of information because we want to, either consciously or unconsciously. **203**

motivation Those variables that arouse, sustain, and direct behavior toward attainment of some goal. **339**

motor neurons (efferent neurons) The neurons that carry signals from the brain and spinal cord to the muscles and glands. **76**

multiple personality An extreme form of dissociation in which a person's personality structure divides into two or more complete behavior organizations, each well defined and distinct from the others. **490**

myelin sheath A fatty, whitish substance that wraps around an axon. **79**

nasal passages Cavities of the nose that are lined with the olfactory membranes. **124**

natural concepts Categories used in daily thought to classify objects. **213**

naturalistic observation The study of subjects in a natural setting without interference or distraction from the investigator. **45**

negative correlation The relationship between two variables in which a high rank on one is accompanied by a low rank on the other. **42**

negative reinforcement Reinforcement that strengthens a response because the response removes some painful or unpleasant stimulus or enables the organism to avoid it. **155**

nerves Bundles of neural fibers and connective and supportive tissues that transmit electrochemical impulses from one part of the body to another. **74-5**

neurons Cells specialized for conducting signals from one part of the body to another; they connect receptor cells to effector cells and integrate their activities. They are also called nerve cells. **73**

neurosis A mental disorder that produces abnormal symptoms, but, unlike the more severe psychosis, affects only part of the personality. **477**

neurotransmitters Chemical substances which diffuse across synapses and activate receptor sites on adjacent cells. **79**

noise Irrelevant, competing stimuli that serve to limit our sensory capacities. **107**

normal curve A line graph of a symmetrical distribution having a bell-shaped curve. **51**

normal distribution A distribution showing a normal curve. **51**

normative distribution (norm) The average performance levels for a test for a given group, usually a group which is considered representative of the population which will be given the test. **442**

norms A set of shared guidelines and standards. **589**

obedience Compliance with the explicit commands of a person in authority. **584**

object concept (concept of object permanence) According to Piaget, the capability, which develops during the sensorimotor period, to understand that an object exists even when it is no longer perceived. **247**

observational learning, imitative learning, or **modeling** The process of learning how to act by watching the behavior of others. **171**

obsession A recurring irrational thought, one that the victim recognizes as senseless and tries to suppress. **488**

occipital lobe A rear portion of each cerebral hemisphere, concerned with the reception and analysis of visual information. **89**

Oedipus conflict According to Freud, a boy's desire to possess his mother sexually, manifested in the phallic stage and thereafter repressed. The female form of the conflict is the Electra conflict. **262**

olfaction The sense of smell. **124**

olfactory membranes Membranes that line the roof of the nasal passages, and contain many receptor cells. **124**

olfactory nerves The nerves along which nerve impulses travel from the receptor cells in the olfactory membranes to the brain. **124**

operant behavior Action that an organism emits spontaneously, of its own accord. **154**

operant conditioning Learning to either make or withhold a particular response because of its positive or negative consequences. **154**

operantly conditioned response A response resulting from a learned association between a particular action and a desirable consequence. **145**

opponent-process theory The theory that three different systems, composed of three types of cells, are responsible for color vision: In one system, some cells are stimulated by red and inhibited by green and others are stimulated by green and inhibited by red. In another system, yellow and blue similarly act in opposition to each other. The other system is achromatic and sensitive to brightness. **116**

optic chiasma The point at which the nerves from each retina meet and then split to opposite sides of the cerebral cortex. **113**

optic nerve The nerve that carries visual information from the eye to the brain for interpretation. **112**

oral stage According to Freud, the first psychosexual stage (occurring during the first eighteen months of life) in which pleasure is focused on the mouth's activities. **412**

organizational psychologists Psychologists who study the relationship between the behavior of individuals in large organizations, such as businesses, and the efficiency of the organization. **23**

organ of Corti A structure of the cochlea containing hair cells that are the receptors for hearing. **122**

orgasm The peak of sexual response, involving involuntary contractions of the muscles around the genitals, the return of blood into the bloodstream, and ejaculation in men. **356**

orienting reflex A response that involves a whole chain of activities—looking, listening, touching, sniffing—designed to ascertain what a new stimulus is about. **145**

ossicles Three small bones (hammer, anvil, and stirrup) in the middle ear that transmit sound from the eardrum to the cochlea. **121**

oval window A membrane-covered opening between the middle ear and the inner ear that transmits sound from the ossicles to the cochlea. **121**

overregularization The erroneous extension of a grammatical rule to instances where it does not apply. **292**

parasympathetic nervous system The division of the autonomic nervous system that dominates under conditions of relaxation and tends to conserve the body's energy. **74**

parietal lobe A portion of the cerebral hemisphere concerned with skin senses and the sense of body position. **88**

partial overlap The illusion, created when one object partially blocks the view of another object, that the second object is farther away. **131**

partial reinforcement schedule Reinforcing a desired behavior only part of the time. **158**

participant modeling A therapeutic technique which has the therapist serve as a model by performing activities feared by a patient and then guiding the client through a series of steps culminating in the same activity. **519**

participant observation A form of naturalistic observation in which a psychologist joins an existing group in order to record thoughts and feelings accessible to only group members. **45**

perceptual constancy The tendency to perceive objects as having certain constant or stable properties. **130**

perceptual set A tendency to ignore certain types of stimuli, while being very sensitive to others. **134**

peripheral nervous system (PNS) The part of the nervous system that conveys signals from the sensory receptors to the central nervous system and transmits messages back out to the muscles and glands. **74**

personality The set of characteristics and tendencies that determine the individuality of a person's responses to a variety of environmental circumstances. **405**

personality disorders Deep-seated maladaptive patterns of relating to others that cause distress either to the victim, those around the victim, or both. **504**

personality psychologists Psychologists who measure and explain individual differences in behavior. **22**

personnel psychology A subfield of industrial psychology that studies and evaluates the performance of employees. **24**

persuasive communications Messages consciously intended to persuade or to promote attitude change. **548**

phallic stage According to Freud, the third psychosexual stage (occurring during the third to fifth or sixth year of life), during which pleasure is focused on the genitals and the Electra and Oedipus complexes arise. **412**

phenomenological approaches Methods of understanding personality that emphasize the potential of human beings for growth, creativity, and spontaneity, and that stress the importance of an individual's unique perception of the world. **406**

phenomenology An individual's unique perception of the world. **428**

phobia An excessive fear of particular objects or situations, often with no basis in reality. **487**

phonemes A class of slightly varying sounds that speakers of a language perceive as linguistically similar. **277**

phonology The study and description of the sounds that make up a language. **277**

phrenology The study of character by assessing the shape of the skull, which, according to nineteenth-century anatomist Franz Joseph Gall, conformed to the shape of the brain beneath. **72**

physiological measures Measures that provide objective, quantitative data on phenomena associated with particular psychological states, such as sleep, that are difficult to assess in other ways. **47**

physiological psychologists Those psychologists concerned with the relationships between physiological activities and mental processes. **21**

pinna The projection of skin-covered cartilage visible on the outside of the head, through which sound enters the outer ear. **121**

pituitary gland A small endocrine gland at the base of the brain which controls a wide range of bodily functions, and which has been called the "master gland." **81**

placebo A substance that has no physiological effect. **56**

plateau phase The second phase of sexual response, involving the full engorgement of the genitals, the retraction of the clitoris into its hood for women, and the enlargement of the glans of the penis for men. **356**

pleasure principle According to psychoanalytic theory, the principle of mental functioning of the id whereby painful tensions are reduced by gratification of instinctual drives without regard for logic, reality, or morality. **409**

polarized Describing cells that are negatively charged inside and positively charged outside. **78**

pons The structure of the brain which transmits motor information from the higher brain areas and spinal cord to the cerebellum, and is vital in integrating movements between the right and left sides of the body. **84**

positive correlation The relationship between two variables in which a high rank on one is accompanied by a high rank on the other. **42**

positive reinforcement Reinforcement that strengthens a response because the response is followed by a positive or pleasant stimulus. **155**

postconventional stage According to Kohlberg, the final stage in moral development, during which a person recognizes that universal ethical principles can transcend specific societal laws. Failure to adhere to these principles brings self-condemnation. **266**

preconventional stage According to Kohlberg, the early stage in moral development during which a child adheres to the rules of society because he or she fears the consequences of breaking them. **266**

prejudice A negative and inflexible attitude based on erroneous or incomplete information. **569**

preoperational period The second of Piaget's periods of intellectual development (from age two through six) during which a child understands complex events but cannot use mental operations or coordinate thoughts into logical systems. **245**

primacy effect The principle that information received early in a series tends to outweigh later information. **556**

primary drive A state of physiological tension that arises automatically due to factors that disrupt the body's normal internal balance. **341**

primary reinforcer The reinforcer that establishes and maintains a conditioned response. **165**

principle of mass action Karl S. Lashley's term for the fact that almost all activity involves many parts of the brain. **100**

principle of multiple control The fact that a specific part of the brain is likely to be involved in the performance of many types of behavior. **100**

principle of reinforcement Skinner's name for Thorndike's law of effect, in which positive and negative rewards are seen as the basic forces controlling human behavior. **154**

proactive interference The fading of memory that occurs when material learned earlier interferes with recall of material learned later. **202**

probability The likelihood of a particuliar event or response occurring, calculated mathematically. **55**

processes Fibers that branch out from the cell body; include **dendrites** and **axons**. **75**

program evaluation A field of psychology that involves the measuring of the variables that go into particular programs, especially in government, and the results they bring about. **29**

programmed instruction Instruction which emphasizes reinforcement by providing the student with immediate feedback for every response, and by not allowing the student to proceed until each subject has been fully understood. **161-2**

projection According to psychoanalytic theory, a defense mechanism that involves the attribution of one's own objectionable impulses to other people. **411**

projective tests Tests in which personality characteristics are revealed by the way a subject responds to and interprets ambiguous material; the best known of these is the Rorschach Inkblot Test. **458**

propositions Unitary ideas that combine to yield the meaning of a sentence. **279**

proximity The principle of Gestalt psychology that stimuli close to each other will tend to be perceived as a group. **128**

psychiatric nurse A registered nurse who has specialized in psychiatric nursing as part of the nursing degree and is usually employed in a mental hospital. **510**

psychiatric social worker Someone who has an M.A. in social work and has specialized in psychiatric social work. **510**

psychiatrists Medical doctors who specialize in the diagnosis and treatment of mental disorders. **510**

psychoactive drugs Drugs that interact with the central nervous system to alter a person's mood, perception, and behavior. **391**

psychoanalysis Freudian psychotherapy which employs techniques such as transference and free association to unlock the thoughts and feelings of the unconscious. **408**

psychoanalyst Usually a psychiatrist (although sometimes a lay person or psychologist) who has had advanced training in psychoanalysis and who has been psychoanalyzed as part of that training. **510**

psychoanalytic approaches Various methods of understanding personality that emphasize childhood experiences and the role of the unconscious. **406**

psychodynamic behavior theory The theory of personality developed by Dollard and Miller in which learning principles are used to explain many of Freud's concepts. **417**

psychological reactance The tendency of people to increase their support for an activity or idea when they feel threatened by attempts to change that idea or behavior. **554**

psychology The study of behavior and mental processes. **6**

psychopharmacology The study of the relationship between drugs and behavior. **21**

psychosis A severe mental disorder marked by a generalized failure of functioning in all areas of a person's life. **477**

psychosurgery The removal or destruction of parts of the brain for the purpose of altering behavior. **313**

psychotherapy A systematic series of interactions between a therapist who is trained to aid in solving psychological problems and a person who is troubled. **509**

puberty The period marking the start of adolescence during which a person's reproductive organs become capable of functioning and secondary sex characteristics develop. **268**

punishment A consequence that results in the suppression (decrease in frequency) of the behavior that brought it about. **154**

pupil The opening in the center of the eye through which light enters and travels to the retina. **111**

quasi-experimental design A design that approximates, but does not meet, the requirements of a true experimental design because subjects cannot be randomly assigned to conditions. **41**

radical behaviorism Skinner's brand of stimulus-response psychology, which posits that humans do not possess free will but instead are shaped and controlled by events in the environment, particularly rewards and punishments. **418**

random sample A sample in which every member of the population has an equal chance of being included. **37**

range The difference between the highest and lowest scores of a set of scores. **50**

reaction formation According to psychoanalytic theory, a defense mechanism which involves the replacement of an unacceptable impulse with its direct opposite. **411**

reaction range An organism's unique array of possible responses to variations in its environment as determined by its genetic makeup. **451**

reality principle The functioning of the ego which confronts the need for gratification of instinctual drives with the realistic demands of the environment, and thereby modifies or delays gratification based on a concern for the safety of the individual. **409**

recall The retrieval of specific pieces of information from long-term memory, usually guided by retrieval cues. **184**

receptor cells Cells embedded in the sense organs that are sensitive to particular forms of physical energy and capable of initiating a neural impulse. **73**

recognition Retrieval from long-term memory in which a specific stimulus causes recognition due to previous memorization. **184**

reference group A group with which a person associates or identifies himself or herself, and to which that person turns for guidance in formulating values, beliefs, and attitudes. **589**

reflex arc The set of connections between neurons that links a sensory input to a motor response. **76**

reflex behavior Behavior produced involuntarily by a specific stimulus. **146**

regression A defense mechanism that attempts to evade anxiety by having the troubled individual act in ways characteristic of an earlier period of life. **411**

rehearsal The conscious repetition of information in an effort to remember it, usually involving speech. **181**

reinforcement (reward) A consequence that produces a repetition (increase in frequency) of the behavior that caused it. **154**

relative size Of two objects thought to be the same size, the one that casts the smaller retinal image is perceived to be farther away; a monocular depth cue. **131**

reliability An essential criterion in determining the value of a test. A test is reliable if it yields, upon repetition, similar results for different parts of the test, for scoring by different judges, and for the same test administered to the same person at two different times. **439**

REM sleep The stage of sleep where a person experiences rapid eye movement. Vivid dreaming appears to take place primarily during this stage. **377**

representativeness A heuristic by which the given information is matched with a stereotype. **228**

representative sample A sample in which people known to possess specified characteristics are randomly selected in proportion to their numbers in the population as a whole. **37**

repression A defense mechanism against guilt and anxiety that involves the unconscious pushing back of unacceptable id impulses into the unconscious. **203**

reproductive thinking The direct application of previous knowledge to a new situation. **214**

resistance Attempts by the therapy client to block treatment. **511**

resolution phase After a sexual peak, the body's gradual return to its normal, unstimulated state. Men require an additional rest period before they can respond again to sexual stimulation. **356**

respondent behavior A term for reflexes, emphasizing that they occur automatically in response to particular stimuli. **154**

resting potential The electrical imbalance that occurs across the cell membrane when a cell is polarized. **78**

reticular formation A complex network of neural fibers and cells that extends from the spinal cord to the thalamus, acting as a sentry system to the higher brain and also affecting the sleep-waking cycle. **85**

retina The light-sensitive, innermost coat of the eyeball. The retina is a predominantly neural structure consisting of several layers, including a layer of rods and cones. **112**

retroactive interference The fading of memory that occurs when information learned later interferes with information learned earlier. **202**

retrograde amnesia A form of amnesia in which the memory deficit involves only a specific segment of the past and does not affect the recollection of new events. **198**

rods Cells in the periphery of the retina that are sensitive to light of low intensity and that function in peripheral and nighttime vision. **112**

role enactment theory The view that hypnosis is not a special state of consciousness, but a special case of role playing. **386**

Rorschach Inkblot Test During this test, which was developed in 1921 by Hermann Rorschach, a subject's responses to ambiguous inkblots are studied for their emotional expression, their focus, and their recurring patterns. **458**

sample A selected segment of the available data, representative of the whole. **37**

scanning hypothesis The theory, proposed by William Dement, that rapid eye movements accompanying dreams may be due to the dreamer's ''watching'' the activity in the dream. **378**

schedule of reinforcement The way in which rewards are given for appropriate behavior. **158**

schizophrenia Any of a group of psychoses characterized by profound disturbances in thinking, inappropriate emotional reactions, and disturbed motor behavior. **497**

Scholastic Aptitude Test (SAT) A verbal and mathematical test developed by the College Entrance Examination Board and designed to measure ''aptitude for college studies.'' **445**

school psychology An applied field of psychology which is concerned with behavior in the school environment. **26**

secondary drive A state of physiological tension that arises due to learned responses to stimuli. **341**

secondary or conditioned reinforcer A stimulus that signals that the primary reinforcer is on its way. **165**

second-order conditioning Classical conditioning in which a second conditioned stimulus is repeatedly paired with the first so that it eventually produces by itself the conditioned response. **167**

selective attention The brain's ability to damp down some information entering a given sensory channel while directing attention to other information entering the same channel. **180**

self-actualization According to Rogers, the striving for the fulfillment of one's own needs and potential. **428**

self-fulfilling prophecy The phenomenon whereby investigators' expectations influence their findings. **57**

self-help groups Groups of people who share a particular problem and meet to discuss it among themselves, without the active involvement of professional therapists. **527**

self-instructional training Donald Meichelbaum's version of cognitive therapy in which clients make a conscious effort to think rational and positive thoughts in stressful situations. **521**

self-serving bias The tendency of an individual to take credit for his or her good deeds and to attribute his or her bad deeds to situational factors. **562**

sensation The response to a stimulus by a sensory organ. **106**

sensorimotor period The first of Piaget's periods of intellectual development (from birth to about two years), during which an infant learns through overt action to function in his or her environment but lacks an understanding of what he or she is doing. **245**

sensory gating The way in which the brain selectively turns up one kind of sensory input while turning down others. **180**

sensory memory The momentary lingering of sensory information we experience after a stimulus has been removed. **177**

sensory neurons (afferent neurons) The neurons that carry information from the sense organs to the brain and spinal cord. **75**

septal area One of three interrelated structures of the limbic system; the others are the hippocampus and amygdala. **86**

serial position curve A graph showing the results of a free recall experiment repeated many times. **195–6**

sexual dysfunction Any problem that prevents a person from successfully engaging in sexual relations or from reaching orgasm druring sex. **356**

shaping A method developed by B. F. Skinner in which an animal is reinforced for displaying closer and closer approximations of a desired behavior. **157**

short-term memory The conscious retention of things we have recently encountered, storing very little and for very short periods. **178**

similarity A Gestalt principle of organization proposing that similar items will be perceived as belonging with each other more than with equally near but different items. **128**

simplicity The concept that simple patterns are more easily perceived than complex ones. **129**

single-blind technique A procedure in which the experimenter knows who is in the experimental group and who is in the control group but the subjects do not. **58**

Skinner box (operant chamber) A box that provides a controlled setting in which an animal may be trained to press a bar for a reward, such as food. **156**

social facilitation The phenomenon that occurs when a person's performance improves because of the presence of others. **593**

socialization The processes through which people learn to behave in a manner appropriate to the values and roles of their culture. **261**

social learning theory The belief of cognitive psychologists that a great deal of learning is accomplished by observation, often in the absence of reinforcement. **171**

social psychologists Psychologists who study the interactions between individuals and groups. **23**

somatic nervous system The division of the peripheral nervous system that controls the skeletal muscles. **74**

somatoform disorders A physical malfunction caused by psychological distress. **489**

source amnesia The recall of certain facts without remembering the context in which they were learned. **385**

source traits According to Cattell, the fundamental elements of personality which underlie all surface traits and give rise to their expression. **423**

spontaneous recovery The reappearance of an extinguished response when an animal is returned to an experimental chamber. **161**

standard deviation The average extent to which all the scores in a particular set vary from the mean. **53**

standardization The administering of a test to a group which is considered representative of the population in which the test will be used, to determine the normative distribution of the test. **442**

standardization group A large, representative group of people to whom a psychological test is given prior to general distribution in order to establish norms. **442**

Stanford-Binet test The Stanford University revision of Binet's test; currently employed, usually with children, to judge intelligence by verbal and performance tests grouped according to the subjects' age levels. **443**

state-dependent memory A form of memory dissociation in which a person can retrieve particular information only if he or she is in the same state as when that information was originally stored. **392**

statistical significance The level of probability that the results of an experiment occurred solely by chance; a convention for deciding when to reject the chance hypothesis. **56**

statistics Mathematical methods for assessing and presenting data in summary form. **50**

stereotype A cluster of preconceived beliefs and expectations about the way members of a group think and act. **569**

Stevens' power law A law formulated by S. S. Stevens that the magnitude of a sensation is equal to the physical magnitude of the stimulus producing the sensation raised to a certain power (exponent). The exponent varies, depending on the sense that is being measured. **109**

stimulants Drugs that produce physiological and mental arousal, enhance endurance, diminish appetite, and elevate mood. **397**

stimulus Any form of energy to which an organism is capable of responding. **106**

stimulus control A condition where the animal has been so well trained that whenever the stimuli are present the learned response will occur. **160**

stimulus discrimination The expression of a learned response to only a particular stimulus. **164**

stimulus generalization The expression of a learned response in the presence of a number of similar stimuli. **164**

stimulus substitution The tendency to react to a previously neutral stimulus as though it were a natural or unconditioned stimulus. **148**

stirrup One of a set of three tiny, interconnected bones in the middle ear that transmit sound from the eardrum to the cochlea. **121**

Strong-Campbell Interest Inventory (SCII) A test designed to measure a subject's pattern of interests in order to aid in occupational choices. **465**

structuralism Developed by Wilhelm Wundt, it is the study of how the constituent elements of the human consciousness form the organization, or structure, of the mind. **13**

subgoal analysis A heuristic by which a problem is analyzed into a set of manageable smaller problems called subgoals. **218**

subjective contour A line or shape that appears to be present but which is not physically there. **126**

sublimation According to psychoanalytic theory, a defense mechanism that involves the redirecting of impulses considered unacceptable into socially desirable goals. **411**

superego According to Freud, the partially unconscious part of the psyche that incorporates parental and social standards of morality and that acts to prohibit thoughts and actions that express instinctual drives. **409**

superstitious behavior Behavior that is strengthened or weakened because by chance it happens to precede reinforcement or punishment. **155**

surface structure The words and organization of a sentence. **279**

surface traits According to Cattell, clusters of behavior that tend to fit together. **423**

survey An attempt to estimate the opinions, characteristics, or behavior of a particular population by investigating a representative sample. **43**

symmetrical Describing a distribution in which scores are distributed similarly on both sides of the middle value. **50–1**

sympathetic nervous system The division of the autonomic nervous system that promotes energy expenditure in an emergency or stress situation. **74**

synapses Tiny gaps that separate axons from adjacent cells. **79**

syndrome A group or pattern of symptoms characterizing a specific disease or condition. **476**

syntax The rules of a language which determine how words are to be combined into grammatical phrases and sentences. **279**

systematic desensitization Developed by Joseph Wolpe, this behavior-therapy technique reduces anxiety or removes phobias by pairing muscle relaxation with the presentation of potentially threatening objects or situations in hierarchical order, from least to most feared. **515**

target organs Organs that particular hormones will act on exclusively. **81**

taste buds Tiny organs located in the surface layer of the tongue that are the receptors for taste. **125**

tectorial membrane A jellylike membrane that covers the organ of Corti in the ear and in which hair cells are embedded. **122**

temporal lobe A portion of each cerebral hemisphere, concerned with hearing and visual processing. **88**

texture gradient The impression of depth created by the graduated differences of texture that occur as distance increases. **131**

thalamus A group of nuclei located in the forebrain, some of which relay information from the sensory organs to the cerebral cortex. **85**

Thematic Apperception Test (TAT) A projective psychological test in which a subject's responses to a series of cards with ambiguous scenes are analyzed on an individual basis. **460**

thyroid gland Located in the neck, this endocrine gland secretes the hormone thyroxin, which plays an important role in regulating the body's metabolism. **82**

time-series design A design in which the researcher repeatedly observes or measures the dependent variable both before and after the independent variable changes. **41**

tip-of-the-tongue phenomenon The knowledge that something is stored somewhere in our memory but cannot be located quickly. **185**

token economies Structured environments in which objects such as poker chips are used as rewards that may be exchanged by patients for desired activities or objects; a technique used in operant-conditioning therapies. **163**

trait According to Guilford, any relatively enduring way in which one individual differs from another. **421**

trait theories Methods of understanding personality that organize human behavior according to characteristics that distinguish a person, or traits. **406**

transactional analysis (TA) A therapeutic approach that is based on the belief that each relationship with others can be seen as a dominance of either a mature or immature part of an individual, and that a growth of the Adult, or mature, part of an individual can help interactions to run more smoothly. **526**

transduction The conversion of one type of energy into another, especially the conversion of sensory information into neural impulses. **110**

transference The transfer to the analyst of feelings of love and hostility that were originally directed toward a client's parents or other authority figures; a basic feature of psychoanalysis. **511**

trichromatic theory The theory that there are three different types of color receptors in the eye for detecting all colors. **115**

unconditioned response (UCR) A response elicited by an unconditioned stimulus without any form of training. **147**

unconditioned stimulus (UCS) A stimulus that elicits an unconditioned response without any form of training. **147**

underlying representation The meaning of a sentence. **279**

validity An essential criterion in determining the value of a test. A test is valid if it measures what it is supposed to measure. **440**

variable-interval schedule An unpredictable and irregular partial reinforcement schedule in which there is no perceived relationship between the time elapsed and the frequency of rewards. **159**

variable-ratio schedule An unpredictable and irregular partial reinforcement schedule in which there is no perceived relationship between the number of responses and the number of rewards. **159**

variables Factors capable of change. **40**

wavelength The distance between the crest of one light wave and the crest of the next; the determinant of color. **111**

Weber's law Formulated by Gustav Fechner, this law states that the amount by which a stimulus must be increased to produce a "just noticeable difference" in sensation is always a constant proportion of the initial stimulus intensity. **108**

Wechsler Intelligence Scales These are the Wechsler Adult Intelligence Scale (WAIS) and the Wechsler Intelligence Scale for Children (WISC). Along with the Stanford-Binet, they are the most frequently used individual intelligence tests; they differ from the Stanford-Binet in several ways, primarily in yielding not a single IQ score but separate scores for each subtest. **444**

white matter The myelinated axons of the nervous system. **79**

References and name index

The boldface number(s) after each entry refers to the page number(s) on which that work is cited in the text.

Abraham, K. Notes on psychoanalytic investigation and treatment of manic-depressive insanity and allied conditions (1911). In D. Bryan and A. Strachey (Trans.), *Selected papers of Karl Abraham,* M.D. London: The Hogarth Press, 1948. **493**

Abraham, K. The first pregenital stage of the libido (1916). In D. Bryan and A. Strachey (Trans.), *Selected papers of Karl Abraham,* M.D. London: The Hogarth Press, 1948. **493**

Abramowitz, C. V., and **Dokecki, P. R.** The politics of clinical judgment: Early empirical returns. *Psychological Bulletin,* 1977, *84,* 460–476. **538**

Abramowitz, S. I., Abramowitz, C. V., Jackson, C., and **Gomes, B.** The politics of clinical judgment: What nonliberal examiners infer about women who don't stifle themselves. *Journal of Consulting and Clinical Psychology,* 1973, *41,* 385–391. **571**

Abramson, L. Y., Seligman, M. E. P., and **Teasdale, J. D.** Learned helplessness in humans: Critique and reformulation. *Journal of Abnormal Psychology,* 1978, *87,* 49–74. **494**

Adams, A. J., Balliet, R., and **McAdams, M.** Color vision: Blue deficiencies in children? *Investigative Ophthalmology,* 1975, *14,* 620–625. **118**

Adler, A. Individual psychology. In C. A. Murchison (Ed.), *Psychologies of 1930.* Worcester, Mass.: Clark University Press, 1930. Pp. 395–405. **415**

Adler, A. *What life should mean to you.* Boston: Little, Brown, 1931. **415**

Adler, A. *Understanding human nature.* New York: Humanities Press, 1962. **342**

Adorno, T. W., Frenkel-Brunswick, E., Levinson, D. J., and **Sanford, R. N.** *The authoritarian personality.* New York: Harper, 1950. **573**

Agras, W. S. Behavior therapy in the management of chronic schizophrenia. *American Journal of Psychiatry,* 1967, *124,* 240–243. **500**

Akiskal, H. S., and **McKinney, W. T., Jr.** Depressive disorders: Toward a unified hypothesis. *Science,* 1973, *182,* 20–29. **496**

Akiskal, H. S., and **McKinney, W. T., Jr.** Overview of recent research in depression. *Archives of General Psychiatry,* 1975, *32,* 285–305. **496**

Albee, G. W. I.Q. tests on trial. *The New York Times,* February 12, 1978, Section E, p. 13. **455**

Allport, F. H. The influence of the group upon association and thought. *Journal of Experimental Psychology,* 1920, *3,* 159–182. **593**

Allport, F. H. *Social Psychology.* Boston: Houghton Mifflin, 1924. **593**

Allport, G. W. *Personality: A psychological interpretation.* New York: Holt, Rinehart and Winston, 1937. **422**

Allport, G. W. *The nature of prejudice.* Cambridge, Mass.: Addison-Wesley, 1954. **569**

Allport, G. W. *Pattern and growth in personality.* New York: Holt, Rinehart and Winston, 1961. **422**

Allport, G. W. Traits revisited. *American Psychologist,* 1966, *21,* 1–10. **422**

Allport, G. W. The historical background of modern social psychology. In G. Lindzey and E. Aronson (Eds.), *Handbook of social psychology* (Vol. 1) (2nd ed.). Reading, Mass.: Addison-Wesley, 1968. Pp. 1–80. **546**

Allport, G. W., and **Odbert, H. S.** Trait-names: A psycho-texical study. *Psychological Monographs,* 1936, *47,* Whole No. 211. **422**

Allport, G. W., and **Postman, L. J.** *The psychology of rumor.* New York: Holt, 1947. **189**

Alper, T. G. Achievement motivation in college women: A now-you-see-it-now-you-don't phenomenon. *American Psychologist,* 1974, *29,* 194–203. **368**

Altman, I. *The environment and social behavior: Privacy, personal space, territory, and crowding.* Monterey, Calif.: Brooks/Cole, 1975. **609**

American Psychiatric Association Task Force on Nomenclature and Statistics. *Diagnostic and statistical manual of mental disorders* (3rd ed.). Washington, D.C.: American Psychiatric Association, 1980. **485, 486**

American Psychological Association. Bylaws of the American Psychological Association. *1968 Directory.* Washington, D.C.: American Psychological Association, 1968. **10**

American Psychological Association. *Ethical principles in the conduct of research with human participants.* Washington, D.C.: American Psychological Association, 1973. **64**

Amoore, J. E., and **Venstrum, D.** Correlations between stereochemical assessments and organoleptic analysis of odorous compounds. In T. Hayashi (Ed.), *Olfaction and taste.* Oxford: Pergamon, 1967. Pp. 3–17. **125**

Andrews, E. A., and **Braveman, N. S.** The combined effects of dosage level and interstimulus interval on the formation of one-trial poison-based aversions in rats. *Animal Learning and Behavior,* 1975, *3,* 287–289. **151**

Anglin, J. A. *Word, object, and conceptual development.* New York: Norton, 1977. **211**

Anisman, H., and **Sklar, L. S.** Catecholamine depletion in mice upon reexposure to stress: Mediation of the escape deficits produced by inescapable shock. *Journal of Comparative and Physiological Psychology,* 1979, *93,* 610–625. **495**

Armstrong, R. H. Gastric secretion during sleep and dreaming. Paper presented at the annual meeting of the Association for the Psychophysiological Study of Sleep, March 1965. **378**

Aronfreed, J. The concept of internalization. In D. A. Goslin (Ed.), *Handbook of socialization theory and research.* Chicago: Rand McNally, 1969. **266**

Aronson, E. *The social animal* (3rd ed.). San Francisco: W. H. Freeman, 1980. **573, 582**

Anand, B. K., and **Brobeck, J. R.** Localization of a feeding center in the hypothalamus of the rat. *Proceedings for the Society of Experimental Biological Medicine,* 1951, *77,* 323–324. **345**

Anand, B. K., Chhina, G. S., and **Singh, B.** Some aspects of electroencephalographic studies in yogis. *Electroencephalography and Clinical Neurophysiology,* 1961, *13,* 452–456. **387**

Anastasi, A. *Psychological testing.* New York: Macmillan, 1976. **445, 450, 459**

Anders, T. F., and **Roffwarg, H. P.** The effects of selective interruption and deprivation of sleep in the human newborn. *Developmental Psychobiology,* 1973, *6,* 77–89. **379**

Anderson, C. R. Coping behaviors as intervening mechanisms in the inverted-U stress-performance relationship. *Journal of Applied Psychology,* 1976, *61,* 30–34. **360**

Anderson, N. H. A simple model of information integration. In R. P. Abelson, E. Aronson, W. J. McGuire, T. M. Newcomb, M. J. Rosenberg, and P. H. Tannenbaum (Eds.), *Theories of cognitive consistency: A sourcebook.* Chicago: Rand McNally, 1968. Pp. 731–743. **557**

Aronson, E., and **Carlsmith, J. M.** The effect of the severity of threat on the devaluation of forbidden behavior. *Journal of Abnormal and Social Psychology,* 1963, *66,* 584–588. **552**

Aronson, E., and **Osherow, N.** Cooperation, prosocial behavior, and academic performance: Experiments in the desegregated classroom. In L. Bickman (Ed.), *Applied social psychology annual* (Vol. 1). Beverly Hills, Calif.: Sage Publications, 1980. **575**

Asch, S. E. Effects of group pressure upon the modification and distortion of judgments. In H. Guetzkow (Ed.), *Groups, leadership, and men.* Pittsburgh: Carnegie Press, 1951. **581**

Asch, S. E. Studies of independence and conformity: A minority of one against a unanimous majority. *Psychological Monographs,* 1956, *70,* 9, Whole No. 416. **581**

Aserinsky, E., and Kleitman, N. Regularly occurring periods of eye motility and concomitant phenomena during sleep. *Science,* 1953, *178,* 273–274. **377**

Astin, H. S. The academic labor market. In P. J. Woods (Ed.), *Career opportunities for psychologists: Expanding and emerging areas.* Washington, D.C.: APA, 1976. **29**

Atkinson, J. W. (Ed.). *Motives in fantasy, action, and society.* New York: Van Nostrand Reinhold, 1958. **364**

Atkinson, J. W. *An introduction to motivation.* Princeton, N.J.: Van Nostrand Reinhold, 1964. **365**

Atkinson, J. W., and Litwin, G. H. Achievement motive and test anxiety conceived as motive to approach success and motive to avoid failure. *Journal of Abnormal and Social Psychology,* 1960, *60,* 52–63. **365**

Atkinson, J. W., and Raynor, J. O. (Eds.). *Motivation and achievement.* Washington, D.C.: Winston, 1974. **365**

Attneave, F. Some information aspects of visual perception. *Psychological Review,* 1954, *61,* 183–193. **129**

Avery, D., and Winokur, G. The efficacy of electroconvulsive therapy and antidepressants in depression. *Biological Psychiatry,* 1977, *12,* 507–523. **534**

Ax, A. F. The physiological differentiation between fear and anger in humans. *Psychosomatic Medicine,* 1953, *15,* 433–442. **316**

Ayllon, T., and Azrin, N. H. *The token economy: A motivational system for therapy and rehabilitation.* New York: Appleton-Century-Crofts, 1968. **518**

Azrin, N. H., and Foxx, R. M. *Toilet training in less than a day.* New York: Simon and Schuster, 1974. **158**

Ball, W., and Tronick, E. Infant responses to impending collision: Optical and real. *Science,* 1971, *171,* 818. **243**

Baltes, P. B., Reese, H. W., and Nesselroade, J. R. *Life-span developmental psychology: Introduction to research methods.* Monterey, Calif.: Brooks/Cole, 1977. **49**

Baltes, P. B., and Schaie, K. W. Aging and IQ: The myth of the twilight years. *Psychology Today,* 1974, *7,* 35–40. **255**

Ban, T. *Recent advances in the biology of schizophrenia.* Springfield, Ill.: Charles C. Thomas, 1973. **501**

Bandura, A. Influence of models' reinforcement contingencies on the acquisition of imitative responses. *Journal of Personality and Social Psychology,* 1965, *1,* 589–595. **598**

Bandura, A. Vicarious processes: A case of no-trial learning. In L. Berkowitz (Ed.), *Advances in experimental social psychology* (Vol. 2). New York: Academic Press, 1966. Pp. 1–55. **420**

Bandura, A. Social learning analysis of aggression. In E. Ribes-Inesta and A. Bandura (Eds.), *Analysis of delinquency and aggression.* Hillsdale, N.J.: Lawrence Erlbaum, 1976. Pp. 202–232. **597**

Bandura, A. *Social learning theory.* Englewood Cliffs, N.J.: Prentice-Hall, 1977. **171, 172**

Bandura, A. Self-efficacy: Toward a unifying theory of behavioral change. *Psychological Review,* 1977, *84,* 191–215. **172, 519**

Bandura, A., Blanchard, E. B., and Ritter, B. Relative efficacy of desensitization and modeling approaches for inducing behavioral, affective, and attitudinal changes. *Journal of Personality and Social Psychology,* 1969, *13,* 173–199. **173, 519**

Bandura, A., Grusec, J. E., and Menlove, F. L. Vicarious extinction of avoidance behavior. *Journal of Personality and Social Psychology,* 1967, *5,* 16–23. **519**

Bandura, A., Ross, D., and Ross, S. Transmission of aggression through imitation of aggressive models. *Journal of Abnormal and Social Psychology,* 1961, *63,* 575–582. **265, 597**

Banks, M. S., Aslin, R. N., and Letson, R. D. Sensitive period for the development of human binocular vision. *Science,* 1975, *190,* 675–677. **137**

Barber, T. X. Measuring "hypnotic-like" suggestibility with and without hypnotic induction: Psychometric properties, norms, and variables influencing response to the Barber suggestibility scale (BSS). *Psychological Reports,* 1965, *16,* 809–844. **384**

Barber, T. X. Responding to "hypnotic" suggestions: An introspective report. *American Journal of Clinical Hypnosis,* 1975, *18,* 6–22. **383**

Barfield, R. A., and Morgan, J. N. *Early retirement: The decision and the experience.* Ann Arbor, Mich.: Institute for Social Research, University of Michigan, 1970. **271**

Barker, R. G., Dembo, T., and Lewin, K. *Frustration and regression: A study of young children.* University of Iowa Studies in Child Welfare, 1941, *18,* 1–314. **599**

Baron, R. A. *Human aggression.* New York: Plenum, 1977. **596, 598**

Barrett, D. The hypnotic dream: Its relation to nocturnal dreams and waking fantasies. *Journal of Abnormal Psychology,* 1979, *88,* 584–591. **381**

Barron, F. H. The psychology of imagination. *Scientific American,* 1958, *199,* 150–170. **224**

Barron, F. H. *Creativity and personal freedom.* New York: Van Nostrand Reinhold, 1968. **449, 450**

Barron, F. H. Behavioral decision theory: A topical bibliography for management scientists. *Interfaces,* 1974, *5,* 56–62. **225**

Bartlett, F. C. *Remembering: A study in experimental and social psychology.* London: Cambridge University Press, 1932. **189**

Bartoshuk, L. M. The chemical senses, I: taste. In J. W. Kling and L. A. Riggs (Eds.), *Woodworth and Schlosberg's experimental psychology* (3rd ed.). New York: Holt, Rinehart and Winston, 1971. **125**

Bartoshuk, L. M. Taste illusions: Some demonstrations. *Annals of the New York Academy of Sciences,* 1974, *237,* 279–285. **125, 126**

Bates, J. A. Extrinsic reward and intrinsic motivation: A review with implications for the classroom. *Review of Educational Research,* 1979, *49,* 557–576. **554**

Bateson, G., Jackson, D., Haley, J., and Weakland, J. Toward a theory of schizophrenia. *Behavioral Science,* 1956, *1,* 251–264. **501**

Baum, A., Aiello, J., and Calesnick, L. Crowding and personal control: social density and the development of learned helplessness. *Journal of Personality and Social Psychology,* 1978, *36,* 1000–1011. **609**

Baum, A., and Gatchel, R. J. Cognitive determinants of reaction to uncontrollable events: Development of reactance and learned helplessness. *Journal of Personality and Social Psychology,* in press.

Baum, A., and Valins, S. *Architecture and social behavior: Psychological studies of social density.* Hillsdale, N.J.: Lawrence Erlbaum, 1977. **609**

Baumrind, D. Some thoughts on the ethics of research: After reading Milgram's "Behavioral study of obedience." *American Psychologist,* 1964, *19,* 421–423. **586**

Bazar, J. Catching up with the ape language debate. *American Psychological Association Monitor,* January 1980, 5ff. **11**

Beach, L. R., Campbell, F. L., and Townes, B. D. Subjective utility and the prediction of birth-planning decisions. *Organizational Behavior and Human Performance,* 1979, *24,* 18–28. **226**

Beck, A. T. *Depression: clinical, experimental and theoretical aspects.* New York: Harper & Row, 1967. **493**

Beck, A. T. The development of depression: A cognitive model. In R. J. Friedman and M. M. Katz (Eds.), *The psychology of depression: Contemporary theory and research.* Washington: Winston-Wiley, 1974. **493**

Beck, A. T. *Cognitive therapy and the emotional disorders.* New York: International Universities Press, 1976. **520–521**

Beck, A. T., Rush, A. J., Show, B. F., and Emery, G. *Cognitive therapy of depression.* New York: Guilford Press, 1979. **520**

Begelman, D. Ethical and legal issues of behavior modification. In M. Hersen, R. Eisler, and P. Miller (Eds.), *Progress in behavior modification* (Vol. 1). New York: Academic Press, 1975. **514**

Beier, E. G. Nonverbal communication: How we send emotional messages. *Psychology Today,* October 1974, 53–56. **300, 301**

Bellugi, U. *The emergence of inflections and negative systems in the speech of two children.* Paper presented at the meeting of the New England Psychological Association, 1964. **292**

Bellugi, U. Learning the language. *Psychology Today,* 1970, *4,* 32–35ff. **292**

Belsky, J., and Steinberg, L. D. The effects of daycare: A critical review. *Child Development,* 1978, *49,* 929–949. **260**

Bem, D. J. Self-perception: An alternative interpretation of cognitive dissonance phenomena. *Psychological Review,* 1967, *74,* 183–200. **553**

Bem, D. J., and **Allen, A.** On predicting some of the people some of the time: The search for cross-situational consistencies in behavior. *Psychological Review,* 1974, *81,* 506–520. **426**

Bem, D. J., and **McConnell, H. K.** Testing the self-perception explanation of dissonance phenomena: On the salience of premanipulation attitudes. *Journal of Personality and Social Psychology,* 1970, *14,* 23–31. **553**

Bem, S. L. The measurement of psychological androgyny. *Journal of Consulting and Clinical Psychology,* 1974, *42,* 155–162. **22**

Bem, S. L. Sex-role adaptability: One consequence of psychological androgyny. *Journal of Personality and Social Psychology,* 1975, *31,* 634–643. **22**

Bem, S. L., and **Bem, D. J.** Case study of a nonconscious ideology: Training the woman to know her place. In D. J. Bem, *Beliefs, attitudes, and human affairs.* Monterey, Calif.: Brooks/Cole, 1970. Pp. 89–99. **571**

Bentler, P. M., and **Woodward, J. A.** A Head-Start re-evaluation: Positive effects are not yet demonstrable. *Evaluation Quarterly,* 1978, *2,* 493–510. **605**

Berger, P. A. Medical treatment of mental illness. *Science,* 1978, *200,* 974–981. **495**

Bergin, A. E. The evaluation of therapeutic outcomes. In A. E. Bergin and S. L. Garfield (Eds.), *Handbook of psychotherapy and behavior change: An empirical analysis.* New York: Wiley, 1971. **528**

Bergin, A. E., and **Lambert, M. J.** The evaluation of therapeutic outcomes. In S. L. Garfield and A. E. Bergin (Eds.), *Handbook of psychotherapy and behavior change: An empirical analysis* (2nd ed.). New York: Wiley, 1978. **529**

Berkman, L. F., and **Syme, S. L.** Social networks, host resistance, and mortality: A nine-year follow-up of Alameda County residents. *American Journal of Epidemiology,* 1979, *109,* 186–204. **330**

Berkowitz, L. *Aggression: A social psychological analysis.* New York: McGraw-Hill, 1962. **600**

Berkowitz, L. The concept of aggressive drive: Some additional considerations. In L. Berkowitz (Ed.), *Advances in experimental social psychology* (Vol. 2). New York: Academic Press, 1965. **600**

Berkowitz, L. (Ed.). *Roots of aggression: A reexamination of the frustration–aggression hypothesis.* New York: Atherton, 1969. **600**

Berkowitz, L., and **Geen, R. G.** Film violence and cue properties of available targets. *Journal of Personality and Social Psychology,* 1966, *3,* 525–530. **600**

Berkowitz, L., and **Lepage, A.** Weapons as aggression-eliciting stimuli. *Journal of Personality and Social Psychology,* 1976, *7,* 202–207. **600**

Berlin, B., and **Kay, P.** *Basic color terms: Their universality and evolution.* Berkeley: University of California Press, 1969. **296, 297**

Bernard, L. L. *Instinct.* New York: Holt, 1924. **340**

Berne, E. *Games people play.* New York: Grove Press, 1964. **526**

Bernstein, I. Learned taste aversions in children receiving chemotherapy. *Science,* 1978, *200,* 1302–1303. **151**

Bever, T. G. The cognitive basis for linguistic structures. In J. R. Hayes (Ed.), *Cognition and the development of language.* New York: Wiley, 1970. Pp. 279–362. **292**

Bexton, W. H. *Some effects of perceptual isolation in human beings.* Unpublished doctoral dissertation, McGill University, 1953. **360**

Bexton, W. H., Heron, W., and **Scott, T. H.** Effects of decreased variation in the sensory environment. *Canadian Journal of Psychology,* 1954, *8,* 70–76. **127, 360**

Birch, H. G., and **Rabinowitz, H. S.** The negative effect of previous experience on productive thinking. *Journal of Experimental Psychology,* 1951, *41,* 121–125. **216**

Birnbaum, I. M., Parker, E. S., Hartley, J. T., and **Noble, E. P.** Alcohol and memory: Retrieval processes. *Journal of Verbal Learning and Verbal Behavior,* 1978, *17,* 325–335. **392**

Blake, R., and **Hirsch, H. V. B.** Deficits in binocular depth perception in cats after alternating monocular deprivation. *Science,* 1975, *190,* 1114–1116. **136**

Blake, R. R., and **Mouton, J.** Intergroup problem solving in organizations: From theory to practice. In W. Austin and S. Worchel (Eds.), *The social psychology of intergroup relations.* Monterey, Calif.: Brooks/Cole, 1979. **594**

Blakemore, C., and **Cooper, G.** Development of the brain depends on the visual environment. *Nature,* 1970, *228,* 477–478. **20, 136**

Blanchard, E. B. Biofeedback and the modification of cardiovascular dysfunctions. In R. J. Gatchel and K. P. Price (Eds.), *Clinical applications of biofeedback: Appraisal and status.* Elmsford, N.Y.: Pergamon, 1979. **390**

Bleuler, E. *Dementia praecox or the group of schizophrenias* (1911). J. Sinkin (Trans.) New York: International Universities Press, 1950. **497, 499**

Block, J. *Lives through time.* Berkeley, Calif.: Bancroft Books, 1971. **427**

Block, J. H. *Another look at sex differentiation in the socialization behaviors of mothers and fathers.* Paper presented at the Conference on New Directions for Research on Women, Madison, Wisconsin, May 1975. **263**

Block, J. H., Block, H., and **Harrington, D. M.** *The relationship of parental teaching strategies in preschool children.* Paper presented at the meeting of the Western Psychological Association, San Francisco, California, April 1974. **264**

Block, N. J., and **Dworkin, G.** (Eds.). *The IQ controversy.* New York: Pantheon, 1976. **254–55**

Blodgett, H. C. The effect of the introduction of reward upon maze performance of rats. *University of California Publications in Psychology,* 1929, *4,* 117–120.

Bloom, F., Segal, D., Ling, N., and **Guillemin, R.** Endorphins: Profound behavioral effects in rats suggest new etiological factors in mental illness. *Science,* 1976, *194,* 630–632. **503**

Bloom, L. M. *Language development: Form and function in emerging grammars.* Cambridge, Mass.: MIT Press, 1970. **288**

Blum, J. M. *Pseudoscience and mental ability.* New York: Monthly Review Press, 1978. **452, 456**

Boehm, V. R. *Changing career patterns for women in the Bell System.* Paper presented at the meeting of the American Psychological Association, New Orleans, August 1974. **572**

Bogen, J. E. Some educational implications of hemispheric specialization. In M. C. Wittrock (Ed.), *The human brain.* Englewood Cliffs, N.J.: Prentice-Hall, 1977. Pp. 133–152. **95**

Bootzin, R. R. *Behavior modification and therapy.* Boston: Winthrop, 1975. **514, 539**

Bootzin, R. R., and **Acocella, J. R.** *Abnormal psychology: Current perspectives* (3rd ed.). New York: Random House, 1980. **539**

Bootzin, R. R., and **Max, D.** Learning and behavioral theories of anxiety and stress. In I. L. Kutash and L. B. Schlesinger (Eds.), *Pressure point: Perspectives on stress and anxiety.* San Francisco: Jossey-Bass, in press. **488**

Bootzin, R. R., and **Nicassio, P. M.** Behavioral treatments for insomnia. In M. Hersen, R. M. Eisler, and P. M. Miller (Eds.), *Progress in behavior modification* (Vol. 6). New York: Academic Press, 1978. **518**

Boring, E. G. *A history of experimental psychology* (2nd ed.). New York: Appleton-Century-Crofts, 1957. **13**

Borke, H. Piaget's mountains revisited: Changes in the egocentric landscape. *Developmental Psychology,* 1975, *11,* 240–243. **249**

Bornstein, M. H. The psychological component of cultural difference in color naming and illusion susceptibility. *Behavior Science Notes,* 1973, *8,* 41–101. **119**

Bornstein, M. H., Kessen, W., and **Weiskopf, B.** The categories of hue in infancy. *Science,* 1976, *191,* 201–202. **118, 296**

Bornstein, P. E., and **Clayton, P. J.** The anniversary reaction. *Diseases of the Nervous System,* 1972, *33,* 470–472. **325**

Bourne, L. E., Dominowski, R. L., and **Loftus, E. F.** *Cognitive processes.* Englewood Cliffs, N.J.: Prentice-Hall, 1979. **218**

Bower, G. H. A selective review of organizational factors in memory. In E. Tulving and W. Donaldson (Eds.), *Organization of memory.* New York: Academic Press, 1972. **187**

Bower, G. H., and **Clark, M. C.** Narrative stories as mediators for serial learning. *Psychonomic Science,* 1969, *14,* 181–182. **187**

Bower, T. G. R., Broughton, J., and **Moore, K. M.** The development of the object concept as manifested by changes in the tracking behavior of infants. *Journal of Experimental Child Psychology,* 1971, *12,* 182–193. **243**

Bowers, K. S. Situationism in psychology: An analysis and critique. *Psychological Review,* 1973, *80,* 307–336. **427**

Bowers, K. S. *Hypnosis for the seriously curious.* Monterey, Calif.: Brooks/Cole, 1976. **383**

Bowers, P. Hypnosis and creativity: The search for the missing link. *Journal of Abnormal Psychology,* 1979, *88,* 564–572. **383**

Brackbill, Y. Arousal level in neonates and preschool children under continuous auditory stimulation. *Journal of Experimental Child Psychology,* 1966, 177–188. **63**

Brackbill, Y. Cumulative effects of continuous stimulation on arousal level in infants. *Child Development,* 1971, *42,* 17–26. **63**

Bradburn, N. M. *The structure of psychological well-being.* Chicago: Aldine, 1969. **334**

Bradley, C., and **Cox, T.** Stress and health. In T. Cox (Ed.), *Stress.* London: Macmillan, 1978. **327**

Bradley, G. W. Self-serving biases in the attribution process: A re-examination of the fact or fiction question. *Journal of Personality and Social Psychology,* 1978, *35,* 56–71. **563**

Bradway, K. I.Q. constancy on the revised Stanford-Binet from the preschool to the junior high school level. *Journal of Genetic Psychology,* 1944, *65,* 197–217. **255**

Branchey, M. H., Charles, J., and **Simpson, G. M.** Extrapyrimidal side effects in lithium maintenance therapy. *American Journal of Psychiatry,* 1976, *133,* 444–445. **534**

Bransford, J. D., and **Johnson, M. K.** Contextual prerequisites for understanding: Some investigations of comprehension and recall. *Journal of Verbal Learning and Verbal Behavior,* 1972, *11,* 717–726. **298**

Bray, G. A., and **Gallagher, T. F., Jr.** Manifestations of hypothalamic obesity in man: A comprehensive investigation of eight patients and a review of the literature. *Medicine,* 1975, *54,* 301–330. **348**

Brehm, J. W. *A theory of psychological reactance.* New York: Academic Press, 1966. **554**

Brickman, P. *Happiness: Can we make it last?* Paper, Northwestern University, April 1978. **332, 333**

Brickman, P., and **Campbell, D. T.** Hedonic relativism and planning the good society. In M. H. Appley (Ed.), *Adaptation level theory.* New York: Academic Press, 1971. **332, 333**

Brickman, P., Coates, D., and **Janoff-Bulman, R.** Lottery winners and accident victims: Is happiness relative? *Journal of Personality and Social Psychology,* 1978, *36,* 917–927. **333**

Brickman, P., Rabinowitz, V. C., Coates, D., Cohn, E., Kidder, L., and **Karuza, J.** *Helping.* Unpublished paper, Institute for Social Research, University of Michigan, 1979. **605**

Broadbent, D. E. *Perception and communication.* London: Pergamon, 1958. **181**

Broadbent, D. E. The current state of noise research: Reply to Poulton. *Psychological Bulletin,* 1978, *85,* 1052–1067. **607**

Broverman, I. K., Broverman, D. M., Clarkson, F. E., Rosenkrantz, P. S., and **Vogel, S. R.** Sex-role stereotypes and clinical judgments of mental health. *Journal of Consulting and Clinical Psychology,* 1970, *34,* 1–7. **538**

Broverman, I. K., Vogel, S. R., Broverman, D. M., Clarkson, F. E., and **Rosenkrantz, P. S.** Sex-role stereotypes: A current appraisal. *Journal of Social Issues,* 1972, *28,* 59–78. **571**

Brown, B. B. *New mind, new body.* New York: Harper & Row, 1974. **391**

Brown, R. *A first language: The early stages.* Cambridge, Mass.: Harvard University Press, 1973. **288**

Brown, R., and **Bellugi, U.** Three processes in the child's acquisition of syntax. *Harvard Educational Review,* 1964, *34,* 133–151. **290**

Brown, R., Cazden, C., and **Bellugi-Klima, U.** The child's grammar from I to III. In J. P. Hill (Ed.), *Minnesota Symposium on Child Development* (Vol. 2). Minneapolis: University of Minnesota Press, 1968. Pp. 28–73. **290, 293**

Brown, R., and **Fraser, C.** The acquisition of syntax. In C. N. Cofer and B. S. Musgrave (Eds.), *Verbal behavior and learning problems and processes.* New York: McGraw-Hill, 1973. **288**

Brown, R., and **Hanlon, C.** Derivational complexity and order of acquisition in child speech. In J. R. Hayes (Ed.), *Cognition and the development of language.* New York: Wiley, 1970. **288**

Brown, R., and **McNeill, D.** The "tip of the tongue" phenomenon. *Journal of Verbal Learning and Verbal Behavior,* 1966, *5,* 325–337. **20, 185**

Bruner, J. S., Goodnow, J. J., and **Austin, G. A.** *A study of thinking.* New York: Wiley, 1956. **212**

Bryan, J. H. Children's cooperation and helping behaviors. In E. M. Hetherington (Ed.), *Review of child development research* (Vol. 5). Chicago: University of Chicago Press, 1975. **265**

Bucher, B., and **Lovaas, O. I.** Use of aversive stimulation in behavior modification. In M. R. Jones (Ed.), *Miami Symposium on the Prediction of Behavior, 1967: Aversive Stimulation.* Coral Gables, Fla.: University of Miami Press, 1968. **518**

Buck, R. A test of nonverbal receiving ability: Preliminary studies. *Human Communication Research,* 1976, *2,* 162–171. **302**

Budzynski, T. H. Biofeedback strategies in headache treatment. In J. V. Basmajian (Ed.), *Biofeedback—principles and practice for clinicians.* Baltimore: Williams & Wilkins, 1979. **390**

Budzynski, T. H., Stoyva, J., and **Adler, C.** Feedback-induced muscle relaxation: Application to tension headaches. *Journal of Behavioral Therapy and Experimental Psychiatry,* 1970, *1,* 205–211.

Bulman, R. J., and **Wortman, C. B.** Attribution of blame and coping in the "real world": Severe accident victims react to their lot. *Journal of Personality and Social Psychology,* 1977, *35,* 351–363. **310**

Burgess, A. W., and **Holmstrom, L. L.** Rape trauma syndrome. *American Journal of Psychiatry,* 1974, *131,* 981–986. **324**

Burgess, A. W., and **Holmstrom, L. L.** Recovery from rape and prior life stress. *Research in Nursing and Health,* 1978, *1,* 165–174. **325, 330**

Burgess, E. W., and **Wallin, P.** *Engagement and marriage.* Philadelphia: Lippincott, 1953.

Burt, C. The genetic determination of differences in intelligence: A study of monozygotic twins reared together and apart. *British Journal of Psychology,* 1966, *57,* 137–153. **451**

Burt, C. Inheritance of general intelligence. *American Psychologist,* 1972, *27,* 175–190. **451**

Byrne, D. *The attraction paradigm.* New York: Academic Press, 1971.

Byrne, D., Ervin, C. R., and **Lambreth, J.** Continuity between the experimental study of attraction and "real life" computer dating. *Journal of Personality and Social Psychology,* 1970, *16,* 157–165. **566**

Cabanac, M. The physiological role of pleasure. *Science,* 1971, *173,* 1103–1107. **343**

Calhoun, J. B. Population density and social pathology. *Scientific American,* 1962, *206,* 139–148. **608**

Calhoun, L. G., Cann, A., Selby, J. W., and **Magee, D. L.** Victim emotional response: Effect on social reaction to victims of rape. *British Journal of Social and Clinical Psychology,* in press. **324**

Cameron, N. *Personality development and psychopathology.* Boston: Houghton Mifflin, 1963. **489, 490**

Cameron, P., Titus, D. G., Kostin, J., and **Kostin, M.** The life satisfaction of nonnormal persons. *Journal of Counseling and Clinical Psychology,* 1973, *41,* 207–214. **333**

Campbell, A. M. G., Evans, M., Thomson, J. L., and **Williams, M. J.** Cerebral atrophy in young cannabis smokers. *Lancet,* 1971, *2,* 1219–1224. **30**

Campbell, D. T. Reforms as experiments. In F. G. Caro (Ed.), *Readings in evaluation research.* New York: Russell Sage Foundation, 1971. **41**

Campbell, D. T., and **Stanley, J. C.** Experimental and quasi-experimental designs for research on teaching. In N. L. Gage (Ed.), *Handbook of research on teaching.* Chicago: Rand McNally, 1963. Pp. 171–246. (Reprinted as *Experimental and quasi-experimental designs for research.* Chicago: Rand McNally, 1966.) **41**

Campos, J. J. Heart rate: A sensitive tool for the study of infant emotional expression. In Lewis P. Lipsitt (Ed.), *Developmental psychobiology: The significance of infancy.* New York: Halsted Press, 1976. **61**

Campos, J. J., Langer, A., and **Karowitz, A.** Cardiac responses on the visual cliff in prelocomotor human infants. *Science,* 1970, *170,* 196–197. **243**

Cannell, C. G., and **Kahn, R. L.** Interviewing. In G. Lindzey and E. Aronson (Eds.), *The handbook of social psychology* (2nd ed.). Vol. 2: Research methods. Reading, Mass.: Addison-Wesley, 1968. **44, 203**

Cannon, W. B. The James-Lange theory of emotions: A critical examination and an alternative theory. *American Journal of Psychology,* 1927, *39,* 106–124. **316**

Cannon, W. B. *Bodily changes in pain, hunger, fear, and rage* (2nd ed.). New York: Appleton-Century-Crofts, 1929. **316**

Cannon, W. B. Hunger and thirst. In C. Murchison (Ed.), *A handbook of general experimental psychology.* Worcester, Mass.: Clark University Press, 1934. **341**

Cannon, W. B., and **Washburn, A. L.** An explanation of hunger. *American Journal of Physiology,* 1912, *29,* 441–454. **343**

Caplan, N., Morrison, A., and **Stambaugh, R. J.** *The use of social science knowledge in* policy decisions at the national level. Ann Arbor: University of Michigan, 1975.

Caramazza, A., and **Zurif, E. B.** Dissociation of algorithmic and heuristic processes in language comprehension: Evidence from aphasia. *Brain and Language,* 1976, *3,* 572–582. **286**

Carmichael, L., Hogan, H. P., and **Walter, A. A.** An experimental study of the effect of language on the reproduction of visually perceived form. *Journal of Experimental Psychology,* 1932, *15,* 73–86. **191**

Carr, R. What marijuana does (and doesn't do). *Human Behavior,* January 1978. **397**

Cartwright, R. D. Happy endings for our dreams. *Psychology Today,* December 1978, 66–76. **382**

Cartwright, R. D. The nature and function of repetitive dreams: A survey of speculation. *Psychiatry,* 1979, *42,* 131–137. **382**

Cates, J. Baccalaureates in psychology: 1969 and 1970. *American Psychologist,* 1973, *28,* 262–264. **30**

Cattell, R. B. *The scientific analysis of personality.* Baltimore: Penguin, 1965. **423**

Cautela, J. R. Treatment of compulsive behavior by covert sensitization. *Psychological Record,* 1966, *16,* 33–41. **516**

Cautela, J. R. Covert sensitization. *Psychological Reports,* 1967, *20,* 459–468. **516**

Chagnon, N. A. Yanomamö social organization and warfare. In M. Fried, M. Harris, and R. Murphy (Eds.), *War: The anthropology of armed conflict and aggression.* New York: Natural History Press, 1967. **597**

Chagnon, N. A. *Yanomamö: The fierce people.* New York: Holt, Rinehart and Winston, 1968. **597**

Chapanis, N. P., and **Chapanis, A. C.** Cognitive dissonance: Five years later. *Psychological Bulletin,* 1964, *61,* 1–22. **552**

Chapman, L. J., and **Chapman, J. P.** Genesis of popular but erroneous diagnostic observations. *Journal of Abnormal Psychology,* 1967, *72,* 193–204. **231**

Cherniss, C., Egnatios, E. S., and **Wacker, S.** Job stress and career development in new public professionals. *Professional Psychology,* 1976, *7,* 428–436. **606**

Cherniss, C., Egnatios, E. S., Wacker, S., and **O'Dowd, B.** The professional mystique and burnout in public sector professionals. *Social Policy,* in press. **606**

Cherry, E. C. Some experiments on the recognition of speech with one and two ears. *Journal of the Acoustical Society of America,* 1953, *25,* 975–979. **180**

Cherry, F., and **Deaux, K.** *Fear of success vs. fear of gender inconsistent behavior: A sex similarity.* Paper presented at the meeting of the Midwestern Psychological Association, Chicago, May 1975. **368**

Chi, M. T. H. Knowledge structures and memory development. In R. S. Siegler (Ed.), *Children's thinking: What develops?* Hillsdale, N.J.: Lawrence Erlbaum, 1978. **253**

Chomsky, N. *Aspects of the theory of syntax.* Cambridge, Mass.: MIT Press, 1965. **279**

Chomsky, N. *Language and mind.* New York: Harcourt Brace Jovanovich, 1972. **286**

Chorover, S. L. *From genesis to genocide.* Cambridge, Mass.: MIT Press, 1979. **452**

Clark, E. V. What's in a word? On the child's acquisition of semantics in his first language. In T. E. Moore (Ed.), *Cognitive development and the acquisition of language.* New York: Academic Press, 1973. Pp. 65–110. **290**

Clarke-Stewart, K. A. Interactions between mothers and their young children. *Monographs of the Society for Research in Child Development,* 1973, *38* (6–7, Serial No. 153). **261**

Clifford, M., and **Walster, E.** The effect of physical attractiveness on teacher expectations. *Sociology of Education,* 1973, *46,* 248–258. **558**

Coates, D., and **Wortman, C. B.** Depression maintenance and interpersonal control. In A. Baum, J. E. Singer, and Y. Epstein (Eds.), *Advances in environmental psychology* (Vol. 2). Hillsdale, N.J.: Lawrence Erlbaum, 1980. **475**

Cobb, S. Social support as a moderator of life stress. *Psychosomatic Medicine,* 1976, *38,* 300–314. **331**

Cohen, F. Personality, stress, and the development of physical illness. In G. Stone, F. Cohen, N. Adler, and associates (Eds.), *Health psychology—A handbook.* San Francisco: Jossey-Bass, 1979. **327, 329**

Cohen, L. B., DeLoache, J. S., and **Stauss, M. S.** Infant visual perception. In J. Osofsky (Ed.), *Handbook of infancy.* New York: Wiley, 1978. **243**

Cohen, S., Evans, G. W., Krantz, D. S., and **Stokols, D.** Physiological, motivational, and cognitive effects of aircraft noise on children: Moving from the laboratory to the field. *American Psychologist,* 1980. **607**

Cohen, S., Evans, G. W., Krantz, D. S., Stokols, D., and **Kelly, S.** Aircraft noise and children: Longitudinal and cross-sectional evidence on adaptation to noise and the effectiveness of noise abatement. *Journal of Personality and Social Psychology,* in press. **608**

Cohen, S., Glass, D. C., and **Phillips, S.** Environment and health. In H. E. Freeman, S. Levine, and L. G. Reeder (Eds.), *Handbook of medical sociology.* Englewood Cliffs, N.J.: Prentice-Hall, 1979. **607**

Cohen, S., and **Stillman, R. C.** (Eds.). *The therapeutic potential of marijuana.* New York: Plenum, 1976. **393**

Cohen, T. Why diets don't work. *New York,* May 1979, 45–51. **350**

Collins, A. M., and **Quillan, M. R.** Retrieval time from semantic memory. *Journal of Verbal Learning and Verbal Behavior,* 1969, *8,* 240–247. **211**

Collins, B. E. *Social psychology.* Reading, Mass.: Addison-Wesley, 1970. **583**

Collins, B. E., and **Hoyt, M. F.** Personal responsibility-for-consequences: An integration and extension of the forced compliance literature. *Journal of Experimental Social Psychology,* 1972, *8,* 558–593. **553**

Collins, R. L., and **Marlatt, G. A.** Social modeling as a determinant of drinking behavior: Implications for prevention and treatment. *Addictive Behaviors,* in press. **45**

Combs, B. J., Hales, D. R., and **Williams,**

B. K. *An invitation to health.* Menlo Park, Calif.: Benjamin/Cummings, 1980. **392, 398**

Condry, J. Enemies of exploration: Self-initiated versus other-initiated learning. *American Psychologist,* 1977, *35,* 459–477. **518**

Condry, J., and **Condry, S.** Sex differences: A study of the eye of the beholder. *Child Development,* 1976, *47,* 812–819. **264**

Condry, J., and **Dyer, S.** Fear of success: Attribution of cause to the victim. *Journal of Social Issues,* 1976, *32,* 63–83. **369**

Coon, C. S. The taxonomy of human variation. *Annals of the New York Academy of Sciences,* 1966, *134,* 516–523. **119**

Coon, C. S., Garn, S. M., and **Birdsell, J. B.** *Races: A study of the problems of race formation in man.* Springfield, Ill.: Charles C. Thomas, 1950. **119**

Cooper, J., and **Worchel, S.** Role of undesired consequences in arousing cognitive dissonance. *Journal of Personality and Social Psychology,* 1970, *16,* 199–206. **553**

Coopersmith, S. *The antecedents of self-esteem.* San Francisco: W. H. Freeman, 1967. **429**

Corsini, R. J. (Ed.). *Current personality theories.* Itasca, Ill.: Peacock, 1977. **420**

Costa, P. T., Jr., and **McCrae, R. R.** Influence of extraversion and neuroticism on subjective well-being: Happy and unhappy people. *Journal of Personality and Social Psychology,* 1980, *38,* 668–678. **331, 333**

Costanzo, P. R., and **Woody, E. Z.** Externality as a function of obesity in children: Persuasive style or eating-specific attribute? *Journal of Personality and Social Psychology,* 1979, *37,* 2286–2296. **347**

Coyne, J. Toward an interactional description of depression. *Psychiatry,* 1976a, *39,* 14–27. **496**

Coyne, J. Depression and the response of others. *Journal of Abnormal Psychology,* 1976b, *85,* 186–193. **496**

Craik, F. I. M. Age differences in human memory. In J. E. Birren and K. W. Schaie (Eds.), *Handbook of the psychology of aging.* New York: Van Nostrand Reinhold, 1977. Pp. 384–420. **255, 256, 257**

Craik, F. I. M., and **Lockhart, R. S.** Levels of processing: A framework for memory research. *Journal of Verbal Learning and Verbal Behavior,* 1972, *11,* 671–684. **183**

Craik, F. I. M., and **Tulving, E.** Depth of processing and the retention of words in episodic memory. *Journal of Experimental Psychology: General,* 1975, *104,* 268–294. **197**

Creese, I., Burt, D. R., and **Snyder, S. H.** Brain's dopamine receptor—labeling with [dopamine-H₃] and [H₂₁ operidol-H₃]. *Psychopharmacology Communications,* 1975, *1,* 663–673. **503**

Cronbach, L. J. Five decades of public controversy over mental testing. *American Psychologist,* 1975, *30,* 1–14. **452**

Csikszentmihalyi, M. *Beyond freedom and anxiety.* San Francisco: Jossey-Bass, 1975. **334**

Curtiss, S. *Genie: A psycholinguistic study of a modern-day "wild child."* New York: Academic Press, 1977. **287**

Dahlstrom, W. G., and Welsh, G. S. *An MMPI handbook: A guide to use in clinical practice and research.* Minneapolis: University of Minnesota Press, 1960. **463**

Darley, C. F., Tinklenberg, J. R., Roth, W. T., Hollister, L. E., and Atkinson, R. C. Influence of marihuana on storage and retrieval processes in memory. *Memory and Cognition,* 1973, *1,* 196–200. **395**

Darley, J. M., and Batson, C. D. "From Jerusalem to Jericho": A study of situational and dispositional variables in helping behavior. *Journal of Personality and Social Psychology,* 1973, *27,* 100–108. **604**

Darley, J. M., and Latane, B. Bystander intervention in emergencies: Diffusion of responsibility. *Journal of Personality and Social Psychology,* 1968, *8,* 377–383. **7, 602, 603**

Darwin, C. *On the origin of species by means of natural selection* (1859). Cambridge, Mass.: Harvard University Press, 1964. **15**

Darwin, C. *The descent of man and selection in relation to sex* (1871). New York: Modern Library. **15**

Darwin, C. *The expression of the emotions in man and animals.* London: Murray, 1872. **301**

David-Neel, A. *Magic and mystery in Tibet.* Baltimore: Penguin, 1971. **389**

Davis, J. D., Gallagher, R. J., Ladove, R. F., and Turausky, A. J. Inhibition of food intake by a humoral factor. *Journal of Comparative and Physiological Psychology,* 1969, *67,* 407–414. **344, 345**

Davis, J. M. Overview: Maintenance therapy in psychiatry: I. Schizophrenia. *American Journal of Psychiatry,* 1975, *132,* 1237–1245. **532**

Dawkins, E. *The selfish gene.* New York: Oxford University Press, 1975. **601**

De Carlo, T. J. *Recreational participation patterns and successful aging: A twin study.* Unpublished doctoral dissertation, Columbia University, 1971. **257**

Deci, E. L. Effects of externally mediated rewards on intrinsic motivation. *Journal of Personality and Social Psychology,* 1971, *18,* 105–115. **554**

Decke, E. Effects of taste on the eating behavior of obese and normal persons. Cited in S. Schachter, *Emotion, obesity, and crime.* New York: Academic Press, 1971. **21, 346**

De Groot, A. D. *Thought and choice in chess.* The Hague: Mouton, 1965. **183**

De Lamater, J. A definition of "group." *Small Group Behavior,* 1974, *5,* 30–44. **588**

Dement, W. C. Dream deprivation. *Science,* 1960, *132,* 1420–1422. **379**

Dement, W. C. *Some must watch while some must sleep: Exploring the world of sleep.* New York: Norton, 1976. **375, 377, 378**

Dement, W. C., and Wolpert, E. A. The relation of eye movements, body mobility, and external stimuli to dream content. *Journal of Experimental Psychology,* 1958, *55,* 543–553. **380**

Dennis, W., and Sayegh, J. The effect of supplementary experiences upon the behavioral development of infants in institutions. *Child Development,* 1965, *36,* 81–90. **260**

Denton, G. G. *The influence of visual pattern on perceived speed.* Crowthorne, England: Road Research Library, 1971. **133**

Depue, R. A., and Evans, R. The psychobiology of depressive disorders. In B. H. Maher (Ed.), *Progress in experimental personality research* (Vol. 8). New York: Academic Press, 1976. **495**

Dermer, M., Cohen, S. J., and Anderson, E. A. *Evaluative aspects of life as a function of vicarious exposure to hedonic extremes.* Unpublished paper, University of Wisconsin-Milwaukee, 1978. **332**

Derogatis, L. R., Abeloff, M. D., and Melisaratos, N. Psychological coping mechanisms and survival time in metastatic breast cancer. *Journal of the American Medical Association,* 1979, *242,* 1504–1508. **327**

De Ropp, R. S. *Drugs and the mind.* New York: Dell, 1976. **391**

Deutsch, M., and Gerard, H. B. A study of normative and informational influences on social judgment. *Journal of Abnormal and Social Psychology,* 1955, *51,* 629–636. **582**

De Valois, R. L. Analysis and coding of color vision in the primate visual system. *Cold Spring Harbor Symposia on Quantitative Biology,* 1965a, *30,* 567–579, **115**

De Valois, R. L. Behavioral and electrophysiological studies of primate vision. In W. D. Neff (Ed.), *Contributions to sensory physiology* (Vol. 1). New York: Academic Press, 1965b. **115**

Dienstbier, R. A. Emotion-attribution theory: Establishing roots and exploring future perspectives. In S. Murray and R. Levine (Eds.), *Nebraska Symposium on Motivation,* 1979, *26.* **317, 323**

Dion, K. Physical attractiveness and evaluations of children's transgressions. *Journal of Personality and Social Psychology,* 1972, *24,* 207–213. **558**

Dion, K. Young children's stereotyping of facial attractiveness. *Developmental Psychology,* 1973, *9,* 183–188. **558**

Dion, K., Berscheid, E., and Walster, E. What is beautiful is good. *Journal of Personality and Social Psychology,* 1972, *24,* 285–290. **558**

Dipboye, R. L., Fromkin, H. L., and Wiback, K. Relative importance of applicant sex, attractiveness, and scholastic standing in evaluation of job applicant resumes. *Journal of Applied Psychology,* 1975, *60,* 39–45. **570**

Dittes, J., and Kelley, H. Effects of different conditions of acceptance upon conformity to group norms. *Journal of Abnormal and Social Psychology,* 1956, *53,* 100–107. **582**

Dollard, J., Doob, L. W., Miller, N. E., Mowrer, O. H., and Sears, R. R. *Frustration and aggression.* New Haven: Yale University Press, 1939. **599**

Dollard, J., and Miller, N. E. *Personality and psychotherapy: An analysis in terms of learning, thinking, and culture.* New York: McGraw-Hill, 1950. **417**

Driscoll, R., Davis, K. E., and Lipetz, M. E. Parental interference and romantic love: The Romeo and Juliet effect. *Journal of Personality and Social Psychology,* 1972, *24,* 1–10. **555**

Du Bois, P. H. Review of the Scholastic Aptitude Test. In O. K. Buros (Ed.), *The seventh mental measurements yearbook.* Highland Park, N.J.: Gryphon Press, 1972. Pp. 646–648. **446**

Duffy, E. The psychological significance of the concept of "arousal" or "activation." *Psychological Review,* 1957, *64,* 265–275. **359**

Duncan, C. P. The retroactive effect of electroshock on learning. *Journal of Comparative and Physiological Psychology,* 1949, *42,* 32–44. **198**

Duncker, K. On problem-solving (1935). L. S. Lees (Trans.). *Psychological Monographs,* 1945, *58,* Whole No. 270. **216, 219**

Dunham, H. W. *Community and schizophrenia: An epidemiological analysis.* Detroit: Wayne State University Press, 1965. **481**

Dutton, D. G., and Aron, A. P. Some evidence for heightened sexual attraction under conditions of high anxiety. *Journal of Personality and Social Psychology,* 1974, *30,* 510–517. **568**

Dweck, C. S. The role of expectations and attributions in the alleviation of learned helplessness. *Journal of Personality and Social Psychology,* 1975, *31,* 674–685. **6**

Dweck, C. S., Goetz, T. E., and Strauss, N. L. Sex differences in learned helplessness: IV. An experimental and naturalistic study of failure generalization and its mediators. *Journal of Personality and Social Psychology,* 1980, *38,* 3, 441–452.

Dweck, C. S., and Reppucci, N. D. Learned helplessness and reinforcement responsibility in children. *Journal of Personality and Social Psychology,* 1973, *25,* 109–116. **6**

Dweck, C. S., and Wortman, C. B. Learned helplessness: Cognitions and coping strategies. In H. W. Krohne and L. Laux (Eds.), *Achievement, stress, and anxiety.* Washington, D.C.: Hemisphere, in press. **521**

Eagley, A. H., and Himmelfarb, S. Attitudes and opinions. In *Annual Review of Psychology,* 1978, *29,* 517–554. **554**

Ebbinghaus, H. *Memory: A contribution to experimental psychology* (1885). H. A. Roger and C. E. Bussenius (Trans.). New York: Teachers College, 1913. **201**

Eccles, J. C., Ito, M., and Szentágotnaik, J. *The cerebellum as a neuronal machine.* New York: Springer, 1967. **85**

Edwards, M. K. *Life crisis and myocardial infarction.* Master of Nursing thesis, University of Washington, Seattle, 1971. **327**

Ehrhardt, A. A., and Baker, S. W. *Hormonal aberrations and their implications for the understanding of normal sex differentiation.* Paper presented at the meeting of the Society for Research in Child Development, Philadelphia, 1973. **83**

Eibl-Eibesfeldt, I. *Ethology: The biology of behavior.* E. Klinghammer (Trans.). New York: Holt, Rinehart and Winston, 1970. **302**

Ekman, P., and Friesen, W. V. The repertoire of nonverbal behavior categories, origins, usage, and coding. *Semiotica,* 1969, *1,* 49–98. **300**

Ekman, P., and Friesen, W. V. Constants across culture in the face and emotion. *Jour-*

nal of Personality and Social Psychology, 1971, *17,* 124–129. **300, 302**

Ekman, P., Friesen, W. V., and **Ellsworth, P.** *Emotion in the human face: Guidelines for research and an integration of findings.* Elmsford, N.Y.: Pergamon, 1972.

Ellis, A. *Reason and emotion in psychotherapy.* Secaucus, N.J.: Lyle Stuart, 1962. **520**

Ennis, B. J., and **Emery, R. D.** *The rights of mental patients.* New York: Avon, 1978. **539**

Epstein, A. N. Water intake without the act of drinking. *Science,* 1960, *131,* 497–498. **344**

Epstein, A. N. The lateral hypothalamic syndrome: Its implications for the physiological psychology of hunger and thirst. In E. Stellar and J. M. Sprague (Eds.), *Progress in physiological psychology* (Vol. 4). New York: Academic Press, 1971. **98**

Epstein, A. N., and **Teitelbaum, P.** Regulation of food intake in the absence of taste, smell, and other oropharyngeal sensations. *Journal of Comparative and Physiological Psychology,* 1962, *55,* 753–759. **344**

Epstein, S. The stability of behavior: II. Implications for psychological research. *American Psychologist,* 1980, *35,* 790–806. **427**

Erikson, E. H. *Childhood and society.* New York: Norton, 1950. **268**

Eron, L. D., Huesmann, L. R., Lefkowitz, M. M., and **Walder, L. O.** Does television violence cause aggression? *American Psychologist,* 1972, *27,* 253–263. **598**

Evans, F. J. Contextual forgetting: Posthypnotic source amnesia. *Journal of Abnormal Psychology,* 1979, *88,* 556–563. **385**

Evans, G. *Behavioral and physiological consequences of crowding in humans.* Unpublished doctoral dissertation, University of Massachusetts, Amherst, 1975. **608**

Evans, R. Behavioral medicine: A new applied challenge to social psychologists. In L. Bickman (Ed.), *Applied social psychology annual* (Vol. 1). Beverly Hills, Calif.: Sage Publications, 1980. **547, 550**

Eysenck, H. J. The effects of psychotherapy: An evaluation. *Journal of Consulting Psychology,* 1952, *16,* 319–324. **528**

Eysenck, H. J. *The effects of psychotherapy.* New York: International Science Press, 1966. **528**

Eysenck, H. J. *The biological basis of personality.* Springfield, Ill.: Charles C. Thomas, 1967. **361**

Eysenck, H. J. *The structure of human personality.* London: Methuen, 1970. **424**

Fairweather, G. W., Sanders, D. H., Maynard, H., and **Cressler, D. L.** *Community life for the mentally ill: An alternative to institutional care.* Chicago: Aldine, 1969. **536**

Fazio, R. H., Zanna, M. P., and **Cooper, J.** Dissonance and self-perception: An integrative view of each theory's proper domain of application. *Journal of Experimental Social Psychology,* 1977, *13,* 464–479.

Fechner, G. T. *Elemente der psychophysik.* Leipzig: Breitkopf und Härtel, 1860. **108**

Fenigstein, A. Does aggression cause a preference for viewing media violence? *Journal of Personality and Social Psychology,* 1979, *37,* 2307–2317. **599**

Fenz, W. D., and **Epstein, S.** Gradients of physiological arousal in parachutists as a function of an approaching jump. *Psychosomatic Medicine,* 1967, *29,* 33–51. **47**

Festinger, L. *A theory of cognitive dissonance.* Stanford, Calif.: Stanford University Press, 1957. **551**

Festinger, L., and **Carlsmith, J. M.** Cognitive consequences of forced compliance. *Journal of Abnormal and Social Psychology,* 1959, *58,* 203–210. **551**

Festinger, L., Riecken, H. W., Jr., and **Schachter, S.** *When prophecy fails.* Minneapolis: University of Minnesota Press, 1956. **45**

Festinger, L., Schachter, S., and **Back, K.** *Social pressures in informal groups: A study of human factors in housing.* New York: Harper & Row, 1950. **564**

Fields, H. L. Secrets of the placebo. *Psychology Today,* November 1978, *12,* 172. **80**

Fishbein, M., and **Ajzen, I.** *Belief, attitude, intention, and behavior: An introduction to theory and research.* Reading, Mass.: Addison-Wesley, 1975. **546**

Fisher, A. E. Maternal and sexual behavior induced by intracranial chemical stimulation. *Science,* 1956, *124,* 228–229. **97, 353**

Fisher, A. E. Chemical stimulation of the brain. In *Psychobiology: The biological bases of behavior.* San Francisco: W. H. Freeman, 1967. **353**

Fisher, S., and **Greenberg, R. P.** *The scientific credibility of Freud's theories and therapy.* New York: Basic Books, 1977. **416, 478**

Fixsen, D. L., Phillips, E. A., and **Wolf, M. M.** The teaching-family model of group home treatment. In W. E. Craighead, A. E. Kazdin, and M. J. Mahoney (Eds.), *Behavior modification: Principles, issues, and applications.* Boston: Houghton Mifflin, 1976. **518**

Flavell, J. H., and **Wellman, H. M.** Metamemory. In R. V. Kail, Jr., and J. W. Hagen (Eds.), *Perspectives on the development of memory and cognition.* Hillsdale, N.J.: Lawrence Erlbaum, 1977. Pp. 3–33. **253**

Flynn, J. P., Vanegas, H., Foote, W., and **Edwards, S.** Neural mechanisms involved in a cat's attack on a rat. In R. E. Whalen (Eds.), *Neural control of behavior.* New York: Academic Press, 1970. Pp. 135–173. **313**

Fodor, J. A., and **Bever, T. G.** The psychological reality of linguistic segments. *Journal of Verbal Learning and Verbal Behavior,* 1965, *4,* 414–420. **281**

Foulkes, D. Theories of dream formation and recent studies of sleep consciousness. *Psychological Bulletin,* 1964, *62,* 236–247. **381**

Fowler, O. S., and **Fowler, L. N.** *Phrenology: A practical guide to your head.* New York: Chelsea House, 1969. **72**

Fraser, A., and **Wilcox, K. J.** Perception of illusory movement. *Nature,* 1979, *281,* 565–566. **133**

Freedman, J. *Happy people: What happiness is, who has it, and why.* New York: Harcourt Brace Jovanovich, 1978. **331, 332, 334, 335**

Freedman, J. L. Long-term behavioral effects of cognitive dissonance. *Journal of Experimental Social Psychology,* 1965, *1,* 145–155. **552**

Freedman, J. L., and **Fraser, S. C.** Compliance without pressure: The foot-in-the-door technique. *Journal of Personal and Social Psychology,* 1966, *4,* 195–202. **64**

Freedman, J. L., and **Staff, I.** Crowding, aggressiveness, and external or internal crowding as an intensifier of internal vs. external pleasantness. In J. L. Freedman (Ed.), *Crowding and behavior.* San Francisco: W. H. Freeman, 1975. **608**

Freeman, R. D., Mitchell, D. E., and **Millodot, M.** A neural effect of partial visual deprivation in humans. *Science,* 1972, *175,* 1384–1386. **136**

Freeman, R. D., and **Thibos, L. N.** Electrophysiological evidence that abnormal early visual experience can modify the human brain. *Science,* 1973, *180,* 876–878. **136**

Freud, A. *The ego and mechanisms of defense.* New York: International Universities Press, 1946. **411**

Freud, S. *The interpretation of dreams* (1900). James Strachey (Ed. and Trans.). New York: Basic Books, 1955. **380, 408**

Freud, S. Mourning and melancholia (1917). In *Collected papers* (Vol. 4). London: The Hogarth Press, 1924. **493**

Freud, S. Beyond the pleasure principle (1920). In James Strachey (Ed. and Trans.), *The standard edition of the complete psychological works of Sigmund Freud* (Vol. 18). London: The Hogarth Press, 1953. **409**

Freud, S. *The ego and the id* (1923). London: The Hogarth Press, 1947. **409**

Freud, S. Some psychical consequences of the anatomical distinction between the sexes (1925). In *The standard edition of the works of Sigmund Freud* (Vol. 19). London: The Hogarth Press, 1961. **413**

Freud, S. *Civilization and its discontents* (1930). James Strachey (Ed. and Trans.). New York: Norton, 1962. **411, 596**

Freud, S. *New introductory lectures on psychoanalysis* (1933). James Strachey (Ed. and Trans.). New York: Norton, 1965. **410**

Freud, S. *A general introduction to psychoanalysis.* New York: Washington Square Press, 1935. **412**

Friedman, M., and **Rosenman, R. H.** Association of a specific overt behavior pattern with blood and cardiovascular findings. *Journal of the American Medical Association,* 1959, *169,* 1286. **327**

Friedman, M., and **Rosenman, R. H.** *Type A behavior and your heart.* New York: Knopf, 1974. **327**

Frisch, H. L. Stereotypes in adult-infant play. *Child Development,* 1977, *48,* 1671–1675. **264**

Frodi, A., Macaulay, J., and **Thome, P. R.** Are women always less aggressive than men? A review of the experimental literature. *Psychological Bulletin,* 1977, *84,* 634–660. **262**

Gal, R., and **Lazarus, R. S.** The role of activity in anticipating and confronting stressful situations. *Journal of Human Stress,* 1975, *1,* 4–20. **330**

Galanter, M., Rabkin, R., Rabkin, J., and **Deutsch, A.** The "Moonies": A psychological study of conversion and membership in a contemporary religious sect. *American Journal of Psychiatry,* 1979, *36,* 165–170. **591**

Galton, F. *Hereditary genius: An inquiry into its laws and consequences* (1869). New York: St. Martin's Press, 1979. **16**

Garcia, J., Ervin, F. R., and **Koelling, R. A.** Learning with prolonged delay of reinforcement. *Psychonomic Science,* 1966, *5,* 121–122. **151**

Garcia, J., Hankins, W. G., and **Rusiniak, K. W.** Behavioral regulation of the milieu interne in man and rat. *Science,* 1974, *185,* 824–831. **149**

Garcia, J., Kimeldorf, D. J., and **Hunt, E. L.** The use of ionizing radiation as a motivating stimulus. *Psychological Review,* 1961, *68,* 383. **149**

Garcia, J., Kimeldorf, D. J., Hunt, E. L., and **Davies, B. P.** Food and water consumption of rats during exposure to gamma radiation. *Radiation Research,* 1956, *4,* 33–41. **149**

Garcia, J., and **Koelling, R. A.** Relation of cue to consequence in avoidance learning. *Psychonometric Science,* 1966, *4,* 123–124. **20, 150**

Gardner, B. T., and **Gardner, R. A.** Two-way communication with an infant chimpanzee. In A. M. Schrier and F. Stollnitz (Eds.), *Behavior of nonhuman primates* (Vol. 4). New York: Academic Press, 1972. **283**

Gardner, E. *Fundamentals of neurology.* Philadelphia: Saunders, 1975. **95**

Gardner, L. I. Deprivation dwarfism. *Scientific American,* 1972, *227,* 76–82. **241**

Gardner, R. A., and **Gardner, B. T.** Teaching sign language to a chimpanzee. *Science,* 1969, *165,* 664–672. **283**

Garrow, J. S. *Energy balance and obesity in man.* Amsterdam: Elsevier/North Holland Biomedical Press, 1978. **351**

Gatchel, R. J., and **Price, K. P.** (Eds.). *Clinical applications of biofeedback: Appraisal and status.* Elmsford, N.Y.: Pergamon, 1979. **391**

Gazzaniga, M. S. The split brain in man. *Scientific American,* 1967, *217,* 24–29. **90, 91, 92**

Gazzaniga, M. S. One brain—two minds? *American Scientist,* 1972, *60,* 311–317.

Gearheart, B. R. *Special education for the '80s.* St. Louis: Mosby, 1980. **447**

Geldard, F. A. *The human senses* (2nd ed.). New York: Wiley, 1972. **107, 124**

Gelenberg, A. J. The rational use of psychotropic drugs: Prescribing antidepressants. *Drug Therapy,* 1979, *9,* 95–112. **534**

Gelman, R. Logical capacity of very young children: Number invariance rules. *Child Development,* 1972, *43,* 75–90. **251**

Gersten, J. C., Langner, T. S., Eisenberg, J. G., and **Orzeck, L.** Child behavior and life events: Undesirable change or change per se? In B. S. Dohrenwend and B. P. Dohrenwend (Eds.), *Stressful life events: Their nature and effects.* New York: Wiley, 1974. **329**

Ghiselin, B. (Ed.). *The creative process.* Berkeley: University of California Press, 1952. **223**

Gholson, B., Levine, M., and **Phillips, S.** Hypotheses, strategies, and stereotypes in discrimination learning. *Journal of Experimental Child Psychology,* 1972, *13,* 423–446. **212, 213**

Giantonio, G. W., Lund, N. L., and **Gerall, A. A.** Effects of diencephalic and rhinencephalic lesions on the male rat's sexual behaviour. *Journal of Comparative Physiological Psychology,* 1970, *73,* 38–46. **353**

Gibson, E. J., and **Walk, R. D.** The "visual cliff." *Scientific American,* 1960, *202,* 64–71. **244**

Gil, D. G. *Violence against children.* Cambridge, Mass.: Harvard University Press, 1970. **427**

Gillie, O. Did Sir Cyril Burt fake his research on heritability of intelligence?—Part I. *Phi Delta Kappan,* February 1977, 469–471. **452**

Ginsberg, A. *Kaddish and other poems: Nineteen fifty-eight to nineteen sixty.* San Francisco: City Lights, 1960. **399**

Glanville, B. G., Best, C. T., and **Levenson, R.** A cardiac measure of cerebral asymmetries in infant auditory perception. *Developmental Psychology,* 1977, *13,* 54–59. **288**

Glass, A. L., Holyoak, K. J., and **Santa, J. L.** *Cognition.* Reading, Mass.: Addison-Wesley, 1979. **181**

Glass, D. C., and **Singer, J. E.** *Urban stress: Experiments on noise and social stressors.* New York: Academic Press, 1972. **607**

Globus, A., Rosenzweig, M. R., Bennett, E. L., and **Diamond, M. C.** Effects of differential experience on dendritic spine counts in rat cerebral cortex. *Journal of Comparative Physiological Psychology,* 1973, *82,* 175–181. **200**

Gluckman, M. L., Hirsch, J., McCully, R. S., Barron, B. A., and **Knittle, J. L.** The response of obese patients to weight reduction. II. A quantitative evaluation of behavior. *Psychosomatic Medicine,* 1968, *30,* 359–373. **350**

Glucksburg, S., and **Danks, J. H.** Effects of discriminative labels and of nonsense labels upon availability of novel function. *Journal of Verbal Learning and Verbal Behavior,* 1968, *7,* 12–16. **216**

Goethals, G. R., and **Cooper, J.** When dissonance is reduced: The timing of self-justificatory attitude change. *Journal of Personality and Social Psychology,* 1975, *32,* 361–387. **553**

Goffman, E. *Behavior in public places: Notes on the social organization of gatherings.* Glencoe, Ill.: Free Press, 1963. **566, 601**

Goldberg, P. Are women prejudiced against women? *Trans-Action,* 1968, *5,* 28–30.

Goldberg, S., and **Lewis, M.** The acquisition and violation of expectancy: An experimental paradigm. *Journal of Experimental Child Psychology,* 1969, *7,* 70–80. **261**

Goldstein, A. P. *Therapist-patient expectancies in psychotherapy.* New York: Macmillan, 1962. **529**

Goleman, D. *The varieties of the meditative experience.* New York: Dutton, 1977. **387**

Goodenough, F. L. Expression of the emotions in a blind-deaf child. *Journal of Abnormal and Social Psychology,* 1932, *27,* 328–333. **301**

Goodglass, H., and **Geschwind, N.** Language disorders (aphasia). In E. C. Carterette and M. Friedman (Eds.), *Handbook of perception* (Vol. 8). New York: Academic Press, 1976. **286**

Goodstein, L., and **Sandler, I.** Using psychology to promote human welfare: A conceptual analysis of the role of community psychology. *American Psychologist,* 1978, *33,* 882–891. **537**

Goranson, R. E. Media violence and aggressive behavior. In L. Berkowitz (Ed.), *Advances in experimental and social psychology* (Vol. 5). New York: Academic Press, 1970. **599**

Gorden, H. W., and **Bogen, G. E.** Hemispheric lateralization of singing after intracarotid sodium amylobarbitone. *Journal of Neurology, Neurosurgery, and Psychiatry,* 1974, *37,* 727–738. **286**

Grover, G. Man has no "killer" instinct. In M. F. A. Montagu (Ed.), *Man and aggression.* New York: Oxford University Press, 1968. Pp. 27–36. **18**

Gould, R. L. The phases of adult life: A study in developmental psychology. *American Journal of Psychiatry,* 1972, *129,* 521–531. **269, 270**

Gould, R. L. *Transformations.* New York: Simon and Schuster, 1978. **269, 270**

Graf, R., and **Torrey, J. W.** Perception of phrase structure in written language. *American Psychological Association Convention Proceedings,* 1966, 83–84. **281**

Graham, S. The sociological approach to epidemiology. *American Journal of Public Health,* 1974, *64,* 1046–1049. **329**

Gregory, R. L. *The intelligent eye.* New York: McGraw-Hill, 1970. **132**

Grinker, J. Behavioral and metabolic consequences of weight reduction. *Journal of the American Dietetic Association,* 1973, *62,* 30–34. **350**

Grinspoon, L., and **Bakalar, J. G.** *Cocaine: A drug and its social evolution.* New York: Basic Books, 1976. **397**

Groen, J. J. Psychosocial influences in bronchial asthma. In L. Levi (Ed.), *Society, stress, and disease* (Vol. 1). London: Oxford University Press, 1971. **327**

Grossman, H. J. (Ed.). *Manual on terminology and classification in mental retardation* (3rd ed.). Washington, D.C.: American Association on Mental Deficiency, 1977. **446**

Grossman, S. P. Eating or drinking elicited by direct adrenergic, or chrolinergic stimulation of hypothalamus. *Science,* 1960, *132,* 301–302. **97**

Grossman, S. P. Role of the hypothalamus in the regulation of food and water intake. *Psychological Review,* 1975, *82,* 200–224. **345**

Guilford, J. P. *Personality.* New York: McGraw-Hill, 1959. **421**

Guilford, J. P., and **Hoepfner, R.** *The analysis of intelligence.* New York: McGraw-Hill, 1971. **450**

Gunderson, J. G., Autry, J. H., and **Mosher, L. R.** Special report: Schizophrenia, 1973. *Schizophrenia Bulletin,* 1974, No. 9, 15–54. **501**

Gunne, L. M., Lindstrom, L., and **Terenius, J.** Naloxone-induced reversal of schizophrenic hallucinations. *Journal of Neural Transmissions,* 1977, *40,* 13–19. **503**

Haber, R. N. Eidetic images. *Scientific American*, 1969, *220*, 36–44. **188**

Haber, R. N., and **Standing, L. G.** Direct measures of short-term visual storage. *Quarterly Journal of Experimental Psychology*, 1969, *21*, 43–45. **185**

Haley, J. *Uncommon therapy*. New York: Norton, 1973. **490, 538**

Haley, J. *Leaving home: The therapy of disturbed young people*. New York: McGraw-Hill, 1980. **480, 522, 523**

Hall, C. S., and **Van de Castle, R. L.** *The content analysis of dreams*. New York: Appleton-Century-Crofts, 1966. **380**

Hall, E. T., interviewed by **Kenneth Friedman.** Learning the Arab's silent language. *Psychology Today*, 1979, *13*, 45–54. **78**

Hall, J. A., Rosenthal, R., Archer, D., Di Matteo, M. R., and **Rogers, P. L.** Decoding wordless messages. *Human Nature*, May 1978, 68–75. **302**

Hamill, W. T., and **Fontana, A. F.** The immediate effects of chlorpromazine in newly admitted schizophrenic patients. *American Journal of Psychiatry*, 1975, *132*, 1023–1026. **533**

Hamilton, J. O. Motivation and risk taking behavior: A test of Atkinson's theory. *Journal of Personality and Social Psychology*, 1974, *29*, 856–864. **365**

Hare, A. P. *Handbook of small group research*. New York: Free Press, 1976. **588**

Hare, R. D. *Psychopathy: Theory and research*. New York: Wiley, 1970. **506**

Hariton, E. B., and **Singer, J. L.** Women's fantasies during sexual intercourse: Normative and theoretical implications. *Journal of Consulting and Clinical Psychology*, 1974, *42*, 313–322. **354**

Harlow, H. F. The nature of love. *American Psychologist*, 1958, *13*, 673–685. **258**

Harlow, H. F., and **Harlow, M. K.** Learning to love. *American Scientist*, 1966, *54*, 244–272. **258, 342**

Harlow, H. F., and **Harlow, M. K.** Effects of various mother-infant relationships on rhesus monkey behaviors. In B. M. Foss (Ed.), *Determinants of infant behavior* (Vol. 4). London: Methuen, 1969. Pp. 15–36. **258**

Harlow, H. F., Harlow, M. K., and **Meyer, D. R.** Learning motivated by a manipulation drive. *Journal of Experimental Psychology*, 1950, *40*, 228–234. **357**

Harlow, H. F., Harlow, M. K., and **Suomi, S. J.** From thought to therapy: Lessons from a private library. *American Scientist*, 1971, *59*, 538–549. **259**

Harlow, H. F., and **Suomi, S. J.** The nature of love—simplified. *American Psychologist*, 1970, *25*, 161–168. **258**

Harlow, H. F., and **Suomi, S. J.** Social recovery by isolation-reared monkeys. *Proceedings of the National Academy of Science*, 1971, *68*, 1534–1538. **259**

Harrington, A. *Psychopaths*. New York: Simon and Schuster, 1972. **505**

Harris, T. *I'm OK—you're OK: A practical guide to transactional analysis*. New York: Harper & Row, 1969. **526**

Harris, V. A., and **Katkin, E. S.** Primary and secondary emotional behavior: An analysis of the role of autonomic feedback on affect,

arousal, and attribution. *Psychological Bulletin*, 1975, *82*, 904–916. **320**

Hartman, E. *The biology of dreaming*. Springfield, Ill.: Charles C. Thomas, 1967. **379**

Hartshorne, H., and **May, M. A.** *Studies in the nature of character. Vol. 1, Studies in deceit*. New York: Macmillan, 1928. **425**

Harwood, E., and **Naylor, G. F. K.** Recall and recognition in elderly and young subjects. *Australian Journal of Psychology*, 1969, *21*, 251–257. **256**

Hashim, S. A., and **Van Itallie, T. B.** Studies in normal and obese subjects using a monitored food-dispensing device. *Annals of the New York Academy of Science*, 1965, *131*, 654–661. **346**

Hathaway, S. R., and **McKinley, J. C.** A multiphasic personality schedule (Minnesota): I. Construction of the schedule. *Journal of Psychology*, 1940, *10*, 249–254. **462**

Hayes, K. J., and **Hayes, C.** The intellectual development of a home-raised chimpanzee. *Proceedings of the American Philosophical Society*, 1951, *95*, 105–109. **283**

Hayes, K. J., and **Hayes, C.** Imitation in a home-raised chimpanzee. *Journal of Comparative and Physiological Psychology*, 1952, *45*, 450–459. **172**

Haynes, S. G., Feinleib, M., and **Kannel, W. B.** The relationship of psychosocial factors to coronary heart disease in the Framingham study: III. Eight-year incidence of coronary heart disease. *American Journal of Epidemiology*, 1980, *111*, 37–58. **327**

Hearst, E., and **Jenkins, H. M.** *Sign-tracking: The stimulus-reinforcer relation and directed action*. Austin: Psychonomic Society, 1974.

Hebb, D. Drives and the CNS. *Psychological Review*, 1955, *62*, 243–253. **342, 359**

Heckhausen, H. Achievement motivation and its constructs: A cognitive model. *Motivation and Emotion*, 1977, *1*, 283–329. **366**

Heider, F. Social perception and phenomenal causality. *Psychological Review*, 1944, *51*, 358–374. **559**

Heider, F. *The psychology of interpersonal relations*. New York: Wiley, 1958. **559**

Heinicke, C. M. Parental deprivation in early childhood: A predisposition to later depression? In J. P. Scott and E. C. Senay (Eds.), *Separation and depression: Clinical and research aspects*. Washington, D.C.: American Association for the Advancement of Science, 1973. **493**

Helmrath, T. A., and **Steinitz, E. M.** Death of an infant: Parental grieving and the failure of social support. *Journal of Family Practice*, 1978, *6*, 785–790. **325**

Helmstadter, G. C. *Research concepts in human behavior*. New York: Appleton-Century-Crofts, 1970. **422**

Helson, H. *Adaptation-level theory*. New York: Harper & Row, 1964. **333**

Hendrick, C., and **Costantini, A. F.** Effects of varying trait inconsistency and response requirements on the primacy effect in impression formation. *Journal of Personality and Social Psychology*, 1970, *15*, 158–164. **556**

Henle, M. On the relation between logic and thinking. *Psychological Review*, 1962, *69*, 366–378. **255**

Henning, H. Die Qualitätenreihe des Geschmacks. *Zeitschrift für Psychologie*, 1916, *74*, 203–319.

Herman, C. P. *Possible costs of successful weight control*. Paper presented at the ninth annual meeting of the Association for the Advancement of Behavior Therapy, 1975. **350**

Herman, C. P., and **Mack, D.** Restrained and unrestrained eating. *Journal of Personality*, 1975, *43*, 647–660. **349**

Herman, C. P., and **Polivy, J.** Anxiety, restraint and eating behavior. *Journal of Abnormal Psychology*, 1975, *84*, 666–672. **348**

Herman, C. P., and **Polivy, J.** Restrained eating. In A. J. Stunkard (Ed.), *Obesity*. Philadelphia: W. B. Saunders, 1980.

Heron, W. The pathology of boredom. *Scientific American*, 1957, *196*, 52–56.

Hershey, M. *Characteristics of gifted children*. Gifted Association Conference, Kansas City, Mo., 1976. **449**

Hess, E. H. Attitude and pupil size. *Scientific American*, 1965, *212*, 46–54. **78, 547**

Hess, E. H., and **Polt, J. M.** Pupil size as related to interest value of visual stimuli. *Science*, 1960, *132*, 349–350. **547**

Hess, E. H., and **Polt, J. M.** Pupil size in relation to mental activity during simple problem solving. *Science*, 1964, *143*, 1190–1192. **547**

Hetherington, A. W., and **Ranson, S. W.** Hypothalamic lesions and adiposity in the rat. *The Anatomical Record*, 1940, *78*, 149–172. **98, 345**

Hibscher, J. A., and **Herman, C. P.** Obesity, dieting, and the expression of "obese" characteristics. *Journal of Comparative and Physiological Psychology*, 1977, *91*, 374–380. **348**

Higbee, K. L. Fifteen years of fear arousal: Research on threat appeals: 1953–1968. *Psychological Bulletin*, 1969, *72*, 426–444. **549**

Hilgard, E. R. *Hypnotic susceptibility*. New York: Harcourt Brace Jovanovich, 1965. **383**

Hilgard, E. R. A neodissociation interpretation of pain reduction in hypnosis. *Psychological Review*, 1973, *80*, 396–411. **385, 386**

Hilgard, E. R. Hypnosis. *Annual Review of Psychology*, 1975, *26*, 19–44. **384**

Hilgard, E. R. *Divided consciousness: Multiple controls in human thought and action*. New York: Wiley, 1977. **385**

Hilgard, E. R. Hypnosis and consciousness. *Human Nature*, 1978, *1*, 42–49. **385**

Hilgard, E. R., and **Hilgard, J. R.** *Hypnosis in the relief of pain*. Los Altos, Calif.: William Kaufmann, 1975. **385**

Hilgard, J. R. *Personality and hypnosis: A study of imaginative involvement*. Chicago: University of Chicago Press, 1970. **383**

Hilgard, J. R. Imaginative involvement: Some characteristics of the highly hypnotizable and the nonhypnotizable. *International Journal of Clinical and Experimental Hypnosis*, 1974, *22*, 128–156. **383**

Hill, C. T., Rubin, Z., and **Peplau, L. A.** Breakups before marriage: The end of 103 affairs. *Journal of Social Issues,* 1976, *32,* 147–168. **568**

Hinkle, L. E., Jr. The effect of exposure to culture change, social change, and changes in interpersonal relationships on health. In B. S. Dohrenwend and B. P. Dohrenwend (Eds.), *Stressful life events: Their nature and effects.* New York: Wiley, 1974. **330**

Hirsh, J., and **Knittle, J. L.** Cellularity of obese and nonobese human adipose tissue. *Federation Proceedings,* 1970, *29,* 1516–1521. **348**

Hirst, W., Neisser, U., and **Spelke, E.** Divided attention. *Human Nature,* June 1978, 54–61. **180**

Hochberg, J. E. *Perception.* Englewood Cliffs, N.J.: Prentice-Hall, 1964. **129**

Hodgson, R., and **Rachman, S.** The modification of compulsive behavior. In H. J. Eysenck (Ed.), *Case studies in behaviour therapy.* Boston: Routledge and Kegan Paul, 1976. **488**

Hoebel, B. G., and **Teitelbaum, P.** Hypothalamic control of feeding and self-stimulation. *Science,* 1962, *135,* 375–377. **345**

Hoffman, M. L. Empathy, role-taking, guilt, and development of altruistic motives. In T. Lickona (Ed.), *Moral development and behavior: Theory, research and social issues.* New York: Holt, Rinehart and Winston, 1976. **265, 266**

Hoffman, M. L. Personality and social development. *Annual Review of Psychology,* 1977, *28,* 295–321. **268**

Hoffman, M. L., and **Saltzstein, H. D.** Parent discipline and the child's moral development. *Journal of Personality and Social Psychology,* 1967, *5,* 45–57. **266**

Hoffman, P. J., Slovic, P., and **Rorer, L. G.** An analysis-of-variance model for the assessment of configural cue utilization in clinical judgment. *Psychological Bulletin,* 1968, *69,* 338–349. **227**

Hohmann, G. W. Some effects of spinal cord lesions on experienced emotional feelings. *Psychophysiology,* 1966, *3,* 143–156. **317**

Hollingshead, A. B., and **Redlich, F. C.** *Social class and mental illness: A community study.* New York: Wiley, 1958. **481**

Holmes, T. H., and **Rahe, R. H.** The social readjustment rating scale. *Journal of Psychosomatic Research,* 1967, *11,* 213–218.

Holstein, C. B. Irreversible, stepwise sequence in the development of moral judgment: A longitudinal study of males and females. *Child Development,* 1976, *47,* 31–61. **268**

Horner, M. S. *Sex differences in achievement motivation and performance in competitive and non-competitive situations.* Unpublished doctoral dissertation, University of Michigan, 1968. **366**

Horner, M. S. *Feminine personality and conflict.* Monterey, Calif.: Brooks/Cole, 1970.

Horney, K. Flight from womanhood. *International Journal of Psychoanalysis,* 1926, *7,* 324–339.

Horney, K. *Our inner conflicts.* New York: Norton, 1945. **415**

Horney, K. *Feminine psychology.* New York: Norton, 1967. **414**

Hovland, C. I., Lumsdaine, A., and **Sheffield, F.** *Experiments on mass communication.* Princeton, N.J.: Princeton University Press, 1949. **548**

Hudgens, R. W. Personal catastrophe and depression. In B. S. Dohrenwend and B. P. Dohrenwend (Eds.), *Stressful life events: Their nature and effects.* New York: Wiley, 1974. **329**

Hull, C. L. *A behavior system.* New Haven: Yale University Press, 1952. **341**

Humphreys, M., Revelle, W. R., Simon, L., and **Gilliland, K.** The interactive effect of personality, time of day and caffeine: A test of the arousal model. *Journal of Experimental Psychology: General,* 1980, *109,* 1–31.

Hunter, E. *Brainwashing in Red China: The calculated destruction of men's minds.* New York: Vanguard, 1951.

Hurley, A. D. Unsystematic desensitization using pleasurable images to inhibit anxiety. *Journal of Behavior Therapy and Experimental Psychiatry,* 1976, *7,* 295. **487**

Hutt, C., and **Vaizey, M. J.** Differential effects of group density on social behavior. *Nature,* 1966, *209,* 1371–1372. **608**

Huxley, A. *Brave new world.* New York: Harper & Row, 1932. **419**

Hydén, H., and **Egyhazi, E.** Nuclear RNA changes of nerve cells during a learning experiment in rats. *Proceedings of the United States Academy of Natural Science,* 1962, *48,* 1366–1373. **200**

Hynes, K. Innovative career opportunities and job placement mechanisms in psychology. In P. J. Woods (Ed.), *Career opportunities for psychologists: Expanding and emerging areas.* Washington, D.C.: American Psychological Association, 1976. **29**

Inhelder, B., and **Piaget, J.** *The growth of logical thinking from childhood to adolescence.* New York: Basic Books, 1958. **245**

Insko, C. A., and **Schopler, J.** Triadic consistency: A statement of affective-cognitive-conative consistency. *Psychological Review,* 1967, *74,* 361–376. **546**

Isaacson, R. L. Relation between achievement, test anxiety, and curricular choices. *Journal of Abnormal and Social Psychology,* 1964, *68,* 447–452. **365**

Jackson, R. L., Maier, S. F., and **Coon, D. J.** Long-term analgesic effects of inescapable shock and learned helplessness. *Science,* 1979, *206,* 91–93.

James, W. *The principles of psychology* (Vol. 2). New York: Holt, 1890. **315, 375**

Janis, I. L. *Victims of groupthink: A psychological study of foreign policy decisions and fiascoes.* Boston: Houghton Mifflin, 1972. **594, 595**

Janis, I. L., and **Feshbach, S.** Effects of fear-arousing communication. *Journal of Abnormal and Social Psychology,* 1953, *48,* 78–92. **548**

Janis, I. L., and **Mann, L.** *Decision making: A psychological analysis of conflict, choice, and commitment.* New York: Free Press, 1977. **595**

Janis, I. L., and **Wheeler, D.** Thinking clearly about career choices. *Psychology Today,* May 1978, 67ff. **227**

Janowitz, H. D. Role of gastrointestinal tract in the regulation of food intake. In C. F. Code (Ed.), *Handbook of physiology: Alimentary canal I.* Washington, D.C.: American Physiological Society, 1967. Pp. 219–224. **343**

Janowitz, H. D., and **Grossman, M. I.** Some factors affecting the food intake of normal dogs and dogs with esophagostomy and gastric fistula. *American Journal of Physiology,* 1949, *159,* 143–148. **343**

Jarvik, L. F. Thoughts on the psychobiology of aging. *American Psychologist,* 1975, 576–583. **256**

Jenkins, J. G., and **Dallenbach, K. M.** Obliv-escence during sleep and waking. *American Journal of Psychology,* 1924, *35,* 605–612. **203**

Jensen, A. R. How much can we boost I.Q. and scholastic achievement? *Harvard Educational Review,* 1969, *39,* 1–123. **451, 605**

Jensen, A. R. The heritability of intelligence. *Saturday Evening Post,* 1972, *244,* 9ff. **448**

Jensen, A. R. Did Sir Cyril Burt fake his research on heritability of intelligence?—Part II. *Phi Delta Kappan,* February 1977, 471. **452**

Jensen, A. R. *Bias in mental testing.* New York: Free Press, 1980. **456**

John, E. R. How the brain works—a new theory. *Psychology Today,* May 1976, 50–52. **100**

Johnson, J. E., and **Leventhal, H.** Effects of accurate expectations and behavioral instructions on reactions during a noxious medical examination. *Journal of Personality and Social Psychology,* 1974, *29,* 710–718. **550**

Johnson, J. E., Rice, V. H., Fuller, S. S., and **Endress, M. P.** Sensory information, instruction, in a coping strategy and recovery from surgery. *Research in Nursing and Health,* 1978, *1,* 4–17. **550**

Jones, E. E., and **Davis, K. E.** From acts to dispositions: The attribution process in person perception. In L. Berkowitz (Ed.), *Advances in experimental social psychology* (Vol. 2). New York: Academic Press, 1965. Pp. 219–266. **560**

Jones, E. E., Davis, K. E., and **Gergen, K. J.** Role playing variations and their informational value for person perception. *Journal of Abnormal and Social Psychology,* 1961, *63,* 302–310. **560**

Jones, E. E., and **Harris, V. A.** The attribution of attitudes. *Journal of Experimental Social Psychology,* 1967, *3,* 1–24. **561**

Jones and Jones chapter. In I. M. Birnbaum and E. S. Parker (Eds.), *Alcohol and human memory.* Hillsdale, N.J.: Lawrence Erlbaum, 1977. **392**

Jones, E. E., and **Nisbett, R. E.** *The actor and observer: Perceptions of the causes of behavior.* New York: General Learning Press, 1971. **562**

Jones, M. Community care for chronic mental patients: The need for a reassessment. *Hospital and Community Psychiatry,* 1975, *26,* 94–98. **536**

Jonides, J., Kahn, R., and **Rozin, P.** Imagery instructions improve memory in blind subjects. *Bulletin of the Psychonomic Society,* 1975, *5,* 424-426. **188**

Jordan, H. A. Voluntary intragastric feeding: Oral and gastric contributions to food intake and hunger in man. *Journal of Comparative and Physiological Psychology,* 1969, *68,* 498-506. **344**

Jouvet, M. The stages of sleep. *Scientific American,* 1967, *216,* 62-72. **379**

Judd, D. B., and **Wyszecki, G.** *Color in business, science, and industry.* New York: Wiley, 1963. **119**

Jung, C. G. *Collected works.* H. Read, M. Fordham, and G. Adler (Eds.). R. F. C. Hull (Trans.). Princeton, N.J.: Princeton University Press, 1953. **414**

Jus, A., Pineau, R., Lachance, R., Pelchat, G., Jus, K., Pires, P., and **Villeneuve, R.** Epidemiology of tardive dyskinesia, Part I. *Diseases of the Nervous System,* 1976, *37,* 210-214. **533**

Kagon, J., Kearsley, R., and **Zelazo, P.** *The effects of infant day care on psychological development.* Paper presented at the meeting of the American Association for the Advancement of Science, Boston, February 1976. **260**

Kahneman, D., and **Tversky, A.** On the psychology of prediction. *Psychological Review,* 1973, *80,* 237-251. **229, 561**

Kalat, J. W., and **Rozin, P.** Role of interference in taste-aversion learning. *Journal of Comparative and Physiological Psychology,* 1971, *77,* 53-58. **151**

Kallmann, F. J. *Heredity in health and mental disorder.* New York: Norton, 1953. **501**

Kaltreider, N. B., Wallace, A., and **Horowitz, M .J.** A field study of the stress response syndrome: Young women after hysterectomy. *Journal of the American Medical Association,* 1979, *242,* 1499-1503. **325**

Kamin, L. *The science and politics of IQ.* New York: Wiley, 1974. **452**

Kamin, L. Heredity, intelligence, politics, and psychology: 1. In N. J. Block and G. Dworkin (Eds.), *The IQ controversy.* New York: Pantheon, 1976. **452**

Kanfer, F. F., and **Phillips, J.** *Learning foundations of behavior therapy.* New York: Wiley, 1970.

Kangas, J., and **Bradway, K.** Intelligence at middle age: A thirty-eight-year follow-up. *Developmental Psychology,* 1971, *5,* 333-337. **255**

Kanizsa, G. Subjective contours. *Scientific American,* 1976, *234,* 48-52. **127**

Kaplan, H. S. *The new sex therapy: Active treatment of sexual dysfunctions.* New York: Brunner-Mazel, 1974. **356**

Kasamatsu, A., and **Hirai, T.** An electroencephalographic study on the Zen meditation (Zayen). *Folia Psychiatrica et Neurologica Japonica,* 1966, *20,* 315-366. **388**

Katz, H., Cadoret, R., Hughes, K., and **Abbey, D.** Physiological correlates of acceptable and unacceptable attitude statements. *Psychological Reports,* 1965, *17,* 78. **546**

Katz, M. L. *Female motive to avoid success: A psychological barrier or a response to deviancy?* Princeton, N.J.: Educational Testing Service, 1973. **368**

Kazdin, A. E. *The token economy: A review and evaluation.* New York: Plenum, 1977. **518, 519**

Kazdin, A. E., and **Wilson, G. T.** *Evaluation of behavior therapy: Issues, evidence, and research strategies.* Cambridge, Mass.: Ballenger, 1978. **516, 530**

Kelley, H. H. Attribution theory in social psychology. In D. Levine (Ed.), *Nebraska Symposium of Motivation,* 1967 (Vol. 15). Lincoln: University of Nebraska Press, 1967. Pp. 192-238. **560**

Kelley, H. H. *Attribution in social interaction.* Morristown, N.J.: General Learning Press, 1971. **560**

Kelley, H. H. *Personal relationships.* Hillsdale, N.J.: Lawrence Erlbaum, 1979. **560, 562**

Kellogg, V. Some silkworm moth reflexes. *Biology Bulletin,* Woods Hole, 1907, *12,* 152-154. **353**

Kelman, H. C. Compliance, identification, and internalization: Three processes of attitude change. *Journal of Conflict Resolution,* 1958, *2,* 51-60. **582, 590**

Kelman, H. C. Processes of opinion change. *Public Opinion Quarterly,* 1961, *25,* 57-78. **582, 590**

Kemper, T. D. *A social interaction theory of emotions.* New York: Wiley, 1978. **322**

Kenrick, D., and **Cialdini, R.** Romantic attraction: Misattribution versus reinforcement explanations. *Journal of Personality and Social Psychology,* 1977, *35,* 381-391. **568**

Kesey, K. *One flew over the cuckoo's nest.* New York: Viking, 1962. **399**

Kety, S. S. Biochemical hypotheses and studies. In L. Bellak and L. Loeb (Eds.), *The schizophrenic syndrome.* New York: Grune & Stratton, 1969. Pp. 155-171. **503**

Kiesler, C. A., and **Kiesler, S. B.** *Conformity.* Reading, Mass.: Addison-Wesley, 1969. **580**

Kiesler, C. A., and **Pallak, M. S.** Arousal properties of dissonance manipulations. *Psychological Bulletin,* 1976, *83,* 1014-1025. **554**

Kimble, G. A. *Hilgard and Marquis conditioning and learning* (2nd ed.). New York: Appleton-Century-Crofts, 1961. **145**

Kimmel, A. J. Ethics and human subjects research: A delicate balance. *American Psychologist,* 1979, *34,* 633-635. **65**

King, S. H. Coping mechanisms in adolescents. *Psychiatric Annals,* 1973, *1,* 10-46. **269**

Kinsey, A. C., Pomeroy, W. B., and **Martin, C. E.** *Sexual behavior in the human male.* Philadelphia: Saunders, 1948. **44, 254**

Kinsey, A. C., Pomeroy, W. B., Martin, C. E., and **Gebhard, P. H.** *Sexual behavior in the human female.* Philadelphia: Saunders, 1953. **44, 254**

Kleiter, G. D., Gachowetz, H., and **Huber, D.** *Bibliography: Decision making.* Salzburg: Psychology Institute, University of Salzburg, 1976. **225**

Kleitman, N. *Sleep and wakefulness* (rev. ed.). Chicago: University of Chicago Press, 1963. **377**

Klineberg, O. Emotional expression in Chinese literature. *Journal of Abnormal and Social Psychology,* 1938, *33,* 517-520. **301**

Klüver, H., and **Bucy, P. C.** Preliminary analysis of functions of the temporal lobes in monkeys. *Archives of Neurology and Psychiatry,* 1939, *42,* 979-1000. **87**

Knittle, J. L., and **Hirsch, J.** Effect of early nutrition on the development of rat epididymal fat pads: Cellularity and metabolism. *Journal of Clinical Investigation,* 1968, *47,* 2091. **344**

Kobasa, S. C. Stressful life events, personality, and health. An inquiry into hardiness. *Journal of Personality and Social Psychology,* 1979, *37,* 1-11. **330**

Kobasigawa, A. Utilization of retrieval cues by children in recall. *Child Development,* 1974, *45,* 127-134. **253**

Kohlberg, L. The development of children's orientation toward a moral order: 1. Sequence in the development of moral thought. *Vita Humana,* 1963, *6,* 11-33. **266, 268**

Kohlberg, L. Stage and sequence: The cognitive-developmental approach to socialization. In D. A. Goslin (Ed.), *Handbook of socialization and research.* Chicago: Rand McNally, 1969. Pp. 347-480. **264, 265, 266**

Köhler, I. Experiment with goggles. *Scientific American,* 1962, *206,* 62-72. **127**

Köhler, W. *The mentality of apes.* New York: Harcourt, Brace, 1925. **222**

Köhler, W. *The task of Gestalt psychology.* Princeton, N.J.: Princeton University Press, 1969.

Kohn, M. L. Social class and schizophrenia: A critical review. In D. Rosenthal and S. S. Kety (Eds.), *The transmission of schizophrenia.* London: Pergamon Press, 1968.

Kolb, L. C., Bernard, V. W., and **Dohrenwend, B. S.** (Eds.). *Urban challenges to psychiatry: The case history of a response.* Boston: Little, Brown, 1969. **481**

Kolodny, R. C., Masters, W. H., Kolodner, R. M., and **Toro, G.** Depression of plasma testosterone after chronic marihuana use. *New England Journal of Medicine,* 1974, *290,* 872-874. **31**

Korchin, S. J. *Modern clinical psychology.* New York: Basic Books, 1976. **510, 514**

Kovel, J. *A complete guide to therapy.* New York: Pantheon, 1976. **522**

Kozol, H., Boucher, R., and **Garofolo, R.** Diagnosis and treatment of dangerousness. *Crime and Delinquency,* 1972, *18,* 371-392. **539**

Krashen, S. D. The critical period for language acquisition and its possible basis. In D. Aaronson and R. W. Rieber (Eds.), *Developmental Psycholinguistics and Communication Disorders.* Annals of the New York Academy of Sciences, Vol. 263, 1975, 211-224. **287**

Krasner, L. The future and the past in the behaviorism-humanism dialogue. *American Psychologist,* 1978, *33,* 799-804. **432**

Kübler-Ross, E. *On death and dying.* New York: Macmillan, 1969. **324**

Kuhn, D., Langer, J., Kohlberg, L., and **Haan, N. S.** The development of formal operations in logical and moral judgment.

Genetic Psychology Monographs, 1977, *95L,* 97–188. **268**

Kulik, J. A., and **McKeachie, W. J.** The evaluation of teachers in higher education. In F. N. Kerlinger (Ed.), *Review of research in education.* Itasca, Ill.: Peacock, 1975. **25**

Kuo, Z. Y. The genesis of the cat's responses to the rat. *Journal of Comparative Psychology,* 1930, *11,* 1–35. **597**

Kurtines, W., and **Greif, E. B.** The development of moral thought: Review and evaluation of Kohlberg's approach. *Psychological Bulletin,* 1974, *81,* 453–470. **268**

La Breque, M. On making sounder judgments. *Psychology Today,* June 1980, 33–42. **230**

Lacey, J. I. Somatic response patterning and stress: Some revisions of activation theory. In M. H. Appley and R. Trumbull (Eds.), *Psychological stress.* New York: Appleton-Century-Crofts, 1967. Pp. 14–42. **326**

Lacey, J. I., and **Lacey, B. C.** The law of initial value in the longitudinal study of autonomic constitution: Reproducibility of autonomic responses and response patterns over a four-year interval. *Annuals of the New York Academy of Science,* 1962, *98,* 1257–1326. **326**

Laing, R. D. Is schizophrenia a disease? *International Journal of Social Psychiatry,* 1964, *10,* 184–193. **501**

Laing, R. D., and **Esterson, A.** *Sanity, madness, and the family* (2nd ed.). New York: Basic Books, 1971. **501**

Lamb, H. R., and **Zusman, J.** Primary prevention in perspective. *American Journal of Psychiatry,* 1979, *136,* 12–17. **537**

Landis, C. A. A statistical evaluation of psychotherapeutic methods. In L. E. Hinsie (Ed.), *Concepts and problems of psychotherapy.* New York: Columbia University Press, 1937. Pp. 155–165. **528**

Landy, D., and **Sigall, H.** Beauty is talent: Task evaluation as a function of the performer's physical attractiveness. *Journal of Personality and Social Psychology,* 1974, *29,* 299–304. **558**

Landy, F. J. The validity of the interview in police officer selection. *Journal of Applied Psychology,* 1976, *61,* 193–198. **466**

Lang, P. J., Rice, D. G., and **Sternbach, R. A.** The psychophysiology of emotion. In N. S. Greenfield and R. A. Sternbach (Eds.), *Handbook of psychophysiology.* New York: Holt, Rinehart and Winston, 1972. **312**

Lange, C. G., and **James, W.** *The emotions.* I. A. Haupt (Trans.). Baltimore: Williams & Wilkins, 1922. **315**

Langer, E. J. Old age: An artifact? In *Biology, behavior, and aging.* National Research Council Publication, 1980. **605**

Lanyon, R. I., and **Lanyon, B.** *Behavior therapy: A clinical introduction.* Reading, Mass.: Addison-Wesley, 1978. **158**

LaPiere, R. T. Attitudes vs. actions. *Social Forces,* 1934, *13,* 230–237. **10, 547**

Lashley, K. S. *Brain mechanisms and intelligence.* Chicago: University of Chicago Press, 1929. **100**

Lashley, K. S. *The neuropsychology of Lashley: Selected papers.* F. A. Beach (Ed.). New York: McGraw-Hill, 1960. **156**

Latané, B., and **Darley, J. M.** Group inhibition of bystander intervention in emergencies. *Journal of Personality and Social Psychology,* 1968, *10,* 215–221. **8, 601**

Latané, B., and **Darley, J. M.** *The unresponsive bystander: Why doesn't he help?* New York: Appleton-Century-Crofts, 1970.

Lawson, N. C. *Depression after spinal cord injury: A multimeasure longitudinal study.* Unpublished doctoral dissertation, University of Houston, 1976. **324**

Lazarus, R. S. *Psychological stress and the coping process.* New York: McGraw-Hill, 1966. **327**

Lazarus, R. S. Psychological stress and coping in adaptation and illness. *International Journal of Psychiatry in Medicine,* 1974, *5,* 321–333. **327**

Lazarus, R. S., Cohen, J. B., Folkman, S., Kanner, A., and **Schaefer, C.** Psychological stress and adaptation: Some unresolved issues. In H. Selye (Ed.), *Guide to stress research.* New York: Van Nostrand Reinhold, 1980. **323, 331**

Leavitt, F. *Drugs and behavior.* Philadelphia: Saunders, 1974. **400**

Lederberg, J. Racial alienation and intelligence. *Harvard Educational Review,* 1969, *39,* 611–615. **453**

Lee, T., and **Seeman, P.** Dopamine receptors in normal and schizophrenic human brains. *Society for Neuroscience Abstracts* (Vol. 3). Bethesda, Md.: Society for Neuroscience, 1977, 443. **503**

Lehmann, E., Beeler, G. W., and **Fender, D. H.** EEG responses during the observation of stabilized and normal retinal images. *Electroencephalograph and Clinical Neurophysiology,* 1967, *22,* 136–142. **389**

Leibowitz, H. W., and **Pick, H. A., Jr.** Cross-cultural and educational aspects of the Ponzo perspective illusion. *Perception and Psychophysics,* 1972, *12,* 430–432. **135**

Levine, M. *A cognitive theory of learning.* Hillsdale, N.J.: Lawrence Erlbaum, 1975. **213**

LeMagnen, J. Advances in studies on the physiological control and regulation of food intake. In E. Stellar and J. M. Sprague (Eds.), *Progress in physiological psychology* (Vol. 4). New York: Academic Press, 1971. **343**

Lenneberg, E. *The biological foundations of language.* New York: Wiley, 1967. **288**

Leopold, R. L., and **Dillon, H.** Psychoanatomy of a disaster: A long-term study of posttraumatic neurosis in survivors of a marine explosion. *American Journal of Psychiatry,* 1963, *119,* 913–921. **478**

Lepper, M. R., and **Greene, D.** (Eds.). *The hidden cost of reward.* Hillsdale, N.J.: Lawrence Erlbaum, 1978. **554**

Lepper, M. R., Greene, D., and **Nisbett, R. E.** Undermining children's intrinsic interest with extrinsic reward: A test of the "overjustification" hypothesis. *Journal of Personality and Social Psychology,* 1973, *28,* 129–137. **554**

Lettvin, J. Y. What the frog's eye tells the frog's brain. *Proceedings of the Institute of Radio Engineers,* 1959, *47,* 1940–1951. **99**

Leventhal, H., Jones, S., and **Trembly, G.** Sex differences in attitude and behavior change under conditions of fear and specific instructions. *Journal of Experimental Social Psychology,* 1966, *2,* 387–399. **549**

Leventhal, H., Meyer, D., and **Nerenz, D.** The common sense representation of illness danger. In S. Rachman (Ed.), *Medical psychology* (Vol. 2). Elmsford, N.Y.: Pergamon, 1980. **550**

Leventhal, H., and **Singer, R.** Affect arousal and positioning of recommendation in persuasive communications. *Journal of Personality and Social Psychology,* 1966, *4,* 137–146. **549**

Leventhal, H., Singer, R., and **Jones, S.** The effects of fear and specificity of recommendation upon attitudes and behavior. *Journal of Personality and Social Psychology,* 1954, *2,* 20–29. **549, 550**

Leventhal, H., Watts, J. C., and **Pagano, F.** Effects of fear and instructions on how to cope with danger. *Journal of Personality and Social Psychology,* 1967, *6,* 313–321. **549**

Levinson, D. J., with **Darrow, C. N., Klein, E. B., Levinson, M. H.,** and **McKee, B.** *The seasons of a man's life.* New York: Knopf, 1978. **270**

Levitin, T. E., Quinn, R. P., and **Staines, G. L.** A woman is 58% of a man. *Psychology Today,* 1973, *6,* 89–92. **570**

Levitsky, A., and **Perls, F. S.** The rules and games of gestalt therapy. In J. Fagan and I. L. Sheperd (Eds.), *Gestalt therapy now.* Palo Alto, Calif.: Science and Behavior Books, 1970. **524**

Lewinsohn, P. M. A behavioral approach to depression. In R. J. Friedman and M. M. Katz (Eds.), *The psychology of depression: Contemporary theory and research.* Washington, D.C.: V. H. Winston, 1974. **493**

Lewinsohn, P. M., Mischel, W., Chaplin, W., and **Barton, R.** Social competence and depression: The role of illusory self-perceptions. *Journal of Abnormal Psychology,* 1980, *89,* 203–212. **493**

Lewis, H. R., and **Papadimitriou, C. H.** The efficiency of algorithms. *Scientific American,* 1978, *238,* 96–109.

Lewis, M., and **Brooks, J.** Self-knowledge and emotional development. In M. Lewis and L. Rosenblum (Eds.), *The development of affect.* New York: Plenum, 1978. Pp. 205–226. **261**

Liberman, R. P., Levine, J., Wheeler, E., Sanders, N., and **Wallace, C. J.** Marital therapy in groups: A comparative evaluation of behavioral and interactional formats. *Acta Psychiatrica Scandinavica,* 1976, Supplementum 266, 1–34.

Lidz, T. *The origin and treatment of schizophrenic disorders.* New York: Basic Books, 1973. **500**

Lidz, T., Cornelison, A., Fleck, S., and **Terry, D.** The intrafamilial environment of schizophrenic patients: II. Marital schism and marital skew. *American Journal of Psychiatry,* 1957, *114,* 241–248. **500**

Liebelt, R. A., Bordelon, C. B., and **Liebelt, A. G.** The adipose tissue system and food intake. In E. Stellar and J. M. Sprague (Eds.), *Progress in physiological psychology.* New York: Academic Press, 1973. **346**

Lieberman, M. A., and **Coplan, A. S.** Distance from death as a variable in the study of aging. *Developmental Psychology,* 1970, 71–84. **271**

Lieberman, M. A., and **Mullan, J. T.** Does help work? The adaptive consequences of obtaining help from professionals and social networks. *American Journal of Community Psychology,* 1978, *6,* 499–517. **605**

Lieberman, M. A., Yalom, I. D., and **Miks, M. B.** *Encounter groups: First facts.* New York: Basic Books, 1973. **527**

Liebert, R. M., Neale, J. M., and **Davidson, E. S.** *The early window: Effects of television on children and youth.* Elmsford, N.Y.: Pergamon, 1973. **598**

Liebowitz, M. R., and **Klein, D. F.** Hysteroid dysphoria. *Psychiatric Clinics of North America,* 1979, *2,* 555–575. **567**

Liem, J. H. Effects of verbal communications of parents and children: A comparison of normal and schizophrenic families. *Journal of Consulting and Clinical Psychology,* 1974, *42,* 438–450. **501**

Linder, D. E., Cooper, J., and **Jones, E. E.** Decision freedom as a determinant of the role of incentive magnitude in attitude change. *Journal of Personality and Social Psychology,* 1967, *6,* 245–254. **553**

Lindholm, E., and **Lowry, S.** Alpha production in humans under conditions of false feedback. *Bulletin of the Psychonomic Society,* 1978, *11,* 106–108. **391**

Lindner, R. *The fifty-minute hour.* New York: Holt, Rinehart and Winston, 1954. **513**

Lindsay, P. H., and **Norman, D. A.** *Human information processing: An introduction to psychology* (2nd ed.). New York: Academic Press, 1977. **189**

Lindsley, D. B. Emotion. In S. S. Stevens (Ed.), *Handbook of experimental psychology.* New York: Wiley, 1951. **359**

Linsenmeier, J. A., and **Wortman, C. B.** Attitudes toward workers and toward their work: More evidence that sex makes a difference. *Journal of Applied Social Psychology,* 1979, *4,* 326–324. **572**

Linton, M. I remember it well. *Psychology Today,* July 1978, 81–86. **201**

Lloyd, G. G., and **Lishman, W. A.** Effect of depression on the speed of recall of pleasant and unpleasant experiences. *Psychological Medicine,* 1975, *5,* 173–180. **494**

Loehlin, J. C., Lindzey, G., and **Spuhler, J. N.** *Racial differences in intelligence.* San Francisco: W. H. Freeman, 1975. **454**

Loftus, E. F. Leading questions and the eyewitness report. *Cognitive Psychology,* 1975, *7,* 560–572. **44, 193**

Loftus, E. F. Shifting human color memory. *Memory and Cognition,* 1977, *5,* 696–699.

Loftus, E. F. Human memory. In G. Lindzey, C. Hall, and R. F. Thompson, *Psychology.* New York: Worth, 1978.

Loftus, E. F. *Eyewitness testimony.* Cambridge, Mass.: Harvard University Press, 1979. **191, 194, 205**

Loftus, E. F. Reactions to blatantly contradictory information. *Memory and Cognition,* 1979, *7,* 368–374.

Loftus, E. F., and **Loftus, G. R.** On the permanence of stored information in the human brain. *American Psychologist,* 1980, *35,* 409–420. **203**

Loftus, E. F., Miller, D. G., and **Burns, H. J.** Semantic integration of verbal information into a visual memory. *Journal of Experimental Psychology,* 1978, *4,* 19–31. **59, 193, 194**

Loftus, G. R., and **Loftus, E. F.** *Human memory: The processing of information.* Hillsdale, N.J.: Lawrence Erlbaum, 1976.

Lorenz, K. *Evolution and modification of behavior.* Chicago: University of Chicago Press, 1965. **287**

Lorenz, K. *The eight deadly sins of civilized man.* Marjorie Kerr-Wilson (Trans.). New York: Harcourt Brace Jovanovich, 1974. **596**

Luborsky, L., Singer, B., and **Luborsky, L.** Comparative studies of psychotherapies. *Archives of General Psychiatry,* 1975, *32,* 995–1008. **529**

Luborsky, L., and **Spence, D. P.** Quantitative research on psychoanalytic therapy. In S. L. Garfield and A. E. Bergin (Eds.), *Handbook of psychotherapy and behavior change: An empirical analysis* (2nd ed.). New York: Wiley, 1978. **513**

Luce, G. G. *Body time.* New York: Random House, 1971. **205**

Luchins, A. S. Classroom experiments on mental set. *American Journal of Psychology,* 1946, *59,* 295–298. **220**

Luchins, A. S. Primacy-recency in impression formation. In C. I. Hovland (Ed.), *The order of presentation in persuasion.* New Haven: Yale University Press, 1957. Pp. 33–61. **556**

Lumsdaine, A., and **Janis, I.** Resistance to "counter-propaganda" produced by one-sided and two-sided "propaganda" presentations. *Public Opinion Quarterly,* 1953, *17,* 311–318. **556**

Luria, A. *The mind of a mnemonist.* Lynn Solotaroff (Trans.). New York: Basic Books, 1968. **205**

Lynch, J. J., Paskewitz, D. A., and **Orne, M. T.** Some factors in the feedback control of human alpha rhythm. *Psychosomatic Medicine,* 1974, *36,* 399–410. **391**

Maccoby, E. E., and **Jacklin, C. N.** *The psychology of sex differences.* Stanford, Calif.: Stanford University Press, 1974. **83, 261, 262, 263, 571**

MacDonald, M. L., Lidsky, T. I., and **Kern, J. M.** Drug instigated effects. In A. P. Goldstein and F. H. Kanfer (Eds.), *Maximizing treatment gains: transfer enhancement in psychotherapy.* New York: Academic Press, 1979. Pp. 429–444. **533**

MacDonald, M. L., and **Tobias, L. L.** Withdrawal causes relapse? Our response. *Psychological Bulletin,* 1976, *83,* 448–451. **532**

Macfarlane, D. A. The role of kinesthesis in maze learning. *University of California Publications in Psychology,* 1930, *4,* 277–305. **170**

MacKinnon, D. W. The nature and nurture of creative talent. *American Psychologist,* 1962, *17,* 484–495. **432, 449**

MacKinnon, D. W. Personality and the realization of creative potential. *American Psychologist,* 1965, *20,* 273–281. **432, 449**

MacLean, P. D. Contrasting function of limbic and neocortical systems of the brain and their relevance to psychophysiological aspects of medicine. *American Journal of Medicine,* 1958, *25,* 611–626. **87**

MacNichol, E. F., Jr. Three-pigment color vision. *Scientific American,* 1964, *211,* 48–56. **115**

Maddi, S. *Personality theories: A comparative analysis* (3rd ed.). Homewood, Ill.: Dorsey, 1976. **405**

Madsen, K. B. *Theories of motivation: A comparative study of modern theories of motivation.* Copenhagen: Munksgaard, 1959. **339**

Magoun, H. W. *The waking brain.* Springfield, Ill.: Charles C. Thomas, 1963. **85**

Maguire, G. P., Lee, E. G., Bevington, D. J., Kuchemann, C. S., Crabtree, R. J., and **Cornell, C. E.** Psychiatric problems in the first year after mastectomy. *British Medical Journal,* 1978, *1,* 963–965. **325**

Mahone, C. H. Fear of failure and unrealistic vocational aspiration. *Journal of Abnormal and Social Psychology,* 1960, *60,* 253–261. **365**

Mahoney M. J., and **Arnkoff, D.** Cognitive and self-control therapies. In S. L. Garfield and A. E. Bergin (Eds.), *Handbook of psychotherapy and behavior change: An empirical analysis* (2nd ed.). New York: Wiley, 1978. **518**

Mahoney, M. J., and **Mahoney, K.** Fight fat with behavior control. *Psychology Today,* 1976, *9,* 39–43, 92–94. **351**

Maier, N. R. F. Reasoning in humans. *Journal of Comparative Psychology,* 1931, *12,* 181–194. **210**

Malinowski, B. *The sexual life of savages in northwestern Melanesia.* New York: Eugenics Press, 1929. **262**

Malsbury, C. W. Facilitation of male rat copulatory behaviour by electrical stimulation of the medial preptic area. *Physiology and Behavior,* 1971, *7,* 797–805. **353**

Marañon, G. Contribution à l'etude de l'action emotive de l'adrenaline. *Revue Francaise d'Endocrinologie,* 1924, *2,* 301–325. **316**

Mark, V. H., and **Ervin, F. R.** *Violence and the brain.* New York: Harper & Row, 1970. **313, 596**

Markman, E. Realizing that you don't understand: A preliminary investigation. *Child Development,* 1977, *48,* 986–992. **254**

Marks, I. M., and **Gelder, M. G.** Transvestism and fetishism: Clinical and psychological changes during faradic aversion. *British Journal of Psychiatry,* 1967, *113,* 711–729. **516**

Marlatt, G. A., and **Nathan, P. E.** (Eds.). *Behavioral approaches to alcoholism.* New Brunswick, N.J.: Rutgers Center for Alcohol Studies, 1978. **45**

Marsh, C. A framework for describing subjective states of consciousness. In N. E. Zinberg (Ed.), *Alternate states of consciousness.* New York: Free Press, 1977. Pp. 145–157. **373**

Marshall, G. D., and **Zimbardo, P. G.** Affective consequences of inadequately explained physiological arousal. *Journal of Personality and Social Psychology,* 1979, *37,* 970–988. **322, 323**

Maslach, C. Burned-out. *Human Behavior,* 1976, *5,* 16–22. **605, 606**

Maslach, C. The client role in staff burn-out. *Journal of Social Issues,* 1978, *34,* 111–124. **605**

Maslach, C. Negative emotional biasing of unexplained arousal. *Journal of Personality and Social Psychology,* 1979, *37,* 359–369. **322**

Maslow, A. H. *Motivation and personality.* New York: Harper & Row, 1954. **342, 431**

Maslow, A. H. *The psychology of science: A reconnaissance.* New York: Harper & Row, 1966. **430**

Maslow, A. H. *Toward a psychology of being* (2nd ed.). New York: Van Nostrand Reinhold, 1968. **430**

Maslow, A. H. *Motivation and personality* (2nd ed.). New York: Harper & Row, 1970. **430**

Maslow, A. H. *The farther reaches of the human mind.* New York: Viking, 1971a. **430**

Maslow, A. H. Some basic propositions of a growth and self-actualization psychology. In S. Maddi (Ed.), *Perspectives on personality.* Boston: Little, Brown, 1971b. **430**

Mason, J. W. A re-evaluation of the concept of "non-specificity" in stress theory. *Journal of Psychiatric Research,* 1971, *8,* 323–333. **327**

Mason, J. W. Specificity in the organization of neuroendocrine response profiles. In P. Seeman and G. M. Brown (Eds.), *Frontiers in neurology and neuroscience research.* First International Symposium of the Neuroscience Institute. Toronto: University of Toronto, 1974. **327**

Mason, J. W. Emotion as reflected in patterns of endocrine regulation. In L. Levi (Ed.), *Emotions: Their parameters and measurement.* New York: Raven Press, 1975. **323, 327**

Mason, J. W., Maher, J. T., Hartley, L. H., Morigey, E., Perlow, M. J., and **Jones, L. G.** Selectivity of corticosteroid and catecholamine response to various natural stimuli. In G. Serban (Ed.), *Psychopathology of human adaptation.* New York: Plenum, 1976. Pp. 141–171. **323**

Mason, M. K. Learning to speak after years of silence. *Journal of Hearing and Speech Disorders,* 1942, *7,* 295–304. **287**

Mason, W. A. The effects of social restriction on the behavior of rhesus monkeys: III. Tests of gregariousness. *Journal of Comparative and Physiological Psychology,* 1961, *54,* 287–290. **303**

Masters, R. E. L., and **Houston, J.** *Psychedelic art.* New York: Grove Press, 1968. **399**

Masters, W. H., and **Johnson, V. E.** *Human sexual response.* Boston: Little, Brown, 1966. **47, 355**

Masters, W. H., and **Johnson, V. E.** *Human sexual inadequacy.* Boston: Little, Brown, 1970. **356, 357**

Mathews, K. E., and **Canon, L. K.** Environmental noise level as a determinant of helping behavior. *Journal of Personality and Social Psychology,* 1975, *32,* 571–577. **607**

May, R. *Love and will.* New York: Norton, 1969. **482**

Mayer-Gross, W., Slater, E., and **Roth, M.** *Clinical psychiatry.* Baltimore: Williams & Wilkins, 1969. **498**

McArthur, L., and **Post, D.** Figural emphasis and person perception. *Journal of Experimental Social Psychology,* 1977, *13,* 520–535. **562**

McCardell, J., and **Murray, E. J.** Nonspecific factors in weekend encounter groups. *Journal of Consulting Clinical Psychology,* 1974, *42,* 337. **530**

McCary, J. L. *McCary's human sexuality* (3rd ed.). New York: Van Nostrand Reinhold, 1978.

McClelland, D. C. Some social consequences of achievement motivation. In M. R. Jones (Ed.), *Nebraska symposium on motivation 1955.* Lincoln: University of Nebraska Press, 1955. **365**

McClelland, D. Testing for competence rather than for "intelligence." *American Psychologist,* 1973, 1–14. **448, 456**

McClelland, D. C. Managing motivation to expand human freedom. *American Psychologist,* 1978, 201–210. **366**

McClelland, D. C., and **Atkinson, J. W.** The projective expression of needs: I. The effects of different intensities of the hunger drive on perception. *Journal of Psychology,* 1948, *25,* 205–232. **134**

McClelland, D. C., Atkinson, J. W., Clark, R. W., and **Lowell, E. L.** *The achievement motive.* New York: Appleton-Century-Crofts, 1953. **342, 364**

McClelland, D. C., and **Winter, D. G.** *Motivating economic achievement.* New York: Free Press, 1969. **366**

McConnell, J. V. *New evidence for "transfer of training" effect in planarians: Symposium on the biological bases of memory traces.* Paper read at the Eighth International Congress of Psychology, Moscow, 1966. **200**

McCulloch, J. W., and **Prins, H. A.** *Signs of stress.* London: Collins, 1975. **487, 488**

McDougall, W. *Social psychology.* New York: Putnam's, 1908.

McGaugh, J. L. Time-dependent processes in memory storage. *Science,* 1966, *153,* 1351–1358. **201**

McGuire, W. J. Some impending reorientations in social psychology: Some thoughts provoked by Kenneth Ring. *Journal of Experimental Social Psychology,* 1976a, *3,* 124–139. **610**

McGuire, W. J. *Theory-oriented research in natural settings: The best of both worlds for social psychology.* Symposium paper presented at Pennsylvania State University, May 1967b. **610**

McGuire, W. J. Theory of the structure of human thought. In R. Abelson, E. Aronson, W. J. McGuire, T. Newcomb, M. Rosenberg, and P. Tannenbaum (Eds.), *Theories of cognitive consistency: A sourcebook.* Chicago: Rand McNally, 1968. Pp. 140–162. **549**

McIntyre, A. Sex differences in children's aggression. *Proceedings of the 80th Annual Convention of the American Psychological Association,* 1972, *7,* 93–94. **261**

McKee, S. P., McCann, J. J., and **Benton, J. L.** Color vision from rod and long-wave cone interactions: Conditions in which rods contribute to multicolored images. *Vision Research,* 1977, *17,* 175–185. **113**

McKinney, F. Fifty years of psychology. *American Psychologist,* 1976, *31,* 834–842. **15**

McNeil, E. B. *The quiet furies.* Englewood Cliffs, N.J.: Prentice-Hall, 1967. **505**

McNeill, D. Developmental psycholinguistics. In F. L. Smith and G. A. Miller (Eds.), *The genesis of language: A psycholinguistic approach.* Cambridge, Mass.: MIT Press, 1966. **294**

McPeak, W. R. Family therapies. In A. P. Goldstein and F. H. Kanfer (Eds.), *Maximizing treatment gains: transfer enhancement in psychotherapy.* New York: Academic Press, 1979. Pp. 155–181. **522, 523**

Mead, M. *Sex and temperament in three primitive societies.* New York: Morrow, 1935. **262**

Mehrabian, A. Relationship of attitude to seated posture, orientation, and distance. *Journal of Personality and Social Psychology,* 1968, *10,* 26–30. **566**

Mehrabian, A. *Nonverbal communication.* Chicago: Aldine-Atherton, 1972. **300**

Meichenbaum, D. H. (Ed.). *Cognitive behavior modification: An integrative approach.* New York: Plenum, 1977. **521**

Meichenbaum, D. H., Henshaw, D., and **Himmel, N.** Coping with stress as a problem-solving process. In W. Krohne and L. Laux (Eds.), *Achievement stress and anxiety.* Washington, D.C.: Hemisphere, in press.

Mellinger, G. D., Balter, M. B., Manheimer, D. I., Cisin, I. H., and **Parry, H. J.** Psychic distress, life crisis, and use of psychotherapeutic medications: National household survey data. *Archives of General Psychiatry,* 1978, *35,* 1045–1052. **531**

Meltzer, H. Individual differences in forgetting pleasant and unpleasant experiences. *Journal of Educational Psychology,* 1930, *21,* 399–409. **203**

Meltzer, H. Y., and **Stahl, S. M.** Dopamine hypothesis of schizophrenia—Review. *Schizophrenic Bulletin,* 1976, *2,* 19–76. **503**

Menyuk, P., and **Bernholtz, N.** Prosodic features and children's language production. *M.I.T. Research Laboratory of Electronics Quarterly Progress Reports,* 1969, *93,* 216–219. **289**

Merton, R. K., and **Kitt, A. S.** Contributions to the theory of reference group behavior. In R. K. Merton and P. F. Lazarsfeld (Eds.), *Continuities in social research: Studies in the scope and method of "The American Soldier."* Glencoe, Ill.: Free Press, 1950. **332**

Meyer, V., Gross, C. G., and **Teuber, H.** Effect knowledge of site of stimulation on the threshold for pressure sensitivity. *Perception and Motor Skills,* 1963, *16,* 637–640. **108**

Milgram, S. *Dynamics of obedience: Experiments in social psychology.* Mimeographed report, National Science Foundation, January 25, 1961. **584, 585**

Milgram, S. Behavioral study of obedience. *Journal of Abnormal and Social Psychology,* 1963, *67,* 371–378. **23, 48, 59, 583, 584, 585, 587**

Milgram, S. Issues in the study of obedience: A reply to Baumrind. *American Psychologist,* 1964, *19,* 848–852. **587**

Milgram, S. Some conditions of obedience and disobedience to authority. In I. D. Steiner and M. Fishbein (Eds.), *Current studies in social psychology.* New York: Holt, Rinehart and Winston, 1965. Pp. 243–262. **583, 586**

Milgram, S. Some conditions of obedience and disobedience to authority. *Human Relations,* 1968, *18,* 56–76. **587**

Milgram, S. The experience of living in cities: A psychological analysis. *Science,* 1970, *167,* 1461–1468. **586, 604**

Milgram, S. *Obedience to authority.* New York: Harper & Row, 1974. **585, 587**

Milgram, S. *The individual in a social world.* Reading, Mass.: Addison-Wesley, 1977. **588**

Miller, D. T., and Ross, M. Self-serving biases in the attribution of causality: Fact or fiction? *Psychological Bulletin,* 1975, *82,* 213–225. **563**

Miller, G. A. The magical number seven, plus or minus two: Some limits on our capacity for processing information. *Psychological Review,* 1956, *63,* 81–97. **182**

Miller, G. A. *Psychology.* New York: Harper & Row, 1962. **17, 442**

Miller, L. L., Cornett, T. L., Brightwell, D. R., McFarland, D. J., Drew, W. G., and Winkler, A. Marijuana: Effects on storage and retrieval of prose material. *Psychopharmacology,* 1977, *51,* 311–316. **396**

Miller, L. L., Cornett, T. L., and McFarland, D. J. Marijuana: An analysis of storage and retrieval deficits in memory with the technique of restricted reminding. *Pharmacology Biochemistry and Behavior,* 1978, *8,* 327–332. **396**

Miller, N. E. The frustration-aggression hypothesis. *Psychological Review,* 1941, *48,* 337–342. **599**

Miller, N. E. Experimental studies of conflict. In J. McV. Hunt (Ed.), *Personality and the behavior disorders* (Vol. 1). New York: Ronald Press, 1944. Pp. 431–465. **417**

Miller, N. E. Theory and experiment relating psychoanalytic displacement to stimulus-response generalization. *Journal of Abnormal and Social Psychology,* 1948, *43,* 155–178. **418**

Miller, N. E. Experiments on motivation. *Science,* 1957, *126,* 1271–1278. **97**

Miller, N. E. Liberalization of basic S-R concepts: Extensions to conflict behavior, social motivation and learning. In S. Koch (Ed.), *Psychology: A study of a science* (Vol. 2). New York: McGraw-Hill, 1959. **418**

Miller, N. E. Biofeedback: Evaluation of a new technic. *New England Journal of Medicine,* 1974, *290,* 684–685. **391**

Miller, N. E., and Bugelski, R. Minor studies of aggression: II. The influence of frustrations imposed by the in-group on attitudes expressed toward out-groups. *Journal of Psychology,* 1948, *25,* 437–452. **573**

Miller, R. E., Caul, W. F., and Mirsky, I. A. Communication of affects between feral and socially isolated monkeys. *Journal of Personality and Social Psychology,* 1967, *7,* 231–239. **303**

Miller, R. G., Rubin, R. T., Clark, B. R., Crawford, W. R., and Arthur, R. J. The stress of aircraft carrier landings: I. Corticosteroid responses in naval aviators. *Psychosomatic Medicine,* 1970, *32,* 581–588. **330**

Mills, K. C., Sobell, M. B., and Schaefer, H. H. Training social drinking as an alternative to abstinence for alcoholics. *Behavior Therapy,* 1971, *2,* 18–27. **516, 518**

Mills, M., and Melhuish, E. Recognition of mother's voice in early infancy. *Nature,* 1974, *252,* 123–124. **243**

Milner, B. Some effects of frontal lobectomy in man. In J. M. Warren and K. Arent (Eds.), *The frontal granular cortex and behavior.* New York: McGraw-Hill, 1964. **88**

Milner, B. Amnesia following operation on the temporal lobes. In C. W. M. Whitty and O. L. Zangwill (Eds.), *Amnesia.* London: Butterworth, 1966. **46, 197**

Milton, K. Women in policing. *Police Foundation,* 1972. **570**

Mintz, E. E. Marathon groups as intensive psychotherapy. In D. S. Milman and G. D. Goldman (Eds.), *Group process today: Evaluation and perspective.* Springfield, Ill.: Charles C. Thomas, 1974. **527**

Minuchin, S. *Families and family therapy.* Cambridge, Mass.: Harvard University Press, 1974. **480**

Minuchin, S., Rosman, B. L., and Baher, L. *Psychosomatic families.* Cambridge, Mass.: Harvard University Press, 1978. **327**

Mischel, W. *Personality and assessment.* New York: Wiley, 1968. **425**

Mitchell, K. M., Bozarth, J. D., and Krauft, C. C. A reappraisal of the therapeutic effectiveness of accurate empathy, nonpossessive warmth, and genuineness. In A. S. Gurman and A. M. Razin (Eds.), *Effective psychotherapy: A handbook of research.* New York: Pergamon, 1977. **524**

Monahan, L., Kuhn, D., and Shaver, P. Intrapsychic versus cultural explanations of the "fear of success" motive. *Journal of Personality and Social Psychology,* 1974, *29,* 60–64. **368**

Monnier, M., Boehmer, A., and Scholer, A. Early habituation, dishabituation, and generalization induced in visual center by color stimuli. *Vision Research,* 1976, *16,* 1497–1504. **246**

Montour, K. William James Sidis, the broken twig. *American Psychologist,* 1977, *32,* 265–279. **448**

Morrell, P., and Norton, W. T. Myelin. *Scientific American,* 1980, *242,* 88ff. **79**

Moss, H. A. Sex, age, and state as determinants of mother-infant interaction. *Merrill-Palmer Quarterly of Behavior and Development,* 1967, *13,* 19–36. **261**

Murray, H. A. *Explorations in personality.* New York: Oxford University Press, 1938. **342, 461**

Murray, H. A. *Thematic Apperception Test: Pictures and manual.* Cambridge, Mass.: Harvard University Press, 1943.

Mussen, P. H. Early sex role development. In D. A. Goslin (Ed.), *Handbook of socialization theory and research.* Chicago: Rand McNally, 1969. Pp. 707–731. **265**

Mussen, P. H., and Eisenberg, N. *The roots of caring.* San Francisco: W. H. Freeman, 1977. **430**

Myers, D. G., and Ridl, J. Can we all be better than average? *Psychology Today,* 1979, *13,* 89–98. **44, 203**

Myers, R. E., and Sperry, R. W. *Anatomical Records,* 1953, *115,* 351, as cited in R. W. Sperry. Some developments in brain lesion studies of learning. In C. G. Gross and H. P. Zeigler (Eds.), *Readings in physiological psychology: Learning and memory.* New York: Harper & Row, 1969. **90**

My Lai: An American tragedy. *Time,* December 5, 1969, *24,* 26–32.

Myrdal, G. *An American dilemma.* New York: Harper, 1944. **570**

Naftulin, D. H., Ware, J. E., Jr., and Donnelly, F. A. The Doctor Fox lecture: A paradigm of educational seduction. *Journal of Medical Education,* 1973, *48,* 630–635. **25**

Nathan, P. E. Alcoholism. In H. Leitenberg (Ed.), *Handbook of behavior modification and behavior therapy.* Englewood Cliffs, N.J.: Prentice-Hall, 1976. **516**

National Science Foundation funded projects controversy: Senator William Proxmire vs. social scientists. *Wisconsin Sociologist,* 1975, *12,* 72–86.

Natterson, J. M., and Knudson, A. G. Observations concerning fear of death in fatally ill children and their mothers. *Psychosomatic Medicine,* 1960, *22,* 456–465. **324**

Needleman, H. L. Lead poisoning in children: Neurologic implications of widespread subclinical intoxication. *Seminars in Psychiatry,* 1973, *5,* 47–53. **453**

Needleman, H. L. Subclinical lead exposure in Philadelphia schoolchildren. *New England Journal of Medicine,* 1974, *290,* 245–248. **453**

Nelson, K. E. Concept, word, and sentence: Interrelations in acquisition and development. *Psychological Review,* 1974, *81,* 267–285. **290**

Nelson, K. E. Facilitating children's syntax acquisition. *Developmental Psychology,* 1977, *13,* 101–107. **294, 421**

Neugarten, B. L. Adaptation and the life cycle. *The Counseling Psychologist,* 1976, *6,* 16–20. **270**

Newell, A., and Simon, H. A. *Human problem solving.* Englewood Cliffs, N.J.: Prentice-Hall, 1972. **218**

Nisbett, R. E. Taste, deprivation, and weight determinants of eating behavior. *Journal of Personality and Social Psychology,* 1968, *10,* 107–116. **346**

Nisbett, R. E. Hunger, obesity, and the ventromedial hypothalamus. *Psychological Review,* 1972, *79,* 433–453. **347, 348**

Nisbett, R. E., and Gurwitz, S. Weight, sex, and the eating behavior of human newborns. *Journal of Comparative and Physiological Psychology,* 1970, *73,* 245–253. **347**

Nisbett, R. E., and Ross, L. *Human inference: Strategies and shortcomings of social judgment.* Englewood Cliffs, N.J.: Prentice-Hall, 1980. **229, 561, 563, 570**

Nisbett, R. E., and **Schachter, S.** Cognitive manipulation of pain. *Journal of Experimental Social Psychology,* 1966, *2,* 227-236. **320**

Nisbett, R. E., and **Wilson, T.** Telling more than we know. *Psychological Review,* 1977, *84,* 231-259. **210, 374**

Novak, M. A., and **Harlow, H. F.** Social recovery of monkeys isolated for the first year of life: I. Rehabilitation and therapy. *Developmental Psychology,* 1975, *11,* 453-465. **259**

Oden, M. H. The fulfillment of promise: Forty-year follow-up of Terman gifted group. *Genetic Psychology Monographs,* 1968, *7,* 3-93. **448**

Olds, J., and **Milner, P.** Positive reinforcement produced by electrical stimulation of septal area and other regions of rat brain. *Journal of Comparative and Physiological Psychology,* 1954, *47,* 411-427. **87**

Olson, G. M. An information-processing analysis of visual memory and habituation in infants. In T. J. Tighe and R. N. Leaton (Eds.), *Habituation: Perspectives from child development, animal behavior, and neurophysiology.* Hillsdale, N.J.: Lawrence Erlbaum, 1976. Pp. 239-277. **246**

Oomura, Y., Ooyama, H., Yamamoto, T., and **Naka, F.** Reciprocal relationship of the lateral and ventromedial hypothalamus in the regulation of food intake. *Physiology and Behavior,* 1967, *2,* 97-115. **345**

Orne, M. T. On the social psychology of the psychological experiment: With particular reference to demand characteristics and their implications. *American Psychologist,* 1962, *17,* 776-783. **58**

Orne, M. T., and **Holland, C. C.** On the ecological validity of laboratory deceptions. *International Journal of Psychiatry,* 1968, *6,* 282-293. **587**

Ornstein, R. *The psychology of consciousness* (2nd ed.). New York: Harcourt Brace Jovanovich, 1977. **95, 389, 390**

Osgood, C. E., and **Tannenbaum, P. H.** The principles of congruity in the prediction of attitude change. *Psychological Review,* 1955, *62,* 42-55. **551**

Overmier, J. B., Payne, R. J., Brackbill, R. M., Linder, B., and **Lawry, J. A.** On the mechanism of the post-asymptotic decrement phenomenon. *Acta Neurobiologiae Experimentalis,* 1979, *39,* 603-620. **362**

Paivio, A. *Imagery and verbal process.* New York: Holt, Rinehart and Winston, 1971. **187**

Papousek, H. Individual variability in learned responses in human infants. In R. J. Robinson (Ed.), *Brain and early behavior: Development in the fetus and infant.* London: Academic Press, 1969. Pp. 251-266. **246**

Parke, R. D., Berkowitz, L., Leyens, J. P., West, S. G., and **Sebastian, R. J.** Some effects of violent and nonviolent movies on the behavior of juvenile delinquents. In L. Berkowitz (Ed.), *Advances in experimental social psychology* (Vol. 10). New York: Academic Press, 1977. Pp. 135-172. **598**

Parker, E. S., Birnbaum, I. M., and **Noble, E. P.** Alcohol and memory: Storage and state

dependency. *Journal of Verbal Learning Behavior,* 1976, *15,* 691-702. **392**

Parker, E. S., and **Noble, E. P.** Alcohol consumption and cognitive functioning in social drinkers. *Journal of Studies on Alcohol,* 1977, *36,* 1224-1232. **393**

Parkes, C. M. The first year of bereavement: A longitudinal study of the reactions of London widows to the death of their husbands. *Psychiatry,* 1970, *33,* 444-467. **325**

Parkes, C. M. Unexpected and untimely bereavement: A statistical study of young Boston widows and widowers. In B. B. Schoenberg, I. Gerber, A. Wiener, A. H. Kutscher, D. Peretz, and A. C. Carr (Eds.), *Bereavement: Its psychosocial aspects.* New York: Columbia University Press, 1975. **325**

Parkes, J. D. Clinical aspects of tardive dyskinesia. In H. F. Bradford and C. D. Marsden (Eds.), *Biochemistry and neurology.* New York: Academic Press, 1976. **532**

Parsons, O. A., and **Prigatano, G. P.** Memory functioning in alcoholics. In I. M. Birnbaum and E. S. Parker (Eds.), *Alcohol and human memory.* Hillsdale, N.J.: Lawrence Erlbaum, 1977. Pp. 185-194. **393**

Patterson, G. R., Littman, R. A., and **Bricker, W.** Assertive behavior in children: A step toward a theory of aggression. *Monographs of the Society for Research in Child Development,* 1967, *32,* Serial No. 113. **598**

Pattie, F. A. A report of attempts to produce uniocular blindness by hypnotic suggestion. *British Journal of Medical Psychology,* 1935, *15,* 230-241. **384**

Pattison, E. M. *The experience of dying.* Englewood Cliffs, N.J.: Prentice-Hall, 1977. **324**

Paul, G. L., and **Lentz, R. J.** *Psychosocial treatment of chronic mental patients: Milieu versus social-learning programs.* Cambridge, Mass.: Harvard University Press, 1977. **518**

Paul, S. M. Movement and madness: Towards a biological model of schizophrenia. In J. D. Maser and M. E. P. Seligman (Eds.), *Psychopathology: Experimental models.* San Francisco: W. H. Freeman, 1977. Pp. 358-386. **503**

Pavlov, I. P. *Conditioned reflexes.* G. V. Anrep (Trans.). London: Oxford University Press, 1927. **146**

Penfield, W. Consciousness, memory, and man's conditioned reflexes. In K. H. Pribram (Ed.), *On the biology of learning.* New York: Harcourt Brace Jovanovich, 1969. Pp. 127-168. **203, 374**

Penfield, W., and **Rasmussen, T.** *The cerebral cortex of man.* New York: Macmillan, 1950. **88, 96**

Penick, S., Smith, G., Wienske, K., and **Hinkle, L.** An experimental evaluation of the relationship between hunger and gastric motility. *American Journal of Physiology,* 1963, *205,* 421-426. **343**

Perloff, M. B. et al. *Assessment of psychosocial treatment of mental health disorders: Current status and prospects.* Report to the National Academy of Sciences, Institute of Medicine, Washington, D.C., 1978.

Perls, F. S. Four lectures. In J. Fagan and I. L. Sheperd (Eds.), *Gestalt therapy now.*

Palo Alto, Calif.: Science and Behavior Books, 1970. **524**

Peterson, L. R., and **Peterson, M.** Short-term retention of individual verbal items. *Journal of Experimental Psychology,* 1959, *58,* 193-198. **182**

Pettigrew, T. Social psychology and desegregation research. *American Psychologist,* 1961, *16,* 105-112. **574**

Phares, E. J. *Clinical psychology: Concepts, methods, and profession.* Homewood, Ill.: Dorsey, 1979. **524, 525**

Phillips, S., with **King, S.,** and **Du Bois, L.** Spontaneous activities of female versus male newborns. *Child Development,* 1978, *49,* 590-597. **261**

Piaget, J. *The language of the child.* M. Warden (Trans.). New York: Harcourt, 1926. **245**

Piaget, J. *The moral judgment of the child* (1932). New York: Free Press, 1948. **24, 266**

Piaget, J. *The origins of intelligence in children.* M. Cook (Trans.). New York: International Universities Press, 1952. **245, 247, 254**

Piaget, J. *The construction of reality in the child.* M. Cook (Trans.). New York: Basic Books, 1954. **245, 247**

Piaget, J. *Biology and knowledge.* B. Walsh (Trans.). Chicago: University of Chicago Press, 1971. **245**

Piaget, J., and **Inhelder, B.** *The child's conception of space.* New York: Humanities Press, 1956.

Piaget, J., and **Inhelder. B.** *The psychology of the child.* New York: Basic Books, 1969. **245, 248, 254**

Pickford, R. W. *Individual differences in colour vision.* London: Routledge and Kegan Paul, 1951. **119**

Piliavin, I. M., Rodin, J., and **Piliavin, J. A.** Good samaritanism: An underground phenomenon? *Journal of Personality and Social Psychology,* 1969, *13,* 289-299. **603**

Piliavin, J. A., and **Piliavin, I. M.** Effect of blood on reactions to a victim. *Journal of Personal and Social Psychology,* 1972, *23,* 353-361. **64**

Pines, A., and **Maslach, C.** Characteristics of staff burnout in mental health settings. *Hospital and Community Psychiatry,* 1978, *29,* 233-237. **606**

Plotkin, W. B., and **Cohen, R.** Occipital alpha and the attributes of the "alpha experience." *Psychological Physiology,* 1976, *13,* 16-21. **391**

Plutchik, R., and **Ax, A. F.** A critique of "determinants of emotional state" by Schachter and Singer (1962). *Psychophysiology,* 1967, *4,* 79-82. **321**

Pollack, I., and **Pickett, J. M.** Intelligibility of excerpts from fluent speech: Auditory vs. structural context. *Journal of Verbal Learning and Verbal Behavior,* 1964, *3,* 79-84. **282**

Pomeroy, W. B. The Masters-Johnson report and the Kinsey tradition. In R. Brecher and E. Brecher (Eds.), *An analysis of "Human sexual response."* New York: New American Library, 1966. **354**

Posner, M. I. *Cognition: An introduction.* Glenview, Ill.: Scott Foresman, 1973. **215, 221, 222**

Prechtl, H. F. R. Problems of behavioral studies in the newborn infant. In D. S. Lehrman, R. A. Hinde, and E. Shaw (Eds.), *Advances in the study of behavior* (Vol. 1). New York: Academic Press, 1965. Pp. 75-98. **242**

Premack, D. Language in the chimpanzee? *Science,* 1971a, *172,* 808-822. **284**

Premack, D. On the assessment of language competence in the chimpanzee. In A. M. Schrier and F. Stollnitz (Eds.), *Behavior of nonhuman primates.* New York: Academic Press, 1971b. Pp. 185-228. **284**

Premack, D. Language and intelligence in ape and man. *American Scientist,* 1976, *64,* 674-683. **284**

Prescott, J. W. Alienation of affection. *Psychology Today,* December 1979, 124. **260**

Rahe, R. H., and **Lind, E.** Psychosocial factors and sudden cardiac death: A pilot study. *Journal of Psychosomatic Research,* 1971, *15,* 19-24. **327**

Rankin, R. E., and **Campbell, D. T.** Galvanic skin response to Negro and white experimenters. *Journal of Applied Social Psychology,* 1955, *51,* 30-33. **547**

Rausch, H. L. Paradox, levels, and junctures in person-situation systems. In D. Magnusson and N. S. Endler (Eds.), *Personality at the crossroads: Current issues in interaction psychology.* Hillsdale, N.J.: Lawrence Erlbaum, 1977. Pp. 287-304.

Raven, B. H., and **French, J.** Legitimate power, coercive power, and observability in social influence. *Sociometry,* 1958, *21,* 83-97. **582**

Ray, O. *Drugs, society, and human behavior* (2nd ed.). St. Louis: Mosby, 1978. **531**

Raymond, B. J., and **Unger, R. K.** "The apparel oft proclaims the man": Cooperation with deviant and conventional youths. *Journal of Social Psychology,* 1972, *87,* 75-82. **582**

Rescorla, R. A. Pavlovian conditioning and its proper control procedures. *Psychological Review,* 1967, *74,* 71-80. **148**

Resnick, R. B., Kestenbaum, R. S., and **Schwartz, L. K.** Acute systemic effects of cocaine in man: A controlled study by intranasal and intravenous routes of administration. *Science,* 1977, *195,* 696-698. **397**

Restak, R. *The brain: The last frontier.* Garden City, N.Y.: Doubleday, 1979. **99**

Revelle, W., Amaral, P., and **Turriff, S.** Introversion/extraversion, time stress, and caffeine: The effect on verbal performance. *Science,* 1976, *192,* 149-150. **361**

Revulsky, S. H., and **Bedarf, E. W.** Association of illness with prior ingestion of novel foods. *Science,* 1967, *155,* 219-220. **151**

Rice, B. Brave new world of intelligence testing. *Psychology Today,* 1979, *13,* 27-41. **446, 455, 457**

Rice, B. Going for the gifted gold. *Psychology Today,* 1980, *13,* 55ff. **449**

Richards, M., Richardson, K., and **Spears, D.** Conclusion: Intelligence and society. In K. Richardson, D. Spears, and M. Richards (Eds.), *Race and intelligence.* Baltimore: Penguin, 1972.

Riesman, D. (in association with **N. Glazer** and **R. Denny**). *The lonely crowd: A study of the changing American character.* New Haven: Yale University Press, 1950. **582**

Rimm, D. C., and **Mahoney, M. J.** The application of reinforcement and participant modeling procedures in the treatment of snake-phobic behavior. *Behavior Research and Therapy,* 1969, *7,* 369-376. **519**

Rimm, D. C., and **Masters, J. C.** *Behavior therapy: Techniques and empirical findings.* New York: Academic Press, 1979. **516**

Rodin, J. Effects of distraction on the performance of obese and normal subjects. *Journal of Comparative and Physiological Psychology,* 1973, *83,* 68-78. **347**

Rodin, J., and **Slochower, J.** Externality in the nonobese: Effects of environmental responsiveness on weight. *Journal of Personality and Social Psychology,* 1976, *33,* 338-344. **347**

Roffwarg, H. P., Muzio, J. N., and **Dement, W. C.** Ontogenetic development of the human sleep-dream cycle. *Science,* 1966, *152,* 604-619. **380**

Rogentine, G. N., Jr., Fox, B. H., and **Boyd, S. C.** Psychological factors in the prognosis of malignant melanoma: A prospective study. *Psychosomatic Medicine,* 1979, *41,* 647-655. **327**

Rogers, C. R. *Client-centered therapy: Its current practice, implications, and theory.* Boston: Houghton Mifflin, 1951. **429, 523**

Rogers, C. R. The actualizing tendency in relation to "motives" and to consciousness. In M. R. Jones (Ed.), *Nebraska symposium on motivation.* Lincoln: University of Nebraska Press, 1963. Pp. 1-24. **432**

Rogers, C. R. *On becoming a person: A therapist's view of psychotherapy.* Boston: Houghton Mifflin, 1970. **428, 482**

Rogers, C. R. A theory of personality. In S. Maddi (Ed.), *Perspectives on personality.* Boston: Little, Brown, 1971. **428**

Rorschach, H. *Psychodiagnostik: Methodik und ergebnisse eines wahrnehmungs-diagnostichen experiments* (2nd ed.). P. Lemkau and B. Fronenberg (Trans.). Berne and Berlin: Huber, 1932. (Republished: New York: Grune & Stratton, 1942.) **458**

Rosch, E. H. Cognitive representations of semantic categories. *Journal of Experimental Psychology: General,* 1975, *104,* 192-233. **213**

Rosenbaum, A. H., Maruta, T., and **Richelson, E.** Drugs that alter mood: I. Tricyclic agents and monoamine oxidase inhibitors. *Mayo Clinic Proceedings,* 1979, *54,* 335-344. **534**

Rosenberg, M. J. When dissonance fails: On eliminating evaluation apprehension from attitude measurement. *Journal of Personality and Social Psychology,* 1965, *1,* 28-42. **552**

Rosenhan, D. L. On being sane in insane places. *Science,* 1973, *179,* 250-258. **26, 483, 484**

Rosenhan, D. L. The contextual nature of psychiatric diagnosis. *Journal of Abnormal Psychology,* 1975, *84,* 462-474. **484, 485**

Rosenman, R. H., Brand, R. J., Jenkins, C. D., Friedman, M., Straus, R., and **Wurm, M.** Coronary heart disease in the Western Collaborative Group Study: Final follow-up experience of 8.5 years. *Journal of the American Medical Association,* 1975, *223,* 872-877. **327**

Rosenman, R. H., Friedman, M., Straus, R., Jenkins, C. D., Zyzanski, S. H., and **Wurm, M.** Coronary heart disease in the Western Collaborative Group Study. *Journal of Chronic Diseases,* 1979, *23,* 173-190.

Rosenthal, D., Wender, P. H., Kety, S. S., Welner, J., and **Schulsinger, F.** The adopted-away offspring of schizophrenics. *American Journal of Psychiatry,* 1971, *128,* 307-311. **502**

Rosenthal, R. *Experimenter effects in behavioral research.* New York: Appleton-Century-Crofts, 1966. **57, 299, 558**

Rosenthal, R., Archer, D., Di Matteo, M. R., Koivumaki, J. H., and **Rogers, P. L.** Body talk and tone of voice: The language without words. *Psychology Today,* September 1974, 64-68. **300**

Rosenthal, T., and **Bandura, A.** Psychological modeling: Theory and practice. In S. L. Garfield and A. E. Bergin (Eds.), *Handbook of psychotherapy and behavior change: An empirical analysis* (2nd ed.). New York: Wiley, 1978. **519**

Rosenzweig, M. R., Bennett, E. L., and **Diamond, M. C.** Brain changes in response to experience. *Scientific American,* 1972, *226,* 22-29. **200**

Ross, L. Obesity and externality. In S. Schachter and J. Rodin (Eds.), *Obese humans and rats.* Potomac, Md.: Lawrence Erlbaum, 1974. **347**

Ross, L. The intuitive psychologist and his shortcomings: Distortions in the attribution process. In L. Berkowitz (Ed.), *Advances in experimental social psychology.* New York: Academic Press, 1977. **561**

Ro-Trock, G., Wellisch, D., and **Schoolar, J. A.** A family therapy outcome study in an inpatient setting. *American Journal of Orthopsychiatry,* 1977, *47,* 514-522. **523**

Roueché, B. All I could do was stand in the woods. *New Yorker,* September 12, 1977, 97-117. **125**

Rubin, H. B., and **Henson, D. E.** Voluntary enhancement of penile erection. *Bulletin of the Psychonomic Society,* 1975, *6,* 158-160. **354**

Rubin, J. L., Provenzano, F. J., and **Luria, Z.** The eye of the beholder: Parents on sex of newborns. *American Journal of Orthopsychiatry,* 1974, *44,* 512-519. **571**

Rubin, Z. Measurement of romantic love. *Journal of Personality and Social Psychology,* 1970, *16,* 265-273. **565**

Rubin, Z. *Liking and loving: An invitation to social psychology.* New York: Holt, Rinehart and Winston, 1973. **565, 566**

Rumbaugh, D. M., Gill, T. V., and **von Glasersfeld, E. C.** Reading and sentence completion by a chimpanzee. *Science,* 1963, *182,* 731-733. **284**

Rush, J., Beck, A., Kovacs, M., and **Hollon, S.** Comparative efficacy of cognitive therapy and pharmacotherapy in the treatment of depressed outpatients. *Cognitive Therapy and Research,* 1977, *1,* 17-38. **521**

Russek, M. Hepatic receptors and the neurophysiological mechanisms controlling feeding behavior. In S. Ehrenpreis (Ed.), *Neurosciences research* (Vol. 4). New York: Academic Press, 1971. **345**

Russo, J. E., Krieser, G., and **Miyashita, S.** An effective display of unit price information. *Journal of Marketing*, 1975, *39*, 11–19. **227**

Rynders, J. *Annual report of the University of Minnesota Institute of Child Development*, 1975. **242**

Saegert, S., Swap, W. C., and **Zajonc, R. B.** Exposure, context, and interpersonal attraction. *Journal of Personality and Social Psychology*, 1973, *25*, 234–242. **564**

Salk, L. Mothers' heartbeat as an imprinting stimulus. *Transactions of the New York Academy of Science*, 1962, *24*, 753–763. **63**

Sarbin, T. R., and **Coe, W. C.** *Hypnosis: A social psychological analysis of influence communication.* New York: Holt, Rinehart and Winston, 1972. **386**

Sassoon, H. F. Blue vision in children. *Clinical Pediatrics*, 1973, *12*, 351. **118**

Sassoon, H. F., and **Tolder, M.** Blue vision and learning difficulties in children. *Federation Proceedings*, 1972, *31*, 384. **118**

Sawatzky, H. L., and **Lehn, W. H.** The arctic mirage and the early North Atlantic. *Science*, 1976, *192*, 1300–1305. **131**

Scarr, S., and **Weinberg, R. A.** IQ test performance of black children adopted by white families. *American Psychologist*, 1976, *3*, 726–739. **454**

Scarr-Salapatek, S. Unknowns in the IQ equation. *Science*, 1971a, *174*, 1223–1228. **451, 453**

Scarr-Salapatek, S. Race, social class, and IQ. *Science*, 1971b, *174*, 1286–1295. **453**

Schachter, S. *The psychology of affiliation.* Stanford, Calif.: Stanford University Press, 1959. **38**

Schachter, S. *Emotion, obesity, and crime.* New York: Academic Press, 1971a. **21, 345, 347**

Schachter, S. Some extraordinary facts about obese humans and rats. *American Psychologist*, 1971b, *26*, 129–144. **21, 351**

Schachter, S., and **Friedman, L. N.** The effects of work and cue prominence on eating behavior. In S. Schachter and J. Rodin (Eds.), *Obese humans and rats.* Potomac, Md.: Lawrence Erlbaum, 1974. **347**

Schachter, S., and **Rodin, J.** (Eds.). *Obese humans and rats.* Potomac, Md.: Lawrence Erlbaum, 1974. **347**

Schachter, S., and **Singer, J. E.** Cognitive, social, and physiological determinants of emotional state. *Psychological Review*, 1962, *69*, 379–399. **318**

Schachter, S., and **Singer, J. E.** Comments on the Maslach and Marshall-Zimbardo experiments. *Journal of Personality and Social Psychology*, 1979, *37*, 989–995. **323**

Schaefer, H. H. Twelve-month follow-up of behaviorally trained ex-alcoholic social drinkers. *Behavior Therapy*, 1972, *3*, 286–289. **516**

Schaps, E. Cost, dependency, and helping. *Journal of Personal and Social Psychology*, 1972, *21*, 74–78. **64**

Scheerer, M. Problem-solving. *Scientific American*, 1963, *208*, 118–128. **215**

Scheff, T. J. *Labeling madness.* Englewood Cliffs, N.J.: Prentice-Hall, 1975. **481, 500**

Schein, E. H. The Chinese indoctrination program for prisoners of war: A study of attempted "brainwashing." *Psychiatry: Journal for the Study of Interpersonal Processes*, 1956, *19*, 149–172. **590, 591**

Schein, E. H. *Coercive persuasion.* New York: Norton, 1961. **590, 591**

Schildkraut, J., and **Freyhan, F. A.** Neuropharmacological studies of mood disorder. In J. Zubin (Ed.), *Disorders of mood.* New York: Grune & Stratton, 1972. **317**

Schildkraut, J., and **Kety, S. S.** Biogenic amines and emotions. *Science*, 1967, *156*, 21–30. **317**

Schmitt, R. C. Density, delinquency, and crime in Honolulu. *Sociology and Social Research*, 1957, *41*, 274–276. **608**

Schmitt, R. C. Implications of density in Hong Kong. *American Institute of Planners Journal*, 1963, *29*, 210–217. **608**

Schmitt, R. C. Density, health, and social disorganization. *American Institute of Planners Journal*, 1966, *32*, 38–40. **608**

Schoenberg, B. B., Carr, A. C., Peretz, D., and **Kutscher, A. H.** Physicians and the bereaved. *General Practitioner*, 1969, *40*, 105–108. **325**

Schoenberg, B. B., Carr, A. C., Peretz, D., Kutscher, A. H., and **Cherico, D. J.** Advice of the bereaved for the bereaved. In B. B. Schoenberg, I. Gerber, A. Wiener, A. H. Kutscher, D. Peretz, and A. C. Carr (Eds.), *Bereavement: Its psychosocial aspects.* New York: Columbia University Press, 1975. **325**

Schreiner, L., and **Kling, A.** Rhinencephalon and behavior. *American Journal of Physiology*, 1956, *184*, 486–490. **354**

Schuessler, K. F. The deterrent influence of the death penalty. *Annals of the American Academy*, 1952, *284*, 54–62. **41**

Schultes, R. E. *Hallucinogenic plants.* New York: Golden Press, 1976. **398**

Schwartz, G. E. Psychosomatic disorders and biofeedback: A psychobiological model of disregulation. In J. D. Maser and M. E. P. Seligman (Eds.), *Psychopathology: Experimental models.* San Francisco: W. H. Freeman, 1977. **531**

Schwartz, S. H., and **Gottlieb, A.** Bystander reactions to a violent theft: Crime in Jerusalem. *Journal of Personality and Social Psychology*, 1976, *34*, 1188–1199.

Schwartz, S. H., and **Gottlieb, A.** Bystander anonymity and reactions to emergencies. *Journal of Personality and Social Psychology*, 1980, *39*, 418–430.

Scovern, A. W., and **Kilmann, P. R.** Status of electroconvulsive therapy: Review of the outcome literature. *Psychological Bulletin*, 1980, *87*, 260–303. **534**

Sears, R. R., Rau, L., and **Alpert, R.** *Identification and child rearing.* Stanford, Calif.: Stanford University Press, 1965. **262**

Seay, B. M., Hansen, E. W., and **Harlow, H. F.** Mother-infant separation in monkeys. *Journal of Child Psychology and Psychiatry*, 1962, *3*, 123–132. **258**

Seay, B. M., and **Harlow, H. F.** Maternal separation in the rhesus monkey. *Journal of Nervous and Mental Disease*, 1965, *140*, 434–441. **258**

Sechrest, L. Testing, measuring, and assessing people. In E. F. Borgatta and W. W. Lambert (Eds.), *Handbook of personality theory and research.* Chicago: Rand McNally, 1968. Pp. 529–578. **460**

Segall, M. H., Campbell, D. T., and **Herskovitz, M.** *The influence of culture on visual perception.* Indianapolis: Bobbs-Merrill, 1966. **135**

Sekuler, R., and **Ball, K.** Mental set alters visibility of moving targets. *Science*, 1977, *198*, 9960–9962. **108**

Sekuler, R., and **Levinson, E.** The perception of moving targets. *Scientific American*, 1977, *286*, 60–73. **133**

Seligman, M. E. P. *Helplessness: On depression development and death.* San Francisco: W. H. Freeman, 1975. **495**

Seligman, M. E. P., Maier, S. F., and **Geer, J.** The alleviation of learned helplessness in the dog. *Journal of Abnormal Psychology*, 1968, *78*, 256–262. **494**

Selman, R. L. Toward a structural analysis of developing interpersonal relations concepts. In A. Pick (Ed.), *Minnesota symposia on child psychology* (Vol. 10). Minneapolis: University of Minnesota, 1976. **268**

Selye, H. *The stress of life.* New York: McGraw-Hill, 1956. **326**

Selye, H., and **Cherry, L.** On the real benefits of eustress. *Psychology Today*, March 1978, 60–63, 69–70. **326**

Senden, M. von. *Space and sight: The perception of space and shape in the congenitally blind before and after operation.* Peter Heath (Trans.). New York: Free Press, 1960. **129**

Serbin, L. A., and **O'Leary, K. D.** How nursery schools teach girls to shut up. *Psychology Today*, 1975, *9*, 56–58ff. **571**

Shachem, S., Leventhal, H., Boothe, C. S., and **Leventhal, E.** *The role of attention in distress control during childbirth.* Unpublished paper, University of Wisconsin, Madison, 1978. **550**

Shashoua, V. E. RNA metabolism in goldfish brain during acquisition of new behavioral patterns. *Proceedings of the National Academy of Science*, 1970, *65*, 160–167. **200**

Shaw, M. E. *Group dynamics: The psychology of small group behavior* (2nd ed.). New York: McGraw-Hill, 1976. **588**

Sheehy, G. *Passages: Predictable crises of adult life.* New York: Dutton, 1976. **269**

Sherif, M., and **Sherif, C. W.** *Groups in harmony and tension.* New York: Harper & Row, 1953. **573**

Sherman, A. R. *In vivo* therapies for phobic reactions, instrumental behavior problems, and interpersonal and communication problems. In A. P. Goldstein and F. H. Kanfer (Eds.), *Maximizing treatment gains: Transfer enhancement in psychotherapy.* New York: Academic Press, 1979. Pp. 25–86. **520**

Sherrod, D. R. Crowding, perceived control, and behavioral after effects. *Journal of Applied Social Psychology*, 1974, *4*, 171–186. **609**

Siegel, R. K. Hallucinations. *Scientific American*, 1977, *237*, 132–140. **398**

Siegel, S., Hinson, R. E., and **Krank, M. D.**

The role of pre-drug signals in morphine analgesic tolerance: Support for a Pavlovian conditioning model of tolerance. *Journal of Experimental Psychology: Animal Behavior Processes*, 1978, *4*, 188–196. **362**

Sigall, H., and Landy, D. Radiating beauty: The effects of having a physically attractive partner on person perception. *Journal of Personality and Social Psychology*, 1973, *28*, 218–224. **558**

Silvar, S. D., and Pollack, R. H. Racial differences in pigmentation of the fundus oculi. *Psychonomic Science*, 1967, *7*, 159–160. **119**

Silveira, J. *Incubation: The effect of interruption timing and length on problem solution and quality of problem processing.* Unpublished doctoral dissertation, University of Oregon, 1971. **221**

Silver, R. L., and Wortman, C. B. Coping with undesirable life events. In J. Garber and M. E. P. Seligman (Eds.), *Human helplessness: Theory and application.* New York: Academic Press, 1980. **323, 325**

Silverman, P. R. Mutual help groups. *Sage human services guide* (Vol. 16). Beverly Hills, Calif.: Sage Publications, 1980. **528**

Simon, C. W., and Emmons, W. H. Response to material presented during various levels of sleep. *Journal of Experimental Psychology*, 1956, *51*, 89–97. **60**

Simon, H., and Gilmartin, K. A simulation of memory for chess positions. *Cognitive Psychology*, 1973, *5*, 29–46. **183**

Singer, M. T. Coming out of the cults. *Psychology Today*, 1979, *12*, 72–82. **588, 591, 592**

Siqueland, E. R., and Lipsitt, L. P. Conditioned head-turning in human newborns. *Journal of Experimental Child Psychology*, 1966, *3*, 356–376. **246**

Skinner, B. F. *Behavior of organisms: An experimental analysis.* New York: Appleton-Century-Crofts, 1938. **12, 156**

Skinner, B. F. Superstitious behavior in the pigeon. *Journal of Experimental Psychology*, 1948, *38*, 168–172. **155**

Skinner, B. F. *Walden two.* New York: Macmillan, 1948. **15, 419**

Skinner, B. F. *Beyond freedom and dignity.* New York: Knopf, 1971. **419**

Skinner, B. F. The ethics of helping people. In L. Wispe (Ed.), *Sympathy, altruism, and helping behavior.* New York: Academic Press, 1978. **605**

Skodak, M., and Skeels, H. M. A final follow-up of one hundred adopted children. *Journal of Genetic Psychology*, 1949, *75*, 85–125. **453**

Slaby, R. G., and Frey, K. S. Development of gender constancy and selective attention to same-sex models. *Child Development*, 1975, *46*, 849–856. **265**

Sloane, R. B., Staples, F. R., Cristal, A. H., Yorkston, W. J., and Whipple, K. *Psychotherapy vs. behavior therapy.* Cambridge, Mass.: Harvard University Press, 1975. **515, 530**

Slobin, D. I. Children and language: They learn the same way all around the world. *Psychology Today*, 1972, *6*, 71–74ff. **292**

Slovic, P., Fischhoff, B., and Lichtenstein, S. Cognitive processes and societal risk taking. *Oregon Research Institute Monograph*, 1976, *15*. **230**

Slovic, P., Fischhoff, B., and Lichtenstein, S. Risky assumptions. *Psychology Today*, June 1980, 44–48. **230**

Slovic, P., Kunreuther, H., and White, G. F. Decision processes, rationality, and adjustment to natural hazards. In C. F. White (Ed.), *Natural hazards, local, national and global.* New York: Oxford University Press, 1974. Pp. 187–205. **227**

Slovic, P., and Lichtenstein, S. Relative importance of probabilities and payoffs in risk taking. *Journal of Experimental Psychology*, 1968, *78*, 1–18. **230**

Slovic, P., and Lichtenstein, S. Comparison of Bayesian and regression approaches to the study of information processing in judgment. *Organic Behavior and Human Performance*, 1971, *5*, 649–744.

Smith, E. E., Shoben, E. J., and Rips, L. J. Structure and process in semantic memory: A feature model for semantic decisions. *Psychological Review*, 1974, *81*, 214–224. **213**

Smith, M. L., and Glass, G. V. Meta-analysis of psychotherapy outcome studies. *American Psychologist*, 1977, *32*, 752–760. **529**

Smith, M. L., Glass, G. V., and Miller, R. L. *The benefits of psychotherapy.* Baltimore: Johns Hopkins University Press, in press. **529**

Snyder, F. Sleep and dreaming: Progress in the new biology of dreaming. *American Journal of Psychiatry*, 1965, *122*, 377–391. **378**

Snyder, F. The phenomenology of dreaming. In L. Madow and L. H. Snow (Eds.), *The psychodynamic implications of the physiological studies on dreams.* Springfield, Ill.: Charles C. Thomas, 1970. **380**

Snyder, M., Tanke, E. D., and Berscheid, E. Social perception and interpersonal behavior: On the self-fulfilling nature of social stereotypes. *Journal of Personality and Social Psychology*, 1977, *35*, 656–666. **558**

Snyder, S., interviewed by D. Golesman. Matter over mind: The big issues raised by newly discovered brain chemicals. *Psychology Today*, 1980, *14*, 66–76. **80**

Solomon, R. L. The opponent-process theory of acquired motivation: The costs of pleasure and the benefits of pain. *American Psychologist*, 1980, *35*, 691–712. **362**

Solomon, R. L., and Corbit, J. D. An opponent-process theory of motivation. *Psychological Review*, 1974, *81*, 119–145. **362**

Sowell, T. "Affirmative action" reconsidered. *Public Interest*, 1976, *42*, 47–65. **605**

Sperling, G. The information available in brief visual presentation. *Psychological Monographs*, 1960, *74*, Whole No. 498. **178**

Sperry, R. W. The great cerebral commissure. *Scientific American*, January 1964. **94**

Sperry, R. W. Lateral specialization of cerebral function in the surgically separated hemispheres. In F. J. McGuigan (Ed.), *The psychophysiology of thinking.* New York: Academic Press, 1973. **95**

Sperry, R. W. Changing concepts of consciousness and free will. *Perspectives in Biology and Medicine*, 1976, *20*, 9–19. **375**

Sperry, R. W. Bridging science and values: A unifying view of mind and brain. *American Psychologist*, 1977, *32*, 237–245.

Spirduso, W. W. Reaction and movement time as a function of age and physical-activity level. *Journal of Gerontology*, 1975, *30*, 435–440. **257**

Spitzer, R. L. On pseudoscience in science, logic in remission, and psychiatric diagnosis: A critique of D. L. Rosenhan's "On being sane in insane places." *Journal of Abnormal Psychology*, 1975, *84*, 442–452. **484, 485**

Spitzer, R. L. More on pseudoscience in science and the case for psychiatric diagnosis: A critique of D. L. Rosenhan's "On being sane in insane places" and "The contextual nature of psychiatric diagnosis." *Archives of General Psychiatry*, 1976, *33*, 459–470. **484**

Spitzer, R. L., and Fleiss, J. L. A reanalysis of the reliability of psychiatric diagnosis. *British Journal of Psychiatry*, 1974, *125*, 341–347. **486**

Stanley, J. C. Test better finder of great math talent than teachers are. *American Psychologist*, 1976, *31*, 313–314. **437**

Stebbins, L. B., St. Pierre, R. G., Proper, E. C., Anderson, R. B., and Cerva, T. R. An evaluation of Follow Through. In T. D. Cook, M. L. Del Rosario, K. M. Hennigan, M. M. Mark, and W. M. K. Trochim (Eds.), *Evaluation studies review annual* (Vol. 3). Beverly Hills, Calif.: Sage Publications, 1978. **605**

Stephan, W. G., Rosenfield, D., and Stephan, C. Egotism in males and females. *Journal of Personality and Social Psychology*, 1976, *34*, 1161–1167.

Stern, W. *The psychological methods of testing intelligence.* G. W. Whipple (Trans.). Baltimore: Warwick & York, 1914. **443**

Stevens, C. F. *Neurophysiology: A primer.* New York: Wiley, 1966.

Stevens, S. S. On the psychophysical law. *Psychological Review*, 1957, *64*, 153–181. **109**

Stevens, S. S. The surprising simplicity of sensory metrics. *American Psychologist*, 1962, *17*, 29–39. **109**

Stewart, K. Dream theory in Malaya. In C. T. Tart (Ed.), *Altered states of consciousness.* New York: Doubleday, 1972. **382**

Stokols, D. Environmental psychology. *Annual Review of Psychology 1978*, 1978, *29*, 253–295. **606**

Stokols, D., Rall, M., Pinner, B., and Schopler, J. Physical, social, and personal determinants of the perception of crowding. *Environment and Behavior*, 1973, *5*, 87–115. **608**

Stolz, W. A study of the ability to decode grammatically novel sentences. *Journal of Verbal Learning and Verbal Behavior*, 1967, *6*, 867–873. **282**

Stoner, C., and Parke, J. A. *All God's children: The cult experience—salvation or slavery?* New York: Penguin, 1979. **591**

Stratton, G. M. Some preliminary experiments on vision without inversion of the retinal image. *Psychological Review*, 1896, *3*, 611–617. **127**

Strickler, D., Bigelow, G., Lawrence, C., and Liebson, I. Moderate drinking as an alternative to alcohol abuse: A nonaversive procedure. *Behavior Research and Therapy*, 1976, *14*, 279–288. **518**

Stuart, R. B. Behavioral control of overeating. *Behavior Research and Therapy*, 1967, *5*, 357–365. **518**

Stunkard, A. J. (Ed.). *Obesity*. Philadelphia: Saunders, 1980.

Suedfeld, P. The benefits of boredom: Sensory deprivation reconsidered. *American Scientist*, 1975, *63*, 60–69. **360**

Sulzbacher, S. Psychotropic medication with children: An evaluation of procedural biases in results of reported studies. *Pediatrics*, 1973, *51*, 513–517. **533**

Sundstrom, E. Crowding as a sequential process: Review of research on the effects of population density on humans. In A. Baum and Y. Epstein (Eds.), *Human response to crowding*. Hillsdale, N.J.: Lawrence Erlbaum, 1978. **608**

Sutcliffe, J. P. "Credulous" and "skeptical" views of hypnotic phenomena: Experiments in esthesia, hallucination, and delusion. *Journal of Abnormal and Social Psychology*, 1961, *62*, 189–200. **62**

Sweet, W. H., Ervin, F., and Mark, V. H. The relationship of violent behavior to focal cerebral disease. In S. Garattini and E. Sigg (Eds.), *Aggressive behavior*. New York: Wiley, 1969. **313**

Swets, J. A., and Sewall, S. Stimulus vs. response uncertainty in recognition. *Journal of Acoustical Society of America*, 1961, *33*, 11, 1586–1592. **107**

Sylvester, J. D., and Liversedge, L. A. Conditioning and the occupational cramps. In H. J. Eysenck (Ed.), *Behavior therapy and the neuroses*. New York: Pergamon, 1960. Pp. 334–348. **167**

Szasz, T. S. *The myth of mental illness: Foundations of a theory of personal conduct*. New York: Harper & Row, 1961. **477**

Tart, C. T. (Ed.). *Altered states of consciousness: A book of readings*. New York: Wiley, 1969.

Tart, C. T. Marijuana intoxication: Common experiences. *Nature*, 1970, *226*, 701–704. **394**

Taylor, I. A. A retrospective view of creativity investigation. In I. A. Taylor and J. W. Getzels (Eds.), *Perspectives in creativity*. Chicago: Aldine, 1975. **450**

Taylor, S. E., Crocker, J., Fiske, S. T., Sprinzen, M., and Winkler, J. D. The generalizability of salience effects. *Journal of Personality and Social Psychology*, 1979, *37*, 357–368. **562**

Taylor, S. E., and Fiske, S. T. Point of view and perceptions of causality. *Journal of Personality and Social Psychology*, 1975, *32*, 439–445. **562**

Taylor, S. E., and Fiske, S. T. Salience, attention, and attribution: Top of the head phenomena. In L. Berkowitz (Ed.), *Advances in experimental social psychology* (Vol. 11). New York: Academic Press, 1978. **562**

Teitelbaum, P. Sensory control of hypothalamic hyperphagia. *Journal of Comparative and Physiological Psychology*, 1955, *48*, 156–163. **346**

Teitelbaum, P. Random and food-directed activity in hyperphagic and normal rats. *Journal of Comparative and Physiological Psychology*, 1957, *50*, 486–490. **346**

Teitelbaum, P. The encephalization of hunger. In E. Stellar and J. M. Sprague (Eds.), *Progress in physiological psychology* (Vol. 4). New York: Academic Press, 1971. **101**

Terman, L. M. *The measurement of intelligence*. Boston: Houghton Mifflin, 1916. **443, 448**

Terman, L. M., and Merrill, M. A. *Stanford-Binet Intelligence Scale: Manual for the third revision, form L-M*. Boston: Houghton Mifflin, 1973. **444**

Terman, L. M., and Oden, M. H. *The gifted child grows up*. Stanford, Calif.: Stanford University Press, 1947. **448**

Terrace, H. S. How Nim Chimpsky changed my mind. *Psychology Today*, November 1979, 65–76. **284**

Tetlock, P. E. Identifying victims of groupthink from public statements of decision makers. *Journal of Personality and Social Psychology*, 1979, *37*, 1314–1324.

Thase, M. E., and Moss, M. K. The relative efficacy of covert modeling procedures and guided participant modeling on the reduction of avoidance behavior. *Journal of Behavior Therapy and Experimental Psychiatry*, 1976, *7*, 7–12. **519**

Thompson, L. C. The spectral sensitivity of the central fovea. *Journal of Physiology*, 1951, *112*, 114–132. **119**

Thompson, S. K. Gender labels and early sex role development. *Child Development*, 1975, *46*, 339–347. **265**

Thompson, T., and Grabowski, J. *Behavior modification of the mentally retarded* (2nd ed.). New York: Oxford University Press, 1977. **518**

Thorndike, E. L. Animal intelligence: An experimental study of the associative processes in animals. *Psychological Review Monograph Supplement*, 1898, *2*. **17**

Thorndike, E. L. *The fundamentals of learning*. New York: Teachers College, 1932. **154**

Tinklenberg, J. R. A clinical view of the amphetamines. *American Family Physician*, 1971, *4*, 82–86. **398**

Tollefson, D. J. *The relationship between the occurrence of fractures and life crisis events*. Master of Nursing thesis, University of Washington, Seattle, 1972. **327**

Tolman, E. C., and Honzik, C. H. Introduction and removal of reward and maze performance in rats. University of California Publications in Psychology, 1930, *4*, 257–275. **170**

Tonkova-Yampol'skaya, R. V. Development of speech intonation in infants during the first two years of life. In C. A. Ferguson and D. I. Slobin (Eds.), *Studies of child language development*. New York: Holt, Rinehart and Winston, 1973. Pp. 128–138. **289**

Trask, C. H., and Cree, E. M. Oximeter studies on patients with chronic obstructive emphysema, awake and during sleep. *New England Journal of Medicine*, 1962, *266*, 639–642. **378**

Treiman, D., and Terrell, K. Sex and the process of status attainment: A comparison of working women and men. *American Sociological Review*, 1975, *40*, 174–200. **570**

Treisman, A. M. Contextual cues in selective listening. *Quarterly Journal of Experimental Psychology*, 1960, *12*, 242–248. **181**

Treisman, A. M. Verbal cues, language and meaning in selective attention. *American Journal of Psychology*, 1964, *77*, 206–219. **181**

Tresemer, D. Fear of success: Popular, but unproven. *Psychology Today*, March 1974, 82–85. **368**

Trimble, J. E. *The consonance of agreement of stereotypic descriptions of the American Indian*. Unpublished manuscript, Oklahoma City University, 1968. **573**

Truex, R. C., and Carpenter, M. B. *Human neuroanatomy*. Baltimore: Williams & Wilkins, 1969.

Tulving, E., and Pearlstone, Z. Availability versus accessibility of information in memory for words. *Journal of Verbal Learning and Verbal Behavior*, 1966, *5*, 381–391. **184**

Tversky, A., and Kahneman, D. Belief in the law of small numbers. *Psychological Bulletin*, 1971, *76*, 105–110. **232**

Tversky, A., and Kahneman, D. Availability: A heuristic for judging frequency and probability. *Cognitive Psychology*, 1973, *5*, 207–232. **228, 230**

Tversky, A., and Kahneman, D. Judgment under uncertainty: Heuristics and biases. *Science*, 1974, *185*, 1124–1131. **229**

Tyhurst, J. S. Individual reactions to community disaster. *American Journal of Psychiatry*, 1951, *10*, 746–769. **360**

Uhlenhuth, E. H., Balter, M. B., and Lipman, R. S. Minor tranquilizers: Clinical correlates of use in an urban population. *Archives of General Psychiatry*, 1978, *35*, 650–655. **531**

Ullman, L. P., and Krasner, L. *A psychological approach to abnormal behavior* (2nd ed.). Englewood Cliffs, N.J.: Prentice-Hall, 1975. **500**

Ullman, M. Dreaming, life-style, and physiology: A comment on Adler's view of the dream. *Journal of Individual Psychology*, 1962, *18*, 18–25. **381**

Ungar, G. Role of proteins and peptides in learning and memory. In G. Ungar (Ed.), *Molecular mechanisms in memory and learning*. New York: Plenum, 1970. **201**

Valenstein, E. S. *Brain control: A critical examination of brain stimulation and psychosurgery*. New York: Wiley, 1973. **97, 535**

Valenstein, E. S. Science-fiction fantasy and the brain. *Psychology Today*, 1978, *12*, 28–39. **503**

Valins, S. Cognitive effects of false heart-rate feedback. *Journal of Personality and Social Psychology*, 1966, *4*, 400–408. **320**

Van Atta, L., and Sutin, J. The response of single lateral hypothalamic neurons to ventromedial nucleus and limbic stimulation. *Physiology and Behavior*, 1971, *6*, 523–536. **345**

Vaughan, E. Misconceptions about psychology among introductory psychology students. *Teaching of Psychology*, 1977, *4*, 138–141. **9, 10**

Vonnegut, M. *The Eden express*. New York: Praeger, 1975. **532**

Waddington, C. H. *The strategy of the genes.* New York: Macmillan, 1957.

Wagemaker, H., Jr., and **Cade, R.** The use of hemodialysis in chronic schizophrenia. *American Journal of Psychiatry,* 1977, *134,* 684–685. **503**

Waggoner, K. Psychocivilization or electroligarchy: Dr. Delgado's amazing world of ESB. *Yale Alumni Magazine,* January 1970, 22. **8**

Wald, G. Molecular basis of visual excitation. *Science,* 1968, *162,* 230–239. **114**

Wallace, R. K., and **Benson, H.** The physiology of meditation. *Scientific American,* 1972, *226,* 84–90. **388**

Wallace, W. L. Review of the Scholastic Aptitude Test. In O. K. Buros (Ed.), *The seventh mental measurements yearbook.* Highland Park, N.J.: Gryphon Press, 1972. Pp. 648–650. **446**

Walls, G. L., and **Judd, H. D.** The intraocular colour filters of vertebrates. *British Journal of Ophthalmology,* 1933, *17,* 641–675, 705–725. **119**

Walster, E., Aronson, V., Abrahams, D., and **Rottman, L.** Importance of physical attractiveness in dating behavior. *Journal of Personality and Social Psychology,* 1966, *4,* 508–516. **557**

Walster, E., and **Walster, W. G.** *A new look at love.* Reading, Mass.: Addison-Wesley, 1978. **320, 353**

Ward, C. H., Beck, A. T., Mendelson, M., Mock, J. E., and **Erbaugh, J. K.** The psychiatric nomenclature: Reasons for diagnostic disagreement. *Archives of General Psychiatry,* 1962, *7,* 198–205. **486**

Warrington, E. K., and **Sanders, H. I.** The fate of old memories. *Quarterly Journal of Experimental Psychology,* 1971, *23,* 432–442. **256**

Wason, P., and **Johnson-Laird, P. N.** *Psychology of reasoning: Structure and content.* Cambridge, Mass.: Harvard University Press, 1972. **255**

Waterman, C. K. The facilitating and interfering effects of cognitive dissonance on simple and complex paired-associate learning tasks. *Journal of Experimental Social Psychology,* 1969, *5,* 31–42. **554**

Waters, H. F., and **Malamud, P.** Drop that gun, Captain Video. *Newsweek,* March 10, 1975, *85,* 81–82. **598**

Watson, J. Some social and psychological situations related to change in attitude. *Human Relations,* 1950, *3,* 15–56. **574**

Watson, J. B. Kinesthetic and organic sensations: Their role in the reactions of the white rat to the maze. *Psychological Monographs,* 1907, Whole No. 33. **17**

Watson, J. B. *Behaviorism.* New York: People's Institute, 1924. **14, 153**

Watson, J. B., and **Rayner, R.** Conditioned emotional reactions. *Journal of Experimental Psychology,* 1920, *3,* 1–14. **143**

Watson, J. S. Smiling, cooing, and "the game." *Merrill-Palmer Quarterly of Behavior and Development,* 1972, *18,* 323–339. **246**

Watzlawick, P., Beavin, J., and **Jackson, D.** *Pragmatics of human communication: A study of interaction patterns, pathologies, and paradoxes.* New York: Norton, 1967. **480**

Watzlawick, P., and **Coyne, J. C.** Depression following stroke: Brief, problem-focused family treatment. *Family Process,* 1980, *19,* 13–18.

Webb, E. J., Campbell, D. T., Schwartz, R. D., and **Sechrest, L.** *Unobtrusive measures: Nonreactive research in the social sciences.* Chicago: Rand McNally, 1966. **47, 48, 547**

Webb, W. B. *Sleep: The gentle tyrant.* Englewood Cliffs, N.J.: Prentice-Hall, 1975. **380**

Weber, D. J., and **Castleman, J.** The time it takes to imagine. *Perception and Psychophysics,* 1970, *8,* 165–168. **182**

Wechsler, D. *Wechsler Adult Intelligence Scale manual.* New York: Psychological Corporation, 1955. **444**

Wechsler, D. *The measurement and appraisal of adult intelligence* (14th ed.). Baltimore: Williams & Wilkins, 1958. **444**

Weil, A. T., Zinberg, N., and **Nelsen, J. M.** Clinical and psychological effects of marijuana in man. *Science,* 1968, *162,* 1234–1242. **394**

Weiner, B. *Theories of motivation: From mechanism to cognition.* Chicago: Markham, 1972. **365**

Weingartner, H., Adefris, W., Eich, J. E., and **Murphy, D. L.** Encoding-imagery specificity in alcohol state-dependent learning. *Journal of Experimental Psychology: Human Learning and Memory,* 1976, *2,* 83–87. **392**

Weisman, A. D., and **Worden, J. W.** Psychosocial analysis of cancer deaths. *Omega: Journal of Death and Dying,* 1975, *6,* 61–75. **331**

Weiss, J. M., Glazer, H. I., and **Pohorecky, L. A.** Coping behavior and neurochemical changes: An alternative explanation for the original "learned helplessness" experiments. In G. Serban and A. Kling (Eds.), *Relevance of the animal model to the human.* New York: Plenum, 1974a (tentative). **495**

Weiss, J. M., Glazer, H. I., and **Pohorecky, L. A.** Neurotransmitters and helplessness: A chemical bridge to depression? *Psychology Today,* 1974b, *8,* 58–62. **495**

Weiss, J. M., Stone, E. A., and **Harrell, N.** Coping behavior and brain norepinephrine in rats. *Journal of Comparative and Physiological Psychology,* 1968, *65,* 413–421. **495**

Weiss, J. M., Stone, E. A., and **Harrell, N.** Coping behavior and brain norepinephrine levels in rats. *Journal of Comparative and Physiological Psychology,* 1970, *72,* 153–160. **495**

Wender, P. H., Rosenthal, D., Kety, S. S., Schulsinger, F., and **Welner, J.** Social class and psychopathology in adoptees: A natural experimental method for separating the roles of genetic and experiential factors. *Archives of General Psychiatry,* 1973, *28,* 318–325. **481**

Wessman, A. E., and **Ricks, D. F.** *Mood and personality.* New York: Holt, Rinehart and Winston, 1966. **334, 490**

Wetheimer, M. Psychomotor coordination of auditory and visual space at birth. *Science,* 1961, *134,* 1692. **243**

Wever, E. G., and **Bray, C. W.** Present possibilities for auditory theory. *Psychological Review,* 1930, *37,* 365–380. **123**

Whorf, B. L. Science and linguistics. In J. B. Carroll (Ed.), *Language, thought, and reality: Selected writings of Benjamin Lee Whorf.* Cambridge, Mass.: MIT Press, 1956. Pp. 207–219. **295**

Whyte, W. H., Jr. *The organization man.* New York: Simon and Schuster, 1956. **582**

Widroe, H. J., and **Heisler, S.** Treatment of tardive dyskinesia. *Diseases of the Nervous System,* 1976, *37,* 162–164. **533**

Wiener, A., Gerber, I., Battin, D., and **Arkin, A. M.** The process and phenomenology of bereavement. In B. B. Schoenberg, I. Gerber, A. Wiener, A. H. Kutscher, D. Peretz, and A. C. Carr (Eds.), *Bereavement: Its psychosocial aspects.* New York: Columbia University Press, 1975. **325**

Williams, M. D. *Retrieval from very long-term memory.* Unpublished doctoral dissertation, University of California, San Diego, 1976. **188**

Williams, P. L., and **Warwick, R.** *Functional neuroanatomy of man.* Philadelphia: Saunders, 1975.

Wilson, E. O. *Sociobiology: The new synthesis.* Cambridge, Mass.: Harvard University Press, 1975. **597, 601, 605**

Wilson, J. Q. *Thinking about crime.* New York: Basic Books, 1975.

Winsborough, H. The social consequences of high population density. *Law and Contemporary Problems,* 1955, *30,* 120–126. **608**

Wittgenstein, L. *Tractatus logico-philosophicus* (2nd ed.). New York: Humanities Press, 1963.

Wold, D. A. *The adjustment of siblings to childhood leukemia.* Medical thesis, University of Washington, Seattle, 1968. **327**

Wolf, S., and **Wolff, H. G.** *Human gastric function.* New York: Oxford University Press, 1947. **316**

Wolfe, J. B. Effectiveness of token-rewards for chimpanzees. *Comparative Psychological Monographs,* 1936, *12,* Whole No. 5. **166**

Wolff, P. The natural history of crying and other vocalizations in early infancy. In B. M. Foss (Ed.), *Determinants of infant behavior* (Vol. 4). London: Methuen, 1969. Pp. 81–109. **289**

Wolpe, J. *Psychotherapy by reciprocal inhibition.* Stanford, Calif.: Stanford University Press, 1958. **515**

Wolpe, J. *The practice of behavior therapy* (2nd ed.). New York: Pergamon, 1973. **515**

Wolpe, J. *Theme and variations: A behavior therapy casebook.* Elmsford, N.Y.: Pergamon, 1976. **515**

Wolpe, J. Cognition and causation in human behavior and its therapy. *American Psychologist,* 1978, *33,* 437–446. **515**

Woods, P. J. (Ed.). *Career opportunities for psychologists: Expanding and emerging areas.* Washington, D.C.: American Psychological Association, 1976. **21**

Woods, W. A., and **Makhoul, J.** Mechanical inference problems in continuous speech understanding. *Proceedings of the Third International Joint Conference on Artificial Intelligence.* Stanford, Calif.: Stanford Research Institute, 1973. Pp. 200–207. **282**

Woodworth, R. S. *Dynamic psychology*. New York: Columbia University Press, 1918.

Woolfolk, R. L. Psychophysiological correlates of meditation. *Archives of General Psychiatry*, 1975, *32*, 1326–1333. **388**

Woolsey, C. N. Organization of the cortical auditory system. In W. A. Rosenblith (Ed.), *Sensory communication*. New York: Wiley, 1961. **99**

Worchel, S., and Brehm, J. W. Effect of threats to attitudinal freedom as a function of agreement with the communicator. *Journal of Personality and Social Psychology*, 1970, *14*, 18–22. **554**

Wortman, C. B., Abbey, A., Holland, A. E., Silver, R. L., and Janoff-Bulman, R. Transitions from the laboratory to the field: Problems and progress. In L. Bickman (Ed.), *Applications in social psychology* (Vol. 1). Beverly Hills, Calif.: Sage Publications, 1980. **48, 610**

Wortman, C. B., and Dintzer, L. Is an attributional analysis of the learned helplessness phenomenon viable? A critique of the Abramson, Seligman, and Teasdale reformulation. *Journal of Abnormal Psychology*, 1978, *87*, 75–90. **495**

Wortman, C. B., and Dunkel-Schetter, C. Interpersonal relationships and cancer: A theoretical analysis. *Journal of Social Issues*, 1979, *35*, 120–154. **324, 528, 606**

Yalom, I. D., and Lieberman, M. A. A study of encounter group casualties. *Archives of General Psychiatry*, 1971, *25*, 16–20. **527**

Yarmey, A. D. I recognize your face but I can't remember your name: Further evidence on the tip-of-the-tongue phenomenon. *Memory and Cognition*, 1973, *1*, 287–290. **185**

Yochelson, S., and Samenow, S. E. *The criminal personality* (Vol. 1). New York: Jason Aronson, 1976. **605**

Young, W. C., Goy, R. W., and Phoenix, C. H. Hormones and sexual behavior. *Science*, 1964, *143*, 212–218. **83**

Zanna, M. P., Higgins, E. T., and Taves, P. A. Is dissonance phenomenologically aversive? *Journal of Experimental Social Psychology*, 1976, *12*, 520–538. **554**

Zax, M., and Stricker, G. *Patterns of psychopathology*. New York: Macmillan, 1963. **497**

Zilbergeld, B., and Evans, M. The inadequacy of Masters and Johnson. *Psychology Today*, 1980, *18*, 29–43. **357**

Zimbardo, P. G., Ebbesen, E. B., and Maslach, C. *Influencing attitudes and changing behavior* (2nd ed.). Reading, Mass.: Addison-Wesley, 1977. **321**

Zimbardo, P. G., Haney, C., and Banks, W. C. A Pirandellian prison. *The New York Times Magazine*, April 8, 1973, pp. 38–60. **545, 592**

Zimbardo, P. G., Haney, C., Banks, W. C., and Jaffe, D. *The psychology of imprisonment: Privation, power, and pathology*. Unpublished paper, Stanford University, 1972. **545, 592, 593**

Zinberg, N. E. The war over marijuana. *Psychology Today*, 1976, *10*, 45ff. **393**

Zubin, J., and Spring, B. Vulnerability—a new view of schizophrenia. *Journal of Abnormal Psychology*, 1977, *86*, 103–126. **504**

Zuckerman, M. The search for high sensation. *Psychology Today*, 1978, *11*, 30–46, 96–99. **364**

Credits and acknowledgments

Chapter 1

13, The Bettmann Archive; *14,* Culver Pictures; *17,* (top and bottom) Culver Pictures; *21,* UPI; *22,* Copyright © 1972 by the American Psychological Association. Reprinted by permission; *28,* Courtesy, C. Scott Moss, Ph.D.

Chapter 2

35, Public Media Center, San Francisco

Chapter 3

91, From "The Split Brain in Man," by Michael S. Gazzaniga. Copyright © 1967 by Scientific American, Inc. All rights reserved; *94,* From "The Bisected Brain," by Michael S. Gazzaniga. New York: Plenum, 1970, p. 99; *98,* Courtesy, Dr. Neal Miller

Chapter 4

114, Jay Braun; *131,* © Frank Siteman/Stock, Boston; *134,* Courtesy, Alex Fraser, F.A.A., University of Cincinnati

Chapter 5

148, From *Psychonomic Science* Journal; *164,* Yale Joel/LIFE Magazine © 1950 Time, Inc.; *166,* Yerkes Regional Primate Research Center, Emory University

Chapter 6

185, (left) Peter Marlow/Sygma; *185,* (center and right) Wide World Photos; *190,* From "Remembering: A Study in Experimental and Social Psychology," by F. C. Bartlett, 1932. Reprinted by permission of Cambridge University Press; *191,* From THE PSYCHOLOGY OF RUMOR by Gordon Allport and Leo Postman. Copyright 1947 by Henry Holt & Co., Inc. Renewal © 1975 by Holt, Rinehart and Winston. Reprinted by permission of Holt, Rinehart and Winston; *193,* Courtesy, Professor Elizabeth F. Loftus

Chapter 7

215 and 222, From "The Task of Gestalt Psychology," by Wolfgang Kohler. With an Introduction by Carroll C. Pratt copyright © 1969 by Princeton University Press (figure 25, p. 146 redrawn, and table on p. 150 in adapted form). Reprinted by permission of Princeton University Press; *224,* The figure preference test and the inkblot test from "The Psychology of Imagination" by Frank Barron. Reprinted by permission; *226,* Reprinted with permission of Macmillan Publishing Co., Inc., from "Thinking Clearly About Career Choices" by Irving Janis and Dan Wheeler. Copyright © 1977 by the Free Press, a division of Macmillan Publishing Co., Inc. and *Psychology Today* Magazine. Copyright © 1978 Ziff Davis Publishing Company; *227,* From "Relative Importance of Probabilities and Payoffs in Risk Taking" by Pat Slovick and S. Lichtenstein. Copyright 1968 by the American Psychological Association. Reprinted by permission; *231,* From "Availability: A Heuristic for Judging Frequency and Probability" by Amos Tversky and Daniel Kahneman. Reprinted by permission.

Chapter 8

242, © Charles Harbutt/Magnum; *244,* Courtesy, Dr. Richard Walk; *246,* Dr. Carolyn Ravel-Collier, Rutgers Department of Psychology; *247,* George Zimbel/Monkmeyer Press Photos; *250,* Steve Wells; *257,* Constantine Manos/Magnum; *259,* Harry F. Harlow, Wisconsin University Primate Laboratory; *263,* © Burk Uzzle/Magnum; *271,* © Elliot Erwitt/Magnum

Chapter 9

278, Whitney Museum of American Art, Collection of Jim Dine. Photograph by Geoffrey Clements; *287,* Thomas McAvoy/Life Magazine © Time, Inc.; *293,* Bill MacDonald; *298,* (top) From "Consideration of Some Problems in Comprehension" by Bransford and Johnson in VISUAL INFORMAT PROCESSING, W. G. Chase, ed., 1973. Reprinted by permission of Academic Press and John D. Bradford; *298,* (bottom) Thomas Höpker/Woodfin Camp & Assoc.

Chapter 10

315, James H. Karales/Peter Arnold, Inc.; *316,* Jack Prelutsky/Stock, Boston; *328,* Reprinted with permission from *Journal of Psychosomatic Research* 11, from Thomas H. Holmes and Richard H. Rahe, "The Social Readjustment Rating Scale," copyright © 1967, Pergamon Press, Ltd.; *329,* © Costa Manos/Magnum

Index